Introduction to Algorithms

Thomas H. Cormen
Charles E. Leiserson
Ronald L. Rivest

Introduction to Algorithms

The MIT Press
Cambridge, Massachusetts   London, England

McGraw-Hill Book Company
New York   St. Louis   San Francisco   Montreal   Toronto

Thirteenth printing, 1994

This book is one of a series of texts written by faculty of the Electrical Engineering and Computer Science Department at the Massachusetts Institute of Technology. It was edited and produced by The MIT Press under a joint production-distribution agreement with the McGraw-Hill Book Company.

Ordering Information:

North America
Text orders should be addressed to the McGraw-Hill Book Company. All other orders should be addressed to The MIT Press.

Outside North America
All orders should be addressed to The MIT Press or its local distributor.

Library of Congress Cataloging-in-Publication Data

Cormen, Thomas H.
    Introduction to Algorithms / Thomas H. Cormen, Charles E.
Leiserson, Ronald L. Rivest.
        p.   cm.—(The MIT electrical engineering and computer
science series)
    Includes bibliographical references.
    ISBN 0-262-03141-8 (MIT Press).—ISBN 0-07-013143-0 (McGraw-Hill)
    1. Electronic digital computers—Programming. 2. Algorithms.
I. Leiserson, Charles Eric.   II. Rivest, Ronald L.   III. Title
IV. Series.
QA76.6.C662   1989
005.1–dc20   89–13027
                                                                      CIP

Contents

Preface   *xiii*

1   **Introduction**   *1*
   1.1   Algorithms   *1*
   1.2   Analyzing algorithms   *6*
   1.3   Designing algorithms   *11*
   1.4   Summary   *16*

I   *Mathematical Foundations*

Introduction   *21*

2   **Growth of Functions**   *23*
   2.1   Asymptotic notation   *23*
   2.2   Standard notations and common functions   *32*

3   **Summations**   *42*
   3.1   Summation formulas and properties   *42*
   3.2   Bounding summations   *46*

4   **Recurrences**   *53*
   4.1   The substitution method   *54*
   4.2   The iteration method   *58*
   4.3   The master method   *61*
  ★ 4.4   Proof of the master theorem   *64*

5   **Sets, Etc.**   *77*
   5.1   Sets   *77*
   5.2   Relations   *81*
   5.3   Functions   *84*
   5.4   Graphs   *86*
   5.5   Trees   *91*

6   Counting and Probability   *99*

6.1   Counting   *99*

6.2   Probability   *104*

6.3   Discrete random variables   *111*

6.4   The geometric and binomial distributions   *115*

★   6.5   The tails of the binomial distribution   *121*

6.6   Probabilistic analysis   *126*

II   Sorting and Order Statistics

Introduction   *137*

7   Heapsort   *140*

7.1   Heaps   *140*

7.2   Maintaining the heap property   *142*

7.3   Building a heap   *145*

7.4   The heapsort algorithm   *147*

7.5   Priority queues   *149*

8   Quicksort   *153*

8.1   Description of quicksort   *153*

8.2   Performance of quicksort   *156*

8.3   Randomized versions of quicksort   *161*

8.4   Analysis of quicksort   *163*

9   Sorting in Linear Time   *172*

9.1   Lower bounds for sorting   *172*

9.2   Counting sort   *175*

9.3   Radix sort   *178*

9.4   Bucket sort   *180*

10   Medians and Order Statistics   *185*

10.1   Minimum and maximum   *185*

10.2   Selection in expected linear time   *187*

10.3   Selection in worst-case linear time   *189*

III *Data Structures*

Introduction *197*

11 **Elementary Data Structures** *200*
    11.1 Stacks and queues *200*
    11.2 Linked lists *204*
    11.3 Implementing pointers and objects *209*
    11.4 Representing rooted trees *213*

12 **Hash Tables** *219*
    12.1 Direct-address tables *219*
    12.2 Hash tables *221*
    12.3 Hash functions *226*
    12.4 Open addressing *232*

13 **Binary Search Trees** *244*
    13.1 What is a binary search tree? *244*
    13.2 Querying a binary search tree *246*
    13.3 Insertion and deletion *250*
★   13.4 Randomly built binary search trees *254*

14 **Red-Black Trees** *263*
    14.1 Properties of red-black trees *263*
    14.2 Rotations *265*
    14.3 Insertion *268*
    14.4 Deletion *272*

15 **Augmenting Data Structures** *281*
    15.1 Dynamic order statistics *281*
    15.2 How to augment a data structure *287*
    15.3 Interval trees *290*

IV *Advanced Design and Analysis Techniques*

Introduction *299*

16 **Dynamic Programming** *301*
    16.1 Matrix-chain multiplication *302*
    16.2 Elements of dynamic programming *309*
    16.3 Longest common subsequence *314*
    16.4 Optimal polygon triangulation *320*

17   Greedy Algorithms   *329*

17.1 An activity-selection problem   *329*

17.2 Elements of the greedy strategy   *333*

17.3 Huffman codes   *337*

★   17.4 Theoretical foundations for greedy methods   *345*

★   17.5 A task-scheduling problem   *350*

18   Amortized Analysis   *356*

18.1 The aggregate method   *357*

18.2 The accounting method   *360*

18.3 The potential method   *363*

18.4 Dynamic tables   *367*

V   *Advanced Data Structures*

Introduction   *379*

19   B-Trees   *381*

19.1 Definition of B-trees   *384*

19.2 Basic operations on B-trees   *387*

19.3 Deleting a key from a B-tree   *395*

20   Binomial Heaps   *400*

20.1 Binomial trees and binomial heaps   *401*

20.2 Operations on binomial heaps   *406*

21   Fibonacci Heaps   *420*

21.1 Structure of Fibonacci heaps   *421*

21.2 Mergeable-heap operations   *423*

21.3 Decreasing a key and deleting a node   *431*

21.4 Bounding the maximum degree   *435*

22   Data Structures for Disjoint Sets   *440*

22.1 Disjoint-set operations   *440*

22.2 Linked-list representation of disjoint sets   *443*

22.3 Disjoint-set forests   *446*

★   22.4 Analysis of union by rank with path compression   *450*

VI Graph Algorithms

Introduction *463*

23 Elementary Graph Algorithms *465*
23.1 Representations of graphs *465*
23.2 Breadth-first search *469*
23.3 Depth-first search *477*
23.4 Topological sort *485*
23.5 Strongly connected components *488*

24 Minimum Spanning Trees *498*
24.1 Growing a minimum spanning tree *499*
24.2 The algorithms of Kruskal and Prim *504*

25 Single-Source Shortest Paths *514*
25.1 Shortest paths and relaxation *518*
25.2 Dijkstra's algorithm *527*
25.3 The Bellman-Ford algorithm *532*
25.4 Single-source shortest paths in directed acyclic graphs *536*
25.5 Difference constraints and shortest paths *539*

26 All-Pairs Shortest Paths *550*
26.1 Shortest paths and matrix multiplication *552*
26.2 The Floyd-Warshall algorithm *558*
26.3 Johnson's algorithm for sparse graphs *565*
★ 26.4 A general framework for solving path problems in directed graphs *570*

27 Maximum Flow *579*
27.1 Flow networks *580*
27.2 The Ford-Fulkerson method *587*
27.3 Maximum bipartite matching *600*
★ 27.4 Preflow-push algorithms *605*
★ 27.5 The lift-to-front algorithm *615*

VII   *Selected Topics*

Introduction   *631*

28   Sorting Networks   *634*

28.1 Comparison networks   *634*

28.2 The zero-one principle   *639*

28.3 A bitonic sorting network   *642*

28.4 A merging network   *646*

28.5 A sorting network   *648*

29   Arithmetic Circuits   *654*

29.1 Combinational circuits   *655*

29.2 Addition circuits   *660*

29.3 Multiplication circuits   *671*

29.4 Clocked circuits   *678*

30   Algorithms for Parallel Computers   *688*

30.1 Pointer jumping   *692*

30.2 CRCW algorithms versus EREW algorithms   *701*

30.3 Brent's theorem and work efficiency   *709*

★   30.4 Work-efficient parallel prefix computation   *714*

30.5 Deterministic symmetry breaking   *720*

31   Matrix Operations   *730*

31.1 Properties of matrices   *730*

31.2 Strassen's algorithm for matrix multiplication   *739*

★   31.3 Algebraic number systems and boolean matrix multiplication   *745*

31.4 Solving systems of linear equations   *749*

31.5 Inverting matrices   *762*

31.6 Symmetric positive-definite matrices and least-squares approximation   *766*

32   Polynomials and the FFT   *776*

32.1 Representation of polynomials   *778*

32.2 The DFT and FFT   *783*

32.3 Efficient FFT implementations   *791*

33   Number-Theoretic Algorithms   *801*

33.1 Elementary number-theoretic notions   *802*

33.2 Greatest common divisor   *808*

33.3 Modular arithmetic   *814*

33.4 Solving modular linear equations *820*

33.5 The Chinese remainder theorem *823*

33.6 Powers of an element *827*

33.7 The RSA public-key cryptosystem *831*

★ 33.8 Primality testing *837*

★ 33.9 Integer factorization *844*

34 String Matching *853*

34.1 The naive string-matching algorithm *855*

34.2 The Rabin-Karp algorithm *857*

34.3 String matching with finite automata *862*

34.4 The Knuth-Morris-Pratt algorithm *869*

★ 34.5 The Boyer-Moore algorithm *876*

35 Computational Geometry *886*

35.1 Line-segment properties *887*

35.2 Determining whether any pair of segments intersects *892*

35.3 Finding the convex hull *898*

35.4 Finding the closest pair of points *908*

36 NP-Completeness *916*

36.1 Polynomial time *917*

36.2 Polynomial-time verification *924*

36.3 NP-completeness and reducibility *929*

36.4 NP-completeness proofs *939*

36.5 NP-complete problems *946*

37 Approximation Algorithms *964*

37.1 The vertex-cover problem *966*

37.2 The traveling-salesman problem *969*

37.3 The set-covering problem *974*

37.4 The subset-sum problem *978*

Bibliography *987*

Index *997*

Preface

This book provides a comprehensive introduction to the modern study of computer algorithms. It presents many algorithms and covers them in considerable depth, yet makes their design and analysis accessible to all levels of readers. We have tried to keep explanations elementary without sacrificing depth of coverage or mathematical rigor.

Each chapter presents an algorithm, a design technique, an application area, or a related topic. Algorithms are described in English and in a "pseudocode" designed to be readable by anyone who has done a little programming. The book contains over 260 figures illustrating how the algorithms work. Since we emphasize *efficiency* as a design criterion, we include careful analyses of the running times of all our algorithms.

The text is intended primarily for use in undergraduate or graduate courses in algorithms or data structures. Because it discusses engineering issues in algorithm design, as well as mathematical aspects, it is equally well suited for self-study by technical professionals.

To the teacher

This book is designed to be both versatile and complete. You will find it useful for a variety of courses, from an undergraduate course in data structures up through a graduate course in algorithms. Because we have provided considerably more material than can fit in a typical one-term course, you should think of the book as a "buffet" or "smorgasbord" from which you can pick and choose the material that best supports the course you wish to teach.

You should find it easy to organize your course around just the chapters you need. We have made chapters relatively self-contained, so that you need not worry about an unexpected and unnecessary dependence of one chapter on another. Each chapter presents the easier material first and the more difficult material later, with section boundaries marking natural stopping points. In an undergraduate course, you might use only the earlier sections from a chapter; in a graduate course, you might cover the entire chapter.

We have included over 900 exercises and over 120 problems. Each section ends with exercises, and each chapter ends with problems. The exercises are generally short questions that test basic mastery of the material. Some are simple self-check thought exercises, whereas others are suitable as assigned homework. The problems are more elaborate case studies that often introduce new material; they typically consist of several questions that lead the student through the steps required to arrive at a solution.

We have starred ($\star$) the sections and exercises that are more suitable for graduate students than for undergraduates. A starred section is not necessarily more difficult than an unstarred one, but it may require an understanding of more advanced mathematics. Likewise, starred exercises may require an advanced background or more than average creativity.

To the student

We hope that this textbook provides you with an enjoyable introduction to the field of algorithms. We have attempted to make every algorithm accessible and interesting. To help you when you encounter unfamiliar or difficult algorithms, we describe each one in a step-by-step manner. We also provide careful explanations of the mathematics needed to understand the analysis of the algorithms. If you already have some familiarity with a topic, you will find the chapters organized so that you can skim introductory sections and proceed quickly to the more advanced material.

This is a large book, and your class will probably cover only a portion of its material. We have tried, however, to make this a book that will be useful to you now as a course textbook and also later in your career as a mathematical desk reference or an engineering handbook.

What are the prerequisites for reading this book?

- You should have some programming experience. In particular, you should understand recursive procedures and simple data structures such as arrays and linked lists.

- You should have some facility with proofs by mathematical induction. A few portions of the book rely on some knowledge of elementary calculus. Beyond that, Part I of this book teaches you all the mathematical techniques you will need.

To the professional

The wide range of topics in this book makes it an excellent handbook on algorithms. Because each chapter is relatively self-contained, you can focus in on the topics that most interest you.

Most of the algorithms we discuss have great practical utility. We therefore address implementation concerns and other engineering issues. We generally provide practical alternatives to the few algorithms that are primarily of theoretical interest.

If you wish to implement any of the algorithms, you will find the translation of our pseudocode into your favorite programming language a fairly straightforward task. The pseudocode is designed to present each algorithm clearly and succinctly. Consequently, we do not address error-handling and other software-engineering issues that require specific assumptions about your programming environment. We attempt to present each algorithm simply and directly without allowing the idiosyncrasies of a particular programming language to obscure its essence.

Errors

A book of this length is certain to contain errors and omissions. If you find any errors or have other constructive suggestions, we would appreciate hearing from you. We particularly welcome suggestions for new exercises and problems, but please include solutions. You can mail your comments to

Introduction to Algorithms
MIT Laboratory for Computer Science
545 Technology Square
Cambridge, Massachusetts 02139

Alternatively, you can use Internet electronic mail to submit bug reports, request a list of known errors, or make constructive suggestions. To receive instructions, send electronic mail to algorithms@theory.lcs.mit.edu with "Subject: help" in the message header. We regret that we cannot personally respond to all mail.

Acknowledgments

Many friends and colleagues have contributed greatly to the quality of this book. We thank all of you for your help and constructive criticisms.

MIT's Laboratory for Computer Science has provided an ideal working environment. Our colleagues in the laboratory's Theory of Computation Group have been particularly supportive and tolerant of our incessant requests for critical appraisal of chapters. We specifically thank Baruch Awerbuch, Shafi Goldwasser, Leo Guibas, Tom Leighton, Albert Meyer, David Shmoys, and Eva Tardos. Thanks to William Ang, Sally Bemus, Ray Hirschfeld, and Mark Reinhold for keeping our machines (DEC Microvaxes, Apple Macintoshes, and Sun Sparcstations) running and for recompiling TEX whenever we exceeded a compile-time limit. Thinking Machines Corporation provided partial support for Charles Leiserson to work on this book during a leave of absence from MIT.

Many colleagues have used drafts of this text in courses at other schools. They have suggested numerous corrections and revisions. We particularly wish to thank Richard Beigel (Yale), Andrew Goldberg (Stanford),

Joan Lucas (Rutgers), Mark Overmars (Utrecht), Alan Sherman (Tufts and Maryland), and Diane Souvaine (Rutgers).

Many teaching assistants in our courses have made significant contributions to the development of this material. We especially thank Alan Baratz, Bonnie Berger, Aditi Dhagat, Burt Kaliski, Arthur Lent, Andrew Moulton, Marios Papaefthymiou, Cindy Phillips, Mark Reinhold, Phil Rogaway, Flavio Rose, Arie Rudich, Alan Sherman, Cliff Stein, Susmita Sur, Gregory Troxel, and Margaret Tuttle.

Additional valuable technical assistance was provided by many individuals. Denise Sergent spent many hours in the MIT libraries researching bibliographic references. Maria Sensale, the librarian of our reading room, was always cheerful and helpful. Access to Albert Meyer's personal library saved many hours of library time in preparing the chapter notes. Shlomo Kipnis, Bill Niehaus, and David Wilson proofread old exercises, developed new ones, and wrote notes on their solutions. Marios Papaefthymiou and Gregory Troxel contributed to the indexing. Over the years, our secretaries Inna Radzihovsky, Denise Sergent, Gayle Sherman, and especially Be Hubbard provided endless support in this project, for which we thank them.

Many errors in the early drafts were reported by students. We particularly thank Bobby Blumofe, Bonnie Eisenberg, Raymond Johnson, John Keen, Richard Lethin, Mark Lillibridge, John Pezaris, Steve Ponzio, and Margaret Tuttle for their careful readings.

Colleagues have also provided critical reviews of specific chapters, or information on specific algorithms, for which we are grateful. We especially thank Bill Aiello, Alok Aggarwal, Eric Bach, Vašek Chvátal, Richard Cole, Johan Hastad, Alex Ishii, David Johnson, Joe Kilian, Dina Kravets, Bruce Maggs, Jim Orlin, James Park, Thane Plambeck, Herschel Safer, Jeff Shallit, Cliff Stein, Gil Strang, Bob Tarjan, and Paul Wang. Several of our colleagues also graciously supplied us with problems; we particularly thank Andrew Goldberg, Danny Sleator, and Umesh Vazirani.

This book was typeset with LaTeX, a macro package for TeX. The figures were drawn on an Apple Macintosh using MacDraw II; thanks to Joanna Terry of Claris Corporation and Michael Mahoney of Advanced Computer Graphics for timely customer support. The index was compiled using Windex, a C program written by the authors. The bibliography was prepared using BibTeX. The book was typeset at the American Mathematical Society with an Autologic phototypesetter; thanks to Ralph Youngen of AMS for his help. The cover for the book was designed by Jeannet Leendertse. The book design was created by Rebecca Daw, and Amy Hendrickson implemented the design in LaTeX.

It has been a pleasure working with The MIT Press and McGraw-Hill in the development of this text. We especially thank Frank Satlow, Terry Ehling, Larry Cohen, and Lorrie Lejeune of The MIT Press and David Shapiro of McGraw-Hill for their encouragement, support, and patience.

We are particularly grateful to Larry Cohen for his outstanding copyediting.

Finally, we thank our wives—Nicole Cormen, Linda Lue Leiserson, and Gail Rivest—and our children—Ricky, William, and Debby Leiserson and Alex and Christopher Rivest—for their love and support during the writing of this book. (Alex Rivest also helped with the "Martian birthday paradox.") The love, patience, and encouragement of our families made this project possible. We affectionately dedicate this book to them.

Cambridge, Massachusetts   THOMAS H. CORMEN
March 1990   CHARLES E. LEISERSON
                                                                          RONALD L. RIVEST

Introduction to Algorithms

1 Introduction

This chapter will familiarize you with the framework we shall use throughout the book to think about the design and analysis of algorithms. It is self-contained, but it does include several references to material that will be introduced in Part I.

We begin with a discussion of computational problems in general and of the algorithms needed to solve them, with the problem of sorting as our running example. We introduce a "pseudocode" that should be familiar to readers who have done computer programming to show how we shall specify our algorithms. Insertion sort, a simple sorting algorithm, serves as an initial example. We analyze the running time of insertion sort, introducing a notation that focuses on how that time increases with the number of items to be sorted. We also introduce the divide-and-conquer approach to the design of algorithms and use it to develop an algorithm called merge sort. We end with a comparison of the two sorting algorithms.

1.1 Algorithms

Informally, an *algorithm* is any well-defined computational procedure that takes some value, or set of values, as *input* and produces some value, or set of values, as *output*. An algorithm is thus a sequence of computational steps that transform the input into the output.

We can also view an algorithm as a tool for solving a well-specified *computational problem*. The statement of the problem specifies in general terms the desired input/output relationship. The algorithm describes a specific computational procedure for achieving that input/output relationship.

We begin our study of algorithms with the problem of sorting a sequence of numbers into nondecreasing order. This problem arises frequently in practice and provides fertile ground for introducing many standard design techniques and analysis tools. Here is how we formally define the *sorting problem*:

Input: A sequence of n numbers $\langle a_1, a_2, \ldots, a_n \rangle$.

Output: A permutation (reordering) $\langle a'_1, a'_2, \ldots, a'_n \rangle$ of the input sequence such that $a'_1 \leq a'_2 \leq \cdots \leq a'_n$.

Given an input sequence such as $\langle 31, 41, 59, 26, 41, 58 \rangle$, a sorting algorithm returns as output the sequence $\langle 26, 31, 41, 41, 58, 59 \rangle$. Such an input sequence is called an ***instance*** of the sorting problem. In general, an ***instance of a problem*** consists of all the inputs (satisfying whatever constraints are imposed in the problem statement) needed to compute a solution to the problem.

Sorting is a fundamental operation in computer science (many programs use it as an intermediate step), and as a result a large number of good sorting algorithms have been developed. Which algorithm is best for a given application depends on the number of items to be sorted, the extent to which the items are already somewhat sorted, and the kind of storage device to be used: main memory, disks, or tapes.

An algorithm is said to be ***correct*** if, for every input instance, it halts with the correct output. We say that a correct algorithm ***solves*** the given computational problem. An incorrect algorithm might not halt at all on some input instances, or it might halt with other than the desired answer. Contrary to what one might expect, incorrect algorithms can sometimes be useful, if their error rate can be controlled. We shall see an example of this in Chapter 33 when we study algorithms for finding large prime numbers. Ordinarily, however, we shall be concerned only with correct algorithms.

An algorithm can be specified in English, as a computer program, or even as a hardware design. The only requirement is that the specification must provide a precise description of the computational procedure to be followed.

In this book, we shall typically describe algorithms as programs written in a ***pseudocode*** that is very much like C, Pascal, or Algol. If you have been introduced to any of these languages, you should have little trouble reading our algorithms. What separates pseudocode from "real" code is that in pseudocode, we employ whatever expressive method is most clear and concise to specify a given algorithm. Sometimes, the clearest method is English, so do not be surprised if you come across an English phrase or sentence embedded within a section of "real" code. Another difference between pseudocode and real code is that pseudocode is not typically concerned with issues of software engineering. Issues of data abstraction, modularity, and error handling are often ignored in order to convey the essence of the algorithm more concisely.

Insertion sort

We start with ***insertion sort***, which is an efficient algorithm for sorting a small number of elements. Insertion sort works the way many people sort a bridge or gin rummy hand. We start with an empty left hand and the

Figure 1.1 Sorting a hand of cards using insertion sort.

cards face down on the table. We then remove one card at a time from the table and insert it into the correct position in the left hand. To find the correct position for a card, we compare it with each of the cards already in the hand, from right to left, as illustrated in Figure 1.1.

Our pseudocode for insertion sort is presented as a procedure called INSERTION-SORT, which takes as a parameter an array $A[1 .. n]$ containing a sequence of length n that is to be sorted. (In the code, the number n of elements in A is denoted by *length*[A].) The input numbers are ***sorted in place***: the numbers are rearranged within the array A, with at most a constant number of them stored outside the array at any time. The input array A contains the sorted output sequence when INSERTION-SORT is finished.

INSERTION-SORT(A)

```
1  for j ← 2 to length[A]
2      do key ← A[j]
3          ▷ Insert A[j] into the sorted sequence A[1 .. j − 1].
4          i ← j − 1
5          while i > 0 and A[i] > key
6              do A[i + 1] ← A[i]
7                  i ← i − 1
8          A[i + 1] ← key
```

Figure 1.2 shows how this algorithm works for $A = \langle 5, 2, 4, 6, 1, 3 \rangle$. The index j indicates the "current card" being inserted into the hand. Array elements $A[1 .. j − 1]$ constitute the currently sorted hand, and elements $A[j + 1 .. n]$ correspond to the pile of cards still on the table. The index j moves left to right through the array. At each iteration of the "outer" **for** loop, the element $A[j]$ is picked out of the array (line 2). Then, starting in

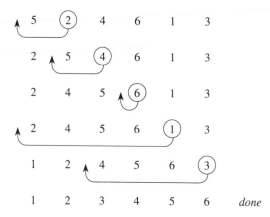

Figure 1.2   The operation of INSERTION-SORT on the array $A = \langle 5, 2, 4, 6, 1, 3 \rangle$. The position of index j is indicated by a circle.

position $j - 1$, elements are successively moved one position to the right until the proper position for $A[j]$ is found (lines 4–7), at which point it is inserted (line 8).

Pseudocode conventions

We use the following conventions in our pseudocode.

1. Indentation indicates block structure. For example, the body of the **for** loop that begins on line 1 consists of lines 2–8, and the body of the **while** loop that begins on line 5 contains lines 6–7 but not line 8. Our indentation style applies to **if-then-else** statements as well. Using indentation instead of conventional indicators of block structure, such as **begin** and **end** statements, greatly reduces clutter while preserving, or even enhancing, clarity.[1]

2. The looping constructs **while**, **for**, and **repeat** and the conditional constructs **if**, **then**, and **else** have the the same interpretation as in Pascal.

3. The symbol "▷" indicates that the remainder of the line is a comment.

4. A multiple assignment of the form $i \leftarrow j \leftarrow e$ assigns to both variables i and j the value of expression e; it should be treated as equivalent to the assignment $j \leftarrow e$ followed by the assignment $i \leftarrow j$.

5. Variables (such as i, j, and *key*) are local to the given procedure. We shall not use global variables without explicit indication.

---

[1]In real programming languages, it is generally not advisable to use indentation alone to indicate block structure, since levels of indentation are hard to determine when code is split across pages.

6. Array elements are accessed by specifying the array name followed by the index in square brackets. For example, $A[i]$ indicates the ith element of the array A. The notation ".." is used to indicate a range of values within an array. Thus, $A[1..j]$ indicates the subarray of A consisting of elements $A[1], A[2], \ldots, A[j]$.

7. Compound data are typically organized into **objects**, which are comprised of **attributes** or **fields**. A particular field is accessed using the field name followed by the name of its object in square brackets. For example, we treat an array as an object with the attribute *length* indicating how many elements it contains. To specify the number of elements in an array A, we write *length*$[A]$. Although we use square brackets for both array indexing and object attributes, it will usually be clear from the context which interpretation is intended.

   A variable representing an array or object is treated as a pointer to the data representing the array or object. For all fields f of an object x, setting $y \leftarrow x$ causes $f[y] = f[x]$. Moreover, if we now set $f[x] \leftarrow 3$, then afterward not only is $f[x] = 3$, but $f[y] = 3$ as well. In other words, x and y point to ("are") the same object after the assignment $y \leftarrow x$.

   Sometimes, a pointer will refer to no object at all. In this case, we give it the special value NIL.

8. Parameters are passed to a procedure **by value**: the called procedure receives its own copy of the parameters, and if it assigns a value to a parameter, the change is *not* seen by the calling routine. When objects are passed, the pointer to the data representing the object is copied, but the object's fields are not. For example, if x is a parameter of a called procedure, the assignment $x \leftarrow y$ within the called procedure is not visible to the calling procedure. The assignment $f[x] \leftarrow 3$, however, is visible.

Exercises

1.1-1
Using Figure 1.2 as a model, illustrate the operation of INSERTION-SORT on the array $A = \langle 31, 41, 59, 26, 41, 58 \rangle$.

1.1-2
Rewrite the INSERTION-SORT procedure to sort into nonincreasing instead of nondecreasing order.

1.1-3
Consider the **searching problem**:

Input: A sequence of n numbers $A = \langle a_1, a_2, \ldots, a_n \rangle$ and a value v.

Output: An index i such that $v = A[i]$ or the special value NIL if v does not appear in A.

Write pseudocode for *linear search*, which scans through the sequence, looking for v.

1.1-4

Consider the problem of adding two n-bit binary integers, stored in two n-element arrays A and B. The sum of the two integers should be stored in binary form in an $(n + 1)$-element array C. State the problem formally and write pseudocode for adding the two integers.

1.2   Analyzing algorithms

Analyzing an algorithm has come to mean predicting the resources that the algorithm requires. Occasionally, resources such as memory, communication bandwidth, or logic gates are of primary concern, but most often it is computational time that we want to measure. Generally, by analyzing several candidate algorithms for a problem, a most efficient one can be easily identified. Such analysis may indicate more than one viable candidate, but several inferior algorithms are usually discarded in the process.

Before we can analyze an algorithm, we must have a model of the implementation technology that will be used, including a model for the resources of that technology and their costs. For most of this book, we shall assume a generic one-processor, *random-access machine* (*RAM*) model of computation as our implementation technology and understand that our algorithms will be implemented as computer programs. In the RAM model, instructions are executed one after another, with no concurrent operations. In later chapters, however, we shall have occasion to investigate models for parallel computers and digital hardware.

Analyzing even a simple algorithm can be a challenge. The mathematical tools required may include discrete combinatorics, elementary probability theory, algebraic dexterity, and the ability to identify the most significant terms in a formula. Because the behavior of an algorithm may be different for each possible input, we need a means for summarizing that behavior in simple, easily understood formulas.

Even though we typically select only one machine model to analyze a given algorithm, we still face many choices in deciding how to express our analysis. One immediate goal is to find a means of expression that is simple to write and manipulate, shows the important characteristics of an algorithm's resource requirements, and suppresses tedious details.

Analysis of insertion sort

The time taken by the INSERTION-SORT procedure depends on the input: sorting a thousand numbers takes longer than sorting three numbers. More-over, INSERTION-SORT can take different amounts of time to sort two input sequences of the same size depending on how nearly sorted they already are. In general, the time taken by an algorithm grows with the size of the input, so it is traditional to describe the running time of a program as a function of the size of its input. To do so, we need to define the terms "running time" and "size of input" more carefully.

The best notion for **input size** depends on the problem being studied. For many problems, such as sorting or computing discrete Fourier transforms, the most natural measure is the *number of items in the input*—for example, the array size n for sorting. For many other problems, such as multiplying two integers, the best measure of input size is the *total number of bits* needed to represent the input in ordinary binary notation. Sometimes, it is more appropriate to describe the size of the input with two numbers rather than one. For instance, if the input to an algorithm is a graph, the input size can be described by the numbers of vertices and edges in the graph. We shall indicate which input size measure is being used with each problem we study.

The **running time** of an algorithm on a particular input is the number of primitive operations or "steps" executed. It is convenient to define the notion of step so that it is as machine-independent as possible. For the moment, let us adopt the following view. A constant amount of time is required to execute each line of our pseudocode. One line may take a different amount of time than another line, but we shall assume that each execution of the ith line takes time c_i, where c_i is a constant. This viewpoint is in keeping with the RAM model, and it also reflects how the pseudocode would be implemented on most actual computers.[2]

In the following discussion, our expression for the running time of INSERTION-SORT will evolve from a messy formula that uses all the statement costs c_i to a much simpler notation that is more concise and more easily manipulated. This simpler notation will also make it easy to determine whether one algorithm is more efficient than another.

We start by presenting the INSERTION-SORT procedure with the time "cost" of each statement and the number of times each statement is executed. For each $j = 2, 3, \ldots, n$, where $n = length[A]$, we let t_j be the number of times the **while** loop test in line 5 is executed for that value of j. We assume that comments are not executable statements, and so they take no time.

---

[2]There are some subtleties here. Computational steps that we specify in English are often variants of a procedure that requires more than just a constant amount of time. For example, later in this book we might say "sort the points by x-coordinate," which, as we shall see, takes more than a constant amount of time. Also, note that a statement that calls a subroutine takes constant time, though the subroutine, once invoked, may take more. That is, we separate the process of **calling** the subroutine—passing parameters to it, etc.—from the process of **executing** the subroutine.

INSERTION-SORT(A)	cost	times
1 **for** $j \leftarrow 2$ **to** $length[A]$	c_1	n
2 **do** $key \leftarrow A[j]$	c_2	$n - 1$
3 $\triangleright$ Insert $A[j]$ into the sorted		
$\triangleright$ sequence $A[1 .. j - 1]$.	0	$n - 1$
4 $i \leftarrow j - 1$	c_4	$n - 1$
5 **while** $i > 0$ and $A[i] > key$	c_5	$\sum_{j=2}^{n} t_j$
6 **do** $A[i + 1] \leftarrow A[i]$	c_6	$\sum_{j=2}^{n}(t_j - 1)$
7 $i \leftarrow i - 1$	c_7	$\sum_{j=2}^{n}(t_j - 1)$
8 $A[i + 1] \leftarrow key$	c_8	$n - 1$

The running time of the algorithm is the sum of running times for each statement executed; a statement that takes c_i steps to execute and is executed n times will contribute $c_i n$ to the total running time.[3] To compute $T(n)$, the running time of INSERTION-SORT, we sum the products of the *cost* and *times* columns, obtaining

$$T(n) = c_1 n + c_2(n - 1) + c_4(n - 1) + c_5 \sum_{j=2}^{n} t_j + c_6 \sum_{j=2}^{n}(t_j - 1)$$
$$+ c_7 \sum_{j=2}^{n}(t_j - 1) + c_8(n - 1) .$$

Even for inputs of a given size, an algorithm's running time may depend on *which* input of that size is given. For example, in INSERTION-SORT, the best case occurs if the array is already sorted. For each $j = 2, 3, \ldots, n$, we then find that $A[i] \leq key$ in line 5 when i has its initial value of $j - 1$. Thus $t_j = 1$ for $j = 2, 3, \ldots, n$, and the best-case running time is

$$T(n) = c_1 n + c_2(n - 1) + c_4(n - 1) + c_5(n - 1) + c_8(n - 1)$$
$$= (c_1 + c_2 + c_4 + c_5 + c_8)n - (c_2 + c_4 + c_5 + c_8) .$$

This running time can be expressed as $an + b$ for *constants* a and b that depend on the statement costs c_i; it is thus a ***linear function*** of n.

If the array is in reverse sorted order—that is, in decreasing order—the worst case results. We must compare each element $A[j]$ with each element in the entire sorted subarray $A[1 .. j - 1]$, and so $t_j = j$ for $j = 2, 3, \ldots, n$. Noting that

$$\sum_{j=2}^{n} j = \frac{n(n + 1)}{2} - 1$$

and

---

[3]This characteristic does not necessarily hold for a resource such as memory. A statement that references m words of memory and is executed n times does not necessarily consume mn words of memory in total.

$$\sum_{j=2}^{n}(j-1) = \frac{n(n-1)}{2}$$

(we shall review these summations in Chapter 3), we find that in the worst case, the running time of INSERTION-SORT is

$$
\begin{aligned}
T(n) &= c_1 n + c_2(n-1) + c_4(n-1) + c_5\left(\frac{n(n+1)}{2} - 1\right) \\
&\quad + c_6\left(\frac{n(n-1)}{2}\right) + c_7\left(\frac{n(n-1)}{2}\right) + c_8(n-1) \\
&= \left(\frac{c_5}{2} + \frac{c_6}{2} + \frac{c_7}{2}\right)n^2 + \left(c_1 + c_2 + c_4 + \frac{c_5}{2} - \frac{c_6}{2} - \frac{c_7}{2} + c_8\right)n \\
&\quad - (c_2 + c_4 + c_5 + c_8) \ .
\end{aligned}
$$

This worst-case running time can be expressed as $an^2 + bn + c$ for constants a, b, and c that again depend on the statement costs c_i; it is thus a **quadratic function** of n.

Typically, as in insertion sort, the running time of an algorithm is fixed for a given input, although in later chapters we shall see some interesting "randomized" algorithms whose behavior can vary even for a fixed input.

Worst-case and average-case analysis

In our analysis of insertion sort, we looked at both the best case, in which the input array was already sorted, and the worst case, in which the input array was reverse sorted. For the remainder of this book, though, we shall usually concentrate on finding only the **worst-case running time**, that is, the longest running time for *any* input of size n. We give three reasons for this orientation.

- The worst-case running time of an algorithm is an upper bound on the running time for any input. Knowing it gives us a guarantee that the algorithm will never take any longer. We need not make some educated guess about the running time and hope that it never gets much worse.

- For some algorithms, the worst case occurs fairly often. For example, in searching a database for a particular piece of information, the searching algorithm's worst case will often occur when the information is not present in the database. In some searching applications, searches for absent information may be frequent.

- The "average case" is often roughly as bad as the worst case. Suppose that we randomly choose n numbers and apply insertion sort. How long does it take to determine where in subarray $A[1 .. j-1]$ to insert element $A[j]$? On average, half the elements in $A[1 .. j-1]$ are less than $A[j]$, and half the elements are greater. On average, therefore, we check half of the subarray $A[1 .. j-1]$, so $t_j = j/2$. If we work out the resulting average-case running time, it turns out to be a quadratic function of the input size, just like the worst-case running time.

In some particular cases, we shall be interested in the ***average-case*** or ***expected*** running time of an algorithm. One problem with performing an average-case analysis, however, is that it may not be apparent what constitutes an "average" input for a particular problem. Often, we shall assume that all inputs of a given size are equally likely. In practice, this assumption may be violated, but a randomized algorithm can sometimes force it to hold.

Order of growth

We have used some simplifying abstractions to ease our analysis of the INSERTION-SORT procedure. First, we ignored the actual cost of each statement, using the constants c_i to represent these costs. Then, we observed that even these constants give us more detail than we really need: the worst-case running time is $an^2 + bn + c$ for some constants a, b, and c that depend on the statement costs c_i. We thus ignored not only the actual statement costs, but also the abstract costs c_i.

We shall now make one more simplifying abstraction. It is the ***rate of growth***, or ***order of growth***, of the running time that really interests us. We therefore consider only the leading term of a formula (e.g., an^2), since the lower-order terms are relatively insignificant for large n. We also ignore the leading term's constant coefficient, since constant factors are less significant than the rate of growth in determining computational efficiency for large inputs. Thus, we write that insertion sort, for example, has a worst-case running time of $\Theta(n^2)$ (pronounced "theta of n-squared"). We shall use Θ-notation informally in this chapter; it will be defined precisely in Chapter 2.

We usually consider one algorithm to be more efficient than another if its worst-case running time has a lower order of growth. This evaluation may be in error for small inputs, but for large enough inputs a $\Theta(n^2)$ algorithm, for example, will run more quickly in the worst case than a $\Theta(n^3)$ algorithm.

Exercises

1.2-1
Consider sorting n numbers stored in array A by first finding the smallest element of A and putting it in the first entry of another array B. Then find the second smallest element of A and put it in the second entry of B. Continue in this manner for the n elements of A. Write pseudocode for this algorithm, which is known as ***selection sort***. Give the best-case and worst-case running times of selection sort in Θ-notation.

1.2-2
Consider linear search again (see Exercise 1.1-3). How many elements of the input sequence need to be checked on the average, assuming that the element being searched for is equally likely to be any element in the array? How about in the worst case? What are the average-case and worst-case running times of linear search in Θ-notation? Justify your answers.

1.2-3
Consider the problem of determining whether an arbitrary sequence $\langle x_1, x_2, \ldots, x_n \rangle$ of n numbers contains repeated occurrences of some number. Show that this can be done in $\Theta(n \lg n)$ time, where $\lg n$ stands for $\log_2 n$.

1.2-4
Consider the problem of evaluating a polynomial at a point. Given n coefficients $a_0, a_1, \ldots, a_{n-1}$ and a real number x, we wish to compute $\sum_{i=0}^{n-1} a_i x^i$. Describe a straightforward $\Theta(n^2)$-time algorithm for this problem. Describe a $\Theta(n)$-time algorithm that uses the following method (called Horner's rule) for rewriting the polynomial:

$$\sum_{i=0}^{n-1} a_i x^i = (\cdots (a_{n-1}x + a_{n-2})x + \cdots + a_1)x + a_0 .$$

1.2-5
Express the function $n^3/1000 - 100n^2 - 100n + 3$ in terms of Θ-notation.

1.2-6
How can we modify almost any algorithm to have a good best-case running time?

1.3 Designing algorithms

There are many ways to design algorithms. Insertion sort uses an *incremental* approach: having sorted the subarray $A[1 .. j-1]$, we insert the single element $A[j]$ into its proper place, yielding the sorted subarray $A[1 .. j]$.

In this section, we examine an alternative design approach, known as "divide-and-conquer." We shall use divide-and-conquer to design a sorting algorithm whose worst-case running time is much less than that of insertion sort. One advantage of divide-and-conquer algorithms is that their running times are often easily determined using techniques that will be introduced in Chapter 4.

1.3.1   The divide-and-conquer approach

Many useful algorithms are *recursive* in structure: to solve a given problem, they call themselves recursively one or more times to deal with closely related subproblems. These algorithms typically follow a *divide-and-conquer* approach: they break the problem into several subproblems that are similar to the original problem but smaller in size, solve the subproblems recursively, and then combine these solutions to create a solution to the original problem.

The divide-and-conquer paradigm involves three steps at each level of the recursion:

Divide the problem into a number of subproblems.

Conquer the subproblems by solving them recursively. If the subproblem sizes are small enough, however, just solve the subproblems in a straightforward manner.

Combine the solutions to the subproblems into the solution for the original problem.

The *merge sort* algorithm closely follows the divide-and-conquer paradigm. Intuitively, it operates as follows.

Divide: Divide the n-element sequence to be sorted into two subsequences of $n/2$ elements each.

Conquer: Sort the two subsequences recursively using merge sort.

Combine: Merge the two sorted subsequences to produce the sorted answer.

We note that the recursion "bottoms out" when the sequence to be sorted has length 1, in which case there is no work to be done, since every sequence of length 1 is already in sorted order.

The key operation of the merge sort algorithm is the merging of two sorted sequences in the "combine" step. To perform the merging, we use an auxiliary procedure MERGE(A, p, q, r), where A is an array and p, q, and r are indices numbering elements of the array such that $p \leq q < r$. The procedure assumes that the subarrays $A[p..q]$ and $A[q+1..r]$ are in sorted order. It *merges* them to form a single sorted subarray that replaces the current subarray $A[p..r]$.

Although we leave the pseudocode as an exercise (see Exercise 1.3-2), it is easy to imagine a MERGE procedure that takes time $\Theta(n)$, where $n = r - p + 1$ is the number of elements being merged. Returning to our card-playing motif, suppose we have two piles of cards face up on a table. Each pile is sorted, with the smallest cards on top. We wish to merge the two piles into a single sorted output pile, which is to be face down on the table. Our basic step consists of choosing the smaller of the two cards on top of the face-up piles, removing it from its pile (which exposes a new top card), and placing this card face down onto the output pile. We repeat this step until one input pile is empty, at which time we just take the remaining input pile and place it face down onto the output pile. Computationally, each basic step takes constant time, since we are checking just two top cards. Since we perform at most n basic steps, merging takes $\Theta(n)$ time.

We can now use the MERGE procedure as a subroutine in the merge sort algorithm. The procedure MERGE-SORT(A, p, r) sorts the elements in the subarray $A[p..r]$. If $p \geq r$, the subarray has at most one element and is therefore already sorted. Otherwise, the divide step simply computes an index q that partitions $A[p..r]$ into two subarrays: $A[p..q]$, containing $\lceil n/2 \rceil$ elements, and $A[q + 1..r]$, containing $\lfloor n/2 \rfloor$ elements.[4]

MERGE-SORT(A, p, r)

1 **if** $p < r$
2   **then** $q \leftarrow \lfloor (p + r)/2 \rfloor$
3   MERGE-SORT(A, p, q)
4   MERGE-SORT($A, q + 1, r$)
5   MERGE(A, p, q, r)

To sort the entire sequence $A = \langle A[1], A[2], \ldots, A[n] \rangle$, we call MERGE-SORT($A, 1, length[A]$), where once again $length[A] = n$. If we look at the operation of the procedure bottom-up when n is a power of two, the algorithm consists of merging pairs of 1-item sequences to form sorted sequences of length 2, merging pairs of sequences of length 2 to form sorted sequences of length 4, and so on, until two sequences of length $n/2$ are merged to form the final sorted sequence of length n. Figure 1.3 illustrates this process.

1.3.2 Analyzing divide-and-conquer algorithms

When an algorithm contains a recursive call to itself, its running time can often be described by a *recurrence equation* or *recurrence*, which describes the overall running time on a problem of size n in terms of the running time on smaller inputs. We can then use mathematical tools to solve the recurrence and provide bounds on the performance of the algorithm.

A recurrence for the running time of a divide-and-conquer algorithm is based on the three steps of the basic paradigm. As before, we let $T(n)$ be the running time on a problem of size n. If the problem size is small enough, say $n \leq c$ for some constant c, the straightforward solution takes constant time, which we write as $\Theta(1)$. Suppose we divide the problem into a subproblems, each of which is $1/b$ the size of the original. If we take $D(n)$ time to divide the problem into subproblems and $C(n)$ time to combine the solutions to the subproblems into the solution to the original problem, we get the recurrence

---

[4]The expression $\lceil x \rceil$ denotes the least integer greater than or equal to x, and $\lfloor x \rfloor$ denotes the greatest integer less than or equal to x. These notations are defined in Chapter 2.

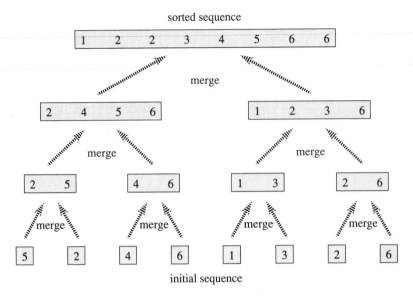

Figure 1.3   The operation of merge sort on the array $A = \langle 5, 2, 4, 6, 1, 3, 2, 6 \rangle$. The lengths of the sorted sequences being merged increase as the algorithm progresses from bottom to top.

$$T(n) = \begin{cases} \Theta(1) & \text{if } n \le c , \\ aT(n/b) + D(n) + C(n) & \text{otherwise .} \end{cases}$$

In Chapter 4, we shall see how to solve common recurrences of this form.

Analysis of merge sort

Although the pseudocode for MERGE-SORT works correctly when the number of elements is not even, our recurrence-based analysis is simplified if we assume that the original problem size is a power of two. Each divide step then yields two subsequences of size exactly $n/2$. In Chapter 4, we shall see that this assumption does not affect the order of growth of the solution to the recurrence.

We reason as follows to set up the recurrence for $T(n)$, the worst-case running time of merge sort on n numbers. Merge sort on just one element takes constant time. When we have $n > 1$ elements, we break down the running time as follows.

Divide: The divide step just computes the middle of the subarray, which takes constant time. Thus, $D(n) = \Theta(1)$.

Conquer: We recursively solve two subproblems, each of size $n/2$, which contributes $2T(n/2)$ to the running time.

Combine: We have already noted that the MERGE procedure on an n-element subarray takes time $\Theta(n)$, so $C(n) = \Theta(n)$.

When we add the functions $D(n)$ and $C(n)$ for the merge sort analysis, we are adding a function that is $\Theta(n)$ and a function that is $\Theta(1)$. This sum is a linear function of n, that is, $\Theta(n)$. Adding it to the $2T(n/2)$ term from the "conquer" step gives the recurrence for the worst-case running time $T(n)$ of merge sort:

$$T(n) = \begin{cases} \Theta(1) & \text{if } n = 1 , \\ 2T(n/2) + \Theta(n) & \text{if } n > 1 . \end{cases}$$

In Chapter 4, we shall show that $T(n)$ is $\Theta(n \lg n)$, where $\lg n$ stands for $\log_2 n$. For large enough inputs, merge sort, with its $\Theta(n \lg n)$ running time, outperforms insertion sort, whose running time is $\Theta(n^2)$, in the worst case.

Exercises

1.3-1
Using Figure 1.3 as a model, illustrate the operation of merge sort on the array $A = \langle 3, 41, 52, 26, 38, 57, 9, 49 \rangle$.

1.3-2
Write pseudocode for MERGE(A, p, q, r).

1.3-3
Use mathematical induction to show that the solution of the recurrence

$$T(n) = \begin{cases} 2 & \text{if } n = 2 , \\ 2T(n/2) + n & \text{if } n = 2^k, k > 1 \end{cases}$$

is $T(n) = n \lg n$.

1.3-4
Insertion sort can be expressed as a recursive procedure as follows. In order to sort $A[1 .. n]$, we recursively sort $A[1 .. n - 1]$ and then insert $A[n]$ into the sorted array $A[1 .. n - 1]$. Write a recurrence for the running time of this recursive version of insertion sort.

1.3-5
Referring back to the searching problem (see Exercise 1.1-3), observe that if the sequence A is sorted, we can check the midpoint of the sequence against v and eliminate half of the sequence from further consideration. **Binary search** is an algorithm that repeats this procedure, halving the size of the remaining portion of the sequence each time. Write pseudocode, either iterative or recursive, for binary search. Argue that the worst-case running time of binary search is $\Theta(\lg n)$.

1.3-6
Observe that the **while** loop of lines 5–7 of the INSERTION-SORT procedure in Section 1.1 uses a linear search to scan (backward) through the sorted subarray $A[1 .. j - 1]$. Can we use a binary search (see Exercise 1.3-5)

instead to improve the overall worst-case running time of insertion sort to $\Theta(n \lg n)$?

1.3-7 ⋆

Describe a $\Theta(n \lg n)$-time algorithm that, given a set S of n real numbers and another real number x, determines whether or not there exist two elements in S whose sum is exactly x.

1.4   Summary

A good algorithm is like a sharp knife—it does exactly what it is supposed to do with a minimum amount of applied effort. Using the wrong algorithm to solve a problem is like trying to cut a steak with a screwdriver: you may eventually get a digestible result, but you will expend considerably more effort than necessary, and the result is unlikely to be aesthetically pleasing.

Algorithms devised to solve the same problem often differ dramatically in their efficiency. These differences can be much more significant than the difference between a personal computer and a supercomputer. As an example, let us pit a supercomputer running insertion sort against a small personal computer running merge sort. They each must sort an array of one million numbers. Suppose the supercomputer executes 100 million instructions per second, while the personal computer executes only one million instructions per second. To make the difference even more dramatic, suppose that the world's craftiest programmer codes insertion sort in machine language for the supercomputer, and the resulting code requires $2n^2$ supercomputer instructions to sort n numbers. Merge sort, on the other hand, is programmed for the personal computer by an average programmer using a high-level language with an inefficient compiler, with the resulting code taking $50n \lg n$ personal computer instructions. To sort a million numbers, the supercomputer takes

$$\frac{2 \cdot (10^6)^2 \text{ instructions}}{10^8 \text{ instructions/second}} = 20{,}000 \text{ seconds} \approx 5.56 \text{ hours},$$

while the personal computer takes

$$\frac{50 \cdot 10^6 \lg 10^6 \text{ instructions}}{10^6 \text{ instructions/second}} \approx 1{,}000 \text{ seconds} \approx 16.67 \text{ minutes}.$$

By using an algorithm whose running time has a lower order of growth, even with a poor compiler, the personal computer runs 20 times faster than the supercomputer!

This example shows that algorithms, like computer hardware, are a **_technology_**. Total system performance depends on choosing efficient algorithms as much as on choosing fast hardware. Just as rapid advances are being made in other computer technologies, they are being made in algorithms as well.

Exercises

1.4-1
Suppose we are comparing implementations of insertion sort and merge sort on the same machine. For inputs of size n, insertion sort runs in $8n^2$ steps, while merge sort runs in $64n \lg n$ steps. For which values of n does insertion sort beat merge sort? How might one rewrite the merge sort pseudocode to make it even faster on small inputs?

1.4-2
What is the smallest value of n such that an algorithm whose running time is $100n^2$ runs faster than an algorithm whose running time is 2^n on the same machine?

Problems

1-1 Comparison of running times
For each function $f(n)$ and time t in the following table, determine the largest size n of a problem that can be solved in time t, assuming that the algorithm to solve the problem takes $f(n)$ microseconds.

	1 second	1 minute	1 hour	1 day	1 month	1 year	1 century
$\lg n$							
$\sqrt{n}$							
n							
$n \lg n$							
n^2							
n^3							
2^n							
$n!$							

1-2 Insertion sort on small arrays in merge sort
Although merge sort runs in $\Theta(n \lg n)$ worst-case time and insertion sort runs in $\Theta(n^2)$ worst-case time, the constant factors in insertion sort make it faster for small n. Thus, it makes sense to use insertion sort within merge sort when subproblems become sufficiently small. Consider a modification to merge sort in which n/k sublists of length k are sorted using insertion

sort and then merged using the standard merging mechanism, where k is a value to be determined.

a. Show that the n/k sublists, each of length k, can be sorted by insertion sort in $\Theta(nk)$ worst-case time.

b. Show that the sublists can be merged in $\Theta(n \lg(n/k))$ worst-case time.

c. Given that the modified algorithm runs in $\Theta(nk + n \lg(n/k))$ worst-case time, what is the largest asymptotic (Θ-notation) value of k as a function of n for which the modified algorithm has the same asymptotic running time as standard merge sort?

d. How should k be chosen in practice?

1-3   Inversions

Let $A[1 \mathbin{..} n]$ be an array of n distinct numbers. If $i < j$ and $A[i] > A[j]$, then the pair (i, j) is called an ***inversion*** of A.

a. List the five inversions of the array $\langle 2, 3, 8, 6, 1 \rangle$.

b. What array with elements from the set $\{1, 2, \ldots, n\}$ has the most inversions? How many does it have?

c. What is the relationship between the running time of insertion sort and the number of inversions in the input array? Justify your answer.

d. Give an algorithm that determines the number of inversions in any permutation on n elements in $\Theta(n \lg n)$ worst-case time. (*Hint:* Modify merge sort.)

Chapter notes

There are many excellent texts on the general topic of algorithms, including those by Aho, Hopcroft, and Ullman [4, 5], Baase [14], Brassard and Bratley [33], Horowitz and Sahni [105], Knuth [121, 122, 123], Manber [142], Mehlhorn [144, 145, 146], Purdom and Brown [164], Reingold, Nievergelt, and Deo [167], Sedgewick [175], and Wilf [201]. Some of the more practical aspects of algorithm design are discussed by Bentley [24, 25] and Gonnet [90].

In 1968, Knuth published the first of three volumes with the general title *The Art of Computer Programming* [121, 122, 123]. The first volume ushered in the modern study of computer algorithms with a focus on the analysis of running time, and the full series remains an engaging and worthwhile reference for many of the topics presented here. According to Knuth, the word "algorithm" is derived from the name "al-Khowârizmî," a ninth-century Persian mathematician.

Aho, Hopcroft, and Ullman [4] advocated the asymptotic analysis of algorithms as a means of comparing relative performance. They also popularized the use of recurrence relations to describe the running times of recursive algorithms.

Knuth [123] provides an encyclopedic treatment of many sorting algorithms. His comparison of sorting algorithms (page 381) includes exact step-counting analyses, like the one we performed here for insertion sort. Knuth's discussion of insertion sort encompasses several variations of the algorithm. The most important of these is Shell's sort, introduced by D. L. Shell, which uses insertion sort on periodic subsequences of the input to produce a faster sorting algorithm.

Merge sort is also described by Knuth. He mentions that a mechanical collator capable of merging two decks of punched cards in a single pass was invented in 1938. J. von Neumann, one of the pioneers of computer science, apparently wrote a program for merge sort on the EDVAC computer in 1945.

I Mathematical Foundations

Introduction

The analysis of algorithms often requires us to draw upon a body of mathematical tools. Some of these tools are as simple as high-school algebra, but others, such as solving recurrences, may be new to you. This part of the book is a compendium of the methods and tools we shall use to analyze algorithms. It is organized primarily for reference, with a tutorial flavor to some of the topics.

We suggest that you not try to digest all of this mathematics at once. Skim the chapters in this part to see what material they contain. You can then proceed directly to the chapters that focus on algorithms. As you read those chapters, though, refer back to this part whenever you need a better understanding of the tools used in the mathematical analyses. At some point, however, you will want to study each of these chapters in its entirety, so that you have a firm foundation in the mathematical techniques.

Chapter 2 precisely defines several asymptotic notations, an example of which is the Θ-notation that you met in Chapter 1. The rest of Chapter 2 is primarily a presentation of mathematical notation. Its purpose is more to ensure that your use of notation matches that in this book than to teach you new mathematical concepts.

Chapter 3 offers methods for evaluating and bounding summations, which occur frequently in the analysis of algorithms. Many of the formulas in this chapter can be found in any calculus text, but you will find it convenient to have these methods compiled in one place.

Methods for solving recurrences, which we used to analyze merge sort in Chapter 1 and which we shall see many times again, are given in Chapter 4. One powerful technique is the "master method," which can be used to solve recurrences that arise from divide-and-conquer algorithms. Much of Chapter 4 is devoted to proving the correctness of the master method, though this proof may be skipped without harm.

Chapter 5 contains basic definitions and notations for sets, relations, functions, graphs, and trees. This chapter also gives some basic properties of these mathematical objects. This material is essential for an understanding of this text but may safely be skipped if you have already had a discrete mathematics course.

Chapter 6 begins with elementary principles of counting: permutations, combinations, and the like. The remainder of the chapter contains definitions and properties of basic probability. Most of the algorithms in this book require no probability for their analysis, and thus you can easily omit the latter sections of the chapter on a first reading, even without skimming them. Later, when you encounter a probabilistic analysis that you want to understand better, you will find Chapter 6 well organized for reference purposes.

2 Growth of Functions

The order of growth of the running time of an algorithm, defined in Chapter 1, gives a simple characterization of the algorithm's efficiency and also allows us to compare the relative performance of alternative algorithms. Once the input size n becomes large enough, merge sort, with its $\Theta(n \lg n)$ worst-case running time, beats insertion sort, whose worst-case running time is $\Theta(n^2)$. Although we can sometimes determine the exact running time of an algorithm, as we did for insertion sort in Chapter 1, the extra precision is not usually worth the effort of computing it. For large enough inputs, the multiplicative constants and lower-order terms of an exact running time are dominated by the effects of the input size itself.

When we look at input sizes large enough to make only the order of growth of the running time relevant, we are studying the *asymptotic* efficiency of algorithms. That is, we are concerned with how the running time of an algorithm increases with the size of the input *in the limit*, as the size of the input increases without bound. Usually, an algorithm that is asymptotically more efficient will be the best choice for all but very small inputs.

This chapter gives several standard methods for simplifying the asymptotic analysis of algorithms. The next section begins by defining several types of "asymptotic notation," of which we have already seen an example in Θ-notation. Several notational conventions used throughout this book are then presented, and finally we review the behavior of functions that commonly arise in the analysis of algorithms.

2.1 Asymptotic notation

The notations we use to describe the asymptotic running time of an algorithm are defined in terms of functions whose domains are the set of natural numbers $\mathbf{N} = \{0, 1, 2, \ldots\}$. Such notations are convenient for describing the worst-case running-time function $T(n)$, which is usually defined only on integer input sizes. It is sometimes convenient, however, to *abuse* asymptotic notation in a variety of ways. For example, the notation is easily extended to the domain of real numbers or, alternatively, restricted to a subset of the natural numbers. It is important, however, to understand the precise meaning of the notation so that when it is abused, it is not *misused*. This section defines the basic asymptotic notations and also introduces some common abuses.

Θ-notation

In Chapter 1, we found that the worst-case running time of insertion sort is $T(n) = \Theta(n^2)$. Let us define what this notation means. For a given function $g(n)$, we denote by $\Theta(g(n))$ the *set of functions*

$$\Theta(g(n)) = \{f(n) : \text{ there exist positive constants } c_1, c_2, \text{ and } n_0 \text{ such that } 0 \le c_1 g(n) \le f(n) \le c_2 g(n) \text{ for all } n \ge n_0\} .$$

A function $f(n)$ belongs to the set $\Theta(g(n))$ if there exist positive constants c_1 and c_2 such that it can be "sandwiched" between $c_1 g(n)$ and $c_2 g(n)$, for sufficiently large n. Although $\Theta(g(n))$ is a set, we write "$f(n) = \Theta(g(n))$" to indicate that $f(n)$ is a member of $\Theta(g(n))$, or "$f(n) \in \Theta(g(n))$." This abuse of equality to denote set membership may at first appear confusing, but we shall see later in this section that it has advantages.

Figure 2.1(a) gives an intuitive picture of functions $f(n)$ and $g(n)$, where $f(n) = \Theta(g(n))$. For all values of n to the right of n_0, the value of $f(n)$ lies at or above $c_1 g(n)$ and at or below $c_2 g(n)$. In other words, for all $n \ge n_0$, the function $f(n)$ is equal to $g(n)$ to within a constant factor. We say that $g(n)$ is an *asymptotically tight bound* for $f(n)$.

The definition of $\Theta(g(n))$ requires that every member of $\Theta(g(n))$ be *asymptotically nonnegative*, that is, that $f(n)$ be nonnegative whenever n is sufficiently large. Consequently, the function $g(n)$ itself must be asymptotically nonnegative, or else the set $\Theta(g(n))$ is empty. We shall therefore assume that every function used within Θ-notation is asymptotically nonnegative. This assumption holds for the other asymptotic notations defined in this chapter as well.

In Chapter 1, we introduced an informal notion of Θ-notation that amounted to throwing away lower-order terms and ignoring the leading coefficient of the highest-order term. Let us briefly justify this intuition by using the formal definition to show that $\frac{1}{2}n^2 - 3n = \Theta(n^2)$. To do so, we must determine positive constants c_1, c_2, and n_0 such that

$$c_1 n^2 \le \frac{1}{2}n^2 - 3n \le c_2 n^2$$

for all $n \ge n_0$. Dividing by n^2 yields

$$c_1 \le \frac{1}{2} - \frac{3}{n} \le c_2 .$$

The right-hand inequality can be made to hold for any value of $n \ge 1$ by choosing $c_2 \ge 1/2$. Likewise, the left-hand inequality can be made to hold for any value of $n \ge 7$ by choosing $c_1 \le 1/14$. Thus, by choosing

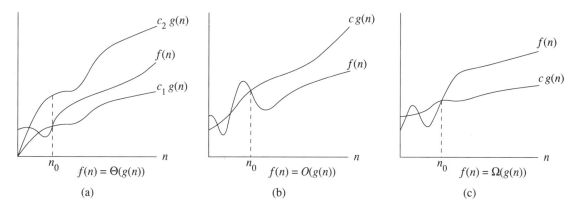

Figure 2.1   Graphic examples of the Θ, O, and Ω notations. In each part, the value of n_0 shown is the minimum possible value; any greater value would also work. **(a)** Θ-notation bounds a function to within constant factors. We write $f(n) = \Theta(g(n))$ if there exist positive constants n_0, c_1, and c_2 such that to the right of n_0, the value of $f(n)$ always lies between $c_1 g(n)$ and $c_2 g(n)$ inclusive. **(b)** O-notation gives an upper bound for a function to within a constant factor. We write $f(n) = O(g(n))$ if there are positive constants n_0 and c such that to the right of n_0, the value of $f(n)$ always lies on or below $cg(n)$. **(c)** Ω-notation gives a lower bound for a function to within a constant factor. We write $f(n) = \Omega(g(n))$ if there are positive constants n_0 and c such that to the right of n_0, the value of $f(n)$ always lies on or above $cg(n)$.

$c_1 = 1/14$, $c_2 = 1/2$, and $n_0 = 7$, we can verify that $\frac{1}{2}n^2 - 3n = \Theta(n^2)$. Certainly, other choices for the constants exist, but the important thing is that some choice exists. Note that these constants depend on the function $\frac{1}{2}n^2 - 3n$; a different function belonging to $\Theta(n^2)$ would usually require different constants.

We can also use the formal definition to verify that $6n^3 \neq \Theta(n^2)$. Suppose for the purpose of contradiction that c_2 and n_0 exist such that $6n^3 \leq c_2 n^2$ for all $n \geq n_0$. But then $n \leq c_2/6$, which cannot possibly hold for arbitrarily large n, since c_2 is constant.

Intuitively, the lower-order terms of an asymptotically positive function can be ignored in determining asymptotically tight bounds because they are insignificant for large n. A tiny fraction of the highest-order term is enough to dominate the lower-order terms. Thus, setting c_1 to a value that is slightly smaller than the coefficient of the highest-order term and setting c_2 to a value that is slightly larger permits the inequalities in the definition of Θ-notation to be satisfied. The coefficient of the highest-order term can likewise be ignored, since it only changes c_1 and c_2 by a constant factor equal to the coefficient.

As an example, consider any quadratic function $f(n) = an^2 + bn + c$, where a, b, and c are constants and $a > 0$. Throwing away the lower-order terms and ignoring the constant yields $f(n) = \Theta(n^2)$. Formally, to show the same thing, we take the constants $c_1 = a/4$, $c_2 = 7a/4$, and

$n_0 = 2 \cdot \max((|b|/a), \sqrt{(|c|/a)})$. The reader may verify that $0 \le c_1 n^2 \le an^2 + bn + c \le c_2 n^2$ for all $n \ge n_0$. In general, for any polynomial $p(n) = \sum_{i=0}^{d} a_i n^i$, where the a_i are constants and $a_d > 0$, we have $p(n) = \Theta(n^d)$ (see Problem 2-1).

Since any constant is a degree-0 polynomial, we can express any constant function as $\Theta(n^0)$, or $\Theta(1)$. This latter notation is a minor abuse, however, because it is not clear what variable is tending to infinity.[1] We shall often use the notation $\Theta(1)$ to mean either a constant or a constant function with respect to some variable.

O-notation

The Θ-notation asymptotically bounds a function from above and below. When we have only an ***asymptotic upper bound***, we use O-notation. For a given function $g(n)$, we denote by $O(g(n))$ the set of functions

$$O(g(n)) = \{f(n) : \text{there exist positive constants } c \text{ and } n_0 \text{ such that}$$
$$0 \le f(n) \le cg(n) \text{ for all } n \ge n_0\} \,.$$

We use O-notation to give an upper bound on a function, to within a constant factor. Figure 2.1(b) shows the intuition behind O-notation. For all values n to the right of n_0, the value of the function $f(n)$ is on or below $g(n)$.

To indicate that a function $f(n)$ is a member of $O(g(n))$, we write $f(n) = O(g(n))$. Note that $f(n) = \Theta(g(n))$ implies $f(n) = O(g(n))$, since Θ-notation is a stronger notion than O-notation. Written set-theoretically, we have $\Theta(g(n)) \subseteq O(g(n))$. Thus, our proof that any quadratic function $an^2 + bn + c$, where $a > 0$, is in $\Theta(n^2)$ also shows that any quadratic function is in $O(n^2)$. What may be more surprising is that any *linear* function $an + b$ is in $O(n^2)$, which is easily verified by taking $c = a + |b|$ and $n_0 = 1$.

Some readers who have seen O-notation before may find it strange that we should write, for example, $n = O(n^2)$. In the literature, O-notation is sometimes used informally to describe asymptotically tight bounds, that is, what we have defined using Θ-notation. In this book, however, when we write $f(n) = O(g(n))$, we are merely claiming that some constant multiple of $g(n)$ is an asymptotic upper bound on $f(n)$, with no claim about how tight an upper bound it is. Distinguishing asymptotic upper bounds from asymptotically tight bounds has now become standard in the algorithms literature.

Using O-notation, we can often describe the running time of an algorithm merely by inspecting the algorithm's overall structure. For example,

---

[1]The real problem is that our ordinary notation for functions does not distinguish functions from values. In λ-calculus, the parameters to a function are clearly specified: the function n^2 could be written as $\lambda n.n^2$, or even $\lambda r.r^2$. Adopting a more rigorous notation, however, would complicate algebraic manipulations, and so we choose to tolerate the abuse.

the doubly nested loop structure of the insertion sort algorithm from Chapter 1 immediately yields an $O(n^2)$ upper bound on the worst-case running time: the cost of the inner loop is bounded from above by $O(1)$ (constant), the indices i and j are both at most n, and the inner loop is executed at most once for each of the n^2 pairs of values for i and j.

Since O-notation describes an upper bound, when we use it to bound the worst-case running time of an algorithm, by implication we also bound the running time of the algorithm on arbitrary inputs as well. Thus, the $O(n^2)$ bound on worst-case running time of insertion sort also applies to its running time on every input. The $\Theta(n^2)$ bound on the worst-case running time of insertion sort, however, does not imply a $\Theta(n^2)$ bound on the running time of insertion sort on *every* input. For example, we saw in Chapter 1 that when the input is already sorted, insertion sort runs in $\Theta(n)$ time.

Technically, it is an abuse to say that the running time of insertion sort is $O(n^2)$, since for a given n, the actual running time depends on the particular input of size n. That is, the running time is not really a function of n. What we mean when we say "the running time is $O(n^2)$" is that the worst-case running time (which is a function of n) is $O(n^2)$, or equivalently, no matter what particular input of size n is chosen for each value of n, the running time on that set of inputs is $O(n^2)$.

Ω-notation

Just as O-notation provides an asymptotic *upper* bound on a function, Ω-notation provides an ***asymptotic lower bound***. For a given function $g(n)$, we denote by $\Omega(g(n))$ the set of functions

$\Omega(g(n)) = \{f(n) :$ there exist positive constants c and n_0 such that $0 \le cg(n) \le f(n)$ for all $n \ge n_0\}$.

The intuition behind Ω-notation is shown in Figure 2.1(c). For all values n to the right of n_0, the value of $f(n)$ is on or above $g(n)$.

From the definitions of the asymptotic notations we have seen thus far, it is easy to prove the following important theorem (see Exercise 2.1-5).

Theorem 2.1
For any two functions $f(n)$ and $g(n)$, $f(n) = \Theta(g(n))$ if and only if $f(n) = O(g(n))$ and $f(n) = \Omega(g(n))$. ∎

As an example of the application of this theorem, our proof that $an^2 + bn + c = \Theta(n^2)$ for any constants a, b, and c, where $a > 0$, immediately implies that $an^2 + bn + c = \Omega(n^2)$ and $an^2 + bn + c = O(n^2)$. In practice, rather than using Theorem 2.1 to obtain asymptotic upper and lower bounds from asymptotically tight bounds, as we did for this example, we usually use it to prove asymptotically tight bounds from asymptotic upper and lower bounds.

Since Ω-notation describes a lower bound, when we use it to bound the best-case running time of an algorithm, by implication we also bound the running time of the algorithm on arbitrary inputs as well. For example, the best-case running time of insertion sort is $\Omega(n)$, which implies that the running time of insertion sort is $\Omega(n)$.

The running time of insertion sort therefore falls between $\Omega(n)$ and $O(n^2)$, since it falls anywhere between a linear function of n and a quadratic function of n. Moreover, these bounds are asymptotically as tight as possible: for instance, the running time of insertion sort is not $\Omega(n^2)$, since insertion sort runs in $\Theta(n)$ time when the input is already sorted. It is not contradictory, however, to say that the *worst-case* running time of insertion sort is $\Omega(n^2)$, since there exists an input that causes the algorithm to take $\Omega(n^2)$ time. When we say that the *running time* (no modifier) of an algorithm is $\Omega(g(n))$, we mean that *no matter what particular input of size n is chosen for each value of n*, the running time on that set of inputs is at least a constant times $g(n)$, for sufficiently large n.

Asymptotic notation in equations

We have already seen how asymptotic notation can be used within mathematical formulas. For example, in introducing O-notation, we wrote "$n = O(n^2)$." We might also write $2n^2 + 3n + 1 = 2n^2 + \Theta(n)$. How do we interpret such formulas?

When the asymptotic notation stands alone on the right-hand side of an equation, as in $n = O(n^2)$, we have already defined the equal sign to mean set membership: $n \in O(n^2)$. In general, however, when asymptotic notation appears in a formula, we interpret it as standing for some anonymous function that we do not care to name. For example, the formula $2n^2 + 3n + 1 = 2n^2 + \Theta(n)$ means that $2n^2 + 3n + 1 = 2n^2 + f(n)$, where $f(n)$ is some function in the set $\Theta(n)$. In this case, $f(n) = 3n + 1$, which indeed is in $\Theta(n)$.

Using asymptotic notation in this manner can help eliminate inessential detail and clutter in an equation. For example, in Chapter 1 we expressed the worst-case running time of merge sort as the recurrence

$$T(n) = 2T(n/2) + \Theta(n) .$$

If we are interested only in the asymptotic behavior of $T(n)$, there is no point in specifying all the lower-order terms exactly; they are all understood to be included in the anonymous function denoted by the term $\Theta(n)$.

The number of anonymous functions in an expression is understood to be equal to the number of times the asymptotic notation appears. For example, in the expression

$$\sum_{i=1}^{n} O(i) \; ,$$

there is only a single anonymous function (a function of i). This expression is thus *not* the same as $O(1) + O(2) + \cdots + O(n)$, which doesn't really have a clean interpretation.

In some cases, asymptotic notation appears on the left-hand side of an equation, as in

$$2n^2 + \Theta(n) = \Theta(n^2) \; .$$

We interpret such equations using the following rule: *No matter how the anonymous functions are chosen on the left of the equal sign, there is a way to choose the anonymous functions on the right of the equal sign to make the equation valid.* Thus, the meaning of our example is that for *any* function $f(n) \in \Theta(n)$, there is *some* function $g(n) \in \Theta(n^2)$ such that $2n^2 + f(n) = g(n)$ for all n. In other words, the right-hand side of an equation provides coarser level of detail than the left-hand side.

A number of such relationships can be chained together, as in

$$
\begin{aligned}
2n^2 + 3n + 1 &= 2n^2 + \Theta(n) \\
&= \Theta(n^2) \; .
\end{aligned}
$$

We can interpret each equation separately by the rule above. The first equation says that there is *some* function $f(n) \in \Theta(n)$ such that $2n^2 + 3n + 1 = 2n^2 + f(n)$ for all n. The second equation says that for *any* function $g(n) \in \Theta(n)$ (such as the $f(n)$ just mentioned), there is *some* function $h(n) \in \Theta(n^2)$ such that $2n^2 + g(n) = h(n)$ for all n. Note that this interpretation implies that $2n^2 + 3n + 1 = \Theta(n^2)$, which is what the chaining of equations intuitively gives us.

o-notation

The asymptotic upper bound provided by O-notation may or may not be asymptotically tight. The bound $2n^2 = O(n^2)$ is asymptotically tight, but the bound $2n = O(n^2)$ is not. We use o-notation to denote an upper bound that is not asymptotically tight. We formally define $o(g(n))$ ("little-oh of g of n") as the set

$$o(g(n)) = \{ f(n) : \text{for any positive constant } c > 0, \text{ there exists a constant} \\ n_0 > 0 \text{ such that } 0 \le f(n) < cg(n) \text{ for all } n \ge n_0 \} \; .$$

For example, $2n = o(n^2)$, but $2n^2 \ne o(n^2)$.

The definitions of O-notation and o-notation are similar. The main difference is that in $f(n) = O(g(n))$, the bound $0 \le f(n) \le cg(n)$ holds for *some* constant $c > 0$, but in $f(n) = o(g(n))$, the bound $0 \le f(n) < cg(n)$ holds for *all* constants $c > 0$. Intuitively, in the o-notation, the function $f(n)$ becomes insignificant relative to $g(n)$ as n approaches infinity; that is,

$$\lim_{n \to \infty} \frac{f(n)}{g(n)} = 0 \ . \tag{2.1}$$

Some authors use this limit as a definition of the o-notation; the definition in this book also restricts the anonymous functions to be asymptotically nonnegative.

ω-notation

By analogy, ω-notation is to Ω-notation as o-notation is to O-notation. We use ω-notation to denote a lower bound that is not asymptotically tight. One way to define it is by

$f(n) \in \omega(g(n))$ if and only if $g(n) \in o(f(n))$.

Formally, however, we define $\omega(g(n))$ ("little-omega of g of n") as the set

$$\omega(g(n)) = \{f(n) : \text{for any positive constant } c > 0, \text{ there exists a constant} \\ n_0 > 0 \text{ such that } 0 \leq cg(n) < f(n) \text{ for all } n \geq n_0\} \ .$$

For example, $n^2/2 = \omega(n)$, but $n^2/2 \neq \omega(n^2)$. The relation $f(n) = \omega(g(n))$ implies that

$$\lim_{n \to \infty} \frac{f(n)}{g(n)} = \infty \ ,$$

if the limit exists. That is, $f(n)$ becomes arbitrarily large relative to $g(n)$ as n approaches infinity.

Comparison of functions

Many of the relational properties of real numbers apply to asymptotic comparisons as well. For the following, assume that $f(n)$ and $g(n)$ are asymptotically positive.

Transitivity:

$$f(n) = \Theta(g(n)) \quad \text{and} \quad g(n) = \Theta(h(n)) \quad \text{imply} \quad f(n) = \Theta(h(n)) \ ,$$
$$f(n) = O(g(n)) \quad \text{and} \quad g(n) = O(h(n)) \quad \text{imply} \quad f(n) = O(h(n)) \ ,$$
$$f(n) = \Omega(g(n)) \quad \text{and} \quad g(n) = \Omega(h(n)) \quad \text{imply} \quad f(n) = \Omega(h(n)) \ ,$$
$$f(n) = o(g(n)) \quad \text{and} \quad g(n) = o(h(n)) \quad \text{imply} \quad f(n) = o(h(n)) \ ,$$
$$f(n) = \omega(g(n)) \quad \text{and} \quad g(n) = \omega(h(n)) \quad \text{imply} \quad f(n) = \omega(h(n)) \ .$$

Reflexivity:

$$f(n) = \Theta(f(n)) \ ,$$
$$f(n) = O(f(n)) \ ,$$
$$f(n) = \Omega(f(n)) \ .$$

Symmetry:

$$f(n) = \Theta(g(n)) \quad \text{if and only if} \quad g(n) = \Theta(f(n)) \ .$$

Transpose symmetry:

$f(n) = O(g(n))$ if and only if $g(n) = \Omega(f(n))$,

$f(n) = o(g(n))$ if and only if $g(n) = \omega(f(n))$.

Because these properties hold for asymptotic notations, one can draw an analogy between the asymptotic comparison of two functions f and g and the comparison of two real numbers a and b:

$$f(n) = O(g(n)) \approx a \le b,$$
$$f(n) = \Omega(g(n)) \approx a \ge b,$$
$$f(n) = \Theta(g(n)) \approx a = b,$$
$$f(n) = o(g(n)) \approx a < b,$$
$$f(n) = \omega(g(n)) \approx a > b.$$

One property of real numbers, however, does not carry over to asymptotic notation:

Trichotomy: For any two real numbers a and b, exactly one of the following must hold: $a < b$, $a = b$, or $a > b$.

Although any two real numbers can be compared, not all functions are asymptotically comparable. That is, for two functions $f(n)$ and $g(n)$, it may be the case that neither $f(n) = O(g(n))$ nor $f(n) = \Omega(g(n))$ holds. For example, the functions n and $n^{1+\sin n}$ cannot be compared using asymptotic notation, since the value of the exponent in $n^{1+\sin n}$ oscillates between 0 and 2, taking on all values in between.

Exercises

2.1-1
Let $f(n)$ and $g(n)$ be asymptotically nonnegative functions. Using the basic definition of Θ-notation, prove that $\max(f(n), g(n)) = \Theta(f(n) + g(n))$.

2.1-2
Show that for any real constants a and b, where $b > 0$,

$$(n + a)^b = \Theta(n^b).\tag{2.2}$$

2.1-3
Explain why the statement, "The running time of algorithm A is at least $O(n^2)$," is content-free.

2.1-4
Is $2^{n+1} = O(2^n)$? Is $2^{2n} = O(2^n)$?

2.1-5
Prove Theorem 2.1.

2.1-6
Prove that the running time of an algorithm is $\Theta(g(n))$ if and only if its worst-case running time is $O(g(n))$ and its best-case running time is $\Omega(g(n))$.

2.1-7
Prove that $o(g(n)) \cap \omega(g(n))$ is the empty set.

2.1-8
We can extend our notation to the case of two parameters n and m that can go to infinity independently at different rates. For a given function $g(n, m)$, we denote by $O(g(n, m))$ the set of functions

$$O(g(n,m)) = \{f(n,m) : \text{there exist positive constants } c, n_0, \text{ and } m_0$$
$$\text{such that } 0 \le f(n,m) \le cg(n,m)$$
$$\text{for all } n \ge n_0 \text{ and } m \ge m_0\} \, .$$

Give corresponding definitions for $\Omega(g(n, m))$ and $\Theta(g(n, m))$.

2.2   Standard notations and common functions

This section reviews some standard mathematical functions and notations and explores the relationships among them. It also illustrates the use of the asymptotic notations.

Monotonicity

A function $f(n)$ is *monotonically increasing* if $m \le n$ implies $f(m) \le f(n)$. Similarly, it is *monotonically decreasing* if $m \le n$ implies $f(m) \ge f(n)$. A function $f(n)$ is *strictly increasing* if $m < n$ implies $f(m) < f(n)$ and *strictly decreasing* if $m < n$ implies $f(m) > f(n)$.

Floors and ceilings

For any real number x, we denote the greatest integer less than or equal to x by $\lfloor x \rfloor$ (read "the floor of x") and the least integer greater than or equal to x by $\lceil x \rceil$ (read "the ceiling of x"). For all real x,

$$x - 1 < \lfloor x \rfloor \le x \le \lceil x \rceil < x + 1 \, .$$

For any integer n,

$$\lceil n/2 \rceil + \lfloor n/2 \rfloor = n \, ,$$

and for any integer n and integers $a \ne 0$ and $b \ne 0$,

$$\lceil \lceil n/a \rceil / b \rceil = \lceil n/ab \rceil \tag{2.3}$$

and

$$\lfloor \lfloor n/a \rfloor /b \rfloor = \lfloor n/ab \rfloor \ . \qquad (2.4)$$

The floor and ceiling functions are monotonically increasing.

Polynomials

Given a positive integer d, a *polynomial in n of degree d* is a function $p(n)$ of the form

$$p(n) = \sum_{i=0}^{d} a_i n^i \ ,$$

where the constants $a_0, a_1, \ldots, a_d$ are the *coefficients* of the polynomial and $a_d \neq 0$. A polynomial is *asymptotically positive* if and only if $a_d > 0$. For an asymptotically positive polynomial $p(n)$ of degree d, we have $p(n) = \Theta(n^d)$. For any real constant $a \geq 0$, the function n^a is monotonically increasing, and for any real constant $a \leq 0$, the function n^a is monotonically decreasing. We say that a function $f(n)$ is *polynomially bounded* if $f(n) = n^{O(1)}$, which is equivalent to saying that $f(n) = O(n^k)$ for some constant k (see Exercise 2.2-2).

Exponentials

For all real $a \neq 0$, m, and n, we have the following identities:

$$
\begin{aligned}
a^0 &= 1 \ , \\
a^1 &= a \ , \\
a^{-1} &= 1/a \ , \\
(a^m)^n &= a^{mn} \ , \\
(a^m)^n &= (a^n)^m \ , \\
a^m a^n &= a^{m+n} \ .
\end{aligned}
$$

For all n and $a \geq 1$, the function a^n is monotonically increasing in n. When convenient, we shall assume $0^0 = 1$.

The rates of growth of polynomials and exponentials can be related by the following fact. For all real constants a and b such that $a > 1$,

$$\lim_{n \to \infty} \frac{n^b}{a^n} = 0 \ , \qquad (2.5)$$

from which we can conclude that

$$n^b = o(a^n) \ .$$

Thus, any positive exponential function grows faster than any polynomial.

Using e to denote $2.71828\ldots$, the base of the natural logarithm function, we have for all real x,

$$e^x = 1 + x + \frac{x^2}{2!} + \frac{x^3}{3!} + \cdots = \sum_{i=0}^{\infty} \frac{x^i}{i!} \, , \tag{2.6}$$

where "!" denotes the factorial function defined later in this section. For all real x, we have the inequality

$$e^x \geq 1 + x \, , \tag{2.7}$$

where equality holds only when $x = 0$. When $|x| \leq 1$, we have the approximation

$$1 + x \leq e^x \leq 1 + x + x^2 \, . \tag{2.8}$$

When $x \to 0$, the approximation of e^x by $1 + x$ is quite good:

$$e^x = 1 + x + \Theta(x^2) \, .$$

(In this equation, the asymptotic notation is used to describe the limiting behavior as $x \to 0$ rather than as $x \to \infty$.) We have for all x,

$$\lim_{n \to \infty} \left(1 + \frac{x}{n}\right)^n = e^x \, .$$

Logarithms

We shall use the following notations:

$$
\begin{aligned}
\lg n &= \log_2 n && \text{(binary logarithm)} \, , \\
\ln n &= \log_e n && \text{(natural logarithm)} \, , \\
\lg^k n &= (\lg n)^k && \text{(exponentiation)} \, , \\
\lg \lg n &= \lg(\lg n) && \text{(composition)} \, .
\end{aligned}
$$

An important notational convention we shall adopt is that *logarithm functions will apply only to the next term in the formula*, so that $\lg n + k$ will mean $(\lg n) + k$ and not $\lg(n + k)$. For $n > 0$ and $b > 1$, the function $\log_b n$ is strictly increasing.

For all real $a > 0$, $b > 0$, $c > 0$, and n,

$$
\begin{aligned}
a &= b^{\log_b a} \, , \\
\log_c(ab) &= \log_c a + \log_c b \, , \\
\log_b a^n &= n \log_b a \, , \\
\log_b a &= \frac{\log_c a}{\log_c b} \, , \\
\log_b(1/a) &= -\log_b a \, , \\
\log_b a &= \frac{1}{\log_a b} \, , \\
a^{\log_b n} &= n^{\log_b a} \, . \tag{2.9}
\end{aligned}
$$

Since changing the base of a logarithm from one constant to another only changes the value of the logarithm by a constant factor, we shall often use the notation "lg n" when we don't care about constant factors, such as in O-notation. Computer scientists find 2 to be the most natural base for logarithms because so many algorithms and data structures involve splitting a problem into two parts.

There is a simple series expansion for $\ln(1 + x)$ when $|x| < 1$:

$$\ln(1 + x) = x - \frac{x^2}{2} + \frac{x^3}{3} - \frac{x^4}{4} + \frac{x^5}{5} - \cdots .$$

We also have the following inequalities for $x > -1$:

$$\frac{x}{1 + x} \leq \ln(1 + x) \leq x , \tag{2.10}$$

where equality holds only for $x = 0$.

We say that a function $f(n)$ is **polylogarithmically bounded** if $f(n) = \lg^{O(1)} n$. We can relate the growth of polynomials and polylogarithms by substituting $\lg n$ for n and 2^a for a in equation (2.5), yielding

$$\lim_{n \to \infty} \frac{\lg^b n}{2^{a \lg n}} = \lim_{n \to \infty} \frac{\lg^b n}{n^a} = 0 .$$

From this limit, we can conclude that

$$\lg^b n = o(n^a)$$

for any constant $a > 0$. Thus, any positive polynomial function grows faster than any polylogarithmic function.

Factorials

The notation $n!$ (read "n factorial") is defined for integers $n \geq 0$ as

$$n! = \begin{cases} 1 & \text{if } n = 0 , \\ n \cdot (n - 1)! & \text{if } n > 0 . \end{cases}$$

Thus, $n! = 1 \cdot 2 \cdot 3 \cdots n$.

A weak upper bound on the factorial function is $n! \leq n^n$, since each of the n terms in the factorial product is at most n. **Stirling's approximation**,

$$n! = \sqrt{2\pi n} \left(\frac{n}{e} \right)^n \left(1 + \Theta \left(\frac{1}{n} \right) \right) , \tag{2.11}$$

where e is the base of the natural logarithm, gives us a tighter upper bound, and a lower bound as well. Using Stirling's approximation, one can prove

$$\begin{aligned} n! &= o(n^n) , \\ n! &= \omega(2^n) , \\ \lg(n!) &= \Theta(n \lg n) . \end{aligned}$$

The following bounds also hold for all n:

$$\sqrt{2\pi n} \left(\frac{n}{e} \right)^n \leq n! \leq \sqrt{2\pi n} \left(\frac{n}{e} \right)^{n+(1/12n)} \tag{2.12}$$

The iterated logarithm function

We use the notation $\lg^* n$ (read "log star of n") to denote the iterated logarithm, which is defined as follows. Let the function $\lg^{(i)} n$ be defined recursively for nonnegative integers i as

$$\lg^{(i)} n = \begin{cases} n & \text{if } i = 0, \\ \lg(\lg^{(i-1)} n) & \text{if } i > 0 \text{ and } \lg^{(i-1)} n > 0, \\ \text{undefined} & \text{if } i > 0 \text{ and } \lg^{(i-1)} n \leq 0 \text{ or } \lg^{(i-1)} n \text{ is undefined}. \end{cases}$$

Be sure to distinguish $\lg^{(i)} n$ (the logarithm function applied i times in succession, starting with argument n) from $\lg^i n$ (the logarithm of n raised to the ith power). The iterated logarithm function is defined as

$$\lg^* n = \min \left\{ i \geq 0 : \lg^{(i)} n \leq 1 \right\}.$$

The iterated logarithm is a *very* slowly growing function:

$$\begin{aligned} \lg^* 2 &= 1, \\ \lg^* 4 &= 2, \\ \lg^* 16 &= 3, \\ \lg^* 65536 &= 4, \\ \lg^* (2^{65536}) &= 5. \end{aligned}$$

Since the number of atoms in the observable universe is estimated to be about 10^{80}, which is much less than 2^{65536}, we rarely encounter a value of n such that $\lg^* n > 5$.

Fibonacci numbers

The *Fibonacci numbers* are defined by the following recurrence:

$$\begin{aligned} F_0 &= 0, \\ F_1 &= 1, \\ F_i &= F_{i-1} + F_{i-2} \qquad \text{for } i \geq 2. \end{aligned} \tag{2.13}$$

Thus, each Fibonacci number is the sum of the two previous ones, yielding the sequence

$$0, 1, 1, 2, 3, 5, 8, 13, 21, 34, 55, \ldots.$$

Fibonacci numbers are related to the *golden ratio* ϕ and to its conjugate $\widehat{\phi}$, which are given by the following formulas:

$$\begin{aligned} \phi &= \frac{1 + \sqrt{5}}{2} \\ &= 1.61803\ldots, \\ \widehat{\phi} &= \frac{1 - \sqrt{5}}{2} \\ &= -.61803\ldots. \end{aligned} \tag{2.14}$$

Specifically, we have

$$F_i = \frac{\phi^i - \widehat{\phi}^i}{\sqrt{5}} \, , \tag{2.15}$$

which can be proved by induction (Exercise 2.2-7). Since $|\widehat{\phi}| < 1$, we have $|\widehat{\phi}^i|/\sqrt{5} < 1/\sqrt{5} < 1/2$, so that the ith Fibonacci number F_i is equal to $\phi^i/\sqrt{5}$ rounded to the nearest integer. Thus, Fibonacci numbers grow exponentially.

Exercises

2.2-1
Show that if $f(n)$ and $g(n)$ are monotonically increasing functions, then so are the functions $f(n) + g(n)$ and $f(g(n))$, and if $f(n)$ and $g(n)$ are in addition nonnegative, then $f(n) \cdot g(n)$ is monotonically increasing.

2.2-2
Use the definition of O-notation to show that $T(n) = n^{O(1)}$ if and only if there exists a constant $k > 0$ such that $T(n) = O(n^k)$.

2.2-3
Prove equation (2.9).

2.2-4
Prove that $\lg(n!) = \Theta(n \lg n)$ and that $n! = o(n^n)$.

2.2-5 ⋆
Is the function $\lceil \lg n \rceil!$ polynomially bounded? Is the function $\lceil \lg \lg n \rceil!$ polynomially bounded?

2.2-6 ⋆
Which is asymptotically larger: $\lg(\lg^* n)$ or $\lg^*(\lg n)$?

2.2-7
Prove by induction that the ith Fibonacci number satisfies the equality $F_i = (\phi^i - \widehat{\phi}^i)/\sqrt{5}$, where ϕ is the golden ratio and $\widehat{\phi}$ is its conjugate.

2.2-8
Prove that for $i \geq 0$, the $(i+2)$nd Fibonacci number satisfies $F_{i+2} \geq \phi^i$.

Problems

2-1 Asymptotic behavior of polynomials
Let

$$p(n) = \sum_{i=0}^{d} a_i n^i ,$$

where $a_d > 0$, be a degree-d polynomial in n, and let k be a constant. Use the definitions of the asymptotic notations to prove the following properties.

a. If $k \geq d$, then $p(n) = O(n^k)$.

b. If $k \leq d$, then $p(n) = \Omega(n^k)$.

c. If $k = d$, then $p(n) = \Theta(n^k)$.

d. If $k > d$, then $p(n) = o(n^k)$.

e. If $k < d$, then $p(n) = \omega(n^k)$.

2-2 Relative asymptotic growths
Indicate, for each pair of expressions (A, B) in the table below, whether A is O, o, Ω, ω, or Θ of B. Assume that $k \geq 1$, $\epsilon > 0$, and $c > 1$ are constants. Your answer should be in the form of the table with "yes" or "no" written in each box.

	A	B	O	o	Ω	ω	Θ
a.	$\lg^k n$	n^ϵ					
b.	n^k	c^n					
c.	$\sqrt{n}$	$n^{\sin n}$					
d.	2^n	$2^{n/2}$					
e.	$n^{\lg m}$	$m^{\lg n}$					
f.	$\lg(n!)$	$\lg(n^n)$					

2-3 Ordering by asymptotic growth rates
a. Rank the following functions by order of growth; that is, find an arrangement $g_1, g_2, \ldots, g_{30}$ of the functions satisfying $g_1 = \Omega(g_2)$, $g_2 = \Omega(g_3)$, $\ldots$, $g_{29} = \Omega(g_{30})$. Partition your list into equivalence classes such that $f(n)$ and $g(n)$ are in the same class if and only if $f(n) = \Theta(g(n))$.

$$\lg(\lg^* n) \quad 2^{\lg^* n} \quad (\sqrt{2})^{\lg n} \quad n^2 \quad n! \quad (\lg n)!$$

$$(\tfrac{3}{2})^n \quad n^3 \quad \lg^2 n \quad \lg(n!) \quad 2^{2^n} \quad n^{1/\lg n}$$

$$\ln\ln n \quad \lg^* n \quad n \cdot 2^n \quad n^{\lg \lg n} \quad \ln n \quad 1$$

$$2^{\lg n} \quad (\lg n)^{\lg n} \quad e^n \quad 4^{\lg n} \quad (n+1)! \quad \sqrt{\lg n}$$

$$\lg^*(\lg n) \quad 2^{\sqrt{2 \lg n}} \quad n \quad 2^n \quad n \lg n \quad 2^{2^{n+1}}$$

b. Give an example of a single nonnegative function $f(n)$ such that for all functions $g_i(n)$ in part (a), $f(n)$ is neither $O(g_i(n))$ nor $\Omega(g_i(n))$.

2-4 *Asymptotic notation properties*

Let $f(n)$ and $g(n)$ be asymptotically positive functions. Prove or disprove each of the following conjectures.

a. $f(n) = O(g(n))$ implies $g(n) = O(f(n))$.

b. $f(n) + g(n) = \Theta(\min(f(n), g(n)))$.

c. $f(n) = O(g(n))$ implies $\lg(f(n)) = O(\lg(g(n)))$, where $\lg(g(n)) > 0$ and $f(n) \geq 1$ for all sufficiently large n.

d. $f(n) = O(g(n))$ implies $2^{f(n)} = O\left(2^{g(n)}\right)$.

e. $f(n) = O\left((f(n))^2\right)$.

f. $f(n) = O(g(n))$ implies $g(n) = \Omega(f(n))$.

g. $f(n) = \Theta(f(n/2))$.

h. $f(n) + o(f(n)) = \Theta(f(n))$.

2-5 *Variations on O and Ω*

Some authors define Ω in a slightly different way than we do; let's use $\overset{\infty}{\Omega}$ (read "omega infinity") for this alternative definition. We say that $f(n) = \overset{\infty}{\Omega}(g(n))$ if there exists a positive constant c such that $f(n) \geq cg(n) \geq 0$ for infinitely many integers n.

a. Show that for any two functions $f(n)$ and $g(n)$ that are asymptotically nonnegative, either $f(n) = O(g(n))$ or $f(n) = \overset{\infty}{\Omega}(g(n))$ or both, whereas this is not true if we use Ω in place of $\overset{\infty}{\Omega}$.

b. Describe the potential advantages and disadvantages of using $\overset{\infty}{\Omega}$ instead of Ω to characterize the running times of programs.

Some authors also define O in a slightly different manner; let's use O' for the alternative definition. We say that $f(n) = O'(g(n))$ if and only if $|f(n)| = O(g(n))$.

c. What happens to each direction of the "if and only if" in Theorem 2.1 under this new definition?

Some authors define $\widetilde{O}$ (read "soft-oh") to mean O with logarithmic factors ignored:

$$\widetilde{O}(g(n)) = \{f(n) : \text{there exist positive constants } c, k, \text{ and } n_0 \text{ such that} \\ 0 \le f(n) \le cg(n)\lg^k(n) \text{ for all } n \ge n_0\} \ .$$

d. Define $\widetilde{\Omega}$ and $\widetilde{\Theta}$ in a similar manner. Prove the corresponding analog to Theorem 2.1.

2-6 *Iterated functions*

The iteration operator "∗" used in the $\lg^*$ function can be applied to monotonically increasing functions over the reals. For a function f satisfying $f(n) < n$, we define the function $f^{(i)}$ recursively for nonnegative integers i by

$$f^{(i)}(n) = \begin{cases} f(f^{(i-1)}(n)) & \text{if } i > 0 \ , \\ n & \text{if } i = 0 \ . \end{cases}$$

For a given constant $c \in \mathbf{R}$, we define the iterated function f_c^* by

$$f_c^*(n) = \min\left\{i \ge 0 : f^{(i)}(n) \le c\right\} \ ,$$

which need not be well-defined in all cases. In other words, the quantity $f_c^*(n)$ is the number of iterated applications of the function f required to reduce its argument down to c or less.

For each of the following functions $f(n)$ and constants c, give as tight a bound as possible on $f_c^*(n)$.

	$f(n)$	c	$f_c^*(n)$
a.	$\lg n$	1	
b.	$n - 1$	0	
c.	$n/2$	1	
d.	$n/2$	2	
e.	$\sqrt{n}$	2	
f.	$\sqrt{n}$	1	
g.	$n^{1/3}$	2	
h.	$n/\lg n$	2	

Chapter notes

Knuth [121] traces the origin of the O-notation to a number-theory text by P. Bachmann in 1892. The o-notation was invented by E. Landau in 1909 for his discussion of the distribution of prime numbers. The Ω and Θ notations were advocated by Knuth [124] to correct the popular, but technically sloppy, practice in the literature of using O-notation for both upper and lower bounds. Many people continue to use the *O*-notation where the Θ-notation is more technically precise. Further discussion of the history and development of asymptotic notations can be found in Knuth [121, 124] and Brassard and Bratley [33].

Not all authors define the asymptotic notations in the same way, although the various definitions agree in most common situations. Some of the alternative definitions encompass functions that are not asymptotically nonnegative, as long as their absolute values are appropriately bounded.

Other properties of elementary mathematical functions can be found in any good mathematical reference, such as Abramowitz and Stegun [1] or Beyer [27], or in a calculus book, such as Apostol [12] or Thomas and Finney [192]. Knuth [121] contains a wealth of material on discrete mathematics as used in computer science.

3 Summations

When an algorithm contains an iterative control construct such as a **while** or **for** loop, its running time can be expressed as the sum of the times spent on each execution of the body of the loop. For example, we found in Section 1.2 that the jth iteration of insertion sort took time proportional to j in the worst case. By adding up the time spent on each iteration, we obtained the summation (or series)

$$\sum_{j=2}^{n} j .$$

Evaluating this summation yielded a bound of $\Theta(n^2)$ on the worst-case running time of the algorithm. This example indicates the general importance of understanding how to manipulate and bound summations. (As we shall see in Chapter 4, summations also arise when we use certain methods to solve recurrences.)

Section 3.1 lists several basic formulas involving summations. Section 3.2 offers useful techniques for bounding summations. The formulas in Section 3.1 are given without proof, though proofs for some of them are presented in Section 3.2 to illustrate the methods of that section. Most of the other proofs can be found in any calculus text.

3.1 Summation formulas and properties

Given a sequence $a_1, a_2, \ldots$ of numbers, the finite sum $a_1 + a_2 + \cdots + a_n$ can be written

$$\sum_{k=1}^{n} a_k .$$

If $n = 0$, the value of the summation is defined to be 0. If n is not an integer, we assume that the upper limit is $\lfloor n \rfloor$. Similarly, if the sum begins with $k = x$, where x is not an integer, we assume that the initial value for the summation is $\lceil x \rceil$. (Generally, we shall put in floors and ceilings explicitly.) The value of a finite series is always well defined, and its terms can be added in any order.

Given a sequence $a_1, a_2, \ldots$ of numbers, the infinite sum $a_1 + a_2 + \cdots$ can be written

$$\sum_{k=1}^{\infty} a_k \, ,$$

which is interpreted to mean

$$\lim_{n \to \infty} \sum_{k=1}^{n} a_k \, .$$

If the limit does not exist, the series **diverges**; otherwise, it **converges**. The terms of a convergent series cannot always be added in any order. We can, however, rearrange the terms of an **absolutely convergent series**, that is, a series $\sum_{k=1}^{\infty} a_k$ for which the series $\sum_{k=1}^{\infty} |a_k|$ also converges.

Linearity

For any real number c and any finite sequences $a_1, a_2, \ldots, a_n$ and $b_1, b_2, \ldots, b_n$,

$$\sum_{k=1}^{n} (c a_k + b_k) = c \sum_{k=1}^{n} a_k + \sum_{k=1}^{n} b_k \, .$$

The linearity property is also obeyed by infinite convergent series.

The linearity property can be exploited to manipulate summations incorporating asymptotic notation. For example,

$$\sum_{k=1}^{n} \Theta(f(k)) = \Theta\left(\sum_{k=1}^{n} f(k)\right) \, .$$

In this equation, the Θ-notation on the left-hand side applies to the variable k, but on the right-hand side, it applies to n. Such manipulations can also be applied to infinite convergent series.

Arithmetic series

The summation

$$\sum_{k=1}^{n} k = 1 + 2 + \cdots + n \, ,$$

which came up when we analyzed insertion sort, is an **arithmetic series** and has the value

$$\sum_{k=1}^{n} k \;=\; \frac{1}{2} n(n+1) \tag{3.1}$$

$$\;=\; \Theta(n^2) \, . \tag{3.2}$$

Geometric series

For real $x \neq 1$, the summation

$$\sum_{k=0}^{n} x^k = 1 + x + x^2 + \cdots + x^n$$

is a **geometric** or **exponential series** and has the value

$$\sum_{k=0}^{n} x^k = \frac{x^{n+1} - 1}{x - 1} . \tag{3.3}$$

When the summation is infinite and $|x| < 1$, we have the infinite decreasing geometric series

$$\sum_{k=0}^{\infty} x^k = \frac{1}{1 - x} . \tag{3.4}$$

Harmonic series

For positive integers n, the nth **harmonic number** is

$$
\begin{aligned}
H_n &= 1 + \frac{1}{2} + \frac{1}{3} + \frac{1}{4} + \cdots + \frac{1}{n} \\
&= \sum_{k=1}^{n} \frac{1}{k} \\
&= \ln n + O(1) .
\end{aligned}
\tag{3.5}
$$

Integrating and differentiating series

Additional formulas can be obtained by integrating or differentiating the formulas above. For example, by differentiating both sides of the infinite geometric series (3.4) and multiplying by x, we get

$$\sum_{k=0}^{\infty} k x^k = \frac{x}{(1 - x)^2} . \tag{3.6}$$

Telescoping series

For any sequence $a_0, a_1, \ldots, a_n$,

$$\sum_{k=1}^{n} (a_k - a_{k-1}) = a_n - a_0 , \tag{3.7}$$

since each of the terms $a_1, a_2, \ldots, a_{n-1}$ is added in exactly once and subtracted out exactly once. We say that the sum **telescopes**. Similarly,

$$\sum_{k=0}^{n-1} (a_k - a_{k+1}) = a_0 - a_n .$$

As an example of a telescoping sum, consider the series

$$\sum_{k=1}^{n-1} \frac{1}{k(k+1)} .$$

Since we can rewrite each term as

$$\frac{1}{k(k+1)} = \frac{1}{k} - \frac{1}{k+1} ,$$

we get

$$\begin{aligned}
\sum_{k=1}^{n-1} \frac{1}{k(k+1)} &= \sum_{k=1}^{n-1} \left(\frac{1}{k} - \frac{1}{k+1} \right) \\
&= 1 - \frac{1}{n} .
\end{aligned}$$

Products

The finite product $a_1 a_2 \cdots a_n$ can be written

$$\prod_{k=1}^{n} a_k .$$

If $n = 0$, the value of the product is defined to be 1. We can convert a formula with a product to a formula with a summation by using the identity

$$\lg \left(\prod_{k=1}^{n} a_k \right) = \sum_{k=1}^{n} \lg a_k .$$

Exercises

3.1-1
Find a simple formula for $\sum_{k=1}^{n} (2k-1)$.

3.1-2 $\star$
Show that $\sum_{k=1}^{n} 1/(2k-1) = \ln(\sqrt{n}) + O(1)$ by manipulating the harmonic series.

3.1-3 $\star$
Show that $\sum_{k=0}^{\infty} (k-1)/2^k = 0$.

3.1-4 $\star$
Evaluate the sum $\sum_{k=1}^{\infty} (2k+1)x^{2k}$.

3.1-5
Use the linearity property of summations to prove that $\sum_{k=1}^{n} O(f_k(n)) = O(\sum_{k=1}^{n} f_k(n))$.

3.1-6
Prove that $\sum_{k=1}^{\infty} \Omega(f(k)) = \Omega\left(\sum_{k=1}^{\infty} f(k)\right)$.

3.1-7
Evaluate the product $\prod_{k=1}^{n} 2 \cdot 4^k$.

3.1-8 $\star$
Evaluate the product $\prod_{k=2}^{n}(1 - 1/k^2)$.

3.2   Bounding summations

There are many techniques available for bounding the summations that describe the running times of algorithms. Here are some of the most frequently used methods.

Mathematical induction

The most basic way to evaluate a series is to use mathematical induction. As an example, let us prove that the arithmetic series $\sum_{k=1}^{n} k$ evaluates to $\frac{1}{2}n(n+1)$. We can easily verify this for $n = 1$, so we make the inductive assumption that it holds for n and prove that it holds for $n + 1$. We have

$$
\begin{aligned}
\sum_{k=1}^{n+1} k &= \sum_{k=1}^{n} k + (n+1) \\
&= \frac{1}{2}n(n+1) + (n+1) \\
&= \frac{1}{2}(n+1)(n+2) .
\end{aligned}
$$

One need not guess the exact value of a summation in order to use mathematical induction. Induction can be used to show a bound as well. As an example, let us prove that the geometric series $\sum_{k=0}^{n} 3^k$ is $O(3^n)$. More specifically, let us prove that $\sum_{k=0}^{n} 3^k \leq c3^n$ for some constant c. For the initial condition $n = 0$, we have $\sum_{k=0}^{0} 3^k = 1 \leq c \cdot 1$ as long as $c \geq 1$. Assuming that the bound holds for n, let us prove that it holds for $n + 1$. We have

$$
\begin{aligned}
\sum_{k=0}^{n+1} 3^k &= \sum_{k=0}^{n} 3^k + 3^{n+1} \\
&\leq c3^n + 3^{n+1} \\
&= \left(\frac{1}{3} + \frac{1}{c}\right) c3^{n+1} \\
&\leq c3^{n+1}
\end{aligned}
$$

as long as $(1/3 + 1/c) \leq 1$ or, equivalently, $c \geq 3/2$. Thus, $\sum_{k=0}^{n} 3^k = O(3^n)$, as we wished to show.

We have to be careful when we use asymptotic notation to prove bounds by induction. Consider the following fallacious proof that $\sum_{k=1}^{n} k = O(n)$. Certainly, $\sum_{k=1}^{1} k = O(1)$. Assuming the bound for n, we now prove it for $n + 1$:

$$
\begin{aligned}
\sum_{k=1}^{n+1} k &= \sum_{k=1}^{n} k + (n + 1) \\
&= O(n) + (n + 1) \qquad \Longleftarrow \textit{wrong!!} \\
&= O(n + 1) \ .
\end{aligned}
$$

The bug in the argument is that the "constant" hidden by the "big-oh" grows with n and thus is not constant. We have not shown that the same constant works for *all* n.

Bounding the terms

Sometimes, a good upper bound on a series can be obtained by bounding each term of the series, and it often suffices to use the largest term to bound the others. For example, a quick upper bound on the arithmetic series (3.1) is

$$
\begin{aligned}
\sum_{k=1}^{n} k &\leq \sum_{k=1}^{n} n \\
&= n^2 \ .
\end{aligned}
$$

In general, for a series $\sum_{k=1}^{n} a_k$, if we let $a_{\max} = \max_{1 \leq k \leq n} a_k$, then

$$
\sum_{k=1}^{n} a_k \leq n a_{\max} \ .
$$

The technique of bounding each term in a series by the largest term is a weak method when the series can in fact be bounded by a geometric series. Given the series $\sum_{k=0}^{n} a_k$, suppose that $a_{k+1}/a_k \leq r$ for all $k \geq 0$, where $r < 1$ is a constant. The sum can be bounded by an infinite decreasing geometric series, since $a_k \leq a_0 r^k$, and thus

$$
\begin{aligned}
\sum_{k=0}^{n} a_k &\leq \sum_{k=0}^{\infty} a_0 r^k \\
&= a_0 \sum_{k=0}^{\infty} r^k \\
&= a_0 \frac{1}{1 - r} \ .
\end{aligned}
$$

We can apply this method to bound the summation $\sum_{k=1}^{\infty}(k/3^k)$. The first term is $1/3$, and the ratio of consecutive terms is

$$\frac{(k+1)/3^{k+1}}{k/3^k} = \frac{1}{3} \cdot \frac{k+1}{k}$$
$$\leq \frac{2}{3}$$

for all $k \geq 1$. Thus, each term is bounded above by $(1/3)(2/3)^k$, so that

$$\sum_{k=1}^{\infty}\frac{k}{3^k} \leq \sum_{k=1}^{\infty}\frac{1}{3}\left(\frac{2}{3}\right)^k$$
$$= \frac{1}{3} \cdot \frac{1}{1-2/3}$$
$$= 1 .$$

A common bug in applying this method is to show that the ratio of consecutive terms is less than 1 and then to assume that the summation is bounded by a geometric series. An example is the infinite harmonic series, which diverges since

$$\sum_{k=1}^{\infty}\frac{1}{k} = \lim_{n\to\infty}\sum_{k=1}^{n}\frac{1}{k}$$
$$= \lim_{n\to\infty}\Theta(\lg n)$$
$$= \infty .$$

The ratio of the $(k+1)$st and kth terms in this series is $k/(k+1) < 1$, but the series is not bounded by a decreasing geometric series. To bound a series by a geometric series, one must show that the ratio is bounded away from 1; that is, there must be an $r < 1$, which is a *constant*, such that the ratio of all pairs of consecutive terms never exceeds r. In the harmonic series, no such r exists because the ratio becomes arbitrarily close to 1.

Splitting summations

One way to obtain bounds on a difficult summation is to express the series as the sum of two or more series by partitioning the range of the index and then to bound each of the resulting series. For example, suppose we try to find a lower bound on the arithmetic series $\sum_{k=1}^{n}k$, which has already been shown to have an upper bound of n^2. We might attempt to bound each term in the summation by the smallest term, but since that term is 1, we get a lower bound of n for the summation—far off from our upper bound of n^2.

We can obtain a better lower bound by first splitting the summation. Assume for convenience that n is even. We have

$$\sum_{k=1}^{n}k = \sum_{k=1}^{n/2}k + \sum_{k=n/2+1}^{n}k$$

$$\geq \sum_{k=1}^{n/2} 0 + \sum_{k=n/2+1}^{n} (n/2)$$

$$\geq (n/2)^2$$

$$= \Omega(n^2) ,$$

which is an asymptotically tight bound, since $\sum_{k=1}^{n} k = O(n^2)$.

For a summation arising from the analysis of an algorithm, we can often split the summation and ignore a constant number of the initial terms. Generally, this technique applies when each term a_k in a summation $\sum_{k=0}^{n} a_k$ is independent of n. Then for any constant $k_0 > 0$, we can write

$$\sum_{k=0}^{n} a_k = \sum_{k=0}^{k_0-1} a_k + \sum_{k=k_0}^{n} a_k$$

$$= \Theta(1) + \sum_{k=k_0}^{n} a_k ,$$

since the initial terms of the summation are all constant and there is a constant number of them. We can then use other methods to bound $\sum_{k=k_0}^{n} a_k$. For example, to find an asymptotic upper bound on

$$\sum_{k=0}^{\infty} \frac{k^2}{2^k} ,$$

we observe that the ratio of consecutive terms is

$$\frac{(k+1)^2/2^{k+1}}{k^2/2^k} = \frac{(k+1)^2}{2k^2}$$

$$\leq \frac{8}{9}$$

if $k \geq 3$. Thus, the summation can be split into

$$\sum_{k=0}^{\infty} \frac{k^2}{2^k} = \sum_{k=0}^{2} \frac{k^2}{2^k} + \sum_{k=3}^{\infty} \frac{k^2}{2^k}$$

$$\leq O(1) + \frac{9}{8} \sum_{k=0}^{\infty} \left(\frac{8}{9}\right)^k$$

$$= O(1) ,$$

since the second summation is a decreasing geometric series.

The technique of splitting summations can be used to determine asymptotic bounds in much more difficult situations. For example, we can obtain a bound of $O(\lg n)$ on the harmonic series (3.5):

$$H_n = \sum_{k=1}^{n} \frac{1}{k} .$$

The idea is to split the range 1 to n into $\lfloor \lg n \rfloor$ pieces and upper bound the contribution of each piece by 1. Thus,

$$
\begin{aligned}
\sum_{k=1}^{n} \frac{1}{k} &\leq \sum_{i=0}^{\lfloor \lg n \rfloor} \sum_{j=0}^{2^i - 1} \frac{1}{2^i + j} \\
&\leq \sum_{i=0}^{\lfloor \lg n \rfloor} \sum_{j=0}^{2^i - 1} \frac{1}{2^i} \\
&\leq \sum_{i=0}^{\lfloor \lg n \rfloor} 1 \\
&\leq \lg n + 1 \ .
\end{aligned}
\tag{3.8}
$$

Approximation by integrals

When a summation can be expressed as $\sum_{k=m}^{n} f(k)$, where $f(k)$ is a monotonically increasing function, we can approximate it by integrals:

$$
\int_{m-1}^{n} f(x)\,dx \leq \sum_{k=m}^{n} f(k) \leq \int_{m}^{n+1} f(x)\,dx \ .
\tag{3.9}
$$

The justification for this approximation is shown in Figure 3.1. The summation is represented as the area of the rectangles in the figure, and the integral is the shaded region under the curve. When $f(k)$ is a monotonically decreasing function, we can use a similar method to provide the bounds

$$
\int_{m}^{n+1} f(x)\,dx \leq \sum_{k=m}^{n} f(k) \leq \int_{m-1}^{n} f(x)\,dx \ .
\tag{3.10}
$$

The integral approximation (3.10) gives a tight estimate for the nth harmonic number. For a lower bound, we obtain

$$
\begin{aligned}
\sum_{k=1}^{n} \frac{1}{k} &\geq \int_{1}^{n+1} \frac{dx}{x} \\
&= \ln(n+1) \ .
\end{aligned}
\tag{3.11}
$$

For the upper bound, we derive the inequality

$$
\begin{aligned}
\sum_{k=2}^{n} \frac{1}{k} &\leq \int_{1}^{n} \frac{dx}{x} \\
&= \ln n \ ,
\end{aligned}
$$

which yields the bound

$$
\sum_{k=1}^{n} \frac{1}{k} \leq \ln n + 1 \ .
\tag{3.12}
$$

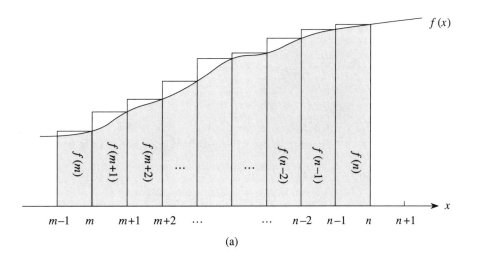

(a)

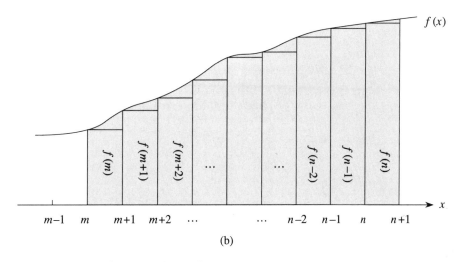

(b)

Figure 3.1 Approximation of $\sum_{k=m}^{n} f(k)$ by integrals. The area of each rectangle is shown within the rectangle, and the total rectangle area represents the value of the summation. The integral is represented by the shaded area under the curve. By comparing areas in (**a**), we get $\int_{m-1}^{n} f(x)\,dx \leq \sum_{k=m}^{n} f(k)$, and then by shifting the rectangles one unit to the right, we get $\sum_{k=m}^{n} f(k) \leq \int_{m}^{n+1} f(x)\,dx$ in (**b**).

Exercises

3.2-1
Show that $\sum_{k=1}^{n} 1/k^2$ is bounded above by a constant.

3.2-2
Find an asymptotic upper bound on the summation

$$\sum_{k=0}^{\lfloor \lg n \rfloor} \lceil n/2^k \rceil .$$

3.2-3
Show that the nth harmonic number is $\Omega(\lg n)$ by splitting the summation.

3.2-4
Approximate $\sum_{k=1}^{n} k^3$ with an integral.

3.2-5
Why didn't we use the integral approximation (3.10) directly on $\sum_{k=1}^{n} 1/k$ to obtain an upper bound on the nth harmonic number?

Problems

3-1   Bounding summations
Give asymptotically tight bounds on the following summations. Assume that $r \geq 0$ and $s \geq 0$ are constants.

a. $\displaystyle\sum_{k=1}^{n} k^r$.

b. $\displaystyle\sum_{k=1}^{n} \lg^s k$.

c. $\displaystyle\sum_{k=1}^{n} k^r \lg^s k$.

Chapter notes

Knuth [121] is an excellent reference for the material presented in this chapter. Basic properties of series can be found in any good calculus book, such as Apostol [12] or Thomas and Finney [192].

4 Recurrences

As noted in Chapter 1, when an algorithm contains a recursive call to itself, its running time can often be described by a recurrence. A *recurrence* is an equation or inequality that describes a function in terms of its value on smaller inputs. For example, we saw in Chapter 1 that the worst-case running time $T(n)$ of the MERGE-SORT procedure could be described by the recurrence

$$T(n) = \begin{cases} \Theta(1) & \text{if } n = 1, \\ 2T(n/2) + \Theta(n) & \text{if } n > 1, \end{cases} \tag{4.1}$$

whose solution was claimed to be $T(n) = \Theta(n \lg n)$.

This chapter offers three methods for solving recurrences—that is, for obtaining asymptotic "Θ" or "O" bounds on the solution. In the *substitution method*, we guess a bound and then use mathematical induction to prove our guess correct. The *iteration method* converts the recurrence into a summation and then relies on techniques for bounding summations to solve the recurrence. The *master method* provides bounds for recurrences of the form

$$T(n) = aT(n/b) + f(n),$$

where $a \geq 1$, $b > 1$, and $f(n)$ is a given function; it requires memorization of three cases, but once you do that, determining asymptotic bounds for many simple recurrences is easy.

Technicalities

In practice, we neglect certain technical details when we state and solve recurrences. A good example of a detail that is often glossed over is the assumption of integer arguments to functions. Normally, the running time $T(n)$ of an algorithm is only defined when n is an integer, since for most algorithms, the size of the input is always an integer. For example, the recurrence describing the worst-case running time of MERGE-SORT is really

$$T(n) = \begin{cases} \Theta(1) & \text{if } n = 1, \\ T(\lceil n/2 \rceil) + T(\lfloor n/2 \rfloor) + \Theta(n) & \text{if } n > 1. \end{cases} \tag{4.2}$$

Boundary conditions represent another class of details that we typically ignore. Since the running time of an algorithm on a constant-sized input is a constant, the recurrences that arise from the running times of algorithms generally have $T(n) = \Theta(1)$ for sufficiently small n. Consequently, for convenience, we shall generally omit statements of the boundary conditions of recurrences and assume that $T(n)$ is constant for small n. For example, we normally state recurrence (4.1) as

$$T(n) = 2T(n/2) + \Theta(n) , \tag{4.3}$$

without explicitly giving values for small n. The reason is that although changing the value of $T(1)$ changes the solution to the recurrence, the solution typically doesn't change by more than a constant factor, so the order of growth is unchanged.

When we state and solve recurrences, we often omit floors, ceilings, and boundary conditions. We forge ahead without these details and later determine whether or not they matter. They usually don't, but it is important to know when they do. Experience helps, and so do some theorems stating that these details don't affect the asymptotic bounds of many recurrences encountered in the analysis of algorithms (see Theorem 4.1 and Problem 4-5). In this chapter, however, we shall address some of these details to show the fine points of recurrence solution methods.

4.1   The substitution method

The substitution method for solving recurrences involves guessing the form of the solution and then using mathematical induction to find the constants and show that the solution works. The name comes from the substitution of the guessed answer for the function when the inductive hypothesis is applied to smaller values. This method is powerful, but it obviously can be applied only in cases when it is easy to guess the form of the answer.

The substitution method can be used to establish either upper or lower bounds on a recurrence. As an example, let us determine an upper bound on the recurrence

$$T(n) = 2T(\lfloor n/2 \rfloor) + n , \tag{4.4}$$

which is similar to recurrences (4.2) and (4.3). We guess that the solution is $T(n) = O(n \lg n)$. Our method is to prove that $T(n) \le cn \lg n$ for an appropriate choice of the constant $c > 0$. We start by assuming that this bound holds for $\lfloor n/2 \rfloor$, that is, that $T(\lfloor n/2 \rfloor) \le c \lfloor n/2 \rfloor \lg(\lfloor n/2 \rfloor)$. Substituting into the recurrence yields

$$
\begin{aligned}
T(n) &\le 2(c \lfloor n/2 \rfloor \lg(\lfloor n/2 \rfloor)) + n \\
&\le cn \lg(n/2) + n \\
&= cn \lg n - cn \lg 2 + n \\
&= cn \lg n - cn + n \\
&\le cn \lg n ,
\end{aligned}
$$

where the last step holds as long as $c \geq 1$.

Mathematical induction now requires us to show that our solution holds for the boundary conditions. That is, we must show that we can choose the constant c large enough so that the bound $T(n) \leq cn \lg n$ works for the boundary conditions as well. This requirement can sometimes lead to problems. Let us assume, for the sake of argument, that $T(1) = 1$ is the sole boundary condition of the recurrence. Then, unfortunately, we can't choose c large enough, since $T(1) \leq c1 \lg 1 = 0$.

This difficulty in proving an inductive hypothesis for a specific boundary condition can be easily overcome. We take advantage of the fact that asymptotic notation only requires us to prove $T(n) \leq cn \lg n$ for $n \geq n_0$, where n_0 is a constant. The idea is to remove the difficult boundary condition $T(1) = 1$ from consideration in the inductive proof and to include $n = 2$ and $n = 3$ as part of the boundary conditions for the proof. We can impose $T(2)$ and $T(3)$ as boundary conditions for the inductive proof because for $n > 3$, the recurrence does not depend directly on $T(1)$. From the recurrence, we derive $T(2) = 4$ and $T(3) = 5$. The inductive proof that $T(n) \leq cn \lg n$ for some constant $c \geq 2$ can now be completed by choosing c large enough so that $T(2) \leq c2 \lg 2$ and $T(3) \leq c3 \lg 3$. As it turns out, any choice of $c \geq 2$ suffices. For most of the recurrences we shall examine, it is straightforward to extend boundary conditions to make the inductive assumption work for small n.

Making a good guess

Unfortunately, there is no general way to guess the correct solutions to recurrences. Guessing a solution takes experience and, occasionally, creativity. Fortunately, though, there are some heuristics that can help you become a good guesser.

If a recurrence is similar to one you have seen before, then guessing a similar solution is reasonable. As an example, consider the recurrence

$$T(n) = 2T(\lfloor n/2 \rfloor + 17) + n \;,$$

which looks difficult because of the added "17" in the argument to T on the right-hand side. Intuitively, however, this additional term cannot substantially affect the solution to the recurrence. When n is large, the difference between $T(\lfloor n/2 \rfloor)$ and $T(\lfloor n/2 \rfloor + 17)$ is not that large: both cut n nearly evenly in half. Consequently, we make the guess that $T(n) = O(n \lg n)$, which you can verify as correct by using the substitution method (see Exercise 4.1-5).

Another way to make a good guess is to prove loose upper and lower bounds on the recurrence and then reduce the range of uncertainty. For example, we might start with a lower bound of $T(n) = \Omega(n)$ for the recurrence (4.4), since we have the term n in the recurrence, and we can prove an initial upper bound of $T(n) = O(n^2)$. Then, we can gradually lower the upper bound and raise the lower bound until we converge on the correct, asymptotically tight solution of $T(n) = \Theta(n \lg n)$.

Subtleties

There are times when you can correctly guess at an asymptotic bound on the solution of a recurrence, but somehow the math doesn't seem to work out in the induction. Usually, the problem is that the inductive assumption isn't strong enough to prove the detailed bound. When you hit such a snag, revising the guess by subtracting a lower-order term often permits the math to go through.

Consider the recurrence

$$T(n) = T(\lfloor n/2 \rfloor) + T(\lceil n/2 \rceil) + 1 \; .$$

We guess that the solution is $O(n)$, and we try to show that $T(n) \leq cn$ for an appropriate choice of the constant c. Substituting our guess in the recurrence, we obtain

$$\begin{aligned} T(n) &\leq c \lfloor n/2 \rfloor + c \lceil n/2 \rceil + 1 \\ &= cn + 1 \; , \end{aligned}$$

which does not imply $T(n) \leq cn$ for any choice of c. It's tempting to try a larger guess, say $T(n) = O(n^2)$, which can be made to work, but in fact, our guess that the solution is $T(n) = O(n)$ is correct. In order to show this, however, we must make a stronger inductive hypothesis.

Intuitively, our guess is nearly right: we're only off by the constant 1, a lower-order term. Nevertheless, mathematical induction doesn't work unless we prove the exact form of the inductive hypothesis. We overcome our difficulty by *subtracting* a lower-order term from our previous guess. Our new guess is $T(n) \leq cn - b$, where $b \geq 0$ is constant. We now have

$$\begin{aligned} T(n) &\leq (c \lfloor n/2 \rfloor - b) + (c \lceil n/2 \rceil - b) + 1 \\ &= cn - 2b + 1 \\ &\leq cn - b \; , \end{aligned}$$

as long as $b \geq 1$. As before, the constant c must be chosen large enough to handle the boundary conditions.

Most people find the idea of subtracting a lower-order term counterintuitive. After all, if the math doesn't work out, shouldn't we be increasing our guess? The key to understanding this step is to remember that we are using mathematical induction: we can prove something stronger for a given value by assuming something stronger for smaller values.

Avoiding pitfalls

It is easy to err in the use of asymptotic notation. For example, in the recurrence (4.4) we can falsely prove $T(n) = O(n)$ by guessing $T(n) \leq cn$

and then arguing

$$
\begin{aligned}
T(n) &\le 2(c \lfloor n/2 \rfloor) + n \\
&\le cn + n \\
&= O(n) , \qquad \Longleftarrow \textit{wrong!!}
\end{aligned}
$$

since c is a constant. The error is that we haven't proved the exact form of the inductive hypothesis, that is, that $T(n) \le cn$.

Changing variables

Sometimes, a little algebraic manipulation can make an unknown recurrence similar to one you have seen before. As an example, consider the recurrence

$$T(n) = 2T(\lfloor \sqrt{n} \rfloor) + \lg n ,$$

which looks difficult. We can simplify this recurrence, though, with a change of variables. For convenience, we shall not worry about rounding off values, such as $\sqrt{n}$, to be integers. Renaming $m = \lg n$ yields

$$T(2^m) = 2T(2^{m/2}) + m .$$

We can now rename $S(m) = T(2^m)$ to produce the new recurrence

$$S(m) = 2S(m/2) + m ,$$

which is very much like recurrence (4.4) and has the same solution: $S(m) = O(m \lg m)$. Changing back from $S(m)$ to $T(n)$, we obtain $T(n) = T(2^m) = S(m) = O(m \lg m) = O(\lg n \lg \lg n)$.

Exercises

4.1-1
Show that the solution of $T(n) = T(\lceil n/2 \rceil) + 1$ is $O(\lg n)$.

4.1-2
Show that the solution of $T(n) = 2T(\lfloor n/2 \rfloor) + n$ is $\Omega(n \lg n)$. Conclude that the solution is $\Theta(n \lg n)$.

4.1-3
Show that by making a different inductive hypothesis, we can overcome the difficulty with the boundary condition $T(1) = 1$ for the recurrence (4.4) without adjusting the boundary conditions for the inductive proof.

4.1-4
Show that $\Theta(n \lg n)$ is the solution to the "exact" recurrence (4.2) for merge sort.

4.1-5
Show that the solution to $T(n) = 2T(\lfloor n/2 \rfloor + 17) + n$ is $O(n \lg n)$.

4.1-6

Solve the recurrence $T(n) = 2T(\sqrt{n}) + 1$ by making a change of variables. Do not worry about whether values are integral.

4.2   The iteration method

The method of iterating a recurrence doesn't require us to guess the answer, but it may require more algebra than the substitution method. The idea is to expand (iterate) the recurrence and express it as a summation of terms dependent only on n and the initial conditions. Techniques for evaluating summations can then be used to provide bounds on the solution.

As an example, consider the recurrence

$$T(n) = 3T(\lfloor n/4 \rfloor) + n .$$

We iterate it as follows:

$$
\begin{aligned}
T(n) &= n + 3T(\lfloor n/4 \rfloor) \\
&= n + 3(\lfloor n/4 \rfloor + 3T(\lfloor n/16 \rfloor)) \\
&= n + 3(\lfloor n/4 \rfloor + 3(\lfloor n/16 \rfloor + 3T(\lfloor n/64 \rfloor))) \\
&= n + 3\lfloor n/4 \rfloor + 9\lfloor n/16 \rfloor + 27T(\lfloor n/64 \rfloor) ,
\end{aligned}
$$

where $\lfloor \lfloor n/4 \rfloor /4 \rfloor = \lfloor n/16 \rfloor$ and $\lfloor \lfloor n/16 \rfloor /4 \rfloor = \lfloor n/64 \rfloor$ follow from the identity (2.4).

How far must we iterate the recurrence before we reach a boundary condition? The ith term in the series is $3^i \lfloor n/4^i \rfloor$. The iteration hits $n = 1$ when $\lfloor n/4^i \rfloor = 1$ or, equivalently, when i exceeds $\log_4 n$. By continuing the iteration until this point and using the bound $\lfloor n/4^i \rfloor \leq n/4^i$, we discover that the summation contains a decreasing geometric series:

$$
\begin{aligned}
T(n) &\leq n + 3n/4 + 9n/16 + 27n/64 + \cdots + 3^{\log_4 n}\Theta(1) \\
&\leq n\sum_{i=0}^{\infty} \left(\frac{3}{4}\right)^i + \Theta(n^{\log_4 3}) \\
&= 4n + o(n) \\
&= O(n) .
\end{aligned}
$$

Here, we have used the identity (2.9) to conclude that $3^{\log_4 n} = n^{\log_4 3}$, and we have used the fact that $\log_4 3 < 1$ to conclude that $\Theta(n^{\log_4 3}) = o(n)$.

The iteration method usually leads to lots of algebra, and keeping everything straight can be a challenge. The key is to focus on two parameters: the number of times the recurrence needs to be iterated to reach the boundary condition, and the sum of the terms arising from each level of the iteration process. Sometimes, in the process of iterating a recurrence, you can guess the solution without working out all the math. Then, the iteration can be abandoned in favor of the substitution method, which usually requires less algebra.

When a recurrence contains floor and ceiling functions, the math can become especially complicated. Often, it helps to assume that the recurrence is defined only on exact powers of a number. In our example, if we had assumed that $n = 4^k$ for some integer k, the floor functions could have been conveniently omitted. Unfortunately, proving the bound $T(n) = O(n)$ solely for exact powers of 4 is technically an abuse of the O-notation. The definitions of asymptotic notation require that bounds be proved for *all* sufficiently large integers, not just those that are powers of 4. We shall see in Section 4.3 that for a large class of recurrences, this technicality can be overcome. Problem 4-5 also gives conditions under which an analysis for exact powers of an integer can be extended to all integers.

Recursion trees

A *recursion tree* is a convenient way to visualize what happens when a recurrence is iterated, and it can help organize the algebraic bookkeeping necessary to solve the recurrence. It is especially useful when the recurrence describes a divide-and-conquer algorithm. Figure 4.1 shows the derivation of the recursion tree for

$$T(n) = 2T(n/2) + n^2 .$$

For convenience, we assume that n is an exact power of 2. Part (a) of the figure shows $T(n)$, which in part (b) has been expanded into an equivalent tree representing the recurrence. The n^2 term is the root (the cost at the top level of recursion), and the two subtrees of the root are the two smaller recurrences $T(n/2)$. Part (c) shows this process carried one step further by expanding $T(n/2)$. The cost for each of the two subnodes at the second level of recursion is $(n/2)^2$. We continue expanding each node in the tree by breaking it into its constituent parts as determined by the recurrence, until a boundary condition is reached. Part (d) shows the resulting tree.

We now evaluate the recurrence by adding the values across each level of the tree. The top level has total value n^2, the second level has value $(n/2)^2 + (n/2)^2 = n^2/2$, the third level has value $(n/4)^2 + (n/4)^2 + (n/4)^2 + (n/4)^2 = n^2/4$, and so on. Since the values decrease geometrically, the total is at most a constant factor more than the largest (first) term, and hence the solution is $\Theta(n^2)$.

As another, more intricate example, Figure 4.2 shows the recursion tree for

$$T(n) = T(n/3) + T(2n/3) + n .$$

(Again, we omit floor and ceiling functions for simplicity.) When we add the values across the levels of the recursion tree, we get a value of n for every level. The longest path from the root to a leaf is $n \to (2/3)n \to (2/3)^2 n \to \cdots \to 1$. Since $(2/3)^k n = 1$ when $k = \log_{3/2} n$, the height of the tree is $\log_{3/2} n$. Thus, the solution to the recurrence is at most $n \log_{3/2} n = O(n \lg n)$.

$T(n)$

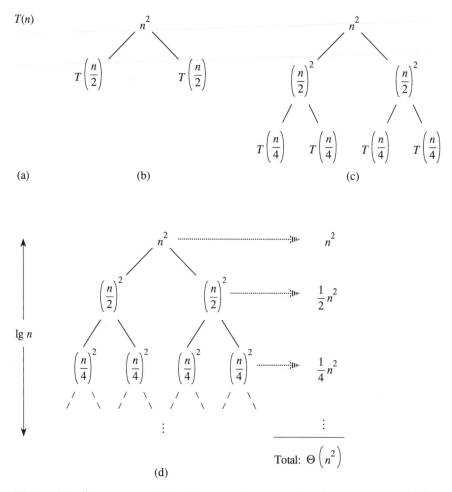

(a)   (b)   (c)

$\lg n$

Total: $\Theta\left(n^2\right)$

(d)

Figure 4.1 The construction of a recursion tree for the recurrence $T(n) = 2T(n/2) + n^2$. Part **(a)** shows $T(n)$, which is progressively expanded in **(b)–(d)** to form the recursion tree. The fully expanded tree in part (d) has height $\lg n$ (it has $\lg n + 1$ levels).

Exercises

4.2-1
Determine a good asymptotic upper bound on the recurrence $T(n) = 3T(\lfloor n/2 \rfloor) + n$ by iteration.

4.2-2
Argue that the solution to the recurrence $T(n) = T(n/3) + T(2n/3) + n$ is $\Omega(n \lg n)$ by appealing to a recursion tree.

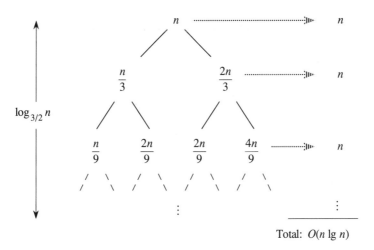

Total: $O(n \lg n)$

Figure 4.2 A recursion tree for the recurrence $T(n) = T(n/3) + T(2n/3) + n$.

4.2-3
Draw the recursion tree for $T(n) = 4T(\lfloor n/2 \rfloor) + n$, and provide tight asymptotic bounds on its solution.

4.2-4
Use iteration to solve the recurrence $T(n) = T(n - a) + T(a) + n$, where $a \geq 1$ is a constant.

4.2-5
Use a recursion tree to solve the recurrence $T(n) = T(\alpha n) + T((1-\alpha)n) + n$, where α is a constant in the range $0 < \alpha < 1$.

4.3 The master method

The master method provides a "cookbook" method for solving recurrences of the form

$$T(n) = aT(n/b) + f(n) , \tag{4.5}$$

where $a \geq 1$ and $b > 1$ are constants and $f(n)$ is an asymptotically positive function. The master method requires memorization of three cases, but then the solution of many recurrences can be determined quite easily, often without pencil and paper.

The recurrence (4.5) describes the running time of an algorithm that divides a problem of size n into a subproblems, each of size n/b, where a and b are positive constants. The a subproblems are solved recursively, each in time $T(n/b)$. The cost of dividing the problem and combining the results of the subproblems is described by the function $f(n)$. (That is, using the notation from Section 1.3.2, $f(n) = D(n) + C(n)$.) For example, the recurrence arising from the MERGE-SORT procedure has $a = 2$, $b = 2$, and $f(n) = \Theta(n)$.

As a matter of technical correctness, the recurrence isn't actually well defined because n/b might not be an integer. Replacing each of the a terms $T(n/b)$ with either $T(\lfloor n/b \rfloor)$ or $T(\lceil n/b \rceil)$ doesn't affect the asymptotic behavior of the recurrence, however. (We'll prove this in the next section.) We normally find it convenient, therefore, to omit the floor and ceiling functions when writing divide-and-conquer recurrences of this form.

The master theorem

The master method depends on the following theorem.

Theorem 4.1 (Master theorem)
Let $a \geq 1$ and $b > 1$ be constants, let $f(n)$ be a function, and let $T(n)$ be defined on the nonnegative integers by the recurrence

$$T(n) = aT(n/b) + f(n) \; ,$$

where we interpret n/b to mean either $\lfloor n/b \rfloor$ or $\lceil n/b \rceil$. Then $T(n)$ can be bounded asymptotically as follows.

1. If $f(n) = O(n^{\log_b a - \epsilon})$ for some constant $\epsilon > 0$, then $T(n) = \Theta(n^{\log_b a})$.
2. If $f(n) = \Theta(n^{\log_b a})$, then $T(n) = \Theta(n^{\log_b a} \lg n)$.
3. If $f(n) = \Omega(n^{\log_b a + \epsilon})$ for some constant $\epsilon > 0$, and if $af(n/b) \leq cf(n)$ for some constant $c < 1$ and all sufficiently large n, then $T(n) = \Theta(f(n))$.   ■

Before applying the master theorem to some examples, let's spend a moment trying to understand what it says. In each of the three cases, we are comparing the function $f(n)$ with the function $n^{\log_b a}$. Intuitively, the solution to the recurrence is determined by the larger of the two functions. If, as in case 1, the function $n^{\log_b a}$ is the larger, then the solution is $T(n) = \Theta(n^{\log_b a})$. If, as in case 3, the function $f(n)$ is the larger, then the solution is $T(n) = \Theta(f(n))$. If, as in case 2, the two functions are the same size, we multiply by a logarithmic factor, and the solution is $T(n) = \Theta(n^{\log_b a} \lg n) = \Theta(f(n) \lg n)$.

Beyond this intuition, there are some technicalities that must be understood. In the first case, not only must $f(n)$ be smaller than $n^{\log_b a}$, it must be *polynomially* smaller. That is, $f(n)$ must be asymptotically smaller than $n^{\log_b a}$ by a factor of n^ϵ for some constant $\epsilon > 0$. In the third case, not only must $f(n)$ be larger than $n^{\log_b a}$, it must be polynomially larger and in addition satisfy the "regularity" condition that $af(n/b) \leq cf(n)$. This condition is satisfied by most of the polynomially bounded functions that we shall encounter.

It is important to realize that the three cases do not cover all the possibilities for $f(n)$. There is a gap between cases 1 and 2 when $f(n)$ is smaller than $n^{\log_b a}$ but not polynomially smaller. Similarly, there is a gap between cases 2 and 3 when $f(n)$ is larger than $n^{\log_b a}$ but not polynomially larger. If the function $f(n)$ falls into one of these gaps, or if the regularity condition in case 3 fails to hold, the master method cannot be used to solve the recurrence.

Using the master method

To use the master method, we simply determine which case (if any) of the master theorem applies and write down the answer.

As a first example, consider

$$T(n) = 9T(n/3) + n \ .$$

For this recurrence, we have $a = 9$, $b = 3$, $f(n) = n$, and thus $n^{\log_b a} = n^{\log_3 9} = \Theta(n^2)$. Since $f(n) = O(n^{\log_3 9 - \epsilon})$, where $\epsilon = 1$, we can apply case 1 of the master theorem and conclude that the solution is $T(n) = \Theta(n^2)$.

Now consider

$$T(n) = T(2n/3) + 1,$$

in which $a = 1$, $b = 3/2$, $f(n) = 1$, and $n^{\log_b a} = n^{\log_{3/2} 1} = n^0 = 1$. Case 2 applies, since $f(n) = \Theta(n^{\log_b a}) = \Theta(1)$, and thus the solution to the recurrence is $T(n) = \Theta(\lg n)$.

For the recurrence

$$T(n) = 3T(n/4) + n \lg n \ ,$$

we have $a = 3$, $b = 4$, $f(n) = n \lg n$, and $n^{\log_b a} = n^{\log_4 3} = O(n^{0.793})$. Since $f(n) = \Omega(n^{\log_4 3 + \epsilon})$, where $\epsilon \approx 0.2$, case 3 applies if we can show that the regularity condition holds for $f(n)$. For sufficiently large n, $af(n/b) = 3(n/4) \lg(n/4) \leq (3/4)n \lg n = cf(n)$ for $c = 3/4$. Consequently, by case 3, the solution to the recurrence is $T(n) = \Theta(n \lg n)$.

The master method does not apply to the recurrence

$$T(n) = 2T(n/2) + n \lg n,$$

even though it has the proper form: $a = 2$, $b = 2$, $f(n) = n \lg n$, and $n^{\log_b a} = n$. It seems that case 3 should apply, since $f(n) = n \lg n$ is asymptotically larger than $n^{\log_b a} = n$ but not *polynomially* larger. The ratio $f(n)/n^{\log_b a} = (n \lg n)/n = \lg n$ is asymptotically less than n^ϵ for any positive constant ϵ. Consequently, the recurrence falls into the gap between case 2 and case 3. (See Exercise 4.4-2 for a solution.)

Exercises

4.3-1
Use the master method to give tight asymptotic bounds for the following recurrences.

a. $T(n) = 4T(n/2) + n$.

b. $T(n) = 4T(n/2) + n^2$.

c. $T(n) = 4T(n/2) + n^3$.

4.3-2
The running time of an algorithm A is described by the recurrence $T(n) = 7T(n/2) + n^2$. A competing algorithm A' has a running time of $T'(n) = aT'(n/4) + n^2$. What is the largest integer value for a such that A' is asymptotically faster than A?

4.3-3
Use the master method to show that the solution to the recurrence $T(n) = T(n/2) + \Theta(1)$ of binary search (see Exercise 1.3-5) is $T(n) = \Theta(\lg n)$.

4.3-4 $\star$
Consider the regularity condition $af(n/b) \le cf(n)$ for some constant $c < 1$, which is part of case 3 of the master theorem. Give an example of a simple function $f(n)$ that satisfies all the conditions in case 3 of the master theorem except the regularity condition.

$\star$ **4.4   Proof of the master theorem**

This section contains a proof of the master theorem (Theorem 4.1) for more advanced readers. The proof need not be understood in order to apply the theorem.

The proof is in two parts. The first part analyzes the "master" recurrence (4.5), under the simplifying assumption that $T(n)$ is defined only on exact powers of $b > 1$, that is, for $n = 1, b, b^2, \ldots$. This part gives all the intuition needed to understand why the master theorem is true. The second part shows how the analysis can be extended to all positive integers n and is merely mathematical technique applied to the problem of handling floors and ceilings.

In this section, we shall sometimes abuse our asymptotic notation slightly by using it to describe the behavior of functions that are only defined over exact powers of b. Recall that the definitions of asymptotic notations require that bounds be proved for all sufficiently large numbers, not just those that are powers of b. Since we could make new asymptotic notations that apply to the set $\{b^i : i = 0, 1, \ldots\}$, instead of the nonnegative integers, this abuse is minor.

Nevertheless, we must always be on guard when we are using asymptotic notation over a limited domain so that we do not draw improper conclusions. For example, proving that $T(n) = O(n)$ when n is an exact power of 2 does not guarantee that $T(n) = O(n)$. The function $T(n)$ could be defined as

$$T(n) = \begin{cases} n & \text{if } n = 1, 2, 4, 8, \ldots , \\ n^2 & \text{otherwise} , \end{cases}$$

in which case the best upper bound that can be proved is $T(n) = O(n^2)$. Because of this sort of drastic consequence, we shall never use asymptotic notation over a limited domain without making it absolutely clear from the context that we are doing so.

4.4.1 The proof for exact powers

The first part of the proof of the master theorem analyzes the master recurrence (4.5),

$$T(n) = aT(n/b) + f(n) ,$$

under the assumption that n is an exact power of $b > 1$, where b need not be an integer. The analysis is broken into three lemmas. The first reduces the problem of solving the master recurrence to the problem of evaluating an expression that contains a summation. The second determines bounds on this summation. The third lemma puts the first two together to prove a version of the master theorem for the case in which n is an exact power of b.

Lemma 4.2
Let $a \geq 1$ and $b > 1$ be constants, and let $f(n)$ be a nonnegative function defined on exact powers of b. Define $T(n)$ on exact powers of b by the recurrence

$$T(n) = \begin{cases} \Theta(1) & \text{if } n = 1 , \\ aT(n/b) + f(n) & \text{if } n = b^i , \end{cases}$$

where i is a positive integer. Then

$$T(n) = \Theta(n^{\log_b a}) + \sum_{j=0}^{\log_b n - 1} a^j f(n/b^j) . \tag{4.6}$$

Proof Iterating the recurrence yields

$$\begin{aligned} T(n) &= f(n) + aT(n/b) \\ &= f(n) + af(n/b) + a^2 T(n/b^2) \\ &= f(n) + af(n/b) + a^2 f(n/b^2) + \cdots \\ &\quad + a^{\log_b n - 1} f(n/b^{\log_b n - 1}) + a^{\log_b n} T(1) . \end{aligned}$$

Since $a^{\log_b n} = n^{\log_b a}$, the last term of this expression becomes

$$a^{\log_b n} T(1) = \Theta(n^{\log_b a}) \, ,$$

using the boundary condition $T(1) = \Theta(1)$. The remaining terms can be expressed as the sum

$$\sum_{j=0}^{\log_b n - 1} a^j f(n/b^j) \, ;$$

thus,

$$T(n) = \Theta(n^{\log_b a}) + \sum_{j=0}^{\log_b n - 1} a^j f(n/b^j) \, ,$$

which completes the proof.   ∎

The recursion tree

Before proceeding, let's try to develop some intuition by using a recursion tree. Figure 4.3 shows the tree corresponding to the iteration of the recurrence in Lemma 4.2. The root of the tree has cost $f(n)$, and it has a children, each with cost $f(n/b)$. (It is convenient to think of a as being an integer, especially when visualizing the recursion tree, but the mathematics does not require it.) Each of these children has a children with cost $f(n/b^2)$, and thus there are a^2 nodes that are distance 2 from the root. In general, there are a^j nodes that are distance j from the root, and each has cost $f(n/b^j)$. The cost of each leaf is $T(1) = \Theta(1)$, and each leaf is distance $\log_b n$ from the root, since $n/b^{\log_b n} = 1$. There are $a^{\log_b n} = n^{\log_b a}$ leaves in the tree.

We can obtain equation (4.6) by summing the costs of each level of the tree, as shown in the figure. The cost for a level j of internal nodes is $a^j f(n/b^j)$, and so the total of all internal node levels is

$$\sum_{j=0}^{\log_b n - 1} a^j f(n/b^j) \, .$$

In the underlying divide-and-conquer algorithm, this sum represents the costs of dividing problems into subproblems and then recombining the subproblems. The cost of all the leaves, which is the cost of doing all $n^{\log_b a}$ subproblems of size 1, is $\Theta(n^{\log_b a})$.

In terms of the recursion tree, the three cases of the master theorem correspond to cases in which the total cost of the tree is (1) dominated by the costs in the leaves, (2) evenly distributed across the levels of the tree, or (3) dominated by the cost of the root.

The summation in equation (4.6) describes the cost of the dividing and combining steps in the underlying divide-and-conquer algorithm. The next lemma provides asymptotic bounds on the summation's growth.

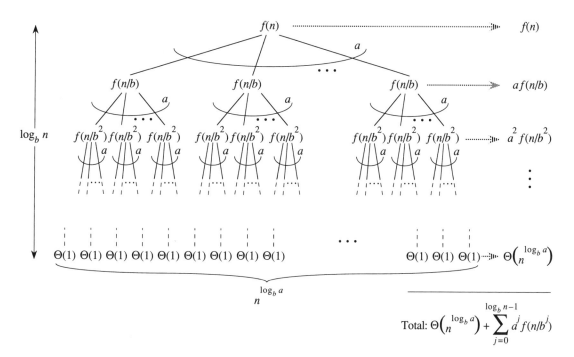

Figure 4.3 The recursion tree generated by $T(n) = aT(n/b) + f(n)$. The tree is a complete a-ary tree with $n^{\log_b a}$ leaves and height $\log_b a$. The cost of each level is shown at the right, and their sum is given in equation (4.6).

Lemma 4.3

Let $a \geq 1$ and $b > 1$ be constants, and let $f(n)$ be a nonnegative function defined on exact powers of b. A function $g(n)$ defined over exact powers of b by

$$g(n) = \sum_{j=0}^{\log_b n - 1} a^j f(n/b^j) \tag{4.7}$$

can then be bounded asymptotically for exact powers of b as follows.

1. If $f(n) = O(n^{\log_b a - \epsilon})$ for some constant $\epsilon > 0$, then $g(n) = O(n^{\log_b a})$.
2. If $f(n) = \Theta(n^{\log_b a})$, then $g(n) = \Theta(n^{\log_b a} \lg n)$.
3. If $af(n/b) \leq cf(n)$ for some constant $c < 1$ and all $n \geq b$, then $g(n) = \Theta(f(n))$.

Proof For case 1, we have $f(n) = O(n^{\log_b a - \epsilon})$, implying that $f(n/b^j) = O((n/b^j)^{\log_b a - \epsilon})$. Substituting into equation (4.7) yields

$$g(n) = O\left(\sum_{j=0}^{\log_b n - 1} a^j \left(\frac{n}{b^j} \right)^{\log_b a - \epsilon} \right). \tag{4.8}$$

We bound the summation within the O-notation by factoring out terms and simplifying, which leaves an increasing geometric series:

$$
\begin{aligned}
\sum_{j=0}^{\log_b n - 1} a^j \left(\frac{n}{b^j} \right)^{\log_b a - \epsilon}
&= n^{\log_b a - \epsilon} \sum_{j=0}^{\log_b n - 1} \left(\frac{ab^\epsilon}{b^{\log_b a}} \right)^j \\
&= n^{\log_b a - \epsilon} \sum_{j=0}^{\log_b n - 1} (b^\epsilon)^j \\
&= n^{\log_b a - \epsilon} \left(\frac{b^{\epsilon \log_b n} - 1}{b^\epsilon - 1} \right) \\
&= n^{\log_b a - \epsilon} \left(\frac{n^\epsilon - 1}{b^\epsilon - 1} \right) .
\end{aligned}
$$

Since b and ϵ are constants, the last expression reduces to $n^{\log_b a - \epsilon} O(n^\epsilon) = O(n^{\log_b a})$. Substituting this expression for the summation in equation (4.8) yields

$$ g(n) = O(n^{\log_b a}) , $$

and case 1 is proved.

Under the assumption that $f(n) = \Theta(n^{\log_b a})$ for case 2, we have that $f(n/b^j) = \Theta((n/b^j)^{\log_b a})$. Substituting into equation (4.7) yields

$$ g(n) = \Theta \left(\sum_{j=0}^{\log_b n - 1} a^j \left(\frac{n}{b^j} \right)^{\log_b a} \right) . \tag{4.9} $$

We bound the summation within the Θ as in case 1, but this time we do not obtain a geometric series. Instead, we discover that every term of the summation is the same:

$$
\begin{aligned}
\sum_{j=0}^{\log_b n - 1} a^j \left(\frac{n}{b^j} \right)^{\log_b a}
&= n^{\log_b a} \sum_{j=0}^{\log_b n - 1} \left(\frac{a}{b^{\log_b a}} \right)^j \\
&= n^{\log_b a} \sum_{j=0}^{\log_b n - 1} 1 \\
&= n^{\log_b a} \log_b n .
\end{aligned}
$$

Substituting this expression for the summation in equation (4.9) yields

$$
\begin{aligned}
g(n) &= \Theta(n^{\log_b a} \log_b n) \\
&= \Theta(n^{\log_b a} \lg n) ,
\end{aligned}
$$

and case 2 is proved.

Case 3 is proved similarly. Since $f(n)$ appears in the definition (4.7) of $g(n)$ and all terms of $g(n)$ are nonnegative, we can conclude that $g(n) = \Omega(f(n))$ for exact powers of b. Under the assumption that $af(n/b) \le cf(n)$ for some constant $c < 1$ and all $n \ge b$, we have $a^j f(n/b^j) \le c^j f(n)$.

Substituting into equation (4.7) and simplifying yields a geometric series, but unlike the series in case 1, this one has decreasing terms:

$$
\begin{aligned}
g(n) &\leq \sum_{j=0}^{\log_b n - 1} a^j f(n/b^j) \\
&\leq \sum_{j=0}^{\log_b n - 1} c^j f(n) \\
&\leq f(n) \sum_{j=0}^{\infty} c^j \\
&= f(n) \left(\frac{1}{1-c} \right) \\
&= O(f(n)) \,,
\end{aligned}
$$

since c is constant. Thus, we can conclude that $g(n) = \Theta(f(n))$ for exact powers of b. Case 3 is proved, which completes the proof of the lemma. ∎

We can now prove a version of the master theorem for the case in which n is an exact power of b.

Lemma 4.4

Let $a \geq 1$ and $b > 1$ be constants, and let $f(n)$ be a nonnegative function defined on exact powers of b. Define $T(n)$ on exact powers of b by the recurrence

$$
T(n) = \begin{cases} \Theta(1) & \text{if } n = 1 \,, \\ aT(n/b) + f(n) & \text{if } n = b^i \,, \end{cases}
$$

where i is a positive integer. Then $T(n)$ can be bounded asymptotically for exact powers of b as follows.

1. If $f(n) = O(n^{\log_b a - \epsilon})$ for some constant $\epsilon > 0$, then $T(n) = \Theta(n^{\log_b a})$.
2. If $f(n) = \Theta(n^{\log_b a})$, then $T(n) = \Theta(n^{\log_b a} \lg n)$.
3. If $f(n) = \Omega(n^{\log_b a + \epsilon})$ for some constant $\epsilon > 0$, and if $af(n/b) \leq cf(n)$ for some constant $c < 1$ and all sufficiently large n, then $T(n) = \Theta(f(n))$.

Proof We use the bounds in Lemma 4.3 to evaluate the summation (4.6) from Lemma 4.2. For case 1, we have

$$
\begin{aligned}
T(n) &= \Theta(n^{\log_b a}) + O(n^{\log_b a}) \\
&= \Theta(n^{\log_b a}) \,,
\end{aligned}
$$

and for case 2,

$$
\begin{aligned}
T(n) &= \Theta(n^{\log_b a}) + \Theta(n^{\log_b a} \lg n) \\
&= \Theta(n^{\log_b a} \lg n) \,.
\end{aligned}
$$

For case 3, the condition $af(n/b) \le cf(n)$ implies $f(n) = \Omega(n^{\log_b a + \epsilon})$ (see Exercise 4.4-3). Consequently,

$$
\begin{aligned}
T(n) &= \Theta(n^{\log_b a}) + \Theta(f(n)) \\
     &= \Theta(f(n)) \,.
\end{aligned}
$$

∎

4.4.2   Floors and ceilings

To complete the proof of the master theorem, we must now extend our analysis to the situation in which floors and ceilings are used in the master recurrence, so that the recurrence is defined for all integers, not just exact powers of b. Obtaining a lower bound on

$$T(n) = aT(\lceil n/b \rceil) + f(n) \tag{4.10}$$

and an upper bound on

$$T(n) = aT(\lfloor n/b \rfloor) + f(n) \tag{4.11}$$

is routine, since the bound $\lceil n/b \rceil \ge n/b$ can be pushed through in the first case to yield the desired result, and the bound $\lfloor n/b \rfloor \le n/b$ can be pushed through in the second case. Lower bounding the recurrence (4.11) requires much the same technique as upper bounding the recurrence (4.10), so we shall only present this latter bound.

We wish to iterate the recurrence (4.10), as was done in Lemma 4.2. As we iterate the recurrence, we obtain a sequence of recursive invocations on the arguments

n ,

$\lceil n/b \rceil$,

$\lceil \lceil n/b \rceil /b \rceil$,

$\lceil \lceil \lceil n/b \rceil /b \rceil /b \rceil$,

$\vdots$

Let us denote the ith element in the sequence by n_i, where

$$
n_i = \begin{cases} n & \text{if } i = 0 \,, \\ \lceil n_{i-1}/b \rceil & \text{if } i > 0 \,. \end{cases} \tag{4.12}
$$

Our first goal is to determine the number of iterations k such that n_k is a constant. Using the inequality $\lceil x \rceil \le x + 1$, we obtain

$$
\begin{aligned}
n_0 &\le n \,, \\
n_1 &\le \frac{n}{b} + 1 \,, \\
n_2 &\le \frac{n}{b^2} + \frac{1}{b} + 1 \,,
\end{aligned}
$$

$$n_3 \ \leq \ \frac{n}{b^3} + \frac{1}{b^2} + \frac{1}{b} + 1 \ ,$$

$$\vdots$$

In general,

$$n_i \ \leq \ \frac{n}{b^i} + \sum_{j=0}^{i-1} \frac{1}{b^j}$$

$$\leq \ \frac{n}{b^i} + \frac{b}{b-1} \ ,$$

and thus, when $i = \lfloor \log_b n \rfloor$, we obtain $n_i \leq b + b/(b-1) = O(1)$.

We can now iterate recurrence (4.10), obtaining

$$
\begin{aligned}
T(n) &= f(n_0) + aT(n_1) \\
&= f(n_0) + af(n_1) + a^2 T(n_2) \\
&\leq f(n_0) + af(n_1) + a^2 f(n_2) + \cdots \\
&\quad + a^{\lfloor \log_b n \rfloor - 1} f(n_{\lfloor \log_b n \rfloor - 1}) + a^{\lfloor \log_b n \rfloor} T(n_{\lfloor \log_b n \rfloor}) \\
&= \Theta(n^{\log_b a}) + \sum_{j=0}^{\lfloor \log_b n \rfloor - 1} a^j f(n_j) \ ,
\end{aligned} \tag{4.13}
$$

which is much the same as equation (4.6), except that n is an arbitrary integer and not restricted to be an exact power of b.

We can now evaluate the summation

$$g(n) = \sum_{j=0}^{\lfloor \log_b n \rfloor - 1} a^j f(n_j) \tag{4.14}$$

from (4.13) in a manner analogous to the proof of Lemma 4.3. Beginning with case 3, if $af(\lceil n/b \rceil) \leq cf(n)$ for $n > b + b/(b-1)$, where $c < 1$ is a constant, then it follows that $a^j f(n_j) \leq c^j f(n)$. Therefore, the sum in equation (4.14) can be evaluated just as in Lemma 4.3. For case 2, we have $f(n) = \Theta(n^{\log_b a})$. If we can show that $f(n_j) = O(n^{\log_b a}/a^j) = O((n/b^j)^{\log_b a})$, then the proof for case 2 of Lemma 4.3 will go through. Observe that $j \leq \lfloor \log_b n \rfloor$ implies $b^j/n \leq 1$. The bound $f(n) = O(n^{\log_b a})$ implies that there exists a constant $c > 0$ such that for sufficiently large n_j,

$$
\begin{aligned}
f(n_j) &\leq c \left(\frac{n}{b^j} + \frac{b}{b-1} \right)^{\log_b a} \\
&= c \left(\frac{n^{\log_b a}}{a^j} \right) \left(1 + \left(\frac{b^j}{n} \cdot \frac{b}{b-1} \right) \right)^{\log_b a} \\
&\leq c \left(\frac{n^{\log_b a}}{a^j} \right) \left(1 + \frac{b}{b-1} \right)^{\log_b a} \\
&\leq O \left(\frac{n^{\log_b a}}{a^j} \right) \ ,
\end{aligned}
$$

since $c(1 + b/(b - 1))^{\log_b a}$ is a constant. Thus, case 2 is proved. The proof of case 1 is almost identical. The key is to prove the bound $f(n_j) = O(n^{\log_b a - \epsilon})$, which is similar to the corresponding proof of case 2, though the algebra is more intricate.

We have now proved the upper bounds in the master theorem for all integers n. The proof of the lower bounds is similar.

Exercises

4.4-1 ★
Give a simple and exact expression for n_i in equation (4.12) for the case in which b is a positive integer instead of an arbitrary real number.

4.4-2 ★
Show that if $f(n) = \Theta(n^{\log_b a} \lg^k n)$, where $k \geq 0$, then the master recurrence has solution $T(n) = \Theta(n^{\log_b a} \lg^{k+1} n)$. For simplicity, confine your analysis to exact powers of b.

4.4-3 ★
Show that case 3 of the master theorem is overstated, in the sense that the regularity condition $af(n/b) \leq cf(n)$ for some constant $c < 1$ implies that there exists a constant $\epsilon > 0$ such that $f(n) = \Omega(n^{\log_b a + \epsilon})$.

Problems

4-1   *Recurrence examples*
Give asymptotic upper and lower bounds for $T(n)$ in each of the following recurrences. Assume that $T(n)$ is constant for $n \leq 2$. Make your bounds as tight as possible, and justify your answers.

a. $T(n) = 2T(n/2) + n^3$.

b. $T(n) = T(9n/10) + n$.

c. $T(n) = 16T(n/4) + n^2$.

d. $T(n) = 7T(n/3) + n^2$.

e. $T(n) = 7T(n/2) + n^2$.

f. $T(n) = 2T(n/4) + \sqrt{n}$.

g. $T(n) = T(n - 1) + n$.

h. $T(n) = T(\sqrt{n}) + 1$.

4-2 *Finding the missing integer*

An array $A[1..n]$ contains all the integers from 0 to n except one. It would be easy to determine the missing integer in $O(n)$ time by using an auxiliary array $B[0..n]$ to record which numbers appear in A. In this problem, however, we cannot access an entire integer in A with a single operation. The elements of A are represented in binary, and the only operation we can use to access them is "fetch the jth bit of $A[i]$," which takes constant time.

Show that if we use only this operation, we can still determine the missing integer in $O(n)$ time.

4-3 *Parameter-passing costs*

Throughout this book, we assume that parameter passing during procedure calls takes constant time, even if an N-element array is being passed. This assumption is valid in most systems because a pointer to the array is passed, not the array itself. This problem examines the implications of three parameter-passing strategies:

1. An array is passed by pointer. Time $= \Theta(1)$.

2. An array is passed by copying. Time $= \Theta(N)$, where N is the size of the array.

3. An array is passed by copying only the subrange that might be accessed by the called procedure. Time $= \Theta(p - q + 1)$ if the subarray $A[p..q]$ is passed.

a. Consider the recursive binary search algorithm for finding a number in a sorted array (see Exercise 1.3-5). Give recurrences for the worst-case running times of binary search when arrays are passed using each of the three methods above, and give good upper bounds on the solutions of the recurrences. Let N be the size of the original problem and n be the size of a subproblem.

b. Redo part (a) for the MERGE-SORT algorithm from Section 1.3.1.

4-4 *More recurrence examples*

Give asymptotic upper and lower bounds for $T(n)$ in each of the following recurrences. Assume that $T(n)$ is constant for $n \leq 2$. Make your bounds as tight as possible, and justify your answers.

a. $T(n) = 3T(n/2) + n \lg n$.

b. $T(n) = 3T(n/3 + 5) + n/2$.

c. $T(n) = 2T(n/2) + n/\lg n$.

d. $T(n) = T(n - 1) + 1/n$.

e. $T(n) = T(n-1) + \lg n$.

f. $T(n) = \sqrt{n} T(\sqrt{n}) + n$.

4-5   *Sloppiness conditions*

Often, we are able to bound a recurrence $T(n)$ at exact powers of an integral constant b. This problem gives sufficient conditions for us to extend the bound to all real $n > 0$.

a. Let $T(n)$ and $h(n)$ be monotonically increasing functions, and suppose that $T(n) \leq h(n)$ when n is an exact power of a constant $b > 1$. Moreover, suppose that $h(n)$ is "slowly growing" in the sense that $h(n) = O(h(n/b))$. Prove that $T(n) = O(h(n))$.

b. Suppose that we have the recurrence $T(n) = aT(n/b) + f(n)$, where $a \geq 1$, $b > 1$, and $f(n)$ is monotonically increasing. Suppose further that the initial conditions for the recurrence are given by $T(n) = g(n)$ for $n \leq n_0$, where $g(n)$ is monotonically increasing and $g(n_0) \leq aT(n_0/b) + f(n_0)$. Prove that $T(n)$ is monotonically increasing.

c. Simplify the proof of the master theorem for the case in which $f(n)$ is monotonically increasing and slowly growing. Use Lemma 4.4.

4-6   *Fibonacci numbers*

This problem develops properties of the Fibonacci numbers, which are defined by recurrence (2.13). We shall use the technique of generating functions to solve the Fibonacci recurrence. Define the ***generating function*** (or ***formal power series***) $\mathcal{F}$ as

$$
\begin{aligned}
\mathcal{F}(z) &= \sum_{i=0}^{\infty} F_i z^i \\
&= 0 + z + z^2 + 2z^3 + 3z^4 + 5z^5 + 8z^6 + 13z^7 + 21z^8 + \cdots .
\end{aligned}
$$

a. Show that $\mathcal{F}(z) = z + z\mathcal{F}(z) + z^2\mathcal{F}(z)$.

b. Show that

$$
\begin{aligned}
\mathcal{F}(z) &= \frac{z}{1 - z - z^2} \\
&= \frac{z}{(1 - \phi z)(1 - \widehat{\phi} z)} \\
&= \frac{1}{\sqrt{5}} \left(\frac{1}{1 - \phi z} - \frac{1}{1 - \widehat{\phi} z} \right) ,
\end{aligned}
$$

where

$$
\phi = \frac{1 + \sqrt{5}}{2} = 1.61803\ldots
$$

and

$$\hat{\phi} = \frac{1 - \sqrt{5}}{2} = -0.61803\ldots .$$

c. Show that

$$\mathcal{F}(z) = \sum_{i=0}^{\infty} \frac{1}{\sqrt{5}} (\phi^i - \hat{\phi}^i) z^i \ .$$

d. Prove that $F_i = \phi^i / \sqrt{5}$ for $i > 0$, rounded to the nearest integer. (*Hint:* $|\hat{\phi}| < 1$.)

e. Prove that $F_{i+2} \geq \phi^i$ for $i \geq 0$.

4-7 *VLSI chip testing*

Professor Diogenes has n supposedly identical VLSI[1] chips that in principle are capable of testing each other. The professor's test jig accommodates two chips at a time. When the jig is loaded, each chip tests the other and reports whether it is good or bad. A good chip always reports accurately whether the other chip is good or bad, but the answer of a bad chip cannot be trusted. Thus, the four possible outcomes of a test are as follows:

Chip A says	Chip B says	Conclusion
B is good	A is good	both are good, or both are bad
B is good	A is bad	at least one is bad
B is bad	A is good	at least one is bad
B is bad	A is bad	at least one is bad

a. Show that if more than $n/2$ chips are bad, the professor cannot necessarily determine which chips are good using any strategy based on this kind of pairwise test. Assume that the bad chips can conspire to fool the professor.

b. Consider the problem of finding a single good chip from among n chips, assuming that more than $n/2$ of the chips are good. Show that $\lfloor n/2 \rfloor$ pairwise tests are sufficient to reduce the problem to one of nearly half the size.

c. Show that the good chips can be identified with $\Theta(n)$ pairwise tests, assuming that more than $n/2$ of the chips are good. Give and solve the recurrence that describes the number of tests.

---

[1] VLSI stands for "very-large-scale integration," which is the integrated-circuit chip technology used to fabricate most microprocessors today.

Chapter notes

Recurrences were studied as early as 1202 by L. Fibonacci, for whom the Fibonacci numbers are named. A. De Moivre introduced the method of generating functions (see Problem 4-6) for solving recurrences. The master method is adapted from Bentley, Haken, and Saxe [26], which provides the extended method justified by Exercise 4.4-2. Knuth [121] and Liu [140] show how to solve linear recurrences using the method of generating functions. Purdom and Brown [164] contains an extended discussion of recurrence solving.

5 Sets, Etc.

In earlier chapters, we touched on the elements of discrete mathematics. This chapter reviews more completely the notations, definitions, and elementary properties of sets, relations, functions, graphs, and trees. Readers already well versed in this material need only skim this chapter.

5.1 Sets

A *set* is a collection of distinguishable objects, called its *members* or *elements*. If an object x is a member of a set S, we write $x \in S$ (read "x is a member of S" or, more briefly, "x is in S"). If x is not a member of S, we write $x \notin S$. We can describe a set by explicitly listing its members as a list inside braces. For example, we can define a set S to contain precisely the numbers 1, 2, and 3 by writing $S = \{1, 2, 3\}$. Since 2 is a member of the set S, we can write $2 \in S$, and since 4 is not a member, we have $4 \notin S$. A set cannot contain the same object more than once, and its elements are not ordered. Two sets A and B are *equal*, written $A = B$, if they contain the same elements. For example, $\{1, 2, 3, 1\} = \{1, 2, 3\} = \{3, 2, 1\}$.

We adopt special notations for frequently encountered sets.

- $\emptyset$ denotes the *empty set*, that is, the set containing no members.
- **Z** denotes the set of *integers*, that is, the set $\{\ldots, -2, -1, 0, 1, 2, \ldots\}$.
- **R** denotes the set of *real numbers*.
- **N** denotes the set of *natural numbers*, that is, the set $\{0, 1, 2, \ldots\}$.[1]

If all the elements of a set A are contained in a set B, that is, if $x \in A$ implies $x \in B$, then we write $A \subseteq B$ and say that A is a *subset* of B. A set A is a *proper subset* of B, written $A \subset B$, if $A \subseteq B$ but $A \neq B$. (Some authors use the symbol "$\subset$" to denote the ordinary subset relation, rather than the proper-subset relation.) For any set A, we have $A \subseteq A$. For two sets A and B, we have $A = B$ if and only if $A \subseteq B$ and $B \subseteq A$. For any

---

[1] Some authors start the natural numbers with 1 instead of 0. The modern trend seems to be to start with 0.

three sets A, B, and C, if $A \subseteq B$ and $B \subseteq C$, then $A \subseteq C$. For any set A, we have $\emptyset \subseteq A$.

We sometimes define sets in terms of other sets. Given a set A, we can define a set $B \subseteq A$ by stating a property that distinguishes the elements of B. For example, we can define the set of even integers by $\{x : x \in \mathbf{Z} \text{ and } x/2 \text{ is an integer}\}$. The colon in this notation is read "such that." (Some authors use a vertical bar in place of the colon.)

Given two sets A and B, we can also define new sets by applying *set operations*:

- The *intersection* of sets A and B is the set
$$A \cap B = \{x : x \in A \text{ and } x \in B\} \ .$$

- The *union* of sets A and B is the set
$$A \cup B = \{x : x \in A \text{ or } x \in B\} \ .$$

- The *difference* between two sets A and B is the set
$$A - B = \{x : x \in A \text{ and } x \notin B\} \ .$$

Set operations obey the following laws.

Empty set laws:
$$\begin{aligned} A \cap \emptyset &= \emptyset \ , \\ A \cup \emptyset &= A \ . \end{aligned}$$

Idempotency laws:
$$\begin{aligned} A \cap A &= A \ , \\ A \cup A &= A \ . \end{aligned}$$

Commutative laws:
$$\begin{aligned} A \cap B &= B \cap A \ , \\ A \cup B &= B \cup A \ . \end{aligned}$$

Associative laws:
$$\begin{aligned} A \cap (B \cap C) &= (A \cap B) \cap C \ , \\ A \cup (B \cup C) &= (A \cup B) \cup C \ . \end{aligned}$$

Distributive laws:
$$\begin{aligned} A \cap (B \cup C) &= (A \cap B) \cup (A \cap C) \ , \\ A \cup (B \cap C) &= (A \cup B) \cap (A \cup C) \ . \end{aligned} \tag{5.1}$$

Absorption laws:
$$\begin{aligned} A \cap (A \cup B) &= A \ , \\ A \cup (A \cap B) &= A \ . \end{aligned}$$

DeMorgan's laws:
$$\begin{aligned} A - (B \cap C) &= (A - B) \cup (A - C) \ , \\ A - (B \cup C) &= (A - B) \cap (A - C) \ . \end{aligned} \tag{5.2}$$

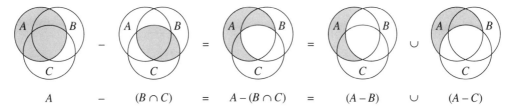

$$A \quad - \quad (B \cap C) \quad = \quad A - (B \cap C) \quad = \quad (A - B) \quad \cup \quad (A - C)$$

Figure 5.1 A Venn diagram illustrating the first of DeMorgan's laws (5.2). Each of the sets A, B, and C is represented as a circle in the plane.

The first of DeMorgan's laws is illustrated in Figure 5.1, using a *Venn diagram*, a graphical picture in which sets are represented as regions of the plane.

Often, all the sets under consideration are subsets of some larger set U called the *universe*. For example, if we are considering various sets made up only of integers, the set $\mathbf{Z}$ of integers is an appropriate universe. Given a universe U, we define the *complement* of a set A as $\overline{A} = U - A$. For any set $A \subseteq U$, we have the following laws:

$$
\begin{aligned}
\overline{\overline{A}} &= A , \\
A \cap \overline{A} &= \emptyset , \\
A \cup \overline{A} &= U .
\end{aligned}
$$

DeMorgan's laws (5.2) can be rewritten with complements. For any two sets $A, B \subseteq U$, we have

$$
\begin{aligned}
\overline{A \cap B} &= \overline{A} \cup \overline{B} , \\
\overline{A \cup B} &= \overline{A} \cap \overline{B} .
\end{aligned}
$$

Two sets A and B are *disjoint* if they have no elements in common, that is, if $A \cap B = \emptyset$. A collection $\mathcal{S} = \{S_i\}$ of nonempty sets forms a *partition* of a set S if

- the sets are *pairwise disjoint*, that is, $S_i, S_j \in \mathcal{S}$ and $i \neq j$ imply $S_i \cap S_j = \emptyset$, and

- their union is S, that is,

$$S = \bigcup_{S_i \in \mathcal{S}} S_i .$$

In other words, $\mathcal{S}$ forms a partition of S if each element of S appears in exactly one $S_i \in \mathcal{S}$.

The number of elements in a set is called the *cardinality* (or *size*) of the set, denoted $|S|$. Two sets have the same cardinality if their elements can be put into a one-to-one correspondence. The cardinality of the empty set is $|\emptyset| = 0$. If the cardinality of a set is a natural number, we say the set is *finite*; otherwise, it is *infinite*. An infinite set that can be put into a one-to-one correspondence with the natural numbers $\mathbf{N}$ is *countably infinite*;

otherwise, it is **uncountable**. The integers **Z** are countable, but the reals **R** are uncountable.

For any two finite sets A and B, we have the identity

$$|A \cup B| = |A| + |B| - |A \cap B| \ , \tag{5.3}$$

from which we can conclude that

$$|A \cup B| \leq |A| + |B| \ .$$

If A and B are disjoint, then $|A \cap B| = 0$ and thus $|A \cup B| = |A| + |B|$. If $A \subseteq B$, then $|A| \leq |B|$.

A finite set of n elements is sometimes called an **n-set**. A 1-set is called a **singleton**. A subset of k elements of a set is sometimes called a **k-subset**.

The set of all subsets of a set S, including the empty set and the set S itself, is denoted 2^S and is called the **power set** of S. For example, $2^{\{a,b\}} = \{\emptyset, \{a\}, \{b\}, \{a,b\}\}$. The power set of a finite set S has cardinality $2^{|S|}$.

We sometimes care about setlike structures in which the elements are ordered. An **ordered pair** of two elements a and b is denoted (a,b) and can be defined formally as the set $(a,b) = \{a, \{a,b\}\}$. Thus, the ordered pair (a,b) is *not* the same as the ordered pair (b,a).

The **Cartesian product** of two sets A and B, denoted $A \times B$, is the set of all ordered pairs such that the first element of the pair is an element of A and the second is an element of B. More formally,

$$A \times B = \{(a,b) : a \in A \text{ and } b \in B\} \ .$$

For example, $\{a,b\} \times \{a,b,c\} = \{(a,a), (a,b), (a,c), (b,a), (b,b), (b,c)\}$. When A and B are finite sets, the cardinality of their Cartesian product is

$$|A \times B| = |A| \cdot |B| \ . \tag{5.4}$$

The Cartesian product of n sets $A_1, A_2, \ldots, A_n$ is the set of **n-tuples**

$$A_1 \times A_2 \times \cdots \times A_n = \{(a_1, a_2, \ldots, a_n) : a_i \in A_i, i = 1, 2, \ldots, n\} \ ,$$

whose cardinality is

$$|A_1 \times A_2 \times \cdots \times A_n| = |A_1| \cdot |A_2| \cdots |A_n|$$

if all sets are finite. We denote an n-fold Cartesian product over a single set A by the set

$$A^n = A \times A \times \cdots \times A \ ,$$

whose cardinality is $|A^n| = |A|^n$ if A is finite. An n-tuple can also be viewed as a finite sequence of length n (see page 84).

Exercises

5.1-1
Draw Venn diagrams that illustrate the first of the distributive laws (5.1).

5.1-2
Prove the generalization of DeMorgan's laws to any finite collection of sets:

$$\overline{A_1 \cap A_2 \cap \cdots \cap A_n} = \overline{A_1} \cup \overline{A_2} \cup \cdots \cup \overline{A_n} ,$$
$$\overline{A_1 \cup A_2 \cup \cdots \cup A_n} = \overline{A_1} \cap \overline{A_2} \cap \cdots \cap \overline{A_n} .$$

5.1-3 ⋆
Prove the generalization of equation (5.3), which is called the ***principle of inclusion and exclusion***:

$$|A_1 \cup A_2 \cup \cdots \cup A_n| =$$
$$\quad |A_1| + |A_2| + \cdots + |A_n|$$
$$\quad - |A_1 \cap A_2| - |A_1 \cap A_3| - \cdots \qquad \text{(all pairs)}$$
$$\quad + |A_1 \cap A_2 \cap A_3| + \cdots \qquad \text{(all triples)}$$
$$\vdots$$
$$\quad + (-1)^{n-1} |A_1 \cap A_2 \cap \cdots \cap A_n| .$$

5.1-4
Show that the set of odd natural numbers is countable.

5.1-5
Show that for any finite set S, the power set 2^S has $2^{|S|}$ elements (that is, there are $2^{|S|}$ distinct subsets of S).

5.1-6
Give an inductive definition for an n-tuple by extending the set-theoretic definition for an ordered pair.

5.2   Relations

A ***binary relation*** R on two sets A and B is a subset of the Cartesian product $A \times B$. If $(a, b) \in R$, we sometimes write $a R b$. When we say that R is a binary relation on a set A, we mean that R is a subset of $A \times A$. For example, the "less than" relation on the natural numbers is the set $\{(a, b) : a, b \in \mathbf{N} \text{ and } a < b\}$. An n-ary relation on sets $A_1, A_2, \ldots, A_n$ is a subset of $A_1 \times A_2 \times \cdots \times A_n$.

A binary relation $R \subseteq A \times A$ is ***reflexive*** if

$$a R a$$

for all $a \in A$. For example, "=" and "≤" are reflexive relations on $\mathbf{N}$, but "<" is not. The relation R is ***symmetric*** if

$$a R b \text{ implies } b R a$$

for all $a, b \in A$. For example, "=" is symmetric, but "<" and "≤" are not. The relation R is **transitive** if

$a \, R \, b$ and $b \, R \, c$ imply $a \, R \, c$

for all $a, b, c \in A$. For example, the relations "<," "≤," and "=" are transitive, but the relation $R = \{(a, b) : a, b \in \mathbf{N} \text{ and } a = b - 1\}$ is not, since $3 R 4$ and $4 R 5$ do not imply $3 R 5$.

A relation that is reflexive, symmetric, and transitive is an **equivalence relation**. For example, "=" is an equivalence relation on the natural numbers, but "<" is not. If R is an equivalence relation on a set A, then for $a \in A$, the **equivalence class** of a is the set $[a] = \{b \in A : a \, R \, b\}$, that is, the set of all elements equivalent to A. For example, if we define $R = \{(a, b) : a, b \in \mathbf{N} \text{ and } a + b \text{ is an even number}\}$, then R is an equivalence relation, since $a + a$ is even (reflexive), $a + b$ is even implies $b + a$ is even (symmetric), and $a + b$ is even and $b + c$ is even imply $a + c$ is even (transitive). The equivalence class of 4 is $[4] = \{0, 2, 4, 6, \ldots\}$, and the equivalence class of 3 is $[3] = \{1, 3, 5, 7, \ldots\}$. A basic theorem of equivalence classes is the following.

Theorem 5.1 (An equivalence relation is the same as a partition)
The equivalence classes of any equivalence relation R on a set A form a partition of A, and any partition of A determines an equivalence relation on A for which the sets in the partition are the equivalence classes.

Proof   For the first part of the proof, we must show that the equivalence classes of R are nonempty, pairwise-disjoint sets whose union is A. Because R is reflexive, $a \in [a]$, and so the equivalence classes are nonempty; moreover, since every element $a \in A$ belongs to the equivalence class $[a]$, the union of the equivalence classes is A. It remains to show that the equivalence classes are pairwise disjoint, that is, if two equivalence classes $[a]$ and $[b]$ have an element c in common, then they are in fact the same set. Now $a \, R \, c$ and $b \, R \, c$, which by symmetry and transitivity imply $a \, R \, b$. Thus, for any arbitrary element $x \in [a]$, we have $x \, R \, a$ implies $x \, R \, b$, and thus $[a] \subseteq [b]$. Similarly, $[b] \subseteq [a]$, and thus $[a] = [b]$.

For the second part of the proof, let $\mathcal{A} = \{A_i\}$ be a partition of A, and define $R = \{(a, b) : \text{there exists } i \text{ such that } a \in A_i \text{ and } b \in A_i\}$. We claim that R is an equivalence relation on A. Reflexivity holds, since $a \in A_i$ implies $a \, R \, a$. Symmetry holds, because if $a \, R \, b$, then a and b are in the same set A_i, and hence $b \, R \, a$. If $a \, R \, b$ and $b \, R \, c$, then all three elements are in the same set, and thus $a \, R \, c$ and transitivity holds. To see that the sets in the partition are the equivalence classes of R, observe that if $a \in A_i$, then $x \in [a]$ implies $x \in A_i$, and $x \in A_i$ implies $x \in [a]$.   ∎

A binary relation R on a set A is **antisymmetric** if

$a \, R \, b$ and $b \, R \, a$ imply $a = b$.

For example, the "$\leq$" relation on the natural numbers is antisymmetric, since $a \leq b$ and $b \leq a$ imply $a = b$. A relation that is reflexive, antisymmetric, and transitive is a ***partial order***, and we call a set on which a partial order is defined a ***partially ordered set***. For example, the relation "is a descendant of" is a partial order on the set of all people (if we view individuals as being their own descendants).

In a partially ordered set A, there may be no single "maximum" element x such that $y\, R\, x$ for all $y \in A$. Instead, there may several ***maximal*** elements x such that for no $y \in A$ is it the case that $x\, R\, y$. For example, in a collection of different-sized boxes there may be several maximal boxes that don't fit inside of any other box, yet no single "maximum" box into which any other box will fit.

A partial order R on a set A is a ***total*** or ***linear order*** if for all $a, b \in A$, we have $a\, R\, b$ or $b\, R\, a$, that is, if every pairing of elements of A can be related by R. For example, the relation "$\leq$" is a total order on the natural numbers, but the "is a descendant of" relation is not a total order on the set of all people, since there are individuals neither of whom is descended from the other.

Exercises

5.2-1
Prove that the subset relation "$\subseteq$" on all subsets of $\mathbf{Z}$ is a partial order but not a total order.

5.2-2
Show that for any positive integer n, the relation "equivalent modulo n" is an equivalence relation on the integers. (We say that $a \equiv b \pmod{n}$ if there exists an integer q such that $a - b = qn$.) Into what equivalence classes does this relation partition the integers?

5.2-3
Give examples of relations that are

a. reflexive and symmetric but not transitive,

b. reflexive and transitive but not symmetric,

c. symmetric and transitive but not reflexive.

5.2-4
Let S be a finite set, and let R be an equivalence relation on $S \times S$. Show that if in addition R is antisymmetric, then the equivalence classes of S with respect to R are singletons.

5.2-5
Professor Narcissus claims that if a relation R is symmetric and transitive, then it is also reflexive. He offers the following proof. By symmetry,

$a \, R \, b$ implies $b \, R \, a$. Transitivity, therefore, implies $a \, R \, a$. Is the professor correct?

5.3   Functions

Given two sets A and B, a ***function*** f is a binary relation on $A \times B$ such that for all $a \in A$, there exists precisely one $b \in B$ such that $(a, b) \in f$. The set A is called the ***domain*** of f, and the set B is called the ***codomain*** of f. We sometimes write $f : A \to B$; and if $(a, b) \in f$, we write $b = f(a)$, since b is uniquely determined by the choice of a.

Intuitively, the function f assigns an element of B to each element of A. No element of A is assigned two different elements of B, but the same element of B can be assigned to two different elements of A. For example, the binary relation

$$f = \{(a, b) : a \in \mathbf{N} \text{ and } b = a \bmod 2\}$$

is a function $f : \mathbf{N} \to \{0, 1\}$, since for each natural number a, there is exactly one value b in $\{0, 1\}$ such that $b = a \bmod 2$. For this example, $0 = f(0)$, $1 = f(1)$, $0 = f(2)$, etc. In contrast, the binary relation

$$g = \{(a, b) : a \in \mathbf{N} \text{ and } a + b \text{ is even}\}$$

is not a function, since $(1, 3)$ and $(1, 5)$ are both in g, and thus for the choice $a = 1$, there is not precisely one b such that $(a, b) \in g$.

Given a function $f : A \to B$, if $b = f(a)$, we say that a is the ***argument*** of f and that b is the ***value*** of f at a. We can define a function by stating its value for every element of its domain. For example, we might define $f(n) = 2n$ for $n \in \mathbf{N}$, which means $f = \{(n, 2n) : n \in \mathbf{N}\}$. Two functions f and g are ***equal*** if they have the same domain and codomain and if, for all a in the domain, $f(a) = g(a)$.

A ***finite sequence*** of length n is a function f whose domain is the set $\{0, 1, \ldots, n - 1\}$. We often denote a finite sequence by listing its values: $\langle f(0), f(1), \ldots, f(n-1) \rangle$. An ***infinite sequence*** is a function whose domain is the set $\mathbf{N}$ of natural numbers. For example, the Fibonacci sequence, defined by (2.13), is the infinite sequence $\langle 0, 1, 1, 2, 3, 5, 8, 13, 21, \ldots \rangle$.

When the domain of a function f is a Cartesian product, we often omit the extra parentheses surrounding the argument of f. For example, if $f : A_1 \times A_2 \times \cdots \times A_n \to B$, we would write $b = f(a_1, a_2, \ldots, a_n)$ instead of $b = f((a_1, a_2, \ldots, a_n))$. We also call each a_i an ***argument*** to the function f, though technically the (single) argument to f is the n-tuple $(a_1, a_2, \ldots, a_n)$.

If $f : A \to B$ is a function and $b = f(a)$, then we sometimes say that b is the ***image*** of a under f. The image of a set $A' \subseteq A$ under f is defined by

$$f(A') = \{b \in B : b = f(a) \text{ for some } a \in A'\} \ .$$

The *range* of f is the image of its domain, that is, $f(A)$. For example, the range of the function $f : \mathbf{N} \to \mathbf{N}$ defined by $f(n) = 2n$ is $f(\mathbf{N}) = \{m : m = 2n \text{ for some } n \in \mathbf{N}\}$.

A function is a *surjection* if its range is its codomain. For example, the function $f(n) = \lfloor n/2 \rfloor$ is a surjective function from $\mathbf{N}$ to $\mathbf{N}$, since every element in $\mathbf{N}$ appears as the value of f for some argument. In contrast, the function $f(n) = 2n$ is not a surjective function from $\mathbf{N}$ to $\mathbf{N}$, since no argument to f can produce 3 as a value. The function $f(n) = 2n$ is, however, a surjective function from the natural numbers to the even numbers. A surjection $f : A \to B$ is sometimes described as mapping A *onto B*. When we say that f is onto, we mean that it is surjective.

A function $f : A \to B$ is an *injection* if distinct arguments to f produce distinct values, that is, if $a \neq a'$ implies $f(a) \neq f(a')$. For example, the function $f(n) = 2n$ is an injective function from $\mathbf{N}$ to $\mathbf{N}$, since each even number b is the image under f of at most one element of the domain, namely $b/2$. The function $f(n) = \lfloor n/2 \rfloor$ is not injective, since the value 1 is produced by two arguments: 2 and 3. An injection is sometimes called a *one-to-one* function.

A function $f : A \to B$ is a *bijection* if it is injective and surjective. For example, the function $f(n) = (-1)^n \lceil n/2 \rceil$ is a bijection from $\mathbf{N}$ to $\mathbf{Z}$:

$$
\begin{aligned}
0 &\to 0, \\
1 &\to -1, \\
2 &\to 1, \\
3 &\to -2, \\
4 &\to 2, \\
&\vdots
\end{aligned}
$$

The function is injective, since no element of $\mathbf{Z}$ is the image of more than one element of $\mathbf{N}$. It is surjective, since every element of $\mathbf{Z}$ appears as the image of some element of $\mathbf{N}$. Hence, the function is bijective. A bijection is sometimes called a *one-to-one correspondence*, since it pairs elements in the domain and codomain. A bijection from a set A to itself is sometimes called a *permutation*.

When a function f is bijective, its *inverse* f^{-1} is defined as

$$f^{-1}(b) = a \text{ if and only if } f(a) = b .$$

For example, the inverse of the function $f(n) = (-1)^n \lceil n/2 \rceil$ is

$$
f^{-1}(m) = \begin{cases} 2m & \text{if } m \geq 0, \\ -2m - 1 & \text{if } m < 0 . \end{cases}
$$

Exercises

5.3-1
Let A and B be finite sets, and let $f : A \to B$ be a function. Show that

a. if f is injective, then $|A| \leq |B|$;

b. if f is surjective, then $|A| \geq |B|$.

5.3-2
Is the function $f(x) = x + 1$ bijective when the domain and the codomain are **N**? Is it bijective when the domain and the codomain are **Z**?

5.3-3
Give a natural definition for the inverse of a binary relation such that if a relation is in fact a bijective function, its relational inverse is its functional inverse.

5.3-4   ⋆
Give a bijection from **Z** to **Z** × **Z**.

5.4   Graphs

This section presents two kinds of graphs: directed and undirected. The reader should be aware that certain definitions in the literature differ from those given here, but for the most part, the differences are slight. Section 23.1 shows how graphs can be represented in computer memory.

A ***directed graph*** (or ***digraph***) G is a pair (V, E), where V is a finite set and E is a binary relation on V. The set V is called the ***vertex set*** of G, and its elements are called ***vertices*** (singular: ***vertex***). The set E is called the ***edge set*** of G, and its elements are called ***edges***. Figure 5.2(a) is a pictorial representation of a directed graph on the vertex set $\{1, 2, 3, 4, 5, 6\}$. Vertices are represented by circles in the figure, and edges are represented by arrows. Note that ***self-loops***—edges from a vertex to itself—are possible.

In an ***undirected graph*** $G = (V, E)$, the edge set E consists of *unordered* pairs of vertices, rather than ordered pairs. That is, an edge is a set $\{u, v\}$, where $u, v \in V$ and $u \neq v$. By convention, we use the notation (u, v) for an edge, rather than the set notation $\{u, v\}$, and (u, v) and (v, u) are considered to be the same edge. In an undirected graph, self-loops are forbidden, and so every edge consists of exactly two distinct vertices. Figure 5.2(b) is a pictorial representation of an undirected graph on the vertex set $\{1, 2, 3, 4, 5, 6\}$.

Many definitions for directed and undirected graphs are the same, although certain terms have slightly different meanings in the two contexts. If (u, v) is an edge in a directed graph $G = (V, E)$, we say that (u, v)

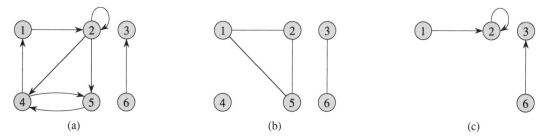

Figure 5.2 Directed and undirected graphs. **(a)** A directed graph $G = (V, E)$, where $V = \{1, 2, 3, 4, 5, 6\}$ and $E = \{(1, 2), (2, 2), (2, 4), (2, 5), (4, 1), (4, 5), (5, 4), (6, 3)\}$. The edge $(2, 2)$ is a self-loop. **(b)** An undirected graph $G = (V, E)$, where $V = \{1, 2, 3, 4, 5, 6\}$ and $E = \{(1, 2), (1, 5), (2, 5), (3, 6)\}$. The vertex 4 is isolated. **(c)** The subgraph of the graph in part (a) induced by the vertex set $\{1, 2, 3, 6\}$.

is *incident from* or *leaves* vertex u and is *incident to* or *enters* vertex v. For example, the edges leaving vertex 2 in Figure 5.2(a) are $(2, 2)$, $(2, 4)$, and $(2, 5)$. The edges entering vertex 2 are $(1, 2)$ and $(2, 2)$. If (u, v) is an edge in an undirected graph $G = (V, E)$, we say that (u, v) is *incident on* vertices u and v. In Figure 5.2(b), the edges incident on vertex 2 are $(1, 2)$ and $(2, 5)$.

If (u, v) is an edge in a graph $G = (V, E)$, we say that vertex v is *adjacent* to vertex u. When the graph is undirected, the adjacency relation is symmetric. When the graph is directed, the adjacency relation is not necessarily symmetric. If v is adjacent to u in a directed graph, we sometimes write $u \rightarrow v$. In parts (a) and (b) of Figure 5.2, vertex 2 is adjacent to vertex 1, since the edge $(1, 2)$ belongs to both graphs. Vertex 1 is *not* adjacent to vertex 2 in Figure 5.2(a), since the edge $(2, 1)$ does not belong to the graph.

The *degree* of a vertex in an undirected graph is the number of edges incident on it. For example, vertex 2 in Figure 5.2(b) has degree 2. In a directed graph, the *out-degree* of a vertex is the number of edges leaving it, and the *in-degree* of a vertex is the number of edges entering it. The *degree* of a vertex in a directed graph is its in-degree plus its out-degree. Vertex 2 in Figure 5.2(a) has in-degree 2, out-degree 3, and degree 5.

A *path* of *length* k from a vertex u to a vertex u' in a graph $G = (V, E)$ is a sequence $\langle v_0, v_1, v_2, \ldots, v_k \rangle$ of vertices such that $u = v_0$, $u' = v_k$, and $(v_{i-1}, v_i) \in E$ for $i = 1, 2, \ldots, k$. The length of the path is the number of edges in the path. The path *contains* the vertices $v_0, v_1, \ldots, v_k$ and the edges $(v_0, v_1), (v_1, v_2), \ldots, (v_{k-1}, v_k)$. If there is a path p from u to u', we say that u' is *reachable* from u via p, which we sometimes write as $u \overset{p}{\rightsquigarrow} u'$ if G is directed. A path is *simple* if all vertices in the path are distinct. In Figure 5.2(a), the path $\langle 1, 2, 5, 4 \rangle$ is a simple path of length 3. The path $\langle 2, 5, 4, 5 \rangle$ is not simple.

A **subpath** of path $p = \langle v_0, v_1, \ldots, v_k \rangle$ is a contiguous subsequence of its vertices. That is, for any $0 \le i \le j \le k$, the subsequence of vertices $\langle v_i, v_{i+1}, \ldots, v_j \rangle$ is a subpath of p.

In a directed graph, a path $\langle v_0, v_1, \ldots, v_k \rangle$ forms a **cycle** if $v_0 = v_k$ and the path contains at least one edge. The cycle is **simple** if, in addition, $v_1, v_2, \ldots, v_k$ are distinct. A self-loop is a cycle of length 1. Two paths $\langle v_0, v_1, v_2, \ldots, v_{k-1}, v_0 \rangle$ and $\langle v_0', v_1', v_2', \ldots, v_{k-1}', v_0' \rangle$ form the same cycle if there exists an integer j such that $v_i' = v_{(i+j) \bmod k}$ for $i = 0, 1, \ldots, k - 1$. In Figure 5.2(a), the path $\langle 1, 2, 4, 1 \rangle$ forms the same cycle as the paths $\langle 2, 4, 1, 2 \rangle$ and $\langle 4, 1, 2, 4 \rangle$. This cycle is simple, but the cycle $\langle 1, 2, 4, 5, 4, 1 \rangle$ is not. The cycle $\langle 2, 2 \rangle$ formed by the edge $(2, 2)$ is a self-loop. A directed graph with no self-loops is **simple**. In an undirected graph, a path $\langle v_0, v_1, \ldots, v_k \rangle$ forms a **cycle** if $v_0 = v_k$ and $v_1, v_2, \ldots, v_k$ are distinct. For example, in Figure 5.2(b), the path $\langle 1, 2, 5, 1 \rangle$ is a cycle. A graph with no cycles is **acyclic**.

An undirected graph is **connected** if every pair of vertices is connected by a path. The **connected components** of a graph are the equivalence classes of vertices under the "is reachable from" relation. The graph in Figure 5.2(b) has three connected components: $\{1, 2, 5\}$, $\{3, 6\}$, and $\{4\}$. Every vertex in $\{1, 2, 5\}$ is reachable from every other vertex in $\{1, 2, 5\}$. An undirected graph is connected if it has exactly one connected component, that is, if every vertex is reachable from every other vertex.

A directed graph is **strongly connected** if every two vertices are reachable from each other. The **strongly connected components** of a graph are the equivalence classes of vertices under the "are mutually reachable" relation. A directed graph is strongly connected if it has only one strongly connected component. The graph in Figure 5.2(a) has three strongly connected components: $\{1, 2, 4, 5\}$, $\{3\}$, and $\{6\}$. All pairs of vertices in $\{1, 2, 4, 5\}$ are mutually reachable. The vertices $\{3, 6\}$ do not form a strongly connected component, since vertex 6 cannot be reached from vertex 3.

Two graphs $G = (V, E)$ and $G' = (V', E')$ are **isomorphic** if there exists a bijection $f : V \rightarrow V'$ such that $(u, v) \in E$ if and only if $(f(u), f(v)) \in E'$. In other words, we can relabel the vertices of G to be vertices of G', maintaining the corresponding edges in G and G'. Figure 5.3(a) shows a pair of isomorphic graphs G and G' with respective vertex sets $V = \{1, 2, 3, 4, 5, 6\}$ and $V' = \{u, v, w, x, y, z\}$. The mapping from V to V' given by $f(1) = u$, $f(2) = v, f(3) = w, f(4) = x, f(5) = y, f(6) = z$ is the required bijective function. The graphs in Figure 5.3(b) are not isomorphic. Although both graphs have 5 vertices and 7 edges, the top graph has a vertex of degree 4 and the bottom graph does not.

We say that a graph $G' = (V', E')$ is a **subgraph** of $G = (V, E)$ if $V' \subseteq V$ and $E' \subseteq E$. Given a set $V' \subseteq V$, the subgraph of G **induced** by V' is the graph $G' = (V', E')$, where

$$E' = \{(u, v) \in E : u, v \in V'\} \ .$$

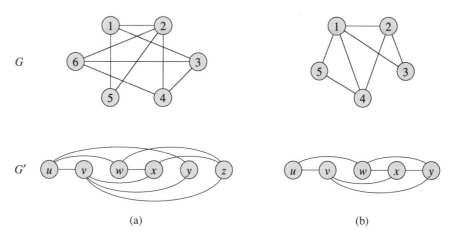

Figure 5.3 (**a**) A pair of isomorphic graphs. The vertices of the top graph are mapped to the vertices of the bottom graph by $f(1) = u, f(2) = v, f(3) = w$, $f(4) = x, f(5) = y, f(6) = z$. (**b**) Two graphs that are not isomorphic, since the top graph has a vertex of degree 4 and the bottom graph does not.

The subgraph induced by the vertex set $\{1, 2, 3, 6\}$ in Figure 5.2(a) appears in Figure 5.2(c) and has the edge set $\{(1, 2), (2, 2), (6, 3)\}$.

Given an undirected graph $G = (V, E)$, the *directed version* of G is the directed graph $G' = (V, E')$, where $(u, v) \in E'$ if and only if $(u, v) \in E$. That is, each undirected edge (u, v) in G is replaced in the directed version by the two directed edges (u, v) and (v, u). Given a directed graph $G = (V, E)$, the *undirected version* of G is the undirected graph $G' = (V, E')$, where $(u, v) \in E'$ if and only if $u \neq v$ and $(u, v) \in E$. That is, the undirected version contains the edges of G "with their directions removed" and with self-loops eliminated. (Since (u, v) and (v, u) are the same edge in an undirected graph, the undirected version of a directed graph contains it only once, even if the directed graph contains both edges (u, v) and (v, u).) In a directed graph $G = (V, E)$, a *neighbor* of a vertex u is any vertex that is adjacent to u in the undirected version of G. That is, v is a neighbor of u if either $(u, v) \in E$ or $(v, u) \in E$. In an undirected graph, u and v are neighbors if they are adjacent.

Several kinds of graphs are given special names. A *complete graph* is an undirected graph in which every pair of vertices is adjacent. A *bipartite graph* is an undirected graph $G = (V, E)$ in which V can be partitioned into two sets V_1 and V_2 such that $(u, v) \in E$ implies either $u \in V_1$ and $v \in V_2$ or $u \in V_2$ and $v \in V_1$. That is, all edges go between the two sets V_1 and V_2. An acyclic, undirected graph is a *forest*, and a connected, acyclic, undirected graph is a *(free) tree* (see Section 5.5). We often take the first letters of "directed acyclic graph" and call such a graph a *dag*.

There are two variants of graphs that you may occasionally encounter. A *multigraph* is like an undirected graph, but it can have both multiple edges between vertices and self-loops. A *hypergraph* is like an undirected graph, but each *hyperedge*, rather than connecting two vertices, connects an arbitrary subset of vertices. Many algorithms written for ordinary directed and undirected graphs can be adapted to run on these graphlike structures.

Exercises

5.4-1
Attendees of a faculty party shake hands to greet each other, and each professor remembers how many times he or she shook hands. At the end of the party, the department head sums up the number of times that each professor shook hands. Show that the result is even by proving the *handshaking lemma*: if $G = (V, E)$ is an undirected graph, then

$$\sum_{v \in V} \text{degree}(v) = 2|E| \ .$$

5.4-2
Show that in an undirected graph, the length of a cycle must be at least 3.

5.4-3
Show that if a directed or undirected graph contains a path between two vertices u and v, then it contains a simple path between u and v. Show that if a directed graph contains a cycle, then it contains a simple cycle.

5.4-4
Show that any connected, undirected graph $G = (V, E)$ satisfies $|E| \geq |V| - 1$.

5.4-5
Verify that in an undirected graph, the "is reachable from" relation is an equivalence relation on the vertices of the graph. Which of the three properties of an equivalence relation hold in general for the "is reachable from" relation on the vertices of a directed graph?

5.4-6
What is the undirected version of the directed graph in Figure 5.2(a)? What is the directed version of the undirected graph in Figure 5.2(b)?

5.4-7 ⋆
Show that a hypergraph can be represented by a bipartite graph if we let incidence in the hypergraph correspond to adjacency in the bipartite graph. (*Hint:* Let one set of vertices in the bipartite graph correspond to vertices of the hypergraph, and let the other set of vertices of the bipartite graph correspond to hyperedges.)

5.5 Trees

As with graphs, there are many related, but slightly different, notions of trees. This section presents definitions and mathematical properties of several kinds of trees. Sections 11.4 and 23.1 describe how trees can be represented in a computer memory.

5.5.1 Free trees

As defined in Section 5.4, a *free tree* is a connected, acyclic, undirected graph. We often omit the adjective "free" when we say that a graph is a tree. If an undirected graph is acyclic but possibly disconnected, it is a *forest*. Many algorithms that work for trees also work for forests. Figure 5.4(a) shows a free tree, and Figure 5.4(b) shows a forest. The forest in Figure 5.4(b) is not a tree because it is not connected. The graph in Figure 5.4(c) is neither a tree nor a forest, because it contains a cycle.

The following theorem captures many important facts about free trees.

Theorem 5.2 (Properties of free trees)
Let $G = (V, E)$ be an undirected graph. The following statements are equivalent.

1. G is a free tree.

2. Any two vertices in G are connected by a unique simple path.

3. G is connected, but if any edge is removed from E, the resulting graph is disconnected.

4. G is connected, and $|E| = |V| - 1$.

5. G is acyclic, and $|E| = |V| - 1$.

6. G is acyclic, but if any edge is added to E, the resulting graph contains a cycle.

Proof $(1) \Rightarrow (2)$: Since a tree is connected, any two vertices in G are connected by at least one simple path. Let u and v be vertices that are

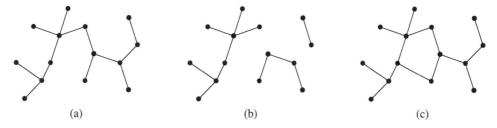

(a)   (b)   (c)

Figure 5.4 **(a)** A free tree. **(b)** A forest. **(c)** A graph that contains a cycle and is therefore neither a tree nor a forest.

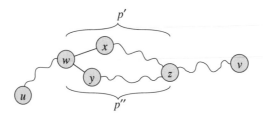

Figure 5.5   A step in the proof of Theorem 5.2: if (1) G is a free tree, then (2) any two vertices in G are connected by a unique simple path. Assume for the sake of contradiction that vertices u and v are connected by two distinct simple paths p_1 and p_2. These paths first diverge at vertex w, and they first reconverge at vertex z. The path p' concatenated with the reverse of the path p'' forms a cycle, which yields the contradiction.

connected by two distinct simple paths p_1 and p_2, as shown in Figure 5.5. Let w be the vertex at which the paths first diverge; that is, w is the first vertex on both p_1 and p_2 whose successor on p_1 is x and whose successor on p_2 is y, where $x \neq y$. Let z be the first vertex at which the paths reconverge; that is, z is the first vertex following w on p_1 that is also on p_2. Let p' be the subpath of p_1 from w through x to z, and let p'' be the subpath of p_2 from w through y to z. Paths p' and p'' share no vertices except their endpoints. Thus, the path obtained by concatenating p' and the reverse of p'' is a cycle. This is a contradiction. Thus, if G is a tree, there can be at most one path between two vertices.

(2) $\Rightarrow$ (3): If any two vertices in G are connected by a unique simple path, then G is connected. Let (u, v) be any edge in E. This edge is a path from u to v, and so it must be the unique path from u to v. If we remove (u, v) from G, there is no path from u to v, and hence its removal disconnects G.

(3) $\Rightarrow$ (4): By assumption, the graph G is connected, and by Exercise 5.4-4, we have $|E| \geq |V| - 1$. We shall prove $|E| \leq |V| - 1$ by induction. A connected graph with $n = 1$ or $n = 2$ vertices has $n - 1$ edges. Suppose that G has $n \geq 3$ vertices and that all graphs satisfying (3) with fewer than n vertices also satisfy $|E| \leq |V| - 1$. Removing an arbitrary edge from G separates the graph into $k \geq 2$ connected components (actually $k = 2$). Each component satisfies (3), or else G would not satisfy (3). Thus, by induction, the number of edges in all components combined is at most $|V| - k \leq |V| - 2$. Adding in the removed edge yields $|E| \leq |V| - 1$.

(4) $\Rightarrow$ (5): Suppose that G is connected and that $|E| = |V| - 1$. We must show that G is acyclic. Suppose that G has a cycle containing k vertices $v_1, v_2, \ldots, v_k$. Let $G_k = (V_k, E_k)$ be the subgraph of G consisting of the cycle. Note that $|V_k| = |E_k| = k$. If $k < |V|$, there must be a vertex $v_{k+1} \in V - V_k$ that is adjacent to some vertex $v_i \in V_k$, since G is connected. Define $G_{k+1} = (V_{k+1}, E_{k+1})$ to be the subgraph of G with $V_{k+1} = V_k \cup \{v_{k+1}\}$ and $E_{k+1} = E_k \cup \{(v_i, v_{k+1})\}$. Note that $|V_{k+1}| = |E_{k+1}| = k+1$. If $k+1 < n$,

we can continue, defining G_{k+2} in the same manner, and so forth, until we obtain $G_n = (V_n, E_n)$, where $n = |V|$, $V_n = V$, and $|E_n| = |V_n| = |V|$. Since G_n is a subgraph of G, we have $E_n \subseteq E$, and hence $|E| \geq |V|$, which contradicts the assumption that $|E| = |V| - 1$. Thus, G is acyclic.

$(5) \Rightarrow (6)$: Suppose that G is acyclic and that $|E| = |V| - 1$. Let k be the number of connected components of G. Each connected component is a free tree by definition, and since (1) implies (5), the sum of all edges in all connected components of G is $|V| - k$. Consequently, we must have $k = 1$, and G is in fact a tree. Since (1) implies (2), any two vertices in G are connected by a unique simple path. Thus, adding any edge to G creates a cycle.

$(6) \Rightarrow (1)$: Suppose that G is acyclic but that if any edge is added to E, a cycle is created. We must show that G is connected. Let u and v be arbitrary vertices in G. If u and v are not already adjacent, adding the edge (u, v) creates a cycle in which all edges but (u, v) belong to G. Thus, there is a path from u to v, and since u and v were chosen arbitrarily, G is connected. ∎

5.5.2 Rooted and ordered trees

A *rooted tree* is a free tree in which one of the vertices is distinguished from the others. The distinguished vertex is called the *root* of the tree. We often refer to a vertex of a rooted tree as a *node*[2] of the tree. Figure 5.6(a) shows a rooted tree on a set of 12 nodes with root 7.

Consider a node x in a rooted tree T with root r. Any node y on the unique path from r to x is called an *ancestor* of x. If y is an ancestor of x, then x is a *descendant* of y. (Every node is both an ancestor and a descendant of itself.) If y is an ancestor of x and $x \neq y$, then y is a *proper ancestor* of x and x is a *proper descendant* of y. The *subtree rooted at x* is the tree induced by descendants of x, rooted at x. For example, the subtree rooted at node 8 in Figure 5.6(a) contains nodes 8, 6, 5, and 9.

If the last edge on the path from the root r of a tree T to a node x is (y, x), then y is the *parent* of x, and x is a *child* of y. The root is the only node in T with no parent. If two nodes have the same parent, they are *siblings*. A node with no children is an *external node* or *leaf*. A nonleaf node is an *internal node*.

---

[2] The term "node" is often used in the graph theory literature as a synonym for "vertex." We shall reserve the term "node" to mean a vertex of a rooted tree.

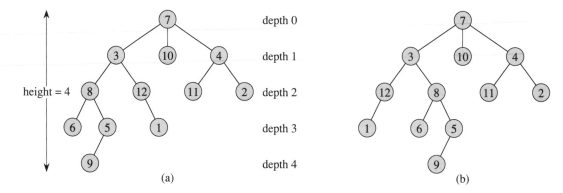

Figure 5.6   Rooted and ordered trees. **(a)** A rooted tree with height 4. The tree is drawn in a standard way: the root (node 7) is at the top, its children (nodes with depth 1) are beneath it, their children (nodes with depth 2) are beneath them, and so forth. If the tree is ordered, the relative left-to-right order of the children of a node matters; otherwise it doesn't. **(b)** Another rooted tree. As a rooted tree, it is identical to the tree in (a), but as an ordered tree it is different, since the children of node 3 appear in a different order.

The number of children of a node x in a rooted tree T is called the **degree** of x.[3] The length of the path from the root r to a node x is the **depth** of x in T. The largest depth of any node in T is the **height** of T.

An **ordered tree** is a rooted tree in which the children of each node are ordered. That is, if a node has k children, then there is a first child, a second child, ..., and a kth child. The two trees in Figure 5.6 are different when considered to be ordered trees, but the same when considered to be just rooted trees.

5.5.3   Binary and positional trees

Binary trees are best described recursively. A **binary tree** T is a structure defined on a finite set of nodes that either

- contains no nodes, or
- is comprised of three disjoint sets of nodes: a **root** node, a binary tree called its **left subtree**, and a binary tree called its **right subtree**.

The binary tree that contains no nodes is called the **empty tree** or **null tree**, sometimes denoted NIL. If the left subtree is nonempty, its root is called the **left child** of the root of the entire tree. Likewise, the root of a nonnull right subtree is the **right child** of the root of the entire tree. If a subtree is

---

[3]Notice that the degree of a node depends on whether T is considered to be a rooted tree or a free tree. The degree of a vertex in a free tree is, as in any undirected graph, the number of adjacent vertices. In a rooted tree, however, the degree is the number of children—the parent of a node does not count toward its degree.

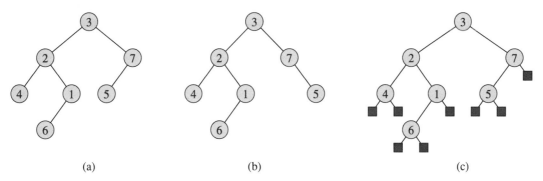

(a) (b) (c)

Figure 5.7 Binary trees. **(a)** A binary tree drawn in a standard way. The left child of a node is drawn beneath the node and to the left. The right child is drawn beneath and to the right. **(b)** A binary tree different from the one in (a). In (a), the left child of node 7 is 5 and the right child is absent. In (b), the left child of node 7 is absent and the right child is 5. As ordered trees, these trees are the same, but as binary trees, they are distinct. **(c)** The binary tree in (a) represented by the internal nodes of a full binary tree: an ordered tree in which each internal node has degree 2. The leaves in the tree are shown as squares.

the null tree NIL, we say that the child is *absent* or *missing*. Figure 5.7(a) shows a binary tree.

A binary tree is not simply an ordered tree in which each node has degree at most 2. For example, in a binary tree, if a node has just one child, the position of the child—whether it is the *left child* or the *right child*—matters. In an ordered tree, there is no distinguishing a sole child as being either left or right. Figure 5.7(b) shows a binary tree that differs from the tree in Figure 5.7(a) because of the position of one node. Considered as ordered trees, however, the two trees are identical.

The positioning information in a binary tree can be represented by the internal nodes of an ordered tree, as shown in Figure 5.7(c). The idea is to replace each missing child in the binary tree with a node having no children. These leaf nodes are drawn as squares in the figure. The tree that results is a *full binary tree*: each node is either a leaf or has degree exactly 2. There are no degree-1 nodes. Consequently, the order of the children of a node preserves the position information.

The positioning information that distinguishes binary trees from ordered trees can be extended to trees with more than 2 children per node. In a *positional tree*, the children of a node are labeled with distinct positive integers. The ith child of a node is *absent* if no child is labeled with integer i. A *k-ary* tree is a positional tree in which for every node, all children with labels greater than k are missing. Thus, a binary tree is a k-ary tree with $k = 2$.

A *complete k-ary tree* is a k-ary tree in which all leaves have the same depth and all internal nodes have degree k. Figure 5.8 shows a complete binary tree of height 3. How many leaves does a complete k-ary tree of

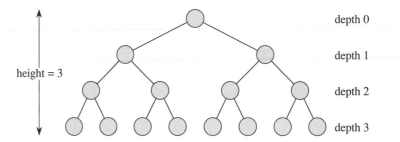

Figure 5.8 A complete binary tree of height 3 with 8 leaves and 7 internal nodes.

height h have? The root has k children at depth 1, each of which has k children at depth 2, etc. Thus, the number of leaves at depth h is k^h. Consequently, the height of a complete k-ary tree with n leaves is $\log_k n$. The number of internal nodes of a complete k-ary tree of height h is

$$
\begin{aligned}
1 + k + k^2 + \cdots + k^{h-1} &= \sum_{i=0}^{h-1} k^i \\
&= \frac{k^h - 1}{k - 1}
\end{aligned}
$$

by equation (3.3). Thus, a complete binary tree has $2^h - 1$ internal nodes.

Exercises

5.5-1
Draw all the free trees composed of the 3 vertices A, B, and C. Draw all the rooted trees with nodes A, B, and C with A as the root. Draw all the ordered trees with nodes A, B, and C with A as the root. Draw all the binary trees with nodes A, B, and C with A as the root.

5.5-2
Show that for $n \geq 7$, there exists a free tree on n nodes such that picking each of the n nodes as a root results in a different rooted tree.

5.5-3
Let $G = (V, E)$ be a directed acyclic graph in which there is a vertex $v_0 \in V$ such that there exists a unique path from v_0 to every vertex $v \in V$. Prove that the undirected version of G forms a tree.

5.5-4
Show by induction that the number of degree-2 nodes in any binary tree is 1 less than the number of leaves.

5.5-5
Show by induction that a binary tree with n nodes has height at least $\lfloor \lg n \rfloor$.

5.5-6 ⋆

The *internal path length* of a full binary tree is the sum, taken over all internal nodes of the tree, of the depth of each node. Likewise, the *external path length* is the sum, taken over all leaves of the tree, of the depth of each leaf. Consider a full binary tree with n internal nodes, internal path length i, and external path length e. Prove that $e = i + 2n$.

5.5-7 ⋆

Let us associate a "weight" $w(x) = 2^{-d}$ with each leaf x of depth d in a binary tree T. Prove that $\sum_x w(x) \leq 1$, where the sum is taken over all leaves x in T. (This is known as the *Kraft inequality*.)

5.5-8 ⋆

Show that every binary tree with L leaves contains a subtree having between $L/3$ and $2L/3$ leaves, inclusive.

Problems

5-1 Graph coloring

A *k-coloring* of an undirected graph $G = (V, E)$ is a function $c : V \rightarrow \{0, 1, \ldots, k - 1\}$ such that $c(u) \neq c(v)$ for every edge $(u, v) \in E$. In other words, the numbers $0, 1, \ldots, k - 1$ represent the k colors, and adjacent vertices must have different colors.

a. Show that any tree is 2-colorable.

b. Show that the following are equivalent:

1. G is bipartite.
2. G is 2-colorable.
3. G has no cycles of odd length.

c. Let d be the maximum degree of any vertex in a graph G. Prove that G can be colored with $d + 1$ colors.

d. Show that if G has $O(|V|)$ edges, then G can be colored with $O(\sqrt{|V|})$ colors.

5-2 Friendly graphs

Reword each of the following statements as a theorem about undirected graphs, and then prove it. Assume that friendship is symmetric but not reflexive.

a. In any group of $n \geq 2$ people, there are two people with the same number of friends in the group.

b. Every group of six people contains either three mutual friends or three mutual strangers.

c. Any group of people can be partitioned into two subgroups such that at least half the friends of each person belong to the subgroup of which that person is *not* a member.

d. If everyone in a group is the friend of at least half the people in the group, then the group can be seated around a table in such a way that everyone is seated between two friends.

5-3   *Bisecting trees*

Many divide-and-conquer algorithms that operate on graphs require that the graph be bisected into two nearly equal-sized subgraphs by removing a small number of edges. This problem investigates bisections of trees.

a. Show that by removing a single edge, we can partition the vertices of any n-vertex binary tree into two sets A and B such that $|A| \le 3n/4$ and $|B| \le 3n/4$.

b. Show that the constant $3/4$ in part (a) is optimal in the worst case by giving an example of a simple tree whose most evenly balanced partition upon removal of a single edge has $|A| = 3n/4$.

c. Show that by removing at most $O(\lg n)$ edges, we can partition the vertices of any n-vertex tree into two sets A and B such that $|A| = \lfloor n/2 \rfloor$ and $|B| = \lceil n/2 \rceil$.

Chapter notes

G. Boole pioneered the development of symbolic logic, and he introduced many of the basic set notations in a book published in 1854. Modern set theory was created by G. Cantor during the period 1874–1895. Cantor focused primarily on sets of infinite cardinality. The term "function" is attributed to G. W. Leibnitz, who used it to refer to several kinds of mathematical formulas. His limited definition has been generalized many times. Graph theory originated in 1736, when L. Euler proved that it was impossible to cross each of the seven bridges in the city of Königsberg exactly once and return to the starting point.

A useful compendium of many definitions and results from graph theory is the book by Harary [94].

6   Counting and Probability

This chapter reviews elementary combinatorics and probability theory. If you have a good background in these areas, you may want to skim the beginning of the chapter lightly and concentrate on the later sections. Most of the chapters do not require probability, but for some chapters it is essential.

Section 6.1 reviews elementary results in counting theory, including standard formulas for counting permutations and combinations. The axioms of probability and basic facts concerning probability distributions are presented in Section 6.2. Random variables are introduced in Section 6.3, along with the properties of expectation and variance. Section 6.4 investigates the geometric and binomial distributions that arise from studying Bernoulli trials. The study of the binomial distribution is continued in Section 6.5, an advanced discussion of the "tails" of the distribution. Finally, Section 6.6 illustrates probabilistic analysis via three examples: the birthday paradox, tossing balls randomly into bins, and winning streaks.

6.1   Counting

Counting theory tries to answer the question "How many?" without actually enumerating how many. For example, we might ask, "How many different n-bit numbers are there?" or "How many orderings of n distinct elements are there?" In this section, we review the elements of counting theory. Since some of the material assumes a basic understanding of sets, the reader is advised to start by reviewing the material in Section 5.1.

Rules of sum and product

A set of items that we wish to count can sometimes be expressed as a union of disjoint sets or as a Cartesian product of sets.

The **rule of sum** says that the number of ways to choose an element from one of two *disjoint* sets is the sum of the cardinalities of the sets. That is, if A and B are two finite sets with no members in common, then

$|A \cup B| = |A| + |B|$, which follows from equation (5.3). For example, each position on a car's license plate is a letter or a digit. The number of possibilities for each position is therefore $26 + 10 = 36$, since there are 26 choices if it is a letter and 10 choices if it is a digit.

The **rule of product** says that the number of ways to choose an ordered pair is the number of ways to choose the first element times the number of ways to choose the second element. That is, if A and B are two finite sets, then $|A \times B| = |A| \cdot |B|$, which is simply equation (5.4). For example, if an ice-cream parlor offers 28 flavors of ice cream and 4 toppings, the number of possible sundaes with one scoop of ice cream and one topping is $28 \cdot 4 = 112$.

Strings

A **string** over a finite set S is a sequence of elements of S. For example, there are 8 binary strings of length 3:

$$000, 001, 010, 011, 100, 101, 110, 111 .$$

We sometimes call a string of length k a **k-string**. A **substring** s' of a string s is an ordered sequence of consecutive elements of s. A **k-substring** of a string is a substring of length k. For example, 010 is a 3-substring of 01101001 (the 3-substring that begins in position 4), but 111 is not a substring of 01101001.

A k-string over a set S can be viewed as an element of the Cartesian product S^k of k-tuples; thus, there are $|S|^k$ strings of length k. For example, the number of binary k-strings is 2^k. Intuitively, to construct a k-string over an n-set, we have n ways to pick the first element; for each of these choices, we have n ways to pick the second element; and so forth k times. This construction leads to the k-fold product $n \cdot n \cdots n = n^k$ as the number of k-strings.

Permutations

A **permutation** of a finite set S is an ordered sequence of all the elements of S, with each element appearing exactly once. For example, if $S = \{a, b, c\}$, there are 6 permutations of S:

$$abc, acb, bac, bca, cab, cba .$$

There are $n!$ permutations of a set of n elements, since the first element of the sequence can be chosen in n ways, the second in $n - 1$ ways, the third in $n - 2$ ways, and so on.

A **k-permutation** of S is an ordered sequence of k elements of S, with no element appearing more than once in the sequence. (Thus, an ordinary permutation is just an n-permutation of an n-set.) The twelve 2-permutations of the set $\{a, b, c, d\}$ are

$ab, ac, ad, ba, bc, bd, ca, cb, cd, da, db, dc$.

The number of k-permutations of an n-set is

$$n(n-1)(n-2)\cdots(n-k+1) = \frac{n!}{(n-k)!} , \tag{6.1}$$

since there are n ways of choosing the first element, $n-1$ ways of choosing the second element, and so on until k elements are selected, the last being a selection from $n-k+1$ elements.

Combinations

A **k-combination** of an n-set S is simply a k-subset of S. There are six 2-combinations of the 4-set $\{a, b, c, d\}$:

ab, ac, ad, bc, bd, cd .

(Here we use the shorthand of denoting the 2-set $\{a, b\}$ by ab, and so on.) We can construct a k-combination of an n-set by choosing k distinct (different) elements from the n-set.

The number of k-combinations of an n-set can be expressed in terms of the number of k-permutations of an n-set. For every k-combination, there are exactly $k!$ permutations of its elements, each of which is a distinct k-permutation of the n-set. Thus, the number of k-combinations of an n-set is the number of k-permutations divided by $k!$; from equation (6.1), this quantity is

$$\frac{n!}{k!\,(n-k)!} . \tag{6.2}$$

For $k = 0$, this formula tells us that the number of ways to choose 0 elements from an n-set is 1 (not 0), since $0! = 1$.

Binomial coefficients

We use the notation $\binom{n}{k}$ (read "n choose k") to denote the number of k-combinations of an n-set. From equation (6.2), we have

$$\binom{n}{k} = \frac{n!}{k!\,(n-k)!} . \tag{6.3}$$

This formula is symmetric in k and $n - k$:

$$\binom{n}{k} = \binom{n}{n-k} . \tag{6.4}$$

These numbers are also known as **binomial coefficients**, due to their appearance in the **binomial expansion**:

$$(x+y)^n = \sum_{k=0}^{n} \binom{n}{k} x^k y^{n-k} . \tag{6.5}$$

A special case of the binomial expansion occurs when $x = y = 1$:

$$2^n = \sum_{k=0}^{n} \binom{n}{k} . \tag{6.6}$$

This formula corresponds to counting the 2^n binary n-strings by the number of 1's they contain: there are $\binom{n}{k}$ binary n-strings containing exactly k 1's, since there are $\binom{n}{k}$ ways to choose k out of the n positions in which to place the 1's.

There are many identities involving binomial coefficients. The exercises at the end of this section give you the opportunity to prove a few.

Binomial bounds

We sometimes need to bound the size of a binomial coefficient. For $1 \leq k \leq n$, we have the lower bound

$$
\begin{aligned}
\binom{n}{k} &= \frac{n(n-1)\cdots(n-k+1)}{k(k-1)\cdots 1} \\
&= \left(\frac{n}{k}\right)\left(\frac{n-1}{k-1}\right)\cdots\left(\frac{n-k+1}{1}\right) \\
&\geq \left(\frac{n}{k}\right)^k .
\end{aligned} \tag{6.7}
$$

Taking advantage of the inequality $k! \geq (k/e)^k$ derived from Stirling's formula (2.12), we obtain the upper bounds

$$
\begin{aligned}
\binom{n}{k} &= \frac{n(n-1)\cdots(n-k+1)}{k(k-1)\cdots 1} \\
&\leq \frac{n^k}{k!} \tag{6.8} \\
&\leq \left(\frac{en}{k}\right)^k . \tag{6.9}
\end{aligned}
$$

For all $0 \leq k \leq n$, we can use induction (see Exercise 6.1-12) to prove the bound

$$\binom{n}{k} \leq \frac{n^n}{k^k(n-k)^{n-k}} , \tag{6.10}$$

where for convenience we assume that $0^0 = 1$. For $k = \lambda n$, where $0 \leq \lambda \leq 1$, this bound can be rewritten as

$$
\begin{aligned}
\binom{n}{\lambda n} &\leq \frac{n^n}{(\lambda n)^{\lambda n}((1-\lambda)n)^{(1-\lambda)n}} \\
&= \left(\left(\frac{1}{\lambda}\right)^{\lambda}\left(\frac{1}{1-\lambda}\right)^{1-\lambda}\right)^n \tag{6.11} \\
&= 2^{n H(\lambda)} , \tag{6.12}
\end{aligned}
$$

where

$$H(\lambda) = -\lambda \lg \lambda - (1 - \lambda) \lg(1 - \lambda) \qquad (6.13)$$

is the *(binary) entropy function* and where, for convenience, we assume that $0 \lg 0 = 0$, so that $H(0) = H(1) = 0$.

Exercises

6.1-1
How many k-substrings does an n-string have? (Consider identical k-substrings at different positions as different.) How many substrings does an n-string have in total?

6.1-2
An n-input, m-output *boolean function* is a function from $\{\text{TRUE}, \text{FALSE}\}^n$ to $\{\text{TRUE}, \text{FALSE}\}^m$. How many n-input, 1-output boolean functions are there? How many n-input, m-output boolean functions are there?

6.1-3
In how many ways can n professors sit around a circular conference table? Consider two seatings to be the same if one can be rotated to form the other.

6.1-4
In how many ways can three distinct numbers be chosen from the set $\{1, 2, \ldots, 100\}$ so that their sum is even?

6.1-5
Prove the identity

$$\binom{n}{k} = \frac{n}{k} \binom{n-1}{k-1} \qquad (6.14)$$

for $0 < k \le n$.

6.1-6
Prove the identity

$$\binom{n}{k} = \frac{n}{n-k} \binom{n-1}{k}$$

for $0 \le k < n$.

6.1-7
To choose k objects from n, you can make one of the objects distinguished and consider whether the distinguished object is chosen. Use this approach to prove that

$$\binom{n}{k} = \binom{n-1}{k} + \binom{n-1}{k-1}.$$

6.1-8

Using the result of Exercise 6.1-7, make a table for $n = 0, 1, \ldots, 6$ and $0 \leq k \leq n$ of the binomial coefficients $\binom{n}{k}$ with $\binom{0}{0}$ at the top, $\binom{1}{0}$ and $\binom{1}{1}$ on the next line, and so forth. Such a table of binomial coefficients is called **Pascal's triangle**.

6.1-9

Prove that

$$\sum_{i=1}^{n} i = \binom{n+1}{2}.$$

6.1-10

Show that for any $n \geq 0$ and $0 \leq k \leq n$, the maximum value of $\binom{n}{k}$ is achieved when $k = \lfloor n/2 \rfloor$ or $k = \lceil n/2 \rceil$.

6.1-11 ⋆

Argue that for any $n \geq 0$, $j \geq 0$, $k \geq 0$, and $j + k \leq n$,

$$\binom{n}{j+k} \leq \binom{n}{j}\binom{n-j}{k}. \tag{6.15}$$

Provide both an algebraic proof and an argument based on a method for choosing $j + k$ items out of n. Give an example in which equality does not hold.

6.1-12 ⋆

Use induction on $k \leq n/2$ to prove inequality (6.10), and use equation (6.4) to extend it to all $k \leq n$.

6.1-13 ⋆

Use Stirling's approximation to prove that

$$\binom{2n}{n} = \frac{2^{2n}}{\sqrt{\pi n}}(1 + O(1/n)). \tag{6.16}$$

6.1-14 ⋆

By differentiating the entropy function $H(\lambda)$, show that it achieves its maximum value at $\lambda = 1/2$. What is $H(1/2)$?

6.2 Probability

Probability is an essential tool for the design and analysis of probabilistic and randomized algorithms. This section reviews basic probability theory.

We define probability in terms of a **sample space** S, which is a set whose elements are called **elementary events**. Each elementary event can be viewed as a possible outcome of an experiment. For the experiment of flipping two distinguishable coins, we can view the sample space as consisting of the set of all possible 2-strings over $\{H, T\}$:

$$S = \{HH, HT, TH, TT\} \ .$$

An *event* is a subset[1] of the sample space S. For example, in the experiment of flipping two coins, the event of obtaining one head and one tail is $\{HT, TH\}$. The event S is called the *certain event*, and the event $\emptyset$ is called the *null event*. We say that two events A and B are *mutually exclusive* if $A \cap B = \emptyset$. We sometimes treat an elementary event $s \in S$ as the event $\{s\}$. By definition, all elementary events are mutually exclusive.

Axioms of probability

A *probability distribution* $\Pr\{\}$ on a sample space S is a mapping from events of S to real numbers such that the following *probability axioms* are satisfied:

1. $\Pr\{A\} \geq 0$ for any event A.
2. $\Pr\{S\} = 1$.
3. $\Pr\{A \cup B\} = \Pr\{A\} + \Pr\{B\}$ for any two mutually exclusive events A and B. More generally, for any (finite or countably infinite) sequence of events $A_1, A_2, \ldots$ that are pairwise mutually exclusive,

$$\Pr\left\{\bigcup_i A_i\right\} = \sum_i \Pr\{A_i\} \ .$$

We call $\Pr\{A\}$ the *probability* of the event A. We note here that axiom 2 is a normalization requirement: there is really nothing fundamental about choosing 1 as the probability of the certain event, except that it is natural and convenient.

Several results follow immediately from these axioms and basic set theory (see Section 5.1). The null event $\emptyset$ has probability $\Pr\{\emptyset\} = 0$. If $A \subseteq B$, then $\Pr\{A\} \leq \Pr\{B\}$. Using $\overline{A}$ to denote the event $S - A$ (the *complement* of A), we have $\Pr\{\overline{A}\} = 1 - \Pr\{A\}$. For any two events A and B,

$$\Pr\{A \cup B\} = \Pr\{A\} + \Pr\{B\} - \Pr\{A \cap B\} \tag{6.17}$$

$$\leq \Pr\{A\} + \Pr\{B\} \ . \tag{6.18}$$

---

[1]For a general probability distribution, there may be some subsets of the sample space S that are not considered to be events. This situation usually arises when the sample space is uncountably infinite. The main requirement is that the set of events of a sample space be closed under the operations of taking the complement of an event, forming the union of a finite or countable number of events, and taking the intersection of a finite or countable number of events. Most of the probability distributions we shall see are over finite or countable sample spaces, and we shall generally consider all subsets of a sample space to be events. A notable exception is the continuous uniform probability distribution, which will be presented shortly.

In our coin-flipping example, suppose that each of the four elementary events has probability $1/4$. Then the probability of getting at least one head is

$$
\begin{aligned}
\Pr\{\text{HH}, \text{HT}, \text{TH}\} &= \Pr\{\text{HH}\} + \Pr\{\text{HT}\} + \Pr\{\text{TH}\} \\
&= 3/4 \ .
\end{aligned}
$$

Alternatively, since the probability of getting strictly less than one head is $\Pr\{\text{TT}\} = 1/4$, the probability of getting at least one head is $1 - 1/4 = 3/4$.

Discrete probability distributions

A probability distribution is **discrete** if it is defined over a finite or countably infinite sample space. Let S be the sample space. Then for any event A,

$$
\Pr\{A\} = \sum_{s \in A} \Pr\{s\} \ ,
$$

since elementary events, specifically those in A, are mutually exclusive. If S is finite and every elementary event $s \in S$ has probability

$$
\Pr\{s\} = 1/|S| \ ,
$$

then we have the **uniform probability distribution** on S. In such a case the experiment is often described as "picking an element of S at random."

As an example, consider the process of flipping a **fair coin**, one for which the probability of obtaining a head is the same as the probability of obtaining a tail, that is, $1/2$. If we flip the coin n times, we have the uniform probability distribution defined on the sample space $S = \{\text{H}, \text{T}\}^n$, a set of size 2^n. Each elementary event in S can be represented as a string of length n over $\{\text{H}, \text{T}\}$, and each occurs with probability $1/2^n$. The event

$$
A = \{\text{exactly } k \text{ heads and exactly } n - k \text{ tails occur}\}
$$

is a subset of S of size $|A| = \binom{n}{k}$, since there are $\binom{n}{k}$ strings of length n over $\{\text{H}, \text{T}\}$ that contain exactly k H's. The probability of event A is thus $\Pr\{A\} = \binom{n}{k}/2^n$.

Continuous uniform probability distribution

The continuous uniform probability distribution is an example of a probability distribution in which all subsets of the sample space are not considered to be events. The continuous uniform probability distribution is defined over a closed interval $[a, b]$ of the reals, where $a < b$. Intuitively, we want each point in the interval $[a, b]$ to be "equally likely." There is an uncountable number of points, however, so if we give all points the same finite, positive probability, we cannot simultaneously satisfy axioms 2 and 3. For this reason, we would like to associate a probability only with *some* of the subsets of S in such a way that the axioms are satisfied for these events.

For any closed interval $[c, d]$, where $a \leq c \leq d \leq b$, the **continuous uniform probability distribution** defines the probability of the event $[c, d]$ to be

$$\Pr\{[c, d]\} = \frac{d - c}{b - a}.$$

Note that for any point $x = [x, x]$, the probability of x is 0. If we remove the endpoints of an interval $[c, d]$, we obtain the open interval (c, d). Since $[c, d] = [c, c] \cup (c, d) \cup [d, d]$, axiom 3 gives us $\Pr\{[c, d]\} = \Pr\{(c, d)\}$. Generally, the set of events for the continuous uniform probability distribution is any subset of $[a, b]$ that can be obtained by a finite or countable union of open and closed intervals.

Conditional probability and independence

Sometimes we have some prior partial knowledge about the outcome of an experiment. For example, suppose that a friend has flipped two fair coins and has told you that at least one of the coins showed a head. What is the probability that both coins are heads? The information given eliminates the possibility of two tails. The three remaining elementary events are equally likely, so we infer that each occurs with probability 1/3. Since only one of these elementary events shows two heads, the answer to our question is 1/3.

Conditional probability formalizes the notion of having prior partial knowledge of the outcome of an experiment. The **conditional probability** of an event A given that another event B occurs is defined to be

$$\Pr\{A \mid B\} = \frac{\Pr\{A \cap B\}}{\Pr\{B\}} \tag{6.19}$$

whenever $\Pr\{B\} \neq 0$. (We read "$\Pr\{A \mid B\}$" as "the probability of A given B.") Intuitively, since we are given that event B occurs, the event that A also occurs is $A \cap B$. That is, $A \cap B$ is the set of outcomes in which both A and B occur. Since the outcome is one of the elementary events in B, we normalize the probabilities of all the elementary events in B by dividing them by $\Pr\{B\}$, so that they sum to 1. The conditional probability of A given B is, therefore, the ratio of the probability of event $A \cap B$ to the probability of event B. In the example above, A is the event that both coins are heads, and B is the event that at least one coin is a head. Thus, $\Pr\{A \mid B\} = (1/4)/(3/4) = 1/3$.

Two events are **independent** if

$$\Pr\{A \cap B\} = \Pr\{A\} \Pr\{B\} ,$$

which is equivalent, if $\Pr\{B\} \neq 0$, to the condition

$$\Pr\{A \mid B\} = \Pr\{A\} .$$

For example, suppose that two fair coins are flipped and that the outcomes are independent. Then the probability of two heads is $(1/2)(1/2) = 1/4$. Now suppose that one event is that the first coin comes up heads and the other event is that the coins come up differently. Each of these events occurs with probability $1/2$, and the probability that both events occur is $1/4$; thus, according to the definition of independence, the events are independent—even though one might think that both events depend on the first coin. Finally, suppose that the coins are welded together so that they both fall heads or both fall tails and that the two possibilities are equally likely. Then the probability that each coin comes up heads is $1/2$, but the probability that they both come up heads is $1/2 \neq (1/2)(1/2)$. Consequently, the event that one comes up heads and the event that the other comes up heads are not independent.

A collection $A_1, A_2, \ldots, A_n$ of events is said to be ***pairwise independent*** if

$$\Pr\{A_i \cap A_j\} = \Pr\{A_i\} \Pr\{A_j\}$$

for all $1 \leq i < j \leq n$. We say that they are ***(mutually) independent*** if every k-subset $A_{i_1}, A_{i_2}, \ldots, A_{i_k}$ of the collection, where $2 \leq k \leq n$ and $1 \leq i_1 < i_2 < \cdots < i_k \leq n$, satisfies

$$\Pr\{A_{i_1} \cap A_{i_2} \cap \cdots \cap A_{i_k}\} = \Pr\{A_{i_1}\} \Pr\{A_{i_2}\} \cdots \Pr\{A_{i_k}\} \ .$$

For example, suppose we flip two fair coins. Let A_1 be the event that the first coin is heads, let A_2 be the event that the second coin is heads, and let A_3 be the event that the two coins are different. We have

$$
\begin{aligned}
\Pr\{A_1\} &= 1/2 \ , \\
\Pr\{A_2\} &= 1/2 \ , \\
\Pr\{A_3\} &= 1/2 \ , \\
\Pr\{A_1 \cap A_2\} &= 1/4 \ , \\
\Pr\{A_1 \cap A_3\} &= 1/4 \ , \\
\Pr\{A_2 \cap A_3\} &= 1/4 \ , \\
\Pr\{A_1 \cap A_2 \cap A_3\} &= 0 \ .
\end{aligned}
$$

Since for $1 \leq i < j \leq 3$, we have $\Pr\{A_i \cap A_j\} = \Pr\{A_i\} \Pr\{A_j\} = 1/4$, the events A_1, A_2, and A_3 are pairwise independent. The events are not mutually independent, however, because $\Pr\{A_1 \cap A_2 \cap A_3\} = 0$ and $\Pr\{A_1\} \Pr\{A_2\} \Pr\{A_3\} = 1/8 \neq 0$.

Bayes's theorem

From the definition of conditional probability (6.19), it follows that for two events A and B, each with nonzero probability,

$$
\begin{aligned}
\Pr\{A \cap B\} &= \Pr\{B\} \Pr\{A \mid B\} \\
&= \Pr\{A\} \Pr\{B \mid A\} \ .
\end{aligned}
\tag{6.20}
$$

Solving for $\Pr\{A \mid B\}$, we obtain

$$\Pr\{A \mid B\} = \frac{\Pr\{A\}\Pr\{B \mid A\}}{\Pr\{B\}} , \tag{6.21}$$

which is known as *Bayes's theorem*. The denominator $\Pr\{B\}$ is a normalizing constant that we can reexpress as follows. Since $B = (B \cap A) \cup (B \cap \overline{A})$ and $B \cap A$ and $B \cap \overline{A}$ are mutually exclusive events,

$$\begin{aligned}\Pr\{B\} &= \Pr\{B \cap A\} + \Pr\{B \cap \overline{A}\} \\ &= \Pr\{A\}\Pr\{B \mid A\} + \Pr\{\overline{A}\}\Pr\{B \mid \overline{A}\} .\end{aligned}$$

Substituting into equation (6.21), we obtain an equivalent form of Bayes's theorem:

$$\Pr\{A \mid B\} = \frac{\Pr\{A\}\Pr\{B \mid A\}}{\Pr\{A\}\Pr\{B \mid A\} + \Pr\{\overline{A}\}\Pr\{B \mid \overline{A}\}} .$$

Bayes's theorem can simplify the computing of conditional probabilities. For example, suppose that we have a fair coin and a biased coin that always comes up heads. We run an experiment consisting of three independent events: one of the two coins is chosen at random, the coin is flipped once, and then it is flipped again. Suppose that the chosen coin comes up heads both times. What is the probability that it is biased?

We solve this problem using Bayes's theorem. Let A be the event that the biased coin is chosen, and let B be the event that the coin comes up heads both times. We wish to determine $\Pr\{A \mid B\}$. We have $\Pr\{A\} = 1/2$, $\Pr\{B \mid A\} = 1$, $\Pr\{\overline{A}\} = 1/2$, and $\Pr\{B \mid \overline{A}\} = 1/4$; hence,

$$\begin{aligned}\Pr\{A \mid B\} &= \frac{(1/2) \cdot 1}{(1/2) \cdot 1 + (1/2) \cdot (1/4)} \\ &= 4/5 .\end{aligned}$$

Exercises

6.2-1
Prove *Boole's inequality*: For any finite or countably infinite sequence of events $A_1, A_2, \ldots,$

$$\Pr\{A_1 \cup A_2 \cup \cdots\} \leq \Pr\{A_1\} + \Pr\{A_2\} + \cdots . \tag{6.22}$$

6.2-2
Professor Rosencrantz flips one fair coin. Professor Guildenstern flips two fair coins. What is the probability that Professor Rosencrantz obtains more heads than Professor Guildenstern?

6.2-3
A deck of 10 cards, each bearing a distinct number from 1 to 10, is shuffled to mix the cards thoroughly. Three cards are removed one at a time from the deck. What is the probability that the three cards are selected in sorted (increasing) order?

6.2-4 ⋆

You are given a biased coin, that when flipped, produces a head with (unknown) probability p, where $0 < p < 1$. Show how a fair "coin flip" can be simulated by looking at multiple flips. (*Hint:* Flip the coin twice and then either output the result of the simulated fair flip or repeat the experiment.) Prove that your answer is correct.

6.2-5 ⋆

Describe a procedure that takes as input two integers a and b such that $0 < a < b$ and, using fair coin flips, produces as output heads with probability a/b and tails with probability $(b - a)/b$. Give a bound on the expected number of coin flips, which should be polynomial in $\lg b$.

6.2-6

Prove that

$$\Pr\{A \mid B\} + \Pr\{\overline{A} \mid B\} = 1 \ .$$

6.2-7

Prove that for any collection of events $A_1, A_2, \ldots, A_n$,

$$\Pr\{A_1 \cap A_2 \cap \cdots \cap A_n\} = \Pr\{A_1\} \cdot \Pr\{A_2 \mid A_1\} \cdot \Pr\{A_3 \mid A_1 \cap A_2\} \cdots$$
$$\Pr\{A_n \mid A_1 \cap A_2 \cap \cdots \cap A_{n-1}\} \ .$$

6.2-8 ⋆

Show how to construct a set of n events that are pairwise independent but such that any subset of $k > 2$ of them are *not* mutually independent.

6.2-9 ⋆

Two events A and B are **conditionally independent**, given C, if

$$\Pr\{A \cap B \mid C\} = \Pr\{A \mid C\} \cdot \Pr\{B \mid C\} \ .$$

Give a simple but nontrivial example of two events that are not independent but are conditionally independent given a third event.

6.2-10 ⋆

You are a contestant in a game show in which a prize is hidden behind one of three curtains. You will win the prize if you select the correct curtain. After you have picked one curtain but before the curtain is lifted, the emcee lifts one of the other curtains, revealing an empty stage, and asks if you would like to switch from your current selection to the remaining curtain. How will your chances change if you switch?

6.2-11 ⋆

A prison warden has randomly picked one prisoner among three to go free. The other two will be executed. The guard knows which one will go free but is forbidden to give any prisoner information regarding his status. Let us call the prisoners X, Y, and Z. Prisoner X asks the guard privately which of Y or Z will be executed, arguing that since he already knows that at least one of them must die, the guard won't be revealing any information about his own status. The guard tells X that Y is to be executed. Prisoner X feels happier now, since he figures that either he or prisoner Z will go free, which means that his probability of going free is now $1/2$. Is he right, or are his chances still $1/3$? Explain.

6.3 Discrete random variables

A *(discrete) random variable* X is a function from a finite or countably infinite sample space S to the real numbers. It associates a real number with each possible outcome of an experiment, which allows us to work with the probability distribution induced on the resulting set of numbers. Random variables can also be defined for uncountably infinite sample spaces, but they raise technical issues that are unnecessary to address for our purposes. Henceforth, we shall assume that random variables are discrete.

For a random variable X and a real number x, we define the event $X = x$ to be $\{s \in S : X(s) = x\}$; thus,

$$\Pr\{X = x\} = \sum_{\{s \in S : X(s) = x\}} \Pr\{s\} \ .$$

The function

$$f(x) = \Pr\{X = x\}$$

is the *probability density function* of the random variable X. From the probability axioms, $\Pr\{X = x\} \geq 0$ and $\sum_x \Pr\{X = x\} = 1$.

As an example, consider the experiment of rolling a pair of ordinary, 6-sided dice. There are 36 possible elementary events in the sample space. We assume that the probability distribution is uniform, so that each elementary event $s \in S$ is equally likely: $\Pr\{s\} = 1/36$. Define the random variable X to be the *maximum* of the two values showing on the dice. We have $\Pr\{X = 3\} = 5/36$, since X assigns a value of 3 to 5 of the 36 possible elementary events, namely, $(1,3)$, $(2,3)$, $(3,3)$, $(3,2)$, and $(3,1)$.

It is common for several random variables to be defined on the same sample space. If X and Y are random variables, the function

$$f(x,y) = \Pr\{X = x \text{ and } Y = y\}$$

is the *joint probability density function* of X and Y. For a fixed value y,

$$\Pr\{Y = y\} = \sum_x \Pr\{X = x \text{ and } Y = y\} \ ,$$

and similarly, for a fixed value x,

$$\Pr\{X = x\} = \sum_y \Pr\{X = x \text{ and } Y = y\} \ .$$

Using the definition (6.19) of conditional probability, we have

$$\Pr\{X = x \mid Y = y\} = \frac{\Pr\{X = x \text{ and } Y = y\}}{\Pr\{Y = y\}} \ .$$

We define two random variables X and Y to be **independent** if for all x and y, the events $X = x$ and $Y = y$ are independent or, equivalently, if for all x and y, we have $\Pr\{X = x \text{ and } Y = y\} = \Pr\{X = x\}\Pr\{Y = y\}$.

Given a set of random variables defined over the same sample space, one can define new random variables as sums, products, or other functions of the original variables.

Expected value of a random variable

The simplest and most useful summary of the distribution of a random variable is the "average" of the values it takes on. The **expected value** (or, synonymously, **expectation** or **mean**) of a discrete random variable X is

$$E[X] = \sum_x x \Pr\{X = x\} \ , \tag{6.23}$$

which is well defined if the sum is finite or converges absolutely. Sometimes the expectation of X is denoted by μ_X or, when the random variable is apparent from context, simply by μ.

Consider a game in which you flip two fair coins. You earn \$3 for each head but lose \$2 for each tail. The expected value of the random variable X representing your earnings is

$$
\begin{aligned}
E[X] &= 6 \cdot \Pr\{2 \text{ н's}\} + 1 \cdot \Pr\{1 \text{ н}, 1 \text{ т}\} - 4 \cdot \Pr\{2 \text{ т's}\} \\
&= 6(1/4) + 1(1/2) - 4(1/4) \\
&= 1 \ .
\end{aligned}
$$

The expectation of the sum of two random variables is the sum of their expectations, that is,

$$E[X + Y] = E[X] + E[Y] \ , \tag{6.24}$$

whenever $E[X]$ and $E[Y]$ are defined. This property extends to finite and absolutely convergent summations of expectations.

If X is any random variable, any function $g(x)$ defines a new random variable $g(X)$. If the expectation of $g(X)$ is defined, then

$$E[g(X)] = \sum_x g(x) \Pr\{X = x\} \ .$$

Letting $g(x) = ax$, we have for any constant a,

$$E[aX] = aE[X] \ . \tag{6.25}$$

Consequently, expectations are linear: for any two random variables X and Y and any constant a,

$$E[aX + Y] = aE[X] + E[Y] .$$ (6.26)

When two random variables X and Y are independent and each has a defined expectation,

$$
\begin{aligned}
E[XY] &= \sum_x \sum_y xy \Pr\{X = x \text{ and } Y = y\} \\
&= \sum_x \sum_y xy \Pr\{X = x\} \Pr\{Y = y\} \\
&= \left(\sum_x x \Pr\{X = x\}\right) \left(\sum_y y \Pr\{Y = y\}\right) \\
&= E[X]E[Y] .
\end{aligned}
$$

In general, when n random variables $X_1, X_2, \ldots, X_n$ are mutually independent,

$$E[X_1 X_2 \cdots X_n] = E[X_1] E[X_2] \cdots E[X_n] .$$ (6.27)

When a random variable X takes on values from the natural numbers $\mathbf{N} = \{0, 1, 2, \ldots\}$, there is a nice formula for its expectation:

$$
\begin{aligned}
E[X] &= \sum_{i=0}^{\infty} i \Pr\{X = i\} \\
&= \sum_{i=0}^{\infty} i(\Pr\{X \geq i\} - \Pr\{X \geq i + 1\}) \\
&= \sum_{i=1}^{\infty} \Pr\{X \geq i\} ,
\end{aligned}
$$ (6.28)

since each term $\Pr\{X \geq i\}$ is added in i times and subtracted out $i - 1$ times (except $\Pr\{X \geq 0\}$, which is added in 0 times and not subtracted out at all).

Variance and standard deviation

The *variance* of a random variable X with mean $E[X]$ is

$$
\begin{aligned}
\text{Var}[X] &= E\left[(X - E[X])^2\right] \\
&= E\left[X^2 - 2XE[X] + E^2[X]\right] \\
&= E\left[X^2\right] - 2E[XE[X]] + E^2[X] \\
&= E\left[X^2\right] - 2E^2[X] + E^2[X] \\
&= E\left[X^2\right] - E^2[X] .
\end{aligned}
$$ (6.29)

The justification for the equalities $E\left[E^2[X]\right] = E^2[X]$ and $E[XE[X]] = E^2[X]$ is that $E[X]$ is not a random variable but simply a real number, which means that equation (6.25) applies (with $a = E[X]$). Equation (6.29) can be rewritten to obtain an expression for the expectation of the square of a random variable:

$$E[X^2] = \text{Var}[X] + E^2[X] \ . \tag{6.30}$$

The variance of a random variable X and the variance of aX are related:

$$\text{Var}[aX] = a^2 \text{Var}[X] \ .$$

When X and Y are independent random variables,

$$\text{Var}[X + Y] = \text{Var}[X] + \text{Var}[Y] \ .$$

In general, if n random variables $X_1, X_2, \ldots, X_n$ are pairwise independent, then

$$\text{Var}\left[\sum_{i=1}^{n} X_i\right] = \sum_{i=1}^{n} \text{Var}[X_i] \ . \tag{6.31}$$

The **standard deviation** of a random variable X is the positive square root of the variance of X. The standard deviation of a random variable X is sometimes denoted σ_X or simply σ when the random variable X is understood from context. With this notation, the variance of X is denoted σ^2.

Exercises

6.3-1
Two ordinary, 6-sided dice are rolled. What is the expectation of the sum of the two values showing? What is the expectation of the maximum of the two values showing?

6.3-2
An array $A[1 \mathinner{.\,.} n]$ contains n distinct numbers that are randomly ordered, with each permutation of the n numbers being equally likely. What is the expectation of the index of the maximum element in the array? What is the expectation of the index of the minimum element in the array?

6.3-3
A carnival game consists of three dice in a cage. A player can bet a dollar on any of the numbers 1 through 6. The cage is shaken, and the payoff is as follows. If the player's number doesn't appear on any of the dice, he loses his dollar. Otherwise, if his number appears on exactly k of the three dice, for $k = 1, 2, 3$, he keeps his dollar and wins k more dollars. What is his expected gain from playing the carnival game once?

6.3-4 ★
Let X and Y be independent random variables. Prove that $f(X)$ and $g(Y)$ are independent for any choice of functions f and g.

6.3-5 ★
Let X be a nonnegative random variable, and suppose that $E[X]$ is well defined. Prove **Markov's inequality**:

$$\Pr\{X \geq t\} \leq \mathrm{E}[X]/t \tag{6.32}$$

for all $t > 0$.

6.3-6 ⋆
Let S be a sample space, and let X and X' be random variables such that $X(s) \geq X'(s)$ for all $s \in S$. Prove that for any real constant t,

$$\Pr\{X \geq t\} \geq \Pr\{X' \geq t\} \ .$$

6.3-7
Which is larger: the expectation of the square of a random variable, or the square of its expectation?

6.3-8
Show that for any random variable X that takes on only the values 0 and 1, we have $\mathrm{Var}[X] = \mathrm{E}[X]\,\mathrm{E}[1 - X]$.

6.3-9
Prove that $\mathrm{Var}[aX] = a^2\mathrm{Var}[x]$ from the definition (6.29) of variance.

6.4   The geometric and binomial distributions

A coin flip is an instance of a **Bernoulli trial**, which is defined as an experiment with only two possible outcomes: **success**, which occurs with probability p, and **failure**, which occurs with probability $q = 1 - p$. When we speak of **Bernoulli trials** collectively, we mean that the trials are mutually independent and, unless we specifically say otherwise, that each has the same probability p for success. Two important distributions arise from Bernoulli trials: the geometric distribution and the binomial distribution.

The geometric distribution

Suppose we have a sequence of Bernoulli trials, each with a probability p of success and a probability $q = 1 - p$ of failure. How many trials occur before we obtain a success? Let the random variable X be the number of trials needed to obtain a success. Then X has values in the range $\{1, 2, \ldots\}$, and for $k \geq 1$,

$$\Pr\{X = k\} = q^{k-1}p \ , \tag{6.33}$$

since we have $k - 1$ failures before the one success. A probability distribution satisfying equation (6.33) is said to be a **geometric distribution**. Figure 6.1 illustrates such a distribution.

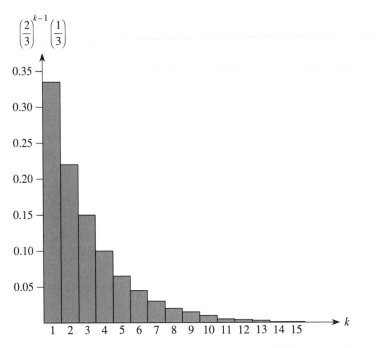

Figure 6.1   A geometric distribution with probability $p = 1/3$ of success and a probability $q = 1 - p$ of failure. The expectation of the distribution is $1/p = 3$.

Assuming $p < 1$, the expectation of a geometric distribution can be calculated using identity (3.6):

$$
\begin{aligned}
\mathrm{E}[X] &= \sum_{k=1}^{\infty} k q^{k-1} p \\
&= \frac{p}{q} \sum_{k=0}^{\infty} k q^{k} \\
&= \frac{p}{q} \cdot \frac{q}{(1-q)^2} \\
&= 1/p \ .
\end{aligned}
\tag{6.34}
$$

Thus, on average, it takes $1/p$ trials before we obtain a success, an intuitive result. The variance, which can be calculated similarly, is

$$
\mathrm{Var}[X] = q/p^2 \ .
\tag{6.35}
$$

As an example, suppose we repeatedly roll two dice until we obtain either a seven or an eleven. Of the 36 possible outcomes, 6 yield a seven and 2 yield an eleven. Thus, the probability of success is $p = 8/36 = 2/9$, and we must roll $1/p = 9/2 = 4.5$ times on average to obtain a seven or eleven.

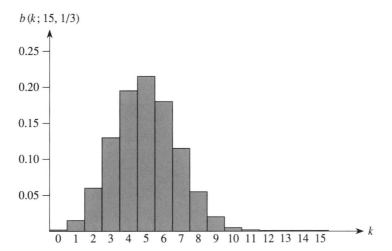

Figure 6.2   The binomial distribution $b(k; 15, 1/3)$ resulting from $n = 15$ Bernoulli trials, each with probability $p = 1/3$ of success. The expectation of the distribution is $np = 5$.

The binomial distribution

How many successes occur during n Bernoulli trials, where a success occurs with probability p and a failure with probability $q = 1 - p$? Define the random variable X to be the number of successes in n trials. Then X has values in the range $\{0, 1, \ldots, n\}$, and for $k = 0, \ldots, n$,

$$\Pr\{X = k\} = \binom{n}{k} p^k q^{n-k} \,, \tag{6.36}$$

since there are $\binom{n}{k}$ ways to pick which k of the n trials are successes, and the probability that each occurs is $p^k q^{n-k}$. A probability distribution satisfying equation (6.36) is said to be a ***binomial distribution***. For convenience, we define the family of binomial distributions using the notation

$$b(k; n, p) = \binom{n}{k} p^k (1 - p)^{n-k} \,. \tag{6.37}$$

Figure 6.2 illustrates a binomial distribution. The name "binomial" comes from the fact that (6.37) is the kth term of the expansion of $(p + q)^n$. Consequently, since $p + q = 1$,

$$\sum_{k=0}^{n} b(k; n, p) = 1 \,, \tag{6.38}$$

as is required by axiom 2 of the probability axioms.

  We can compute the expectation of a random variable having a binomial distribution from equations (6.14) and (6.38). Let X be a random variable that follows the binomial distribution $b(k; n, p)$, and let $q = 1 - p$. By the definition of expectation, we have

$$
\begin{aligned}
\mathrm{E}[X] &= \sum_{k=0}^{n} k\, b(k;n,p) \\
&= \sum_{k=1}^{n} k \binom{n}{k} p^k q^{n-k} \\
&= np \sum_{k=1}^{n} \binom{n-1}{k-1} p^{k-1} q^{n-k} \\
&= np \sum_{k=0}^{n-1} \binom{n-1}{k} p^k q^{(n-1)-k} \\
&= np \sum_{k=0}^{n-1} b(k;n-1,p) \\
&= np \ .
\end{aligned}
\tag{6.39}
$$

By using the linearity of expectation, we can obtain the same result with substantially less algebra. Let X_i be the random variable describing the number of successes in the ith trial. Then $\mathrm{E}[X_i] = p \cdot 1 + q \cdot 0 = p$, and by linearity of expectation (6.26), the expected number of successes for n trials is

$$
\begin{aligned}
\mathrm{E}[X] &= \mathrm{E}\!\left[\sum_{i=1}^{n} X_i\right] \\
&= \sum_{i=1}^{n} \mathrm{E}[X_i] \\
&= \sum_{i=1}^{n} p \\
&= np \ .
\end{aligned}
$$

The same approach can be used to calculate the variance of the distribution. Using equation (6.29), we have $\mathrm{Var}[X_i] = \mathrm{E}\left[X_i^2\right] - \mathrm{E}^2[X_i]$. Since X_i only takes on the values 0 and 1, we have $\mathrm{E}\left[X_i^2\right] = \mathrm{E}[X_i] = p$, and hence

$$
\mathrm{Var}[X_i] = p - p^2 = pq \ .
\tag{6.40}
$$

To compute the variance of X, we take advantage of the independence of the n trials; thus, by equation (6.31),

$$
\begin{aligned}
\mathrm{Var}[X] &= \mathrm{Var}\!\left[\sum_{i=1}^{n} X_i\right] \\
&= \sum_{i=1}^{n} \mathrm{Var}[X_i] \\
&= \sum_{i=1}^{n} pq \\
&= npq \ .
\end{aligned}
\tag{6.41}
$$

As can be seen from Figure 6.2, the binomial distribution $b(k; n, p)$ increases as k runs from 0 to n until it reaches the mean np, and then it decreases. We can prove that the distribution always behaves in this manner by looking at the ratio of successive terms:

$$
\begin{aligned}
\frac{b(k; n, p)}{b(k - 1; n, p)} &= \frac{\binom{n}{k} p^k q^{n-k}}{\binom{n}{k-1} p^{k-1} q^{n-k+1}} \\
&= \frac{n!(k-1)!(n-k+1)!p}{k!(n-k)!n!q} \\
&= \frac{(n-k+1)p}{kq} \\
&= 1 + \frac{(n+1)p - k}{kq} .
\end{aligned}
\tag{6.42}
$$

This ratio is greater than 1 precisely when $(n + 1)p - k$ is positive. Consequently, $b(k; n, p) > b(k - 1; n, p)$ for $k < (n + 1)p$ (the distribution increases), and $b(k; n, p) < b(k - 1; n, p)$ for $k > (n + 1)p$ (the distribution decreases). If $k = (n + 1)p$ is an integer, then $b(k; n, p) = b(k - 1; n, p)$, so the distribution has two maxima: at $k = (n + 1)p$ and at $k - 1 = (n + 1)p - 1 = np - q$. Otherwise, it attains a maximum at the unique integer k that lies in the range $np - q < k < (n + 1)p$.

The following lemma provides an upper bound on the binomial distribution.

Lemma 6.1
Let $n \geq 0$, let $0 < p < 1$, let $q = 1 - p$, and let $0 \leq k \leq n$. Then

$$
b(k; n, p) \leq \left(\frac{np}{k} \right)^k \left(\frac{nq}{n-k} \right)^{n-k} .
$$

Proof Using equation (6.10), we have

$$
\begin{aligned}
b(k; n, p) &= \binom{n}{k} p^k q^{n-k} \\
&\leq \left(\frac{n}{k} \right)^k \left(\frac{n}{n-k} \right)^{n-k} p^k q^{n-k} \\
&= \left(\frac{np}{k} \right)^k \left(\frac{nq}{n-k} \right)^{n-k} . \quad \blacksquare
\end{aligned}
$$

Exercises

6.4-1
Verify axiom 2 of the probability axioms for the geometric distribution.

6.4-2
How many times on average must we flip 6 fair coins before we obtain 3 heads and 3 tails?

6.4-3

Show that $b(k; n, p) = b(n - k; n, q)$, where $q = 1 - p$.

6.4-4

Show that value of the maximum of the binomial distribution $b(k; n, p)$ is approximately $1/\sqrt{2\pi npq}$, where $q = 1 - p$.

6.4-5 ★

Show that the probability of no successes in n Bernoulli trials, each with probability $p = 1/n$, is approximately $1/e$. Show that the probability of exactly one success is also approximately $1/e$.

6.4-6 ★

Professor Rosencrantz flips a fair coin n times, and so does Professor Guildenstern. Show that the probability that they get the same number of heads is $\binom{2n}{n}/4^n$. (*Hint:* For Professor Rosencrantz, call a head a success; for Professor Guildenstern, call a tail a success.) Use your argument to verify the identity

$$\sum_{k=0}^{n} \binom{n}{k}^2 = \binom{2n}{n} .$$

6.4-7 ★

Show that for $0 \le k \le n$,

$$b(k; n, 1/2) \le 2^{n\,H(k/n)-n} ,$$

where $H(x)$ is the entropy function (6.13).

6.4-8 ★

Consider n Bernoulli trials, where for $i = 1, 2, \ldots, n$, the ith trial has probability p_i of success, and let X be the random variable denoting the total number of successes. Let $p \ge p_i$ for all $i = 1, 2, \ldots, n$. Prove that for $1 \le k \le n$,

$$\Pr\{X < k\} \le \sum_{i=0}^{k-1} b(i; n, p) .$$

6.4-9 ★

Let X be the random variable for the total number of successes in a set A of n Bernoulli trials, where the ith trial has a probability p_i of success, and let X' be the random variable for the total number of successes in a second set A' of n Bernoulli trials, where the ith trial has a probability $p_i' \ge p_i$ of success. Prove that for $0 \le k \le n$,

$$\Pr\{X' \ge k\} \ge \Pr\{X \ge k\} .$$

(*Hint:* Show how to obtain the Bernoulli trials in A' by an experiment involving the trials of A, and use the result of Exercise 6.3-6.)

⋆ 6.5 The tails of the binomial distribution

The probability of having at least, or at most, k successes in n Bernoulli trials, each with probability p of success, is often of more interest than the probability of having exactly k successes. In this section, we investigate the *tails* of the binomial distribution: the two regions of the distribution $b(k; n, p)$ that are far from the mean np. We shall prove several important bounds on (the sum of all terms in) a tail.

We first provide a bound on the right tail of the distribution $b(k; n, p)$. Bounds on the left tail can be determined by inverting the roles of successes and failures.

Theorem 6.2
Consider a sequence of n Bernoulli trials, where success occurs with probability p. Let X be the random variable denoting the total number of successes. Then for $0 \le k \le n$, the probability of at least k successes is

$$\Pr\{X \ge k\} = \sum_{i=k}^{n} b(i; n, p)$$

$$\le \binom{n}{k} p^k .$$

Proof We make use of the inequality (6.15)

$$\binom{n}{k+i} \le \binom{n}{k}\binom{n-k}{i} .$$

We have

$$\Pr\{X \ge k\} = \sum_{i=k}^{n} b(i; n, p)$$

$$= \sum_{i=0}^{n-k} b(k + i; n, p)$$

$$= \sum_{i=0}^{n-k} \binom{n}{k+i} p^{k+i}(1 - p)^{n-(k+i)}$$

$$\le \sum_{i=0}^{n-k} \binom{n}{k}\binom{n-k}{i} p^{k+i}(1 - p)^{n-(k+i)}$$

$$= \binom{n}{k} p^k \sum_{i=0}^{n-k} \binom{n-k}{i} p^i(1 - p)^{(n-k)-i}$$

$$= \binom{n}{k} p^k \sum_{i=0}^{n-k} b(i; n - k, p)$$

$$= \binom{n}{k} p^k ,$$

since $\sum_{i=0}^{n-k} b(i; n - k, p) = 1$ by equation (6.38).   ∎

The following corollary restates the theorem for the left tail of the binomial distribution. In general, we shall leave it to the reader to adapt the bounds from one tail to the other.

Corollary 6.3

Consider a sequence of n Bernoulli trials, where success occurs with probability p. If X is the random variable denoting the total number of successes, then for $0 \le k \le n$, the probability of at most k successes is

$$
\begin{aligned}
\Pr\{X \le k\} &= \sum_{i=0}^{k} b(i; n, p) \\
&\le \binom{n}{n-k}(1 - p)^{n-k} \\
&= \binom{n}{k}(1 - p)^{n-k} .
\end{aligned}
$$

∎

Our next bound focuses on the left tail of the binomial distribution. Far from the mean, the number of successes in the left tail diminishes exponentially, as the following theorem shows.

Theorem 6.4

Consider a sequence of n Bernoulli trials, where success occurs with probability p and failure with probability $q = 1 - p$. Let X be the random variable denoting the total number of successes. Then for $0 < k < np$, the probability of fewer than k successes is

$$
\begin{aligned}
\Pr\{X < k\} &= \sum_{i=0}^{k-1} b(i; n, p) \\
&< \frac{kq}{np - k} b(k; n, p) .
\end{aligned}
$$

Proof   We bound the series $\sum_{i=0}^{k-1} b(i; n, p)$ by a geometric series using the technique from Section 3.2, page 47. For $i = 1, 2, \ldots, k$, we have from equation (6.42),

$$
\begin{aligned}
\frac{b(i - 1; n, p)}{b(i; n, p)} &= \frac{iq}{(n - i + 1)p} \\
&< \left(\frac{i}{n - i}\right)\left(\frac{q}{p}\right) \\
&\le \left(\frac{k}{n - k}\right)\left(\frac{q}{p}\right) .
\end{aligned}
$$

If we let

$$x = \left(\frac{k}{n-k}\right)\left(\frac{q}{p}\right) < 1 ,$$

it follows that

$$b(i-1;n,p) < x\, b(i;n,p)$$

for $0 < i \le k$. Iterating, we obtain

$$b(i;n,p) < x^{k-i}\, b(k;n,p)$$

for $0 \le i < k$, and hence

$$
\begin{aligned}
\sum_{i=0}^{k-1} b(i;n,p) &< \sum_{i=0}^{k-1} x^{k-i} b(k;n,p) \\
&< b(k;n,p) \sum_{i=1}^{\infty} x^i \\
&= \frac{x}{1-x}\, b(k;n,p) \\
&= \frac{kq}{np-k}\, b(k;n,p) .
\end{aligned}
$$

$\blacksquare$

When $k \le np/2$, we have $kq/(np-k) \le 1$, which means that $b(k;n,p)$ bounds the sum of all terms smaller than k. As an example, suppose we flip n fair coins. Using $p = 1/2$ and $k = n/4$, Theorem 6.4 tells us that the probability of obtaining fewer than $n/4$ heads is less than the probability of obtaining exactly $n/4$ heads. Furthermore, for any $r \ge 4$, the probability of obtaining fewer than n/r heads is less than that of obtaining exactly n/r heads. Theorem 6.4 can also be quite useful in conjunction with upper bounds on the binomial distribution, such as Lemma 6.1.

A bound on the right tail can be determined similarly.

Corollary 6.5
Consider a sequence of n Bernoulli trials, where success occurs with probability p. Let X be the random variable denoting the total number of successes. Then for $np < k < n$, the probability of more than k successes is

$$
\begin{aligned}
\Pr\{X > k\} &= \sum_{i=k+1}^{n} b(i;n,p) \\
&< \frac{(n-k)p}{k-np}\, b(k;n,p) .
\end{aligned}
$$

$\blacksquare$

The next theorem considers n Bernoulli trials, each with a probability p_i of success, for $i = 1, 2, \ldots, n$. As the subsequent corollary shows, we can use the theorem to provide a bound on the right tail of the binomial distribution by setting $p_i = p$ for each trial.

Theorem 6.6

Consider a sequence of n Bernoulli trials, where in the ith trial, for $i = 1, 2, \ldots, n$, success occurs with probability p_i and failure occurs with probability $q_i = 1 - p_i$. Let X be the random variable describing the total number of successes, and let $\mu = \mathrm{E}[X]$. Then for $r > \mu$,

$$\Pr\{X - \mu \geq r\} \leq \left(\frac{\mu e}{r}\right)^r .$$

Proof   Since for any $\alpha > 0$, the function $e^{\alpha x}$ is strictly increasing in x,

$$\Pr\{X - \mu \geq r\} = \Pr\{e^{\alpha(X-\mu)} \geq e^{\alpha r}\} ,$$

where α will be determined later. Using Markov's inequality (6.32), we obtain

$$\Pr\{X - \mu \geq r\} \leq \mathrm{E}\left[e^{\alpha(X-\mu)}\right] e^{-\alpha r} . \tag{6.43}$$

The bulk of the proof consists of bounding $\mathrm{E}\left[e^{\alpha(X-\mu)}\right]$ and substituting a suitable value for α in inequality (6.43). First, we evaluate $\mathrm{E}\left[e^{\alpha(X-\mu)}\right]$. For $i = 1, 2, \ldots, n$, let X_i be the random variable that is 1 if the ith Bernoulli trial is a success and 0 if it is a failure. Thus,

$$X = \sum_{i=1}^{n} X_i$$

and

$$X - \mu = \sum_{i=1}^{n} (X_i - p_i) .$$

Substituting for $X - \mu$, we obtain

$$
\begin{aligned}
\mathrm{E}\left[e^{\alpha(X-\mu)}\right] &= \mathrm{E}\left[\prod_{i=1}^{n} e^{\alpha(X_i - p_i)}\right] \\
&= \prod_{i=1}^{n} \mathrm{E}\left[e^{\alpha(X_i - p_i)}\right] ,
\end{aligned}
$$

which follows from (6.27), since the mutual independence of the random variables X_i implies the mutual independence of the random variables $e^{\alpha(X_i - p_i)}$ (see Exercise 6.3-4). By the definition of expectation,

$$
\begin{aligned}
\mathrm{E}\left[e^{\alpha(X_i - p_i)}\right] &= e^{\alpha(1-p_i)} p_i + e^{\alpha(0-p_i)} q_i \\
&= p_i e^{\alpha q_i} + q_i e^{-\alpha p_i} \\
&\leq p_i e^{\alpha} + 1 \\
&\leq \exp(p_i e^{\alpha}) ,
\end{aligned}
\tag{6.44}
$$

where $\exp(x)$ denotes the exponential function: $\exp(x) = e^x$. (Inequality (6.44) follows from the inequalities $\alpha > 0$, $q \leq 1$, $e^{\alpha q} \leq e^{\alpha}$, and

$e^{-\alpha p} \leq 1$, and the last line follows from inequality (2.7)). Consequently,

$$
\begin{aligned}
\mathrm{E}\left[e^{\alpha(X-\mu)}\right] &\leq \prod_{i=1}^{n} \exp(p_i e^{\alpha}) \\
&= \exp(\mu e^{\alpha}) ,
\end{aligned}
$$

since $\mu = \sum_{i=1}^{n} p_i$. Hence, from inequality (6.43), it follows that

$$
\Pr\{X - \mu \geq r\} \leq \exp(\mu e^{\alpha} - \alpha r) . \tag{6.45}
$$

Choosing $\alpha = \ln(r/\mu)$ (see Exercise 6.5-6), we obtain

$$
\begin{aligned}
\Pr\{X - \mu \geq r\} &\leq \exp(\mu e^{\ln(r/\mu)} - r\ln(r/\mu)) \\
&= \exp(r - r\ln(r/\mu)) \\
&= \frac{e^r}{(r/\mu)^r} \\
&= \left(\frac{\mu e}{r}\right)^r .
\end{aligned}
$$

∎

When applied to Bernoulli trials in which each trial has the same probability of success, Theorem 6.6 yields the following corollary bounding the right tail of a binomial distribution.

Corollary 6.7
Consider a sequence of n Bernoulli trials, where in each trial success occurs with probability p and failure occurs with probability $q = 1 - p$. Then for $r > np$,

$$
\begin{aligned}
\Pr\{X - np \geq r\} &= \sum_{k=\lceil np+r\rceil}^{n} b(k; n, p) \\
&\leq \left(\frac{npe}{r}\right)^r .
\end{aligned}
$$

Proof For a binomial distribution, equation (6.39) implies that $\mu = \mathrm{E}[X] = np$. ∎

Exercises

6.5-1 ⋆
Which is less likely: obtaining no heads when you flip a fair coin n times, or obtaining fewer than n heads when you flip the coin $4n$ times?

6.5-2 ⋆
Show that

$$
\sum_{i=0}^{k-1} \binom{n}{i} a^i < (a+1)^n \frac{k}{na - k(a+1)} b(k; n, a/(a+1))
$$

for all $a > 0$ and all k such that $0 < k < n$.

6.5-3   ⋆

Prove that if $0 < k < np$, where $0 < p < 1$ and $q = 1 - p$, then

$$\sum_{i=0}^{k-1} p^i q^{n-i} < \frac{kq}{np - k} \left(\frac{np}{k}\right)^k \left(\frac{nq}{n - k}\right)^{n-k} .$$

6.5-4   ⋆

Show that the conditions of Theorem 6.6 imply that

$$\Pr\{\mu - X \geq r\} \leq \left(\frac{(n - \mu)e}{r}\right)^r .$$

Similarly, show that the conditions of Corollary 6.7 imply that

$$\Pr\{np - X \geq r\} \leq \left(\frac{nqe}{r}\right)^r .$$

6.5-5   ⋆

Consider a sequence of n Bernoulli trials, where in the ith trial, for $i = 1, 2, \ldots, n$, success occurs with probability p_i and failure occurs with probability $q_i = 1 - p_i$. Let X be the random variable describing the total number of successes, and let $\mu = \mathrm{E}[X]$. Show that for $r \geq 0$,

$$\Pr\{X - \mu \geq r\} \leq e^{-r^2/2n} .$$

(*Hint:* Prove that $p_i e^{\alpha q_i} + q_i e^{-\alpha p_i} \leq e^{-\alpha^2/2}$. Then follow the outline of the proof of Theorem 6.6, using this inequality in place of inequality (6.44).)

6.5-6   ⋆

Show that choosing $\alpha = \ln(r/\mu)$ minimizes the right-hand side of inequality (6.45).

6.6   Probabilistic analysis

This section uses three examples to illustrate probabilistic analysis. The first determines the probability that in a room of k people, some pair shares the same birthday. The second example examines the random tossing of balls into bins. The third investigates "streaks" of consecutive heads in coin flipping.

6.6.1   The birthday paradox

A good example to illustrate probabilistic reasoning is the classical **birthday paradox**. How many people must there be in a room before there is a good chance two of them were born on the same day of the year? The answer is surprisingly few. The paradox is that it is in fact far fewer than the number of days in the year, as we shall see.

To answer the question, we index the people in the room with the integers $1, 2, \ldots, k$, where k is the number of people in the room. We ignore the issue of leap years and assume that all years have $n = 365$ days. For $i = 1, 2, \ldots, k$, let b_i be the day of the year on which i's birthday falls, where $1 \leq b_i \leq n$. We also assume that birthdays are uniformly distributed across the n days of the year, so that $\Pr\{b_i = r\} = 1/n$ for $i = 1, 2, \ldots, k$ and $r = 1, 2, \ldots, n$.

The probability that two people i and j have matching birthdays depends on whether the random selection of birthdays is independent. If birthdays are independent, then the probability that i's birthday and j's birthday both fall on day r is

$$
\begin{aligned}
\Pr\{b_i = r \text{ and } b_j = r\} &= \Pr\{b_i = r\}\Pr\{b_j = r\} \\
&= 1/n^2 \ .
\end{aligned}
$$

Thus, the probability that they both fall on the same day is

$$
\begin{aligned}
\Pr\{b_i = b_j\} &= \sum_{r=1}^{n} \Pr\{b_i = r \text{ and } b_j = r\} \\
&= \sum_{r=1}^{n} (1/n^2) \\
&= 1/n \ .
\end{aligned}
$$

More intuitively, once b_i is chosen, the probability that b_j is chosen the same is $1/n$. Thus, the probability that i and j have the same birthday is the same as the probability that the birthday of one of them falls on a given day. Notice, however, that this coincidence depends on the assumption that the birthdays are independent.

We can analyze the probability of at least 2 out of k people having matching birthdays by looking at the complementary event. The probability that at least two of the birthdays match is 1 minus the probability that all the birthdays are different. The event that k people have distinct birthdays is

$$
B_k = \bigcap_{i=1}^{k-1} A_i \ ,
$$

where A_i is the event that person $(i+1)$'s birthday is different from person j's for all $j \leq i$, that is,

$$
A_i = \{b_{i+1} \neq b_j : j = 1, 2 \ldots, i\} \ .
$$

Since we can write $B_k = A_{k-1} \cap B_{k-1}$, we obtain from equation (6.20) the recurrence

$$
\Pr\{B_k\} = \Pr\{B_{k-1}\}\Pr\{A_{k-1} \mid B_{k-1}\} \ , \tag{6.46}
$$

where we take $\Pr\{B_1\} = 1$ as an initial condition. In other words, the probability that $b_1, b_2, \ldots, b_k$ are distinct birthdays is the probability that $b_1, b_2, \ldots, b_{k-1}$ are distinct birthdays times the probability that $b_k \neq b_i$ for $i = 1, 2, \ldots, k - 1$, given that $b_1, b_2, \ldots, b_{k-1}$ are distinct.

If $b_1, b_2, \ldots, b_{k-1}$ are distinct, the conditional probability that $b_k \neq b_i$ for $i = 1, 2, \ldots, k - 1$ is $(n - k + 1)/n$, since out of the n days, there are $n - (k - 1)$ that are not taken. By iterating the recurrence (6.46), we obtain

$$
\begin{aligned}
\Pr\{B_k\} &= \Pr\{B_1\}\Pr\{A_1 \mid B_1\}\Pr\{A_2 \mid B_2\} \cdots \Pr\{A_{k-1} \mid B_{k-1}\} \\
&= 1 \cdot \left(\frac{n-1}{n}\right)\left(\frac{n-2}{n}\right) \cdots \left(\frac{n-k+1}{n}\right) \\
&= 1 \cdot \left(1 - \frac{1}{n}\right)\left(1 - \frac{2}{n}\right) \cdots \left(1 - \frac{k-1}{n}\right) .
\end{aligned}
$$

The inequality (2.7), $1 + x \leq e^x$, gives us

$$
\begin{aligned}
\Pr\{B_k\} &\leq e^{-1/n}e^{-2/n} \cdots e^{-(k-1)/n} \\
&= e^{-\sum_{i=1}^{k-1} i/n} \\
&= e^{-k(k-1)/2n} \\
&\leq 1/2
\end{aligned}
$$

when $-k(k - 1)/2n \leq \ln(1/2)$. The probability that all k birthdays are distinct is at most $1/2$ when $k(k - 1) \geq 2n \ln 2$ or, solving the quadratic equation, when $k \geq (1 + \sqrt{1 + (8 \ln 2)n})/2$. For $n = 365$, we must have $k \geq 23$. Thus, if at least 23 people are in a room, the probability is at least $1/2$ that at least two people have the same birthday. On Mars, a year is 669 Martian days long; it therefore takes 31 Martians to get the same effect.

Another method of analysis

We can use the linearity of expectation (equation (6.26)) to provide a simpler but approximate analysis of the birthday paradox. For each pair (i, j) of the k people in the room, let us define the random variable X_{ij}, for $1 \leq i < j \leq k$, by

$$
X_{ij} = \begin{cases} 1 & \text{if person } i \text{ and person } j \text{ have the same birthday ,} \\ 0 & \text{otherwise .} \end{cases}
$$

The probability that two people have matching birthdays is $1/n$, and thus by the definition of expectation (6.23),

$$
\begin{aligned}
E[X_{ij}] &= 1 \cdot (1/n) + 0 \cdot (1 - 1/n) \\
&= 1/n .
\end{aligned}
$$

The expected number of pairs of individuals having the same birthday is, by equation (6.24), just the sum of the individual expectations of the pairs, which is

$$\sum_{i=2}^{k}\sum_{j=1}^{i-1}\mathrm{E}\,[X_{ij}] \;=\; \binom{k}{2}\frac{1}{n}$$
$$=\; \frac{k(k-1)}{2n}\;.$$

When $k(k-1) \geq 2n$, therefore, the expected number of pairs of birthdays is at least 1. Thus, if we have at least $\sqrt{2n}$ individuals in a room, we can expect at least two to have the same birthday. For $n = 365$, if $k = 28$, the expected number of pairs with the same birthday is $(28 \cdot 27)/(2 \cdot 365) \approx 1.0356$. Thus, with at least 28 people, we expect to find at least one matching pair of birthdays. On Mars, where a year is 669 Martian days long, we need at least 38 Martians.

The first analysis determined the number of people required for the probability to exceed $1/2$ that a matching pair of birthdays exists, and the second analysis determined the number such that the expected number of matching birthdays is 1. Although the numbers of people differ for the two situations, they are the same asymptotically: $\Theta(\sqrt{n})$.

6.6.2 Balls and bins

Consider the process of randomly tossing identical balls into b bins, numbered $1, 2, \ldots, b$. The tosses are independent, and on each toss the ball is equally likely to end up in any bin. The probability that a tossed ball lands in any given bin is $1/b$. Thus, the ball-tossing process is a sequence of Bernoulli trials with a probability $1/b$ of success, where success means that the ball falls in the given bin. A variety of interesting questions can be asked about the ball-tossing process.

How many balls fall in a given bin? The number of balls that fall in a given bin follows the binomial distribution $b(k; n, 1/b)$. If n balls are tossed, the expected number of balls that fall in the given bin is n/b.

How many balls must one toss, on the average, until a given bin contains a ball? The number of tosses until the given bin receives a ball follows the geometric distribution with probability $1/b$, and thus the expected number of tosses until success is $1/(1/b) = b$.

How many balls must one toss until every bin contains at least one ball? Let us call a toss in which a ball falls into an empty bin a "hit." We want to know the average number n of tosses required to get b hits.

The hits can be used to partition the n tosses into stages. The ith stage consists of the tosses after the $(i-1)$st hit until the ith hit. The first stage consists of the first toss, since we are guaranteed to have a hit when all bins are empty. For each toss during the ith stage, there are $i - 1$ bins that contain balls and $b - i + 1$ empty bins. Thus, for all tosses in the ith stage, the probability of obtaining a hit is $(b - i + 1)/b$.

Let n_i denote the number of tosses in the ith stage. Thus, the number of tosses required to get b hits is $n = \sum_{i=1}^{b} n_i$. Each random variable n_i has a geometric distribution with probability of success $(b-i+1)/b$, and therefore

$$E[n_i] = \frac{b}{b-i+1} \ .$$

By linearity of expectation,

$$
\begin{aligned}
E[n] &= E\left[\sum_{i=1}^{b} n_i\right] \\
&= \sum_{i=1}^{b} E[n_i] \\
&= \sum_{i=1}^{b} \frac{b}{b-i+1} \\
&= b \sum_{i=1}^{b} \frac{1}{i} \\
&\leq b(\ln b + O(1)) \ .
\end{aligned}
$$

The last line follows from the bound (3.5) on the harmonic series. It therefore takes approximately $b \ln b$ tosses before we can expect that every bin has a ball.

6.6.3   Streaks

Suppose you flip a fair coin n times. What is the longest streak of consecutive heads that you expect to see? The answer is $\Theta(\lg n)$, as the following analysis shows.

We first prove that the expected length of the longest streak of heads is $O(\lg n)$. Let A_{ik} be the event that a streak of heads of length at least k begins with the ith coin flip or, more precisely, the event that the k consecutive coin flips $i, i+1, \ldots, i+k-1$ yield only heads, where $1 \leq k \leq n$ and $1 \leq i \leq n-k+1$. For any given event A_{ik}, the probability that all k flips are heads has a geometric distribution with $p = q = 1/2$:

$$\Pr\{A_{ik}\} = 1/2^k \ . \tag{6.47}$$

For $k = 2\lceil \lg n \rceil$,

$$
\begin{aligned}
\Pr\{A_{i,2\lceil \lg n \rceil}\} &= 1/2^{2\lceil \lg n \rceil} \\
&\leq 1/2^{2 \lg n} \\
&= 1/n^2 \ ,
\end{aligned}
$$

and thus the probability that a streak of heads of length at least $\lceil 2 \lg n \rceil$ begins in position i is quite small, especially considering that there are at most n positions (actually $n - 2\lceil \lg n \rceil + 1$) where the streak can begin. The probability that a streak of heads of length at least $\lceil 2 \lg n \rceil$ begins anywhere is therefore

$$\Pr \left\{ \bigcup_{i=1}^{n - 2\lceil \lg n \rceil + 1} A_{i, 2\lceil \lg n \rceil} \right\} \leq \sum_{i=1}^{n} 1/n^2$$
$$= 1/n ,$$

since by Boole's inequality (6.22), the probability of a union of events is at most the sum of the probabilities of the individual events. (Note that Boole's inequality holds even for events such as these that are not independent.)

The probability is therefore at most $1/n$ that any streak has length at least $2\lceil \lg n \rceil$; hence, the probability is at least $1 - 1/n$ that the longest streak has length less than $2\lceil \lg n \rceil$. Since every streak has length at most n, the expected length of the longest streak is bounded above by

$$(2\lceil \lg n \rceil)(1 - 1/n) + n(1/n) = O(\lg n) .$$

The chances that a streak of heads exceeds $r\lceil \lg n \rceil$ flips diminish quickly with r. For $r \geq 1$, the probability that a streak of $r\lceil \lg n \rceil$ heads starts in position i is

$$\Pr \{A_{i, r\lceil \lg n \rceil}\} = 1/2^{r\lceil \lg n \rceil}$$
$$\leq 1/n^r .$$

Thus, the probability is at most $n/n^r = 1/n^{r-1}$ that the longest streak is at least $r\lceil \lg n \rceil$, or equivalently, the probability is at least $1 - 1/n^{r-1}$ that the longest streak has length less than $r\lceil \lg n \rceil$.

As an example, for $n = 1000$ coin flips, the probability of having a streak of at least $2\lceil \lg n \rceil = 20$ heads is at most $1/n = 1/1000$. The chances of having a streak longer than $3\lceil \lg n \rceil = 30$ heads is at most $1/n^2 = 1/1,000,000$.

We now prove a complementary lower bound: the expected length of the longest streak of heads in n coin flips is $\Omega(\lg n)$. To prove this bound, we look for streaks of length $\lfloor \lg n \rfloor / 2$. From equation (6.47), we have

$$\Pr \{A_{i, \lfloor \lg n \rfloor / 2}\} = 1/2^{\lfloor \lg n \rfloor / 2}$$
$$\geq 1/\sqrt{n} .$$

The probability that a streak of heads of length at least $\lfloor \lg n \rfloor / 2$ does not begin in position i is therefore at most $1 - 1/\sqrt{n}$. We can partition the n coin flips into at least $\lfloor 2n/\lfloor \lg n \rfloor \rfloor$ groups of $\lfloor \lg n \rfloor / 2$ consecutive coin flips. Since these groups are formed from mutually exclusive, independent coin flips, the probability that every one of these groups *fails* to be a streak of length $\lfloor \lg n \rfloor / 2$ is

$$\left(1 - 1/\sqrt{n}\right)^{\lfloor 2n/\lfloor \lg n \rfloor \rfloor} \leq \left(1 - 1/\sqrt{n}\right)^{2n/\lg n - 1}$$
$$\leq e^{-(2n/\lg n - 1)/\sqrt{n}}$$
$$\leq e^{-\lg n}$$
$$\leq 1/n .$$

For this argument, we used inequality (2.7), $1+x \leq e^x$, and the fact, which you might want to verify, that $(2n/\lg n - 1)/\sqrt{n} \geq \lg n$ for $n \geq 2$. (For $n = 1$, the probability that every group fails to be a streak is trivially at most $1/n = 1$.)

Thus, the probability that the longest streak exceeds $\lfloor \lg n \rfloor /2$ is at least $1 - 1/n$. Since the longest streak has length at least 0, the expected length of the longest streak is at least

$$(\lfloor \lg n \rfloor /2)(1 - 1/n) + 0 \cdot (1/n) = \Omega(\lg n) \ .$$

Exercises

6.6-1
Suppose that balls are tossed into b bins. Each toss is independent, and each ball is equally likely to end up in any bin. What is the expected number of ball tosses before at least one of the bins contains two balls?

6.6-2 ★
For the analysis of the birthday paradox, is it important that the birthdays be mutually independent, or is pairwise independence sufficient? Justify your answer.

6.6-3 ★
How many people should be invited to a party in order to make it likely that there are *three* people with the same birthday?

6.6-4 ★
What is the probability that a k-string over a set of size n is actually a k-permutation? How does this question relate to the birthday paradox?

6.6-5 ★
Suppose that n balls are tossed into n bins, where each toss is independent and the ball is equally likely to end up in any bin. What is the expected number of empty bins? What is the expected number of bins with exactly one ball?

6.6-6 ★
Sharpen the lower bound on streak length by showing that in n flips of a fair coin, the probability is less than $1/n$ that no streak longer than $\lg n - 2 \lg \lg n$ consecutive heads occurs.

Problems

6-1 Balls and bins

In this problem, we investigate the effect of various assumptions on the number of ways of placing n balls into b distinct bins.

a. Suppose that the n balls are distinct and that their order within a bin does not matter. Argue that the number of ways of placing the balls in the bins is b^n.

b. Suppose that the balls are distinct and that the balls in each bin are ordered. Prove that the number of ways of placing the balls in the bins is $(b+n-1)!/(b-1)!$. (*Hint:* Consider the number of ways of arranging n distinct balls and $b-1$ indistinguishable sticks in a row.)

c. Suppose that the balls are identical, and hence their order within a bin does not matter. Show that the number of ways of placing the balls in the bins is $\binom{b+n-1}{n}$. (*Hint:* Of the arrangements in part (b), how many are repeated if the balls are made identical?)

d. Suppose that the balls are identical and that no bin may contain more than one ball. Show that the number of ways of placing the balls is $\binom{b}{n}$.

e. Suppose that the balls are identical and that no bin may be left empty. Show that the number of ways of placing the balls is $\binom{n-1}{b-1}$.

6-2 Analysis of max program

The following program determines the maximum value in an unordered array $A[1 .. n]$.

```
1  max ← −∞
2  for i ← 1 to n
3      do ▷ Compare A[i] to max.
4          if A[i] > max
5              then max ← A[i]
```

We want to determine the average number of times the assignment in line 5 is executed. Assume that all numbers in A are randomly drawn from the interval $[0, 1]$.

a. If a number x is randomly chosen from a set of n distinct numbers, what is the probability that x is the largest number in the set?

b. When line 5 of the program is executed, what is the relationship between $A[i]$ and $A[j]$ for $1 \le j \le i$?

c. For each i in the range $1 \le i \le n$, what is the probability that line 5 is executed?

d. Let $s_1, s_2, \ldots, s_n$ be n random variables, where s_i represents the number of times (0 or 1) that line 5 is executed during the ith iteration of the **for** loop. What is $E[s_i]$?

e. Let $s = s_1 + s_2 + \cdots + s_n$ be the total number of times that line 5 is executed during some run of the program. Show that $E[s] = \Theta(\lg n)$.

6-3   Hiring problem

Professor Dixon needs to hire a new research assistant. She has arranged interviews with n applicants and would like to base her decision solely on their qualifications. Unfortunately, university regulations require that after each interview she immediately reject or offer the position to the applicant.

Professor Dixon decides to adopt the strategy of selecting a positive integer $k < n$, interviewing and then rejecting the first k applicants, and hiring the first applicant thereafter who is better qualified than all preceding applicants. If the best-qualified applicant is among the first k interviewed, then she will hire the nth applicant. Show that Professor Dixon maximizes her chances of hiring the best-qualified applicant by choosing k approximately equal to n/e and that her chances of hiring the best-qualified applicant are then approximately $1/e$.

6-4   Probabilistic counting

With a t-bit counter, we can ordinarily only count up to $2^t - 1$. With R. Morris's *probabilistic counting*, we can count up to a much larger value at the expense of some loss of precision.

We let a counter value of i represent a count of n_i for $i = 0, 1, \ldots, 2^t - 1$, where the n_i form an increasing sequence of nonnegative values. We assume that the initial value of the counter is 0, representing a count of $n_0 = 0$. The INCREMENT operation works on a counter containing the value i in a probabilistic manner. If $i = 2^t - 1$, then an overflow error is reported. Otherwise, the counter is increased by 1 with probability $1/(n_{i+1} - n_i)$, and it remains unchanged with probability $1 - 1/(n_{i+1} - n_i)$.

If we select $n_i = i$ for all $i \geq 0$, then the counter is an ordinary one. More interesting situations arise if we select, say, $n_i = 2^{i-1}$ for $i > 0$ or $n_i = F_i$ (the ith Fibonacci number—see Section 2.2).

For this problem, assume that $n_{2^t - 1}$ is large enough that the probability of an overflow error is negligible.

a. Show that the expected value represented by the counter after n INCREMENT operations have been performed is exactly n.

b. The analysis of the variance of the count represented by the counter depends on the sequence of the n_i. Let us consider a simple case: $n_i = 100i$ for all $i \geq 0$. Estimate the variance in the value represented by the register after n INCREMENT operations have been performed.

Chapter notes

The first general methods for solving probability problems were discussed in a famous correspondence between B. Pascal and P. de Fermat, which began in 1654, and in a book by C. Huygens in 1657. Rigorous probability theory began with the work of J. Bernoulli in 1713 and A. De Moivre in 1730. Further developments of the theory were provided by P. S. de Laplace, S.-D. Poisson, and C. F. Gauss.

Sums of random variables were originally studied by P. L. Chebyshev and A. A. Markov. Probability theory was axiomatized by A. N. Kolmogorov in 1933. Bounds on the tails of distributions were provided by Chernoff [40] and Hoeffding [99]. Seminal work in random combinatorial structures was done by P. Erdös.

Knuth [121] and Liu [140] are good references for elementary combinatorics and counting. Standard textbooks such as Billingsley [28], Chung [41], Drake [57], Feller [66], and Rozanov [171] offer comprehensive introductions to probability. Bollobás [30], Hofri [100], and Spencer [179] contain a wealth of advanced probabilistic techniques.

II Sorting and Order Statistics

Introduction

This part presents several algorithms that solve the following *sorting problem*:

Input: A sequence of n numbers $\langle a_1, a_2, \ldots, a_n \rangle$.

Output: A permutation (reordering) $\langle a_1', a_2', \ldots, a_n' \rangle$ of the input sequence such that $a_1' \leq a_2' \leq \cdots \leq a_n'$.

The input sequence is usually an n-element array, although it may be represented in some other fashion, such as a linked list.

The structure of the data

In practice, the numbers to be sorted are rarely isolated values. Each is usually part of a collection of data called a *record*. Each record contains a *key*, which is the value to be sorted, and the remainder of the record consists of *satellite data*, which are usually carried around with the key. In practice, when a sorting algorithm permutes the keys, it must permute the satellite data as well. If each record includes a large amount of satellite data, we often permute an array of pointers to the records rather than the records themselves in order to minimize data movement.

In a sense, it is these implementation details that distinguish an algorithm from a full-blown program. Whether we sort individual numbers or large records that contain numbers is irrelevant to the *method* by which a sorting procedure determines the sorted order. Thus, when focusing on the problem of sorting, we typically assume that the input consists only of numbers. The translation of an algorithm for sorting numbers into a program for sorting records is conceptually straightforward, although in a given engineering situation there may be other subtleties that make the actual programming task a challenge.

Sorting algorithms

We introduced two algorithms that sort n real numbers in Chapter 1. Insertion sort takes $\Theta(n^2)$ time in the worst case. Because its inner loops are tight, however, it is a fast in-place sorting algorithm for small input sizes. (Recall that a sorting algorithm sorts ***in place*** if only a constant number of elements of the input array are ever stored outside the array.) Merge sort has a better asymptotic running time, $\Theta(n \lg n)$, but the MERGE procedure it uses does not operate in place.

In this part, we shall introduce two more algorithms that sort arbitrary real numbers. Heapsort, presented in Chapter 7, sorts n numbers in place in $O(n \lg n)$ time. It uses an important data structure, called a heap, to implement a priority queue.

Quicksort, in Chapter 8, also sorts n numbers in place, but its worst-case running time is $\Theta(n^2)$. Its average-case running time is $\Theta(n \lg n)$, though, and it generally outperforms heapsort in practice. Like insertion sort, quicksort has tight code, so the hidden constant factor in its running time is small. It is a popular algorithm for sorting large input arrays.

Insertion sort, merge sort, heapsort, and quicksort are all comparison sorts: they determine the sorted order of an input array by comparing elements. Chapter 9 begins by introducing the decision-tree model in order to study the performance limitations of comparison sorts. Using this model, we prove a lower bound of $\Omega(n \lg n)$ on the worst-case running time of any comparison sort on n inputs, thus showing that heapsort and merge sort are asymptotically optimal comparison sorts.

Chapter 9 then goes on to show that we can beat this lower bound of $\Omega(n \lg n)$ if we can gather information about the sorted order of the input by means other than comparing elements. The counting sort algorithm, for example, assumes that the input numbers are in the set $\{1, 2, \ldots, k\}$. By using array indexing as a tool for determining relative order, counting sort can sort n numbers in $O(k + n)$ time. Thus, when $k = O(n)$, counting sort runs in time that is linear in the size of the input array. A related algorithm, radix sort, can be used to extend the range of counting sort. If there are n integers to sort, each integer has d digits, and each digit is in the set $\{1, 2, \ldots, k\}$, radix sort can sort the numbers in $O(d(n + k))$ time. When d is a constant and k is $O(n)$, radix sort runs in linear time. A third algorithm, bucket sort, requires knowledge of the probabilistic distribution of numbers in the input array. It can sort n real numbers uniformly distributed in the half-open interval $[0, 1)$ in average-case $O(n)$ time.

Order statistics

The ith order statistic of a set of n numbers is the ith smallest number in the set. One can, of course, select the ith order statistic by sorting the input and indexing the ith element of the output. With no assumptions about the input distribution, this method runs in $\Omega(n \lg n)$ time, as the lower bound proved in Chapter 9 shows.

In Chapter 10, we show that we can find the ith smallest element in $O(n)$ time, even when the elements are arbitrary real numbers. We present an algorithm with tight pseudocode that runs in $O(n^2)$ time in the worst case, but linear time on average. We also give a more complicated algorithm that runs in $O(n)$ worst-case time.

Background

Although most of this part does not rely on difficult mathematics, some sections do require mathematical sophistication. In particular, the average-case analyses of quicksort, bucket sort, and the order-statistic algorithm use probability, which is reviewed in Chapter 6. The analysis of the worst-case linear-time algorithm for the order statistic involves somewhat more sophisticated mathematics than the other worst-case analyses in this part.

7   Heapsort

In this chapter, we introduce another sorting algorithm. Like merge sort, but unlike insertion sort, heapsort's running time is $O(n \lg n)$. Like insertion sort, but unlike merge sort, heapsort sorts in place: only a constant number of array elements are stored outside the input array at any time. Thus, heapsort combines the better attributes of the two sorting algorithms we have already discussed.

Heapsort also introduces another algorithm design technique: the use of a data structure, in this case one we call a "heap," to manage information during the execution of the algorithm. Not only is the heap data structure useful for heapsort, it also makes an efficient priority queue. The heap data structure will reappear in algorithms in later chapters.

We note that the term "heap" was originally coined in the context of heapsort, but it has since come to refer to "garbage-collected storage," such as the programming language Lisp provides. Our heap data structure is *not* garbage-collected storage, and whenever we refer to heaps in this book, we shall mean the structure defined in this chapter.

7.1   Heaps

The *(binary) heap* data structure is an array object that can be viewed as a complete binary tree (see Section 5.5.3), as shown in Figure 7.1. Each node of the tree corresponds to an element of the array that stores the value in the node. The tree is completely filled on all levels except possibly the lowest, which is filled from the left up to a point. An array A that represents a heap is an object with two attributes: *length*[A], which is the number of elements in the array, and *heap-size*[A], the number of elements in the heap stored within array A. That is, although $A[1 \mathinner{.\,.} length[A]]$ may contain valid numbers, no element past $A[heap\text{-}size[A]]$, where $heap\text{-}size[A] \leq length[A]$, is an element of the heap. The root of the tree is $A[1]$, and given the index i of a node, the indices of its parent PARENT(i), left child LEFT(i), and right child RIGHT(i) can be computed simply:

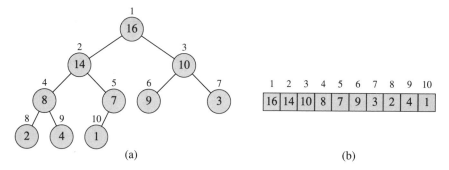

Figure 7.1 A heap viewed as **(a)** a binary tree and **(b)** an array. The number within the circle at each node in the tree is the value stored at that node. The number next to a node is the corresponding index in the array.

PARENT(i)

   return $\lfloor i/2 \rfloor$

LEFT(i)

   return $2i$

RIGHT(i)

   return $2i + 1$

On most computers, the LEFT procedure can compute $2i$ in one instruction by simply shifting the binary representation of i left one bit position. Similarly, the RIGHT procedure can quickly compute $2i + 1$ by shifting the binary representation of i left one bit position and shifting in a 1 as the low-order bit. The PARENT procedure can compute $\lfloor i/2 \rfloor$ by shifting i right one bit position. In a good implementation of heapsort, these three procedures are often implemented as "macros" or "in-line" procedures.

   Heaps also satisfy the ***heap property***: for every node i other than the root,

$$A[\text{PARENT}(i)] \geq A[i] \,, \tag{7.1}$$

that is, the value of a node is at most the value of its parent. Thus, the largest element in a heap is stored at the root, and the subtrees rooted at a node contain smaller values than does the node itself.

   We define the ***height*** of a node in a tree to be the number of edges on the longest simple downward path from the node to a leaf, and we define the height of the tree to be the height of its root. Since a heap of n elements is based on a complete binary tree, its height is $\Theta(\lg n)$ (see Exercise 7.1-2). We shall see that the basic operations on heaps run in time at most proportional to the height of the tree and thus take $O(\lg n)$ time. The remainder of this chapter presents five basic procedures and shows how they are used in a sorting algorithm and a priority-queue data structure.

- The HEAPIFY procedure, which runs in $O(\lg n)$ time, is the key to maintaining the heap property (7.1).

- The BUILD-HEAP procedure, which runs in linear time, produces a heap from an unordered input array.

- The HEAPSORT procedure, which runs in $O(n \lg n)$ time, sorts an array in place.

- The EXTRACT-MAX and INSERT procedures, which run in $O(\lg n)$ time, allow the heap data structure to be used as a priority queue.

Exercises

_7.1-1_
What are the minimum and maximum numbers of elements in a heap of height h?

_7.1-2_
Show that an n-element heap has height $\lfloor \lg n \rfloor$.

_7.1-3_
Show that the largest element in a subtree of a heap is at the root of the subtree.

_7.1-4_
Where in a heap might the smallest element reside?

_7.1-5_
Is an array that is in reverse sorted order a heap?

_7.1-6_
Is the sequence $\langle 23, 17, 14, 6, 13, 10, 1, 5, 7, 12 \rangle$ a heap?

7.2 Maintaining the heap property

HEAPIFY is an important subroutine for manipulating heaps. Its inputs are an array A and an index i into the array. When HEAPIFY is called, it is assumed that the binary trees rooted at LEFT(i) and RIGHT(i) are heaps, but that $A[i]$ may be smaller than its children, thus violating the heap property (7.1). The function of HEAPIFY is to let the value at $A[i]$ "float down" in the heap so that the subtree rooted at index i becomes a heap.

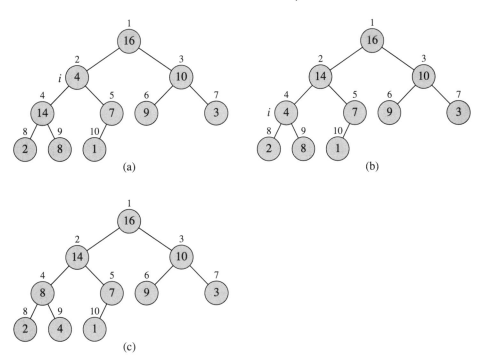

Figure 7.2   The action of HEAPIFY($A, 2$), where *heap-size*[A] = 10. (**a**) The initial configuration of the heap, with $A[2]$ at node $i = 2$ violating the heap property since it is not larger than both children. The heap property is restored for node 2 in (**b**) by exchanging $A[2]$ with $A[4]$, which destroys the heap property for node 4. The recursive call HEAPIFY($A, 4$) now sets $i = 4$. After swapping $A[4]$ with $A[9]$, as shown in (**c**), node 4 is fixed up, and the recursive call HEAPIFY($A, 9$) yields no further change to the data structure.

HEAPIFY(A, i)

```
 1   l ← LEFT(i)
 2   r ← RIGHT(i)
 3   if l ≤ heap-size[A] and A[l] > A[i]
 4       then largest ← l
 5       else largest ← i
 6   if r ≤ heap-size[A] and A[r] > A[largest]
 7       then largest ← r
 8   if largest ≠ i
 9       then exchange A[i] ↔ A[largest]
10               HEAPIFY(A, largest)
```

Figure 7.2 illustrates the action of HEAPIFY. At each step, the largest of the elements $A[i]$, $A[\text{LEFT}(i)]$, and $A[\text{RIGHT}(i)]$ is determined, and its index is stored in *largest*. If $A[i]$ is largest, then the subtree rooted at node i is a heap and the procedure terminates. Otherwise, one of the two children has the largest element, and $A[i]$ is swapped with $A[largest]$, which causes node i and its children to satisfy the heap property. The node *largest*, however, now has the original value $A[i]$, and thus the subtree rooted at *largest* may violate the heap property. Consequently, HEAPIFY must be called recursively on that subtree.

The running time of HEAPIFY on a subtree of size n rooted at given node i is the $\Theta(1)$ time to fix up the relationships among the elements $A[i]$, $A[\text{LEFT}(i)]$, and $A[\text{RIGHT}(i)]$, plus the time to run HEAPIFY on a subtree rooted at one of the children of node i. The children's subtrees each have size at most $2n/3$—the worst case occurs when the last row of the tree is exactly half full—and the running time of HEAPIFY can therefore be described by the recurrence

$$T(n) \leq T(2n/3) + \Theta(1) \; .$$

The solution to this recurrence, by case 2 of the master theorem (Theorem 4.1), is $T(n) = O(\lg n)$. Alternatively, we can characterize the running time of HEAPIFY on a node of height h as $O(h)$.

Exercises

7.2-1
Using Figure 7.2 as a model, illustrate the operation of HEAPIFY($A, 3$) on the array $A = \langle 27, 17, 3, 16, 13, 10, 1, 5, 7, 12, 4, 8, 9, 0 \rangle$.

7.2-2
What is the effect of calling HEAPIFY(A, i) when the element $A[i]$ is larger than its children?

7.2-3
What is the effect of calling HEAPIFY(A, i) for $i > heap\text{-}size[A]/2$?

7.2-4
The code for HEAPIFY is quite efficient in terms of constant factors, except possibly for the recursive call in line 10, which might cause some compilers to produce inefficient code. Write an efficient HEAPIFY that uses an iterative control construct (a loop) instead of recursion.

7.2-5
Show that the worst-case running time of HEAPIFY on a heap of size n is $\Omega(\lg n)$. (*Hint:* For a heap with n nodes, give node values that cause HEAPIFY to be called recursively at every node on a path from the root down to a leaf.)

7.3 Building a heap

We can use the procedure HEAPIFY in a bottom-up manner to convert an array $A[1 .. n]$, where $n = length[A]$, into a heap. Since the elements in the subarray $A[(\lfloor n/2 \rfloor + 1) .. n]$ are all leaves of the tree, each is a 1-element heap to begin with. The procedure BUILD-HEAP goes through the remaining nodes of the tree and runs HEAPIFY on each one. The order in which the nodes are processed guarantees that the subtrees rooted at children of a node i are heaps before HEAPIFY is run at that node.

BUILD-HEAP(A)

1 $heap\text{-}size[A] \leftarrow length[A]$
2 **for** $i \leftarrow \lfloor length[A]/2 \rfloor$ **downto** 1
3   **do** HEAPIFY(A, i)

Figure 7.3 shows an example of the action of BUILD-HEAP.

We can compute a simple upper bound on the running time of BUILD-HEAP as follows. Each call to HEAPIFY costs $O(\lg n)$ time, and there are $O(n)$ such calls. Thus, the running time is at most $O(n \lg n)$. This upper bound, though correct, is not asymptotically tight.

We can derive a tighter bound by observing that the time for HEAPIFY to run at a node varies with the height of the node in the tree, and the heights of most nodes are small. Our tighter analysis relies on the property that in an n-element heap there are at most $\lceil n/2^{h+1} \rceil$ nodes of height h (see Exercise 7.3-3).

The time required by HEAPIFY when called on a node of height h is $O(h)$, so we can express the total cost of BUILD-HEAP as

$$\sum_{h=0}^{\lfloor \lg n \rfloor} \left\lceil \frac{n}{2^{h+1}} \right\rceil O(h) = O\left(n \sum_{h=0}^{\lfloor \lg n \rfloor} \frac{h}{2^h} \right) . \tag{7.2}$$

The last summation can be evaluated by substituting $x = 1/2$ in the formula (3.6), which yields

$$\sum_{h=0}^{\infty} \frac{h}{2^h} = \frac{1/2}{(1 - 1/2)^2}$$
$$= 2 .$$

Thus, the running time of BUILD-HEAP can be bounded as

$$O\left(n \sum_{h=0}^{\lfloor \lg n \rfloor} \frac{h}{2^h} \right) = O\left(n \sum_{h=0}^{\infty} \frac{h}{2^h} \right)$$
$$= O(n) .$$

Hence, we can build a heap from an unordered array in linear time.

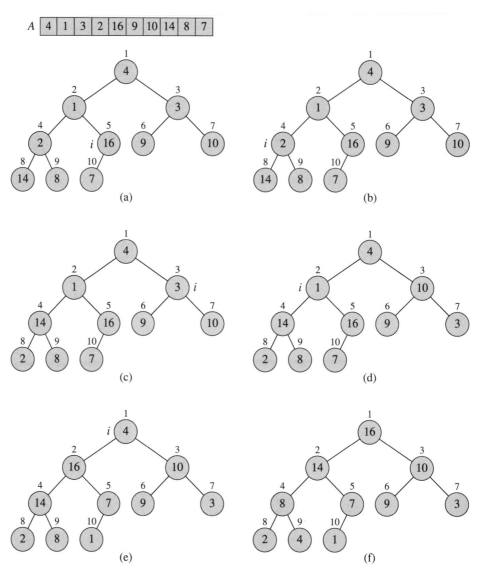

Figure 7.3 The operation of BUILD-HEAP, showing the data structure before the call to HEAPIFY in line 3 of BUILD-HEAP. (a) A 10-element input array A and the binary tree it represents. The figure shows that the loop index i points to node 5 before the call HEAPIFY(A, i). (b) The data structure that results. The loop index i for the next iteration points to node 4. (c)–(e) Subsequent iterations of the **for** loop in BUILD-HEAP. Observe that whenever HEAPIFY is called on a node, the two subtrees of that node are both heaps. (f) The heap after BUILD-HEAP finishes.

Exercises

7.3-1
Using Figure 7.3 as a model, illustrate the operation of BUILD-HEAP on the array $A = \langle 5, 3, 17, 10, 84, 19, 6, 22, 9 \rangle$.

7.3-2
Why do we want the loop index i in line 2 of BUILD-HEAP to decrease from $\lfloor length[A]/2 \rfloor$ to 1 rather than increase from 1 to $\lfloor length[A]/2 \rfloor$?

7.3-3
Show that there are at most $\lceil n/2^{h+1} \rceil$ nodes of height h in any n-element heap.

7.4 The heapsort algorithm

The heapsort algorithm starts by using BUILD-HEAP to build a heap on the input array $A[1 .. n]$, where $n = length[A]$. Since the maximum element of the array is stored at the root $A[1]$, it can be put into its correct final position by exchanging it with $A[n]$. If we now "discard" node n from the heap (by decrementing *heap-size*$[A]$), we observe that $A[1 .. (n-1)]$ can easily be made into a heap. The children of the root remain heaps, but the new root element may violate the heap property (7.1). All that is needed to restore the heap property, however, is one call to HEAPIFY$(A, 1)$, which leaves a heap in $A[1 .. (n-1)]$. The heapsort algorithm then repeats this process for the heap of size $n - 1$ down to a heap of size 2.

HEAPSORT(A)

```
1  BUILD-HEAP(A)
2  for i ← length[A] downto 2
3      do exchange A[1] ↔ A[i]
4         heap-size[A] ← heap-size[A] − 1
5         HEAPIFY(A, 1)
```

Figure 7.4 shows an example of the operation of heapsort after the heap is initially built. Each heap is shown at the beginning of an iteration of the **for** loop in line 2.

The HEAPSORT procedure takes time $O(n \lg n)$, since the call to BUILD-HEAP takes time $O(n)$ and each of the $n - 1$ calls to HEAPIFY takes time $O(\lg n)$.

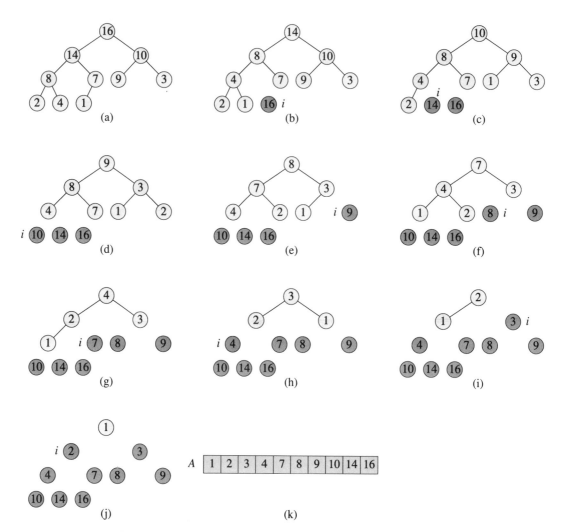

Figure 7.4 The operation of HEAPSORT. (**a**) The heap data structure just after it has been built by BUILD-HEAP. (**b**)–(**j**) The heap just after each call of HEAPIFY in line 5. The value of *i* at that time is shown. Only lightly shaded nodes remain in the heap. (**k**) The resulting sorted array *A*.

Exercises

7.4-1
Using Figure 7.4 as a model, illustrate the operation of HEAPSORT on the array $A = \langle 5, 13, 2, 25, 7, 17, 20, 8, 4 \rangle$.

7.4-2
What is the running time of heapsort on an array A of length n that is already sorted in increasing order? What about decreasing order?

7.4-3
Show that the running time of heapsort is $\Omega(n \lg n)$.

7.5 Priority queues

Heapsort is an excellent algorithm, but a good implementation of quicksort, presented in Chapter 8, usually beats it in practice. Nevertheless, the heap data structure itself has enormous utility. In this section, we present one of the most popular applications of a heap: its use as an efficient priority queue.

A *priority queue* is a data structure for maintaining a set S of elements, each with an associated value called a *key*. A priority queue supports the following operations.

INSERT(S, x) inserts the element x into the set S. This operation could be written as $S \leftarrow S \cup \{x\}$.

MAXIMUM(S) returns the element of S with the largest key.

EXTRACT-MAX(S) removes and returns the element of S with the largest key.

One application of priority queues is to schedule jobs on a shared computer. The priority queue keeps track of the jobs to be performed and their relative priorities. When a job is finished or interrupted, the highest-priority job is selected from those pending using EXTRACT-MAX. A new job can be added to the queue at any time using INSERT.

A priority queue can also be used in an event-driven simulator. The items in the queue are events to be simulated, each with an associated time of occurrence that serves as its key. The events must be simulated in order of their time of occurrence, because the simulation of an event can cause other events to be simulated in the future. For this application, it is natural to reverse the linear order of the priority queue and support the operations MINIMUM and EXTRACT-MIN instead of MAXIMUM and EXTRACT-MAX. The simulation program uses EXTRACT-MIN at each step to choose the next event to simulate. As new events are produced, they are inserted into the priority queue using INSERT.

Not surprisingly, we can use a heap to implement a priority queue. The operation HEAP-MAXIMUM returns the maximum heap element in $\Theta(1)$ time by simply returning the value $A[1]$ in the heap. The HEAP-EXTRACT-MAX procedure is similar to the **for** loop body (lines 3–5) of the HEAPSORT procedure:

HEAP-EXTRACT-MAX(A)

```
1  if heap-size[A] < 1
2      then error "heap underflow"
3  max ← A[1]
4  A[1] ← A[heap-size[A]]
5  heap-size[A] ← heap-size[A] − 1
6  HEAPIFY(A, 1)
7  return max
```

The running time of HEAP-EXTRACT-MAX is $O(\lg n)$, since it performs only a constant amount of work on top of the $O(\lg n)$ time for HEAPIFY.

The HEAP-INSERT procedure inserts a node into heap A. To do so, it first expands the heap by adding a new leaf to the tree. Then, in a manner reminiscent of the insertion loop (lines 5–7) of INSERTION-SORT from Section 1.1, it traverses a path from this leaf toward the root to find a proper place for the new element.

HEAP-INSERT(A, *key*)

```
1  heap-size[A] ← heap-size[A] + 1
2  i ← heap-size[A]
3  while i > 1 and A[PARENT(i)] < key
4      do A[i] ← A[PARENT(i)]
5          i ← PARENT(i)
6  A[i] ← key
```

Figure 7.5 shows an example of a HEAP-INSERT operation. The running time of HEAP-INSERT on an n-element heap is $O(\lg n)$, since the path traced from the new leaf to the root has length $O(\lg n)$.

In summary, a heap can support any priority-queue operation on a set of size n in $O(\lg n)$ time.

Exercises

7.5-1
Using Figure 7.5 as a model, illustrate the operation of HEAP-INSERT(A, 3) on the heap $A = \langle 15, 13, 9, 5, 12, 8, 7, 4, 0, 6, 2, 1 \rangle$.

7.5-2
Illustrate the operation of HEAP-EXTRACT-MAX on the heap $A = \langle 15, 13, 9, 5, 12, 8, 7, 4, 0, 6, 2, 1 \rangle$.

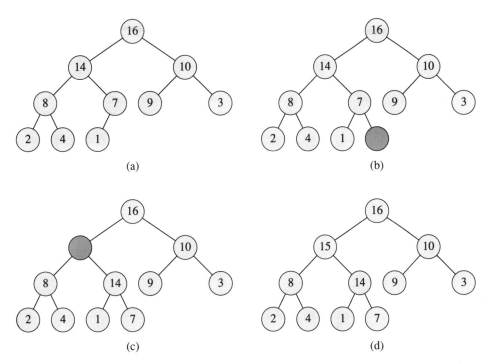

Figure 7.5   The operation of HEAP-INSERT. **(a)** The heap of Figure 7.4(a) before we insert a node with key 15. **(b)** A new leaf is added to the tree. **(c)** Values on the path from the new leaf to the root are copied down until a place for the key 15 is found. **(d)** The key 15 is inserted.

7.5-3

Show how to implement a first-in, first-out queue with a priority queue. Show how to implement a stack with a priority queue. (FIFO's and stacks are defined in Section 11.1.)

7.5-4

Give an $O(\lg n)$-time implementation of the procedure HEAP-INCREASE-KEY(A, i, k), which sets $A[i] \leftarrow \max(A[i], k)$ and updates the heap structure appropriately.

7.5-5

The operation HEAP-DELETE(A, i) deletes the item in node i from heap A. Give an implementation of HEAP-DELETE that runs in $O(\lg n)$ time for an n-element heap.

7.5-6

Give an $O(n \lg k)$-time algorithm to merge k sorted lists into one sorted list, where n is the total number of elements in all the input lists. (*Hint:* Use a heap for k-way merging.)

Problems

7-1   *Building a heap using insertion*

The procedure BUILD-HEAP in Section 7.3 can be implemented by repeatedly using HEAP-INSERT to insert the elements into the heap. Consider the following implementation:

BUILD-HEAP$'(A)$

1 *heap-size*$[A] \leftarrow 1$
2 **for** $i \leftarrow 2$ **to** *length*$[A]$
3   **do** HEAP-INSERT$(A, A[i])$

a. Do the procedures BUILD-HEAP and BUILD-HEAP$'$ always create the same heap when run on the same input array? Prove that they do, or provide a counterexample.

b. Show that in the worst case, BUILD-HEAP$'$ requires $\Theta(n \lg n)$ time to build an n-element heap.

7-2   *Analysis of d-ary heaps*

A ***d-ary heap*** is like a binary heap, but instead of 2 children, nodes have d children.

a. How would you represent a d-ary heap in an array?

b. What is the height of a d-ary heap of n elements in terms of n and d?

c. Give an efficient implementation of EXTRACT-MAX. Analyze its running time in terms of d and n.

d. Give an efficient implementation of INSERT. Analyze its running time in terms of d and n.

e. Give an efficient implementation of HEAP-INCREASE-KEY(A, i, k), which sets $A[i] \leftarrow \max(A[i], k)$ and updates the heap structure appropriately. Analyze its running time in terms of d and n.

Chapter notes

The heapsort algorithm was invented by Williams [202], who also described how to implement a priority queue with a heap. The BUILD-HEAP procedure was suggested by Floyd [69].

8 Quicksort

Quicksort is a sorting algorithm whose worst-case running time is $\Theta(n^2)$ on an input array of n numbers. In spite of this slow worst-case running time, quicksort is often the best practical choice for sorting because it is remarkably efficient on the average: its expected running time is $\Theta(n \lg n)$, and the constant factors hidden in the $\Theta(n \lg n)$ notation are quite small. It also has the advantage of sorting in place (see page 3), and it works well even in virtual memory environments.

Section 8.1 describes the algorithm and an important subroutine used by quicksort for partitioning. Because the behavior of quicksort is complex, we start with an intuitive discussion of its performance in Section 8.2 and postpone its precise analysis to the end of the chapter. Section 8.3 presents two versions of quicksort that use a random-number generator. These "randomized" algorithms have many desirable properties. Their average-case running time is good, and no particular input elicits their worst-case behavior. One of the randomized versions of quicksort is analyzed in Section 8.4, where it is shown to run in $O(n^2)$ time in the worst case and in $O(n \lg n)$ time on average.

8.1 Description of quicksort

Quicksort, like merge sort, is based on the divide-and-conquer paradigm introduced in Section 1.3.1. Here is the three-step divide-and-conquer process for sorting a typical subarray $A[p \mathrel{.\,.} r]$.

Divide: The array $A[p \mathrel{.\,.} r]$ is partitioned (rearranged) into two nonempty subarrays $A[p \mathrel{.\,.} q]$ and $A[q + 1 \mathrel{.\,.} r]$ such that each element of $A[p \mathrel{.\,.} q]$ is less than or equal to each element of $A[q + 1 \mathrel{.\,.} r]$. The index q is computed as part of this partitioning procedure.

Conquer: The two subarrays $A[p \mathrel{.\,.} q]$ and $A[q + 1 \mathrel{.\,.} r]$ are sorted by recursive calls to quicksort.

Combine: Since the subarrays are sorted in place, no work is needed to combine them: the entire array $A[p \mathrel{.\,.} r]$ is now sorted.

The following procedure implements quicksort.

QUICKSORT(A, p, r)

1 **if** $p < r$
2   **then** $q \leftarrow$ PARTITION(A, p, r)
3   QUICKSORT(A, p, q)
4   QUICKSORT($A, q + 1, r$)

To sort an entire array A, the initial call is QUICKSORT($A, 1, length[A]$).

Partitioning the array

The key to the algorithm is the PARTITION procedure, which rearranges the subarray $A[p..r]$ in place.

PARTITION(A, p, r)

1   $x \leftarrow A[p]$
2   $i \leftarrow p - 1$
3   $j \leftarrow r + 1$
4   **while** TRUE
5   **do repeat** $j \leftarrow j - 1$
6   **until** $A[j] \leq x$
7   **repeat** $i \leftarrow i + 1$
8   **until** $A[i] \geq x$
9   **if** $i < j$
10   **then** exchange $A[i] \leftrightarrow A[j]$
11   **else return** j

Figure 8.1 shows how PARTITION works. It first selects an element $x = A[p]$ from $A[p..r]$ as a "pivot" element around which to partition $A[p..r]$. It then grows two regions $A[p..i]$ and $A[j..r]$ from the top and bottom of $A[p..r]$, respectively, such that every element in $A[p..i]$ is less than or equal to x and every element in $A[j..r]$ is greater than or equal to x. Initially, $i = p - 1$ and $j = r + 1$, so the two regions are empty.

Within the body of the **while** loop, the index j is decremented and the index i is incremented, in lines 5–8, until $A[i] \geq x \geq A[j]$. Assuming that these inequalities are strict, $A[i]$ is too large to belong to the bottom region and $A[j]$ is too small to belong to the top region. Thus, by exchanging $A[i]$ and $A[j]$ as is done in line 10, we can extend the two regions. (If the inequalities are not strict, the exchange can be performed anyway.)

The body of the **while** loop repeats until $i \geq j$, at which point the entire array $A[p..r]$ has been partitioned into two subarrays $A[p..q]$ and $A[q + 1 ..r]$, where $p \leq q < r$, such that no element of $A[p..q]$ is larger than any element of $A[q + 1..r]$. The value $q = j$ is returned at the end of the procedure.

Conceptually, the partitioning procedure performs a simple function: it puts elements smaller than x into the bottom region of the array and

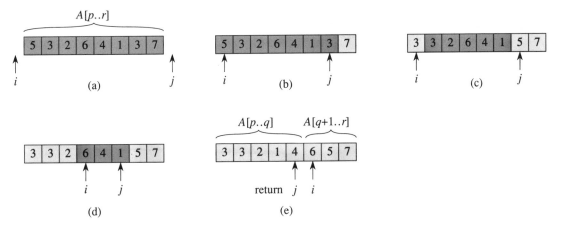

Figure 8.1 The operation of PARTITION on a sample array. Lightly shaded array elements have been placed into the correct partitions, and heavily shaded elements are not yet in their partitions. (a) The input array, with the initial values of i and j just off the left and right ends of the array. We partition around $x = A[p] = 5$. (b) The positions of i and j at line 9 of the first iteration of the **while** loop. (c) The result of exchanging the elements pointed to by i and j in line 10. (d) The positions of i and j at line 9 of the second iteration of the **while** loop. (e) The positions of i and j at line 9 of the third and last iteration of the **while** loop. The procedure terminates because $i \geq j$, and the value $q = j$ is returned. Array elements up to and including $A[j]$ are less than or equal to $x = 5$, and array elements after $A[j]$ are greater than or equal to $x = 5$.

elements larger than x into the top region. There are technicalities that make the pseudocode of PARTITION a little tricky, however. For example, the indices i and j never index the subarray $A[p \mathinner{\ldotp\ldotp} r]$ out of bounds, but this isn't entirely apparent from the code. As another example, it is important that $A[p]$ be used as the pivot element x. If $A[r]$ is used instead and it happens that $A[r]$ is also the largest element in the subarray $A[p \mathinner{\ldotp\ldotp} r]$, then PARTITION returns to QUICKSORT the value $q = r$, and QUICKSORT loops forever. Problem 8-1 asks you to prove PARTITION correct.

The running time of PARTITION on an array $A[p \mathinner{\ldotp\ldotp} r]$ is $\Theta(n)$, where $n = r - p + 1$ (see Exercise 8.1-3).

Exercises

8.1-1
Using Figure 8.1 as a model, illustrate the operation of PARTITION on the array $A = \langle 13, 19, 9, 5, 12, 8, 7, 4, 11, 2, 6, 21 \rangle$.

8.1-2
What value of q does PARTITION return when all elements in the array $A[p \mathinner{\ldotp\ldotp} r]$ have the same value?

8.1-3

Give a brief argument that the running time of PARTITION on a subarray of size n is $\Theta(n)$.

8.1-4

How would you modify QUICKSORT to sort in nonincreasing order?

8.2   Performance of quicksort

The running time of quicksort depends on whether the partitioning is balanced or unbalanced, and this in turn depends on which elements are used for partitioning. If the partitioning is balanced, the algorithm runs asymptotically as fast as merge sort. If the partitioning is unbalanced, however, it can run asymptotically as slow as insertion sort. In this section, we shall informally investigate how quicksort performs under the assumptions of balanced versus unbalanced partitioning.

Worst-case partitioning

The worst-case behavior for quicksort occurs when the partitioning routine produces one region with $n - 1$ elements and one with only 1 element. (This claim is proved in Section 8.4.1.) Let us assume that this unbalanced partitioning arises at every step of the algorithm. Since partitioning costs $\Theta(n)$ time and $T(1) = \Theta(1)$, the recurrence for the running time is

$$T(n) = T(n - 1) + \Theta(n) .$$

To evaluate this recurrence, we observe that $T(1) = \Theta(1)$ and then iterate:

$$
\begin{aligned}
T(n) &= T(n - 1) + \Theta(n) \\
&= \sum_{k=1}^{n} \Theta(k) \\
&= \Theta\left(\sum_{k=1}^{n} k\right) \\
&= \Theta(n^2) .
\end{aligned}
$$

We obtain the last line by observing that $\sum_{k=1}^{n} k$ is the arithmetic series (3.2). Figure 8.2 shows a recursion tree for this worst-case execution of quicksort. (See Section 4.2 for a discussion of recursion trees.)

Thus, if the partitioning is maximally unbalanced at every recursive step of the algorithm, the running time is $\Theta(n^2)$. Therefore the worst-case running time of quicksort is no better than that of insertion sort. Moreover, the $\Theta(n^2)$ running time occurs when the input array is already

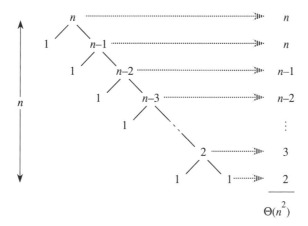

Figure 8.2   A recursion tree for QUICKSORT in which the PARTITION procedure always puts only a single element on one side of the partition (the worst case). The resulting running time is $\Theta(n^2)$.

completely sorted—a common situation in which insertion sort runs in $O(n)$ time.

Best-case partitioning

If the partitioning procedure produces two regions of size $n/2$, quicksort runs much faster. The recurrence is then

$$T(n) = 2T(n/2) + \Theta(n) \, ,$$

which by case 2 of the master theorem (Theorem 4.1) has solution $T(n) = \Theta(n \lg n)$. Thus, this best-case partitioning produces a much faster algorithm. Figure 8.3 shows the recursion tree for this best-case execution of quicksort.

Balanced partitioning

The average-case running time of quicksort is much closer to the best case than to the worst case, as the analyses in Section 8.4 will show. The key to understanding why this might be true is to understand how the balance of the partitioning is reflected in the recurrence that describes the running time.

Suppose, for example, that the partitioning algorithm always produces a 9-to-1 proportional split, which at first blush seems quite unbalanced. We then obtain the recurrence

$$T(n) = T(9n/10) + T(n/10) + n$$

on the running time of quicksort, where we have replaced $\Theta(n)$ by n for convenience. Figure 8.4 shows the recursion tree for this recurrence. No-

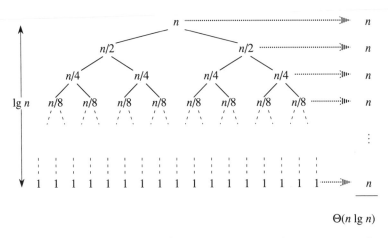

Figure 8.3   A recursion tree for QUICKSORT in which PARTITION always balances the two sides of the partition equally (the best case). The resulting running time is $\Theta(n \lg n)$.

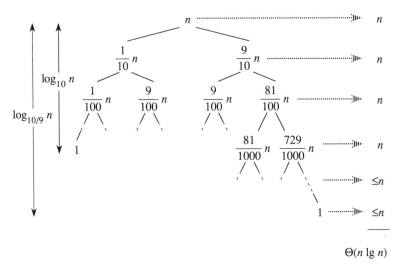

Figure 8.4   A recursion tree for QUICKSORT in which PARTITION always produces a 9-to-1 split, yielding a running time of $\Theta(n \lg n)$.

tice that every level of the tree has cost n, until a boundary condition is reached at depth $\log_{10} n = \Theta(\lg n)$, and then the levels have cost at most n. The recursion terminates at depth $\log_{10/9} n = \Theta(\lg n)$. The total cost of quicksort is therefore $\Theta(n \lg n)$. Thus, with a 9-to-1 proportional split at every level of recursion, which intuitively seems quite unbalanced, quicksort runs in $\Theta(n \lg n)$ time—asymptotically the same as if the split were right down the middle. In fact, even a 99-to-1 split yields an $O(n \lg n)$ running time. The reason is that any split of *constant* proportionality yields a recursion tree of depth $\Theta(\lg n)$, where the cost at each level is $O(n)$. The running time is therefore $\Theta(n \lg n)$ whenever the split has constant proportionality.

Intuition for the average case

To develop a clear notion of the average case for quicksort, we must make an assumption about how frequently we expect to encounter the various inputs. A common assumption is that all permutations of the input numbers are equally likely. We shall discuss this assumption in the next section, but first let's explore its ramifications.

When we run quicksort on a random input array, it is unlikely that the partitioning always happens in the same way at every level, as our informal analysis has assumed. We expect that some of the splits will be reasonably well balanced and that some will be fairly unbalanced. For example, Exercise 8.2-5 asks to you show that about 80 percent of the time PARTITION produces a split that is more balanced than 9 to 1, and about 20 percent of the time it produces a split that is less balanced than 9 to 1.

In the average case, PARTITION produces a mix of "good" and "bad" splits. In a recursion tree for an average-case execution of PARTITION, the good and bad splits are distributed randomly throughout the tree. Suppose for the sake of intuition, however, that the good and bad splits alternate levels in the tree, and that the good splits are best-case splits and the bad splits are worst-case splits. Figure 8.5(a) shows the splits at two consecutive levels in the recursion tree. At the root of the tree, the cost is n for partitioning and the subarrays produced have sizes $n - 1$ and 1: the worst case. At the next level, the subarray of size $n-1$ is best-case partitioned into two subarrays of size $(n - 1)/2$. Let's assume that the boundary-condition cost is 1 for the subarray of size 1.

The combination of the bad split followed by the good split produces three subarrays of sizes 1, $(n - 1)/2$, and $(n - 1)/2$ at a combined cost of $2n - 1 = \Theta(n)$. Certainly, this situation is no worse than that in Figure 8.5(b), namely a single level of partitioning that produces two subarrays of sizes $(n - 1)/2 + 1$ and $(n - 1)/2$ at a cost of $n = \Theta(n)$. Yet this latter situation is very nearly balanced, certainly better than 9 to 1. Intuitively, the $\Theta(n)$ cost of the bad split can be absorbed into the $\Theta(n)$ cost of the good split, and the resulting split is good. Thus, the running time of quick-

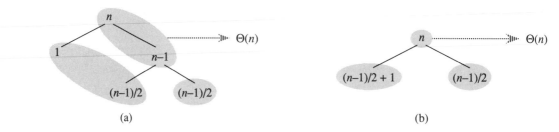

Figure 8.5   (a) Two levels of a recursion tree for quicksort. The partitioning at the root costs n and produces a "bad" split: two subarrays of sizes 1 and $n - 1$. The partitioning of the subarray of size $n - 1$ costs $n - 1$ and produces a "good" split: two subarrays of size $(n - 1)/2$. (b) A single level of a recursion tree that is worse than the combined levels in (a), yet very well balanced.

sort, when levels alternate between good and bad splits, is like the running time for good splits alone: still $O(n \lg n)$, but with a slightly larger constant hidden by the O-notation. We shall give a rigorous analysis of the average case in Section 8.4.2.

Exercises

8.2-1
Show that the running time of QUICKSORT is $\Theta(n \lg n)$ when all elements of array A have the same value.

8.2-2
Show that the running time of QUICKSORT is $\Theta(n^2)$ when the array A is sorted in nonincreasing order.

8.2-3
Banks often record transactions on an account in order of the times of the transactions, but many people like to receive their bank statements with checks listed in order by check number. People usually write checks in order by check number, and merchants usually cash them with reasonable dispatch. The problem of converting time-of-transaction ordering to check-number ordering is therefore the problem of sorting almost-sorted input. Argue that the procedure INSERTION-SORT would tend to beat the procedure QUICKSORT on this problem.

8.2-4
Suppose that the splits at every level of quicksort are in the proportion $1 - \alpha$ to α, where $0 < \alpha \leq 1/2$ is a constant. Show that the minimum depth of a leaf in the recursion tree is approximately $-\lg n / \lg \alpha$ and the maximum depth is approximately $-\lg n / \lg(1 - \alpha)$. (Don't worry about integer round-off.)

8.2-5 ★

Argue that for any constant $0 < \alpha \leq 1/2$, the probability is approximately $1 - 2\alpha$ that on a random input array, PARTITION produces a split more balanced than $1 - \alpha$ to α. For what value of α are the odds even that the split is more balanced than less balanced?

8.3 Randomized versions of quicksort

In exploring the average-case behavior of quicksort, we have made an assumption that all permutations of the input numbers are equally likely. When this assumption on the distribution of the inputs is valid, many people regard quicksort as the algorithm of choice for large enough inputs. In an engineering situation, however, we cannot always expect it to hold. (See Exercise 8.2-3.) This section introduces the notion of a randomized algorithm and presents two randomized versions of quicksort that overcome the assumption that all permutations of the input numbers are equally likely.

An alternative to *assuming* a distribution of inputs is to *impose* a distribution. For example, suppose that before sorting the input array, quicksort randomly permutes the elements to enforce the property that every permutation is equally likely. (Exercise 8.3-4 asks for an algorithm that randomly permutes the elements of an array of size n in time $O(n)$.) This modification does not improve the worst-case running time of the algorithm, but it does make the running time independent of the input ordering.

We call an algorithm *randomized* if its behavior is determined not only by the input but also by values produced by a *random-number generator*. We shall assume that we have at our disposal a random-number generator RANDOM. A call to RANDOM(a, b) returns an integer between a and b, inclusive, with each such integer being equally likely. For example, RANDOM$(0, 1)$ produces a 0 with probability $1/2$ and a 1 with probability $1/2$. Each integer returned by RANDOM is independent of the integers returned on previous calls. You may imagine RANDOM as rolling a $(b - a + 1)$-sided die to obtain its output. (In practice, most programming environments offer a *pseudorandom-number generator*: a deterministic algorithm that returns numbers that "look" statistically random.)

This randomized version of quicksort has an interesting property that is also possessed by many other randomized algorithms: *no particular input elicits its worst-case behavior*. Instead, its worst case depends on the random-number generator. Even intentionally, you cannot produce a bad input array for quicksort, since the random permutation makes the input order irrelevant. The randomized algorithm performs badly only if the random-number generator produces an unlucky permutation to be sorted. Exercise 13.4-4 shows that almost all permutations cause quicksort to perform nearly as well as the average case: there are *very* few permutations that cause near-worst-case behavior.

A randomized strategy is typically useful when there are many ways in which an algorithm can proceed but it is difficult to determine a way that is guaranteed to be good. If many of the alternatives are good, simply choosing one randomly can yield a good strategy. Often, an algorithm must make many choices during its execution. If the benefits of good choices outweigh the costs of bad choices, a random selection of good and bad choices can yield an efficient algorithm. We noted in Section 8.2 that a mixture of good and bad splits yields a good running time for quicksort, and thus it makes sense that randomized versions of the algorithm should perform well.

By modifying the PARTITION procedure, we can design another random-ized version of quicksort that uses this random-choice strategy. At each step of the quicksort algorithm, before the array is partitioned, we ex-change element $A[p]$ with an element chosen at random from $A[p \mathrel{.\,.} r]$. This modification ensures that the pivot element $x = A[p]$ is equally likely to be any of the $r - p + 1$ elements in the subarray. Thus, we expect the split of the input array to be reasonably well balanced on average. The randomized algorithm based on randomly permuting the input array also works well on average, but it is somewhat more difficult to analyze than this version.

The changes to PARTITION and QUICKSORT are small. In the new parti-tion procedure, we simply implement the swap before actually partitioning:

RANDOMIZED-PARTITION(A, p, r)

1   $i \leftarrow$ RANDOM(p, r)
2   exchange $A[p] \leftrightarrow A[i]$
3   **return** PARTITION(A, p, r)

We now make the new quicksort call RANDOMIZED-PARTITION in place of PARTITION:

RANDOMIZED-QUICKSORT(A, p, r)

1   **if** $p < r$
2   **then** $q \leftarrow$ RANDOMIZED-PARTITION(A, p, r)
3   RANDOMIZED-QUICKSORT(A, p, q)
4   RANDOMIZED-QUICKSORT$(A, q + 1, r)$

We analyze this algorithm in the next section.

Exercises

8.3-1

Why do we analyze the average-case performance of a randomized algo-rithm and not its worst-case performance?

8.3-2
During the running of the procedure RANDOMIZED-QUICKSORT, how many calls are made to the random-number generator RANDOM in the worst case? How does the answer change in the best case?

8.3-3 ★
Describe an implementation of the procedure RANDOM(a, b) that uses only fair coin flips. What is the expected running time of your procedure?

8.3-4 ★
Give a $\Theta(n)$-time, randomized procedure that takes as input an array $A[1 .. n]$ and performs a random permutation on the array elements.

8.4 Analysis of quicksort

Section 8.2 gave some intuition for the worst-case behavior of quicksort and for why we expect it to run quickly. In this section, we analyze the behavior of quicksort more rigorously. We begin with a worst-case analysis, which applies to either QUICKSORT or RANDOMIZED-QUICKSORT, and conclude with an average-case analysis of RANDOMIZED-QUICKSORT.

8.4.1 Worst-case analysis

We saw in Section 8.2 that a worst-case split at every level of recursion in quicksort produces a $\Theta(n^2)$ running time, which, intuitively, is the worst-case running time of the algorithm. We now prove this assertion.

Using the substitution method (see Section 4.1), we can show that the running time of quicksort is $O(n^2)$. Let $T(n)$ be the worst-case time for the procedure QUICKSORT on an input of size n. We have the recurrence

$$T(n) = \max_{1 \leq q \leq n-1} (T(q) + T(n-q)) + \Theta(n) , \tag{8.1}$$

where the parameter q ranges from 1 to $n-1$ because the procedure PARTITION produces two regions, each having size at least 1. We guess that $T(n) \leq cn^2$ for some constant c. Substituting this guess into (8.1), we obtain

$$
\begin{aligned}
T(n) &\leq \max_{1 \leq q \leq n-1} (cq^2 + c(n-q)^2) + \Theta(n) \\
&= c \cdot \max_{1 \leq q \leq n-1} (q^2 + (n-q)^2) + \Theta(n) .
\end{aligned}
$$

The expression $q^2 + (n-q)^2$ achieves a maximum over the range $1 \leq q \leq n-1$ at one of the endpoints, as can be seen since the second derivative of the expression with respect to q is positive (see Exercise 8.4-2). This gives us the bound $\max_{1 \leq q \leq n-1}(q^2 + (n-q)^2) \leq 1^2 + (n-1)^2 = n^2 - 2(n-1)$.

Continuing with our bounding of $T(n)$, we obtain

$$
\begin{aligned}
T(n) &\leq cn^2 - 2c(n-1) + \Theta(n) \\
&\leq cn^2,
\end{aligned}
$$

since we can pick the constant c large enough so that the $2c(n-1)$ term dominates the $\Theta(n)$ term. Thus, the (worst-case) running time of quicksort is $\Theta(n^2)$.

8.4.2   Average-case analysis

We have already given an intuitive argument why the average-case running time of RANDOMIZED-QUICKSORT is $\Theta(n \lg n)$: if the split induced by RANDOMIZED-PARTITION puts any constant fraction of the elements on one side of the partition, then the recursion tree has depth $\Theta(\lg n)$ and $\Theta(n)$ work is performed at $\Theta(\lg n)$ of these levels. We can analyze the expected running time of RANDOMIZED-QUICKSORT precisely by first understanding how the partitioning procedure operates. We can then develop a recurrence for the average time required to sort an n-element array and solve this recurrence to determine bounds on the expected running time. As part of the process of solving the recurrence, we shall develop tight bounds on an interesting summation.

Analysis of partitioning

We first make some observations about the operation of PARTITION. When PARTITION is called in line 3 of the procedure RANDOMIZED-PARTITION, the element $A[p]$ has already been exchanged with a random element in $A[p \mathinner{.\,.} r]$. To simplify the analysis, we assume that all input numbers are distinct. If all input numbers are not distinct, it is still true that quicksort's average-case running time is $O(n \lg n)$, but a somewhat more intricate analysis than we present here is required.

Our first observation is that the value of q returned by PARTITION depends only on the rank of $x = A[p]$ among the elements in $A[p \mathinner{.\,.} r]$. (The *rank* of a number in a set is the number of elements less than or equal to it.) If we let $n = r - p + 1$ be the number of elements in $A[p \mathinner{.\,.} r]$, swapping $A[p]$ with a random element from $A[p \mathinner{.\,.} r]$ yields a probability $1/n$ that $\mathrm{rank}(x) = i$ for $i = 1, 2, \ldots, n$.

We next compute the likelihoods of the various outcomes of the partitioning. If $\mathrm{rank}(x) = 1$, then the first time through the **while** loop in lines 4–11 of PARTITION, index i stops at $i = p$ and index j stops at $j = p$. Thus, when $q = j$ is returned, the "low" side of the partition contains the sole element $A[p]$. This event occurs with probability $1/n$ since that is the probability that $\mathrm{rank}(x) = 1$.

If $\mathrm{rank}(x) \geq 2$, then there is at least one element smaller than $x = A[p]$. Consequently, the first time through the **while** loop, index i stops at $i = p$

but j stops before reaching p. An exchange with $A[p]$ is then made to put $A[p]$ in the high side of the partition. When PARTITION terminates, each of the rank$(x) - 1$ elements in the low side of the partition is strictly less than x. Thus, for each $i = 1, 2, \ldots, n - 1$, when rank$(x) \geq 2$, the probability is $1/n$ that the low side of the partition has i elements.

Combining these two cases, we conclude that the size $q - p + 1$ of the low side of the partition is 1 with probability $2/n$ and that the size is i with probability $1/n$ for $i = 2, 3, \ldots, n - 1$.

A recurrence for the average case

We now establish a recurrence for the expected running time of RANDOMIZED-QUICKSORT. Let $T(n)$ denote the average time required to sort an n-element input array. A call to RANDOMIZED-QUICKSORT with a 1-element array takes constant time, so we have $T(1) = \Theta(1)$. A call to RANDOMIZED-QUICKSORT with an array $A[1 .. n]$ of length n uses time $\Theta(n)$ to partition the array. The PARTITION procedure returns an index q, and then RANDOMIZED-QUICKSORT is called recursively with subarrays of length q and $n - q$. Consequently, the average time to sort an array of length n can be expressed as

$$T(n) = \frac{1}{n} \left(T(1) + T(n - 1) + \sum_{q=1}^{n-1} (T(q) + T(n - q)) \right) + \Theta(n) . \qquad (8.2)$$

The value of q has an almost uniform distribution, except that the value $q = 1$ is twice as likely as the others, as was noted above. Using the facts that $T(1) = \Theta(1)$ and $T(n - 1) = O(n^2)$ from our worst-case analysis, we have

$$\begin{aligned} \frac{1}{n}(T(1) + T(n - 1)) &= \frac{1}{n}(\Theta(1) + O(n^2)) \\ &= O(n) , \end{aligned}$$

and the term $\Theta(n)$ in equation (8.2) can therefore absorb the expression $\frac{1}{n}(T(1) + T(n - 1))$. We can thus restate recurrence (8.2) as

$$T(n) = \frac{1}{n} \sum_{q=1}^{n-1} (T(q) + T(n - q)) + \Theta(n) . \qquad (8.3)$$

Observe that for $k = 1, 2, \ldots, n - 1$, each term $T(k)$ of the sum occurs once as $T(q)$ and once as $T(n - q)$. Collapsing the two terms of the sum yields

$$T(n) = \frac{2}{n} \sum_{k=1}^{n-1} T(k) + \Theta(n) . \qquad (8.4)$$

Solving the recurrence

We can solve the recurrence (8.4) using the substitution method. Assume inductively that $T(n) \leq an \lg n + b$ for some constants $a > 0$ and $b > 0$ to be determined. We can pick a and b sufficiently large so that $an \lg n + b$ is greater than $T(1)$. Then for $n > 1$, we have by substitution

$$
\begin{aligned}
T(n) &= \frac{2}{n} \sum_{k=1}^{n-1} T(k) + \Theta(n) \\
&\leq \frac{2}{n} \sum_{k=1}^{n-1} (ak \lg k + b) + \Theta(n) \\
&= \frac{2a}{n} \sum_{k=1}^{n-1} k \lg k + \frac{2b}{n}(n-1) + \Theta(n) .
\end{aligned}
$$

We show below that the summation in the last line can be bounded by

$$
\sum_{k=1}^{n-1} k \lg k \leq \frac{1}{2} n^2 \lg n - \frac{1}{8} n^2 . \tag{8.5}
$$

Using this bound, we obtain

$$
\begin{aligned}
T(n) &\leq \frac{2a}{n} \left(\frac{1}{2} n^2 \lg n - \frac{1}{8} n^2 \right) + \frac{2b}{n}(n-1) + \Theta(n) \\
&\leq an \lg n - \frac{a}{4} n + 2b + \Theta(n) \\
&= an \lg n + b + \left(\Theta(n) + b - \frac{a}{4} n \right) \\
&\leq an \lg n + b ,
\end{aligned}
$$

since we can choose a large enough so that $\frac{a}{4} n$ dominates $\Theta(n) + b$. We conclude that quicksort's average running time is $O(n \lg n)$.

Tight bounds on the key summation

It remains to prove the bound (8.5) on the summation

$$
\sum_{k=1}^{n-1} k \lg k .
$$

Since each term is at most $n \lg n$, we have the bound

$$
\sum_{k=1}^{n-1} k \lg k \leq n^2 \lg n ,
$$

which is tight to within a constant factor. This bound is not strong enough to solve the recurrence as $T(n) = O(n \lg n)$, however. Specifically, we need a bound of $\frac{1}{2} n^2 \lg n - \Omega(n^2)$ for the solution of the recurrence to work out.

We can get this bound on the summation by splitting it into two parts, as discussed in Section 3.2 on page 48. We obtain

$$\sum_{k=1}^{n-1} k \lg k = \sum_{k=1}^{\lceil n/2 \rceil - 1} k \lg k + \sum_{k=\lceil n/2 \rceil}^{n-1} k \lg k .$$

The $\lg k$ in the first summation on the right is bounded above by $\lg(n/2) = \lg n - 1$. The $\lg k$ in the second summation is bounded above by $\lg n$. Thus,

$$
\begin{aligned}
\sum_{k=1}^{n-1} k \lg k &\le (\lg n - 1) \sum_{k=1}^{\lceil n/2 \rceil - 1} k + \lg n \sum_{k=\lceil n/2 \rceil}^{n-1} k \\
&= \lg n \sum_{k=1}^{n-1} k - \sum_{k=1}^{\lceil n/2 \rceil - 1} k \\
&\le \frac{1}{2} n(n-1) \lg n - \frac{1}{2} \left(\frac{n}{2} - 1 \right) \frac{n}{2} \\
&\le \frac{1}{2} n^2 \lg n - \frac{1}{8} n^2
\end{aligned}
$$

if $n \ge 2$. This is the bound (8.5).

Exercises

8.4-1
Show that quicksort's best-case running time is $\Omega(n \lg n)$.

8.4-2
Show that $q^2 + (n - q)^2$ achieves a maximum over $q = 1, 2, \ldots, n - 1$ when $q = 1$ or $q = n - 1$.

8.4-3
Show that RANDOMIZED-QUICKSORT's expected running time is $\Omega(n \lg n)$.

8.4-4
The running time of quicksort can be improved in practice by taking advantage of the fast running time of insertion sort when its input is "nearly" sorted. When quicksort is called on a subarray with fewer than k elements, let it simply return without sorting the subarray. After the top-level call to quicksort returns, run insertion sort on the entire array to finish the sorting process. Argue that this sorting algorithm runs in $O(nk + n \lg(n/k))$ expected time. How should k be picked, both in theory and in practice?

8.4-5 ⋆
Prove the identity

$$\int x \ln x \, dx = \frac{1}{2} x^2 \ln x - \frac{1}{4} x^2 ,$$

and then use the integral approximation method to give a tighter upper bound than (8.5) on the summation $\sum_{k=1}^{n-1} k \lg k$.

8.4-6 ⋆

Consider modifying the PARTITION procedure by randomly picking three elements from array A and partitioning about their median. Approximate the probability of getting at worst an α-to-$(1 - \alpha)$ split, as a function of α in the range $0 < \alpha < 1$.

Problems

8-1 *Partition correctness*

Give a careful argument that the procedure PARTITION in Section 8.1 is correct. Prove the following:

a. The indices i and j never reference an element of A outside the interval $[p..r]$.

b. The index j is not equal to r when PARTITION terminates (so that the split is always nontrivial).

c. Every element of $A[p..j]$ is less than or equal to every element of $A[j+1..r]$ when PARTITION terminates.

8-2 *Lomuto's partitioning algorithm*

Consider the following variation of PARTITION, due to N. Lomuto. To partition $A[p..r]$, this version grows two regions, $A[p..i]$ and $A[i+1..j]$, such that every element in the first region is less than or equal to $x = A[r]$ and every element in the second region is greater than x.

LOMUTO-PARTITION(A, p, r)

```
1   x ← A[r]
2   i ← p − 1
3   for j ← p to r
4       do if A[j] ≤ x
5             then i ← i + 1
6                  exchange A[i] ↔ A[j]
7   if i < r
8       then return i
9       else return i − 1
```

a. Argue that LOMUTO-PARTITION is correct.

b. What are the maximum numbers of times that an element can be moved by PARTITION and by LOMUTO-PARTITION?

c. Argue that LOMUTO-PARTITION, like PARTITION, runs in $\Theta(n)$ time on an n-element subarray.

d. How does replacing PARTITION by LOMUTO-PARTITION affect the running time of QUICKSORT when all input values are equal?

e. Define a procedure RANDOMIZED-LOMUTO-PARTITION that exchanges $A[r]$ with a randomly chosen element in $A[p..r]$ and then calls LOMUTO-PARTITION. Show that the probability that a given value q is returned by RANDOMIZED-LOMUTO-PARTITION is equal to the probability that $p + r - q$ is returned by RANDOMIZED-PARTITION.

8-3 *Stooge sort*

Professors Howard, Fine, and Howard have proposed the following "elegant" sorting algorithm:

STOOGE-SORT(A, i, j)

```
1  if A[i] > A[j]
2      then exchange A[i] ↔ A[j]
3  if i + 1 ≥ j
4      then return
5  k ← ⌊(j − i + 1)/3⌋           ▷ Round down.
6  STOOGE-SORT(A, i, j − k)       ▷ First two-thirds.
7  STOOGE-SORT(A, i + k, j)       ▷ Last two-thirds.
8  STOOGE-SORT(A, i, j − k)       ▷ First two-thirds again.
```

a. Argue that STOOGE-SORT$(A, 1, length[A])$ correctly sorts the input array $A[1..n]$, where $n = length[A]$.

b. Give a recurrence for the worst-case running time of STOOGE-SORT and a tight asymptotic (Θ-notation) bound on the worst-case running time.

c. Compare the worst-case running time of STOOGE-SORT with that of insertion sort, merge sort, heapsort, and quicksort. Do the professors deserve tenure?

8-4 *Stack depth for quicksort*

The QUICKSORT algorithm of Section 8.1 contains two recursive calls to itself. After the call to PARTITION, the left subarray is recursively sorted and then the right subarray is recursively sorted. The second recursive call in QUICKSORT is not really necessary; it can be avoided by using an iterative control structure. This technique, called ***tail recursion***, is provided automatically by good compilers. Consider the following version of quicksort, which simulates tail recursion.

QUICKSORT$'(A, p, r)$

```
1  while p < r
2      do ▷ Partition and sort left subarray
3          q ← PARTITION(A, p, r)
4          QUICKSORT'(A, p, q)
5          p ← q + 1
```

a. Argue that QUICKSORT$'(A, 1, length[A])$ correctly sorts the array A.

Compilers usually execute recursive procedures by using a ***stack*** that contains pertinent information, including the parameter values, for each recursive call. The information for the most recent call is at the top of the stack, and the information for the initial call is at the bottom. When a procedure is invoked, its information is ***pushed*** onto the stack; when it terminates, its information is ***popped***. Since we assume that array parameters are actually represented by pointers, the information for each procedure call on the stack requires $O(1)$ stack space. The ***stack depth*** is the maximum amount of stack space used at any time during a computation.

b. Describe a scenario in which the stack depth of QUICKSORT$'$ is $\Theta(n)$ on an n-element input array.

c. Modify the code for QUICKSORT$'$ so that the worst-case stack depth is $\Theta(\lg n)$.

8-5   Median-of-3 partition

One way to improve the RANDOMIZED-QUICKSORT procedure is to partition around an element x that is chosen more carefully than by picking a random element from the subarray. One common approach is the ***median-of-3*** method: choose x as the median (middle element) of a set of 3 elements randomly selected from the subarray. For this problem, let us assume that the elements in the input array $A[1 .. n]$ are distinct and that $n \geq 3$. We denote the sorted output array by $A'[1 .. n]$. Using the median-of-3 method to choose the pivot element x, define $p_i = \Pr\{x = A'[i]\}$.

a. Give an exact formula for p_i as a function of n and i for $i = 2, 3, \ldots,$ $n - 1$. (Note that $p_1 = p_n = 0$.)

b. By what amount have we increased the likelihood of choosing $x = A'[\lfloor (n + 1)/2 \rfloor]$, the median of $A[1 .. n]$, compared to the ordinary implementation? Assume that $n \to \infty$, and give the limiting ratio of these probabilities.

c. If we define a "good" split to mean choosing $x = A'[i]$, where $n/3 \leq i \leq$ $2n/3$, by what amount have we increased the likelihood of getting a good split compared to the ordinary implementation? (*Hint:* Approximate the sum by an integral.)

d. Argue that the median-of-3 method affects only the constant factor in the $\Omega(n \lg n)$ running time of quicksort.

Chapter notes

The quicksort procedure was invented by Hoare [98]. Sedgewick [174] provides a good reference on the details of implementation and how they matter. The advantages of randomized algorithms were articulated by Rabin [165].

9   Sorting in Linear Time

We have now introduced several algorithms that can sort n numbers in $O(n \lg n)$ time. Merge sort and heapsort achieve this upper bound in the worst case; quicksort achieves it on average. Moreover, for each of these algorithms, we can produce a sequence of n input numbers that causes the algorithm to run in $\Omega(n \lg n)$ time.

These algorithms share an interesting property: *the sorted order they determine is based only on comparisons between the input elements.* We call such sorting algorithms ***comparison sorts***. All the sorting algorithms introduced thus far are comparison sorts.

In Section 9.1, we shall prove that any comparison sort must make $\Omega(n \lg n)$ comparisons in the worst case to sort a sequence of n elements. Thus, merge sort and heapsort are asymptotically optimal, and no comparison sort exists that is faster by more than a constant factor.

Sections 9.2, 9.3, and 9.4 examine three sorting algorithms—counting sort, radix sort, and bucket sort—that run in linear time. Needless to say, these algorithms use operations other than comparisons to determine the sorted order. Consequently, the $\Omega(n \lg n)$ lower bound does not apply to them.

9.1   Lower bounds for sorting

In a comparison sort, we use only comparisons between elements to gain order information about an input sequence $\langle a_1, a_2, \ldots, a_n \rangle$. That is, given two elements a_i and a_j, we perform one of the tests $a_i < a_j$, $a_i \le a_j$, $a_i = a_j$, $a_i \ge a_j$, or $a_i > a_j$ to determine their relative order. We may not inspect the values of the elements or gain order information about them in any other way.

In this section, we assume without loss of generality that all of the input elements are distinct. Given this assumption, comparisons of the form $a_i = a_j$ are useless, so we can assume that no comparisons of this form are made. We also note that the comparisons $a_i \le a_j$, $a_i \ge a_j$, $a_i > a_j$, and $a_i < a_j$ are all equivalent in that they yield identical information about

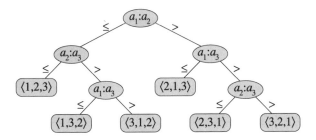

Figure 9.1 The decision tree for insertion sort operating on three elements. There are $3! = 6$ possible permutations of the input elements, so the decision tree must have at least 6 leaves.

the relative order of a_i and a_j. We therefore assume that all comparisons have the form $a_i \le a_j$.

The decision-tree model

Comparison sorts can be viewed abstractly in terms of ***decision trees***. A decision tree represents the comparisons performed by a sorting algorithm when it operates on an input of a given size. Control, data movement, and all other aspects of the algorithm are ignored. Figure 9.1 shows the decision tree corresponding to the insertion sort algorithm from Section 1.1 operating on an input sequence of three elements.

In a decision tree, each internal node is annotated by $a_i : a_j$ for some i and j in the range $1 \le i, j \le n$, where n is the number of elements in the input sequence. Each leaf is annotated by a permutation $\langle \pi(1), \pi(2), \ldots, \pi(n) \rangle$. (See Section 6.1 for background on permutations.) The execution of the sorting algorithm corresponds to tracing a path from the root of the decision tree to a leaf. At each internal node, a comparison $a_i \le a_j$ is made. The left subtree then dictates subsequent comparisons for $a_i \le a_j$, and the right subtree dictates subsequent comparisons for $a_i > a_j$. When we come to a leaf, the sorting algorithm has established the ordering $a_{\pi(1)} \le a_{\pi(2)} \le \cdots \le a_{\pi(n)}$. Each of the $n!$ permutations on n elements must appear as one of the leaves of the decision tree for the sorting algorithm to sort properly.

A lower bound for the worst case

The length of the longest path from the root of a decision tree to any of its leaves represents the worst-case number of comparisons the sorting algorithm performs. Consequently, the worst-case number of comparisons for a comparison sort corresponds to the height of its decision tree. A lower bound on the heights of decision trees is therefore a lower bound on the running time of any comparison sort algorithm. The following theorem establishes such a lower bound.

Theorem 9.1
Any decision tree that sorts n elements has height $\Omega(n \lg n)$.

Proof   Consider a decision tree of height h that sorts n elements. Since there are $n!$ permutations of n elements, each permutation representing a distinct sorted order, the tree must have at least $n!$ leaves. Since a binary tree of height h has no more than 2^h leaves, we have

$$n! \leq 2^h ,$$

which, by taking logarithms, implies

$$h \geq \lg(n!) ,$$

since the lg function is monotonically increasing. From Stirling's approximation (2.11), we have

$$n! > \left(\frac{n}{e}\right)^n ,$$

where $e = 2.71828\ldots$ is the base of natural logarithms; thus

$$
\begin{aligned}
h &\geq \lg\left(\frac{n}{e}\right)^n \\
  &= n \lg n - n \lg e \\
  &= \Omega(n \lg n) .
\end{aligned}
$$ ∎

Corollary 9.2
Heapsort and merge sort are asymptotically optimal comparison sorts.

Proof   The $O(n \lg n)$ upper bounds on the running times for heapsort and merge sort match the $\Omega(n \lg n)$ worst-case lower bound from Theorem 9.1.   ∎

Exercises

9.1-1
What is the smallest possible depth of a leaf in a decision tree for a sorting algorithm?

9.1-2
Obtain asymptotically tight bounds on $\lg(n!)$ without using Stirling's approximation. Instead, evaluate the summation $\sum_{k=1}^{n} \lg k$ using techniques from Section 3.2.

9.1-3

Show that there is no comparison sort whose running time is linear for at least half of the $n!$ inputs of length n. What about a fraction of $1/n$ of the inputs of length n? What about a fraction $1/2^n$?

9.1-4

Professor Solomon claims that the $\Omega(n \lg n)$ lower bound for sorting n numbers does not apply to his computer environment, in which the control flow of a program can split three ways after a single comparison $a_i : a_j$, according to whether $a_i < a_j$, $a_i = a_j$, or $a_i > a_j$. Show that the professor is wrong by proving that the number of three-way comparisons required to sort n elements is still $\Omega(n \lg n)$.

9.1-5

Prove that $2n - 1$ comparisons are necessary in the worst case to merge two sorted lists containing n elements each.

9.1-6

You are given a sequence of n elements to sort. The input sequence consists of n/k subsequences, each containing k elements. The elements in a given subsequence are all smaller than the elements in the succeeding subsequence and larger than the elements in the preceding subsequence. Thus, all that is needed to sort the whole sequence of length n is to sort the k elements in each of the n/k subsequences. Show an $\Omega(n \lg k)$ lower bound on the number of comparisons needed to solve this variant of the sorting problem. (*Hint:* It is not rigorous to simply combine the lower bounds for the individual subsequences.)

9.2 Counting sort

Counting sort assumes that each of the n input elements is an integer in the range 1 to k, for some integer k. When $k = O(n)$, the sort runs in $O(n)$ time.

The basic idea of counting sort is to determine, for each input element x, the number of elements less than x. This information can be used to place element x directly into its position in the output array. For example, if there are 17 elements less than x, then x belongs in output position 18. This scheme must be modified slightly to handle the situation in which several elements have the same value, since we don't want to put them all in the same position.

In the code for counting sort, we assume that the input is an array $A[1 .. n]$, and thus $length[A] = n$. We require two other arrays: the array $B[1 .. n]$ holds the sorted output, and the array $C[1 .. k]$ provides temporary working storage.

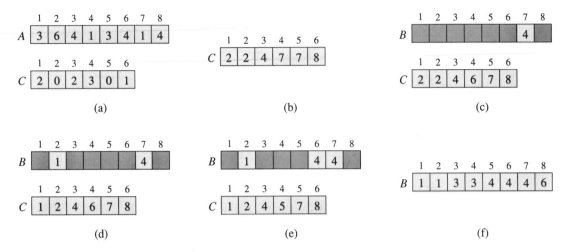

Figure 9.2 The operation of COUNTING-SORT on an input array $A[1..8]$, where each element of A is a positive integer no larger than $k = 6$. **(a)** The array A and the auxiliary array C after line 4. **(b)** The array C after line 7. **(c)–(e)** The output array B and the auxiliary array C after one, two, and three iterations of the loop in lines 9–11, respectively. Only the lightly shaded elements of array B have been filled in. **(f)** The final sorted output array B.

COUNTING-SORT(A, B, k)
```
 1  for i ← 1 to k
 2       do C[i] ← 0
 3  for j ← 1 to length[A]
 4       do C[A[j]] ← C[A[j]] + 1
 5  ▷ C[i] now contains the number of elements equal to i.
 6  for i ← 2 to k
 7       do C[i] ← C[i] + C[i − 1]
 8  ▷ C[i] now contains the number of elements less than or equal to i.
 9  for j ← length[A] downto 1
10       do B[C[A[j]]] ← A[j]
11          C[A[j]] ← C[A[j]] − 1
```

Counting sort is illustrated in Figure 9.2. After the initialization in lines 1–2, we inspect each input element in lines 3–4. If the value of an input element is i, we increment $C[i]$. Thus, after lines 3–4, $C[i]$ holds the number of input elements equal to i for each integer $i = 1, 2, \ldots, k$. In lines 6–7, we determine for each $i = 1, 2, \ldots, k$, how many input elements are less than or equal to i; this is done by keeping a running sum of the array C.

Finally, in lines 9–11, we place each element $A[j]$ in its correct sorted position in the output array B. If all n elements are distinct, then when we first enter line 9, for each $A[j]$, the value $C[A[j]]$ is the correct final position of $A[j]$ in the output array, since there are $C[A[j]]$ elements less than or equal to $A[j]$. Because the elements might not be distinct, we decrement $C[A[j]]$ each time we place a value $A[j]$ into the B array; this causes the next input element with a value equal to $A[j]$, if one exists, to go to the position immediately before $A[j]$ in the output array.

How much time does counting sort require? The **for** loop of lines 1–2 takes time $O(k)$, the **for** loop of lines 3–4 takes time $O(n)$, the **for** loop of lines 6–7 takes time $O(k)$, and the **for** loop of lines 9–11 takes time $O(n)$. Thus, the overall time is $O(k + n)$. In practice, we usually use counting sort when we have $k = O(n)$, in which case the running time is $O(n)$.

Counting sort beats the lower bound of $\Omega(n \lg n)$ proved in Section 9.1 because it is not a comparison sort. In fact, no comparisons between input elements occur anywhere in the code. Instead, counting sort uses the actual values of the elements to index into an array. The $\Omega(n \lg n)$ lower bound for sorting does not apply when we depart from the comparison-sort model.

An important property of counting sort is that it is *stable*: numbers with the same value appear in the output array in the same order as they do in the input array. That is, ties between two numbers are broken by the rule that whichever number appears first in the input array appears first in the output array. Of course, the property of stability is important only when satellite data are carried around with the element being sorted. We shall see why stability is important in the next section.

Exercises

9.2-1
Using Figure 9.2 as a model, illustrate the operation of COUNTING-SORT on the array $A = \langle 7, 1, 3, 1, 2, 4, 5, 7, 2, 4, 3 \rangle$.

9.2-2
Prove that COUNTING-SORT is stable.

9.2-3
Suppose that the **for** loop in line 9 of the COUNTING-SORT procedure is rewritten:

9   **for** $j \leftarrow 1$ **to** $length[A]$

Show that the algorithm still works properly. Is the modified algorithm stable?

9.2-4
Suppose that the output of the sorting algorithm is a data stream such as a graphics display. Modify COUNTING-SORT to produce the output in sorted order without using any substantial additional storage besides that in A and C. (*Hint:* Link elements of A that have the same key into lists. Where is a "free" place to keep the pointers for the linked list?)

9.2-5
Describe an algorithm that, given n integers in the range 1 to k, preprocesses its input and then answers any query about how many of the n integers fall into a range $[a..b]$ in $O(1)$ time. Your algorithm should use $O(n + k)$ preprocessing time.

9.3 Radix sort

Radix sort is the algorithm used by the card-sorting machines you now find only in computer museums. The cards are organized into 80 columns, and in each column a hole can be punched in one of 12 places. The sorter can be mechanically "programmed" to examine a given column of each card in a deck and distribute the card into one of 12 bins depending on which place has been punched. An operator can then gather the cards bin by bin, so that cards with the first place punched are on top of cards with the second place punched, and so on.

For decimal digits, only 10 places are used in each column. (The other two places are used for encoding nonnumeric characters.) A d-digit number would then occupy a field of d columns. Since the card sorter can look at only one column at a time, the problem of sorting n cards on a d-digit number requires a sorting algorithm.

Intuitively, one might want to sort numbers on their *most significant* digit, sort each of the resulting bins recursively, and then combine the decks in order. Unfortunately, since the cards in 9 of the 10 bins must be put aside to sort each of the bins, this procedure generates many intermediate piles of cards that must be kept track of. (See Exercise 9.3-5.)

Radix sort solves the problem of card sorting counterintuitively by sorting on the *least significant* digit first. The cards are then combined into a single deck, with the cards in the 0 bin preceding the cards in the 1 bin preceding the cards in the 2 bin, and so on. Then the entire deck is sorted again on the second least-significant digit and recombined in a like manner. The process continues until the cards have been sorted on all d digits. Remarkably, at that point the cards are fully sorted on the d-digit number. Thus, only d passes through the deck are required to sort. Figure 9.3 shows how radix sort operates on a "deck" of seven 3-digit numbers.

It is essential that the digit sorts in this algorithm be stable. The sort performed by a card sorter is stable, but the operator has to be wary about not changing the order of the cards as they come out of a bin, even though all the cards in a bin have the same digit in the chosen column.

In a typical computer, which is a sequential random-access machine, radix sort is sometimes used to sort records of information that are keyed by multiple fields. For example, we might wish to sort dates by three keys: year, month, and day. We could run a sorting algorithm with a compar-

```
329        720        720        329
457        355        329        355
657        436        436        436
839   ⇒    457   ⇒    839   ⇒    457
436        657        355        657
720        329        457        720
355        839        657        839
            ↑          ↑          ↑
```

Figure 9.3 The operation of radix sort on a list of seven 3-digit numbers. The first column is the input. The remaining columns show the list after successive sorts on increasingly significant digit positions. The vertical arrows indicate the digit position sorted on to produce each list from the previous one.

ison function that, given two dates, compares years, and if there is a tie, compares months, and if another tie occurs, compares days. Alternatively, we could sort the information three times with a stable sort: first on day, next on month, and finally on year.

The code for radix sort is straightforward. The following procedure assumes that each element in the n-element array A has d digits, where digit 1 is the lowest-order digit and digit d is the highest-order digit.

RADIX-SORT(A, d)

1 **for** $i \leftarrow 1$ **to** d
2   **do** use a stable sort to sort array A on digit i

The correctness of radix sort follows by induction on the column being sorted (see Exercise 9.3-3). The analysis of the running time depends on the stable sort used as the intermediate sorting algorithm. When each digit is in the range 1 to k, and k is not too large, counting sort is the obvious choice. Each pass over n d-digit numbers then takes time $\Theta(n + k)$. There are d passes, so the total time for radix sort is $\Theta(dn + kd)$. When d is constant and $k = O(n)$, radix sort runs in linear time.

Some computer scientists like to think of the number of bits in a computer word as being $\Theta(\lg n)$. For concreteness, let's say that $d \lg n$ is the number of bits, where d is a positive constant. Then, if each number to be sorted fits in one computer word, we can treat it as a d-digit number in radix-n notation. As a concrete example, consider sorting 1 million 64-bit numbers. By treating these numbers as four-digit, radix-2^{16} numbers, we can sort them in just four passes using radix sort. This compares favorably with a typical $\Theta(n \lg n)$ comparison sort, which requires approximately $\lg n = 20$ operations per number to be sorted. Unfortunately, the version of radix sort that uses counting sort as the intermediate stable sort does not sort in place, which many of the $\Theta(n \lg n)$ comparison sorts do. Thus, when primary memory storage is at a premium, an algorithm such as quicksort may be preferable.

Exercises

9.3-1
Using Figure 9.3 as a model, illustrate the operation of RADIX-SORT on
the following list of English words: COW, DOG, SEA, RUG, ROW, MOB,
BOX, TAB, BAR, EAR, TAR, DIG, BIG, TEA, NOW, FOX.

9.3-2
Which of the following sorting algorithms are stable: insertion sort, merge
sort, heapsort, and quicksort? Give a simple scheme that makes any sorting
algorithm stable. How much additional time and space does your scheme
entail?

9.3-3
Use induction to prove that radix sort works. Where does your proof need
the assumption that the intermediate sort is stable?

9.3-4
Show how to sort n integers in the range 1 to n^2 in $O(n)$ time.

9.3-5 ★
In the first card-sorting algorithm in this section, exactly how many sorting
passes are needed to sort d-digit decimal numbers in the worst case? How
many piles of cards would an operator need to keep track of in the worst
case?

9.4   Bucket sort

Bucket sort runs in linear time on the average. Like counting sort, bucket
sort is fast because it assumes something about the input. Whereas counting sort assumes that the input consists of integers in a small range, bucket
sort assumes that the input is generated by a random process that distributes elements uniformly over the interval $[0, 1)$. (See Section 6.2 for a
definition of uniform distribution.)

The idea of bucket sort is to divide the interval $[0, 1)$ into n equal-sized
subintervals, or ***buckets***, and then distribute the n input numbers into the
buckets. Since the inputs are uniformly distributed over $[0, 1)$, we don't
expect many numbers to fall into each bucket. To produce the output, we
simply sort the numbers in each bucket and then go through the buckets
in order, listing the elements in each.

Our code for bucket sort assumes that the input is an n-element array A
and that each element $A[i]$ in the array satisfies $0 \leq A[i] < 1$. The code
requires an auxiliary array $B[0 .. n - 1]$ of linked lists (buckets) and as-

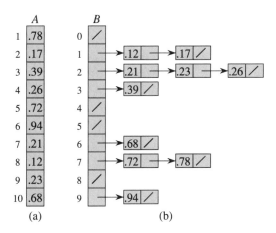

Figure 9.4 The operation of BUCKET-SORT. **(a)** The input array $A[1 .. 10]$. **(b)** The array $B[0 .. 9]$ of sorted lists (buckets) after line 5 of the algorithm. Bucket i holds values in the interval $[i/10, (i + 1)/10)$. The sorted output consists of a concatenation in order of the lists $B[0], B[1], \ldots, B[9]$.

sumes that there is a mechanism for maintaining such lists. (Section 11.2 describes how to implement basic operations on linked lists.)

BUCKET-SORT(A)

1 $n \leftarrow length[A]$
2 **for** $i \leftarrow 1$ **to** n
3   **do** insert $A[i]$ into list $B[\lfloor nA[i] \rfloor]$
4 **for** $i \leftarrow 0$ **to** $n - 1$
5   **do** sort list $B[i]$ with insertion sort
6 concatenate the lists $B[0], B[1], \ldots, B[n - 1]$ together in order

Figure 9.4 shows the operation of bucket sort on an input array of 10 numbers.

To see that this algorithm works, consider two elements $A[i]$ and $A[j]$. If these elements fall in the same bucket, they appear in the proper relative order in the output sequence because their bucket is sorted by insertion sort. Suppose they fall into different buckets, however. Let these buckets be $B[i']$ and $B[j']$, respectively, and assume without loss of generality that $i' < j'$. When the lists of B are concatenated in line 6, elements of bucket $B[i']$ come before elements of $B[j']$, and thus $A[i]$ precedes $A[j]$ in the output sequence. Hence, we must show that $A[i] \leq A[j]$. Assuming the contrary, we have

$$
\begin{aligned}
i' &= \lfloor nA[i] \rfloor \\
&\geq \lfloor nA[j] \rfloor \\
&= j',
\end{aligned}
$$

which is a contradiction, since $i' < j'$. Thus, bucket sort works.

To analyze the running time, observe that all lines except line 5 take $O(n)$ time in the worst case. The total time to examine all buckets in line 5 is $O(n)$, and so the only interesting part of the analysis is the time taken by the insertion sorts in line 5.

To analyze the cost of the insertion sorts, let n_i be the random variable denoting the number of elements placed in bucket $B[i]$. Since insertion sort runs in quadratic time (see Section 1.2), the expected time to sort the elements in bucket $B[i]$ is $E\left[O(n_i^2)\right] = O\left(E\left[n_i^2\right]\right)$. The total expected time to sort all the elements in all the buckets is therefore

$$\sum_{i=0}^{n-1} O\left(E\left[n_i^2\right]\right) = O\left(\sum_{i=0}^{n-1} E\left[n_i^2\right]\right) . \tag{9.1}$$

In order to evaluate this summation, we must determine the distribution of each random variable n_i. We have n elements and n buckets. The probability that a given element falls into bucket $B[i]$ is $1/n$, since each bucket is responsible for $1/n$ of the interval $[0, 1)$. Thus, the situation is analogous to the ball-tossing example of Section 6.6.2: we have n balls (elements) and n bins (buckets), and each ball is thrown independently with probability $p = 1/n$ of falling into any particular bucket. Thus, the probability that $n_i = k$ follows the binomial distribution $b(k; n, p)$, which has mean $E[n_i] = np = 1$ and variance $\text{Var}[n_i] = np(1 - p) = 1 - 1/n$. For any random variable X, equation (6.30) gives

$$
\begin{aligned}
E\left[n_i^2\right] &= \text{Var}[n_i] + E^2[n_i] \\
&= 1 - \frac{1}{n} + 1^2 \\
&= 2 - \frac{1}{n} \\
&= \Theta(1) .
\end{aligned}
$$

Using this bound in equation (9.1), we conclude that the expected time for insertion sorting is $O(n)$. Thus, the entire bucket sort algorithm runs in linear expected time.

Exercises

9.4-1
Using Figure 9.4 as a model, illustrate the operation of BUCKET-SORT on the array $A = \langle .79, .13, .16, .64, .39, .20, .89, .53, .71, .42 \rangle$.

9.4-2
What is the worst-case running time for the bucket-sort algorithm? What simple change to the algorithm preserves its linear expected running time and makes its worst-case running time $O(n \lg n)$?

9.4-3 ⋆

We are given n points in the unit circle, $p_i = (x_i, y_i)$, such that $0 < x_i^2 + y_i^2 \leq 1$ for $i = 1, 2, \ldots, n$. Suppose that the points are uniformly distributed; that is, the probability of finding a point in any region of the circle is proportional to the area of that region. Design a $\Theta(n)$ expected-time algorithm to sort the n points by their distances $d_i = \sqrt{x_i^2 + y_i^2}$ from the origin. (*Hint:* Design the bucket sizes in BUCKET-SORT to reflect the uniform distribution of the points in the unit circle.)

9.4-4 ⋆

A *probability distribution function* $P(x)$ for a random variable X is defined by $P(x) = \Pr\{X \leq x\}$. Suppose a list of n numbers has a continuous probability distribution function P that is computable in $O(1)$ time. Show how to sort the numbers in linear expected time.

Problems

9-1 *Average-case lower bounds on comparison sorting*

In this problem, we prove an $\Omega(n \lg n)$ lower bound on the expected running time of any deterministic or randomized comparison sort on n inputs. We begin by examining a deterministic comparison sort A with decision tree T_A. We assume that every permutation of A's inputs is equally likely.

a. Suppose that each leaf of T_A is labeled with the probability that it is reached given a random input. Prove that exactly $n!$ leaves are labeled $1/n!$ and that the rest are labeled 0.

b. Let $D(T)$ denote the external path length of a tree T; that is, $D(T)$ is the sum of the depths of all the leaves of T. Let T be a tree with $k > 1$ leaves, and let RT and LT be the right and left subtrees of T. Show that $D(T) = D(RT) + D(LT) + k$.

c. Let $d(m)$ be the minimum value of $D(T)$ over all trees T with m leaves. Show that $d(k) = \min_{1 \leq i \leq k} \{d(i) + d(k - i) + k\}$. (*Hint:* Consider a tree T with k leaves that achieves the minimum. Let i be the number of leaves in RT and $k - i$ the number of leaves in LT.)

d. Prove that for a given value of k, the function $i \lg i + (k - i) \lg(k - i)$ is minimized at $i = k/2$. Conclude that $d(k) = \Omega(k \lg k)$.

e. Prove that $D(T_A) = \Omega(n! \lg(n!))$ for T_A, and conclude that the expected time to sort n elements is $\Omega(n \lg n)$.

Now, consider a *randomized* comparison sort B. We can extend the decision-tree model to handle randomization by incorporating two kinds of nodes: ordinary comparison nodes and "randomization" nodes. A randomization node models a random choice of the form RANDOM$(1, r)$ made by algorithm B; the node has r children, each of which is equally likely to be chosen during an execution of the algorithm.

f. Show that for any randomized comparison sort B, there exists a deterministic comparison sort A that makes no more comparisons on the average than B does.

9-2   *Sorting in place in linear time*

a. Suppose that we have an array of n data records to sort and that the key of each record has the value 0 or 1. Give a simple, linear-time algorithm for sorting the n data records in place. Use no storage of more than constant size in addition to the storage provided by the array.

b. Can your sort from part (a) be used to radix sort n records with b-bit keys in $O(bn)$ time? Explain how or why not.

c. Suppose that the n records have keys in the range from 1 to k. Show how to modify counting sort so that the records can be sorted in place in $O(n + k)$ time. You may use $O(k)$ storage outside the input array. (*Hint:* How would you do it for $k = 3$?)

Chapter notes

The decision-tree model for studying comparison sorts was introduced by Ford and Johnson [72]. Knuth's comprehensive treatise on sorting [123] covers many variations on the sorting problem, including the information-theoretic lower bound on the complexity of sorting given here. Lower bounds for sorting using generalizations of the decision-tree model were studied comprehensively by Ben-Or [23].

Knuth credits H. H. Seward with inventing counting sort in 1954, and also with the idea of combining counting sort with radix sort. Radix sorting by the least-significant digit first appears to be a folk algorithm widely used by operators of mechanical card-sorting machines. According to Knuth, the first published reference to the method is a 1929 document by L. J. Comrie describing punched-card equipment. Bucket sorting has been in use since 1956, when the basic idea was proposed by E. J. Isaac and R. C. Singleton.

10   Medians and Order Statistics

The ith *order statistic* of a set of n elements is the ith smallest element. For example, the *minimum* of a set of elements is the first order statistic ($i = 1$), and the *maximum* is the nth order statistic ($i = n$). A *median*, informally, is the "halfway point" of the set. When n is odd, the median is unique, occurring at $i = (n + 1)/2$. When n is even, there are two medians, occurring at $i = n/2$ and $i = n/2 + 1$. Thus, regardless of the parity of n, medians occur at $i = \lfloor (n + 1)/2 \rfloor$ and $i = \lceil (n + 1)/2 \rceil$.

This chapter addresses the problem of selecting the ith order statistic from a set of n distinct numbers. We assume for convenience that the set contains distinct numbers, although virtually everything that we do extends to the situation in which a set contains repeated values. The *selection problem* can be specified formally as follows:

Input: A set A of n (distinct) numbers and a number i, with $1 \leq i \leq n$.

Output: The element $x \in A$ that is larger than exactly $i - 1$ other elements of A.

The selection problem can be solved in $O(n \lg n)$ time, since we can sort the numbers using heapsort or merge sort and then simply index the ith element in the output array. There are faster algorithms, however.

In Section 10.1, we examine the problem of selecting the minimum and maximum of a set of elements. More interesting is the general selection problem, which is investigated in the subsequent two sections. Section 10.2 analyzes a practical algorithm that achieves an $O(n)$ bound on the running time in the average case. Section 10.3 contains an algorithm of more theoretical interest that achieves the $O(n)$ running time in the worst case.

10.1   Minimum and maximum

How many comparisons are necessary to determine the minimum of a set of n elements? We can easily obtain an upper bound of $n - 1$ comparisons: examine each element of the set in turn and keep track of the smallest element seen so far. In the following procedure, we assume that the set resides in array A, where $length[A] = n$.

MINIMUM(*A*)

1   *min* ← *A*[1]
2   **for** *i* ← 2 **to** *length*[*A*]
3   **do if** *min* > *A*[*i*]
4   **then** *min* ← *A*[*i*]
5   **return** *min*

Finding the maximum can, of course, be accomplished with $n - 1$ comparisons as well.

Is this the best we can do? Yes, since we can obtain a lower bound of $n - 1$ comparisons for the problem of determining the minimum. Think of any algorithm that determines the minimum as a tournament among the elements. Each comparison is a match in the tournament in which the smaller of the two elements wins. The key observation is that every element except the winner must lose at least one match. Hence, $n - 1$ comparisons are necessary to determine the minimum, and the algorithm MINIMUM is optimal with respect to the number of comparisons performed.

An interesting fine point of the analysis is the determination of the expected number of times that line 4 is executed. Problem 6-2 asks you to show that this expectation is $\Theta(\lg n)$.

Simultaneous minimum and maximum

In some applications, we must find both the minimum and the maximum of a set of n elements. For example, a graphics program may need to scale a set of (x, y) data to fit onto a rectangular display screen or other graphical output device. To do so, the program must first determine the minimum and maximum of each coordinate.

It is not too difficult to devise an algorithm that can find both the minimum and the maximum of n elements using the asymptotically optimal $\Omega(n)$ number of comparisons. Simply find the minimum and maximum independently, using $n - 1$ comparisons for each, for a total of $2n - 2$ comparisons.

In fact, only $3 \lceil n/2 \rceil$ comparisons are necessary to find both the minimum and the maximum. To do this, we maintain the minimum and maximum elements seen thus far. Rather than processing each element of the input by comparing it against the current minimum and maximum, however, at a cost of two comparisons per element, we process elements in pairs. We compare pairs of elements from the input first with *each other*, and then compare the smaller to the current minimum and the larger to the current maximum, at a cost of three comparisons for every two elements.

Exercises

10.1-1
Show that the second smallest of n elements can be found with $n + \lceil \lg n \rceil - 2$
comparisons in the worst case. (*Hint:* Also find the smallest element.)

10.1-2 ⋆
Show that $\lceil 3n/2 \rceil - 2$ comparisons are necessary in the worst case to find
both the maximum and minimum of n numbers. (*Hint:* Consider how
many numbers are potentially either the maximum or minimum, and investigate how a comparison affects these counts.)

10.2 Selection in expected linear time

The general selection problem appears more difficult than the simple problem of finding a minimum, yet, surprisingly, the asymptotic running time
for both problems is the same: $\Theta(n)$. In this section, we present a divide-
and-conquer algorithm for the selection problem. The algorithm RAN-
DOMIZED-SELECT is modeled after the quicksort algorithm of Chapter 8.
As in quicksort, the idea is to partition the input array recursively. But
unlike quicksort, which recursively processes both sides of the partition,
RANDOMIZED-SELECT only works on one side of the partition. This difference shows up in the analysis: whereas quicksort has an expected running
time of $\Theta(n \lg n)$, the expected time of RANDOMIZED-SELECT is $\Theta(n)$.

RANDOMIZED-SELECT uses the procedure RANDOMIZED-PARTITION introduced in Section 8.3. Thus, like RANDOMIZED-QUICKSORT, it is a randomized algorithm, since its behavior is determined in part by the output
of a random-number generator. The following code for RANDOMIZED-
SELECT returns the ith smallest element of the array $A[p \mathinner{.\,.} r]$.

RANDOMIZED-SELECT(A, p, r, i)

1   **if** $p = r$
2   **then return** $A[p]$
3   $q \leftarrow$ RANDOMIZED-PARTITION(A, p, r)
4   $k \leftarrow q - p + 1$
5   **if** $i \leq k$
6   **then return** RANDOMIZED-SELECT(A, p, q, i)
7   **else return** RANDOMIZED-SELECT$(A, q + 1, r, i - k)$

After RANDOMIZED-PARTITION is executed in line 3 of the algorithm, the
array $A[p \mathinner{.\,.} r]$ is partitioned into two nonempty subarrays $A[p \mathinner{.\,.} q]$ and
$A[q + 1 \mathinner{.\,.} r]$ such that each element of $A[p \mathinner{.\,.} q]$ is less than each element of
$A[q + 1 \mathinner{.\,.} r]$. Line 4 of the algorithm computes the number k of elements
in the subarray $A[p \mathinner{.\,.} q]$. The algorithm now determines in which of the

two subarrays $A[p \mathinner{\ldotp\ldotp} q]$ and $A[q + 1 \mathinner{\ldotp\ldotp} r]$ the ith smallest element lies. If $i \leq k$, then the desired element lies on the low side of the partition, and it is recursively selected from the subarray in line 6. If $i > k$, however, then the desired element lies on the high side of the partition. Since we already know k values that are smaller than the ith smallest element of $A[p \mathinner{\ldotp\ldotp} r]$—namely, the elements of $A[p \mathinner{\ldotp\ldotp} q]$—the desired element is the $(i - k)$th smallest element of $A[q + 1 \mathinner{\ldotp\ldotp} r]$, which is found recursively in line 7.

The worst-case running time for RANDOMIZED-SELECT is $\Theta(n^2)$, even to find the minimum, because we could be extremely unlucky and always partition around the largest remaining element. The algorithm works well in the average case, though, and because it is randomized, no particular input elicits the worst-case behavior.

We can obtain an upper bound $T(n)$ on the expected time required by RANDOMIZED-SELECT on an input array of n elements as follows. We observed in Section 8.4 that the algorithm RANDOMIZED-PARTITION produces a partition whose low side has 1 element with probability $2/n$ and i elements with probability $1/n$ for $i = 2, 3, \ldots, n - 1$. Assuming that $T(n)$ is monotonically increasing, in the worst case RANDOMIZED-SELECT is always unlucky in that the ith element is determined to be on the larger side of the partition. Thus, we get the recurrence

$$
\begin{aligned}
T(n) &\leq \frac{1}{n} \left(T(\max(1, n - 1)) + \sum_{k=1}^{n-1} T(\max(k, n - k)) \right) + O(n) \\
&\leq \frac{1}{n} \left(T(n - 1) + 2 \sum_{k=\lceil n/2 \rceil}^{n-1} T(k) \right) + O(n) \\
&= \frac{2}{n} \sum_{k=\lceil n/2 \rceil}^{n-1} T(k) + O(n) \ .
\end{aligned}
$$

The second line follows from the first since $\max(1, n - 1) = n - 1$ and

$$
\max(k, n - k) = \begin{cases} k & \text{if } k \geq \lceil n/2 \rceil \ , \\ n - k & \text{if } k < \lceil n/2 \rceil \ . \end{cases}
$$

If n is odd, each term $T(\lceil n/2 \rceil), T(\lceil n/2 \rceil + 1), \ldots, T(n - 1)$ appears twice in the summation, and if n is even, each term $T(\lceil n/2 \rceil + 1), T(\lceil n/2 \rceil + 2), \ldots, T(n - 1)$ appears twice and the term $T(\lceil n/2 \rceil)$ appears once. In either case, the summation of the first line is bounded from above by the summation of the second line. The third line follows from the second since in the worst case $T(n - 1) = O(n^2)$, and thus the term $\frac{1}{n}T(n - 1)$ can be absorbed by the term $O(n)$.

We solve the recurrence by substitution. Assume that $T(n) \leq cn$ for some constant c that satisfies the initial conditions of the recurrence. Using this inductive hypothesis, we have

$$
\begin{aligned}
T(n) \;&\leq\; \frac{2}{n}\sum_{k=\lceil n/2\rceil}^{n-1} ck + O(n) \\[2mm]
&\leq\; \frac{2c}{n}\left(\sum_{k=1}^{n-1} k - \sum_{k=1}^{\lceil n/2\rceil -1} k\right) + O(n) \\[2mm]
&=\; \frac{2c}{n}\left(\frac{1}{2}(n-1)n - \frac{1}{2}\left(\left\lceil\frac{n}{2}\right\rceil - 1\right)\left\lceil\frac{n}{2}\right\rceil\right) + O(n) \\[2mm]
&\leq\; c(n-1) - \frac{c}{n}\left(\frac{n}{2}-1\right)\left(\frac{n}{2}\right) + O(n) \\[2mm]
&=\; c\left(\frac{3}{4}n - \frac{1}{2}\right) + O(n) \\[2mm]
&\leq\; cn\,,
\end{aligned}
$$

since we can pick c large enough so that $c(n/4 + 1/2)$ dominates the $O(n)$ term.

Thus, any order statistic, and in particular the median, can be determined on average in linear time.

Exercises

10.2-1
Write an iterative version of RANDOMIZED-SELECT.

10.2-2
Suppose we use RANDOMIZED-SELECT to select the minimum element of the array $A = \langle 3, 2, 9, 0, 7, 5, 4, 8, 6, 1\rangle$. Describe a sequence of partitions that results in a worst-case performance of RANDOMIZED-SELECT.

10.2-3
Recall that in the presence of equal elements, the RANDOMIZED-PARTITION procedure partitions the subarray $A[p \mathinner{\ldotp\ldotp} r]$ into two nonempty subarrays $A[p \mathinner{\ldotp\ldotp} q]$ and $A[q + 1 \mathinner{\ldotp\ldotp} r]$ such that each element in $A[p \mathinner{\ldotp\ldotp} q]$ is less than *or equal to* every element in $A[q + 1 \mathinner{\ldotp\ldotp} r]$. If equal elements are present, does the RANDOMIZED-SELECT procedure work correctly?

10.3 Selection in worst-case linear time

We now examine a selection algorithm whose running time is $O(n)$ in the worst case. Like RANDOMIZED-SELECT, the algorithm SELECT finds the desired element by recursively partitioning the input array. The idea behind the algorithm, however, is to *guarantee* a good split when the array is partitioned. SELECT uses the deterministic partitioning algorithm PARTITION

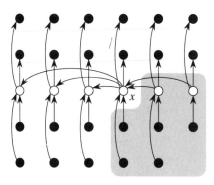

Figure 10.1 Analysis of the algorithm SELECT. The n elements are represented by small circles, and each group occupies a column. The medians of the groups are whitened, and the median-of-medians x is labeled. Arrows are drawn from larger elements to smaller, from which it can be seen that 3 out of every group of 5 elements to the right of x are greater than x, and 3 out of every group of 5 elements to the left of x are less than x. The elements greater than x are shown on a shaded background.

from quicksort (see Section 8.1), modified to take the element to partition around as an input parameter.

The SELECT algorithm determines the ith smallest of an input array of n elements by executing the following steps.

1. Divide the n elements of the input array into $\lfloor n/5 \rfloor$ groups of 5 elements each and at most one group made up of the remaining n mod 5 elements.

2. Find the median of each of the $\lceil n/5 \rceil$ groups by insertion sorting the elements of each group (of which there are 5 at most) and taking its middle element. (If the group has an even number of elements, take the larger of the two medians.)

3. Use SELECT recursively to find the median x of the $\lceil n/5 \rceil$ medians found in step 2.

4. Partition the input array around the median-of-medians x using a modified version of PARTITION. Let k be the number of elements on the low side of the partition, so that $n - k$ is the number of elements on the high side.

5. Use SELECT recursively to find the ith smallest element on the low side if $i \leq k$, or the $(i - k)$th smallest element on the high side if $i > k$.

To analyze the running time of SELECT, we first determine a lower bound on the number of elements that are greater than the partitioning element x. Figure 10.1 is helpful in visualizing this bookkeeping. At least half of the medians found in step 2 are greater than or equal to the median-of-medians x. Thus, at least half of the $\lceil n/5 \rceil$ groups contribute 3 elements that are greater than x, except for the one group that has fewer than 5 elements if 5 does not divide n exactly, and the one group containing x

itself. Discounting these two groups, it follows that the number of elements greater than x is at least

$$3 \left(\left\lceil \frac{1}{2} \left\lceil \frac{n}{5} \right\rceil \right\rceil - 2 \right) \geq \frac{3n}{10} - 6 \; .$$

Similarly, the number of elements that are less than x is at least $3n/10 - 6$. Thus, in the worst case, SELECT is called recursively on at most $7n/10 + 6$ elements in step 5.

We can now develop a recurrence for the worst-case running time $T(n)$ of the algorithm SELECT. Steps 1, 2, and 4 take $O(n)$ time. (Step 2 consists of $O(n)$ calls of insertion sort on sets of size $O(1)$.) Step 3 takes time $T(\lceil n/5 \rceil)$, and step 5 takes time at most $T(7n/10 + 6)$, assuming that T is monotonically increasing. Note that $7n/10 + 6 < n$ for $n > 20$ and that any input of 80 or fewer elements requires $O(1)$ time. We can therefore obtain the recurrence

$$T(n) \leq \begin{cases} \Theta(1) & \text{if } n \leq 80 \; , \\ T(\lceil n/5 \rceil) + T(7n/10 + 6) + O(n) & \text{if } n > 80 \; . \end{cases}$$

We show that the running time is linear by substitution. Assume that $T(n) \leq cn$ for some constant c and all $n \leq 80$. Substituting this inductive hypothesis into the right-hand side of the recurrence yields

$$
\begin{aligned}
T(n) &\leq c \lceil n/5 \rceil + c(7n/10 + 6) + O(n) \\
&\leq cn/5 + c + 7cn/10 + 6c + O(n) \\
&\leq 9cn/10 + 7c + O(n) \\
&\leq cn \; ,
\end{aligned}
$$

since we can pick c large enough so that $c(n/10 - 7)$ is larger than the function described by the $O(n)$ term for all $n > 80$. The worst-case running time of SELECT is therefore linear.

As in a comparison sort (see Section 9.1), SELECT and RANDOMIZED-SELECT determine information about the relative order of elements only by comparing elements. Thus, the linear-time behavior is not a result of assumptions about the input, as was the case for the sorting algorithms in Chapter 9. Sorting requires $\Omega(n \lg n)$ time in the comparison model, even on average (see Problem 9-1), and thus the method of sorting and indexing presented in the introduction to this chapter is asymptotically inefficient.

Exercises

10.3-1

In the algorithm SELECT, the input elements are divided into groups of 5. Will the algorithm work in linear time if they are divided into groups of 7? How about groups of 3?

10.3-2

Analyze SELECT to show that the number of elements greater than the median-of-medians x and the number of elements less than x is at least $\lceil n/4 \rceil$ if $n \geq 38$.

10.3-3

Show how quicksort can be made to run in $O(n \lg n)$ time in the worst case.

10.3-4 ⋆

Suppose that an algorithm uses only comparisons to find the ith smallest element in a set of n elements. Show that it can also find the $i - 1$ smaller elements and the $n - i$ larger elements without performing any additional comparisons.

10.3-5

Given a "black-box" worst-case linear-time median subroutine, give a simple, linear-time algorithm that solves the selection problem for an arbitrary order statistic.

10.3-6

The kth **quantiles** of an n-element set are the $k - 1$ order statistics that divide the sorted set into k equal-sized sets (to within 1). Give an $O(n \lg k)$-time algorithm to list the kth quantiles of a set.

10.3-7

Describe an $O(n)$-time algorithm that, given a set S of n distinct numbers and a positive integer $k \leq n$, determines the k numbers in S that are closest to the median of S.

10.3-8

Let $X[1 .. n]$ and $Y[1 .. n]$ be two arrays, each containing n numbers already in sorted order. Give an $O(\lg n)$-time algorithm to find the median of all $2n$ elements in arrays X and Y.

10.3-9

Professor Olay is consulting for an oil company, which is planning a large pipeline running east to west through an oil field of n wells. From each well, a spur pipeline is to be connected directly to the main pipeline along a shortest path (either north or south), as shown in Figure 10.2. Given x- and y-coordinates of the wells, how should the professor pick the optimal location of the main pipeline (the one that minimizes the total length of the spurs)? Show that the optimal location can be determined in linear time.

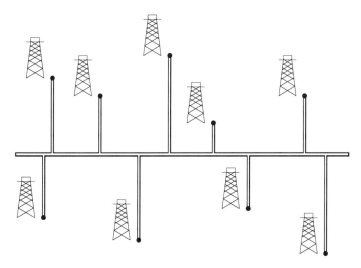

Figure 10.2 We want to determine the position of the east-west oil pipeline that minimizes the total length of the north-south spurs.

Problems

10-1 Largest i numbers in sorted order

Given a set of n numbers, we wish to find the i largest in sorted order using a comparison-based algorithm. Find the algorithm that implements each of the following methods with the best asymptotic worst-case running time, and analyze the running times of the methods in terms of n and i.

a. Sort the numbers and list the i largest.

b. Build a priority queue from the numbers and call EXTRACT-MAX i times.

c. Use an order-statistic algorithm to find the ith largest number, partition, and sort the i largest numbers.

10-2 Weighted median

For n distinct elements $x_1, x_2, \ldots, x_n$ with positive weights $w_1, w_2, \ldots, w_n$ such that $\sum_{i=1}^{n} w_i = 1$, the ***weighted median*** is the element x_k satisfying

$$\sum_{x_i < x_k} w_i \leq \frac{1}{2}$$

and

$$\sum_{x_i > x_k} w_i \leq \frac{1}{2} \ .$$

a. Argue that the median of $x_1, x_2, \ldots, x_n$ is the weighted median of the x_i with weights $w_i = 1/n$ for $i = 1, 2, \ldots, n$.

b. Show how to compute the weighted median of n elements in $O(n \lg n)$ worst-case time using sorting.

c. Show how to compute the weighted median in $\Theta(n)$ worst-case time using a linear-time median algorithm such as SELECT from Section 10.3.

The ***post-office location problem*** is defined as follows. We are given n points $p_1, p_2, \ldots, p_n$ with associated weights $w_1, w_2, \ldots, w_n$. We wish to find a point p (not necessarily one of the input points) that minimizes the sum $\sum_{i=1}^{n} w_i \, d(p, p_i)$, where $d(a, b)$ is the distance between points a and b.

d. Argue that the weighted median is a best solution for the 1-dimensional post-office location problem, in which points are simply real numbers and the distance between points a and b is $d(a, b) = |a - b|$.

e. Find the best solution for the 2-dimensional post-office location problem, in which the points are (x, y) coordinate pairs and the distance between points $a = (x_1, y_1)$ and $b = (x_2, y_2)$ is the ***Manhattan distance***: $d(a, b) = |x_1 - x_2| + |y_1 - y_2|$.

10-3 *Small order statistics*
The worst-case number $T(n)$ of comparisons used by SELECT to select the ith order statistic from n numbers was shown to satisfy $T(n) = \Theta(n)$, but the constant hidden by the Θ-notation is rather large. When i is small relative to n, we can implement a different procedure that uses SELECT as a subroutine but makes fewer comparisons in the worst case.

a. Describe an algorithm that uses $U_i(n)$ comparisons to find the ith smallest of n elements, where $i \le n/2$ and

$$U_i(n) = \begin{cases} T(n) & \text{if } n \le 2i , \\ n/2 + U_i(n/2) + T(2i) & \text{otherwise .} \end{cases}$$

(*Hint:* Begin with $\lfloor n/2 \rfloor$ disjoint pairwise comparisons, and recurse on the set containing the smaller element from each pair.)

b. Show that $U_i(n) = n + O(T(2i) \lg(n/i))$.

c. Show that if i is a constant, then $U_i(n) = n + O(\lg n)$.

d. Show that if $i = n/k$ for $k \ge 2$, then $U_i(n) = n + O(T(2n/k) \lg k)$.

Chapter notes

The worst-case median-finding algorithm was invented by Blum, Floyd, Pratt, Rivest, and Tarjan [29]. The fast average-time version is due to Hoare [97]. Floyd and Rivest [70] have developed an improved average-time version that partitions around an element recursively selected from a small sample of the elements.

III   Data Structures

Introduction

Sets are as fundamental to computer science as they are to mathematics. Whereas mathematical sets are unchanging, the sets manipulated by algorithms can grow, shrink, or otherwise change over time. We call such sets *dynamic*. The next five chapters present some basic techniques for representing finite dynamic sets and manipulating them on a computer.

Algorithms may require several different types of operations to be performed on sets. For example, many algorithms need only the ability to insert elements into, delete elements from, and test membership in a set. A dynamic set that supports these operations is called a *dictionary*. Other algorithms require more complicated operations. For example, priority queues, which were introduced in Chapter 7 in the context of the heap data structure, support the operations of inserting an element into and extracting the smallest element from a set. Not surprisingly, the best way to implement a dynamic set depends upon the operations that must be supported.

Elements of a dynamic set

In a typical implementation of a dynamic set, each element is represented by an object whose fields can be examined and manipulated if we have a pointer to the object. (Chapter 11 discusses the implementation of objects and pointers in programming environments that do not contain them as basic data types.) Some kinds of dynamic sets assume that one of the object's fields is an identifying *key* field. If the keys are all different, we can think of the dynamic set as being a set of key values. The object may contain *satellite data*, which are carried around in other object fields but are otherwise unused by the set implementation. It may also have fields that are manipulated by the set operations; these fields may contain data or pointers to other objects in the set.

Some dynamic sets presuppose that the keys are drawn from a totally ordered set, such as the real numbers, or the set of all words under the usual alphabetic ordering. (A totally ordered set satisfies the trichotomy property, defined on page 31.) A total ordering allows us to define the minimum element of the set, for example, or speak of the next element larger than a given element in a set.

Operations on dynamic sets

Operations on a dynamic set can be grouped into two categories: *queries*, which simply return information about the set, and *modifying operations*, which change the set. Here is a list of typical operations. Any specific application will usually require only a few of these to be implemented.

SEARCH(S, k)   A query that, given a set S and a key value k, returns a pointer x to an element in S such that $key[x] = k$, or NIL if no such element belongs to S.

INSERT(S, x)   A modifying operation that augments the set S with the element pointed to by x. We usually assume that any fields in element x needed by the set implementation have already been initialized.

DELETE(S, x)   A modifying operation that, given a pointer x to an element in the set S, removes x from S. (Note that this operation uses a pointer to an element x, not a key value.)

MINIMUM(S)   A query on a totally ordered set S that returns the element of S with the smallest key.

MAXIMUM(S)   A query on a totally ordered set S that returns the element of S with the largest key.

SUCCESSOR(S, x)   A query that, given an element x whose key is from a totally ordered set S, returns the next larger element in S, or NIL if x is the maximum element.

PREDECESSOR(S, x)   A query that, given an element x whose key is from a totally ordered set S, returns the next smaller element in S, or NIL if x is the minimum element.

The queries SUCCESSOR and PREDECESSOR are often extended to sets with nondistinct keys. For a set on n keys, the normal presumption is that a call to MINIMUM followed by $n - 1$ calls to SUCCESSOR enumerates the elements in the set in sorted order.

The time taken to execute a set operation is usually measured in terms of the size of the set given as one of its arguments. For example, Chapter 14 describes a data structure that can support any of the operations listed above on a set of size n in time $O(\lg n)$.

Overview of Part III

Chapters 11–15 describe several data structures that can be used to implement dynamic sets; many of these will be used later to construct efficient algorithms for a variety of problems. Another important data structure—the heap—has already been introduced in Chapter 7.

Chapter 11 presents the essentials of working with simple data structures such as stacks, queues, linked lists, and rooted trees. It also shows how objects and pointers can be implemented in programming environments that do not support them as primitives. Much of this material should be familiar to anyone who has taken an introductory programming course.

Chapter 12 introduces hash tables, which support the dictionary operations INSERT, DELETE, and SEARCH. In the worst case, hashing requires $\Theta(n)$ time to perform a SEARCH operation, but the expected time for hash-table operations is $O(1)$. The analysis of hashing relies on probability, but most of the chapter requires no background in the subject.

Binary search trees, which are covered in Chapter 13, support all the dynamic-set operations listed above. In the worst case, each operation takes $\Theta(n)$ time on a tree with n elements, but on a randomly built binary search tree, the expected time for each operation is $O(\lg n)$. Binary search trees serve as the basis for many other data structures.

Red-black trees, a variant of binary search trees, are introduced in Chapter 14. Unlike ordinary binary search trees, red-black trees are guaranteed to perform well: operations take $O(\lg n)$ time in the worst case. A red-black tree is a balanced search tree; Chapter 19 presents another kind of balanced search tree, called a B-tree. Although the mechanics of red-black trees are somewhat intricate, you can glean most of their properties from the chapter without studying the mechanics in detail. Nevertheless, walking through the code can be quite instructive.

In Chapter 15, we show how to augment red-black trees to support operations other than the basic ones listed above. First, we augment them so that we can dynamically maintain order statistics for a set of keys. Then, we augment them in a different way to maintain intervals of real numbers.

11 Elementary Data Structures

In this chapter, we examine the representation of dynamic sets by simple data structures that use pointers. Although many complex data structures can be fashioned using pointers, we present only the rudimentary ones: stacks, queues, linked lists, and rooted trees. We also discuss a method by which objects and pointers can be synthesized from arrays.

11.1 Stacks and queues

Stacks and queues are dynamic sets in which the element removed from the set by the DELETE operation is prespecified. In a *stack*, the element deleted from the set is the one most recently inserted: the stack implements a *last-in, first-out*, or *LIFO*, policy. Similarly, in a *queue*, the element deleted is always the one that has been in the set for the longest time: the queue implements a *first-in, first-out*, or *FIFO*, policy. There are several efficient ways to implement stacks and queues on a computer. In this section we show how to use a simple array to implement each.

Stacks

The INSERT operation on a stack is often called PUSH, and the DELETE operation, which does not take an element argument, is often called POP. These names are allusions to physical stacks, such as the spring-loaded stacks of plates used in cafeterias. The order in which plates are popped from the stack is the reverse of the order in which they were pushed onto the stack, since only the top plate is accessible.

As shown in Figure 11.1, we can implement a stack of at most n elements with an array $S[1 .. n]$. The array has an attribute $top[S]$ that indexes the most recently inserted element. The stack consists of elements $S[1 .. top[S]]$, where $S[1]$ is the element at the bottom of the stack and $S[top[S]]$ is the element at the top.

When $top[S] = 0$, the stack contains no elements and is *empty*. The stack can be tested for emptiness by the query operation STACK-EMPTY. If an

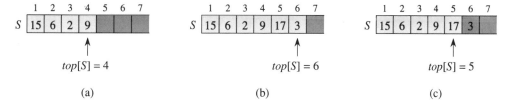

Figure 11.1 An array implementation of a stack S. Stack elements appear only in the lightly shaded positions. **(a)** Stack S has 4 elements. The top element is 9. **(b)** Stack S after the calls PUSH($S, 17$) and PUSH($S, 3$). **(c)** Stack S after the call POP(S) has returned the element 3, which is the one most recently pushed. Although element 3 still appears in the array, it is no longer in the stack; the top is element 17.

empty stack is popped, we say the stack ***underflows***, which is normally an error. If $top[S]$ exceeds n, the stack ***overflows***. (In our pseudocode implementation, we don't worry about stack overflow.)

The stack operations can each be implemented with a few lines of code.

STACK-EMPTY(S)

1   **if** $top[S] = 0$
2   **then return** TRUE
3   **else return** FALSE

PUSH(S, x)

1   $top[S] \leftarrow top[S] + 1$
2   $S[top[S]] \leftarrow x$

POP(S)

1   **if** STACK-EMPTY(S)
2   **then error** "underflow"
3   **else** $top[S] \leftarrow top[S] - 1$
4   **return** $S[top[S] + 1]$

Figure 11.1 shows the effects of the modifying operations PUSH and POP. Each of the three stack operations takes $O(1)$ time.

Queues

We call the INSERT operation on a queue ENQUEUE, and we call the DELETE operation DEQUEUE; like the stack operation POP, DEQUEUE takes no element argument. The FIFO property of a queue causes it to operate like a line of people in the registrar's office. The queue has a ***head*** and a ***tail***. When an element is enqueued, it takes its place at the tail of the queue, like a newly arriving student takes a place at the end of the line. The ele-

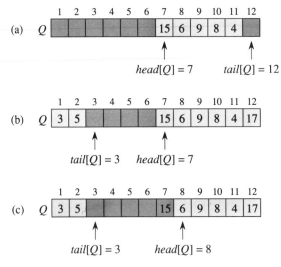

Figure 11.2 A queue implemented using an array $Q[1..12]$. Queue elements appear only in the lightly shaded positions. **(a)** The queue has 5 elements, in locations $Q[7..11]$. **(b)** The configuration of the queue after the calls ENQUEUE($Q, 17$), ENQUEUE($Q, 3$), and ENQUEUE($Q, 5$). **(c)** The configuration of the queue after the call DEQUEUE(Q) returns the key value 15 formerly at the head of the queue. The new head has key 6.

ment dequeued is always the one at the head of the queue, like the student at the head of the line who has waited the longest. (Fortunately, we don't have to worry about computational elements cutting into line.)

Figure 11.2 shows one way to implement a queue of at most $n - 1$ elements using an array $Q[1..n]$. The queue has an attribute $head[Q]$ that indexes, or points to, its head. The attribute $tail[Q]$ indexes the next location at which a newly arriving element will be inserted into the queue. The elements in the queue are in locations $head[Q], head[Q]+1, \ldots, tail[Q]-1$, where we "wrap around" in the sense that location 1 immediately follows location n in a circular order. When $head[Q] = tail[Q]$, the queue is empty. Initially, we have $head[Q] = tail[Q] = 1$. When the queue is empty, an attempt to dequeue an element causes the queue to underflow. When $head[Q] = tail[Q] + 1$, the queue is full, and an attempt to enqueue an element causes the queue to overflow.

In our procedures ENQUEUE and DEQUEUE, the error checking for underflow and overflow has been omitted. (Exercise 11.1-4 asks you to supply code that checks for these two error conditions.)

ENQUEUE(Q, x)

```
1  Q[tail[Q]] ← x
2  if tail[Q] = length[Q]
3     then tail[Q] ← 1
4     else tail[Q] ← tail[Q] + 1
```

DEQUEUE(Q)
1 $x \leftarrow Q[head[Q]]$
2 **if** $head[Q] = length[Q]$
3   **then** $head[Q] \leftarrow 1$
4   **else** $head[Q] \leftarrow head[Q] + 1$
5 **return** x

Figure 11.2 shows the effects of the ENQUEUE and DEQUEUE operations. Each operation takes $O(1)$ time.

Exercises

11.1-1
Using Figure 11.1 as a model, illustrate the result of each of the operations PUSH(S, 4), PUSH(S, 1), PUSH(S, 3), POP(S), PUSH(S, 8), and POP(S) on an initially empty stack S stored in array $S[1..6]$.

11.1-2
Explain how to implement two stacks in one array $A[1..n]$ in such a way that neither stack overflows unless the total number of elements in both stacks together is n. The PUSH and POP operations should run in $O(1)$ time.

11.1-3
Using Figure 11.2 as a model, illustrate the result of each of the operations ENQUEUE(Q, 4), ENQUEUE(Q, 1), ENQUEUE(Q, 3), DEQUEUE(Q), ENQUEUE(Q, 8), and DEQUEUE(Q) on an initially empty queue Q stored in array $Q[1..6]$.

11.1-4
Rewrite ENQUEUE and DEQUEUE to detect underflow and overflow of a queue.

11.1-5
Whereas a stack allows insertion and deletion of elements at only one end, and a queue allows insertion at one end and deletion at the other end, a *deque* (double-ended queue) allows insertion and deletion at both ends. Write four $O(1)$-time procedures to insert elements into and delete elements from both ends of a deque constructed from an array.

11.1-6
Show how to implement a queue using two stacks. Analyze the running time of the queue operations.

11.1-7

Show how to implement a stack using two queues. Analyze the running time of the stack operations.

11.2   Linked lists

A *linked list* is a data structure in which the objects are arranged in a linear order. Unlike an array, though, in which the linear order is determined by the array indices, the order in a linked list is determined by a pointer in each object. Linked lists provide a simple, flexible representation for dynamic sets, supporting (though not necessarily efficiently) all the operations listed on page 198.

As shown in Figure 11.3, each element of a *doubly linked list* L is an object with a *key* field and two other pointer fields: *next* and *prev*. The object may also contain other satellite data. Given an element x in the list, $next[x]$ points to its successor in the linked list, and $prev[x]$ points to its predecessor. If $prev[x] = $ NIL, the element x has no predecessor and is therefore the first element, or *head*, of the list. If $next[x] = $ NIL, the element x has no successor and is therefore the last element, or *tail*, of the list. An attribute $head[L]$ points to the first element of the list. If $head[L] = $ NIL, the list is empty.

A list may have one of several forms. It may be either singly linked or doubly linked, it may be sorted or not, and it may be circular or not. If a list is *singly linked*, we omit the *prev* pointer in each element. If a list is *sorted*, the linear order of the list corresponds to the linear order of keys stored in elements of the list; the minimum element is the head of the list, and the maximum element is the tail. If the list is *unsorted*, the elements can appear in any order. In a *circular list*, the *prev* pointer of the head of the list points to the tail, and the *next* pointer of the tail of the list points to the head. The list may thus be viewed as a ring of elements. In the remainder of this section, we assume that the lists with which we are working are unsorted and doubly linked.

Searching a linked list

The procedure LIST-SEARCH(L, k) finds the first element with key k in list L by a simple linear search, returning a pointer to this element. If no object with key k appears in the list, then NIL is returned. For the linked list in Figure 11.3(a), the call LIST-SEARCH($L, 4$) returns a pointer to the third element, and the call LIST-SEARCH($L, 7$) returns NIL.

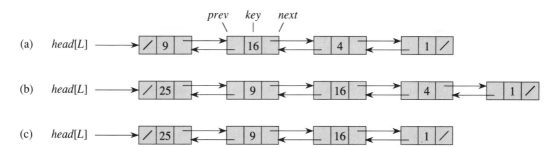

Figure 11.3 **(a)** A doubly linked list L representing the dynamic set $\{1, 4, 9, 16\}$. Each element in the list is an object with fields for the key and pointers (shown by arrows) to the next and previous objects. The *next* field of the tail and the *prev* field of the head are NIL, indicated by a diagonal slash. The attribute *head*[L] points to the head. **(b)** Following the execution of LIST-INSERT(L, x), where *key*[x] = 25, the linked list has a new object with key 25 as the new head. This new object points to the old head with key 9. **(c)** The result of the subsequent call LIST-DELETE(L, x), where x points to the object with key 4.

LIST-SEARCH(L, k)

1   $x \leftarrow head[L]$
2   **while** $x \neq$ NIL and $key[x] \neq k$
3   **do** $x \leftarrow next[x]$
4   **return** x

To search a list of n objects, the LIST-SEARCH procedure takes $\Theta(n)$ time in the worst case, since it may have to search the entire list.

Inserting into a linked list

Given an element x whose *key* field has already been set, the LIST-INSERT procedure "splices" x onto the front of the linked list, as shown in Figure 11.3(b).

LIST-INSERT(L, x)

1   $next[x] \leftarrow head[L]$
2   **if** $head[L] \neq$ NIL
3   **then** $prev[head[L]] \leftarrow x$
4   $head[L] \leftarrow x$
5   $prev[x] \leftarrow$ NIL

The running time for LIST-INSERT on a list of n elements is $O(1)$.

Deleting from a linked list

The procedure LIST-DELETE removes an element x from a linked list L. It must be given a pointer to x, and it then "splices" x out of the list by updating pointers. If we wish to delete an element with a given key, we must first call LIST-SEARCH to retrieve a pointer to the element.

LIST-DELETE(L, x)

```
1  if prev[x] ≠ NIL
2     then next[prev[x]] ← next[x]
3     else head[L] ← next[x]
4  if next[x] ≠ NIL
5     then prev[next[x]] ← prev[x]
```

Figure 11.3(c) shows how an element is deleted from a linked list. LIST-DELETE runs in $O(1)$ time, but if we wish to delete an element with a given key, $\Theta(n)$ time is required in the worst case because we must first call LIST-SEARCH.

Sentinels

The code for LIST-DELETE would be simpler if we could ignore the boundary conditions at the head and tail of the list.

LIST-DELETE$'$(L, x)

```
1  next[prev[x]] ← next[x]
2  prev[next[x]] ← prev[x]
```

A *sentinel* is a dummy object that allows us to simplify boundary conditions. For example, suppose that we provide with list L an object $nil[L]$ that represents NIL but has all the fields of the other list elements. Wherever we have a reference to NIL in list code, we replace it by a reference to the sentinel $nil[L]$. As shown in Figure 11.4, this turns a regular doubly linked list into a circular list, with the sentinel $nil[L]$ placed between the head and tail; the field $next[nil[L]]$ points to the head of the list, and $prev[nil[L]]$ points to the tail. Similarly, both the *next* field of the tail and the *prev* field of the head point to $nil[L]$. Since $next[nil[L]]$ points to the head, we can eliminate the attribute $head[L]$ altogether, replacing references to it by references to $next[nil[L]]$. An empty list consists of just the sentinel, since both $next[nil[L]]$ and $prev[nil[L]]$ can be set to $nil[L]$.

The code for LIST-SEARCH remains the same as before, but with the references to NIL and $head[L]$ changed as specified above.

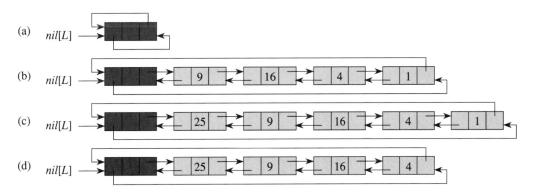

Figure 11.4   A linked list *L* that uses a sentinel *nil*[*L*] (heavily shaded) is the regular doubly linked list turned into a circular list with *nil*[*L*] appearing between the head and tail. The attribute *head*[*L*] is no longer needed, since we can access the head of the list by *next*[*nil*[*L*]]. **(a)** An empty list. **(b)** The linked list from Figure 11.3(a), with key 9 at the head and key 1 at the tail. **(c)** The list after executing LIST-INSERT′(*L*, *x*), where *key*[*x*] = 25. The new object becomes the head of the list. **(d)** The list after deleting the object with key 1. The new tail is the object with key 4.

LIST-SEARCH′(*L*, *k*)

1   *x* ← *next*[*nil*[*L*]]
2   **while** *x* ≠ *nil*[*L*] and *key*[*x*] ≠ *k*
3   **do** *x* ← *next*[*x*]
4   **return** *x*

We use the two-line procedure LIST-DELETE′ to delete an element from the list. We use the following procedure to insert an element into the list.

LIST-INSERT′(*L*, *x*)

1   *next*[*x*] ← *next*[*nil*[*L*]]
2   *prev*[*next*[*nil*[*L*]]] ← *x*
3   *next*[*nil*[*L*]] ← *x*
4   *prev*[*x*] ← *nil*[*L*]

Figure 11.4 shows the effects of LIST-INSERT′ and LIST-DELETE′ on a sample list.

Sentinels rarely reduce the asymptotic time bounds of data structure operations, but they can reduce constant factors. The gain from using sentinels within loops is usually a matter of clarity of code rather than speed; the linked list code, for example, is simplified by the use of sentinels, but we save only *O*(1) time in the LIST-INSERT′ and LIST-DELETE′ procedures. In other situations, however, the use of sentinels helps to tighten the code in a loop, thus reducing the coefficient of, say, *n* or *n*² in the running time.

Sentinels should not be used indiscriminately. If there are many small lists, the extra storage used by their sentinels can represent significant wasted memory. In this book, we only use sentinels when they truly simplify the code.

Exercises

11.2-1
Can the dynamic-set operation INSERT be implemented on a singly linked list in $O(1)$ time? How about DELETE?

11.2-2
Implement a stack using a singly linked list L. The operations PUSH and POP should still take $O(1)$ time.

11.2-3
Implement a queue by a singly linked list L. The operations ENQUEUE and DEQUEUE should still take $O(1)$ time.

11.2-4
Implement the dictionary operations INSERT, DELETE, and SEARCH using singly linked, circular lists. What are the running times of your procedures?

11.2-5
The dynamic-set operation UNION takes two disjoint sets S_1 and S_2 as input, and it returns a set $S = S_1 \cup S_2$ consisting of all the elements of S_1 and S_2. The sets S_1 and S_2 are usually destroyed by the operation. Show how to support UNION in $O(1)$ time using a suitable list data structure.

11.2-6
Write a procedure that merges two singly linked, sorted lists into one singly linked, sorted list without using sentinels. Then, write a similar procedure using a sentinel with key ∞ to mark the end of each list. Compare the simplicity of code for the two procedures.

11.2-7
Give a $\Theta(n)$-time nonrecursive procedure that reverses a singly linked list of n elements. The procedure should use no more than constant storage beyond that needed for the list itself.

11.2-8 ⋆
Explain how to implement doubly linked lists using only one pointer value $np[x]$ per item instead of the usual two (*next* and *prev*). Assume that all index values can be interpreted as k-bit integers, and define $np[x]$ to be $np[x] = next[x]$ XOR $prev[x]$, the k-bit "exclusive-or" of $next[x]$ and $prev[x]$. (The value NIL is represented by 0.) Be sure to describe what information is needed to access the head of the list. Show how to implement the SEARCH, INSERT, and DELETE operations on such a list. Also show how to reverse such a list in $O(1)$ time.

11.3 Implementing pointers and objects

How do we implement pointers and objects in languages, such as Fortran, that do not provide them? In this section, we shall see two ways of implementing linked data structures without an explicit pointer data type. We shall synthesize objects and pointers from arrays and array indices.

A multiple-array representation of objects

We can represent a collection of objects that have the same fields by using an array for each field. As an example, Figure 11.5 shows how we can implement the linked list of Figure 11.3(a) with three arrays. The array *key* holds the values of the keys currently in the dynamic set, and the pointers are stored in the arrays *next* and *prev*. For a given array index *x*, *key*[*x*], *next*[*x*], and *prev*[*x*] represent an object in the linked list. Under this interpretation, a pointer *x* is simply a common index into the *key*, *next*, and *prev* arrays.

In Figure 11.3(a), the object with key 4 follows the object with key 16 in the linked list. In Figure 11.5, key 4 appears in *key*[2], and key 16 appears in *key*[5], so we have *next*[5] = 2 and *prev*[2] = 5. Although the constant NIL appears in the *next* field of the tail and the *prev* field of the head, we usually use an integer (such as 0 or −1) that cannot possibly represent an actual index into the arrays. A variable *L* holds the index of the head of the list.

In our pseudocode, we have been using square brackets to denote both the indexing of an array and the selection of a field (attribute) of an object. Either way, the meanings of *key*[*x*], *next*[*x*], and *prev*[*x*] are consistent with implementation practice.

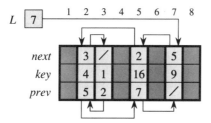

Figure 11.5 The linked list of Figure 11.3(a) represented by the arrays *key*, *next*, and *prev*. Each vertical slice of the arrays represents a single object. Stored pointers correspond to the array indices shown at the top; the arrows show how to interpret them. Lightly shaded object positions contain list elements. The variable *L* keeps the index of the head.

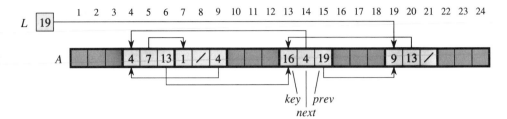

Figure 11.6 The linked list of Figures 11.3(a) and 11.5 represented in a single array *A*. Each list element is an object that occupies a contiguous subarray of length 3 within the array. The three fields *key*, *next*, and *prev* correspond to the offsets 0, 1, and 2, respectively. A pointer to an object is an index of the first element of the object. Objects containing list elements are lightly shaded, and arrows show the list ordering.

A single-array representation of objects

The words in a computer memory are typically addressed by integers from 0 to $M - 1$, where M is a suitably large integer. In many programming languages, an object occupies a contiguous set of locations in the computer memory. A pointer is simply the address of the first memory location of the object, and other memory locations within the object can be indexed by adding an offset to the pointer.

We can use the same strategy for implementing objects in programming environments that do not provide explicit pointer data types. For example, Figure 11.6 shows how a single array *A* can be used to store the linked list from Figures 11.3(a) and 11.5. An object occupies a contiguous subarray $A[j .. k]$. Each field of the object corresponds to an offset in the range from 0 to $k - j$, and a pointer to the object is the index j. In Figure 11.6, the offsets corresponding to *key*, *next*, and *prev* are 0, 1, and 2, respectively. To read the value of *prev*[*i*], given a pointer *i*, we add the value *i* of the pointer to the offset 2, thus reading $A[i + 2]$.

The single-array representation is flexible in that it permits objects of different lengths to be stored in the same array. The problem of managing such a heterogeneous collection of objects is more difficult than the problem of managing a homogeneous collection, where all objects have the same fields. Since most of the data structures we shall consider are composed of homogeneous elements, it will be sufficient for our purposes to use the multiple-array representation of objects.

Allocating and freeing objects

To insert a key into a dynamic set represented by a doubly linked list, we must allocate a pointer to a currently unused object in the linked-list representation. Thus, it is useful to manage the storage of objects not

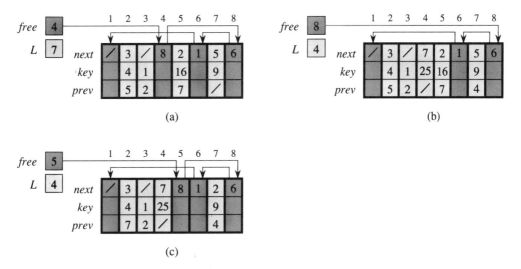

Figure 11.7 The effect of the ALLOCATE-OBJECT and FREE-OBJECT procedures. **(a)** The list of Figure 11.5 (lightly shaded) and a free list (heavily shaded). Arrows show the free-list structure. **(b)** The result of calling ALLOCATE-OBJECT() (which returns index 4), setting *key*[4] to 25, and calling LIST-INSERT(L, 4). The new free-list head is object 8, which had been *next*[4] on the free list. **(c)** After executing LIST-DELETE(L, 5), we call FREE-OBJECT(5). Object 5 becomes the new free-list head, with object 8 following it on the free list.

currently used in the linked-list representation so that one can be allocated. In some systems, a **garbage collector** is responsible for determining which objects are unused. Many applications, however, are simple enough that they can bear responsibility for returning an unused object to a storage manager. We shall now explore the problem of allocating and freeing (or deallocating) homogeneous objects using the example of a doubly linked list represented by multiple arrays.

Suppose that the arrays in the multiple-array representation have length m and that at some moment the dynamic set contains $n \leq m$ elements. Then n objects represent elements currently in the dynamic set, and the remaining $m - n$ objects are **free**; the free objects can be used to represent elements inserted into the dynamic set in the future.

We keep the free objects in a singly linked list, which we call the **free list**. The free list uses only the *next* array, which stores the *next* pointers within the list. The head of the free list is held in the global variable *free*. When the dynamic set represented by linked list L is nonempty, the free list may be intertwined with list L, as shown in Figure 11.7. Note that each object in the representation is either in list L or in the free list, but not in both.

The free list is a stack: the next object allocated is the last one freed. We can use a list implementation of the stack operations PUSH and POP to implement the procedures for allocating and freeing objects, respectively.

Figure 11.8   Two linked lists, L_1 (lightly shaded) and L_2 (heavily shaded), and a free list (darkened) intertwined.

We assume that the global variable *free* used in the following procedures points to the first element of the free list.

ALLOCATE-OBJECT()

```
1  if free = NIL
2      then error "out of space"
3      else  x ← free
4            free ← next[x]
5            return x
```

FREE-OBJECT(x)

```
1  next[x] ← free
2  free ← x
```

The free list initially contains all n unallocated objects. When the free list has been exhausted, the ALLOCATE-OBJECT procedure signals an error. It is common to use a single free list to service several linked lists. Figure 11.8 shows three linked lists and a free list intertwined through *key*, *next*, and *prev* arrays.

The two procedures run in $O(1)$ time, which makes them quite practical. They can be modified to work for any homogeneous collection of objects by letting any one of the fields in the object act like a *next* field in the free list.

Exercises

11.3-1
Draw a picture of the sequence $\langle 13, 4, 8, 19, 5, 11 \rangle$ stored as a doubly linked list using the multiple-array representation. Do the same for the single-array representation.

11.3-2
Write the procedures ALLOCATE-OBJECT and FREE-OBJECT for a homogeneous collection of objects implemented by the single-array representation.

11.3-3

Why don't we need to set or reset the *prev* fields of objects in the implementation of the ALLOCATE-OBJECT and FREE-OBJECT procedures?

11.3-4

It is often desirable to keep all elements of a doubly linked list compact in storage, using, for example, the first m index locations in the multiple-array representation. (This is the case in a paged, virtual-memory computing environment.) Explain how the procedures ALLOCATE-OBJECT and FREE-OBJECT can be implemented so that the representation is compact. Assume that there are no pointers to elements of the linked list outside the list itself. (*Hint:* Use the array implementation of a stack.)

11.3-5

Let L be a doubly linked list of length m stored in arrays *key*, *prev*, and *next* of length n. Suppose that these arrays are managed by ALLOCATE-OBJECT and FREE-OBJECT procedures that keep a doubly linked free list F. Suppose further that of the n items, exactly m are on list L and $n - m$ are on the free list. Write a procedure COMPACTIFY-LIST(L, F) that, given the list L and the free list F, moves the items in L so that they occupy array positions $1, 2, \ldots, m$ and adjusts the free list F so that it remains correct, occupying array positions $m + 1, m + 2, \ldots, n$. The running time of your procedure should be $\Theta(m)$, and it should use only a constant amount of extra space. Give a careful argument for the correctness of your procedure.

11.4 Representing rooted trees

The methods for representing lists given in the previous section extend to any homogeneous data structure. In this section, we look specifically at the problem of representing rooted trees by linked data structures. We first look at binary trees, and then we present a method for rooted trees in which nodes can have an arbitrary number of children.

We represent each node of a tree by an object. As with linked lists, we assume that each node contains a *key* field. The remaining fields of interest are pointers to other nodes, and they vary according to the type of tree.

Binary trees

As shown in Figure 11.9, we use the fields p, *left*, and *right* to store pointers to the parent, left child, and right child of each node in a binary tree T. If $p[x] = $ NIL, then x is the root. If node x has no left child, then $left[x] = $ NIL, and similarly for the right child. The root of the entire tree T is pointed to by the attribute $root[T]$. If $root[T] = $ NIL, then the tree is empty.

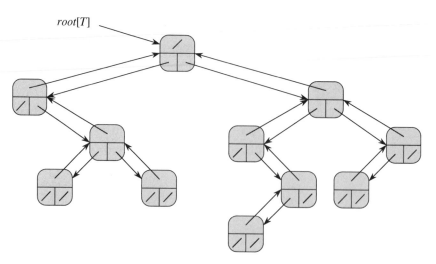

Figure 11.9 The representation of a binary tree T. Each node x has the fields $p[x]$ (top), *left*$[x]$ (lower left), and *right*$[x]$ (lower right). The *key* fields are not shown.

Rooted trees with unbounded branching

The scheme for representing a binary tree can be extended to any class of trees in which the number of children of each node is at most some constant k: we replace the *left* and *right* fields by $child_1, child_2, \ldots, child_k$. This scheme no longer works when the number of children of a node is unbounded, since we do not know how many fields (arrays in the multiple-array representation) to allocate in advance. Moreover, even if the number of children k is bounded by a large constant but most nodes have a small number of children, we may waste a lot of memory.

Fortunately, there is a clever scheme for using binary trees to represent trees with arbitrary numbers of children. It has the advantage of using only $O(n)$ space for any n-node rooted tree. The ***left-child, right-sibling representation*** is shown in Figure 11.10. As before, each node contains a parent pointer p, and *root*$[T]$ points to the root of tree T. Instead of having a pointer to each of its children, however, each node x has only two pointers:

1. *left-child*$[x]$ points to the leftmost child of node x, and

2. *right-sibling*$[x]$ points to the sibling of x immediately to the right.

If node x has no children, then *left-child*$[x] = $ NIL, and if node x is the rightmost child of its parent, then *right-sibling*$[x] = $ NIL.

Other tree representations

We sometimes represent rooted trees in other ways. In Chapter 7, for example, we represented a heap, which is based on a complete binary

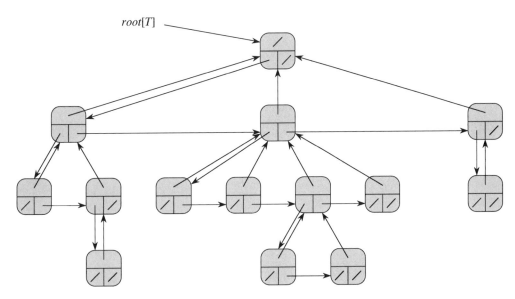

Figure 11.10 The left-child, right-sibling representation of a tree T. Each node x has fields $p[x]$ (top), *left-child*$[x]$ (lower left), and *right-sibling*$[x]$ (lower right). Keys are not shown.

tree, by a single array plus an index. The trees that appear in Chapter 22 are only traversed toward the root, so only the parent pointers are present; there are no pointers to children. Many other schemes are possible. Which scheme is best depends on the application.

Exercises

11.4-1

Draw the binary tree rooted at index 6 that is represented by the following fields.

index	*key*	*left*	*right*
1	12	7	3
2	15	8	NIL
3	4	10	NIL
4	10	5	9
5	2	NIL	NIL
6	18	1	4
7	7	NIL	NIL
8	14	6	2
9	21	NIL	NIL
10	5	NIL	NIL

11.4-2

Write an $O(n)$-time recursive procedure that, given an n-node binary tree, prints out the key of each node in the tree.

11.4-3

Write an $O(n)$-time nonrecursive procedure that, given an n-node binary tree, prints out the key of each node in the tree. Use a stack as an auxiliary data structure.

11.4-4

Write an $O(n)$-time procedure that prints all the keys of an arbitrary rooted tree with n nodes, where the tree is stored using the left-child, right-sibling representation.

11.4-5 ⋆

Write an $O(n)$-time nonrecursive procedure that, given an n-node binary tree, prints out the key of each node. Use no more than constant extra space outside of the tree itself and do not modify the tree, even temporarily, during the procedure.

11.4-6 ⋆

The left-child, right-sibling representation of an arbitrary rooted tree uses three pointers in each node: *left-child*, *right-sibling*, and *parent*. From any node, the parent and all the children of the node can be reached and identified. Show how to achieve the same effect using only two pointers and one boolean value in each node.

Problems

11-1 *Comparisons among lists*

For each of the four types of lists in the following table, what is the asymptotic worst-case running time for each dynamic-set operation listed?

	unsorted, singly linked	sorted, singly linked	unsorted, doubly linked	sorted, doubly linked
Search(L, k)				
Insert(L, x)				
Delete(L, x)				
Successor(L, x)				
Predecessor(L, x)				
Minimum(L)				
Maximum(L)				

11-2 Mergeable heaps using linked lists

A *mergeable heap* supports the following operations: MAKE-HEAP (which creates an empty mergeable heap), INSERT, MINIMUM, EXTRACT-MIN, and UNION. Show how to implement mergeable heaps using linked lists in each of the following cases. Try to make each operation as efficient as possible. Analyze the running time of each operation in terms of the size of the dynamic set(s) being operated on.

a. Lists are sorted.

b. Lists are unsorted.

c. Lists are unsorted, and dynamic sets to be merged are disjoint.

11-3 Searching a sorted compact list

Exercise 11.3-4 asked how we might maintain an n-element list compactly in the first n positions of an array. We shall assume that all keys are distinct and that the compact list is also sorted, that is, $key[i] < key[next[i]]$ for all $i = 1, 2, \ldots, n$ such that $next[i] \neq$ NIL. Under these assumptions, we expect that the following randomized algorithm can be used to search the list much faster than linear time.

COMPACT-LIST-SEARCH(L, k)

```
 1  i ← head[L]
 2  n ← length[L]
 3  while i ≠ NIL and key[i] < k
 4      do j ← RANDOM(1, n)
 5         if key[i] < key[j] and key[j] < k
 6            then i ← j
 7         i ← next[i]
 8         if key[i] = k
 9            then return i
10  return NIL
```

If we ignore lines 4–6 of the procedure, we have the usual algorithm for searching a sorted linked list, in which index i points to each position of the list in turn. Lines 4–6 attempt to skip ahead to a randomly chosen position j. Such a skip is beneficial if $key[j]$ is larger than $key[i]$ and smaller than k; in such a case, j marks a position in the list that i would have to pass by during an ordinary list search. Because the list is compact, we know that any choice of j between 1 and n indexes some object in the list rather than a slot on the free list.

a. Why do we assume that all keys are distinct in COMPACT-LIST-SEARCH? Argue that random skips do not necessarily help asymptotically when the list contains repeated key values.

We can analyze the performance of COMPACT-LIST-SEARCH by breaking its execution into two phases. During the first phase, we discount any progress toward finding k that is accomplished by lines 7–9. That is, phase 1 consists of moving ahead in the list by random skips only. Likewise, phase 2 discounts progress accomplished by lines 4–6, and thus it operates like ordinary linear search.

Let X_t be the random variable that describes the distance in the linked list (that is, through the chain of *next* pointers) from position i to the desired key k after t iterations of phase 1.

b. Argue that the expected running time of COMPACT-LIST-SEARCH is $O(t + \text{E}[X_t])$ for all $t \geq 0$.

c. Show that $\text{E}[X_t] \leq \sum_{r=1}^{n}(1 - r/n)^t$. (*Hint:* Use equation (6.28).)

d. Show that $\sum_{r=0}^{n-1} r^t \leq n^{t+1}/(t+1)$.

e. Prove that $\text{E}[X_t] \leq n/(t+1)$, and explain why this formula makes intuitive sense.

f. Show that COMPACT-LIST-SEARCH runs in $O(\sqrt{n})$ expected time.

Chapter notes

Aho, Hopcroft, and Ullman [5] and Knuth [121] are excellent references for elementary data structures. Gonnet [90] provides experimental data on the performance of many data structure operations.

The origin of stacks and queues as data structures in computer science is unclear, since corresponding notions already existed in mathematics and paper-based business practices before the introduction of digital computers. Knuth [121] cites A. M. Turing for the development of stacks for subroutine linkage in 1947.

Pointer-based data structures also seem to be a folk invention. According to Knuth, pointers were apparently used in early computers with drum memories. The A-1 language developed by G. M. Hopper in 1951 represented algebraic formulas as binary trees. Knuth credits the IPL-II language, developed in 1956 by A. Newell, J. C. Shaw, and H. A. Simon, for recognizing the importance and promoting the use of pointers. Their IPL-III language, developed in 1957, included explicit stack operations.

12   Hash Tables

Many applications require a dynamic set that supports only the dictionary operations INSERT, SEARCH, and DELETE. For example, a compiler for a computer language maintains a symbol table, in which the keys of elements are arbitrary character strings that correspond to identifiers in the language. A hash table is an effective data structure for implementing dictionaries. Although searching for an element in a hash table can take as long as searching for an element in a linked list—$\Theta(n)$ time in the worst case—in practice, hashing performs extremely well. Under reasonable assumptions, the expected time to search for an element in a hash table is $O(1)$.

A hash table is a generalization of the simpler notion of an ordinary array. Directly addressing into an ordinary array makes effective use of our ability to examine an arbitrary position in an array in $O(1)$ time. Section 12.1 discusses direct addressing in more detail. Direct addressing is applicable when we can afford to allocate an array that has one position for every possible key.

When the number of keys actually stored is small relative to the total number of possible keys, hash tables become an effective alternative to directly addressing an array, since a hash table typically uses an array of size proportional to the number of keys actually stored. Instead of using the key as an array index directly, the array index is *computed* from the key. Section 12.2 presents the main ideas, and Section 12.3 describes how array indices can be computed from keys using hash functions. Several variations on the basic theme are presented and analyzed; the "bottom line" is that hashing is an extremely effective and practical technique: the basic dictionary operations require only $O(1)$ time on the average.

12.1   Direct-address tables

Direct addressing is a simple technique that works well when the universe U of keys is reasonably small. Suppose that an application needs a dynamic set in which each element has a key drawn from the universe $U = \{0, 1, \ldots, m - 1\}$, where m is not too large. We shall assume that no two elements have the same key.

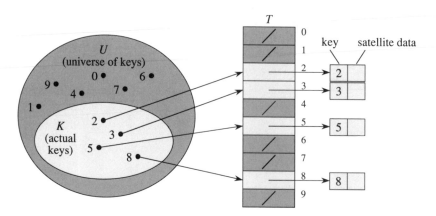

Figure 12.1 Implementing a dynamic set by a direct-address table T. Each key in the universe $U = \{0, 1, \ldots, 9\}$ corresponds to an index in the table. The set $K = \{2, 3, 5, 8\}$ of actual keys determines the slots in the table that contain pointers to elements. The other slots, heavily shaded, contain NIL.

To represent the dynamic set, we use an array, or ***direct-address table***, $T[0 \mathinner{.\,.} m - 1]$, in which each position, or ***slot***, corresponds to a key in the universe U. Figure 12.1 illustrates the approach; slot k points to an element in the set with key k. If the set contains no element with key k, then $T[k] = \text{NIL}$.

The dictionary operations are trivial to implement.

DIRECT-ADDRESS-SEARCH(T, k)
    return $T[k]$

DIRECT-ADDRESS-INSERT(T, x)
    $T[key[x]] \leftarrow x$

DIRECT-ADDRESS-DELETE(T, x)
    $T[key[x]] \leftarrow \text{NIL}$

Each of these operations is fast: only $O(1)$ time is required.

For some applications, the elements in the dynamic set can be stored in the direct-address table itself. That is, rather than storing an element's key and satellite data in an object external to the direct-address table, with a pointer from a slot in the table to the object, we can store the object in the slot itself, thus saving space. Moreover, it is often unnecessary to store the key field of the object, since if we have the index of an object in the table, we have its key. If keys are not stored, however, we must have some way to tell if the slot is empty.

Exercises

12.1-1
Consider a dynamic set S that is represented by a direct-address table T of length m. Describe a procedure that finds the maximum element of S. What is the worst-case performance of your procedure?

12.1-2
A *bit vector* is simply an array of bits (0's and 1's). A bit vector of length m takes much less space than an array of m pointers. Describe how to use a bit vector to represent a dynamic set of distinct elements with no satellite data. Dictionary operations should run in $O(1)$ time.

12.1-3
Suggest how to implement a direct-address table in which the keys of stored elements do not need to be distinct and the elements can have satellite data. All three dictionary operations (INSERT, DELETE, and SEARCH) should run in $O(1)$ time. (Don't forget that DELETE takes as an argument a pointer to an object to be deleted, not a key.)

12.1-4 ⋆
We wish to implement a dictionary by using direct addressing on a *huge* array. At the start, the array entries may contain garbage, and initializing the entire array is impractical because of its size. Describe a scheme for implementing a direct-address dictionary on a huge array. Each stored object should use $O(1)$ space; the operations SEARCH, INSERT, and DELETE should take $O(1)$ time each; and the initialization of the data structure should take $O(1)$ time. (*Hint:* Use an additional stack, whose size is the number of keys actually stored in the dictionary, to help determine whether a given entry in the huge array is valid or not.)

12.2   Hash tables

The difficulty with direct addressing is obvious: if the universe U is large, storing a table T of size $|U|$ may be impractical, or even impossible, given the memory available on a typical computer. Furthermore, the set K of keys *actually stored* may be so small relative to U that most of the space allocated for T would be wasted.

When the set K of keys stored in a dictionary is much smaller than the universe U of all possible keys, a hash table requires much less storage than a direct-address table. Specifically, the storage requirements can be reduced to $\Theta(|K|)$, even though searching for an element in the hash table still requires only $O(1)$ time. (The only catch is that this bound is for

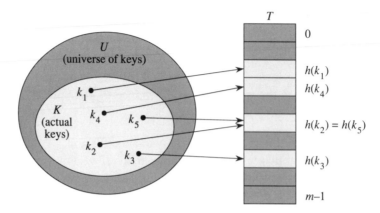

Figure 12.2   Using a hash function h to map keys to hash-table slots. Keys k_2 and k_5 map to the same slot, so they collide.

the *average time*, whereas for direct addressing it holds for the *worst-case time*.)

With direct addressing, an element with key k is stored in slot k. With hashing, this element is stored in slot $h(k)$; that is, a **hash function** h is used to compute the slot from the key k. Here h maps the universe U of keys into the slots of a **hash table** $T[0 .. m - 1]$:

$$h : U \rightarrow \{0, 1, \ldots, m - 1\} \ .$$

We say that an element with key k **hashes** to slot $h(k)$; we also say that $h(k)$ is the **hash value** of key k. Figure 12.2 illustrates the basic idea. The point of the hash function is to reduce the range of array indices that need to be handled. Instead of $|U|$ values, we need to handle only m values. Storage requirements are correspondingly reduced.

The fly in the ointment of this beautiful idea is that two keys may hash to the same slot—a **collision**. Fortunately, there are effective techniques for resolving the conflict created by collisions.

Of course, the ideal solution would be to avoid collisions altogether. We might try to achieve this goal by choosing a suitable hash function h. One idea is to make h appear to be "random," thus avoiding collisions or at least minimizing their number. The very term "to hash," evoking images of random mixing and chopping, captures the spirit of this approach. (Of course, a hash function h must be deterministic in that a given input k should always produce the same output $h(k)$.) Since $|U| > m$, however, there must be two keys that have the same hash value; avoiding collisions altogether is therefore impossible. Thus, while a well-designed, "random"-looking hash function can minimize the number of collisions, we still need a method for resolving the collisions that do occur.

The remainder of this section presents the simplest collision resolution technique, called chaining. Section 12.4 introduces an alternative method for resolving collisions, called open addressing.

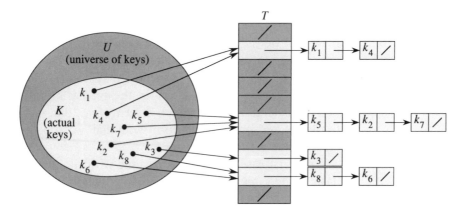

Figure 12.3   Collision resolution by chaining. Each hash-table slot $T[j]$ contains a linked list of all the keys whose hash value is j. For example, $h(k_1) = h(k_4)$ and $h(k_5) = h(k_2) = h(k_7)$.

Collision resolution by chaining

In *chaining*, we put all the elements that hash to the same slot in a linked list, as shown in Figure 12.3. Slot j contains a pointer to the head of the list of all stored elements that hash to j; if there are no such elements, slot j contains NIL.

The dictionary operations on a hash table T are easy to implement when collisions are resolved by chaining.

CHAINED-HASH-INSERT(T, x)

   insert x at the head of list $T[h(key[x])]$

CHAINED-HASH-SEARCH(T, k)

   search for an element with key k in list $T[h(k)]$

CHAINED-HASH-DELETE(T, x)

   delete x from the list $T[h(key[x])]$

The worst-case running time for insertion is $O(1)$. For searching, the worst-case running time is proportional to the length of the list; we shall analyze this more closely below. Deletion of an element x can be accomplished in $O(1)$ time if the lists are doubly linked. (If the lists are singly linked, we must first find x in the list $T[h(key[x])]$, so that the *next* link of x's predecessor can be properly set to splice x out; in this case, deletion and searching have essentially the same running time.)

Analysis of hashing with chaining

How well does hashing with chaining perform? In particular, how long does it take to search for an element with a given key?

Given a hash table T with m slots that stores n elements, we define the *load factor* α for T as n/m, that is, the average number of elements stored in a chain. Our analysis will be in terms of α; that is, we imagine α staying fixed as n and m go to infinity. (Note that α can be less than, equal to, or greater than 1.)

The worst-case behavior of hashing with chaining is terrible: all n keys hash to the same slot, creating a list of length n. The worst-case time for searching is thus $\Theta(n)$ plus the time to compute the hash function—no better than if we used one linked list for all the elements. Clearly, hash tables are not used for their worst-case performance.

The average performance of hashing depends on how well the hash function h distributes the set of keys to be stored among the m slots, on the average. Section 12.3 discusses these issues, but for now we shall assume that any given element is equally likely to hash into any of the m slots, independently of where any other element has hashed to. We call this the assumption of *simple uniform hashing*.

We assume that the hash value $h(k)$ can be computed in $O(1)$ time, so that the time required to search for an element with key k depends linearly on the length of the list $T[h(k)]$. Setting aside the $O(1)$ time required to compute the hash function and access slot $h(k)$, let us consider the expected number of elements examined by the search algorithm, that is, the number of elements in the list $T[h(k)]$ that are checked to see if their keys are equal to k. We shall consider two cases. In the first, the search is unsuccessful: no element in the table has key k. In the second, the search successfully finds an element with key k.

Theorem 12.1
In a hash table in which collisions are resolved by chaining, an unsuccessful search takes time $\Theta(1+\alpha)$, on the average, under the assumption of simple uniform hashing.

Proof Under the assumption of simple uniform hashing, any key k is equally likely to hash to any of the m slots. The average time to search unsuccessfully for a key k is thus the average time to search to the end of one of the m lists. The average length of such a list is the load factor $\alpha = n/m$. Thus, the expected number of elements examined in an unsuccessful search is α, and the total time required (including the time for computing $h(k)$) is $\Theta(1 + \alpha)$. ∎

Theorem 12.2
In a hash table in which collisions are resolved by chaining, a successful search takes time $\Theta(1+\alpha)$, on the average, under the assumption of simple uniform hashing.

Proof   We assume that the key being searched for is equally likely to be any of the n keys stored in the table. We also assume that the CHAINED-HASH-INSERT procedure inserts a new element at the end of the list instead of the front. (By Exercise 12.2-3, the average successful search time is the same whether new elements are inserted at the front of the list or at the end.)   The expected number of elements examined during a successful search is 1 more than the number of elements examined when the sought-for element was inserted (since every new element goes at the end of the list).   To find the expected number of elements examined, we therefore take the average, over the n items in the table, of 1 plus the expected length of the list to which the ith element is added.   The expected length of that list is $(i-1)/m$, and so the expected number of elements examined in a successful search is

$$
\begin{aligned}
\frac{1}{n}\sum_{i=1}^{n}\left(1+\frac{i-1}{m}\right) &= 1+\frac{1}{nm}\sum_{i=1}^{n}(i-1) \\
&= 1+\left(\frac{1}{nm}\right)\left(\frac{(n-1)n}{2}\right) \\
&= 1+\frac{\alpha}{2}-\frac{1}{2m} \, .
\end{aligned}
$$

Thus, the total time required for a successful search (including the time for computing the hash function) is $\Theta(2+\alpha/2-1/2m) = \Theta(1+\alpha)$.   ∎

What does this analysis mean? If the number of hash-table slots is at least proportional to the number of elements in the table, we have $n = O(m)$ and, consequently, $\alpha = n/m = O(m)/m = O(1)$. Thus, searching takes constant time on average. Since insertion takes $O(1)$ worst-case time (see Exercise 12.2-3), and deletion takes $O(1)$ worst-case time when the lists are doubly linked, all dictionary operations can be supported in $O(1)$ time on average.

Exercises

12.2-1
Suppose we use a random hash function h to hash n distinct keys into an array T of length m. What is the expected number of collisions? More precisely, what is the expected cardinality of $\{(x,y) : h(x) = h(y)\}$?

12.2-2

Demonstrate the insertion of the keys 5, 28, 19, 15, 20, 33, 12, 17, 10 into a hash table with collisions resolved by chaining. Let the table have 9 slots, and let the hash function be $h(k) = k \bmod 9$.

12.2-3

Argue that the expected time for a successful search with chaining is the same whether new elements are inserted at the front or at the end of a list. (*Hint:* Show that the expected successful search time is the same for *any* two orderings of any list.)

12.2-4

Professor Marley hypothesizes that substantial performance gains can be obtained if we modify the chaining scheme so that each list is kept in sorted order. How does the professor's modification affect the running time for successful searches, unsuccessful searches, insertions, and deletions?

12.2-5

Suggest how storage for elements can be allocated and deallocated within the hash table itself by linking all unused slots into a free list. Assume that one slot can store a flag and either one element plus a pointer or two pointers. All dictionary and free-list operations should run in $O(1)$ expected time. Does the free list need to be doubly linked, or does a singly linked free list suffice?

12.2-6

Show that if $|U| > nm$, there is a subset of U of size n consisting of keys that all hash to the same slot, so that the worst-case searching time for hashing with chaining is $\Theta(n)$.

12.3   Hash functions

In this section, we discuss some issues regarding the design of good hash functions and then present three schemes for their creation: hashing by division, hashing by multiplication, and universal hashing.

What makes a good hash function?

A good hash function satisfies (approximately) the assumption of simple uniform hashing: each key is equally likely to hash to any of the m slots. More formally, let us assume that each key is drawn independently from U according to a probability distribution P; that is, $P(k)$ is the probability that k is drawn. Then the assumption of simple uniform hashing is that

$$\sum_{k:h(k)=j} P(k) = \frac{1}{m} \qquad \text{for } j = 0, 1, \ldots, m - 1 \; . \qquad (12.1)$$

Unfortunately, it is generally not possible to check this condition, since P is usually unknown.

Sometimes (rarely) we do know the distribution P. For example, suppose the keys are known to be random real numbers k independently and uniformly distributed in the range $0 \le k < 1$. In this case, the hash function

$$h(k) = \lfloor km \rfloor$$

can be shown to satisfy equation (12.1).

In practice, heuristic techniques can be used to create a hash function that is likely to perform well. Qualitative information about P is sometimes useful in this design process. For example, consider a compiler's symbol table, in which the keys are arbitrary character strings representing identifiers in a program. It is common for closely related symbols, such as pt and pts, to occur in the same program. A good hash function would minimize the chance that such variants hash to the same slot.

A common approach is to derive the hash value in a way that is expected to be independent of any patterns that might exist in the data. For example, the "division method" (discussed further below) computes the hash value as the remainder when the key is divided by a specified prime number. Unless that prime is somehow related to patterns in the probability distribution P, this method gives good results.

Finally, we note that some applications of hash functions might require stronger properties than are provided by simple uniform hashing. For example, we might want keys that are "close" in some sense to yield hash values that are far apart. (This property is especially desirable when we are using linear probing, defined in Section 12.4.)

Interpreting keys as natural numbers

Most hash functions assume that the universe of keys is the set $\mathbf{N} = \{0, 1, 2, \ldots\}$ of natural numbers. Thus, if the keys are not natural numbers, a way must be found to interpret them as natural numbers. For example, a key that is a character string can be interpreted as an integer expressed in suitable radix notation. Thus, the identifier pt might be interpreted as the pair of decimal integers $(112, 116)$, since p $= 112$ and t $= 116$ in the ASCII character set; then, expressed as a radix-128 integer, pt becomes $(112 \cdot 128) + 116 = 14452$. It is usually straightforward in any given application to devise some such simple method for interpreting each key as a (possibly large) natural number. In what follows, we shall assume that the keys are natural numbers.

12.3.1   The division method

In the *division method* for creating hash functions, we map a key k into one of m slots by taking the remainder of k divided by m. That is, the hash function is

$$h(k) = k \bmod m \ .$$

For example, if the hash table has size $m = 12$ and the key is $k = 100$, then $h(k) = 4$. Since it requires only a single division operation, hashing by division is quite fast.

When using the division method, we usually avoid certain values of m. For example, m should not be a power of 2, since if $m = 2^p$, then $h(k)$ is just the p lowest-order bits of k. Unless it is known a priori that the probability distribution on keys makes all low-order p-bit patterns equally likely, it is better to make the hash function depend on all the bits of the key. Powers of 10 should be avoided if the application deals with decimal numbers as keys, since then the hash function does not depend on all the decimal digits of k. Finally, it can be shown that when $m = 2^p - 1$ and k is a character string interpreted in radix 2^p, two strings that are identical except for a transposition of two adjacent characters will hash to the same value.

Good values for m are primes not too close to exact powers of 2. For example, suppose we wish to allocate a hash table, with collisions resolved by chaining, to hold roughly $n = 2000$ character strings, where a character has 8 bits. We don't mind examining an average of 3 elements in an unsuccessful search, so we allocate a hash table of size $m = 701$. The number 701 is chosen because it is a prime near $\alpha = 2000/3$ but not near any power of 2. Treating each key k as an integer, our hash function would be

$$h(k) = k \bmod 701 \ .$$

As a precautionary measure, we could check how evenly this hash function distributes sets of keys among the slots, where the keys are chosen from "real" data.

12.3.2   The multiplication method

The *multiplication method* for creating hash functions operates in two steps. First, we multiply the key k by a constant A in the range $0 < A < 1$ and extract the fractional part of kA. Then, we multiply this value by m and take the floor of the result. In short, the hash function is

$$h(k) = \lfloor m (k A \bmod 1) \rfloor \ ,$$

where "$k A \bmod 1$" means the fractional part of kA, that is, $kA - \lfloor kA \rfloor$.

An advantage of the multiplication method is that the value of m is not critical. We typically choose it to be a power of 2—$m = 2^p$ for some

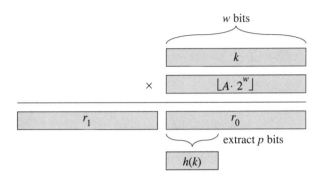

Figure 12.4 The multiplication method of hashing. The w-bit representation of the key k is multiplied by the w-bit value $\lfloor A \cdot 2^w \rfloor$, where $0 < A < 1$ is a suitable constant. The p highest-order bits of the lower w-bit half of the product form the desired hash value $h(k)$.

integer p—since we can then easily implement the function on most computers as follows. Suppose that the word size of the machine is w bits and that k fits into a single word. Referring to Figure 12.4, we first multiply k by the w-bit integer $\lfloor A \cdot 2^w \rfloor$. The result is a $2w$-bit value $r_1 2^w + r_0$, where r_1 is the high-order word of the product and r_0 is the low-order word of the product. The desired p-bit hash value consists of the p most significant bits of r_0.

Although this method works with any value of the constant A, it works better with some values than with others. The optimal choice depends on the characteristics of the data being hashed. Knuth [123] discusses the choice of A in some detail and suggests that

$$A \approx (\sqrt{5} - 1)/2 = 0.6180339887\ldots \tag{12.2}$$

is likely to work reasonably well.

As an example, if we have $k = 123456$, $m = 10000$, and A as in equation (12.2), then

$$
\begin{aligned}
h(k) &= \lfloor 10000 \cdot (123456 \cdot 0.61803\ldots \bmod 1) \rfloor \\
&= \lfloor 10000 \cdot (76300.0041151\ldots \bmod 1) \rfloor \\
&= \lfloor 10000 \cdot 0.0041151\ldots \rfloor \\
&= \lfloor 41.151\ldots \rfloor \\
&= 41 \ .
\end{aligned}
$$

12.3.3 Universal hashing

If a malicious adversary chooses the keys to be hashed, then he can choose n keys that all hash to the same slot, yielding an average retrieval time of $\Theta(n)$. Any fixed hash function is vulnerable to this sort of worst-case behavior; the only effective way to improve the situation is to choose the hash function *randomly* in a way that is *independent* of the keys that are actually going to be stored. This approach, called **universal hashing**, yields good performance on the average, no matter what keys are chosen by the adversary.

The main idea behind universal hashing is to select the hash function at random at run time from a carefully designed class of functions. As in the case of quicksort, randomization guarantees that no single input will always evoke worst-case behavior. Because of the randomization, the algorithm can behave differently on each execution, even for the same input. This approach guarantees good average-case performance, no matter what keys are provided as input. Returning to the example of a compiler's symbol table, we find that the programmer's choice of identifiers cannot now cause consistently poor hashing performance. Poor performance occurs only if the compiler chooses a random hash function that causes the set of identifiers to hash poorly, but the probability of this occurring is small and is the same for any set of identifiers of the same size.

Let $\mathcal{H}$ be a finite collection of hash functions that map a given universe U of keys into the range $\{0, 1, \ldots, m - 1\}$. Such a collection is said to be **universal** if for each pair of distinct keys $x, y \in U$, the number of hash functions $h \in \mathcal{H}$ for which $h(x) = h(y)$ is precisely $|\mathcal{H}| / m$. In other words, with a hash function randomly chosen from $\mathcal{H}$, the chance of a collision between x and y when $x \neq y$ is exactly $1/m$, which is exactly the chance of a collision if $h(x)$ and $h(y)$ are randomly chosen from the set $\{0, 1, \ldots, m - 1\}$.

The following theorem shows that a universal class of hash functions gives good average-case behavior.

Theorem 12.3

If h is chosen from a universal collection of hash functions and is used to hash n keys into a table of size m, where $n \leq m$, the expected number of collisions involving a particular key x is less than 1.

Proof For each pair y, z of distinct keys, let c_{yz} be a random variable that is 1 if $h(y) = h(z)$ (i.e., if y and z collide using h) and 0 otherwise. Since, by definition, a single pair of keys collides with probability $1/m$, we have

$$E[c_{yz}] = 1/m \; .$$

Let C_x be the total number of collisions involving key x in a hash table T of size m containing n keys. Equation (6.24) gives

$$
\begin{aligned}
E[C_x] &= \sum_{\substack{y \in T \\ y \neq x}} E[c_{xy}] \\
&= \frac{n-1}{m} \; .
\end{aligned}
$$

Since $n \leq m$, we have $\mathrm{E}[C_x] < 1$.   ■

But how easy is it to design a universal class of hash functions? It is quite easy, as a little number theory will help us prove. Let us choose our table size m to be prime (as in the division method). We decompose a key x into $r+1$ bytes (i.e., characters, or fixed-width binary substrings), so that $x = \langle x_0, x_1, \ldots, x_r \rangle$; the only requirement is that the maximum value of a byte should be less than m. Let $a = \langle a_0, a_1, \ldots, a_r \rangle$ denote a sequence of $r + 1$ elements chosen randomly from the set $\{0, 1, \ldots, m - 1\}$. We define a corresponding hash function $h_a \in \mathcal{H}$:

$$h_a(x) = \sum_{i=0}^{r} a_i x_i \bmod m \ . \tag{12.3}$$

With this definition,

$$\mathcal{H} = \bigcup_a \{h_a\} \tag{12.4}$$

has m^{r+1} members.

Theorem 12.4
The class $\mathcal{H}$ defined by equations (12.3) and (12.4) is a universal class of hash functions.

Proof   Consider any pair of distinct keys x, y. Assume that $x_0 \neq y_0$. (A similar argument can be made for a difference in any other byte position.) For any fixed values of $a_1, a_2, \ldots, a_r$, there is exactly one value of a_0 that satisfies the equation $h(x) = h(y)$; this a_0 is the solution to

$$a_0(x_0 - y_0) \equiv -\sum_{i=1}^{r} a_i(x_i - y_i) \pmod{m} \ .$$

To see this property, note that since m is prime, the nonzero quantity $x_0 - y_0$ has a multiplicative inverse modulo m, and thus there is a unique solution for a_0 modulo m. (See Section 33.4.) Therefore, each pair of keys x and y collides for exactly m^r values of a, since they collide exactly once for each possible value of $\langle a_1, a_2, \ldots, a_r \rangle$ (i.e., for the unique value of a_0 noted above). Since there are m^{r+1} possible values for the sequence a, keys x and y collide with probability exactly $m^r / m^{r+1} = 1/m$. Therefore, $\mathcal{H}$ is universal.   ■

Exercises

12.3-1
Suppose we wish to search a linked list of length n, where each element contains a key k along with a hash value $h(k)$. Each key is a long character

string. How might we take advantage of the hash values when searching the list for an element with a given key?

12.3-2

Suppose a string of r characters is hashed into m slots by treating it as a radix-128 number and then using the division method. The number m is easily represented as a 32-bit computer word, but the string of r characters, treated as a radix-128 number, takes many words. How can we apply the division method to compute the hash value of the character string without using more than a constant number of words of storage outside the string itself?

12.3-3

Consider a version of the division method in which $h(k) = k \bmod m$, where $m = 2^p - 1$ and k is a character string interpreted in radix 2^p. Show that if string x can be derived from string y by permuting its characters, then x and y hash to the same value. Give an example of an application in which this property would be undesirable in a hash function.

12.3-4

Consider a hash table of size $m = 1000$ and the hash function $h(k) = \lfloor m(k A \bmod 1) \rfloor$ for $A = (\sqrt{5} - 1)/2$. Compute the locations to which the keys 61, 62, 63, 64, and 65 are mapped.

12.3-5

Show that if we restrict each component a_i of a in equation (12.3) to be nonzero, then the set $\mathcal{H} = \{h_a\}$ as defined in equation (12.4) is not universal. (*Hint:* Consider the keys $x = 0$ and $y = 1$.)

12.4   Open addressing

In **open addressing**, all elements are stored in the hash table itself. That is, each table entry contains either an element of the dynamic set or NIL. When searching for an element, we systematically examine table slots until the desired element is found or it is clear that the element is not in the table. There are no lists and no elements stored outside the table, as there are in chaining. Thus, in open addressing, the hash table can "fill up" so that no further insertions can be made; the load factor α can never exceed 1.

Of course, we could store the linked lists for chaining inside the hash table, in the otherwise unused hash-table slots (see Exercise 12.2-5), but the advantage of open addressing is that it avoids pointers altogether. Instead of following pointers, we *compute* the sequence of slots to be examined. The extra memory freed by not storing pointers provides the hash table with a larger number of slots for the same amount of memory, potentially yielding fewer collisions and faster retrieval.

To perform insertion using open addressing, we successively examine, or **probe**, the hash table until we find an empty slot in which to put the key. Instead of being fixed in the order $0, 1, \ldots, m-1$ (which requires $\Theta(n)$ search time), the sequence of positions probed *depends upon the key being inserted*. To determine which slots to probe, we extend the hash function to include the probe number (starting from 0) as a second input. Thus, the hash function becomes

$$h : U \times \{0, 1, \ldots, m - 1\} \rightarrow \{0, 1, \ldots, m - 1\} \ .$$

With open addressing, we require that for every key k, the **probe sequence**

$$\langle h(k, 0), h(k, 1), \ldots, h(k, m - 1) \rangle$$

be a permutation of $\langle 0, 1, \ldots, m - 1 \rangle$, so that every hash-table position is eventually considered as a slot for a new key as the table fills up. In the following pseudocode, we assume that the elements in the hash table T are keys with no satellite information; the key k is identical to the element containing key k. Each slot contains either a key or NIL (if the slot is empty).

HASH-INSERT(T, k)

```
1  i ← 0
2  repeat j ← h(k, i)
3          if T[j] = NIL
4              then T[j] ← k
5                   return j
6              else i ← i + 1
7      until i = m
8  error "hash table overflow"
```

The algorithm for searching for key k probes the same sequence of slots that the insertion algorithm examined when key k was inserted. Therefore, the search can terminate (unsuccessfully) when it finds an empty slot, since k would have been inserted there and not later in its probe sequence. (Note that this argument assumes that keys are not deleted from the hash table.) The procedure HASH-SEARCH takes as input a hash table T and a key k, returning j if slot j is found to contain key k, or NIL if key k is not present in table T.

HASH-SEARCH(T, k)

```
1  i ← 0
2  repeat j ← h(k, i)
3          if T[j] = k
4              then return j
5          i ← i + 1
6  until  T[j] = NIL or i = m
7  return NIL
```

Deletion from an open-address hash table is difficult. When we delete a key from slot i, we cannot simply mark that slot as empty by storing NIL in it. Doing so might make it impossible to retrieve any key k during whose insertion we had probed slot i and found it occupied. One solution is to mark the slot by storing in it the special value DELETED instead of NIL. We would then modify the procedure HASH-SEARCH so that it keeps on looking when it sees the value DELETED, while HASH-INSERT would treat such a slot as if it were empty so that a new key can be inserted. When we do this, though, the search times are no longer dependent on the load factor α, and for this reason chaining is more commonly selected as a collision resolution technique when keys must be deleted.

In our analysis, we make the assumption of *uniform hashing*: we assume that each key considered is equally likely to have any of the $m!$ permutations of $\{0, 1, \ldots, m - 1\}$ as its probe sequence. Uniform hashing generalizes the notion of simple uniform hashing defined earlier to the situation in which the hash function produces not just a single number, but a whole probe sequence. True uniform hashing is difficult to implement, however, and in practice suitable approximations (such as double hashing, defined below) are used.

Three techniques are commonly used to compute the probe sequences required for open addressing: linear probing, quadratic probing, and double hashing. These techniques all guarantee that $\langle h(k, 1), h(k, 2), \ldots, h(k, m)\rangle$ is a permutation of $\langle 0, 1, \ldots, m - 1 \rangle$ for each key k. None of these techniques fulfills the assumption of uniform hashing, however, since none of them is capable of generating more than m^2 different probe sequences (instead of the $m!$ that uniform hashing requires). Double hashing has the greatest number of probe sequences and, as one might expect, seems to give the best results.

Linear probing

Given an ordinary hash function $h' : U \rightarrow \{0, 1, \ldots, m - 1\}$, the method of *linear probing* uses the hash function

$$h(k, i) = (h'(k) + i) \bmod m$$

for $i = 0, 1, \ldots, m - 1$. Given key k, the first slot probed is $T[h'(k)]$. We next probe slot $T[h'(k) + 1]$, and so on up to slot $T[m - 1]$. Then we wrap around to slots $T[0], T[1], \ldots$, until we finally probe slot $T[h'(k) - 1]$. Since the initial probe position determines the entire probe sequence, only m distinct probe sequences are used with linear probing.

Linear probing is easy to implement, but it suffers from a problem known as **primary clustering**. Long runs of occupied slots build up, increasing the average search time. For example, if we have $n = m/2$ keys in the table, where every even-indexed slot is occupied and every odd-indexed slot is empty, then the average unsuccessful search takes 1.5 probes. If the first $n = m/2$ locations are the ones occupied, however, the average number of probes increases to about $n/4 = m/8$. Clusters are likely to arise, since if an empty slot is preceded by i full slots, then the probability that the empty slot is the next one filled is $(i + 1)/m$, compared with a probability of $1/m$ if the preceding slot was empty. Thus, runs of occupied slots tend to get longer, and linear probing is not a very good approximation to uniform hashing.

Quadratic probing

Quadratic probing uses a hash function of the form

$$h(k, i) = (h'(k) + c_1 i + c_2 i^2) \bmod m , \qquad (12.5)$$

where (as in linear probing) h' is an auxiliary hash function, c_1 and $c_2 \neq 0$ are auxiliary constants, and $i = 0, 1, \ldots, m - 1$. The initial position probed is $T[h'(k)]$; later positions probed are offset by amounts that depend in a quadratic manner on the probe number i. This method works much better than linear probing, but to make full use of the hash table, the values of c_1, c_2, and m are constrained. Problem 12-4 shows one way to select these parameters. Also, if two keys have the same initial probe position, then their probe sequences are the same, since $h(k_1, 0) = h(k_2, 0)$ implies $h(k_1, i) = h(k_2, i)$. This leads to a milder form of clustering, called **secondary clustering**. As in linear probing, the initial probe determines the entire sequence, so only m distinct probe sequences are used.

Double hashing

Double hashing is one of the best methods available for open addressing because the permutations produced have many of the characteristics of randomly chosen permutations. **Double hashing** uses a hash function of the form

$$h(k, i) = (h_1(k) + i h_2(k)) \bmod m ,$$

where h_1 and h_2 are auxiliary hash functions. The initial position probed is $T[h_1(k)]$; successive probe positions are offset from previous positions by

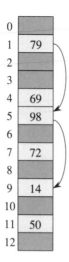

Figure 12.5 Insertion by double hashing. Here we have a hash table of size 13 with $h_1(k) = k \bmod 13$ and $h_2(k) = 1 + (k \bmod 11)$. Since $14 \equiv 1 \bmod 13$ and $14 \equiv 3 \bmod 11$, the key 14 will be inserted into empty slot 9, after slots 1 and 5 have been examined and found to be already occupied.

the amount $h_2(k)$, modulo m. Thus, unlike the case of linear or quadratic probing, the probe sequence here depends in two ways upon the key k, since the initial probe position, the offset, or both, may vary. Figure 12.5 gives an example of insertion by double hashing.

The value $h_2(k)$ must be relatively prime to the hash-table size m for the entire hash table to be searched. Otherwise, if m and $h_2(k)$ have greatest common divisor $d > 1$ for some key k, then a search for key k would examine only $(1/d)$th of the hash table. (See Chapter 33.) A convenient way to ensure this condition is to let m be a power of 2 and to design h_2 so that it always produces an odd number. Another way is to let m be prime and to design h_2 so that it always returns a positive integer less than m. For example, we could choose m prime and let

$$
\begin{aligned}
h_1(k) &= k \bmod m , \\
h_2(k) &= 1 + (k \bmod m') ,
\end{aligned}
$$

where m' is chosen to be slightly less than m (say, $m - 1$ or $m - 2$). For example, if $k = 123456$ and $m = 701$, we have $h_1(k) = 80$ and $h_2(k) = 257$, so the first probe is to position 80, and then every 257th slot (modulo m) is examined until the key is found or every slot is examined.

Double hashing represents an improvement over linear or quadratic probing in that $\Theta(m^2)$ probe sequences are used, rather than $\Theta(m)$, since each possible $(h_1(k), h_2(k))$ pair yields a distinct probe sequence, and as we vary the key, the initial probe position $h_1(k)$ and the offset $h_2(k)$ may vary independently. As a result, the performance of double hashing appears to be very close to the performance of the "ideal" scheme of uniform hashing.

Analysis of open-address hashing

Our analysis of open addressing, like our analysis of chaining, is expressed in terms of the load factor α of the hash table, as n and m go to infinity. Recall that if n elements are stored in a table with m slots, the average number of elements per slot is $\alpha = n/m$. Of course, with open addressing, we have at most one element per slot, and thus $n \leq m$, which implies $\alpha \leq 1$.

We assume that uniform hashing is used. In this idealized scheme, the probe sequence $\langle h(k,0), h(k,1), \ldots, h(k, m-1) \rangle$ for each key k is equally likely to be any permutation on $\langle 0, 1, \ldots, m-1 \rangle$. That is, each possible probe sequence is equally likely to be used as the probe sequence for an insertion or a search. Of course, a given key has a unique fixed probe sequence associated with it; what is meant here is that, considering the probability distribution on the space of keys and the operation of the hash function on the keys, each possible probe sequence is equally likely.

We now analyze the expected number of probes for hashing with open addressing under the assumption of uniform hashing, beginning with an analysis of the number of probes made in an unsuccessful search.

Theorem 12.5
Given an open-address hash table with load factor $\alpha = n/m < 1$, the expected number of probes in an unsuccessful search is at most $1/(1 - \alpha)$, assuming uniform hashing.

Proof In an unsuccessful search, every probe but the last accesses an occupied slot that does not contain the desired key, and the last slot probed is empty. Let us define

$p_i = \text{Pr}\{\text{exactly } i \text{ probes access occupied slots}\}$

for $i = 0, 1, 2, \ldots$ For $i > n$, we have $p_i = 0$, since we can find at most n slots already occupied. Thus, the expected number of probes is

$$1 + \sum_{i=0}^{\infty} i \, p_i . \tag{12.6}$$

To evaluate equation (12.6), we define

$q_i = \text{Pr}\{\text{at least } i \text{ probes access occupied slots}\}$

for $i = 0, 1, 2, \ldots$ We can then use identity (6.28):

$$\sum_{i=0}^{\infty} i \, p_i = \sum_{i=1}^{\infty} q_i .$$

What is the value of q_i for $i \geq 1$? The probability that the first probe accesses an occupied slot is n/m; thus,

$$q_1 = \frac{n}{m} \; .$$

With uniform hashing, a second probe, if necessary, is to one of the remaining $m - 1$ unprobed slots, $n - 1$ of which are occupied. We make a second probe only if the first probe accesses an occupied slot; thus,

$$q_2 = \left(\frac{n}{m}\right) \left(\frac{n-1}{m-1}\right) \; .$$

In general, the ith probe is made only if the first $i - 1$ probes access occupied slots, and the slot probed is equally likely to be any of the remaining $m - i + 1$ slots, $n - i + 1$ of which are occupied. Thus,

$$
\begin{aligned}
q_i &= \left(\frac{n}{m}\right) \left(\frac{n-1}{m-1}\right) \cdots \left(\frac{n-i+1}{m-i+1}\right) \\
&\leq \left(\frac{n}{m}\right)^i \\
&= \alpha^i
\end{aligned}
$$

for $i = 1, 2, \ldots, n$, since $(n - j)/(m - j) \leq n/m$ if $n \leq m$ and $j \geq 0$. After n probes, all n occupied slots have been seen and will not be probed again, and thus $q_i = 0$ for $i > n$.

We are now ready to evaluate equation (12.6). Given the assumption that $\alpha < 1$, the average number of probes in an unsuccessful search is

$$
\begin{aligned}
1 + \sum_{i=0}^{\infty} i \, p_i &= 1 + \sum_{i=1}^{\infty} q_i \\
&\leq 1 + \alpha + \alpha^2 + \alpha^3 + \cdots \\
&= \frac{1}{1 - \alpha} \; .
\end{aligned}
\tag{12.7}
$$

Equation (12.7) has an intuitive interpretation: one probe is always made, with probability approximately α a second probe is needed, with probability approximately α^2 a third probe is needed, and so on.   ∎

If α is a constant, Theorem 12.5 predicts that an unsuccessful search runs in $O(1)$ time. For example, if the hash table is half full, the average number of probes in an unsuccessful search is $1/(1 - .5) = 2$. If it is 90 percent full, the average number of probes is $1/(1 - .9) = 10$.

Theorem 12.5 gives us the performance of the HASH-INSERT procedure almost immediately.

Corollary 12.6
Inserting an element into an open-address hash table with load factor α requires at most $1/(1 - \alpha)$ probes on average, assuming uniform hashing.

Proof An element is inserted only if there is room in the table, and thus $\alpha < 1$. Inserting a key requires an unsuccessful search followed by placement of the key in the first empty slot found. Thus, the expected number of probes is $1/(1 - \alpha)$. ∎

Computing the expected number of probes for a successful search requires a little more work.

Theorem 12.7
Given an open-address hash table with load factor $\alpha < 1$, the expected number of probes in a successful search is at most

$$\frac{1}{\alpha} \ln \frac{1}{1 - \alpha} + \frac{1}{\alpha},$$

assuming uniform hashing and assuming that each key in the table is equally likely to be searched for.

Proof A search for a key k follows the same probe sequence as was followed when the element with key k was inserted. By Corollary 12.6, if k was the $(i + 1)$st key inserted into the hash table, the expected number of probes made in a search for k is at most $1/(1 - i/m) = m/(m - i)$. Averaging over all n keys in the hash table gives us the average number of probes in a successful search:

$$\frac{1}{n} \sum_{i=0}^{n-1} \frac{m}{m - i} = \frac{m}{n} \sum_{i=0}^{n-1} \frac{1}{m - i}$$

$$= \frac{1}{\alpha} (H_m - H_{m-n}),$$

where $H_i = \sum_{j=1}^{i} 1/j$ is the ith harmonic number (as defined in equation (3.5)). Using the bounds $\ln i \leq H_i \leq \ln i + 1$ from equations (3.11) and (3.12), we obtain

$$\frac{1}{\alpha}(H_m - H_{m-n}) \leq \frac{1}{\alpha}(\ln m + 1 - \ln(m - n))$$

$$= \frac{1}{\alpha} \ln \frac{m}{m - n} + \frac{1}{\alpha}$$

$$= \frac{1}{\alpha} \ln \frac{1}{1 - \alpha} + \frac{1}{\alpha}$$

for a bound on the expected number of probes in a successful search. ∎

If the hash table is half full, the expected number of probes is less than 3.387. If the hash table is 90 percent full, the expected number of probes is less than 3.670.

Exercises

12.4-1
Consider inserting the keys $10, 22, 31, 4, 15, 28, 17, 88, 59$ into a hash table of length $m = 11$ using open addressing with the primary hash function $h'(k) = k \bmod m$. Illustrate the result of inserting these keys using linear probing, using quadratic probing with $c_1 = 1$ and $c_2 = 3$, and using double hashing with $h_2(k) = 1 + (k \bmod (m-1))$.

12.4-2
Write pseudocode for HASH-DELETE as outlined in the text, and modify HASH-INSERT and HASH-SEARCH to incorporate the special value DELETED.

12.4-3 ⋆
Suppose that we use double hashing to resolve collisions; that is, we use the hash function $h(k, i) = (h_1(k) + ih_2(k)) \bmod m$. Show that the probe sequence $\langle h(k, 0), h(k, 1), \ldots, h(k, m-1) \rangle$ is a permutation of the slot sequence $\langle 0, 1, \ldots, m-1 \rangle$ if and only if $h_2(k)$ is relatively prime to m. (*Hint:* See Chapter 33.)

12.4-4
Consider an open-address hash table with uniform hashing and a load factor $\alpha = 1/2$. What is the expected number of probes in an unsuccessful search? What is the expected number of probes in a successful search? Repeat these calculations for the load factors $3/4$ and $7/8$.

12.4-5 ⋆
Suppose that we insert n keys into a hash table of size m using open addressing and uniform hashing. Let $p(n, m)$ be the probability that no collisions occur. Show that $p(n, m) \le e^{-n(n-1)/2m}$. (*Hint:* See equation (2.7).) Argue that when n exceeds $\sqrt{m}$, the probability of avoiding collisions goes rapidly to zero.

12.4-6 ⋆
The bound on the harmonic series can be improved to

$$H_n = \ln n + \gamma + \frac{\epsilon}{2n} , \qquad (12.8)$$

where $\gamma = 0.5772156649\ldots$ is known as ***Euler's constant*** and ϵ satisfies $0 < \epsilon < 1$. (See Knuth [121] for a derivation.) How does this improved approximation for the harmonic series affect the statement and proof of Theorem 12.7?

12.4-7 ⋆
Consider an open-address hash table with a load factor α. Find the nonzero value α for which the expected number of probes in an unsuccessful search equals twice the expected number of probes in a successful search. Use

the estimate $(1/\alpha)\ln(1/(1-\alpha))$ for the number of probes required for a successful search.

Problems

12-1 Longest-probe bound for hashing

A hash table of size m is used to store n items, with $n \le m/2$. Open addressing is used for collision resolution.

a. Assuming uniform hashing, show that for $i = 1, 2, \ldots, n$, the probability that the ith insertion requires strictly more than k probes is at most 2^{-k}.

b. Show that for $i = 1, 2, \ldots, n$, the probability that the ith insertion requires more than $2\lg n$ probes is at most $1/n^2$.

Let the random variable X_i denote the number of probes required by the ith insertion. You have shown in part (b) that $\Pr\{X_i > 2\lg n\} \le 1/n^2$. Let the random variable $X = \max_{1 \le i \le n} X_i$ denote the maximum number of probes required by any of the n insertions.

c. Show that $\Pr\{X > 2\lg n\} \le 1/n$.

d. Show that the expected length of the longest probe sequence is $\mathrm{E}[X] = O(\lg n)$.

12-2 Searching a static set

You are asked to implement a dynamic set of n elements in which the keys are numbers. The set is static (no INSERT or DELETE operations), and the only operation required is SEARCH. You are given an arbitrary amount of time to preprocess the n elements so that SEARCH operations run quickly.

a. Show that SEARCH can be implemented in $O(\lg n)$ worst-case time using no extra storage beyond what is needed to store the elements of the set themselves.

b. Consider implementing the set by open-address hashing on m slots, and assume uniform hashing. What is the minimum amount of extra storage $m - n$ required to make the average performance of an unsuccessful SEARCH operation be at least as good as the bound in part (a)? Your answer should be an asymptotic bound on $m - n$ in terms of n.

12-3 Slot-size bound for chaining

Suppose that we have a hash table with n slots, with collisions resolved by chaining, and suppose that n keys are inserted into the table. Each key is equally likely to be hashed to each slot. Let M be the maximum number of keys in any slot after all the keys have been inserted. Your mission is to prove an $O(\lg n / \lg\lg n)$ upper bound on $\mathrm{E}[M]$, the expected value of M.

a. Argue that the probability Q_k that k keys hash to a particular slot is given by

$$Q_k = \left(\frac{1}{n}\right)^k \left(1 - \frac{1}{n}\right)^{n-k} \binom{n}{k}.$$

b. Let P_k be the probability that $M = k$, that is, the probability that the slot containing the most keys contains k keys. Show that $P_k \leq nQ_k$.

c. Use Stirling's approximation, equation (2.11), to show that $Q_k < e^k/k^k$.

d. Show that there exists a constant $c > 1$ such that $Q_{k_0} < 1/n^3$ for $k_0 = c \lg n / \lg \lg n$. Conclude that $P_{k_0} < 1/n^2$ for $k_0 = c \lg n / \lg \lg n$.

e. Argue that

$$\mathrm{E}\,[M] \leq \Pr\left\{M > \frac{c \lg n}{\lg \lg n}\right\} \cdot n + \Pr\left\{M \leq \frac{c \lg n}{\lg \lg n}\right\} \cdot \frac{c \lg n}{\lg \lg n}.$$

Conclude that $\mathrm{E}\,[M] = O(\lg n / \lg \lg n)$.

12-4   *Quadratic probing*

Suppose that we are given a key k to search for in a hash table with positions $0, 1, \ldots, m - 1$, and suppose that we have a hash function h mapping the key space into the set $\{0, 1, \ldots, m - 1\}$. The search scheme is as follows.

1. Compute the value $i \leftarrow h(k)$, and set $j \leftarrow 0$.

2. Probe in position i for the desired key k. If you find it, or if this position is empty, terminate the search.

3. Set $j \leftarrow (j + 1) \bmod m$ and $i \leftarrow (i + j) \bmod m$, and return to step 2.

Assume that m is a power of 2.

a. Show that this scheme is an instance of the general "quadratic probing" scheme by exhibiting the appropriate constants c_1 and c_2 for equation (12.5).

b. Prove that this algorithm examines every table position in the worst case.

12-5   *k-universal hashing*

Let $\mathcal{H} = \{h\}$ be a class of hash functions in which each h maps the universe U of keys to $\{0, 1, \ldots, m - 1\}$. We say that $\mathcal{H}$ is ***k-universal*** if, for every fixed sequence of k distinct keys $\langle x_1, x_2, \ldots, x_k \rangle$ and for any h chosen at random from $\mathcal{H}$, the sequence $\langle h(x_1), h(x_2), \ldots, h(x_k) \rangle$ is equally likely to be any of the m^k sequences of length k with elements drawn from $\{0, 1, \ldots, m - 1\}$.

a. Show that if $\mathcal{H}$ is 2-universal, then it is universal.

b. Show that the class $\mathcal{H}$ defined in Section 12.3.3 is not 2-universal.

    c. Show that if we modify the definition of $\mathcal{H}$ in Section 12.3.3 so that each
    function also contains a constant term b, that is, if we replace $h(x)$ with

$$h_{a,b}(x) = a \cdot x + b \, ,$$

    then $\mathcal{H}$ is 2-universal.

Chapter notes

Knuth [123] and Gonnet [90] are excellent references for the analysis of
hashing algorithms. Knuth credits H. P. Luhn (1953) for inventing hash
tables, along with the chaining method for resolving collisions. At about
the same time, G. M. Amdahl originated the idea of open addressing.

13 Binary Search Trees

Search trees are data structures that support many dynamic-set operations, including SEARCH, MINIMUM, MAXIMUM, PREDECESSOR, SUCCESSOR, INSERT, and DELETE. Thus, a search tree can be used both as a dictionary and as a priority queue.

Basic operations on a binary search tree take time proportional to the height of the tree. For a complete binary tree with n nodes, such operations run in $\Theta(\lg n)$ worst-case time. If the tree is a linear chain of n nodes, however, the same operations take $\Theta(n)$ worst-case time. We shall see in Section 13.4 that the height of a randomly built binary search tree is $O(\lg n)$, so that basic dynamic-set operations take $\Theta(\lg n)$ time.

In practice, we can't always guarantee that binary search trees are built randomly, but there are variations of binary search trees whose worst-case performance on basic operations can be guaranteed to be good. Chapter 14 presents one such variation, red-black trees, which have height $O(\lg n)$. Chapter 19 introduces B-trees, which are particularly good for maintaining data bases on random-access, secondary (disk) storage.

After presenting the basic properties of binary search trees, the following sections show how to walk a binary search tree to print its values in sorted order, how to search for a value in a binary search tree, how to find the minimum or maximum element, how to find the predecessor or successor of an element, and how to insert into or delete from a binary search tree. The basic mathematical properties of trees were introduced in Chapter 5.

13.1 What is a binary search tree?

A binary search tree is organized, as the name suggests, in a binary tree, as shown in Figure 13.1. Such a tree can be represented by a linked data structure in which each node is an object. In addition to a *key* field, each node contains fields *left*, *right*, and *p* that point to the nodes corresponding to its left child, its right child, and its parent, respectively. If a child or the parent is missing, the appropriate field contains the value NIL. The root node is the only node in the tree whose parent field is NIL.

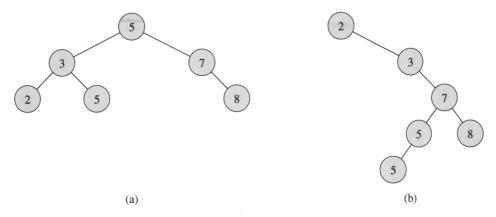

Figure 13.1 Binary search trees. For any node x, the keys in the left subtree of x are at most $key[x]$, and the keys in the right subtree of x are at least $key[x]$. Different binary search trees can represent the same set of values. The worst-case running time for most search-tree operations is proportional to the height of the tree. **(a)** A binary search tree on 6 nodes with height 2. **(b)** A less efficient binary search tree with height 4 that contains the same keys.

The keys in a binary search tree are always stored in such a way as to satisfy the ***binary-search-tree property***:

> Let x be a node in a binary search tree. If y is a node in the left subtree of x, then $key[y] \le key[x]$. If y is a node in the right subtree of x, then $key[x] \le key[y]$.

Thus, in Figure 13.1(a), the key of the root is 5, the keys 2, 3, and 5 in its left subtree are no larger than 5, and the keys 7 and 8 in its right subtree are no smaller than 5. The same property holds for every node in the tree. For example, the key 3 in Figure 13.1(a) is no smaller than the key 2 in its left subtree and no larger than the key 5 in its right subtree.

The binary-search-tree property allows us to print out all the keys in a binary search tree in sorted order by a simple recursive algorithm, called an ***inorder tree walk***. This algorithm derives its name from the fact that the key of the root of a subtree is printed between the values in its left subtree and those in its right subtree. (Similarly, a ***preorder tree walk*** prints the root before the values in either subtree, and a ***postorder tree walk*** prints the root after the values in its subtrees.) To use the following procedure to print all the elements in a binary search tree T, we call INORDER-TREE-WALK($root[T]$).

INORDER-TREE-WALK(x)

1 **if** $x \ne$ NIL
2   **then** INORDER-TREE-WALK($left[x]$)
3   print $key[x]$
4   INORDER-TREE-WALK($right[x]$)

As an example, the inorder tree walk prints the keys in each of the two binary search trees from Figure 13.1 in the order $2, 3, 5, 5, 7, 8$. The correctness of the algorithm follows by induction directly from the binary-search-tree property. It takes $\Theta(n)$ time to walk an n-node binary search tree, since after the initial call, the procedure is called recursively exactly twice for each node in the tree—once for its left child and once for its right child.

Exercises

13.1-1
Draw binary search trees of height $2, 3, 4, 5$, and 6 on the set of keys $\{1, 4, 5, 10, 16, 17, 21\}$.

13.1-2
What is the difference between the binary-search-tree property and the heap property (7.1)? Can the heap property be used to print out the keys of an n-node tree in sorted order in $O(n)$ time? Explain how or why not.

13.1-3
Give a nonrecursive algorithm that performs an inorder tree walk. (*Hint:* There is an easy solution that uses a stack as an auxiliary data structure and a more complicated but elegant solution that uses no stack but assumes that two pointers can be tested for equality.)

13.1-4
Give recursive algorithms that perform preorder and postorder tree walks in $\Theta(n)$ time on a tree of n nodes.

13.1-5
Argue that since sorting n elements takes $\Omega(n \lg n)$ time in the worst case in the comparison model, any comparison-based algorithm for constructing a binary search tree from an arbitrary list of n elements takes $\Omega(n \lg n)$ time in the worst case.

13.2   Querying a binary search tree

The most common operation performed on a binary search tree is searching for a key stored in the tree. Besides the SEARCH operation, binary search trees can support such queries as MINIMUM, MAXIMUM, SUCCESSOR, and PREDECESSOR. In this section, we shall examine these operations and show that each can be supported in time $O(h)$ on a binary search tree of height h.

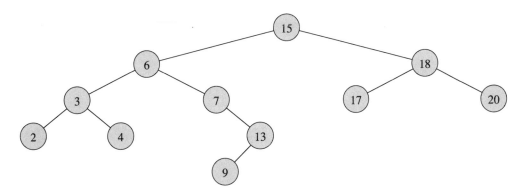

Figure 13.2 Queries on a binary search tree. To search for the key 13 in the tree, the path $15 \rightarrow 6 \rightarrow 7 \rightarrow 13$ is followed from the root. The minimum key in the tree is 2, which can be found by following *left* pointers from the root. The maximum key 20 is found by following *right* pointers from the root. The successor of the node with key 15 is the node with key 17, since it is the minimum key in the right subtree of 15. The node with key 13 has no right subtree, and thus its successor is its lowest ancestor whose left child is also an ancestor. In this case, the node with key 15 is its successor.

Searching

We use the following procedure to search for a node with a given key in a binary search tree. Given a pointer to the root of the tree and a key k, TREE-SEARCH returns a pointer to a node with key k if one exists; otherwise, it returns NIL.

TREE-SEARCH(x, k)

```
1   if x = NIL or k = key[x]
2       then return x
3   if k < key[x]
4       then return TREE-SEARCH(left[x], k)
5       else return TREE-SEARCH(right[x], k)
```

The procedure begins its search at the root and traces a path downward in the tree, as shown in Figure 13.2. For each node x it encounters, it compares the key k with $key[x]$. If the two keys are equal, the search terminates. If k is smaller than $key[x]$, the search continues in the left subtree of x, since the binary-search-tree property implies that k could not be stored in the right subtree. Symmetrically, if k is larger than $key[k]$, the search continues in the right subtree. The nodes encountered during the recursion form a path downward from the root of the tree, and thus the running time of TREE-SEARCH is $O(h)$, where h is the height of the tree.

The same procedure can be written iteratively by "unrolling" the recursion into a **while** loop. On most computers, this version is more efficient.

ITERATIVE-TREE-SEARCH(x, k)

```
1  while x ≠ NIL and k ≠ key[x]
2      do if k < key[x]
3            then x ← left[x]
4            else x ← right[x]
5  return x
```

Minimum and maximum

An element in a binary search tree whose key is a minimum can always be found by following *left* child pointers from the root until a NIL is encountered, as shown in Figure 13.2. The following procedure returns a pointer to the minimum element in the subtree rooted at a given node x.

TREE-MINIMUM(x)

```
1  while left[x] ≠ NIL
2      do x ← left[x]
3  return x
```

The binary-search-tree property guarantees that TREE-MINIMUM is correct. If a node x has no left subtree, then since every key in the right subtree of x is at least as large as $key[x]$, the minimum key in the subtree rooted at x is $key[x]$. If node x has a left subtree, then since no key in the right subtree is smaller than $key[x]$ and every key in the left subtree is not larger than $key[x]$, the minimum key in the subtree rooted at x can be found in the subtree rooted at $left[x]$.

The pseudocode for TREE-MAXIMUM is symmetric.

TREE-MAXIMUM(x)

```
1  while right[x] ≠ NIL
2      do x ← right[x]
3  return x
```

Both of these procedures run in $O(h)$ time on a tree of height h, since they trace paths downward in the tree.

Successor and predecessor

Given a node in a binary search tree, it is sometimes important to be able to find its successor in the sorted order determined by an inorder tree walk. If all keys are distinct, the successor of a node x is the node with the smallest key greater than $key[x]$. The structure of a binary search tree allows us to determine the successor of a node without ever comparing keys. The following procedure returns the successor of a node x in a binary search tree if it exists, and NIL if x has the largest key in the tree.

TREE-SUCCESSOR(x)

```
1  if right[x] ≠ NIL
2     then return TREE-MINIMUM(right[x])
3  y ← p[x]
4  while y ≠ NIL and x = right[y]
5     do x ← y
6        y ← p[y]
7  return y
```

The code for TREE-SUCCESSOR is broken into two cases. If the right subtree of node x is nonempty, then the successor of x is just the leftmost node in the right subtree, which is found in line 2 by calling TREE-MINIMUM($right[x]$). For example, the successor of the node with key 15 in Figure 13.2 is the node with key 17.

On the other hand, if the right subtree of node x is empty and x has a successor y, then y is the lowest ancestor of x whose left child is also an ancestor of x. In Figure 13.2, the successor of the node with key 13 is the node with key 15. To find y, we simply go up the tree from x until we encounter a node that is the left child of its parent; this is accomplished by lines 3–7 of TREE-SUCCESSOR.

The running time of TREE-SUCCESSOR on a tree of height h is $O(h)$, since we either follow a path up the tree or follow a path down the tree. The procedure TREE-PREDECESSOR, which is symmetric to TREE-SUCCESSOR, also runs in time $O(h)$.

In summary, we have proved the following theorem.

Theorem 13.1

The dynamic-set operations SEARCH, MINIMUM, MAXIMUM, SUCCESSOR, and PREDECESSOR can be made to run in $O(h)$ time on a binary search tree of height h. ∎

Exercises

13.2-1

Suppose that we have numbers between 1 and 1000 in a binary search tree and want to search for the number 363. Which of the following sequences could *not* be the sequence of nodes examined?

a. 2, 252, 401, 398, 330, 344, 397, 363.

b. 924, 220, 911, 244, 898, 258, 362, 363.

c. 925, 202, 911, 240, 912, 245, 363.

d. 2, 399, 387, 219, 266, 382, 381, 278, 363.

e. 935, 278, 347, 621, 299, 392, 358, 363.

13.2-2

Professor Bunyan thinks he has discovered a remarkable property of binary search trees. Suppose that the search for key k in a binary search tree ends up in a leaf. Consider three sets: A, the keys to the left of the search path; B, the keys on the search path; and C, the keys to the right of the search path. Professor Bunyan claims that any three keys $a \in A$, $b \in B$, and $c \in C$ must satisfy $a \le b \le c$. Give a smallest possible counterexample to the professor's claim.

13.2-3

Use the binary-search-tree property to prove rigorously that the code for TREE-SUCCESSOR is correct.

13.2-4

An inorder tree walk of an n-node binary search tree can be implemented by finding the minimum element in the tree with TREE-MINIMUM and then making $n - 1$ calls to TREE-SUCCESSOR. Prove that this algorithm runs in $\Theta(n)$ time.

13.2-5

Prove that no matter what node we start at in a height-h binary search tree, k successive calls to TREE-SUCCESSOR take $O(k + h)$ time.

13.2-6

Let T be a binary search tree, let x be a leaf node, and let y be its parent. Show that $key[y]$ is either the smallest key in T larger than $key[x]$ or the largest key in the tree smaller than $key[x]$.

13.3   Insertion and deletion

The operations of insertion and deletion cause the dynamic set represented by a binary search tree to change. The data structure must be modified to reflect this change, but in such a way that the binary-search-tree property continues to hold. As we shall see, modifying the tree to insert a new element is relatively straightforward, but handling deletion is somewhat more intricate.

Insertion

To insert a new value v into a binary search tree T, we use the procedure TREE-INSERT. The procedure is passed a node z for which $key[z] = v$, $left[z] = \text{NIL}$, and $right[z] = \text{NIL}$. It modifies T and some of the fields of z in such a way that z is inserted into an appropriate position in the tree.

TREE-INSERT(*T*, *z*)

```
 1   y ← NIL
 2   x ← root[T]
 3   while x ≠ NIL
 4       do y ← x
 5           if key[z] < key[x]
 6               then x ← left[x]
 7               else  x ← right[x]
 8   p[z] ← y
 9   if y = NIL
10       then root[T] ← z
11       else  if key[z] < key[y]
12               then left[y] ← z
13               else  right[y] ← z
```

Figure 13.3 shows how TREE-INSERT works. Like the procedures TREE-SEARCH and ITERATIVE-TREE-SEARCH, TREE-INSERT begins at the root of the tree and traces a path downward. The pointer *x* traces the path, and the pointer *y* is maintained as the parent of *x*. After initialization, the **while** loop in lines 3–7 causes these two pointers to move down the tree, going left or right depending on the comparison of *key*[*z*] with *key*[*x*], until *x* is set to NIL. This NIL occupies the position where we wish to place the input item *z*. Lines 8–13 set the pointers that cause *z* to be inserted.

Like the other primitive operations on search trees, the procedure TREE-INSERT runs in $O(h)$ time on a tree of height *h*.

Deletion

The procedure for deleting a given node *z* from a binary search tree takes as an argument a pointer to *z*. The procedure considers the three cases shown in Figure 13.4. If *z* has no children, we modify its parent *p*[*z*] to replace *z* with NIL as its child. If the node has only a single child, we "splice out" *z* by making a new link between its child and its parent. Finally, if the node has two children, we splice out *z*'s successor *y*, which has no left child (see Exercise 13.3-4) and replace the contents of *z* with the contents of *y*.

The code for TREE-DELETE organizes these three cases a little differently.

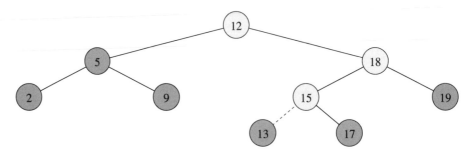

Figure 13.3 Inserting an item with key 13 into a binary search tree. Lightly shaded nodes indicate the path from the root down to the position where the item is inserted. The dashed line indicates the link in the tree that is added to insert the item.

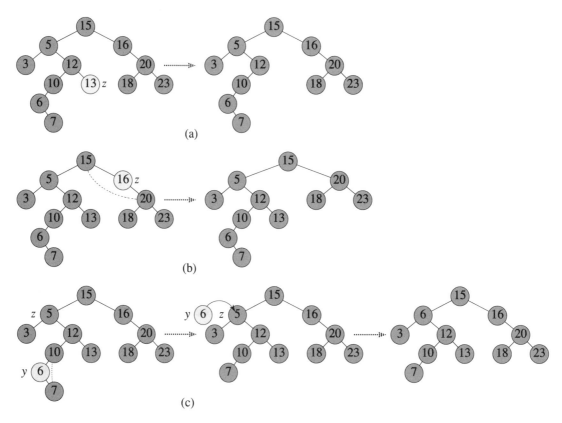

Figure 13.4 Deleting a node z from a binary search tree. In each case, the node actually removed is lightly shaded. **(a)** If z has no children, we just remove it. **(b)** If z has only one child, we splice out z. **(c)** If z has two children, we splice out its successor y, which has at most one child, and then replace the contents of z with the contents of y.

TREE-DELETE(*T*, *z*)

```
 1   if left[z] = NIL or right[z] = NIL
 2      then y ← z
 3      else  y ← TREE-SUCCESSOR(z)
 4   if left[y] ≠ NIL
 5      then x ← left[y]
 6      else  x ← right[y]
 7   if x ≠ NIL
 8      then p[x] ← p[y]
 9   if p[y] = NIL
10      then root[T] ← x
11      else  if y = left[p[y]]
12              then left[p[y]] ← x
13              else right[p[y]] ← x
14   if y ≠ z
15      then key[z] ← key[y]
16            ▷ If y has other fields, copy them, too.
17   return y
```

In lines 1–3, the algorithm determines a node y to splice out. The node y is either the input node z (if z has at most 1 child) or the successor of z (if z has two children). Then, in lines 4–6, x is set to the non-NIL child of y, or to NIL if y has no children. The node y is spliced out in lines 7–13 by modifying pointers in $p[y]$ and x. Splicing out y is somewhat complicated by the need for proper handling of the boundary conditions, which occur when $x = $ NIL or when y is the root. Finally, in lines 14–16, if the successor of z was the node spliced out, the contents of z are moved from y to z, overwriting the previous contents. The node y is returned in line 17 so that the calling procedure can recycle it via the free list. The procedure runs in $O(h)$ time on a tree of height h.

In summary, we have proved the following theorem.

Theorem 13.2
The dynamic-set operations INSERT and DELETE can be made to run in $O(h)$ time on a binary search tree of height h. ∎

Exercises

13.3-1
Give a recursive version of the TREE-INSERT procedure.

13.3-2
Suppose that a binary search tree is constructed by repeatedly inserting distinct values into the tree. Argue that the number of nodes examined in

searching for a value in the tree is one plus the number of nodes examined when the value was first inserted into the tree.

13.3-3

We can sort a given set of n numbers by first building a binary search tree containing these numbers (using TREE-INSERT repeatedly to insert the numbers one by one) and then printing the numbers by an inorder tree walk. What are the worst-case and best-case running times for this sorting algorithm?

13.3-4

Show that if a node in a binary search tree has two children, then its successor has no left child and its predecessor has no right child.

13.3-5

Suppose that another data structure contains a pointer to a node y in a binary search tree, and suppose that y's predecessor z is deleted from the tree by the procedure TREE-DELETE. What problem can arise? How can TREE-DELETE be rewritten to solve this problem?

13.3-6

Is the operation of deletion "commutative" in the sense that deleting x and then y from a binary search tree leaves the same tree as deleting y and then x? Argue why it is or give a counterexample.

13.3-7

When node z in TREE-DELETE has two children, we could splice out its predecessor rather than its successor. Some have argued that a fair strategy, giving equal priority to predecessor and successor, yields better empirical performance. How might TREE-DELETE be changed to implement such a fair strategy?

★ 13.4   Randomly built binary search trees

We have shown that all the basic operations on a binary search tree run in $O(h)$ time, where h is the height of the tree. The height of a binary search tree varies, however, as items are inserted and deleted. In order to analyze the behavior of binary search trees in practice, it is reasonable to make statistical assumptions about the distribution of keys and the sequence of insertions and deletions.

Unfortunately, little is known about the average height of a binary search tree when both insertion and deletion are used to create it. When the tree is created by insertion alone, the analysis becomes more tractable. Let us therefore define a *randomly built binary search tree* on n distinct keys as one that arises from inserting the keys in random order into an initially empty tree, where each of the $n!$ permutations of the input keys is equally likely. (Exercise 13.4-2 asks you to show that this notion is different from assuming that every binary search tree on n keys is equally likely.) The goal of this section is to show that the expected height of a randomly built binary search tree on n keys is $O(\lg n)$.

We begin by investigating the structure of binary search trees that are built by insertion alone.

Lemma 13.3

Let T be the tree that results from inserting n distinct keys $k_1, k_2, \ldots, k_n$ (in order) into an initially empty binary search tree. Then k_i is an ancestor of k_j in T, for $1 \leq i < j \leq n$, if and only if

$$k_i = \min\{k_l : 1 \leq l \leq i \text{ and } k_l > k_j\}$$

or

$$k_i = \max\{k_l : 1 \leq l \leq i \text{ and } k_l < k_j\} \ .$$

Proof $\Rightarrow$: Suppose that k_i is an ancestor of k_j. Consider the tree T_i that results after the keys $k_1, k_2, \ldots, k_i$ have been inserted. The path in T_i from the root to k_i is the same as the path in T from the root to k_i. Thus, if k_j were inserted into T_i, it would become either the left or the right child of k_i. Consequently (see Exercise 13.2-6), k_i is either the smallest key among $k_1, k_2, \ldots, k_i$ that is larger than k_j or the largest key among $k_1, k_2, \ldots, k_i$ that is smaller than k_j.

$\Leftarrow$: Suppose that k_i is the smallest key among $k_1, k_2, \ldots, k_i$ that is larger than k_j. (The case in which k_i is the largest key among $k_1, k_2, \ldots, k_i$ that is smaller than k_j is handled symmetrically.) Comparing k_j to any of the keys on the path in T from the root to k_i yields the same results as comparing k_i to the keys. Hence, when k_j is inserted, it follows a path through k_i and is inserted as a descendant of k_i. $\blacksquare$

As a corollary of Lemma 13.3, we can precisely characterize the depth of a key based on the input permutation.

Corollary 13.4

Let T be the tree that results from inserting n distinct keys $k_1, k_2, \ldots, k_n$ (in order) into an initially empty binary search tree. For a given key k_j, where $1 \leq j \leq n$, define

$$G_j = \{k_i : 1 \leq i < j \text{ and } k_l > k_i > k_j \text{ for all } l < i \text{ such that } k_l > k_j\}$$

and

$$L_j = \{k_i : 1 \leq i < j \text{ and } k_l < k_i < k_j \text{ for all } l < i \text{ such that } k_l < k_j\} \ .$$

Then the keys on the path from the root to k_j are exactly the keys in $G_j \cup L_j$, and the depth in T of any key k_j is

$$d(k_j, T) = |G_j| + |L_j| \ . \qquad\qquad\qquad\qquad\blacksquare$$

Figure 13.5 illustrates the two sets G_j and L_j. The set G_j contains any key k_i inserted before k_j such that k_i is the smallest key among $k_1, k_2, \ldots, k_i$ that is larger than k_j. (The structure of L_j is symmetric.) To better understand the set G_j, let us explore a method by which we can enumerate its elements. Among the keys $k_1, k_2, \ldots, k_{j-1}$, consider in order those that are larger than k_j. These keys are shown as G'_j in the figure. As each key is considered in turn, keep a running account of the minimum. The set G_j consists of those elements that update the running minimum.

Let us simplify this scenario somewhat for the purpose of analysis. Suppose that n distinct numbers are inserted one at a time into a dynamic set. If all permutations of the numbers are equally likely, how many times on average does the minimum of the set change? To answer this question, suppose that the ith number inserted is k_i, for $i = 1, 2, \ldots, n$. The probability is $1/i$ that k_i is the minimum of the first i numbers, since the rank of k_i among the first i numbers is equally likely to be any of the i possible ranks. Consequently, the expected number of changes to the minimum of the set is

$$\sum_{i=1}^{n} \frac{1}{i} = H_n \ ,$$

where $H_n = \ln n + O(1)$ is the nth harmonic number (see equation (3.5) and Problem 6-2).

We therefore expect the number of changes to the minimum to be approximately $\ln n$, and the following lemma shows that the probability that it is much greater is very small.

Lemma 13.5
Let $k_1, k_2, \ldots, k_n$ be a random permutation of n distinct numbers, and let $|S|$ be the random variable that is the cardinality of the set

$$S = \{k_i : 1 \leq i \leq n \text{ and } k_l > k_i \text{ for all } l < i\} \ . \qquad (13.1)$$

Then $\Pr\{|S| \geq (\beta + 1)H_n\} \leq 1/n^2$, where H_n is the nth harmonic number and $\beta \approx 4.32$ satisfies the equation $(\ln \beta - 1)\beta = 2$.

Proof   We can view the cardinality of the set S as being determined by n Bernoulli trials, where a success occurs in the ith trial when k_i is smaller than the elements $k_1, k_2, \ldots, k_{i-1}$. Success in the ith trial occurs with probability $1/i$. The trials are independent, since the probability that k_i is the minimum of $k_1, k_2, \ldots, k_i$ is independent of the relative ordering of $k_1, k_2, \ldots, k_{i-1}$.

We can use Theorem 6.6 to bound the probability that $|S| \geq (\beta + 1)H_n$. The expectation of $|S|$ is $\mu = H_n \geq \ln n$. Since $\beta > 1$, Theorem 6.6 yields

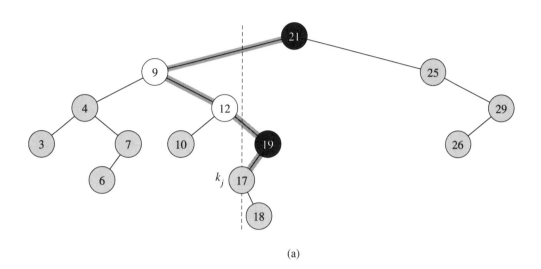

(a)

keys	21	9	4	25	7	12	3	10	19	29	17	6	26	18
G_j'	21			25					19	29				
G_j	21								19					
L_j'		9	4		7	12	3	10						
L_j		9				12								

(b)

Figure 13.5   Illustrating the two sets G_j and L_j that comprise the keys on a path from the root of a binary search tree to a key $k_j = 17$. (**a**) The nodes with keys in G_j are black, and the nodes with keys in L_j are white. All other nodes are shaded. The path from the root down to the node with key k_j is shaded. Keys to the left of the dashed line are less than k_j, and keys to the right are greater. The tree is constructed by inserting the keys shown in the topmost list in (**b**). The set $G_j' = \{21, 25, 19, 29\}$ consists of those elements that are inserted before 17 and are greater than 17. The set $G_j = \{21, 19\}$ consists of those elements that update a running minimum of the elements in G_j'. Thus, the key 21 is in G_j, since it is the first element. The key 25 is not in G_j, since it is larger than the running minimum 21. The key 19 is in G_j, since it is smaller than the running minimum 21. The key 29 is not in G_j, since it is larger than the running minimum 19. The structures of L_j' and L_j are symmetric.

$$\begin{aligned}
\Pr\{|S| \geq (\beta+1)H_n\} &= \Pr\{|S| - \mu \geq \beta H_n\} \\
&\leq \left(\frac{eH_n}{\beta H_n}\right)^{\beta H_n} \\
&= e^{(1-\ln\beta)\beta H_n} \\
&\leq e^{-(\ln\beta-1)\beta \ln n} \\
&= n^{-(\ln\beta-1)\beta} \\
&= 1/n^2 ,
\end{aligned}$$

which follows from the definition of β.   ∎

We now have the tools to bound the height of a randomly built binary search tree.

Theorem 13.6

The average height of a randomly built binary search tree on n distinct keys is $O(\lg n)$.

Proof   Let $k_1, k_2, \ldots, k_n$ be a random permutation on the n keys, and let T be the binary search tree that results from inserting the keys in order into an initially empty tree. We first consider the probability that the depth $d(k_j, T)$ of a given key k_j is at least t, for an arbitrary value t. By the characterization of $d(k_j, T)$ in Corollary 13.4, if the depth of k_j is at least t, then the cardinality of one of the two sets G_j and L_j must be at least $t/2$. Thus,

$$\Pr\{d(k_j, T) \geq t\} \leq \Pr\{|G_j| \geq t/2\} + \Pr\{|L_j| \geq t/2\} . \tag{13.2}$$

Let us examine $\Pr\{|G_j| \geq t/2\}$ first. We have

$$\begin{aligned}
&\Pr\{|G_j| \geq t/2\} \\
&\quad = \Pr\{|\{k_i : 1 \leq i < j \text{ and } k_l > k_i > k_j \text{ for all } l < i\}| \geq t/2\} \\
&\quad \leq \Pr\{|\{k_i : i \leq n \text{ and } k_l > k_i \text{ for all } l < i\}| \geq t/2\} \\
&\quad = \Pr\{|S| \geq t/2\} ,
\end{aligned}$$

where S is defined as in equation (13.1). To justify this argument, note that the probability does not decrease if we extend the range of i from $i < j$ to $i \leq n$, since more elements are added to the set. Likewise, the probability does not decrease if we remove the condition that $k_i > k_j$, since we are substituting a random permutation on possibly fewer than n elements (those k_i that are greater than k_j) for a random permutation on n elements.

Using a symmetric argument, we can prove that

$$\Pr\{|L_j| \geq t/2\} \leq \Pr\{|S| \geq t/2\} \;,$$

and thus, by inequality (13.2), we obtain

$$\Pr\{d(k_j, T) \geq t\} \leq 2\Pr\{|S| \geq t/2\} \;.$$

If we choose $t = 2(\beta + 1)H_n$, where H_n is the nth harmonic number and $\beta \approx 4.32$ satisfies $(\ln \beta - 1)\beta = 2$, we can apply Lemma 13.5 to conclude that

$$\begin{aligned} \Pr\{d(k_j, T) \geq 2(\beta + 1)H_n\} &\leq 2\Pr\{|S| \geq (\beta + 1)H_n\} \\ &\leq 2/n^2 \;. \end{aligned}$$

Since there are at most n nodes in a randomly built binary search tree, the probability that *any* node's depth is at least $2(\beta + 1)H_n$ is therefore, by Boole's inequality (6.22), at most $n(2/n^2) = 2/n$. Thus, at least $1 - 2/n$ of the time, the height of a randomly built binary search tree is less than $2(\beta + 1)H_n$, and at most $2/n$ of the time, it is at most n. The expected height is therefore at most $(2(\beta + 1)H_n)(1 - 2/n) + n(2/n) = O(\lg n)$. ■

Exercises

13.4-1
Describe a binary search tree on n nodes such that the average depth of a node in the tree is $\Theta(\lg n)$ but the height of the tree is $\omega(\lg n)$. How large can the height of an n-node binary search tree be if the average depth of a node is $\Theta(\lg n)$?

13.4-2
Show that the notion of a randomly chosen binary search tree on n keys, where each binary search tree of n keys is equally likely to be chosen, is different from the notion of a randomly built binary search tree given in this section. (*Hint:* List the possibilities when $n = 3$.)

13.4-3 ⋆
Given a constant $r \geq 1$, determine t such that the probability is less than $1/n^r$ that the height of a randomly built binary search tree is at least tH_n.

13.4-4 ⋆
Consider RANDOMIZED-QUICKSORT operating on a sequence of n input numbers. Prove that for any constant $k > 0$, all but $O(1/n^k)$ of the $n!$ input permutations yield an $O(n \lg n)$ running time.

Problems

13-1 Binary search trees with equal keys
Equal keys pose a problem for the implementation of binary search trees.

a. What is the asymptotic performance of Tree-Insert when used to insert *n* items with identical keys into an initially empty binary search tree?

We propose to improve Tree-Insert by testing before line 5 whether or not $key[z] = key[x]$ and by testing before line 11 whether or not $key[z] = key[y]$. If equality holds, we implement one of the following strategies. For each strategy, find the asymptotic performance of inserting *n* items with identical keys into an initially empty binary search tree. (The strategies are described for line 5, in which we compare the keys of *z* and *x*. Substitute *y* for *x* to arrive at the strategies for line 11.)

b. Keep a boolean flag $b[x]$ at node *x*, and set *x* to either $left[x]$ or $right[x]$ based on the value of $b[x]$, which alternates between FALSE and TRUE each time the node is visited during Tree-Insert.

c. Keep a list of nodes with equal keys at *x*, and insert *z* into the list.

d. Randomly set *x* to either $left[x]$ or $right[x]$. (Give the worst-case performance and informally derive the average-case performance.)

13-2   *Radix trees*

Given two strings $a = a_0 a_1 \ldots a_p$ and $b = b_0 b_1 \ldots b_q$, where each a_i and each b_j is in some ordered set of characters, we say that string *a* is ***lexicographically less than*** string *b* if either

1. there exists an integer *j*, $0 \le j \le \min(p, q)$, such that $a_i = b_i$ for all $i = 0, 1, \ldots, j - 1$ and $a_j < b_j$, or

2. $p < q$ and $a_i = b_i$ for all $i = 0, 1, \ldots, p$.

For example, if *a* and *b* are bit strings, then $10100 < 10110$ by rule 1 (letting $j = 3$) and $10100 < 101000$ by rule 2. This is similar to the ordering used in English-language dictionaries.

The ***radix tree*** data structure shown in Figure 13.6 stores the bit strings 1011, 10, 011, 100, and 0. When searching for a key $a = a_0 a_1 \ldots a_p$, we go left at a node of depth *i* if $a_i = 0$ and right if $a_i = 1$. Let *S* be a set of distinct binary strings whose lengths sum to *n*. Show how to use a radix tree to sort *S* lexicographically in $\Theta(n)$ time. For the example in Figure 13.6, the output of the sort should be the sequence 0, 011, 10, 100, 1011.

13-3   *Average node depth in a randomly built binary search tree*

In this problem, we prove that the average depth of a node in a randomly built binary search tree with *n* nodes is $O(\lg n)$. Although this result is weaker than that of Theorem 13.6, the technique we shall use reveals a surprising similarity between the building of a binary search tree and the running of Randomized-Quicksort from Section 8.3.

We start by recalling from Chapter 5 that the internal path length $P(T)$ of a binary tree *T* is the sum, over all nodes *x* in *T*, of the depth of node *x*, which we denote by $d(x, T)$.

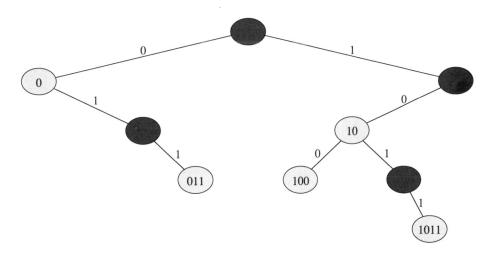

Figure 13.6 A radix tree storing the bit strings 1011, 10, 011, 100, and 0. Each node's key can be determined by traversing the path from the root to that node. There is no need, therefore, to store the keys in the nodes; the keys are shown here for illustrative purposes only. Nodes are heavily shaded if the keys corresponding to them are not in the tree; such nodes are present only to establish a path to other nodes.

a. Argue that the average depth of a node in T is

$$\frac{1}{n}\sum_{x \in T} d(x, T) = \frac{1}{n}P(T) .$$

Thus, we wish to show that the expected value of $P(T)$ is $O(n \lg n)$.

b. Let T_L and T_R denote the left and right subtrees of tree T, respectively. Argue that if T has n nodes, then

$$P(T) = P(T_L) + P(T_R) + n - 1 .$$

c. Let $P(n)$ denote the average internal path length of a randomly built binary search tree with n nodes. Show that

$$P(n) = \frac{1}{n}\sum_{i=0}^{n-1}(P(i) + P(n - i - 1) + n - 1) .$$

d. Show that $P(n)$ can be rewritten as

$$P(n) = \frac{2}{n}\sum_{k=1}^{n-1} P(k) + \Theta(n) .$$

e. Recalling the analysis of the randomized version of quicksort, conclude that $P(n) = O(n \lg n)$.

At each recursive invocation of quicksort, we choose a random pivot element to partition the set of elements being sorted. Each node of a binary search tree partitions the set of elements that fall into the subtree rooted at that node.

f. Describe an implementation of quicksort in which the comparisons to sort a set of elements are exactly the same as the comparisons to insert the elements into a binary search tree. (The order in which comparisons are made may differ, but the same comparisons must be made.)

13-4   *Number of different binary trees*

Let b_n denote the number of different binary trees with n nodes. In this problem, you will find a formula for b_n as well as an asymptotic estimate.

a. Show that $b_0 = 1$ and that, for $n \geq 1$,

$$b_n = \sum_{k=0}^{n-1} b_k b_{n-1-k} \ .$$

b. Let $B(x)$ be the generating function

$$B(x) = \sum_{n=0}^{\infty} b_n x^n$$

(see Problem 4-6 for the definition of generating functions). Show that $B(x) = xB(x)^2 + 1$ and hence

$$B(x) = \frac{1}{2x} \left(1 - \sqrt{1 - 4x} \right) \ .$$

The *Taylor expansion* of $f(x)$ around the point $x = a$ is given by

$$f(x) = \sum_{k=0}^{\infty} \frac{f^{(k)}(x - a)}{k!} (x - a)^k \ ,$$

where $f^{(k)}(x)$ is the kth derivative of f evaluated at x.

c. Show that

$$b_n = \frac{1}{n+1} \binom{2n}{n}$$

(the nth *Catalan number*) by using the Taylor expansion of $\sqrt{1 - 4x}$ around $x = 0$. (If you wish, instead of using the Taylor expansion, you may use the generalization of the binomial expansion (6.5) to non-integral exponents n, where for any real number n and integer k, we interpret $\binom{n}{k}$ to be $n(n-1)\cdots(n-k+1)/k!$ if $k \geq 0$, and 0 otherwise.)

d. Show that

$$b_n = \frac{4^n}{\sqrt{\pi} n^{3/2}} \left(1 + O(1/n) \right) \ .$$

Chapter notes

Knuth [123] contains a good discussion of simple binary search trees as well as many variations. Binary search trees seem to have been independently discovered by a number of people in the late 1950's.

14 Red-Black Trees

Chapter 13 showed that a binary search tree of height h can implement any of the basic dynamic-set operations—such as SEARCH, PREDECESSOR, SUCCESSOR, MINIMUM, MAXIMUM, INSERT, and DELETE—in $O(h)$ time. Thus, the set operations are fast if the height of the search tree is small; but if its height is large, their performance may be no better than with a linked list. Red-black trees are one of many search-tree schemes that are "balanced" in order to guarantee that basic dynamic-set operations take $O(\lg n)$ time in the worst case.

14.1 Properties of red-black trees

A *red-black tree* is a binary search tree with one extra bit of storage per node: its *color*, which can be either RED or BLACK. By constraining the way nodes can be colored on any path from the root to a leaf, red-black trees ensure that no such path is more than twice as long as any other, so that the tree is approximately *balanced*.

Each node of the tree now contains the fields *color*, *key*, *left*, *right*, and *p*. If a child or the parent of a node does not exist, the corresponding pointer field of the node contains the value NIL. We shall regard these NIL's as being pointers to external nodes (leaves) of the binary search tree and the normal, key-bearing nodes as being internal nodes of the tree.

A binary search tree is a red-black tree if it satisfies the following *red-black properties*:

1. Every node is either red or black.

2. Every leaf (NIL) is black.

3. If a node is red, then both its children are black.

4. Every simple path from a node to a descendant leaf contains the same number of black nodes.

An example of a red-black tree is shown in Figure 14.1.

We call the number of black nodes on any path from, but not including, a node x to a leaf the *black-height* of the node, denoted bh(x). By property 4, the notion of black-height is well defined, since all descending paths from

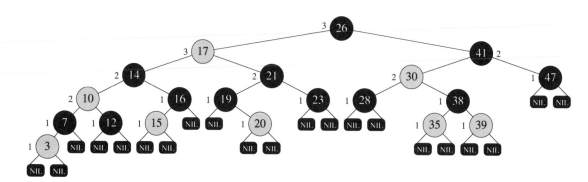

Figure 14.1 A red-black tree with black nodes darkened and red nodes shaded. Every node in a red-black tree is either red or black, every leaf (NIL) is black, the children of a red node are both black, and every simple path from a node to a descendant leaf contains the same number of black nodes. Each non-NIL node is marked with its black-height; NIL's have black-height 0.

the node have the same number of black nodes. We define the black-height of a red-black tree to be the black-height of its root.

The following lemma shows why red-black trees make good search trees.

Lemma 14.1
A red-black tree with n internal nodes has height at most $2\lg(n+1)$.

Proof We first show that the subtree rooted at any node x contains at least $2^{\mathrm{bh}(x)} - 1$ internal nodes. We prove this claim by induction on the height of x. If the height of x is 0, then x must be a leaf (NIL), and the subtree rooted at x indeed contains at least $2^{\mathrm{bh}(x)} - 1 = 2^0 - 1 = 0$ internal nodes. For the inductive step, consider a node x that has positive height and is an internal node with two children. Each child has a black-height of either $\mathrm{bh}(x)$ or $\mathrm{bh}(x) - 1$, depending on whether its color is red or black, respectively. Since the height of a child of x is less than the height of x itself, we can apply the inductive hypothesis to conclude that each child has at least $2^{\mathrm{bh}(x)-1} - 1$ internal nodes. Thus, the subtree rooted at x contains at least $(2^{\mathrm{bh}(x)-1} - 1) + (2^{\mathrm{bh}(x)-1} - 1) + 1 = 2^{\mathrm{bh}(x)} - 1$ internal nodes, which proves the claim.

To complete the proof of the lemma, let h be the height of the tree. According to property 3, at least half the nodes on any simple path from the root to a leaf, not including the root, must be black. Consequently, the black-height of the root must be at least $h/2$; thus,

$$n \geq 2^{h/2} - 1 .$$

Moving the 1 to the left-hand side and taking logarithms on both sides yields $\lg(n+1) \geq h/2$, or $h \leq 2\lg(n+1)$. ∎

An immediate consequence of this lemma is that the dynamic-set operations SEARCH, MINIMUM, MAXIMUM, SUCCESSOR, and PREDECESSOR can be implemented in $O(\lg n)$ time on red-black trees, since they can be made to run in $O(h)$ time on a search tree of height h (as shown in Chapter 13) and any red-black tree on n nodes is a search tree with height $O(\lg n)$. Although the algorithms TREE-INSERT and TREE-DELETE from Chapter 13 run in $O(\lg n)$ time when given a red-black tree as input, they do not directly support the dynamic-set operations INSERT and DELETE, since they do not guarantee that the modified binary search tree will be a red-black tree. We shall see in Sections 14.3 and 14.4, however, that these two operations can indeed be supported in $O(\lg n)$ time.

Exercises

14.1-1
Draw the complete binary search tree of height 3 on the keys $\{1, 2, \ldots, 15\}$. Add the NIL leaves and color the nodes in three different ways such that the black-heights of the resulting red-black trees are 2, 3, and 4.

14.1-2
Suppose that the root of a red-black tree is red. If we make it black, does the tree remain a red-black tree?

14.1-3
Show that the longest simple path from a node x in a red-black tree to a descendant leaf has length at most twice that of the shortest simple path from node x to a descendant leaf.

14.1-4
What is the largest possible number of internal nodes in a red-black tree with black-height k? What is the smallest possible number?

14.1-5
Describe a red-black tree on n keys that realizes the largest possible ratio of red internal nodes to black internal nodes. What is this ratio? What tree has the smallest possible ratio, and what is the ratio?

14.2 Rotations

The search-tree operations TREE-INSERT and TREE-DELETE, when run on a red-black tree with n keys, take $O(\lg n)$ time. Because they modify the tree, the result may violate the red-black properties enumerated in Section 14.1. To restore these properties, we must change the colors of some of the nodes in the tree and also change the pointer structure.

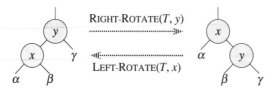

Figure 14.2 The rotation operations on a binary search tree. The operation RIGHT-ROTATE(T, x) transforms the configuration of the two nodes on the left into the configuration on the right by changing a constant number of pointers. The configuration on the right can be transformed into the configuration on the left by the inverse operation LEFT-ROTATE(T, y). The two nodes might occur anywhere in a binary search tree. The letters α, β, and γ represent arbitrary subtrees. A rotation operation preserves the inorder ordering of keys: the keys in α precede *key*[x], which precedes the keys in β, which precede *key*[y], which precedes the keys in γ.

We change the pointer structure through ***rotation***, which is a local operation in a search tree that preserves the inorder key ordering. Figure 14.2 shows the two kinds of rotations: left rotations and right rotations. When we do a left rotation on a node x, we assume that its right child y is non-NIL. The left rotation "pivots" around the link from x to y. It makes y the new root of the subtree, with x as y's left child and y's left child as x's right child.

The pseudocode for LEFT-ROTATE assumes that *right*[x] $\neq$ NIL.

LEFT-ROTATE(T, x)

```
 1   y ← right[x]              ▷ Set y.
 2   right[x] ← left[y]        ▷ Turn y's left subtree into x's right subtree.
 3   if left[y] ≠ NIL
 4      then p[left[y]] ← x
 5   p[y] ← p[x]               ▷ Link x's parent to y.
 6   if p[x] = NIL
 7      then root[T] ← y
 8      else if x = left[p[x]]
 9              then left[p[x]] ← y
10              else right[p[x]] ← y
11   left[y] ← x               ▷ Put x on y's left.
12   p[x] ← y
```

Figure 14.3 shows how LEFT-ROTATE operates. The code for RIGHT-ROTATE is similar. Both LEFT-ROTATE and RIGHT-ROTATE run in $O(1)$ time. Only pointers are changed by a rotation; all other fields in a node remain the same.

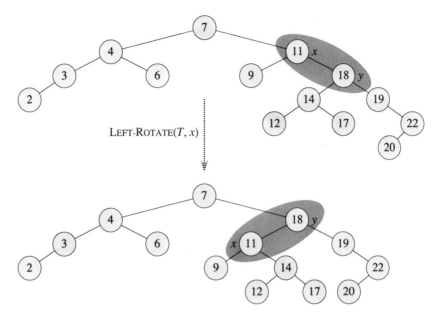

Figure 14.3 An example of how the procedure LEFT-ROTATE(T, x) modifies a binary search tree. The NIL leaves are omitted. Inorder tree walks of the input tree and the modified tree produce the same listing of key values.

Exercises

14.2-1
Draw the red-black tree that results after TREE-INSERT is called on the tree in Figure 14.1 with key 36. If the inserted node is colored red, is the resulting tree a red-black tree? What if it is colored black?

14.2-2
Write pseudocode for RIGHT-ROTATE.

14.2-3
Argue that rotation preserves the inorder key ordering of a binary tree.

14.2-4
Let a, b, and c be arbitrary nodes in subtrees α, β, and γ, respectively, in the left tree of Figure 14.2. How do the depths of a, b, and c change when a left rotation is performed on node x in the figure?

14.2-5
Show that any arbitrary n-node tree can be transformed into any other arbitrary n-node tree using $O(n)$ rotations. (*Hint:* First show that at most $n - 1$ right rotations suffice to transform any tree into a right-going chain.)

14.3   Insertion

Insertion of a node into an n-node red-black tree can be accomplished in $O(\lg n)$ time. We use the TREE-INSERT procedure (Section 13.3) to insert node x into the tree T as if it were an ordinary binary search tree, and then we color x red. To guarantee that the red-black properties are preserved, we then fix up the modified tree by recoloring nodes and performing rotations. Most of the code for RB-INSERT handles the various cases that can arise as we fix up the modified tree.

RB-INSERT(T, x)

```
 1  TREE-INSERT(T, x)
 2  color[x] ← RED
 3  while x ≠ root[T] and color[p[x]] = RED
 4      do if p[x] = left[p[p[x]]]
 5          then y ← right[p[p[x]]]
 6              if color[y] = RED
 7                  then color[p[x]] ← BLACK          ▷ Case 1
 8                      color[y] ← BLACK              ▷ Case 1
 9                      color[p[p[x]]] ← RED          ▷ Case 1
10                      x ← p[p[x]]                   ▷ Case 1
11                  else if x = right[p[x]]
12                      then x ← p[x]                 ▷ Case 2
13                          LEFT-ROTATE(T, x)         ▷ Case 2
14                      color[p[x]] ← BLACK           ▷ Case 3
15                      color[p[p[x]]] ← RED          ▷ Case 3
16                      RIGHT-ROTATE(T, p[p[x]])      ▷ Case 3
17          else (same as then clause
                  with "right" and "left" exchanged)
18  color[root[T]] ← BLACK
```

The code for RB-INSERT is less imposing than it looks. We shall break our examination of the code into three major steps. First, we shall determine what violations of the red-black properties are introduced in lines 1–2 when the node x is inserted and colored red. Second, we shall examine the overall goal of the **while** loop in lines 3–17. Finally, we shall explore each of the three cases into which the **while** loop is broken and see how they accomplish the goal. Figure 14.4 shows how RB-INSERT operates on a sample red-black tree.

Which of the red-black properties can be violated after lines 1–2? Property 1 certainly continues to hold, as does property 2, since the newly inserted red node has NIL's for children. Property 4, which says that the number of blacks is the same on every path from a given node, is satisfied as well, because node x replaces a (black) NIL, and node x is red with NIL children. Thus, the only property that might be violated is property 3,

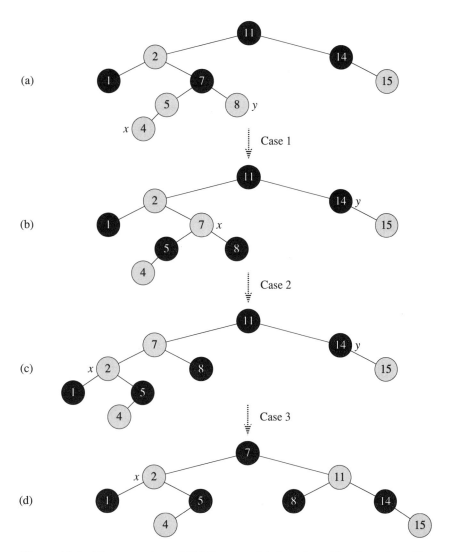

Figure 14.4 The operation of RB-INSERT. (**a**) A node x after insertion. Since x and its parent $p[x]$ are both red, a violation of property 3 occurs. Since x's uncle y is red, case 1 in the code can be applied. Nodes are recolored and the pointer x is moved up the tree, resulting in the tree shown in (**b**). Once again, x and its parent are both red, but x's uncle y is black. Since x is the right child of $p[x]$, case 2 can be applied. A left rotation is performed, and the tree that results is shown in (**c**). Now x is the left child of its parent, and case 3 can be applied. A right rotation yields the tree in (**d**), which is a legal red-black tree.

which says that a red node cannot have a red child. Specifically, property 3 is violated if x's parent is red, since x is itself colored red in line 2. Figure 14.4(a) shows such a violation after the node x has been inserted.

The goal of the **while** loop in lines 3–17 is to move the one violation of property 3 up the tree while maintaining property 4 as an invariant. At the beginning of each iteration of the loop, x points to a red node with a red parent—the only violation in the tree. There are two possible outcomes of each iteration of the loop: the pointer x moves up the tree, or some rotations are performed and the loop terminates.

There are actually six cases to consider in the **while** loop, but three of them are symmetric to the other three, depending on whether x's parent $p[x]$ is a left child or a right child of x's grandparent $p[p[x]]$, which is determined in line 4. We have given the code only for the situation in which $p[x]$ is a left child. We have made the important assumption that the root of the tree is black—a property we guarantee in line 18 each time we terminate—so that $p[x]$ is not the root and $p[p[x]]$ exists.

Case 1 is distinguished from cases 2 and 3 by the color of x's parent's sibling, or "uncle." Line 5 makes y point to x's uncle $right[p[p[x]]]$, and a test is made in line 6. If y is red, then case 1 is executed. Otherwise, control passes to cases 2 and 3. In all three cases, x's grandparent $p[p[x]]$ is black, since its parent $p[x]$ is red, and property 3 is violated only between x and $p[x]$.

The situation for case 1 (lines 7–10) is shown in Figure 14.5. Case 1 is executed when both $p[x]$ and y are red. Since $p[p[x]]$ is black, we can color both $p[x]$ and y black, thereby fixing the problem of x and $p[x]$ both being red, and color $p[p[x]]$ red, thereby maintaining property 4. The only problem that might arise is that $p[p[x]]$ might have a red parent; hence, we must repeat the **while** loop with $p[p[x]]$ as the new node x.

In cases 2 and 3, the color of x's uncle y is black. The two cases are distinguished by whether x is a right or left child of $p[x]$. Lines 12–13 constitute case 2, which is shown in Figure 14.6 together with case 3. In case 2, node x is a right child of its parent. We immediately use a left rotation to transform the situation into case 3 (lines 14–16), in which node x is a left child. Because both x and $p[x]$ are red, the rotation affects neither the black-height of nodes nor property 4. Whether we enter case 3 directly or through case 2, x's uncle y is black, since otherwise we would have executed case 1. We execute some color changes and a right rotation, which preserve property 4, and then, since we no longer have two red nodes in a row, we are done. The body of the **while** loop is not executed another time, since $p[x]$ is now black.

What is the running time of RB-INSERT? Since the height of a red-black tree on n nodes is $O(\lg n)$, the call to TREE-INSERT takes $O(\lg n)$ time. The **while** loop only repeats if case 1 is executed, and then the pointer x moves up the tree. The total number of times the **while** loop can be executed is therefore $O(\lg n)$. Thus, RB-INSERT takes a total of $O(\lg n)$

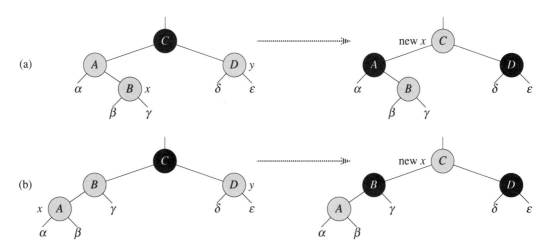

Figure 14.5   Case 1 of the procedure RB-INSERT. Property 3 is violated, since x and its parent $p[x]$ are both red. The same action is taken whether (**a**) x is a right child or (**b**) x is a left child. Each of the subtrees α, β, γ, δ, and ε has a black root, and each has the same black-height. The code for case 1 changes the colors of some nodes, preserving property 4: all downward paths from a node to a leaf have the same number of blacks. The **while** loop continues with node x's grandparent $p[p[x]]$ as the new x. Any violation of property 3 can now occur only between the new x, which is red, and its parent, if it is red as well.

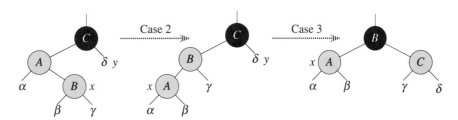

Figure 14.6   Cases 2 and 3 of the procedure RB-INSERT. As in case 1, property 3 is violated in either case 2 or case 3 because x and its parent $p[x]$ are both red. Each of the subtrees α, β, γ, and δ has a black root, and each has the same black-height. Case 2 is transformed into case 3 by a left rotation, which preserves property 4: all downward paths from a node to a leaf have the same number of blacks. Case 3 causes some color changes and a right rotation, which also preserve property 4. The **while** loop then terminates, because property 3 is satisfied: there are no longer two red nodes in a row.

time. Interestingly, it never performs more than two rotations, since the **while** loop terminates if case 2 or case 3 is executed.

Exercises

14.3-1

In line 2 of RB-INSERT, we set the color of the newly inserted node x to red. Notice that if we had chosen to set x's color to black, then property 3 of a red-black tree would not be violated. Why didn't we choose to set x's color to black?

14.3-2

In line 18 of RB-INSERT, we set the root's color to black. What is the advantage of doing so?

14.3-3

Show the red-black trees that result after successively inserting the keys $41, 38, 31, 12, 19, 8$ into an initially empty red-black tree.

14.3-4

Suppose that the black-height of each of the subtrees $\alpha, \beta, \gamma, \delta, \varepsilon$ in Figures 14.5 and 14.6 is k. Label each node in each figure with its black-height to verify that property 4 is preserved by the indicated transformation.

14.3-5

Consider a red-black tree formed by inserting n nodes with RB-INSERT. Argue that if $n > 1$, the tree has at least one red node.

14.3-6

Suggest how to implement RB-INSERT efficiently if the representation for red-black trees includes no storage for parent pointers.

14.4   Deletion

Like the other basic operations on an n-node red-black tree, deletion of a node takes time $O(\lg n)$. Deleting a node from a red-black tree is only slightly more complicated than inserting a node.

In order to simplify boundary conditions in the code, we use a sentinel to represent NIL (see page 206). For a red-black tree T, the sentinel $nil[T]$ is an object with the same fields as an ordinary node in the tree. Its *color* field is BLACK, and its other fields—p, *left*, *right*, and *key*—can be set to arbitrary values. In the red-black tree, all pointers to NIL are replaced by pointers to the sentinel $nil[T]$.

We use sentinels so that we can treat a NIL child of a node x as an ordinary node whose parent is x. We could add a distinct sentinel node for each NIL in the tree, so that the parent of each NIL is well defined, but that would waste space. Instead, we use the one sentinel $nil[T]$ to represent all the NIL's. When we wish to manipulate a child of a node x, however, we must be careful to set $p[nil[T]]$ to x first.

The procedure RB-DELETE is a minor modification of the TREE-DELETE procedure (Section 13.3). After splicing out a node, it calls an auxiliary procedure RB-DELETE-FIXUP that changes colors and performs rotations to restore the red-black properties.

RB-DELETE(T, z)

```
 1   if left[z] = nil[T] or right[z] = nil[T]
 2      then y ← z
 3      else y ← TREE-SUCCESSOR(z)
 4   if left[y] ≠ nil[T]
 5      then x ← left[y]
 6      else x ← right[y]
 7   p[x] ← p[y]
 8   if p[y] = nil[T]
 9      then root[T] ← x
10      else if y = left[p[y]]
11              then left[p[y]] ← x
12              else right[p[y]] ← x
13   if y ≠ z
14      then key[z] ← key[y]
15              ▷ If y has other fields, copy them, too.
16   if color[y] = BLACK
17      then RB-DELETE-FIXUP(T, x)
18   return y
```

There are three differences between the procedures TREE-DELETE and RB-DELETE. First, all references to NIL in TREE-DELETE have been replaced by references to the sentinel $nil[T]$ in RB-DELETE. Second, the test for whether x is NIL in line 7 of TREE-DELETE has been removed, and the assignment $p[x] \leftarrow p[y]$ is performed unconditionally in line 7 of RB-DELETE. Thus, if x is the sentinel $nil[T]$, its parent pointer points to the parent of the spliced-out node y. Third, a call to RB-DELETE-FIXUP is made in lines 16–17 if y is black. If y is red, the red-black properties still hold when y is spliced out, since no black-heights in the tree have changed and no red nodes have been made adjacent. The node x passed to RB-DELETE-FIXUP is the node that was y's sole child before y was spliced out if y had a non-NIL child, or the sentinel $nil[T]$ if y had no children. In the latter case, the unconditional assignment in line 7 guarantees that x's parent is now the node that was previously y's parent, whether x is a key-bearing internal node or the sentinel $nil[T]$.

We can now examine how the procedure RB-DELETE-FIXUP restores the red-black properties to the search tree.

RB-DELETE-FIXUP(T, x)

```
 1  while x ≠ root[T] and color[x] = BLACK
 2      do if x = left[p[x]]
 3          then w ← right[p[x]]
 4              if color[w] = RED
 5                  then color[w] ← BLACK               ▷ Case 1
 6                      color[p[x]] ← RED               ▷ Case 1
 7                      LEFT-ROTATE(T, p[x])            ▷ Case 1
 8                      w ← right[p[x]]                 ▷ Case 1
 9              if color[left[w]] = BLACK and color[right[w]] = BLACK
10                  then color[w] ← RED                 ▷ Case 2
11                      x ← p[x]                        ▷ Case 2
12                  else if color[right[w]] = BLACK
13                      then color[left[w]] ← BLACK     ▷ Case 3
14                          color[w] ← RED              ▷ Case 3
15                          RIGHT-ROTATE(T, w)          ▷ Case 3
16                          w ← right[p[x]]             ▷ Case 3
17                      color[w] ← color[p[x]]          ▷ Case 4
18                      color[p[x]] ← BLACK             ▷ Case 4
19                      color[right[w]] ← BLACK         ▷ Case 4
20                      LEFT-ROTATE(T, p[x])            ▷ Case 4
21                      x ← root[T]                     ▷ Case 4
22          else (same as then clause
                    with "right" and "left" exchanged)
23  color[x] ← BLACK
```

If the spliced-out node y in RB-DELETE is black, its removal causes any path that previously contained node y to have one fewer black node. Thus, property 4 is now violated by any ancestor of y in the tree. We can correct this problem by thinking of node x as having an "extra" black. That is, if we add 1 to the count of black nodes on any path that contains x, then under this interpretation, property 4 holds. When we splice out the black node y, we "push" its blackness onto its child. The only problem is that now node x may be "doubly black," thereby violating property 1.

The procedure RB-DELETE-FIXUP attempts to restore property 1. The goal of the **while** loop in lines 1–22 is to move the extra black up the tree until (1) x points to a red node, in which case we color the node black in line 23, (2) x points to the root, in which case the extra black can be simply "removed," or (3) suitable rotations and recolorings can be performed.

Within the **while** loop, x always points to a nonroot black node that has the extra black. We determine in line 2 whether x is a left child or a right child of its parent $p[x]$. (We have given the code for the situation in which x is a left child; the situation in which x is a right child—line 22—is symmetric.) We maintain a pointer w to the sibling of x. Since node x is doubly black, node w cannot be *nil[T]*; otherwise, the number of blacks on the path from $p[x]$ to the NIL leaf w would be smaller than the number on the path from $p[x]$ to x.

The four cases in the code are illustrated in Figure 14.7. Before examining each case in detail, let's look more generally at how we can verify that the transformation in each of the cases preserves property 4. The key idea is that in each case the number of black nodes from (and including) the root of the subtree shown to each of the subtrees $\alpha, \beta, \ldots, \zeta$ is preserved by the transformation. For example, in Figure 14.7(a), which illustrates case 1, the number of black nodes from the root to either subtree α or β is 3, both before and after the transformation. (Remember, the pointer x adds an extra black.) Similarly, the number of black nodes from the root to any of γ, δ, ε, and ζ is 2, both before and after the transformation. In Figure 14.7(b), the counting must involve the color c, which can be either red or black. If we define count(RED) = 0 and count(BLACK) = 1, then the number of black nodes from the root to α is $2 + \text{count}(c)$, both before and after the transformation. The other cases can be verified similarly (Exercise 14.4-5).

Case 1 (lines 5–8 of RB-DELETE-FIXUP and Figure 14.7(a)) occurs when node w, the sibling of node x, is red. Since w must have black children, we can switch the colors of w and $p[x]$ and then perform a left-rotation on $p[x]$ without violating any of the red-black properties. The new sibling of x, one of w's children, is now black, and thus we have converted case 1 into case 2, 3, or 4.

Cases 2, 3, and 4 occur when node w is black; they are distinguished by the colors of w's children. In case 2 (lines 10–11 of RB-DELETE-FIXUP and Figure 14.7(b)), both of w's children are black. Since w is also black, we take one black off both x and w, leaving x with only one black and leaving w red, and add an extra black to $p[x]$. We then repeat the **while** loop with $p[x]$ as the new node x. Observe that if we enter case 2 through case 1, the color c of the new node x is red, since the original $p[x]$ was red, and thus the loop terminates when it tests the loop condition.

Case 3 (lines 13–16 and Figure 14.7(c)) occurs when w is black, its left child is red, and its right child is black. We can switch the colors of w and its left child *left[w]* and then perform a right rotation on w without violating any of the red-black properties. The new sibling w of x is now a black node with a red right child, and thus we have transformed case 3 into case 4.

Case 4 (lines 17–21 and Figure 14.7(d)) occurs when node x's sibling w is black and w's right child is red. By making some color changes and performing a left rotation on $p[x]$, we can remove the extra black on x without violating any of the red-black properties. Setting x to be the root causes the **while** loop to terminate when it tests the loop condition.

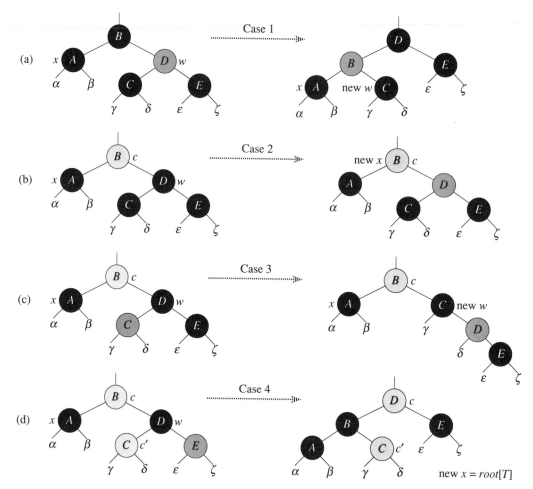

Figure 14.7 The cases in the **while** loop of the procedure RB-DELETE. Darkened nodes are black, heavily shaded nodes are red, and lightly shaded nodes, which may be either red or black, are represented by c and c'. The letters $\alpha, \beta, \ldots, \zeta$ represent arbitrary subtrees. In each case, the configuration on the left is transformed into the configuration on the right by changing some colors and/or performing a rotation. A node pointed to by x has an extra black. The only case that causes the loop to repeat is case 2. **(a)** Case 1 is transformed to case 2, 3, or 4 by exchanging the colors of nodes B and D and performing a left rotation. **(b)** In case 2, the extra black represented by the pointer x is moved up the tree by coloring node D red and setting x to point to node B. If we enter case 2 through case 1, the **while** loop terminates, since the color c is red. **(c)** Case 3 is transformed to case 4 by exchanging the colors of nodes C and D and performing a right rotation. **(d)** In case 4, the extra black represented by x can be removed by changing some colors and performing a left rotation (without violating the red-black properties), and the loop terminates.

What is the running time of RB-Delete? Since the height of a red-black tree of n nodes is $O(\lg n)$, the total cost of the procedure without the call to RB-Delete-Fixup takes $O(\lg n)$ time. Within RB-Delete-Fixup, cases 1, 3, and 4 each terminate after performing a constant number of color changes and at most three rotations. Case 2 is the only case in which the **while** loop can be repeated, and then the pointer x moves up the tree at most $O(\lg n)$ times and no rotations are performed. Thus, the procedure RB-Delete-Fixup takes $O(\lg n)$ time and performs at most three rotations, and the overall time for RB-Delete is therefore also $O(\lg n)$.

Exercises

14.4-1
Argue that the root of the red-black tree is always black after RB-Delete executes.

14.4-2
In Exercise 14.3-3, you found the red-black tree that results from successively inserting the keys $41, 38, 31, 12, 19, 8$ into an initially empty tree. Now show the red-black trees that result from the successive deletion of the keys in the order $8, 12, 19, 31, 38, 41$.

14.4-3
In which lines of the code for RB-Delete-Fixup might we examine or modify the sentinel $nil[T]$?

14.4-4
Simplify the code for Left-Rotate by using a sentinel for NIL and another sentinel to hold the pointer to the root.

14.4-5
In each of the cases of Figure 14.7, give the count of black nodes from the root of the subtree shown to each of the subtrees $\alpha, \beta, \ldots, \zeta$, and verify that each count remains the same after the transformation. When a node has a color c or c', use the notation count(c) or count(c') symbolically in your count.

14.4-6
Suppose that a node x is inserted into a red-black tree with RB-Insert and then immediately deleted with RB-Delete. Is the resulting red-black tree the same as the initial red-black tree? Justify your answer.

Problems

14-1   *Persistent dynamic sets*

During the course of an algorithm, we sometimes find that we need to maintain past versions of a dynamic set as it is updated. Such a set is called **persistent**. One way to implement a persistent set is to copy the entire set whenever it is modified, but this approach can slow down a program and also consume much space. Sometimes, we can do much better.

Consider a persistent set S with the operations INSERT, DELETE, and SEARCH, which we implement using binary search trees as shown in Figure 14.8(a). We maintain a separate root for every version of the set. In order to insert the key 5 into the set, we create a new node with key 5. This node becomes the left child of a new node with key 7, since we cannot modify the existing node with key 7. Similarly, the new node with key 7 becomes the left child of a new node with key 8 whose right child is the existing node with key 10. The new node with key 8 becomes, in turn, the right child of a new root r' with key 4 whose left child is the existing node with key 3. We thus copy only part of the tree and share some of the nodes with the original tree, as shown in Figure 14.8(b).

a. For a general persistent binary search tree, identify the nodes that need to be changed to insert a key k or delete a node y.

b. Write a procedure PERSISTENT-TREE-INSERT that, given a persistent tree T and a key k to insert, returns a new persistent tree T' that is the result of inserting k into T. Assume that each tree node has the fields *key*, *left*, and *right* but no parent field. (See also Exercise 14.3-6.)

c. If the height of the persistent binary search tree T is h, what are the time and space requirements of your implementation of PERSISTENT-TREE-INSERT? (The space requirement is proportional to the number of new nodes allocated.)

d. Suppose that we had included the parent field in each node. In this case, PERSISTENT-TREE-INSERT would need to perform additional copying. Prove that PERSISTENT-TREE-INSERT would then require $\Omega(n)$ time and space, where n is the number of nodes in the tree.

e. Show how to use red-black trees to guarantee that the worst-case running time and space is $O(\lg n)$ per insertion or deletion.

14-2   *Join operation on red-black trees*

The **join** operation takes two dynamic sets S_1 and S_2 and an element x such that for any $x_1 \in S_1$ and $x_2 \in S_2$, we have $key[x_1] \leq key[x] \leq key[x_2]$. It returns a set $S = S_1 \cup \{x\} \cup S_2$. In this problem, we investigate how to implement the join operation on red-black trees.

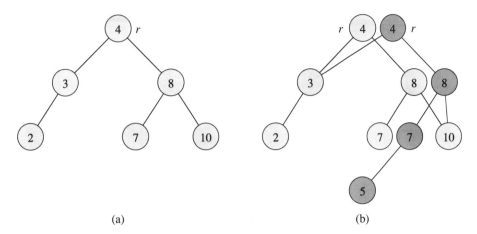

Figure 14.8 (a) A binary search tree with keys 2, 3, 4, 7, 8, 10. (b) The persistent binary search tree that results from the insertion of key 5. The most recent version of the set consists of the nodes reachable from the root r', and the previous version consists of the nodes reachable from r. Heavily shaded nodes are added when key 5 is inserted.

a. Given a red-black tree T, we store its black-height as the field $bh[T]$. Argue that this field can be maintained by RB-INSERT and RB-DELETE without requiring extra storage in the tree and without increasing the asymptotic running times. Show that while descending through T, we can determine the black-height of each node we visit in $O(1)$ time per node visited.

We wish to implement the operation RB-JOIN(T_1, x, T_2), which destroys T_1 and T_2 and returns a red-black tree $T = T_1 \cup \{x\} \cup T_2$. Let n be the total number of nodes in T_1 and T_2.

b. Assume without loss of generality that $bh[T_1] \geq bh[T_2]$. Describe an $O(\lg n)$-time algorithm that finds a black node y in T_1 with the largest key from among those nodes whose black-height is $bh[T_2]$.

c. Let T_y be the subtree rooted at y. Describe how T_y can be replaced by $T_y \cup \{x\} \cup T_2$ in $O(1)$ time without destroying the binary-search-tree property.

d. What color should we make x so that red-black properties 1, 2, and 4 are maintained? Describe how property 3 can be enforced in $O(\lg n)$ time.

e. Argue that the running time of RB-JOIN is $O(\lg n)$.

Chapter notes

The idea of balancing a search tree is due to Adel'son-Vel'skiĭ and Landis [2], who introduced a class of balanced search trees called "AVL trees" in 1962. Balance is maintained in AVL trees by rotations, but as many as $\Theta(\lg n)$ rotations may be required after an insertion to maintain balance in an n-node tree. Another class of search trees, called "2-3 trees," was introduced by J. E. Hopcroft (unpublished) in 1970. Balance is maintained in a 2-3 tree by manipulating the degrees of nodes in the tree. A generalization of 2-3 trees introduced by Bayer and McCreight [18], called B-trees, is the topic of Chapter 19.

Red-black trees were invented by Bayer [17] under the name "symmetric binary B-trees." Guibas and Sedgewick [93] studied their properties at length and introduced the red/black color convention.

Of the many other variations on balanced binary trees, perhaps the most intriguing are the "splay trees" introduced by Sleator and Tarjan [177], which are "self-adjusting." (A good description of splay trees is given by Tarjan [188].) Splay trees maintain balance without any explicit balance condition such as color. Instead, "splay operations" (which involve rotations) are performed within the tree every time an access is made. The amortized cost (see Chapter 18) of each operation on an n-node tree is $O(\lg n)$.

15   Augmenting Data Structures

There are some engineering situations that require no more than a "text-book" data structure—such as a doubly linked list, a hash table, or a binary search tree—but many others require a dash of creativity. Only in rare situations will you need to create an entirely new type of data structure, though. More often, it will suffice to augment a textbook data structure by storing additional information in it. You can then program new operations for the data structure to support the desired application. Augmenting a data structure is not always straightforward, however, since the added information must be updated and maintained by the ordinary operations on the data structure.

This chapter discusses two data structures that are constructed by augmenting red-black trees. Section 15.1 describes a data structure that supports general order-statistic operations on a dynamic set. We can then quickly find the ith smallest number in a set or the rank of a given element in the total ordering of the set. Section 15.2 abstracts the process of augmenting a data structure and provides a theorem that can simplify the augmentation of red-black trees. Section 15.3 uses this theorem to help design a data structure for maintaining a dynamic set of intervals, such as time intervals. Given a query interval, we can then quickly find an interval in the set that overlaps it.

15.1   Dynamic order statistics

Chapter 10 introduced the notion of an order statistic. Specifically, the ith order statistic of a set of n elements, where $i \in \{1, 2, \ldots, n\}$, is simply the element in the set with the ith smallest key. We saw that any order statistic could be retrieved in $O(n)$ time from an unordered set. In this section, we shall see how red-black trees can be modified so that any order statistic can be determined in $O(\lg n)$ time. We shall also see how the *rank* of an element—its position in the linear order of the set—can likewise be determined in $O(\lg n)$ time.

A data structure that can support fast order-statistic operations is shown in Figure 15.1. An *order-statistic tree* T is simply a red-black tree with

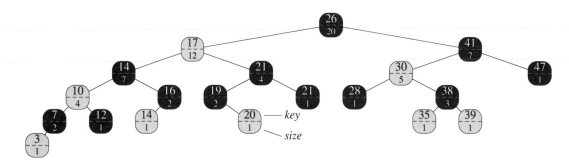

Figure 15.1 An order-statistic tree, which is an augmented red-black tree. Shaded nodes are red, and darkened nodes are black. In addition to its usual fields, each node x has a field $size[x]$, which is the number of nodes in the subtree rooted at x.

additional information stored in each node. Besides the usual red-black tree fields $key[x]$, $color[x]$, $p[x]$, $left[x]$, and $right[x]$ in a node x, we have another field $size[x]$. This field contains the number of (internal) nodes in the subtree rooted at x (including x itself), that is, the size of the subtree. If we define $size[\text{NIL}]$ to be 0, then we have the identity

$$size[x] = size[left[x]] + size[right[x]] + 1 .$$

(To handle the boundary condition for NIL properly, an actual implementation might test explicitly for NIL each time the $size$ field is accessed or, more simply, as in Section 14.4, use a sentinel $nil[T]$ to represent NIL, where $size[nil[T]] = 0$.)

Retrieving an element with a given rank

Before we show how to maintain this size information during insertion and deletion, let us examine the implementation of two order-statistic queries that use this additional information. We begin with an operation that retrieves an element with a given rank. The procedure OS-SELECT(x, i) returns a pointer to the node containing the ith smallest key in the subtree rooted at x. To find the ith smallest key in an order-statistic tree T, we call OS-SELECT$(root[T], i)$.

OS-SELECT(x, i)

1 $r \leftarrow size[left[x]]+1$
2 **if** $i = r$
3   **then return** x
4 **elseif** $i < r$
5   **then return** OS-SELECT$(left[x], i)$
6 **else return** OS-SELECT$(right[x], i - r)$

The idea behind OS-SELECT is similar to that of the selection algorithms in Chapter 10. The value of $size[left[x]]$ is the number of nodes that come before x in an inorder tree walk of the subtree rooted at x. Thus, $size[left[x]] + 1$ is the rank of x within the subtree rooted at x.

In line 1 of OS-SELECT, we compute r, the rank of node x within the subtree rooted at x. If $i = r$, then node x is the ith smallest element, so we return x in line 3. If $i < r$, then the ith smallest element is in x's left subtree, so we recurse on $left[x]$ in line 5. If $i > r$, then the ith smallest element is in x's right subtree. Since there are r elements in the subtree rooted at x that come before x's right subtree in an inorder tree walk, the ith smallest element in the subtree rooted at x is the $(i - r)$th smallest element in the subtree rooted at $right[x]$. This element is determined recursively in line 6.

To see how OS-SELECT operates, consider a search for the 17th smallest element in the order-statistic tree of Figure 15.1. We begin with x as the root, whose key is 26, and with $i = 17$. Since the size of 26's left subtree is 12, its rank is 13. Thus, we know that the node with rank 17 is the $17 - 13 = 4$th smallest element in 26's right subtree. After the recursive call, x is the node with key 41, and $i = 4$. Since the size of 41's left subtree is 5, its rank within its subtree is 6. Thus, we know that the node with rank 4 is in the 4th smallest element in 41's left subtree. After the recursive call, x is the node with key 30, and its rank within its subtree is 2. Thus, we recurse once again to find the $4 - 2 = 2$nd smallest element in the subtree rooted at the node with key 38. We now find that its left subtree has size 1, which means it is the second smallest element. Thus, a pointer to the node with key 38 is returned by the procedure.

Because each recursive call goes down one level in the order-statistic tree, the total time for OS-SELECT is at worst proportional to the height of the tree. Since the tree is a red-black tree, its height is $O(\lg n)$, where n is the number of nodes. Thus, the running time of OS-SELECT is $O(\lg n)$ for a dynamic set of n elements.

Determining the rank of an element

Given a pointer to a node x in an order-statistic tree T, the procedure OS-RANK returns the position of x in the linear order determined by an inorder tree walk of T.

OS-RANK(T, x)

```
1   r ← size[left[x]] + 1
2   y ← x
3   while y ≠ root[T]
4       do if y = right[p[y]]
5           then r ← r + size[left[p[y]]] + 1
6           y ← p[y]
7   return r
```

The procedure works as follows. The rank of x can be viewed as the number of nodes preceding x in an inorder tree walk, plus 1 for x itself. The following invariant is maintained: at the top of the **while** loop of lines 3–6, r is the rank of $key[x]$ in the subtree rooted at node y. We maintain this invariant as follows. In line 1, we set r to be the rank of $key[x]$ within the subtree rooted at x. Setting $y \leftarrow x$ in line 2 makes the invariant true the first time the test in line 3 executes. In each iteration of the **while** loop, we consider the subtree rooted at $p[y]$. We have already counted the number of nodes in the subtree rooted at node y that precede x in an inorder walk, so we must add the nodes in the subtree rooted at y's sibling that precede x in an inorder walk, plus 1 for $p[y]$ if it, too, precedes x. If y is a left child, then neither $p[y]$ nor any node in $p[y]$'s right subtree precedes x, so we leave r alone. Otherwise, y is a right child and all the nodes in $p[y]$'s left subtree precede x, as does $p[y]$ itself. Thus, in line 5, we add $size[left[y]] + 1$ to the current value of r. Setting $y \leftarrow p[y]$ makes the invariant true for the next iteration. When $y = root[T]$, the procedure returns the value of r, which is now the rank of $key[x]$.

As an example, when we run OS-RANK on the order-statistic tree of Figure 15.1 to find the rank of the node with key 38, we get the following sequence of values of $key[y]$ and r at the top of the **while** loop:

iteration	$key[y]$	r
1	38	2
2	30	4
3	41	4
4	26	17

The rank 17 is returned.

Since each iteration of the **while** loop takes $O(1)$ time, and y goes up one level in the tree with each iteration, the running time of OS-RANK is at worst proportional to the height of the tree: $O(\lg n)$ on an n-node order-statistic tree.

Maintaining subtree sizes

Given the *size* field in each node, OS-SELECT and OS-RANK can quickly compute order-statistic information. But unless these fields can be efficiently maintained by the basic modifying operations on red-black trees, our work will have been for naught. We shall now show that subtree sizes can be maintained for both insertion and deletion without affecting the asymptotic running times of either operation.

We noted in Section 14.3 that insertion into a red-black tree consists of two phases. The first phase goes down the tree from the root, inserting the new node as a child of an existing node. The second phase goes up the tree, changing colors and ultimately performing rotations to maintain the red-black properties.

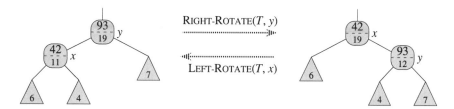

Figure 15.2 Updating subtree sizes during rotations. The two *size* fields that need to be updated are the ones incident on the link around which the rotation is performed. The updates are local, requiring only the *size* information stored in x, y, and the roots of the subtrees shown as triangles.

To maintain the subtree sizes in the first phase, we simply increment *size*[x] for each node x on the path traversed from the root down toward the leaves. The new node added gets a *size* of 1. Since there are $O(\lg n)$ nodes on the traversed path, the additional cost of maintaining the *size* fields is $O(\lg n)$.

In the second phase, the only structural changes to the underlying red-black tree are caused by rotations, of which there are at most two. Moreover, a rotation is a local operation: it invalidates only the two *size* fields in the nodes incident on the link around which the rotation is performed. Referring to the code for LEFT-ROTATE(T, x) in Section 14.2, we add the following lines:

```
13   size[y] ← size[x]
14   size[x] ← size[left[x]] + size[right[x]] + 1
```

Figure 15.2 illustrates how the fields are updated. The change to RIGHT-ROTATE is symmetric.

Since at most two rotations are performed during insertion into a red-black tree, only $O(1)$ additional time is spent updating *size* fields in the second phase. Thus, the total time for insertion into an n-node order-statistic tree is $O(\lg n)$—asymptotically the same as for an ordinary red-black tree.

Deletion from a red-black tree also consists of two phases: the first operates on the underlying search tree, and the second causes at most three rotations and otherwise performs no structural changes. (See Section 14.4.) The first phase splices out one node y. To update the subtree sizes, we simply traverse a path from node y up to the root, decrementing the *size* field of each node on the path. Since this path has length $O(\lg n)$ in an n-node red-black tree, the additional time spent maintaining *size* fields in the first phase is $O(\lg n)$. The $O(1)$ rotations in the second phase of deletion can be handled in the same manner as for insertion. Thus, both insertion and deletion, including the maintenance of the *size* fields, take $O(\lg n)$ time for an n-node order-statistic tree.

Exercises

15.1-1
Show how OS-SELECT($T, 10$) operates on the red-black tree T of Figure 15.2.

15.1-2
Show how OS-RANK(T, x) operates on the red-black tree T of Figure 15.2 and the node x with $key[x] = 35$.

15.1-3
Write a nonrecursive version of OS-SELECT.

15.1-4
Write a recursive procedure OS-KEY-RANK(T, k) that takes as input an order-statistic tree T and a key k and returns the rank of k in the dynamic set represented by T. Assume that the keys of T are distinct.

15.1-5
Given an element x in an n-node order-statistic tree and a natural number i, how can the ith successor of x in the linear order of the tree be determined in $O(\lg n)$ time?

15.1-6
Observe that whenever the *size* field is referenced in either OS-SELECT or OS-RANK, it is only used to compute the rank of x in the subtree rooted at x. Accordingly, suppose we store in each node its rank in the subtree of which it is the root. Show how this information can be maintained during insertion and deletion. (Remember that these two operations can cause rotations.)

15.1-7
Show how to use an order-statistic tree to to count the number of inversions (see Problem 1-3) in an array of size n in time $O(n \lg n)$.

15.1-8 ⋆
Consider n chords on a circle, each defined by its endpoints. Describe an $O(n \lg n)$-time algorithm for determining the number of pairs of chords that intersect inside the circle. (For example, if the n chords are all diameters that meet at the center, then the correct answer is $\binom{n}{2}$.) Assume that no two chords share an endpoint.

15.2 How to augment a data structure

The process of augmenting a basic data structure to support additional functionality occurs quite frequently in algorithm design. It will be used again in the next section to design a data structure that supports operations on intervals. In this section, we shall examine the steps involved in such augmentation. We shall also prove a theorem that allows us to augment red-black trees easily in many cases.

Augmenting a data structure can be broken into four steps:

1. choosing an underlying data structure,

2. determining additional information to be maintained in the underlying data structure,

3. verifying that the additional information can be maintained for the basic modifying operations on the underlying data structure, and

4. developing new operations.

As with any prescriptive design method, you should not blindly follow the steps in the order given. Most design work contains an element of trial and error, and progress on all steps usually proceeds in parallel. There is no point, for example, in determining additional information and developing new operations (steps 2 and 4) if we will not be able to maintain the additional information efficiently. Nevertheless, this four-step method provides a good focus for your efforts in augmenting a data structure, and it is also a good way to organize the documentation of an augmented data structure.

We followed these steps in Section 15.1 to design our order-statistic trees. For step 1, we chose red-black trees as the underlying data structure. A clue to the suitability of red-black trees comes from their efficient support of other dynamic-set operations on a total order, such as MINIMUM, MAXIMUM, SUCCESSOR, and PREDECESSOR.

For step 2, we provided the *size* fields, which in each node x stores the size of the subtree rooted at x. Generally, the additional information makes operations more efficient. For example, we could have implemented OS-SELECT and OS-RANK using just the keys stored in the tree, but they would not have run in $O(\lg n)$ time. Sometimes, the additional information is pointer information rather than data, as in Exercise 15.2-1.

For step 3, we ensured that insertion and deletion could maintain the *size* fields while still running in $O(\lg n)$ time. Ideally, a small number of changes to the data structure should suffice to maintain the additional information. For example, if we simply stored in each node its rank in the tree, the OS-SELECT and OS-RANK procedures would run quickly, but inserting a new minimum element would cause a change to this information in every node of the tree. When we store subtree sizes instead, inserting a new element causes information to change in only $O(\lg n)$ nodes.

For step 4, we developed the operations OS-SELECT and OS-RANK. After all, the need for new operations is why we bother to augment a data
structure in the first place. Occasionally, rather than developing new operations, we use the additional information to expedite existing ones, as in
Exercise 15.2-1.

Augmenting red-black trees

When red-black trees underlie an augmented data structure, we can prove
that certain kinds of additional information can always be efficiently maintained by insertion and deletion, thereby making step 3 very easy. The
proof of the following theorem is similar to the argument from Section 15.1
that the *size* field can be maintained for order-statistic trees.

Theorem 15.1 (Augmenting a red-black tree)
Let f be a field that augments a red-black tree T of n nodes, and suppose
that the contents of f for a node x can be computed using only the information in nodes x, *left*[x], and *right*[x], including $f[left[x]]$ and $f[right[x]]$.
Then, we can maintain the values of f in all nodes of T during insertion
and deletion without asymptotically affecting the $O(\lg n)$ performance of
these operations.

Proof   The main idea of the proof is that a change to an f field in a
node x propagates only to ancestors of x in the tree. That is, changing
$f[x]$ may require $f[p[x]]$ to be updated, but nothing else; updating $f[p[x]]$
may require $f[p[p[x]]]$ to be updated, but nothing else; and so on up the
tree. When $f[root[T]]$ is updated, no other node depends on the new
value, so the process terminates. Since the height of a red-black tree is
$O(\lg n)$, changing an f field in a node costs $O(\lg n)$ time in updating nodes
dependent on the change.

   Insertion of a node x into T consists of two phases. (See Section 14.3.)
During the first phase, x is inserted as a child of an existing node $p[x]$.
The value for $f[x]$ can be computed in $O(1)$ time since, by supposition,
it depends only on information in the other fields of x itself and the information in x's children, but x's children are both NIL. Once $f[x]$ is
computed, the change propagates up the tree. Thus, the total time for
the first phase of insertion is $O(\lg n)$. During the second phase, the only
structural changes to the tree come from rotations. Since only two nodes
change in a rotation, the total time for updating the f fields is $O(\lg n)$ per
rotation. Since the number of rotations during insertion is at most two,
the total time for insertion is $O(\lg n)$.

   Like insertion, deletion has two phases. (See Section 14.4.) In the first
phase, changes to the tree occur if the deleted node is replaced by its
successor, and then again when either the deleted node or its successor is
spliced out. Propagating the updates to f caused by these changes costs

at most $O(\lg n)$ since the changes modify the tree locally. Fixing up the red-black tree during the second phase requires at most three rotations, and each rotation requires at most $O(\lg n)$ time to propagate the updates to f. Thus, like insertion, the total time for deletion is $O(\lg n)$. ∎

In many cases, such as maintenance of the *size* fields in order-statistic trees, the cost of updating after a rotation is $O(1)$, rather than the $O(\lg n)$ derived in the proof of Theorem 15.1. Exercise 15.2-4 gives an example.

Exercises

15.2-1
Show how the dynamic-set queries MINIMUM, MAXIMUM, SUCCESSOR, and PREDECESSOR can each be supported in $O(1)$ worst-case time on an augmented order-statistic tree. The asymptotic performance of other operations on order-statistic trees should not be affected.

15.2-2
Can the black-heights of nodes in a red-black tree be maintained as fields in the nodes of the tree without affecting the asymptotic performance of any of the red-black tree operations? Show how, or argue why not.

15.2-3
Can the depths of nodes in a red-black tree be efficiently maintained as fields in the nodes of the tree? Show how, or argue why not.

15.2-4 ⋆
Let $\otimes$ be an associative binary operator, and let a be a field maintained in each node of a red-black tree. Suppose that we want to include in each node x an additional field f such that $f[x] = a[x_1] \otimes a[x_2] \otimes \cdots \otimes a[x_m]$, where $x_1, x_2, \ldots, x_m$ is the inorder listing of nodes in the subtree rooted at x. Show that the f fields can be properly updated in $O(1)$ time after a rotation. Modify your argument slightly to show that the *size* fields in order-statistic trees can be maintained in $O(1)$ time per rotation.

15.2-5 ⋆
We wish to augment red-black trees with an operation RB-ENUMERATE(x, a, b) that outputs all the keys k such that $a \leq k \leq b$ in a red-black tree rooted at x. Describe how RB-ENUMERATE can be implemented in $\Theta(m + \lg n)$ time, where m is the number of keys that are output and n is the number of internal nodes in the tree. (*Hint:* There is no need to add new fields to the red-black tree.)

15.3   Interval trees

In this section, we shall augment red-black trees to support operations on dynamic sets of intervals. A ***closed interval*** is an ordered pair of real numbers $[t_1, t_2]$, with $t_1 \leq t_2$. The interval $[t_1, t_2]$ represents the set $\{t \in \mathbf{R} : t_1 \leq t \leq t_2\}$. ***Open*** and ***half-open*** intervals omit both or one of the endpoints from the set, respectively. In this section, we shall assume that intervals are closed; extending the results to open and half-open intervals is conceptually straightforward.

Intervals are convenient for representing events that each occupy a continuous period of time. We might, for example, wish to query a database of time intervals to find out what events occurred during a given interval. The data structure in this section provides an efficient means for maintaining such an interval database.

We can represent an interval $[t_1, t_2]$ as an object i, with fields $low[i] = t_1$ (the ***low endpoint***) and $high[i] = t_2$ (the ***high endpoint***). We say that intervals i and i' ***overlap*** if $i \cap i' \neq \emptyset$, that is, if $low[i] \leq high[i']$ and $low[i'] \leq high[i]$. Any two intervals i and i' satisfy the ***interval trichotomy***; that is, exactly one of the following three properties holds:

a. i and i' overlap,

b. $high[i] < low[i']$,

c. $high[i'] < low[i]$.

Figure 15.3 shows the three possibilities.

An ***interval tree*** is a red-black tree that maintains a dynamic set of elements, with each element x containing an interval $int[x]$. Interval trees support the following operations.

INTERVAL-INSERT(T, x) adds the element x, whose int field is assumed to contain an interval, to the interval tree T.

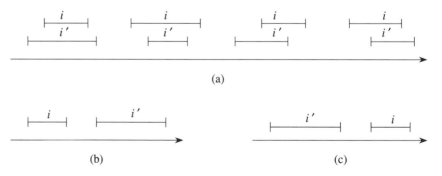

(a)

(b)   (c)

Figure 15.3   The interval trichotomy for two closed intervals i and i'. **(a)** If i and i' overlap, there are four situations; in each, $low[i] \leq high[i']$ and $low[i'] \leq high[i]$. **(b)** $high[i] < low[i']$. **(c)** $high[i'] < low[i]$.

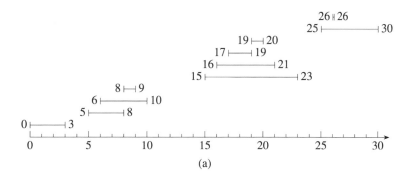

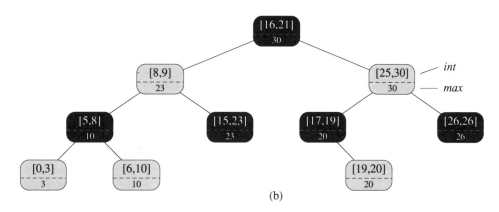

Figure 15.4   An interval tree. **(a)** A set of 10 intervals, shown sorted bottom to top by left endpoint. **(b)** The interval tree that represents them. An inorder tree walk of the tree lists the nodes in sorted order by left endpoint.

INTERVAL-DELETE(T, x) removes the element x from the interval tree T.

INTERVAL-SEARCH(T, i) returns a pointer to an element x in the interval tree T such that $int[x]$ overlaps interval i, or NIL if no such element is in the set.

Figure 15.4 shows how an interval tree represents a set of intervals. We shall track the four-step method from Section 15.2 as we review the design of an interval tree and the operations that run on it.

Step 1: Underlying data structure

We choose a red-black tree in which each node x contains an interval $int[x]$ and the key of x is the low endpoint, $low[int[x]]$, of the interval. Thus, an inorder tree walk of the data structure lists the intervals in sorted order by low endpoint.

Step 2: Additional information

In addition to the intervals themselves, each node x contains a value $max[x]$, which is the maximum value of any interval endpoint stored in the subtree rooted at x. Since any interval's high endpoint is at least as large as its low endpoint, $max[x]$ is the maximum value of all right endpoints in the subtree rooted at x.

Step 3: Maintaining the information

We must verify that insertion and deletion can be performed in $O(\lg n)$ time on an interval tree of n nodes. We can determine $max[x]$ given interval $int[x]$ and the max values of node x's children:

$$max[x] = \max(high[int[x]], max[left[x]], max[right[x]]) \ .$$

Thus, by Theorem 15.1, insertion and deletion run in $O(\lg n)$ time. In fact, updating the max fields after a rotation can be accomplished in $O(1)$ time, as is shown in Exercises 15.2-4 and 15.3-1.

Step 4: Developing new operations

The only new operation we need is INTERVAL-SEARCH(T, i), which finds an interval in tree T that overlaps interval i. If there is no interval that overlaps i in the tree, NIL is returned.

INTERVAL-SEARCH(T, i)

```
1  x ← root[T]
2  while x ≠ NIL and i does not overlap int[x]
3      do if left[x] ≠ NIL and max[left[x]] ≥ low[i]
4            then x ← left[x]
5            else  x ← right[x]
6  return x
```

The search for an interval that overlaps i starts with x at the root of the tree and proceeds downward. It terminates when either an overlapping interval is found or x becomes NIL. Since each iteration of the basic loop takes $O(1)$ time, and since the height of an n-node red-black tree is $O(\lg n)$, the INTERVAL-SEARCH procedure takes $O(\lg n)$ time.

Before we see why INTERVAL-SEARCH is correct, let's examine how it works on the interval tree in Figure 15.4. Suppose we wish to find an interval that overlaps the interval $i = [22, 25]$. We begin with x as the root, which contains $[16, 21]$ and does not overlap i. Since $max[left[x]] = 23$ is greater than $low[i] = 22$, the loop continues with x as the left child of the root—the node containing $[8, 9]$, which also does not overlap i. This time, $max[left[x]] = 10$ is less than $low[i] = 22$, so the loop continues with the right child of x as the new x. The interval $[15, 23]$ stored in this node overlaps i, so the procedure returns this node.

As an example of an unsuccessful search, suppose we wish to find an interval that overlaps $i = [11, 14]$ in the interval tree of Figure 15.4. We once again begin with x as the root. Since the root's interval $[16, 21]$ does not overlap i, and since $max[left[x]] = 23$ is greater than $low[i] = 11$, we go left to the node containing $[8, 9]$. (Note that no interval in the right subtree overlaps i—we shall see why later.) Interval $[8, 9]$ does not overlap i, and $max[left[x]] = 10$ is less than $low[i] = 11$, so we go right. (Note that no interval in the left subtree overlaps i.) Interval $[15, 23]$ does not overlap i, and its left child is NIL, so we go right, the loop terminates, and NIL is returned.

To see why INTERVAL-SEARCH is correct, we must understand why it suffices to examine a single path from the root. The basic idea is that at any node x, if $int[x]$ does not overlap i, the search always proceeds in a safe direction: an overlapping interval will definitely be found if there is one in the tree. The following theorem states this property more precisely.

Theorem 15.2
Consider any iteration of the **while** loop during the execution of INTERVAL-SEARCH(T, i).

1. If line 4 is executed (the search goes left), then x's left subtree contains an interval that overlaps i or no interval in x's right subtree overlaps i.

2. If line 5 is executed (the search goes right), then x's left subtree contains no interval that overlaps i.

Proof The proof of both cases depend on the interval trichotomy. We prove case 2 first, since it is simpler. Observe that if line 5 is executed, then because of the branch condition in line 3, we have $left[x] = $ NIL, or $max[left[x]] < low[i]$. If $left[x] = $ NIL, the subtree rooted at $left[x]$ clearly contains no interval that overlaps i, because it contains no intervals at all. Suppose, therefore, that $left[x] \neq $ NIL and $max[left[x]] < low[i]$. Let i' be an interval in x's left subtree. (See Figure 15.5(a).) Since $max[left[x]]$ is the largest endpoint in x's left subtree, we have

$$
\begin{aligned}
high[i'] \quad &\leq \quad max[left[x]] \\
&< \quad low[i] \, ,
\end{aligned}
$$

and thus, by the interval trichotomy, i' and i do not overlap, which completes the proof of case 2.

To prove case 1, we may assume that no intervals in x's left subtree overlap i (since if any do, we are done), and thus we need only prove that no intervals in x's right subtree overlap i under this assumption. Observe that if line 4 is executed, then because of the branch condition in line 3, we have $max[left[x]] \geq low[i]$. Moreover, by definition of the *max* field,

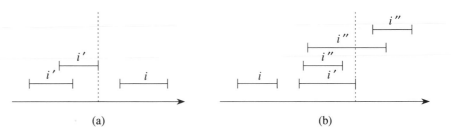

Figure 15.5 Intervals in the proof of Theorem 15.2. The value of *max*[*left*[*x*]] is shown in each case as a dashed line. **(a)** Case 2: the search goes right. No interval *i'* can overlap *i*. **(b)** Case 1: the search goes left. The left subtree of *x* contains an interval that overlaps *i* (situation not shown), or there is an interval *i'* in *x*'s left subtree such that *high*[*i'*] = *max*[*left*[*x*]]. Since *i* does not overlap *i'*, neither does it overlap any interval *i''* in *x*'s right subtree, since *low*[*i'*] ≤ *low*[*i''*].

there must be some interval *i'* in *x*'s left subtree such that

$$high[i'] = max[left[x]]$$
$$\geq low[i] \,.$$

(Figure 15.5(b) illustrates the situation.) Since *i* and *i'* do not overlap, and since it is not true that *high*[*i'*] < *low*[*i*], it follows by the interval trichotomy that *high*[*i*] < *low*[*i'*]. Interval trees are keyed on the low endpoints of intervals, and thus the search-tree property implies that for any interval *i''* in *x*'s right subtree,

$$high[i] < low[i']$$
$$\leq low[i''] \,.$$

By the interval trichotomy, *i* and *i''* do not overlap.   ∎

Theorem 15.2 guarantees that if INTERVAL-SEARCH continues with one of *x*'s children and no overlapping interval is found, a search starting with *x*'s other child would have been equally fruitless.

Exercises

15.3-1
Write pseudocode for LEFT-ROTATE that operates on nodes in an interval tree and updates the *max* fields in $O(1)$ time.

15.3-2
Rewrite the code for INTERVAL-SEARCH so that it works properly when all intervals are assumed to be open.

15.3-3
Describe an efficient algorithm that, given an interval i, returns an interval overlapping i that has the minimum low endpoint, or NIL if no such interval exists.

15.3-4
Given an interval tree T and an interval i, describe how all intervals in T that overlap i can be listed in $O(\min(n, k \lg n))$ time, where k is the number of intervals in the output list. (*Optional:* Find a solution that does not modify the tree.)

15.3-5
Suggest modifications to the interval-tree procedures to support the operation INTERVAL-SEARCH-EXACTLY(T, i), which returns a pointer to a node x in interval tree T such that $low[int[x]] = low[i]$ and $high[int[x]] = high[i]$, or NIL if T contains no such node. All operations, including INTERVAL-SEARCH-EXACTLY, should run in $O(\lg n)$ time on an n-node tree.

15.3-6
Show how to maintain a dynamic set Q of numbers that supports the operation MIN-GAP, which gives the magnitude of the difference of the two closest numbers in Q. For example, if $Q = \{1, 5, 9, 15, 18, 22\}$, then MIN-GAP$(Q)$ returns $18 - 15 = 3$, since 15 and 18 are the two closest numbers in Q. Make the operations INSERT, DELETE, SEARCH, and MIN-GAP as efficient as possible, and analyze their running times.

15.3-7 $\star$
VLSI databases commonly represent an integrated circuit as a list of rectangles. Assume that each rectangle is rectilinearly oriented (sides parallel to the x- and y-axis), so that a representation of a rectangle consists of its minimum and maximum x- and y-coordinates. Give an $O(n \lg n)$-time algorithm to decide whether or not a set of rectangles so represented contains two rectangles that overlap. Your algorithm need not report all intersecting pairs, but it must report that an overlap exists if one rectangle entirely covers another, even if the boundary lines do not intersect. (*Hint:* Move a "sweep" line across the set of rectangles.)

Problems

15-1 *Point of maximum overlap*
Suppose that we wish to keep track of a *point of maximum overlap* in a set of intervals—a point that has the largest number of intervals in the database overlapping it. Show how the point of maximum overlap can be maintained efficiently while intervals are inserted and deleted.

15-2   Josephus permutation

The *Josephus problem* is defined as follows. Suppose that n people are arranged in a circle and that we are given a positive integer $m \leq n$. Beginning with a designated first person, we proceed around the circle, removing every mth person. After each person is removed, counting continues around the circle that remains. This process continues until all n people have been removed. The order in which the people are removed from the circle defines the *(n, m)-Josephus permutation* of the integers $1, 2, \ldots, n$. For example, the $(7, 3)$-Josephus permutation is $\langle 3, 6, 2, 7, 5, 1, 4 \rangle$.

a. Suppose that m is a constant. Describe an $O(n)$-time algorithm that, given an integer n, outputs the (n, m)-Josephus permutation.

b. Suppose that m is not a constant. Describe an $O(n \lg n)$-time algorithm that, given integers n and m, outputs the (n, m)-Josephus permutation.

Chapter notes

Preparata and Shamos [160] describe several of the interval trees that appear in the literature. Among the more important theoretically are those due independently to H. Edelsbrunner (1980) and E. M. McCreight (1981), which, in a database of n intervals, allow all k intervals that overlap a given query interval to be enumerated in $O(k + \lg n)$ time.

IV Advanced Design and Analysis Techniques

Introduction

This part covers three important techniques for the design and analysis of efficient algorithms: dynamic programming (Chapter 16), greedy algorithms (Chapter 17), and amortized analysis (Chapter 18). Earlier parts have presented other widely applicable techniques, such as divide-and-conquer, randomization, and the solution of recurrences. The new techniques are somewhat more sophisticated, but they are essential for effectively attacking many computational problems. The themes introduced in this part will recur later in the book.

Dynamic programming typically applies to optimization problems in which a set of choices must be made in order to arrive at an optimal solution. As choices are made, subproblems of the same form often arise. Dynamic programming is effective when a given subproblem may arise from more than one partial set of choices; the key technique is to store, or "memoize," the solution to each such subproblem in case it should reappear. Chapter 16 shows how this simple idea can easily transform exponential-time algorithms into polynomial-time algorithms.

Like dynamic-programming algorithms, greedy algorithms typically apply to optimization problems in which a set of choices must be made in order to arrive at an optimal solution. The idea of a greedy algorithm is to make each choice in a locally optimal manner. A simple example is coin-changing: to minimize the number of U.S. coins needed to make change for a given amount, it suffices to select repeatedly the largest-denomination coin that is not larger than the amount still owed. There are many such problems for which a greedy approach provides an optimal solution much more quickly than would a dynamic-programming approach. It is not always easy to tell whether a greedy approach will be effective, however. Chapter 17 reviews matroid theory, which can often be helpful in making such a determination.

Amortized analysis is a tool for analyzing algorithms that perform a sequence of similar operations. Instead of bounding the cost of the sequence of operations by bounding the actual cost of each operation separately, an amortized analysis can be used to provide a bound on the actual cost of the entire sequence. One reason this idea can be effective is that it may be impossible in a sequence of operations for all of the individual operations to run in their known worst-case time bounds. While some operations are expensive, many others might be cheap. Amortized analysis is not just an analysis tool, however; it is also a way of thinking about the design of algorithms, since the design of an algorithm and the analysis of its running time are often closely intertwined. Chapter 18 introduces three equivalent ways to perform an amortized analysis of an algorithm.

16   Dynamic Programming

Dynamic programming, like the divide-and-conquer method, solves problems by combining the solutions to subproblems. ("Programming" in this context refers to a tabular method, not to writing computer code.) As we saw in Chapter 1, divide-and-conquer algorithms partition the problem into independent subproblems, solve the subproblems recursively, and then combine their solutions to solve the original problem. In contrast, dynamic programming is applicable when the subproblems are not independent, that is, when subproblems share subsubproblems. In this context, a divide-and-conquer algorithm does more work than necessary, repeatedly solving the common subsubproblems. A dynamic-programming algorithm solves every subsubproblem just once and then saves its answer in a table, thereby avoiding the work of recomputing the answer every time the subsubproblem is encountered.

Dynamic programming is typically applied to *optimization problems*. In such problems there can be many possible solutions. Each solution has a value, and we wish to find a solution with the optimal (minimum or maximum) value. We call such a solution *an* optimal solution to the problem, as opposed to *the* optimal solution, since there may be several solutions that achieve the optimal value.

The development of a dynamic-programming algorithm can be broken into a sequence of four steps.

1. Characterize the structure of an optimal solution.

2. Recursively define the value of an optimal solution.

3. Compute the value of an optimal solution in a bottom-up fashion.

4. Construct an optimal solution from computed information.

Steps 1–3 form the basis of a dynamic-programming solution to a problem. Step 4 can be omitted if only the value of an optimal solution is required. When we do perform step 4, we sometimes maintain additional information during the computation in step 3 to ease the construction of an optimal solution.

The sections that follow use the dynamic-programming method to solve some optimization problems. Section 16.1 asks how we can multiply a chain of matrices so that the fewest total scalar multiplications are performed. Given this example of dynamic programming, Section 16.2 discusses two key characteristics that a problem must have for dynamic programming to be a viable solution technique. Section 16.3 then shows how to find the longest common subsequence of two sequences. Finally, Section 16.4 uses dynamic programming to find an optimal triangulation of a convex polygon, a problem that is surprisingly similar to matrix-chain multiplication.

16.1   Matrix-chain multiplication

Our first example of dynamic programming is an algorithm that solves the problem of matrix-chain multiplication. We are given a sequence (chain) $\langle A_1, A_2, \ldots, A_n \rangle$ of n matrices to be multiplied, and we wish to compute the product

$$A_1 A_2 \cdots A_n \, . \tag{16.1}$$

We can evaluate the expression (16.1) using the standard algorithm for multiplying pairs of matrices as a subroutine once we have parenthesized it to resolve all ambiguities in how the matrices are multiplied together. A product of matrices is ***fully parenthesized*** if it is either a single matrix or the product of two fully parenthesized matrix products, surrounded by parentheses. Matrix multiplication is associative, and so all parenthesizations yield the same product. For example, if the chain of matrices is $\langle A_1, A_2, A_3, A_4 \rangle$, the product $A_1 A_2 A_3 A_4$ can be fully parenthesized in five distinct ways:

$(A_1(A_2(A_3 A_4)))$,
$(A_1((A_2 A_3)A_4))$,
$((A_1 A_2)(A_3 A_4))$,
$((A_1(A_2 A_3))A_4)$,
$(((A_1 A_2)A_3)A_4)$.

The way we parenthesize a chain of matrices can have a dramatic impact on the cost of evaluating the product. Consider first the cost of multiplying two matrices. The standard algorithm is given by the following pseudocode. The attributes *rows* and *columns* are the numbers of rows and columns in a matrix.

MATRIX-MULTIPLY(*A*, *B*)

```
1  if columns[A] ≠ rows[B]
2     then error "incompatible dimensions"
3     else for i ← 1 to rows[A]
4             do for j ← 1 to columns[B]
5                     do C[i, j] ← 0
6                        for k ← 1 to columns[A]
7                            do C[i, j] ← C[i, j] + A[i, k] · B[k, j]
8            return C
```

We can multiply two matrices A and B only if the number of columns of A is equal to the number of rows of B. If A is a $p \times q$ matrix and B is a $q \times r$ matrix, the resulting matrix C is a $p \times r$ matrix. The time to compute C is dominated by the number of scalar multiplications in line 7, which is pqr. In what follows, we shall express running times in terms of the number of scalar multiplications.

To illustrate the different costs incurred by different parenthesizations of a matrix product, consider the problem of a chain $\langle A_1, A_2, A_3 \rangle$ of three matrices. Suppose that the dimensions of the matrices are 10×100, 100×5, and 5×50, respectively. If we multiply according to the parenthesization $((A_1 A_2) A_3)$, we perform $10 \cdot 100 \cdot 5 = 5000$ scalar multiplications to compute the 10×5 matrix product $A_1 A_2$, plus another $10 \cdot 5 \cdot 50 = 2500$ scalar multiplications to multiply this matrix by A_3, for a total of 7500 scalar multiplications. If instead we multiply according to the parenthesization $(A_1 (A_2 A_3))$, we perform $100 \cdot 5 \cdot 50 = 25{,}000$ scalar multiplications to compute the 100×50 matrix product $A_2 A_3$, plus another $10 \cdot 100 \cdot 50 = 50{,}000$ scalar multiplications to multiply A_1 by this matrix, for a total of 75,000 scalar multiplications. Thus, computing the product according to the first parenthesization is 10 times faster.

The **matrix-chain multiplication problem** can be stated as follows: given a chain $\langle A_1, A_2, \ldots, A_n \rangle$ of n matrices, where for $i = 1, 2, \ldots, n$, matrix A_i has dimension $p_{i-1} \times p_i$, fully parenthesize the product $A_1 A_2 \cdots A_n$ in a way that minimizes the number of scalar multiplications.

Counting the number of parenthesizations

Before solving the matrix-chain multiplication problem by dynamic programming, we should convince ourselves that exhaustively checking all possible parenthesizations does not yield an efficient algorithm. Denote the number of alternative parenthesizations of a sequence of n matrices by $P(n)$. Since we can split a sequence of n matrices between the kth and $(k + 1)$st matrices for any $k = 1, 2, \ldots, n - 1$ and then parenthesize the two resulting subsequences independently, we obtain the recurrence

$$P(n) = \begin{cases} 1 & \text{if } n = 1, \\ \sum_{k=1}^{n-1} P(k)P(n-k) & \text{if } n \geq 2. \end{cases}$$

Problem 13-4 asked you to show that the solution to this recurrence is the sequence of *Catalan numbers*:

$$P(n) = C(n-1),$$

where

$$\begin{aligned} C(n) &= \frac{1}{n+1}\binom{2n}{n} \\ &= \Omega(4^n/n^{3/2}). \end{aligned}$$

The number of solutions is thus exponential in n, and the brute-force method of exhaustive search is therefore a poor strategy for determining the optimal parenthesization of a matrix chain.

The structure of an optimal parenthesization

The first step of the dynamic-programming paradigm is to characterize the structure of an optimal solution. For the matrix-chain multiplication problem, we can perform this step as follows. For convenience, let us adopt the notation $A_{i..j}$ for the matrix that results from evaluating the product $A_i A_{i+1} \cdots A_j$. An optimal parenthesization of the product $A_1 A_2 \cdots A_n$ splits the product between A_k and A_{k+1} for some integer k in the range $1 \leq k < n$. That is, for some value of k, we first compute the matrices $A_{1..k}$ and $A_{k+1..n}$ and then multiply them together to produce the final product $A_{1..n}$. The cost of this optimal parenthesization is thus the cost of computing the matrix $A_{1..k}$, plus the cost of computing $A_{k+1..n}$, plus the cost of multiplying them together.

The key observation is that the parenthesization of the "prefix" subchain $A_1 A_2 \cdots A_k$ within this optimal parenthesization of $A_1 A_2 \cdots A_n$ must be an *optimal* parenthesization of $A_1 A_2 \cdots A_k$. Why? If there were a less costly way to parenthesize $A_1 A_2 \dots A_k$, substituting that parenthesization in the optimal parenthesization of $A_1 A_2 \cdots A_n$ would produce another parenthesization of $A_1 A_2 \cdots A_n$ whose cost was lower than the optimum: a contradiction. A similar observation holds for the the parenthesization of the subchain $A_{k+1} A_{k+2} \cdots A_n$ in the optimal parenthesization of $A_1 A_2 \cdots A_n$: it must be an optimal parenthesization of $A_{k+1} A_{k+2} \cdots A_n$.

Thus, an optimal solution to an instance of the matrix-chain multiplication problem contains within it optimal solutions to subproblem instances. Optimal substructure within an optimal solution is one of the hallmarks of the applicability of dynamic programming, as we shall see in Section 16.2.

A recursive solution

The second step of the dynamic-programming paradigm is to define the value of an optimal solution recursively in terms of the optimal solutions to subproblems. For the matrix-chain multiplication problem, we pick as our subproblems the problems of determining the minimum cost of a parenthesization of $A_i A_{i+1} \cdots A_j$ for $1 \leq i \leq j \leq n$. Let $m[i, j]$ be the minimum number of scalar multiplications needed to compute the matrix $A_{i..j}$; the cost of a cheapest way to compute $A_{1..n}$ would thus be $m[1, n]$.

We can define $m[i, j]$ recursively as follows. If $i = j$, the chain consists of just one matrix $A_{i..i} = A_i$, so no scalar multiplications are necessary to compute the product. Thus, $m[i, i] = 0$ for $i = 1, 2, \ldots, n$. To compute $m[i, j]$ when $i < j$, we take advantage of the structure of an optimal solution from step 1. Let us assume that the optimal parenthesization splits the product $A_i A_{i+1} \cdots A_j$ between A_k and A_{k+1}, where $i \leq k < j$. Then, $m[i, j]$ is equal to the minimum cost for computing the subproducts $A_{i..k}$ and $A_{k+1..j}$, plus the cost of multiplying these two matrices together. Since computing the matrix product $A_{i..k} A_{k+1..j}$ takes $p_{i-1} p_k p_j$ scalar multiplications, we obtain

$$m[i, j] = m[i, k] + m[k + 1, j] + p_{i-1} p_k p_j \ .$$

This recursive equation assumes that we know the value of k, which we don't. There are only $j - i$ possible values for k, however, namely $k = i, i + 1, \ldots, j - 1$. Since the optimal parenthesization must use one of these values for k, we need only check them all to find the best. Thus, our recursive definition for the minimum cost of parenthesizing the product $A_i A_{i+1} \cdots A_j$ becomes

$$m[i, j] = \begin{cases} 0 & \text{if } i = j \ , \\ \min_{i \leq k < j} \{ m[i, k] + m[k + 1, j] + p_{i-1} p_k p_j \} & \text{if } i < j \ . \end{cases} \quad (16.2)$$

The $m[i, j]$ values give the costs of optimal solutions to subproblems. To help us keep track of how to construct an optimal solution, let us define $s[i, j]$ to be a value of k at which we can split the product $A_i A_{i+1} \cdots A_j$ to obtain an optimal parenthesization. That is, $s[i, j]$ equals a value k such that $m[i, j] = m[i, k] + m[k + 1, j] + p_{i-1} p_k p_j$.

Computing the optimal costs

At this point, it is a simple matter to write a recursive algorithm based on recurrence (16.2) to compute the minimum cost $m[1, n]$ for multiplying $A_1 A_2 \cdots A_n$. As we shall see in Section 16.2, however, this algorithm takes exponential time—no better than the brute-force method of checking each way of parenthesizing the product.

The important observation that we can make at this point is that we have relatively few subproblems: one problem for each choice of i and j

satisfying $1 \le i \le j \le n$, or $\binom{n}{2} + n = \Theta(n^2)$ total. A recursive algorithm may encounter each subproblem many times in different branches of its recursion tree. This property of overlapping subproblems is the second hallmark of the applicability of dynamic programming.

Instead of computing the solution to recurrence (16.2) recursively, we perform the third step of the dynamic-programming paradigm and compute the optimal cost by using a bottom-up approach. The following pseudocode assumes that matrix A_i has dimensions $p_{i-1} \times p_i$ for $i = 1, 2, \ldots, n$. The input is a sequence $\langle p_0, p_1, \ldots, p_n \rangle$, where $length[p] = n + 1$. The procedure uses an auxiliary table $m[1 .. n, 1 .. n]$ for storing the $m[i, j]$ costs and an auxiliary table $s[1 .. n, 1 .. n]$ that records which index of k achieved the optimal cost in computing $m[i, j]$.

MATRIX-CHAIN-ORDER(p)

```
1   n ← length[p] − 1
2   for i ← 1 to n
3       do m[i, i] ← 0
4   for l ← 2 to n
5       do for i ← 1 to n − l + 1
6           do j ← i + l − 1
7               m[i, j] ← ∞
8               for k ← i to j − 1
9                   do q ← m[i, k] + m[k + 1, j] + p_{i-1} p_k p_j
10                      if q < m[i, j]
11                          then m[i, j] ← q
12                              s[i, j] ← k
13  return m and s
```

The algorithm fills in the table m in a manner that corresponds to solving the parenthesization problem on matrix chains of increasing length. Equation (16.2) shows that the cost $m[i, j]$ of computing a matrix-chain product of $j - i + 1$ matrices depends only on the costs of computing matrix-chain products of fewer than $j - i + 1$ matrices. That is, for $k = i, i+1, \ldots, j-1$, the matrix $A_{i..k}$ is a product of $k - i + 1 < j - i + 1$ matrices and the matrix $A_{k+1..j}$ is a product of $j - k < j - i + 1$ matrices.

The algorithm first computes $m[i, i] \leftarrow 0$ for $i = 1, 2, \ldots, n$ (the minimum costs for chains of length 1) in lines 2–3. It then uses recurrence (16.2) to compute $m[i, i + 1]$ for $i = 1, 2, \ldots, n - 1$ (the minimum costs for chains of length $l = 2$) during the first execution of the loop in lines 4–12. The second time through the loop, it computes $m[i, i + 2]$ for $i = 1, 2, \ldots, n - 2$ (the minimum costs for chains of length $l = 3$), and so forth. At each step, the $m[i, j]$ cost computed in lines 9–12 depends only on table entries $m[i, k]$ and $m[k + 1, j]$ already computed.

Figure 16.1 illustrates this procedure on a chain of $n = 6$ matrices. Since we have defined $m[i, j]$ only for $i \le j$, only the portion of the table m strictly above the main diagonal is used. The figure shows the table

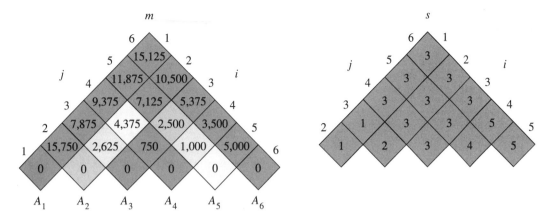

Figure 16.1 The m and s tables computed by MATRIX-CHAIN-ORDER for $n = 6$ and the following matrix dimensions:

matrix	dimension
A_1	30×35
A_2	35×15
A_3	15×5
A_4	5×10
A_5	10×20
A_6	20×25

The tables are rotated so that the main diagonal runs horizontally. Only the main diagonal and upper triangle are used in the m table, and only the upper triangle is used in the s table. The minimum number of scalar multiplications to multiply the 6 matrices is $m[1,6] = 15{,}125$. Of the lightly shaded entries, the pairs that have the same shading are taken together in line 9 when computing

$$m[2,5] = \min \begin{cases} m[2,2] + m[3,5] + p_1 p_2 p_5 = 0 + 2500 + 35 \cdot 15 \cdot 20 & = 13000 , \\ m[2,3] + m[4,5] + p_1 p_3 p_5 = 2625 + 1000 + 35 \cdot 5 \cdot 20 & = 7125 , \\ m[2,4] + m[5,5] + p_1 p_4 p_5 = 4375 + 0 + 35 \cdot 10 \cdot 20 & = 11375 \end{cases}$$
$$= 7125 .$$

rotated to make the main diagonal run horizontally. The matrix chain is listed along the bottom. Using this layout, the minimum cost $m[i, j]$ for multiplying a subchain $A_i A_{i+1} \cdots A_j$ of matrices can be found at the intersection of lines running northeast from A_i and northwest from A_j. Each horizontal row in the table contains the entries for matrix chains of the same length. MATRIX-CHAIN-ORDER computes the rows from bottom to top and from left to right within each row. An entry $m[i, j]$ is computed using the products $p_{i-1} p_k p_j$ for $k = i, i+1, \ldots, j-1$ and all entries southwest and southeast from $m[i, j]$.

A simple inspection of the nested loop structure of MATRIX-CHAIN-ORDER yields a running time of $O(n^3)$ for the algorithm. The loops are nested three deep, and each loop index (l, i, and k) takes on at most n values. Exercise 16.1-3 asks you to show that the running time of this algorithm is in fact also $\Omega(n^3)$. The algorithm requires $\Theta(n^2)$ space to store the m and s tables. Thus, MATRIX-CHAIN-ORDER is much more efficient than the exponential-time method of enumerating all possible parenthesizations and checking each one.

Constructing an optimal solution

Although MATRIX-CHAIN-ORDER determines the optimal number of scalar multiplications needed to compute a matrix-chain product, it does not directly show how to multiply the matrices. Step 4 of the dynamic-programming paradigm is to construct an optimal solution from computed information.

In our case, we use the table $s[1 \mathrel{..} n, 1 \mathrel{..} n]$ to determine the best way to multiply the matrices. Each entry $s[i, j]$ records the value of k such that the optimal parenthesization of $A_i A_{i+1} \cdots A_j$ splits the product between A_k and A_{k+1}. Thus, we know that the final matrix multiplication in computing $A_{1 \mathrel{..} n}$ optimally is $A_{1 \mathrel{..} s[1,n]} A_{s[1,n]+1 \mathrel{..} n}$. The earlier matrix multiplications can be computed recursively, since $s[1, s[1, n]]$ determines the last matrix multiplication in computing $A_{1 \mathrel{..} s[1,n]}$, and $s[s[1, n] + 1, n]$ determines the last matrix multiplication in computing $A_{s[1,n]+1 \mathrel{..} n}$. The following recursive procedure computes the matrix-chain product $A_{i \mathrel{..} j}$ given the matrices $A = \langle A_1, A_2, \ldots, A_n \rangle$, the s table computed by MATRIX-CHAIN-ORDER, and the indices i and j. The initial call is MATRIX-CHAIN-MULTIPLY$(A, s, 1, n)$.

MATRIX-CHAIN-MULTIPLY(A, s, i, j)

```
1  if j > i
2     then X ← MATRIX-CHAIN-MULTIPLY(A, s, i, s[i, j])
3          Y ← MATRIX-CHAIN-MULTIPLY(A, s, s[i, j] + 1, j)
4          return MATRIX-MULTIPLY(X, Y)
5     else return A_i
```

In the example of Figure 16.1, the call MATRIX-CHAIN-MULTIPLY$(A, s, 1, 6)$ computes the matrix-chain product according to the parenthesization

$$((A_1(A_2 A_3))((A_4 A_5)A_6)) \,. \tag{16.3}$$

Exercises

16.1-1
Find an optimal parenthesization of a matrix-chain product whose sequence of dimensions is $\langle 5, 10, 3, 12, 5, 50, 6 \rangle$.

16.1-2
Give an efficient algorithm PRINT-OPTIMAL-PARENS to print the optimal parenthesization of a matrix chain given the table s computed by MATRIX-CHAIN-ORDER. Analyze your algorithm.

16.1-3

Let $R(i, j)$ be the number of times that table entry $m[i, j]$ is referenced by MATRIX-CHAIN-ORDER in computing other table entries. Show that the total number of references for the entire table is

$$\sum_{i=1}^{n} \sum_{j=i}^{n} R(i, j) = \frac{n^3 - n}{3} .$$

(*Hint:* You may find the identity $\sum_{i=1}^{n} i^2 = n(n + 1)(2n + 1)/6$ useful.)

16.1-4

Show that a full parenthesization of an n-element expression has exactly $n - 1$ pairs of parentheses.

16.2 Elements of dynamic programming

Although we have just worked through an example of the dynamic-programming method, you might still be wondering just when the method applies. From an engineering perspective, when should we look for a dynamic-programming solution to a problem? In this section, we examine the two key ingredients that an optimization problem must have for dynamic programming to be applicable: optimal substructure and overlapping subproblems. We also look at a variant method, called memoization, for taking advantage of the overlapping-subproblems property.

Optimal substructure

The first step in solving an optimization problem by dynamic programming is to characterize the structure of an optimal solution. We say that a problem exhibits *optimal substructure* if an optimal solution to the problem contains within it optimal solutions to subproblems. Whenever a problem exhibits optimal substructure, it is a good clue that dynamic programming might apply. (It also might mean that a greedy strategy applies, however. See Chapter 17.)

In Section 16.1, we discovered that the problem of matrix-chain multiplication exhibits optimal substructure. We observed that an optimal parenthesization of $A_1 A_2 \cdots A_n$ that splits the product between A_k and A_{k+1} contains within it optimal solutions to the problems of parenthesizing $A_1 A_2 \cdots A_k$ and $A_{k+1} A_{k+2} \cdots A_n$. The technique that we used to show that subproblems have optimal solutions is typical. We assume that there is a better solution to the subproblem and show how this assumption contradicts the optimality of the solution to the original problem.

The optimal substructure of a problem often suggests a suitable space of subproblems to which dynamic programming can be applied. Typically, there are several classes of subproblems that might be considered "natural" for a problem. For example, the space of subproblems that we considered for matrix-chain multiplication contained all subchains of the input chain. We could equally well have chosen as our space of subproblems arbitrary sequences of matrices from the input chain, but this space of subproblems is unnecessarily large. A dynamic-programming algorithm based on this space of subproblems solves many more problems than it has to.

Investigating the optimal substructure of a problem by iterating on subproblem instances is a good way to infer a suitable space of subproblems for dynamic programming. For example, after looking at the structure of an optimal solution to a matrix-chain problem, we might iterate and look at the structure of optimal solutions to subproblems, subsubproblems, and so forth. We discover that all subproblems consist of subchains of $\langle A_1, A_2, \ldots, A_n \rangle$. Thus, the set of chains of the form $\langle A_i, A_{i+1}, \ldots, A_j \rangle$ for $1 \le i \le j \le n$ makes a natural and reasonable space of subproblems to use.

Overlapping subproblems

The second ingredient that an optimization problem must have for dynamic programming to be applicable is that the space of subproblems must be "small" in the sense that a recursive algorithm for the problem solves the same subproblems over and over, rather than always generating new subproblems. Typically, the total number of distinct subproblems is a polynomial in the input size. When a recursive algorithm revisits the same problem over and over again, we say that the optimization problem has **overlapping subproblems**. In contrast, a problem for which a divide-and-conquer approach is suitable usually generates brand-new problems at each step of the recursion. Dynamic-programming algorithms typically take advantage of overlapping subproblems by solving each subproblem once and then storing the solution in a table where it can be looked up when needed, using constant time per lookup.

To illustrate the overlapping-subproblems property, let us reexamine the matrix-chain multiplication problem. Referring back to Figure 16.1, observe that MATRIX-CHAIN-ORDER repeatedly looks up the solution to subproblems in lower rows when solving subproblems in higher rows. For example, entry $m[3, 4]$ is referenced 4 times: during the computations of $m[2, 4]$, $m[1, 4]$, $m[3, 5]$, and $m[3, 6]$. If $m[3, 4]$ were recomputed each time, rather than just being looked up, the increase in running time would be dramatic. To see this, consider the following (inefficient) recursive procedure that determines $m[i, j]$, the minimum number of scalar multiplications needed to compute the matrix-chain product $A_{i..j} = A_i A_{i+1} \cdots A_j$. The procedure is based directly on the recurrence (16.2).

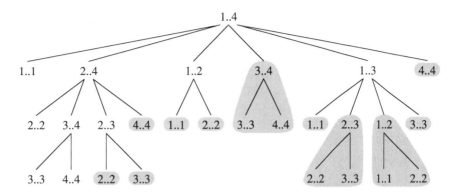

Figure 16.2   The recursion tree for the computation of RECURSIVE-MATRIX-CHAIN($p, 1, 4$). Each node contains the parameters i and j. The computations performed in a shaded subtree are replaced by a single table lookup in MEMOIZED-MATRIX-CHAIN($p, 1, 4$).

RECURSIVE-MATRIX-CHAIN(p, i, j)

```
1  if i = j
2     then return 0
3  m[i, j] ← ∞
4  for k ← i to j − 1
5     do q ← RECURSIVE-MATRIX-CHAIN(p, i, k)
               + RECURSIVE-MATRIX-CHAIN(p, k + 1, j) + p_{i−1}p_k p_j
6        if q < m[i, j]
7           then m[i, j] ← q
8  return m[i, j]
```

Figure 16.2 shows the recursion tree produced by the call RECURSIVE-MATRIX-CHAIN($p, 1, 4$). Each node is labeled by the values of the parameters i and j. Observe that some pairs of values occur many times.

In fact, we can show that the running time $T(n)$ to compute $m[1, n]$ by this recursive procedure is at least exponential in n. Let us assume that the execution of lines 1–2 and of lines 6–7 each take at least unit time. Inspection of the procedure yields the recurrence

$$T(1) \geq 1 ,$$
$$T(n) \geq 1 + \sum_{k=1}^{n-1} (T(k) + T(n-k) + 1) \qquad \text{for } n > 1 .$$

Noting that for $i = 1, 2, \ldots, n - 1$, each term $T(i)$ appears once as $T(k)$ and once as $T(n - k)$, and collecting the $n - 1$ 1's in the summation together with the 1 out front, we can rewrite the recurrence as

$$T(n) \geq 2 \sum_{i=1}^{n-1} T(i) + n . \qquad (16.4)$$

We shall prove that $T(n) = \Omega(2^n)$ using the substitution method. Specifically, we shall show that $T(n) \geq 2^{n-1}$ for all $n \geq 1$. The basis is easy, since $T(1) \geq 1 = 2^0$. Inductively, for $n \geq 2$ we have

$$
\begin{aligned}
T(n) &\geq 2 \sum_{i=1}^{n-1} 2^{i-1} + n \\
&= 2 \sum_{i=0}^{n-2} 2^i + n \\
&= 2(2^{n-1} - 1) + n \\
&= (2^n - 2) + n \\
&\geq 2^{n-1},
\end{aligned}
$$

which completes the proof. Thus, the total amount of work performed by the call RECURSIVE-MATRIX-CHAIN$(p, 1, n)$ is at least exponential in n.

Compare this top-down, recursive algorithm with the bottom-up, dynamic-programming algorithm. The latter is more efficient because it takes advantage of the overlapping-subproblems property. There are only $\Theta(n^2)$ different subproblems, and the dynamic-programming algorithm solves each exactly once. The recursive algorithm, on the other hand, must repeatedly resolve each subproblem each time it reappears in the recursion tree. Whenever a recursion tree for the natural recursive solution to a problem contains the same subproblem repeatedly, and the total number of different subproblems is small, it is a good idea to see if dynamic programming can be made to work.

Memoization

There is a variation of dynamic programming that often offers the efficiency of the usual dynamic-programming approach while maintaining a top-down strategy. The idea is to *memoize* the natural, but inefficient, recursive algorithm. As in ordinary dynamic programming, we maintain a table with subproblem solutions, but the control structure for filling in the table is more like the recursive algorithm.

A memoized recursive algorithm maintains an entry in a table for the solution to each subproblem. Each table entry initially contains a special value to indicate that the entry has yet to be filled in. When the subproblem is first encountered during the execution of the recursive algorithm, its solution is computed and then stored in the table. Each subsequent time that the subproblem is encountered, the value stored in the table is simply looked up and returned.[1]

---

[1] This approach presupposes that the set of all possible subproblem parameters is known and that the relation between table positions and subproblems is established. Another approach is to memoize by using hashing with the subproblem parameters as keys.

The following procedure is a memoized version of RECURSIVE-MATRIX-CHAIN.

MEMOIZED-MATRIX-CHAIN(p)

```
1  n ← length[p] − 1
2  for i ← 1 to n
3      do for j ← i to n
4          do m[i, j] ← ∞
5  return LOOKUP-CHAIN(p, 1, n)
```

LOOKUP-CHAIN(p, i, j)

```
1  if m[i, j] < ∞
2      then return m[i, j]
3  if i = j
4      then m[i, j] ← 0
5      else for k ← i to j − 1
6          do q ← LOOKUP-CHAIN(p, i, k)
                  + LOOKUP-CHAIN(p, k + 1, j) + p_{i−1}p_k p_j
7              if q < m[i, j]
8                  then m[i, j] ← q
9  return m[i, j]
```

MEMOIZED-MATRIX-CHAIN, like MATRIX-CHAIN-ORDER, maintains a table $m[1 .. n, 1 .. n]$ of computed values of $m[i, j]$, the minimum number of scalar multiplications needed to compute the matrix $A_{i..j}$. Each table entry initially contains the value ∞ to indicate that the entry has yet to be filled in. When the call LOOKUP-CHAIN(p, i, j) is executed, if $m[i, j] < \infty$ in line 1, the procedure simply returns the previously computed cost $m[i, j]$ (line 2). Otherwise, the cost is computed as in RECURSIVE-MATRIX-CHAIN, stored in $m[i, j]$, and returned. (The value ∞ is convenient to use for an unfilled table entry since it is the value used to initialize $m[i, j]$ in line 3 of RECURSIVE-MATRIX-CHAIN.) Thus, LOOKUP-CHAIN(p, i, j) always returns the value of $m[i, j]$, but it only computes it if this is the first time that LOOKUP-CHAIN has been called with the parameters i and j.

Figure 16.2 illustrates how MEMOIZED-MATRIX-CHAIN saves time over RECURSIVE-MATRIX-CHAIN. Shaded subtrees represent values that are looked up rather than computed.

Like the dynamic-programming algorithm MATRIX-CHAIN-ORDER, the procedure MEMOIZED-MATRIX-CHAIN runs in $O(n^3)$ time. Each of $\Theta(n^2)$ table entries is initialized once in line 4 of MEMOIZED-MATRIX-CHAIN and filled in for good by just one call of LOOKUP-CHAIN. Each of these $\Theta(n^2)$ calls to LOOKUP-CHAIN takes $O(n)$ time, excluding the time spent in computing other table entries, so a total of $O(n^3)$ is spent altogether. Memoization thus turns an $\Omega(2^n)$ algorithm into an $O(n^3)$ algorithm.

In summary, the matrix-chain multiplication problem can be solved in $O(n^3)$ time by either a top-down, memoized algorithm or a bottom-up, dynamic-programming algorithm. Both methods take advantage of the overlapping-subproblems property. There are only $\Theta(n^2)$ different subproblems in total, and either of these methods computes the solution to each subproblem once. Without memoization, the natural recursive algorithm runs in exponential time, since solved subproblems are repeatedly solved.

In general practice, if all subproblems must be solved at least once, a bottom-up dynamic-programming algorithm usually outperforms a top-down memoized algorithm by a constant factor, because there is no overhead for recursion and less overhead for maintaining the table. Moreover, there are some problems for which the regular pattern of table accesses in the dynamic-programming another algorithm can be exploited to reduce time or space requirements even further. Alternatively, if some subproblems in the subproblem space need not be solved at all, the memoized solution has the advantage of only solving those subproblems that are definitely required.

Exercises

16.2-1
Compare the recurrence (16.4) with the recurrence (8.4) that arose in the analysis of the average-case running time of quicksort. Explain intuitively why the solutions to the two recurrences should be so dramatically different.

16.2-2
Which is a more efficient way to determine the optimal number of multiplications in a chain-matrix multiplication problem: enumerating all the ways of parenthesizing the product and computing the number of multiplications for each, or running RECURSIVE-MATRIX-CHAIN? Justify your answer.

16.2-3
Draw the recursion tree for the MERGE-SORT procedure from Section 1.3.1 on an array of 16 elements. Explain why memoization is ineffective in speeding up a good divide-and-conquer algorithm such as MERGE-SORT.

16.3   Longest common subsequence

The next problem we shall consider is the longest-common-subsequence problem. A subsequence of a given sequence is just the given sequence with some elements (possibly none) left out. Formally, given a sequence $X = \langle x_1, x_2, \ldots, x_m \rangle$, another sequence $Z = \langle z_1, z_2, \ldots, z_k \rangle$ is a **subsequence** of X if there exists a strictly increasing sequence $\langle i_1, i_2, \ldots, i_k \rangle$ of indices of X such that for all $j = 1, 2, \ldots, k$, we have $x_{i_j} = z_j$. For example, $Z = \langle B, C, D, B \rangle$ is a subsequence of $X = \langle A, B, C, B, D, A, B \rangle$ with corresponding index sequence $\langle 2, 3, 5, 7 \rangle$.

Given two sequences X and Y, we say that a sequence Z is a *common subsequence* of X and Y if Z is a subsequence of both X and Y. For example, if $X = \langle A, B, C, B, D, A, B \rangle$ and $Y = \langle B, D, C, A, B, A \rangle$, the sequence $\langle B, C, A \rangle$ is a common subsequence of both X and Y. The sequence $\langle B, C, A \rangle$ is not a *longest* common subsequence (LCS) of X and Y, however, since it has length 3 and the sequence $\langle B, C, B, A \rangle$, which is also common to both X and Y, has length 4. The sequence $\langle B, C, B, A \rangle$ is an LCS of X and Y, as is the sequence $\langle B, D, A, B \rangle$, since there is no common subsequence of length 5 or greater.

In the *longest-common-subsequence problem*, we are given two sequences $X = \langle x_1, x_2, \ldots, x_m \rangle$ and $Y = \langle y_1, y_2, \ldots, y_n \rangle$ and wish to find a maximum-length common subsequence of X and Y. This section shows that the LCS problem can be solved efficiently using dynamic programming.

Characterizing a longest common subsequence

A brute-force approach to solving the LCS problem is to enumerate all subsequences of X and check each subsequence to see if it is also a subsequence of Y, keeping track of the longest subsequence found. Each subsequence of X corresponds to a subset of the indices $\{1, 2, \ldots, m\}$ of X. There are 2^m subsequences of X, so this approach requires exponential time, making it impractical for long sequences.

The LCS problem has an optimal-substructure property, however, as the following theorem shows. As we shall see, the natural class of subproblems correspond to pairs of "prefixes" of the two input sequences. To be precise, given a sequence $X = \langle x_1, x_2, \ldots, x_m \rangle$, we define the ith *prefix* of X, for $i = 0, 1, \ldots, m$, as $X_i = \langle x_1, x_2, \ldots, x_i \rangle$. For example, if $X = \langle A, B, C, B, D, A, B \rangle$, then $X_4 = \langle A, B, C, B \rangle$ and X_0 is the empty sequence.

Theorem 16.1 (Optimal substructure of an LCS)
Let $X = \langle x_1, x_2, \ldots, x_m \rangle$ and $Y = \langle y_1, y_2, \ldots, y_n \rangle$ be sequences, and let $Z = \langle z_1, z_2, \ldots, z_k \rangle$ be any LCS of X and Y.

1. If $x_m = y_n$, then $z_k = x_m = y_n$ and Z_{k-1} is an LCS of X_{m-1} and Y_{n-1}.
2. If $x_m \neq y_n$, then $z_k \neq x_m$ implies that Z is an LCS of X_{m-1} and Y.
3. If $x_m \neq y_n$, then $z_k \neq y_n$ implies that Z is an LCS of X and Y_{n-1}.

Proof   (1) If $z_k \neq x_m$, then we could append $x_m = y_n$ to Z to obtain a common subsequence of X and Y of length $k + 1$, contradicting the supposition that Z is a *longest* common subsequence of X and Y. Thus, we must have $z_k = x_m = y_n$. Now, the prefix Z_{k-1} is a length-$(k - 1)$ common subsequence of X_{m-1} and Y_{n-1}. We wish to show that it is an

LCS. Suppose for the purpose of contradiction that there is a common subsequence W of X_{m-1} and Y_{n-1} with length greater than $k - 1$. Then, appending $x_m = y_n$ to W produces a common subsequence of X and Y whose length is greater than k, which is a contradiction.

(2) If $z_k \neq x_m$, then Z is a common subsequence of X_{m-1} and Y. If there were a common subsequence W of X_{m-1} and Y with length greater than k, then W would also be a common subsequence of X_m and Y, contradicting the assumption that Z is an LCS of X and Y.

(3) The proof is symmetric to (2).   ■

The characterization of Theorem 16.1 shows that an LCS of two sequences contains within it an LCS of prefixes of the two sequences. Thus, the LCS problem has an optimal-substructure property. A recursive solution also has the overlapping-subproblems property, as we shall see in a moment.

A recursive solution to subproblems

Theorem 16.1 implies that there are either one or two subproblems to examine when finding an LCS of $X = \langle x_1, x_2, \ldots, x_m \rangle$ and $Y = \langle y_1, y_2, \ldots, y_n \rangle$. If $x_m = y_n$, we must find an LCS of X_{m-1} and Y_{n-1}. Appending $x_m = y_n$ to this LCS yields an LCS of X and Y. If $x_m \neq y_n$, then we must solve two subproblems: finding an LCS of X_{m-1} and Y and finding an LCS of X and Y_{n-1}. Whichever of these two LCS's is longer is an LCS of X and Y.

We can readily see the overlapping-subproblems property in the LCS problem. To find an LCS of X and Y, we may need to find the LCS's of X and Y_{n-1} and of X_{m-1} and Y. But each of these subproblems has the subsubproblem of finding the LCS of X_{m-1} and Y_{n-1}. Many other subproblems share subsubproblems.

Like the matrix-chain multiplication problem, our recursive solution to the LCS problem involves establishing a recurrence for the cost of an optimal solution. Let us define $c[i, j]$ to be the length of an LCS of the sequences X_i and Y_j. If either $i = 0$ or $j = 0$, one of the sequences has length 0, so the LCS has length 0. The optimal substructure of the LCS problem gives the recursive formula

$$c[i, j] = \begin{cases} 0 & \text{if } i = 0 \text{ or } j = 0, \\ c[i-1, j-1] + 1 & \text{if } i, j > 0 \text{ and } x_i = y_j, \\ \max(c[i, j-1], c[i-1, j]) & \text{if } i, j > 0 \text{ and } x_i \neq y_j. \end{cases} \quad (16.5)$$

Computing the length of an LCS

Based on equation (16.5), we could easily write an exponential-time recursive algorithm to compute the length of an LCS of two sequences. Since there are only $\Theta(mn)$ distinct subproblems, however, we can use dynamic programming to compute the solutions bottom up.

Procedure LCS-LENGTH takes two sequences $X = \langle x_1, x_2, \ldots, x_m \rangle$ and $Y = \langle y_1, y_2, \ldots, y_n \rangle$ as inputs. It stores the $c[i, j]$ values in a table $c[0 \mathbin{.\,.} m, 0 \mathbin{.\,.} n]$ whose entries are computed in row-major order. (That is, the first row of c is filled in from left to right, then the second row, and so on.) It also maintains the table $b[1 \mathbin{.\,.} m, 1 \mathbin{.\,.} n]$ to simplify construction of an optimal solution. Intuitively, $b[i, j]$ points to the table entry corresponding to the optimal subproblem solution chosen when computing $c[i, j]$. The procedure returns the b and c tables; $c[m, n]$ contains the length of an LCS of X and Y.

LCS-LENGTH(X, Y)

```
 1  m ← length[X]
 2  n ← length[Y]
 3  for i ← 1 to m
 4      do c[i, 0] ← 0
 5  for j ← 0 to n
 6      do c[0, j] ← 0
 7  for i ← 1 to m
 8      do for j ← 1 to n
 9          do if x_i = y_j
10              then c[i, j] ← c[i − 1, j − 1] + 1
11                  b[i, j] ← "↖"
12              else if c[i − 1, j] ≥ c[i, j − 1]
13                  then c[i, j] ← c[i − 1, j]
14                      b[i, j] ← "↑"
15                  else c[i, j] ← c[i, j − 1]
16                      b[i, j] ← "←"
17  return c and b
```

Figure 16.3 shows the tables produced by LCS-LENGTH on the sequences $X = \langle A, B, C, B, D, A, B \rangle$ and $Y = \langle B, D, C, A, B, A \rangle$. The running time of the procedure is $O(mn)$, since each table entry takes $O(1)$ time to compute.

Constructing an LCS

The b table returned by LCS-LENGTH can be used to quickly construct an LCS of $X = \langle x_1, x_2, \ldots, x_m \rangle$ and $Y = \langle y_1, y_2, \ldots, y_n \rangle$. We simply begin at $b[m, n]$ and trace through the table following the arrows. Whenever we encounter a "↖" in entry $b[i, j]$, it implies that $x_i = y_j$ is an element of the LCS. The elements of the LCS are encountered in reverse order by this method. The following recursive procedure prints out an LCS of X and Y in the proper, forward order. The initial invocation is PRINT-LCS$(b, X, length[X], length[Y])$.

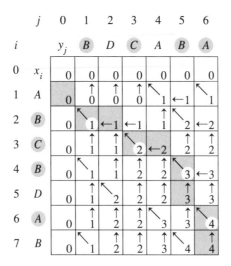

Figure 16.3 The c and b tables computed by LCS-LENGTH on the sequences $X = \langle A, B, C, B, D, A, B \rangle$ and $Y = \langle B, D, C, A, B, A \rangle$. The square in row i and column j contains the value of $c[i, j]$ and the appropriate arrow for the value of $b[i, j]$. The entry 4 in $c[7, 6]$—the lower right-hand corner of the table—is the length of an LCS $\langle B, C, B, A \rangle$ of X and Y. For $i, j > 0$, entry $c[i, j]$ depends only on whether $x_i = y_j$ and the values in entries $c[i - 1, j]$, $c[i, j - 1]$, and $c[i - 1, j - 1]$, which are computed before $c[i, j]$. To reconstruct the elements of an LCS, follow the $b[i, j]$ arrows from the lower right-hand corner; the path is shaded. Each "$\nwarrow$" on the path corresponds to an entry (highlighted) for which $x_i = y_j$ is a member of an LCS.

PRINT-LCS(b, X, i, j)

```
1  if i = 0 or j = 0
2      then return
3  if b[i, j] = "↖"
4      then PRINT-LCS(b, X, i − 1, j − 1)
5          print xᵢ
6  elseif b[i, j] = "↑"
7      then PRINT-LCS(b, X, i − 1, j)
8  else PRINT-LCS(b, X, i, j − 1)
```

For the b table in Figure 16.3, this procedure prints "$BCBA$." The procedure takes time $O(m + n)$, since at least one of i and j is decremented in each stage of the recursion.

Improving the code

Once you have developed an algorithm, you will often find that you can improve on the time or space it uses. This is especially true of straightforward dynamic-programming algorithms. Some changes can simplify the code and improve constant factors but otherwise yield no asymptotic improvement in performance. Others can yield substantial asymptotic savings in time and space.

For example, we can eliminate the b table altogether. Each $c[i, j]$ entry depends on only three other c table entries: $c[i-1, j-1]$, $c[i-1, j]$, and $c[i, j-1]$. Given the value of $c[i, j]$, we can determine in $O(1)$ time which of these three values was used to compute $c[i, j]$, without inspecting table b. Thus, we can reconstruct an LCS in $O(m + n)$ time using a procedure similar to PRINT-LCS. (Exercise 16.3-2 asks you to give the pseudocode.) Although we save $\Theta(mn)$ space by this method, the auxiliary space requirement for computing an LCS does not asymptotically decrease, since we need $\Theta(mn)$ space for the c table anyway.

We can, however, reduce the asymptotic space requirements for LCS-LENGTH, since it needs only two rows of table c at a time: the row being computed and the previous row. (In fact, we can use only slightly more than the space for one row of c to compute the length of an LCS. See Exercise 16.3-4.) This improvement works if we only need the length of an LCS; if we need to reconstruct the elements of an LCS, the smaller table does not keep enough information to retrace our steps in $O(m + n)$ time.

Exercises

16.3-1
Determine an LCS of $\langle 1, 0, 0, 1, 0, 1, 0, 1 \rangle$ and $\langle 0, 1, 0, 1, 1, 0, 1, 1, 0 \rangle$.

16.3-2
Show how to reconstruct an LCS from the completed c table and the original sequences $X = \langle x_1, x_2, \ldots, x_m \rangle$ and $Y = \langle y_1, y_2, \ldots, y_n \rangle$ in $O(m + n)$ time, without using the b table.

16.3-3
Give a memoized version of LCS-LENGTH that runs in $O(mn)$ time.

16.3-4
Show how to compute the length of an LCS using only $2 \min(m, n)$ entries in the c table plus $O(1)$ additional space. Then, show how to do this using $\min(m, n)$ entries plus $O(1)$ additional space.

16.3-5
Give an $O(n^2)$-time algorithm to find the longest monotonically increasing subsequence of a sequence of n numbers.

16.3-6 ⋆
Give an $O(n \lg n)$-time algorithm to find the longest monotonically increasing subsequence of a sequence of n numbers. (*Hint:* Observe that the last element of a candidate subsequence of length i is at least as large as the last

element of a candidate subsequence of length $i - 1$. Maintain candidate subsequences by linking them through the input sequence.)

16.4   Optimal polygon triangulation

In this section, we investigate the problem of optimally triangulating a convex polygon. Despite its outward appearance, we shall see that this geometric problem has a strong similarity to matrix-chain multiplication.

A *polygon* is a piecewise-linear, closed curve in the plane. That is, it is a curve ending on itself that is formed by a sequence of straight-line segments, called the *sides* of the polygon. A point joining two consecutive sides is called a *vertex* of the polygon. If the polygon is *simple*, as we shall generally assume, it does not cross itself. The set of points in the plane enclosed by a simple polygon forms the *interior* of the polygon, the set of points on the polygon itself forms its *boundary*, and the set of points surrounding the polygon forms its *exterior*. A simple polygon is *convex* if, given any two points on its boundary or in its interior, all points on the line segment drawn between them are contained in the polygon's boundary or interior.

We can represent a convex polygon by listing its vertices in counterclockwise order. That is, if $P = \langle v_0, v_1, \ldots, v_{n-1} \rangle$ is a convex polygon, it has n sides $\overline{v_0 v_1}, \overline{v_1 v_2}, \ldots, \overline{v_{n-1} v_n}$, where we interpret v_n as v_0. (In general, we shall implicitly assume arithmetic on vertex indices is taken modulo the number of vertices.)

Given two nonadjacent vertices v_i and v_j, the segment $\overline{v_i v_j}$ is a *chord* of the polygon. A chord $\overline{v_i v_j}$ divides the polygon into two polygons: $\langle v_i, v_{i+1}, \ldots, v_j \rangle$ and $\langle v_j, v_{j+1}, \ldots, v_i \rangle$. A *triangulation* of a polygon is a set T of chords of the polygon that divide the polygon into disjoint *triangles* (polygons with 3 sides). Figure 16.4 shows two ways of triangulating a 7-sided polygon. In a triangulation, no chords intersect (except at endpoints) and the set T of chords is maximal: every chord not in T intersects some chord in T. The sides of triangles produced by the triangulation are either chords in the triangulation or sides of the polygon. Every triangulation of an n-vertex convex polygon has $n - 3$ chords and divides the polygon into $n - 2$ triangles.

In the *optimal (polygon) triangulation problem*, we are given a convex polygon $P = \langle v_0, v_1, \ldots, v_{n-1} \rangle$ and a weight function w defined on triangles formed by sides and chords of P. The problem is to find a triangulation that minimizes the sum of the weights of the triangles in the triangulation. One weight function on triangles that comes to mind naturally is

$$w(\triangle v_i v_j v_k) = |v_i v_j| + |v_j v_k| + |v_k v_i| \; ,$$

where $|v_i v_j|$ is the euclidean distance from v_i to v_j. The algorithm we shall develop works for an arbitrary choice of weight function.

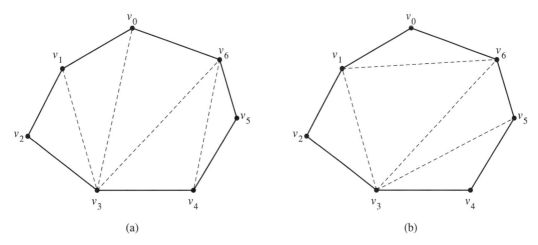

Figure 16.4 Two ways of triangulating a convex polygon. Every triangulation of this 7-sided polygon has $7 - 3 = 4$ chords and divides the polygon into $7 - 2 = 5$ triangles.

Correspondence to parenthesization

There is a surprising correspondence between the triangulation of a polygon and the parenthesization of an expression such as a matrix-chain product. This correspondence is best explained using trees.

A full parenthesization of an expression corresponds to a full binary tree, sometimes called the *parse tree* of the expression. Figure 16.5(a) shows a parse tree for the parenthesized matrix-chain product

$$((A_1(A_2A_3))(A_4(A_5A_6))) \ . \tag{16.6}$$

Each leaf of a parse tree is labeled by one of the atomic elements (matrices) in the expression. If the root of a subtree of the parse tree has a left subtree representing an expression E_l and a right subtree representing an expression E_r, then the subtree itself represents the expression (E_lE_r). There is a one-to-one correspondence between parse trees and fully parenthesized expressions on n atomic elements.

A triangulation of a convex polygon $\langle v_0, v_1, \ldots, v_{n-1} \rangle$ can also be represented by a parse tree. Figure 16.5(b) shows the parse tree for the triangulation of the polygon from Figure 16.4(a). The internal nodes of the parse tree are the chords of the triangulation plus the side $\overline{v_0v_6}$, which is the root. The leaves are the other sides of the polygon. The root $\overline{v_0v_6}$ is one side of the triangle $\triangle v_0v_3v_6$. This triangle determines the children of the root: one is the chord $\overline{v_0v_3}$, and the other is the chord $\overline{v_3v_6}$. Notice that this triangle divides the original polygon into three parts: the triangle $\triangle v_0v_3v_6$ itself, the polygon $\langle v_0, v_1, \ldots, v_3 \rangle$, and the polygon $\langle v_3, v_4, \ldots, v_6 \rangle$. Moreover, the two subpolygons are formed entirely by sides of the original polygon, except for their roots, which are the chords $\overline{v_0v_3}$ and $\overline{v_3v_6}$.

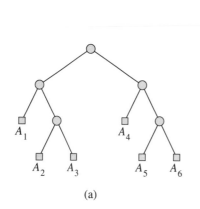
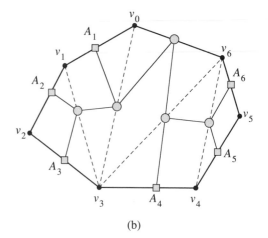

(a)   (b)

Figure 16.5 Parse trees. **(a)** The parse tree for the parenthesized product $((A_1(A_2A_3))(A_4(A_5A_6)))$ and for the triangulation of the 7-sided polygon from Figure 16.4(a). **(b)** The triangulation of the polygon with the parse tree overlaid. Each matrix A_i corresponds to the side $\overline{v_{i-1}v_i}$ for $i = 1, 2, \ldots, 6$.

In recursive fashion, the polygon $\langle v_0, v_1, \ldots, v_3 \rangle$ contains the left subtree of the root of the parse tree, and the polygon $\langle v_3, v_4, \ldots, v_6 \rangle$ contains the right subtree.

In general, therefore, a triangulation of an n-sided polygon corresponds to a parse tree with $n - 1$ leaves. By an inverse process, one can produce a triangulation from a given parse tree. There is a one-to-one correspondence between parse trees and triangulations.

Since a fully parenthesized product of n matrices corresponds to a parse tree with n leaves, it therefore also corresponds to a triangulation of an $(n + 1)$-vertex polygon. Figures 16.5(a) and (b) illustrate this correspondence. Each matrix A_i in a product $A_1 A_2 \cdots A_n$ corresponds to a side $\overline{v_{i-1}v_i}$ of an $(n + 1)$-vertex polygon. A chord $\overline{v_i v_j}$, where $i < j$, corresponds to a matrix $A_{i+1..j}$ computed during the evaluation of the product.

In fact, the matrix-chain multiplication problem is a special case of the optimal triangulation problem. That is, every instance of matrix-chain multiplication can be cast as an optimal triangulation problem. Given a matrix-chain product $A_1 A_2 \cdots A_n$, we define an $(n + 1)$-vertex convex polygon $P = \langle v_0, v_1, \ldots, v_n \rangle$. If matrix A_i has dimensions $p_{i-1} \times p_i$ for $i = 1, 2, \ldots, n$, we define the weight function for the triangulation as

$$w(\triangle v_i v_j v_k) = p_i p_j p_k \ .$$

An optimal triangulation of P with respect to this weight function gives the parse tree for an optimal parenthesization of $A_1 A_2 \cdots A_n$.

Although the reverse is not true—the optimal triangulation problem is *not* a special case of the matrix-chain multiplication problem—it turns out that our code MATRIX-CHAIN-ORDER from Section 16.1, with minor modifications, solves the optimal triangulation problem on an $(n + 1)$-vertex polygon. We simply replace the sequence $\langle p_0, p_1, \ldots, p_n \rangle$ of matrix dimensions with the sequence $\langle v_0, v_1, \ldots, v_n \rangle$ of vertices, change references to p to references to v, and change line 9 to read:

9   **do** $q \leftarrow m[i, k] + m[k + 1, j] + w(\triangle v_{i-1} v_k v_j)$

After running the algorithm, the element $m[1, n]$ contains the weight of an optimal triangulation. Let us see why this is so.

The substructure of an optimal triangulation

Consider an optimal triangulation T of an $(n + 1)$-vertex polygon $P = \langle v_0, v_1, \ldots, v_n \rangle$ that includes the triangle $\triangle v_0 v_k v_n$ for some k, where $1 \leq k \leq n - 1$. The weight of T is just the sum of the weights of $\triangle v_0 v_k v_n$ and triangles in the triangulation of the two subpolygons $\langle v_0, v_1, \ldots, v_k \rangle$ and $\langle v_k, v_{k+1}, \ldots, v_n \rangle$. The triangulations of the subpolygons determined by T must therefore be optimal, since a lesser-weight triangulation of either subpolygon would contradict the minimality of the weight of T.

A recursive solution

Just as we defined $m[i, j]$ to be the minimum cost of computing the matrix-chain subproduct $A_i A_{i+1} \cdots A_j$, let us define $t[i, j]$, for $1 \leq i < j \leq n$, to be the weight of an optimal triangulation of the polygon $\langle v_{i-1}, v_i, \ldots, v_j \rangle$. For convenience, we consider a degenerate polygon $\langle v_{i-1}, v_i \rangle$ to have weight 0. The weight of an optimal triangulation of polygon P is given by $t[1, n]$.

Our next step is to define $t[i, j]$ recursively. The basis is the degenerate case of a 2-vertex polygon: $t[i, i] = 0$ for $i = 1, 2, \ldots, n$. When $j - i \geq 1$, we have a polygon $\langle v_{i-1}, v_i, \ldots, v_j \rangle$ with at least 3 vertices. We wish to minimize over all vertices v_k, for $k = i, i + 1, \ldots, j - 1$, the weight of $\triangle v_{i-1} v_k v_j$ plus the weights of the optimal triangulations of the polygons $\langle v_{i-1}, v_i, \ldots, v_k \rangle$ and $\langle v_k, v_{k+1}, \ldots, v_j \rangle$. The recursive formulation is thus

$$t[i, j] = \begin{cases} 0 & \text{if } i = j \,, \\ \min_{i \leq k \leq j-1} \{t[i, k] + t[k + 1, j] + w(\triangle v_{i-1} v_k v_j)\} & \text{if } i < j \,. \end{cases} \quad (16.7)$$

Compare this recurrence with the recurrence (16.2) that we developed for the minimum number $m[i, j]$ of scalar multiplications needed to compute $A_i A_{i+1} \cdots A_j$. Except for the weight function, the recurrences are identical, and thus, with the minor changes to the code mentioned above, the procedure MATRIX-CHAIN-ORDER can compute the weight of an optimal triangulation. Like MATRIX-CHAIN-ORDER, the optimal triangulation procedure runs in time $\Theta(n^3)$ and uses $\Theta(n^2)$ space.

Exercises

16.4-1
Prove that every triangulation of an *n*-vertex convex polygon has $n - 3$ chords and divides the polygon into $n - 2$ triangles.

16.4-2
Professor Guinevere suggests that a faster algorithm to solve the optimal triangulation problem might exist for the special case in which the weight of a triangle is its area. Is the professor's intuition accurate?

16.4-3
Suppose that a weight function w is defined on the chords of a triangulation instead of on the triangles. The weight of a triangulation with respect to w is then the sum of the weights of the chords in the triangulation. Show that the optimal triangulation problem with weighted chords is just a special case of the optimal triangulation problem with weighted triangles.

16.4-4
Find an optimal triangulation of a regular octagon with unit-length sides. Use the weight function

$$w(\triangle v_i v_j v_k) = |v_i v_j| + |v_j v_k| + |v_k v_i| \ ,$$

where $|v_i v_j|$ is the euclidean distance from v_i to v_j. (A regular polygon is one with equal sides and equal interior angles.)

Problems

16-1   Bitonic euclidean traveling-salesman problem
The *euclidean traveling-salesman problem* is the problem of determining the shortest closed tour that connects a given set of *n* points in the plane. Figure 16.6(a) shows the solution to a 7-point problem. The general problem is NP-complete, and its solution is therefore believed to require more than polynomial time (see Chapter 36).

J. L. Bentley has suggested that we simplify the problem by restricting our attention to *bitonic tours*, that is, tours that start at the leftmost point, go strictly left to right to the rightmost point, and then go strictly right to left back to the starting point. Figure 16.6(b) shows the shortest bitonic tour of the same 7 points. In this case, a polynomial-time algorithm is possible.

Describe an $O(n^2)$-time algorithm for determining an optimal bitonic tour. You may assume that no two points have the same *x*-coordinate. (*Hint:* Scan left to right, maintaining optimal possibilities for the two parts of the tour.)

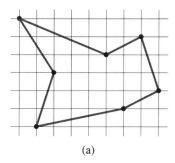 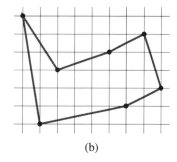

(a)   (b)

Figure 16.6 Seven points in the plane, shown on a unit grid. **(a)** The shortest closed tour, with length 24.88…. This tour is not bitonic. **(b)** The shortest bitonic tour for the same set of points. Its length is 25.58….

16-2 Printing neatly

Consider the problem of neatly printing a paragraph on a printer. The input text is a sequence of n words of lengths $l_1, l_2, \dots, l_n$, measured in characters. We want to print this paragraph neatly on a number of lines that hold a maximum of M characters each. Our criterion of "neatness" is as follows. If a given line contains words i through j and we leave exactly one space between words, the number of extra space characters at the end of the line is $M - j + i - \sum_{k=i}^{j} l_k$. We wish to minimize the sum, over all lines except the last, of the cubes of the numbers of extra space characters at the ends of lines. Give a dynamic-programming algorithm to print a paragraph of n words neatly on a printer. Analyze the running time and space requirements of your algorithm.

16-3 Edit distance

When a "smart" terminal updates a line of text, replacing an existing "source" string $x[1 \mathinner{.\,.} m]$ with a new "target" string $y[1 \mathinner{.\,.} n]$, there are several ways in which the changes can be made. A single character of the source string can be deleted, replaced by another character, or copied to the target string; characters can be inserted; or two adjacent characters of the source string can be interchanged ("twiddled") while being copied to the target string. After all the other operations have occurred, an entire suffix of the source string can be deleted, an operation known as "kill to end of line."

As an example, one way to transform the source string `algorithm` to the target string `altruistic` is to use the following sequence of operations.

Operation	Target string	Source string
copy a	a	lgorithm
copy l	al	gorithm
replace g by t	alt	orithm
delete o	alt	rithm
copy r	altr	ithm
insert u	altru	ithm
insert i	altrui	ithm
insert s	altruis	ithm
twiddle it into ti	altruisti	hm
insert c	altruistic	hm
kill hm	altruistic	

There are many other sequences of operations that accomplish the same result.

Each of the operations delete, replace, copy, insert, twiddle, and kill has an associated cost. (Presumably, the cost of replacing a character is less than the combined costs of deletion and insertion; otherwise, the replace operation would not be used.) The cost of a given sequence of transformation operations is the sum of the costs of the individual operations in the sequence. For the sequence above, the cost of converting `algorithm` to `altruistic` is

$$(3 \cdot \text{cost(copy)}) + \text{cost(replace)} + \text{cost(delete)} + (3 \cdot \text{cost(insert)})$$
$$+ \text{cost(twiddle)} + \text{cost(kill)} \ .$$

Given two sequences $x[1 .. m]$ and $y[1 .. n]$ and a given set of operation costs, the **_edit distance_** from x to y is the cost of the least expensive transformation sequence that converts x to y. Describe a dynamic-programming algorithm to find the edit distance from $x[1 .. m]$ to $y[1 .. n]$ and print an optimal transformation sequence. Analyze the running time and space requirements of your algorithm.

16-4   *Planning a company party*

Professor McKenzie is consulting for the president of A.-B. Corporation, which is planning a company party. The company has a hierarchical structure; that is, the supervisor relation forms a tree rooted at the president. The personnel office has ranked each employee with a conviviality rating, which is a real number. In order to make the party fun for all attendees, the president does not want both an employee and his or her immediate supervisor to attend.

a. Describe an algorithm to make up the guest list. The goal should be to maximize the sum of the conviviality ratings of the guests. Analyze the running time of your algorithm.

b. How can the professor ensure that the president gets invited to his own party?

16-5 Viterbi algorithm

We can use dynamic programming on a directed graph $G = (V, E)$ for speech recognition. Each edge $(u, v) \in E$ is labeled with a sound $\sigma(u, v)$ from a finite set Σ of sounds. The labeled graph is a formal model of a person speaking a restricted language. Each path in the graph starting from a distinguished vertex $v_0 \in V$ corresponds to a possible sequence of sounds produced by the model. The label of a directed path is defined to be the concatenation of the labels of the edges on that path.

a. Describe an efficient algorithm that, given an edge-labeled graph G with distinguished vertex v_0 and a sequence $s = \langle \sigma_1, \sigma_2, \ldots, \sigma_k \rangle$ of characters from Σ, returns a path in G that begins at v_0 and has s as its label, if any such path exists. Otherwise, the algorithm should return NO-SUCH-PATH. Analyze the running time of your algorithm. (*Hint:* You may find concepts from Chapter 23 useful.)

Now, suppose that every edge $(u, v) \in E$ has also been given an associated nonnegative probability $p(u, v)$ of traversing the edge (u, v) from vertex u and producing the corresponding sound. The sum of the probabilities of the edges leaving any vertex equals 1. The probability of a path is defined to be the product of the probabilities of its edges. We can view the probability of a path beginning at v_0 as the probability that a "random walk" beginning at v_0 will follow the specified path, where the choice of which edge to take at a vertex u is made probabilistically according to the probabilities of the available edges leaving u.

b. Extend your answer to part (a) so that if a path is returned, it is a *most probable path* starting at v_0 and having label s. Analyze the running time of your algorithm.

Chapter notes

R. Bellman began the systematic study of dynamic programming in 1955. The word "programming," both here and in linear programming, refers to the use of a tabular solution method. Although optimization techniques incorporating elements of dynamic programming were known earlier, Bellman provided the area with a solid mathematical basis [21].

Hu and Shing [106] give an $O(n \lg n)$-time algorithm for the matrix-chain multiplication problem. They also demonstrate the correspondence between the optimal polygon triangulation problem and the matrix-chain multiplication problem.

The $O(mn)$-time algorithm for the longest-common-subsequence problem seems to be a folk algorithm. Knuth [43] posed the question of whether subquadratic algorithms for the LCS problem exist. Masek and Paterson [143] answered this question in the affirmative by giving an algorithm that runs in $O(mn / \lg n)$ time, where $n \leq m$ and the sequences are drawn from a set of bounded size. For the special case in which no element appears more than once in an input sequence, Szymanski [184] shows that the problem can be solved in $O((n+m)\lg(n+m))$ time. Many of these results extend to the problem of computing string edit distances (Problem 16-3).

17   Greedy Algorithms

Algorithms for optimization problems typically go through a sequence of steps, with a set of choices at each step. For many optimization problems, using dynamic programming to determine the best choices is overkill; simpler, more efficient algorithms will do. A *greedy algorithm* always makes the choice that looks best at the moment. That is, it makes a locally optimal choice in the hope that this choice will lead to a globally optimal solution. This chapter explores optimization problems that are solvable by greedy algorithms.

Greedy algorithms do not always yield optimal solutions, but for many problems they do. We shall first examine in Section 17.1 a simple but nontrivial problem, the activity-selection problem, for which a greedy algorithm efficiently computes a solution. Next, Section 17.2 reviews some of the basic elements of the greedy approach. Section 17.3 presents an important application of greedy techniques: the design of data-compression (Huffman) codes. In Section 17.4, we investigate some of the theory underlying combinatorial structures called "matroids" for which a greedy algorithm always produces an optimal solution. Finally, Section 17.5 illustrates the application of matroids using the problem of scheduling unit-time tasks with deadlines and penalties.

The greedy method is quite powerful and works well for a wide range of problems. Later chapters will present many algorithms that can be viewed as applications of the greedy method, including minimum-spanning-tree algorithms (Chapter 24), Dijkstra's algorithm for shortest paths from a single source (Chapter 25), and Chvátal's greedy set-covering heuristic (Chapter 37). Minimum spanning trees form a classic example of the greedy method. Although this chapter and Chapter 24 can be read independently of each other, you may find it useful to read them together.

17.1   An activity-selection problem

Our first example is the problem of scheduling a resource among several competing activities. We shall find that a greedy algorithm provides an elegant and simple method for selecting a maximum-size set of mutually compatible activities.

Suppose we have a set $S = \{1, 2, \ldots, n\}$ of n proposed *activities* that wish to use a resource, such as a lecture hall, which can be used by only one activity at a time. Each activity i has a *start time* s_i and a *finish time* f_i, where $s_i \le f_i$. If selected, activity i takes place during the half-open time interval $[s_i, f_i)$. Activities i and j are *compatible* if the intervals $[s_i, f_i)$ and $[s_j, f_j)$ do not overlap (i.e., i and j are compatible if $s_i \ge f_j$ or $s_j \ge f_i$). The *activity-selection problem* is to select a maximum-size set of mutually compatible activities.

A greedy algorithm for the activity-selection problem is given in the following pseudocode. We assume that the input activities are in order by increasing finishing time:

$$f_1 \le f_2 \le \cdots \le f_n .\qquad(17.1)$$

If not, we can sort them into this order in time $O(n \lg n)$, breaking ties arbitrarily. The pseudocode assumes that inputs s and f are represented as arrays.

GREEDY-ACTIVITY-SELECTOR(s, f)
```
1  n ← length[s]
2  A ← {1}
3  j ← 1
4  for i ← 2 to n
5      do if s_i ≥ f_j
6          then A ← A ∪ {i}
7              j ← i
8  return A
```

The operation of the algorithm is shown in Figure 17.1. The set A collects the selected activities. The variable j specifies the most recent addition to A. Since the activities are considered in order of nondecreasing finishing time, f_j is always the maximum finishing time of any activity in A. That is,

$$f_j = \max \{f_k : k \in A\} .\qquad(17.2)$$

Lines 2–3 select activity 1, initialize A to contain just this activity, and initialize j to this activity. Lines 4–7 consider each activity i in turn and add i to A if it is compatible with all previously selected activities. To see if activity i is compatible with every activity currently in A, it suffices by equation (17.2) to check (line 5) that its start time s_i is not earlier than the finish time f_j of the activity most recently added to A. If activity i is compatible, then lines 6–7 add it to A and update j. The GREEDY-ACTIVITY-SELECTOR procedure is quite efficient. It can schedule a set S of n activities in $\Theta(n)$ time, assuming that the activities were already sorted initially by their finish times.

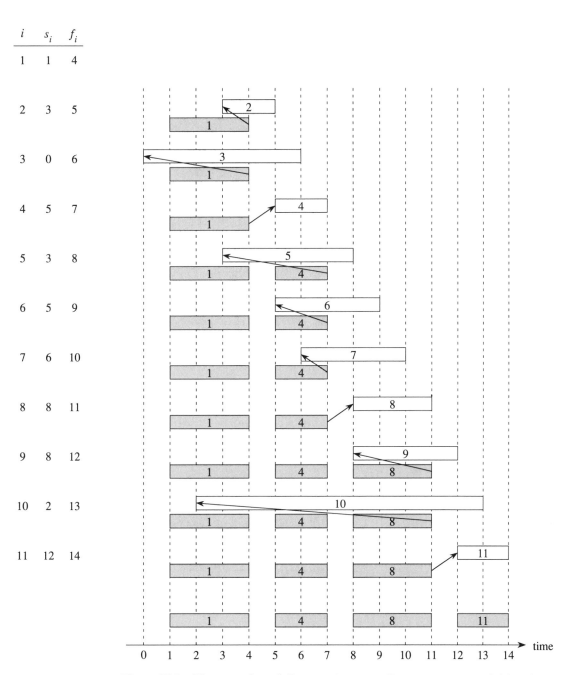

Figure 17.1 The operation of GREEDY-ACTIVITY-SELECTOR on 11 activities given at the left. Each row of the figure corresponds to an iteration of the **for** loop in lines 4–7. The activities that have been selected to be in set A are shaded, and activity i, shown in white, is being considered. If the starting time s_i of activity i occurs before the finishing time f_j of the most recently selected activity j (the arrow between them points left), it is rejected. Otherwise (the arrow points directly up or to the right), it is accepted and put into set A.

The activity picked next by GREEDY-ACTIVITY-SELECTOR is always the one with the earliest finish time that can be legally scheduled. The activity picked is thus a "greedy" choice in the sense that, intuitively, it leaves as much opportunity as possible for the remaining activities to be scheduled. That is, the greedy choice is the one that maximizes the amount of unscheduled time remaining.

Proving the greedy algorithm correct

Greedy algorithms do not always produce optimal solutions. However, GREEDY-ACTIVITY-SELECTOR always finds an optimal solution to an instance of the activity-selection problem.

Theorem 17.1
Algorithm GREEDY-ACTIVITY-SELECTOR produces solutions of maximum size for the activity-selection problem.

Proof   Let $S = \{1, 2, \ldots, n\}$ be the set of activities to schedule. Since we are assuming that the activities are in order by finish time, activity 1 has the earliest finish time. We wish to show that there is an optimal solution that begins with a greedy choice, that is, with activity 1.

Suppose that $A \subseteq S$ is an optimal solution to the given instance of the activity-selection problem, and let us order the activities in A by finish time. Suppose further that the first activity in A is activity k. If $k = 1$, then schedule A begins with a greedy choice. If $k \neq 1$, we want to show that there is another optimal solution B to S that begins with the greedy choice, activity 1. Let $B = A - \{k\} \cup \{1\}$. Because $f_1 \leq f_k$, the activities in B are disjoint, and since B has the same number of activities as A, it is also optimal. Thus, B is an optimal solution for S that contains the greedy choice of activity 1. Therefore, we have shown that there always exists an optimal schedule that begins with a greedy choice.

Moreover, once the greedy choice of activity 1 is made, the problem reduces to finding an optimal solution for the activity-selection problem over those activities in S that are compatible with activity 1. That is, if A is an optimal solution to the original problem S, then $A' = A - \{1\}$ is an optimal solution to the activity-selection problem $S' = \{i \in S : s_i \geq f_1\}$. Why? If we could find a solution B' to S' with more activities than A', adding activity 1 to B' would yield a solution B to S with more activities than A, thereby contradicting the optimality of A. Therefore, after each greedy choice is made, we are left with an optimization problem of the same form as the original problem. By induction on the number of choices made, making the greedy choice at every step produces an optimal solution.   ∎

Exercises

17.1-1
Give a dynamic-programming algorithm for the activity-selection problem, based on computing m_i iteratively for $i = 1, 2, \ldots, n$, where m_i is the size of the largest set of mutually compatible activities among activities $\{1, 2, \ldots, i\}$. Assume that the inputs have been sorted as in equation (17.1). Compare the running time of your solution to the running time of GREEDY-ACTIVITY-SELECTOR.

17.1-2
Suppose that we have a set of activities to schedule among a large number of lecture halls. We wish to schedule all the activities using as few lecture halls as possible. Give an efficient greedy algorithm to determine which activity should use which lecture hall.

(This is also known as the *interval-graph coloring problem*. We can create an interval graph whose vertices are the given activities and whose edges connect incompatible activities. The smallest number of colors required to color every vertex so that no two adjacent vertices are given the same color corresponds to finding the fewest lecture halls needed to schedule all of the given activities.)

17.1-3
Not just any greedy approach to the activity-selection problem produces a maximum-size set of mutually compatible activities. Give an example to show that the approach of selecting the activity of least duration from those that are compatible with previously selected activities does not work. Do the same for the approach of always selecting the activity that overlaps the fewest other remaining activities.

17.2 Elements of the greedy strategy

A greedy algorithm obtains an optimal solution to a problem by making a sequence of choices. For each decision point in the algorithm, the choice that seems best at the moment is chosen. This heuristic strategy does not always produce an optimal solution, but as we saw in the activity-selection problem, sometimes it does. This section discusses some of the general properties of greedy methods.

How can one tell if a greedy algorithm will solve a particular optimization problem? There is no way in general, but there are two ingredients that are exhibited by most problems that lend themselves to a greedy strategy: the greedy-choice property and optimal substructure.

Greedy-choice property

The first key ingredient is the *greedy-choice property*: a globally optimal solution can be arrived at by making a locally optimal (greedy) choice. Here is where greedy algorithms differ from dynamic programming. In dynamic programming, we make a choice at each step, but the choice may depend on the solutions to subproblems. In a greedy algorithm, we make whatever choice seems best at the moment and then solve the subproblems arising after the choice is made. The choice made by a greedy algorithm may depend on choices so far, but it cannot depend on any future choices or on the solutions to subproblems. Thus, unlike dynamic programming, which solves the subproblems bottom up, a greedy strategy usually progresses in a top-down fashion, making one greedy choice after another, iteratively reducing each given problem instance to a smaller one.

Of course, we must prove that a greedy choice at each step yields a globally optimal solution, and this is where cleverness may be required. Typically, as in the case of Theorem 17.1, the proof examines a globally optimal solution. It then shows that the solution can be modified so that a greedy choice is made as the first step, and that this choice reduces the problem to a similar but smaller problem. Then, induction is applied to show that a greedy choice can be used at every step. Showing that a greedy choice results in a similar but smaller problem reduces the proof of correctness to demonstrating that an optimal solution must exhibit optimal substructure.

Optimal substructure

A problem exhibits *optimal substructure* if an optimal solution to the problem contains within it optimal solutions to subproblems. This property is a key ingredient of assessing the applicability of dynamic programming as well as greedy algorithms. As an example of optimal substructure, recall that the proof of Theorem 17.1 demonstrated that if an optimal solution A to the activity-selection problem begins with activity 1, then the set of activities $A' = A - \{1\}$ is an optimal solution to the activity-selection problem $S' = \{i \in S : s_i \geq f_1\}$.

Greedy versus dynamic programming

Because the optimal-substructure property is exploited by both greedy and dynamic-programming strategies, one might be tempted to generate a dynamic-programming solution to a problem when a greedy solution suffices, or one might mistakenly think that a greedy solution works when in fact a dynamic-programming solution is required. To illustrate the subtleties between the two techniques, let us investigate two variants of a classical optimization problem.

The *0-1 knapsack problem* is posed as follows. A thief robbing a store finds n items; the ith item is worth v_i dollars and weighs w_i pounds, where v_i and w_i are integers. He wants to take as valuable a load as possible, but he can carry at most W pounds in his knapsack for some integer W. What items should he take? (This is called the 0-1 knapsack problem because each item must either be taken or left behind; the thief cannot take a fractional amount of an item or take an item more than once.)

In the *fractional knapsack problem*, the setup is the same, but the thief can take fractions of items, rather than having to make a binary (0-1) choice for each item. You can think of an item in the 0-1 knapsack problem as being like a gold ingot, while an item in the fractional knapsack problem is more like gold dust.

Both knapsack problems exhibit the optimal-substructure property. For the 0-1 problem, consider the most valuable load that weighs at most W pounds. If we remove item j from this load, the remaining load must be the most valuable load weighing at most $W - w_j$ that the thief can take from the $n - 1$ original items excluding j. For the comparable fractional problem, consider that if we remove a weight w of one item j from the optimal load, the remaining load must be the most valuable load weighing at most $W - w$ that the thief can take from the $n - 1$ original items plus $w_j - w$ pounds of item j.

Although the problems are similar, the fractional knapsack problem is solvable by a greedy strategy, whereas the 0-1 problem is not. To solve the fractional problem, we first compute the value per pound v_i/w_i for each item. Obeying a greedy strategy, the thief begins by taking as much as possible of the item with the greatest value per pound. If the supply of that item is exhausted and he can still carry more, he takes as much as possible of the item with the next greatest value per pound, and so forth until he can't carry any more. Thus, by sorting the items by value per pound, the greedy algorithm runs in $O(n \lg n)$ time. The proof that the fractional knapsack problem has the greedy-choice property is left as Exercise 17.2-1.

To see that this greedy strategy does not work for the 0-1 knapsack problem, consider the problem instance illustrated in Figure 17.2(a). There are 3 items, and the knapsack can hold 50 pounds. Item 1 weighs 10 pounds and is worth 60 dollars. Item 2 weighs 20 pounds and is worth 100 dollars. Item 3 weighs 30 pounds and is worth 120 dollars. Thus, the value per pound of item 1 is 6 dollars per pound, which is greater than the value per pound of either item 2 (5 dollars per pound) or item 3 (4 dollars per pound). The greedy strategy, therefore, would take item 1 first. As can be seen from the case analysis in Figure 17.2(b), however, the optimal solution takes items 2 and 3, leaving 1 behind. The two possible solutions that involve item 1 are both suboptimal.

For the comparable fractional problem, however, the greedy strategy, which takes item 1 first, does yield an optimal solution, as shown in Fig-

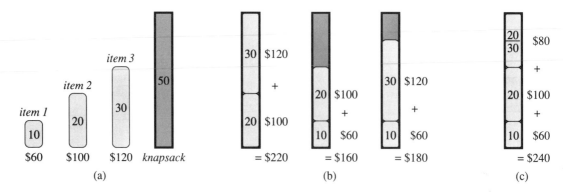

Figure 17.2 The greedy strategy does not work for the 0-1 knapsack problem.
(a) The thief must select a subset of the three items shown whose weight must not
exceed 50 pounds. (b) The optimal subset includes items 2 and 3. Any solution
with item 1 is suboptimal, even though item 1 has the greatest value per pound.
(c) For the fractional knapsack problem, taking the items in order of greatest value
per pound yields an optimal solution.

ure 17.2(c). Taking item 1 doesn't work in the 0-1 problem because the
thief is unable to fill his knapsack to capacity, and the empty space lowers
the effective value per pound of his load. In the 0-1 problem, when we
consider an item for inclusion in the knapsack, we must compare the solution to the subproblem in which the item is included with the solution
to the subproblem in which the item is excluded before we can make the
choice. The problem formulated in this way gives rise to many overlapping
subproblems—a hallmark of dynamic programming, and indeed, dynamic
programming can be used to solve the 0-1 problem. (See Exercise 17.2-2.)

Exercises

17.2-1
Prove that the fractional knapsack problem has the greedy-choice property.

17.2-2
Give a dynamic-programming solution to the 0-1 knapsack problem that
runs in $O(nW)$ time, where n is number of items and W is the maximum
weight of items that the thief can put in his knapsack.

17.2-3
Suppose that in a 0-1 knapsack problem, the order of the items when sorted
by increasing weight is the same as their order when sorted by decreasing
value. Give an efficient algorithm to find an optimal solution to this variant
of the knapsack problem, and argue that your algorithm is correct.

17.2-4

Professor Midas drives an automobile from Newark to Reno along Interstate 80. His car's gas tank, when full, holds enough gas to travel n miles, and his map gives the distances between gas stations on his route. The professor wishes to make as few gas stops as possible along the way. Give an efficient method by which Professor Midas can determine at which gas stations he should stop, and prove that your strategy yields an optimal solution.

17.2-5

Describe an efficient algorithm that, given a set $\{x_1, x_2, \ldots, x_n\}$ of points on the real line, determines the smallest set of unit-length closed intervals that contains all of the given points. Argue that your algorithm is correct.

17.2-6 ⋆

Show how to solve the fractional knapsack problem in $O(n)$ time. Assume that you have a solution to Problem 10-2.

17.3 Huffman codes

Huffman codes are a widely used and very effective technique for compressing data; savings of 20% to 90% are typical, depending on the characteristics of the file being compressed. Huffman's greedy algorithm uses a table of the frequencies of occurrence of each character to build up an optimal way of representing each character as a binary string.

Suppose we have a 100,000-character data file that we wish to store compactly. We observe that the characters in the file occur with the frequencies given by Figure 17.3. That is, only six different characters appear, and the character a occurs 45,000 times.

There are many ways to represent such a file of information. We consider the problem of designing a ***binary character code*** (or ***code*** for short) wherein each character is represented by a unique binary string. If we use a ***fixed-length code***, we need 3 bits to represent six characters: a = 000, b = 001,

	a	b	c	d	e	f
Frequency (in thousands)	45	13	12	16	9	5
Fixed-length codeword	000	001	010	011	100	101
Variable-length codeword	0	101	100	111	1101	1100

Figure 17.3 A character-coding problem. A data file of 100,000 characters contains only the characters a–f, with the frequencies indicated. If each character is assigned a 3-bit codeword, the file can be encoded in 300,000 bits. Using the variable-length code shown, the file can be encoded in 224,000 bits.

..., $f = 101$. This method requires 300,000 bits to code the entire file. Can we do better?

A **variable-length code** can do considerably better than a fixed-length code, by giving frequent characters short codewords and infrequent characters long codewords. Figure 17.3 shows such a code; here the 1-bit string 0 represents a, and the 4-bit string 1100 represents f. This code requires

$$(45 \cdot 1 + 13 \cdot 3 + 12 \cdot 3 + 16 \cdot 3 + 9 \cdot 4 + 5 \cdot 4) \cdot 1{,}000 = 224{,}000 \text{ bits}$$

to represent the file, a savings of approximately 25%. In fact, this is an optimal character code for this file, as we shall see.

Prefix codes

We consider here only codes in which no codeword is also a prefix of some other codeword. Such codes are called **prefix codes**.[1] It is possible to show (although we won't do so here) that the optimal data compression achievable by a character code can always be achieved with a prefix code, so there is no loss of generality in restricting attention to prefix codes.

Prefix codes are desirable because they simplify encoding (compression) and decoding. Encoding is always simple for any binary character code; we just concatenate the codewords representing each character of the file. For example, with the variable-length prefix code of Figure 17.3, we code the 3-character file abc as $0 \cdot 101 \cdot 100 = 0101100$, where we use "·" to denote concatenation.

Decoding is also quite simple with a prefix code. Since no codeword is a prefix of any other, the codeword that begins an encoded file is unambiguous. We can simply identify the initial codeword, translate it back to the original character, remove it from the encoded file, and repeat the decoding process on the remainder of the encoded file. In our example, the string 001011101 parses uniquely as $0 \cdot 0 \cdot 101 \cdot 1101$, which decodes to aabe.

The decoding process needs a convenient representation for the prefix code so that the initial codeword can be easily picked off. A binary tree whose leaves are the given characters provides one such representation. We interpret the binary codeword for a character as the path from the root to that character, where 0 means "go to the left child" and 1 means "go to the right child." Figure 17.4 shows the trees for the two codes of our example. Note that these are not binary search trees, since the leaves need not appear in sorted order and internal nodes do not contain character keys.

An optimal code for a file is always represented by a *full* binary tree, in which every nonleaf node has two children (see Exercise 17.3-1). The

---

[1] Perhaps "prefix-free codes" would be a better name, but the term "prefix codes" is standard in the literature.

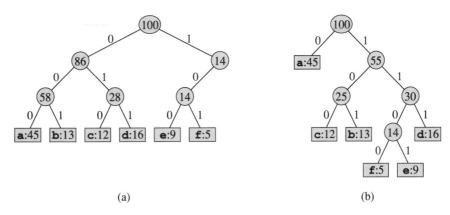

Figure 17.4 Trees corresponding to the coding schemes in Figure 17.3. Each leaf is labeled with a character and its frequency of occurrence. Each internal node is labeled with the sum of the weights of the leaves in its subtree. **(a)** The tree corresponding to the fixed-length code a = 000, ..., f = 100. **(b)** The tree corresponding to the optimal prefix code a = 0, b = 101, ..., f = 1100.

fixed-length code in our example is not optimal since its tree, shown in Figure 17.4(a), is not a full binary tree: there are codewords beginning 10..., but none beginning 11.... Since we can now restrict our attention to full binary trees, we can say that if C is the alphabet from which the characters are drawn, then the tree for an optimal prefix code has exactly $|C|$ leaves, one for each letter of the alphabet, and exactly $|C| - 1$ internal nodes.

Given a tree T corresponding to a prefix code, it is a simple matter to compute the number of bits required to encode a file. For each character c in the alphabet C, let $f(c)$ denote the frequency of c in the file and let $d_T(c)$ denote the depth of c's leaf in the tree. Note that $d_T(c)$ is also the length of the codeword for character c. The number of bits required to encode a file is thus

$$B(T) = \sum_{c \in C} f(c) d_T(c) \,, \tag{17.3}$$

which we define as the **cost** of the tree T.

Constructing a Huffman code

Huffman invented a greedy algorithm that constructs an optimal prefix code called a **Huffman code**. The algorithm builds the tree T corresponding to the optimal code in a bottom-up manner. It begins with a set of $|C|$ leaves and performs a sequence of $|C| - 1$ "merging" operations to create the final tree.

In the pseudocode that follows, we assume that C is a set of n characters and that each character $c \in C$ is an object with a defined frequency $f[c]$.

A priority queue Q, keyed on f, is used to identify the two least-frequent objects to merge together. The result of the merger of two objects is a new object whose frequency is the sum of the frequencies of the two objects that were merged.

HUFFMAN(C)

```
1  n ← |C|
2  Q ← C
3  for i ← 1 to n − 1
4      do z ← ALLOCATE-NODE()
5         x ← left[z] ← EXTRACT-MIN(Q)
6         y ← right[z] ← EXTRACT-MIN(Q)
7         f[z] ← f[x] + f[y]
8         INSERT(Q, z)
9  return EXTRACT-MIN(Q)
```

For our example, Huffman's algorithm proceeds as shown in Figure 17.5. Since there are 6 letters in the alphabet, the initial queue size is $n = 6$, and 5 merge steps are required to build the tree. The final tree represents the optimal prefix code. The codeword for a letter is the sequence of edge labels on the path from the root to the letter.

Line 2 initializes the priority queue Q with the characters in C. The **for** loop in lines 3–8 repeatedly extracts the two nodes x and y of lowest frequency from the queue, and replaces them in the queue with a new node z representing their merger. The frequency of z is computed as the sum of the frequencies of x and y in line 7. The node z has x as its left child and y as its right child. (This order is arbitrary; switching the left and right child of any node yields a different code of the same cost.) After $n - 1$ mergers, the one node left in the queue—the root of the code tree—is returned in line 9.

The analysis of the running time of Huffman's algorithm assumes that Q is implemented as a binary heap (see Chapter 7). For a set C of n characters, the initialization of Q in line 2 can be performed in $O(n)$ time using the BUILD-HEAP procedure in Section 7.3. The **for** loop in lines 3–8 is executed exactly $|n| - 1$ times, and since each heap operation requires time $O(\lg n)$, the loop contributes $O(n \lg n)$ to the running time. Thus, the total running time of HUFFMAN on a set of n characters is $O(n \lg n)$.

Correctness of Huffman's algorithm

To prove that the greedy algorithm HUFFMAN is correct, we show that the problem of determining an optimal prefix code exhibits the greedy-choice and optimal-substructure properties. The next lemma shows that the greedy-choice property holds.

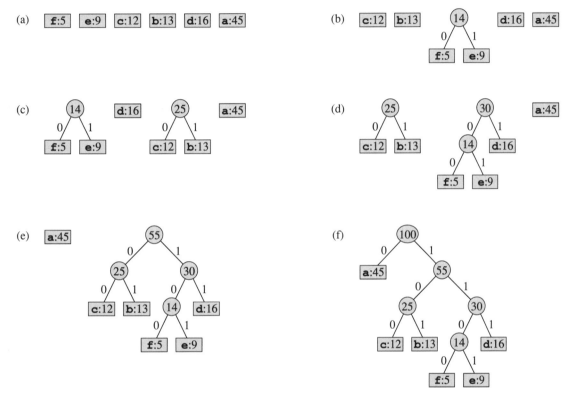

Figure 17.5 The steps of Huffman's algorithm for the frequencies given in Figure 17.3. Each part shows the contents of the queue sorted into increasing order by frequency. At each step, the two trees with lowest frequencies are merged. Leaves are shown as rectangles containing a character and its frequency. Internal nodes are shown as circles containing the sum of the frequencies of its children. An edge connecting an internal node with its children is labeled 0 if it is an edge to a left child and 1 if it is an edge to a right child. The codeword for a letter is the sequence of labels on the edges connecting the root to the leaf for that letter. **(a)** The initial set of $n = 6$ nodes, one for each letter. **(b)**–**(e)** Intermediate stages. **(f)** The final tree.

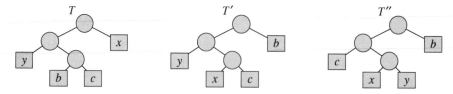

Figure 17.6   An illustration of the key step in the proof of Lemma 17.2. In the optimal tree T, leaves b and c are two of the deepest leaves and are siblings. Leaves x and y are the two leaves that Huffman's algorithm merges together first; they appear in arbitrary positions in T. Leaves b and x are swapped to obtain tree T'. Then, leaves c and y are swapped to obtain tree T''. Since each swap does not increase the cost, the resulting tree T'' is also an optimal tree.

Lemma 17.2
Let C be an alphabet in which each character $c \in C$ has frequency $f[c]$. Let x and y be two characters in C having the lowest frequencies. Then there exists an optimal prefix code for C in which the codewords for x and y have the same length and differ only in the last bit.

Proof   The idea of the proof is to take the tree T representing an arbitrary optimal prefix code and modify it to make a tree representing another optimal prefix code such that the characters x and y appear as sibling leaves of maximum depth in the new tree. If we can do this, then their codewords will have the same length and differ only in the last bit.

Let b and c be two characters that are sibling leaves of maximum depth in T. Without loss of generality, we assume that $f[b] \leq f[c]$ and $f[x] \leq f[y]$. Since $f[x]$ and $f[y]$ are the two lowest leaf frequencies, in order, and $f[b]$ and $f[c]$ are two arbitrary frequencies, in order, we have $f[x] \leq f[b]$ and $f[y] \leq f[c]$. As shown in Figure 17.6, we exchange the positions in T of b and x to produce a tree T', and then we exchange the positions in T' of c and y to produce a tree T''. By equation (17.3), the difference in cost between T and T' is

$$
\begin{aligned}
B(T) - B(T') &= \sum_{c \in C} f(c)d_T(c) - \sum_{c \in C} f(c)d_{T'}(c) \\
&= f[x]d_T(x) + f[b]d_T(b) - f[x]d_{T'}(x) - f[b]d_{T'}(b) \\
&= f[x]d_T(x) + f[b]d_T(b) - f[x]d_T(b) - f[b]d_T(x) \\
&= (f[b] - f[x])(d_T(b) - d_T(x)) \\
&\geq 0 \ ,
\end{aligned}
$$

because both $f[b] - f[x]$ and $d_T[b] - d_T[x]$ are nonnegative. More specifically, $f[b] - f[x]$ is nonnegative because x is a minimum-frequency leaf, and $d_T[b] - d_T[x]$ is nonnegative because b is a leaf of maximum depth in T. Similarly, because exchanging y and c does not increase the cost, $B(T') - B(T'')$ is nonnegative. Therefore, $B(T'') \leq B(T)$, and since T is optimal, $B(T) \leq B(T'')$, which implies $B(T'') = B(T)$. Thus, T'' is an optimal tree in which x and y appear as sibling leaves of maximum depth, from which the lemma follows. ■

Lemma 17.2 implies that the process of building up an optimal tree by mergers can, without loss of generality, begin with the greedy choice of merging together those two characters of lowest frequency. Why is this a greedy choice? We can view the cost of a single merger as being the sum of the frequencies of the two items being merged. Exercise 17.3-3 shows that the total cost of the tree constructed is the sum of the costs of its mergers. Of all possible mergers at each step, HUFFMAN chooses the one that incurs the least cost.

The next lemma shows that the problem of constructing optimal prefix codes has the optimal-substructure property.

Lemma 17.3
Let T be a full binary tree representing an optimal prefix code over an alphabet C, where frequency $f[c]$ is defined for each character $c \in C$. Consider any two characters x and y that appear as sibling leaves in T, and let z be their parent. Then, considering z as a character with frequency $f[z] = f[x] + f[y]$, the tree $T' = T - \{x, y\}$ represents an optimal prefix code for the alphabet $C' = C - \{x, y\} \cup \{z\}$.

Proof We first show that the cost $B(T)$ of tree T can be expressed in terms of the cost $B(T')$ of tree T' by considering the component costs in equation (17.3). For each $c \in C - \{x, y\}$, we have $d_T(c) = d_{T'}(c)$, and hence $f[c]d_T(c) = f[c]d_{T'}(c)$. Since $d_T(x) = d_T(y) = d_{T'}(z) + 1$, we have

$$
\begin{aligned}
f[x]d_T(x) + f[y]d_T(y) &= (f[x] + f[y])(d_{T'}(z) + 1) \\
&= f[z]d_{T'}(z) + (f[x] + f[y]) ,
\end{aligned}
$$

from which we conclude that

$$B(T) = B(T') + f[x] + f[y] .$$

If T' represents a nonoptimal prefix code for the alphabet C', then there exists a tree T'' whose leaves are characters in C' such that $B(T'') < B(T')$. Since z is treated as a character in C', it appears as a leaf in T''. If we add x and y as children of z in T'', then we obtain a prefix code for C with cost $B(T'') + f[x] + f[y] < B(T)$, contradicting the optimality of T. Thus, T' must be optimal for the alphabet C'. ■

Theorem 17.4
Procedure HUFFMAN produces an optimal prefix code.

Proof Immediate from Lemmas 17.2 and 17.3. ■

Exercises

17.3-1
Prove that a binary tree that is not full cannot correspond to an optimal prefix code.

17.3-2
What is an optimal Huffman code for the following set of frequencies, based on the first 8 Fibonacci numbers?

a:1 b:1 c:2 d:3 e:5 f:8 g:13 h:21

Can you generalize your answer to find the optimal code when the frequencies are the first n Fibonacci numbers?

17.3-3
Prove the total cost of a tree for a code can also be computed as the sum, over all internal nodes, of the combined frequencies of the two children of the node.

17.3-4
Prove that for an optimal code, if the characters are ordered so that their frequencies are nonincreasing, then their codeword lengths are nondecreasing.

17.3-5
Let $C = \{0, 1, \ldots, n - 1\}$ be a set of characters. Show that any optimal prefix code on C can be represented by a sequence of

$$2n - 1 + n \lceil \lg n \rceil$$

bits. (*Hint:* Use $2n - 1$ bits to specify the structure of the tree, as discovered by a walk of the tree.)

17.3-6
Generalize Huffman's algorithm to ternary codewords (i.e., codewords using the symbols 0, 1, and 2), and prove that it yields optimal ternary codes.

17.3-7
Suppose a data file contains a sequence of 8-bit characters such that all 256 characters are about as common: the maximum character frequency is less than twice the minimum character frequency. Prove that Huffman coding in this case is no more efficient than using an ordinary 8-bit fixed-length code.

17.3-8
Show that no compression scheme can expect to compress a file of randomly chosen 8-bit characters by even a single bit. (*Hint:* Compare the number of files with the number of possible encoded files.)

★ 17.4 Theoretical foundations for greedy methods

There is a beautiful theory about greedy algorithms, which we sketch in this section. This theory is useful in determining when the greedy method yields optimal solutions. It involves combinatorial structures known as "matroids." Although this theory does not cover all cases for which a greedy method applies (for example, it does not cover the activity-selection problem of Section 17.1 or the Huffman coding problem of Section 17.3), it does cover many cases of practical interest. Furthermore, this theory is being rapidly developed and extended to cover many more applications; see the notes at the end of this chapter for references.

17.4.1 Matroids

A *matroid* is an ordered pair $M = (S, \mathcal{I})$ satisfying the following conditions.

1. S is a finite nonempty set.

2. $\mathcal{I}$ is a nonempty family of subsets of S, called the *independent* subsets of S, such that if $B \in \mathcal{I}$ and $A \subseteq B$, then $A \in \mathcal{I}$. We say that $\mathcal{I}$ is *hereditary* if it satisfies this property. Note that the empty set $\emptyset$ is necessarily a member of $\mathcal{I}$.

3. If $A \in \mathcal{I}$, $B \in \mathcal{I}$, and $|A| < |B|$, then there is some element $x \in B - A$ such that $A \cup \{x\} \in \mathcal{I}$. We say that M satisfies the *exchange property*.

The word "matroid" is due to Hassler Whitney. He was studying *matric matroids*, in which the elements of S are the rows of a given matrix and a set of rows is independent if they are linearly independent in the usual sense. It is easy to show that this structure defines a matroid (see Exercise 17.4-2).

As another illustration of matroids, consider the *graphic matroid* $M_G = (S_G, \mathcal{I}_G)$ defined in terms of a given undirected graph $G = (V, E)$ as follows.

- The set S_G is defined to be E, the set of edges of G.

- If A is a subset of E, then $A \in \mathcal{I}_G$ if and only if A is acyclic. That is, a set of edges is independent if and only if it forms a forest.

The graphic matroid M_G is closely related to the minimum-spanning-tree problem, which is covered in detail in Chapter 24.

Theorem 17.5
If G is an undirected graph, then $M_G = (S_G, \mathcal{I}_G)$ is a matroid.

Proof Clearly, $S_G = E$ is a finite set. Furthermore, $\mathcal{I}_G$ is hereditary, since a subset of a forest is a forest. Putting it another way, removing edges from an acyclic set of edges cannot create cycles.

Thus, it remains to show that M_G satisfies the exchange property. Suppose that A and B are forests of G and that $|B| > |A|$. That is, A and B are acyclic sets of edges, and B contains more edges than A does.

It follows from Theorem 5.2 that a forest having k edges contains exactly $|V| - k$ trees. (To prove this another way, begin with $|V|$ trees and no edges. Then, each edge that is added to the forest reduces the number of trees by one.) Thus, forest A contains $|V| - |A|$ trees, and forest B contains $|V| - |B|$ trees.

Since forest B has fewer trees than forest A does, forest B must contain some tree T whose vertices are in two different trees in forest A. Moreover, since T is connected, it must contain an edge (u, v) such that vertices u and v are in different trees in forest A. Since the edge (u, v) connects vertices in two different trees in forest A, the edge (u, v) can be added to forest A without creating a cycle. Therefore, M_G satisfies the exchange property, completing the proof that M_G is a matroid. ∎

Given a matroid $M = (S, \mathcal{I})$, we call an element $x \notin A$ an **extension** of $A \in \mathcal{I}$ if x can be added to A while preserving independence; that is, x is an extension of A if $A \cup \{x\} \in \mathcal{I}$. As an example, consider a graphic matroid M_G. If A is an independent set of edges, then edge e is an extension of A if and only if e is not in A and the addition of x to A does not create a cycle.

If A is an independent subset in a matroid M, we say that A is **maximal** if it has no extensions. That is, A is maximal if it is not contained in any larger independent subset of M. The following property is often useful.

Theorem 17.6
All maximal independent subsets in a matroid have the same size.

Proof Suppose to the contrary that A is a maximal independent subset of M and there exists another larger maximal independent subset B of M. Then, the exchange property implies that A is extendable to a larger independent set $A \cup \{x\}$ for some $x \in B - A$, contradicting the assumption that A is maximal. ∎

As an illustration of this theorem, consider a graphic matroid M_G for a connected, undirected graph G. Every maximal independent subset of M_G must be a free tree with exactly $|V| - 1$ edges that connects all the vertices of G. Such a tree is called a **spanning tree** of G.

We say that a matroid $M = (S, \mathcal{I})$ is **weighted** if there is an associated weight function w that assigns a strictly positive weight $w(x)$ to each element $x \in S$. The weight function w extends to subsets of S by summation:

$$w(A) = \sum_{x \in A} w(x)$$

for any $A \subseteq S$. For example, if we let $w(e)$ denote the length of an edge e in a graphic matroid M_G, then $w(A)$ is the total length of the edges in edge set A.

17.4.2 Greedy algorithms on a weighted matroid

Many problems for which a greedy approach provides optimal solutions can be formulated in terms of finding a maximum-weight independent subset in a weighted matroid. That is, we are given a weighted matroid $M = (S, \mathcal{I})$, and we wish to find an independent set $A \in \mathcal{I}$ such that $w(A)$ is maximized. We call such a subset that is independent and has maximum possible weight an *optimal* subset of the matroid. Because the weight $w(x)$ of any element $x \in S$ is positive, an optimal subset is always a maximal independent subset—it always helps to make A as large as possible.

For example, in the *minimum-spanning-tree problem*, we are given a connected undirected graph $G = (V, E)$ and a length function w such that $w(e)$ is the (positive) length of edge e. (We use the term "length" here to refer to the original edge weights for the graph, reserving the term "weight" to refer to the weights in the associated matroid.) We are asked to find a subset of the edges that connects all of the vertices together and has minimum total length. To view this as a problem of finding an optimal subset of a matroid, consider the weighted matroid M_G with weight function w', where $w'(e) = w_0 - w(e)$ and w_0 is larger than the maximum length of any edge. In this weighted matroid, all weights are positive and an optimal subset is a spanning tree of minimum total length in the original graph. More specifically, each maximal independent subset A corresponds to a spanning tree, and since

$$w'(A) = (|V| - 1)w_0 - w(A)$$

for any maximal independent subset A, the independent subset that maximizes $w'(A)$ must minimize $w(A)$. Thus, any algorithm that can find an optimal subset A in an arbitrary matroid can solve the minimum-spanning-tree problem.

Chapter 24 gives algorithms for the minimum-spanning-tree problem, but here we give a greedy algorithm that works for any weighted matroid. The algorithm takes as input a weighted matroid $M = (S, \mathcal{I})$ with an an associated positive weight function w, and it returns an optimal subset A. In our pseudocode, we denote the components of M by $S[M]$ and $\mathcal{I}[M]$ and the weight function by w. The algorithm is greedy because it considers each element $x \in S$ in turn in order of nonincreasing weight and immediately adds it to the set A being accumulated if $A \cup \{x\}$ is independent.

GREEDY(M, w)

1 $A \leftarrow \emptyset$
2 sort $S[M]$ into nonincreasing order by weight w
3 **for** each $x \in S[M]$, taken in nonincreasing order by weight $w(x)$
4   **do if** $A \cup \{x\} \in \mathcal{I}[M]$
5   **then** $A \leftarrow A \cup \{x\}$
6 **return** A

The elements of S are considered in turn, in order of nonincreasing weight. If the element x being considered can be added to A while maintaining A's independence, it is. Otherwise, x is discarded. Since the empty set is independent by the definition of a matroid, and since x is only added to A if $A \cup \{x\}$ is independent, the subset A is always independent, by induction. Therefore, GREEDY always returns an independent subset A. We shall see in a moment that A is a subset of maximum possible weight, so that A is an optimal subset.

The running time of GREEDY is easy to analyze. Let n denote $|S|$. The sorting phase of GREEDY takes time $O(n \lg n)$. Line 4 is executed exactly n times, once for each element of S. Each execution of line 4 requires a check on whether or not the set $A \cup \{x\}$ is independent. If each such check takes time $O(f(n))$, the entire algorithm runs in time $O(n \lg n + n f(n))$.

We now prove that GREEDY returns an optimal subset.

Lemma 17.7 (Matroids exhibit the greedy-choice property)
Suppose that $M = (S, \mathcal{I})$ is a weighted matroid with weight function w and that S is sorted into nonincreasing order by weight. Let x be the first element of S such that $\{x\}$ is independent, if any such x exists. If x exists, then there exists an optimal subset A of S that contains x.

Proof   If no such x exists, then the only independent subset is the empty set and we're done. Otherwise, let B be any nonempty optimal subset. Assume that $x \notin B$; otherwise, we let $A = B$ and we're done.

No element of B has weight greater than $w(x)$. To see this, observe that $y \in B$ implies that $\{y\}$ is independent, since $B \in \mathcal{I}$ and $\mathcal{I}$ is hereditary. Our choice of x therefore ensures that $w(x) \geq w(y)$ for any $y \in B$.

Construct the set A as follows. Begin with $A = \{x\}$. By the choice of x, A is independent. Using the exchange property, repeatedly find a new element of B that can be added to A until $|A| = |B|$ while preserving the independence of A. Then, $A = B - \{y\} \cup \{x\}$ for some $y \in B$, and so

$$
\begin{aligned}
w(A) &= w(B) - w(y) + w(x) \\
&\geq w(B) .
\end{aligned}
$$

Because B is optimal, A must also be optimal, and because $x \in A$, the lemma is proven.   ∎

We next show that if an element is not an option initially, then it cannot be an option later.

Lemma 17.8
Let $M = (S, \mathcal{I})$ be any matroid. If x is an element of S such that x is not an extension of $\emptyset$, then x is not an extension of any independent subset A of S.

Proof   The proof is by contradiction. Assume that x is an extension of A but not of $\emptyset$. Since x is an extension of A, we have that $A \cup \{x\}$ is independent. Since $\mathcal{I}$ is hereditary, $\{x\}$ must be independent, which contradicts the assumption that x is not an extension of $\emptyset$.   ∎

Lemma 17.8 says that any element that cannot be used immediately can never be used. Therefore, GREEDY cannot make an error by passing over any initial elements in S that are not an extension of $\emptyset$, since they can never be used.

Lemma 17.9 (Matroids exhibit the optimal-substructure property)
Let x be the first element of S chosen by GREEDY for the weighted matroid $M = (S, \mathcal{I})$. The remaining problem of finding a maximum-weight independent subset containing x reduces to finding a maximum-weight independent subset of the weighted matroid $M' = (S', \mathcal{I}')$, where

$$
\begin{aligned}
S' &= \{y \in S : \{x, y\} \in \mathcal{I}\} \ , \\
\mathcal{I}' &= \{B \subseteq S - \{x\} : B \cup \{x\} \in \mathcal{I}\} \ , \text{ and}
\end{aligned}
$$

the weight function for M' is the weight function for M, restricted to S'. (We call M' the **contraction** of M by the element x.)

Proof   If A is any maximum-weight independent subset of M containing x, then $A' = A - \{x\}$ is an independent subset of M'. Conversely, any independent subset A' of M' yields an independent subset $A = A' \cup \{x\}$ of M. Since we have in both cases that $w(A) = w(A') + w(x)$, a maximum-weight solution in M containing x yields a maximum-weight solution in M', and vice versa.   ∎

Theorem 17.10 (Correctness of the greedy algorithm on matroids)
If $M = (S, \mathcal{I})$ is a weighted matroid with weight function w, then the call GREEDY(M, w) returns an optimal subset.

Proof   By Lemma 17.8, any elements that are passed over initially because they are not extensions of $\emptyset$ can be forgotten about, since they can never be useful. Once the first element x is selected, Lemma 17.7 implies that GREEDY does not err by adding x to A, since there exists an optimal subset containing x. Finally, Lemma 17.9 implies that the remaining problem is one of finding an optimal subset in the matroid M' that is the contraction of M by x. After the procedure GREEDY sets A to $\{x\}$, all of its remaining steps can be interpreted as acting in the matroid $M' = (S', \mathcal{I}')$, because B is independent in M' if and only if $B \cup \{x\}$ is independent in M, for all sets $B \in \mathcal{I}'$. Thus, the subsequent operation of GREEDY will find a maximum-weight independent subset for M', and the overall operation of GREEDY will find a maximum-weight independent subset for M.   ∎

Exercises

17.4-1
Show that $(S, \mathcal{I}_k)$ is a matroid, where S is any finite set and $\mathcal{I}_k$ is the set of all subsets of S of size at most k, where $k \leq |S|$.

17.4-2 ⋆
Given an $n \times n$ real-valued matrix T, show that $(S, \mathcal{I})$ is a matroid, where S is the set of columns of T and $A \in \mathcal{I}$ if and only if the columns in A are linearly independent.

17.4-3 ⋆
Show that if $(S, \mathcal{I})$ is a matroid, then $(S, \mathcal{I}')$ is a matroid, where $\mathcal{I}' = \{A' : S - A'$ contains some maximal $A \in \mathcal{I}\}$. That is, the maximal independent sets of $(S', \mathcal{I}')$ are just the complements of the maximal independent sets of $(S, \mathcal{I})$.

17.4-4 ⋆
Let S be a finite set and let $S_1, S_2, \dots, S_k$ be a partition of S into nonempty disjoint subsets. Define the structure $(S, \mathcal{I})$ by the condition that $\mathcal{I} = \{A : |A \cap S_i| \leq 1$ for $i = 1, 2, \dots, k\}$. Show that $(S, \mathcal{I})$ is a matroid. That is, the set of all sets A that contain at most one member in each block of the partition determines the independent sets of a matroid.

17.4-5
Show how to transform the weight function of a weighted matroid problem, where the desired optimal solution is a *minimum-weight* maximal independent subset, to make it an standard weighted-matroid problem. Argue carefully that your transformation is correct.

⋆ **17.5   A task-scheduling problem**

An interesting problem that can be solved using matroids is the problem of optimally scheduling unit-time tasks on a single processor, where each task has a deadline and a penalty that must be paid if the deadline is missed.

The problem looks complicated, but it can be solved in a surprisingly simple manner using a greedy algorithm.

A ***unit-time task*** is a job, such as a program to be run on a computer, that requires exactly one unit of time to complete. Given a finite set S of unit-time tasks, a ***schedule*** for S is a permutation of S specifying the order in which these tasks are to be performed. The first task in the schedule begins at time 0 and finishes at time 1, the second task begins at time 1 and finishes at time 2, and so on.

The problem of ***scheduling unit-time tasks with deadlines and penalties for a single processor*** has the following inputs:

- a set $S = \{1, 2, \dots, n\}$ of n unit-time tasks;

- a set of n integer ***deadlines*** $d_1, d_2, \dots, d_n$, such that each d_i satisfies $1 \le d_i \le n$ and task i is supposed to finish by time d_i; and

- a set of n nonnegative weights or ***penalties*** $w_1, w_2, \dots, w_n$, such that a penalty w_i is incurred if task i is not finished by time d_i and no penalty is incurred if a task finishes by its deadline.

We are asked to find a schedule for S that minimizes the total penalty incurred for missed deadlines.

Consider a given schedule. We say that a task is ***late*** in this schedule if it finishes after its deadline. Otherwise, the task is ***early*** in the schedule. An arbitrary schedule can always be put into ***early-first form***, in which the early tasks precede the late tasks. To see this, note that if some early task x follows some late task y, then we can switch the positions of x and y without affecting x being early or y being late.

We similarly claim that an arbitrary schedule can always be put into ***canonical form***, in which the early tasks precede the late tasks and the early tasks are scheduled in order of nondecreasing deadlines. To do so, we put the schedule into early-first form. Then, as long as there are two early tasks i and j finishing at respective times k and $k+1$ in the schedule such that $d_j < d_i$, we swap the positions of i and j. Since task j is early before the swap, $k + 1 \le d_j$. Therefore, $k + 1 < d_i$, and so task i is still early after the swap. Task j is moved earlier in the schedule, so it also still early after the swap.

The search for an optimal schedule thus reduces to finding a set A of tasks that are to be early in the optimal schedule. Once A is determined, we can create the actual schedule by listing the elements of A in order of nondecreasing deadline, then listing the late tasks (i.e., $S - A$) in any order, producing a canonical ordering of the optimal schedule.

We say that a set A of tasks is ***independent*** if there exists a schedule for these tasks such that no tasks are late. Clearly, the set of early tasks for a schedule forms an independent set of tasks. Let $\mathcal{I}$ denote the set of all independent sets of tasks.

Consider the problem of determining whether a given set A of tasks is independent. For $t = 1, 2, \dots, n$, let $N_t(A)$ denote the number of tasks in A whose deadline is t or earlier.

Lemma 17.11
For any set of tasks A, the following statements are equivalent.

1. The set A is independent.

2. For $t = 1, 2, \ldots, n$, we have $N_t(A) \le t$.

3. If the tasks in A are scheduled in order of nondecreasing deadlines, then no task is late.

Proof   Clearly, if $N_t(A) > t$ for some t, then there is no way to make a schedule with no late tasks for set A, because there are more than t tasks to finish before time t. Therefore, (1) implies (2). If (2) holds, then (3) must follow: there is no way to "get stuck" when scheduling the tasks in order of nondecreasing deadlines, since (2) implies that the ith largest deadline is at most i. Finally, (3) trivially implies (1).   ■

Using property 2 of Lemma 17.11, we can easily compute whether or not a given set of tasks is independent (see Exercise 17.5-2).

The problem of minimizing the sum of the penalties of the late tasks is the same as the problem of maximizing the sum of the penalties of the early tasks. The following theorem thus ensures that we can use the greedy algorithm to find an independent set A of tasks with the maximum total penalty.

Theorem 17.12
If S is a set of unit-time tasks with deadlines, and $\mathcal{I}$ is the set of all independent sets of tasks, then the corresponding system $(S, \mathcal{I})$ is a matroid.

Proof   Every subset of an independent set of tasks is certainly independent. To prove the exchange property, suppose that B and A are independent sets of tasks and that $|B| > |A|$. Let k be the largest t such that $N_t(B) \le N_t(A)$. Since $N_n(B) = |B|$ and $N_n(A) = |A|$, but $|B| > |A|$, we must have that $k < n$ and that $N_j(B) > N_j(A)$ for all j in the range $k + 1 \le j \le n$. Therefore, B contains more tasks with deadline $k + 1$ than A does. Let x be a task in $B - A$ with deadline $k + 1$. Let $A' = A \cup \{x\}$.

We now show that A' must be independent by using property 2 of Lemma 17.11. For $1 \le t \le k$, we have $N_t(A') = N_t(A) \le t$, since A is independent. For $k < t \le n$, we have $N_t(A') \le N_t(B) \le t$, since B is independent. Therefore, A' is independent, completing our proof that $(S, \mathcal{I})$ is a matroid.   ■

By Theorem 17.10, we can use a greedy algorithm to find a maximum-weight independent set of tasks A. We can then create an optimal schedule having the tasks in A as its early tasks. This method is an efficient algorithm for scheduling unit-time tasks with deadlines and penalties for a single processor. The running time is $O(n^2)$ using GREEDY, since each of the

				Task			
	1	2	3	4	5	6	7
d_i	4	2	4	3	1	4	6
w_i	70	60	50	40	30	20	10

Figure 17.7 An instance of the problem of scheduling unit-time tasks with deadlines and penalties for a single processor.

$O(n)$ independence checks made by that algorithm takes time $O(n)$ (see Exercise 17.5-2). A faster implementation is given in Problem 17-3.

Figure 17.7 gives an example of a problem of scheduling unit-time tasks with deadlines and penalties for a single processor. In this example, the greedy algorithm selects tasks 1, 2, 3, and 4, then rejects tasks 5 and 6, and finally accepts task 7. The final optimal schedule is

$$\langle 2, 4, 1, 3, 7, 5, 6 \rangle \,,$$

which has a total penalty incurred of $w_5 + w_6 = 50$.

Exercises

17.5-1
Solve the instance of the scheduling problem given in Figure 17.7, but with each penalty w_i replaced by $80 - w_i$.

17.5-2
Show how to use property 2 of Lemma 17.11 to determine in time $O(|A|)$ whether or not a given set A of tasks is independent.

Problems

17-1 Coin changing
Consider the problem of making change for n cents using the least number of coins.

a. Describe a greedy algorithm to make change consisting of quarters, dimes, nickels, and pennies. Prove that your algorithm yields an optimal solution.

b. Suppose that the available coins are in the denominations $c^0, c^1, \ldots, c^k$ for some integers $c > 1$ and $k \geq 1$. Show that the greedy algorithm always yields an optimal solution.

c. Give a set of coin denominations for which the greedy algorithm does not yield an optimal solution.

17-2   Acyclic subgraphs

a. Let $G = (V, E)$ be an undirected graph. Using the definition of a matroid, show that $(E, \mathcal{I})$ is a matroid, where $A \in \mathcal{I}$ if and only if A is an acyclic subset of E.

b. The **incidence matrix** for an undirected graph $G = (V, E)$ is a $|V| \times |E|$ matrix M such that $M_{ve} = 1$ if edge e is incident on vertex v, and $M_{ve} = 0$ otherwise. Argue that a set of columns of M is linearly independent if and only if the corresponding set of edges is acyclic. Then, use the result of Exercise 17.4-2 to provide an alternate proof that $(E, \mathcal{I})$ of part (a) is matroid.

c. Suppose that a nonnegative weight $w(e)$ is associated with each edge in an undirected graph $G = (V, E)$. Give an efficient algorithm to find an an acyclic subset of E of maximum total weight.

d. Let $G(V, E)$ be an arbitrary directed graph, and let $(E, \mathcal{I})$ be defined so that $A \in \mathcal{I}$ if and only if A does not contain any directed cycles. Give an example of a directed graph G such that the associated system $(E, \mathcal{I})$ is not a matroid. Specify which defining condition for a matroid fails to hold.

e. The **incidence matrix** for a directed graph $G = (V, E)$ is a $|V| \times |E|$ matrix M such that $M_{ve} = -1$ if edge e leaves vertex v, $M_{ve} = 1$ if edge e enters vertex v, and and $M_{ve} = 0$ otherwise. Argue that if a set of edges of G is linearly independent, then the corresponding set of edges does not contain a directed cycle.

f. Exercise 17.4-2 tells us that the set of linearly independent sets of columns of any matrix M forms a matroid. Explain carefully why the results of parts (d) and (e) are not contradictory. How can there fail to be a perfect correspondence between the notion of a set of edges being acyclic and the notion of the associated set of columns of the incidence matrix being linearly independent?

17-3   Scheduling variations

Consider the following algorithm for solving the problem in Section 17.5 of scheduling unit-time tasks with deadlines and penalties. Let all n time slots be initially empty, where time slot i is the unit-length slot of time that finishes at time i. We consider the jobs in order of monotonically decreasing penalty. When considering job j, if there exists a time slot at or before j's deadline d_j that is still empty, assign job j to the latest such slot, filling it. If there is no such slot, assign job j to the latest of the as yet unfilled slots.

a. Argue that this algorithm always gives an optimal answer.

b. Use the fast disjoint-set forest presented in Section 22.3 to implement the algorithm efficiently. Assume that the set of input jobs has already been sorted into monotonically decreasing order by penalty. Analyze the running time of your implementation.

Chapter notes

Much more material on greedy algorithms and matroids can be found in Lawler [132] and Papadimitriou and Steiglitz [154].

The greedy algorithm first appeared in the combinatorial optimization literature in a 1971 article by Edmonds [62], though the theory of matroids dates back to a 1935 article by Whitney [200].

Our proof of the correctness of the greedy algorithm for the activity-selection problem follows that of Gavril [80]. The task-scheduling problem is studied in Lawler [132], Horowitz and Sahni [105], and Brassard and Bratley [33].

Huffman codes were invented in 1952 [107]; Lelewer and Hirschberg [136] surveys data-compression techniques known as of 1987.

An extension of matroid theory to greedoid theory was pioneered by Korte and Lovász [127, 128, 129, 130], who greatly generalize the theory presented here.

18   Amortized Analysis

In an ***amortized analysis***, the time required to perform a sequence of data-structure operations is averaged over all the operations performed. Amortized analysis can be used to show that the average cost of an operation is small, if one averages over a sequence of operations, even though a single operation might be expensive. Amortized analysis differs from average-case analysis in that probability is not involved; an amortized analysis guarantees the *average performance of each operation in the worst case*.

The first three sections of this chapter cover the three most common techniques used in amortized analysis. Section 18.1 starts with the aggregate method, in which we determine an upper bound $T(n)$ on the total cost of a sequence of n operations. The amortized cost per operation is then $T(n)/n$.

Section 18.2 covers the accounting method, in which we determine an amortized cost of each operation. When there is more than one type of operation, each type of operation may have a different amortized cost. The accounting method overcharges some operations early in the sequence, storing the overcharge as "prepaid credit" on specific objects in the data structure. The credit is used later in the sequence to pay for operations that are charged less than they actually cost.

Section 18.3 discusses the potential method, which is like the accounting method in that we determine the amortized cost of each operation and may overcharge operations early on to compensate for undercharges later. The potential method maintains the credit as the "potential energy" of the data structure instead of associating the credit with individual objects within the data structure.

We shall use two examples to examine these three models. One is a stack with the additional operation MULTIPOP, which pops several objects at once. The other is a binary counter that counts up from 0 by means of the single operation INCREMENT.

While reading this chapter, bear in mind that the charges assigned during an amortized analysis are for analysis purposes only. They should not appear in the code. If, for example, a credit is assigned to an object x when using the accounting method, there is no need to assign an appropriate amount to some attribute *credit*[x] in the code.

The insight into a particular data structure gained by performing an amortized analysis can help in optimizing the design. In Section 18.4, for example, we shall use the potential method to analyze a dynamically expanding and contracting table.

18.1 The aggregate method

In the **aggregate method** of amortized analysis, we show that for all n, a sequence of n operations takes *worst-case* time $T(n)$ in total. In the worst case, the average cost, or **amortized cost**, per operation is therefore $T(n)/n$. Note that this amortized cost applies to each operation, even when there are several types of operations in the sequence. The other two methods we shall study in this chapter, the accounting method and the potential method, may assign different amortized costs to different types of operations.

Stack operations

In our first example of the aggregate method, we analyze stacks that have been augmented with a new operation. Section 11.1 presented the two fundamental stack operations, each of which takes $O(1)$ time:

PUSH(S, x) pushes object x onto stack S.

POP(S) pops the top of stack S and returns the popped object.

Since each of these operations runs in $O(1)$ time, let us consider the cost of each to be 1. The total cost of a sequence of n PUSH and POP operations is therefore n, and the actual running time for n operations is therefore $\Theta(n)$.

The situation becomes more interesting if we add the stack operation MULTIPOP(S, k), which removes the k top objects of stack S, or pops the entire stack if it contains less than k objects. In the following pseudocode, the operation STACK-EMPTY returns TRUE if there are no objects currently on the stack, and FALSE otherwise.

MULTIPOP(S, k)

1 **while** not STACK-EMPTY(S) and $k \neq 0$
2   **do** POP(S)
3          $k \leftarrow k - 1$

Figure 18.1 shows an example of MULTIPOP.

What is the running time of MULTIPOP(S, k) on a stack of s objects? The actual running time is linear in the number of POP operations actually executed, and thus it suffices to analyze MULTIPOP in terms of the abstract costs of 1 each for PUSH and POP. The number of iterations of the **while** loop is the number $\min(s, k)$ of objects popped off the stack. For each iteration of the loop, one call is made to POP in line 2. Thus, the total cost

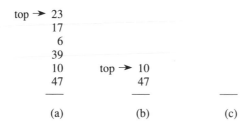

Figure 18.1   The action of MULTIPOP on a stack S, shown initially in (**a**). The top 4 objects are popped by MULTIPOP$(S, 4)$, whose result is shown in (**b**). The next operation is MULTIPOP$(S, 7)$, which empties the stack—shown in (**c**)—since there were fewer than 7 objects remaining.

of MULTIPOP is $\min(s, k)$, and the actual running time is a linear function of this cost.

Let us analyze a sequence of n PUSH, POP, and MULTIPOP operations on an initially empty stack. The worst-case cost of a MULTIPOP operation in the sequence is $O(n)$, since the stack size is at most n. The worst-case time of any stack operation is therefore $O(n)$, and hence a sequence of n operations costs $O(n^2)$, since we may have $O(n)$ MULTIPOP operations costing $O(n)$ each. Although this analysis is correct, the $O(n^2)$ result, obtained by considering the worst-case cost of each operation individually, is not tight.

Using the aggregate method of amortized analysis, we can obtain a better upper bound that considers the entire sequence of n operations. In fact, although a single MULTIPOP operation can be expensive, any sequence of n PUSH, POP, and MULTIPOP operations on an initially empty stack can cost at most $O(n)$. Why? Each object can be popped at most once for each time it is pushed. Therefore, the number of times that POP can be called on a nonempty stack, including calls within MULTIPOP, is at most the number of PUSH operations, which is at most n. For any value of n, any sequence of n PUSH, POP, and MULTIPOP operations takes a total of $O(n)$ time. The amortized cost of an operation is the average: $O(n)/n = O(1)$.

We emphasize again that although we have just shown that the average cost, and hence running time, of a stack operation is $O(1)$, no probabilistic reasoning was involved. We actually showed a *worst-case* bound of $O(n)$ on a sequence of n operations. Dividing this total cost by n yielded the average cost per operation, or the amortized cost.

Incrementing a binary counter

As another example of the aggregate method, consider the problem of implementing a k-bit binary counter that counts upward from 0. We use an array $A[0 . . k - 1]$ of bits, where $length[A] = k$, as the counter. A binary number x that is stored in the counter has its lowest-order bit in $A[0]$ and its highest-order bit in $A[k - 1]$, so that $x = \sum_{i=0}^{k-1} A[i] \cdot 2^i$. Initially, $x = 0$,

Counter value	$A[7]$	$A[6]$	$A[5]$	$A[4]$	$A[3]$	$A[2]$	$A[1]$	$A[0]$	Total cost
0	0	0	0	0	0	0	0	0	0
1	0	0	0	0	0	0	0	1	1
2	0	0	0	0	0	0	1	0	3
3	0	0	0	0	0	0	1	1	4
4	0	0	0	0	0	1	0	0	7
5	0	0	0	0	0	1	0	1	8
6	0	0	0	0	0	1	1	0	10
7	0	0	0	0	0	1	1	1	11
8	0	0	0	0	1	0	0	0	15
9	0	0	0	0	1	0	0	1	16
10	0	0	0	0	1	0	1	0	18
11	0	0	0	0	1	0	1	1	19
12	0	0	0	0	1	1	0	0	22
13	0	0	0	0	1	1	0	1	23
14	0	0	0	0	1	1	1	0	25
15	0	0	0	0	1	1	1	1	26
16	0	0	0	1	0	0	0	0	31

Figure 18.2 An 8-bit binary counter as its value goes from 0 to 16 by a sequence of 16 INCREMENT operations. Bits that flip to achieve the next value are shaded. The running cost for flipping bits is shown at the right. Notice that the total cost is never more than twice the total number of INCREMENT operations.

and thus $A[i] = 0$ for $i = 0, 1, \ldots, k - 1$. To add 1 (modulo 2^k) to the value in the counter, we use the following procedure.

INCREMENT(A)

```
1  i ← 0
2  while i < length[A] and A[i] = 1
3      do A[i] ← 0
4         i ← i + 1
5  if i < length[A]
6      then A[i] ← 1
```

This algorithm is essentially the same one implemented in hardware by a ripple-carry counter (see Section 29.2.1). Figure 18.2 shows what happens to a binary counter as it is incremented 16 times, starting with the initial value 0 and ending with the value 16. At the start of each iteration of the **while** loop in lines 2–4, we wish to add a 1 into position i. If $A[i] = 1$, then adding 1 flips the bit to 0 in position i and yields a carry of 1, to be added into position $i + 1$ on the next iteration of the loop. Otherwise, the loop ends, and then, if $i < k$, we know that $A[i] = 0$, so that adding a 1 into position i, flipping the 0 to a 1, is taken care of in line 6. The cost of each INCREMENT operation is linear in the number of bits flipped.

As with the stack example, a cursory analysis yields a bound that is correct but not tight. A single execution of INCREMENT takes time $\Theta(k)$ in the worst case, in which array A contains all 1's. Thus, a sequence of

n INCREMENT operations on an initially zero counter takes time $O(nk)$ in the worst case.

We can tighten our analysis to yield a worst-case cost of $O(n)$ for a sequence of n INCREMENT's by observing that not all bits flip each time INCREMENT is called. As Figure 18.2 shows, $A[0]$ does flip each time INCREMENT is called. The next-highest-order bit, $A[1]$, flips only every other time: a sequence of n INCREMENT operations on an initially zero counter causes $A[1]$ to flip $\lfloor n/2 \rfloor$ times. Similarly, bit $A[2]$ flips only every fourth time, or $\lfloor n/4 \rfloor$ times in a sequence of n INCREMENT's. In general, for $i = 0, 1, \ldots, \lfloor \lg n \rfloor$, bit $A[i]$ flips $\lfloor n/2^i \rfloor$ times in a sequence of n INCREMENT operations on an initially zero counter. For $i > \lfloor \lg n \rfloor$, bit $A[i]$ never flips at all. The total number of flips in the sequence is thus

$$\sum_{i=0}^{\lfloor \lg n \rfloor} \left\lfloor \frac{n}{2^i} \right\rfloor \;<\; n \sum_{i=0}^{\infty} \frac{1}{2^i}$$
$$= \; 2n \, ,$$

by equation (3.4). The worst-case time for a sequence of n INCREMENT operations on an initially zero counter is therefore $O(n)$, so the amortized cost of each operation is $O(n)/n = O(1)$.

Exercises

18.1-1
If a MULTIPUSH operation were included in the set of stack operations, would the $O(1)$ bound on the amortized cost of stack operations continue to hold?

18.1-2
Show that if a DECREMENT operation were included in the k-bit counter example, n operations could cost as much as $\Theta(nk)$ time.

18.1-3
A sequence of n operations is performed on a data structure. The ith operation costs i if i is an exact power of 2, and 1 otherwise. Use an aggregate method of analysis to determine the amortized cost per operation.

18.2   The accounting method

In the ***accounting method*** of amortized analysis, we assign differing charges to different operations, with some operations charged more or less than they actually cost. The amount we charge an operation is called its ***amortized cost***. When an operation's amortized cost exceeds its actual cost, the difference is assigned to specific objects in the data structure as ***credit***.

Credit can be used later on to help pay for operations whose amortized cost is less than their actual cost. Thus, one can view the amortized cost of an operation as being split between its actual cost and credit that is either deposited or used up. This is very different from the aggregate method, in which all operations have the same amortized cost.

One must choose the amortized costs of operations carefully. If we want analysis with amortized costs to show that in the worst case the average cost per operation is small, the total amortized cost of a sequence of operations must be an upper bound on the total actual cost of the sequence. Moreover, as in the aggregate method, this relationship must hold for all sequences of operations. Thus, the total credit associated with the data structure must be nonnegative at all times, since it represents the amount by which the total amortized costs incurred exceed the total actual costs incurred. If the total credit were ever allowed to become negative (the result of undercharging early operations with the promise of repaying the account later on), then the total amortized costs incurred at that time would be below the total actual costs incurred; for the sequence of operations up to that time, the total amortized cost would not be an upper bound on the total actual cost. Thus, we must take care that the total credit in the data structure never becomes negative.

Stack operations

To illustrate the accounting method of amortized analysis, let us return to the stack example. Recall that the actual costs of the operations were

PUSH   1 ,
POP   1 ,
MULTIPOP $\min(k, s)$,

where k is the argument supplied to MULTIPOP and s is the stack size when it is called. Let us assign the following amortized costs:

PUSH   2 ,
POP   0 ,
MULTIPOP   0 .

Note that the amortized cost of MULTIPOP is a constant (0), whereas the actual cost is variable. Here, all three amortized costs are $O(1)$, although in general the amortized costs of the operations under consideration may differ asymptotically.

We shall now show that we can pay for any sequence of stack operations by charging the amortized costs. Suppose we use a dollar bill to represent each unit of cost. We start with an empty stack. Recall the analogy of Section 11.1 between the stack data structure and a stack of plates in a cafeteria. When we push a plate on the stack, we use 1 dollar to pay the actual cost of the push and are left with a credit of 1 dollar (out of the 2 dollars charged), which we put on top of the plate. At any point in time, every plate on the stack has a dollar of credit on it.

The dollar stored on the plate is prepayment for the cost of popping it from the stack. When we execute a POP operation, we charge the operation nothing and pay its actual cost using the credit stored in the stack. To pop a plate, we take the dollar of credit off the plate and use it to pay the actual cost of the operation. Thus, by charging the PUSH operation a little bit more, we needn't charge the POP operation anything.

Moreover, we needn't charge MULTIPOP operations anything either. To pop the first plate, we take the dollar of credit off the plate and use it to pay the actual cost of a POP operation. To pop a second plate, we again have a dollar of credit on the plate to pay for the POP operation, and so on. Thus, we have always charged at least enough up front to pay for MULTIPOP operations. In other words, since each plate on the stack has 1 dollar of credit on it, and the stack always has a nonnegative number of plates, we have ensured that the amount of credit is always nonnegative. Thus, for *any* sequence of n PUSH, POP, and MULTIPOP operations, the total amortized cost is an upper bound on the total actual cost. Since the total amortized cost is $O(n)$, so is the total actual cost.

Incrementing a binary counter

As another illustration of the accounting method, we analyze the INCRE-MENT operation on a binary counter that starts at zero. As we observed earlier, the running time of this operation is proportional to the number of bits flipped, which we shall use as our cost for this example. Let us once again use a dollar bill to represent each unit of cost (the flipping of a bit in this example).

For the amortized analysis, let us charge an amortized cost of 2 dollars to set a bit to 1. When a bit is set, we use 1 dollar (out of the 2 dollars charged) to pay for the actual setting of the bit, and we place the other dollar on the bit as credit. At any point in time, every 1 in the counter has a dollar of credit on it, and thus we needn't charge anything to reset a bit to 0; we just pay for the reset with the dollar bill on the bit.

The amortized cost of INCREMENT can now be determined. The cost of resetting the bits within the **while** loop is paid for by the dollars on the bits that are reset. At most one bit is set, in line 6 of INCREMENT, and therefore the amortized cost of an INCREMENT operation is at most 2 dollars. The number of 1's in the counter is never negative, and thus the amount of credit is always nonnegative. Thus, for n INCREMENT operations, the total amortized cost is $O(n)$, which bounds the total actual cost.

Exercises

18.2-1

A sequence of stack operations is performed on a stack whose size never exceeds k. After every k operations, a copy of the entire stack is made for backup purposes. Show that the cost of n stack operations, including copying the stack, is $O(n)$ by assigning suitable amortized costs to the various stack operations.

18.2-2

Redo Exercise 18.1-3 using an accounting method of analysis.

18.2-3

Suppose we wish not only to increment a counter but also to reset it to zero (i.e., make all bits in it 0). Show how to implement a counter as a bit vector so that any sequence of n INCREMENT and RESET operations takes time $O(n)$ on an initially zero counter. (*Hint:* Keep a pointer to the high-order 1.)

18.3   The potential method

Instead of representing prepaid work as credit stored with specific objects in the data structure, the *potential method* of amortized analysis represents the prepaid work as "potential energy," or just "potential," that can be released to pay for future operations. The potential is associated with the data structure as a whole rather than with specific objects within the data structure.

The potential method works as follows. We start with an initial data structure D_0 on which n operations are performed. For each $i = 1, 2, \ldots, n$, we let c_i be the actual cost of the ith operation and D_i be the data structure that results after applying the ith operation to data structure D_{i-1}. A *potential function* Φ maps each data structure D_i to a real number $\Phi(D_i)$, which is the *potential* associated with data structure D_i. The *amortized cost* $\widehat{c}_i$ of the ith operation with respect to potential function Φ is defined by

$$\widehat{c}_i = c_i + \Phi(D_i) - \Phi(D_{i-1}) . \tag{18.1}$$

The amortized cost of each operation is therefore its actual cost plus the increase in potential due to the operation. By equation (18.1), the total amortized cost of the n operations is

$$\sum_{i=1}^{n} \widehat{c}_i = \sum_{i=1}^{n} (c_i + \Phi(D_i) - \Phi(D_{i-1}))$$

$$= \sum_{i=1}^{n} c_i + \Phi(D_n) - \Phi(D_0) . \qquad (18.2)$$

The second equality follows from equation (3.7), since the $\Phi(D_i)$ telescope.

If we can define a potential function Φ so that $\Phi(D_n) \geq \Phi(D_0)$, then the total amortized cost $\sum_{i=1}^{n} \widehat{c}_i$ is an upper bound on the total actual cost. In practice, we do not always know how many operations might be performed. Therefore, if we require that $\Phi(D_i) \geq \Phi(D_0)$ for all i, then we guarantee, as in the accounting method, that we pay in advance. It is often convenient to define $\Phi(D_0)$ to be 0 and then to show that $\Phi(D_i) \geq 0$ for all i. (See Exercise 18.3-1 for an easy way to handle cases in which $\Phi(D_0) \neq 0$.)

Intuitively, if the potential difference $\Phi(D_i) - \Phi(D_{i-1})$ of the ith operation is positive, then the amortized cost $\widehat{c}_i$ represents an overcharge to the ith operation, and the potential of the data structure increases. If the potential difference is negative, then the amortized cost represents an undercharge to the ith operation, and the actual cost of the operation is paid by the decrease in the potential.

The amortized costs defined by equations (18.1) and (18.2) depend on the choice of the potential function Φ. Different potential functions may yield different amortized costs yet still be upper bounds on the actual costs. There are often trade-offs that can be made in choosing a potential function; the best potential function to use depends on the desired time bounds.

Stack operations

To illustrate the potential method, we return once again to the example of the stack operations PUSH, POP, and MULTIPOP. We define the potential function Φ on a stack to be the number of objects in the stack. For the empty stack D_0 with which we start, we have $\Phi(D_0) = 0$. Since the number of objects in the stack is never negative, the stack D_i that results after the ith operation has nonnegative potential, and thus

$$\begin{aligned} \Phi(D_i) &\geq 0 \\ &= \Phi(D_0) . \end{aligned}$$

The total amortized cost of n operations with respect to Φ therefore represents an upper bound on the actual cost.

Let us now compute the amortized costs of the various stack operations. If the ith operation on a stack containing s objects is a PUSH operation, then the potential difference is

$$\begin{aligned} \Phi(D_i) - \Phi(D_{i-1}) &= (s+1) - s \\ &= 1 . \end{aligned}$$

By equation (18.1), the amortized cost of this PUSH operation is

$$\widehat{c}_i = c_i + \Phi(D_i) - \Phi(D_{i-1})$$

$$= 1 + 1$$
$$= 2 \; .$$

Suppose that the ith operation on the stack is MULTIPOP(S, k) and that $k' = \min(k, s)$ objects are popped off the stack. The actual cost of the operation is k', and the potential difference is

$$\Phi(D_i) - \Phi(D_{i-1}) = -k' \; .$$

Thus, the amortized cost of the MULTIPOP operation is

$$\begin{aligned} \widehat{c_i} &= c_i + \Phi(D_i) - \Phi(D_{i-1}) \\ &= k' - k' \\ &= 0 \; . \end{aligned}$$

Similarly, the amortized cost of an ordinary POP operation is 0.

The amortized cost of each of the three operations is $O(1)$, and thus the total amortized cost of a sequence of n operations is $O(n)$. Since we have already argued that $\Phi(D_i) \geq \Phi(D_0)$, the total amortized cost of n operations is an upper bound on the total actual cost. The worst-case cost of n operations is therefore $O(n)$.

Incrementing a binary counter

As another example of the potential method, we again look at incrementing a binary counter. This time, we define the potential of the counter after the ith INCREMENT operation to be b_i, the number of 1's in the counter after the ith operation.

Let us compute the amortized cost of an INCREMENT operation. Suppose that the ith INCREMENT operation resets t_i bits. The actual cost of the operation is therefore at most $t_i + 1$, since in addition to resetting t_i bits, it sets at most one bit to a 1. The number of 1's in the counter after the ith operation is therefore $b_i \leq b_{i-1} - t_i + 1$, and the potential difference is

$$\begin{aligned} \Phi(D_i) - \Phi(D_{i-1}) &\leq (b_{i-1} - t_i + 1) - b_{i-1} \\ &= 1 - t_i \; . \end{aligned}$$

The amortized cost is therefore

$$\begin{aligned} \widehat{c_i} &= c_i + \Phi(D_i) - \Phi(D_{i-1}) \\ &\leq (t_i + 1) + (1 - t_i) \\ &= 2 \; . \end{aligned}$$

If the counter starts at zero, then $\Phi(D_0) = 0$. Since $\Phi(D_i) \geq 0$ for all i, the total amortized cost of a sequence of n INCREMENT operations is an upper bound on the total actual cost, and so the worst-case cost of n INCREMENT operations is $O(n)$.

The potential method gives us an easy way to analyze the counter even when it does not start at zero. There are initially b_0 1's, and after n

INCREMENT operations there are b_n 1's, where $0 \le b_0, b_n \le k$. We can rewrite equation (18.2) as

$$\sum_{i=1}^{n} c_i = \sum_{i=1}^{n} \widehat{c}_i - \Phi(D_n) + \Phi(D_0) \,. \tag{18.3}$$

We have $\widehat{c}_i \le 2$ for all $1 \le i \le n$. Since $\Phi(D_0) = b_0$ and $\Phi(D_n) = b_n$, the total actual cost of n INCREMENT operations is

$$\begin{aligned}
\sum_{i=1}^{n} c_i &\le \sum_{i=1}^{n} 2 - b_n + b_0 \\
&= 2n - b_n + b_0 \,.
\end{aligned}$$

Note in particular that since $b_0 \le k$, if we execute at least $n = \Omega(k)$ INCREMENT operations, the total actual cost is $O(n)$, no matter what initial value the counter contains.

Exercises

18.3-1
Suppose we have a potential function Φ such that $\Phi(D_i) \ge \Phi(D_0)$ for all i, but $\Phi(D_0) \ne 0$. Show that there exists a potential function Φ' such that $\Phi'(D_0) = 0$, $\Phi'(D_i) \ge 0$ for all $i \ge 1$, and the amortized costs using Φ' are the same as the amortized costs using Φ.

18.3-2
Redo Exercise 18.1-3 using a potential method of analysis.

18.3-3
Consider an ordinary binary heap data structure with n elements that supports the instructions INSERT and EXTRACT-MIN in $O(\lg n)$ worst-case time. Give a potential function Φ such that the amortized cost of INSERT is $O(\lg n)$ and the amortized cost of EXTRACT-MIN is $O(1)$, and show that it works.

18.3-4
What is the total cost of executing n of the stack operations PUSH, POP, and MULTIPOP, assuming that the stack begins with s_0 objects and finishes with s_n objects?

18.3-5
Suppose that a counter begins at a number with b 1's in its binary representation, rather than at 0. Show that the cost of performing n INCREMENT operations is $O(n)$ if $n = \Omega(b)$. (Do not assume that b is constant.)

18.3-6
Show how to implement a queue with two ordinary stacks (Exercise 11.1-6) so that the amortized cost of each ENQUEUE and each DEQUEUE operation is $O(1)$.

18.4 Dynamic tables

In some applications, we do not know in advance how many objects will be stored in a table. We might allocate space for a table, only to find out later that it is not enough. The table must then be reallocated with a larger size, and all objects stored in the original table must be copied over into the new, larger table. Similarly, if many objects have been deleted from the table, it may be worthwhile to reallocate the table with a smaller size. In this section, we study this problem of dynamically expanding and contracting a table. Using amortized analysis, we shall show that the amortized cost of insertion and deletion is only $O(1)$, even though the actual cost of an operation is large when it triggers an expansion or a contraction. Moreover, we shall see how to guarantee that the unused space in a dynamic table never exceeds a constant fraction of the total space.

We assume that the dynamic table supports the operations TABLE-INSERT and TABLE-DELETE. TABLE-INSERT inserts into the table an item that occupies a single *slot*, that is, a space for one item. Likewise, TABLE-DELETE can be thought of as removing an item from the table, thereby freeing a slot. The details of the data-structuring method used to organize the table are unimportant; we might use a stack (Section 11.1), a heap (Section 7.1), or a hash table (Chapter 12). We might also use an array or collection of arrays to implement object storage, as we did in Section 11.3.

We shall find it convenient to use a concept introduced in our analysis of hashing (Chapter 12). We define the *load factor* $\alpha(T)$ of a nonempty table T to be the number of items stored in the table divided by the size (number of slots) of the table. We assign an empty table (one with no items) size 0, and we define its load factor to be 1. If the load factor of a dynamic table is bounded below by a constant, the unused space in the table is never more than a constant fraction of the total amount of space.

We start by analyzing a dynamic table in which only insertions are performed. We then consider the more general case in which both insertions and deletions are allowed.

18.4.1 Table expansion

Let us assume that storage for a table is allocated as an array of slots. A table fills up when all slots have been used or, equivalently, when its load factor is 1.[1] In some software environments, if an attempt is made to insert an item into a full table, there is no alternative but to abort with an error. We shall assume, however, that our software environment, like many modern ones, provides a memory-management system that can allocate and free blocks of storage on request. Thus, when an item is inserted into a full table, we can *expand* the table by allocating a new table with more slots than the old table had and then copy items from the old table into the new one.

A common heuristic is to allocate a new table that has twice as many slots as the old one. If only insertions are performed, the load factor of a table is always at least $1/2$, and thus the amount of wasted space never exceeds half the total space in the table.

In the following pseudocode, we assume that T is an object representing the table. The field $table[T]$ contains a pointer to the block of storage representing the table. The field $num[T]$ contains the number of items in the table, and the field $size[T]$ is the total number of slots in the table. Initially, the table is empty: $num[T] = size[T] = 0$.

TABLE-INSERT(T, x)
```
 1   if size[T] = 0
 2      then allocate table[T] with 1 slot
 3           size[T] ← 1
 4   if num[T] = size[T]
 5      then allocate new-table with 2 · size[T] slots
 6           insert all items in table[T] into new-table
 7           free table[T]
 8           table[T] ← new-table
 9           size[T] ← 2 · size[T]
10   insert x into table[T]
11   num[T] ← num[T] + 1
```

Notice that we have two "insertion" procedures here: the TABLE-INSERT procedure itself and the *elementary insertion* into a table in lines 6 and 10. We can analyze the running time of TABLE-INSERT in terms of the number of elementary insertions by assigning a cost of 1 to each elementary insertion. We assume that the actual running time of TABLE-INSERT is linear in the time to insert individual items, so that the overhead for allocating an initial table in line 2 is constant and the overhead for allocating and freeing storage in lines 5 and 7 is dominated by the cost of transferring items in line 6. We call the event in which the **then** clause in lines 5–9 is executed an *expansion*.

---

[1]In some situations, such as an open-address hash table, we may wish to consider a table to be full if its load factor equals some constant strictly less than 1. (See Exercise 18.4-2.)

Let us analyze a sequence of n TABLE-INSERT operations on an initially empty table. What is the cost c_i of the ith operation? If there is room in the current table (or if this is the first operation), then $c_i = 1$, since we need only perform the one elementary insertion in line 10. If the current table is full, however, and an expansion occurs, then $c_i = i$: the cost is 1 for the elementary insertion in line 10 plus $i - 1$ for the items that must be copied from the old table to the new table in line 6. If n operations are performed, the worst-case cost of an operation is $O(n)$, which leads to an upper bound of $O(n^2)$ on the total running time for n operations.

This bound is not tight, because the cost of expanding the table is not borne often in the course of n TABLE-INSERT operations. Specifically, the ith operation causes an expansion only when $i - 1$ is an exact power of 2. The amortized cost of an operation is in fact $O(1)$, as we can show using the aggregate method. The cost of the ith operation is

$$c_i = \begin{cases} i & \text{if } i - 1 \text{ is an exact power of 2 ,} \\ 1 & \text{otherwise .} \end{cases}$$

The total cost of n TABLE-INSERT operations is therefore

$$\begin{aligned} \sum_{i=1}^{n} c_i & \leq n + \sum_{j=0}^{\lfloor \lg n \rfloor} 2^j \\ & < n + 2n \\ & = 3n , \end{aligned}$$

since there are at most n operations that cost 1 and the costs of the remaining operations form a geometric series. Since the total cost of n TABLE-INSERT operations is $3n$, the amortized cost of a single operation is 3.

By using the accounting method, we can gain some feeling for why the amortized cost of a TABLE-INSERT operation should be 3. Intuitively, each item pays for 3 elementary insertions: inserting itself in the current table, moving itself when the table is expanded, and moving another item that has already been moved once when the table is expanded. For example, suppose that the size of the table is m immediately after an expansion. Then, the number of items in the table is $m/2$, and the table contains no credit. We charge 3 dollars for each insertion. The elementary insertion that occurs immediately costs 1 dollar. Another dollar is placed as credit on the item inserted. The third dollar is placed as credit on one of the $m/2$ items already in the table. Filling the table requires $m/2$ additional insertions, and thus, by the time the table contains m items and is full, each item has a dollar to pay for its reinsertion during the expansion.

The potential method can also be used to analyze a sequence of n TABLE-INSERT operations, and we shall use it in Section 18.4.2 to design a TABLE-DELETE operation that has $O(1)$ amortized cost as well. We start by defining a potential function Φ that is 0 immediately after an expansion but builds to the table size by the time the table is full, so that the next expansion can be paid for by the potential. The function

$$\Phi(T) = 2 \cdot num[T] - size[T] \tag{18.4}$$

is one possibility. Immediately after an expansion, we have $num[T] = size[T]/2$, and thus $\Phi(T) = 0$, as desired. Immediately before an expansion, we have $num[T] = size[T]$, and thus $\Phi(T) = num[T]$, as desired. The initial value of the potential is 0, and since the table is always at least half full, $num[T] \geq size[T]/2$, which implies that $\Phi(T)$ is always nonnegative. Thus, the sum of the amortized costs of n TABLE-INSERT operations is an upper bound on the sum of the actual costs.

To analyze the amortized cost of the ith TABLE-INSERT operation, we let num_i denote the number of items stored in the table after the ith operation, $size_i$ denote the total size of the table after the ith operation, and Φ_i denote the potential after the ith operation. Initially, we have $num_0 = 0$, $size_0 = 0$, and $\Phi_0 = 0$.

If the ith TABLE-INSERT operation does not trigger an expansion, then $size_i = size_{i-1}$ and the amortized cost of the operation is

$$\begin{aligned}
\widehat{c}_i &= c_i + \Phi_i - \Phi_{i-1} \\
&= 1 + (2 \cdot num_i - size_i) - (2 \cdot num_{i-1} - size_{i-1}) \\
&= 1 + (2 \cdot num_i - size_i) - (2(num_i - 1) - size_i) \\
&= 3 .
\end{aligned}$$

If the ith operation does trigger an expansion, then $size_i/2 = size_{i-1} = num_i - 1$, and the amortized cost of the operation is

$$\begin{aligned}
\widehat{c}_i &= c_i + \Phi_i - \Phi_{i-1} \\
&= num_i + (2 \cdot num_i - size_i) - (2 \cdot num_{i-1} - size_{i-1}) \\
&= num_i + (2 \cdot num_i - (2 \cdot num_i - 2)) - (2(num_i - 1) - (num_i - 1)) \\
&= num_i + 2 - (num_i - 1) \\
&= 3 .
\end{aligned}$$

Figure 18.3 plots the values of num_i, $size_i$, and Φ_i against i. Notice how the potential builds to pay for the expansion of the table.

18.4.2 Table expansion and contraction

To implement a TABLE-DELETE operation, it is simple enough to remove the specified item from the table. It is often desirable, however, to *contract* the table when the load factor of the table becomes too small, so that the wasted space is not exorbitant. Table contraction is analogous to table expansion: when the number of items in the table drops too low, we allocate a new, smaller table and then copy the items from the old table into the new one. The storage for the old table can then be freed by returning it to the memory-management system. Ideally, we would like to preserve two properties:

• the load factor of the dynamic table is bounded below by a constant, and

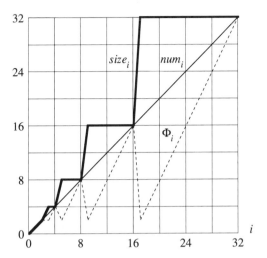

Figure 18.3   The effect of a sequence of n TABLE-INSERT operations on the number num_i of items in the table, the number $size_i$ of slots in the table, and the potential $\Phi_i = 2 \cdot num_i - size_i$, each being measured after the ith operation. The thin line shows num_i, the thick line shows $size_i$, and the dashed line shows Φ_i. Notice that immediately before an expansion, the potential has built up to the number of items in the table, and therefore it can pay for moving all the items to the new table. Afterwards, the potential drops to 0, but it is immediately increased by 2 when the item that caused the expansion is inserted.

- the amortized cost of a table operation is bounded above by a constant.

We assume that cost can be measured in terms of elementary insertions and deletions.

A natural strategy for expansion and contraction is to double the table size when an item is inserted into a full table and halve the size when a deletion would cause the table to become less than half full. This strategy guarantees that the load factor of the table never drops below $1/2$, but unfortunately, it can cause the amortized cost of an operation to be quite large. Consider the following scenario. We perform n operations on a table T, where n is an exact power of 2. The first $n/2$ operations are insertions, which by our previous analysis cost a total of $\Theta(n)$. At the end of this sequence of insertions, $num[T] = size[T] = n/2$. For the second $n/2$ operations, we perform the following sequence:

I, D, D, I, I, D, D, I, I, ... ,

where I stands for an insertion and D stands for a deletion. The first insertion causes an expansion of the table to size n. The two following deletions cause a contraction of the table back to size $n/2$. Two further insertions cause another expansion, and so forth. The cost of each expansion and contraction is $\Theta(n)$, and there are $\Theta(n)$ of them. Thus, the total cost of the n operations is $\Theta(n^2)$, and the amortized cost of an operation is $\Theta(n)$.

The difficulty with this strategy is obvious: after an expansion, we do not perform enough deletions to pay for a contraction. Likewise, after a contraction, we do not perform enough insertions to pay for an expansion.

We can improve upon this strategy by allowing the load factor of the table to drop below $1/2$. Specifically, we continue to double the table size when an item is inserted into a full table, but we halve the table size when a deletion causes the table to become less than $1/4$ full, rather than $1/2$ full as before. The load factor of the table is therefore bounded below by the constant $1/4$. The idea is that after an expansion, the load factor of the table is $1/2$. Thus, half the items in the table must be deleted before a contraction can occur, since contraction does not occur unless the load factor would fall below $1/4$. Likewise, after a contraction, the load factor of the table is also $1/2$. Thus, the number of items in the table must be doubled by insertions before an expansion can occur, since expansion occurs only when the load factor would exceed 1.

We omit the code for TABLE-DELETE, since it is analogous to TABLE-INSERT. It is convenient to assume for analysis, however, that if the number of items in the table drops to 0, the storage for the table is freed. That is, if $num[T] = 0$, then $size[T] = 0$.

We can now use the potential method to analyze the cost of a sequence of n TABLE-INSERT and TABLE-DELETE operations. We start by defining a potential function Φ that is 0 immediately after an expansion or contraction and builds as the load factor increases to 1 or decreases to $1/4$. Let us denote the load factor of a nonempty table T by $\alpha(T) = num[T]/size[T]$. Since for an empty table, $num[T] = size[T] = 0$ and $\alpha[T] = 1$, we always have $num[T] = \alpha(T) \cdot size[T]$, whether the table is empty or not. We shall use as our potential function

$$\Phi(T) = \begin{cases} 2 \cdot num[T] - size[T] & \text{if } \alpha(T) \geq 1/2 \;, \\ size[T]/2 - num[T] & \text{if } \alpha(T) < 1/2 \;. \end{cases} \quad (18.5)$$

Observe that the potential of an empty table is 0 and that the potential is never negative. Thus, the total amortized cost of a sequence of operations with respect to Φ is an upper bound on their actual cost.

Before proceeding with a precise analysis, we pause to observe some properties of the potential function. Notice that when the load factor is $1/2$, the potential is 0. When it is 1, we have $size[T] = num[T]$, which implies $\Phi(T) = num[T]$, and thus the potential can pay for an expansion if an item is inserted. When the load factor is $1/4$, we have $size[T] = 4 \cdot num[T]$, which implies $\Phi(T) = num[T]$, and thus the potential can pay for a contraction if an item is deleted. Figure 18.4 illustrates how the potential behaves for a sequence of operations.

To analyze a sequence of n TABLE-INSERT and TABLE-DELETE operations, we let c_i denote the actual cost of the ith operation, $\hat{c}_i$ denote its amortized cost with respect to Φ, num_i denote the number of items stored in the table after the ith operation, $size_i$ denote the total size of the table after the ith operation, α_i denote the load factor of the table after the ith

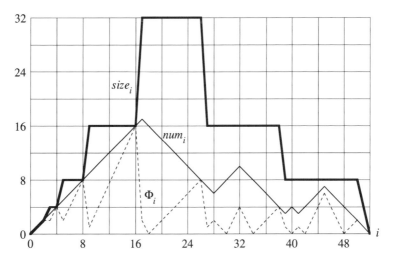

Figure 18.4   The effect of a sequence of n TABLE-INSERT and TABLE-DELETE operations on the number num_i of items in the table, the number $size_i$ of slots in the table, and the potential

$$\Phi_i = \begin{cases} 2 \cdot num_i - size_i & \text{if } \alpha_i \geq 1/2 , \\ size_i/2 - num_i & \text{if } \alpha_i < 1/2 , \end{cases}$$

each being measured after the ith operation. The thin line shows num_i, the thick line shows $size_i$, and the dashed line shows Φ_i. Notice that immediately before an expansion, the potential has built up to the number of items in the table, and therefore it can pay for moving all the items to the new table. Likewise, immediately before a contraction, the potential has built up to the number of items in the table.

operation, and Φ_i denote the potential after the ith operation. Initially, $num_0 = 0$, $size_0 = 0$, $\alpha_0 = 1$, and $\Phi_0 = 0$.

We start with the case in which the ith operation is TABLE-INSERT. If $\alpha_{i-1} \geq 1/2$, the analysis is identical to that for table expansion in Section 18.4.1. Whether the table expands or not, the amortized cost $\widehat{c}_i$ of the operation is at most 3. If $\alpha_{i-1} < 1/2$, the table cannot expand as a result of the operation, since expansion occurs only when $\alpha_{i-1} = 1$. If $\alpha_i < 1/2$ as well, then the amortized cost of the ith operation is

$$\begin{aligned} \widehat{c}_i &= c_i + \Phi_i - \Phi_{i-1} \\ &= 1 + (size_i/2 - num_i) - (size_{i-1}/2 - num_{i-1}) \\ &= 1 + (size_i/2 - num_i) - (size_i/2 - (num_i - 1)) \\ &= 0 . \end{aligned}$$

If $\alpha_{i-1} < 1/2$ but $\alpha_i \geq 1/2$, then

$$\begin{aligned} \widehat{c}_i &= c_i + \Phi_i - \Phi_{i-1} \\ &= 1 + (2 \cdot num_i - size_i) - (size_{i-1}/2 - num_{i-1}) \\ &= 1 + (2(num_{i-1} + 1) - size_{i-1}) - (size_{i-1}/2 - num_{i-1}) \end{aligned}$$

$$= \quad 3 \cdot num_{i-1} - \frac{3}{2}size_{i-1} + 3$$

$$= \quad 3\alpha_{i-1}size_{i-1} - \frac{3}{2}size_{i-1} + 3$$

$$< \quad \frac{3}{2}size_{i-1} - \frac{3}{2}size_{i-1} + 3$$

$$= \quad 3 \ .$$

Thus, the amortized cost of a TABLE-INSERT operation is at most 3.

We now turn to the case in which the ith operation is TABLE-DELETE. In this case, $num_i = num_{i-1} - 1$. If $\alpha_{i-1} < 1/2$, then we must consider whether the operation causes a contraction. If it does not, then $size_i = size_{i-1}$ and the amortized cost of the operation is

$$\begin{aligned}
\widehat{c}_i &= c_i + \Phi_i - \Phi_{i-1} \\
&= 1 + (size_i/2 - num_i) - (size_{i-1}/2 - num_{i-1}) \\
&= 1 + (size_i/2 - num_i) - (size_i/2 - (num_i + 1)) \\
&= 2 \ .
\end{aligned}$$

If $\alpha_{i-1} < 1/2$ and the ith operation does trigger a contraction, then the actual cost of the operation is $c_i = num_i + 1$, since we delete one item and move num_i items. We have $size_i/2 = size_{i-1}/4 = num_i + 1$, and the amortized cost of the operation is

$$\begin{aligned}
\widehat{c}_i &= c_i + \Phi_i - \Phi_{i-1} \\
&= (num_i + 1) + (size_i/2 - num_i) - (size_{i-1}/2 - num_{i-1}) \\
&= (num_i + 1) + ((num_i + 1) - num_i) - ((2 \cdot num_i + 2) - (num_i + 1)) \\
&= 1 \ .
\end{aligned}$$

When the ith operation is a TABLE-DELETE and $\alpha_{i-1} \geq 1/2$, the amortized cost is also bounded above by a constant. The analysis is left as Exercise 18.4-3.

In summary, since the amortized cost of each operation is bounded above by a constant, the actual time for any sequence of n operations on a dynamic table is $O(n)$.

Exercises

18.4-1
Argue intuitively that if $\alpha_{i-1} \leq 1/2$ and $\alpha_i \leq 1/2$, then the amortized cost of a TABLE-INSERT operation is 0.

18.4-2
Suppose that we wish to implement a dynamic, open-address hash table. Why might we consider the table to be full when its load factor reaches some value α that is strictly less than 1? Describe briefly how to make insertion into a dynamic, open-address hash table run in such a way that

the expected value of the amortized cost per insertion is $O(1)$. Why is the expected value of the actual cost per insertion not necessarily $O(1)$ for all insertions?

18.4-3
Show that if the ith operation on a dynamic table is TABLE-DELETE and $\alpha_{i-1} \geq 1/2$, then the amortized cost of the operation with respect to the potential function (18.5) is bounded above by a constant.

18.4-4
Suppose that instead of contracting a table by halving its size when its load factor drops below $1/4$, we contract it by multiplying its size by $2/3$ when its load factor drops below $1/3$. Using the potential function

$$\Phi(T) = |2 \cdot num[T] - size[T]| \; ,$$

show that the amortized cost of a TABLE-DELETE that uses this strategy is bounded above by a constant.

Problems

18-1 *Bit-reversed binary counter*
Chapter 32 examines an important algorithm called the Fast Fourier Transform, or FFT. The first step of the FFT algorithm performs a *bit-reversal permutation* on an input array $A[0 .. n - 1]$ whose length is $n = 2^k$ for some nonnegative integer k. This permutation swaps elements whose indices have binary representations that are the reverse of each other.

We can express each index a as a k-bit sequence $\langle a_{k-1}, a_{k-2}, \ldots, a_0 \rangle$, where $a = \sum_{i=0}^{k-1} a_i 2^i$. We define

$$\mathrm{rev}_k(\langle a_{k-1}, a_{k-2}, \ldots, a_0 \rangle) = \langle a_0, a_1, \ldots, a_{k-1} \rangle \; ;$$

thus,

$$\mathrm{rev}_k(a) = \sum_{i=0}^{k-1} a_{k-i-1} 2^i \; .$$

For example, if $n = 16$ (or, equivalently, $k = 4$), then $\mathrm{rev}_k(3) = 12$, since the 4-bit representation of 3 is 0011, which when reversed gives 1100, the 4-bit representation of 12.

a. Given a function rev_k that runs in $\Theta(k)$ time, write an algorithm to perform the bit-reversal permutation on an array of length $n = 2^k$ in $O(nk)$ time.

We can use an algorithm based on an amortized analysis to improve the running time of the bit-reversal permutation. We maintain a "bit-reversed counter" and a procedure BIT-REVERSED-INCREMENT that, when given a bit-reversed-counter value a, produces $rev_k(rev_k(a) + 1)$. If $k = 4$, for example, and the bit-reversed counter starts at 0, then successive calls to BIT-REVERSED-INCREMENT produce the sequence

$$0000, 1000, 0100, 1100, 0010, 1010, \ldots = 0, 8, 4, 12, 2, 10, \ldots .$$

b. Assume that the words in your computer store k-bit values and that in unit time, your computer can manipulate the binary values with operations such as shifting left or right by arbitrary amounts, bitwise-AND, bitwise-OR, etc. Describe an implementation of the BIT-REVERSED-INCREMENT procedure that allows the bit-reversal permutation on an n-element array to be performed in a total of $O(n)$ time.

c. Suppose that you can shift a word left or right by only one bit in unit time. Is it still possible to implement an $O(n)$-time bit-reversal permutation?

18-2   *Making binary search dynamic*

Binary search of a sorted array takes logarithmic search time, but the time to insert a new element is linear in the size of the array. We can improve the time for insertion by keeping several sorted arrays.

Specifically, suppose that we wish to support SEARCH and INSERT on a set of n elements. Let $k = \lceil \lg(n + 1) \rceil$, and let the binary representation of n be $\langle n_{k-1}, n_{k-2}, \ldots, n_0 \rangle$. We have k sorted arrays $A_0, A_1, \ldots, A_{k-1}$, where for $i = 0, 1, \ldots, k - 1$, the length of array A_i is 2^i. Each array is either full or empty, depending on whether $n_i = 1$ or $n_i = 0$, respectively. The total number of elements held in all k arrays is therefore $\sum_{i=0}^{k-1} n_i 2^i = n$. Although each individual array is sorted, there is no particular relationship between elements in different arrays.

a. Describe how to perform the SEARCH operation for this data structure. Analyze its worst-case running time.

b. Describe how to insert a new element into this data structure. Analyze its worst-case and amortized running times.

c. Discuss how to implement DELETE.

18-3   *Amortized weight-balanced trees*

Consider an ordinary binary search tree augmented by adding to each node x the field $size[x]$ giving the number of keys stored in the subtree rooted at x. Let α be a constant in the range $1/2 \le \alpha < 1$. We say that a given node x is α-***balanced*** if

$$size[left[x]] \le \alpha \cdot size[x]$$

and

$$size[right[x]] \le \alpha \cdot size[x] .$$

The tree as a whole is α-***balanced*** if every node in the tree is α-balanced. The following amortized approach to maintaining weight-balanced trees was suggested by G. Varghese.

a. A 1/2-balanced tree is, in a sense, as balanced as it can be. Given a node x in an arbitrary binary search tree, show how to rebuild the subtree rooted at x so that it becomes 1/2-balanced. Your algorithm should run in time $\Theta(size[x])$, and it can use $O(size[x])$ auxiliary storage.

b. Show that performing a search in an n-node α-balanced binary search tree takes $O(\lg n)$ worst-case time.

For the remainder of this problem, assume that the constant α is strictly greater than 1/2. Suppose that INSERT and DELETE are implemented as usual for an n-node binary search tree, except that after every such operation, if any node in the tree is no longer α-balanced, then the subtree rooted at the highest such node in the tree is "rebuilt" so that it becomes 1/2-balanced.

We shall analyze this rebuilding scheme using the potential method. For a node x in a binary search tree T, we define

$$\Delta(x) = |size[left[x]] - size[right[x]]|\ ,$$

and we define the potential of T as

$$\Phi(T) = c \sum_{x \in T : \Delta(x) \geq 2} \Delta(x)\ ,$$

where c is a sufficiently large constant that depends on α.

c. Argue that any binary search tree has nonnegative potential and that a 1/2-balanced tree has potential 0.

d. Suppose that m units of potential can pay for rebuilding an m-node subtree. How large must c be in terms of α in order for it to take $O(1)$ amortized time to rebuild a subtree that is not α-balanced?

e. Show that inserting a node into or deleting a node from an n-node α-balanced tree costs $O(\lg n)$ amortized time.

Chapter notes

The aggregate method of amortized analysis was used by Aho, Hopcroft, and Ullman [4]. Tarjan [189] surveys the accounting and potential methods of amortized analysis and presents several applications. He attributes the accounting method to several authors, including M. R. Brown, R. E. Tarjan, S. Huddleston, and K. Mehlhorn. He attributes the potential method to D. D. Sleator. The term "amortized" is due to D. D. Sleator and R. E. Tarjan.

V   Advanced Data Structures

Introduction

This part returns to the examination of data structures that support operations on dynamic sets but at a more advanced level than Part III. Two of the chapters, for example, make extensive use of the amortized analysis techniques we saw in Chapter 18.

Chapter 19 presents B-trees, which are balanced search trees designed to be stored on magnetic disks. Because magnetic disks operate much more slowly than random-access memory, we measure the performance of B-trees not only by how much computing time the dynamic-set operations consume but also by how many disk accesses are performed. For each B-tree operation, the number of disk accesses increases with the height of the B-tree, which is kept low by the B-tree operations.

Chapters 20 and 21 give implementations of mergeable heaps, which support the operations INSERT, MINIMUM, EXTRACT-MIN, and UNION. The UNION operation unites, or merges, two heaps. The data structures in these chapters also support the operations DELETE and DECREASE-KEY.

Binomial heaps, which appear in Chapter 20, support each of these operations in $O(\lg n)$ worst-case time, where n is the total number of elements in the input heap (or in the two input heaps together in the case of UNION). It is when the UNION operation must be supported that binomial heaps are superior to the binary heaps introduced in Chapter 7, because it takes $\Theta(n)$ time to unite two binary heaps in the worst case.

Fibonacci heaps, in Chapter 21, improve upon binomial heaps, at least in a theoretical sense. We use amortized time bounds to measure the performance of Fibonacci heaps. The operations INSERT, MINIMUM, and UNION take only $O(1)$ actual and amortized time on Fibonacci heaps, and the operations EXTRACT-MIN and DELETE take $O(\lg n)$ amortized time. The most significant advantage of Fibonacci heaps, however, is that DECREASE-KEY takes only $O(1)$ amortized time. The low amortized time of the DECREASE-KEY operation is why Fibonacci heaps are at the heart of some of the asymptotically fastest algorithms to date for graph problems.

Finally, Chapter 22 presents data structures for disjoint sets. We have a universe of n elements that are grouped into dynamic sets. Initially, each element belongs to its own singleton set. The operation UNION unites two sets, and the query FIND-SET identifies the set that a given element is in at the moment. By representing each set by a simple rooted tree, we obtain surprisingly fast operations: a sequence of m operations runs in $O(m \, \alpha(m, n))$ time, where $\alpha(m, n)$ is an incredibly slowly growing function—as long as n is no more than the estimated number of atoms in the entire known universe, $\alpha(m, n)$ is at most 4. The amortized analysis that proves this time bound is as complex as the data structure is simple. Chapter 22 proves an interesting but somewhat simpler bound on the running time.

The topics covered in this part are by no means the only examples of "advanced" data structures. Other advanced data structures include the following.

- A data structure invented by van Emde Boas [194] supports the operations MINIMUM, MAXIMUM, INSERT, DELETE, SEARCH, EXTRACT-MIN, EXTRACT-MAX, PREDECESSOR, and SUCCESSOR in worst-case time $O(\lg \lg n)$, subject to the restriction that the universe of keys is the set $\{1, 2, \ldots, n\}$.

- *Dynamic trees*, introduced by Sleator and Tarjan [177] and discussed by Tarjan [188], maintain a forest of disjoint rooted trees. Each edge in each tree has a real-valued cost. Dynamic trees support queries to find parents, roots, edge costs, and the minimum edge cost on a path from a node up to a root. Trees may be manipulated by cutting edges, updating all edge costs on a path from a node up to a root, linking a root into another tree, and making a node the root of the tree it appears in. One implementation of dynamic trees gives an $O(\lg n)$ amortized time bound for each operation; a more complicated implementation yields $O(\lg n)$ worst-case time bounds.

- *Splay trees*, developed by Sleator and Tarjan [178] and discussed by Tarjan [188], are a form of binary search tree on which the standard search-tree operations run in $O(\lg n)$ amortized time. One application of splay trees simplifies dynamic trees.

- *Persistent* data structures allow queries, and sometimes updates as well, on past versions of a data structure. Driscoll, Sarnak, Sleator, and Tarjan [59] present techniques for making linked data structures persistent with only a small time and space cost. Problem 14-1 gives a simple example of a persistent dynamic set.

19 B-Trees

B-trees are balanced search trees designed to work well on magnetic disks or other direct-access secondary storage devices. B-trees are similar to red-black trees (Chapter 14), but they are better at minimizing disk I/O operations.

B-trees differ significantly from red-black trees in that B-tree nodes may have many children, from a handful to thousands. That is, the "branching factor" of a B-tree can be quite large, although it is usually determined by characteristics of the disk unit used. B-trees are similar to red-black trees in that every n-node B-tree has height $O(\lg n)$, although the height of a B-tree can be considerably less than that of a red-black tree because its branching factor can be much larger. Therefore, B-trees can also be used to implement many dynamic-set operations in time $O(\lg n)$.

B-trees generalize binary search trees in a natural manner. Figure 19.1 shows a simple B-tree. If a B-tree node x contains $n[x]$ keys, then x has $n[x] + 1$ children. The keys in node x are used as dividing points separating the range of keys handled by x into $n[x] + 1$ subranges, each handled by one child of x. When searching for a key in a B-tree, we make an $(n[x]+1)$-way decision based on comparisons with the $n[x]$ keys stored at node x.

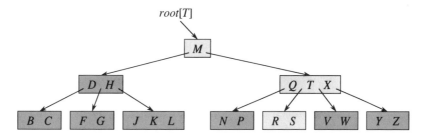

Figure 19.1   A B-tree whose keys are the consonants of English. An internal node x containing $n[x]$ keys has $n[x] + 1$ children. All leaves are at the same depth in the tree. The lightly shaded nodes are examined in a search for the letter R.

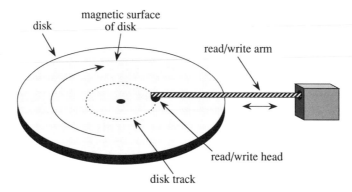

disk

magnetic surface
of disk

read/write arm

read/write head

disk track

Figure 19.2   A typical disk drive.

Section 19.1 gives a precise definition of B-trees and proves that the height of a B-tree grows only logarithmically with the number of nodes it contains. Section 19.2 describes how to search for a key and insert a key into a B-tree, and Section 19.3 discusses deletion. Before proceeding, however, we need to ask why data structures designed to work on a magnetic disk are evaluated differently than data structures designed to work in main random-access memory.

Data structures on secondary storage

There are many different technologies available for providing memory capacity in a computer system. The *primary memory* (or *main memory*) of a computer system typically consists of silicon memory chips, each of which can hold 1 million bits of data. This technology is more expensive per bit stored than magnetic storage technology, such as tapes or disks. A typical computer system has *secondary storage* based on magnetic disks; the amount of such secondary storage often exceeds the amount of primary memory by several orders of magnitude.

Figure 19.2 shows a typical disk drive. The disk surface is covered with a magnetizable material. The read/write head can read or write data magnetically on the rotating disk surface. The read/write arm can position the head at different distances from the center of the disk. When the head is stationary, the surface that passes underneath it is called a *track*. The information stored on each track is often divided into a fixed number of equal-sized *pages*; for a typical disk, a page might be 2048 bytes in length. The basic unit of information storage and retrieval is usually a page of information—that is, disk reads and writes are typically of entire pages. The *access time*—the time required to position the read/write head and to wait for a given page of information to pass underneath the head—may be large (e.g., 20 milliseconds), while the time to read or write a page, once accessed, is small. The price paid for the low cost of magnetic storage techniques is thus the relatively long time it takes to access the data. Since moving electrons is much easier than moving large (or even small) objects, storage devices that are entirely electronic, such as silicon memory chips, have a much smaller access time than storage devices that have moving parts, such as magnetic disk drives. However, once everything is positioned correctly, reading or writing a magnetic disk is entirely electronic (aside from the rotation of the disk), and large amounts of data can be read or written quickly.

Often, it takes more time to access a page of information and read it from a disk than it takes for the computer to examine all the information read. For this reason, in this chapter we shall look separately at the two principal components of the running time:

- the number of disk accesses, and
- the CPU (computing) time.

The number of disk accesses is measured in terms of the number of pages of information that need to be read from or written to the disk. We note that disk access time is not constant—it depends on the distance between the current track and the desired track and also on the initial rotational state of the disk. We shall nonetheless use the number of pages read or written as a crude first-order approximation of the total time spent accessing the disk.

In a typical B-tree application, the amount of data handled is so large that all the data do not fit into main memory at once. The B-tree algorithms copy selected pages from disk into main memory as needed and write back onto disk pages that have changed. Since the B-tree algorithms only need a constant number of pages in main memory at any time, the size of main memory does not limit the size of B-trees that can be handled.

We model disk operations in our pseudocode as follows. Let x be a pointer to an object. If the object is currently in the computer's main memory, then we can refer to the fields of the object as usual: $key[x]$, for example. If the object referred to by x resides on disk, however, then we must perform the operation DISK-READ(x) to read object x into main memory before its fields can be referred to. (We assume that if x is already in main memory, then DISK-READ(x) requires no disk accesses; it is a "no-op.") Similarly, the operation DISK-WRITE(x) is used to save any changes that have been made to the fields of object x. That is, the typical pattern for working with an object is as follows.

```
1  ...
2  x ← a pointer to some object
3  DISK-READ(x)
4  operations that access and/or modify the fields of x
5  DISK-WRITE(x)          ▷ Omitted if no fields of x were changed.
6  other operations that access but do not modify fields of x
7  ...
```

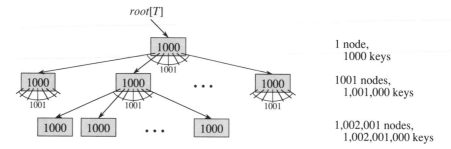

Figure 19.3 A B-tree of height 2 containing over one billion keys. Each internal node and leaf contains 1000 keys. There are 1001 nodes at depth 1 and over one million leaves at depth 2. Shown inside each node x is $n[x]$, the number of keys in x.

The system can only keep a limited number of pages in main memory at any one time. We shall assume that pages no longer in use are flushed from main memory by the system; our B-tree algorithms will ignore this issue.

Since in most systems the running time of a B-tree algorithm is determined mainly by the number of DISK-READ and DISK-WRITE operations it performs, it is sensible to use these operations intensively by having them read or write as much information as possible. Thus, a B-tree node is usually as large as a whole disk page. The number of children a B-tree node can have is therefore limited by the size of a disk page.

For a large B-tree stored on a disk, branching factors between 50 and 2000 are often used, depending on the size of a key relative to the size of a page. A large branching factor dramatically reduces both the height of the tree and the number of disk accesses required to find any key. Figure 19.3 shows a B-tree with a branching factor of 1001 and height 2 that can store over one billion keys; nevertheless, since the root node can be kept permanently in main memory, only *two* disk accesses at most are required to find any key in this tree!

19.1   Definition of B-trees

To keep things simple, we assume, as we have for binary search trees and red-black trees, that any "satellite information" associated with a key is stored in the same node as the key. In practice, one might actually store with each key just a pointer to another disk page containing the satellite information for that key. The pseudocode in this chapter implicitly assumes that the satellite information associated with a key, or the pointer to such satellite information, travels with the key whenever the key is moved from node to node. Another commonly used B-tree organization stores all the satellite information in the leaves and only stores keys and child pointers in the internal nodes, thus maximizing the branching factor of the internal nodes.

A **B-tree** T is a rooted tree (with root $root[T]$) having the following properties.

1. Every node x has the following fields:

   a. $n[x]$, the number of keys currently stored in node x,

   b. the $n[x]$ keys themselves, stored in nondecreasing order: $key_1[x] \leq key_2[x] \leq \cdots \leq key_{n[x]}[x]$, and

   c. $leaf[x]$, a boolean value that is TRUE if x is a leaf and FALSE if x is an internal node.

2. If x is an internal node, it also contains $n[x] + 1$ pointers $c_1[x], c_2[x], \ldots, c_{n[x]+1}[x]$ to its children. Leaf nodes have no children, so their c_i fields are undefined.

3. The keys $key_i[x]$ separate the ranges of keys stored in each subtree: if k_i is any key stored in the subtree with root $c_i[x]$, then

$$k_1 \leq key_1[x] \leq k_2 \leq key_2[x] \leq \cdots \leq key_{n[x]}[x] \leq k_{n[x]+1} \ .$$

4. Every leaf has the same depth, which is the tree's height h.

5. There are lower and upper bounds on the number of keys a node can contain. These bounds can be expressed in terms of a fixed integer $t \geq 2$ called the **minimum degree** of the B-tree:

   a. Every node other than the root must have at least $t - 1$ keys. Every internal node other than the root thus has at least t children. If the tree is nonempty, the root must have at least one key.

   b. Every node can contain at most $2t - 1$ keys. Therefore, an internal node can have at most $2t$ children. We say that a node is **full** if it contains exactly $2t - 1$ keys.

The simplest B-tree occurs when $t = 2$. Every internal node then has either 2, 3, or 4 children, and we have a **2-3-4 tree**. In practice, however, much larger values of t are typically used.

The height of a B-tree

The number of disk accesses required for most operations on a B-tree is proportional to the height of the B-tree. We now analyze the worst-case height of a B-tree.

Theorem 19.1
If $n \geq 1$, then for any n-key B-tree T of height h and minimum degree $t \geq 2$,

$$h \leq \log_t \frac{n + 1}{2} \ .$$

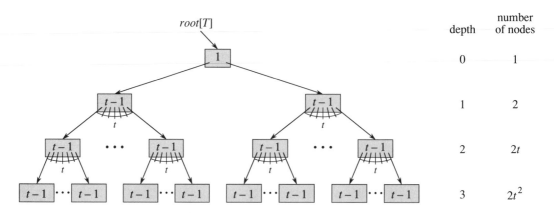

Figure 19.4 A B-tree of height 3 containing a minimum possible number of keys. Shown inside each node x is $n[x]$.

Proof If a B-tree has height h, the number of its nodes is minimized when the root contains one key and all other nodes contain $t - 1$ keys. In this case, there are 2 nodes at depth 1, $2t$ nodes at depth 2, $2t^2$ nodes at depth 3, and so on, until at depth h there are $2t^{h-1}$ nodes. Figure 19.4 illustrates such a tree for $h = 3$. Thus, the number n of keys satisfies the inequality

$$
\begin{aligned}
n &\geq 1 + (t - 1) \sum_{i=1}^{h} 2t^{i-1} \\
&= 1 + 2(t - 1) \left(\frac{t^h - 1}{t - 1} \right) \\
&= 2t^h - 1 \,,
\end{aligned}
$$

which implies the theorem.   ∎

Here we see the power of B-trees, as compared to red-black trees. Although the height of the tree grows as $O(\lg n)$ in both cases (recall that t is a constant), for B-trees the base of the logarithm can be many times larger. Thus, B-trees save a factor of about $\lg t$ over red-black trees in the number of nodes examined for most tree operations. Since examining an arbitrary node in a tree usually requires a disk access, the number of disk accesses is substantially reduced.

Exercises

19.1-1
Why don't we allow a minimum degree of $t = 1$?

19.1-2
For what values of t is the tree of Figure 19.1 a legal B-tree?

19.1-3
Show all legal B-trees of minimum degree 2 that represent $\{1, 2, 3, 4, 5\}$.

19.1-4
Derive a tight upper bound on the number of keys that can be stored in a B-tree of height h as a function of the minimum degree t.

19.1-5
Describe the data structure that would result if each black node in a red-black tree were to absorb its red children, incorporating their children with its own.

19.2 Basic operations on B-trees

In this section, we present the details of the operations B-TREE-SEARCH, B-TREE-CREATE, and B-TREE-INSERT. In these procedures, we adopt two conventions:

- The root of the B-tree is always in main memory, so that a DISK-READ on the root is never required; a DISK-WRITE of the root is required, however, whenever the root node is changed.

- Any nodes that are passed as parameters must already have had a DISK-READ operation performed on them.

The procedures we present are all "one-pass" algorithms that proceed downward from the root of the tree, without having to back up.

Searching a B-tree

Searching a B-tree is much like searching a binary search tree, except that instead of making a binary, or "two-way," branching decision at each node, we make a multiway branching decision according to the number of the node's children. More precisely, at each internal node x, we make an $(n[x] + 1)$-way branching decision.

B-TREE-SEARCH is a straightforward generalization of the TREE-SEARCH procedure defined for binary search trees. B-TREE-SEARCH takes as input a pointer to the root node x of a subtree and a key k to be searched for in that subtree. The top-level call is thus of the form B-TREE-SEARCH($root[T], k$). If k is in the B-tree, B-TREE-SEARCH returns the ordered pair (y, i) consisting of a node y and an index i such that $key_i[y] = k$. Otherwise, the value NIL is returned.

B-TREE-SEARCH(x, k)

```
1  i ← 1
2  while i ≤ n[x] and k > key_i[x]
3      do i ← i + 1
4  if i ≤ n[x] and k = key_i[x]
5     then return (x, i)
6  if leaf[x]
7     then return NIL
8     else DISK-READ(c_i[x])
9          return B-TREE-SEARCH(c_i[x], k)
```

Using a linear-search procedure, lines 1–3 find the smallest i such that $k \le key_i[x]$, or else they set i to $n[x]+1$. Lines 4–5 check to see if we have now discovered the key, returning if we have. Lines 6–9 either terminate the search unsuccessfully (if x is a leaf) or recurse to search the appropriate subtree of x, after performing the necessary DISK-READ on that child.

Figure 19.1 illustrates the operation of B-TREE-SEARCH; the lightly shaded nodes are examined during a search for the key R.

As in the TREE-SEARCH procedure for binary search trees, the nodes encountered during the recursion form a path downward from the root of the tree. The number of disk pages accessed by B-TREE-SEARCH is therefore $\Theta(h) = \Theta(\log_t n)$, where h is the height of the B-tree and n is the number of keys in the B-tree. Since $n[x] < 2t$, the time taken by the **while** loop of lines 2–3 within each node is $O(t)$, and the total CPU time is $O(th) = O(t \log_t n)$.

Creating an empty B-tree

To build a B-tree T, we first use B-TREE-CREATE to create an empty root node and then call B-TREE-INSERT to add new keys. Both of these procedures use an auxiliary procedure ALLOCATE-NODE, which allocates one disk page to be used as a new node in $O(1)$ time. We can assume that a node created by ALLOCATE-NODE requires no DISK-READ, since there is as yet no useful information stored on the disk for that node.

B-TREE-CREATE(T)

```
1  x ← ALLOCATE-NODE()
2  leaf[x] ← TRUE
3  n[x] ← 0
4  DISK-WRITE(x)
5  root[T] ← x
```

B-TREE-CREATE requires $O(1)$ disk operations and $O(1)$ CPU time.

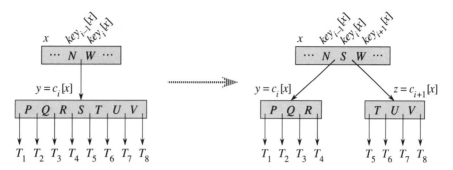

Figure 19.5 Splitting a node with $t = 4$. Node y is split into two nodes, y and z, and the median key S of y is moved up into y's parent.

Splitting a node in a B-tree

Inserting a key into a B-tree is significantly more complicated than inserting a key into a binary search tree. A fundamental operation used during insertion is the ***splitting*** of a full node y (having $2t - 1$ keys) around its ***median key*** $key_t[y]$ into two nodes having $t - 1$ keys each. The median key moves up into y's parent—which must be nonfull prior to the splitting of y—to identify the dividing point between the two new trees; if y has no parent, then the tree grows in height by one. Splitting, then, is the means by which the tree grows.

The procedure B-TREE-SPLIT-CHILD takes as input a *nonfull* internal node x (assumed to be in main memory), an index i, and a node y such that $y = c_i[x]$ is a *full* child of x. The procedure then splits this child in two and adjusts x so that it now has an additional child.

Figure 19.5 illustrates this process. The full node y is split about its median key S, which is moved up into y's parent node x. Those keys in y that are greater than the median key are placed in a new node z, which is made a new child of x.

B-Tree-Split-Child(x, i, y)

```
 1   z ← Allocate-Node()
 2   leaf[z] ← leaf[y]
 3   n[z] ← t − 1
 4   for j ← 1 to t − 1
 5       do key_j[z] ← key_{j+t}[y]
 6   if not leaf[y]
 7       then for j ← 1 to t
 8                do c_j[z] ← c_{j+t}[y]
 9   n[y] ← t − 1
10   for j ← n[x] + 1 downto i + 1
11       do c_{j+1}[x] ← c_j[x]
12   c_{i+1}[x] ← z
13   for j ← n[x] downto i
14       do key_{j+1}[x] ← key_j[x]
15   key_i[x] ← key_t[y]
16   n[x] ← n[x] + 1
17   Disk-Write(y)
18   Disk-Write(z)
19   Disk-Write(x)
```

B-Tree-Split-Child works by straightforward "cutting and pasting." Here, y is the ith child of x and is the node being split. Node y originally has $2t - 1$ children but is reduced to $t - 1$ children by this operation. Node z "adopts" the $t - 1$ largest children of y, and z becomes a new child of x, positioned just after y in x's table of children. The median key of y moves up to become the key in x that separates y and z.

Lines 1–8 create node z and give it the larger $t - 1$ keys and corresponding t children of y. Line 9 adjusts the key count for y. Finally, lines 10–16 insert z as a child of x, move the median key from y up to x in order to separate y from z, and adjust x's key count. Lines 17-19 write out all modified disk pages. The CPU time used by B-Tree-Split-Child is $\Theta(t)$, due to the loops on lines 4–5 and 7–8. (The other loops run for at most t iterations.)

Inserting a key into a B-tree

Inserting a key k into a B-tree T of height h is done in a single pass down the tree, requiring $O(h)$ disk accesses. The CPU time required is $O(th) = O(t \log_t n)$. The B-Tree-Insert procedure uses B-Tree-Split-Child to guarantee that the recursion never descends to a full node.

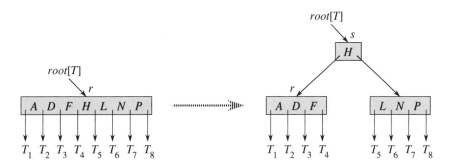

Figure 19.6 Splitting the root with $t = 4$. Root node r is split in two, and a new root node s is created. The new root contains the median key of r and has the two halves of r as children. The B-tree grows in height by one when the root is split.

B-TREE-INSERT(T, k)

```
 1  r ← root[T]
 2  if n[r] = 2t − 1
 3      then s ← ALLOCATE-NODE()
 4           root[T] ← s
 5           leaf[s] ← FALSE
 6           n[s] ← 0
 7           c₁[s] ← r
 8           B-TREE-SPLIT-CHILD(s, 1, r)
 9           B-TREE-INSERT-NONFULL(s, k)
10      else B-TREE-INSERT-NONFULL(r, k)
```

Lines 3–9 handle the case in which the root node r is full: the root is split and a new node s (having two children) becomes the root. Splitting the root is the only way to increase the height of a B-tree. Figure 19.6 illustrates this case. Unlike a binary search tree, a B-tree increases in height at the top instead of at the bottom. The procedure finishes by calling B-TREE-INSERT-NONFULL to perform the insertion of key k in the tree rooted at the nonfull root node. B-TREE-INSERT-NONFULL recurses as necessary down the tree, at all times guaranteeing that the node to which it recurses is not full by calling B-TREE-SPLIT-CHILD as necessary.

The auxiliary recursive procedure B-TREE-INSERT-NONFULL inserts key k into node x, which is assumed to be nonfull when the procedure is called. The operation of B-TREE-INSERT and the recursive operation of B-TREE-INSERT-NONFULL guarantee that this assumption is true.

B-TREE-INSERT-NONFULL(x, k)

```
 1  i ← n[x]
 2  if leaf[x]
 3     then while i ≥ 1 and k < key_i[x]
 4              do key_{i+1}[x] ← key_i[x]
 5                 i ← i − 1
 6           key_{i+1}[x] ← k
 7           n[x] ← n[x] + 1
 8           DISK-WRITE(x)
 9     else while i ≥ 1 and k < key_i[x]
10              do i ← i − 1
11           i ← i + 1
12           DISK-READ(c_i[x])
13           if n[c_i[x]] = 2t − 1
14              then B-TREE-SPLIT-CHILD(x, i, c_i[x])
15                   if k > key_i[x]
16                      then i ← i + 1
17           B-TREE-INSERT-NONFULL(c_i[x], k)
```

The B-TREE-INSERT-NONFULL procedure works as follows. Lines 3–8 handle the case in which x is a leaf node by inserting key k into x. If x is not a leaf node, then we must insert k into the appropriate leaf node in the subtree rooted at internal node x. In this case, lines 9–11 determine the child of x to which the recursion descends. Line 13 detects whether the recursion would descend to a full child, in which case line 14 uses B-TREE-SPLIT-CHILD to split that child into two nonfull children, and lines 15–16 determine which of the two children is now the correct one to descend to. (Note that there is no need for a DISK-READ$(c_i[x])$ after line 16 increments i, since the recursion will descend in this case to a child that was just created by B-TREE-SPLIT-CHILD.) The net effect of lines 13–16 is thus to guarantee that the procedure never recurses to a full node. Line 17 then recurses to insert k into the appropriate subtree. Figure 19.7 illustrates the various cases of inserting into a B-tree.

The number of disk accesses performed by B-TREE-INSERT is $O(h)$ for a B-tree of height h, since only $O(1)$ DISK-READ and DISK-WRITE operations are performed between calls to B-TREE-INSERT-NONFULL. The total CPU time used is $O(th) = O(t \log_t n)$. Since B-TREE-INSERT-NONFULL is tail-recursive, it can be alternatively implemented as a **while** loop, demonstrating that the number of pages that need to be in main memory at any time is $O(1)$.

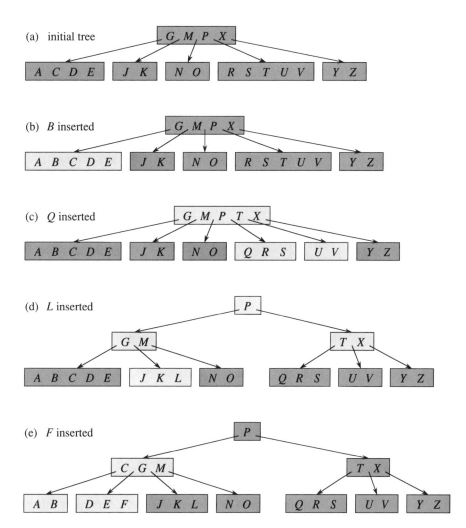

Figure 19.7 Inserting keys into a B-tree. The minimum degree t for this B-tree is 3, so a node can hold at most 5 keys. Nodes that are modified by the insertion process are lightly shaded. (**a**) The initial tree for this example. (**b**) The result of inserting B into the initial tree; this is a simple insertion into a leaf node. (**c**) The result of inserting Q into the previous tree. The node $RSTUV$ is split into two nodes containing RS and UV, the key T is moved up to the root, and Q is inserted in the leftmost of the two halves (the RS node). (**d**) The result of inserting L into the previous tree. The root is split right away, since it is full, and the B-tree grows in height by one. Then L is inserted into the leaf containing JK. (**e**) The result of inserting F into the previous tree. The node $ABCDE$ is split before F is inserted into the rightmost of the two halves (the DE node).

Exercises

19.2-1
Show the results of inserting the keys

$$F, S, Q, K, C, L, H, T, V, W, M, R, N, P, A, B, X, Y, D, Z, E$$

in order into an empty B-tree. Only draw the configurations of the tree just before some node must split, and also draw the final configuration.

19.2-2
Explain under what circumstances, if any, redundant DISK-READ or DISK-WRITE operations are performed during the course of executing a call to B-TREE-INSERT. (A redundant DISK-READ is a DISK-READ for a page that is already in memory. A redundant DISK-WRITE writes to disk a page of information that is identical to what is already stored there.)

19.2-3
Explain how to find the minimum key stored in a B-tree and how to find the predecessor of a given key stored in a B-tree.

19.2-4 $\star$
Suppose that the keys $\{1, 2, \ldots, n\}$ are inserted into an empty B-tree with minimum degree 2. How many nodes does the final B-tree have?

19.2-5
Since leaf nodes require no pointers to children, they could conceivably use a different (larger) t value than internal nodes for the same disk page size. Show how to modify the procedures for creating and inserting into a B-tree to handle this variation.

19.2-6
Suppose that B-TREE-SEARCH is implemented to use binary search rather than linear search within each node. Show that this makes the CPU time required $O(\lg n)$, independently of how t might be chosen as a function of n.

19.2-7
Suppose that disk hardware allows us to choose the size of a disk page arbitrarily, but that the time it takes to read the disk page is $a + bt$, where a and b are specified constants and t is the minimum degree for a B-tree using pages of the selected size. Describe how to choose t so as to minimize (approximately) the B-tree search time. Suggest an optimal value of t for the case in which $a = 30$ milliseconds and $b = 40$ microseconds.

19.3 Deleting a key from a B-tree

Deletion from a B-tree is analogous to insertion but a little more complicated. We sketch how it works instead of presenting the complete pseudocode.

Assume that procedure B-TREE-DELETE is asked to delete the key k from the subtree rooted at x. This procedure is structured to guarantee that whenever B-TREE-DELETE is called recursively on a node x, the number of keys in x is at least the minimum degree t. Note that this condition requires one more key than the minimum required by the usual B-tree conditions, so that sometimes a key may have to be moved into a child node before recursion descends to that child. This strengthened condition allows us to delete a key from the tree in one downward pass without having to "back up" (with one exception, which we'll explain). The following specification for deletion from a B-tree should be interpreted with the understanding that if it ever happens that the root node x becomes an internal node having no keys, then x is deleted and x's only child $c_1[x]$ becomes the new root of the tree, decreasing the height of the tree by one and preserving the property that the root of the tree contains at least one key (unless the tree is empty).

Figure 19.8 illustrates the various cases of deleting keys from a B-tree.

1. If the key k is in node x and x is a leaf, delete the key k from x.

2. If the key k is in node x and x is an internal node, do the following.

   a. If the child y that precedes k in node x has at least t keys, then find the predecessor k' of k in the subtree rooted at y. Recursively delete k', and replace k by k' in x. (Finding k' and deleting it can be performed in a single downward pass.)

   b. Symmetrically, if the child z that follows k in node x has at least t keys, then find the successor k' of k in the subtree rooted at z. Recursively delete k', and replace k by k' in x. (Finding k' and deleting it can be performed in a single downward pass.)

   c. Otherwise, if both y and z have only $t - 1$ keys, merge k and all of z into y, so that x loses both k and the pointer to z, and y now contains $2t - 1$ keys. Then, free z and recursively delete k from y.

3. If the key k is not present in internal node x, determine the root $c_i[x]$ of the appropriate subtree that must contain k, if k is in the tree at all. If $c_i[x]$ has only $t - 1$ keys, execute step 3a or 3b as necessary to guarantee that we descend to a node containing at least t keys. Then, finish by recursing on the appropriate child of x.

   a. If $c_i[x]$ has only $t - 1$ keys but has a sibling with t keys, give $c_i[x]$ an extra key by moving a key from x down into $c_i[x]$, moving a key from $c_i[x]$'s immediate left or right sibling up into x, and moving the appropriate child from the sibling into $c_i[x]$.

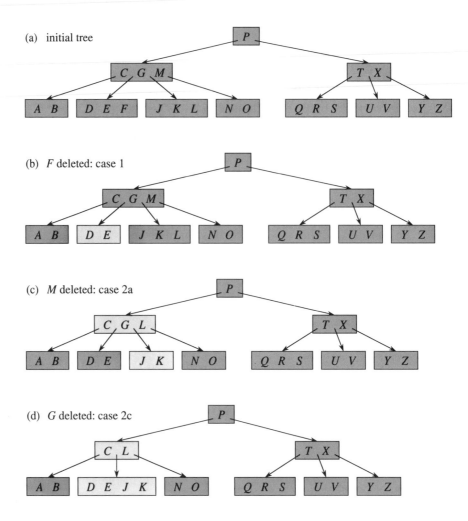

Figure 19.8 Deleting keys from a B-tree. The minimum degree for this B-tree is $t = 3$, so a node (other than the root) cannot have less than 2 keys. Nodes that are modified are lightly shaded. **(a)** The B-tree of Figure 19.7(e). **(b)** Deletion of F. This is case 1: simple deletion from a leaf. **(c)** Deletion of M. This is case 2a: the predecessor L of M is moved up to take M's position. **(d)** Deletion of G. This is case 2c: G is pushed down to make node $DEGJK$, and then G is deleted from this leaf (case 1). **(e)** Deletion of D. This is case 3b: the recursion can't descend to node CL because it has only 2 keys, so P is pushed down and merged with CL and TX to form $CLPTX$; then, D is deleted from a leaf (case 1). **(e′)** After (d), the root is deleted and the tree shrinks in height by one. **(f)** Deletion of B. This is case 3a: C is moved to fill B's position and E is moved to fill C's position.

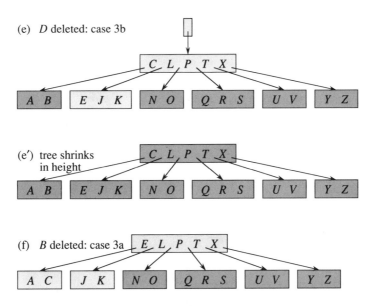

(e) *D* deleted: case 3b

(e′) tree shrinks in height

(f) *B* deleted: case 3a

b. If $c_i[x]$ and all of $c_i[x]$'s siblings have $t-1$ keys, merge c_i with one sibling, which involves moving a key from x down into the new merged node to become the median key for that node.

Since most of the keys in a B-tree are in the leaves, we may expect that in practice, deletion operations are most often used to delete keys from leaves. The B-TREE-DELETE procedure then acts in one downward pass through the tree, without having to back up. When deleting a key in an internal node, however, the procedure makes a downward pass through the tree but may have to return to the node from which the key was deleted to replace the key with its predecessor or successor (cases 2a and 2b).

Although this procedure seems complicated, it involves only $O(h)$ disk operations for a B-tree of height h, since only $O(1)$ calls to DISK-READ and DISK-WRITE are made between recursive invocations of the procedure. The CPU time required is $O(th) = O(t \log_t n)$.

Exercises

19.3-1
Show the results of deleting C, P, and V, in order, from the tree of Figure 19.8(f).

19.3-2
Write pseudocode for B-TREE-DELETE.

Problems

19-1   Stacks on secondary storage

Consider implementing a stack in a computer that has a relatively small amount of fast primary memory and a relatively large amount of slower disk storage. The operations PUSH and POP are supported on single-word values. The stack we wish to support can grow to be much larger than can fit in memory, and thus most of it must be stored on disk.

A simple, but inefficient, stack implementation keeps the entire stack on disk. We maintain in memory a stack pointer, which is the disk address of the top element on the stack. If the pointer has value p, the top element is the $(p \bmod m)$th word on page $\lfloor p/m \rfloor$ of the disk, where m is the number of words per page.

To implement the PUSH operation, we increment the stack pointer, read the appropriate page into memory from disk, copy the element to be pushed to the appropriate word on the page, and write the page back to disk. A POP operation is similar. We decrement the stack pointer, read in the appropriate page from disk, and return the top of the stack. We need not write back the page, since it was not modified.

Because disk operations are relatively expensive, we use the total number of disk accesses as a figure of merit for any implementation. We also count CPU time, but we charge $\Theta(m)$ for any disk access to a page of m words.

a. Asymptotically, what is the worst-case number of disk accesses for n stack operations using this simple implementation? What is the CPU time for n stack operations? (Express your answer in terms of m and n for this and subsequent parts.)

Now, consider a stack implementation in which we keep one page of the stack in memory. (We also maintain a small amount of memory to keep track of which page is currently in memory.) We can perform a stack operation only if the relevant disk page resides in memory. If necessary, the page currently in memory can be written to the disk and the new page read in from the disk to memory. If the relevant disk page is already in memory, then no disk accesses are required.

b. What is the worst-case number of disk accesses required for n PUSH operations? What is the CPU time?

c. What is the worst-case number of disk accesses required for n stack operations? What is the CPU time?

Suppose that we now implement the stack by keeping two pages in memory (in addition to a small number of words for bookkeeping).

d. Describe how to manage the stack pages so that the amortized number of disk accesses for any stack operation is $O(1/m)$ and the amortized CPU time for any stack operation is $O(1)$.

19-2 *Joining and splitting 2-3-4 trees*

The *join* operation takes two dynamic sets S' and S'' and an element x such that for any $x' \in S'$ and $x'' \in S''$, we have $key[x'] < key[x] < key[x'']$. It returns a set $S = S' \cup \{x\} \cup S''$. The *split* operation is like an "inverse" join: given a dynamic set S and an element $x \in S$, it creates a set S' consisting of all elements in $S - \{x\}$ whose keys are less than $key[x]$ and a set S'' consisting of all elements in $S - \{x\}$ whose keys are greater than $key[x]$. In this problem, we investigate how to implement these operations on 2-3-4 trees. We assume for convenience that elements consist only of keys and that all key values are distinct.

a. Show how to maintain, for every node x of a 2-3-4 tree, the height of the subtree rooted at x as a field $height[x]$. Make sure that your implementation does not affect the asymptotic running times of searching, insertion, and deletion.

b. Show how to implement the join operation. Given two 2-3-4 trees T' and T'' and a key k, the join should run in $O(|h' - h''|)$ time, where h' and h'' are the heights of T' and T'', respectively.

c. Consider the path p from the root of a 2-3-4 tree T to a given key k, the set S' of keys in T that are less than k, and the set S'' of keys in T that are greater than k. Show that p breaks S' into a set of trees $\{T_0', T_1', \ldots, T_m'\}$ and a set of keys $\{k_1', k_2', \ldots, k_m'\}$, where, for $i = 1, 2, \ldots, m$, we have $y < k_i' < z$ for any keys $y \in T_{i-1}'$ and $z \in T_i'$. What is the relationship between the heights of T_{i-1}' and T_i'? Describe how p breaks S'' into sets of trees and keys.

d. Show how to implement the split operation on T. Use the join operation to assemble the keys in S' into a single 2-3-4 tree T' and the keys in S'' into a single 2-3-4 tree T''. The running time of the split operation should be $O(\lg n)$, where n is the number of keys in T. (*Hint:* The costs for joining should telescope.)

Chapter notes

Knuth [123], Aho, Hopcroft, and Ullman [4], and Sedgewick [175] give further discussions of balanced-tree schemes and B-trees. Comer [48] provides a comprehensive survey of B-trees. Guibas and Sedgewick [93] discuss the relationships among various kinds of balanced-tree schemes, including red-black trees and 2-3-4 trees.

In 1970, J. E. Hopcroft invented 2-3 trees, a precursor to B-trees and 2-3-4 trees, in which every internal node has either two or three children. B-trees were introduced by Bayer and McCreight in 1972 [18]; they did not explain their choice of name.

20   Binomial Heaps

This chapter and Chapter 21 present data structures known as *mergeable heaps*, which support the following five operations.

MAKE-HEAP() creates and returns a new heap containing no elements.

INSERT(H, x) inserts node x, whose *key* field has already been filled in, into heap H.

MINIMUM(H) returns a pointer to the node in heap H whose key is minimum.

EXTRACT-MIN(H) deletes the node from heap H whose key is minimum, returning a pointer to the node.

UNION(H_1, H_2) creates and returns a new heap that contains all the nodes of heaps H_1 and H_2. Heaps H_1 and H_2 are "destroyed" by this operation.

In addition, the data structures in these chapters also support the following two operations.

DECREASE-KEY(H, x, k) assigns to node x within heap H the new key value k, which is assumed to be no greater than its current key value.

DELETE(H, x) deletes node x from heap H.

As the table in Figure 20.1 shows, if we don't need the UNION operation, ordinary binary heaps, as used in heapsort (Chapter 7), work well. Operations other than UNION run in worst-case time $O(\lg n)$ (or better) on a binary heap. If the UNION operation must be supported, however, binary heaps perform poorly. By concatenating the two arrays that hold the binary heaps to be merged and then running HEAPIFY, the UNION operation takes $\Theta(n)$ time in the worst case.

In this chapter, we shall examine "binomial heaps," whose worst-case time bounds are also shown in Figure 20.1. In particular, the UNION operation takes only $O(\lg n)$ time to merge two binomial heaps with a total of n elements.

In Chapter 21, we shall explore Fibonacci heaps, which have even better time bounds for some operations. Note, however, that the running times for Fibonacci heaps in Figure 20.1 are amortized time bounds, not worst-case per operation time bounds.

Procedure	Binary heap (worst-case)	Binomial heap (worst-case)	Fibonacci heap (amortized)
MAKE-HEAP	$\Theta(1)$	$\Theta(1)$	$\Theta(1)$
INSERT	$\Theta(\lg n)$	$O(\lg n)$	$\Theta(1)$
MINIMUM	$\Theta(1)$	$O(\lg n)$	$\Theta(1)$
EXTRACT-MIN	$\Theta(\lg n)$	$\Theta(\lg n)$	$O(\lg n)$
UNION	$\Theta(n)$	$O(\lg n)$	$\Theta(1)$
DECREASE-KEY	$\Theta(\lg n)$	$\Theta(\lg n)$	$\Theta(1)$
DELETE	$\Theta(\lg n)$	$\Theta(\lg n)$	$O(\lg n)$

Figure 20.1 Running times for operations on three implementations of mergeable heaps. The number of items in the heap(s) at the time of an operation is denoted by n.

This chapter ignores issues of allocating nodes prior to insertion and freeing nodes following deletion. We assume that the code that calls the heap procedures handles these details.

Binary heaps, binomial heaps, and Fibonacci heaps are all inefficient in their support of the operation SEARCH; it can take a while to find a node with a given key. For this reason, operations such as DECREASE-KEY and DELETE that refer to a given node require a pointer to that node as part of their input. This requirement poses no problem in many applications.

Section 20.1 defines binomial heaps after first defining their constituent binomial trees. It also introduces a particular representation of binomial heaps. Section 20.2 shows how we can implement operations on binomial heaps in the time bounds given in Figure 20.1.

20.1 Binomial trees and binomial heaps

A binomial heap is a collection of binomial trees, so this section starts by defining binomial trees and proving some key properties. We then define binomial heaps and show how they can be represented.

20.1.1 Binomial trees

The **binomial tree** B_k is an ordered tree (see Section 5.5.2) defined recursively. As shown in Figure 20.2(a), the binomial tree B_0 consists of a single node. The binomial tree B_k consists of two binomial trees B_{k-1} that are **linked** together: the root of one is the leftmost child of the root of the other. Figure 20.2(b) shows the binomial trees B_0 through B_4.

Some properties of binomial trees are given by the following lemma.

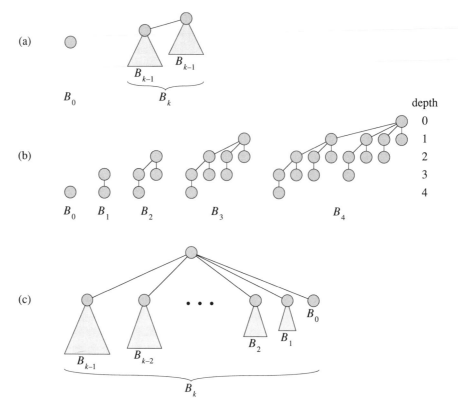

Figure 20.2   (a) The recursive definition of the binomial tree B_k. Triangles represent rooted subtrees. (b) The binomial trees B_0 through B_4. Node depths in B_4 are shown. (c) Another way of looking at the binomial tree B_k.

Lemma 20.1 (Properties of binomial trees)
For the binomial tree B_k,

1. there are 2^k nodes,

2. the height of the tree is k,

3. there are exactly $\binom{k}{i}$ nodes at depth i for $i = 0, 1, \ldots, k$, and

4. the root has degree k, which is greater than that of any other node; moreover if the children of the root are numbered from left to right by $k - 1, k - 2, \ldots, 0$, child i is the root of a subtree B_i.

Proof   The proof is by induction on k. For each property, the basis is the binomial tree B_0. Verifying that each property holds for B_0 is trivial.
   For the inductive step, we assume that the lemma holds for B_{k-1}.

1. Binomial tree B_k consists of two copies of B_{k-1}, so B_k has $2^{k-1} + 2^{k-1} = 2^k$ nodes.

2. Because of the way in which the two copies of B_{k-1} are linked to form B_k, the maximum depth of a node in B_k is one greater than the maxi-

mum depth in B_{k-1}. By the inductive hypothesis, this maximum depth is $(k-1) + 1 = k$.

3. Let $D(k, i)$ be the number of nodes at depth i of binomial tree B_k. Since B_k is composed of two copies of B_{k-1} linked together, a node at depth i in B_{k-1} appears in B_k once at depth i and once at depth $i + 1$. In other words, the number of nodes at depth i in B_k is the number of nodes at depth i in B_{k-1} plus the number of nodes at depth $i - 1$ in B_{k-1}. Thus,

$$
\begin{aligned}
D(k, i) &= D(k - 1, i) + D(k - 1, i - 1) \\
&= \binom{k-1}{i} + \binom{k-1}{i-1} \\
&= \binom{k}{i} .
\end{aligned}
$$

The second equality follows from the inductive hypothesis, and the third equality follows from Exercise 6.1-7.

4. The only node with greater degree in B_k than in B_{k-1} is the root, which has one more child than in B_{k-1}. Since the root of B_{k-1} has degree $k-1$, the root of B_k has degree k. Now by the inductive hypothesis, and as Figure 20.2(c) shows, from left to right, the children of the root of B_{k-1} are roots of $B_{k-2}, B_{k-3}, \ldots, B_0$. When B_{k-1} is linked to B_{k-1}, therefore, the children of the resulting root are roots of $B_{k-1}, B_{k-2}, \ldots, B_0$. ∎

Corollary 20.2
The maximum degree of any node in an n-node binomial tree is $\lg n$.

Proof Immediate from properties 1 and 4 of Lemma 20.1. ∎

The term "binomial tree" comes from property 3 of Lemma 20.1, since the terms $\binom{k}{i}$ are the binomial coefficients. Exercise 20.1-3 gives further justification for the term.

20.1.2 Binomial heaps

A ***binomial heap*** H is a set of binomial trees that satisfies the following ***binomial-heap properties***.

1. Each binomial tree in H is ***heap-ordered***: the key of a node is greater than or equal to the key of its parent.

2. There is at most one binomial tree in H whose root has a given degree.

The first property tells us that the root of a heap-ordered tree contains the smallest key in the tree.

The second property implies that an n-node binomial heap H consists of at most $\lfloor \lg n \rfloor + 1$ binomial trees. To see why, observe that the binary representation of n has $\lfloor \lg n \rfloor + 1$ bits, say $\langle b_{\lfloor \lg n \rfloor}, b_{\lfloor \lg n \rfloor - 1}, \ldots, b_0 \rangle$, so that $n = \sum_{i=0}^{\lfloor \lg n \rfloor} b_i 2^i$. By property 1 of Lemma 20.1, therefore, binomial tree B_i

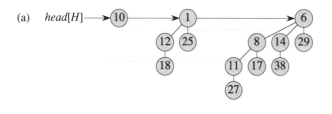

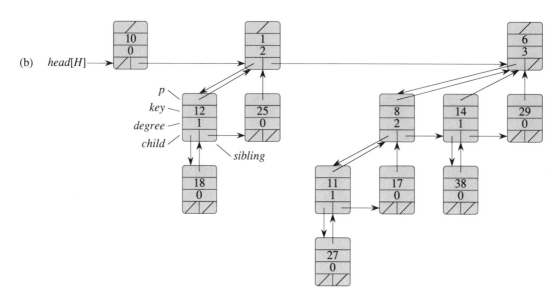

Figure 20.3   A binomial heap H with $n = 13$ nodes. **(a)** The heap consists of binomial trees B_0, B_2, and B_3, which have 1, 4, and 8 nodes respectively, totaling $n = 13$ nodes. Since each binomial tree is heap-ordered, the key of any node is no less than the key of its parent. Also shown is the root list, which is a linked list of roots in order of increasing degree. **(b)** A more detailed representation of binomial heap H. Each binomial tree is stored in the left-child, right-sibling representation, and each node stores its degree.

appears in H if and only if bit $b_i = 1$. Thus, binomial heap H contains at most $\lfloor \lg n \rfloor + 1$ binomial trees.

Figure 20.3(a) shows a binomial heap H with 13 nodes. The binary representation of 13 is $\langle 1101 \rangle$, and H consists of heap-ordered binomial trees B_3, B_2, and B_0, having 8, 4, and 1 nodes respectively, for a total of 13 nodes.

Representing binomial heaps

As shown in Figure 20.3(b), each binomial tree within a binomial heap is stored in the left-child, right-sibling representation of Section 11.4. Each node has a *key* field and any other satellite information required by the application. In addition, each node x contains pointers $p[x]$ to its parent,

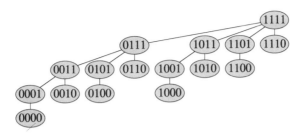

Figure 20.4   The binomial tree B_4 with nodes labeled in binary by a postorder walk.

child[x] to its leftmost child, and *sibling*[x] to the sibling of x immediately to its right. If node x is a root, then $p[x]$ = NIL. If node x has no children, then *child*[x] = NIL, and if x is the rightmost child of its parent, then *sibling*[x] = NIL. Each node x also contains the field *degree*[x], which is the number of children of x.

As Figure 20.3 also shows, the roots of the binomial trees within a binomial heap are organized in a linked list, which we refer to as the ***root list***. The degrees of the roots strictly increase as we traverse the root list. By the second binomial-heap property, in an n-node binomial heap the degrees of the roots are a subset of $\{0, 1, \ldots, \lfloor \lg n \rfloor\}$. The *sibling* field has a different meaning for roots than for nonroots. If x is a root, then *sibling*[x] points to the next root in the root list. (As usual, *sibling*[x] = NIL if x is the last root in the root list.)

A given binomial heap H is accessed by the field *head*[H], which is simply a pointer to the first root in the root list of H. If binomial heap H has no elements, then *head*[H] = NIL.

Exercises

20.1-1

Suppose that x is a node in a binomial tree within a binomial heap, and assume that *sibling*[x] $\neq$ NIL. If x is not a root, how does *degree*[*sibling*[x]] compare to *degree*[x]? How about if x is a root?

20.1-2

If x is a nonroot node in a binomial tree within a binomial heap, how does *degree*[$p[x]$] compare to *degree*[x]?

20.1-3

Suppose we label the nodes of binomial tree B_k in binary by a postorder walk, as in Figure 20.4. Consider a node x labeled l at depth i, and let $j = k - i$. Show that x has j 1's in its binary representation. How many binary k-strings are there that contain exactly j 1's? Show that the degree of x is equal to the number of 1's to the right of the rightmost 0 in the binary representation of l.

20.2   Operations on binomial heaps

In this section, we show how to perform operations on binomial heaps in the time bounds shown in Figure 20.1. We shall only show the upper bounds; the lower bounds are left as Exercise 20.2-10.

Creating a new binomial heap

To make an empty binomial heap, the MAKE-BINOMIAL-HEAP procedure simply allocates and returns an object H, where $head[H] = \text{NIL}$. The running time is $\Theta(1)$.

Finding the minimum key

The procedure BINOMIAL-HEAP-MINIMUM returns a pointer to the node with the minimum key in an n-node binomial heap H. This implementation assumes that there are no keys with value ∞. (See Exercise 20.2-5.)

BINOMIAL-HEAP-MINIMUM(H)

```
1   y ← NIL
2   x ← head[H]
3   min ← ∞
4   while x ≠ NIL
5       do if key[x] < min
6           then min ← key[x]
7                   y ← x
8           x ← sibling[x]
9   return y
```

Since a binomial heap is heap-ordered, the minimum key must reside in a root node. The BINOMIAL-HEAP-MINIMUM procedure checks all roots, which number at most $\lfloor \lg n \rfloor + 1$, saving the current minimum in *min* and a pointer to the current minimum in y. When called on the binomial heap of Figure 20.3, BINOMIAL-HEAP-MINIMUM returns a pointer to the node with key 1.

Because there are at most $\lfloor \lg n \rfloor + 1$ roots to check, the running time of BINOMIAL-HEAP-MINIMUM is $O(\lg n)$.

Uniting two binomial heaps

The operation of uniting two binomial heaps is used as a subroutine by most of the remaining operations. The BINOMIAL-HEAP-UNION procedure repeatedly links binomial trees whose roots have the same degree. The following procedure links the B_{k-1} tree rooted at node y to the B_{k-1} tree rooted at node z; that is, it makes z the parent of y. Node z thus becomes the root of a B_k tree.

BINOMIAL-LINK(y, z)

1 $p[y] \leftarrow z$
2 $sibling[y] \leftarrow child[z]$
3 $child[z] \leftarrow y$
4 $degree[z] \leftarrow degree[z] + 1$

The BINOMIAL-LINK procedure makes node y the new head of the linked list of node z's children in $O(1)$ time. It works because the left-child, right-sibling representation of each binomial tree matches the ordering property of the tree: in a B_k tree, the leftmost child of the root is the root of a B_{k-1} tree.

The following procedure unites binomial heaps H_1 and H_2, returning the resulting heap. It destroys the representations of H_1 and H_2 in the process. Besides BINOMIAL-LINK, the procedure uses an auxiliary procedure BINOMIAL-HEAP-MERGE that merges the root lists of H_1 and H_2 into a single linked list that is sorted by degree into monotonically increasing order. The BINOMIAL-HEAP-MERGE procedure, whose pseudocode we leave as Exercise 20.2-2, is similar to the MERGE procedure in Section 1.3.1.

BINOMIAL-HEAP-UNION(H_1, H_2)
```
 1   H ← MAKE-BINOMIAL-HEAP()
 2   head[H] ← BINOMIAL-HEAP-MERGE(H₁, H₂)
 3   free the objects H₁ and H₂ but not the lists they point to
 4   if head[H] = NIL
 5       then return H
 6   prev-x ← NIL
 7   x ← head[H]
 8   next-x ← sibling[x]
 9   while next-x ≠ NIL
10       do if (degree[x] ≠ degree[next-x]) or
                 (sibling[next-x] ≠ NIL
                  and degree[sibling[next-x]] = degree[x])
11           then prev-x ← x                              ▷ Cases 1 and 2
12                x ← next-x                              ▷ Cases 1 and 2
13           else if key[x] ≤ key[next-x]
14                   then sibling[x] ← sibling[next-x]    ▷ Case 3
15                        BINOMIAL-LINK(next-x, x)        ▷ Case 3
16                   else if prev-x = NIL                 ▷ Case 4
17                           then head[H] ← next-x        ▷ Case 4
18                           else sibling[prev-x] ← next-x ▷ Case 4
19                        BINOMIAL-LINK(x, next-x)        ▷ Case 4
20                        x ← next-x                      ▷ Case 4
21           next-x ← sibling[x]
22   return H
```

Figure 20.5 shows an example of BINOMIAL-HEAP-UNION in which all four cases given in the pseudocode occur.

The BINOMIAL-HEAP-UNION procedure has two phases. The first phase, performed by the call of BINOMIAL-HEAP-MERGE, merges the root lists of binomial heaps H_1 and H_2 into a single linked list H that is sorted by degree into monotonically increasing order. There might be as many as two roots (but no more) of each degree, however, so the second phase links roots of equal degree until at most one root remains of each degree. Because the linked list H is sorted by degree, we can perform all the link operations quickly.

In detail, the procedure works as follows. Lines 1–3 start by merging the root lists of binomial heaps H_1 and H_2 into a single root list H. The root lists of H_1 and H_2 are sorted by strictly increasing degree, and BINOMIAL-HEAP-MERGE returns a root list H that is sorted by monotonically increasing degree. If the root lists of H_1 and H_2 have m roots altogether, BINOMIAL-HEAP-MERGE runs in $O(m)$ time by repeatedly examining the roots at the heads of the two root lists and appending the root with the lower degree to the output root list, removing it from its input root list in the process.

The BINOMIAL-HEAP-UNION procedure next initializes some pointers into the root list of H. First, it simply returns in lines 4–5 if it happens to be uniting two empty binomial heaps. From line 6 on, therefore, we know that H has at least one root. Throughout the procedure, we maintain three pointers into the root list:

- x points to the root currently being examined,
- *prev-x* points to the root preceding x on the root list: *sibling[prev-x]* = x, and
- *next-x* points to the root following x on the root list: *sibling[x]* = *next-x*.

Initially, there are at most two roots on the root list H of a given degree: because H_1 and H_2 were binomial heaps, they each had only one root of a given degree. Moreover, BINOMIAL-HEAP-MERGE guarantees us that if two roots in H have the same degree, they are adjacent in the root list.

In fact, during the execution of BINOMIAL-HEAP-UNION, there may be three roots of a given degree appearing on the root list H at some time. We shall see in a moment how this situation could occur. At each iteration of the **while** loop of lines 9–21, therefore, we decide whether to link x and *next-x* based on their degrees and possibly the degree of *sibling[next-x]*. An invariant of the loop is that each time we start the body of the loop, both x and *next-x* are non-NIL.

Case 1, shown in Figure 20.6(a), occurs when *degree[x]* $\neq$ *degree[next-x]*, that is, when x is the root of a B_k-tree and *next-x* is the root of a B_l-tree for some $l > k$. Lines 11–12 handle this case. We don't link x and *next-x*, so we simply march the pointers one position further down the list. Updating *next-x* to point to the node following the new node x is handled in line 21, which is common to every case.

Case 2, shown in Figure 20.6(b), occurs when x is the first of three roots of equal degree, that is, when

$$degree[x] = degree[next\text{-}x] = degree[sibling[next\text{-}x]] \ .$$

We handle this case in the same manner as case 1: we just march the pointers one position further down the list. Line 10 tests for both cases 1 and 2, and lines 11–12 handle both cases.

Cases 3 and 4 occur when x is the first of two roots of equal degree, that is, when

$$degree[x] = degree[next\text{-}x] \neq degree[sibling[next\text{-}x]] \ .$$

These cases may occur on the next iteration after any case, but one of them always occurs immediately following case 2. In cases 3 and 4, we link x and *next-x*. The two cases are distinguished by whether x or *next-x* has the smaller key, which determines the node that will be the root after the two are linked.

In case 3, shown in Figure 20.6(c), *key[x]* $\leq$ *key[next-x]*, so *next-x* is linked to x. Line 14 removes *next-x* from the root list, and line 15 makes *next-x* the leftmost child of x.

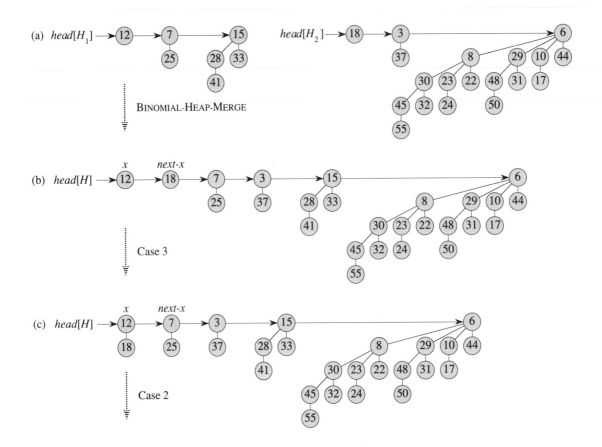

Figure 20.5 The execution of BINOMIAL-HEAP-UNION. **(a)** Binomial heaps H_1 and H_2. **(b)** Binomial heap H is the output of BINOMIAL-HEAP-MERGE(H_1, H_2). Initially, x is the first root on the root list of H. Because both x and *next-x* have degree 0 and *key[x]* < *key[next-x]*, case 3 applies. **(c)** After the link occurs, x is the first of three roots with the same degree, so case 2 applies. **(d)** After all the pointers move down one position in the root list, case 4 applies, since x is the first of two roots of equal degree. **(e)** After the link occurs, case 3 applies. **(f)** After another link, case 1 applies, because x has degree 3 and *next-x* has degree 4. This iteration of the **while** loop is the last, because after the pointers move down one position in the root list, *next-x* = NIL.

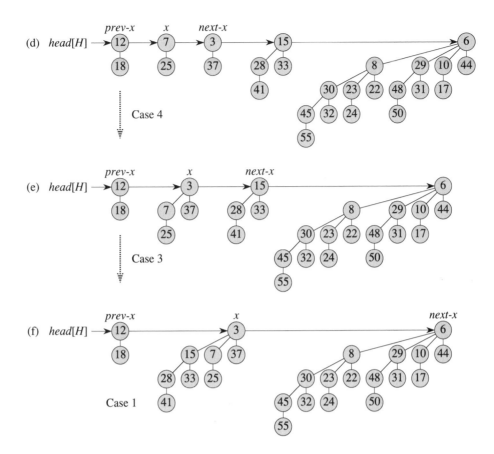

In case 4, shown in Figure 20.6(d), *next-x* has the smaller key, so x is linked to *next-x*. Lines 16–18 remove x from the root list, which has two cases depending on whether x is the first root on the list (line 17) or is not (line 18). Line 19 then makes x the leftmost child of *next-x*, and line 20 updates x for the next iteration.

Following either case 3 or case 4, the setup for the next iteration of the **while** loop is the same. We have just linked two B_k-trees to form a B_{k+1}-tree, which x now points to. There were already zero, one, or two other B_{k+1}-trees on the root list from the output of BINOMIAL-HEAP-MERGE, so x is now the first of either one, two, or three B_{k+1}-trees on the root list. If x is the only one, then we enter case 1 in the next iteration: $degree[x] \neq degree[next-x]$. If x is the first of two, then we enter either case 3 or case 4 in the next iteration. It is when x is the first of three that we enter case 2 in the next iteration.

The running time of BINOMIAL-HEAP-UNION is $O(\lg n)$, where n is the total number of nodes in binomial heaps H_1 and H_2. We can see this as follows. Let H_1 contain n_1 nodes and H_2 contain n_2 nodes, so that $n = n_1 + n_2$. Then, H_1 contains at most $\lfloor \lg n_1 \rfloor + 1$ roots and H_2 contains at most $\lfloor \lg n_2 \rfloor + 1$ roots, so H contains at most $\lfloor \lg n_1 \rfloor + \lfloor \lg n_2 \rfloor + 2 \leq 2 \lfloor \lg n \rfloor + 2 = O(\lg n)$ roots immediately after the call of BINOMIAL-HEAP-

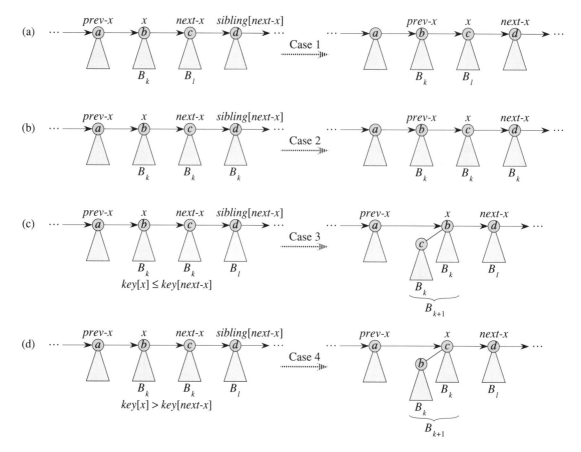

Figure 20.6 The four cases that occur in BINOMIAL-HEAP-UNION. Labels a, b, c, and d serve only to identify the roots involved; they do not indicate the degrees or keys of these roots. In each case, x is the root of a B_k-tree and $l > k$. **(a)** Case 1: $degree[x] \neq degree[next\text{-}x]$. The pointers move one position further down the root list. **(b)** Case 2: $degree[x] = degree[next\text{-}x] = degree[sibling[next\text{-}x]]$. Again, the pointers move one position further down the list, and the next iteration executes either case 3 or case 4. **(c)** Case 3: $degree[x] = degree[next\text{-}x] \neq degree[sibling[next\text{-}x]]$ and $key[x] \leq key[next\text{-}x]$. We remove $next\text{-}x$ from the root list and link it to x, creating a B_{k+1}-tree. **(d)** Case 4: $degree[x] = degree[next\text{-}x] \neq degree[sibling[next\text{-}x]]$ and $key[next\text{-}x] \leq key[x]$. We remove x from the root list and link it to $next\text{-}x$, again creating a B_{k+1}-tree.

MERGE. The time to perform BINOMIAL-HEAP-MERGE is thus $O(\lg n)$. Each iteration of the **while** loop takes $O(1)$ time, and there are at most $\lfloor \lg n_1 \rfloor + \lfloor \lg n_2 \rfloor + 2$ iterations because each iteration either advances the pointers one position down the root list of H or removes a root from the root list. The total time is thus $O(\lg n)$.

Inserting a node

The following procedure inserts node x into binomial heap H, assuming of course that node x has already been allocated and $key[x]$ has already been filled in.

BINOMIAL-HEAP-INSERT(H, x)

```
1  H′ ← MAKE-BINOMIAL-HEAP()
2  p[x] ← NIL
3  child[x] ← NIL
4  sibling[x] ← NIL
5  degree[x] ← 0
6  head[H′] ← x
7  H ← BINOMIAL-HEAP-UNION(H, H′)
```

The procedure simply makes a one-node binomial heap H' in $O(1)$ time and unites it with the n-node binomial heap H in $O(\lg n)$ time. The call to BINOMIAL-HEAP-UNION takes care of freeing the temporary binomial heap H'. (A direct implementation that does not call BINOMIAL-HEAP-UNION is given as Exercise 20.2-8.)

Extracting the node with minimum key

The following procedure extracts the node with the minimum key from binomial heap H and returns a pointer to the extracted node.

BINOMIAL-HEAP-EXTRACT-MIN(H)

```
1  find the root x with the minimum key in the root list of H,
        and remove x from the root list of H
2  H′ ← MAKE-BINOMIAL-HEAP()
3  reverse the order of the linked list of x's children,
        and set head[H′] to point to the head of the resulting list
4  H ← BINOMIAL-HEAP-UNION(H, H′)
5  return x
```

This procedure works as shown in Figure 20.7. The input binomial heap H is shown in Figure 20.7(a). Figure 20.7(b) shows the situation after line 1: the root x with the minimum key has been removed from the root list of H. If x is the root of a B_k-tree, then by property 4 of Lemma 20.1, x's children, from left to right, are roots of $B_{k-1}\text{-}, B_{k-2}\text{-}, \ldots, B_0$-trees. Fig-

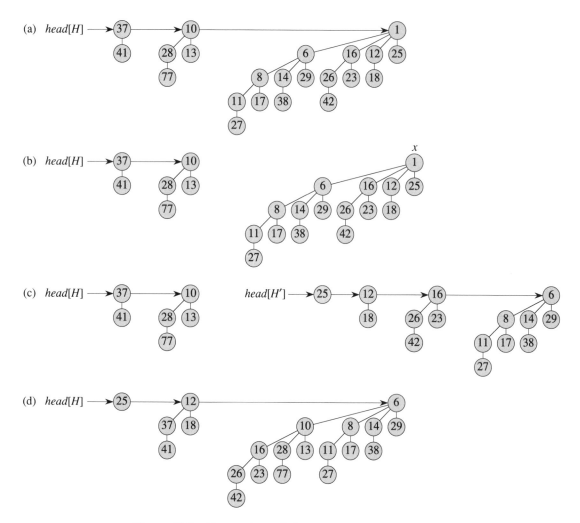

Figure 20.7 The action of BINOMIAL-HEAP-EXTRACT-MIN. (a) A binomial heap H. (b) The root x with minimum key is removed from the root list of H. (c) The linked list of x's children is reversed, giving another binomial heap H'. (d) The result of uniting H and H'.

ure 20.7(c) shows that by reversing the list of x's children in line 3, we have a binomial heap H' that contains every node in x's tree except for x itself. Because x's tree is removed from H in line 1, the binomial heap that results from uniting H and H' in line 4, shown in Figure 20.7(d), contains all the nodes originally in H except for x. Finally, line 5 returns x.

Since each of lines 1–4 takes $O(\lg n)$ time if H has n nodes, BINOMIAL-HEAP-EXTRACT-MIN runs in $O(\lg n)$ time.

Decreasing a key

The following procedure decreases the key of a node x in a binomial heap H to a new value k. It signals an error if k is greater than x's current key.

BINOMIAL-HEAP-DECREASE-KEY(H, x, k)

```
 1  if k > key[x]
 2      then error "new key is greater than current key"
 3  key[x] ← k
 4  y ← x
 5  z ← p[y]
 6  while z ≠ NIL and key[y] < key[z]
 7      do exchange key[y] ↔ key[z]
 8          ▷ If y and z have satellite fields, exchange them, too.
 9          y ← z
10          z ← p[y]
```

As shown in Figure 20.8, this procedure decreases a key in the same manner as in a binary heap: by "bubbling up" the key in the heap. After ensuring that the new key is in fact no greater than the current key and then assigning the new key to x, the procedure goes up the tree, with y initially pointing to node x. In each iteration of the **while** loop of lines 6–10, $key[y]$ is checked against the key of y's parent z. If y is the root or $key[y] \geq key[z]$, the binomial tree is now heap-ordered. Otherwise, node y violates heap ordering, so its key is exchanged with the key of its parent z, along with any other satellite information. The procedure then sets y to z, going up one level in the tree, and continues with the next iteration.

The BINOMIAL-HEAP-DECREASE-KEY procedure takes $O(\lg n)$ time. By property 2 of Lemma 20.1, the maximum depth of x is $\lfloor \lg n \rfloor$, so the **while** loop of lines 6–10 iterates at most $\lfloor \lg n \rfloor$ times.

Deleting a key

It is easy to delete a node x's key and satellite information from binomial heap H in $O(\lg n)$ time. The following implementation assumes that no node currently in the binomial heap has a key of $-\infty$.

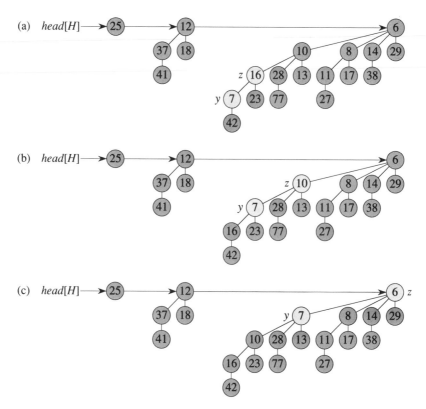

Figure 20.8 The action of Binomial-Heap-Decrease-Key. **(a)** The situation just before line 5 of the first iteration of the **while** loop. Node y has had its key decreased to 7, which is less than the key of y's parent z. **(b)** The keys of the two nodes are exchanged, and the situation just before line 5 of the second iteration is shown. Pointers y and z have moved up one level in the tree, but heap order is still violated. **(c)** After another exchange and moving pointers y and z up one more level, we finally find that heap order is satisfied, so the **while** loop terminates.

Binomial-Heap-Delete(H, x)

1 Binomial-Heap-Decrease-Key($H, x, -\infty$)
2 Binomial-Heap-Extract-Min(H)

The Binomial-Heap-Delete procedure makes node x have the unique minimum key in the entire binomial heap by giving it a key of $-\infty$. (Exercise 20.2-6 deals with the situation in which $-\infty$ cannot appear as a key, even temporarily.) It then bubbles this key and the associated satellite information up to a root by calling Binomial-Heap-Decrease-Key. This root is then removed from H by a call of Binomial-Heap-Extract-Min.

The Binomial-Heap-Delete procedure takes $O(\lg n)$ time.

Exercises

20.2-1
Give an example of two *binary* heaps with n elements each such that BUILD-HEAP takes $\Theta(n)$ time on the concatenation of their arrays.

20.2-2
Write pseudocode for BINOMIAL-HEAP-MERGE.

20.2-3
Show the binomial heap that results when a node with key 24 is inserted into the binomial heap shown in Figure 20.7(d).

20.2-4
Show the binomial heap that results when the node with key 28 is deleted from the binomial heap shown in Figure 20.8(c).

20.2-5
Explain why the BINOMIAL-HEAP-MINIMUM procedure might not work correctly if keys can have the value ∞. Rewrite the pseudocode to make it work correctly in such cases.

20.2-6
Suppose there is no way to represent the key $-\infty$. Rewrite the BINOMIAL-HEAP-DELETE procedure to work correctly in this situation. It should still take $O(\lg n)$ time.

20.2-7
Discuss the relationship between inserting into a binomial heap and incrementing a binary number and the relationship between uniting two binomial heaps and adding two binary numbers.

20.2-8
In light of Exercise 20.2-7, rewrite BINOMIAL-HEAP-INSERT to insert a node directly into a binomial heap without calling BINOMIAL-HEAP-UNION.

20.2-9
Show that if root lists are kept in strictly decreasing order by degree (instead of strictly increasing order), each of the binomial heap operations can be implemented without changing its asymptotic running time.

20.2-10
Find inputs that cause BINOMIAL-HEAP-EXTRACT-MIN, BINOMIAL-HEAP-DECREASE-KEY, and BINOMIAL-HEAP-DELETE to run in $\Omega(\lg n)$ time. Explain why the worst-case running times of BINOMIAL-HEAP-INSERT, BINOMIAL-HEAP-MINIMUM, and BINOMIAL-HEAP-UNION are $\overset{\infty}{\Omega}(\lg n)$ but not $\Omega(\lg n)$. (See Problem 2-5.)

Problems

20-1 *2-3-4 heaps*

Chapter 19 introduced the 2-3-4 tree, in which every internal node (other than possibly the root) has two, three, or four children and all leaves have the same depth. In this problem, we shall implement *2-3-4 heaps*, which support the mergeable-heap operations.

The 2-3-4 heaps differ from 2-3-4 trees in the following ways. In 2-3-4 heaps, only leaves store keys, and each leaf x stores exactly one key in the field $key[x]$. There is no particular ordering of the keys in the leaves; that is, from left to right, the keys may be in any order. Each internal node x contains a value $small[x]$ that is equal to the smallest key stored in any leaf in the subtree rooted at x. The root r contains a field $height[r]$ that is the height of the tree. Finally, 2-3-4 heaps are intended to be kept in main memory, so that disk reads and writes are not needed.

Implement the following 2-3-4 heap operations. Each of the operations in parts (a)–(e) should run in $O(\lg n)$ time on a 2-3-4 heap with n elements. The UNION operation in part (f) should run in $O(\lg n)$ time, where n is the number of elements in the two input heaps.

a. MINIMUM, which returns a pointer to the leaf with the smallest key.

b. DECREASE-KEY, which decreases the key of a given leaf x to a given value $k \le key[x]$.

c. INSERT, which inserts leaf x with key k.

d. DELETE, which deletes a given leaf x.

e. EXTRACT-MIN, which extracts the leaf with the smallest key.

f. UNION, which unites two 2-3-4 heaps, returning a single 2-3-4 heap and destroying the input heaps.

20-2 *Minimum-spanning-tree algorithm using mergeable heaps*

Chapter 24 presents two algorithms to solve the problem of finding a minimum spanning tree of an undirected graph. Here, we shall see how mergeable heaps can be used to devise a different minimum-spanning-tree algorithm.

We are given a connected, undirected graph $G = (V, E)$ with a weight function $w : E \to \mathbf{R}$. We call $w(u, v)$ the weight of edge (u, v). We wish to find a minimum spanning tree for G: an acyclic subset $T \subseteq E$ that connects all the vertices in V and whose total weight

$$w(T) = \sum_{(u,v) \in T} w(u, v)$$

is minimized.

The following pseudocode, which can be proven correct using techniques from Section 24.1, constructs a minimum spanning tree T. It maintains a partition $\{V_i\}$ of the vertices of V and, with each set V_i, a set

$$E_i \subseteq \{(u,v) : u \in V_i \text{ or } v \in V_i\}$$

of edges incident on vertices in V_i.

MST-MERGEABLE-HEAP(G)

```
 1  T ← ∅
 2  for each vertex v_i ∈ V[G]
 3      do V_i ← {v_i}
 4         E_i ← {(v_i, v) ∈ E[G]}
 5  while there is more than one set V_i
 6      do choose any set V_i
 7         extract the minimum-weight edge (u, v) from E_i
 8         assume without loss of generality that u ∈ V_i and v ∈ V_j
 9         if i ≠ j
10            then T ← T ∪ {(u, v)}
11                 V_i ← V_i ∪ V_j, destroying V_j
12                 E_i ← E_i ∪ E_j
```

Describe how to implement this algorithm using the mergeable-heap operations given in Figure 20.1. Give the running time of your implementation, assuming that the mergeable heaps are implemented by binomial heaps.

Chapter notes

Binomial heaps were introduced in 1978 by Vuillemin [196]. Brown [36, 37] studied their properties in detail.

21 Fibonacci Heaps

In Chapter 20, we saw how binomial heaps support in $O(\lg n)$ worst-case time the mergeable-heap operations INSERT, MINIMUM, EXTRACT-MIN, and UNION, plus the operations DECREASE-KEY and DELETE. In this chapter, we shall examine Fibonacci heaps, which support the same operations but have the advantage that operations that do not involve deleting an element run in $O(1)$ amortized time.

From a theoretical standpoint, Fibonacci heaps are especially desirable when the number of EXTRACT-MIN and DELETE operations is small relative to the number of other operations performed. This situation arises in many applications. For example, some algorithms for graph problems may call DECREASE-KEY once per edge. For dense graphs, which have many edges, the $O(1)$ amortized time of each call of DECREASE-KEY adds up to a big improvement over the $\Theta(\lg n)$ worst-case time of binary or binomial heaps. The asymptotically fastest algorithms to date for problems such as computing minimum spanning trees (Chapter 24) and finding single-source shortest paths (Chapter 25) make essential use of Fibonacci heaps.

From a practical point of view, however, the constant factors and programming complexity of Fibonacci heaps make them less desirable than ordinary binary (or k-ary) heaps for most applications. Thus, Fibonacci heaps are predominantly of theoretical interest. If a much simpler data structure with the same amortized time bounds as Fibonacci heaps were developed, it would be of great practical use as well.

Like a binomial heap, a Fibonacci heap is a collection of trees. Fibonacci heaps, in fact, are loosely based on binomial heaps. If neither DECREASE-KEY nor DELETE is ever invoked on a Fibonacci heap, each tree in the heap is like a binomial tree. Fibonacci heaps differ from binomial heaps, however, in that they have a more relaxed structure, allowing for improved asymptotic time bounds. Work that maintains the structure can be delayed until it is convenient to perform.

Like the dynamic tables of Section 18.4, Fibonacci heaps offer a good example of a data structure designed with amortized analysis in mind. The intuition and analyses of Fibonacci heap operations in the remainder of this chapter rely heavily on the potential method of Section 18.3.

The exposition in this chapter assumes that you have read Chapter 20 on binomial heaps. The specifications for the operations appear in that chapter, as does the table in Figure 20.1, which summarizes the time bounds for operations on binary heaps, binomial heaps, and Fibonacci heaps. Our presentation of the structure of Fibonacci heaps relies on that of binomial-heap structure. You will also find that some of the operations performed on Fibonacci heaps are similar to those performed on binomial heaps.

Like binomial heaps, Fibonacci heaps are not designed to give efficient support to the operation SEARCH; operations that refer to a given node therefore require a pointer to that node as part of their input.

Section 21.1 defines Fibonacci heaps, discusses their representation, and presents the potential function used for their amortized analysis. Section 21.2 shows how to implement the mergeable-heap operations and achieve the amortized time bounds shown in Figure 20.1. The remaining two operations, DECREASE-KEY and DELETE, are presented in Section 21.3. Finally, Section 21.4 finishes off a key part of the analysis.

21.1 Structure of Fibonacci heaps

Like a binomial heap, a *Fibonacci heap* is a collection of heap-ordered trees. The trees in a Fibonacci heap are not constrained to be binomial trees, however. Figure 21.1(a) shows an example of a Fibonacci heap.

Unlike trees within binomial heaps, which are ordered, trees within Fibonacci heaps are rooted but unordered. As Figure 21.1(b) shows, each node x contains a pointer $p[x]$ to its parent and a pointer $child[x]$ to any one of its children. The children of x are linked together in a circular, doubly linked list, which we call the *child list* of x. Each child y in a child list has pointers $left[y]$ and $right[y]$ that point to y's left and right siblings, respectively. If node y is an only child, then $left[y] = right[y] = y$. The order in which siblings appear in a child list is arbitrary.

Circular, doubly linked lists (see Section 11.2) have two advantages for use in Fibonacci heaps. First, we can remove a node from a circular, doubly linked list in $O(1)$ time. Second, given two such lists, we can concatenate them (or "splice" them together) into one circular, doubly linked list in $O(1)$ time. In the descriptions of Fibonacci heap operations, we shall refer to these operations informally, letting the reader fill in the details of their implementations.

Two other fields in each node will be of use. The number of children in the child list of node x is stored in $degree[x]$. The boolean-valued field $mark[x]$ indicates whether node x has lost a child since the last time x was made the child of another node. We won't worry about the details of marking nodes until Section 21.3. Newly created nodes are unmarked, and a node x becomes unmarked whenever it is made the child of another node.

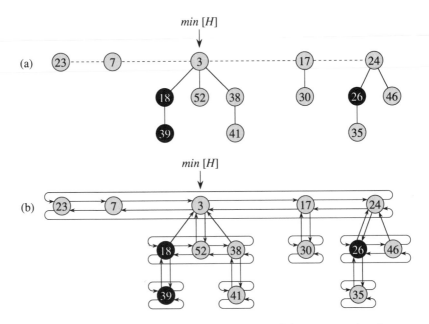

Figure 21.1   (**a**) A Fibonacci heap consisting of five heap-ordered trees and 14 nodes. The dashed line indicates the root list. The minimum node of the heap is the node containing the key 3. The three marked nodes are blackened. The potential of this particular Fibonacci heap is $5 + 2 \cdot 3 = 11$. (**b**) A more complete representation showing pointers p (up arrows), *child* (down arrows), and *left* and *right* (sideways arrows). These details are omitted in the remaining figures in this chapter, since all the information shown here can be determined from what appears in part (a).

A given Fibonacci heap H is accessed by a pointer $min[H]$ to the root of the tree containing a minimum key; this node is called the ***minimum node*** of the Fibonacci heap. If a Fibonacci heap H is empty, then $min[H] = \text{NIL}$.

The roots of all the trees in a Fibonacci heap are linked together using their *left* and *right* pointers into a circular, doubly linked list called the ***root list*** of the Fibonacci heap. The pointer $min[H]$ thus points to the node in the root list whose key is minimum. The order of the trees within a root list is arbitrary.

We rely on one other attribute for a Fibonacci heap H: the number of nodes currently in H is kept in $n[H]$.

Potential function

As mentioned, we shall use the potential method of Section 18.3 to analyze the performance of Fibonacci heap operations. For a given Fibonacci heap H, we indicate by $t(H)$ the number of trees in the root list of H and by $m(H)$ the number of marked nodes in H. The potential of Fibonacci heap H is then defined by

$$\Phi(H) = t(H) + 2\,m(H)\ . \tag{21.1}$$

For example, the potential of the Fibonacci heap shown in Figure 21.1 is $5 + 2 \cdot 3 = 11$. The potential of a set of Fibonacci heaps is the sum of the potentials of its constituent Fibonacci heaps. We shall assume that a unit of potential can pay for a constant amount of work, where the constant is sufficiently large to cover the cost of any of the specific constant-time pieces of work that we might encounter.

We assume that a Fibonacci heap application begins with no heaps. The initial potential, therefore, is 0, and by equation (21.1), the potential is nonnegative at all subsequent times. From equation (18.2), an upper bound on the total amortized cost is thus an upper bound on the total actual cost for the sequence of operations.

Maximum degree

The amortized analyses we shall perform in the remaining sections of this chapter assume that there is a known upper bound $D(n)$ on the maximum degree of any node in an n-node Fibonacci heap. Exercise 21.2-3 shows that when only the mergeable-heap operations are supported, $D(n) = \lfloor \lg n \rfloor$. In Section 21.3, we shall show that when we support DECREASE-KEY and DELETE as well, $D(n) = O(\lg n)$.

21.2 Mergeable-heap operations

In this section, we describe and analyze the mergeable-heap operations as implemented for Fibonacci heaps. If only these operations—MAKE-HEAP, INSERT, MINIMUM, EXTRACT-MIN, and UNION—are to be supported, each Fibonacci heap is simply a collection of "unordered" binomial trees. An *unordered binomial tree* is like a binomial tree, and it, too, is defined recursively. The unordered binomial tree U_0 consists of a single node, and an unordered binomial tree U_k consists of two unordered binomial trees U_{k-1} for which the root of one is made into *any* child of the root of the other. Lemma 20.1, which gives properties of binomial trees, holds for unordered binomial trees as well, but with the following variation on property 4 (see Exercise 21.2-2):

4′. For the unordered binomial tree U_k, the root has degree k, which is greater than that of any other node. The children of the root are roots of subtrees $U_0, U_1, \dots, U_{k-1}$ in some order.

Thus, if an n-node Fibonacci heap is a collection of unordered binomial trees, then $D(n) = \lg n$.

The key idea in the mergeable-heap operations on Fibonacci heaps is to delay work as long as possible. There is a performance trade-off among implementations of the various operations. If the number of trees in a

Fibonacci heap is small, then we can quickly determine the new minimum node during an EXTRACT-MIN operation. However, as we saw with binomial heaps in Exercise 20.2-10, we pay a price for ensuring that the number of trees is small: it can take up to $\Omega(\lg n)$ time to insert a node into a binomial heap or to unite two binomial heaps. As we shall see, we do not attempt to consolidate trees in a Fibonacci heap when we insert a new node or unite two heaps. We save the consolidation for the EXTRACT-MIN operation, which is when we really need to find the new minimum node.

Creating a new Fibonacci heap

To make an empty Fibonacci heap, the MAKE-FIB-HEAP procedure allocates and returns the Fibonacci heap object H, where $n[H] = 0$ and $min[H] = $ NIL; there are no trees in H. Because $t(H) = 0$ and $m(H) = 0$, the potential of the empty Fibonacci heap is $\Phi(H) = 0$. The amortized cost of MAKE-FIB-HEAP is thus equal to its $O(1)$ actual cost.

Inserting a node

The following procedure inserts node x into Fibonacci heap H, assuming of course that the node has already been allocated and that $key[x]$ has already been filled in.

FIB-HEAP-INSERT(H, x)

```
 1   degree[x] ← 0
 2   p[x] ← NIL
 3   child[x] ← NIL
 4   left[x] ← x
 5   right[x] ← x
 6   mark[x] ← FALSE
 7   concatenate the root list containing x with root list H
 8   if min[H] = NIL or key[x] < key[min[H]]
 9       then min[H] ← x
10   n[H] ← n[H] + 1
```

After lines 1–6 initialize the structural fields of node x, making it its own circular, doubly linked list, line 7 adds x to the root list of H in $O(1)$ actual time. Thus, node x becomes a single-node heap-ordered tree, and thus an unordered binomial tree, in the Fibonacci heap. It has no children and is unmarked. Lines 8–9 then update the pointer to the minimum node of Fibonacci heap H if necessary. Finally, line 10 increments $n[H]$ to reflect the addition of the new node. Figure 21.2 shows a node with key 21 inserted into the Fibonacci heap of Figure 21.1.

Unlike the BINOMIAL-HEAP-INSERT procedure, FIB-HEAP-INSERT makes no attempt to consolidate the trees within the Fibonacci heap. If k con-

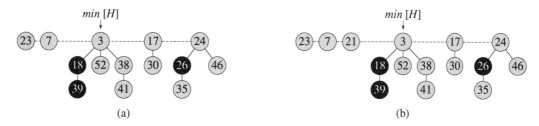

Figure 21.2 Inserting a node into a Fibonacci heap. **(a)** A Fibonacci heap H. **(b)** Fibonacci heap H after the node with key 21 has been inserted. The node becomes its own heap-ordered tree and is then added to the root list, becoming the left sibling of the root.

secutive FIB-HEAP-INSERT operations occur, then k single-node trees are added to the root list.

To determine the amortized cost of FIB-HEAP-INSERT, let H be the input Fibonacci heap and H' be the resulting Fibonacci heap. Then, $t(H') = t(H) + 1$ and $m(H') = m(H)$, and the increase in potential is

$$((t(H) + 1) + 2\,m(H)) - (t(H) + 2\,m(H)) = 1 .$$

Since the actual cost is $O(1)$, the amortized cost is $O(1) + 1 = O(1)$.

Finding the minimum node

The minimum node of a Fibonacci heap H is given by the pointer $min[H]$, so we can find the minimum node in $O(1)$ actual time. Because the potential of H does not change, the amortized cost of this operation is equal to its $O(1)$ actual cost.

Uniting two Fibonacci heaps

The following procedure unites Fibonacci heaps H_1 and H_2, destroying H_1 and H_2 in the process.

FIB-HEAP-UNION(H_1, H_2)
1 $H \leftarrow$ MAKE-FIB-HEAP()
2 $min[H] \leftarrow min[H_1]$
3 concatenate the root list of H_2 with the root list of H
4 **if** ($min[H_1] =$ NIL) or ($min[H_2] \neq$ NIL and $min[H_2] < min[H_1]$)
5   **then** $min[H] \leftarrow min[H_2]$
6 $n[H] \leftarrow n[H_1] + n[H_2]$
7 free the objects H_1 and H_2
8 **return** H

Lines 1–3 concatenate the root lists of H_1 and H_2 into a new root list H. Lines 2, 4, and 5 set the minimum node of H, and line 6 sets $n[H]$ to the

total number of nodes. The Fibonacci heap objects H_1 and H_2 are freed
in line 7, and line 8 returns the resulting Fibonacci heap H. As in the
FIB-HEAP-INSERT procedure, no consolidation of trees occurs.

The change in potential is

$$\Phi(H) - (\Phi(H_1) + \Phi(H_2))$$
$$= (t(H) + 2\,m(H)) - ((t(H_1) + 2\,m(H_1)) + (t(H_2) + 2\,m(H_2)))$$
$$= 0,$$

because $t(H) = t(H_1) + t(H_2)$ and $m(H) = m(H_1) + m(H_2)$. The amortized
cost of FIB-HEAP-UNION is therefore equal to its $O(1)$ actual cost.

Extracting the minimum node

The process of extracting the minimum node is the most complicated of the
operations presented in this section. It is also where the delayed work of
consolidating trees in the root list finally occurs. The following pseudocode
extracts the minimum node. The code assumes for convenience that when
a node is removed from a linked list, pointers remaining in the list are
updated, but pointers in the extracted node are left unchanged. It also uses
the auxiliary procedure CONSOLIDATE, which will be presented shortly.

FIB-HEAP-EXTRACT-MIN(H)

```
 1   z ← min[H]
 2   if z ≠ NIL
 3      then for each child x of z
 4              do add x to the root list of H
 5                 p[x] ← NIL
 6           remove z from the root list of H
 7           if z = right[z]
 8              then min[H] ← NIL
 9              else min[H] ← right[z]
10                   CONSOLIDATE(H)
11           n[H] ← n[H] − 1
12   return z
```

As shown in Figure 21.3, FIB-HEAP-EXTRACT-MIN works by first making
a root out of each of the minimum node's children and removing the
minimum node from the root list. It then consolidates the root list by
linking roots of equal degree until at most one root remains of each degree.

We start in line 1 by saving a pointer z to the minimum node; this
pointer is returned at the end. If $z = $ NIL, then Fibonacci heap H is already
empty and we are done. Otherwise, as in the BINOMIAL-HEAP-EXTRACT-
MIN procedure, we delete node z from H by making all of z's children
roots of H in lines 3–5 (putting them into the root list) and removing z
from the root list in line 6. If $z = right[z]$ after line 6, then z was the only
node on the root list and it had no children, so all that remains is to make

the Fibonacci heap empty in line 8 before returning z. Otherwise, we set the pointer $min[H]$ into the root list to point to a node other than z (in this case, $right[z]$). Figure 21.3(b) shows the Fibonacci heap of Figure 21.3(a) after line 9 has been performed.

The next step, in which we reduce the number of trees in the Fibonacci heap, is **consolidating** the root list of H; this is performed by the call CONSOLIDATE(H). Consolidating the root list consists of repeatedly executing the following steps until every root in the root list has a distinct *degree* value.

1. Find two roots x and y in the root list with the same degree, where $key[x] \leq key[y]$.

2. **Link** y to x: remove y from the root list, and make y a child of x. This operation is performed by the FIB-HEAP-LINK procedure. The field $degree[x]$ is incremented, and the mark on y, if any, is cleared.

The procedure CONSOLIDATE uses an auxiliary array $A[0 .. D(n[H])]$; if $A[i] = y$, then y is currently a root with $degree[y] = i$.

CONSOLIDATE(H)

```
 1  for i ← 0 to D(n[H])
 2      do A[i] ← NIL
 3  for each node w in the root list of H
 4      do x ← w
 5          d ← degree[x]
 6          while A[d] ≠ NIL
 7              do y ← A[d]
 8                  if key[x] > key[y]
 9                      then exchange x ↔ y
10                  FIB-HEAP-LINK(H, y, x)
11                  A[d] ← NIL
12                  d ← d + 1
13          A[d] ← x
14  min[H] ← NIL
15  for i ← 0 to D(n[H])
16      do if A[i] ≠ NIL
17          then add A[i] to the root list of H
18              if min[H] = NIL or key[A[i]] < key[min[H]]
19                  then min[H] ← A[i]
```

FIB-HEAP-LINK(H, y, x)

```
1  remove y from the root list of H
2  make y a child of x, incrementing degree[x]
3  mark[y] ← FALSE
```

In detail, the CONSOLIDATE procedure works as follows. In lines 1–2, we initialize A by making each entry NIL. When we are done processing

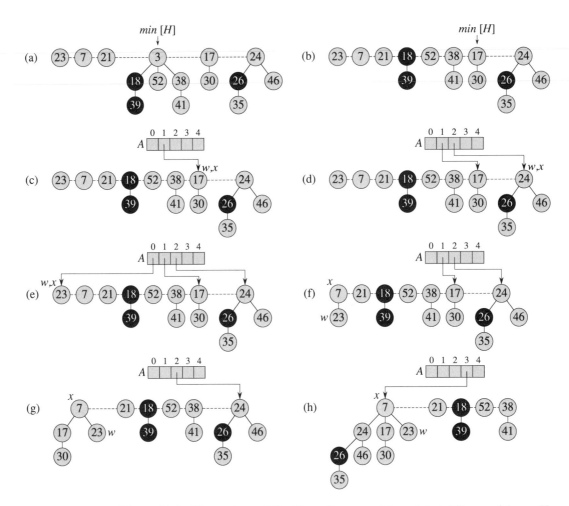

Figure 21.3 The action of FIB-HEAP-EXTRACT-MIN. (a) A Fibonacci heap H. (b) The situation after the minimum node z is removed from the root list and its children are added to the root list. (c)–(e) The array A and the trees after each of the first three iterations of the **for** loop of lines 3–13 of the procedure CONSOLIDATE. The root list is processed by starting at the minimum node and following *right* pointers. Each part shows the values of w and x at the end of an iteration. (f)–(h) The next iteration of the **for** loop, with the values of w and x shown at the end of each iteration of the **while** loop of lines 6–12. Part (f) shows the situation after the first time through the **while** loop. The node with key 23 has been linked to the node with key 7, which is now pointed to by x. In part (g), the node with key 17 has been linked to the node with key 7, which is still pointed to by x. In part (h), the node with key 24 has been linked to the node with key 7. Since no node was previously pointed to by $A[3]$, at the end of the **for** loop iteration, $A[3]$ is set to point to the root of the resulting tree. (i)–(l) The situation after each of the next four iterations of the **while** loop. (m) Fibonacci heap H after reconstruction of the root list from the array A and determination of the new $min[H]$ pointer.

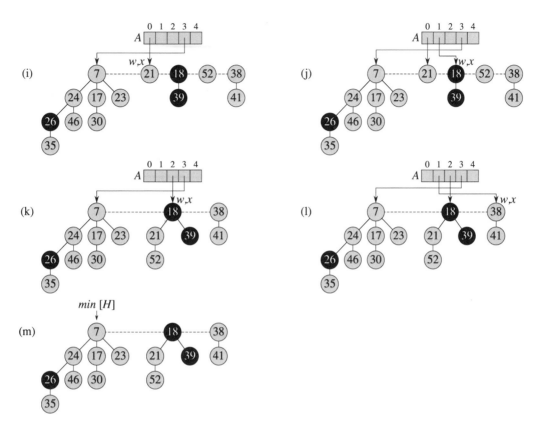

each root w, it ends up in a tree rooted at some node x, which may or may not be identical to w. Array entry $A[degree[x]]$ will then be set to point to x. In the **for** loop of lines 3–13, we examine each root w in the root list. The invariant maintained during each iteration of the **for** loop is that node x is the root of the tree containing node w. The **while** loop of lines 6–12 maintains the invariant that $d = degree[x]$ (except in line 11, as we shall see in a moment). In each iteration of the **while** loop, $A[d]$ points to some root y. Because $d = degree[x] = degree[y]$, we want to link x and y. Whichever of x and y has the smaller key becomes the parent of the other as a result of the link operation, and so lines 8–9 exchange the pointers to x and y if necessary. Next, we link y to x by the call FIB-HEAP-LINK(H, y, x) in line 10. This call increments $degree[x]$ but leaves $degree[y]$ as d. Because node y is no longer a root, the pointer to it in array A is removed in line 11. Because the value of $degree[x]$ is incremented by the call of FIB-HEAP-LINK, line 12 restores the invariant that $d = degree[x]$. We repeat the **while** loop until $A[d] = $ NIL, in which case there is no other root with the same degree as x. We set $A[d]$ to x in line 13 and perform the next iteration of the **for** loop. Figures 21.3(c)–(e) show the array A and the resulting trees after the first three iterations of the **for** loop of lines 3–13. In the next iteration of the **for** loop, three links occur; their results are shown in Figures 21.3(f)–(h). Figures 21.3(i)–(l) show the result of the next four iterations of the **for** loop.

All that remains is to clean up. Once the **for** loop of lines 3–13 completes, line 14 empties the root list, and lines 15–19 reconstruct it. The resulting Fibonacci heap is shown in Figure 21.3(m). After consolidating the root list, FIB-HEAP-EXTRACT-MIN finishes up by decrementing $n[H]$ in line 11 and returning a pointer to the deleted node z in line 12.

Observe that if all trees in the Fibonacci heap are unordered binomial trees before FIB-HEAP-EXTRACT-MIN is executed, then they are all unordered binomial trees afterward. There are two ways in which trees are changed. First, in lines 3–5 of FIB-HEAP-EXTRACT-MIN, each child x of root z becomes a root. By Exercise 21.2-2, each new tree is itself an unordered binomial tree. Second, trees are linked by FIB-HEAP-LINK only if they have the same degree. Since all trees are unordered binomial trees before the link occurs, two trees whose roots each have k children must have the structure of U_k. The resulting tree therefore has the structure of U_{k+1}.

We are now ready to show that the amortized cost of extracting the minimum node of an n-node Fibonacci heap is $O(D(n))$. Let H denote the Fibonacci heap just prior to the FIB-HEAP-EXTRACT-MIN operation.

The actual cost of extracting the minimum node can be accounted for as follows. An $O(D(n))$ contribution comes from there being at most $D(n)$ children of the minimum node that are processed in FIB-HEAP-EXTRACT-MIN and from the work in lines 1–2 and 14–19 of CONSOLIDATE. It remains to analyze the contribution from the **for** loop of lines 3–13. The size of the root list upon calling CONSOLIDATE is at most $D(n) + t(H) - 1$, since it consists of the original $t(H)$ root-list nodes, minus the extracted root node, plus the children of the extracted node, which number at most $D(n)$. Every time through the **while** loop of lines 6–12, one of the roots is linked to another, and thus the total amount of work performed in the **for** loop is at most proportional to $D(n) + t(H)$. Thus, the total actual work is $O(D(n) + t(H))$.

The potential before extracting the minimum node is $t(H) + 2m(H)$, and the potential afterward is at most $(D(n) + 1) + 2m(H)$, since at most $D(n) + 1$ roots remain and no nodes become marked during the operation. The amortized cost is thus at most

$$O(D(n) + t(H)) + ((D(n) + 1) + 2m(H)) - (t(H) + 2m(H))$$
$$= O(D(n)) + O(t(H)) - t(H)$$
$$= O(D(n)) ,$$

since we can scale up the units of potential to dominate the constant hidden in $O(t(H))$. Intuitively, the cost of performing each link is paid for by the reduction in potential due to the link reducing the number of roots by one.

Exercises

21.2-1
Show the Fibonacci heap that results from calling FIB-HEAP-EXTRACT-MIN
on the Fibonacci heap shown in Figure 21.3(m).

21.2-2
Prove that Lemma 20.1 holds for unordered binomial trees, but with property 4' in place of property 4.

21.2-3
Show that if only the mergeable-heap operations are supported, the maximum degree $D(n)$ in an n-node Fibonacci heap is at most $\lfloor \lg n \rfloor$.

21.2-4
Professor McGee has devised a new data structure based on Fibonacci
heaps. A McGee heap has the same structure as a Fibonacci heap and
supports the mergeable-heap operations. The implementations of the operations are the same as for Fibonacci heaps, except that insertion and
union perform consolidation as their last step. What are the worst-case
running time of operations on McGee heaps? How novel is the professor's
data structure?

21.2-5
Argue that when the only operations on keys are comparing two keys (as
is the case for all the implementations in this chapter), not all of the
mergeable-heap operations can run in $O(1)$ amortized time.

21.3 Decreasing a key and deleting a node

In this section, we show how to decrease the key of a node in a Fibonacci
heap in $O(1)$ amortized time and how to delete any node from an n-
node Fibonacci heap in $O(D(n))$ amortized time. These operations do not
preserve the property that all trees in the Fibonacci heap are unordered
binomial trees. They are close enough, however, that we can bound the
maximum degree $D(n)$ by $O(\lg n)$. Proving this bound will imply that
FIB-HEAP-EXTRACT-MIN and FIB-HEAP-DELETE run in $O(\lg n)$ amortized
time.

Decreasing a key

In the following pseudocode for the operation FIB-HEAP-DECREASE-KEY,
we assume as before that removing a node from a linked list does not
change any of the structural fields in the removed node.

FIB-HEAP-DECREASE-KEY(H, x, k)

1 **if** $k > key[x]$
2   **then error** "new key is greater than current key"
3 $key[x] \leftarrow k$
4 $y \leftarrow p[x]$
5 **if** $y \neq$ NIL **and** $key[x] < key[y]$
6   **then** CUT(H, x, y)
7   CASCADING-CUT(H, y)
8 **if** $key[x] < key[min[H]]$
9   **then** $min[H] \leftarrow x$

CUT(H, x, y)

1 remove x from the child list of y, decrementing $degree[y]$
2 add x to the root list of H
3 $p[x] \leftarrow$ NIL
4 $mark[x] \leftarrow$ FALSE

CASCADING-CUT(H, y)

1 $z \leftarrow p[y]$
2 **if** $z \neq$ NIL
3   **then if** $mark[y] =$ FALSE
4   **then** $mark[y] \leftarrow$ TRUE
5   **else** CUT(H, y, z)
6   CASCADING-CUT(H, z)

The FIB-HEAP-DECREASE-KEY procedure works as follows. Lines 1–3 ensure that the new key is no greater than the current key of x and then assign the new key to x. If x is a root or if $key[x] \geq key[y]$, where y is x's parent, then no structural changes need occur, since heap order has not been violated. Lines 4–5 test for this condition.

If heap order has been violated, many changes may occur. We start by *cutting* x in line 6. The CUT procedure "cuts" the link between x and its parent y, making x a root.

We use the *mark* fields to obtain the desired time bounds. They help to produce the following effect. Suppose that x is a node that has undergone the following history:

1. at some time, x was a root,

2. then x was linked to another node,

3. then two children of x were removed by cuts.

As soon as the second child has been lost, x is cut from its parent, making it a new root. The field $mark[x]$ is TRUE if steps 1 and 2 have occurred and one child of x has been cut. The CUT procedure, therefore, clears $mark[x]$ in line 4, since it performs step 1. (We can now see why line 3 of FIB-HEAP-LINK clears *mark*[*y*]: node *y* is being linked to another node, and so step 2 is being performed. The next time a child of *y* is cut, *mark*[*y*] will be set to TRUE.)

We are not yet done, because *x* might be the second child cut from its parent *y* since the time that *y* was linked to another node. Therefore, line 7 of FIB-HEAP-DECREASE-KEY performs a *cascading-cut* operation on *y*. If *y* is a root, then the test in line 2 of CASCADING-CUT causes the procedure to just return. If *y* is unmarked, the procedure marks it in line 4, since its first child has just been cut, and returns. If *y* is marked, however, it has just lost its second child; *y* is cut in line 5, and CASCADING-CUT calls itself recursively in line 6 on *y*'s parent *z*. The CASCADING-CUT procedure recurses its way up the tree until either a root or an unmarked node is found.

Once all the cascading cuts have occurred, lines 8–9 of FIB-HEAP-DE-CREASE-KEY finish up by updating *min*[*H*] if necessary.

Figure 21.4 shows the execution of two calls of FIB-HEAP-DECREASE-KEY, starting with the Fibonacci heap shown in Figure 21.4(a). The first call, shown in Figure 21.4(b), involves no cascading cuts. The second call, shown in Figures 21.4(c)–(e), invokes two cascading cuts.

We shall now show that the amortized cost of FIB-HEAP-DECREASE-KEY is only $O(1)$. We start by determining its actual cost. The FIB-HEAP-DECREASE-KEY procedure takes $O(1)$ time, plus the time to perform the cascading cuts. Suppose that CASCADING-CUT is recursively called c times from a given invocation of FIB-HEAP-DECREASE-KEY. Each call of CASCADING-CUT takes $O(1)$ time exclusive of recursive calls. Thus, the actual cost of FIB-HEAP-DECREASE-KEY, including all recursive calls, is $O(c)$.

We next compute the change in potential. Let H denote the Fibonacci heap just prior to the FIB-HEAP-DECREASE-KEY operation. Each recursive call of CASCADING-CUT, except for the last one, cuts a marked node and clears the mark bit. Afterward, there are $t(H) + c$ trees (the original $t(H)$ trees, $c - 1$ trees produced by cascading cuts, and the tree rooted at x) and at most $m(H) - c + 2$ marked nodes ($c - 1$ were unmarked by cascading cuts and the last call of CASCADING-CUT may have marked a node). The change in potential is therefore at most

$$((t(H) + c) + 2(m(H) - c + 2)) - (t(H) + 2m(H)) = 4 - c .$$

Thus, the amortized cost of FIB-HEAP-DECREASE-KEY is at most

$$O(c) + 4 - c = O(1) ,$$

since we can scale up the units of potential to dominate the constant hidden in $O(c)$.

You can now see why the potential function was defined to include a term that is twice the number of marked nodes. When a marked node *y* is cut by a cascading cut, its mark bit is cleared, so the potential is reduced by 2. One unit of potential pays for the cut and the clearing of the mark

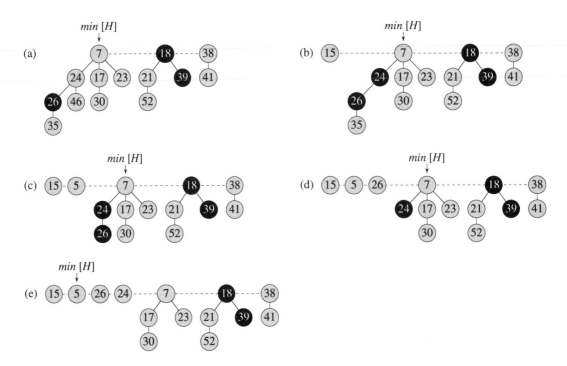

Figure 21.4 Two calls of FIB-HEAP-DECREASE-KEY. **(a)** The initial Fibonacci heap. **(b)** The node with key 46 has its key decreased to 15. The node becomes a root, and its parent (with key 24), which had previously been unmarked, becomes marked. **(c)–(e)** The node with key 35 has its key decreased to 5. In part (c), the node, now with key 5, becomes a root. Its parent, with key 26, is marked, so a cascading cut occurs. The node with key 26 is cut from its parent and made an unmarked root in (d). Another cascading cut occurs, since the node with key 24 is marked as well. This node is cut from its parent and made an unmarked root in part (e). The cascading cuts stop at this point, since the node with key 7 is a root. (Even if this node were not a root, the cascading cuts would stop, since it is unmarked.) The result of the FIB-HEAP-DECREASE-KEY operation is shown in part (e), with $min[H]$ pointing to the new minimum node.

bit, and the other unit compensates for the unit increase in potential due to node y becoming a root.

Deleting a node

It is easy to delete a node from an n-node Fibonacci heap in $O(D(n))$ amortized time, as is done by the following pseudocode. We assume that there is no key value of $-\infty$ currently in the Fibonacci heap.

FIB-HEAP-DELETE(H, x)

1   FIB-HEAP-DECREASE-KEY($H, x, -\infty$)
2   FIB-HEAP-EXTRACT-MIN(H)

FIB-HEAP-DELETE is analogous to BINOMIAL-HEAP-DELETE. It makes x become the minimum node in the Fibonacci heap by giving it a uniquely small key of $-\infty$. Node x is then removed from the Fibonacci heap by the FIB-HEAP-EXTRACT-MIN procedure. The amortized time of FIB-HEAP-DELETE is the sum of the $O(1)$ amortized time of FIB-HEAP-DECREASE-KEY and the $O(D(n))$ amortized time of FIB-HEAP-EXTRACT-MIN.

Exercises

21.3-1
Suppose that a root x in a Fibonacci heap is marked. Explain how x came to be a marked root. Argue that it doesn't matter to the analysis that x is marked, even though it is not a root that was first linked to another node and then lost one child.

21.3-2
Justify the $O(1)$ amortized time of FIB-HEAP-DECREASE-KEY using the aggregate method of Section 18.1.

21.4 Bounding the maximum degree

To prove that the amortized time of FIB-HEAP-EXTRACT-MIN and FIB-HEAP-DELETE is $O(\lg n)$, we must show that the upper bound $D(n)$ on the degree of any node of an n-node Fibonacci heap is $O(\lg n)$. By Exercise 21.2-3, when all trees in the Fibonacci heap are unordered binomial trees, $D(n) = \lfloor \lg n \rfloor$. The cuts that occur in FIB-HEAP-DECREASE-KEY, however, may cause trees within the Fibonacci heap to violate the unordered binomial tree properties. In this section, we shall show that because we cut a node from its parent as soon as it loses two children, $D(n)$ is $O(\lg n)$. In particular, we shall show that $D(n) \leq \lfloor \log_\phi n \rfloor$, where $\phi = (1 + \sqrt{5})/2$.

The key to the analysis is as follows. For each node x within a Fibonacci heap, define size(x) to be the number of nodes, including x itself, in the subtree rooted at x. (Note that x need not be in the root list—it can be any node at all.) We shall show that size(x) is exponential in *degree*[x]. Bear in mind that *degree*[x] is always maintained as an accurate count of the degree of x.

Lemma 21.1
Let x be any node in a Fibonacci heap, and suppose that *degree*[x] = k. Let $y_1, y_2, \ldots, y_k$ denote the children of x in the order in which they were linked to x, from the earliest to the latest. Then, *degree*[y_1] ≥ 0 and *degree*[y_i] $\geq i - 2$ for $i = 2, 3, \ldots, k$.

Proof   Obviously, $degree[y_1] \geq 0$.

For $i \geq 2$, we note that when y_i was linked to x, all of $y_1, y_2, \ldots, y_{i-1}$ were children of x, so we must have had $degree[x] \geq i - 1$. Node y_i is linked to x only if $degree[x] = degree[y_i]$, so we must have also had $degree[y_i] \geq i - 1$ at that time. Since then, node y_i has lost at most one child, since it would have been cut from x if it had lost two children. We conclude that $degree[y_i] \geq i - 2$.   ∎

We finally come to the part of the analysis that explains the name "Fibonacci heaps." Recall from Section 2.2 that for $k = 0, 1, 2, \ldots$, the kth Fibonacci number is defined by the recurrence

$$F_k = \begin{cases} 0 & \text{if } k = 0 \text{,} \\ 1 & \text{if } k = 1 \text{,} \\ F_{k-1} + F_{k-2} & \text{if } k \geq 2 \text{.} \end{cases}$$

The following lemma gives another way to express F_k.

Lemma 21.2
For all integers $k \geq 0$,

$$F_{k+2} = 1 + \sum_{i=0}^{k} F_i \text{ .}$$

Proof   The proof is by induction on k. When $k = 0$,

$$\begin{aligned} 1 + \sum_{i=0}^{0} F_i &= 1 + F_0 \\ &= 1 + 0 \\ &= 1 \\ &= F_2 \text{ .} \end{aligned}$$

We now assume the inductive hypothesis that $F_{k+1} = 1 + \sum_{i=0}^{k-1} F_i$, and we have

$$\begin{aligned} F_{k+2} &= F_k + F_{k+1} \\ &= F_k + \left(1 + \sum_{i=0}^{k-1} F_i \right) \\ &= 1 + \sum_{i=0}^{k} F_i \text{ .} \end{aligned}$$ ∎

The following lemma and its corollary complete the analysis. It uses the inequality (proved in Exercise 2.2-8)

$$F_{k+2} \geq \phi^k \text{ ,}$$

where ϕ is the golden ratio defined in equation (2.14) as $\phi = (1 + \sqrt{5})/2 = 1.61803\ldots$.

Lemma 21.3
Let x be any node in a Fibonacci heap, and let $k = degree[x]$. Then, $\text{size}(x) \geq F_{k+2} \geq \phi^k$, where $\phi = (1 + \sqrt{5})/2$.

Proof Let s_k denote the minimum possible value of $\text{size}(z)$ over all nodes z such that $degree[z] = k$. Trivially, $s_0 = 1$, $s_1 = 2$, and $s_2 = 3$. The number s_k is at most $\text{size}(x)$. As in Lemma 21.1, let $y_1, y_2, \ldots, y_k$ denote the children of x in the order in which they were linked to x. To compute a lower bound on $\text{size}(x)$, we count one for x itself and one for the first child y_1 (for which $\text{size}(y_1) \geq 1$) and then apply Lemma 21.1 for the other children. We thus have

$$
\begin{aligned}
\text{size}(x) &\geq s_k \\
&\geq 2 + \sum_{i=2}^{k} s_{i-2} .
\end{aligned}
$$

We now show by induction on k that $s_k \geq F_{k+2}$ for all nonnegative integer k. The bases, for $k = 0$ and $k = 1$, are trivial. For the inductive step, we assume that $k \geq 2$ and that $s_i \geq F_{i+2}$ for $i = 0, 1, \ldots, k-1$. We have

$$
\begin{aligned}
s_k &\geq 2 + \sum_{i=2}^{k} s_{i-2} \\
&\geq 2 + \sum_{i=2}^{k} F_i \\
&= 1 + \sum_{i=0}^{k} F_i \\
&= F_{k+2} .
\end{aligned}
$$

The last equality follows from Lemma 21.2.

Thus, we have shown that $\text{size}(x) \geq s_k \geq F_{k+2} \geq \phi^k$. ∎

Corollary 21.4
The maximum degree $D(n)$ of any node in an n-node Fibonacci heap is $O(\lg n)$.

Proof Let x be any node in an n-node Fibonacci heap, and let $k = degree[x]$. By Lemma 21.3, we have $n \geq \text{size}(x) \geq \phi^k$. Taking base-$\phi$ logarithms yields $k \leq \log_\phi n$. (In fact, because k is an integer, $k \leq \lfloor \log_\phi n \rfloor$.) The maximum degree $D(n)$ of any node is thus $O(\lg n)$. ∎

Exercises

21.4-1
Professor Pinocchio claims that the height of an n-node Fibonacci heap is $O(\lg n)$. Show that the professor is mistaken by exhibiting, for any positive integer n, a sequence of Fibonacci-heap operations that creates a Fibonacci heap consisting of just one tree that is a linear chain of n nodes.

21.4-2
Suppose we generalize the cascading-cut rule to cut a node x from its parent as soon as it loses its kth child, for some integer constant k. (The rule in Section 21.3 uses $k = 2$.) For what values of k is $D(n) = O(\lg n)$?

Problems

21-1   Alternative implementation of deletion
Professor Pisano has proposed the following variant of the FIB-HEAP-DELETE procedure, claiming that it runs faster when the node being deleted is not the node pointed to by $min[H]$.

PISANO-DELETE(H, x)

```
1   if x = min[H]
2      then FIB-HEAP-EXTRACT-MIN(H)
3      else y ← p[x]
4           if y ≠ NIL
5              then CUT(H, x, y)
6                   CASCADING-CUT(H, y)
7           add x's child list to the root list of H
8           remove x from the root list of H
```

a. The professor's claim that this procedure runs faster is based partly on the assumption that line 7 can be performed in $O(1)$ actual time. What is wrong with this assumption?

b. Give a good upper bound on the actual time of PISANO-DELETE when $x \neq min[H]$. Your bound should be in terms of $degree[x]$ and the number c of calls to the CASCADING-CUT procedure.

c. Let H' be the Fibonacci heap that results from an execution of PISANO-DELETE(H, x). Assuming that node x is not a root, bound the potential of H' in terms of $degree[x]$, c, $t(H)$, and $m(H)$.

d. Conclude that the amortized time for PISANO-DELETE is asymptotically no better than for FIB-HEAP-DELETE, even when $x \neq min[H]$.

21-2 *More Fibonacci-heap operations*

We wish to augment a Fibonacci heap H to support two new operations without changing the amortized running time of any other Fibonacci-heap operations.

a. Give an efficient implementation of the operation FIB-HEAP-CHANGE-KEY(H, x, k), which changes the key of node x to the value k. Analyze the amortized running time of your implementation for the cases in which k is greater than, less than, or equal to $key[x]$.

b. Give an efficient implementation of FIB-HEAP-PRUNE(H, r), which deletes $\min(r, n[H])$ nodes from H. Which nodes are deleted should be arbitrary. Analyze the amortized running time of your implementation. (*Hint:* You may need to modify the data structure and potential function.)

Chapter notes

Fibonacci heaps were introduced by Fredman and Tarjan [75]. Their paper also describes the application of Fibonacci heaps to the problems of single-source shortest paths, all-pairs shortest pairs, weighted bipartite matching, and the minimum-spanning-tree problem.

Subsequently, Driscoll, Sarnak, Sleator, and Tarjan [58] developed "relaxed heaps" as an alternative to Fibonacci heaps. There are two varieties of relaxed heaps. One gives the same amortized time bounds as Fibonacci heaps. The other allows DECREASE-KEY to run in $O(1)$ worst-case (not amortized) time and EXTRACT-MIN and DELETE to run in $O(\lg n)$ worst-case time. Relaxed heaps also have some advantages over Fibonacci heaps in parallel algorithms.

22 Data Structures for Disjoint Sets

Some applications involve grouping n distinct elements into a collection of disjoint sets. Two important operations are then finding which set a given element belongs to and uniting two sets. This chapter explores methods for maintaining a data structure that supports these operations.

Section 22.1 describes the operations supported by a disjoint-set data structure and presents a simple application. In Section 22.2, we look at a simple linked-list implementation for disjoint sets. A more efficient representation using rooted trees is given in Section 22.3. The running time using the tree representation is linear for all practical purposes but is theoretically superlinear. Section 22.4 defines and discusses Ackermann's function and its very slowly growing inverse, which appears in the running time of operations on the tree-based implementation, and then uses amortized analysis to prove a slightly weaker upper bound on the running time.

22.1 Disjoint-set operations

A *disjoint-set data structure* maintains a collection $\mathcal{S} = \{S_1, S_2, \ldots, S_k\}$ of disjoint dynamic sets. Each set is identified by a *representative*, which is some member of the set. In some applications, it doesn't matter which member is used as the representative; we only care that if we ask for the representative of a dynamic set twice without modifying the set between the requests, we get the same answer both times. In other applications, there may be a prespecified rule for choosing the representative, such as choosing the smallest member in the set (assuming, of course, that the elements can be ordered).

As in the other dynamic-set implementations we have studied, each element of a set is represented by an object. Letting x denote an object, we wish to support the following operations.

MAKE-SET(x) creates a new set whose only member (and thus representative) is pointed to by x. Since the sets are disjoint, we require that x not already be in a set.

UNION(x, y) unites the dynamic sets that contain x and y, say S_x and S_y, into a new set that is the union of these two sets. The two sets are assumed to be disjoint prior to the operation. The representative of the resulting set is some member of $S_x \cup S_y$, although many implementations of UNION choose the representative of either S_x or S_y as the new representative. Since we require the sets in the collection to be disjoint, we "destroy" sets S_x and S_y, removing them from the collection S.

FIND-SET(x) returns a pointer to the representative of the (unique) set containing x.

Throughout this chapter, we shall analyze the running times of disjoint-set data structures in terms of two parameters: n, the number of MAKE-SET operations, and m, the total number of MAKE-SET, UNION, and FIND-SET operations. Since the sets are disjoint, each UNION operation reduces the number of sets by one. After $n - 1$ UNION operations, therefore, only one set remains. The number of UNION operations is thus at most $n - 1$. Note also that since the MAKE-SET operations are included in the total number of operations m, we have $m \geq n$.

An application of disjoint-set data structures

One of the many applications of disjoint-set data structures arises in determining the connected components of an undirected graph (see Section 5.4). Figure 22.1(a), for example, shows a graph with four connected components.

The procedure CONNECTED-COMPONENTS that follows uses the disjoint-set operations to compute the connected components of a graph. Once CONNECTED-COMPONENTS has been run as a preprocessing step, the procedure SAME-COMPONENT answers queries about whether two vertices are in the same connected component.[1] (The set of vertices of a graph G is denoted by $V[G]$, and the set of edges is denoted by $E[G]$.)

CONNECTED-COMPONENTS(G)

```
1  for each vertex v ∈ V[G]
2      do MAKE-SET(v)
3  for each edge (u, v) ∈ E[G]
4      do if FIND-SET(u) ≠ FIND-SET(v)
5          then UNION(u, v)
```

---

[1]When the edges of the graph are "static"—not changing over time—the connected components can be computed faster by using depth-first search (Exercise 23.3-9). Sometimes, however, the edges are added "dynamically" and we need to maintain the connected components as each edge is added. In this case, the implementation given here can be more efficient than running a new depth-first search for each new edge.

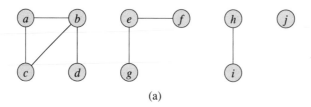

(a)

Edge processed	Collection of disjoint sets									
initial sets	$\{a\}$	$\{b\}$	$\{c\}$	$\{d\}$	$\{e\}$	$\{f\}$	$\{g\}$	$\{h\}$	$\{i\}$	$\{j\}$
(b,d)	$\{a\}$	$\{b,d\}$	$\{c\}$		$\{e\}$	$\{f\}$	$\{g\}$	$\{h\}$	$\{i\}$	$\{j\}$
(e,g)	$\{a\}$	$\{b,d\}$	$\{c\}$		$\{e,g\}$	$\{f\}$		$\{h\}$	$\{i\}$	$\{j\}$
(a,c)	$\{a,c\}$	$\{b,d\}$			$\{e,g\}$	$\{f\}$		$\{h\}$	$\{i\}$	$\{j\}$
(h,i)	$\{a,c\}$	$\{b,d\}$			$\{e,g\}$	$\{f\}$		$\{h,i\}$		$\{j\}$
(a,b)	$\{a,b,c,d\}$				$\{e,g\}$	$\{f\}$		$\{h,i\}$		$\{j\}$
(e,f)	$\{a,b,c,d\}$				$\{e,f,g\}$			$\{h,i\}$		$\{j\}$
(b,c)	$\{a,b,c,d\}$				$\{e,f,g\}$			$\{h,i\}$		$\{j\}$

(b)

Figure 22.1   **(a)** A graph with four connected components: $\{a,b,c,d\}$, $\{e,f,g\}$, $\{h,i\}$, and $\{j\}$. **(b)** The collection of disjoint sets after each edge is processed.

SAME-COMPONENT(u, v)

1 **if** FIND-SET(u) = FIND-SET(v)
2   **then return** TRUE
3   **else return** FALSE

The procedure CONNECTED-COMPONENTS initially places each vertex v in its own set. Then, for each edge (u, v), it unites the sets containing u and v. By Exercise 22.1-2, after all the edges are processed, two vertices are in the same connected component if and only if the corresponding objects are in the same set. Thus, CONNECTED-COMPONENTS computes sets in such a way that the procedure SAME-COMPONENT can determine whether two vertices are in the same connected component. Figure 22.1(b) illustrates how the disjoint sets are computed by CONNECTED-COMPONENTS.

Exercises

22.1-1
Suppose that CONNECTED-COMPONENTS is run on the undirected graph $G = (V, E)$, where $V = \{a, b, c, d, e, f, g, h, i, j, k\}$ and the edges of E are processed in the following order: $(d, i), (f, k), (g, i), (b, g), (a, h), (i, j), (d, k), (b, j), (d, f), (g, j), (a, e), (i, d)$. List the vertices in each connected component after each iteration of lines 3–5.

22.1-2
Show that after all edges are processed by CONNECTED-COMPONENTS, two vertices are in the same connected component if and only if they are in the same set.

22.1-3
During the execution of CONNECTED-COMPONENTS on an undirected graph $G = (V, E)$ with k connected components, how many times is FIND-SET called? How many times is UNION called? Express your answers in terms of $|V|$, $|E|$, and k.

22.2 Linked-list representation of disjoint sets

A simple way to implement a disjoint-set data structure is to represent each set by a linked list. The first object in each linked list serves as its set's representative. Each object in the linked list contains a set member, a pointer to the object containing the next set member, and a pointer back to the representative. Figure 22.2(a) shows two sets. Within each linked list, the objects may appear in any order (subject to our assumption that the first object in each list is the representative).

With this linked-list representation, both MAKE-SET and FIND-SET are easy, requiring $O(1)$ time. To carry out MAKE-SET(x), we create a new linked list whose only object is x. For FIND-SET(x), we just return the pointer from x back to the representative.

A simple implementation of union

The simplest implementation of the UNION operation using the linked-list set representation takes significantly more time than MAKE-SET or FIND-SET. As Figure 22.2(b) shows, we perform UNION(x, y) by appending x's list onto the end of y's list. The representative of the new set is the element that was originally the representative of the set containing y. Unfortunately, we must update the pointer to the representative for each object originally on x's list, which takes time linear in the length of x's list.

In fact, it is not difficult to come up with a sequence of m operations that requires $\Theta(m^2)$ time. We let $n = \lceil m/2 \rceil + 1$ and $q = m - n = \lfloor m/2 \rfloor - 1$ and suppose that we have objects $x_1, x_2, \ldots, x_n$. We then execute the sequence of $m = n + q$ operations shown in Figure 22.3. We spend $\Theta(n)$ time performing the n MAKE-SET operations. Because the ith UNION operation updates i objects, the total number of objects updated by all the UNION operations is

$$\sum_{i=1}^{q-1} i = \Theta(q^2) \ .$$

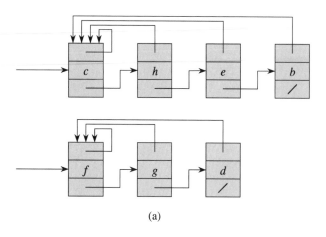

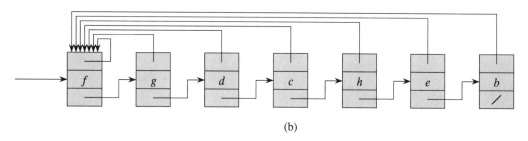

(b)

Figure 22.2   **(a)** Linked-list representations of two sets. One contains objects b, c, e, and h, with c as the representative, and the other contains objects d, f, and g, with f as the representative. Each object on the list contains a set member, a pointer to the next object on the list, and a pointer back to the first object on the list, which is the representative. **(b)** The result of UNION(e, g). The representative of the resulting set is f.

Operation	Number of objects updated
MAKE-SET(x_1)	1
MAKE-SET(x_2)	1
$\vdots$	$\vdots$
MAKE-SET(x_n)	1
UNION(x_1, x_2)	1
UNION(x_2, x_3)	2
UNION(x_3, x_4)	3
$\vdots$	$\vdots$
UNION(x_{q-1}, x_q)	$q - 1$

Figure 22.3   A sequence of m operations that takes $O(m^2)$ time using the linked-list set representation and the simple implementation of UNION. For this example, $n = \lceil m/2 \rceil + 1$ and $q = m - n$.

The total time spent is therefore $\Theta(n+q^2)$, which is $\Theta(m^2)$ since $n = \Theta(m)$ and $q = \Theta(m)$. Thus, on the average, each operation requires $\Theta(m)$ time. That is, the amortized time of an operation is $\Theta(m)$.

A weighted-union heuristic

The above implementation of the UNION procedure requires an average of $\Theta(m)$ time per call because we may be appending a longer list onto a shorter list; we must update the pointer to the representative for each member of the longer list. Suppose instead that each representative also includes the length of the list (which is easily maintained) and that we always append the smaller list onto the longer, with ties broken arbitrarily. With this simple *weighted-union heuristic*, a single UNION operation can still take $\Omega(m)$ time if both sets have $\Omega(m)$ members. As the following theorem shows, however, a sequence of m MAKE-SET, UNION, and FIND-SET operations, n of which are MAKE-SET operations, takes $O(m + n \lg n)$ time.

Theorem 22.1
Using the linked-list representation of disjoint sets and the weighted-union heuristic, a sequence of m MAKE-SET, UNION, and FIND-SET operations, n of which are MAKE-SET operations, takes $O(m + n \lg n)$ time.

Proof We start by computing, for each object in a set of size n, an upper bound on the number of times the object's pointer back to the representative has been updated. Consider a fixed object x. We know that each time x's representative pointer was updated, x must have started in the smaller set. The first time x's representative pointer was updated, therefore, the resulting set must have had at least 2 members. Similarly, the next time x's representative pointer was updated, the resulting set must have had at least 4 members. Continuing on, we observe that for any $k \leq n$, after x's representative pointer has been updated $\lceil \lg k \rceil$ times, the resulting set must have at least k members. Since the largest set has at most n members, each object's representative pointer has been updated at most $\lceil \lg n \rceil$ times over all the UNION operations. The total time used in updating the n objects is thus $O(n \lg n)$.

The time for the entire sequence of m operations follows easily. Each MAKE-SET and FIND-SET operation takes $O(1)$ time, and there are $O(m)$ of them. The total time for the entire sequence is thus $O(m + n \lg n)$. ∎

Exercises

22.2-1
Write pseudocode for MAKE-SET, FIND-SET, and UNION using the linked-list representation and the weighted-union heuristic. Assume that each object x has attributes $rep[x]$ pointing to the representative of the set containing x, $last[x]$ pointing to the last object in the linked list containing x, and $size[x]$ giving the size of the set containing x. Your pseudocode can assume that $last[x]$ and $size[x]$ are correct only if x is a representative.

22.2-2
Show the data structure that results and the answers returned by the FIND-SET operations in the following program. Use the linked-list representation with the weighted-union heuristic.

```
1   for i ← 1 to 16
2       do MAKE-SET(xi)
3   for i ← 1 to 15 by 2
4       do UNION(xi, xi+1)
5   for i ← 1 to 13 by 4
6       do UNION(xi, xi+2)
7   UNION(x1, x5)
8   UNION(x11, x13)
9   UNION(x1, x10)
10  FIND-SET(x2)
11  FIND-SET(x9)
```

22.2-3
Argue on the basis of Theorem 22.1 that we can obtain amortized time bounds of $O(1)$ for MAKE-SET and FIND-SET and $O(\lg n)$ for UNION using the linked-list representation and the weighted-union heuristic.

22.2-4
Give a tight asymptotic bound on the running time of the sequence of operations in Figure 22.3 assuming the linked-list representation and the weighted-union heuristic.

22.3   Disjoint-set forests

In a faster implementation of disjoint sets, we represent sets by rooted trees, with each node containing one member and each tree representing one set. In a ***disjoint-set forest***, illustrated in Figure 22.4(a), each member points only to its parent. The root of each tree contains the representative and is its own parent. As we shall see, although the straightforward

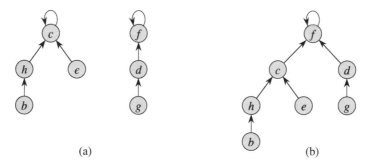

Figure 22.4 A disjoint-set forest. (**a**) Two trees representing the two sets of Figure 22.2. The tree on the left represents the set $\{b, c, e, h\}$, with c as the representative, and the tree on the right represents the set $\{d, f, g\}$, with f as the representative. (**b**) The result of UNION(e, g).

algorithms that use this representation are no faster than ones that use the linked-list representation, by introducing two heuristics—"union by rank" and "path compression"—we can achieve the asymptotically fastest disjoint-set data structure known.

We perform the three disjoint-set operations as follows. A MAKE-SET operation simply creates a tree with just one node. We perform a FIND-SET operation by chasing parent pointers until we find the root of the tree. The nodes visited on this path toward the root constitute the *find path*. A UNION operation, shown in Figure 22.4(b), causes the root of one tree to point to the root of the other.

Heuristics to improve the running time

So far, we have not improved on the linked-list implementation. A sequence of $n - 1$ UNION operations may create a tree that is just a linear chain of n nodes. By using two heuristics, however, we can achieve a running time that is almost linear in the total number of operations m.

The first heuristic, ***union by rank***, is similar to the weighted-union heuristic we used with the linked-list representation. The idea is to make the root of the tree with fewer nodes point to the root of the tree with more nodes. Rather than explicitly keeping track of the size of the subtree rooted at each node, we shall use an approach that eases the analysis. For each node, we maintain a ***rank*** that approximates the logarithm of the subtree size and is also an upper bound on the height of the node. In union by rank, the root with smaller rank is made to point to the root with larger rank during a UNION operation.

The second heuristic, ***path compression***, is also quite simple and very effective. As shown in Figure 22.5, we use it during FIND-SET operations to make each node on the find path point directly to the root. Path compression does not change any ranks.

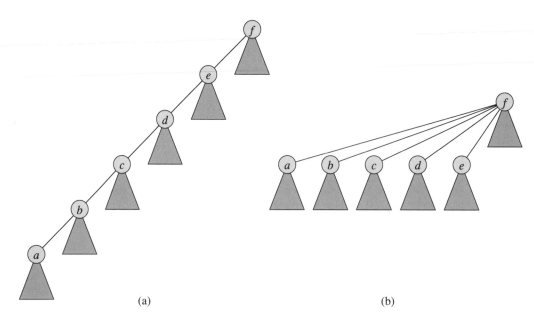

(a)   (b)

Figure 22.5 Path compression during the operation FIND-SET. Arrows and self-loops at roots are omitted. **(a)** A tree representing a set prior to executing FIND-SET(a). Triangles represent subtrees whose roots are the nodes shown. Each node has a pointer to its parent. **(b)** The same set after executing FIND-SET(a). Each node on the find path now points directly to the root.

Pseudocode for disjoint-set forests

To implement a disjoint-set forest with the union-by-rank heuristic, we must keep track of ranks. With each node x, we maintain the integer value $rank[x]$, which is an upper bound on the height of x (the number of edges in the longest path between x and a descendant leaf). When a singleton set is created by MAKE-SET, the initial rank of the single node in the corresponding tree is 0. Each FIND-SET operation leaves all ranks unchanged. When applying UNION to two trees, we make the root of higher rank the parent of the root of lower rank. In case of a tie, we arbitrarily choose one of the roots as the parent and increment its rank.

Let us put this method into pseudocode. We designate the parent of node x by $p[x]$. The LINK procedure, a subroutine called by UNION, takes pointers to two roots as inputs.

MAKE-SET(x)
1   $p[x] \leftarrow x$
2   $rank[x] \leftarrow 0$

UNION(x, y)
1   LINK(FIND-SET(x), FIND-SET(y))

LINK(x, y)

1 **if** $rank[x] > rank[y]$
2   **then** $p[y] \leftarrow x$
3   **else** $p[x] \leftarrow y$
4   **if** $rank[x] = rank[y]$
5   **then** $rank[y] \leftarrow rank[y] + 1$

The FIND-SET procedure with path compression is quite simple.

FIND-SET(x)

1 **if** $x \neq p[x]$
2   **then** $p[x] \leftarrow$ FIND-SET$(p[x])$
3 **return** $p[x]$

The FIND-SET procedure is a ***two-pass method***: it makes one pass up the find path to find the root, and it makes a second pass back down the find path to update each node so that it points directly to the root. Each call of FIND-SET(x) returns $p[x]$ in line 3. If x is the root, then line 2 is not executed and $p[x] = x$ is returned. This is the case in which the recursion bottoms out. Otherwise, line 2 is executed, and the recursive call with parameter $p[x]$ returns a pointer to the root. Line 2 updates node x to point directly to the root, and this pointer is returned in line 3.

Effect of the heuristics on the running time

Separately, either union by rank or path compression improves the running time of the operations on disjoint-set forests, and the improvement is even greater when the two heuristics are used together. Alone, union by rank yields the same running time as we achieved with the weighted union heuristic for the list representation: the resulting implementation runs in time $O(m \lg n)$ (see Exercise 22.4-3). This bound is tight (see Exercise 22.3-3). Although we shall not prove it here, if there are n MAKE-SET operations (and hence at most $n - 1$ UNION operations) and f FIND-SET operations, the path-compression heuristic alone gives a worst-case running time of $\Theta(f \log_{(1+f/n)} n)$ if $f \geq n$ and $\Theta(n + f \lg n)$ if $f < n$.

When we use both union by rank and path compression, the worst-case running time is $O(m \, \alpha(m, n))$, where $\alpha(m, n)$ is the *very* slowly growing inverse of Ackermann's function, which we define in Section 22.4. In any conceivable application of a disjoint-set data structure, $\alpha(m, n) \leq 4$; thus, we can view the running time as linear in m in all practical situations. In Section 22.4, we prove the slightly weaker bound of $O(m \lg^* n)$.

Exercises

22.3-1
Do Exercise 22.2-2 using a disjoint-set forest with union by rank and path compression.

22.3-2
Write a nonrecursive version of FIND-SET with path compression.

22.3-3
Give a sequence of m MAKE-SET, UNION, and FIND-SET operations, n of which are MAKE-SET operations, that takes $\Omega(m \lg n)$ time when we use union by rank only.

22.3-4 $\star$
Show that any sequence of m MAKE-SET, FIND-SET, and UNION operations, where all the UNION operations appear before any of the FIND-SET operations, takes only $O(m)$ time if both path compression and union by rank are used. What happens in the same situation if only the path-compression heuristic is used?

$\star$ **22.4   Analysis of union by rank with path compression**

As noted in Section 22.3, the running time of the combined union-by-rank and path-compression heuristic is $O(m \, \alpha(m, n))$ for m disjoint-set operations on n elements. In this section, we shall examine the function α to see just how slowly it grows. Then, rather than presenting the very complex proof of the $O(m \, \alpha(m, n))$ running time, we shall offer a simpler proof of a slightly weaker upper bound on the running time: $O(m \lg^* n)$.

Ackermann's function and its inverse

To understand Ackermann's function and its inverse α, it helps to have a notation for repeated exponentiation. For an integer $i \geq 0$, the expression

$$2^{2^{\cdot^{\cdot^{\cdot^{2}}}}} \Big\} i$$

stands for the function $g(i)$, defined recursively by

$$g(i) = \begin{cases} 2^1 & \text{if } i = 0 \text{ ,} \\ 2^2 & \text{if } i = 1 \text{ ,} \\ 2^{g(i-1)} & \text{if } i > 1 \text{ .} \end{cases}$$

Intuitively, the parameter i gives the "height of the stack of 2's" that make up the exponent. For example,

	$j = 1$	$j = 2$	$j = 3$	$j = 4$
$i = 1$	2^1	2^2	2^3	2^4
$i = 2$	2^2	2^{2^2}	$2^{2^{2^2}}$	$2^{2^{2^{2^2}}}$
$i = 3$	2^{2^2}	$\left.2^{2^{\cdot^{\cdot^{\cdot^2}}}}\right\}16$	$\left.2^{2^{\cdot^{\cdot^{\cdot^2}}}}\right\}2^{\left.2^{\cdot^{\cdot^{\cdot^2}}}\right\}16}$	$\left.2^{2^{\cdot^{\cdot^{\cdot^2}}}}\right\}2^{\left.2^{\cdot^{\cdot^{\cdot^2}}}\right\}2^{2^{\cdot^{\cdot^{\cdot^2}}}}\}16}$

Figure 22.6 Values of $A(i, j)$ for small values of i and j.

$$\left. 2^{2^{\cdot^{\cdot^{\cdot^2}}}} \right\}4 = 2^{2^{2^2}} = 2^{65536} .$$

Recall the definition of the function $\lg^*$ (page 36) in terms of the functions $\lg^{(i)}$ defined for integer $i \geq 0$:

$$\lg^{(i)} n = \begin{cases} n & \text{if } i = 0 , \\ \lg(\lg^{(i-1)} n) & \text{if } i > 0 \text{ and } \lg^{(i-1)} n > 0 , \\ \text{undefined} & \text{if } i > 0 \text{ and } \lg^{(i-1)} n \leq 0 \text{ or } \lg^{(i-1)} n \text{ is undefined} ; \end{cases}$$

$$\lg^* n = \min \left\{ i \geq 0 : \lg^{(i)} n \leq 1 \right\} .$$

The $\lg^*$ function is essentially the inverse of repeated exponentiation:

$$\lg^* 2^{2^{\cdot^{\cdot^{\cdot^2}}}}\}n = n + 1 .$$

We are now ready to show Ackermann's function, which is defined for integers $i, j \geq 1$ by

$$\begin{aligned} A(1, j) &= 2^j && \text{for } j \geq 1 , \\ A(i, 1) &= A(i - 1, 2) && \text{for } i \geq 2 , \\ A(i, j) &= A(i - 1, A(i, j - 1)) && \text{for } i, j \geq 2 . \end{aligned}$$

Figure 22.6 shows the value of the function for small values of i and j.

Figure 22.7 shows schematically why Ackermann's function has such explosive growth. The first row, exponential in the column number j, is already rapidly growing. The second row consists of the widely spaced subset of columns $2, 2^2, 2^{2^2}, 2^{2^{2^2}}, \ldots$ of the first row. Lines between adjacent rows indicate columns in the lower-numbered row that are in the subset included in the higher-numbered row. The third row consists of the even more widely spaced subset of columns $2, 2^{2^2}, 2^{2^{\cdot^{\cdot^{\cdot^2}}}}\}16, 2^{2^{\cdot^{\cdot^{\cdot^2}}}}\}2^{2^{\cdot^{\cdot^{\cdot^2}}}}\}16, \ldots$ of the second row, which is an even sparser subset of columns of the first row. In general, the spacing between columns of row $i - 1$ appearing in

column

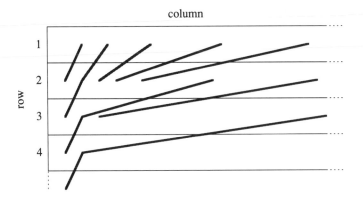

Figure 22.7 The explosive growth of Ackermann's function. Lines between rows $i - 1$ and i indicate entries of row $i - 1$ appearing in row i. Due to the explosive growth, the horizontal spacing is not to scale. The horizontal spacing between entries of row $i - 1$ appearing in row i greatly increases with the column number and row number. If we trace the entries in row i to their original appearance in row 1, the explosive growth is even more evident.

row i increases dramatically with both the column number and the row number. Observe that $A(2, j) = 2^{2^{\cdot^{\cdot^{\cdot^{2}}}}} \big\} j$ for all integers $j \geq 1$. Thus, for $i > 2$, the function $A(i, j)$ grows even more quickly than $2^{2^{\cdot^{\cdot^{\cdot^{2}}}}} \big\} j$.

We define the inverse of Ackermann's function by[2]

$$\alpha(m, n) = \min\{i \geq 1 : A(i, \lfloor m/n \rfloor) > \lg n\} \ .$$

If we fix a value of n, then as m increases, the function $\alpha(m, n)$ is monotonically decreasing. To see this property, note that $\lfloor m/n \rfloor$ is monotonically increasing as m increases; therefore, since n is fixed, the smallest value of i needed to bring $A(i, \lfloor m/n \rfloor)$ above $\lg n$ is monotonically decreasing. This property corresponds to our intuition about disjoint-set forests with path compression: for a given number of distinct elements n, as the number of operations m increases, we would expect the average find-path length to decrease due to path compression. If we perform m operations in time $O(m\,\alpha(m, n))$, then the average time per operation is $O(\alpha(m, n))$, which is monotonically decreasing as m increases.

To back up our earlier claim that $\alpha(m, n) \leq 4$ for all practical purposes, we first note that the quantity $\lfloor m/n \rfloor$ is at least 1, since $m \geq n$. Since Ackermann's function is strictly increasing with each argument, $\lfloor m/n \rfloor \geq 1$ implies $A(i, \lfloor m/n \rfloor) \geq A(i, 1)$ for all $i \geq 1$. In particular, $A(4, \lfloor m/n \rfloor) \geq$

---

[2]Although this function is not the inverse of Ackermann's function in the true mathematical sense, it captures the spirit of the inverse in its growth, which is as slow as Ackermann's function is fast. The reason we use the mysterious $\lg n$ threshold is revealed in the proof of the $O(m\,\alpha(m, n))$ running time, which is beyond the scope of this book.

$A(4, 1)$. But we also have that

$$A(4, 1) = A(3, 2)$$
$$= 2^{2^{\cdot^{\cdot^{\cdot^2}}}} \Big\} 16 \ ,$$

which is far greater than the estimated number of atoms in the observable universe (roughly 10^{80}). It is only for impractically large values of n that $A(4, 1) \leq \lg n$, and thus $\alpha(m, n) \leq 4$ for all practical purposes. Note that the $O(m \lg^* n)$ bound is only slightly weaker than the $O(m \alpha(m, n))$ bound; $\lg^* 65536 = 4$ and $\lg^* 2^{65536} = 5$, so $\lg^* n \leq 5$ for all practical purposes.

Properties of ranks

In the remainder of this section, we prove an $O(m \lg^* n)$ bound on the running time of the disjoint-set operations with union by rank and path compression. In order to prove this bound, we first prove some simple properties of ranks.

Lemma 22.2
For all nodes x, we have $rank[x] \leq rank[p[x]]$, with strict inequality if $x \neq p[x]$. The value of $rank[x]$ is initially 0 and increases through time until $x \neq p[x]$; from then on, $rank[x]$ does not change. The value of $rank[p[x]]$ is a monotonically increasing function of time.

Proof The proof is a straightforward induction on the number of operations, using the implementations of MAKE-SET, UNION, and FIND-SET that appear in Section 22.3. We leave it as Exercise 22.4-1. ∎

We define $size(x)$ to be the number of nodes in the tree rooted at node x, including node x itself.

Lemma 22.3
For all tree roots x, $size(x) \geq 2^{rank[x]}$.

Proof The proof is by induction on the number of LINK operations. Note that FIND-SET operations change neither the rank of a tree root nor the size of its tree.
Basis: The lemma is true before the first LINK, since ranks are initially 0 and each tree contains at least one node.
Inductive step: Assume that the lemma holds before performing the operation LINK(x, y). Let $rank$ denote the rank just before the LINK, and let $rank'$ denote the rank just after the LINK. Define size and size' similarly.
If $rank[x] \neq rank[y]$, assume without loss of generality that $rank[x] < rank[y]$. Node y is the root of the tree formed by the LINK operation, and

$$size'(y) = size(x) + size(y)$$

$$\geq \quad 2^{rank[x]} + 2^{rank[y]}$$
$$\geq \quad 2^{rank[y]}$$
$$= \quad 2^{rank'[y]} .$$

No ranks or sizes change for any nodes other than y.

If $rank[x] = rank[y]$, node y is again the root of the new tree, and

$$
\begin{aligned}
size'(y) \quad &= \quad size(x) + size(y) \\
&\geq \quad 2^{rank[x]} + 2^{rank[y]} \\
&= \quad 2^{rank[y]+1} \\
&= \quad 2^{rank'[y]} .
\end{aligned}
$$

■

Lemma 22.4
For any integer $r \geq 0$, there are at most $n/2^r$ nodes of rank r.

Proof   Fix a particular value of r. Suppose that when we assign a rank r to a node x (in line 2 of MAKE-SET or in line 5 of LINK), we attach a label x to each node in the tree rooted at x. By Lemma 22.3, at least 2^r nodes are labeled each time. Suppose that the root of the tree containing node x changes. Lemma 22.2 assures us that the rank of the new root (or, in fact, of any proper ancestor of x) is at least $r + 1$. Since we assign labels only when a root is assigned a rank r, no node in this new tree will ever again be labeled. Thus, each node is labeled at most once, when its root is first assigned rank r. Since there are n nodes, there are at most n labeled nodes, with at least 2^r labels assigned for each node of rank r. If there were more than $n/2^r$ nodes of rank r, then more than $2^r \cdot (n/2^r) = n$ nodes would be labeled by a node of rank r, which is a contradiction. Therefore, at most $n/2^r$ nodes are ever assigned rank r.   ■

Corollary 22.5
Every node has rank at most $\lfloor \lg n \rfloor$.

Proof   If we let $r > \lg n$, then there are at most $n/2^r < 1$ nodes of rank r. Since ranks are natural numbers, the corollary follows.   ■

Proving the time bound

We shall use the aggregate method of amortized analysis (see Section 18.1) to prove the $O(m \lg^* n)$ time bound. In performing the amortized analysis, it is convenient to assume that we invoke the LINK operation rather than the UNION operation. That is, since the parameters of the LINK procedure are pointers to two roots, we assume that the appropriate FIND-SET operations are performed if necessary. The following lemma shows that even if we count the extra FIND-SET operations, the asymptotic running time remains unchanged.

Lemma 22.6

Suppose we convert a sequence S' of m' MAKE-SET, UNION, and FIND-SET operations into a sequence S of m MAKE-SET, LINK, and FIND-SET operations by turning each UNION into two FIND-SET operations followed by a LINK. Then, if sequence S runs in $O(m \lg^* n)$ time, sequence S' runs in $O(m' \lg^* n)$ time.

Proof Since each UNION operation in sequence S' is converted into three operations in S, we have $m' \leq m \leq 3m'$. Since $m = O(m')$, an $O(m \lg^* n)$ time bound for the converted sequence S implies an $O(m' \lg^* n)$ time bound for the original sequence S'. ∎

In the remainder of this section, we shall assume that the initial sequence of m' MAKE-SET, UNION, and FIND-SET operations has been converted to a sequence of m MAKE-SET, LINK, and FIND-SET operations. We now prove an $O(m \lg^* n)$ time bound for the converted sequence and appeal to Lemma 22.6 to prove the $O(m' \lg^* n)$ running time of the original sequence of m' operations.

Theorem 22.7

A sequence of m MAKE-SET, LINK, and FIND-SET operations, n of which are MAKE-SET operations, can be performed on a disjoint-set forest with union by rank and path compression in worst-case time $O(m \lg^* n)$.

Proof We assess *charges* corresponding to the actual cost of each set operation and compute the total number of charges assessed once the entire sequence of set operations has been performed. This total then gives us the actual cost of all the set operations.

The charges assessed to the MAKE-SET and LINK operations are simple: one charge per operation. Since these operations each take $O(1)$ actual time, the charges assessed equal the actual costs of the operations.

Before discussing charges assessed to the FIND-SET operations, we partition node ranks into *blocks* by putting rank r into block $\lg^* r$ for $r = 0, 1, \ldots, \lfloor \lg n \rfloor$. (Recall that $\lfloor \lg n \rfloor$ is the maximum rank.) The highest-numbered block is therefore block $\lg^*(\lg n) = \lg^* n - 1$. For notational convenience, we define for integers $j \geq -1$,

$$B(j) = \begin{cases} -1 & \text{if } j = -1 , \\ 1 & \text{if } j = 0 , \\ 2 & \text{if } j = 1 , \\ 2^{2^{\cdot^{\cdot^{\cdot^2}}}} \Big\} j-1 & \text{if } j \geq 2 . \end{cases}$$

Then, for $j = 0, 1, \ldots, \lg^* n - 1$, the jth block consists of the set of ranks

$$\{B(j-1)+1, B(j-1)+2, \ldots, B(j)\} \ .$$

We use two types of charges for a FIND-SET operation: ***block charges*** and ***path charges***. Suppose that the FIND-SET starts at node x_0 and that the find path consists of nodes $x_0, x_1, \ldots, x_l$, where for $i = 1, 2, \ldots, l$, node x_i is $p[x_{i-1}]$ and x_l (a root) is $p[x_l]$. For $j = 0, 1, \ldots, \lg^* n - 1$, we assess one block charge to the *last* node with rank in block j on the path. (Note that Lemma 22.2 implies that on any find path, the nodes with ranks in a given block are consecutive.) We also assess one block charge to the child of the root, that is, to x_{l-1}. Because ranks strictly increase along any find path, an equivalent formulation assesses one block charge to each node x_i such that $p[x_i] = x_l$ (x_i is the root or its child) or $\lg^* rank[x_i] < \lg^* rank[x_{i+1}]$ (the block of x_i's rank differs from that of its parent). At each node on the find path for which we do not assess a block charge, we assess one path charge.

Once a node other than the root or its child is assessed block charges, it will never again be assessed path charges. To see why, observe that each time path compression occurs, the rank of a node x_i for which $p[x_i] \neq x_l$ remains the same, but the new parent of x_i has a rank strictly greater than that of x_i's old parent. The difference between the ranks of x_i and its parent is a monotonically increasing function of time. Thus, the difference between $\lg^* rank[p[x_i]]$ and $\lg^* rank[x_i]$ is also a monotonically increasing function of time. Once x_i and its parent have ranks in different blocks, they will always have ranks in different blocks, and so x_i will never again be assessed a path charge.

Since we have charged once for each node visited in each FIND-SET operation, the total number of charges assessed is the total number of nodes visited in all the FIND-SET operations; this total represents the actual cost of all the FIND-SET operations. We wish to show that this total is $O(m \lg^* n)$.

The number of block charges is easy to bound. There is at most one block charge assessed for each block number on the given find path, plus one block charge for the child of the root. Since block numbers range from 0 to $\lg^* n - 1$, there are at most $\lg^* n + 1$ block charges assessed for each FIND-SET operation. Thus, there are at most $m(\lg^* n + 1)$ block charges assessed over all FIND-SET operations.

Bounding the path charges is a little trickier. We start by observing that if a node x_i is assessed a path charge, then $p[x_i] \neq x_l$ before path compression, so that x_i will be assigned a new parent during path compression. Moreover, as we have observed, x_i's new parent has a higher rank than its old parent. Suppose that node x_i's rank is in block j. How many times can x_i be assigned a new parent, and thus assessed a path charge, before x_i is assigned a parent whose rank is in a different block (after which x_i will never again be assessed a path charge)? This number of times is maximized if x_i has the lowest rank in its block, namely $B(j-1)+1$, and its parents' ranks successively take on the values $B(j-1)+2, B(j-1)+3, \ldots, B(j)$.

Since there are $B(j) - B(j - 1) - 1$ such ranks, we conclude that a vertex can be assessed at most $B(j) - B(j - 1) - 1$ path charges while its rank is in block j.

Our next step in bounding the path charges is to bound the number of nodes that have ranks in block j for integers $j \geq 0$. (Recall that by Lemma 22.2, the rank of a node is fixed once it becomes a child of another node.) Let the number of nodes whose ranks are in block j be denoted by $N(j)$. Then, by Lemma 22.4,

$$N(j) \leq \sum_{r=B(j-1)+1}^{B(j)} \frac{n}{2^r} .$$

For $j = 0$, this sum evaluates to

$$
\begin{aligned}
N(0) &= n/2^0 + n/2^1 \\
&= 3n/2 \\
&= 3n/2B(0) .
\end{aligned}
$$

For $j \geq 1$, we have

$$
\begin{aligned}
N(j) &\leq \frac{n}{2^{B(j-1)+1}} \sum_{r=0}^{B(j)-(B(j-1)+1)} \frac{1}{2^r} \\
&< \frac{n}{2^{B(j-1)+1}} \sum_{r=0}^{\infty} \frac{1}{2^r} \\
&= \frac{n}{2^{B(j-1)}} \\
&= \frac{n}{B(j)} .
\end{aligned}
$$

Thus, $N(j) \leq 3n/2B(j)$ for all integers $j \geq 0$.

We finish bounding the path charges by summing over all blocks the product of the maximum number of nodes with ranks in the block and the maximum number of path charges per node of that block. Denoting by $P(n)$ the overall number of path charges, we have

$$
\begin{aligned}
P(n) &\leq \sum_{j=0}^{\lg^* n - 1} \frac{3n}{2B(j)} (B(j) - B(j-1) - 1) \\
&\leq \sum_{j=0}^{\lg^* n - 1} \frac{3n}{2B(j)} \cdot B(j) \\
&= \frac{3}{2} n \lg^* n .
\end{aligned}
$$

Thus, the total number of charges incurred by FIND-SET operations is $O(m(\lg^* n + 1) + n \lg^* n)$, which is $O(m \lg^* n)$ since $m \geq n$. Since there are $O(n)$ MAKE-SET and LINK operations, with one charge each, the total time is $O(m \lg^* n)$. ∎

Corollary 22.8
A sequence of m Make-Set, Union, and Find-Set operations, n of which are Make-Set operations, can be performed on a disjoint-set forest with union by rank and path compression in worst-case time $O(m \lg^* n)$.

Proof Immediate from Theorem 22.7 and Lemma 22.6.   ■

Exercises

22.4-1
Prove Lemma 22.2.

22.4-2
For each node x, how many bits are necessary to store $size(x)$? How about $rank[x]$?

22.4-3
Using Lemma 22.2 and Corollary 22.5, give a simple proof that operations on a disjoint-set forest with union by rank but without path compression run in $O(m \lg n)$ time.

22.4-4 ⋆
Suppose we modify the rule about assessing charges so that we assess one block charge to the last node on the find path whose rank is in block j for $j = 0, 1, \ldots, \lg^* n - 1$. Otherwise, we assess one path charge to the node. Thus, if a node is a child of the root and is not the last node of a block, it is assessed a path charge, not a block charge. Show that $\Omega(m)$ path charges could be assessed a given node while its rank is in a given block j.

Problems

22-1   Off-line minimum
The ***off-line minimum problem*** asks us to maintain a dynamic set T of elements from the domain $\{1, 2, \ldots, n\}$ under the operations Insert and Extract-Min. We are given a sequence S of n Insert and m Extract-Min calls, where each key in $\{1, 2, \ldots, n\}$ is inserted exactly once. We wish to determine which key is returned by each Extract-Min call. Specifically, we wish to fill in an array *extracted*$[1 .. m]$, where for $i = 1, 2, \ldots, m$, *extracted*$[i]$ is the key returned by the ith Extract-Min call. The problem is "off-line" in the sense that we are allowed to process the entire sequence S before determining any of the returned keys.

a. In the following instance of the off-line minimum problem, each INSERT
is represented by a number and each EXTRACT-MIN is represented by
the letter E:

$4, 8, E, 3, E, 9, 2, 6, E, E, E, 1, 7, E, 5$.

Fill in the correct values in the *extracted* array.

To develop an algorithm for this problem, we break the sequence S into
homogeneous subsequences. That is, we represent S by

$I_1, E, I_2, E, I_3, \ldots, I_m, E, I_{m+1}$,

where each E represents a single EXTRACT-MIN call and each I_j represents
a (possibly empty) sequence of INSERT calls. For each subsequence I_j, we
initially place the keys inserted by these operations into a set K_j, which is
empty if I_j is empty. We then do the following.

OFF-LINE-MINIMUM(m, n)

```
1  for i ← 1 to n
2      do determine j such that i ∈ K_j
3          if j ≠ m + 1
4              then extracted[j] ← i
5                  let l be the smallest value greater than j
                        for which set K_l exists
6                  K_l ← K_j ∪ K_l, destroying K_j
7  return extracted
```

b. Argue that the array *extracted* returned by OFF-LINE-MINIMUM is correct.

c. Describe how to use a disjoint-set data structure to implement OFF-
LINE-MINIMUM efficiently. Give a tight bound on the worst-case running
time of your implementation.

22-2 Depth determination

In the ***depth-determination problem***, we maintain a forest $\mathcal{F} = \{T_i\}$ of
rooted trees under three operations:

MAKE-TREE(v) creates a tree whose only node is v.

FIND-DEPTH(v) returns the depth of node v within its tree.

GRAFT(r, v) makes node r, which is assumed to be the root of a tree,
become the child of node v, which is assumed to be in a different tree
than r but may or may not itself be a root.

a. Suppose that we use a tree representation similar to a disjoint-set forest:
$p[v]$ is the parent of node v, except that $p[v] = v$ if v is a root. If
we implement GRAFT(r, v) by setting $p[r] \leftarrow v$ and FIND-DEPTH(v) by
following the find path up to the root, returning a count of all nodes

other than v encountered, show that the worst-case running time of a sequence of m MAKE-TREE, FIND-DEPTH, and GRAFT operations is $\Theta(m^2)$.

By using the union-by-rank and path-compression heuristics, we can reduce the worst-case running time. We use the disjoint-set forest $S = \{S_i\}$, where each set S_i (which is itself a tree) corresponds to a tree T_i in the forest $\mathcal{F}$. The tree structure within a set S_i, however, does not necessarily correspond to that of T_i. In fact, the implementation of S_i does not record the exact parent-child relationships but nevertheless allows us to determine any node's depth in T_i.

The key idea is to maintain in each node v a "pseudodistance" $d[v]$, which is defined so that the sum of the pseudodistances along the path from v to the root of its set S_i equals the depth of v in T_i. That is, if the path from v to its root in S_i is $v_0, v_1, \ldots, v_k$, where $v_0 = v$ and v_k is S_i's root, then the depth of v in T_i is $\sum_{j=0}^{k} d[v_j]$.

b. Give an implementation of MAKE-TREE.

c. Show how to modify FIND-SET to implement FIND-DEPTH. Your implementation should perform path compression, and its running time should be linear in the length of the find path. Make sure that your implementation updates pseudodistances correctly.

d. Show how to modify the UNION and LINK procedures to implement GRAFT(r, v), which combines the sets containing r and v. Make sure that your implementation updates pseudodistances correctly. Note that the root of a set S_i is not necessarily the root of the corresponding tree T_i.

e. Give a tight bound on the worst-case running time of a sequence of m MAKE-TREE, FIND-DEPTH, and GRAFT operations, n of which are MAKE-TREE operations.

22-3 *Tarjan's off-line least-common-ancestors algorithm*

The *least common ancestor* of two nodes u and v in a rooted tree T is the node w that is an ancestor of both u and v and that has the greatest depth in T. In the *off-line least-common-ancestors problem*, we are given a rooted tree T and an arbitrary set $P = \{\{u, v\}\}$ of unordered pairs of nodes in T, and we wish to determine the least common ancestor of each pair in P.

To solve the off-line least-common-ancestors problem, the following procedure performs a tree walk of T with the initial call LCA($root[T]$). Each node is assumed to be colored WHITE prior to the walk.

LCA(u)

```
1   MAKE-SET(u)
2   ancestor[FIND-SET(u)] ← u
3   for each child v of u in T
4       do LCA(v)
5           UNION(u, v)
6           ancestor[FIND-SET(u)] ← u
7   color[u] ← BLACK
8   for each node v such that {u, v} ∈ P
9       do if color[v] = BLACK
10              then print "The least common ancestor of"
                        u "and" v "is" ancestor[FIND-SET(v)]
```

a. Argue that line 10 is executed exactly once for each pair $\{u, v\} \in P$.

b. Argue that at the time of the call LCA(u), the number of sets in the disjoint-set data structure is equal to the depth of u in T.

c. Prove that LCA correctly prints the least common ancestor of u and v for each pair $\{u, v\} \in P$.

d. Analyze the running time of LCA, assuming that we use the implementation of the disjoint-set data structure in Section 22.3.

Chapter notes

Many of the important results for disjoint-set data structures are due at least in part to R. E. Tarjan. The upper bound of $O(m\,\alpha(m, n))$ was first given by Tarjan [186, 188]. The $O(m\lg^* n)$ upper bound was proven earlier by Hopcroft and Ullman [4, 103]. Tarjan and van Leeuwen [190] discuss variants on the path-compression heuristic, including "one-pass methods," which sometimes offer better constant factors in their performance than do two-pass methods. Gabow and Tarjan [76] show that in certain applications, the disjoint-set operations can be made to run in $O(m)$ time.

Tarjan [187] showed that a lower bound of $\Omega(m\alpha(m, n))$ time is required for operations on any disjoint-set data structure satisfying certain technical conditions. This lower bound was later generalized by Fredman and Saks [74], who showed that in the worst case, $\Omega(m\,\alpha(m, n))$ $(\lg n)$-bit words of memory must be accessed.

VI   Graph Algorithms

Introduction

Graphs are a pervasive data structure in computer science, and algorithms for working with them are fundamental to the field. There are hundreds of interesting computational problems defined in terms of graphs. In this part, we touch on a few of the more significant ones.

Chapter 23 shows how we can represent a graph on a computer and then discusses algorithms based on searching a graph using either breadth-first search or depth-first search. Two applications of depth-first search are given: topologically sorting a directed acyclic graph and decomposing a directed graph into its strongly connected components.

Chapter 24 describes how to compute a minimum-weight spanning tree of a graph. Such a tree is defined as the least-weight way of connecting all of the vertices together when each edge has an associated weight. The algorithms for computing minimum spanning trees are good examples of greedy algorithms (see Chapter 17).

Chapters 25 and 26 consider the problem of computing shortest paths between vertices when each edge has an associated length or "weight." Chapter 25 considers the computation of shortest paths from a given source vertex to all other vertices, and Chapter 26 considers the computation of shortest paths between every pair of vertices.

Finally, Chapter 27 shows how to compute a maximum flow of material in a network (directed graph) having a specified source of material, a specified sink, and specified capacities for the amount of material that can traverse each directed edge. This general problem arises in many forms, and a good algorithm for computing maximum flows can be used to solve a variety of related problems efficiently.

In describing the running time of a graph algorithm on a given graph $G = (V, E)$, we usually measure the size of the input in terms of the number of vertices $|V|$ and the number of edges $|E|$ of the graph. That is, there are two relevant parameters describing the size of the input, not just one. We adopt a common notational convention for these parameters. Inside asymptotic notation (such as O-notation or Θ-notation), and *only* inside such notation, the symbol V denotes $|V|$ and the symbol E denotes $|E|$. For example, we might say, "the algorithm runs in time $O(VE)$," meaning that the algorithm runs in time $O(|V||E|)$. This convention makes the running-time formulas easier to read, without risk of ambiguity.

Another convention we adopt appears in pseudocode. We denote the vertex set of a graph G by $V[G]$ and its edge set by $E[G]$. That is, the pseudocode views vertex and edge sets as attributes of a graph.

23 Elementary Graph Algorithms

This chapter presents methods for representing a graph and for searching a graph. Searching a graph means systematically following the edges of the graph so as to visit the vertices of the graph. A graph-searching algorithm can discover much about the structure of a graph. Many algorithms begin by searching their input graph to obtain this structural information. Other graph algorithms are organized as simple elaborations of basic graph-searching algorithms. Techniques for searching a graph are at the heart of the field of graph algorithms.

Section 23.1 discusses the two most common computational representations of graphs: as adjacency lists and as adjacency matrices. Section 23.2 presents a simple graph-searching algorithm called breadth-first search and shows how to create a breadth-first tree. Section 23.3 presents depth-first search and proves some standard results about the order in which depth-first search visits vertices. Section 23.4 provides our first real application of depth-first search: topologically sorting a directed acyclic graph. A second application of depth-first search, finding the strongly connected components of a directed graph, is given in Section 23.5.

23.1 Representations of graphs

There are two standard ways to represent a graph $G = (V, E)$: as a collection of adjacency lists or as an adjacency matrix. The adjacency-list representation is usually preferred, because it provides a compact way to represent *sparse* graphs—those for which $|E|$ is much less than $|V|^2$. Most of the graph algorithms presented in this book assume that an input graph is represented in adjacency-list form. An adjacency-matrix representation may be preferred, however, when the graph is *dense*—$|E|$ is close to $|V|^2$—or when we need to be able to tell quickly if there is an edge connecting two given vertices. For example, two of the all-pairs shortest-paths algorithms presented in Chapter 26 assume that their input graphs are represented by adjacency matrices.

The *adjacency-list representation* of a graph $G = (V, E)$ consists of an array *Adj* of $|V|$ lists, one for each vertex in V. For each $u \in V$, the

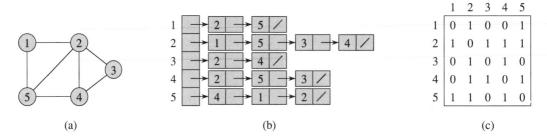

Figure 23.1 Two representations of an undirected graph. **(a)** An undirected graph G having five vertices and seven edges. **(b)** An adjacency-list representation of G. **(c)** The adjacency-matrix representation of G.

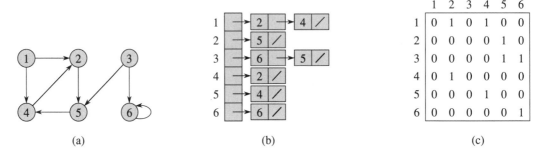

Figure 23.2 Two representations of a directed graph. **(a)** A directed graph G having six vertices and eight edges. **(b)** An adjacency-list representation of G. **(c)** The adjacency-matrix representation of G.

adjacency list *Adj*[u] contains (pointers to) all the vertices v such that there is an edge $(u,v) \in E$. That is, *Adj*[u] consists of all the vertices adjacent to u in G. The vertices in each adjacency list are typically stored in an arbitrary order. Figure 23.1(b) is an adjacency-list representation of the undirected graph in Figure 23.1(a). Similarly, Figure 23.2(b) is an adjacency-list representation of the directed graph in Figure 23.2(a).

If G is a directed graph, the sum of the lengths of all the adjacency lists is $|E|$, since an edge of the form (u,v) is represented by having v appear in *Adj*[u]. If G is an undirected graph, the sum of the lengths of all the adjacency lists is $2|E|$, since if (u,v) is an undirected edge, then u appears in v's adjacency list and vice versa. Whether a graph is directed or not, the adjacency-list representation has the desirable property that the amount of memory it requires is $O(\max(V,E)) = O(V + E)$.

Adjacency lists can readily be adapted to represent ***weighted graphs***, that is, graphs for which each edge has an associated ***weight***, typically given by a ***weight function*** $w : E \to \mathbf{R}$. For example, let $G = (V, E)$ be a weighted graph with weight function w. The weight $w(u,v)$ of the edge $(u,v) \in E$ is simply stored with vertex v in u's adjacency list. The adjacency-list representation is quite robust in that it can be modified to support many other graph variants.

A potential disadvantage of the adjacency-list representation is that there is no quicker way to determine if a given edge (u, v) is present in the graph than to search for v in the adjacency list *Adj[u]*. This disadvantage can be remedied by an adjacency-matrix representation of the graph, at the cost of using asymptotically more memory.

For the ***adjacency-matrix representation*** of a graph $G = (V, E)$, we assume that the vertices are numbered $1, 2, \ldots, |V|$ in some arbitrary manner. The adjacency-matrix representation of a graph G then consists of a $|V| \times |V|$ matrix $A = (a_{ij})$ such that

$$a_{ij} = \begin{cases} 1 & \text{if } (i, j) \in E \text{ ,} \\ 0 & \text{otherwise .} \end{cases}$$

Figures 23.1(c) and 23.2(c) are the adjacency matrices of the undirected and directed graphs in Figures 23.1(a) and 23.2(a), respectively. The adjacency matrix of a graph requires $\Theta(V^2)$ memory, independent of the number of edges in the graph.

Observe the symmetry along the main diagonal of the adjacency matrix in Figure 23.1(c). We define the the ***transpose*** of a matrix $A = (a_{ij})$ to be the matrix $A^\mathrm{T} = (a_{ij}^\mathrm{T})$ given by $a_{ij}^\mathrm{T} = a_{ji}$. Since in an undirected graph, (u, v) and (v, u) represent the same edge, the adjacency matrix A of an undirected graph is its own transpose: $A = A^\mathrm{T}$. In some applications, it pays to store only the entries on and above the diagonal of the adjacency matrix, thereby cutting the memory needed to store the graph almost in half.

Like the adjacency-list representation of a graph, the adjacency-matrix representation can be used for weighted graphs. For example, if $G = (V, E)$ is a weighted graph with edge-weight function w, the weight $w(u, v)$ of the edge $(u, v) \in E$ is simply stored as the entry in row u and column v of the adjacency matrix. If an edge does not exist, a NIL value can be stored as its corresponding matrix entry, though for many problems it is convenient to use a value such as 0 or ∞.

Although the adjacency-list representation is asymptotically at least as efficient as the adjacency-matrix representation, the simplicity of an adjacency matrix may make it preferable when graphs are reasonably small. Moreover, if the graph is unweighted, there is an additional advantage in storage for the adjacency-matrix representation. Rather than using one word of computer memory for each matrix entry, the adjacency matrix uses only one bit per entry.

Exercises

23.1-1
Given an adjacency-list representation of a directed graph, how long does it take to compute the out-degree of every vertex? How long does it take to compute the in-degrees?

23.1-2
Give an adjacency-list representation for a complete binary tree on 7 vertices. Give an equivalent adjacency-matrix representation. Assume that vertices are numbered from 1 to 7 as in a binary heap.

23.1-3
The ***transpose*** of a directed graph $G = (V, E)$ is the graph $G^T = (V, E^T)$, where $E^T = \{(v, u) \in V \times V : (u, v) \in E\}$. Thus, G^T is G with all its edges reversed. Describe efficient algorithms for computing G^T from G, for both the adjacency-list and adjacency-matrix representations of G. Analyze the running times of your algorithms.

23.1-4
Given an adjacency-list representation of a multigraph $G = (V, E)$, describe an $O(V + E)$-time algorithm to compute the adjacency-list representation of the "equivalent" undirected graph $G' = (V, E')$, where E' consists of the edges in E with all multiple edges between two vertices replaced by a single edge and with all self-loops removed.

23.1-5
The ***square*** of a directed graph $G = (V, E)$ is the graph $G^2 = (V, E^2)$ such that $(u, w) \in E^2$ if and only if for some $v \in V$, both $(u, v) \in E$ and $(v, w) \in E$. That is, G^2 contains an edge between u and w whenever G contains a path with exactly two edges between u and w. Describe efficient algorithms for computing G^2 from G for both the adjacency-list and adjacency-matrix representations of G. Analyze the running times of your algorithms.

23.1-6
When an adjacency-matrix representation is used, most graph algorithms require time $\Theta(V^2)$, but there are some exceptions. Show that determining whether a directed graph contains a ***sink***—a vertex with in-degree $|V| - 1$ and out-degree 0—can be determined in time $O(V)$, even if an adjacency-matrix representation is used.

23.1-7
The ***incidence matrix*** of a directed graph $G = (V, E)$ is a $|V| \times |E|$ matrix $B = (b_{ij})$ such that

$$b_{ij} = \begin{cases} -1 & \text{if edge } j \text{ leaves vertex } i \text{,} \\ 1 & \text{if edge } j \text{ enters vertex } i \text{,} \\ 0 & \text{otherwise .} \end{cases}$$

Describe what the entries of the matrix product BB^{T} represent, where B^{T} is the transpose of B.

23.2 Breadth-first search

Breadth-first search is one of the simplest algorithms for searching a graph and the archetype for many important graph algorithms. Dijkstra's single-source shortest-paths algorithm (Chapter 25) and Prim's minimum-spanning-tree algorithm (Section 24.2) use ideas similar to those in breadth-first search.

Given a graph $G = (V, E)$ and a distinguished ***source*** vertex s, breadth-first search systematically explores the edges of G to "discover" every vertex that is reachable from s. It computes the distance (fewest number of edges) from s to all such reachable vertices. It also produces a "breadth-first tree" with root s that contains all such reachable vertices. For any vertex v reachable from s, the path in the breadth-first tree from s to v corresponds to a "shortest path" from s to v in G, that is, a path containing the fewest number of edges. The algorithm works on both directed and undirected graphs.

Breadth-first search is so named because it expands the frontier between discovered and undiscovered vertices uniformly across the breadth of the frontier. That is, the algorithm discovers all vertices at distance k from s before discovering any vertices at distance $k + 1$.

To keep track of progress, breadth-first search colors each vertex white, gray, or black. All vertices start out white and may later become gray and then black. A vertex is ***discovered*** the first time it is encountered during the search, at which time it becomes nonwhite. Gray and black vertices, therefore, have been discovered, but breadth-first search distinguishes between them to ensure that the search proceeds in a breadth-first manner. If $(u, v) \in E$ and vertex u is black, then vertex v is either gray or black; that is, all vertices adjacent to black vertices have been discovered. Gray vertices may have some adjacent white vertices; they represent the frontier between discovered and undiscovered vertices.

Breadth-first search constructs a breadth-first tree, initially containing only its root, which is the source vertex s. Whenever a white vertex v is discovered in the course of scanning the adjacency list of an already discovered vertex u, the vertex v and the edge (u, v) are added to the tree. We say that u is the ***predecessor*** or ***parent*** of v in the breadth-first tree. Since a vertex is discovered at most once, it has at most one parent. Ancestor and descendant relationships in the breadth-first tree are defined relative to the root s as usual: if u is on a path in the tree from the root s to vertex v, then u is an ancestor of v and v is a descendant of u.

The breadth-first-search procedure BFS below assumes that the input graph $G = (V, E)$ is represented using adjacency lists. It maintains several additional data structures with each vertex in the graph. The color of each vertex $u \in V$ is stored in the variable *color*[u], and the predecessor of u is stored in the variable $\pi[u]$. If u has no predecessor (for example, if $u = s$ or u has not been discovered), then $\pi[u] = $ NIL. The distance from the source s to vertex u computed by the algorithm is stored in $d[u]$. The algorithm also uses a first-in, first-out queue Q (see Section 11.1) to manage the set of gray vertices.

BFS(G, s)

```
 1  for each vertex u ∈ V[G] − {s}
 2      do color[u] ← WHITE
 3         d[u] ← ∞
 4         π[u] ← NIL
 5  color[s] ← GRAY
 6  d[s] ← 0
 7  π[s] ← NIL
 8  Q ← {s}
 9  while Q ≠ ∅
10      do u ← head[Q]
11         for each v ∈ Adj[u]
12             do if color[v] = WHITE
13                 then color[v] ← GRAY
14                      d[v] ← d[u] + 1
15                      π[v] ← u
16                      ENQUEUE(Q, v)
17         DEQUEUE(Q)
18         color[u] ← BLACK
```

Figure 23.3 illustrates the progress of BFS on a sample graph.

The procedure BFS works as follows. Lines 1–4 paint every vertex white, set $d[u]$ to be infinity for every vertex u, and set the parent of every vertex to be NIL. Line 5 paints the source vertex s gray, since it is considered to be discovered when the procedure begins. Line 6 initializes $d[s]$ to 0, and line 7 sets the predecessor of the source to be NIL. Line 8 initializes Q to the queue containing just the vertex s; thereafter, Q always contains the set of gray vertices.

The main loop of the program is contained in lines 9–18. The loop iterates as long as there remain gray vertices, which are discovered vertices that have not yet had their adjacency lists fully examined. Line 10 determines the gray vertex u at the head of the queue Q. The **for** loop of lines 11–16 considers each vertex v in the adjacency list of u. If v is white, then it has not yet been discovered, and the algorithm discovers it

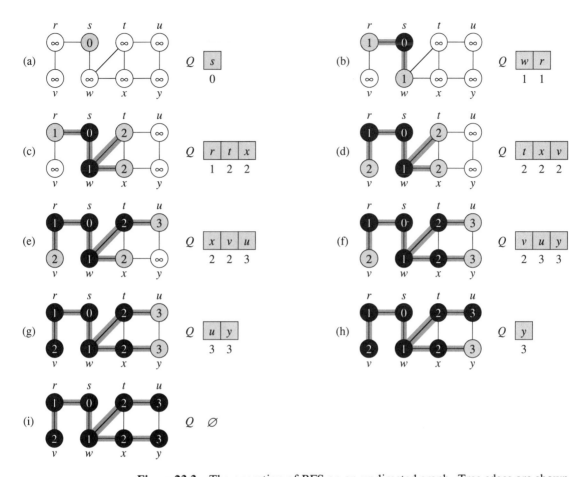

Figure 23.3   The operation of BFS on an undirected graph. Tree edges are shown shaded as they are produced by BFS. Within each vertex u is shown $d[u]$. The queue Q is shown at the beginning of each iteration of the **while** loop of lines 9–18. Vertex distances are shown next to vertices in the queue.

by executing lines 13–16. It is first grayed, and its distance $d[v]$ is set to $d[u] + 1$. Then, u is recorded as its parent. Finally, it is placed at the tail of the queue Q. When all the vertices on u's adjacency list have been examined, u is removed from Q and blackened in lines 17–18.

Analysis

Before proving all the various properties of breadth-first search, we take on the somewhat easier job of analyzing its running time on an input graph $G = (V, E)$. After initialization, no vertex is ever whitened, and thus the test in line 12 ensures that each vertex is enqueued at most once, and hence dequeued at most once. The operations of enqueuing and dequeuing take $O(1)$ time, so the total time devoted to queue operations is $O(V)$.

Because the adjacency list of each vertex is scanned only when the vertex is dequeued, the adjacency list of each vertex is scanned at most once. Since the sum of the lengths of all the adjacency lists is $\Theta(E)$, at most $O(E)$ time is spent in total scanning adjacency lists. The overhead for initialization is $O(V)$, and thus the total running time of BFS is $O(V + E)$. Thus, breadth-first search runs in time linear in the size of the adjacency-list representation of G.

Shortest paths

At the beginning of this section, we claimed that breadth-first search finds the distance to each reachable vertex in a graph $G = (V, E)$ from a given source vertex $s \in V$. Define the ***shortest-path distance*** $\delta(s, v)$ from s to v as the minimum number of edges in any path from vertex s to vertex v, or else ∞ if there is no path from s to v. A path of length $\delta(s, v)$ from s to v is said to be a ***shortest path***[1] from s to v. Before showing that breadth-first search actually computes shortest-path distances, we investigate an important property of shortest-path distances.

Lemma 23.1
Let $G = (V, E)$ be a directed or undirected graph, and let $s \in V$ be an arbitrary vertex. Then, for any edge $(u, v) \in E$,

$$\delta(s, v) \leq \delta(s, u) + 1 \ .$$

Proof   If u is reachable from s, then so is v. In this case, the shortest path from s to v cannot be longer than the shortest path from s to u followed by the edge (u, v), and thus the inequality holds. If u is not reachable from s, then $\delta(s, u) = \infty$, and the inequality holds. ∎

We want to show that BFS properly computes $d[v] = \delta(s, v)$ for each vertex $v \in V$. We first show that $d[v]$ bounds $\delta(s, v)$ from above.

Lemma 23.2
Let $G = (V, E)$ be a directed or undirected graph, and suppose that BFS is run on G from a given source vertex $s \in V$. Then upon termination, for each vertex $v \in V$, the value $d[v]$ computed by BFS satisfies $d[v] \geq \delta(s, v)$.

Proof   We use induction on the number of times a vertex is placed in the queue Q. Our inductive hypothesis is that $d[v] \geq \delta(s, v)$ for all $v \in V$.

---

[1] In Chapters 25 and 26, we shall generalize our study of shortest paths to weighted graphs, in which every edge has a real-valued weight and the weight of a path is the sum of the weights of its constituent edges. The graphs considered in the present chapter are unweighted.

The basis of the induction is the situation immediately after s is placed in Q in line 8 of BFS. The inductive hypothesis holds here, because $d[s] = 0 = \delta(s, s)$ and $d[v] = \infty \geq \delta(s, v)$ for all $v \in V - \{s\}$.

For the inductive step, consider a white vertex v that is discovered during the search from a vertex u. The inductive hypothesis implies that $d[u] \geq \delta(s, u)$. From the assignment performed by line 14 and from Lemma 23.1, we obtain

$$
\begin{aligned}
d[v] &= d[u] + 1 \\
&\geq \delta(s, u) + 1 \\
&\geq \delta(s, v) \ .
\end{aligned}
$$

Vertex v is then inserted into the queue Q, and it is never inserted again because it is also grayed and the **then** clause of lines 13–16 is executed only for white vertices. Thus, the value of $d[v]$ never changes again, and the inductive hypothesis is maintained.   ∎

To prove that $d[v] = \delta(s, v)$, we must first show more precisely how the queue Q operates during the course of BFS. The next lemma shows that at all times, there are at most two distinct d values in the queue.

Lemma 23.3

Suppose that during the execution of BFS on a graph $G = (V, E)$, the queue Q contains the vertices $\langle v_1, v_2, \ldots, v_r \rangle$, where v_1 is the head of Q and v_r is the tail. Then, $d[v_r] \leq d[v_1] + 1$ and $d[v_i] \leq d[v_{i+1}]$ for $i = 1, 2, \ldots, r - 1$.

Proof   The proof is by induction on the number of queue operations. Initially, when the queue contains only s, the lemma certainly holds.

For the inductive step, we must prove the lemma holds after both dequeuing and enqueuing a vertex. If the head v_1 of the queue is dequeued, the new head is v_2. (If the queue becomes empty, then the lemma holds vacuously.) But then we have $d[v_r] \leq d[v_1] + 1 \leq d[v_2] + 1$, and the remaining inequalities are unaffected. Thus, the lemma follows with v_2 as the head. Enqueuing a vertex requires closer examination of the code. In line 16 of BFS, when the vertex v is enqueued, thus becoming v_{r+1}, the head v_1 of Q is in fact the vertex u whose adjacency list is currently being scanned. Thus, $d[v_{r+1}] = d[v] = d[u] + 1 = d[v_1] + 1$. We also have $d[v_r] \leq d[v_1] + 1 = d[u] + 1 = d[v] = d[v_{r+1}]$, and the remaining inequalities are unaffected. Thus, the lemma follows when v is enqueued.   ∎

We can now prove that breadth-first search correctly finds shortest-path distances.

Theorem 23.4 (Correctness of breadth-first search)

Let $G = (V, E)$ be a directed or undirected graph, and suppose that BFS is run on G from a given source vertex $s \in V$. Then, during its execution,

BFS discovers every vertex $v \in V$ that is reachable from the source s, and upon termination, $d[v] = \delta(s, v)$ for all $v \in V$. Moreover, for any vertex $v \neq s$ that is reachable from s, one of the shortest paths from s to v is the shortest path from s to $\pi[v]$ followed by the edge $(\pi[v], v)$.

Proof We start with the case in which v is unreachable from s. Since Lemma 23.2 gives $d[v] \geq \delta(s, v) = \infty$, vertex v cannot have $d[v]$ set to a finite value in line 14. By induction, there cannot be a first vertex whose d value is set to ∞ by line 14. Line 14 is therefore only executed only for vertices with finite d values. Thus, if v is unreachable, it is never discovered.

The main part of the proof is for vertices reachable from s. Let V_k denote the set of vertices at distance k from s; that is, $V_k = \{v \in V : \delta(s, v) = k\}$. The proof proceeds by induction on k. As an inductive hypothesis, we assume that for each vertex $v \in V_k$, there is exactly one point during the execution of BFS at which

- v is grayed,
- $d[v]$ is set to k,
- if $v \neq s$, then $\pi[v]$ is set to u for some $u \in V_{k-1}$, and
- v is inserted into the queue Q.

As we have noted before, there is certainly at most one such point.

The basis is for $k = 0$. We have $V_0 = \{s\}$, since the source s is the only vertex at distance 0 from s. During the initialization, s is grayed, $d[s]$ is set to 0, and s is placed into Q, so the inductive hypothesis holds.

For the inductive step, we start by noting that the queue Q is never empty until the algorithm terminates and that, once a vertex u is inserted into the queue, neither $d[u]$ nor $\pi[u]$ ever changes. By Lemma 23.3, therefore, if vertices are inserted into the queue over the course of the algorithm in the order $v_1, v_2, \ldots, v_r$, then the sequence of distances is monotonically increasing: $d[v_i] \leq d[v_{i+1}]$ for $i = 1, 2, \ldots, r - 1$.

Now let us consider an arbitrary vertex $v \in V_k$, where $k \geq 1$. The monotonicity property, combined with $d[v] \geq k$ (by Lemma 23.2) and the inductive hypothesis, implies that v must be discovered after all vertices in V_{k-1} are enqueued, if it is discovered at all.

Since $\delta(s, v) = k$, there is a path of k edges from s to v, and thus there exists a vertex $u \in V_{k-1}$ such that $(u, v) \in E$. Without loss of generality, let u be the first such vertex grayed, which must happen since, by induction, all vertices in V_{k-1} are grayed. The code for BFS enqueues every grayed vertex, and hence u must ultimately appear as the head of the queue in line 10. When u appears as the head, its adjacency list is scanned and v is discovered. (The vertex v could not have been discovered earlier, since it is not adjacent to any vertex in V_j for $j < k - 1$—otherwise, v could not belong to V_k—and by assumption, u is the first vertex discovered in V_{k-1} to which v is adjacent.) Line 13 grays v, line 14 establishes $d[v] =$

$d[u] + 1 = k$, line 15 sets $\pi[v]$ to u, and line 16 inserts v into the queue. Since v is an arbitrary vertex in V_k, the inductive hypothesis is proved.

To conclude the proof of the lemma, observe that if $v \in V_k$, then by what we have just seen, $\pi[v] \in V_{k-1}$. Thus, we can obtain a shortest path from s to v by taking a shortest path from s to $\pi[v]$ and then traversing the edge $(\pi[v], v)$.   ■

Breadth-first trees

The procedure BFS builds a breadth-first tree as it searches the graph, as illustrated in Figure 23.3. The tree is represented by the π field in each vertex. More formally, for a graph $G = (V, E)$ with source s, we define the *predecessor subgraph* of G as $G_\pi = (V_\pi, E_\pi)$, where

$$V_\pi = \{v \in V : \pi[v] \neq \text{NIL}\} \cup \{s\}$$

and

$$E_\pi = \{(\pi[v], v) \in E : v \in V_\pi - \{s\}\} \ .$$

The predecessor subgraph G_π is a *breadth-first tree* if V_π consists of the vertices reachable from s and, for all $v \in V_\pi$, there is a unique simple path from s to v in G_π that is also a shortest path from s to v in G. A breadth-first tree is in fact a tree, since it is connected and $|E_\pi| = |V_\pi| - 1$ (see Theorem 5.2). The edges in E_π are called *tree edges*.

After BFS has been run from a source s on a graph G, the following lemma shows that the predecessor subgraph is a breadth-first tree.

Lemma 23.5
When applied to a directed or undirected graph $G = (V, E)$, procedure BFS constructs π so that the predecessor subgraph $G_\pi = (V_\pi, E_\pi)$ is a breadth-first tree.

Proof   Line 15 of BFS only sets $\pi[v] = u$ if $(u, v) \in E$ and $\delta(s, v) < \infty$— that is, if v is reachable from s—and thus V_π consists of the vertices in V reachable from v. Since G_π forms a tree, it contains a unique path from s to each vertex in V_π. By applying Theorem 23.4 inductively, we conclude that every such path is a shortest path.   ■

The following procedure prints out the vertices on a shortest path from s to v, assuming that BFS has already been run to compute the shortest-path tree.

PRINT-PATH(G, s, v)
1 **if** $v = s$
2   **then** print s
3   **else if** $\pi[v] = $ NIL
4   **then** print "no path from" s "to" v "exists"
5   **else** PRINT-PATH($G, s, \pi[v]$)
6   print v

This procedure runs in time linear in the number of vertices in the path printed, since each recursive call is for a path one vertex shorter.

Exercises

23.2-1
Show the result of running breadth-first search on the directed graph of Figure 23.2(a), using vertex 3 as the source.

23.2-2
Show the result of running breadth-first search on the undirected graph of Figure 23.3, using vertex u as the source.

23.2-3
What is the running time of BFS if its input graph is represented by an adjacency matrix and the algorithm is modified to handle this form of input?

23.2-4
Argue that in a breadth-first search, the value $d[u]$ assigned to a vertex u is independent of the order in which the vertices in each adjacency list are given.

23.2-5
Give an example of a directed graph $G = (V, E)$, a source vertex $s \in V$, and a set of tree edges $E_\pi \subseteq E$ such that for each vertex $v \in V$, the unique path in E_π from s to v is a shortest path in G, yet the set of edges E_π cannot be produced by running BFS on G, no matter how the vertices are ordered in each adjacency list.

23.2-6
Give an efficient algorithm to determine if an undirected graph is bipartite.

23.2-7 ★
The *diameter* of a tree $T = (V, E)$ is given by

$$\max_{u,v \in V} \delta(u, v) \; ;$$

that is, the diameter is the largest of all shortest-path distances in the tree. Give an efficient algorithm to compute the diameter of a tree, and analyze the running time of your algorithm.

23.2-8
Let $G = (V, E)$ be an undirected graph. Give an $O(V + E)$-time algorithm to compute a path in G that traverses each edge in E exactly once in each direction. Describe how you can find your way out of a maze if you are given a large supply of pennies.

23.3 Depth-first search

The strategy followed by depth-first search is, as its name implies, to search "deeper" in the graph whenever possible. In depth-first search, edges are explored out of the most recently discovered vertex v that still has unexplored edges leaving it. When all of v's edges have been explored, the search "backtracks" to explore edges leaving the vertex from which v was discovered. This process continues until we have discovered all the vertices that are reachable from the original source vertex. If any undiscovered vertices remain, then one of them is selected as a new source and the search is repeated from that source. This entire process is repeated until all vertices are discovered.

As in breadth-first search, whenever a vertex v is discovered during a scan of the adjacency list of an already discovered vertex u, depth-first search records this event by setting v's predecessor field $\pi[v]$ to u. Unlike breadth-first search, whose predecessor subgraph forms a tree, the predecessor subgraph produced by a depth-first search may be composed of several trees, because the search may be repeated from multiple sources. The ***predecessor subgraph*** of a depth-first search is therefore defined slightly differently from that of a breadth-first search: we let $G_\pi = (V, E_\pi)$, where

$$E_\pi = \{(\pi[v], v) : v \in V \text{ and } \pi[v] \neq \text{NIL}\} .$$

The predecessor subgraph of a depth-first search forms a ***depth-first forest*** composed of several ***depth-first trees***. The edges in E_π are called ***tree edges***.

As in breadth-first search, vertices are colored during the search to indicate their state. Each vertex is initially white, is grayed when it is ***discovered*** in the search, and is blackened when it is ***finished***, that is, when its adjacency list has been examined completely. This technique guarantees that each vertex ends up in exactly one depth-first tree, so that these trees are disjoint.

Besides creating a depth-first forest, depth-first search also ***timestamps*** each vertex. Each vertex v has two timestamps: the first timestamp $d[v]$ records when v is first discovered (and grayed), and the second timestamp $f[v]$ records when the search finishes examining v's adjacency list (and blackens v). These timestamps are used in many graph algorithms and are generally helpful in reasoning about the behavior of depth-first search.

The procedure DFS below records when it discovers vertex u in the variable $d[u]$ and when it finishes vertex u in the variable $f[u]$. These timestamps are integers between 1 and $2|V|$, since there is one discovery event and one finishing event for each of the $|V|$ vertices. For every vertex u,

$$d[u] < f[u] .\tag{23.1}$$

Vertex u is WHITE before time $d[u]$, GRAY between time $d[u]$ and time $f[u]$, and BLACK thereafter.

The following pseudocode is the basic depth-first-search algorithm. The input graph G may be undirected or directed. The variable *time* is a global variable that we use for timestamping.

DFS(G)

```
1   for each vertex u ∈ V[G]
2       do color[u] ← WHITE
3           π[u] ← NIL
4   time ← 0
5   for each vertex u ∈ V[G]
6       do if color[u] = WHITE
7           then DFS-VISIT(u)
```

DFS-VISIT(u)

```
1   color[u] ← GRAY          ▷ White vertex u has just been discovered.
2   d[u] ← time ← time + 1
3   for each v ∈ Adj[u]       ▷ Explore edge (u, v).
4       do if color[v] = WHITE
5           then π[v] ← u
6               DFS-VISIT(v)
7   color[u] ← BLACK          ▷ Blacken u; it is finished.
8   f[u] ← time ← time + 1
```

Figure 23.4 illustrates the progress of DFS on the graph shown in Figure 23.2.

Procedure DFS works as follows. Lines 1–3 paint all vertices white and initialize their π fields to NIL. Line 4 resets the global time counter. Lines 5–7 check each vertex in V in turn and, when a white vertex is found, visit it using DFS-VISIT. Every time DFS-VISIT(u) is called in line 7, vertex u becomes the root of a new tree in the depth-first forest. When DFS returns, every vertex u has been assigned a discovery time $d[u]$ and a finishing time $f[u]$.

In each call DFS-VISIT(u), vertex u is initially white. Line 1 paints u gray, and line 2 records the discovery time $d[u]$ by incrementing and saving

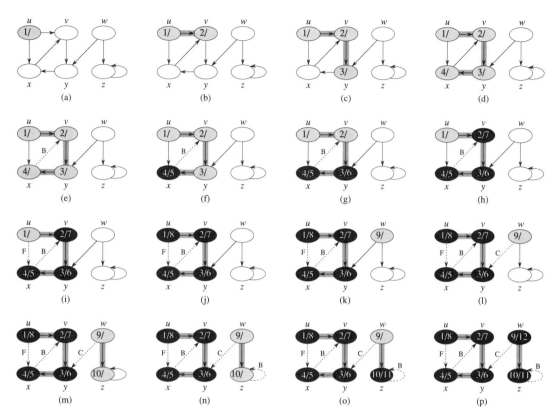

Figure 23.4 The progress of the depth-first-search algorithm DFS on a directed graph. As edges are explored by the algorithm, they are shown as either shaded (if they are tree edges) or dashed (otherwise). Nontree edges are labeled B, C, or F according to whether they are back, cross, or forward edges. Vertices are timestamped by discovery time/finishing time.

the global variable *time*. Lines 3–6 examine each vertex v adjacent to u and recursively visit v if it is white. As each vertex $v \in Adj[u]$ is considered in line 3, we say that edge (u, v) is **explored** by the depth-first search. Finally, after every edge leaving u has been explored, lines 7–8 paint u black and record the finishing time in $f[u]$.

What is the running time of DFS? The loops on lines 1–2 and lines 5–7 of DFS take time $\Theta(V)$, exclusive of the time to execute the calls to DFS-VISIT. The procedure DFS-VISIT is called exactly once for each vertex $v \in V$, since DFS-VISIT is invoked only on white vertices and the first thing it does is paint the vertex gray. During an execution of DFS-VISIT(v), the loop on lines 3–6 is executed $|Adj[v]|$ times. Since

$$\sum_{v \in V} |Adj[v]| = \Theta(E) \ ,$$

the total cost of executing lines 2–5 of DFS-VISIT is $\Theta(E)$. The running time of DFS is therefore $\Theta(V + E)$.

Properties of depth-first search

Depth-first search yields much information about the structure of a graph. Perhaps the most basic property of depth-first search is that the predecessor subgraph G_π does indeed form a forest of trees, since the structure of the depth-first trees exactly mirrors the structure of recursive calls of DFS-VISIT. That is, $u = \pi[v]$ if and only if DFS-VISIT(v) was called during a search of u's adjacency list.

Another important property of depth-first search is that discovery and finishing times have *parenthesis structure*. If we represent the discovery of vertex u with a left parenthesis "(u" and represent its finishing by a right parenthesis "u)," then the history of discoveries and finishings makes a well-formed expression in the sense that the parentheses are properly nested. For example, the depth-first search of Figure 23.5(a) corresponds to the parenthesization shown in Figure 23.5(b). Another way of stating the condition of parenthesis structure is given in the following theorem.

Theorem 23.6 (Parenthesis theorem)
In any depth-first search of a (directed or undirected) graph $G = (V, E)$, for any two vertices u and v, exactly one of the following three conditions holds:

- the intervals $[d[u], f[u]]$ and $[d[v], f[v]]$ are entirely disjoint,
- the interval $[d[u], f[u]]$ is contained entirely within the interval $[d[v], f[v]]$, and u is a descendant of v in the depth-first tree, or
- the interval $[d[v], f[v]]$ is contained entirely within the interval $[d[u], f[u]]$, and v is a descendant of u in the depth-first tree.

Proof   We begin with the case in which $d[u] < d[v]$. There are two subcases to consider, according to whether $d[v] < f[u]$ or not. In the first subcase, $d[v] < f[u]$, so v was discovered while u was still gray. This implies that v is a descendant of u. Moreover, since v was discovered more recently than u, all of its outgoing edges are explored, and v is finished, before the search returns to and finishes u. In this case, therefore, the interval $[d[v], f[v]]$ is entirely contained within the interval $[d[u], f[u]]$. In the other subcase, $f[u] < d[v]$, and inequality (23.1) implies that the intervals $[d[u], f[u]]$ and $[d[v], f[v]]$ are disjoint.

The case in which $d[v] < d[u]$ is similar, with the roles of u and v reversed in the above argument.   ■

Corollary 23.7 (Nesting of descendants' intervals)
Vertex v is a proper descendant of vertex u in the depth-first forest for a (directed or undirected) graph G if and only if $d[u] < d[v] < f[v] < f[u]$.

Proof   Immediate from Theorem 23.6.   ■

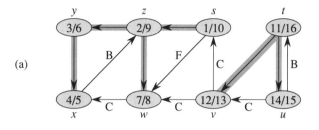

(a)

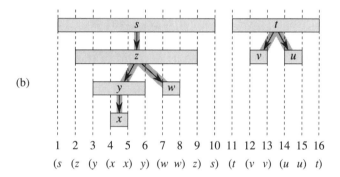

(b)

$(s \; (z \; (y \; (x \; x) \; y) \; (w \; w) \; z) \; s) \; (t \; (v \; v) \; (u \; u) \; t)$

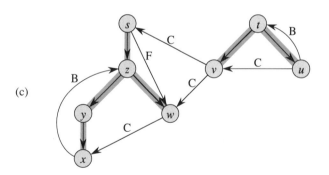

(c)

Figure 23.5 Properties of depth-first search. **(a)** The result of a depth-first search of a directed graph. Vertices are timestamped and edge types are indicated as in Figure 23.4. **(b)** Intervals for the discovery time and finishing time of each vertex correspond to the parenthesization shown. Each rectangle spans the interval given by the discovery and finishing times of the corresponding vertex. Tree edges are shown. If two intervals overlap, then one is nested within the other, and the vertex corresponding to the smaller interval is a descendant of the vertex corresponding to the larger. **(c)** The graph of part (a) redrawn with all tree and forward edges going down within a depth-first tree and all back edges going up from a descendant to an ancestor.

The next theorem gives another important characterization of when one vertex is a descendant of another in the depth-first forest.

Theorem 23.8 (White-path theorem)

In a depth-first forest of a (directed or undirected) graph $G = (V, E)$, vertex v is a descendant of vertex u if and only if at the time $d[u]$ that the search discovers u, vertex v can be reached from u along a path consisting entirely of white vertices.

Proof   ⇒: Assume that v is a descendant of u. Let w be any vertex on the path between u and v in the depth-first tree, so that w is a descendant of u. By Corollary 23.7, $d[u] < d[w]$, and so w is white at time $d[u]$.

⇐: Suppose that vertex v is reachable from u along a path of white vertices at time $d[u]$, but v does not become a descendant of u in the depth-first tree. Without loss of generality, assume that every other vertex along the path becomes a descendant of u. (Otherwise, let v be the closest vertex to u along the path that doesn't become a descendant of u.) Let w be the predecessor of v in the path, so that w is a descendant of u (w and u may in fact be the same vertex) and, by Corollary 23.7, $f[w] \leq f[u]$. Note that v must be discovered after u is discovered, but before w is finished. Therefore, $d[u] < d[v] < f[w] \leq f[u]$. Theorem 23.6 then implies that the interval $[d[v], f[v]]$ is contained entirely within the interval $[d[u], f[u]]$. By Corollary 23.7, v must after all be a descendant of u.   ∎

Classification of edges

Another interesting property of depth-first search is that the search can be used to classify the edges of the input graph $G = (V, E)$. This edge classification can be used to glean important information about a graph. For example, in the next section, we shall see that a directed graph is acyclic if and only if a depth-first search yields no "back" edges (Lemma 23.10).

We can define four edge types in terms of the depth-first forest G_π produced by a depth-first search on G.

1. ***Tree edges*** are edges in the depth-first forest G_π. Edge (u, v) is a tree edge if v was first discovered by exploring edge (u, v).

2. ***Back edges*** are those edges (u, v) connecting a vertex u to an ancestor v in a depth-first tree. Self-loops are considered to be back edges.

3. ***Forward edges*** are those nontree edges (u, v) connecting a vertex u to a descendant v in a depth-first tree.

4. ***Cross edges*** are all other edges. They can go between vertices in the same depth-first tree, as long as one vertex is not an ancestor of the other, or they can go between vertices in different depth-first trees.

In Figures 23.4 and 23.5, edges are labeled to indicate their type. Figure 23.5(c) also shows how the graph of Figure 23.5(a) can be redrawn so that all tree and forward edges head downward in a depth-first tree and all back edges go up. Any graph can be redrawn in this fashion.

The DFS algorithm can be modified to classify edges as it encounters them. The key idea is that each edge (u, v) can be classified by the color of the vertex v that is reached when the edge is first explored (except that forward and cross edges are not distinguished):

1. WHITE indicates a tree edge,

2. GRAY indicates a back edge, and

3. BLACK indicates a forward or cross edge.

The first case is immediate from the specification of the algorithm. For the second case, observe that the gray vertices always form a linear chain of descendants corresponding to the stack of active DFS-VISIT invocations; the number of gray vertices is one more than the depth in the depth-first forest of the vertex most recently discovered. Exploration always proceeds from the deepest gray vertex, so an edge that reaches another gray vertex reaches an ancestor. The third case handles the remaining possibility; it can be shown that such an edge (u, v) is a forward edge if $d[u] < d[v]$ and a cross edge if $d[u] > d[v]$. (See Exercise 23.3-4.)

In an undirected graph, there may be some ambiguity in the type classification, since (u, v) and (v, u) are really the same edge. In such a case, the edge is classified as the *first* type in the classification list that applies. Equivalently (see Exercise 23.3-5), the edge is classified according to whichever of (u, v) or (v, u) is encountered first during the execution of the algorithm.

We now show that forward and cross edges never occur in a depth-first search of an undirected graph.

Theorem 23.9
In a depth-first search of an undirected graph G, every edge of G is either a tree edge or a back edge.

Proof Let (u, v) be an arbitrary edge of G, and suppose without loss of generality that $d[u] < d[v]$. Then, v must be discovered and finished before we finish u, since v is on u's adjacency list. If the edge (u, v) is explored first in the direction from u to v, then (u, v) becomes a tree edge. If (u, v) is explored first in the direction from v to u, then (u, v) is a back edge, since u is still gray at the time the edge is first explored. ∎

We shall see many applications of these theorems in the following sections.

Exercises

23.3-1
Make a 3-by-3 chart with row and column labels WHITE, GRAY, and BLACK. In each cell (i, j), indicate whether, at any point during a depth-first search

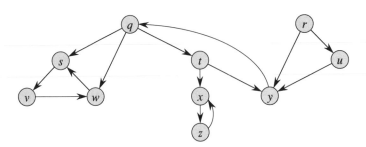

Figure 23.6   A directed graph for use in Exercises 23.3-2 and 23.5-2.

of a directed graph, there can be an edge from a vertex of color i to a vertex of color j. For each possible edge, indicate what edge types it can be. Make a second such chart for depth-first search of an undirected graph.

23.3-2
Show how depth-first search works on the graph of Figure 23.6. Assume that the **for** loop of lines 5–7 of the DFS procedure considers the vertices in alphabetical order, and assume that each adjacency list is ordered alphabetically. Show the discovery and finishing times for each vertex, and show the classification of each edge.

23.3-3
Show the parenthesis structure of the depth-first search shown in Figure 23.4.

23.3-4
Show that edge (u, v) is

a. a tree edge or forward edge if and only if $d[u] < d[v] < f[v] < f[u]$,

b. a back edge if and only if $d[v] < d[u] < f[u] < f[v]$, and

c. a cross edge if and only if $d[v] < f[v] < d[u] < f[u]$.

23.3-5
Show that in an undirected graph, classifying an edge (u, v) as a tree edge or a back edge according to whether (u, v) or (v, u) is encountered first during the depth-first search is equivalent to classifying it according to the priority of types in the classification scheme.

23.3-6
Give a counterexample to the conjecture that if there is a path from u to v in a directed graph G, and if $d[u] < d[v]$ in a depth-first search of G, then v is a descendant of u in the depth-first forest produced.

23.3-7
Modify the pseudocode for depth-first search so that it prints out every edge in the directed graph G, together with its type. Show what modifications, if any, must be made if G is undirected.

23.3-8
Explain how a vertex u of a directed graph can end up in a depth-first tree containing only u, even though u has both incoming and outgoing edges in G.

23.3-9
Show that a depth-first search of an undirected graph G can be used to identify the connected components of G, and that the depth-first forest contains as many trees as G has connected components. More precisely, show how to modify depth-first search so that each vertex v is assigned an integer label $cc[v]$ between 1 and k, where k is the number of connected components of G, such that $cc[u] = cc[v]$ if and only if u and v are in the same connected component.

23.3-10 ⋆
A directed graph $G = (V, E)$ is ***singly connected*** if $u \rightsquigarrow v$ implies that there is at most one simple path from u to v for all vertices $u, v \in V$. Give an efficient algorithm to determine whether or not a directed graph is singly connected.

23.4 Topological sort

This section shows how depth-first search can be used to perform topological sorts of directed acyclic graphs, or "dags" as they are sometimes called. A ***topological sort*** of a dag $G = (V, E)$ is a linear ordering of all its vertices such that if G contains an edge (u, v), then u appears before v in the ordering. (If the graph is not acyclic, then no linear ordering is possible.) A topological sort of a graph can be viewed as an ordering of its vertices along a horizontal line so that all directed edges go from left to right. Topological sorting is thus different from the usual kind of "sorting" studied in Part II.

Directed acyclic graphs are used in many applications to indicate precedences among events. Figure 23.7 gives an example that arises when Professor Bumstead gets dressed in the morning. The professor must don certain garments before others (e.g., socks before shoes). Other items may be put on in any order (e.g., socks and pants). A directed edge (u, v) in the dag of Figure 23.7(a) indicates that garment u must be donned before garment v. A topological sort of this dag therefore gives an order for getting dressed. Figure 23.7(b) shows the topologically sorted dag as an ordering

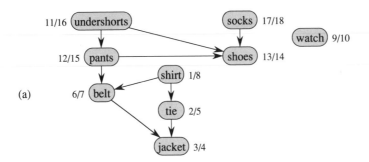

(a)

(b)

Figure 23.7 (a) Professor Bumstead topologically sorts his clothing when getting dressed. Each directed edge (u, v) means that garment u must be put on before garment v. The discovery and finishing times from a depth-first search are shown next to each vertex. (b) The same graph shown topologically sorted. Its vertices are arranged from left to right in order of decreasing finishing time. Note that all directed edges go from left to right.

of vertices along a horizontal line such that all directed edges go from left to right.

The following simple algorithm topologically sorts a dag.

TOPOLOGICAL-SORT(G)

1   call DFS(G) to compute finishing times $f[v]$ for each vertex v
2   as each vertex is finished, insert it onto the front of a linked list
3   **return** the linked list of vertices

Figure 23.7(b) shows how the topologically sorted vertices appear in reverse order of their finishing times.

We can perform a topological sort in time $\Theta(V + E)$, since depth-first search takes $\Theta(V + E)$ time and it takes $O(1)$ time to insert each of the $|V|$ vertices onto the front of the linked list.

We prove the correctness of this algorithm using the following key lemma characterizing directed acyclic graphs.

Lemma 23.10
A directed graph G is acyclic if and only if a depth-first search of G yields no back edges.

Proof   ⇒: Suppose that there is a back edge (u, v). Then, vertex v is an ancestor of vertex u in the depth-first forest. There is thus a path from v to u in G, and the back edge (u, v) completes a cycle.

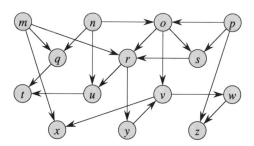

Figure 23.8 A dag for topological sorting.

⇐: Suppose that G contains a cycle c. We show that a depth-first search of G yields a back edge. Let v be the first vertex to be discovered in c, and let (u, v) be the preceding edge in c. At time $d[v]$, there is a path of white vertices from v to u. By the white-path theorem, vertex u becomes a descendant of v in the depth-first forest. Therefore, (u, v) is a back edge. ■

Theorem 23.11
TOPOLOGICAL-SORT(G) produces a topological sort of a directed acyclic graph G.

Proof Suppose that DFS is run on a given dag $G = (V, E)$ to determine finishing times for its vertices. It suffices to show that for any pair of distinct vertices $u, v \in V$, if there is an edge in G from u to v, then $f[v] < f[u]$. Consider any edge (u, v) explored by DFS(G). When this edge is explored, v cannot be gray, since then v would be an ancestor of u and (u, v) would be a back edge, contradicting Lemma 23.10. Therefore, v must be either white or black. If v is white, it becomes a descendant of u, and so $f[v] < f[u]$. If v is black, then $f[v] < f[u]$ as well. Thus, for any edge (u, v) in the dag, we have $f[v] < f[u]$, proving the theorem. ■

Exercises

23.4-1
Show the ordering of vertices produced by TOPOLOGICAL-SORT when it is run on the dag of Figure 23.8.

23.4-2
There are many different orderings of the vertices of a directed graph G that are topological sorts of G. TOPOLOGICAL-SORT produces the ordering that is the reverse of the depth-first finishing times. Show that not all topological sorts can be produced in this way: there exists a graph G such that one of the topological sorts of G cannot be produced by TOPOLOGICAL-SORT, no matter what adjacency-list structure is given for G. Show also

that there exists a graph for which two distinct adjacency-list representations yield the same topological sort.

23.4-3
Give an algorithm that determines whether or not a given undirected graph $G = (V, E)$ contains a cycle. Your algorithm should run in $O(V)$ time, independent of $|E|$.

23.4-4
Prove or disprove: If a directed graph G contains cycles, then TOPOLOGICAL-SORT(G) produces a vertex ordering that minimizes the number of "bad" edges that are inconsistent with the ordering produced.

23.4-5
Another way to perform topological sorting on a directed acyclic graph $G = (V, E)$ is to repeatedly find a vertex of in-degree 0, output it, and remove it and all of its outgoing edges from the graph. Explain how to implement this idea so that it runs in time $O(V + E)$. What happens to this algorithm if G has cycles?

23.5   Strongly connected components

We now consider a classic application of depth-first search: decomposing a directed graph into its strongly connected components. This section shows how to do this decomposition using two depth-first searches. Many algorithms that work with directed graphs begin with such a decomposition; this approach often allows the original problem to be divided into subproblems, one for each strongly connected component. Combining the solutions to the subproblems follows the structure of connections between strongly connected components; this structure can be represented by a graph known as the "component" graph, defined in Exercise 23.5-4.

Recall from Chapter 5 that a strongly connected component of a directed graph $G = (V, E)$ is a maximal set of vertices $U \subseteq V$ such that for every pair of vertices u and v in U, we have both $u \rightsquigarrow v$ and $v \rightsquigarrow u$; that is, vertices u and v are reachable from each other. Figure 23.9 shows an example.

Our algorithm for finding strongly connected components of a graph $G = (V, E)$ uses the transpose of G, which is defined in Exercise 23.1-3 to be the graph $G^{\mathrm{T}} = (V, E^{\mathrm{T}})$, where $E^{\mathrm{T}} = \{(u, v) : (v, u) \in E\}$. That is, E^{T} consists of the edges of G with their directions reversed. Given an adjacency-list representation of G, the time to create G^{T} is $O(V + E)$. It is interesting to observe that G and G^{T} have exactly the same strongly connected components: u and v are reachable from each other in G if and only if they are reachable from each other in G^{T}. Figure 23.9(b) shows

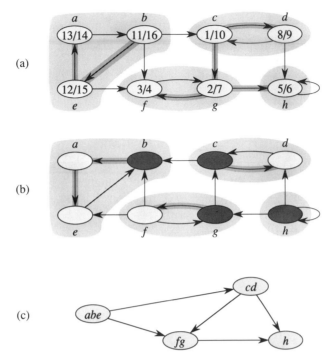

Figure 23.9   (a) A directed graph G. The strongly connected components of G are shown as shaded regions. Each vertex is labeled with its discovery and finishing times. Tree edges are shaded. (b) The graph G^{T}, the transpose of G. The depth-first tree computed in line 3 of STRONGLY-CONNECTED-COMPONENTS is shown, with tree edges shaded. Each strongly connected component corresponds to one depth-first tree. Vertices b, c, g, and h, which are heavily shaded, are forefathers of every vertex in their strongly connected component; these vertices are also the roots of the depth-first trees produced by the depth-first search of G^{T}. (c) The acyclic component graph G^{SCC} obtained by shrinking each strongly connected component of G to a single vertex.

the transpose of the graph in Figure 23.9(a), with the strongly connected components shaded.

The following linear-time (i.e., $\Theta(V + E)$-time) algorithm computes the strongly connected components of a directed graph $G = (V, E)$ using two depth-first searches, one on G and one on G^{T}.

STRONGLY-CONNECTED-COMPONENTS(G)

1 call DFS(G) to compute finishing times $f[u]$ for each vertex u
2 compute G^{T}
3 call DFS(G^{T}), but in the main loop of DFS, consider the vertices
          in order of decreasing $f[u]$ (as computed in line 1)
4 output the vertices of each tree in the depth-first forest of step 3 as a
          separate strongly connected component

This simple-looking algorithm seems to have nothing to do with strongly connected components. In the remainder of this section, we unravel the mystery of its design and prove its correctness. We begin with two useful observations.

Lemma 23.12

If two vertices are in the same strongly connected component, then no path between them ever leaves the strongly connected component.

Proof Let u and v be two vertices in the same strongly connected component. By the definition of strongly connected component, there are paths from u to v and from v to u. Let vertex w be on some path $u \rightsquigarrow w \rightsquigarrow v$, so that w is reachable from u. Moreover, since there is a path $v \rightsquigarrow u$, we know that u is reachable from w by the path $w \rightsquigarrow v \rightsquigarrow u$. Therefore, u and w are in the same strongly connected component. Since w was chosen arbitrarily, the theorem is proved.   ∎

Theorem 23.13

In any depth-first search, all vertices in the same strongly connected component are placed in the same depth-first tree.

Proof Of the vertices in the strongly connected component, let r be the first discovered. Because r is first, the other vertices in the strongly connected component are white at the time it is discovered. There are paths from r to every other vertex in the strongly connected component; because these paths never leave the strongly connected component (by Lemma 23.12), all vertices on them are white. Thus, by the white-path theorem, every vertex in the strongly connected component becomes a descendant of r in the depth-first tree.   ∎

In the rest of this section, the notations $d[u]$ and $f[u]$ refer to the discovery and finishing times as computed by the first depth-first search in line 1 of STRONGLY-CONNECTED-COMPONENTS. Similarly, the notation $u \rightsquigarrow v$ refers to the existence of a path in G, not in G^T.

To prove STRONGLY-CONNECTED-COMPONENTS correct, we introduce the notion of the ***forefather*** $\phi(u)$ of a vertex u, which is the vertex w reachable from u that finished last in the depth-first search of line 1. In other words,

$$\phi(u) = \text{that vertex } w \text{ such that } u \rightsquigarrow w \text{ and } f[w] \text{ is maximized } .$$

Note that $\phi(u) = u$ is possible because u is reachable from itself, and hence

$$f[u] \le f[\phi(u)] . \tag{23.2}$$

We can also show that $\phi(\phi(u)) = \phi(u)$, by the following reasoning. For any vertices $u, v \in V$,

$$u \rightsquigarrow v \text{ implies } f[\phi(v)] \le f[\phi(u)] , \tag{23.3}$$

since $\{w : v \leadsto w\} \subseteq \{w : u \leadsto w\}$ and the forefather has the maximum finishing time of all reachable vertices. Since $\phi(u)$ is reachable from u, formula (23.3) implies that $f[\phi(\phi(u))] \leq f[\phi(u)]$. We also have $f[\phi(u)] \leq f[\phi(\phi(u))]$, by inequality (23.2). Thus, $f[\phi(\phi(u))] = f[\phi(u)]$, and so we have $\phi(\phi(u)) = \phi(u)$, since two vertices that finish at the same time are in fact the same vertex.

As we shall see, every strongly connected component has one vertex that is the forefather of every vertex in the strongly connected component; this forefather is a "representative vertex" for the strongly connected component. In the depth-first search of G, it is the first vertex of the strongly connected component to be discovered, and it is the last vertex of the strongly connected component to be finished. In the depth-first search of G^{T}, it is the root of a depth-first tree. We now prove these properties.

The first theorem justifies calling $\phi(u)$ a "forefather" of u.

Theorem 23.14
In a directed graph $G = (V, E)$, the forefather $\phi(u)$ of any vertex $u \in V$ in any depth-first search of G is an ancestor of u.

Proof If $\phi(u) = u$, the theorem is trivially true. If $\phi(u) \neq u$, consider the colors of the vertices at time $d[u]$. If $\phi(u)$ is black, then $f[\phi(u)] < f[u]$, contradicting inequality (23.2). If $\phi(u)$ is gray, then it is an ancestor of u, and the theorem is proved.

It thus remains to prove that $\phi(u)$ is not white. There are two cases, according to the colors of the intermediate vertices, if any, on the path from u to $\phi(u)$.

1. If every intermediate vertex is white, then $\phi(u)$ becomes a descendant of u, by the white-path theorem. But then $f[\phi(u)] < f[u]$, contradicting inequality (23.2).

2. If some intermediate vertex is nonwhite, let t be the last nonwhite vertex on the path from u to $\phi(u)$. Then, t must be gray, since there is never an edge from a black vertex to a white vertex, and t's successor is white. But then there is a path of white vertices from t to $\phi(u)$, and so $\phi(u)$ is a descendant of t by the white-path theorem. This implies that $f[t] > f[\phi(u)]$, contradicting our choice of $\phi(u)$, since there is a path from u to t. ∎

Corollary 23.15
In any depth-first search of a directed graph $G = (V, E)$, vertices u and $\phi(u)$, for all $u \in V$, lie in the same strongly connected component.

Proof We have $u \leadsto \phi(u)$, by the definition of forefather, and $\phi(u) \leadsto u$, since $\phi(u)$ is an ancestor of u. ∎

The following theorem gives a stronger result relating forefathers to strongly connected components.

Theorem 23.16
In a directed graph $G = (V, E)$, two vertices $u, v \in V$ lie in the same strongly connected component if and only if they have the same forefather in a depth-first search of G.

Proof $\Rightarrow$: Assume that u and v are in the same strongly connected component. Every vertex reachable from u is reachable from v and vice versa, since there are paths in both directions between u and v. By the definition of forefather, then, we conclude that $\phi(u) = \phi(v)$.

$\Leftarrow$: Assume that $\phi(u) = \phi(v)$. By Corollary 23.15, u is in the same strongly connected component as $\phi(u)$, and v is in the same strongly connected component as $\phi(v)$. Therefore, u and v are in the same strongly connected component.   ∎

With Theorem 23.16 in hand, the structure of the algorithm STRONGLY-CONNECTED-COMPONENTS can be more readily understood. The strongly connected components are sets of vertices with the same forefather. Moreover, by Theorem 23.14 and the parenthesis theorem (Theorem 23.6), during the depth-first search in line 1 of STRONGLY-CONNECTED-COMPONENTS a forefather is both the first vertex discovered and the last vertex finished in its strongly connected component.

To understand why we run the depth-first search in line 3 of STRONGLY-CONNECTED-COMPONENTS on G^{T}, consider the vertex r with the largest finishing time computed by the depth-first search in line 1. By the definition of forefather, vertex r must be a forefather, since it is its own forefather: it can reach itself, and no vertex in the graph has a higher finishing time. What are the other vertices in r's strongly connected component? They are those vertices that have r as a forefather—those that can reach r but cannot reach any vertex with a finishing time greater than $f[r]$. But r's finishing time is the maximum of any vertex in G; thus, r's strongly connected component consists simply of those vertices that can reach r. Equivalently, *r's strongly connected component consists of those vertices that r can reach in G^{T}.* Thus, the depth-first search in line 3 identifies all the vertices in r's strongly connected component and blackens them. (A breadth-first search, or *any* search for reachable vertices, could identify this set just as easily.)

After the depth-first search in line 3 is done identifying r's strongly connected component, it begins at the vertex r' with the largest finishing time of any vertex not in r's strongly connected component. Vertex r' must be its own forefather, since it can't reach anything with a higher finishing time (otherwise, it would have been included in r's strongly connected component). By similar reasoning, any vertex that can reach r' that is not already black must be in r''s strongly connected component. Thus, as the depth-first search in line 3 continues, it identifies and blackens every vertex in r''s strongly connected component by searching from r' in G^{T}.

Thus, the depth-first search in line 3 "peels off" strongly connected components one by one. Each component is identified in line 7 of DFS by a call to DFS-VISIT with the forefather of the component as an argument. Recursive calls within DFS-VISIT ultimately blacken each vertex within the component. When DFS-VISIT returns to DFS, the entire component has been blackened and "peeled off." Then, DFS finds the vertex with maximum finishing time among those that have not been blackened; this vertex is the forefather of another component, and the process continues.

The following theorem formalizes this argument.

Theorem 23.17
STRONGLY-CONNECTED-COMPONENTS(G) correctly computes the strongly connected components of a directed graph G.

Proof We argue by induction on the number of depth-first trees found in the depth-first search of G^{T} that the vertices of each tree form a strongly connected component. Each step of the inductive argument proves that a tree formed in the depth-first search of G^{T} is a strongly connected component, assuming that all previous trees produced are strongly connected components. The basis for the induction is trivial, since for the first tree produced there are no previous trees, and hence this assumption is trivially true.

Consider a depth-first tree T with root r produced in the depth-first search of G^{T}. Let $C(r)$ denote the set of vertices with forefather r:

$$C(r) = \{v \in V : \phi(v) = r\} \ .$$

We now prove that a vertex u is placed in T if and only if $u \in C(r)$.

$\Leftarrow$: Theorem 23.13 implies that every vertex in $C(r)$ ends up in the same depth-first tree. Since $r \in C(r)$ and r is the root of T, every element of $C(r)$ ends up in T.

$\Rightarrow$: We show that any vertex w such that $f[\phi(w)] > f[r]$ or $f[\phi(w)] < f[r]$ is not placed in T, by considering these two cases separately. By induction on the number of trees found, any vertex w such that $f[\phi(w)] > f[r]$ is not placed in tree T, since at the time r is selected w will have already been placed in the tree with root $\phi(w)$. Any vertex w such that $f[\phi(w)] < f[r]$ cannot be placed in T, since such a placement would imply $w \rightsquigarrow r$; thus, by formula (23.3) and the property that $r = \phi(r)$, we obtain $f[\phi(w)] \geq f[\phi(r)] = f[r]$, which contradicts $f[\phi(w)] < f[r]$.

Therefore, T contains just those vertices u for which $\phi(u) = r$. That is, T is exactly equal to the strongly connected component $C(r)$, which completes the inductive proof. ∎

Exercises

23.5-1
How can the number of strongly connected components of a graph change if a new edge is added?

23.5-2
Show how the procedure STRONGLY-CONNECTED-COMPONENTS works on the graph of Figure 23.6. Specifically, show the finishing times computed in line 1 and the forest produced in line 3. Assume that the loop of lines 5–7 of DFS considers vertices in alphabetical order and that the adjacency lists are in alphabetical order.

23.5-3
Professor Deaver claims that the algorithm for strongly connected components can be simplified by using the original (instead of the transpose) graph in the second depth-first search and scanning the vertices in order of *increasing* finishing times. Is the professor correct?

23.5-4
We denote the ***component graph*** of $G = (V, E)$ by $G^{\text{SCC}} = (V^{\text{SCC}}, E^{\text{SCC}})$, where V^{SCC} contains one vertex for each strongly connected component of G and E^{SCC} contains the edge (u, v) if there is a directed edge from a vertex in the strongly connected component of G corresponding to u to a vertex in the strongly connected component of G corresponding to v. Figure 23.9(c) shows an example. Prove that G^{SCC} is a dag.

23.5-5
Give an $O(V + E)$-time algorithm to compute the component graph of a directed graph $G = (V, E)$. Make sure that there is at most one edge between two vertices in the component graph your algorithm produces.

23.5-6
Given a directed graph $G = (V, E)$, explain how to create another graph $G' = (V, E')$ such that (a) G' has the same strongly connected components as G, (b) G' has the same component graph as G, and (c) E' is as small as possible. Describe a fast algorithm to compute G'.

23.5-7
A directed graph $G = (V, E)$ is said to be ***semiconnected*** if, for any two vertices $u, v \in V$, we have $u \rightsquigarrow v$ or $v \rightsquigarrow u$. Give an efficient algorithm to determine whether or not G is semiconnected. Prove that your algorithm is correct, and analyze its running time.

Problems

23-1 *Classifying edges by breadth-first search*

A depth-first forest classifies the edges of a graph into tree, back, forward, and cross edges. A breadth-first tree can also be used to classify the edges reachable from the source of the search into the same four categories.

a. Prove that in a breadth-first search of an undirected graph, the following properties hold:

1. There are no back edges and no forward edges.
2. For each tree edge (u, v), we have $d[v] = d[u] + 1$.
3. For each cross edge (u, v), we have $d[v] = d[u]$ or $d[v] = d[u] + 1$.

b. Prove that in a breadth-first search of a directed graph, the following properties hold:

1. There are no forward edges.
2. For each tree edge (u, v), we have $d[v] = d[u] + 1$.
3. For each cross edge (u, v), we have $d[v] \leq d[u] + 1$.
4. For each back edge (u, v), we have $0 \leq d[v] < d[u]$.

23-2 *Articulation points, bridges, and biconnected components*

Let $G = (V, E)$ be a connected, undirected graph. An ***articulation point*** of G is a vertex whose removal disconnects G. A ***bridge*** of G is an edge whose removal disconnects G. A ***biconnected component*** of G is a maximal set of edges such that any two edges in the set lie on a common simple cycle. Figure 23.10 illustrates these definitions. We can determine articulation points, bridges, and biconnected components using depth-first search. Let $G_\pi = (V, E_\pi)$ be a depth-first tree of G.

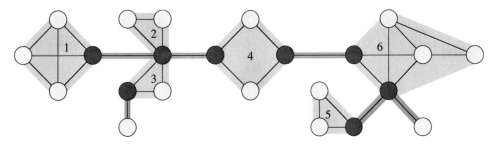

Figure 23.10 The articulation points, bridges, and biconnected components of a connected, undirected graph for use in Problem 23-2. The articulation points are the heavily shaded vertices, the bridges are the heavily shaded edges, and the biconnected components are the edges in the shaded regions, with a *bcc* numbering shown.

a. Prove that the root of G_π is an articulation point of G if and only if it has at least two children in G_π.

b. Let v be a nonroot vertex in G_π. Prove that v is an articulation point of G if and only if there is no back edge (u, w) such that in G_π, u is a descendant of v and w is a proper ancestor of v.

c. Let

$$low[v] = \min \begin{cases} d[v]\,, \\ \{d[w] : (u, w) \text{ is a back edge} \\ \qquad\qquad \text{for some descendant } u \text{ of } v\}\,. \end{cases}$$

Show how to compute $low[v]$ for all vertices $v \in V$ in $O(E)$ time.

d. Show how to compute all articulation points in $O(E)$ time.

e. Prove that an edge of G is a bridge if and only if it does not lie on any simple cycle of G.

f. Show how to compute all the bridges of G in $O(E)$ time.

g. Prove that the biconnected components of G partition the nonbridge edges of G.

h. Give an $O(E)$-time algorithm to label each edge e of G with a positive integer $bcc[e]$ such that $bcc[e] = bcc[e']$ if and only if e and e' are in the same biconnected component.

23-3   *Euler tour*

An ***Euler tour*** of a connected, directed graph $G = (V, E)$ is a cycle that traverses each edge of G exactly once, although it may visit a vertex more than once.

a. Show that G has an Euler tour if and only if

in-degree$(v) = $ out-degree(v)

for each vertex $v \in V$.

b. Describe an $O(E)$-time algorithm to find an Euler tour of G if one exists. (*Hint:* Merge edge-disjoint cycles.)

Chapter notes

Even [65] and Tarjan [188] are excellent references for graph algorithms.

Breadth-first search was discovered by Moore [150] in the context of finding paths through mazes. Lee [134] independently discovered the same algorithm in the context of routing wires on circuit boards.

Hopcroft and Tarjan [102] advocated the use of the adjacency-list representation over the adjacency-matrix representation for sparse graphs and were the first to recognize the algorithmic importance of depth-first search. Depth-first search has been widely used since the late 1950's, especially in artificial intelligence programs.

Tarjan [185] gave a linear-time algorithm for finding strongly connected components. The algorithm for strongly connected components in Section 23.5 is adapted from Aho, Hopcroft, and Ullman [5], who credit it to S. R. Kosaraju and M. Sharir. Knuth [121] was the first to give a linear-time algorithm for topological sorting.

24 Minimum Spanning Trees

In the design of electronic circuitry, it is often necessary to make the pins of several components electrically equivalent by wiring them together. To interconnect a set of n pins, we can use an arrangement of $n - 1$ wires, each connecting two pins. Of all such arrangements, the one that uses the least amount of wire is usually the most desirable.

We can model this wiring problem with a connected, undirected graph $G = (V, E)$, where V is the set of pins, E is the set of possible interconnections between pairs of pins, and for each edge $(u, v) \in E$, we have a weight $w(u, v)$ specifying the cost (amount of wire needed) to connect u and v. We then wish to find an acyclic subset $T \subseteq E$ that connects all of the vertices and whose total weight

$$w(T) = \sum_{(u,v) \in T} w(u, v)$$

is minimized. Since T is acyclic and connects all of the vertices, it must form a tree, which we call a *spanning tree* since it "spans" the graph G. We call the problem of determining the tree T the *minimum-spanning-tree problem*.[1] Figure 24.1 shows an example of a connected graph and its minimum spanning tree.

In this chapter, we shall examine two algorithms for solving the minimum-spanning-tree problem: Kruskal's algorithm and Prim's algorithm. Each can easily be made to run in time $O(E \lg V)$ using ordinary binary heaps. By using Fibonacci heaps, Prim's algorithm can be sped up to run in time $O(E + V \lg V)$, which is an improvement if $|V|$ is much smaller than $|E|$.

The two algorithms also illustrate a heuristic for optimization called the "greedy" strategy. At each step of an algorithm, one of several possible choices must be made. The greedy strategy advocates making the choice that is the best at the moment. Such a strategy is not generally guaranteed to find globally optimal solutions to problems. For the minimum-spanning-

---

[1] The phrase "minimum spanning tree" is a shortened form of the phrase "minimum-weight spanning tree." We are not, for example, minimizing the number of edges in T, since all spanning trees have exactly $|V| - 1$ edges by Theorem 5.2.

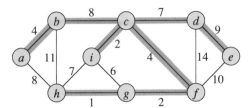

Figure 24.1   A minimum spanning tree for a connected graph. The weights on edges are shown, and the edges in a minimum spanning tree are shaded. The total weight of the tree shown is 37. The tree is not unique: removing the edge (b, c) and replacing it with the edge (a, h) yields another spanning tree with weight 37.

tree problem, however, we can prove that certain greedy strategies do yield a spanning tree with minimum weight. Greedy strategies are discussed at length in Chapter 17. Although the present chapter can be read independently of Chapter 17, the greedy methods presented here are a classic application of the theoretical notions introduced there.

Section 24.1 introduces a "generic" minimum-spanning-tree algorithm that grows a spanning tree by adding one edge at a time. Section 24.2 gives two ways to implement the generic algorithm. The first algorithm, due to Kruskal, is similar to the connected-components algorithm from Section 22.1. The second, due to Prim, is similar to Dijkstra's shortest-paths algorithm (Section 25.2).

24.1   Growing a minimum spanning tree

Assume that we have a connected, undirected graph $G = (V, E)$ with a weight function $w : E \to \mathbf{R}$ and wish to find a minimum spanning tree for G. The two algorithms we consider in this chapter use a greedy approach to the problem, although they differ in how they apply this approach.

This greedy strategy is captured by the following "generic" algorithm, which grows the minimum spanning tree one edge at a time. The algorithm manages a set A that is always a subset of some minimum spanning tree. At each step, an edge (u, v) is determined that can be added to A without violating this invariant, in the sense that $A \cup \{(u, v)\}$ is also a subset of a minimum spanning tree. We call such an edge a *safe edge* for A, since it can be safely added to A without destroying the invariant.

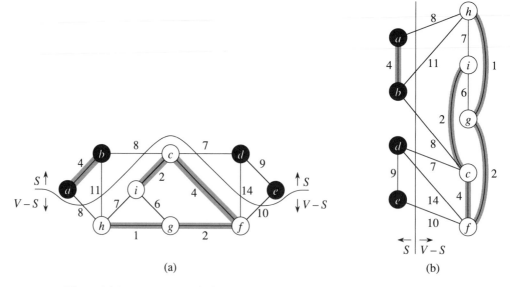

Figure 24.2   Two ways of viewing a cut $(S, V - S)$ of the graph from Figure 24.1.
(**a**) The vertices in the set S are shown in black, and those in $V - S$ are shown in
white. The edges crossing the cut are those connecting white vertices with black
vertices. The edge (d, c) is the unique light edge crossing the cut. A subset A of
the edges is shaded; note that the cut $(S, V - S)$ respects A, since no edge of A
crosses the cut. (**b**) The same graph with the vertices in the set S on the left and
the vertices in the set $V - S$ on the right. An edge crosses the cut if it connects a
vertex on the left with a vertex on the right.

GENERIC-MST(G, w)

1 $A \leftarrow \emptyset$
2 **while** A does not form a spanning tree
3   **do** find an edge (u, v) that is safe for A
4              $A \leftarrow A \cup \{(u, v)\}$
5 **return** A

Note that after line 1, the set A trivially satisfies the invariant that it is
a subset of a minimum spanning tree. The loop in lines 2–4 maintains
the invariant. When the set A is returned in line 5, therefore, it must be
a minimum spanning tree. The tricky part is, of course, finding a safe
edge in line 3. One must exist, since when line 3 is executed, the invariant
dictates that there is a spanning tree T such that $A \subseteq T$, and if there is an
edge $(u, v) \in T$ such that $(u, v) \notin A$, then (u, v) is safe for A.

In the remainder of this section, we provide a rule (Theorem 24.1) for
recognizing safe edges. The next section describes two algorithms that use
this rule to find safe edges efficiently.

We first need some definitions. A **cut** $(S, V - S)$ of an undirected graph
$G = (V, E)$ is a partition of V. Figure 24.2 illustrates this notion. We say

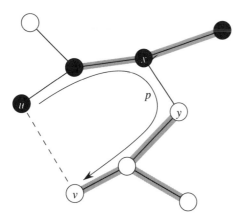

Figure 24.3 The proof of Theorem 24.1. The vertices in S are black, and the vertices in $V - S$ are white. The edges in the minimum spanning tree T are shown, but the edges in the graph G are not. The edges in A are shaded, and (u, v) is a light edge crossing the cut $(S, V - S)$. The edge (x, y) is an edge on the unique path p from u to v in T. A minimum spanning tree T' that contains (u, v) is formed by removing the edge (x, y) from T and adding the edge (u, v).

that an edge $(u, v) \in E$ ***crosses*** the cut $(S, V - S)$ if one of its endpoints is in S and the other is in $V - S$. We say that a cut ***respects*** the set A of edges if no edge in A crosses the cut. An edge is a ***light edge*** crossing a cut if its weight is the minimum of any edge crossing the cut. Note that there can be more than one light edge crossing a cut in the case of ties. More generally, we say that an edge is a ***light edge*** satisfying a given property if its weight is the minimum of any edge satisfying the property.

Our rule for recognizing safe edges is given by the following theorem.

Theorem 24.1
Let $G = (V, E)$ be a connected, undirected graph with a real-valued weight function w defined on E. Let A be a subset of E that is included in some minimum spanning tree for G, let $(S, V - S)$ be any cut of G that respects A, and let (u, v) be a light edge crossing $(S, V - S)$. Then, edge (u, v) is safe for A.

Proof Let T be a minimum spanning tree that includes A, and assume that T does not contain the light edge (u, v), since if it does, we are done. We shall construct another minimum spanning tree T' that includes $A \cup \{(u, v)\}$ by using a cut-and-paste technique, thereby showing that (u, v) is a safe edge for A.

The edge (u, v) forms a cycle with the edges on the path p from u to v in T, as illustrated in Figure 24.3. Since u and v are on opposite sides of the cut $(S, V - S)$, there is at least one edge in T on the path p that also crosses the cut. Let (x, y) be any such edge. The edge (x, y) is not in A, because the cut respects A. Since (x, y) is on the unique path from

u to v in T, removing (x, y) breaks T into two components. Adding (u, v) reconnects them to form a new spanning tree $T' = T - \{(x, y)\} \cup \{(u, v)\}$.

We next show that T' is a minimum spanning tree. Since (u, v) is a light edge crossing $(S, V - S)$ and (x, y) also crosses this cut, $w(u, v) \leq w(x, y)$. Therefore,

$$
\begin{aligned}
w(T') &= w(T) - w(x, y) + w(u, v) \\
&\leq w(T) .
\end{aligned}
$$

But T is a minimum spanning tree, so that $w(T) \leq w(T')$; thus, T' must be a minimum spanning tree also.

It remains to show that (u, v) is actually a safe edge for A. We have $A \subseteq T'$, since $A \subseteq T$ and $(x, y) \notin A$; thus, $A \cup \{(u, v)\} \subseteq T'$. Consequently, since T' is a minimum spanning tree, (u, v) is safe for A. ∎

Theorem 24.1 gives us a better understanding of the workings of the GENERIC-MST algorithm on a connected graph $G = (V, E)$. As the algorithm proceeds, the set A is always acyclic; otherwise, a minimum spanning tree including A would contain a cycle, which is a contradiction. At any point in the execution of the algorithm, the graph $G_A = (V, A)$ is a forest, and each of the connected components of G_A is a tree. (Some of the trees may contain just one vertex, as is the case, for example, when the algorithm begins: A is empty and the forest contains $|V|$ trees, one for each vertex.) Moreover, any safe edge (u, v) for A connects distinct components of G_A, since $A \cup \{(u, v)\}$ must be acyclic.

The loop in lines 2–4 of GENERIC-MST is executed $|V| - 1$ times as each of the $|V| - 1$ edges of a minimum spanning tree is successively determined. Initially, when $A = \emptyset$, there are $|V|$ trees in G_A, and each iteration reduces that number by 1. When the forest contains only a single tree, the algorithm terminates.

The two algorithms in Section 24.2 use the following corollary to Theorem 24.1.

Corollary 24.2

Let $G = (V, E)$ be a connected, undirected graph with a real-valued weight function w defined on E. Let A be a subset of E that is included in some minimum spanning tree for G, and let C be a connected component (tree) in the forest $G_A = (V, A)$. If (u, v) is a light edge connecting C to some other component in G_A, then (u, v) is safe for A.

Proof   The cut $(C, V - C)$ respects A, and (u, v) is therefore a light edge for this cut. ∎

Exercises

24.1-1
Let (u, v) be a minimum-weight edge in a graph G. Show that (u, v) belongs to some minimum spanning tree of G.

24.1-2
Professor Sabatier conjectures the following converse of Theorem 24.1. Let $G = (V, E)$ be a connected, undirected graph with a real-valued weight function w defined on E. Let A be a subset of E that is included in some minimum spanning tree for G, let $(S, V - S)$ be any cut of G that respects A, and let (u, v) be a safe edge for A crossing $(S, V - S)$. Then, (u, v) is a light edge for the cut. Show that the professor's conjecture is incorrect by giving a counterexample.

24.1-3
Show that if an edge (u, v) is contained in some minimum spanning tree, then it is a light edge crossing some cut of the graph.

24.1-4
Give a simple example of a graph such that the set of all edges that are light edges crossing some cut in the graph does not form a minimum spanning tree.

24.1-5
Let e be a maximum-weight edge on some cycle of $G = (V, E)$. Prove that there is a minimum spanning tree of $G' = (V, E - \{e\})$ that is also a minimum spanning tree of G.

24.1-6
Show that a graph has a unique minimum spanning tree if, for every cut of the graph, there is a unique light edge crossing the cut. Show that the converse is not true by giving a counterexample.

24.1-7
Argue that if all of the edge weights of a graph are positive, then any subset of edges that connects all of the vertices and has minimum total weight must be a tree. Give an example to show that the same conclusion does not follow if we allow some weights to be nonpositive.

24.1-8
Let T be a minimum spanning tree of a graph G, and let L be the sorted list of the edge weights of T. Show that for any other minimum spanning tree T' of G, the list L is also the sorted list of edge weights of T'.

24.1-9

Let T be a minimum spanning tree of a graph $G = (V, E)$, and let V' be a subset of V. Let T' be the subgraph of T induced by V', and let G' be the subgraph of G induced by V'. Show that if T' is connected, then T' is a minimum spanning tree of G'.

24.2   The algorithms of Kruskal and Prim

The two minimum-spanning-tree algorithms described in this section are elaborations of the generic algorithm. They each use a specific rule to determine a safe edge in line 3 of GENERIC-MST. In Kruskal's algorithm, the set A is a forest. The safe edge added to A is always a least-weight edge in the graph that connects two distinct components. In Prim's algorithm, the set A forms a single tree. The safe edge added to A is always a least-weight edge connecting the tree to a vertex not in the tree.

Kruskal's algorithm

Kruskal's algorithm is based directly on the generic minimum-spanning-tree algorithm given in Section 24.1. It finds a safe edge to add to the growing forest by finding, of all the edges that connect any two trees in the forest, an edge (u, v) of least weight. Let C_1 and C_2 denote the two trees that are connected by (u, v). Since (u, v) must be a light edge connecting C_1 to some other tree, Corollary 24.2 implies that (u, v) is a safe edge for C_1. Kruskal's algorithm is a greedy algorithm, because at each step it adds to the forest an edge of least possible weight.

Our implementation of Kruskal's algorithm is like the algorithm to compute connected components from Section 22.1. It uses a disjoint-set data structure to maintain several disjoint sets of elements. Each set contains the vertices in a tree of the current forest. The operation FIND-SET(u) returns a representative element from the set that contains u. Thus, we can determine whether two vertices u and v belong to the same tree by testing whether FIND-SET(u) equals FIND-SET(v). The combining of trees is accomplished by the UNION procedure.

MST-KRUSKAL(G, w)

```
1  A ← ∅
2  for each vertex v ∈ V[G]
3       do MAKE-SET(v)
4  sort the edges of E by nondecreasing weight w
5  for each edge (u, v) ∈ E, in order by nondecreasing weight
6       do if FIND-SET(u) ≠ FIND-SET(v)
7            then A ← A ∪ {(u, v)}
8                 UNION(u, v)
9  return A
```

Kruskal's algorithm works as shown in Figure 24.4. Lines 1–3 initialize the set A to the empty set and create $|V|$ trees, one containing each vertex. The edges in E are sorted into order by nondecreasing weight in line 4. The **for** loop in lines 5–8 checks, for each edge (u, v), whether the endpoints u and v belong to the same tree. If they do, then the edge (u, v) cannot be added to the forest without creating a cycle, and the edge is discarded. Otherwise, the two vertices belong to different trees, and the edge (u, v) is added to A in line 7, and the vertices in the two trees are merged in line 8.

The running time of Kruskal's algorithm for a graph $G = (V, E)$ depends on the implementation of the disjoint-set data structure. We shall assume the disjoint-set-forest implementation of Section 22.3 with the union-by-rank and path-compression heuristics, since it is the asymptotically fastest implementation known. Initialization takes time $O(V)$, and the time to sort the edges in line 4 is $O(E \lg E)$. There are $O(E)$ operations on the disjoint-set forest, which in total take $O(E \, \alpha(E, V))$ time, where α is the functional inverse of Ackermann's function defined in Section 22.4. Since $\alpha(E, V) = O(\lg E)$, the total running time of Kruskal's algorithm is $O(E \lg E)$.

Prim's algorithm

Like Kruskal's algorithm, Prim's algorithm is a special case of the generic minimum-spanning-tree algorithm from Section 24.1. Prim's algorithm operates much like Dijkstra's algorithm for finding shortest paths in a graph. (See Section 25.2.) Prim's algorithm has the property that the edges in the set A always form a single tree. As is illustrated in Figure 24.5, the tree starts from an arbitrary root vertex r and grows until the tree spans all the vertices in V. At each step, a light edge connecting a vertex in A to a vertex in $V - A$ is added to the tree. By Corollary 24.2, this rule adds only edges that are safe for A; therefore, when the algorithm terminates, the edges in A form a minimum spanning tree. This strategy is "greedy" since the tree is augmented at each step with an edge that contributes the minimum amount possible to the tree's weight.

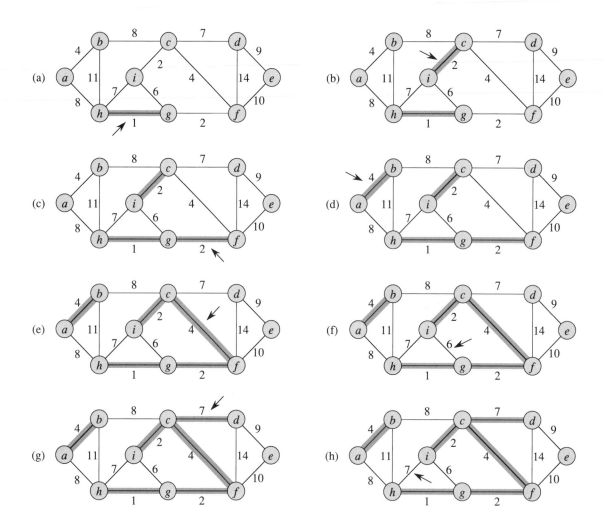

Figure 24.4 The execution of Kruskal's algorithm on the graph from Figure 24.1. Shaded edges belong to the forest A being grown. The edges are considered by the algorithm in sorted order by weight. An arrow points to the edge under consideration at each step of the algorithm. If the edge joins two distinct trees in the forest, it is added to the forest, thereby merging the two trees.

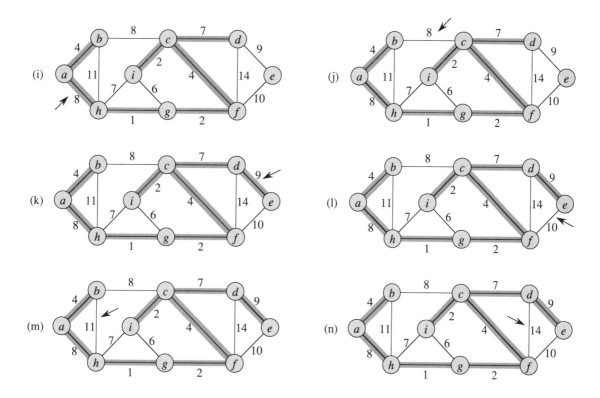

The key to implementing Prim's algorithm efficiently is to make it easy to select a new edge to be added to the tree formed by the edges in A. In the pseudocode below, the connected graph G and the root r of the minimum spanning tree to be grown are inputs to the algorithm. During execution of the algorithm, all vertices that are *not* in the tree reside in a priority queue Q based on a *key* field. For each vertex v, *key*$[v]$ is the minimum weight of any edge connecting v to a vertex in the tree; by convention, *key*$[v] = \infty$ if there is no such edge. The field $\pi[v]$ names the "parent" of v in the tree. During the algorithm, the set A from GENERIC-MST is kept implicitly as

$$A = \{(v, \pi[v]) : v \in V - \{r\} - Q\} \ .$$

When the algorithm terminates, the priority queue Q is empty; the minimum spanning tree A for G is thus

$$A = \{(v, \pi[v]) : v \in V - \{r\}\} \ .$$

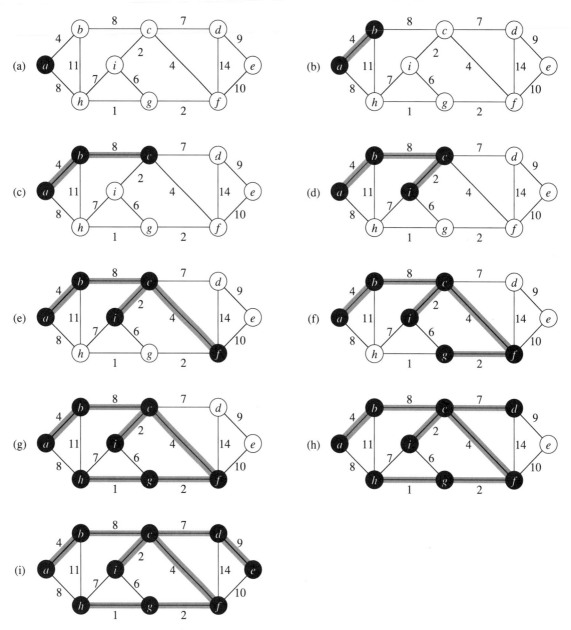

Figure 24.5 The execution of Prim's algorithm on the graph from Figure 24.1. The root vertex is a. Shaded edges are in the tree being grown, and the vertices in the tree are shown in black. At each step of the algorithm, the vertices in the tree determine a cut of the graph, and a light edge crossing the cut is added to the tree. In the second step, for example, the algorithm has a choice of adding either edge (b, c) or edge (a, h) to the tree since both are light edges crossing the cut.

MST-PRIM(G, w, r)

```
1   Q ← V[G]
2   for each u ∈ Q
3       do key[u] ← ∞
4   key[r] ← 0
5   π[r] ← NIL
6   while Q ≠ ∅
7       do u ← EXTRACT-MIN(Q)
8          for each v ∈ Adj[u]
9              do if v ∈ Q and w(u, v) < key[v]
10                    then π[v] ← u
11                         key[v] ← w(u, v)
```

Prim's algorithm works as shown in Figure 24.5. Lines 1–4 initialize the priority queue Q to contain all the vertices and set the key of each vertex to ∞, except for the root r, whose key is set to 0. Line 5 initializes $\pi[r]$ to NIL, since the root r has no parent. Throughout the algorithm, the set $V - Q$ contains the vertices in the tree being grown. Line 7 identifies a vertex $u \in Q$ incident on a light edge crossing the cut $(V - Q, Q)$ (with the exception of the first iteration, in which $u = r$ due to line 4). Removing u from the set Q adds it to the set $V - Q$ of vertices in the tree. Lines 8–11 update the *key* and π fields of every vertex v adjacent to u but not in the tree. The updating maintains the invariants that $key[v] = w(v, \pi[v])$ and that $(v, \pi[v])$ is a light edge connecting v to some vertex in the tree.

The performance of Prim's algorithm depends on how we implement the priority queue Q. If Q is implemented as a binary heap (see Chapter 7), we can use the BUILD-HEAP procedure to perform the initialization in lines 1–4 in $O(V)$ time. The loop is executed $|V|$ times, and since each EXTRACT-MIN operation takes $O(\lg V)$ time, the total time for all calls to EXTRACT-MIN is $O(V \lg V)$. The **for** loop in lines 8–11 is executed $O(E)$ times altogether, since the sum of the lengths of all adjacency lists is $2|E|$. Within the **for** loop, the test for membership in Q in line 9 can be implemented in constant time by keeping a bit for each vertex that tells whether or not it is in Q, and updating the bit when the vertex is removed from Q. The assignment in line 11 involves an implicit DECREASE-KEY operation on the heap, which can be implemented in a binary heap in $O(\lg V)$ time. Thus, the total time for Prim's algorithm is $O(V \lg V + E \lg V) = O(E \lg V)$, which is asymptotically the same as for our implementation of Kruskal's algorithm.

The asymptotic running time of Prim's algorithm can be improved, however, by using Fibonacci heaps. Chapter 21 shows that if $|V|$ elements are organized into a Fibonacci heap, we can perform an EXTRACT-MIN operation in $O(\lg V)$ amortized time and a DECREASE-KEY operation (to implement line 11) in $O(1)$ amortized time. Therefore, if we use a Fibonacci heap to implement the priority queue Q, the running time of Prim's algorithm improves to $O(E + V \lg V)$.

Exercises

24.2-1
Kruskal's algorithm can return different spanning trees for the same input graph G, depending on how ties are broken when the edges are sorted into order. Show that for each minimum spanning tree T of G, there is a way to sort the edges of G in Kruskal's algorithm so that the algorithm returns T.

24.2-2
Suppose that the graph $G = (V, E)$ is represented as an adjacency matrix. Give a simple implementation of Prim's algorithm for this case that runs in $O(V^2)$ time.

24.2-3
Is the Fibonacci-heap implementation of Prim's algorithm asymptotically faster than the binary-heap implementation for a sparse graph $G = (V, E)$, where $|E| = \Theta(V)$? What about for a dense graph, where $|E| = \Theta(V^2)$? How must $|E|$ and $|V|$ be related for the Fibonacci-heap implementation to be asymptotically faster than the binary-heap implementation?

24.2-4
Suppose that all edge weights in a graph are integers in the range from 1 to $|V|$. How fast can you make Kruskal's algorithm run? What if the edge weights are integers in the range from 1 to W for some constant W?

24.2-5
Suppose that all edge weights in a graph are integers in the range from 1 to $|V|$. How fast can you make Prim's algorithm run? What if the edge weights are integers in the range from 1 to W for some constant W?

24.2-6
Describe an efficient algorithm that, given an undirected graph G, determines a spanning tree of G whose largest edge weight is minimum over all spanning trees of G.

24.2-7 ⋆
Suppose that the edge weights in a graph are uniformly distributed over the half-open interval $[0, 1)$. Which algorithm, Kruskal's or Prim's, can you make run faster?

24.2-8 ⋆
Suppose that a graph G has a minimum spanning tree already computed. How quickly can the minimum spanning tree be updated if a new vertex and incident edges are added to G?

Problems

24-1 *Second-best minimum spanning tree*
Let $G = (V, E)$ be an undirected, connected graph with weight function $w : E \rightarrow \mathbf{R}$, and suppose that $|E| \geq |V|$.

a. Let T be a minimum spanning tree of G. Prove that there exist edges $(u, v) \in T$ and $(x, y) \notin T$ such that $T - \{(u, v)\} \cup \{(x, y)\}$ is a second-best minimum spanning tree of G.

b. Let T be a spanning tree of G and, for any two vertices $u, v \in V$, let $max[u, v]$ be an edge of maximum weight on the unique path between u and v in T. Describe an $O(V^2)$-time algorithm that, given T, computes $max[u, v]$ for all $u, v \in V$.

c. Give an efficient algorithm to compute the second-best minimum spanning tree of G.

24-2 *Minimum spanning tree in sparse graphs*
For a very sparse connected graph $G = (V, E)$, we can improve upon the $O(E + V \lg V)$ running time of Prim's algorithm with Fibonacci heaps by "preprocessing" G to decrease the number of vertices before running Prim's algorithm. The following procedure takes as input a weighted graph G and returns a "contracted" version of G, having added some edges to the minimum spanning tree T under construction. Initially, for each edge $(u, v) \in E$, we assume that $orig[u, v] = (u, v)$ and that $w[u, v]$ is the weight of the edge.

MST-REDUCE(G, T)

```
 1  for each v ∈ V[G]
 2      do mark[v] ← FALSE
 3          MAKE-SET(v)
 4  for each u ∈ V[G]
 5      do if mark[u] = FALSE
 6          then choose v ∈ Adj[u] such that w[u, v] is minimized
 7              UNION(u, v)
 8              T ← T ∪ {orig[u, v]}
 9              mark[u] ← mark[v] ← TRUE
10  V[G'] ← {FIND-SET(v) : v ∈ V[G]}
11  E[G'] ← ∅
12  for each (x, y) ∈ E[G]
13      do u ← FIND-SET(x)
14          v ← FIND-SET(y)
15          if (u, v) ∉ E[G']
16              then E[G'] ← E[G'] ∪ {(u, v)}
17                  orig[u, v] ← orig[x, y]
18                  w[u, v] ← w[x, y]
19              else if w[x, y] < w[u, v]
20                  then orig[u, v] ← orig[x, y]
21                      w[u, v] ← w[x, y]
22  construct adjacency lists Adj for G'
23  return G' and T
```

a. Let T be the set of edges returned by MST-REDUCE, and let T' be a minimum spanning tree of the graph G' returned by the procedure. Prove that $T \cup \{orig[x, y] : (x, y) \in T'\}$ is a minimum spanning tree of G.

b. Argue that $|V[G']| \leq |V|/2$.

c. Show how to implement MST-REDUCE so that it runs in $O(E)$ time. (*Hint:* Use simple data structures.)

d. Suppose that we run k phases of MST-REDUCE, using the graph produced by one phase as input to the next and accumulating edges in T. Argue that the overall running time of the k phases is $O(kE)$.

e. Suppose that after running k phases of MST-REDUCE, we run Prim's algorithm on the graph returned by the last phase. Show how to pick k so that the overall running time is $O(E \lg \lg V)$. Argue that your choice of k minimizes the overall asymptotic running time.

f. For what values of $|E|$ (in terms of $|V|$) does Prim's algorithm with preprocessing asymptotically beat Prim's algorithm without preprocessing?

Chapter notes

Tarjan [188] surveys the minimum-spanning-tree problem and provides excellent advanced material. A history of the minimum-spanning-tree problem has been written by Graham and Hell [92].

Tarjan attributes the first minimum-spanning-tree algorithm to a 1926 paper by O. Borůvka. Kruskal's algorithm was reported by Kruskal [131] in 1956. The algorithm commonly known as Prim's algorithm was indeed invented by Prim [163], but it was also invented earlier by V. Jarník in 1930.

The reason why greedy algorithms are effective at finding minimum spanning trees is that the set of forests of a graph forms a graphic matroid. (See Section 17.4.)

The fastest minimum-spanning-tree algorithm to date for the case in which $|E| = \Omega(V \lg V)$ is Prim's algorithm implemented with Fibonacci heaps. For sparser graphs, Fredman and Tarjan [75] give an algorithm that runs in $O(E \, \beta(|E|, |V|))$ time, where $\beta(|E|, |V|) = \min\{i : \lg^{(i)} |V| \le |E| / |V|\}$. The fact that $|E| \ge |V|$ implies that their algorithm runs in time $O(E \lg^* V)$.

25   Single-Source Shortest Paths

A motorist wishes to find the shortest possible route from Chicago to Boston. Given a road map of the United States on which the distance between each pair of adjacent intersections is marked, how can we determine this shortest route?

One possible way is to enumerate all the routes from Chicago to Boston, add up the distances on each route, and select the shortest. It is easy to see, however, that even if we disallow routes that contain cycles, there are millions of possibilities, most of which are simply not worth considering. For example, a route from Chicago to Houston to Boston is obviously a poor choice, because Houston is about a thousand miles out of the way.

In this chapter and in Chapter 26, we show how to solve such problems efficiently. In a *shortest-paths problem*, we are given a weighted, directed graph $G = (V, E)$, with weight function $w : E \rightarrow \mathbf{R}$ mapping edges to real-valued weights. The *weight* of path $p = \langle v_0, v_1, \ldots, v_k \rangle$ is the sum of the weights of its constituent edges:

$$w(p) = \sum_{i=1}^{k} w(v_{i-1}, v_i) .$$

We define the *shortest-path weight* from u to v by

$$\delta(u, v) = \begin{cases} \min\{w(p) : u \overset{p}{\leadsto} v\} & \text{if there is a path from } u \text{ to } v , \\ \infty & \text{otherwise .} \end{cases}$$

A *shortest path* from vertex u to vertex v is then defined as any path p with weight $w(p) = \delta(u, v)$.

In the Chicago-to-Boston example, we can model the road map as a graph: vertices represent intersections, edges represent road segments between intersections, and edge weights represent road distances. Our goal is to find a shortest path from a given intersection in Chicago (say, Clark St. and Addison Ave.) to a given intersection in Boston (say, Brookline Ave. and Yawkey Way).

Edge weights can be interpreted as metrics other than distances. They are often used to represent time, cost, penalties, lossage, or any other quantity that accumulates linearly along a path and that one wishes to minimize.

The breadth-first-search algorithm from Section 23.2 is a shortest-paths algorithm that works on unweighted graphs, that is, graphs in which each edge can be considered to have unit weight. Because many of the concepts from breadth-first search arise in the study of shortest paths in weighted graphs, the reader is encouraged to review Section 23.2 before proceeding.

Variants

In this chapter, we shall focus on the *single-source shortest-paths problem*: given a graph $G = (V, E)$, we want to find a shortest path from a given *source* vertex $s \in V$ to every vertex $v \in V$. Many other problems can be solved by the algorithm for the single-source problem, including the following variants.

Single-destination shortest-paths problem: Find a shortest path to a given *destination* vertex t from every vertex v. By reversing the direction of each edge in the graph, we can reduce this problem to a single-source problem.

Single-pair shortest-path problem: Find a shortest path from u to v for given vertices u and v. If we solve the single-source problem with source vertex u, we solve this problem also. Moreover, no algorithms for this problem are known that run asymptotically faster than the best single-source algorithms in the worst case.

All-pairs shortest-paths problem: Find a shortest path from u to v for every pair of vertices u and v. This problem can be solved by running a single-source algorithm once from each vertex; but it can usually be solved faster, and its structure is of interest in its own right. Chapter 26 addresses the all-pairs problem in detail.

Negative-weight edges

In some instances of the single-source shortest-paths problem, there may be edges whose weights are negative. If the graph $G = (V, E)$ contains no negative-weight cycles reachable from the source s, then for all $v \in V$, the shortest-path weight $\delta(s, v)$ remains well defined, even if it has a negative value. If there is a negative-weight cycle reachable from s, however, shortest-path weights are not well defined. No path from s to a vertex on the cycle can be a shortest path—a lesser-weight path can always be found that follows the proposed "shortest" path and then traverses the negative-weight cycle. If there is a negative-weight cycle on some path from s to v, we define $\delta(s, v) = -\infty$.

Figure 25.1 illustrates the effect of negative weights on shortest-path weights. Because there is only one path from s to a (the path $\langle s, a \rangle$), $\delta(s, a) = w(s, a) = 3$. Similarly, there is only one path from s to b, and so $\delta(s, b) = w(s, a) + w(a, b) = 3 + (-4) = -1$. There are infinitely many paths from s to c: $\langle s, c \rangle$, $\langle s, c, d, c \rangle$, $\langle s, c, d, c, d, c \rangle$, and so on. Because the cycle $\langle c, d, c \rangle$ has weight $6 + (-3) = 3 > 0$, the shortest path from s to c is

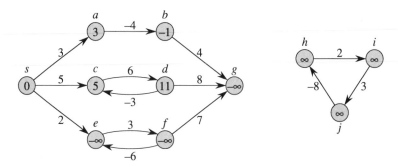

Figure 25.1 Negative edge weights in a directed graph. Shown within each vertex is its shortest-path weight from source s. Because vertices e and f form a negative-weight cycle reachable from s, they have shortest-path weights of $-\infty$. Because vertex g is reachable from a vertex whose shortest-path weight is $-\infty$, it, too, has a shortest-path weight of $-\infty$. Vertices such as h, i, and j are not reachable from s, and so their shortest-path weights are ∞, even though they lie on a negative-weight cycle.

$\langle s, c \rangle$, with weight $\delta(s, c) = 5$. Similarly, the shortest path from s to d is $\langle s, c, d \rangle$, with weight $\delta(s, d) = w(s, c) + w(c, d) = 11$. Analogously, there are infinitely many paths from s to e: $\langle s, e \rangle$, $\langle s, e, f, e \rangle$, $\langle s, e, f, e, f, e \rangle$, and so on. Since the cycle $\langle e, f, e \rangle$ has weight $3 + (-6) = -3 < 0$, however, there is no shortest path from s to e. By traversing the negative-weight cycle $\langle e, f, e \rangle$ arbitrarily many times, we can find paths from s to e with arbitrarily large negative weights, and so $\delta(s, e) = -\infty$. Similarly, $\delta(s, f) = -\infty$. Because g is reachable from f, we can also find paths with arbitrarily large negative weights from s to g, and $\delta(s, g) = -\infty$. Vertices h, i, and j also form a negative-weight cycle. They are not reachable from s, however, and so $\delta(s, h) = \delta(s, i) = \delta(s, j) = \infty$.

Some shortest-paths algorithms, such as Dijkstra's algorithm, assume that all edge weights in the input graph are nonnegative, as in the road-map example. Others, such as the Bellman-Ford algorithm, allow negative-weight edges in the input graph and produce a correct answer as long as no negative-weight cycles are reachable from the source. Typically, if there is such a negative-weight cycle, the algorithm can detect and report its existence.

Representing shortest paths

We often wish to compute not only shortest-path weights, but the vertices on the shortest paths as well. The representation we use for shortest paths is similar to the one we used for breadth-first trees in Section 23.2. Given a graph $G = (V, E)$, we maintain for each vertex $v \in V$ a ***predecessor*** $\pi[v]$ that is either another vertex or NIL. The shortest-paths algorithms in this chapter set the π attributes so that the chain of predecessors originating at a vertex v runs backwards along a shortest path from s to v. Thus, given a vertex v for which $\pi[v] \neq \text{NIL}$, the procedure PRINT-PATH(G, s, v) from Section 23.2 can be used to print a shortest path from s to v.

During the execution of a shortest-paths algorithm, however, the π values need not indicate shortest paths. As in breadth-first search, we shall be interested in the **predecessor subgraph** $G_\pi = (V_\pi, E_\pi)$ induced by the π values. Here again, we define the vertex set V_π to be the set of vertices of G with non-NIL predecessors, plus the source s:

$$V_\pi = \{v \in V : \pi[v] \neq \text{NIL}\} \cup \{s\} \ .$$

The directed edge set E_π is the set of edges induced by the π values for vertices in V_π:

$$E_\pi = \{(\pi[v], v) \in E : v \in V_\pi - \{s\}\} \ .$$

We shall prove that the π values produced by the algorithms in this chapter have the property that at termination G_π is a "shortest-paths tree"—informally, a rooted tree containing a shortest path from a source s to every vertex that is reachable from s. A shortest-paths tree is like the breadth-first tree from Section 23.2, but it contains shortest paths from the source defined in terms of edge weights instead of numbers of edges. To be precise, let $G = (V, E)$ be a weighted, directed graph with weight function $w : E \rightarrow \mathbf{R}$, and assume that G contains no negative-weight cycles reachable from the source vertex $s \in V$, so that shortest paths are well defined. A **shortest-paths tree** rooted at s is a directed subgraph $G' = (V', E')$, where $V' \subseteq V$ and $E' \subseteq E$, such that

1. V' is the set of vertices reachable from s in G,

2. G' forms a rooted tree with root s, and

3. for all $v \in V'$, the unique simple path from s to v in G' is a shortest path from s to v in G.

Shortest paths are not necessarily unique, and neither are shortest-paths trees. For example, Figure 25.2 shows a weighted, directed graph and two shortest-paths trees with the same root.

Chapter outline

The single-source shortest-paths algorithms in this chapter are all based on a technique known as relaxation. Section 25.1 begins by proving some important properties of shortest paths in general and then proves some important facts about relaxation-based algorithms. Dijkstra's algorithm, which solves the single-source shortest-paths problem when all edges have nonnegative weight, is given in Section 25.2. Section 25.3 presents the Bellman-Ford algorithm, which is used in the more general case in which edges can have negative weight. If the graph contains a negative-weight cycle reachable from the source, the Bellman-Ford algorithm detects its

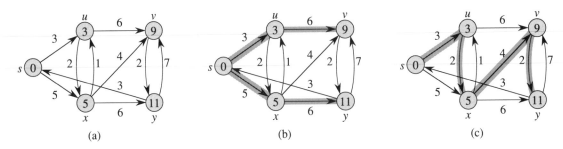

Figure 25.2 (a) A weighted, directed graph with shortest-path weights from source s. (b) The shaded edges form a shortest-paths tree rooted at the source s. (c) Another shortest-paths tree with the same root.

presence. Section 25.4 gives a linear-time algorithm for computing shortest paths from a single source in directed acyclic graphs. Finally, Section 25.5 shows how the Bellman-Ford algorithm can be used to solve a special case of "linear programming."

Our analysis will require some conventions for doing arithmetic with infinities. We shall assume that for any real number $a \neq -\infty$, we have $a + \infty = \infty + a = \infty$. Also, to make our proofs hold in the presence of negative-weight cycles, we shall assume that for any real number $a \neq \infty$, we have $a + (-\infty) = (-\infty) + a = -\infty$.

25.1 Shortest paths and relaxation

To understand single-source shortest-paths algorithms, it is helpful to understand the techniques that they use and the properties of shortest paths that they exploit. The main technique used by the algorithms in this chapter is relaxation, a method that repeatedly decreases an upper bound on the actual shortest-path weight of each vertex until the upper bound equals the shortest-path weight. In this section, we shall see how relaxation works and formally prove several properties it maintains.

On a first reading of this section, you may wish to omit proofs of theorems—reading only their statements—and then proceed immediately to the algorithms in Sections 25.2 and 25.3. Pay particular attention, however, to Lemma 25.7, which is a key to understanding the shortest-paths algorithms in this chapter. On a first reading, you may also wish to ignore completely the lemmas concerning predecessor subgraphs and shortest-paths trees (Lemmas 25.8 and 25.9), concentrating instead on the earlier lemmas, which pertain to shortest-path weights.

Optimal substructure of a shortest path

Shortest-paths algorithms typically exploit the property that a shortest path between two vertices contains other shortest paths within it. This optimal-substructure property is a hallmark of the applicability of both dynamic programming (Chapter 16) and the greedy method (Chapter 17). In fact, Dijkstra's algorithm is a greedy algorithm, and the Floyd-Warshall algorithm, which finds shortest paths between all pairs of vertices (see Chapter 26), is a dynamic-programming algorithm. The following lemma and its corollary state the optimal-substructure property of shortest paths more precisely.

Lemma 25.1 (Subpaths of shortest paths are shortest paths)
Given a weighted, directed graph $G = (V, E)$ with weight function $w : E \rightarrow \mathbf{R}$, let $p = \langle v_1, v_2, \ldots, v_k \rangle$ be a shortest path from vertex v_1 to vertex v_k and, for any i and j such that $1 \leq i \leq j \leq k$, let $p_{ij} = \langle v_i, v_{i+1}, \ldots, v_j \rangle$ be the subpath of p from vertex v_i to vertex v_j. Then, p_{ij} is a shortest path from v_i to v_j.

Proof If we decompose path p into $v_1 \overset{p_{1i}}{\rightsquigarrow} v_i \overset{p_{ij}}{\rightsquigarrow} v_j \overset{p_{jk}}{\rightsquigarrow} v_k$, then $w(p) = w(p_{1i}) + w(p_{ij}) + w(p_{jk})$. Now, assume that there is a path p'_{ij} from v_i to v_j with weight $w(p'_{ij}) < w(p_{ij})$. Then, $v_1 \overset{p_{1i}}{\rightsquigarrow} v_i \overset{p'_{ij}}{\rightsquigarrow} v_j \overset{p_{jk}}{\rightsquigarrow} v_k$ is a path from v_1 to v_k whose weight $w(p_{1i}) + w(p'_{ij}) + w(p_{jk})$ is less than $w(p)$, which contradicts the premise that p is a shortest path from v_1 to v_k. ∎

In studying breadth-first search (Section 23.2), we proved as Lemma 23.1 a simple property of shortest distances in unweighted graphs. The following corollary to Lemma 25.1 generalizes the property to weighted graphs.

Corollary 25.2
Let $G = (V, E)$ be a weighted, directed graph with weight function $w : E \rightarrow \mathbf{R}$. Suppose that a shortest path p from a source s to a vertex v can be decomposed into $s \overset{p'}{\rightsquigarrow} u \rightarrow v$ for some vertex u and path p'. Then, the weight of a shortest path from s to v is $\delta(s, v) = \delta(s, u) + w(u, v)$.

Proof By Lemma 25.1, subpath p' is a shortest path from source s to vertex u. Thus,

$$
\begin{aligned}
\delta(s, v) &= w(p) \\
&= w(p') + w(u, v) \\
&= \delta(s, u) + w(u, v) \, .
\end{aligned}
$$

∎

The next lemma gives a simple but useful property of shortest-path weights.

Lemma 25.3
Let $G = (V, E)$ be a weighted, directed graph $G = (V, E)$ with weight function $w : E \rightarrow \mathbf{R}$ and source vertex s. Then, for all edges $(u, v) \in E$, we have $\delta(s, v) \leq \delta(s, u) + w(u, v)$.

Proof   A shortest path p from source s to vertex v has no more weight than any other path from s to v. Specifically, path p has no more weight than the particular path that takes a shortest path from source s to vertex u and then takes edge (u, v).   ∎

Relaxation

The algorithms in this chapter use the technique of **relaxation**. For each vertex $v \in V$, we maintain an attribute $d[v]$, which is an upper bound on the weight of a shortest path from source s to v. We call $d[v]$ a **shortest-path estimate**. We initialize the shortest-path estimates and predecessors by the following procedure.

INITIALIZE-SINGLE-SOURCE(G, s)

1   **for** each vertex $v \in V[G]$
2   **do** $d[v] \leftarrow \infty$
3            $\pi[v] \leftarrow \text{NIL}$
4    $d[s] \leftarrow 0$

After initialization, $\pi[v] = \text{NIL}$ for all $v \in V$, $d[v] = 0$ for $v = s$, and $d[v] = \infty$ for $v \in V - \{s\}$.

The process of **relaxing**[1] an edge (u, v) consists of testing whether we can improve the shortest path to v found so far by going through u and, if so, updating $d[v]$ and $\pi[v]$. A relaxation step may decrease the value of the shortest-path estimate $d[v]$ and update v's predecessor field $\pi[v]$. The following code performs a relaxation step on edge (u, v).

RELAX(u, v, w)

1   **if** $d[v] > d[u] + w(u, v)$
2   **then** $d[v] \leftarrow d[u] + w(u, v)$
3            $\pi[v] \leftarrow u$

Figure 25.3 shows two examples of relaxing an edge, one in which a shortest-path estimate decreases and one in which no estimate changes.

---

[1]It may seem strange that the term "relaxation" is used for an operation that tightens an upper bound. The use of the term is historical. The outcome of a relaxation step can be viewed as a relaxation of the constraint $d[v] \leq d[u] + w(u, v)$, which, by Lemma 25.3, must be satisfied if $d[u] = \delta(s, u)$ and $d[v] = \delta(s, v)$. That is, if $d[v] \leq d[u] + w(u, v)$, there is no "pressure" to satisfy this constraint, so the constraint is "relaxed."

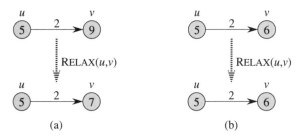

Figure 25.3 Relaxation of an edge (u, v). The shortest-path estimate of each vertex is shown within the vertex. **(a)** Because $d[v] > d[u] + w(u, v)$ prior to relaxation, the value of $d[v]$ decreases. **(b)** Here, $d[v] \leq d[u] + w(u, v)$ before the relaxation step, so $d[v]$ is unchanged by relaxation.

Each algorithm in this chapter calls INITIALIZE-SINGLE-SOURCE and then repeatedly relaxes edges. Moreover, relaxation is the only means by which shortest-path estimates and predecessors change. The algorithms in this chapter differ in how many times they relax each edge and the order in which they relax edges. In Dijkstra's algorithm and the shortest-paths algorithm for directed acyclic graphs, each edge is relaxed exactly once. In the Bellman-Ford algorithm, each edge is relaxed several times.

Properties of relaxation

The correctness of the algorithms in this chapter depends on important properties of relaxation that are summarized in the next few lemmas. Most of the lemmas describe the outcome of executing a sequence of relaxation steps on the edges of a weighted, directed graph that has been initialized by INITIALIZE-SINGLE-SOURCE. Except for Lemma 25.9, these lemmas apply to *any* sequence of relaxation steps, not just those that produce shortest-path values.

Lemma 25.4
Let $G = (V, E)$ be a weighted, directed graph with weight function $w : E \to \mathbf{R}$, and let $(u, v) \in E$. Then, immediately after relaxing edge (u, v) by executing RELAX(u, v, w), we have $d[v] \leq d[u] + w(u, v)$.

Proof If, just prior to relaxing edge (u, v), we have $d[v] > d[u] + w(u, v)$, then $d[v] = d[u] + w(u, v)$ afterward. If, instead, $d[v] \leq d[u] + w(u, v)$ just before the relaxation, then neither $d[u]$ nor $d[v]$ changes, and so $d[v] \leq d[u] + w(u, v)$ afterward. ∎

Lemma 25.5
Let $G = (V, E)$ be a weighted, directed graph with weight function $w : E \to \mathbf{R}$. Let $s \in V$ be the source vertex, and let the graph be initialized by INITIALIZE-SINGLE-SOURCE(G, s). Then, $d[v] \geq \delta(s, v)$ for all $v \in V$, and

this invariant is maintained over any sequence of relaxation steps on the edges of G. Moreover, once $d[v]$ achieves its lower bound $\delta(s, v)$, it never changes.

Proof   The invariant $d[v] \geq \delta(s, v)$ is certainly true after initialization, since $d[s] = 0 \geq \delta(s, s)$ (note that $\delta(s, s)$ is $-\infty$ if s is on a negative-weight cycle and 0 otherwise) and $d[v] = \infty$ implies $d[v] \geq \delta(s, v)$ for all $v \in V - \{s\}$. We shall use proof by contradiction to show that the invariant is maintained over any sequence of relaxation steps. Let v be the first vertex for which a relaxation step of an edge (u, v) causes $d[v] < \delta(s, v)$. Then, just after relaxing edge (u, v), we have

$$
\begin{aligned}
d[u] + w(u, v) &= d[v] \\
&< \delta(s, v) \\
&\leq \delta(s, u) + w(u, v) \quad \text{(by Lemma 25.3)} ,
\end{aligned}
$$

which implies that $d[u] < \delta(s, u)$. But because relaxing edge (u, v) does not change $d[u]$, this inequality must have been true just before we relaxed the edge, which contradicts the choice of v as the first vertex for which $d[v] < \delta(s, v)$. We conclude that the invariant $d[v] \geq \delta(s, v)$ is maintained for all $v \in V$.

To see that the value of $d[v]$ never changes once $d[v] = \delta(s, v)$, note that having achieved its lower bound, $d[v]$ cannot decrease because we have just shown that $d[v] \geq \delta(s, v)$, and it cannot increase because relaxation steps do not increase d values.   ∎

Corollary 25.6
Suppose that in a weighted, directed graph $G = (V, E)$ with weight function $w : E \to \mathbf{R}$, no path connects a source vertex $s \in V$ to a given vertex $v \in V$. Then, after the graph is initialized by INITIALIZE-SINGLE-SOURCE(G, s), we have $d[v] = \delta(s, v)$, and this equality is maintained as an invariant over any sequence of relaxation steps on the edges of G.

Proof   By Lemma 25.5, we always have $\infty = \delta(s, v) \leq d[v]$; thus, so $d[v] = \infty = \delta(s, v)$.   ∎

The following lemma is crucial to proving the correctness of the shortest-paths algorithms that appear later in this chapter. It gives sufficient conditions for relaxation to cause a shortest-path estimate to converge to a shortest-path weight.

Lemma 25.7
Let $G = (V, E)$ be a weighted, directed graph with weight function $w : E \to \mathbf{R}$, let $s \in V$ be a source vertex, and let $s \rightsquigarrow u \to v$ be a shortest path in G for some vertices $u, v \in V$. Suppose that G is initialized by INITIALIZE-SINGLE-SOURCE(G, s) and then a sequence of relaxation steps that includes the call RELAX(u, v, w) is executed on the edges of G. If

$d[u] = \delta(s, u)$ at any time prior to the call, then $d[v] = \delta(s, v)$ at all times after the call.

Proof By Lemma 25.5, if $d[u] = \delta(s, u)$ at some point prior to relaxing edge (u, v), then this equality holds thereafter. In particular, after relaxing edge (u, v), we have

$$
\begin{aligned}
d[v] \;\; &\le \;\; d[u] + w(u, v) \qquad \text{(by Lemma 25.4)} \\
&= \;\; \delta(s, u) + w(u, v) \\
&= \;\; \delta(s, v) \qquad\qquad\quad \text{(by Corollary 25.2) .}
\end{aligned}
$$

By Lemma 25.5, $\delta(s, v)$ bounds $d[v]$ from below, from which we conclude that $d[v] = \delta(s, v)$, and this equality is maintained thereafter. ∎

Shortest-paths trees

So far, we have shown that relaxation causes the shortest-path estimates to descend monotonically toward the actual shortest-path weights. We would also like to show that once a sequence of relaxations has computed the actual shortest-path weights, the predecessor subgraph G_π induced by the resulting π values is a shortest-paths tree for G. We start with the following lemma, which shows that the predecessor subgraph always forms a rooted tree whose root is the source.

Lemma 25.8
Let $G = (V, E)$ be a weighted, directed graph with weight function $w : E \to \mathbf{R}$ and source vertex $s \in V$, and assume that G contains no negative-weight cycles that are reachable from s. Then, after the graph is initialized by INITIALIZE-SINGLE-SOURCE(G, s), the predecessor subgraph G_π forms a rooted tree with root s, and any sequence of relaxation steps on edges of G maintains this property as an invariant.

Proof Initially, the only vertex in G_π is the source vertex, and the lemma is trivially true. Consider a predecessor subgraph G_π that arises after a sequence of relaxation steps. We shall first prove that G_π is acyclic. Suppose for the sake of contradiction that some relaxation step creates a cycle in the graph G_π. Let the cycle be $c = \langle v_0, v_1, \ldots, v_k \rangle$, where $v_k = v_0$. Then, $\pi[v_i] = v_{i-1}$ for $i = 1, 2, \ldots, k$ and, without loss of generality, we can assume that it was the relaxation of edge (v_{k-1}, v_k) that created the cycle in G_π.

We claim that all vertices on cycle c are reachable from the source s. Why? Each vertex on c has a non-NIL predecessor, and so each vertex on c was assigned a finite shortest-path estimate when it was assigned its non-NIL π value. By Lemma 25.5, each vertex on cycle c has a finite shortest-path weight, which implies that it is reachable from s.

We shall examine the shortest-path estimates on c just prior to the call $\text{RELAX}(v_{k-1}, v_k, w)$ and show that c is a negative-weight cycle, thereby contradicting the assumption that G contains no negative-weight cycles that are reachable from the source. Just before the call, we have $\pi[v_i] = v_{i-1}$ for $i = 1, 2, \ldots, k-1$. Thus, for $i = 1, 2, \ldots, k-1$, the last update to $d[v_i]$ was by the assignment $d[v_i] \leftarrow d[v_{i-1}] + w(v_i, v_{i-1})$. If $d[v_{i-1}]$ changed since then, it decreased. Therefore, just before the call $\text{RELAX}(v_{k-1}, v_k, w)$, we have

$$d[v_i] \geq d[v_{i-1}] + w(v_{i-1}, v_i) \qquad \text{for all } i = 1, 2, \ldots, k-1 \ . \qquad (25.1)$$

Because $\pi[v_k]$ is changed by the call, immediately beforehand we also have the strict inequality

$$d[v_k] > d[v_{k-1}] + w(v_{k-1}, v_k) \ .$$

Summing this strict inequality with the $k-1$ inequalities (25.1), we obtain the sum of the shortest-path estimates around cycle c:

$$
\begin{aligned}
\sum_{i=1}^{k} d[v_i] \ &> \ \sum_{i=1}^{k} (d[v_{i-1}] + w(v_{i-1}, v_i)) \\
&= \ \sum_{i=1}^{k} d[v_{i-1}] + \sum_{i=1}^{k} w(v_{i-1}, v_i) \ .
\end{aligned}
$$

But

$$\sum_{i=1}^{k} d[v_i] = \sum_{i=1}^{k} d[v_{i-1}] \ ,$$

since each vertex in the cycle c appears exactly once in each summation. This implies

$$0 > \sum_{i=1}^{k} w(v_{i-1}, v_i) \ .$$

Thus, the sum of weights around the cycle c is negative, thereby providing the desired contradiction.

We have now proved that G_π is a directed, acyclic graph. To show that it forms a rooted tree with root s, it suffices (see Exercise 5.5-3) to prove that for each vertex $v \in V_\pi$, there is a unique path from s to v in G_π.

We first must show that a path from s exists for each vertex in V_π. The vertices in V_π are those with non-NIL π values, plus s. The idea here is to prove by induction that a path exists from s to all vertices in V_π. The details are left as Exercise 25.1-6.

To complete the proof of the lemma, we must now show that for any vertex $v \in V_\pi$, there is at most one path from s to v in the graph G_π. Suppose otherwise. That is, suppose that there are two simple paths from s to some vertex v: p_1, which can be decomposed into $s \rightsquigarrow u \rightsquigarrow x \rightarrow z \rightsquigarrow v$,

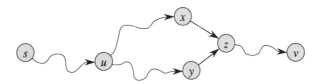

Figure 25.4 Showing that a path in G_π from source s to vertex v is unique. If there are two paths p_1 $(s \rightsquigarrow u \rightsquigarrow x \rightarrow z \rightsquigarrow v)$ and p_2 $(s \rightsquigarrow u \rightsquigarrow y \rightarrow z \rightsquigarrow v)$, where $x \neq y$, then $\pi[z] = x$ and $\pi[z] = y$, a contradiction.

and p_2, which can be decomposed into $s \rightsquigarrow u \rightsquigarrow y \rightarrow z \rightsquigarrow v$, where $x \neq y$. (See Figure 25.4.) But then, $\pi[z] = x$ and $\pi[z] = y$, which implies the contradiction that $x = y$. We conclude that there exists a unique simple path in G_π from s to v, and thus G_π forms a rooted tree with root s. ∎

We can now show that if, after we have performed a sequence of relaxation steps, all vertices have been assigned their true shortest-path weights, then the predecessor subgraph G_π is a shortest-paths tree.

Lemma 25.9
Let $G = (V, E)$ be a weighted, directed graph with weight function $w : E \rightarrow \mathbf{R}$ and source vertex $s \in V$, and assume that G contains no negative-weight cycles that are reachable from s. Let us call INITIALIZE-SINGLE-SOURCE(G, s) and then execute any sequence of relaxation steps on edges of G that produces $d[v] = \delta(s, v)$ for all $v \in V$. Then, the predecessor subgraph G_π is a shortest-paths tree rooted at s.

Proof We must prove that the three properties of shortest-paths trees hold for G_π. To show the first property, we must show that V_π is the set of vertices reachable from s. By definition, a shortest-path weight $\delta(s, v)$ is finite if and only if v is reachable from s, and thus the vertices that are reachable from s are exactly those with finite d values. But a vertex $v \in V - \{s\}$ has been assigned a finite value for $d[v]$ if and only if $\pi[v] \neq$ NIL. Thus, the vertices in V_π are exactly those reachable from s.

The second property follows directly from Lemma 25.8.

It remains, therefore, to prove the last property of shortest-paths trees: for all $v \in V_\pi$, the unique simple path $s \overset{p}{\rightsquigarrow} v$ in G_π is a shortest path from s to v in G. Let $p = \langle v_0, v_1, \ldots, v_k \rangle$, where $v_0 = s$ and $v_k = v$. For $i = 1, 2, \ldots, k$, we have both $d[v_i] = \delta(s, v_i)$ and $d[v_i] \geq d[v_{i-1}] + w(v_{i-1}, v_i)$, from which we conclude $w(v_{i-1}, v_i) \leq \delta(s, v_i) - \delta(s, v_{i-1})$. Summing the weights along path p yields

$$w(p) = \sum_{i=1}^{k} w(v_{i-1}, v_i)$$

$$
\begin{aligned}
&\leq \quad \sum_{i=1}^{k} (\delta(s, v_i) - \delta(s, v_{i-1})) \\
&= \quad \delta(s, v_k) - \delta(s, v_0) \\
&= \quad \delta(s, v_k) \ .
\end{aligned}
$$

The third line comes from the telescoping sum on the second line, and the fourth line follows from $\delta(s, v_0) = \delta(s, s) = 0$. Thus, $w(p) \leq \delta(s, v_k)$. Since $\delta(s, v_k)$ is a lower bound on the weight of any path from s to v_k, we conclude that $w(p) = \delta(s, v_k)$, and thus p is a shortest path from s to $v = v_k$.   ■

Exercises

25.1-1
Give two shortest-paths trees for the directed graph of Figure 25.2 other than the two shown.

25.1-2
Give an example of a weighted, directed graph $G = (V, E)$ with weight function $w : E \to \mathbf{R}$ and source s such that G satisfies the following property: For every edge $(u, v) \in E$, there is a shortest-paths tree rooted at s that contains (u, v) and another shortest-paths tree rooted at s that does not contain (u, v).

25.1-3
Embellish the proof of Lemma 25.3 to handle cases in which shortest-path weights are ∞ or $-\infty$.

25.1-4
Let $G = (V, E)$ be a weighted, directed graph with source vertex s, and let G be initialized by INITIALIZE-SINGLE-SOURCE(G, s). Prove that if a sequence of relaxation steps sets $\pi[s]$ to a non-NIL value, then G contains a negative-weight cycle.

25.1-5
Let $G = (V, E)$ be a weighted, directed graph with no negative-weight edges. Let $s \in V$ be the source vertex, and let us define $\pi[v]$ as usual: $\pi[v]$ is the predecessor of v on some shortest path to v from source s if $v \in V - \{s\}$ is reachable from s, and NIL otherwise. Give an example of such a graph G and an assignment of π values that produces a cycle in G_π. (By Lemma 25.8, such an assignment cannot be produced by a sequence of relaxation steps.)

25.1-6

Let $G = (V, E)$ be a weighted, directed graph with weight function $w : E \to \mathbf{R}$ and no negative-weight cycles. Let $s \in V$ be the source vertex, and let G be initialized by INITIALIZE-SINGLE-SOURCE(G, s). Prove that for every vertex $v \in V_\pi$, there exists a path from s to v in G_π and that this property is maintained as an invariant over any sequence of relaxations.

25.1-7

Let $G = (V, E)$ be a weighted, directed graph that contains no negative-weight cycles. Let $s \in V$ be the source vertex, and let G be initialized by INITIALIZE-SINGLE-SOURCE(G, s). Prove that there is a sequence of $|V| - 1$ relaxation steps that produces $d[v] = \delta(s, v)$ for all $v \in V$.

25.1-8

Let G be an arbitrary weighted, directed graph with a negative-weight cycle reachable from the source vertex s. Show that an infinite sequence of relaxations of the edges of G can always be constructed such that every relaxation causes a shortest-path estimate to change.

25.2 Dijkstra's algorithm

Dijkstra's algorithm solves the single-source shortest-paths problem on a weighted, directed graph $G = (V, E)$ for the case in which all edge weights are nonnegative. In this section, therefore, we assume that $w(u, v) \geq 0$ for each edge $(u, v) \in E$.

Dijkstra's algorithm maintains a set S of vertices whose final shortest-path weights from the source s have already been determined. That is, for all vertices $v \in S$, we have $d[v] = \delta(s, v)$. The algorithm repeatedly selects the vertex $u \in V - S$ with the minimum shortest-path estimate, inserts u into S, and relaxes all edges leaving u. In the following implementation, we maintain a priority queue Q that contains all the vertices in $V - S$, keyed by their d values. The implementation assumes that graph G is represented by adjacency lists.

DIJKSTRA(G, w, s)

```
1  INITIALIZE-SINGLE-SOURCE(G, s)
2  S ← ∅
3  Q ← V[G]
4  while Q ≠ ∅
5      do u ← EXTRACT-MIN(Q)
6          S ← S ∪ {u}
7          for each vertex v ∈ Adj[u]
8              do RELAX(u, v, w)
```

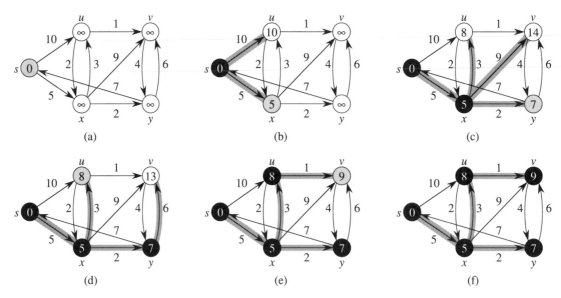

Figure 25.5 The execution of Dijkstra's algorithm. The source is the leftmost vertex. The shortest-path estimates are shown within the vertices, and shaded edges indicate predecessor values: if edge (u, v) is shaded, then $\pi[v] = u$. Black vertices are in the set S, and white vertices are in the priority queue $Q = V - S$. **(a)** The situation just before the first iteration of the **while** loop of lines 4–8. The shaded vertex has the minimum d value and is chosen as vertex u in line 5. **(b)**–**(f)** The situation after each successive iteration of the **while** loop. The shaded vertex in each part is chosen as vertex u in line 5 of the next iteration. The d and π values shown in part (f) are the final values.

Dijkstra's algorithm relaxes edges as shown in Figure 25.5. Line 1 performs the usual initialization of d and π values, and line 2 initializes the set S to the empty set. Line 3 then initializes the priority queue Q to contain all the vertices in $V - S = V - \emptyset = V$. Each time through the **while** loop of lines 4–8, a vertex u is extracted from $Q = V - S$ and inserted into set S. (The first time through this loop, $u = s$.) Vertex u, therefore, has the smallest shortest-path estimate of any vertex in $V - S$. Then, lines 7–8 relax each edge (u, v) leaving u, thus updating the estimate $d[v]$ and the predecessor $\pi[v]$ if the shortest path to v can be improved by going through u. Observe that vertices are never inserted into Q after line 3 and that each vertex is extracted from Q and inserted into S exactly once, so that the **while** loop of lines 4–8 iterates exactly $|V|$ times.

Because Dijkstra's algorithm always chooses the "lightest" or "closest" vertex in $V - S$ to insert into set S, we say that it uses a greedy strategy. Greedy strategies are presented in detail in Chapter 17, but you need not have read that chapter to understand Dijkstra's algorithm. Greedy strategies do not always yield optimal results in general, but as the following theorem and its corollary show, Dijkstra's algorithm does indeed compute

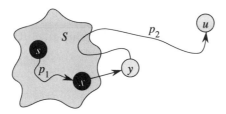

Figure 25.6 The proof of Theorem 25.10. Set S is nonempty just before vertex u is inserted into it. A shortest path p from source s to vertex u can be decomposed into $s \overset{p_1}{\leadsto} x \to y \overset{p_2}{\leadsto} u$, where y is the first vertex on the path that is not in $V - S$ and $x \in S$ immediately precedes y. Vertices x and y are distinct, but we may have $s = x$ or $y = u$. Path p_2 may or may not reenter set S.

shortest paths. The key is to show that each time a vertex u is inserted into set S, we have $d[u] = \delta(s, u)$.

Theorem 25.10 (Correctness of Dijkstra's algorithm)
If we run Dijkstra's algorithm on a weighted, directed graph $G = (V, E)$ with nonnegative weight function w and source s, then at termination, $d[u] = \delta(s, u)$ for all vertices $u \in V$.

Proof We shall show that for each vertex $u \in V$, we have $d[u] = \delta(s, u)$ at the time when u is inserted into set S and that this equality is maintained thereafter.

For the purpose of contradiction, let u be the first vertex for which $d[u] \neq \delta(s, u)$ when it is inserted into set S. We shall focus our attention on the situation at the beginning of the iteration of the **while** loop in which u is inserted into S and derive the contradiction that $d[u] = \delta(s, u)$ at that time by examining a shortest path from s to u. We must have $u \neq s$ because s is the first vertex inserted into set S and $d[s] = \delta(s, s) = 0$ at that time. Because $u \neq s$, we also have that $S \neq \emptyset$ just before u is inserted into S. There must be some path from s to u, for otherwise $d[u] = \delta(s, u) = \infty$ by Corollary 25.6, which would violate our assumption that $d[u] \neq \delta(s, u)$. Because there is at least one path, there is a shortest path p from s to u. Path p connects a vertex in S, namely s, to a vertex in $V - S$, namely u. Let us consider the first vertex y along p such that $y \in V - S$, and let $x \in V$ be y's predecessor. Thus, as shown in Figure 25.6, path p can be decomposed as $s \overset{p_1}{\leadsto} x \to y \overset{p_2}{\leadsto} u$.

We claim that $d[y] = \delta(s, y)$ when u is inserted into S. To prove this claim, observe that $x \in S$. Then, because u is chosen as the first vertex for which $d[u] \neq \delta(s, u)$ when it is inserted into S, we had $d[x] = \delta(s, x)$ when x was inserted into S. Edge (x, y) was relaxed at that time, so the claim follows from Lemma 25.7.

We can now obtain a contradiction to prove the theorem. Because y occurs before u on a shortest path from s to u and all edge weights are nonnegative (notably those on path p_2), we have $\delta(s, y) \leq \delta(s, u)$, and thus

$$
\begin{aligned}
d[y] &= \delta(s, y) \\
&\leq \delta(s, u) \\
&\leq d[u] \quad \text{(by Lemma 25.5)} .
\end{aligned}
\tag{25.2}
$$

But because both vertices u and y were in $V - S$ when u was chosen in line 5, we have $d[u] \leq d[y]$. Thus, the two inequalities in (25.2) are in fact equalities, giving

$$
d[y] = \delta(s, y) = \delta(s, u) = d[u] .
$$

Consequently, $d[u] = \delta(s, u)$, which contradicts our choice of u. We conclude that at the time each vertex $u \in V$ is inserted into set S, we have $d[u] = \delta(s, u)$, and by Lemma 25.5, this equality holds thereafter.   ∎

Corollary 25.11
If we run Dijkstra's algorithm on a weighted, directed graph $G = (V, E)$ with nonnegative weight function w and source s, then at termination, the predecessor subgraph G_π is a shortest-paths tree rooted at s.

Proof   Immediate from Theorem 25.10 and Lemma 25.9.   ∎

Analysis

How fast is Dijkstra's algorithm? Consider first the case in which we maintain the priority queue $Q = V - S$ as a linear array. For such an implementation, each EXTRACT-MIN operation takes time $O(V)$, and there are $|V|$ such operations, for a total EXTRACT-MIN time of $O(V^2)$. Each vertex $v \in V$ is inserted into set S exactly once, so each edge in the adjacency list $Adj[v]$ is examined in the **for** loop of lines 4–8 exactly once during the course of the algorithm. Since the total number of edges in all the adjacency lists is $|E|$, there are a total of $|E|$ iterations of this **for** loop, with each iteration taking $O(1)$ time. The running time of the entire algorithm is thus $O(V^2 + E) = O(V^2)$.

If the graph is sparse, however, it is practical to implement the priority queue Q with a binary heap. The resulting algorithm is sometimes called the ***modified Dijkstra algorithm***. Each EXTRACT-MIN operation then takes time $O(\lg V)$. As before, there are $|V|$ such operations. The time to build the binary heap is $O(V)$. The assignment $d[v] \leftarrow d[u] + w(u, v)$ in RELAX is accomplished by the call DECREASE-KEY($Q, v, d[u] + w(u, v)$), which takes time $O(\lg V)$ (see Exercise 7.5-4), and there are still at most $|E|$ such operations. The total running time is therefore $O((V + E) \lg V)$, which is $O(E \lg V)$ if all vertices are reachable from the source.

We can in fact achieve a running time of $O(V \lg V + E)$ by implementing the priority queue Q with a Fibonacci heap (see Chapter 21). The amortized cost of each of the $|V|$ EXTRACT-MIN operations is $O(\lg V)$, and each of the $|E|$ DECREASE-KEY calls takes only $O(1)$ amortized time. Historically, the development of Fibonacci heaps was motivated by the observation that in the modified Dijkstra algorithm there are potentially many more DECREASE-KEY calls than EXTRACT-MIN calls, so any method of reducing the amortized time of each DECREASE-KEY operation to $o(\lg V)$ without increasing the amortized time of EXTRACT-MIN would yield an asymptotically faster implementation.

Dijkstra's algorithm bears some similarity to both breadth-first search (see Section 23.2) and Prim's algorithm for computing minimum spanning trees (see Section 24.2). It is like breadth-first search in that set S corresponds to the set of black vertices in a breadth-first search; just as vertices in S have their final shortest-path weights, so black vertices in a breadth-first search have their correct breadth-first distances. Dijkstra's algorithm is like Prim's algorithm in that both algorithms use a priority queue to find the "lightest" vertex outside a given set (the set S in Dijkstra's algorithm and the tree being grown in Prim's algorithm), insert this vertex into the set, and adjust the weights of the remaining vertices outside the set accordingly.

Exercises

25.2-1
Run Dijkstra's algorithm on the directed graph of Figure 25.2, first using vertex s as the source and then using vertex y as the source. In the style of Figure 25.5, show the d and π values and the vertices in set S after each iteration of the **while** loop.

25.2-2
Give a simple example of a directed graph with negative-weight edges for which Dijkstra's algorithm produces incorrect answers. Why doesn't the proof of Theorem 25.10 go through when negative-weight edges are allowed?

25.2-3
Suppose we change line 4 of Dijkstra's algorithm to the following.

 4   **while** $|Q| > 1$

This change causes the **while** loop to execute $|V| - 1$ times instead of $|V|$ times. Is this proposed algorithm correct?

25.2-4
We are given a directed graph $G = (V, E)$ on which each edge $(u, v) \in E$ has an associated value $r(u, v)$, which is a real number in the range $0 \leq r(u, v) \leq 1$ that represents the reliability of a communication channel from vertex u to vertex v. We interpret $r(u, v)$ as the probability that the channel from u to v will not fail, and we assume that these probabilities are

independent. Give an efficient algorithm to find the most reliable path between two given vertices.

25.2-5
Let $G = (V, E)$ be a weighted, directed graph with weight function $w : E \rightarrow \{0, 1, \ldots, W - 1\}$ for some nonnegative integer W. Modify Dijkstra's algorithm to compute the shortest paths from a given source vertex s in $O(WV + E)$ time.

25.2-6
Modify your algorithm from Exercise 25.2-5 to run in $O((V + E) \lg W)$ time. (*Hint:* How many distinct shortest-path estimates can there be in $V - S$ at any point in time?)

25.3 The Bellman-Ford algorithm

The ***Bellman-Ford algorithm*** solves the single-source shortest-paths problem in the more general case in which edge weights can be negative. Given a weighted, directed graph $G = (V, E)$ with source s and weight function $w : E \rightarrow \mathbf{R}$, the Bellman-Ford algorithm returns a boolean value indicating whether or not there is a negative-weight cycle that is reachable from the source. If there is such a cycle, the algorithm indicates that no solution exists. If there is no such cycle, the algorithm produces the shortest paths and their weights.

Like Dijkstra's algorithm, the Bellman-Ford algorithm uses the technique of relaxation, progressively decreasing an estimate $d[v]$ on the weight of a shortest path from the source s to each vertex $v \in V$ until it achieves the actual shortest-path weight $\delta(s, v)$. The algorithm returns TRUE if and only if the graph contains no negative-weight cycles that are reachable from the source.

BELLMAN-FORD(G, w, s)
```
1  INITIALIZE-SINGLE-SOURCE(G, s)
2  for i ← 1 to |V[G]| − 1
3      do for each edge (u, v) ∈ E[G]
4          do RELAX(u, v, w)
5  for each edge (u, v) ∈ E[G]
6      do if d[v] > d[u] + w(u, v)
7          then return FALSE
8  return TRUE
```

Figure 25.7 shows how the execution of the Bellman-Ford algorithm works on a graph with 5 vertices. After performing the usual initialization, the algorithm makes $|V| - 1$ passes over the edges of the graph. Each pass is one iteration of the **for** loop of lines 2–4 and consists of relaxing each

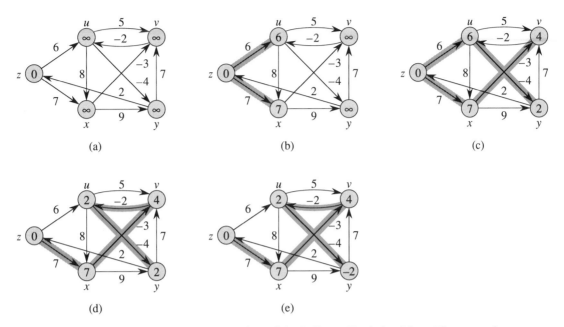

Figure 25.7   The execution of the Bellman-Ford algorithm. The source is vertex z. The d values are shown within the vertices, and shaded edges indicate the π values. In this particular example, each pass relaxes the edges in lexicographic order: $(u, v), (u, x), (u, y), (v, u), (x, v), (x, y), (y, v), (y, z), (z, u), (z, x)$. **(a)** The situation just before the first pass over the edges. **(b)–(e)** The situation after each successive pass over the edges. The d and π values in part (e) are the final values. The Bellman-Ford algorithm returns TRUE in this example.

edge of the graph once. Figures 25.7(b)–(e) show the state of the algorithm after each of the four passes over the edges. After making $|V| - 1$ passes, lines 5–8 check for a negative-weight cycle and return the appropriate boolean value. (We shall see a little later why this check works.)

The Bellman-Ford algorithm runs in time $O(VE)$, since the initialization in line 1 takes $\Theta(V)$ time, each of the $|V| - 1$ passes over the edges in lines 2–4 takes $O(E)$ time, and the **for** loop of lines 5–7 takes $O(E)$ time.

To prove the correctness of the Bellman-Ford algorithm, we start by showing that if there are no negative-weight cycles, the algorithm computes correct shortest-path weights for all vertices reachable from the source. The proof of this lemma contains the intuition behind the algorithm.

Lemma 25.12

Let $G = (V, E)$ be a weighted, directed graph with source s and weight function $w : E \rightarrow \mathbf{R}$, and assume that G contains no negative-weight cycles that are reachable from s. Then, at the termination of BELLMAN-FORD, we have $d[v] = \delta(s, v)$ for all vertices v that are reachable from s.

Proof   Let v be a vertex reachable from s, and let $p = \langle v_0, v_1, \ldots, v_k \rangle$ be a shortest path from s to v, where $v_0 = s$ and $v_k = v$. The path p is simple, and so $k \leq |V| - 1$. We want to prove by induction that for $i = 0, 1, \ldots, k$, we have $d[v_i] = \delta(s, v_i)$ after the ith pass over the edges of G and that this equality is maintained thereafter. Because there are $|V| - 1$ passes, this claim suffices to prove the lemma.

For the basis, we have $d[v_0] = \delta(s, v_0) = 0$ after initialization, and by Lemma 25.5, this equality is maintained thereafter.

For the inductive step, we assume that $d[v_{i-1}] = \delta(s, v_{i-1})$ after the $(i-1)$st pass. Edge (v_{i-1}, v_i) is relaxed in the ith pass, so by Lemma 25.7, we conclude that $d[v_i] = \delta(s, v_i)$ after the ith pass and at all subsequent times, thus completing the proof.   ■

Corollary 25.13

Let $G = (V, E)$ be a weighted, directed graph with source vertex s and weight function $w : E \rightarrow \mathbf{R}$. Then for each vertex $v \in V$, there is a path from s to v if and only if BELLMAN-FORD terminates with $d[v] < \infty$ when it is run on G.

Proof   The proof is similar to that of Lemma 25.12 and is left as Exercise 25.3-2.   ■

Theorem 25.14 (Correctness of the Bellman-Ford algorithm)

Let BELLMAN-FORD be run on a weighted, directed graph $G = (V, E)$ with source s and weight function $w : E \rightarrow \mathbf{R}$. If G contains no negative-weight cycles that are reachable from s, then the algorithm returns TRUE, we have $d[v] = \delta(s, v)$ for all vertices $v \in V$, and the predecessor subgraph G_π is a shortest-paths tree rooted at s. If G does contain a negative-weight cycle reachable from S, then the algorithm returns FALSE.

Proof   Suppose that graph G contains no negative-weight cycles that are reachable from the source s. We first prove the claim that at termination, $d[v] = \delta(s, v)$ for all vertices $v \in V$. If vertex v is reachable from s, then Lemma 25.12 proves this claim. If v is not reachable from s, then the claim follows from Corollary 25.6. Thus, the claim is proven. Lemma 25.9, along with the claim, implies that G_π is a shortest-paths tree. Now we use the claim to show that BELLMAN-FORD returns TRUE. At termination, we have for all edges $(u, v) \in E$,

$$
\begin{aligned}
d[v] &= \delta(s, v) \\
&\leq \delta(s, u) + w(u, v) \qquad \text{(by Lemma 25.3)} \\
&= d[u] + w(u, v) \, ,
\end{aligned}
$$

and so none of the tests in line 6 causes BELLMAN-FORD to return FALSE. It therefore returns TRUE.

Conversely, suppose that graph G contains a negative-weight cycle $c = \langle v_0, v_1, \ldots, v_k \rangle$, where $v_0 = v_k$, that is reachable from the source s. Then,

$$\sum_{i=1}^{k} w(v_{i-1}, v_i) < 0 \ . \tag{25.3}$$

Assume for the purpose of contradiction that the Bellman-Ford algorithm returns TRUE. Thus, $d[v_i] \le d[v_{i-1}] + w(v_{i-1}, v_i)$ for $i = 1, 2, \ldots, k$. Summing the inequalities around cycle c gives us

$$\sum_{i=1}^{k} d[v_i] \le \sum_{i=1}^{k} d[v_{i-1}] + \sum_{i=1}^{k} w(v_{i-1}, v_i) \ .$$

As in the proof of Lemma 25.8, each vertex in c appears exactly once in each of the first two summations. Thus,

$$\sum_{i=1}^{k} d[v_i] = \sum_{i=1}^{k} d[v_{i-1}] \ .$$

Moreover, by Corollary 25.13, $d[v_i]$ is finite for $i = 1, 2, \ldots, k$. Thus,

$$0 \le \sum_{i=1}^{k} w(v_{i-1}, v_i) \ ,$$

which contradicts inequality (25.3). We conclude that the Bellman-Ford algorithm returns TRUE if graph G contains no negative-weight cycles reachable from the source, and FALSE otherwise. ∎

Exercises

25.3-1
Run the Bellman-Ford algorithm on the directed graph of Figure 25.7, using vertex y as the source. Relax edges in lexicographic order in each pass, and show the d and π values after each pass. Now, change the weight of edge (y, v) to 4 and run the algorithm again, using z as the source.

25.3-2
Prove Corollary 25.13.

25.3-3
Given a weighted, directed graph $G = (V, E)$ with no negative-weight cycles, let m be the maximum over all pairs of vertices $u, v \in V$ of the minimum number of edges in a shortest path from u to v. (Here, the shortest path is by weight, not the number of edges.) Suggest a simple change to the Bellman-Ford algorithm that allows it to terminate in $m + 1$ passes.

25.3-4
Modify the Bellman-Ford algorithm so that it sets $d[v]$ to $-\infty$ for all vertices v for which there is a negative-weight cycle on some path from the source to v.

25.3-5

Let $G = (V, E)$ be a weighted, directed graph with weight function $w : E \rightarrow \mathbf{R}$. Give an $O(VE)$-time algorithm to find, for each vertex $v \in V$, the value $\delta^*(v) = \min_{u \in V} \{\delta(u, v)\}$.

25.3-6 $\star$

Suppose that a weighted, directed graph $G = (V, E)$ has a negative-weight cycle. Give an efficient algorithm to list the vertices of one such cycle. Prove that your algorithm is correct.

25.4   Single-source shortest paths in directed acyclic graphs

By relaxing the edges of a weighted dag (directed acyclic graph) $G = (V, E)$ according to a topological sort of its vertices, we can compute shortest paths from a single source in $\Theta(V + E)$ time. Shortest paths are always well defined in a dag, since even if there are negative-weight edges, no negative-weight cycles can exist.

The algorithm starts by topologically sorting the dag (see Section 23.4) to impose a linear ordering on the vertices. If there is a path from vertex u to vertex v, then u precedes v in the topological sort. We make just one pass over the vertices in the topologically sorted order. As each vertex is processed, all the edges that leave the vertex are relaxed.

DAG-SHORTEST-PATHS(G, w, s)

1 topologically sort the vertices of G
2 INITIALIZE-SINGLE-SOURCE(G, s)
3 **for** each vertex u taken in topologically sorted order
4   **do for** each vertex $v \in Adj[u]$
5   **do** RELAX(u, v, w)

An example of the execution of this algorithm is shown in Figure 25.8.

The running time of this algorithm is determined by line 1 and by the **for** loop of lines 3–5. As shown in Section 23.4, the topological sort can be performed in $\Theta(V + E)$ time. In the **for** loop of lines 3–5, as in Dijkstra's algorithm, there is one iteration per vertex. For each vertex, the edges that leave the vertex are each examined exactly once. Unlike Dijkstra's algorithm, however, we use only $O(1)$ time per edge. The running time is thus $\Theta(V + E)$, which is linear in the size of an adjacency-list representation of the graph.

The following theorem shows that the DAG-SHORTEST-PATHS procedure correctly computes the shortest paths.

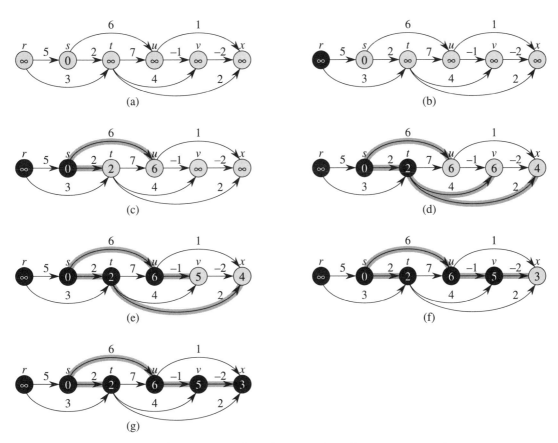

Figure 25.8   The execution of the algorithm for shortest paths in a directed acyclic graph. The vertices are topologically sorted from left to right. The source vertex is s. The d values are shown within the vertices, and shaded edges indicate the π values. **(a)** The situation before the first iteration of the **for** loop of lines 3–5. **(b)–(g)** The situation after each iteration of the **for** loop of lines 3–5. The newly blackened vertex in each iteration was used as v in that iteration. The values shown in part (g) are the final values.

Theorem 25.15

If a weighted, directed graph $G = (V, E)$ has source vertex s and no cycles, then at the termination of the DAG-SHORTEST-PATHS procedure, $d[v] = \delta(s, v)$ for all vertices $v \in V$, and the predecessor subgraph G_π is a shortest-paths tree.

Proof   We first show that $d[v] = \delta(s, v)$ for all vertices $v \in V$ at termination. If v is not reachable from s, then $d[v] = \delta(s, v) = \infty$ by Corollary 25.6. Now, suppose that v is reachable from s, so that there is a shortest path $p = \langle v_0, v_1, \ldots, v_k \rangle$, where $v_0 = s$ and $v_k = v$. Because we process the vertices in topologically sorted order, the edges on p are relaxed in the order $(v_0, v_1), (v_1, v_2), \ldots, (v_{k-1}, v_k)$. A simple induction using Lemma 25.7 (as in the proof of Lemma 25.12) shows that $d[v_i] = \delta(s, v_i)$

at termination for $i = 0, 1, \ldots, k$. Finally, by Lemma 25.9, G_π is a shortest-paths tree. ∎

An interesting application of this algorithm arises in determining critical paths in **PERT chart**[2] analysis. Edges represent jobs to be performed, and edge weights represent the times required to perform particular jobs. If edge (u, v) enters vertex v and edge (v, x) leaves v, then job (u, v) must be performed prior to job (v, x). A path through this dag represents a sequence of jobs that must be performed in a particular order. A **critical path** is a *longest* path through the dag, corresponding to the longest time to perform an ordered sequence of jobs. The weight of a critical path is a lower bound on the total time to perform all the jobs. We can find a critical path by either

- negating the edge weights and running DAG-SHORTEST-PATHS, or
- running DAG-SHORTEST-PATHS, replacing "∞" by "$-\infty$" in line 2 of INITIALIZE-SINGLE-SOURCE and "$>$" by "$<$" in the RELAX procedure.

Exercises

25.4-1
Run DAG-SHORTEST-PATHS on the directed graph of Figure 25.8, using vertex r as the source.

25.4-2
Suppose we change line 3 of DAG-SHORTEST-PATHS to read

3 **for** the first $|V| - 1$ vertices, taken in topologically sorted order

Show that the procedure would remain correct.

25.4-3
The PERT chart formulation given above is somewhat unnatural. It would be more natural for vertices to represent jobs and edges to represent sequencing constraints; that is, edge (u, v) would indicate that job u must be performed before job v. Weights would then be assigned to vertices, not edges. Modify the DAG-SHORTEST-PATHS procedure so that it finds a longest path in a directed acyclic graph with weighted vertices in linear time.

25.4-4
Give an efficient algorithm to count the total number of paths in a directed acyclic graph. Analyze your algorithm and comment on its practicality.

---

[2]"PERT" is an acronym for "program evaluation and review technique."

25.5 Difference constraints and shortest paths

In the general linear-programming problem, we wish to optimize a linear function subject to a set of linear inequalities. In this section, we investigate a special case of linear programming that can be reduced to finding shortest paths from a single source. The single-source shortest-paths problem that results can then be solved using the Bellman-Ford algorithm, thereby also solving the linear-programming problem.

Linear programming

In the general *linear-programming problem*, we are given an $m \times n$ matrix A, an m-vector b, and an n-vector c. We wish to find a vector x of n elements that maximizes the *objective function* $\sum_{i=1}^{n} c_i x_i$ subject to the m constraints given by $Ax \le b$.

Many problems can be expressed as linear programs, and for this reason much work has gone into algorithms for linear programming. The *simplex algorithm*[3] solves general linear programs very quickly in practice. With some carefully contrived inputs, however, the simplex method can require exponential time. General linear programs can be solved in polynomial time by either the *ellipsoid algorithm*, which runs slowly in practice, or *Karmarkar's algorithm*, which in practice is often competitive with the simplex method.

Due to the mathematical investment needed to understand and analyze them, this text does not cover general linear-programming algorithms. For several reasons, though, it is important to understand the setup of linear-programming problems. First, knowing that a given problem can be cast as a polynomial-sized linear-programming problem immediately means that there is a polynomial-time algorithm for the problem. Second, there are many special cases of linear programming for which faster algorithms exist. For example, as shown in this section, the single-source shortest-paths problem is a special case of linear programming. Other problems that can be cast as linear programming include the single-pair shortest-path problem (Exercise 25.5-4) and the maximum-flow problem (Exercise 27.1-8).

---

[3]The simplex algorithm finds an optimal solution to a linear programming problem by examining a sequence of points in the feasible region—the region in n-space that satisfies $Ax \le b$. The algorithm is based on the fact that a solution that maximizes the objective function over the feasible region occurs at some "extreme point," or "corner," of the feasible region. The simplex algorithm proceeds from corner to corner of the feasible region until no further improvement of the objective function is possible. A "simplex" is the convex hull (see Section 35.3) of $d + 1$ points in d-dimensional space (such as a triangle in the plane, or a tetrahedron in 3-space). According to Dantzig [53], it is possible to view the operation of moving from one corner to another as an operation on a simplex derived from a "dual" interpretation of the linear programming problem—hence the name "simplex method."

Sometimes we don't really care about the objective function; we just wish to find any *feasible solution*, that is, any vector x that satisfies $Ax \leq b$, or to determine that no feasible solution exists. We shall focus on one such *feasibility problem*.

Systems of difference constraints

In a *system of difference constraints*, each row of the linear-programming matrix A contains one 1 and one -1, and all other entries of A are 0. Thus, the constraints given by $Ax \leq b$ are a set of m *difference constraints* involving n unknowns, in which each constraint is a simple linear inequality of the form

$$x_j - x_i \leq b_k ,$$

where $1 \leq i, j \leq n$ and $1 \leq k \leq m$.

For example, consider problem of finding the 5-vector $x = (x_i)$ that satisfies

$$\begin{pmatrix} 1 & -1 & 0 & 0 & 0 \\ 1 & 0 & 0 & 0 & -1 \\ 0 & 1 & 0 & 0 & -1 \\ -1 & 0 & 1 & 0 & 0 \\ -1 & 0 & 0 & 1 & 0 \\ 0 & 0 & -1 & 1 & 0 \\ 0 & 0 & -1 & 0 & 1 \\ 0 & 0 & 0 & -1 & 1 \end{pmatrix} \begin{pmatrix} x_1 \\ x_2 \\ x_3 \\ x_4 \\ x_5 \end{pmatrix} \leq \begin{pmatrix} 0 \\ -1 \\ 1 \\ 5 \\ 4 \\ -1 \\ -3 \\ -3 \end{pmatrix} .$$

This problem is equivalent to finding the unknowns x_i, for $i = 1, 2, \dots, 5$, such that the following 8 difference constraints are satisfied:

$$\begin{aligned} x_1 - x_2 &\leq 0 , \\ x_1 - x_5 &\leq -1 , \\ x_2 - x_5 &\leq 1 , \\ x_3 - x_1 &\leq 5 , \\ x_4 - x_1 &\leq 4 , \\ x_4 - x_3 &\leq -1 , \\ x_5 - x_3 &\leq -3 , \\ x_5 - x_4 &\leq -3 . \end{aligned} \qquad (25.4)$$

One solution to this problem is $x = (-5, -3, 0, -1, -4)$, as can be verified directly by checking each inequality. In fact, there is more than one solution to this problem. Another is $x' = (0, 2, 5, 4, 1)$. These two solutions are related: each component of x' is 5 larger than the corresponding component of x. This fact is not mere coincidence.

Lemma 25.16

Let $x = (x_1, x_2, \ldots, x_n)$ be a solution to a system $Ax \le b$ of difference constraints, and let d be any constant. Then $x + d = (x_1 + d, x_2 + d, \ldots, x_n + d)$ is a solution to $Ax \le b$ as well.

Proof For each x_i and x_j, we have $(x_j + d) - (x_i + d) = x_j - x_i$. Thus, if x satisfies $Ax \le b$, so does $x + d$. ∎

Systems of difference constraints occur in many different applications. For example, the unknowns x_i may be times at which events are to occur. Each constraint can be viewed as stating that one event cannot occur too much later than another event. Perhaps the events are jobs to be performed during the construction of a house. If the digging of the foundation begins at time x_1 and takes 3 days and the pouring of the concrete for the foundation begins at time x_2, we may well desire that $x_2 \ge x_1 + 3$ or, equivalently, that $x_1 - x_2 \le -3$. Thus, the relative timing constraint can be expressed as a difference constraint.

Constraint graphs

It is beneficial to interpret systems of difference constraints from a graph-theoretic point of view. The idea is that in a system $Ax \le b$ of difference constraints, the $n \times m$ linear-programming matrix A can be viewed as an incidence matrix (see Exercise 23.1-7) for a graph with n vertices and m edges. Each vertex v_i in the graph, for $i = 1, 2, \ldots, n$, corresponds to one of the n unknown variables x_i. Each directed edge in the graph corresponds to one of the m inequalities involving two unknowns.

More formally, given a system $Ax \le b$ of difference constraints, the corresponding ***constraint graph*** is a weighted, directed graph $G = (V, E)$, where

$$V = \{v_0, v_1, \ldots, v_n\}$$

and

$$E = \{(v_i, v_j) : x_j - x_i \le b_k \text{ is a constraint}\}$$
$$\cup \{(v_0, v_1), (v_0, v_2), (v_0, v_3), \ldots, (v_0, v_n)\} .$$

The additional vertex v_0 is incorporated, as we shall see shortly, to guarantee that every other vertex is reachable from it. Thus, the vertex set V consists of a vertex v_i for each unknown x_i, plus an additional vertex v_0. The edge set E contains an edge for each difference constraint, plus an edge (v_0, v_i) for each unknown x_i. If $x_j - x_i \le b_k$ is a difference constraint, then the weight of edge (v_i, v_j) is $w(v_i, v_j) = b_k$. The weight of each edge leaving v_0 is 0. Figure 25.9 shows the constraint graph for the system (25.4) of difference constraints.

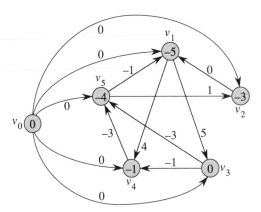

Figure 25.9 The constraint graph corresponding to the system (25.4) of difference constraints. The value of $\delta(v_0, v_i)$ is shown in each vertex v_i. A feasible solution to the system is $x = (-5, -3, 0, -1, -4)$.

The following theorem shows that a solution to a system of difference constraints can be obtained by finding shortest-path weights in the corresponding constraint graph.

Theorem 25.17

Given a system $Ax \le b$ of difference constraints, let $G = (V, E)$ be the corresponding constraint graph. If G contains no negative-weight cycles, then

$$x = (\delta(v_0, v_1), \delta(v_0, v_2), \delta(v_0, v_3), \ldots, \delta(v_0, v_n)) \tag{25.5}$$

is a feasible solution for the system. If G contains a negative-weight cycle, then there is no feasible solution for the system.

Proof   We first show that if the constraint graph contains no negative-weight cycles, then equation (25.5) gives a feasible solution. Consider any edge $(v_i, v_j) \in E$. By Lemma 25.3, $\delta(v_0, v_j) \le \delta(v_0, v_i) + w(v_i, v_j)$ or, equivalently, $\delta(v_0, v_j) - \delta(v_0, v_i) \le w(v_i, v_j)$. Thus, letting $x_i = \delta(v_0, v_i)$ and $x_j = \delta(v_0, v_j)$ satisfies the difference constraint $x_j - x_i \le w(v_i, v_j)$ that corresponds to edge (v_i, v_j).

Now we show that if the constraint graph contains a negative-weight cycle, then the system of difference constraints has no feasible solution. Without loss of generality, let the negative-weight cycle be $c = \langle v_1, v_2, \ldots, v_k \rangle$, where $v_1 = v_k$. (The vertex v_0 cannot be on cycle c, because it has no entering edges.) Cycle c corresponds to the following difference constraints:

$$
\begin{aligned}
x_2 - x_1 &\leq w(v_1, v_2)\,, \\
x_3 - x_2 &\leq w(v_2, v_3)\,, \\
&\vdots \\
x_k - x_{k-1} &\leq w(v_{k-1}, v_k)\,, \\
x_1 - x_k &\leq w(v_k, v_1)\,.
\end{aligned}
$$

Since any solution for x must satisfy each of these k inequalities, any solution must also satisfy the inequality that results when we sum them together. If we sum the left-hand sides, each unknown x_i is added in once and subtracted out once, so that the left-hand side of the sum is 0. The right-hand side sums to $w(c)$, and thus we obtain $0 \leq w(c)$. But since c is a negative-weight cycle, $w(c) < 0$, and hence any solution for the x must satisfy $0 \leq w(c) < 0$, which is impossible. ∎

Solving systems of difference constraints

Theorem 25.17 tells us that we can use the Bellman-Ford algorithm to solve a system of difference constraints. Because there are edges from the source vertex v_0 to all other vertices in the constraint graph, any negative-weight cycle in the constraint graph is reachable from v_0. If the Bellman-Ford algorithm returns TRUE, then the shortest-path weights give a feasible solution to the system. In Figure 25.9, for example, the shortest-path weights provide the feasible solution $x = (-5, -3, 0, -1, -4)$, and by Lemma 25.16, $x = (d - 5, d - 3, d, d - 1, d - 4)$ is also a feasible solution for any constant d. If the Bellman-Ford algorithm returns FALSE, there is no feasible solution to the system of difference constraints.

A system of difference constraints with m constraints on n unknowns produces a graph with $n + 1$ vertices and $n + m$ edges. Thus, using the Bellman-Ford algorithm, we can solve the system in $O((n + 1)(n + m)) = O(n^2 + nm)$ time. Exercise 25.5-5 asks you to show that the algorithm actually runs in $O(nm)$ time, even if m is much less than n.

Exercises

25.5-1
Find a feasible solution or determine that no feasible solution exists for the following system of difference constraints:

$$x_1 - x_2 \leq 1 \, ,$$
$$x_1 - x_4 \leq -4 \, ,$$
$$x_2 - x_3 \leq 2 \, ,$$
$$x_2 - x_5 \leq 7 \, ,$$
$$x_2 - x_6 \leq 5 \, ,$$
$$x_3 - x_6 \leq 10 \, ,$$
$$x_4 - x_2 \leq 2 \, ,$$
$$x_5 - x_1 \leq -1 \, ,$$
$$x_5 - x_4 \leq 3 \, ,$$
$$x_6 - x_3 \leq -8 \, .$$

25.5-2

Find a feasible solution or determine that no feasible solution exists for the following system of difference constraints:

$$x_1 - x_2 \leq 4 \, ,$$
$$x_1 - x_5 \leq 5 \, ,$$
$$x_2 - x_4 \leq -6 \, ,$$
$$x_3 - x_2 \leq 1 \, ,$$
$$x_4 - x_1 \leq 3 \, ,$$
$$x_4 - x_3 \leq 5 \, ,$$
$$x_4 - x_5 \leq 10 \, ,$$
$$x_5 - x_3 \leq -4 \, ,$$
$$x_5 - x_4 \leq -8 \, .$$

25.5-3

Can any shortest-path weight from the new vertex v_0 in a constraint graph be positive? Explain.

25.5-4

Express the single-pair shortest-path problem as a linear program.

25.5-5

Show how to modify the Bellman-Ford algorithm slightly so that when it is used to solve a system of difference constraints with m inequalities on n unknowns, the running time is $O(nm)$.

25.5-6

Show how a system of difference constraints can be solved by a Bellman-Ford-like algorithm that runs on a constraint graph without the extra vertex v_0.

25.5-7 ⋆

Let $Ax \leq b$ be a system of m difference constraints in n unknowns. Show that the Bellman-Ford algorithm, when run on the corresponding constraint graph, maximizes $\sum_{i=1}^{n} x_i$ subject to $Ax \leq b$ and $x_i \leq 0$ for all x_i.

25.5-8 ⋆

Show that the Bellman-Ford algorithm, when run on the constraint graph for a system $Ax \leq b$ of difference constraints, minimizes the quantity $(\max\{x_i\} - \min\{x_i\})$ subject to $Ax \leq b$. Explain how this fact might come in handy if the algorithm is used to schedule construction jobs.

25.5-9

Suppose that every row in the matrix A of a linear program $Ax \leq b$ corresponds to a difference constraint, a single-variable constraint of the form $x_i \leq b_k$, or a single-variable constraint of the form $-x_i \leq b_k$. Show how the Bellman-Ford algorithm can be adapted to solve this variety of constraint system.

25.5-10

Suppose that in addition to a system of difference constraints, we want to handle equality constraints of the form $x_i = x_j + b_k$. Show how the Bellman-Ford algorithm can be adapted to solve this variety of constraint system.

25.5-11

Give an efficient algorithm to solve a system $Ax \leq b$ of difference constraints when all of the elements of b are real-valued and all of the unknowns x_i must be integers.

25.5-12 ⋆

Give an efficient algorithm to solve a system $Ax \leq b$ of difference constraints when all of the elements of b are real-valued and some, but not necessarily all, of the unknowns x_i must be integers.

Problems

25-1 *Yen's improvement to Bellman-Ford*

Suppose that we order the edge relaxations in each pass of the Bellman-Ford algorithm as follows. Before the first pass, we assign an arbitrary linear order $v_1, v_2, \ldots, v_{|V|}$ to the vertices of the input graph $G = (V, E)$. Then, we partition the edge set E into $E_f \cup E_b$, where $E_f = \{(v_i, v_j) \in E : i < j\}$ and $E_b = \{(v_i, v_j) \in E : i > j\}$. Define $G_f = (V, E_f)$ and $G_b = (V, E_b)$.

a. Prove that G_f is acyclic with topological sort $\langle v_1, v_2, \ldots, v_{|V|} \rangle$ and that G_b is acyclic with topological sort $\langle v_{|V|}, v_{|V|-1}, \ldots, v_1 \rangle$.

Suppose that we implement each pass of the Bellman-Ford algorithm in the following way. We visit each vertex in the order $v_1, v_2, \ldots, v_{|V|}$, relaxing edges of E_f that leave the vertex. We then visit each vertex in the order $v_{|V|}, v_{|V|-1}, \ldots, v_1$, relaxing edges of E_b that leave the vertex.

b. Prove that with this scheme, if G contains no negative-weight cycles that are reachable from the source vertex s, then after only $\lceil |V|/2 \rceil$ passes over the edges, $d[v] = \delta(s, v)$ for all vertices $v \in V$.

c. How does this scheme affect the running time of the Bellman-Ford algorithm?

25-2   *Nesting boxes*

A d-dimensional box with dimensions $(x_1, x_2, \ldots, x_d)$ **nests** within another box with dimensions $(y_1, y_2, \ldots, y_d)$ if there exists a permutation π on $\{1, 2, \ldots, d\}$ such that $x_{\pi(1)} < y_1$, $x_{\pi(2)} < y_2$, $\ldots$, $x_{\pi(d)} < y_d$.

a. Argue that the nesting relation is transitive.

b. Describe an efficient method to determine whether or not one d-dimensional box nests inside another.

c. Suppose that you are given a set of n d-dimensional boxes $\{B_1, B_2, \ldots, B_n\}$. Describe an efficient algorithm to determine the longest sequence $\langle B_{i_1}, B_{i_2}, \ldots, B_{i_k} \rangle$ of boxes such that B_{i_j} nests within $B_{i_{j+1}}$ for $j = 1, 2, \ldots, k - 1$. Express the running time of your algorithm in terms of n and d.

25-3   *Arbitrage*

Arbitrage is the use of discrepancies in currency exchange rates to transform one unit of a currency into more than one unit of the same currency. For example, suppose that 1 U.S. dollar buys 0.7 British pound, 1 British pound buys 9.5 French francs, and 1 French franc buys 0.16 U.S. dollar. Then, by converting currencies, a trader can start with 1 U.S. dollar and buy $0.7 \times 9.5 \times 0.16 = 1.064$ U.S. dollars, thus turning a profit of 6.4 percent.

Suppose that we are given n currencies $c_1, c_2, \ldots, c_n$ and an $n \times n$ table R of exchange rates, such that one unit of currency c_i buys $R[i, j]$ units of currency c_j.

a. Give an efficient algorithm to determine whether or not there exists a sequence of currencies $\langle c_{i_1}, c_{i_2}, \ldots, c_{i_k} \rangle$ such that

$$R[i_1, i_2] \cdot R[i_2, i_3] \cdots R[i_{k-1}, i_k] \cdot R[i_k, i_1] > 1 .$$

Analyze the running time of your algorithm.

b. Give an efficient algorithm to print out such a sequence if one exists. Analyze the running time of your algorithm.

25-4 *Gabow's scaling algorithm for single-source shortest paths*

A *scaling* algorithm solves a problem by initially considering only the highest-order bit of each relevant input value (such as an edge weight). It then refines the initial solution by looking at the two highest-order bits. It progressively looks at more and more high-order bits, refining the solution each time, until all bits have been considered and the correct solution has been computed.

In this problem, we examine an algorithm for computing the shortest paths from a single source by scaling edge weights. We are given a directed graph $G = (V, E)$ with nonnegative integer edge weights w. Let $W = \max_{(u,v) \in E} \{w(u, v)\}$. Our goal is to develop an algorithm that runs in $O(E \lg W)$ time.

The algorithm uncovers the bits in the binary representation of the edge weights one at a time, from the most significant bit to the least significant bit. Specifically, let $k = \lceil \lg(W + 1) \rceil$ be the number of bits in the binary representation of W, and for $i = 1, 2, \ldots, k$, let $w_i(u, v) = \lfloor w(u, v)/2^{k-i} \rfloor$. That is, $w_i(u, v)$ is the "scaled-down" version of $w(u, v)$ given by the i most significant bits of $w(u, v)$. (Thus, $w_k(u, v) = w(u, v)$ for all $(u, v) \in E$.) For example, if $k = 5$ and $w(u, v) = 25$, which has the binary representation $\langle 11001 \rangle$, then $w_3(u, v) = \langle 110 \rangle = 6$. As another example with $k = 5$, if $w(u, v) = \langle 00100 \rangle = 4$, then $w_3(u, v) = \langle 001 \rangle = 1$. Let us define $\delta_i(u, v)$ as the shortest-path weight from vertex u to vertex v using weight function w_i. Thus, $\delta_k(u, v) = \delta(u, v)$ for all $u, v \in V$. For a given source vertex s, the scaling algorithm first computes the shortest-path weights $\delta_1(s, v)$ for all $v \in V$, then computes $\delta_2(s, v)$ for all $v \in V$, and so on, until it computes $\delta_k(s, v)$ for all $v \in V$. We assume throughout that $|E| \geq |V| - 1$, and we shall see that computing δ_i from δ_{i-1} takes $O(E)$ time, so that the entire algorithm takes $O(kE) = O(E \lg W)$ time.

a. Suppose that for all vertices $v \in V$, we have $\delta(s, v) \leq |E|$. Show that we can compute $\delta(s, v)$ for all $v \in V$ in $O(E)$ time.

b. Show that we can compute $\delta_1(s, v)$ for all $v \in V$ in $O(E)$ time.

Let us now concentrate on computing δ_i from δ_{i-1}.

c. Prove that for $i = 2, 3, \ldots, k$, either $w_i(u, v) = 2w_{i-1}(u, v)$ or $w_i(u, v) = 2w_{i-1}(u, v) + 1$. Then, prove that

$$2\delta_{i-1}(s, v) \leq \delta_i(s, v) \leq 2\delta_{i-1}(s, v) + |V| - 1$$

for all $v \in V$.

d. Define for $i = 2, 3, \ldots, k$ and all $(u, v) \in E$,

$$\widehat{w}_i(u, v) = w_i(u, v) + 2\delta_{i-1}(s, u) - 2\delta_{i-1}(s, v) .$$

Prove that for $i = 2, 3, \ldots, k$ and all $u, v \in V$, the "reweighted" value $\widehat{w}_i(u, v)$ of edge (u, v) is a nonnegative integer.

e. Now, define $\widehat{\delta}_i(s, v)$ as the shortest-path weight from s to v using the weight function $\widehat{w}_i$. Prove that for $i = 2, 3, \ldots, k$ and all $v \in V$,

$$\delta_i(s, v) = \widehat{\delta}_i(s, v) + 2\delta_{i-1}(s, v)$$

and that $\widehat{\delta}_i(s, v) \leq |E|$.

f. Show how to compute $\delta_i(s, v)$ from $\delta_{i-1}(s, v)$ for all $v \in V$ in $O(E)$ time, and conclude that $\delta(s, v)$ can be computed for all $v \in V$ in $O(E \lg W)$ time.

25-5 *Karp's minimum mean-weight cycle algorithm*

Let $G = (V, E)$ be a directed graph with weight function $w : E \to \mathbf{R}$, and let $n = |V|$. We define the **mean weight** of a cycle $c = \langle e_1, e_2, \ldots, e_k \rangle$ of edges in E to be

$$\mu(c) = \frac{1}{k} \sum_{i=1}^{k} w(e_i) \, .$$

Let $\mu^* = \min_c \mu(c)$, where c ranges over all directed cycles in G. A cycle c for which $\mu(c) = \mu^*$ is called a **minimum mean-weight cycle**. This problem investigates an efficient algorithm for computing μ^*.

Assume without loss of generality that every vertex $v \in V$ is reachable from a source vertex $s \in V$. Let $\delta(s, v)$ be the weight of a shortest path from s to v, and let $\delta_k(s, v)$ be the weight of a shortest path from s to v consisting of *exactly* k edges. If there is no path from s to v with exactly k edges, then $\delta_k(s, v) = \infty$.

a. Show that if $\mu^* = 0$, then G contains no negative-weight cycles and $\delta(s, v) = \min_{0 \leq k \leq n-1} \delta_k(s, v)$ for all vertices $v \in V$.

b. Show that if $\mu^* = 0$, then

$$\max_{0 \leq k \leq n-1} \frac{\delta_n(s, v) - \delta_k(s, v)}{n - k} \geq 0$$

for all vertices $v \in V$. (*Hint:* Use both properties from part (a).)

c. Let c be a 0-weight cycle, and let u and v be any two vertices on c. Suppose that the weight of the path from u to v along the cycle is x. Prove that $\delta(s, v) = \delta(s, u) + x$. (*Hint:* The weight of the path from v to u along the cycle is $-x$.)

d. Show that if $\mu^* = 0$, then there exists a vertex v on the minimum mean-weight cycle such that

$$\max_{0 \leq k \leq n-1} \frac{\delta_n(s, v) - \delta_k(s, v)}{n - k} = 0 \, .$$

(*Hint:* Show that a shortest path to any vertex on the minimum mean-weight cycle can be extended along the cycle to make a shortest path to the next vertex on the cycle.)

e. Show that if $\mu^* = 0$, then

$$\min_{v \in V} \max_{0 \le k \le n-1} \frac{\delta_n(s, v) - \delta_k(s, v)}{n - k} = 0 \ .$$

f. Show that if we add a constant t to the weight of each edge of G, then μ^* is increased by t. Use this to show that

$$\mu^* = \min_{v \in V} \max_{0 \le k \le n-1} \frac{\delta_n(s, v) - \delta_k(s, v)}{n - k} \ .$$

g. Give an $O(VE)$-time algorithm to compute μ^*.

Chapter notes

Dijkstra's algorithm [55] appeared in 1959, but it contained no mention of a priority queue. The Bellman-Ford algorithm is based on separate algorithms by Bellman [22] and Ford [71]. Bellman describes the relation of shortest paths to difference constraints. Lawler [132] describes the linear-time algorithm for shortest paths in a dag, which he considers part of the folklore.

When edge weights are relatively small integers, more efficient algorithms can be used to solve the single-source shortest-paths problem. Ahuja, Mehlhorn, Orlin, and Tarjan [6] give an algorithm that runs in $O(E + V\sqrt{\lg W})$ time on graphs with nonnegative edge weights, where W is the largest weight of any edge in the graph. They also give an easily programmed algorithm that runs in $O(E + V \lg W)$ time. For graphs with negative edge weights, the algorithm due to Gabow and Tarjan [77] runs in $O(\sqrt{V}E \lg(VW))$ time, where W is the magnitude of the largest-magnitude weight of any edge in the graph.

Papadimitriou and Steiglitz [154] have a good discussion of the simplex method and the ellipsoid algorithm as well as other algorithms related to linear programming. The simplex algorithm for linear programming was invented by G. Danzig in 1947. Variants of simplex remain the most popular methods for solving linear-programming problems. The ellipsoid algorithm is due to L. G. Khachian in 1979, based on earlier work by N. Z. Shor, D. B. Judin, and A. S. Nemirovskii. Karmarkar describes his algorithm in [115].

26   All-Pairs Shortest Paths

In this chapter, we consider the problem of finding shortest paths between all pairs of vertices in a graph. This problem might arise in making a table of distances between all pairs of cities for a road atlas. As in Chapter 25, we are given a weighted, directed graph $G = (V, E)$ with a weight function $w : E \rightarrow \mathbf{R}$ that maps edges to real-valued weights. We wish to find, for every pair of vertices $u, v \in V$, a shortest (least-weight) path from u to v, where the weight of a path is the sum of the weights of its constituent edges. We typically want the output in tabular form: the entry in u's row and v's column should be the weight of a shortest path from u to v.

We can solve an all-pairs shortest-paths problem by running a single-source shortest-paths algorithm $|V|$ times, once for each vertex as the source. If all edge weights are nonnegative, we can use Dijkstra's algorithm. If we use the linear-array implementation of the priority queue, the running time is $O(V^3 + VE) = O(V^3)$. The binary-heap implementation of the priority queue yields a running time of $O(VE \lg V)$, which is an improvement if the graph is sparse. Alternatively, we can implement the priority queue with a Fibonacci heap, yielding a running time of $O(V^2 \lg V + VE)$.

If negative-weight edges are allowed, Dijkstra's algorithm can no longer be used. Instead, we must run the slower Bellman-Ford algorithm once from each vertex. The resulting running time is $O(V^2 E)$, which on a dense graph is $O(V^4)$. In this chapter we shall see how to do better. We shall also investigate the relation of the all-pairs shortest-paths problem to matrix multiplication and study its algebraic structure.

Unlike the single-source algorithms, which assume an adjacency-list representation of the graph, most of the algorithms in this chapter use an adjacency-matrix representation. (Johnson's algorithm for sparse graphs uses adjacency lists.) The input is an $n \times n$ matrix W representing the edge weights of an n-vertex directed graph $G = (V, E)$. That is, $W = (w_{ij})$, where

$$w_{ij} = \begin{cases} 0 & \text{if } i = j \text{ ,} \\ \text{the weight of directed edge } (i, j) & \text{if } i \neq j \text{ and } (i, j) \in E \text{ ,} \\ \infty & \text{if } i \neq j \text{ and } (i, j) \notin E \text{ .} \end{cases} \quad (26.1)$$

Negative-weight edges are allowed, but we assume for the time being that the input graph contains no negative-weight cycles.

The tabular output of the all-pairs shortest-paths algorithms presented in this chapter is an $n \times n$ matrix $D = (d_{ij})$, where entry d_{ij} contains the weight of a shortest path from vertex i to vertex j. That is, if we let $\delta(i, j)$ denote the shortest-path weight from vertex i to vertex j (as in Chapter 25), then $d_{ij} = \delta(i, j)$ at termination.

To solve the all-pairs shortest-paths problem on an input adjacency matrix, we need to compute not only the shortest-path weights but also a ***predecessor matrix*** $\Pi = (\pi_{ij})$, where π_{ij} is NIL if either $i = j$ or there is no path from i to j, and otherwise π_{ij} is some predecessor of j on a shortest path from i. Just as the predecessor subgraph G_π from Chapter 25 is a shortest-paths tree for a given source vertex, the subgraph induced by the ith row of the Π matrix should be a shortest-paths tree with root i. For each vertex $i \in V$, we define the ***predecessor subgraph*** of G for i as $G_{\pi,i} = (V_{\pi,i}, E_{\pi,i})$, where

$$V_{\pi,i} = \{j \in V : \pi_{ij} \neq \text{NIL}\} \cup \{i\}$$

and

$$E_{\pi,i} = \{(\pi_{ij}, j) : j \in V_{\pi,i} \text{ and } \pi_{ij} \neq \text{NIL}\} \ .$$

If $G_{\pi,i}$ is a shortest-paths tree, then the following procedure, which is a modified version of the PRINT-PATH procedure from Chapter 23, prints a shortest path from vertex i to vertex j.

PRINT-ALL-PAIRS-SHORTEST-PATH(Π, i, j)

```
1  if i = j
2     then print i
3     else if π_ij = NIL
4              then print "no path from" i "to" j "exists"
5              else PRINT-ALL-PAIRS-SHORTEST-PATH(Π, i, π_ij)
6                   print j
```

In order to highlight the essential features of the all-pairs algorithms in this chapter, we won't cover the creation and properties of predecessor matrices as extensively as we dealt with predecessor subgraphs in Chapter 25. The basics are covered by some of the exercises.

Chapter outline

Section 26.1 presents a dynamic-programming algorithm based on matrix multiplication to solve the all-pairs shortest-paths problem. Using the technique of "repeated squaring," this algorithm can be made to run in $\Theta(V^3 \lg V)$ time. Another dynamic-programming algorithm, the Floyd-Warshall algorithm, is given in Section 26.2. The Floyd-Warshall algorithm runs in time $\Theta(V^3)$. Section 26.2 also covers the problem of finding the transitive closure of a directed graph, which is related to the all-pairs shortest-paths problem. Johnson's algorithm is presented in Section 26.3. Unlike the other algorithms in this chapter, Johnson's algorithm uses the adjacency-list representation of a graph. It solves the all-pairs shortest-paths problem in $O(V^2 \lg V + VE)$ time, which makes it a good algorithm for large, sparse graphs. Finally, in Section 26.4, we examine an algebraic structure called a "closed semiring," which allows many shortest-paths algorithms to be applied to a host of other all-pairs problems not involving shortest paths.

Before proceeding, we need to establish some conventions for adjacency-matrix representations. First, we shall generally assume that the input graph $G = (V, E)$ has n vertices, so that $n = |V|$. Second, we shall use the convention of denoting matrices by uppercase letters, such as W or D, and their individual elements by subscripted lowercase letters, such as w_{ij} or d_{ij}. Some matrices will have parenthesized superscripts, as in $D^{(m)} = \left(d_{ij}^{(m)}\right)$, to indicate iterates. Finally, for a given $n \times n$ matrix A, we shall assume that the value of n is stored in the attribute *rows*[A].

26.1 Shortest paths and matrix multiplication

This section presents a dynamic-programming algorithm for the all-pairs shortest-paths problem on a directed graph $G = (V, E)$. Each major loop of the dynamic program will invoke an operation that is very similar to matrix multiplication, so that the algorithm will look like repeated matrix multiplication. We shall start by developing a $\Theta(V^4)$-time algorithm for the all-pairs shortest-paths problem and then improve its running time to $\Theta(V^3 \lg V)$.

Before proceeding, let us briefly recap the steps given in Chapter 16 for developing a dynamic-programming algorithm.

1. Characterize the structure of an optimal solution.

2. Recursively define the value of an optimal solution.

3. Compute the value of an optimal solution in a bottom-up fashion.

(The fourth step, constructing an optimal solution from computed information, is dealt with in the exercises.)

The structure of a shortest path

We start by characterizing the structure of an optimal solution. For the all-pairs shortest-paths problem on a graph $G = (V, E)$, we have proved (Lemma 25.1) that all subpaths of a shortest path are shortest paths. Suppose that the graph is represented by an adjacency matrix $W = (w_{ij})$. Consider a shortest path p from vertex i to vertex j, and suppose that p contains at most m edges. Assuming that there are no negative-weight cycles, m is finite. If $i = j$, then p has weight 0 and no edges. If vertices i and j are distinct, then we decompose path p into $i \overset{p'}{\leadsto} k \rightarrow j$, where path p' now contains at most $m - 1$ edges. Moreover, by Lemma 25.1, p' is a shortest path from i to k. Thus, by Corollary 25.2, we have $\delta(i, j) = \delta(i, k) + w_{kj}$.

A recursive solution to the all-pairs shortest-paths problem

Now, let $d_{ij}^{(m)}$ be the minimum weight of any path from vertex i to vertex j that contains at most m edges. When $m = 0$, there is a shortest path from i to j with no edges if and only if $i = j$. Thus,

$$d_{ij}^{(0)} = \begin{cases} 0 & \text{if } i = j \,, \\ \infty & \text{if } i \neq j \,. \end{cases}$$

For $m \geq 1$, we compute $d_{ij}^{(m)}$ as the minimum of $d_{ij}^{(m-1)}$ (the weight of the shortest path from i to j consisting of at most $m - 1$ edges) and the minimum weight of any path from i to j consisting of at most m edges, obtained by looking at all possible predecessors k of j. Thus, we recursively define

$$\begin{aligned} d_{ij}^{(m)} &= \min \left(d_{ij}^{(m-1)}, \min_{1 \leq k \leq n} \left\{ d_{ik}^{(m-1)} + w_{kj} \right\} \right) \\ &= \min_{1 \leq k \leq n} \left\{ d_{ik}^{(m-1)} + w_{kj} \right\} \,. \end{aligned} \tag{26.2}$$

The latter equality follows since $w_{jj} = 0$ for all j.

What are the actual shortest-path weights $\delta(i, j)$? If the graph contains no negative-weight cycles, then all shortest paths are simple and thus contain at most $n - 1$ edges. A path from vertex i to vertex j with more than $n - 1$ edges cannot have less weight than a shortest path from i to j. The actual shortest-path weights are therefore given by

$$\delta(i, j) = d_{ij}^{(n-1)} = d_{ij}^{(n)} = d_{ij}^{(n+1)} = \cdots \,. \tag{26.3}$$

Computing the shortest-path weights bottom up

Taking as our input the matrix $W = (w_{ij})$, we now compute a series of matrices $D^{(1)}, D^{(2)}, \ldots, D^{(n-1)}$, where for $m = 1, 2, \ldots, n - 1$, we have $D^{(m)} = \left(d_{ij}^{(m)} \right)$. The final matrix $D^{(n-1)}$ contains the actual shortest-path weights. Observe that since $d_{ij}^{(1)} = w_{ij}$ for all vertices $i, j \in V$, we have $D^{(1)} = W$.

The heart of the algorithm is the following procedure, which, given matrices $D^{(m-1)}$ and W, returns the matrix $D^{(m)}$. That is, it extends the shortest paths computed so far by one more edge.

EXTEND-SHORTEST-PATHS(D, W)

```
1  n ← rows[D]
2  let D' = (d'ᵢⱼ) be an n × n matrix
3  for i ← 1 to n
4      do for j ← 1 to n
5          do d'ᵢⱼ ← ∞
6              for k ← 1 to n
7                  do d'ᵢⱼ ← min(d'ᵢⱼ, dᵢₖ + wₖⱼ)
8  return D'
```

The procedure computes a matrix $D' = (d'_{ij})$, which it returns at the end. It does so by computing equation (26.2) for all i and j, using D for $D^{(m-1)}$ and D' for $D^{(m)}$. (It is written without the superscripts to make its input and output matrices independent of m.) Its running time is $\Theta(n^3)$ due to the three nested **for** loops.

We can now see the relation to matrix multiplication. Suppose we wish to compute the matrix product $C = A \cdot B$ of two $n \times n$ matrices A and B. Then, for $i, j = 1, 2, \ldots, n$, we compute

$$c_{ij} = \sum_{k=1}^{n} a_{ik} \cdot b_{kj} \ . \tag{26.4}$$

Observe that if we make the substitutions

$$
\begin{aligned}
d^{(m-1)} &\rightarrow a \ , \\
w &\rightarrow b \ , \\
d^{(m)} &\rightarrow c \ , \\
\min &\rightarrow + \ , \\
+ &\rightarrow \cdot
\end{aligned}
$$

in equation (26.2), we obtain equation (26.4). Thus, if we make these changes to EXTEND-SHORTEST-PATHS and also replace ∞ (the identity for min) by 0 (the identity for +), we obtain the straightforward $\Theta(n^3)$-time procedure for matrix multiplication.

MATRIX-MULTIPLY(A, B)

```
1  n ← rows[A]
2  let C be an n × n matrix
3  for i ← 1 to n
4      do for j ← 1 to n
5          do cᵢⱼ ← 0
6              for k ← 1 to n
7                  do cᵢⱼ ← cᵢⱼ + aᵢₖ · bₖⱼ
8  return C
```

Returning to the all-pairs shortest-paths problem, we compute the short-est-path weights by extending shortest paths edge by edge. Letting $A \cdot B$

denote the matrix "product" returned by Extend-Shortest-Paths(A, B), we compute the sequence of $n - 1$ matrices

$$
\begin{aligned}
D^{(1)} &= D^{(0)} \cdot W &= W , \\
D^{(2)} &= D^{(1)} \cdot W &= W^2 , \\
D^{(3)} &= D^{(2)} \cdot W &= W^3 , \\
&\quad\vdots \\
D^{(n-1)} &= D^{(n-2)} \cdot W &= W^{n-1} .
\end{aligned}
$$

As we argued above, the matrix $D^{(n-1)} = W^{n-1}$ contains the shortest-path weights. The following procedure computes this sequence in $\Theta(n^4)$ time.

Slow-All-Pairs-Shortest-Paths(W)

```
1  n ← rows[W]
2  D⁽¹⁾ ← W
3  for m ← 2 to n − 1
4      do D⁽ᵐ⁾ ← Extend-Shortest-Paths(D⁽ᵐ⁻¹⁾, W)
5  return D⁽ⁿ⁻¹⁾
```

Figure 26.1 shows a graph and the matrices $D^{(m)}$ computed by the procedure Slow-All-Pairs-Shortest-Paths.

Improving the running time

Our goal, however, is not to compute *all* the $D^{(m)}$ matrices: we are interested only in matrix $D^{(n-1)}$. Recall that in the absence of negative-weight cycles, equation (26.3) implies $D^{(m)} = D^{(n-1)}$ for all integers $m \geq n-1$. We can compute $D^{(n-1)}$ with only $\lceil \lg(n - 1) \rceil$ matrix products by computing the sequence

$$
\begin{aligned}
D^{(1)} &= W , \\
D^{(2)} &= W^2 &= W \cdot W , \\
D^{(4)} &= W^4 &= W^2 \cdot W^2 , \\
D^{(8)} &= W^8 &= W^4 \cdot W^4 , \\
&\quad\vdots \\
D^{(2^{\lceil \lg(n-1) \rceil})} &= W^{2^{\lceil \lg(n-1) \rceil}} &= W^{2^{\lceil \lg(n-1) \rceil - 1}} \cdot W^{2^{\lceil \lg(n-1) \rceil - 1}} .
\end{aligned}
$$

Since $2^{\lceil \lg(n-1) \rceil} \geq n - 1$, the final product $D^{(2^{\lceil \lg(n-1) \rceil})}$ is equal to $D^{(n-1)}$.

The following procedure computes the above sequence of matrices by using this technique of *repeated squaring*.

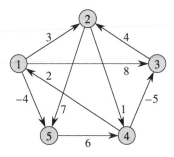

$$D^{(1)} = \begin{pmatrix} 0 & 3 & 8 & \infty & -4 \\ \infty & 0 & \infty & 1 & 7 \\ \infty & 4 & 0 & \infty & \infty \\ 2 & \infty & -5 & 0 & \infty \\ \infty & \infty & \infty & 6 & 0 \end{pmatrix} \quad D^{(2)} = \begin{pmatrix} 0 & 3 & 8 & 2 & -4 \\ 3 & 0 & -4 & 1 & 7 \\ \infty & 4 & 0 & 5 & 11 \\ 2 & -1 & -5 & 0 & -2 \\ 8 & \infty & 1 & 6 & 0 \end{pmatrix}$$

$$D^{(3)} = \begin{pmatrix} 0 & 3 & -3 & 2 & -4 \\ 3 & 0 & -4 & 1 & -1 \\ 7 & 4 & 0 & 5 & 11 \\ 2 & -1 & -5 & 0 & -2 \\ 8 & 5 & 1 & 6 & 0 \end{pmatrix} \quad D^{(4)} = \begin{pmatrix} 0 & 1 & -3 & 2 & -4 \\ 3 & 0 & -4 & 1 & -1 \\ 7 & 4 & 0 & 5 & 3 \\ 2 & -1 & -5 & 0 & -2 \\ 8 & 5 & 1 & 6 & 0 \end{pmatrix}$$

Figure 26.1 A directed graph and the sequence of matrices $D^{(m)}$ computed by SLOW-ALL-PAIRS-SHORTEST-PATHS. The reader may verify that $D^{(5)} = D^{(4)} \cdot W$ is equal to $D^{(4)}$, and thus $D^{(m)} = D^{(4)}$ for all $m \geq 4$.

FASTER-ALL-PAIRS-SHORTEST-PATHS(W)

1 $n \leftarrow rows[W]$
2 $D^{(1)} \leftarrow W$
3 $m \leftarrow 1$
4 **while** $n - 1 > m$
5   **do** $D^{(2m)} \leftarrow$ EXTEND-SHORTEST-PATHS($D^{(m)}, D^{(m)}$)
6          $m \leftarrow 2m$
7 **return** $D^{(m)}$

In each iteration of the **while** loop of lines 4–6, we compute $D^{(2m)} = \left(D^{(m)}\right)^2$, starting with $m = 1$. At the end of each iteration, we double the value of m. The final iteration computes $D^{(n-1)}$ by actually computing $D^{(2m)}$ for some $n - 1 \leq 2m < 2n - 2$. By equation (26.3), $D^{(2m)} = D^{(n-1)}$. The next time the test in line 4 is performed, m has been doubled, so now $n - 1 \leq m$, the test fails, and the procedure returns the last matrix it computed.

The running time of FASTER-ALL-PAIRS-SHORTEST-PATHS is $\Theta(n^3 \lg n)$ since each of the $\lceil \lg(n - 1) \rceil$ matrix products takes $\Theta(n^3)$ time. Observe

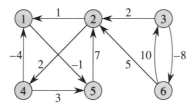

Figure 26.2 A weighted, directed graph for use in Exercises 26.1-1, 26.2-1, and 26.3-1.

that the code is tight, containing no elaborate data structures, and the constant hidden in the Θ-notation is therefore small.

Exercises

26.1-1
Run SLOW-ALL-PAIRS-SHORTEST-PATHS on the weighted, directed graph of Figure 26.2, showing the matrices that result for each iteration of the respective loops. Then do the same for FASTER-ALL-PAIRS-SHORTEST-PATHS.

26.1-2
Why do we require that $w_{ii} = 0$ for all $1 \leq i \leq n$?

26.1-3
What does the matrix

$$D^{(0)} = \begin{pmatrix} 0 & \infty & \infty & \cdots & \infty \\ \infty & 0 & \infty & \cdots & \infty \\ \infty & \infty & 0 & \cdots & \infty \\ \vdots & \vdots & \vdots & \ddots & \vdots \\ \infty & \infty & \infty & \cdots & 0 \end{pmatrix}$$

used in the shortest-paths algorithms correspond to in regular matrix multiplication?

26.1-4
Show how to express the single-source shortest-paths problem as a product of matrices and a vector. Describe how evaluating this product corresponds to a Bellman-Ford-like algorithm (see Section 25.3).

26.1-5
Suppose we also wish to compute the vertices on shortest paths in the algorithms of this section. Show how to compute the predecessor matrix Π from the completed matrix D of shortest-path weights in $O(n^3)$ time.

26.1-6

The vertices on shortest paths can also be computed at the same time as the shortest-path weights. Let us define $\pi_{ij}^{(m)}$ to be the predecessor of vertex j on any minimum-weight path from i to j that contains at most m edges. Modify Extend-Shortest-Paths and Slow-All-Pairs-Shortest-Paths to compute the matrices $\Pi^{(1)}, \Pi^{(2)}, \dots, \Pi^{(n-1)}$ as the matrices $D^{(1)}, D^{(2)}, \dots, D^{(n-1)}$ are computed.

26.1-7

The Faster-All-Pairs-Shortest-Paths procedure, as written, requires us to store $\lceil \lg(n-1) \rceil$ matrices, each with n^2 elements, for a total space requirement of $\Theta(n^2 \lg n)$. Modify the procedure to require only $\Theta(n^2)$ space by using only two $n \times n$ matrices.

26.1-8

Modify Faster-All-Pairs-Shortest-Paths to detect the presence of a negative-weight cycle.

26.1-9

Give an efficient algorithm to find the length (number of edges) of a minimum-length negative-weight cycle in a graph.

26.2   The Floyd-Warshall algorithm

In this section, we shall use a different dynamic-programming formulation to solve the all-pairs shortest-paths problem on a directed graph $G = (V, E)$. The resulting algorithm, known as the ***Floyd-Warshall algorithm***, runs in $\Theta(V^3)$ time. As before, negative-weight edges may be present, but we shall assume that there are no negative-weight cycles. As in Section 26.1, we shall follow the dynamic-programming process to develop the algorithm. After studying the resulting algorithm, we shall present a similar method for finding the transitive closure of a directed graph.

The structure of a shortest path

In the Floyd-Warshall algorithm, we use a different characterization of the structure of a shortest path than we used in the matrix-multiplication-based all-pairs algorithms. The algorithm considers the "intermediate" vertices of a shortest path, where an ***intermediate*** vertex of a simple path $p = \langle v_1, v_2, \dots, v_l \rangle$ is any vertex of p other than v_1 or v_l, that is, any vertex in the set $\{v_2, v_3, \dots, v_{l-1}\}$.

The Floyd-Warshall algorithm is based on the following observation. Let the vertices of G be $V = \{1, 2, \dots, n\}$, and consider a subset $\{1, 2, \dots, k\}$ of vertices for some k. For any pair of vertices $i, j \in V$, consider all paths

all intermediate vertices in $\{1,2,\ldots,k-1\}$ all intermediate vertices in $\{1,2,\ldots,k-1\}$

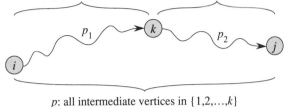

p: all intermediate vertices in $\{1,2,\ldots,k\}$

Figure 26.3   Path p is a shortest path from vertex i to vertex j, and k is the highest-numbered intermediate vertex of p. Path p_1, the portion of path p from vertex i to vertex k, has all intermediate vertices in the set $\{1,2,\ldots,k-1\}$. The same holds for path p_2 from vertex k to vertex j.

from i to j whose intermediate vertices are all drawn from $\{1,2,\ldots,k\}$, and let p be a minimum-weight path from among them. (Path p is simple, since we assume that G contains no negative-weight cycles.) The Floyd-Warshall algorithm exploits a relationship between path p and shortest paths from i to j with all intermediate vertices in the set $\{1,2,\ldots,k-1\}$. The relationship depends on whether or not k is an intermediate vertex of path p.

- If k is not an intermediate vertex of path p, then all intermediate vertices of path p are in the set $\{1,2,\ldots,k-1\}$. Thus, a shortest path from vertex i to vertex j with all intermediate vertices in the set $\{1,2,\ldots,k-1\}$ is also a shortest path from i to j with all intermediate vertices in the set $\{1,2,\ldots,k\}$.

- If k is an intermediate vertex of path p, then we break p down into $i \overset{p_1}{\leadsto} k \overset{p_2}{\leadsto} j$ as shown in Figure 26.3. By Lemma 25.1, p_1 is a shortest path from i to k with all intermediate vertices in the set $\{1,2,\ldots,k\}$. In fact, vertex k is not an intermediate vertex of path p_1, and so p_1 is a shortest path from i to k with all intermediate vertices in the set $\{1,2,\ldots,k-1\}$. Similarly, p_2 is a shortest path from vertex k to vertex j with all intermediate vertices in the set $\{1,2,\ldots,k-1\}$.

A recursive solution to the all-pairs shortest-paths problem

Based on the above observations, we define a different recursive formulation of shortest-path estimates than we did in Section 26.1. Let $d_{ij}^{(k)}$ be the weight of a shortest path from vertex i to vertex j with all intermediate vertices in the set $\{1,2,\ldots,k\}$. When $k=0$, a path from vertex i to vertex j with no intermediate vertex numbered higher than 0 has no intermediate vertices at all. It thus has at most one edge, and hence $d_{ij}^{(0)} = w_{ij}$. A recursive definition is given by

$$d_{ij}^{(k)} = \begin{cases} w_{ij} & \text{if } k = 0 , \\ \min\left(d_{ij}^{(k-1)}, d_{ik}^{(k-1)} + d_{kj}^{(k-1)}\right) & \text{if } k \geq 1 . \end{cases} \qquad (26.5)$$

The matrix $D^{(n)} = \left(d_{ij}^{(n)} \right)$ gives the final answer—$d_{ij}^{(n)} = \delta(i, j)$ for all $i, j \in V$—because all intermediate vertices are in the set $\{1, 2, \ldots, n\}$.

Computing the shortest-path weights bottom up

Based on recurrence (26.5), the following bottom-up procedure can be used to compute the values $d_{ij}^{(k)}$ in order of increasing values of k. Its input is an $n \times n$ matrix W defined as in equation (26.1). The procedure returns the matrix $D^{(n)}$ of shortest-path weights.

FLOYD-WARSHALL(W)

```
1  n ← rows[W]
2  D⁽⁰⁾ ← W
3  for k ← 1 to n
4      do for i ← 1 to n
5          do for j ← 1 to n
6              d_ij^(k) ← min (d_ij^(k-1), d_ik^(k-1) + d_kj^(k-1))
7  return D⁽ⁿ⁾
```

Figure 26.4 shows a directed graph and the matrices $D^{(k)}$ computed by the Floyd-Warshall algorithm.

The running time of the Floyd-Warshall algorithm is determined by the triply nested **for** loops of lines 3–6. Each execution of line 6 takes $O(1)$ time. The algorithm thus runs in time $\Theta(n^3)$. As in the final algorithm in Section 26.1, the code is tight, with no elaborate data structures, and so the constant hidden in the Θ-notation is small. Thus, the Floyd-Warshall algorithm is quite practical for even moderate-sized input graphs.

Constructing a shortest path

There are a variety of different methods for constructing shortest paths in the Floyd-Warshall algorithm. One way is to compute the matrix D of shortest-path weights and then construct the predecessor matrix Π from the D matrix. This method can be implemented to run in $O(n^3)$ time (Exercise 26.1-5). Given the predecessor matrix Π, the PRINT-ALL-PAIRS-SHORTEST-PATH procedure can be used to print the vertices on a given shortest path.

We can compute the predecessor matrix Π "on-line" just as the Floyd-Warshall algorithm computes the matrices $D^{(k)}$. Specifically, we compute a sequence of matrices $\Pi^{(0)}, \Pi^{(1)}, \ldots, \Pi^{(n)}$, where $\Pi = \Pi^{(n)}$ and $\pi_{ij}^{(k)}$ is defined to be the predecessor of vertex j on a shortest path from vertex i with all intermediate vertices in the set $\{1, 2, \ldots, k\}$.

We can give a recursive formulation of $\pi_{ij}^{(k)}$. When $k = 0$, a shortest path from i to j has no intermediate vertices at all. Thus,

$$D^{(0)} = \begin{pmatrix} 0 & 3 & 8 & \infty & -4 \\ \infty & 0 & \infty & 1 & 7 \\ \infty & 4 & 0 & \infty & \infty \\ 2 & \infty & -5 & 0 & \infty \\ \infty & \infty & \infty & 6 & 0 \end{pmatrix} \quad \Pi^{(0)} = \begin{pmatrix} \text{NIL} & 1 & 1 & \text{NIL} & 1 \\ \text{NIL} & \text{NIL} & \text{NIL} & 2 & 2 \\ \text{NIL} & 3 & \text{NIL} & \text{NIL} & \text{NIL} \\ 4 & \text{NIL} & 4 & \text{NIL} & \text{NIL} \\ \text{NIL} & \text{NIL} & \text{NIL} & 5 & \text{NIL} \end{pmatrix}$$

$$D^{(1)} = \begin{pmatrix} 0 & 3 & 8 & \infty & -4 \\ \infty & 0 & \infty & 1 & 7 \\ \infty & 4 & 0 & \infty & \infty \\ 2 & 5 & -5 & 0 & -2 \\ \infty & \infty & \infty & 6 & 0 \end{pmatrix} \quad \Pi^{(1)} = \begin{pmatrix} \text{NIL} & 1 & 1 & \text{NIL} & 1 \\ \text{NIL} & \text{NIL} & \text{NIL} & 2 & 2 \\ \text{NIL} & 3 & \text{NIL} & \text{NIL} & \text{NIL} \\ 4 & 1 & 4 & \text{NIL} & 1 \\ \text{NIL} & \text{NIL} & \text{NIL} & 5 & \text{NIL} \end{pmatrix}$$

$$D^{(2)} = \begin{pmatrix} 0 & 3 & 8 & 4 & -4 \\ \infty & 0 & \infty & 1 & 7 \\ \infty & 4 & 0 & 5 & 11 \\ 2 & 5 & -5 & 0 & -2 \\ \infty & \infty & \infty & 6 & 0 \end{pmatrix} \quad \Pi^{(2)} = \begin{pmatrix} \text{NIL} & 1 & 1 & 2 & 1 \\ \text{NIL} & \text{NIL} & \text{NIL} & 2 & 2 \\ \text{NIL} & 3 & \text{NIL} & 2 & 2 \\ 4 & 1 & 4 & \text{NIL} & 1 \\ \text{NIL} & \text{NIL} & \text{NIL} & 5 & \text{NIL} \end{pmatrix}$$

$$D^{(3)} = \begin{pmatrix} 0 & 3 & 8 & 4 & -4 \\ \infty & 0 & \infty & 1 & 7 \\ \infty & 4 & 0 & 5 & 11 \\ 2 & -1 & -5 & 0 & -2 \\ \infty & \infty & \infty & 6 & 0 \end{pmatrix} \quad \Pi^{(3)} = \begin{pmatrix} \text{NIL} & 1 & 1 & 2 & 1 \\ \text{NIL} & \text{NIL} & \text{NIL} & 2 & 2 \\ \text{NIL} & 3 & \text{NIL} & 2 & 2 \\ 4 & 3 & 4 & \text{NIL} & 1 \\ \text{NIL} & \text{NIL} & \text{NIL} & 5 & \text{NIL} \end{pmatrix}$$

$$D^{(4)} = \begin{pmatrix} 0 & 3 & -1 & 4 & -4 \\ 3 & 0 & -4 & 1 & -1 \\ 7 & 4 & 0 & 5 & 3 \\ 2 & -1 & -5 & 0 & -2 \\ 8 & 5 & 1 & 6 & 0 \end{pmatrix} \quad \Pi^{(4)} = \begin{pmatrix} \text{NIL} & 1 & 4 & 2 & 1 \\ 4 & \text{NIL} & 4 & 2 & 1 \\ 4 & 3 & \text{NIL} & 2 & 1 \\ 4 & 3 & 4 & \text{NIL} & 1 \\ 4 & 3 & 4 & 5 & \text{NIL} \end{pmatrix}$$

$$D^{(5)} = \begin{pmatrix} 0 & 1 & -3 & 2 & -4 \\ 3 & 0 & -4 & 1 & -1 \\ 7 & 4 & 0 & 5 & 3 \\ 2 & -1 & -5 & 0 & -2 \\ 8 & 5 & 1 & 6 & 0 \end{pmatrix} \quad \Pi^{(5)} = \begin{pmatrix} \text{NIL} & 3 & 4 & 5 & 1 \\ 4 & \text{NIL} & 4 & 2 & 1 \\ 4 & 3 & \text{NIL} & 2 & 1 \\ 4 & 3 & 4 & \text{NIL} & 1 \\ 4 & 3 & 4 & 5 & \text{NIL} \end{pmatrix}$$

Figure 26.4   The sequence of matrices $D^{(k)}$ and $\Pi^{(k)}$ computed by the Floyd-Warshall algorithm for the graph in Figure 26.1.

$$\pi_{ij}^{(0)} = \begin{cases} \text{NIL} & \text{if } i = j \text{ or } w_{ij} = \infty , \\ i & \text{if } i \neq j \text{ and } w_{ij} < \infty . \end{cases} \qquad (26.6)$$

For $k \geq 1$, if we take the path $i \rightsquigarrow k \rightsquigarrow j$, then the predecessor of j we choose is the same as the predecessor of j we chose on a shortest path from k with all intermediate vertices in the set $\{1, 2, \dots, k-1\}$. Otherwise, we choose the same predecessor of j that we chose on a shortest path from i with all intermediate vertices in the set $\{1, 2, \dots, k-1\}$. Formally, for $k \geq 1$,

$$\pi_{ij}^{(k)} = \begin{cases} \pi_{ij}^{(k-1)} & \text{if } d_{ij}^{(k-1)} \leq d_{ik}^{(k-1)} + d_{kj}^{(k-1)} , \\ \pi_{kj}^{(k-1)} & \text{if } d_{ij}^{(k-1)} > d_{ik}^{(k-1)} + d_{kj}^{(k-1)} . \end{cases} \qquad (26.7)$$

We leave the incorporation of the $\Pi^{(k)}$ matrix computations into the FLOYD-WARSHALL procedure as Exercise 26.2-3. Figure 26.4 shows the sequence of $\Pi^{(k)}$ matrices that the resulting algorithm computes for the graph of Figure 26.1. The exercise also asks for the more difficult task of proving that the predecessor subgraph $G_{\pi,i}$ is a shortest-paths tree with root i. Yet another way to reconstruct shortest paths is given as Exercise 26.2-6.

Transitive closure of a directed graph

Given a directed graph $G = (V, E)$ with vertex set $V = \{1, 2, \dots, n\}$, we may wish to find out whether there is a path in G from i to j for all vertex pairs $i, j \in V$. The *transitive closure* of G is defined as the graph $G^* = (V, E^*)$, where

$E^* = \{(i, j) : \text{there is a path from vertex } i \text{ to vertex } j \text{ in } G\}$.

One way to compute the transitive closure of a graph in $\Theta(n^3)$ time is to assign a weight of 1 to each edge of E and run the Floyd-Warshall algorithm. If there is a path from vertex i to vertex j, we get $d_{ij} < n$. Otherwise, we get $d_{ij} = \infty$.

There is another, similar way to compute the transitive closure of G in $\Theta(n^3)$ time that can save time and space in practice. This method involves substitution of the logical operations $\vee$ and $\wedge$ for the arithmetic operations min and $+$ in the Floyd-Warshall algorithm. For $i, j, k = 1, 2, \dots, n$, we define $t_{ij}^{(k)}$ to be 1 if there exists a path in graph G from vertex i to vertex j with all intermediate vertices in the set $\{1, 2, \dots, k\}$, and 0 otherwise. We construct the transitive closure $G^* = (V, E^*)$ by putting edge (i, j) into E^* if and only if $t_{ij}^{(n)} = 1$. A recursive definition of $t_{ij}^{(k)}$, analogous to recurrence (26.5), is

$$t_{ij}^{(0)} = \begin{cases} 0 & \text{if } i \neq j \text{ and } (i, j) \notin E , \\ 1 & \text{if } i = j \text{ or } (i, j) \in E , \end{cases}$$

and for $k \geq 1$,

$$t_{ij}^{(k)} = t_{ij}^{(k-1)} \vee \left(t_{ik}^{(k-1)} \wedge t_{kj}^{(k-1)} \right) \ . \tag{26.8}$$

As in the Floyd-Warshall algorithm, we compute the matrices $T^{(k)} = \left(t_{ij}^{(k)} \right)$ in order of increasing k.

TRANSITIVE-CLOSURE(G)

```
 1   n ← |V[G]|
 2   for i ← 1 to n
 3       do for j ← 1 to n
 4              do if i = j or (i, j) ∈ E[G]
 5                     then t_ij^(0) ← 1
 6                     else t_ij^(0) ← 0
 7   for k ← 1 to n
 8       do for i ← 1 to n
 9              do for j ← 1 to n
10                     do t_ij^(k) ← t_ij^(k-1) ∨ ( t_ik^(k-1) ∧ t_kj^(k-1) )
11   return T^(n)
```

Figure 26.5 shows the matrices $T^{(k)}$ computed by the TRANSITIVE-CLO-SURE procedure on a sample graph. Like the Floyd-Warshall algorithm, the running time of the TRANSITIVE-CLOSURE procedure is $\Theta(n^3)$. On some computers, though, logical operations on single-bit values execute faster than arithmetic operations on integer words of data. Moreover, because the direct transitive-closure algorithm uses only boolean values rather than integer values, its space requirement is less than the Floyd-Warshall algorithm's by a factor corresponding to the size of a word of computer storage.

In Section 26.4, we shall see that the correspondence between FLOYD-WARSHALL and TRANSITIVE-CLOSURE is more than coincidence. Both algorithms are based on a type of algebraic structure called a "closed semiring."

Exercises

26.2-1

Run the Floyd-Warshall algorithm on the weighted, directed graph of Figure 26.2. Show the matrix $D^{(k)}$ that results for each iteration of the outer loop.

26.2-2

As it appears above, the Floyd-Warshall algorithm requires $\Theta(n^3)$ space, since we compute $d_{ij}^{(k)}$ for $i, j, k = 1, 2, \ldots, n$. Show that the following procedure, which simply drops all the superscripts, is correct, and thus only $\Theta(n^2)$ space is required.

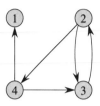

$$T^{(0)} = \begin{pmatrix} 1 & 0 & 0 & 0 \\ 0 & 1 & 1 & 1 \\ 0 & 1 & 1 & 0 \\ 1 & 0 & 1 & 1 \end{pmatrix} \quad T^{(1)} = \begin{pmatrix} 1 & 0 & 0 & 0 \\ 0 & 1 & 1 & 1 \\ 0 & 1 & 1 & 0 \\ 1 & 0 & 1 & 1 \end{pmatrix} \quad T^{(2)} = \begin{pmatrix} 1 & 0 & 0 & 0 \\ 0 & 1 & 1 & 1 \\ 0 & 1 & 1 & 1 \\ 1 & 0 & 1 & 1 \end{pmatrix}$$

$$T^{(3)} = \begin{pmatrix} 1 & 0 & 0 & 0 \\ 0 & 1 & 1 & 1 \\ 0 & 1 & 1 & 1 \\ 1 & 1 & 1 & 1 \end{pmatrix} \quad T^{(4)} = \begin{pmatrix} 1 & 0 & 0 & 0 \\ 1 & 1 & 1 & 1 \\ 1 & 1 & 1 & 1 \\ 1 & 1 & 1 & 1 \end{pmatrix}$$

Figure 26.5 A directed graph and the matrices $T^{(k)}$ computed by the transitive-closure algorithm.

FLOYD-WARSHALL$'(W)$

```
1   n ← rows[W]
2   D ← W
3   for k ← 1 to n
4       do for i ← 1 to n
5           do for j ← 1 to n
6               d_{ij} ← min (d_{ij}, d_{ik} + d_{kj})
7   return D
```

26.2-3

Modify the FLOYD-WARSHALL procedure to include computation of the $\Pi^{(k)}$ matrices according to equations (26.6) and (26.7). Prove rigorously that for all $i \in V$, the predecessor subgraph $G_{\pi,i}$ is a shortest-paths tree with root i. (*Hint:* To show that $G_{\pi,i}$ is acyclic, first show that $\pi_{ij}^{(k)} = l$ implies $d_{ij}^{(k)} \geq d_{il}^{(k-1)} + w_{lj}$. Then, adapt the proof of Lemma 25.8.)

26.2-4

Suppose that we modify the way in which equality is handled in equation (26.7):

$$\pi_{ij}^{(k)} = \begin{cases} \pi_{ij}^{(k-1)} & \text{if } d_{ij}^{(k-1)} < d_{ik}^{(k-1)} + d_{kj}^{(k-1)} , \\ \pi_{kj}^{(k-1)} & \text{if } d_{ij}^{(k-1)} \geq d_{ik}^{(k-1)} + d_{kj}^{(k-1)} . \end{cases}$$

Is this alternative definition of the predecessor matrix Π correct?

26.2-5
How can the output of the Floyd-Warshall algorithm be used to detect the presence of a negative-weight cycle?

26.2-6
Another way to reconstruct shortest paths in the Floyd-Warshall algorithm uses values $\phi_{ij}^{(k)}$ for $i, j, k = 1, 2, \ldots, n$, where $\phi_{ij}^{(k)}$ is the highest-numbered intermediate vertex of a shortest path from i to j. Give a recursive formulation for $\phi_{ij}^{(k)}$, modify the FLOYD-WARSHALL procedure to compute the $\phi_{ij}^{(k)}$ values, and rewrite the PRINT-ALL-PAIRS-SHORTEST-PATH procedure to take the matrix $\Phi = \left(\phi_{ij}^{(n)} \right)$ as an input. How is the matrix Φ like the s table in the matrix-chain multiplication problem of Section 16.1?

26.2-7
Give an $O(VE)$-time algorithm for computing the transitive closure of a directed graph $G = (V, E)$.

26.2-8
Suppose that the transitive closure of a directed acyclic graph can be computed in $f(V, E)$ time, where $f(V, E) = \Omega(V + E)$ and f is monotonically increasing. Show that the time to compute the transitive closure of a general directed graph is $O(f(V, E))$.

26.3 Johnson's algorithm for sparse graphs

Johnson's algorithm finds shortest paths between all pairs in $O(V^2 \lg V + VE)$ time; it is thus asymptotically better than either repeated squaring of matrices or the Floyd-Warshall algorithm for sparse graphs. The algorithm either returns a matrix of shortest-path weights for all pairs or reports that the input graph contains a negative-weight cycle. Johnson's algorithm uses as subroutines both Dijkstra's algorithm and the Bellman-Ford algorithm, which are described in Chapter 25.

Johnson's algorithm uses the technique of ***reweighting***, which works as follows. If all edge weights w in a graph $G = (V, E)$ are nonnegative, we can find shortest paths between all pairs of vertices by running Dijkstra's algorithm once from each vertex; with the Fibonacci-heap priority queue, the running time of this all-pairs algorithm is $O(V^2 \lg V + VE)$. If G has negative-weight edges, we simply compute a new set of nonnegative edge weights that allows us to use the same method. The new set of edge weights $\widehat{w}$ must satisfy two important properties.

1. For all pairs of vertices $u, v \in V$, a shortest path from u to v using weight function w is also a shortest path from u to v using weight function $\widehat{w}$.

2. For all edges (u, v), the new weight $\widehat{w}(u, v)$ is nonnegative.

As we shall see in a moment, the preprocessing of G to determine the new weight function $\widehat{w}$ can be performed in $O(VE)$ time.

Preserving shortest paths by reweighting

As the following lemma shows, it is easy to come up with a reweighting of the edges that satisfies the first property above. We use δ to denote shortest-path weights derived from weight function w and $\widehat{\delta}$ to denote shortest-path weights derived from weight function $\widehat{w}$.

Lemma 26.1 (Reweighting doesn't change shortest paths)
Given a weighted, directed graph $G = (V, E)$ with weight function $w : E \rightarrow \mathbf{R}$, let $h : V \rightarrow \mathbf{R}$ be any function mapping vertices to real numbers. For each edge $(u, v) \in E$, define

$$\widehat{w}(u, v) = w(u, v) + h(u) - h(v) . \tag{26.9}$$

Let $p = \langle v_0, v_1, \ldots, v_k \rangle$ be a path from vertex v_0 to vertex v_k. Then, $w(p) = \delta(v_0, v_k)$ if and only if $\widehat{w}(p) = \widehat{\delta}(v_0, v_k)$. Also, G has a negative-weight cycle using weight function w if and only if G has a negative-weight cycle using weight function $\widehat{w}$.

Proof We start by showing that

$$\widehat{w}(p) = w(p) + h(v_0) - h(v_k) . \tag{26.10}$$

We have

$$\begin{aligned}
\widehat{w}(p) &= \sum_{i=1}^{k} \widehat{w}(v_{i-1}, v_i) \\
&= \sum_{i=1}^{k} (w(v_{i-1}, v_i) + h(v_{i-1}) - h(v_i)) \\
&= \sum_{i=1}^{k} w(v_{i-1}, v_i) + h(v_0) - h(v_k) \\
&= w(p) + h(v_0) - h(v_k) .
\end{aligned}$$

The third equality follows from the telescoping sum on the second line.

We now show by contradiction that $w(p) = \delta(v_0, v_k)$ implies $\widehat{w}(p) = \widehat{\delta}(v_0, v_k)$. Suppose that there is a shorter path p' from v_0 to v_k using weight function $\widehat{w}$. Then, $\widehat{w}(p') < \widehat{w}(p)$. By equation (26.10),

$$\begin{aligned}
w(p') + h(v_0) - h(v_k) &= \widehat{w}(p') \\
&< \widehat{w}(p) \\
&= w(p) + h(v_0) - h(v_k) ,
\end{aligned}$$

which implies that $w(p') < w(p)$. But this contradicts our assumption that p is a shortest path from u to v using w. The proof of the converse is similar.

Finally, we show that G has a negative-weight cycle using weight function w if and only if G has a negative-weight cycle using weight function $\widehat{w}$. Consider any cycle $c = \langle v_0, v_1, \ldots, v_k \rangle$, where $v_0 = v_k$. By equation (26.10),

$$
\begin{aligned}
\widehat{w}(c) &= w(c) + h(v_0) - h(v_k) \\
&= w(c) ,
\end{aligned}
$$

and thus c has negative weight using w if and only if it has negative weight using $\widehat{w}$. ∎

Producing nonnegative weights by reweighting

Our next goal is to ensure that the second property holds: we want $\widehat{w}(u, v)$ to be nonnegative for all edges $(u, v) \in E$. Given a weighted, directed graph $G = (V, E)$ with weight function $w : E \to \mathbf{R}$, we make a new graph $G' = (V', E')$, where $V' = V \cup \{s\}$ for some new vertex $s \notin V$ and $E' = E \cup \{(s, v) : v \in V\}$. We extend the weight function w so that $w(s, v) = 0$ for all $v \in V$. Note that because s has no edges that enter it, no shortest paths in G', other than those with source s, contain s. Moreover, G' has no negative-weight cycles if and only if G has no negative-weight cycles. Figure 26.6(a) shows the graph G' corresponding to the graph G of Figure 26.1.

Now suppose that G and G' have no negative-weight cycles. Let us define $h(v) = \delta(s, v)$ for all $v \in V'$. By Lemma 25.3, we have $h(v) \le h(u) + w(u, v)$ for all edges $(u, v) \in E'$. Thus, if we define the new weights $\widehat{w}$ according to equation (26.9), we have $\widehat{w}(u, v) = w(u, v) + h(u) - h(v) \ge 0$, and the second property is satisfied. Figure 26.6(b) shows the graph G' from Figure 26.6(a) with reweighted edges.

Computing all-pairs shortest paths

Johnson's algorithm to compute all-pairs shortest paths uses the Bellman-Ford algorithm (Section 25.3) and Dijkstra's algorithm (Section 25.2) as subroutines. It assumes that the edges are stored in adjacency lists. The algorithm returns the usual $|V| \times |V|$ matrix $D = d_{ij}$, where $d_{ij} = \delta(i, j)$, or it reports that the input graph contains a negative-weight cycle. (In order for the indices into the D matrix to make any sense, we assume that the vertices are numbered from 1 to $|V|$.)

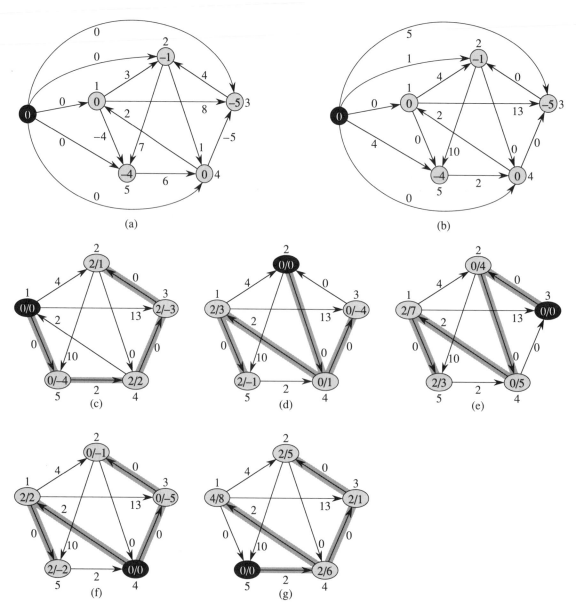

Figure 26.6 Johnson's all-pairs shortest-paths algorithm run on the graph of Figure 26.1. (a) The graph G' with the original weight function w. The new vertex s is black. Within each vertex v is $h(v) = \delta(s, v)$. (b) Each edge (u, v) is reweighted with weight function $\widehat{w}(u, v) = w(u, v) + h(u) - h(v)$. (c)–(g) The result of running Dijkstra's algorithm on each vertex of G using weight function $\widehat{w}$. In each part, the source vertex u is black. Within each vertex v are the values $\widehat{\delta}(u, v)$ and $\delta(u, v)$, separated by a slash. The value $d_{uv} = \delta(u, v)$ is equal to $\widehat{\delta}(u, v) + h(v) - h(u)$.

JOHNSON(G)

```
 1  compute G', where V[G'] = V[G] ∪ {s} and
        E[G'] = E[G] ∪ {(s,v) : v ∈ V[G]}
 2  if BELLMAN-FORD(G', w, s) = FALSE
 3     then print "the input graph contains a negative-weight cycle"
 4     else for each vertex v ∈ V[G']
 5              do set h(v) to the value of δ(s,v)
                     computed by the Bellman-Ford algorithm
 6           for each edge (u,v) ∈ E[G']
 7              do ŵ(u,v) ← w(u,v) + h(u) − h(v)
 8           for each vertex u ∈ V[G]
 9              do run DIJKSTRA(G, ŵ, u) to compute
                     δ̂(u,v) for all v ∈ V[G]
10                 for each vertex v ∈ V[G]
11                    do d_uv ← δ̂(u,v) + h(v) − h(u)
12  return D
```

This code simply performs the actions we specified earlier. Line 1 produces G'. Line 2 runs the Bellman-Ford algorithm on G' with weight function w. If G', and hence G, contains a negative-weight cycle, line 3 reports the problem. Lines 4–11 assume that G' contains no negative-weight cycles. Lines 4–5 set $h(v)$ to the shortest-path weight $\delta(s,v)$ computed by the Bellman-Ford algorithm for all $v \in V'$. Lines 6–7 compute the new weights $\widehat{w}$. For each pair of vertices $u, v \in V$, the **for** loop of lines 8–11 computes the shortest-path weight $\widehat{\delta}(u,v)$ by calling Dijkstra's algorithm once from each vertex in V. Line 11 stores in matrix entry d_{uv} the correct shortest-path weight $\delta(u,v)$, calculated using equation (26.10). Finally, line 12 returns the completed D matrix. Figure 26.6 shows the execution of Johnson's algorithm.

The running time of Johnson's algorithm is easily seen to be $O(V^2 \lg V + VE)$ if the priority queue in Dijkstra's algorithm is implemented by a Fibonacci heap. The simpler binary-heap implementation yields a running time of $O(VE \lg V)$, which is still asymptotically faster than the Floyd-Warshall algorithm if the graph is sparse.

Exercises

26.3-1

Use Johnson's algorithm to find the shortest paths between all pairs of vertices in the graph of Figure 26.2. Show the values of h and $\widehat{w}$ computed by the algorithm.

26.3-2

What is the purpose of adding the new vertex s to V, yielding V'?

26.3-3
Suppose that $w(u, v) \geq 0$ for all edges $(u, v) \in E$. What is the relationship between the weight functions w and $\widehat{w}$?

★ 26.4   A general framework for solving path problems in directed graphs

In this section, we examine "closed semirings," an algebraic structure that yields a general framework for solving path problems in directed graphs. We start by defining closed semirings and discussing how they relate to a calculus of directed paths. We then show some examples of closed semirings and a "generic" algorithm for computing all-pairs path information. Both the Floyd-Warshall algorithm and the transitive-closure algorithm from Section 26.2 are instantiations of this generic algorithm.

Definition of closed semirings

A *closed semiring* is a system $(S, \oplus, \odot, \overline{0}, \overline{1})$, where S is a set of elements, $\oplus$ (the *summary operator*) and $\odot$ (the *extension operator*) are binary operations on S, and $\overline{0}$ and $\overline{1}$ are elements of S, satisfying the following eight properties:

1. $(S, \oplus, \overline{0})$ is a *monoid*:

   - S is *closed* under $\oplus$: $a \oplus b \in S$ for all $a, b \in S$.
   - $\oplus$ is *associative*: $a \oplus (b \oplus c) = (a \oplus b) \oplus c$ for all $a, b, c \in S$.
   - $\overline{0}$ is an *identity* for $\oplus$: $a \oplus \overline{0} = \overline{0} \oplus a = a$ for all $a \in S$.

   Likewise, $(S, \odot, \overline{1})$ is a monoid.

2. $\overline{0}$ is an *annihilator*: $a \odot \overline{0} = \overline{0} \odot a = \overline{0}$ for all $a \in S$.

3. $\oplus$ is *commutative*: $a \oplus b = b \oplus a$ for all $a, b \in S$.

4. $\oplus$ is *idempotent*: $a \oplus a = a$ for all $a \in S$.

5. $\odot$ *distributes* over $\oplus$: $a \odot (b \oplus c) = (a \odot b) \oplus (a \odot c)$ and $(b \oplus c) \odot a = (b \odot a) \oplus (c \odot a)$ for all $a, b, c \in S$.

6. If $a_1, a_2, a_3, \ldots$ is a countable sequence of elements of S, then $a_1 \oplus a_2 \oplus a_3 \oplus \cdots$ is well defined and in S.

7. Associativity, commutativity, and idempotence apply to infinite summaries. (Thus, any infinite summary can be rewritten as an infinite summary in which each term of the summary is included just once and the order of evaluation is arbitrary.)

8. $\odot$ distributes over infinite summaries: $a \odot (b_1 \oplus b_2 \oplus b_3 \oplus \cdots) = (a \odot b_1) \oplus (a \odot b_2) \oplus (a \odot b_3) \oplus \cdots$ and $(a_1 \oplus a_2 \oplus a_3 \oplus \cdots) \odot b = (a_1 \odot b) \oplus (a_2 \odot b) \oplus (a_3 \odot b) \oplus \cdots$.

A calculus of paths in directed graphs

Although the closed-semiring properties may seem abstract, they can be related to a calculus of paths in directed graphs. Suppose we are given a directed graph $G = (V, E)$ and a ***labeling function*** $\lambda : V \times V \to S$ mapping all ordered pairs of vertices into some codomain S. The ***label of edge*** $(u, v) \in E$ is denoted $\lambda(u, v)$. Since λ is defined over the domain $V \times V$, the label $\lambda(u, v)$ is usually taken as $\bar{0}$ if (u, v) is not an edge of G (we shall see why in a moment).

We use the associative extension operator $\odot$ to extend the notion of labels to paths. The ***label of path*** $p = \langle v_1, v_2, \ldots, v_k \rangle$ is

$$\lambda(p) = \lambda(v_1, v_2) \odot \lambda(v_2, v_3) \odot \cdots \odot \lambda(v_{k-1}, v_k) \, .$$

The identity $\bar{1}$ for $\odot$ serves as the label of the empty path.

As a running example of an application of closed semirings, we shall use shortest paths with nonnegative edge weights. The codomain S is $\mathbf{R}^{\geq 0} \cup \{\infty\}$, where $\mathbf{R}^{\geq 0}$ is the set of nonnegative reals, and $\lambda(i, j) = w_{ij}$ for all $i, j \in V$. The extension operator $\odot$ corresponds to the arithmetic operator $+$, and the label of path $p = \langle v_1, v_2, \ldots, v_k \rangle$ is therefore

$$
\begin{aligned}
\lambda(p) &= \lambda(v_1, v_2) \odot \lambda(v_2, v_3) \odot \cdots \odot \lambda(v_{k-1}, v_k) \\
&= w_{v_1, v_2} + w_{v_2, v_3} + \cdots + w_{v_{k-1}, v_k} \\
&= w(p) \, .
\end{aligned}
$$

Not surprisingly, the role of $\bar{1}$, the identity for $\odot$, is taken by 0, the identity for $+$. We denote the empty path by ε, and its label is $\lambda(\varepsilon) = w(\varepsilon) = 0 = \bar{1}$.

Because the extension operator $\odot$ is associative, we can define the label of the concatenation of two paths in a natural way. Given paths $p_1 = \langle v_1, v_2, \ldots, v_k \rangle$ and $p_2 = \langle v_k, v_{k+1}, \ldots, v_l \rangle$, their ***concatenation*** is

$$p_1 \circ p_2 = \langle v_1, v_2, \ldots, v_k, v_{k+1}, \ldots, v_l \rangle \, ,$$

and the label of their concatenation is

$$
\begin{aligned}
\lambda(p_1 \circ p_2) &= \lambda(v_1, v_2) \odot \lambda(v_2, v_3) \odot \cdots \odot \lambda(v_{k-1}, v_k) \odot \\
&\qquad \lambda(v_k, v_{k+1}) \odot \lambda(v_{k+1}, v_{k+2}) \odot \cdots \odot \lambda(v_{l-1}, v_l) \\
&= (\lambda(v_1, v_2) \odot \lambda(v_2, v_3) \odot \cdots \odot \lambda(v_{k-1}, v_k)) \odot \\
&\qquad (\lambda(v_k, v_{k+1}) \odot \lambda(v_{k+1}, v_{k+2}) \odot \cdots \odot \lambda(v_{l-1}, v_l)) \\
&= \lambda(p_1) \odot \lambda(p_2) \, .
\end{aligned}
$$

The summary operator $\oplus$, which is both commutative and associative, is used to ***summarize*** path labels. That is, the value $\lambda(p_1) \oplus \lambda(p_2)$ gives a summary, the semantics of which are specific to the application, of the labels of paths p_1 and p_2.

Our goal will be to compute, for all pairs of vertices $i, j \in V$, the summary of all path labels from i to j:

$$l_{ij} = \bigoplus_{i \overset{p}{\leadsto} j} \lambda(p) \ . \tag{26.11}$$

We require commutativity and associativity of $\oplus$ because the order in which paths are summarized should not matter. Because we use the annihilator $\overline{0}$ as the label of an ordered pair (u, v) that is not an edge in the graph, any path that attempts to take an absent edge has label $\overline{0}$.

For shortest paths, we use min as the summary operator $\oplus$. The identity for min is ∞, and ∞ is indeed an annihilator for $+$: $a + \infty = \infty + a = \infty$ for all $a \in \mathbf{R}^{\geq 0} \cup \{\infty\}$. Absent edges have weight ∞, and if any edge of a path has weight ∞, so does the path.

We want the summary operator $\oplus$ to be idempotent, because from equation (26.11), we see that $\oplus$ should summarize the labels of a set of paths. If p is a path, then $\{p\} \cup \{p\} = \{p\}$; if we summarize path p with itself, the resulting label should be the label of p: $\lambda(p) \oplus \lambda(p) = \lambda(p)$.

Because we consider paths that may not be simple, there may be a countably infinite number of paths in a graph. (Each path, simple or not, has a finite number of edges.) The operator $\oplus$ should therefore be applicable to a countably infinite number of path labels. That is, if $a_1, a_2, a_3, \ldots$ is a countable sequence of elements in codomain S, then the label $a_1 \oplus a_2 \oplus a_3 \oplus \cdots$ should be well defined and in S. It should not matter in which order we summarize path labels, and thus associativity and commutativity should hold for infinite summaries. Furthermore, if we summarize the same path label a a countably infinite number of times, we should get a as the result, and thus idempotence should hold for infinite summaries.

Returning to the shortest-paths example, we ask if min is applicable to an infinite sequence of values in $\mathbf{R}^{\geq 0} \cup \{\infty\}$. For example, is the value of $\min_{k=1}^{\infty} \{1/k\}$ well defined? It is, if we think of the min operator as actually returning the greatest lower bound (infimum) of its arguments, in which case we get $\min_{k=1}^{\infty} \{1/k\} = 0$.

To compute labels of diverging paths, we need distributivity of the extension operator $\odot$ over the summary operator $\oplus$. As shown in Figure 26.7, suppose that we have paths $u \overset{p_1}{\leadsto} v$, $v \overset{p_2}{\leadsto} x$, and $v \overset{p_3}{\leadsto} y$. By distributivity, we can summarize the labels of paths $p_1 \circ p_2$ and $p_1 \circ p_3$ by computing either $(\lambda(p_1) \odot \lambda(p_2)) \oplus (\lambda(p_1) \odot \lambda(p_3))$ or $\lambda(p_1) \odot (\lambda(p_2) \oplus \lambda(p_3))$.

Because there may be a countably infinite number of paths in a graph, $\odot$ should distribute over infinite summaries as well as finite ones. Figure 26.8, for example, contains paths $u \overset{p_1}{\leadsto} v$ and $v \overset{p_2}{\leadsto} x$, along with the cycle $v \overset{c}{\leadsto} v$. We must be able to summarize the paths $p_1 \circ p_2$, $p_1 \circ c \circ p_2$, $p_1 \circ c \circ c \circ p_2$, ... Distributivity of $\odot$ over countably infinite summaries gives us

$$
\begin{aligned}
&(\lambda(p_1) \odot \lambda(p_2)) \ \oplus \ (\lambda(p_1) \odot \lambda(c) \odot \lambda(p_2)) \\
&\qquad \oplus \ (\lambda(p_1) \odot \lambda(c) \odot \lambda(c) \odot \lambda(p_2)) \ \oplus \ \cdots \\
&= \ \lambda(p_1) \odot (\lambda(p_2) \ \oplus \ (\lambda(c) \odot \lambda(p_2)) \ \oplus \ (\lambda(c) \odot \lambda(c) \odot \lambda(p_2)) \ \oplus \ \cdots) \\
&= \ \lambda(p_1) \odot (\overline{1} \ \oplus \ c \ \oplus \ (c \odot c) \ \oplus \ (c \odot c \odot c) \ \oplus \ \cdots) \odot \lambda(p_2) \ .
\end{aligned}
$$

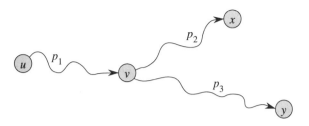

Figure 26.7   Using distributivity of $\odot$ over $\oplus$. To summarize the labels of paths $p_1 \circ p_2$ and $p_1 \circ p_3$, we may compute either $(\lambda(p_1) \odot \lambda(p_2)) \oplus (\lambda(p_1) \odot \lambda(p_3))$ or $\lambda(p_1) \odot (\lambda(p_2) \oplus \lambda(p_3))$.

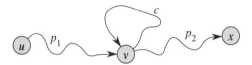

Figure 26.8   Distributivity of $\odot$ over countably infinite summaries of $\oplus$. Because of cycle c, there are a countably infinite number of paths from vertex v to vertex x. We must be able to summarize the paths $p_1 \circ p_2,\ p_1 \circ c \circ p_2,\ p_1 \circ c \circ c \circ p_2,\ \ldots$.

We use a special notation to denote the label of a cycle that may be traversed any number of times. Suppose that we have a cycle c with label $\lambda(c) = a$. We may traverse c zero times for a label of $\lambda(\varepsilon) = \overline{1}$, once for a label of $\lambda(c) = a$, twice for a label of $\lambda(c) \odot \lambda(c) = a \odot a$, and so on. The label we get by summarizing this infinite number of traversals of cycle c is the **closure** of a, defined by

$$a^* = \overline{1} \oplus a \oplus (a \odot a) \oplus (a \odot a \odot a) \oplus (a \odot a \odot a \odot a) \oplus \cdots .$$

Thus, in Figure 26.8, we want to compute $\lambda(p_1) \odot (\lambda(c))^* \odot \lambda(p_2)$.

For the shortest-paths example, for any nonnegative real $a \in \mathbf{R}^{\geq 0} \cup \{\infty\}$,

$$
\begin{aligned}
a^* &= \min_{k=0}^{\infty} \{ka\} \\
    &= 0 \, .
\end{aligned}
$$

The interpretation of this property is that since all cycles have nonnegative weight, no shortest path ever needs to traverse an entire cycle.

Examples of closed semirings

We have already seen one example of a closed semiring, namely $S_1 = (\mathbf{R}^{\geq 0} \cup \{\infty\}, \min, +, \infty, 0)$, which we used for shortest paths with nonnegative edge weights. (As previously noted, the min operator actually returns the greatest lower bound of its arguments.) We have also shown that $a^* = 0$ for all $a \in \mathbf{R}^{\geq 0} \cup \{\infty\}$.

We claimed, however, that even if there are negative-weight edges, the Floyd-Warshall algorithm computes shortest-path weights as long as no negative-weight cycles are present. By adding the appropriate closure operator and extending the codomain of labels to $\mathbf{R} \cup \{-\infty, +\infty\}$, we can find a closed semiring to handle negative-weight cycles. Using min for $\oplus$ and $+$ for $\odot$, the reader may verify that the closure of $a \in \mathbf{R} \cup \{-\infty, +\infty\}$ is

$$a^* = \begin{cases} 0 & \text{if } a \geq 0, \\ -\infty & \text{if } a < 0. \end{cases}$$

The second case $(a < 0)$ models the situation in which we can traverse a negative-weight cycle an infinite number of times to obtain a weight of $-\infty$ on any path containing the cycle. Thus, the closed semiring to use for the Floyd-Warshall algorithm with negative edge weights is $S_2 = (\mathbf{R} \cup \{-\infty, +\infty\}, \min, +, +\infty, 0)$. (See Exercise 26.4-3.)

For transitive closure, we use the closed semiring $S_3 = (\{0, 1\}, \vee, \wedge, 0, 1)$, where $\lambda(i, j) = 1$ if $(i, j) \in E$, and $\lambda(i, j) = 0$ otherwise. Here we have $0^* = 1^* = 1$.

A dynamic-programming algorithm for directed-path labels

Suppose we are given a directed graph $G = (V, E)$ with labeling function $\lambda : V \times V \to S$. The vertices are numbered 1 through n. For each pair of vertices $i, j \in V$, we want to compute equation (26.11):

$$l_{ij} = \bigoplus_{i \overset{p}{\leadsto} j} \lambda(p) ,$$

which is the result of summarizing all paths from i to j using the summary operator $\oplus$. For shortest paths, for example, we wish to compute

$$l_{ij} = \delta(i, j) = \min_{i \overset{p}{\leadsto} j} \{w(p)\} .$$

There is a dynamic-programming algorithm to solve this problem, and its form is very similar to the Floyd-Warshall algorithm and the transitive-closure algorithm. Let $Q_{ij}^{(k)}$ be the set of paths from vertex i to vertex j with all intermediate vertices in the set $\{1, 2, \ldots, k\}$. We define

$$l_{ij}^{(k)} = \bigoplus_{p \in Q_{ij}^{(k)}} \lambda(p) .$$

Note the analogy to the definitions of $d_{ij}^{(k)}$ in the Floyd-Warshall algorithm and $t_{ij}^{(k)}$ in the transitive-closure algorithm. We can define $l_{ij}^{(k)}$ recursively by

$$l_{ij}^{(k)} = l_{ij}^{(k-1)} \oplus \left(l_{ik}^{(k-1)} \odot (l_{kk}^{(k-1)})^* \odot l_{kj}^{(k-1)} \right) . \tag{26.12}$$

Recurrence (26.12) is reminiscent of recurrences (26.5) and (26.8), but with an additional factor of $(l_{kk}^{(k-1)})^*$ included. This factor represents the summary of all cycles that pass through vertex k and have all other vertices in the set $\{1, 2, \ldots, k - 1\}$. (When we assume no negative-weight cycles in the Floyd-Warshall algorithm, $(c_{kk}^{(k-1)})^*$ is 0, corresponding to $\overline{1}$, the weight of an empty cycle. In the transitive-closure algorithm, the empty path from k to k gives us $(t_{kk}^{(k-1)})^* = 1 = \overline{1}$. Thus, for both of these algorithms, we can ignore the factor of $(l_{kk}^{(k-1)})^*$, since it is just the identity for $\odot$.) The basis of the recursive definition is

$$l_{ij}^{(0)} = \begin{cases} \lambda(i, j) & \text{if } i \neq j, \\ \overline{1} \oplus \lambda(i, j) & \text{if } i = j, \end{cases}$$

which we can see as follows. The label of the one-edge path $\langle i, j \rangle$ is simply $\lambda(i, j)$ (which is equal to $\overline{0}$ if (i, j) is not an edge in E). If, in addition, $i = j$, then $\overline{1}$ is the label of the empty path from i to i.

The dynamic-programming algorithm computes the values $l_{ij}^{(k)}$ in order of increasing k. It returns the matrix $L^{(n)} = \left(l_{ij}^{(n)} \right)$.

COMPUTE-SUMMARIES(λ, V)

```
1   n ← |V|
2   for i ← 1 to n
3       do for j ← 1 to n
4           do if i = j
5               then l_{ij}^{(0)} ← 1̄ ⊕ λ(i, j)
6               else  l_{ij}^{(0)} ← λ(i, j)
7   for k ← 1 to n
8       do for i ← 1 to n
9           do for j ← 1 to n
10              do l_{ij}^{(k)} ← l_{ij}^{(k-1)} ⊕ (l_{ik}^{(k-1)} ⊙ (l_{kk}^{(k-1)})* ⊙ l_{kj}^{(k-1)})
11  return L^{(n)}
```

The running time of this algorithm depends on the time to compute $\odot$, $\oplus$, and $*$. If we let $T_\odot$, $T_\oplus$, and T_* represent these times, then the running time of COMPUTE-SUMMARIES is $\Theta(n^3(T_\odot + T_\oplus + T_*))$, which is $\Theta(n^3)$ if each of the three operations takes $O(1)$ time.

Exercises

26.4-1
Verify that $S_1 = (\mathbf{R}^{\geq 0} \cup \{\infty\}, \min, +, \infty, 0)$ and $S_3 = (\{0, 1\}, \vee, \wedge, 0, 1)$ are closed semirings.

26.4-2
Verify that $S_2 = (\mathbf{R} \cup \{-\infty, +\infty\}, \min, +, +\infty, 0)$ is a closed semiring. What is the value of $a + (-\infty)$ for $a \in \mathbf{R}$? What about $(-\infty) + (+\infty)$?

26.4-3
Rewrite the COMPUTE-SUMMARIES procedure to use closed semiring S_2, so that it implements the Floyd-Warshall algorithm. What should be the value of $-\infty + \infty$?

26.4-4
Is the system $S_4 = (\mathbf{R}, +, \cdot, 0, 1)$ a closed semiring?

26.4-5
Can we use an arbitrary closed semiring for Dijkstra's algorithm? What about for the Bellman-Ford algorithm? What about for the FASTER-ALL-PAIRS-SHORTEST-PATHS procedure?

26.4-6
A trucking firm wishes to send a truck from Castroville to Boston laden as heavily as possible with artichokes, but each road in the United States has a maximum weight limit on trucks that use the road. Model this problem with a directed graph $G = (V, E)$ and an appropriate closed semiring, and give an efficient algorithm to solve it.

Problems

26-1 *Transitive closure of a dynamic graph*
Suppose that we wish to maintain the transitive closure of a directed graph $G = (V, E)$ as we insert edges into E. That is, after each edge has been inserted, we want to update the transitive closure of the edges inserted so far. Assume that the graph G has no edges initially and that the transitive closure is to be represented as a boolean matrix.

a. Show how the transitive closure $G^* = (V, E^*)$ of a graph $G = (V, E)$ can be updated in $O(V^2)$ time when a new edge is added to G.

b. Give an example of a graph G and an edge e such that $\Omega(V^2)$ time is required to update the transitive closure after the insertion of e into G.

c. Describe an efficient algorithm for updating the transitive closure as edges are inserted into the graph. For any sequence of n insertions, your algorithm should run in total time $\sum_{i=1}^{n} t_i = O(V^3)$, where t_i is the time to update the transitive closure when the ith edge is inserted. Prove that your algorithm attains this time bound.

26-2 *Shortest paths in ϵ-dense graphs*
A graph $G = (V, E)$ is ϵ-*dense* if $|E| = \Theta(V^{1+\epsilon})$ for some constant ϵ in the range $0 < \epsilon \le 1$. By using d-ary heaps (see Problem 7-2) in shortest-paths algorithms on ϵ-dense graphs, we can match the running

times of Fibonacci-heap-based algorithms without using as complicated a data structure.

a. What are the asymptotic running times for INSERT, EXTRACT-MIN, and DECREASE-KEY, as a function of d and the number n of elements in a d-ary heap? What are these running times if we choose $d = \Theta(n^\alpha)$ for some constant $0 < \alpha \le 1$? Compare these running times to the amortized costs of these operations for a Fibonacci heap.

b. Show how to compute shortest paths from a single source on an ϵ-dense directed graph $G = (V, E)$ with no negative-weight edges in $O(E)$ time. (*Hint:* Pick d as a function of ϵ.)

c. Show how to solve the all-pairs shortest-paths problem on an ϵ-dense directed graph $G = (V, E)$ with no negative-weight edges in $O(VE)$ time.

d. Show how to solve the all-pairs shortest-paths problem in $O(VE)$ time on an ϵ-dense directed graph $G = (V, E)$ that may have negative-weight edges but has no negative-weight cycles.

26-3 *Minimum spanning tree as a closed semiring*

Let $G = (V, E)$ be a connected, undirected graph with weight function $w : E \to \mathbf{R}$. Let the vertex set be $V = \{1, 2, \ldots, n\}$, where $n = |V|$, and assume that all edge weights $w(i, j)$ are unique. Let T be the unique (see Exercise 24.1-6) minimum spanning tree of G. In this problem, we shall determine T by using a closed semiring, as suggested by B. M. Maggs and S. A. Plotkin. We first determine, for each pair of vertices $i, j \in V$, the *minimax* weight

$$m_{ij} = \min_{i \overset{p}{\leadsto} j} \max_{\text{edges } e \text{ on } p} w(e) .$$

a. Briefly justify the assertion that $S = (\mathbf{R} \cup \{-\infty, \infty\}, \min, \max, \infty, -\infty)$ is a closed semiring.

Since S is a closed semiring, we can use the COMPUTE-SUMMARIES procedure to determine the minimax weights m_{ij} in graph G. Let $m_{ij}^{(k)}$ be the minimax weight over all paths from vertex i to vertex j with all intermediate vertices in the set $\{1, 2, \ldots, k\}$.

b. Give a recurrence for $m_{ij}^{(k)}$, where $k \ge 0$.

c. Let $T_m = \{(i, j) \in E : w(i, j) = m_{ij}\}$. Prove that the edges in T_m form a spanning tree of G.

d. Show that $T_m = T$. (*Hint:* Consider the effect of adding edge (i, j) to T and removing an edge on another path from i to j. Consider also the effect of removing edge (i, j) from T and replacing it with another edge.)

Chapter notes

Lawler [132] has a good discussion of the all-pairs shortest-paths problem, although he does not analyze solutions for sparse graphs. He attributes the matrix-multiplication algorithm to the folklore. The Floyd-Warshall algorithm is due to Floyd [68], who based it on a theorem of Warshall [198] that describes how to compute the transitive closure of boolean matrices. The closed-semiring algebraic structure appears in Aho, Hopcroft, and Ullman [4]. Johnson's algorithm is taken from [114].

27   Maximum Flow

Just as we can model a road map as a directed graph in order to find the shortest path from one point to another, we can also interpret a directed graph as a "flow network" and use it to answer questions about material flows. Imagine a material coursing through a system from a source, where the material is produced, to a sink, where it is consumed. The source produces the material at some steady rate, and the sink consumes the material at the same rate. The "flow" of the material at any point in the system is intuitively the rate at which the material moves. Flow networks can be used to model liquids flowing through pipes, parts through assembly lines, current through electrical networks, information through communication networks, and so forth.

Each directed edge in a flow network can be thought of as a conduit for the material. Each conduit has a stated capacity, given as a maximum rate at which the material can flow through the conduit, such as 200 gallons of liquid per hour through a pipe or 20 amperes of electrical current through a wire. Vertices are conduit junctions, and other than the source and sink, material flows through the vertices without collecting in them. In other words, the rate at which material enters a vertex must equal the rate at which it leaves the vertex. We call this property "flow conservation," and it is the same as Kirchhoff's Current Law when the material is electrical current.

The maximum-flow problem is the simplest problem concerning flow networks. It asks, What is the greatest rate at which material can be shipped from the source to the sink without violating any capacity constraints? As we shall see in this chapter, this problem can be solved by efficient algorithms. Moreover, the basic techniques used by these algorithms can be adapted to solve other network-flow problems.

This chapter presents two general methods for solving the maximum-flow problem. Section 27.1 formalizes the notions of flow networks and flows, formally defining the maximum-flow problem. Section 27.2 describes the classical method of Ford and Fulkerson for finding maximum flows. An application of this method, finding a maximum matching in an undirected bipartite graph, is given in Section 27.3. Section 27.4 presents the preflow-push method, which underlies many of the fastest algorithms for network-flow problems. Section 27.5 covers the "lift-to-front" algorithm, a particular implementation of the preflow-push method that runs in time $O(V^3)$. Although this algorithm is not the fastest algorithm known, it illustrates some of the techniques used in the asymptotically fastest algorithms, and it is reasonably efficient in practice.

27.1   Flow networks

In this section, we give a graph-theoretic definition of flow networks, discuss their properties, and define the maximum-flow problem precisely. We also introduce some helpful notation.

Flow networks and flows

A *flow network* $G = (V, E)$ is a directed graph in which each edge $(u, v) \in E$ has a nonnegative *capacity* $c(u, v) \geq 0$. If $(u, v) \notin E$, we assume that $c(u, v) = 0$. We distinguish two vertices in a flow network: a *source* s and a *sink* t. For convenience, we assume that every vertex lies on some path from the source to the sink. That is, for every vertex $v \in V$, there is a path $s \rightsquigarrow v \rightsquigarrow t$. The graph is therefore connected, and $|E| \geq |V| - 1$. Figure 27.1 shows an example of a flow network.

We are now ready to define flows more formally. Let $G = (V, E)$ be a flow network (with an implied capacity function c). Let s be the source of the network, and let t be the sink. A *flow* in G is a real-valued function $f : V \times V \to \mathbf{R}$ that satisfies the following three properties:

Capacity constraint: For all $u, v \in V$, we require $f(u, v) \leq c(u, v)$.

Skew symmetry: For all $u, v \in V$, we require $f(u, v) = -f(v, u)$.

Flow conservation: For all $u \in V - \{s, t\}$, we require

$$\sum_{v \in V} f(u, v) = 0 .$$

The quantity $f(u, v)$, which can be positive or negative, is called the *net flow* from vertex u to vertex v. The *value* of a flow f is defined as

$$|f| = \sum_{v \in V} f(s, v) , \tag{27.1}$$

that is, the total net flow out of the source. (Here, the $|\cdot|$ notation denotes flow value, not absolute value or cardinality.) In the *maximum-flow problem*, we are given a flow network G with source s and sink t, and we wish to find a flow of maximum value from s to t.

Before seeing an example of a network-flow problem, let us briefly explore the three flow properties. The capacity constraint simply says that the net flow from one vertex to another must not exceed the given capacity. Skew symmetry says that the net flow from a vertex u to a vertex v

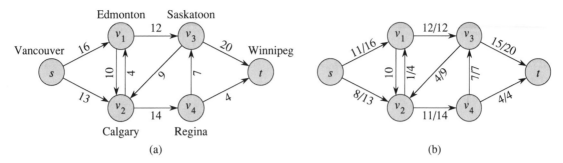

Figure 27.1   (a) A flow network $G = (V, E)$ for the Lucky Puck Company's trucking problem. The Vancouver factory is the source s, and the Winnipeg warehouse is the sink t. Pucks are shipped through intermediate cities, but only $c(u, v)$ crates per day can go from city u to city v. Each edge is labeled with its capacity. **(b)** A flow f in G with value $|f| = 19$. Only positive net flows are shown. If $f(u, v) > 0$, edge (u, v) is labeled by $f(u, v)/c(u, v)$. (The slash notation is used merely to separate the flow and capacity; it does not indicate division.) If $f(u, v) \leq 0$, edge (u, v) is labeled only by its capacity.

is the negative of the net flow in the reverse direction. Thus, the net flow from a vertex to itself is 0, since for all $u \in V$, we have $f(u, u) = -f(u, u)$, which implies that $f(u, u) = 0$. The flow-conservation property says that the total net flow out of a vertex other than the source or sink is 0. By skew symmetry, we can rewrite the flow-conservation property as

$$\sum_{u \in V} f(u, v) = 0$$

for all $v \in V - \{s, t\}$. That is, the total net flow into a vertex is 0.

Observe also that there can be no net flow between u and v if there is no edge between them. If neither $(u, v) \in E$ nor $(v, u) \in E$, then $c(u, v) = c(v, u) = 0$. Hence, by the capacity constraint, $f(u, v) \leq 0$ and $f(v, u) \leq 0$. But since $f(u, v) = -f(v, u)$, by skew symmetry, we have $f(u, v) = f(v, u) = 0$. Thus, nonzero net flow from vertex u to vertex v implies that $(u, v) \in E$ or $(v, u) \in E$ (or both).

Our last observation concerning the flow properties deals with net flows that are positive. The ***positive net flow*** entering a vertex v is defined by

$$\sum_{\substack{u \in V \\ f(u,v) > 0}} f(u, v) \ . \tag{27.2}$$

The positive net flow leaving a vertex is defined symmetrically. One interpretation of the flow-conservation property is that the positive net flow entering a vertex other than the source or sink must equal the positive net flow leaving the vertex.

An example of network flow

A flow network can model the trucking problem shown in Figure 27.1. The Lucky Puck Company has a factory (source s) in Vancouver that manufactures hockey pucks, and it has a warehouse (sink t) in Winnipeg that stocks them. Lucky Puck leases space on trucks from another firm to ship the pucks from the factory to the warehouse. Because the trucks travel over specified routes between cities and have a limited capacity, Lucky Puck can ship at most $c(u, v)$ crates per day between each pair of cities u and v in Figure 27.1(a). Lucky Puck has no control over these routes and capacities and so cannot alter the flow network shown in Figure 27.1(a). Their goal is to determine the largest number p of crates per day that can be shipped and then to produce this amount, since there is no point in producing more pucks than they can ship to their warehouse.

The rate at which pucks are shipped along any truck route is a flow. The pucks emanate from the factory at the rate of p crates per day, and p crates must arrive at the warehouse each day. Lucky Puck is not concerned with how long it takes for a given puck to get from the factory to the warehouse; they care only that p crates per day leave the factory and p crates per day arrive at the warehouse. The capacity constraints are given by the restriction that the flow $f(u, v)$ from city u to city v to be at most $c(u, v)$ crates per day. In a steady state, the rate at which pucks enter an intermediate city in the shipping network must equal the rate at which they leave; otherwise, they would pile up. Flow conservation is therefore obeyed. Thus, a maximum flow in the network determines the maximum number p of crates per day that can be shipped.

Figure 27.1(b) shows a possible flow in the network that is represented in a way that naturally corresponds to shipments. For any two vertices u and v in the network, the net flow $f(u, v)$ corresponds to a shipment of $f(u, v)$ crates per day from u to v. If $f(u, v)$ is 0 or negative, then there is no shipment from u to v. Thus, in Figure 27.1(b), only edges with positive net flow are shown, followed by a slash and the capacity of the edge.

We can understand the relationship between net flows and shipments somewhat better by focusing on the shipments between two vertices. Figure 27.2(a) shows the subgraph induced by vertices v_1 and v_2 in the flow network of Figure 27.1. If Lucky Puck ships 8 crates per day from v_1 to v_2, the result is shown in Figure 27.2(b): the net flow from v_1 to v_2 is 8 crates per day. By skew symmetry, we also say that the net flow in the reverse direction, from v_2 to v_1, is -8 crates per day, even though we do not ship any pucks from v_2 to v_1. In general, the net flow from v_1 to v_2 is the number of crates per day shipped from v_1 to v_2 minus the number per day shipped from v_2 to v_1. Our convention for representing net flows is to show only positive net flows, since they indicate the actual shipments; thus, only an 8 appears in the figure, without the corresponding -8.

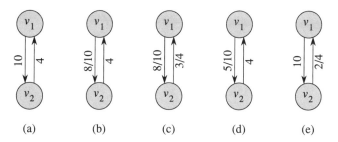

(a)   (b)   (c)   (d)   (e)

Figure 27.2 Cancellation. **(a)** Vertices v_1 and v_2, with $c(v_1, v_2) = 10$ and $c(v_2, v_1) = 4$. **(b)** How we indicate the net flow when 8 crates per day are shipped from v_1 to v_2. **(c)** An additional shipment of 3 crates per day is made from v_2 to v_1. **(d)** By cancelling flow going in opposite directions, we can represent the situation in (c) with positive net flow in one direction only. **(e)** Another 7 crates per day is shipped from v_2 to v_1.

Now let's add another shipment, this time of 3 crates per day from v_2 to v_1. One natural representation of the result is shown in Figure 27.2(c). We now have a situation in which there are shipments in both directions between v_1 and v_2. We ship 8 crates per day from v_1 to v_2 and 3 crates per day from v_2 to v_1. What are the net flows between the two vertices? The net flow from v_1 to v_2 is $8 - 3 = 5$ crates per day, and the net flow from v_2 to v_1 is $3 - 8 = -5$ crates per day.

The situation is equivalent in its result to the situation shown in Figure 27.2(d), in which 5 crates per day are shipped from v_1 to v_2 and no shipments are made from v_2 to v_1. In effect, the 3 crates per day from v_2 to v_1 are *cancelled* by 3 of the 8 crates per day from v_1 to v_2. In both situations, the net flow from v_1 to v_2 is 5 crates per day, but in (d), actual shipments are made in one direction only.

In general, cancellation allows us to represent the shipments between two cities by a positive net flow along at most one of the two edges between the corresponding vertices. If there is zero or negative net flow from one vertex to another, no shipments need be made in that direction. That is, any situation in which pucks are shipped in both directions between two cities can be transformed using cancellation into an equivalent situation in which pucks are shipped in one direction only: the direction of positive net flow. Capacity constraints are not violated by this transformation, since we reduce the shipments in both directions, and conservation constraints are not violated, since the net flow between the two vertices is the same.

Continuing with our example, let us determine the effect of shipping another 7 crates per day from v_2 to v_1. Figure 27.2(e) shows the result using the convention of representing only positive net flows. The net flow from v_1 to v_2 becomes $5 - 7 = -2$, and the net flow from v_2 to v_1 becomes $7 - 5 = 2$. Since the net flow from v_2 to v_1 is positive, it represents a shipment of 2 crates per day from v_2 to v_1. The net flow from v_1 to v_2 is -2 crates per day, and since the net flow is not positive, no pucks are

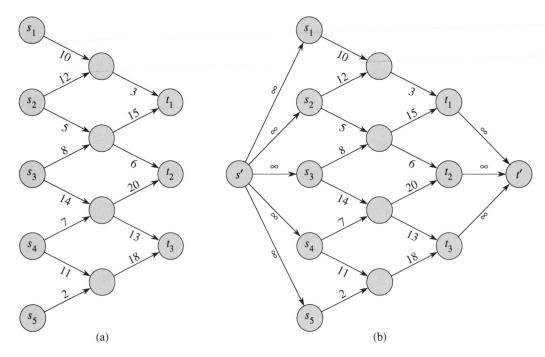

(a)   (b)

Figure 27.3 Converting a multiple-source, multiple-sink maximum-flow problem into a problem with a single source and a single sink. **(a)** A flow network with five sources $S = \{s_1, s_2, s_3, s_4, s_5\}$ and three sinks $T = \{t_1, t_2, t_3\}$. **(b)** An equivalent single-source, single-sink flow network. We add a supersource s' and an edge with infinite capacity from s' to each of the multiple sources. We also add a supersink t' and an edge with infinite capacity from each of the multiple sinks to t'.

shipped in this direction. Alternatively, of the 7 additional crates per day from v_2 to v_1, we can view 5 of them as cancelling the shipment of 5 per day from v_1 to v_2, which leaves 2 crates as the actual shipment per day from v_2 to v_1.

Networks with multiple sources and sinks

A maximum-flow problem may have several sources and sinks, rather than just one of each. The Lucky Puck Company, for example, might actually have a set of m factories $\{s_1, s_2, \ldots, s_m\}$ and a set of n warehouses $\{t_1, t_2, \ldots, t_n\}$, as shown in Figure 27.3(a). Fortunately, this problem is no harder than ordinary maximum flow.

We can reduce the problem of determining a maximum flow in a network with multiple sources and multiple sinks to an ordinary maximum-flow problem. Figure 27.3(b) shows how the network from (a) can be converted to an ordinary flow network with only a single source and a single sink. We add a ***supersource*** s and add a directed edge (s, s_i) with capacity $c(s, s_i) = \infty$ for each $i = 1, 2, \ldots, m$. We also create a new ***supersink*** t and add a directed edge (t_j, t) with capacity $c(t_j, t) = \infty$ for each $i = 1, 2, \ldots, n$. Intuitively, any flow in the network in (a) corresponds to a flow in the network in (b), and vice versa. The single source s simply provides as much flow as desired for the multiple sources s_i, and the single sink t likewise consumes as much flow as desired for the multiple sinks t_i. Exercise 27.1-3 asks you to prove formally that the two problems are equivalent.

Working with flows

We shall be dealing with several functions (like f) that take as arguments two vertices in a flow network. In this chapter, we shall use an ***implicit summation notation*** in which either argument, or both, may be a *set* of vertices, with the interpretation that the value denoted is the sum of all possible ways of replacing the arguments with their members. For example, if X and Y are sets of vertices, then

$$f(X, Y) = \sum_{x \in X} \sum_{y \in Y} f(x, y) \, .$$

As another example, the flow-conservation constraint can be expressed as the condition that $f(u, V) = 0$ for all $u \in V - \{s, t\}$. Also, for convenience, we shall typically omit set braces when they would otherwise be used in the implicit summation notation. For example, in the equation $f(s, V - s) = f(s, V)$, the term $V - s$ means the set $V - \{s\}$.

The implicit set notation often simplifies equations involving flows. The following lemma, whose proof is left as Exercise 27.1-4, captures several of the most commonly occurring identities that involve flows and the implicit set notation.

Lemma 27.1
Let $G = (V, E)$ be a flow network, and let f be a flow in G. Then, for $X \subseteq V$,

$$f(X, X) = 0 \, .$$

For $X, Y \subseteq V$,

$$f(X, Y) = -f(Y, X) \, .$$

For $X, Y, Z \subseteq V$ with $X \cap Y = \emptyset$,

$$f(X \cup Y, Z) = f(X, Z) + f(Y, Z)$$

and

$$f(Z, X \cup Y) = f(Z, X) + f(Z, Y) \, . \qquad \blacksquare$$

As an example of working with the implicit summation notation, we can prove that the value of a flow is the total net flow into the sink; that is,

$$|f| = f(V, t) .\tag{27.3}$$

This is intuitively true, since all vertices other than the source and sink
have a net flow of 0 by flow conservation, and thus the sink is the only
other vertex that can have a nonzero net flow to match the source's nonzero
net flow. Our formal proof goes as follows:

$$
\begin{aligned}
|f| &= f(s, V) & \text{(by definition)} \\
&= f(V, V) - f(V - s, V) & \text{(by Lemma 27.1)} \\
&= f(V, V - s) & \text{(by Lemma 27.1)} \\
&= f(V, t) + f(V, V - s - t) & \text{(by Lemma 27.1)} \\
&= f(V, t) & \text{(by flow conservation) .}
\end{aligned}
$$

Later in this chapter, we shall generalize this result (Lemma 27.5).

Exercises

27.1-1
Given vertices u and v in a flow network, where $c(u, v) = 5$ and $c(v, u) = 8$,
suppose that 3 units of flow are shipped from u to v and 4 units are shipped
from v to u. What is the net flow from u to v? Draw the situation in the
style of Figure 27.2.

27.1-2
Verify each of the three flow properties for the flow f shown in Figure 27.1(b).

27.1-3
Extend the flow properties and definitions to the multiple-source, multiple-
sink problem. Show that any flow in a multiple-source, multiple-sink flow
network corresponds to a flow of identical value in the single-source, single-
sink network obtained by adding a supersource and a supersink, and vice
versa.

27.1-4
Prove Lemma 27.1.

27.1-5
For the flow network $G = (V, E)$ and flow f shown in Figure 27.1(b), find
a pair of subsets $X, Y \subseteq V$ for which $f(X, Y) = -f(V - X, Y)$. Then, find
a pair of subsets $X, Y \subseteq V$ for which $f(X, Y) \neq -f(V - X, Y)$.

27.1-6
Given a flow network $G = (V, E)$, let f_1 and f_2 be functions from $V \times V$
to $\mathbf{R}$. The *flow sum* $f_1 + f_2$ is the function from $V \times V$ to $\mathbf{R}$ defined by

$$(f_1 + f_2)(u, v) = f_1(u, v) + f_2(u, v)\tag{27.4}$$

for all $u, v \in V$. If f_1 and f_2 are flows in G, which of the three flow properties must the flow sum $f_1 + f_2$ satisfy, and which might it violate?

27.1-7
Let f be a flow in a network, and let α be a real number. The **scalar flow product** αf is a function from $V \times V$ to **R** defined by

$$(\alpha f)(u, v) = \alpha \cdot f(u, v) .$$

Prove that the flows in a network form a convex set by showing that if f_1 and f_2 are flows, then so is $\alpha f_1 + (1 - \alpha)f_2$ for all α in the range $0 \leq \alpha \leq 1$.

27.1-8
State the maximum-flow problem as a linear-programming problem.

27.1-9
The flow-network model introduced in this section supports the flow of one commodity; a **multicommodity flow network** supports the flow of p commodities between a set of p **source vertices** $S = \{s_1, s_2, \ldots, s_p\}$ and a set of p **sink vertices** $T = \{t_1, t_2, \ldots, t_p\}$. The net flow of the ith commodity from u to v is denoted $f_i(u, v)$. For the ith commodity, the only source is s_i and the only sink is t_i. There is flow conservation independently for each commodity: the net flow of each commodity out of each vertex is zero unless the vertex is the source or sink for the commodity. The sum of the net flows of all commodities from u to v must not exceed $c(u, v)$, and in this way the commodity flows interact. The **value** of the flow of each commodity is the net flow out of the source for that commodity. The **total flow value** is the sum of the values of all p commodity flows. Prove that there is a polynomial-time algorithm that solves the problem of finding the maximum total flow value of a multicommodity flow network by formulating the problem as a linear program.

27.2 The Ford-Fulkerson method

This section presents the Ford-Fulkerson method for solving the maximum-flow problem. We call it a "method" rather than an "algorithm" because it encompasses several implementations with differing running times. The Ford-Fulkerson method depends on three important ideas that transcend the method and are relevant to many flow algorithms and problems: residual networks, augmenting paths, and cuts. These ideas are essential to the important max-flow min-cut theorem (Theorem 27.7), which characterizes the value of a maximum flow in terms of cuts of the flow network. We end this section by presenting one specific implementation of the Ford-Fulkerson method and analyzing its running time.

The Ford-Fulkerson method is iterative. We start with $f(u, v) = 0$ for all $u, v \in V$, giving an initial flow of value 0. At each iteration, we increase the flow value by finding an "augmenting path," which we can think of simply as a path from the source s to the sink t along which we can push more flow, and then augmenting the flow along this path. We repeat this process until no augmenting path can be found. The max-flow min-cut theorem will show that upon termination, this process yields a maximum flow.

FORD-FULKERSON-METHOD(G, s, t)

1   initialize flow f to 0
2   **while** there exists an augmenting path p
3   **do** augment flow f along p
4   **return** f

Residual networks

Intuitively, given a flow network and a flow, the residual network consists of edges that can admit more net flow. More formally, suppose that we have a flow network $G = (V, E)$ with source s and sink t. Let f be a flow in G, and consider a pair of vertices $u, v \in V$. The amount of *additional* net flow we can push from u to v before exceeding the capacity $c(u, v)$ is the **residual capacity** of (u, v), given by

$$c_f(u, v) = c(u, v) - f(u, v) . \tag{27.5}$$

For example, if $c(u, v) = 16$ and $f(u, v) = 11$, then we can ship $c_f(u, v) = 5$ more units of flow before we exceed the capacity constraint on edge (u, v). When the net flow $f(u, v)$ is negative, the residual capacity $c_f(u, v)$ is greater than the capacity $c(u, v)$. For example, if $c(u, v) = 16$ and $f(u, v) = -4$, then the residual capacity $c_f(u, v)$ is 20. We can interpret this as follows. There is a net flow of 4 units from v to u, which we can cancel by pushing a net flow of 4 units from u to v. We can then push another 16 units from u to v before violating the capacity constraint on edge (u, v). We have thus pushed an additional 20 units of flow, starting with a net flow $f(u, v) = -4$, before reaching the capacity constraint.

Given a flow network $G = (V, E)$ and a flow f, the **residual network** of G induced by f is $G_f = (V, E_f)$, where

$$E_f = \{(u, v) \in V \times V : c_f(u, v) > 0\} .$$

That is, as promised above, each edge of the residual network, or **residual edge**, can admit a strictly positive net flow. Figure 27.4(a) repeats the flow network G and flow f of Figure 27.1(b), and Figure 27.4(b) shows the corresponding residual network G_f.

Notice that (u, v) may be a residual edge in E_f even if it was not an edge in E. In other words, it may very well be the case that $E_f \nsubseteq E$. The residual network in Figure 27.4(b) includes several such edges not in the original flow network, such as (v_1, s) and (v_2, v_3). Such an edge (u, v) appears in G_f

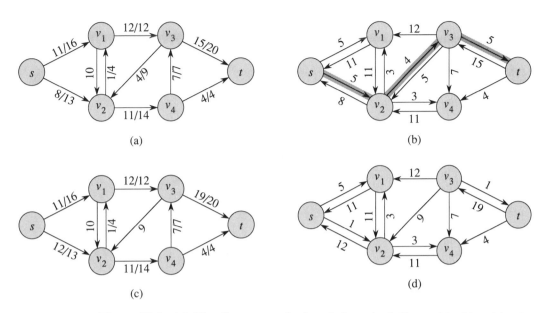

Figure 27.4 (a) The flow network G and flow f of Figure 27.1(b). (b) The residual network G_f with augmenting path p shaded; its residual capacity is $c_f(p) = c(v_2, v_3) = 4$. (c) The flow in G that results from augmenting along path p by its residual capacity 4. (d) The residual network induced by the flow in (c).

only if $(v, u) \in E$ and there is positive net flow from v to u. Because the net flow $f(u, v)$ from u to v is negative, $c_f(u, v) = c(u, v) - f(u, v)$ is positive and $(u, v) \in E_f$. Because an edge (u, v) can appear in a residual network only if at least one of (u, v) and (v, u) appears in the original network, we have the bound

$$|E_f| \le 2|E| .$$

Observe that the residual network G_f is itself a flow network with capacities given by c_f. The following lemma shows how a flow in a residual network relates to a flow in the original flow network.

Lemma 27.2
Let $G = (V, E)$ be a flow network with source s and sink t, and let f be a flow in G. Let G_f be the residual network of G induced by f, and let f' be a flow in G_f. Then, the flow sum $f + f'$ defined by equation (27.4) is a flow in G with value $|f + f'| = |f| + |f'|$.

Proof We must verify that skew symmetry, the capacity constraints, and flow conservation are obeyed. For skew symmetry, note that for all $u, v \in V$, we have

$$
\begin{aligned}
(f + f')(u, v) &= f(u, v) + f'(u, v) \\
&= -f(v, u) - f'(v, u) \\
&= -(f(v, u) + f'(v, u))
\end{aligned}
$$

$$= -(f + f')(v, u) .$$

For the capacity constraints, note that $f'(u, v) \leq c_f(u, v)$ for all $u, v \in V$. By equation (27.5), therefore,

$$
\begin{aligned}
(f + f')(u, v) &= f(u, v) + f'(u, v) \\
&\leq f(u, v) + (c(u, v) - f(u, v)) \\
&= c(u, v) .
\end{aligned}
$$

For flow conservation, note that for all $u \in V - \{s, t\}$, we have

$$
\begin{aligned}
\sum_{v \in V} (f + f')(u, v) &= \sum_{v \in V} (f(u, v) + f'(u, v)) \\
&= \sum_{v \in V} f(u, v) + \sum_{v \in V} f'(u, v) \\
&= 0 + 0 \\
&= 0 .
\end{aligned}
$$

Finally, we have

$$
\begin{aligned}
|f + f'| &= \sum_{v \in V} (f + f')(s, v) \\
&= \sum_{v \in V} (f(s, v) + f'(s, v)) \\
&= \sum_{v \in V} f(s, v) + \sum_{v \in V} f'(s, v) \\
&= |f| + |f'| . \qquad \blacksquare
\end{aligned}
$$

Augmenting paths

Given a flow network $G = (V, E)$ and a flow f, an ***augmenting path*** p is a simple path from s to t in the residual network G_f. By the definition of the residual network, each edge (u, v) on an augmenting path admits some additional positive net flow from u to v without violating the capacity constraint on the edge.

The shaded path in Figure 27.4(b) is an augmenting path. Treating the residual network G_f in the figure as a flow network, we can ship up to 4 units of additional net flow through each edge of this path without violating a capacity constraint, since the smallest residual capacity on this path is $c_f(v_2, v_3) = 4$. We call the maximum amount of net flow that we can ship along the edges of an augmenting path p the ***residual capacity*** of p, given by

$$c_f(p) = \min \{c_f(u, v) : (u, v) \text{ is on } p\} .$$

The following lemma, whose proof is left as Exercise 27.2-7, makes the above argument more precise.

Lemma 27.3
Let $G = (V, E)$ be a flow network, let f be a flow in G, and let p be an augmenting path in G_f. Define a function $f_p : V \times V \to \mathbf{R}$ by

$$f_p(u, v) = \begin{cases} c_f(p) & \text{if } (u, v) \text{ is on } p\ , \\ -c_f(p) & \text{if } (v, u) \text{ is on } p\ , \\ 0 & \text{otherwise}\ . \end{cases} \tag{27.6}$$

Then, f_p is a flow in G_f with value $|f_p| = c_f(p) > 0$. ∎

The following corollary shows that if we add f_p to f, we get another flow in G whose value is closer to the maximum. Figure 27.4(c) shows the result of adding f_p in Figure 27.4(b) to f from Figure 27.4(a).

Corollary 27.4
Let $G = (V, E)$ be a flow network, let f be a flow in G, and let p be an augmenting path in G_f. Let f_p be defined as in equation (27.6). Define a function $f' : V \times V \to \mathbf{R}$ by $f' = f + f_p$. Then, f' is a flow in G with value $|f'| = |f| + |f_p| > |f|$.

Proof Immediate from Lemmas 27.2 and 27.3. ∎

Cuts of flow networks

The Ford-Fulkerson method repeatedly augments the flow along augmenting paths until a maximum flow has been found. The max-flow min-cut theorem, which we shall prove shortly, tells us that a flow is maximum if and only if its residual network contains no augmenting path. To prove this theorem, though, we must first explore the notion of a cut of a flow network.

A ***cut*** (S, T) of flow network $G = (V, E)$ is a partition of V into S and $T = V - S$ such that $s \in S$ and $t \in T$. (This definition is like the definition of "cut" that we used for minimum spanning trees in Chapter 24, except that here we are cutting a directed graph rather than an undirected graph, and we insist that $s \in S$ and $t \in T$.) If f is a flow, then the ***net flow*** across the cut (S, T) is defined to be $f(S, T)$. The ***capacity*** of the cut (S, T) is $c(S, T)$.

Figure 27.5 shows the cut $(\{s, v_1, v_2\}, \{v_3, v_4, t\})$ in the flow network of Figure 27.1(b). The net flow across this cut is

$$\begin{aligned} f(v_1, v_3) + f(v_2, v_3) + f(v_2, v_4) &= 12 + (-4) + 11 \\ &= 19\ , \end{aligned}$$

and its capacity is

$$\begin{aligned} c(v_1, v_3) + c(v_2, v_4) &= 12 + 14 \\ &= 26\ . \end{aligned}$$

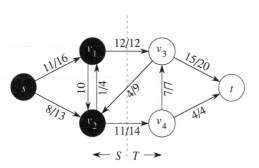

Figure 27.5 A cut (S, T) in the flow network of Figure 27.1(b), where $S = \{s, v_1, v_2\}$ and $T = \{v_3, v_4, t\}$. The vertices in S are black, and the vertices in T are white. The net flow across (S, T) is $f(S, T) = 19$, and the capacity is $c(S, T) = 26$.

Observe that the net flow across a cut can include negative net flows between vertices, but that the capacity of a cut is composed entirely of nonnegative values.

The following lemma shows that the value of a flow in a network is the net flow across any cut of the network.

Lemma 27.5
Let f be a flow in a flow network G with source s and sink t, and let (S, T) be a cut of G. Then, the net flow across (S, T) is $f(S, T) = |f|$.

Proof   Using Lemma 27.1 extensively, we have

$$
\begin{aligned}
f(S, T) &= f(S, V) - f(S, S) \\
&= f(S, V) \\
&= f(s, V) + f(S - s, V) \\
&= f(s, V) \\
&= |f| \ .
\end{aligned}
$$
∎

An immediate corollary to Lemma 27.5 is the result we proved earlier—equation (27.3)—that the value of a flow is the net flow into the sink.

Another corollary to Lemma 27.5 shows how cut capacities can be used to bound the value of a flow.

Corollary 27.6
The value of any flow f in a flow network G is bounded from above by the capacity of any cut of G.

Proof   Let (S, T) be any cut of G and let f be any flow. By Lemma 27.5 and the capacity constraints,

$$
|f| = f(S, T)
$$

$$= \sum_{u \in S} \sum_{v \in T} f(u, v)$$

$$\leq \sum_{u \in S} \sum_{v \in T} c(u, v)$$

$$= c(S, T) .$$ ∎

We are now ready to prove the important max-flow min-cut theorem.

Theorem 27.7 (Max-flow min-cut theorem)
If f is a flow in a flow network $G = (V, E)$ with source s and sink t, then the following conditions are equivalent:

1. f is a maximum flow in G.

2. The residual network G_f contains no augmenting paths.

3. $|f| = c(S, T)$ for some cut (S, T) of G.

Proof $(1) \Rightarrow (2)$: Suppose for the sake of contradiction that f is a maximum flow in G but that G_f has an augmenting path p. Then, by Corollary 27.4, the flow sum $f + f_p$, where f_p is given by equation (27.6), is a flow in G with value strictly greater than $|f|$, contradicting the assumption that f is a maximum flow.

$(2) \Rightarrow (3)$: Suppose that G_f has no augmenting path, that is, that G_f contains no path from s to t. Define

$$S = \{v \in V : \text{there exists a path from } s \text{ to } v \text{ in } G_f\}$$

and $T = V - S$. The partition (S, T) is a cut: we have $s \in S$ trivially and $t \notin S$ because there is no path from s to T in G_f. For each pair of vertices u and v such that $u \in S$ and $v \in T$, we have $f(u, v) = c(u, v)$, since otherwise $(u, v) \in E_f$ and v is in set S. By Lemma 27.5, therefore, $|f| = f(S, T) = c(S, T)$.

$(3) \Rightarrow (1)$: By Corollary 27.6, $|f| \leq c(S, T)$ for all cuts (S, T). The condition $|f| = c(S, T)$ thus implies that f is a maximum flow. ∎

The basic Ford-Fulkerson algorithm

In each iteration of the Ford-Fulkerson method, we find *any* augmenting path p and augment flow f along p by the residual capacity $c_f(p)$. The following implementation of the method computes the maximum flow in a graph $G = (V, E)$ by updating the net flow $f[u, v]$ between each pair u, v of vertices that are connected by an edge.[1] If u and v are not connected

---

[1] We use square brackets when we treat an identifier—such as f—as a mutable field, and we use parentheses when we treat it as a function.

by an edge in either direction, we assume implicitly that $f[u, v] = 0$. The code assumes that the capacity from u to v is provided by a constant-time function $c(u, v)$, with $c(u, v) = 0$ if $(u, v) \notin E$. (In a typical implementation, $c(u, v)$ might be derived from fields stored within vertices and their adjacency lists.) The residual capacity $c_f(u, v)$ is computed in accordance with the formula (27.5). The expression $c_f(p)$ in the code is actually just a temporary variable that stores the residual capacity of the path p.

FORD-FULKERSON(G, s, t)

```
1  for each edge (u, v) ∈ E[G]
2      do f[u, v] ← 0
3         f[v, u] ← 0
4  while there exists a path p from s to t in the residual network G_f
5      do c_f(p) ← min {c_f(u, v) : (u, v) is in p}
6         for each edge (u, v) in p
7             do f[u, v] ← f[u, v] + c_f(p)
8                f[v, u] ← -f[u, v]
```

The FORD-FULKERSON algorithm simply expands on the FORD-FULKERSON-METHOD pseudocode given earlier. Figure 27.6 shows the result of each iteration in a sample run. Lines 1–3 initialize the flow f to 0. The **while** loop of lines 4–8 repeatedly finds an augmenting path p in G_f and augments flow f along p by the residual capacity $c_f(p)$. When no augmenting paths exist, the flow f is a maximum flow.

Analysis of Ford-Fulkerson

The running time of FORD-FULKERSON depends on how the augmenting path p in line 4 is determined. If it is chosen poorly, the algorithm might not even terminate: the value of the flow will increase with successive augmentations, but it need not even converge to the maximum flow value. If the augmenting path is chosen by using a breadth-first search (Section 23.2), however, the algorithm runs in polynomial time. Before proving this, however, we obtain a simple bound for the case in which the augmenting path is chosen arbitrarily and all capacities are integers.

Most often in practice, the maximum-flow problem arises with integral capacities. If the capacities are rational numbers, an appropriate scaling transformation can be used to make them all integral. Under this assumption, a straightforward implementation of FORD-FULKERSON runs in time $O(E |f^*|)$, where f^* is the maximum flow found by the algorithm. The analysis is as follows. Lines 1–3 take time $\Theta(E)$. The **while** loop of lines 4–8 is executed at most $|f^*|$ times, since the flow value increases by at least one unit in each iteration.

The work done within the **while** loop can be made efficient if we efficiently manage the data structure used to implement the network $G = (V, E)$. Let us assume that we keep a data structure corresponding to a

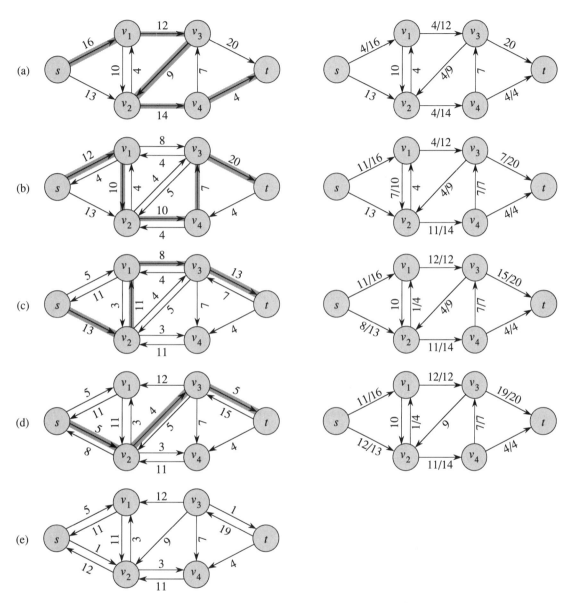

Figure 27.6   The execution of the basic Ford-Fulkerson algorithm. **(a)–(d)** Successive iterations of the **while** loop. The left side of each part shows the residual network G_f from line 4 with a shaded augmenting path p. The right side of each part shows the new flow f that results from adding f_p to f. The residual network in (a) is the input network G. **(e)** The residual network at the last **while** loop test. It has no augmenting paths, and the flow f shown in (d) is therefore a maximum flow.

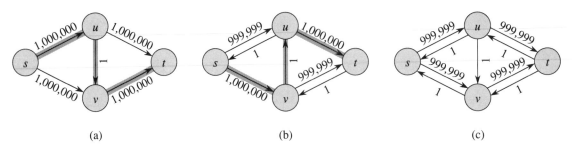

Figure 27.7   (a) A flow network for which FORD-FULKERSON can take $\Theta(E \, |f^*|)$ time, where f^* is a maximum flow, shown here with $|f^*| = 2,000,000$. An augmenting path with residual capacity 1 is shown. (b) The resulting residual network. Another augmenting path with residual capacity 1 is shown. (c) The resulting residual network.

directed graph $G' = (V, E')$, where $E' = \{(u, v) : (u, v) \in E \text{ or } (v, u) \in E\}$. Edges in the network G are also edges in G', and it is therefore a simple matter to maintain capacities and flows in this data structure. Given a flow f on G, the edges in the residual network G_f consist of all edges (u, v) of G' such that $c(u, v) - f[u, v] \neq 0$. The time to find a path in a residual network is therefore $O(E') = O(E)$ if we use either depth-first search or breadth-first search. Each iteration of the **while** loop thus takes $O(E)$ time, making the total running time of FORD-FULKERSON $O(E \, |f^*|)$.

When the capacities are integral and the optimal flow value $|f^*|$ is small, the running time of the Ford-Fulkerson algorithm is good. Figure 27.7(a) shows an example of what can happen on a simple flow network for which $|f^*|$ is large. A maximum flow in this network has value 2,000,000: 1,000,000 units of flow traverse the path $s \rightarrow u \rightarrow t$, and another 1,000,000 units traverse the path $s \rightarrow v \rightarrow t$. If the first augmenting path found by FORD-FULKERSON is $s \rightarrow u \rightarrow v \rightarrow t$, shown in Figure 27.7(a), the flow has value 1 after the first iteration. The resulting residual network is shown in Figure 27.7(b). If the second iteration finds the augmenting path $s \rightarrow v \rightarrow u \rightarrow t$, as shown in Figure 27.7(b), the flow then has value 2. Figure 27.7(c) shows the resulting residual network. We can continue, choosing the augmenting path $s \rightarrow u \rightarrow v \rightarrow t$ in the odd-numbered iterations and the augmenting path $s \rightarrow v \rightarrow u \rightarrow t$ in the even-numbered iterations. We would perform a total of 2,000,000 augmentations, increasing the flow value by only 1 unit in each.

The bound on FORD-FULKERSON can be improved if we implement the computation of the augmenting path p in line 4 with a breadth-first search, that is, if the augmenting path is a *shortest* path from s to t in the residual network, where each edge has unit distance (weight). We call the Ford-Fulkerson method so implemented the ***Edmonds-Karp algorithm***. We now prove that the Edmonds-Karp algorithm runs in $O(VE^2)$ time.

The analysis depends on the distances to vertices in the residual network G_f. The following lemma uses the notation $\delta_f(u, v)$ for the shortest-path distance from u to v in G_f, where each edge has unit distance.

Lemma 27.8
If the Edmonds-Karp algorithm is run on a flow network $G = (V, E)$ with source s and sink t, then for all vertices $v \in V - \{s, t\}$, the shortest-path distance $\delta_f(s, v)$ in the residual network G_f increases monotonically with each flow augmentation.

Proof   Suppose for the purpose of contradiction that for some vertex $v \in V - \{s, t\}$, there is a flow augmentation that causes $\delta_f(s, v)$ to decrease. Let f be the flow just before the augmentation, and let f' be the flow just afterward. Then,

$$\delta_{f'}(s, v) < \delta_f(s, v) \; .$$

We can assume without loss of generality that $\delta_{f'}(s, v) \leq \delta_{f'}(s, u)$ for all vertices $u \in V - \{s, t\}$ such that $\delta_{f'}(s, u) < \delta_f(s, u)$. Equivalently, we can assume that for all vertices $u \in V - \{s, t\}$,

$$\delta_{f'}(s, u) < \delta_{f'}(s, v) \text{ implies } \delta_f(s, u) \leq \delta_{f'}(s, u) \; . \tag{27.7}$$

We now take a shortest path p' in $G_{f'}$ of the form $s \leadsto u \to v$ and consider the vertex u that precedes v on this path. We must have $\delta_{f'}(s, u) = \delta_{f'}(s, v) - 1$ by Corollary 25.2, since (u, v) is an edge on p', which is a shortest path from s to v. By our assumption (27.7), therefore,

$$\delta_f(s, u) \leq \delta_{f'}(s, u) \; .$$

With vertices v and u thus established, we can consider the net flow f from u to v before the augmentation of flow in G_f. If $f[u, v] < c(u, v)$, then we have

$$
\begin{aligned}
\delta_f(s, v) &\leq \delta_f(s, u) + 1 \quad \text{(by Lemma 25.3)} \\
&\leq \delta_{f'}(s, u) + 1 \\
&= \delta_{f'}(s, v) \; ,
\end{aligned}
$$

which contradicts our assumption that the flow augmentation decreases the distance from s to v.

Thus, we must have $f[u, v] = c(u, v)$, which means $(u, v) \notin E_f$. Now, the augmenting path p that was chosen in G_f to produce $G_{f'}$ must contain the edge (v, u) *in the direction from v to u*, since $(u, v) \in E_{f'}$ (by supposition) and $(u, v) \notin E_f$ as we have just shown. That is, augmenting flow along the path p pushes flow *back* along (u, v), and v appears before u on p. Since p is a shortest path from s to t, its subpaths are shortest paths (Lemma 25.1), and thus we have $\delta_f(s, u) = \delta_f(s, v) + 1$. Consequently,

$$\delta_f(s, v) = \delta_f(s, u) - 1$$

$$
\begin{aligned}
&\leq \; \delta_{f'}(s,u) - 1 \\
&= \; \delta_{f'}(s,v) - 2 \\
&< \; \delta_{f'}(s,v) \, ,
\end{aligned}
$$

which contradicts our initial assumption.   ■

The next theorem bounds the number of iterations of the Edmonds-Karp algorithm.

Theorem 27.9
If the Edmonds-Karp algorithm is run on a flow network $G = (V, E)$ with source s and sink t, then the total number of flow augmentations performed by the algorithm is at most $O(VE)$.

Proof   We say that an edge (u, v) in a residual network G_f is **critical** on an augmenting path p if the residual capacity of p is the residual capacity of (u, v), that is, if $c_f(p) = c_f(u, v)$. After we have augmented flow along an augmenting path, any critical edge on the path disappears from the residual network. Moreover, at least one edge on any augmenting path must be critical.

Let u and v be vertices in V that are connected by an edge in E. How many times can (u, v) be a critical edge during the execution of the Edmonds-Karp algorithm? Since augmenting paths are shortest paths, when (u, v) is critical for the first time, we have

$$\delta_f(s,v) = \delta_f(s,u) + 1 \, .$$

Once the flow is augmented, the edge (u, v) disappears from the residual network. It cannot reappear later on another augmenting path until after the net flow from u to v is decreased, and this only happens if (v, u) appears on an augmenting path. If f' is the flow in G when this event occurs, then we have

$$\delta_{f'}(s,u) = \delta_{f'}(s,v) + 1 \, .$$

Since $\delta_f(s,v) \leq \delta_{f'}(s,v)$ by Lemma 27.8, we have

$$
\begin{aligned}
\delta_{f'}(s,u) &= \; \delta_{f'}(s,v) + 1 \\
&\geq \; \delta_f(s,v) + 1 \\
&= \; \delta_f(s,u) + 2 \, .
\end{aligned}
$$

Consequently, from the time (u, v) becomes critical to the time when it next becomes critical, the distance of u from the source increases by at least 2. The distance of u from the source is initially at least 1, and until it becomes unreachable from the source, if ever, its distance is at most $|V| - 2$. Thus, (u, v) can become critical at most $O(V)$ times. Since there are $O(E)$ pairs of vertices that can have an edge between them in a residual graph, the total number of critical edges during the entire execution of the

Edmonds-Karp algorithm is $O(VE)$. Each augmenting path has at least one critical edge, and hence the theorem follows. ∎

Since each iteration of FORD-FULKERSON can be implemented in $O(E)$ time when the augmenting path is found by breadth-first search, the total running time of the Edmonds-Karp algorithm is $O(VE^2)$. The algorithm of Section 27.4 gives a method for achieving an $O(V^2E)$ running time, which forms the basis for the $O(V^3)$-time algorithm of Section 27.5.

Exercises

27.2-1
In Figure 27.1(b), what is the flow across the cut $(\{s, v_2, v_4\}, \{v_1, v_3, t\})$? What is the capacity of this cut?

27.2-2
Show the execution of the Edmonds-Karp algorithm on the flow network of Figure 27.1(a).

27.2-3
In the example of Figure 27.6, what is the minimum cut corresponding to the maximum flow shown? Of the augmenting paths appearing in the example, which two cancel flow that was previously shipped?

27.2-4
Prove that for any pair of vertices u and v and any capacity and flow functions c and f, we have $c_f(u, v) + c_f(v, u) = c(u, v) + c(v, u)$.

27.2-5
Recall that the construction in Section 27.1 that converts a multisource, multisink flow network into a single-source, single-sink network adds edges with infinite capacity. Prove that any flow in the resulting network has a finite value if the edges of the original multisource, multisink network have finite capacity.

27.2-6
Suppose that each source s_i in a multisource, multisink problem produces exactly p_i units of flow, so that $f(s_i, V) = p_i$. Suppose also that each sink t_j consumes exactly q_j units, so that $f(V, t_j) = q_j$, where $\sum_i p_i = \sum_j q_j$. Show how to convert the problem of finding a flow f that obeys these additional constraints into the problem of finding a maximum flow in a single-source, single-sink flow network.

27.2-7
Prove Lemma 27.3.

27.2-8
Show that a maximum flow in a network $G = (V, E)$ can always be found by a sequence of at most $|E|$ augmenting paths. (*Hint:* Determine the paths *after* finding the maximum flow.)

27.2-9
The *edge connectivity* of an undirected graph is the minimum number k of edges that must be removed to disconnect the graph. For example, the edge connectivity of a tree is 1, and the edge connectivity of a cyclic chain of vertices is 2. Show how the edge connectivity of an undirected graph $G = (V, E)$ can be determined by running a maximum-flow algorithm on at most $|V|$ flow networks, each having $O(V)$ vertices and $O(E)$ edges.

27.2-10
Show that the Edmonds-Karp algorithm terminates after at most $|V| \, |E| \, /4$ iterations. (*Hint:* For any edge (u, v), consider how both $\delta(s, u)$ and $\delta(u, t)$ change between times at which (u, v) is critical.)

27.3   Maximum bipartite matching

Some combinatorial problems can easily be cast as maximum-flow problems. The multiple-source, multiple-sink maximum-flow problem from Section 27.1 gave us one example. There are other combinatorial problems that seem on the surface to have little to do with flow networks, but can in fact be reduced to a maximum-flow problem. This section presents one such problem: finding a maximum matching in a bipartite graph (see Section 5.4). In order to solve this problem, we shall take advantage of an integrality property provided by the Ford-Fulkerson method. We shall also see that the Ford-Fulkerson method can be made to solve the maximum-bipartite-matching problem on a graph $G = (V, E)$ in $O(VE)$ time.

The maximum-bipartite-matching problem

Given an undirected graph $G = (V, E)$, a *matching* is a subset of edges $M \subseteq E$ such that for all vertices $v \in V$, at most one edge of M is incident on v. We say that a vertex $v \in V$ is *matched* by matching M if some edge in M is incident on v; otherwise, v is *unmatched*. A *maximum matching* is a matching of maximum cardinality, that is, a matching M such that for any matching M', we have $|M| \geq |M'|$. In this section, we shall restrict our attention to finding maximum matchings in bipartite graphs. We assume that the vertex set can be partitioned into $V = L \cup R$, where L and R are disjoint and all edges in E go between L and R. Figure 27.8 illustrates the notion of a matching.

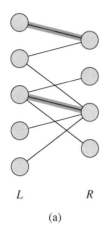 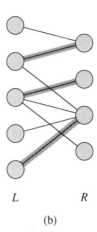

L   R   L   R

(a)   (b)

Figure 27.8 A bipartite graph $G = (V, E)$ with vertex partition $V = L \cup R$. **(a)** A matching with cardinality 2. **(b)** A maximum matching with cardinality 3.

The problem of finding a maximum matching in a bipartite graph has many practical applications. As an example, we might consider matching a set L of machines with a set R of tasks to be performed simultaneously. We take the presence of edge (u, v) in E to mean that a particular machine $u \in L$ is capable of performing a particular task $v \in R$. A maximum matching provides work for as many machines as possible.

Finding a maximum bipartite matching

We can use the Ford-Fulkerson method to find a maximum matching in an undirected bipartite graph $G = (V, E)$ in time polynomial in $|V|$ and $|E|$. The trick is to construct a flow network in which flows correspond to matchings, as shown in Figure 27.9. We define the ***corresponding flow network*** $G' = (V', E')$ for the bipartite graph G as follows. We let the source s and sink t be new vertices not in V, and we let $V' = V \cup \{s, t\}$. If the vertex partition of G is $V = L \cup R$, the directed edges of G' are given by

$$
\begin{aligned}
E' \quad = \quad & \{(s, u) : u \in L\} \\
& \cup \{(u, v) : u \in L, \, v \in R, \text{ and } (u, v) \in E\} \\
& \cup \{(v, t) : v \in R\} \ .
\end{aligned}
$$

To complete the construction, we assign unit capacity to each edge in E'.

The following theorem shows that a matching in G corresponds directly to a flow in G's corresponding flow network G'. We say that a flow f on a flow network $G = (V, E)$ is ***integer-valued*** if $f(u, v)$ is an integer for all $(u, v) \in V \times V$.

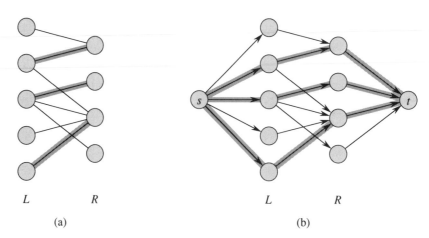

Figure 27.9   The flow network corresponding to a bipartite graph. **(a)** The bipartite graph $G = (V, E)$ with vertex partition $V = L \cup R$ from Figure 27.8. A maximum matching is shown by shaded edges. **(b)** The corresponding flow network G' with a maximum flow shown. Each edge has unit capacity. Shaded edges have a flow of 1, and all other edges carry no flow. The shaded edges from L to R correspond to those in a maximum matching of the bipartite graph.

Lemma 27.10

Let $G = (V, E)$ be a bipartite graph with vertex partition $V = L \cup R$, and let $G' = (V', E')$ be its corresponding flow network. If M is a matching in G, then there is an integer-valued flow f in G' with value $|f| = |M|$. Conversely, if f is an integer-valued flow in G', then there is a matching M in G with cardinality $|M| = |f|$.

Proof   We first show that a matching M in G corresponds to an integer-valued flow in G'. Define f as follows. If $(u, v) \in M$, then $f(s, u) = f(u, v) = f(v, t) = 1$ and $f(u, s) = f(v, u) = f(t, v) = -1$. For all other edges $(u, v) \in E'$, we define $f(u, v) = 0$.

Intuitively, each edge $(u, v) \in M$ corresponds to 1 unit of flow in G' that traverses the path $s \to u \to v \to t$. Moreover, the paths induced by edges in m are vertex-disjoint, except for s and t. To verify that f indeed satisfies skew symmetry, the capacity constraints, and flow conservation, we need only observe that f can be obtained by flow augmentation along each such path. The net flow across cut $(L \cup \{s\}, R \cup \{t\})$ is equal to $|M|$; thus, by Lemma 27.5, the value of the flow is $|f| = |M|$.

To prove the converse, let f be an integer-valued flow in G' and let

$$M = \{(u, v) : u \in L, v \in R, \text{ and } f(u, v) > 0\} \ .$$

Each vertex $u \in L$ has only one entering edge, namely (s, u), and its capacity is 1. Thus, each $u \in L$ has at most one unit of positive net flow entering it. Since f is integer-valued, for each $u \in L$, 1 unit of positive net flow enters u if and only if there is exactly one vertex $v \in R$ such that

$f(u, v) = 1$. Thus, at most one edge leaving each $u \in L$ carries positive net flow. A symmetric argument can be made for each $v \in R$. The set M defined in the statement of the theorem is therefore a matching.

To see that $|M| = |f|$, observe that for every matched vertex $u \in L$, we have $f(s, u) = 1$, and for every edge $(u, v) \in E - M$, we have $f(u, v) = 0$. Consequently, using Lemma 27.1, skew symmetry, and there being no edges from L to t, we obtain

$$
\begin{aligned}
|M| &= f(L, R) \\
&= f(L, V') - f(L, L) - f(L, s) - f(L, t) \\
&= 0 - 0 + f(s, L) - 0 \\
&= f(s, V') \\
&= |f| \ . \qquad \blacksquare
\end{aligned}
$$

It is intuitive that a maximum matching in a bipartite graph G corresponds to a maximum flow in its corresponding flow network G'. Thus, we can compute a maximum matching in G by running a maximum-flow algorithm on G'. The only hitch in this reasoning is that the maximum-flow algorithm might return a flow in G' that consists of nonintegral amounts. The following theorem shows that if we use the Ford-Fulkerson method, this difficulty cannot arise.

Theorem 27.11 *(Integrality theorem)*
If the capacity function c takes on only integral values, then the maximum flow f produced by the Ford-Fulkerson method has the property that $|f|$ is integer-valued. Moreover, for all vertices u and v, the value of $f(u, v)$ is an integer.

Proof The proof is by induction on the number of iterations. We leave it as Exercise 27.3-2. $\blacksquare$

We can now prove the following corollary to Lemma 27.10.

Corollary 27.12
The cardinality of a maximum matching in a bipartite graph G is the value of a maximum flow in its corresponding flow network G'.

Proof We use the nomenclature from Lemma 27.10. Suppose that M is a maximum matching in G and that the corresponding flow f in G' is not maximum. Then there is a maximum flow f' in G' such that $|f'| > |f|$. Since the capacities in G' are integer-valued, by Theorem 27.11, so is f'. Thus, f' corresponds to a matching M' in G with cardinality $|M'| = |f'| > |f| = |M|$, contradicting the maximality of M. In a similar manner, we can show that if f is a maximum flow in G', its corresponding matching is a maximum matching on G. $\blacksquare$

Thus, given a bipartite undirected graph G, we can find a maximum matching by creating the flow network G', running the Ford-Fulkerson method, and directly obtaining a maximum matching M from the integer-valued maximum flow f found. Since any matching in a bipartite graph has cardinality at most $\min(L, R) = O(V)$, the value of the maximum flow in G' is $O(V)$. We can therefore find a maximum matching in a bipartite graph in time $O(VE)$.

Exercises

27.3-1
Run the Ford-Fulkerson algorithm on the flow network in Figure 27.9(b) and show the residual network after each flow augmentation. Number the vertices in L top to bottom from 1 to 5 and in R top to bottom from 6 to 9. For each iteration, pick the augmenting path that is lexicographically smallest.

27.3-2
Prove Theorem 27.11.

27.3-3
Let $G = (V, E)$ be a bipartite graph with vertex partition $V = L \cup R$, and let G' be its corresponding flow network. Give a good upper bound on the length of any augmenting path found in G' during the execution of FORD-FULKERSON.

27.3-4 ⋆
A **perfect matching** is a matching in which every vertex is matched. Let $G = (V, E)$ be an undirected bipartite graph with vertex partition $V = L \cup R$, where $|L| = |R|$. For any $X \subseteq V$, define the **neighborhood** of X as

$$N(X) = \{y \in V : (x, y) \in E \text{ for some } x \in X\} \ ,$$

that is, the set of vertices adjacent to some member of X. Prove **Hall's theorem**: there exists a perfect matching in G if and only if $|A| \leq |N(A)|$ for every subset $A \subseteq L$.

27.3-5 ⋆
A bipartite graph $G = (V, E)$, where $V = L \cup R$, is **d-regular** if every vertex $v \in V$ has degree exactly d. Every d-regular bipartite graph has $|L| = |R|$. Prove that every d-regular bipartite graph has a matching of cardinality $|L|$ by arguing that a minimum cut of the corresponding flow network has capacity $|L|$.

★ 27.4 Preflow-push algorithms

In this section, we present the "preflow-push" approach to computing maximum flows. The fastest maximum-flow algorithms to date are preflow-push algorithms, and other flow problems, such as the minimum-cost flow problem, can be solved efficiently by preflow-push methods. This section introduces Goldberg's "generic" maximum-flow algorithm, which has a simple implementation that runs in $O(V^2 E)$ time, thereby improving upon the $O(VE^2)$ bound of the Edmonds-Karp algorithm. Section 27.5 refines the generic algorithm to obtain another preflow-push algorithm that runs in $O(V^3)$ time.

Preflow-push algorithms work in a more localized manner than the Ford-Fulkerson method. Rather than examine the entire residual network $G = (V, E)$ to find an augmenting path, preflow-push algorithms work on one vertex at a time, looking only at the vertex's neighbors in the residual network. Furthermore, unlike the Ford-Fulkerson method, preflow-push algorithms do not maintain the flow-conservation property throughout their execution. They do, however, maintain a *preflow*, which is a function $f : V \times V \to \mathbf{R}$ that satisfies skew symmetry, capacity constraints, and the following relaxation of flow conservation: $f(V, u) \geq 0$ for all vertices $u \in V - \{s\}$. That is, the net flow into each vertex other than the source is nonnegative. We call the net flow into a vertex u the *excess flow* into u, given by

$$e(u) = f(V, u) . \tag{27.8}$$

We say that a vertex $u \in V - \{s, t\}$ is *overflowing* if $e(u) > 0$.

We shall start this section by describing the intuition behind the preflow-push method. We shall then investigate the two operations employed by the method: "pushing" preflow and "lifting" a vertex. Finally, we shall present a generic preflow-push algorithm and analyze its correctness and running time.

Intuition

The intuition behind the preflow-push method is probably best understood in terms of fluid flows: we consider a flow network $G = (V, E)$ to be a system of interconnected pipes of given capacities. Applying this analogy to the Ford-Fulkerson method, we might say that each augmenting path in the network gives rise to an additional stream of fluid, with no branch points, flowing from the source to the sink. The Ford-Fulkerson method iteratively adds more streams of flow until no more can be added.

The generic preflow-push algorithm has a somewhat different intuition. As before, directed edges correspond to pipes. Vertices, which are pipe junctions, have two interesting properties. First, to accommodate excess flow, each vertex has an outflow pipe leading to an arbitrarily large reservoir that can accumulate fluid. Second, each vertex, its reservoir, and all its pipe connections are on a platform whose height increases as the algorithm progresses.

Vertex heights determine how flow is pushed: we only push flow down-hill, that is, from a higher vertex to a lower vertex. There may be positive net flow from a lower vertex to a higher vertex, but operations that push flow always push it downhill. The height of the source is fixed at $|V|$, and the height of the sink is fixed at 0. All other vertex heights start at 0 and increase with time. The algorithm first sends as much flow as possible downhill from the source toward the sink. The amount it sends is exactly enough to fill each outgoing pipe from the source to capacity; that is, it sends the capacity of the cut $(s, V - s)$. When flow first enters an intermediate vertex, it collects in the vertex's reservoir. From there, it is eventually pushed downhill.

It may eventually happen that the only pipes that leave a vertex u and are not already saturated with flow connect to vertices that are on the same level as u or are uphill from u. In this case, to rid an overflowing vertex u of its excess flow, we must increase its height—an operation called "lifting" vertex u. Its height is increased to one unit more than the height of the lowest of its neighbors to which it has an unsaturated pipe. After a vertex is lifted, therefore, there is at least one outgoing pipe through which more flow can be pushed.

Eventually, all the flow that can possibly get through to the sink has arrived there. No more can arrive, because the pipes obey the capacity constraints; the amount of flow across any cut is still limited by the capacity of the cut. To make the preflow a "legal" flow, the algorithm then sends the excess collected in the reservoirs of overflowing vertices back to the source by continuing to lift vertices to above the fixed height $|V|$ of the source. (Shipping the excess back to the source is actually accomplished by canceling the flows that cause the excess.) As we shall see, once all the reservoirs have been emptied, the preflow is not only a "legal" flow, it is also a maximum flow.

The basic operations

From the preceding discussion, we see that there are two basic operations performed by a preflow-push algorithm: pushing flow excess from a vertex to one of its neighbors and lifting a vertex. The applicability of these operations depends on the heights of vertices, which we now define precisely.

Let $G = (V, E)$ be a flow network with source s and sink t, and let f be a preflow in G. A function $h : V \rightarrow \mathbf{N}$ is a ***height function*** if $h(s) = |V|$, $h(t) = 0$, and

$$h(u) \leq h(v) + 1$$

for every residual edge $(u, v) \in E_f$. We immediately obtain the following lemma.

Lemma 27.13
Let $G = (V, E)$ be a flow network, let f be a preflow in G, and let h be a height function on V. For any two vertices $u, v \in V$, if $h(u) > h(v) + 1$, then (u, v) is not an edge in the residual graph.   ∎

The basic operation PUSH(u, v) can be applied if u is an overflowing vertex, $c_f(u, v) > 0$, and $h(u) = h(v) + 1$. The pseudocode below updates the preflow f in an implied network $G = (V, E)$. It assumes that the capacities are given by a constant-time function c and that residual capacities can also be computed in constant time given c and f. The excess flow stored at a vertex u is maintained as $e[u]$, and the height of u is maintained as $h[u]$. The expression $d_f(u, v)$ is a temporary variable that stores the amount of flow that can be pushed from u to v.

PUSH(u, v)

1 ▷ **Applies when:** u is overflowing, $c_f[u, v] > 0$, and $h[u] = h[v] + 1$.
2 ▷ **Action:** Push $d_f(u, v) = \min(e[u], c_f(u, v))$ units of flow
　　　　　　　　from u to v.
3 $d_f(u, v) \leftarrow \min(e[u], c_f(u, v))$
4 $f[u, v] \leftarrow f[u, v] + d_f(u, v)$
5 $f[v, u] \leftarrow -f[u, v]$
6 $e[u] \leftarrow e[u] - d_f(u, v)$
7 $e[v] \leftarrow e[v] + d_f(u, v)$

The code for PUSH operates as follows. Vertex u is assumed to have a positive excess $e[u]$, and the residual capacity of (u, v) is positive. Thus, we can ship up to $d_f(u, v) = \min(e[u], c_f(u, v))$ units of flow from u to v without causing $e[u]$ to become negative or the capacity $c(u, v)$ to be exceeded. This value is computed in line 3. We move the flow from u to v by updating f in lines 4–5 and e in lines 6–7. Thus, if f is a preflow before PUSH is called, it remains a preflow afterward.

Observe that nothing in the code for PUSH depends on the heights of u and v, yet we prohibit it from being invoked unless $h[u] = h[v] + 1$. Thus, excess flow is only pushed downhill by a height differential of 1. By Lemma 27.13, no residual edges exist between two vertices whose heights differ by more than 1, and thus there is nothing to be gained by allowing flow to be pushed downhill by a height differential of more than 1.

We call the operation PUSH(u, v) a ***push*** from u to v. If a push operation applies to some edge (u, v) leaving a vertex u, we also say that the push operation applies to u. It is a ***saturating push*** if edge (u, v) becomes ***saturated*** ($c_f(u, v) = 0$ afterward); otherwise, it is a ***nonsaturating push***. If an edge is saturated, it does not appear in the residual network.

The basic operation LIFT(u) applies if u is overflowing and if $c_f(u, v) > 0$ implies $h[u] \leq h[v]$ for all vertices v. In other words, we can lift an overflowing vertex u if for every vertex v for which there is residual capacity from u to v, flow cannot be pushed from u to v because v is not downhill from u. (Recall that by definition, neither the source s nor the sink t can be overflowing, so neither s nor t can be lifted.)

LIFT(u)

1 ▷ **Applies when:** u is overflowing and for all $v \in V$,
$$(u, v) \in E_f \text{ implies } h[u] \leq h[v].$$
2 ▷ **Action:** Increase the height of u.
3 $h[u] \leftarrow 1 + \min \{h[v] : (u, v) \in E_f\}$

When we call the operation LIFT(u), we say that vertex u is **lifted**. It is important to note that when u is lifted, E_f must contain at least one edge that leaves u, so that the minimization in the code is over a nonempty set. This fact follows from the assumption that u is overflowing. Since $e[u] > 0$, we have $e[u] = f[V, u] > 0$, and hence there must be at least one vertex v such that $f[v, u] > 0$. But then,

$$
\begin{aligned}
c_f(u, v) &= c(u, v) - f[u, v] \\
&= c(u, v) + f[v, u] \\
&> 0,
\end{aligned}
$$

which implies that $(u, v) \in E_f$. The operation LIFT(u) thus gives u the greatest height allowed by the constraints on height functions.

The generic algorithm

The generic preflow-push algorithm uses the following subroutine to create an initial preflow in the flow network.

INITIALIZE-PREFLOW(G, s)

1 **for** each vertex $u \in V[G]$
2   **do** $h[u] \leftarrow 0$
3          $e[u] \leftarrow 0$
4 **for** each edge $(u, v) \in E[G]$
5   **do** $f[u, v] \leftarrow 0$
6          $f[v, u] \leftarrow 0$
7 $h[s] \leftarrow |V[G]|$
8 **for** each vertex $u \in Adj[s]$
9   **do** $f[s, u] \leftarrow c(s, u)$
10        $f[u, s] \leftarrow -c(s, u)$
11        $e[u] \leftarrow c(s, u)$

INITIALIZE-PREFLOW creates an initial preflow f defined by

$$
f[u, v] = \begin{cases} c(u, v) & \text{if } u = s, \\ -c(v, u) & \text{if } v = s, \\ 0 & \text{otherwise}. \end{cases} \tag{27.9}
$$

That is, each edge leaving the source is filled to capacity, and all other edges carry no flow. For each vertex v adjacent to the source, we initially have $e[v] = c(s, v)$. The generic algorithm also begins with an initial height function h, given by

$$h[u] = \begin{cases} |V| & \text{if } u = s , \\ 0 & \text{otherwise} . \end{cases}$$

This is a height function because the only edges (u, v) for which $h[u] > h[v] + 1$ are those for which $u = s$, and those edges are saturated, which means that they are not in the residual network.

The following algorithm typifies the preflow-push method.

GENERIC-PREFLOW-PUSH(G)

1 INITIALIZE-PREFLOW(G, s)
2 **while** there exists an applicable push or lift operation
3   **do** select an applicable push or lift operation and perform it

After initializing the flow, the generic algorithm repeatedly applies, in any order, the basic operations wherever they are applicable. The following lemma tells us that as long as an overflowing vertex exists, at least one of the two operations applies.

Lemma 27.14 (An overflowing vertex can be either pushed or lifted)
Let $G = (V, E)$ be a flow network with source s and sink t, let f be a preflow, and let h be any height function for f. If u is any overflowing vertex, then either a push or lift operation applies to it.

Proof For any residual edge (u, v), we have $h(u) \le h(v) + 1$ because h is a height function. If a push operation does not apply to u, then for all residual edges (u, v), we must have $h(u) < h(v) + 1$, which implies $h(u) \le h(v)$. Thus, a lift operation can be applied to u. ∎

Correctness of the preflow-push method

To show that the generic preflow-push algorithm solves the maximum-flow problem, we shall first prove that if it terminates, the preflow f is a maximum flow. We shall later prove that it terminates. We start with some observations about the height function h.

Lemma 27.15 (Vertex heights never decrease)
During the execution of GENERIC-PREFLOW-PUSH on a flow network $G = (V, E)$, for each vertex $u \in V$, the height $h[u]$ never decreases. Moreover, whenever a lift operation is applied to a vertex u, its height $h[u]$ increases by at least 1.

Proof Because vertex heights change only during lift operations, it suffices to prove the second statement of the lemma. If vertex u is lifted, then for all vertices v such that $(u, v) \in E_f$, we have $h[u] \le h[v]$; this implies that $h[u] < 1 + \min\{h[v] : (u, v) \in E_f\}$, and so the operation must increase $h[u]$.   ∎

Lemma 27.16
Let $G = (V, E)$ be a flow network with source s and sink t. During the execution of GENERIC-PREFLOW-PUSH on G, the attribute h is maintained as a height function.

Proof   The proof is by induction on the number of basic operations performed. Initially, h is a height function, as we have already observed.

We claim that if h is a height function, then an operation LIFT(u) leaves h a height function. If we look at a residual edge $(u, v) \in E_f$ that leaves u, then the operation LIFT(u) ensures that $h[u] \le h[v] + 1$ afterward. Now consider a residual edge (w, u) that enters u. By Lemma 27.15, $h[w] \le h[u] + 1$ before the operation LIFT(u) implies $h[w] < h[u] + 1$ afterward. Thus, the operation LIFT(u) leaves h a height function.

Now, consider an operation PUSH(u, v). This operation may add the edge (v, u) to E_f, and it may remove (u, v) from E_f. In the former case, we have $h[v] = h[u] - 1$, and so h remains a height function. In the latter case, the removal of (u, v) from the residual network removes the corresponding constraint, and h again remains a height function.   ∎

The following lemma gives an important property of height functions.

Lemma 27.17
Let $G = (V, E)$ be a flow network with source s and sink t, let f be a preflow in G, and let h be a height function on V. Then, there is no path from the source s to the sink t in the residual network G_f.

Proof   Assume for the sake of contradiction that there is a path $p = \langle v_0, v_1, \dots, v_k \rangle$ from s to t in G_f, where $v_0 = s$ and $v_k = t$. Without loss of generality, p is a simple path, and so $k < |V|$. For $i = 0, 1, \dots, k - 1$, edge $(v_i, v_{i+1}) \in E_f$. Because h is a height function, $h(v_i) \le h(v_{i+1}) + 1$ for $i = 0, 1, \dots, k - 1$. Combining these inequalities over path p yields $h(s) \le h(t) + k$. But because $h(t) = 0$, we have $h(s) \le k < |V|$, which contradicts the requirement that $h(s) = |V|$ in a height function.   ∎

We are now ready to show that if the generic preflow-push algorithm terminates, the preflow it computes is a maximum flow.

Theorem 27.18 (Correctness of the generic preflow-push algorithm)
If the algorithm GENERIC-PREFLOW-PUSH terminates when run on a flow network $G = (V, E)$ with source s and sink t, then the preflow f it computes is a maximum flow for G.

Proof If the generic algorithm terminates, then each vertex in $V - \{s, t\}$ must have an excess of 0, because by Lemmas 27.14 and 27.16 and the invariant that f is always a preflow, there are no overflowing vertices. Therefore, f is a flow. Because h is a height function, by Lemma 27.17 there is no path from s to t in the residual network G_f. By the max-flow min-cut theorem, therefore, f is a maximum flow. ∎

Analysis of the preflow-push method

To show that the generic preflow-push algorithm indeed terminates, we shall bound the number of operations it performs. Each of the three types of operations—lifts, saturating pushes, and nonsaturating pushes—is bounded separately. With knowledge of these bounds, it is a straightforward problem to construct an algorithm that runs in $O(V^2 E)$ time. Before beginning the analysis, however, we prove an important lemma.

Lemma 27.19
Let $G = (V, E)$ be a flow network with source s and sink t, and let f be a preflow in G. Then, for any overflowing vertex u, there is a simple path from u to s in the residual network G_f.

Proof Let $U = \{v :$ there exists a simple path from u to v in $G_f\}$, and suppose for the sake of contradiction that $s \notin U$. Let $\overline{U} = V - U$.

We claim for each pair of vertices $v \in U$ and $w \in \overline{U}$ that $f(w, v) \le 0$. Why? If $f(w, v) > 0$, then $f(v, w) < 0$, which implies that $c_f(v, w) = c(v, w) - f(v, w) > 0$. Hence, there exists an edge $(v, w) \in E_f$, and therefore a simple path of the form $u \rightsquigarrow v \rightarrow w$ in G_f, contradicting our choice of w.

Thus, we must have $f(\overline{U}, U) \le 0$, since every term in this implicit summation is nonpositive. Thus, from equation (27.8) and Lemma 27.1, we can conclude that

$$
\begin{aligned}
e(U) &= f(V, U) \\
&= f(\overline{U}, U) + f(U, U) \\
&= f(\overline{U}, U) \\
&\le 0 .
\end{aligned}
$$

Excesses are nonnegative for all vertices in $V - \{s\}$; because we have assumed that $U \subseteq V - \{s\}$, we must therefore have $e(v) = 0$ for all vertices $v \in U$. In particular, $e(u) = 0$, which contradicts the assumption that u is overflowing. ∎

The next lemma bounds the heights of vertices, and its corollary bounds the number of lift operations that are performed in total.

Lemma 27.20

Let $G = (V, E)$ be a flow network with source s and sink t. At any time during the execution of GENERIC-PREFLOW-PUSH on G, we have $h[u] \leq 2|V| - 1$ for all vertices $u \in V$.

Proof   The heights of the source s and the sink t never change because these vertices are by definition not overflowing. Thus, we always have $h[s] = |V|$ and $h[t] = 0$.

Because a vertex is lifted only when it is overflowing, we can consider any overflowing vertex $u \in V - \{s, t\}$. Lemma 27.19 tells us that there is a simple path p from u to s in G_f. Let $p = \langle v_0, v_1, \ldots, v_k \rangle$, where $v_0 = u$, $v_k = s$, and $k \leq |V| - 1$ because p is simple. For $i = 0, 1, \ldots, k - 1$, we have $(v_i, v_{i+1}) \in E_f$, and therefore, by Lemma 27.16, $h[v_i] \leq h[v_{i+1}] + 1$. Expanding these inequalities over path p yields $h[u] = h[v_0] \leq h[v_k] + k \leq h[s] + (|V| - 1) = 2|V| - 1$.   ∎

Corollary 27.21 (Bound on lift operations)

Let $G = (V, E)$ be a flow network with source s and sink t. Then, during the execution of GENERIC-PREFLOW-PUSH on G, the number of lift operations is at most $2|V| - 1$ per vertex and at most $(2|V| - 1)(|V| - 2) < 2|V|^2$ overall.

Proof   Only vertices in $V - \{s, t\}$, which number $|V| - 2$, may be lifted. Let $u \in V - \{s, t\}$. The operation LIFT(u) increases $h[u]$. The value of $h[u]$ is initially 0 and by Lemma 27.20 grows to at most $2|V| - 1$. Thus, each vertex $u \in V - \{s, t\}$ is lifted at most $2|V| - 1$ times, and the total number of lift operations performed is at most $(2|V| - 1)(|V| - 2) < 2|V|^2$.   ∎

Lemma 27.20 also helps us to bound the number of saturating pushes.

Lemma 27.22 (Bound on saturating pushes)

During the execution of GENERIC-PREFLOW-PUSH on any flow network $G = (V, E)$, the number of saturating pushes is at most $2|V||E|$.

Proof   For any pair of vertices $u, v \in V$, consider the saturating pushes from u to v and from v to u. If there are any such pushes, at least one of (u, v) and (v, u) is actually an edge in E. Now, suppose that a saturating push from u to v has occurred. In order for another push from u to v to occur later, the algorithm must first push flow from v to u, which cannot happen until $h[v]$ increases by at least 2. Likewise, $h[u]$ must increase by at least 2 between saturating pushes from v to u.

Consider the sequence A of integers given by $h[u] + h[v]$ for each saturating push that occurs between vertices u and v. We wish to bound the length of this sequence. When the first push in either direction between u and v occurs, we must have $h[u] + h[v] \geq 1$; thus, the first integer in A is at least 1. When the last such push occurs, we have $h[u] + h[v] \leq (2|V| - 1) + (2|V| - 2) = 4|V| - 3$ by Lemma 27.20; the last integer in A is thus at most $4|V| - 3$. By the argument from the previous paragraph, at most every other integer can occur in A. Thus, the number of integers in A is at most $((4|V| - 3) - 1)/2 + 1 = 2|V| - 1$. (We add 1 to make sure that both ends of the sequence are counted.) The total number of saturating pushes between vertices u and v is therefore at most $2|V| - 1$. Multiplying by the number of edges gives a total number of saturating pushes of at most $(2|V| - 1)|E| < 2|V||E|$. ∎

The following lemma bounds the number of nonsaturating pushes in the generic preflow-push algorithm.

Lemma 27.23 (Bound on nonsaturating pushes)
During the execution of GENERIC-PREFLOW-PUSH on any flow network $G = (V, E)$, the number of nonsaturating pushes is at most $4|V|^2 (|V|+|E|)$.

Proof Define a potential function $\Phi = \sum_{v \in X} h[v]$, where $X \subseteq V$ is the set of overflowing vertices. Initially, $\Phi = 0$. Observe that lifting a vertex u increases Φ by at most $2|V|$, since the set over which the sum is taken is the same and u cannot be lifted by more than its maximum possible height, which, by Lemma 27.20, is at most $2|V|$. Also, a saturating push from a vertex u to a vertex v increases Φ by at most $2|V|$, since no heights change and only vertex v, whose height is at most $2|V|$, can possibly become overflowing. Finally, observe that a nonsaturating push from u to v decreases Φ by at least 1, since u is no longer overflowing after the push, v is overflowing afterward even if it wasn't beforehand, and $h[v] - h[u] = -1$.

Thus, during the course of the algorithm, the total amount of increase in Φ is constrained by Corollary 27.21 and Lemma 27.22 to be at most $(2|V|)(2|V|^2) + (2|V|)(2|V||E|) = 4|V|^2 (|V| + |E|)$. Since $\Phi \geq 0$, the total amount of decrease, and therefore the total number of nonsaturating pushes, is at most $4|V|^2 (|V| + |E|)$. ∎

We have now set the stage for the following analysis of the GENERIC-PREFLOW-PUSH procedure, and hence of any algorithm based on the preflow-push method.

Theorem 27.24
During the execution of GENERIC-PREFLOW-PUSH on any flow network $G = (V, E)$, the number of basic operations is $O(V^2 E)$.

Proof Immediate from Corollary 27.21 and Lemmas 27.22 and 27.23. ∎

Corollary 27.25
There is an implementation of the generic preflow-push algorithm that runs in $O(V^2 E)$ time on any flow network $G = (V, E)$.

Proof Exercise 27.4-1 asks you to show how to implement the generic algorithm with an overhead of $O(V)$ per lift operation and $O(1)$ per push. The corollary then follows.   ∎

Exercises

27.4-1
Show how to implement the generic preflow-push algorithm using $O(V)$ time per lift operation and $O(1)$ time per push, for a total time of $O(V^2 E)$.

27.4-2
Prove that the generic preflow-push algorithm spends a total of only $O(VE)$ time in performing all the $O(V^2)$ lift operations.

27.4-3
Suppose that a maximum flow has been found in a flow network $G = (V, E)$ using a preflow-push algorithm. Give a fast algorithm to find a minimum cut in G.

27.4-4
Give an efficient preflow-push algorithm to find a maximum matching in a bipartite graph. Analyze your algorithm.

27.4-5
Suppose that all edge capacities in a flow network $G = (V, E)$ are in the set $\{1, 2, \ldots, k\}$. Analyze the running time of the generic preflow-push algorithm in terms of $|V|$, $|E|$, and k. (*Hint:* How many times can each edge support a nonsaturating push before it becomes saturated?)

27.4-6
Show that line 7 of INITIALIZE-PREFLOW can be changed to

$$h[s] \leftarrow |V[G]| - 2$$

without affecting the correctness or asymptotic performance of the generic preflow-push algorithm.

27.4-7
Let $\delta_f(u, v)$ be the distance (number of edges) from u to v in the residual network G_f. Show that GENERIC-PREFLOW-PUSH maintains the properties that $h[u] < |V|$ implies $h[u] \leq \delta_f(u, t)$ and that $h[u] \geq |V|$ implies $h[u] - |V| \leq \delta_f(u, s)$.

27.4-8 ⋆

As in the previous exercise, let $\delta_f(u, v)$ be the distance from u to v in the residual network G_f. Show how the generic preflow-push algorithm can be modified to maintain the property that $h[u] < |V|$ implies $h[u] = \delta_f(u, t)$ and that $h[u] \geq |V|$ implies $h[u] - |V| = \delta_f(u, s)$. The total time that your implementation dedicates to maintaining this property should be $O(VE)$.

27.4-9

Show that the number of nonsaturating pushes executed by GENERIC-PREFLOW-PUSH on a flow network $G = (V, E)$ is at most $4|V|^2|E|$ for $|V| \geq 4$.

⋆ **27.5 The lift-to-front algorithm**

The preflow-push method allows us to apply the basic operations in any order at all. By choosing the order carefully and managing the network data structure efficiently, however, we can solve the maximum-flow problem faster than the $O(V^2E)$ bound given by Corollary 27.25. We shall now examine the lift-to-front algorithm, a preflow-push algorithm whose running time is $O(V^3)$, which is asymptotically at least as good as $O(V^2E)$.

The lift-to-front algorithm maintains a list of the vertices in the network. Beginning at the front, the algorithm scans the list, repeatedly selecting an overflowing vertex u and then "discharging" it, that is, performing push and lift operations until u no longer has a positive excess. Whenever a vertex is lifted, it is moved to the front of the list (hence the name "lift-to-front") and the algorithm begins its scan anew.

The correctness and analysis of the lift-to-front algorithm depend on the notion of "admissible" edges: those edges in the residual network through which flow can be pushed. After proving some properties about the network of admissible edges, we shall investigate the discharge operation and then present and analyze the lift-to-front algorithm itself.

Admissible edges and networks

If $G = (V, E)$ is a flow network with source s and sink t, f is a preflow in G, and h is a height function, then we say that (u, v) is an ***admissible edge*** if $c_f(u, v) > 0$ and $h(u) = h(v) + 1$. Otherwise, (u, v) is ***inadmissible***. The ***admissible network*** is $G_{f,h} = (V, E_{f,h})$, where $E_{f,h}$ is the set of admissible edges.

The admissible network consists of those edges through which flow can be pushed. The following lemma shows that this network is a directed acyclic graph (dag).

Lemma 27.26 (The admissible network is acyclic)

If $G = (V, E)$ is a flow network, f is a preflow in G, and h is a height function on G, then the admissible network $G_{f,h} = (V, E_{f,h})$ is acyclic.

Proof The proof is by contradiction. Suppose that $G_{f,h}$ contains a cycle $p = \langle v_0, v_1, \ldots, v_k \rangle$, where $v_0 = v_k$ and $k > 0$. Since each edge in p is admissible, we have $h(v_{i-1}) = h(v_i) + 1$ for $i = 1, 2, \ldots, k$. Summing around the cycle gives

$$\sum_{i=1}^{k} h(v_{i-1}) = \sum_{i=1}^{k} (h(v_i) + 1)$$

$$= \sum_{i=1}^{k} h(v_i) + k .$$

Because each vertex in cycle p appears once in each of the summations, we derive the contradiction that $0 = k$. ∎

The next two lemmas show how push and lift operations change the admissible network.

Lemma 27.27

Let $G = (V, E)$ be a flow network, let f be a preflow in G, and let h be a height function. If a vertex u is overflowing and (u, v) is an admissible edge, then PUSH(u, v) applies. The operation does not create any new admissible edges, but it may cause (u, v) to become inadmissible.

Proof By the definition of an admissible edge, flow can be pushed from u to v. Since u is overflowing, the operation PUSH(u, v) applies. The only new residual edge that can be created by pushing flow from u to v is the edge (v, u). Since $h(v) = h(u) - 1$, edge (v, u) cannot become admissible. If the operation is a saturating push, then $c_f(u, v) = 0$ afterward and (u, v) becomes inadmissible. ∎

Lemma 27.28

Let $G = (V, E)$ be a flow network, let f be a preflow in G, and let h be a height function. If a vertex u is overflowing and there are no admissible edges leaving u, then LIFT(u) applies. After the lift operation, there is at least one admissible edge leaving u, but there are no admissible edges entering u.

Proof If u is overflowing, then by Lemma 27.14, either a push or a lift operation applies to it. If there are no admissible edges leaving u, no flow can be pushed from u and LIFT(u) applies. After the lift operation, $h[u] = 1 + \min\{h[v] : (u, v) \in E_f\}$. Thus, if v is a vertex that realizes the minimum in this set, the edge (u, v) becomes admissible. Hence, after the lift, there is at least one admissible edge leaving u.

To show that no admissible edges enter u after a lift operation, suppose that there is a vertex v such that (v, u) is admissible. Then, $h[v] = h[u] + 1$ after the lift, and therefore $h[v] > h[u] + 1$ just before the lift. But by Lemma 27.13, no residual edges exist between vertices whose heights differ by more than 1. Moreover, lifting a vertex does not change the residual network. Thus, (v, u) is not in the residual network, and hence it cannot be in the admissible network. ∎

Neighbor lists

Edges in the lift-to-front algorithm are organized into "neighbor lists." Given a flow network $G = (V, E)$, the ***neighbor list*** $N[u]$ for a vertex $u \in V$ is a singly linked list of the neighbors of u in G. Thus, vertex v appears in the list $N[u]$ if $(u, v) \in E$ or $(v, u) \in E$. The neighbor list $N[u]$ contains exactly those vertices v for which there may be a residual edge (u, v). The first vertex in $N[u]$ is pointed to by $head[N[u]]$. The vertex following v in a neighbor list is pointed to by $next\text{-}neighbor[v]$; this pointer is NIL if v is the last vertex in the neighbor list.

The lift-to-front algorithm cycles through each neighbor list in an arbitrary order that is fixed throughout the execution of the algorithm. For each vertex u, the field $current[u]$ points to the vertex currently under consideration in $N[u]$. Initially, $current[u]$ is set to $head[N[u]]$.

Discharging an overflowing vertex

An overflowing vertex u is ***discharged*** by pushing all of its excess flow through admissible edges to neighboring vertices, lifting u as necessary to cause edges leaving u to become admissible. The pseudocode goes as follows.

DISCHARGE(u)

```
1  while e[u] > 0
2      do v ← current[u]
3          if v = NIL
4              then LIFT(u)
5                  current[u] ← head[N[u]]
6              elseif c_f(u, v) > 0 and h[u] = h[v] + 1
7                  then PUSH(u, v)
8              else current[u] ← next-neighbor[v]
```

Figure 27.10 steps through several iterations of the **while** loop of lines 1–8, which executes as long as vertex u has positive excess. Each iteration performs exactly one of three actions, depending on the current vertex v in the neighbor list $N[u]$.

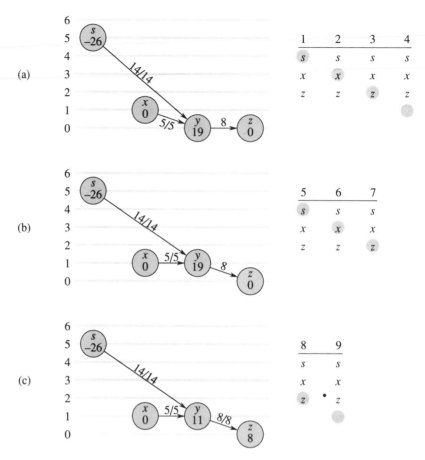

Figure 27.10 Discharging a vertex. It takes 15 iterations of the **while** loop of DISCHARGE to push all the excess flow from vertex y. Only the neighbors of y and edges entering or leaving y are shown. In each part, the number inside each vertex is its excess at the beginning of the first iteration shown in the part, and each vertex is shown at its height throughout the part. To the right is shown the neighbor list $N[y]$ at the beginning of each iteration, with the iteration number on top. The shaded neighbor is *current*$[y]$. **(a)** Initially, there are 19 units of excess to push from y, and *current*$[y] = s$. Iterations 1, 2, and 3 just advance *current*$[y]$, since there are no admissible edges leaving y. In iteration 4, *current*$[y] = $ NIL (shown by the shading being below the neighbor list), and so y is lifted and *current*$[y]$ is reset to the head of the neighbor list. **(b)** After lifting, vertex y has height 1. In iterations 5 and 6, edges (y, s) and (y, x) are found to be inadmissible, but 8 units of excess flow are pushed from y to z in iteration 7. Because of the push, *current*$[y]$ is not advanced in this iteration. **(c)** Because the push in iteration 7 saturated edge (y, z), it is found inadmissible in iteration 8. In iteration 9, *current*$[y] = $ NIL, and so vertex y is again lifted and *current*$[y]$ is reset. **(d)** In iteration 10, (y, s) is inadmissible, but 5 units of excess flow are pushed from y to x in iteration 11. **(e)** Because *current*$[y]$ was not advanced in iteration 11, iteration 12 finds (y, x) to be inadmissible. Iteration 13 finds (y, z) inadmissible, and iteration 14 lifts vertex y and resets *current*$[y]$. **(f)** Iteration 15 pushes 6 units of excess flow from y to s. **(g)** Vertex y now has no excess flow, and DISCHARGE terminates. In this example, DISCHARGE both starts and finishes with the current pointer at the head of the neighbor list, but in general this need not be the case.

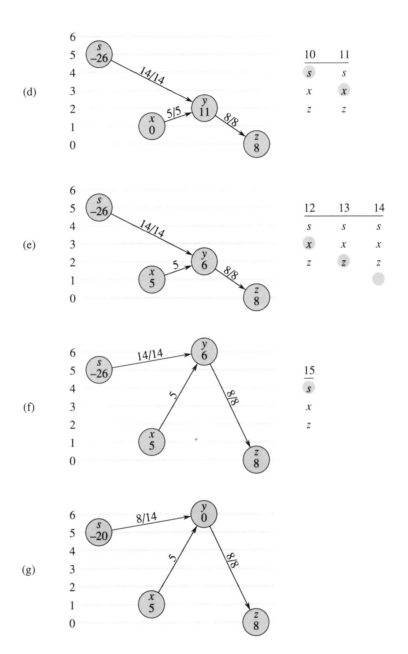

1. If v is NIL, then we have run off the end of $N[u]$. Line 4 lifts vertex u, and then line 5 resets the current neighbor of u to be the first one in $N[u]$. (Lemma 27.29 below states that the lift operation applies in this situation.)

2. If v is non-NIL and (u, v) is an admissible edge (determined by the test in line 6), then line 7 pushes some (or possibly all) of u's excess to vertex v.

3. If v is non-NIL but (u, v) is inadmissible, then line 8 **advances** $current[u]$ one position further in the neighbor list $N[u]$.

Observe that if DISCHARGE is called on an overflowing vertex u, then the last action performed by DISCHARGE must be a push from u. Why? The procedure terminates only when $e[u]$ becomes zero, and neither the lift operation nor the advancing of the pointer $current[u]$ affects the value of $e[u]$.

We must be sure that when PUSH or LIFT is called by DISCHARGE, the operation applies. The next lemma proves this fact.

Lemma 27.29
If DISCHARGE calls PUSH(u, v) in line 7, then a push operation applies to (u, v). If DISCHARGE calls LIFT(u) in line 4, then a lift operation applies to u.

Proof   The tests in lines 1 and 6 ensure that a push operation occurs only if the operation applies, which proves the first statement in the lemma.

To prove the second statement, according to the test in line 1 and Lemma 27.28, we need only show that all edges leaving u are inadmissible. Observe that as DISCHARGE(u) is repeatedly called, the pointer $current[u]$ moves down the list $N[u]$. Each "pass" begins at the head of $N[u]$ and finishes with $current[u] = $ NIL, at which point u is lifted and a new pass begins. For the $current[u]$ pointer to advance past a vertex $v \in N[u]$ during a pass, the edge (u, v) must be deemed inadmissible by the test in line 6. Thus, by the time the pass completes, every edge leaving u has been determined to be inadmissible at some time during the pass. The key observation is that at the end of the pass, every edge leaving u is still inadmissible. Why? By Lemma 27.27, pushes cannot create any admissible edges, let alone one leaving u. Thus, any admissible edge must be created by a lift operation. But the vertex u is not lifted during the pass, and by Lemma 27.28, any other vertex v that is lifted during the pass has no entering admissible edges. Thus, at the end of the pass, all edges leaving u remain inadmissible, and the lemma is proved.   ■

The lift-to-front algorithm

In the lift-to-front algorithm, we maintain a linked list L consisting of all vertices in $V - \{s, t\}$. A key property is that the vertices in L are topologically sorted according to the admissible network. (Recall from Lemma 27.26 that the admissible network is a dag.)

The pseudocode for the lift-to-front algorithm assumes that the neighbor lists $N[u]$ have already been created for each vertex u. It also assumes that $next[u]$ points to the vertex that follows u in list L and that, as usual, $next[u] = $ NIL if u is the last vertex in the list.

LIFT-TO-FRONT(G, s, t)

```
 1   INITIALIZE-PREFLOW(G, s)
 2   L ← V[G] − {s, t}, in any order
 3   for each vertex u ∈ V[G] − {s, t}
 4       do current[u] ← head[N[u]]
 5   u ← head[L]
 6   while u ≠ NIL
 7       do old-height ← h[u]
 8          DISCHARGE(u)
 9          if h[u] > old-height
10             then move u to the front of list L
11          u ← next[u]
```

The lift-to-front algorithm works as follows. Line 1 initializes the preflow and heights to the same values as in the generic preflow-push algorithm. Line 2 initializes the list L to contain all potentially overflowing vertices, in any order. Lines 3–4 initialize the *current* pointer of each vertex u to the first vertex in u's neighbor list.

As shown in Figure 27.11, the **while** loop of lines 6–11 runs through the list L, discharging vertices. Line 5 makes it start with the first vertex in the list. Each time through the loop, a vertex u is discharged in line 8. If u was lifted by the DISCHARGE procedure, line 10 moves it to the front of list L. This determination is made by saving u's height in the variable *old-height* before the discharge operation (line 7) and comparing this saved height to u's height afterward (line 9). Line 11 makes the next iteration of the **while** loop use the vertex following u in list L. If u was moved to the front of the list, the vertex used in the next iteration is the one following u in its new position in the list.

To show that LIFT-TO-FRONT computes a maximum flow, we shall show that it is an implementation of the generic preflow-push algorithm. First, observe that it only performs push and lift operation when they apply, since Lemma 27.29 guarantees that DISCHARGE only performs them when they apply. It remains to show that when LIFT-TO-FRONT terminates, no basic operations apply. Observe that if u reaches the end of L, every vertex in L must have been discharged without causing a lift. Lemma 27.30, which we shall prove in a moment, states that the list L is maintained as a topological sort of the admissible network. Thus, a push operation causes excess flow to move to vertices further down the list (or to s or t). If the

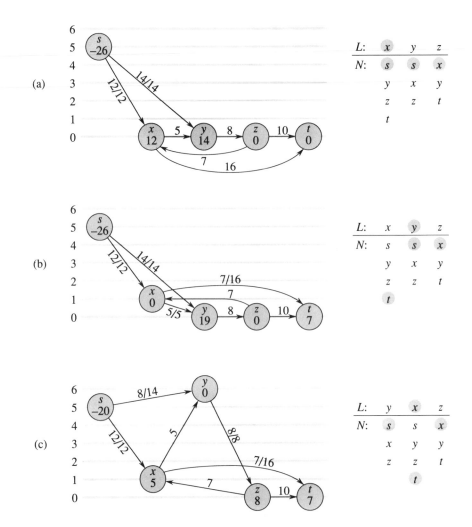

Figure 27.11 The action of LIFT-TO-FRONT. **(a)** A flow network just before the first iteration of the **while** loop. Initially, 26 units of flow leave source s. On the right is shown the initial list $L = \langle x, y, z \rangle$, where initially $u = x$. Under each vertex in list L is its neighbor list, with the current neighbor shaded. Vertex x is discharged. It is lifted to height 1, 5 units of excess flow are pushed to y, and the 7 remaining units of excess are pushed to the sink t. Because x is lifted, it is moved to the head of L, which in this case does not change the structure of L. **(b)** After x, the next vertex in L that is discharged is y. Figure 27.10 shows the detailed action of discharging y in this situation. Because y is lifted, it is moved to the head of L. **(c)** Vertex x now follows y in L, and so it is again discharged, pushing all 5 units of excess flow to t. Because vertex x is not lifted in this discharge operation, it remains in place in list L. **(d)** Since vertex z follows vertex x in L, it is discharged. It is lifted to height 1 and all 8 units of excess flow are pushed to t. Because z is lifted, it is moved to the front of L. **(e)** Vertex y now follows vertex z in L and is therefore discharged. But because y has no excess, DISCHARGE immediately returns, and y remains in place in L. Vertex x is then discharged. Because it, too, has no excess, DISCHARGE again returns, and x remains in place in list L. LIFT-TO-FRONT has reached the end of list L and terminates. There are no overflowing vertices, and the preflow is a maximum flow.

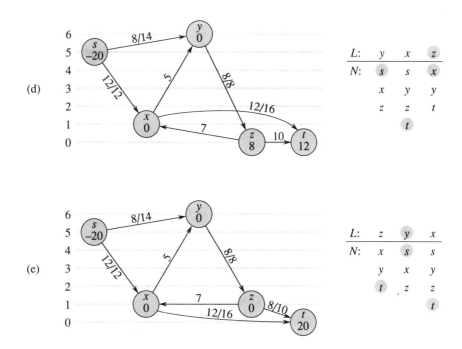

pointer u reaches the end of the list, therefore, the excess of every vertex is 0, and no basic operations apply.

Lemma 27.30

If we run LIFT-TO-FRONT on a flow network $G = (V, E)$ with source s and sink t, then each iteration of the **while** loop in lines 6–11 maintains the invariant that list L is a topological sort of the vertices in the admissible network $G_{f,h} = (V, E_{f,h})$.

Proof   Immediately after INITIALIZE-PREFLOW has been run, $h[s] = |V|$ and $h[v] = 0$ for all $v \in V - \{s\}$. Since $|V| \geq 2$ (because it contains at least s and t), no edge can be admissible. Thus, $E_{f,h} = \emptyset$, and any ordering of $V - \{s, t\}$ is a topological sort of $G_{f,h}$.

We now show that the invariant is maintained by each iteration of the **while** loop. The admissible network is changed only by push and lift operations. By Lemma 27.27, push operations only make edges inadmissible. Thus, admissible edges can be created only by lift operations. After a vertex is lifted, however, Lemma 27.28 states that there are no admissible edges entering u but there may be admissible edges leaving u. Thus, by moving u to the front of L, the algorithm ensures that any admissible edges leaving u satisfy the topological sort ordering.   ∎

Analysis

We shall now show that Lift-To-Front runs in $O(V^3)$ time on any flow network $G = (V, E)$. Since the algorithm is an implementation of the generic preflow-push algorithm, we shall take advantage of Corollary 27.21, which provides an $O(V)$ bound on the number of lift operations executed per vertex and an $O(V^2)$ bound on the total number of lifts overall. In addition, Exercise 27.4-2 provides an $O(VE)$ bound on the total time spent performing lift operations, and Lemma 27.22 provides an $O(VE)$ bound on the total number of saturating push operations.

Theorem 27.31
The running time of Lift-To-Front on any flow network $G = (V, E)$ is $O(V^3)$.

Proof Let us consider a "phase" of the lift-to-front algorithm to be the time between two consecutive lift operations. There are $O(V^2)$ phases, since there are $O(V^2)$ lift operations. Each phase consists of at most $|V|$ calls to Discharge, which can be seen as follows. If Discharge does not perform a lift operation, the next call to Discharge is further down the list L, and the length of L is less than $|V|$. If Discharge does perform a lift, the next call to Discharge belongs to a different phase. Since each phase contains at most $|V|$ calls to Discharge and there are $O(V^2)$ phases, the number of times Discharge is called in line 8 of Lift-To-Front is $O(V^3)$. Thus, the total work performed by the **while** loop in Lift-To-Front, excluding the work performed within Discharge, is at most $O(V^3)$.

We must now bound the work performed within Discharge during the execution of the algorithm. Each iteration of the **while** loop within Discharge performs one of three actions. We shall analyze the total amount of work involved in performing each of these actions.

We start with lift operations (lines 4–5). Exercise 27.4-2 provides an $O(VE)$ time bound on all the $O(V^2)$ lifts that are performed.

Now, suppose that the action updates the *current*[u] pointer in line 8. This action occurs $O(\text{degree}(u))$ times each time a vertex u is lifted, and $O(V \cdot \text{degree}(u))$ times overall for the vertex. For all vertices, therefore, the total amount of work done in advancing pointers in neighbor lists is $O(VE)$ by the handshaking lemma (Exercise 5.4-1).

The third type of action performed by Discharge is a push operation (line 7). We already know that the total number of saturating push operations is $O(VE)$. Observe that if a nonsaturating push is executed, Discharge immediately returns, since the push reduces the excess to 0. Thus, there can be at most one nonsaturating push per call to Discharge. As we have observed, Discharge is called $O(V^3)$ times, and thus the total time spent performing nonsaturating pushes is $O(V^3)$.

The running time of LIFT-TO-FRONT is therefore $O(V^3 + VE)$, which is $O(V^3)$.   ∎

Exercises

27.5-1
Illustrate the execution of LIFT-TO-FRONT in the manner of Figure 27.11 for the flow network in Figure 27.1(a). Assume that the initial ordering of vertices in L is $\langle v_1, v_2, v_3, v_4 \rangle$ and that the neighbor lists are

$$
\begin{aligned}
N[v_1] &= \langle s, v_2, v_3 \rangle, \\
N[v_2] &= \langle s, v_1, v_3, v_4 \rangle, \\
N[v_3] &= \langle v_1, v_2, v_4, t \rangle, \\
N[v_4] &= \langle v_2, v_3, t \rangle.
\end{aligned}
$$

27.5-2 ⋆
We would like to implement a preflow-push algorithm in which we maintain a first-in, first-out queue of overflowing vertices. The algorithm repeatedly discharges the vertex at the head of the queue, and any vertices that were not overflowing before the discharge but are overflowing afterward are placed at the end of the queue. After the vertex at the head of the queue is discharged, it is removed. When the queue is empty, the algorithm terminates. Show that this algorithm can be implemented to compute a maximum flow in $O(V^3)$ time.

27.5-3
Show that the generic algorithm still works if LIFT updates $h[u]$ by simply computing $h[u] \leftarrow h[u] + 1$. How does this change affect the analysis of LIFT-TO-FRONT?

27.5-4 ⋆
Show that if we always discharge a highest overflowing vertex, the preflow-push method can be made to run in $O(V^3)$ time.

Problems

27-1 *Escape problem*
An $n \times n$ **grid** is an undirected graph consisting of n rows and n columns of vertices, as shown in Figure 27.12. We denote the vertex in the ith row and the jth column by (i, j). All vertices in a grid have exactly four neighbors, except for the boundary vertices, which are the points (i, j) for which $i = 1$, $i = n$, $j = 1$, or $j = n$.

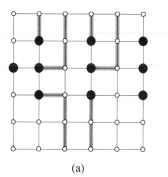
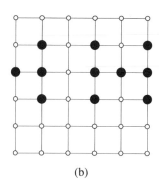

(a)   (b)

Figure 27.12 Grids for the escape problem. Starting points are black, and other grid vertices are white. **(a)** A grid with an escape, shown by shaded paths. **(b)** A grid with no escape.

Given $m \leq n^2$ starting points $(x_1, y_1), (x_2, y_2), \ldots, (x_m, y_m)$ in the grid, the **escape problem** is to determine whether or not there are m vertex-disjoint paths from the starting points to any m different points on the boundary. For example, the grid in Figure 27.12(a) has an escape, but the grid in Figure 27.12(b) does not.

a. Consider a flow network in which vertices, as well as edges, have capacities. That is, the positive net flow entering any given vertex is subject to a capacity constraint. Show that determining the maximum flow in a network with edge and vertex capacities can be reduced to an ordinary maximum-flow problem on a flow network of comparable size.

b. Describe an efficient algorithm to solve the escape problem, and analyze its running time.

27-2 *Minimum path cover*

A **path cover** of a directed graph $G = (V, E)$ is a set P of vertex-disjoint paths such that every vertex in V is included in exactly one path in P. Paths may start and end anywhere, and they may be of any length, including 0. A **minimum path cover** of G is a path cover containing the fewest possible paths.

a. Give an efficient algorithm to find a minimum path cover of a directed acyclic graph $G = (V, E)$. (*Hint:* Assuming that $V = \{1, 2, \ldots, n\}$, construct the graph $G' = (V', E')$, where

$$V' = \{x_0, x_1, \ldots, x_n\} \cup \{y_0, y_1, \ldots, y_n\} \ ,$$
$$E' = \{(x_0, x_i) : i \in V\} \cup \{(y_i, y_0) : i \in V\} \cup \{(x_i, y_j) : (i, j) \in E\} \ ,$$

and run a maximum-flow algorithm.)

b. Does your algorithm work for directed graphs that contain cycles? Explain.

27-3 Space shuttle experiments

Professor Spock is consulting for NASA, which is planning a series of space shuttle flights and must decide which commercial experiments to perform and which instruments to have on board each flight. For each flight, NASA considers a set $E = \{E_1, E_2, \ldots, E_m\}$ of experiments, and the commercial sponsor of experiment E_j has agreed to pay NASA p_j dollars for the results of the experiment. The experiments use a set $I = \{I_1, I_2, \ldots, I_n\}$ of instruments; each experiment E_j requires all the instruments in a subset $R_j \subseteq I$. The cost of carrying instrument I_k is c_k dollars. The professor's job is to find an efficient algorithm to determine which experiments to perform and which instruments to carry for a given flight in order to maximize the net revenue, which is the total income from experiments performed minus the total cost of all instruments carried.

Consider the following network G. The network contains a source vertex s, vertices $I_1, I_2, \ldots, I_n$, vertices $E_1, E_2, \ldots, E_m$, and a sink vertex t. For $k = 1, 2 \ldots, n$, there is an edge (s, I_k) of capacity c_k, and for $j = 1, 2, \ldots, m$, there is an edge (E_j, t) of capacity p_j. For $k = 1, 2, \ldots, n$ and $j = 1, 2, \ldots, m$, if $I_k \in R_j$, then there is an edge (I_k, E_j) of infinite capacity.

a. Show that if $E_j \in T$ for a finite-capacity cut (S, T) of G, then $I_k \in T$ for each $I_k \in R_j$.

b. Show how to determine the maximum net revenue from the capacity of the minimum cut of G and the given p_j values.

c. Give an efficient algorithm to determine which experiments to perform and which instruments to carry. Analyze the running time of your algorithm in terms of m, n, and $r = \sum_{j=1}^{m} |R_j|$.

27-4 Updating maximum flow

Let $G = (V, E)$ be a flow network with source s, sink t, and integer capacities. Suppose that we are given a maximum flow in G.

a. Suppose that the capacity of a single edge $(u, v) \in E$ is increased by 1. Give an $O(V + E)$-time algorithm to update the maximum flow.

b. Suppose that the capacity of a single edge $(u, v) \in E$ is decreased by 1. Give an $O(V + E)$-time algorithm to update the maximum flow.

27-5 Maximum flow by scaling

Let $G = (V, E)$ be a flow network with source s, sink t, and an integer capacity $c(u, v)$ on each edge $(u, v) \in E$. Let $C = \max_{(u,v) \in E} c(u, v)$.

a. Argue that a minimum cut of G has capacity at most $C|E|$.

b. For a given number K, show that an augmenting path of capacity at least K can be found in $O(E)$ time, if such a path exists.

The following modification of FORD-FULKERSON-METHOD can be used to compute a maximum flow in G.

MAX-FLOW-BY-SCALING(G, s, t)

1 $C \leftarrow \max_{(u,v) \in E} c(u, v)$
2 initialize flow f to 0
3 $K \leftarrow 2^{\lfloor \lg C \rfloor}$
4 **while** $K \geq 1$
5   **do while** there exists an augmenting path p of capacity at least K
6   **do** augment flow f along p
7      $K \leftarrow K/2$
8 **return** f

c. Argue that MAX-FLOW-BY-SCALING returns a maximum flow.

d. Show that the residual capacity of a minimum cut of G is at most $2K |E|$ each time line 4 is executed.

e. Argue that the inner **while** loop of lines 5–6 is executed $O(E)$ times for each value of K.

f. Conclude that MAX-FLOW-BY-SCALING can be implemented to run in $O(E^2 \lg C)$ time.

27-6 *Maximum flow with upper and lower capacity bounds*

Suppose that each edge (u, v) in a flow network $G = (V, E)$ has not only an upper bound $c(u, v)$ on the net flow from u to v, but also a lower bound $b(u, v)$. That is, any flow f on the network must satisfy $b(u, v) \leq f(u, v) \leq c(u, v)$. It may be the case for such a network that no feasible flow exists.

a. Prove that if f is a flow on G, then $|f| \leq c(S, T) - b(T, S)$ for any cut (S, T) of G.

b. Prove that the value of a maximum flow in the network, if it exists, is the minimum value of $c(S, T) - b(T, S)$ over all cuts (S, T) of the network.

Let $G = (V, E)$ be a flow network with upper and lower bound functions c and b, and let s and t be the source and sink of G. Construct the ordinary flow network $G' = (V', E')$ with upper bound function c', source s', and sink t' as follows:

$$V' = V \cup \{s', t'\} ,$$
$$E' = E \cup \{(s', v) : v \in V\} \cup \{(u, t') : u \in V\} \cup \{(s, t), (t, s)\} .$$

We assign capacities to edges as follows. For each edge $(u, v) \in E$, we set $c'(u, v) = c(u, v) - b(u, v)$. For each vertex $u \in V$, we set $c'(s', u) = b(V, u)$ and $c'(u, t') = b(u, V)$. We also set $c'(s, t) = c'(t, s) = \infty$.

c. Prove that there exists a feasible flow in G if and only if there exists a maximum flow in G' such that all edges into the sink t' are saturated.

d. Give an algorithm that finds a maximum flow in a network with upper and lower bounds or determines that no feasible flow exists. Analyze the running time of your algorithm.

Chapter notes

Even [65], Lawler [132], Papadimitriou and Steiglitz [154], and Tarjan [188] are good references for network flow and related algorithms. Goldberg, Tardos, and Tarjan [83] provide a nice survey of algorithms for network-flow problems.

The Ford-Fulkerson method is due to Ford and Fulkerson [71], who originated many of the problems in the area of network flow, including the maximum-flow and bipartite-matching problems. Many early implementations of the Ford-Fulkerson method found augmenting paths using breadth-first search; Edmonds and Karp [63] proved that this strategy yields a polynomial-time algorithm. Karzanov [119] developed the idea of preflows. The preflow-push method is due to Goldberg [82]. The fastest preflow-push algorithm to date is due to Goldberg and Tarjan [85], who achieve a running time of $O(VE \lg(V^2/E))$. The best algorithm to date for maximum bipartite matching, discovered by Hopcroft and Karp [101], runs in $O(\sqrt{V}E)$ time.

VII   Selected Topics

Introduction

This part contains a selection of algorithmic topics that extend and complement earlier material in this book. Some chapters introduce new models of computation such as combinational circuits or parallel computers. Others cover specialized domains such as computational geometry or number theory. The last two chapters discuss some of the known limitations to the design of efficient algorithms and introduce techniques for coping with those limitations.

Chapter 28 presents our first parallel model of computation: comparison networks. Roughly speaking, a comparison network is an algorithm that allows many comparisons to be made simultaneously. This chapter shows how to build a comparison network that can sort n numbers in $O(\lg^2 n)$ time.

Chapter 29 introduces another parallel model of computation: combinational circuits. This chapter shows that two n-bit numbers can be added in $O(\lg n)$ time using a combinational circuit called a carry-lookahead adder. It also shows how to multiply two n-bit numbers in $O(\lg n)$ time.

Chapter 30 introduces a general model of parallel computation called the PRAM. The chapter presents basic parallel techniques, including pointer jumping, prefix computations, and the Euler-tour technique. Most of the techniques are illustrated on simple data structures, including lists and trees. The chapter also discusses general issues in parallel computation, including work efficiency and concurrent access to shared memory. It proves Brent's theorem, which shows how a parallel computer can efficiently simulate a combinational circuit. The chapter concludes with a work-efficient, randomized algorithm for list ranking and a remarkably efficient deterministic algorithm for symmetry breaking in a list.

Chapter 31 studies efficient algorithms for operating on matrices. It begins with Strassen's algorithm, which can multiply two $n \times n$ matrices in $O(n^{2.81})$ time. It then presents two general methods—LU decomposition and LUP decomposition—for solving linear equations by Gaussian elimination in $O(n^3)$ time. It also shows that Strassen's algorithm can be used to solve linear systems faster and that, asymptotically, matrix inversion and matrix multiplication can be performed equally fast. The chapter concludes by showing how a least-squares approximate solution can be computed when a set of linear equations has no exact solution.

Chapter 32 studies operations on polynomials and shows that a well-known signal-processing technique—the Fast Fourier Transform (FFT)—can be used to multiply two degree-n polynomials in $O(n \lg n)$ time. It also investigates efficient implementations of the FFT, including a parallel circuit.

Chapter 33 presents number-theoretic algorithms. After a review of elementary number theory, it presents Euclid's algorithm for computing greatest common divisors. Algorithms for solving modular linear equations and for raising one number to a power modulo another number are presented next. An interesting application of number-theoretic algorithms is presented next: the RSA public-key cryptosystem. This cryptosystem not only can be used to encrypt messages so that an adversary cannot read them, it also can be used to provide digital signatures. The chapter then presents the Miller-Rabin randomized primality test, which can be used to find large primes efficiently—an essential requirement for the RSA system. Finally, the chapter covers Pollard's "rho" heuristic for factoring integers and discusses the state of the art of integer factorization.

Chapter 34 studies the problem of finding all occurrences of a given pattern string in a given text string, a problem that arises frequently in text-editing programs. An elegant approach due to Rabin and Karp is considered first. Then, after examining an efficient solution based on finite automata, the chapter presents the Knuth-Morris-Pratt algorithm, which achieves efficiency by cleverly preprocessing the pattern. The chapter closes with a presentation of a string-matching heuristic due to Boyer and Moore.

Computational geometry is the topic of Chapter 35. After discussing basic primitives of computational geometry, the chapter shows how a "sweeping" method can efficiently determine whether or not a set of line segments contains any intersections. Two clever algorithms for finding the convex hull of a set of points—Graham's scan and Jarvis's march—also illustrate the power of sweeping methods. The chapter closes with an efficient algorithm for finding the closest pair from among a given set of points in the plane.

Chapter 36 concerns NP-complete problems. Many interesting computational problems are NP-complete, but no polynomial-time algorithm is known for solving any of them. This chapter presents techniques for determining when a problem is NP-complete. Several classic problems are proved to be NP-complete: determining if a graph has a hamiltonian cycle, determining if a boolean formula is satisfiable, and determining if a given set of numbers has a subset that adds up to a given target value.

The chapter also proves that the famous traveling-salesman problem is NP-complete.

Chapter 37 shows how approximation algorithms can be used to find approximate solutions to NP-complete problems efficiently. For some NP-complete problems, approximate solutions that are near optimal are quite easy to produce, but for others even the best approximation algorithms known work progressively more poorly as the problem size increases. Then, there are some problems for which one can invest increasing amounts of computation time in return for increasingly better approximate solutions. This chapter illustrates these possibilities with the vertex-cover problem, the traveling-salesman problem, the set-covering problem, and the subset-sum problem.

28 Sorting Networks

In Part II, we examined sorting algorithms for serial computers (random-access machines, or RAM's) that allow only one operation to be executed at a time. In this chapter, we investigate sorting algorithms based on a comparison network model of computation in which many comparison operations can be performed simultaneously.

Comparison networks differ from RAM's in two important respects. First, they can only perform comparisons. Thus, an algorithm such as counting sort (see Section 9.2) cannot be implemented on a comparison network. Second, unlike the RAM model, in which operations occur serially—that is, one after another—operations in a comparison network may occur at the same time, or "in parallel." As we shall see, this characteristic allows the construction of comparison networks that sort n values in sublinear time.

We begin in Section 28.1 by defining comparison networks and sorting networks. We also give a natural definition for the "running time" of a comparison network in terms of the depth of the network. Section 28.2 proves the "zero-one principle," which greatly eases the task of analyzing the correctness of sorting networks.

The efficient sorting network that we shall design is essentially a parallel version of the merge-sort algorithm from Section 1.3.1. Our construction will have three steps. Section 28.3 presents the design of a "bitonic" sorter that will be our basic building block. We modify the bitonic sorter slightly in Section 28.4 to produce a merging network that can merge two sorted sequences into one sorted sequence. Finally, in Section 28.5, we assemble these merging networks into a sorting network that can sort n values in $O(\lg^2 n)$ time.

28.1 Comparison networks

Sorting networks are comparison networks that always sort their inputs, so it makes sense to begin our discussion with comparison networks and their characteristics. A comparison network is comprised solely of wires and comparators. A *comparator*, shown in Figure 28.1(a), is a device with two

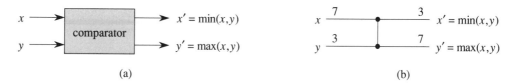

Figure 28.1   (**a**) A comparator with inputs x and y and outputs x' and y'. (**b**) The same comparator, drawn as a single vertical line. Inputs $x = 7, y = 3$ and outputs $x' = 3, y' = 7$ are shown.

inputs, x and y, and two outputs, x' and y', that performs the following function:

$$x' = \min(x, y) \,,$$
$$y' = \max(x, y) \,.$$

Because the pictorial representation of a comparator in Figure 28.1(a) is too bulky for our purposes, we shall adopt the convention of drawing comparators as single vertical lines, as shown in Figure 28.1(b). Inputs appear on the left and outputs on the right, with the smaller input value appearing on the top output and the larger input value appearing on the bottom output. We can thus think of a comparator as sorting its two inputs.

We shall assume that each comparator operates in $O(1)$ time. In other words, we assume that the time between the appearance of the input values x and y and the production of the output values x' and y' is a constant.

A **wire** transmits a value from place to place. Wires can connect the output of one comparator to the input of another, but otherwise they are either network input wires or network output wires. Throughout this chapter, we shall assume that a comparison network contains n **input wires** $a_1, a_2, \ldots, a_n$, through which the values to be sorted enter the network, and n **output wires** $b_1, b_2, \ldots, b_n$, which produce the results computed by the network. Also, we shall speak of the **input sequence** $\langle a_1, a_2, \ldots, a_n \rangle$ and the **output sequence** $\langle b_1, b_2, \ldots, b_n \rangle$, referring to the values on the input and output wires. That is, we use the same name for both a wire and the value it carries. Our intention will always be clear from the context.

Figure 28.2 shows a **comparison network**, which is a set of comparators interconnected by wires. We draw a comparison network on n inputs as a collection of n horizontal **lines** with comparators stretched vertically. Note that a line does *not* represent a single wire, but rather a sequence of distinct wires connecting various comparators. The top line in Figure 28.2, for example, represents three wires: input wire a_1, which connects to an input of comparator A; a wire connecting the top output of comparator A to an input of comparator C; and output wire b_1, which comes from the top output of comparator C. Each comparator input is connected to a wire that is either one of the network's n input wires $a_1, a_2, \ldots, a_n$ or is connected

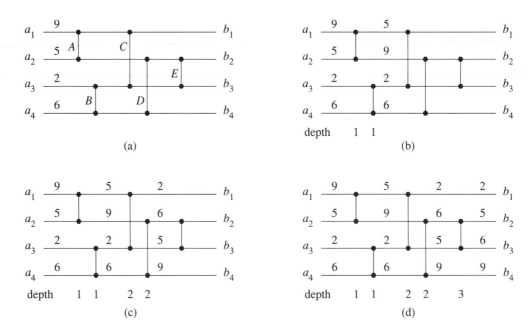

Figure 28.2 (a) A 4-input, 4-output comparison network, which is in fact a sorting network. At time 0, the input values shown appear on the four input wires. (b) At time 1, the values shown appear on the outputs of comparators A and B, which are at depth 1. (c) At time 2, the values shown appear on the outputs of comparators C and D, at depth 2. Output wires b_1 and b_4 now have their final values, but output wires b_2 and b_3 do not. (d) At time 3, the values shown appear on the outputs of comparator E, at depth 3. Output wires b_2 and b_3 now have their final values.

to the output of another comparator. Similarly, each comparator output is connected to a wire that is either one of the network's n output wires $b_1, b_2, \ldots, b_n$ or is connected to the input of another comparator. The main requirement for interconnecting comparators is that the graph of interconnections must be acyclic: if we trace a path from the output of a given comparator to the input of another to output to input, etc., the path we trace must never cycle back on itself and go through the same comparator twice. Thus, as in Figure 28.2, we can draw a comparison network with network inputs on the left and network outputs on the right; data move through the network from left to right.

Each comparator produces its output values only when both of its input values are available to it. In Figure 28.2(a), for example, suppose that the sequence $\langle 9, 5, 2, 6 \rangle$ appears on the input wires at time 0. At time 0, then, only comparators A and B have all their input values available. Assuming that each comparator requires one time unit to compute its output values, comparators A and B produce their outputs at time 1; the resulting values are shown in Figure 28.2(b). Note that comparators A and B produce their values at the same time, or "in parallel." Now, at time 1, comparators C and D, but not E, have all their input values available. One time unit later, at time 2, they produce their outputs, as shown in Figure 28.2(c). Comparators C and D operate in parallel as well. The top output of comparator C and the bottom output of comparator D connect to output wires b_1 and b_4, respectively, of the comparison network, and these network output wires therefore carry their final values at time 2. Meanwhile, at time 2, comparator E has its inputs available, and Figure 28.2(d) shows that it produces its output values at time 3. These values are carried on network output wires b_2 and b_3, and the output sequence $\langle 2, 5, 6, 9 \rangle$ is now complete.

Under the assumption that each comparator takes unit time, we can define the "running time" of a comparison network, that is, the time it takes for all the output wires to receive their values once the input wires receive theirs. Informally, this time is the largest number of comparators that any input element can pass through as it travels from an input wire to an output wire. More formally, we define the **depth** of a wire as follows. An input wire of a comparison network has depth 0. Now, if a comparator has two input wires with depths d_x and d_y, then its output wires have depth $\max(d_x, d_y) + 1$. Because there are no cycles of comparators in a comparison network, the depth of a wire is well defined, and we define the depth of a comparator to be the depth of its output wires. Figure 28.2 shows comparator depths. The depth of a comparison network is the maximum depth of an output wire or, equivalently, the maximum depth of a comparator. The comparison network of Figure 28.2, for example, has depth 3 because comparator E has depth 3. If each comparator takes one time unit to produce its output value, and if network inputs appear at time 0, a comparator at depth d produces its outputs at time d; the depth of the network therefore equals the time for the network to produce values at all of its output wires.

A **sorting network** is a comparison network for which the output sequence is monotonically increasing (that is, $b_1 \leq b_2 \leq \cdots \leq b_n$) for *every* input sequence. Of course, not every comparison network is a sorting network, but the network of Figure 28.2 is. To see why, observe that after time 1, the minimum of the four input values has been produced by either the top output of comparator A or the top output of comparator B. After time 2, therefore, it must be on the top output of comparator C. A symmetrical argument shows that after time 2, the maximum of the four input values has been produced by the bottom output of comparator D. All that remains is for comparator E to ensure that the middle two values occupy their correct output positions, which happens at time 3.

A comparison network is like a procedure in that it specifies how comparisons are to occur, but it is unlike a procedure in that its physical size depends on the number of inputs and outputs. Therefore, we shall actually be describing "families" of comparison networks. For example, the goal of this chapter is to develop a family SORTER of efficient sorting networks. We specify a given network within a family by the family name and

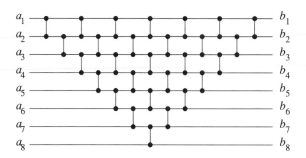

Figure 28.3   A sorting network based on insertion sort for use in Exercise 28.1-6.

the number of inputs (which equals the number of outputs). For example, the n-input, n-output sorting network in the family SORTER is named SORTER[n].

Exercises

28.1-1
Show the values that appear on all the wires of the network of Figure 28.2 when it is given the input sequence $\langle 9, 6, 5, 2 \rangle$.

28.1-2
Let n be an exact power of 2. Show how to construct an n-input, n-output comparison network of depth $\lg n$ in which the top output wire always carries the minimum input value and the bottom output wire always carries the maximum input value.

28.1-3
Professor Nielsen claims that if we add a comparator anywhere in a sorting network, the resulting network also sorts. Show that the professor is mistaken by adding a comparator to the network of Figure 28.2 in such a way that the resulting network does not sort every input permutation.

28.1-4
Prove that any sorting network on n inputs has depth at least $\lg n$.

28.1-5
Prove that the number of comparators in any sorting network is at least $\Omega(n \lg n)$.

28.1-6
Consider the comparison network shown in Figure 28.3. Prove that it is in fact a sorting network, and describe how its structure is related to that of insertion sort (Section 1.1).

28.1-7

We can represent an n-input comparison network with c comparators as a list of c pairs of integers in the range from 1 to n. If two pairs contain an integer in common, the order of the corresponding comparators in the network is determined by the order of the pairs in the list. Given this representation, describe an $O(n+c)$-time (serial) algorithm for determining the depth of a comparison network.

28.1-8   ⋆

Suppose that in addition to the standard kind of comparator, we introduce an "upside-down" comparator that produces its minimum output on the bottom wire and its maximum output on the top wire. Show how to convert any sorting network that uses a total of c standard and upside-down comparators to one that uses c standard ones. Prove that your conversion method is correct.

28.2   The zero-one principle

The **zero-one principle** says that if a sorting network works correctly when each input is drawn from the set $\{0, 1\}$, then it works correctly on arbitrary input numbers. (The numbers can be integers, reals, or, in general, any set of values from any linearly ordered set.) As we construct sorting networks and other comparison networks, the zero-one principle will allow us to focus on their operation for input sequences consisting solely of 0's and 1's. Once we have constructed a sorting network and proved that it can sort all zero-one sequences, we shall appeal to the zero-one principle to show that it properly sorts sequences of arbitrary values.

The proof of the zero-one principle relies on the notion of a monotonically increasing function (Section 2.2).

Lemma 28.1

If a comparison network transforms the input sequence $a = \langle a_1, a_2, \ldots, a_n \rangle$ into the output sequence $b = \langle b_1, b_2, \ldots, b_n \rangle$, then for any monotonically increasing function f, the network transforms the input sequence $f(a) = \langle f(a_1), f(a_2), \ldots, f(a_n) \rangle$ into the output sequence $f(b) = \langle f(b_1), f(b_2), \ldots, f(b_n) \rangle$.

Proof   We shall first prove the claim that if f is a monotonically increasing function, then a single comparator with inputs $f(x)$ and $f(y)$ produces outputs $f(\min(x, y))$ and $f(\max(x, y))$. We shall then use induction to prove the lemma.

To prove the claim, consider a comparator whose input values are x and y. The upper output of the comparator is $\min(x, y)$ and the lower output is $\max(x, y)$. Suppose we now apply $f(x)$ and $f(y)$ to the inputs

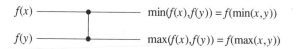

Figure 28.4   The operation of the comparator in the proof of Lemma 28.1. The function f is monotonically increasing.

of the comparator, as is shown in Figure 28.4. The operation of the comparator yields the value $\min(f(x), f(y))$ on the upper output and the value $\max(f(x), f(y))$ on the lower output. Since f is monotonically increasing, $x \le y$ implies $f(x) \le f(y)$. Consequently, we have the identities

$$\min(f(x), f(y)) \;=\; f(\min(x, y)) ,$$
$$\max(f(x), f(y)) \;=\; f(\max(x, y)) .$$

Thus, the comparator produces the values $f(\min(x, y))$ and $f(\max(x, y))$ when $f(x)$ and $f(y)$ are its inputs, which completes the proof of the claim.

We can use induction on the depth of each wire in a general comparison network to prove a stronger result than the statement of the lemma: if a wire assumes the value a_i when the input sequence a is applied to the network, then it assumes the value $f(a_i)$ when the input sequence $f(a)$ is applied. Because the output wires are included in this statement, proving it will prove the lemma.

For the basis, consider a wire at depth 0, that is, an input wire a_i. The result follows trivially: when $f(a)$ is applied to the network, the input wire carries $f(a_i)$. For the inductive step, consider a wire at depth d, where $d \ge 1$. The wire is the output of a comparator at depth d, and the input wires to this comparator are at a depth strictly less than d. By the inductive hypothesis, therefore, if the input wires to the comparator carry values a_i and a_j when the input sequence a is applied, then they carry $f(a_i)$ and $f(a_j)$ when the input sequence $f(a)$ is applied. By our earlier claim, the output wires of this comparator then carry $f(\min(a_i, a_j))$ and $f(\max(a_i, a_j))$. Since they carry $\min(a_i, a_j)$ and $\max(a_i, a_j)$ when the input sequence is a, the lemma is proved.   ∎

As an example of the application of Lemma 28.1, Figure 28.5 shows the sorting network from Figure 28.2 with the monotonically increasing function $f(x) = \lceil x/2 \rceil$ applied to the inputs. The value on every wire is f applied to the value on the same wire in Figure 28.2.

When a comparison network is a sorting network, Lemma 28.1 allows us to prove the following remarkable result.

Theorem 28.2 (Zero-one principle)
If a comparison network with n inputs sorts all 2^n possible sequences of 0's and 1's correctly, then it sorts all sequences of arbitrary numbers correctly.

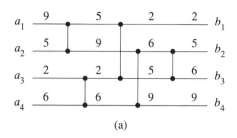
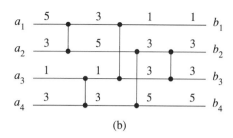

Figure 28.5 **(a)** The sorting network from Figure 28.2 with input sequence $\langle 9, 5, 2, 6 \rangle$. **(b)** The same sorting network with the monotonically increasing function $f(x) = f(\lceil x/2 \rceil)$ applied to the inputs. Each wire in this network has the value of f applied to the value on the corresponding wire in (a).

Proof   Suppose for the purpose of contradiction that the network sorts all zero-one sequences, but there exists a sequence of arbitrary numbers that the network does not correctly sort. That is, there exists an input sequence $\langle a_1, a_2, \ldots, a_n \rangle$ containing elements a_i and a_j such that $a_i < a_j$, but the network places a_j before a_i in the output sequence. We define a monotonically increasing function f as

$$f(x) = \begin{cases} 0 & \text{if } x \le a_i \,, \\ 1 & \text{if } x > a_i \,. \end{cases}$$

Since the network places a_j before a_i in the output sequence when $\langle a_1, a_2, \ldots, a_n \rangle$ is input, it follows from Lemma 28.1 that it places $f(a_j)$ before $f(a_i)$ in the output sequence when $\langle f(a_1), f(a_2), \ldots, f(a_n) \rangle$ is input. But since $f(a_j) = 1$ and $f(a_i) = 0$, we obtain the contradiction that the network fails to sort the zero-one sequence $\langle f(a_1), f(a_2), \ldots, f(a_n) \rangle$ correctly.   ∎

Exercises

28.2-1

Prove that applying a monotonically increasing function to a sorted sequence produces a sorted sequence.

28.2-2

Prove that a comparison network with n inputs correctly sorts the input sequence $\langle n, n-1, \ldots, 1 \rangle$ if and only if it correctly sorts the $n-1$ zero-one sequences $\langle 1, 0, 0, \ldots, 0, 0 \rangle$, $\langle 1, 1, 0, \ldots, 0, 0 \rangle$, $\ldots$, $\langle 1, 1, 1, \ldots, 1, 0 \rangle$.

28.2-3

Use the zero-one principle to prove that the comparison network shown in Figure 28.6 is a sorting network.

28.2-4

State and prove an analog of the zero-one principle for a decision-tree model. (*Hint:* Be sure to handle equality properly.)

Figure 28.6   A sorting network for sorting 4 numbers.

28.2-5

Prove that an n-input sorting network must contain at least one comparator between the ith and $(i + 1)$st lines for all $i = 1, 2, \ldots, n - 1$.

28.3   A bitonic sorting network

The first step in our construction of an efficient sorting network is to construct a comparison network that can sort any ***bitonic sequence***: a sequence that either monotonically increases and then monotonically decreases, or else monotonically decreases and then monotonically increases. For example, the sequences $\langle 1, 4, 6, 8, 3, 2 \rangle$ and $\langle 9, 8, 3, 2, 4, 6 \rangle$ are both bitonic. The zero-one sequences that are bitonic have a simple structure. They have the form $0^i 1^j 0^k$ or the form $1^i 0^j 1^k$, for some $i, j, k \geq 0$. Note that a sequence that is either monotonically increasing or monotonically decreasing is also bitonic.

The bitonic sorter that we shall construct is a comparison network that sorts bitonic sequences of 0's and 1's. Exercise 28.3-6 asks you to show that the bitonic sorter can sort bitonic sequences of arbitrary numbers.

The half-cleaner

A bitonic sorter is comprised of several stages, each of which is called a ***half-cleaner***. Each half-cleaner is a comparison network of depth 1 in which input line i is compared with line $i + n/2$ for $i = 1, 2, \ldots, n/2$. (We assume that n is even.) Figure 28.7 shows HALF-CLEANER[8], the half-cleaner with 8 inputs and 8 outputs.

When a bitonic sequence of 0's and 1's is applied as input to a half-cleaner, the half-cleaner produces an output sequence in which smaller values are in the top half, larger values are in the bottom half, and both halves are bitonic. In fact, at least one of the halves is ***clean***—consisting of either all 0's or all 1's—and it is from this property that we derive the name "half-cleaner." (Note that all clean sequences are bitonic.) The next lemma proves these properties of half-cleaners.

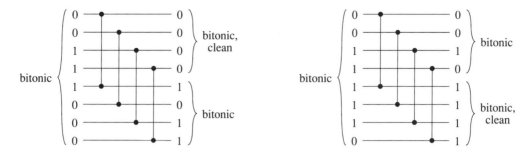

Figure 28.7 The comparison network HALF-CLEANER[8]. Two different sample zero-one input and output values are shown. The input is assumed to be bitonic. A half-cleaner ensures that every output element of the top half is at least as small as every output element of the bottom half. Moreover, both halves are bitonic, and at least one half is clean.

Lemma 28.3

If the input to a half-cleaner is a bitonic sequence of 0's and 1's, then the output satisfies the following properties: both the top half and the bottom half are bitonic, every element in the top half is at least as small as every element of the bottom half, and at least one half is clean.

Proof The comparison network HALF-CLEANER[n] compares inputs i and $i + n/2$ for $i = 1, 2, \ldots, n/2$. Without loss of generality, suppose that the input is of the form $00 \ldots 011 \ldots 100 \ldots 0$. (The situation in which the input is of the form $11 \ldots 100 \ldots 011 \ldots 1$ is symmetric.) There are three possible cases depending upon the block of consecutive 0's or 1's in which the midpoint $n/2$ falls, and one of these cases (the one in which the midpoint occurs in the block of 1's) is further split into two cases. The four cases are shown in Figure 28.8. In each case shown, the lemma holds.   ∎

The bitonic sorter

By recursively combining half-cleaners, as shown in Figure 28.9, we can build a ***bitonic sorter***, which is a network that sorts bitonic sequences. The first stage of BITONIC-SORTER[n] consists of HALF-CLEANER[n], which, by Lemma 28.3, produces two bitonic sequences of half the size such that every element in the top half is at least as small as every element in the bottom half. Thus, we can complete the sort by using two copies of BITONIC-SORTER[$n/2$] to sort the two halves recursively. In Figure 28.9(a), the recursion has been shown explicitly, and in Figure 28.9(b), the recursion has been unrolled to show the progressively smaller half-cleaners that make up the remainder of the bitonic sorter. The depth $D(n)$ of BITONIC-SORTER[n] is given by the recurrence

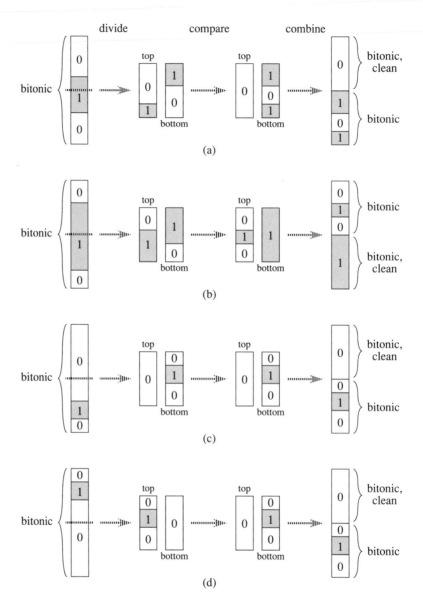

Figure 28.8 The possible comparisons in HALF-CLEANER[n]. The input sequence is assumed to be a bitonic sequence of 0's and 1's, and without loss of generality, we assume that it is of the form $00\ldots011\ldots100\ldots0$. Subsequences of 0's are white, and subsequences of 1's are gray. We can think of the n inputs as being divided into two halves such that for $i = 1, 2, \ldots, n/2$, inputs i and $i + n/2$ are compared. **(a)–(b)** Cases in which the division occurs in the middle subsequence of 1's. **(c)–(d)** Cases in which the division occurs in a subsequence of 0's. For all cases, every element in the top half is at least as small as every element in the bottom half, both halves are bitonic, and at least one half is clean.

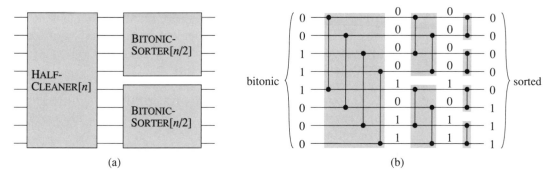

Figure 28.9 The comparison network BITONIC-SORTER[n], shown here for $n = 8$. **(a)** The recursive construction: HALF-CLEANER[n] followed by two copies of BITONIC-SORTER[$n/2$] that operate in parallel. **(b)** The network after unrolling the recursion. Each half-cleaner is shaded. Sample zero-one values are shown on the wires.

$$D(n) = \begin{cases} 0 & \text{if } n = 1 \text{ ,} \\ D(n/2) + 1 & \text{if } n = 2^k \text{ and } k \geq 1 \text{ ,} \end{cases}$$

whose solution is $D(n) = \lg n$.

Thus, a zero-one bitonic sequence can be sorted by BITONIC-SORTER, which has a depth of $\lg n$. It follows by the analog of the zero-one principle given as Exercise 28.3-6 that any bitonic sequence of arbitrary numbers can be sorted by this network.

Exercises

28.3-1
How many bitonic sequences of 0's and 1's are there?

28.3-2
Show that BITONIC-SORTER[n], where n is an exact power of 2, contains $\Theta(n \lg n)$ comparators.

28.3-3
Describe how an $O(\lg n)$-depth bitonic sorter can be constructed when the number n of inputs is not an exact power of 2.

28.3-4
If the input to a half-cleaner is a bitonic sequence of arbitrary numbers, prove that the output satisfies the following properties: both the top half and the bottom half are bitonic, and every element in the top half is at least as small as every element in the bottom half.

28.3-5

Consider two sequences of 0's and 1's. Prove that if every element in one sequence is at least as small as every element in the other sequence, then one of the two sequences is clean.

28.3-6

Prove the following analog of the zero-one principle for bitonic sorting networks: a comparison network that can sort any bitonic sequence of 0's and 1's can sort any bitonic sequence of arbitrary numbers.

28.4   A merging network

Our sorting network will be constructed from *merging networks*, which are networks that can merge two sorted input sequences into one sorted output sequence. We modify BITONIC-SORTER[n] to create the merging network MERGER[n]. As with the bitonic sorter, we shall prove the correctness of the merging network only for inputs that are zero-one sequences. Exercise 28.4-1 asks you to show how the proof can be extended to arbitrary input values.

The merging network is based on the following intuition. Given two sorted sequences, if we reverse the order of the second sequence and then concatenate the two sequences, the resulting sequence is bitonic. For example, given the sorted zero-one sequences $X = 00000111$ and $Y = 00001111$, we reverse Y to get $Y^R = 11110000$. Concatenating X and Y^R yields 0000011111110000, which is bitonic. Thus, to merge the two input sequences X and Y, it suffices to perform a bitonic sort on X concatenated with Y^R.

We can construct MERGER[n] by modifying the first half-cleaner of BITONIC-SORTER[n]. The key is to perform the reversal of the the second half of the inputs implicitly. Given two sorted sequences $\langle a_1, a_2, \ldots, a_{n/2} \rangle$ and $\langle a_{n/2+1}, a_{n/2+2}, \ldots, a_n \rangle$ to be merged, we want the effect of bitonically sorting the sequence $\langle a_1, a_2, \ldots, a_{n/2}, a_n, a_{n-1}, \ldots, a_{n/2+1} \rangle$. Since the half-cleaner of BITONIC-SORTER[n] compares inputs i and $n/2 + i$, for $i = 1, 2, \ldots, n/2$, we make the first stage of the merging network compare inputs i and $n - i + 1$. Figure 28.10 shows the correspondence. The only subtlety is that the order of the outputs from the bottom of the first stage of MERGER[n] are reversed compared with the order of outputs from an ordinary half-cleaner. Since the reversal of a bitonic sequence is bitonic, however, the top and bottom outputs of the first stage of the merging network satisfy the properties in Lemma 28.3, and thus the top and bottom can be bitonically sorted in parallel to produce the sorted output of the merging network.

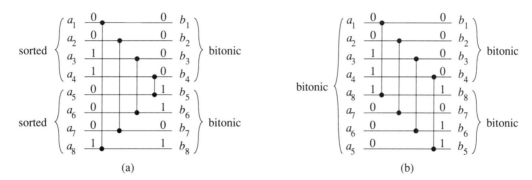

Figure 28.10 Comparing the first stage of MERGER[n] with HALF-CLEANER[n], for $n = 8$. **(a)** The first stage of MERGER[n] transforms the two monotonic input sequences $\langle a_1, a_2, \ldots, a_{n/2} \rangle$ and $\langle a_{n/2+1}, a_{n/2+2}, \ldots, a_n \rangle$ into two bitonic sequences $\langle b_1, b_2, \ldots, b_{n/2} \rangle$ and $\langle b_{n/2+1}, b_{n/2+2}, \ldots, b_n \rangle$. **(b)** The equivalent operation for HALF-CLEANER[n]. The bitonic input sequence $\langle a_1, a_2, \ldots, a_{n/2-1}, a_{n/2}, a_n, a_{n-1}, \ldots, a_{n/2+2}, a_{n/2+1} \rangle$ is transformed into the two bitonic sequences $\langle b_1, b_2, \ldots, b_{n/2} \rangle$ and $\langle b_n, b_{n-1}, \ldots, b_{n/2+1} \rangle$.

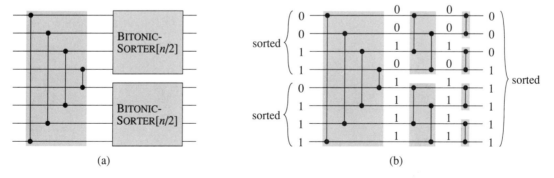

Figure 28.11 A network that merges two sorted input sequences into one sorted output sequence. The network MERGER[n] can be viewed as BITONIC-SORTER[n] with the first half-cleaner altered to compare inputs i and $n - i + 1$ for $i = 1, 2, \ldots, n/2$. Here, $n = 8$. **(a)** The network decomposed into the first stage followed by two parallel copies of BITONIC-SORTER[$n/2$]. **(b)** The same network with the recursion unrolled. Sample zero-one values are shown on the wires, and the stages are shaded.

The resulting merging network is shown in Figure 28.11. Only the first stage of MERGER[n] is different from BITONIC-SORTER[n]. Consequently, the depth of MERGER[n] is lg n, the same as that of BITONIC-SORTER[n].

Exercises

28.4-1
Prove an analog of the zero-one principle for merging networks. Specifically, show that a comparison network that can merge any two monotonically increasing sequences of 0's and 1's can merge any two monotonically increasing sequences of arbitrary numbers.

28.4-2
How many different zero-one input sequences must be applied to the input of a comparison network to verify that it is a merging network?

28.4-3
Show that any network that can merge 1 item with $n - 1$ items to produce a sorted sequence of length n must have depth at least lg n.

28.4-4 ★
Consider a merging network with inputs $a_1, a_2, \ldots, a_n$, for n an exact power of 2, in which the two monotonic sequences to be merged are $\langle a_1, a_3, \ldots, a_{n-1} \rangle$ and $\langle a_2, a_4, \ldots, a_n \rangle$. Prove that the number of comparators in this kind of merging network is $\Omega(n \lg n)$. Why is this an interesting lower bound? (*Hint:* Partition the comparators into three sets.)

28.4-5 ★
Prove that any merging network, regardless of the order of inputs, requires $\Omega(n \lg n)$ comparators.

28.5 A sorting network

We now have all the necessary tools to construct a network that can sort any input sequence. The sorting network SORTER[n] uses the merging network to implement a parallel version of merge sort from Section 1.3.1. The construction and operation of the sorting network are illustrated in Figure 28.12.

Figure 28.12(a) shows the recursive construction of SORTER[n]. The n input elements are sorted by using two copies of SORTER[$n/2$] recursively to sort (in parallel) two subsequences of length $n/2$ each. The two resulting sequences are then merged by MERGER[n]. The boundary case for the recursion is when $n = 1$, in which case we can use a wire to sort the 1-element sequence, since a 1-element sequence is already sorted. Figure 28.12(b)

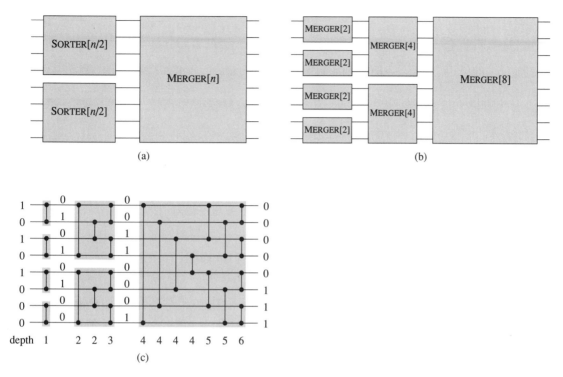

Figure 28.12   The sorting network SORTER[n] constructed by recursively combining merging networks. **(a)** The recursive construction. **(b)** Unrolling the recursion. **(c)** Replacing the MERGER boxes with the actual merging networks. The depth of each comparator is indicated, and sample zero-one values are shown on the wires.

shows the result of unrolling the recursion, and Figure 28.12(c) shows the actual network obtained by replacing the MERGER boxes in Figure 28.12(b) with the actual merging networks.

Data pass through $\lg n$ stages in the network SORTER[n]. Each of the individual inputs to the network is already a sorted 1-element sequence. The first stage of SORTER[n] consists of $n/2$ copies of MERGER[2] that work in parallel to merge pairs of 1-element sequences to produce sorted sequences of length 2. The second stage consists of $n/4$ copies of MERGER[4] that merge pairs of these 2-element sorted sequences to produce sorted sequences of length 4. In general, for $k = 1, 2, \ldots, \lg n$, stage k consists of $n/2^k$ copies of MERGER[2^k] that merge pairs of the 2^{k-1}-element sorted sequences to produce sorted sequences of length 2^k. At the final stage, one sorted sequence consisting of all the input values is produced. This sorting network can be shown by induction to sort zero-one sequences, and consequently, by the zero-one principle (Theorem 28.2), it can sort arbitrary values.

We can analyze the depth of the sorting network recursively. The depth $D(n)$ of SORTER[n] is the depth $D(n/2)$ of SORTER[$n/2$] (there are two copies of SORTER[$n/2$], but they operate in parallel) plus the depth $\lg n$

of MERGER[n]. Consequently, the depth of SORTER[n] is given by the recurrence

$$D(n) = \begin{cases} 0 & \text{if } n = 1 , \\ D(n/2) + \lg n & \text{if } n = 2^k \text{ and } k \geq 1 , \end{cases}$$

whose solution is $D(n) = \Theta(\lg^2 n)$. Thus, we can sort n numbers in parallel in $O(\lg^2 n)$ time.

Exercises

28.5-1
How many comparators are there in SORTER[n]?

28.5-2
Show that the depth of SORTER[n] is exactly $(\lg n)(\lg n + 1)/2$.

28.5-3
Suppose we modify a comparator to take two sorted lists of length k as inputs, merge them, and output the largest k to its "max" output and the smallest k to its "min" output. Show that any sorting network on n inputs with comparators modified in this fashion can sort nk numbers, assuming that each input to the network is a sorted list of length k.

28.5-4
Suppose that we have $2n$ elements $\langle a_1, a_2, \ldots, a_{2n} \rangle$ and wish to partition them into the n smallest and the n largest. Prove that we can do this in constant additional depth after separately sorting $\langle a_1, a_2, \ldots, a_n \rangle$ and $\langle a_{n+1}, a_{n+2}, \ldots, a_{2n} \rangle$.

28.5-5 $\star$
Let $S(k)$ be the depth of a sorting network with k inputs, and let $M(k)$ be the depth of a merging network with $2k$ inputs. Suppose that we have a sequence of n numbers to be sorted and know that every number is within k positions of its correct position in the sorted order. Show that we can sort the n numbers in depth $S(k) + 2M(k)$.

28.5-6 $\star$
We can sort the elements of an $m \times m$ matrix by repeating the following procedure k times:

1. Sort each odd-numbered row into monotonically increasing order.

2. Sort each even-numbered row into monotonically decreasing order.

3. Sort each column into monotonically increasing order.

How many iterations k are required for this procedure to sort, and what is the pattern of the sorted output?

Problems

28-1 Transposition sorting networks

A comparison network is a ***transposition network*** if each comparator connects adjacent lines, as in the network in Figure 28.3.

a. Show that any transposition network with n inputs that sorts has $\Omega(n^2)$ comparators.

b. Prove that a transposition network with n inputs is a sorting network if and only if it sorts the sequence $\langle n, n-1, \ldots, 1 \rangle$. (*Hint:* Use an induction argument analogous to the one in the proof of Lemma 28.1.)

An ***odd-even sorting network*** on n inputs $\langle a_1, a_2, \ldots, a_n \rangle$ has n levels of comparators. Figure 28.13 shows an odd-even transposition network on 8 inputs. As can be seen in the figure, for $i = 2, 3, \ldots, n-1$ and $d = 1, 2, \ldots, n$, line i is connected by a depth-d comparator to line $j = i + (-1)^{i+d}$ if $1 \leq j \leq n$.

c. Prove that the family of odd-even sorting networks is indeed a family of sorting networks.

28-2 Batcher's odd-even merging network

In Section 28.4, we saw how to construct a merging network based on bitonic sorting. In this problem, we shall construct an ***odd-even merging network***. We assume that n is an exact power of 2, and we wish to merge the sorted sequence of elements on lines $\langle a_1, a_2, \ldots, a_n \rangle$ with those on lines $\langle a_{n+1}, a_{n+2}, \ldots, a_{2n} \rangle$. We recursively construct two odd-even merging networks that merge sorted subsequences in parallel. The first merges the sequence on lines $\langle a_1, a_3, \ldots, a_{n-1} \rangle$ with the sequence on lines $\langle a_{n+1}, a_{n+3}, \ldots, a_{2n-1} \rangle$ (the odd elements). The second merges $\langle a_2, a_4, \ldots, a_n \rangle$ with $\langle a_{n+2}, a_{n+4}, \ldots, a_{2n} \rangle$ (the even elements). To combine the two sorted subsequences, we put a comparator between a_{2i-1} and a_{2i} for $i = 1, 2, \ldots, n$.

a. Draw a $2n$-input merging network for $n = 4$.

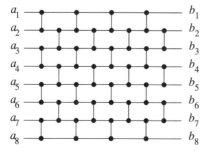

Figure 28.13 An odd-even sorting network on 8 inputs.

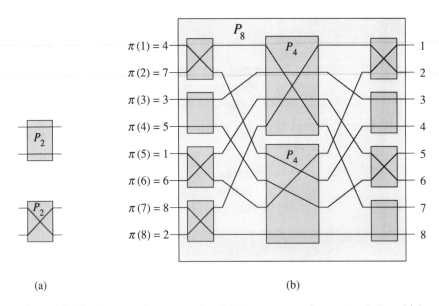

(a)   (b)

Figure 28.14   Permutation networks. (a) The permutation network P_2, which consists of a single switch that can be set in either of the two ways shown. (b) The recursive construction of P_8 from 8 switches and two P_4's. The switches and P_4's are set to realize the permutation $\pi = \langle 4, 7, 3, 5, 1, 6, 8, 2 \rangle$.

b. Use the zero-one principle to prove that any $2n$-input odd-even merging network is indeed a merging network.

c. What is the depth of a $2n$-input odd-even merging network? What is its size?

28-3   Permutation networks

A **permutation network** on n inputs and n outputs has switches that allow it to connect its inputs to its outputs according to any of the $n!$ possible permutations. Figure 28.14(a) shows the 2-input, 2-output permutation network P_2, which consists of a single switch that can be set either to feed its inputs straight through to its outputs or to cross them.

a. Argue that if we replace each comparator in a sorting network with the switch of Figure 28.14(a), the resulting network is a permutation network. That is, for any permutation π, there is a way to set the switches in the network so that input i is connected to output $\pi(i)$.

Figure 28.14(b) shows the recursive construction of an 8-input, 8-output permutation network P_8 that uses two copies of P_4 and 8 switches. The switches have been set to realize the permutation $\pi = \langle 4, 7, 3, 5, 1, 6, 8, 2 \rangle$, which requires (recursively) that the top P_4 realize $\langle 4, 2, 3, 1 \rangle$ and the bottom P_4 realize $\langle 2, 3, 1, 4 \rangle$.

b. Show how to realize the permutation $\langle 5, 3, 4, 6, 1, 8, 2, 7 \rangle$ on P_8 by drawing the switch settings and the permutations performed by the two P_4's.

Let n be an exact power of 2. Define P_n recursively in terms of two $P_{n/2}$'s in a manner similar to the way we defined P_8.

c. Describe an $O(n)$-time (ordinary random-access machine) algorithm that sets the n switches connected to the inputs and outputs of P_n and specifies the permutations that must be realized by each $P_{n/2}$ in order to accomplish any given n-element permutation. Prove that your algorithm is correct.

d. What are the depth and size of P_n? How long does it take on an ordinary random-access machine to compute all switch settings, including those within the $P_{n/2}$'s?

e. Argue that for $n > 2$, any permutation network—not just P_n—must realize some permutation by two distinct combinations of switch settings.

Chapter notes

Knuth [123] contains a discussion of sorting networks and charts their history. They apparently were first explored in 1954 by P. N. Armstrong, R. J. Nelson, and D. J. O'Connor. In the early 1960's, K. E. Batcher discovered the first network capable of merging two sequences of n numbers in $O(\lg n)$ time. He used odd-even merging (see Problem 28-2), and he also showed how this technique could be used to sort n numbers in $O(\lg^2 n)$ time. Shortly afterwards, he discovered an $O(\lg n)$-depth bitonic sorter similar to the one presented in Section 28.3. Knuth attributes the zero-one principle to W. G. Bouricius (1954), who proved it in the context of decision trees.

For a long time, the question remained open as to whether a sorting network with depth $O(\lg n)$ exists. In 1983, the answer was shown to be a somewhat unsatisfying yes. The AKS sorting network (named after its developers, Ajtai, Komlós, and Szemerédi [8]) can sort n numbers in depth $O(\lg n)$ using $O(n \lg n)$ comparators. Unfortunately, the constants hidden by the O-notation are quite large (many, many thousands), and thus it cannot be considered practical.

29 Arithmetic Circuits

The model of computation provided by an ordinary computer assumes that the basic arithmetic operations—addition, subtraction, multiplication, and division—can be performed in constant time. This abstraction is reasonable, since most basic operations on a random-access machine have similar costs. When it comes to designing the circuitry that implements these operations, however, we soon discover that performance depends on the magnitudes of the numbers being operated on. For example, we all learned in grade school how to add two natural numbers, expressed as n-digit decimal numbers, in $\Theta(n)$ steps (although teachers usually do not emphasize the number of steps required).

This chapter introduces circuits that perform arithmetic functions. With serial processes, $\Theta(n)$ is the best asymptotic time bound we can hope to achieve for adding two n-digit numbers. With circuits that operate in parallel, however, we can do better. In this chapter, we shall design circuits that can quickly perform addition and multiplication. (Subtraction is essentially the same as addition, and division is deferred to Problem 29-1.) We shall assume that all inputs are n-bit natural numbers, expressed in binary.

We start in Section 29.1 by presenting combinational circuits. We shall see how the depth of a circuit corresponds to its "running time." The full adder, which is a building block of most of the circuits in this chapter, serves as our first example of a combinational circuit. Section 29.2 presents two combinational circuits for addition: the ripple-carry adder, which works in $\Theta(n)$ time, and the carry-lookahead adder, which takes only $O(\lg n)$ time. It also presents the carry-save adder, which can reduce the problem of summing three numbers to the problem of summing two numbers in $\Theta(1)$ time. Section 29.3 introduces two combinational multipliers: the array multiplier, which takes $\Theta(n)$ time, and the Wallace-tree multiplier, which requires only $\Theta(\lg n)$ time. Finally, Section 29.4 presents circuits with clocked storage elements (registers) and shows how hardware can be saved by reusing combinational circuitry.

29.1 Combinational circuits

Like the comparison networks of Chapter 28, combinational circuits operate in *parallel*: many elements can compute values simultaneously as a single step. In this section, we define combinational circuits and investigate how larger combinational circuits can be built up from elementary gates.

Combinational elements

Arithmetic circuits in real computers are built from combinational elements that are interconnected by wires. A *combinational element* is any circuit element that has a constant number of inputs and outputs and that performs a well-defined function. Some of the elements we shall deal with in this chapter are *boolean combinational elements*—their inputs and outputs are all drawn from the set $\{0, 1\}$, where 0 represents FALSE and 1 represents TRUE.

A boolean combinational element that computes a simple boolean function is called a *logic gate*. Figure 29.1 shows the four basic logic gates that will serve as combinational elements in this chapter: the *NOT gate* (or *inverter*), the *AND gate*, the *OR gate*, and the *XOR gate*. (It also shows two other logic gates—the *NAND gate* and the *NOR gate*—that are required by some of the exercises.) The NOT gate takes a single binary *input* x, whose value is either 0 or 1, and produces a binary *output* z whose value is opposite that of the input value. Each of the other three gates takes two binary inputs x and y and produces a single binary output z.

The operation of each gate, and of any boolean combinational element, can be described by a *truth table*, shown under each gate in Figure 29.1. A truth table gives the outputs of the combinational element for each possible setting of the inputs. For example, the truth table for the XOR gate tells us that when the inputs are $x = 0$ and $y = 1$, the output value is $z = 1$; it computes the "exclusive OR" of its two inputs. We use the symbols $\neg$ to denote the NOT function, $\wedge$ to denote the AND function, $\vee$ to denote the OR function, and $\oplus$ to denote the XOR function. Thus, for example, $0 \oplus 1 = 1$.

Combinational elements in real circuits do not operate instantaneously. Once the input values entering a combinational element *settle*, or become *stable*—that is, hold steady for a long enough time—the element's output value is guaranteed to become both stable and correct a fixed amount of time later. We call this time differential the *propagation delay* of the element. We assume in this chapter that all combinational elements have constant propagation delay.

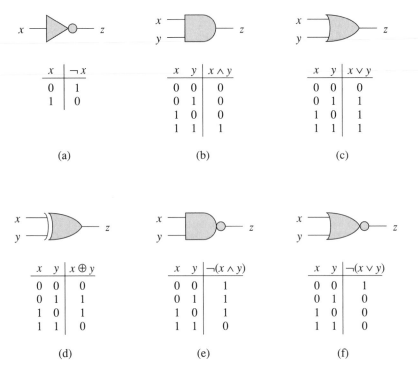

Figure 29.1   Six basic logic gates, with binary inputs and outputs. Under each gate is the truth table that describes the gate's operation. **(a)** The NOT gate. **(b)** The AND gate. **(c)** The OR gate. **(d)** The XOR (exclusive-OR) gate. **(e)** The NAND (NOT-AND) gate. **(f)** The NOR (NOT-OR) gate.

Combinational circuits

A *combinational circuit* consists of one or more combinational elements interconnected in an acyclic fashion.   The interconnections are called *wires*. A wire can connect the output of one element to the input of another, thereby providing the output value of the first element as an input value of the second. Although a single wire may have no more than one combinational-element output connected to it, it can feed several element inputs. The number of element inputs fed by a wire is called the *fan-out* of the wire. If no element output is connected to a wire, the wire is a *circuit input*, accepting input values from an external source. If no element input is connected to a wire, the wire is a *circuit output*, providing the results of the circuit's computation to the outside world. (An internal wire can also fan out to a circuit output.) Combinational circuits contain no cycles and have no memory elements (such as the registers described in Section 29.4).

Full adders

As an example, Figure 29.2 shows a combinational circuit, called a *full adder*, that takes as input three bits x, y, and z. It outputs two bits, s and c, according to the following truth table:

x	y	z	c	s
0	0	0	0	0
0	0	1	0	1
0	1	0	0	1
0	1	1	1	0
1	0	0	0	1
1	0	1	1	0
1	1	0	1	0
1	1	1	1	1

Output s is the *parity* of the input bits,

$$s = \text{parity}(x, y, z) = x \oplus y \oplus z , \tag{29.1}$$

and output c is the *majority* of the input bits,

$$c = \text{majority}(x, y, z) = (x \wedge y) \vee (y \wedge z) \vee (x \wedge z) . \tag{29.2}$$

(In general, the parity and majority functions can take any number of input bits. The parity is 1 if and only if an odd number of the inputs are 1's. The majority is 1 if and only if more than half the inputs are 1's.) Note that the c and s bits, taken together, give the sum of x, y, and z. For example, if $x = 1$, $y = 0$, and $z = 1$, then $\langle c, s \rangle = \langle 10 \rangle$,[1] which is the binary representation of 2, the sum of x, y, and z.

Each of the inputs x, y, and z to the full adder has a fan-out of 3. When the operation performed by a combinational element is commutative and associative with respect to its inputs (such as the functions AND, OR, and XOR), we call the number of inputs the *fan-in* of the element. Although the fan-in of each gate in Figure 29.2 is 2, we could redraw the full adder to replace XOR gates A and E by a single 3-input XOR gate and OR gates F and G by a single 3-input OR gate.

To examine how the full adder operates, assume that each gate operates in unit time. Figure 29.2(a) shows a set of inputs that becomes stable at time 0. Gates A–D, and no other gates, have all their input values stable at that time and therefore produce the values shown in Figure 29.2(b) at time 1. Note that gates A–D operate in parallel. Gates E and F, but not gate G, have stable inputs at time 1 and produce the values shown in Figure 29.2(c) at time 2. The output of gate E is bit s, and so the s output from the full adder is ready at time 2. The c output is not yet ready, however. Gate G finally has stable inputs at time 2, and it produces the c output shown in Figure 29.2(d) at time 3.

---

[1] For clarity, we omit the commas between sequence elements when they are bits.

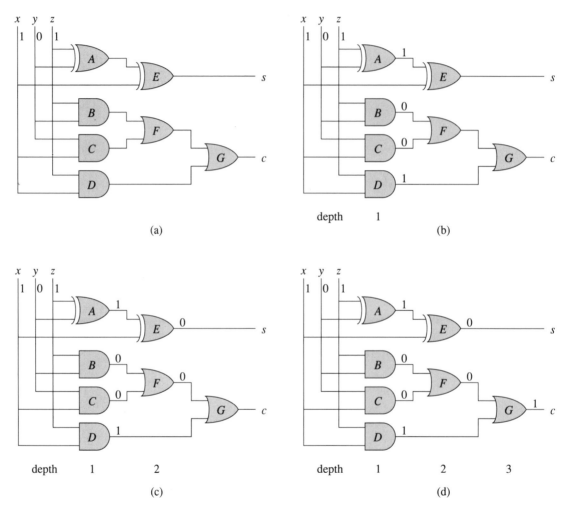

Figure 29.2 A full-adder circuit. **(a)** At time 0, the input bits shown appear on the three input wires. **(b)** At time 1, the values shown appear on the outputs of gates A–D, which are at depth 1. **(c)** At time 2, the values shown appear on the outputs of gates E and F, at depth 2. **(d)** At time 3, gate G produces its output, which is also the circuit output.

Circuit depth

As in the case of the comparison networks discussed in Chapter 28, we measure the propagation delay of a combinational circuit in terms of the largest number of combinational elements on any path from the inputs to the outputs. Specifically, we define the ***depth*** of a circuit, which corresponds to its worst-case "running time," inductively in terms of the depths of its constituent wires. The depth of an input wire is 0. If a combinational element has inputs $x_1, x_2, \ldots, x_n$ at depths $d_1, d_2, \ldots, d_n$ respectively, then its outputs have depth $\max \{d_1, d_2, \ldots, d_n\} + 1$. The depth of a combinational element is the depth of its outputs. The depth of a combinational circuit is the maximum depth of any combinational element. Since we prohibit combinational circuits from containing cycles, the various notions of depth are well defined.

If each combinational element takes constant time to compute its output values, then the worst-case propagation delay through a combinational circuit is proportional to its depth. Figure 29.2 shows the depth of each gate in the full adder. Since the gate with the largest depth is gate G, the full adder itself has depth 3, which is proportional to the worst-case time it takes for the circuit to perform its function.

A combinational circuit can sometimes compute faster than its depth. Suppose that a large subcircuit feeds into one input of a 2-input AND gate but that the other input of the AND gate has value 0. The output of the gate will then be 0, independent of the input from the large subcircuit. In general, however, we cannot count on specific inputs being applied to the circuit, and the abstraction of depth as the "running time" of the circuit is therefore quite reasonable.

Circuit size

Besides circuit depth, there is another resource that we typically wish to minimize when designing circuits. The ***size*** of a combinational circuit is the number of combinational elements it contains. Intuitively, circuit size corresponds to the memory space used by an algorithm. The full adder of Figure 29.2 has size 7, for example, since it uses 7 gates.

This definition of circuit size is not particularly useful for small circuits. After all, since a full adder has a constant number of inputs and outputs and computes a well-defined function, it satisfies the definition of a combinational element. A full adder built from a single full-adder combinational element therefore has size 1. In fact, according to this definition, *any* combinational element has size 1.

The definition of circuit size is intended to apply to families of circuits that compute similar functions. For example, we shall soon see an addition circuit that takes two *n*-bit inputs. We are really not talking about a single circuit here, but rather a family of circuits—one for each size of input.

In this context, the definition of circuit size makes good sense. It allows us to define convenient circuit elements without affecting the size of any implementation of the circuit by more than a constant factor. Of course, in practice, measurements of size are much more complicated, involving not only the choice of combinational elements, but also concerns such as the area the circuit requires when integrated on a silicon chip.

Exercises

29.1-1
In Figure 29.2, change input y to a 1. Show the resulting value carried on each wire.

29.1-2
Show how to construct an n-input parity circuit with $n - 1$ XOR gates and depth $\lceil \lg n \rceil$.

29.1-3
Show that any boolean combinational element can be constructed from a constant number of AND, OR, and NOT gates. (*Hint:* Implement the truth table for the element.)

29.1-4
Show that any boolean function can be constructed entirely out of NAND gates.

29.1-5
Construct a combinational circuit that performs the exclusive-or function using only four 2-input NAND gates.

29.1-6
Let C be an n-input, n-output combinational circuit of depth d. If two copies of C are connected, with the outputs of one feeding directly into the inputs of the other, what is the maximum possible depth of this tandem circuit? What is the minimum possible depth?

29.2 Addition circuits

We now investigate the problem of adding numbers represented in binary. We present three combinational circuits for this problem. First, we look at ripple-carry addition, which can add two n-bit numbers in $\Theta(n)$ time using a circuit with $\Theta(n)$ size. This time bound can be improved to $O(\lg n)$ using a carry-lookahead adder, which also has $\Theta(n)$ size. Finally, we present carry-save addition, which in $O(1)$ time can reduce the sum of 3 n-bit

8	7	6	5	4	3	2	1	0		i
1	1	0	1	1	1	0	0	0	=	c
	0	1	0	1	1	1	1	0	=	a
	1	1	0	1	0	1	0	1	=	b
1	0	0	1	1	0	0	1	1	=	s

Figure 29.3 Adding two 8-bit numbers $a = \langle 01011110 \rangle$ and $b = \langle 11010101 \rangle$ to produce a 9-bit sum $s = \langle 100110011 \rangle$. Each bit c_i is a carry bit. Each column of bits represents, from top to bottom, c_i, a_i, b_i, and s_i for some i. Carry-in c_0 is always 0.

numbers to the sum of an n-bit number and an $(n + 1)$-bit number. The circuit has $\Theta(n)$ size.

29.2.1 Ripple-carry addition

We start with the ordinary method of summing binary numbers. We assume that a nonnegative integer a is represented in binary by a sequence of n bits $\langle a_{n-1}, a_{n-2}, \ldots, a_0 \rangle$, where $n \geq \lceil \lg(a + 1) \rceil$ and

$$a = \sum_{i=0}^{n-1} a_i 2^i \ .$$

Given two n-bit numbers $a = \langle a_{n-1}, a_{n-2}, \ldots, a_0 \rangle$ and $b = \langle b_{n-1}, b_{n-2}, \ldots, b_0 \rangle$, we wish to produce an $(n + 1)$-bit sum $s = \langle s_n, s_{n-1}, \ldots, s_0 \rangle$. Figure 29.3 shows an example of adding two 8-bit numbers. We sum columns right to left, propagating any carry from column i to column $i + 1$, for $i = 0, 1, \ldots, n - 1$. In the ith bit position, we take as inputs bits a_i and b_i and a *carry-in bit* c_i, and we produce a *sum bit* s_i and a *carry-out* bit c_{i+1}. The carry-out bit c_{i+1} from the ith position is the carry-in bit into the $(i + 1)$st position. Since there is no carry-in for position 0, we assume that $c_0 = 0$. The carry-out c_n is bit s_n of the sum.

Observe that each sum bit s_i is the parity of bits a_i, b_i, and c_i (see equation (29.1)). Moreover, the carry-out bit c_{i+1} is the majority of a_i, b_i, and c_i (see equation (29.2)). Thus, each stage of the addition can be performed by a full adder.

An n-bit *ripple-carry adder* is formed by cascading n full adders FA_0, $FA_1, \ldots, FA_{n-1}$, feeding the carry-out c_{i+1} of FA_i directly into the carry-in input of FA_{i+1}. Figure 29.4 shows an 8-bit ripple-carry adder. The carry bits "ripple" from right to left. The carry-in c_0 to full adder FA_1 is *hardwired* to 0, that is, it is 0 no matter what values the other inputs take on. The output is the $(n + 1)$-bit number $s = \langle s_n, s_{n-1}, \ldots, s_0 \rangle$, where s_n equals c_n, the carry-out bit from full adder FA_n.

Because the carry bits ripple through all n full adders, the time required by an n-bit ripple-carry adder is $\Theta(n)$. More precisely, full adder FA_i is at

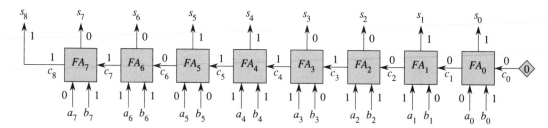

Figure 29.4 An 8-bit ripple-carry adder performing the addition of Figure 29.3. Carry bit c_0 is hardwired to 0, indicated by the diamond, and carry bits ripple from right to left.

depth $i + 1$ in the circuit. Because FA_{n-1} is at the largest depth of any full adder in the circuit, the depth of the ripple-carry adder is n. The size of the circuit is $\Theta(n)$ because it contains n combinational elements.

29.2.2   Carry-lookahead addition

Ripple-carry addition requires $\Theta(n)$ time because of the rippling of carry bits through the circuit. Carry-lookahead addition avoids this $\Theta(n)$-time delay by accelerating the computation of carries using a treelike circuit. A carry-lookahead adder can sum two n-bit numbers in $O(\lg n)$ time.

The key observation is that in ripple-carry addition, for $i \geq 1$, full adder FA_i has two of its input values, namely a_i and b_i, ready long before the carry-in c_i is ready. The idea behind the carry-lookahead adder is to exploit this partial information.

As an example, let $a_{i-1} = b_{i-1}$. Since the carry-out c_i is the majority function, we have $c_i = a_{i-1} = b_{i-1}$ *regardless of the carry-in* c_{i-1}. If $a_{i-1} = b_{i-1} = 0$, we can **kill** the carry-out c_i by forcing it to 0 without waiting for the value of c_{i-1} to be computed. Likewise, if $a_{i-1} = b_{i-1} = 1$, we can **generate** the carry-out $c_i = 1$, irrespective of the value of c_{i-1}.

If $a_{i-1} \neq b_{i-1}$, however, then c_i depends on c_{i-1}. Specifically, $c_i = c_{i-1}$, because the carry-in c_{i-1} casts the deciding "vote" in the majority election that determines c_i. In this case, we **propagate** the carry, since the carry-out is the carry-in.

Figure 29.5 summarizes these relationships in terms of **carry statuses**, where k is "carry kill," g is "carry generate," and p is "carry propagate."

Consider two consecutive full adders FA_{i-1} and FA_i together as a combined unit. The carry-in to the unit is c_{i-1}, and the carry-out is c_{i+1}. We can view the combined unit as killing, generating, or propagating carries, much as for a single full adder. The combined unit kills its carry if FA_i kills its carry or if FA_{i-1} kills its carry and FA_i propagates it. Similarly, the combined unit generates a carry if FA_i generates a carry or if FA_{i-1} generates a carry and FA_i propagates it. The combined unit propagates the carry, setting $c_{i+1} = c_{i-1}$, if both full adders propagate carries. The

a_{i-1}	b_{i-1}	c_i	carry status
0	0	0	k
0	1	c_{i-1}	p
1	0	c_{i-1}	p
1	1	1	g

Figure 29.5 The carry-out bit c_i and carry status corresponding to inputs a_{i-1}, b_{i-1}, and c_{i-1} of full adder FA_{i-1} in ripple-carry addition.

			FA_i	
$\otimes$		k	p	g
	k	k	k	g
FA_{i-1} p		k	p	g
	g	k	g	g

Figure 29.6 The carry status of the combination of full adders FA_{i-1} and FA_i in terms of their individual carry statuses, given by the carry-status operator $\otimes$ over the domain $\{k, p, g\}$.

table in Figure 29.6 summarizes how carry statuses are combined when full adders are juxtaposed. We can view this table as the definition of the **carry-status operator** $\otimes$ over the domain $\{k, p, g\}$. An important property of this operator is that it is associative, as Exercise 29.2-2 asks you to verify.

We can use the carry-status operator to express each carry bit c_i in terms of the inputs. We start by defining $x_0 = k$ and

$$x_i = \begin{cases} k & \text{if } a_{i-1} = b_{i-1} = 0, \\ p & \text{if } a_{i-1} \neq b_{i-1}, \\ g & \text{if } a_{i-1} = b_{i-1} = 1, \end{cases} \tag{29.3}$$

for $i = 1, 2, \ldots, n$. Thus, for $i = 1, 2, \ldots, n$, the value of x_i is the carry status given by Figure 29.5.

The carry-out c_i of a given full adder FA_{i-1} can depend on the carry status of every full adder FA_j for $j = 0, 1, \ldots, i - 1$. Let us define $y_0 = x_0 = k$ and

$$\begin{aligned} y_i &= y_{i-1} \otimes x_i \\ &= x_0 \otimes x_1 \otimes \cdots \otimes x_i \end{aligned} \tag{29.4}$$

for $i = 1, 2, \ldots, n$. We can think of y_i as a "prefix" of $x_0 \otimes x_1 \otimes \cdots \otimes x_n$; we call the process of computing the values $y_0, y_1, \ldots, y_n$ a **prefix computation**. (Chapter 30 discusses prefix computations in a more general parallel context.) Figure 29.7 shows the values of x_i and y_i corresponding to the binary addition shown in Figure 29.3. The following lemma gives the significance of the y_i values for carry-lookahead addition.

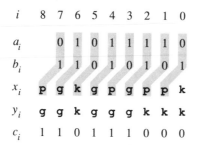

i	8	7	6	5	4	3	2	1	0
a_i		0	1	0	1	1	1	1	0
b_i		1	1	0	1	0	1	0	1
x_i	p	g	k	g	p	g	p	p	k
y_i	g	g	k	g	g	g	k	k	k
c_i	1	1	0	1	1	1	0	0	0

Figure 29.7 The values of x_i and y_i for $i = 0, 1, \ldots, 8$ that correspond to the values of a_i, b_i, and c_i in the binary-addition problem of Figure 29.3. Each value of x_i is shaded with the values of a_{i-1} and b_{i-1} that it depends on.

Lemma 29.1
Define $x_0, x_1, \ldots, x_n$ and $y_0, y_1, \ldots, y_n$ by equations (29.3) and (29.4). For $i = 0, 1, \ldots, n$, the following conditions hold:

1. $y_i = k$ implies $c_i = 0$,

2. $y_i = g$ implies $c_i = 1$, and

3. $y_i = p$ does not occur.

Proof   The proof is by induction on i. For the basis, $i = 0$. We have $y_0 = x_0 = k$ by definition, and also $c_0 = 0$. For the inductive step, assume that the lemma holds for $i - 1$. There are three cases depending on the value of y_i.

1. If $y_i = k$, then since $y_i = y_{i-1} \otimes x_i$, the definition of the carry-status operator $\otimes$ from Figure 29.6 implies either that $x_i = k$ or that $x_i = p$ and $y_{i-1} = k$. If $x_i = k$, then equation (29.3) implies that $a_{i-1} = b_{i-1} = 0$, and thus $c_i = \text{majority}(a_{i-1}, b_{i-1}, c_{i-1}) = 0$. If $x_i = p$ and $y_{i-1} = k$, then $a_{i-1} \neq b_{i-1}$ and, by induction, $c_{i-1} = 0$. Thus, $\text{majority}(a_{i-1}, b_{i-1}, c_{i-1}) = 0$, and thus $c_i = 0$.

2. If $y_i = g$, then either we have $x_i = g$ or we have $x_i = p$ and $y_{i-1} = g$. If $x_i = g$, then $a_{i-1} = b_{i-1} = 1$, which implies $c_i = 1$. If $x_i = p$ and $y_{i-1} = g$, then $a_{i-1} \neq b_{i-1}$ and, by induction, $c_{i-1} = 1$, which implies $c_i = 1$.

3. If $y_i = p$, then Figure 29.6 implies that $y_{i-1} = p$, which contradicts the inductive hypothesis.   ■

Lemma 29.1 implies that we can compute each carry bit c_i by computing each carry status y_i. Once we have all the carry bits, we can compute the entire sum in $\Theta(1)$ time by computing in parallel the sum bits $s_i = \text{parity}(a_i, b_i, c_i)$ for $i = 0, 1, \ldots, n$ (taking $a_n = b_n = 0$). Thus, the problem of quickly adding two numbers reduces to the prefix computation of the carry statuses $y_0, y_1, \ldots, y_n$.

Computing carry statuses with a parallel prefix circuit

By using a prefix circuit that operates in parallel, as opposed to a ripple-carry circuit that produces its outputs one by one, we can compute all n carry statuses $y_0, y_1, \ldots, y_n$ more quickly. Specifically, we shall design a parallel prefix circuit with $O(\lg n)$ depth. The circuit has $\Theta(n)$ size—asymptotically the same amount of hardware as a ripple-carry adder.

Before constructing the parallel prefix circuit, we introduce a notation that will aid our understanding of how the circuit operates. For integers i and j in the range $0 \le i \le j \le n$, we define

$$[i, j] = x_i \otimes x_{i+1} \otimes \cdots \otimes x_j \ .$$

Thus, for $i = 0, 1, \ldots, n$, we have $[i, i] = x_i$, since the composition of just one carry status x_i is itself. For i, j, and k satisfying $0 \le i < j \le k \le n$, we also have the identity

$$[i, k] = [i, j - 1] \otimes [j, k] \ , \tag{29.5}$$

since the carry-status operator is associative. The goal of a prefix computation, in terms of this notation, is to compute $y_i = [0, i]$ for $i = 0, 1, \ldots, n$.

The only combinational element used in the parallel prefix circuit is a circuit that computes the $\otimes$ operator. Figure 29.8 shows how pairs of $\otimes$ elements are organized to form the internal nodes of a complete binary tree, and Figure 29.9 illustrates the parallel prefix circuit for $n = 8$. Note that the wires in the circuit follow the structure of a tree, but the circuit itself is not a tree, although it is purely combinational. The inputs $x_1, x_2, \ldots, x_n$ are supplied at the leaves, and the input x_0 is provided at the root. The outputs $y_0, y_1, \ldots, y_{n-1}$ are produced at leaves, and the output y_n is produced at the root. (For ease in understanding the prefix computation, variable indices increase from left to right in Figures 29.8 and 29.9, rather than from right to left as in other figures of this section.)

The two $\otimes$ elements in each node typically operate at different times and have different depths in the circuit. As shown in Figure 29.8, if the subtree rooted at a given node spans some range $x_i, x_{i+1}, \ldots, x_k$ of inputs, its left subtree spans the range $x_i, x_{i+1}, \ldots, x_{j-1}$, and its right subtree spans the range $x_j, x_{j+1}, \ldots, x_k$, then the node must produce for its parent the product $[i, k]$ of all inputs spanned by its subtree. Since we can assume inductively that the node's left and right children produce the products $[i, j - 1]$ and $[j, k]$, the node simply uses one of its two elements to compute $[i, k] \leftarrow [i, j - 1] \otimes [j, k]$.

Some time after this upward phase of computation, the node receives from its parent the product $[0, i - 1]$ of all inputs that come before the leftmost input x_i that it spans. The node now likewise computes values for its children. The leftmost input spanned by the node's left child is also x_i, and so it passes the value $[0, i - 1]$ to the left child unchanged. The leftmost input spanned by its right child is x_j, and so it must produce $[0, j - 1]$. Since the node receives the value $[0, i - 1]$ from its parent and the value

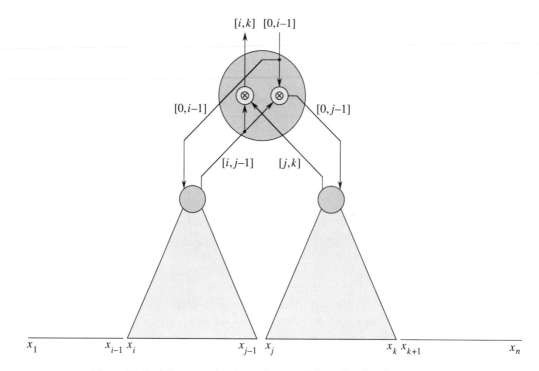

Figure 29.8   The organization of a parallel prefix circuit. The node shown is the root of a subtree whose leaves input the values x_i to x_k. The node's left subtree spans inputs x_i to x_{j-1}, and its right subtree spans inputs x_j to x_k. The node consists of two $\otimes$ elements, which operate at different times during the operation of the circuit. One element computes $[i, k] \leftarrow [i, j - 1] \otimes [j, k]$, and the other element computes $[0, j - 1] \leftarrow [0, i - 1] \otimes [i, j - 1]$. The values computed are shown on the wires.

$[i, j - 1]$ from its left child, it simply computes $[0, j - 1] \leftarrow [0, i - 1] \otimes [i, k]$ and sends this value to the right child.

Figure 29.9 shows the resulting circuit, including the boundary case that arises at the root. The value $x_0 = [0, 0]$ is provided as input at the root, and one more $\otimes$ element is used to compute (in general) the value $y_n = [0, n] = [0, 0] \otimes [1, n]$.

If n is an exact power of 2, then the parallel prefix circuit uses $2n - 1 \otimes$ elements. It takes only $O(\lg n)$ time to compute all $n + 1$ prefixes, since the computation proceeds up the tree and then back down. Exercise 29.2-5 studies the depth of the circuit in more detail.

Completing the carry-lookahead adder

Now that we have a parallel prefix circuit, we can complete the description of the carry-lookahead adder. Figure 29.10 shows the construction. An n-bit ***carry-lookahead adder*** consists of $n + 1$ ***KPG boxes***, each of $\Theta(1)$ size, and a parallel prefix circuit with inputs $x_0, x_1, \ldots, x_n$ (x_0 is hardwired

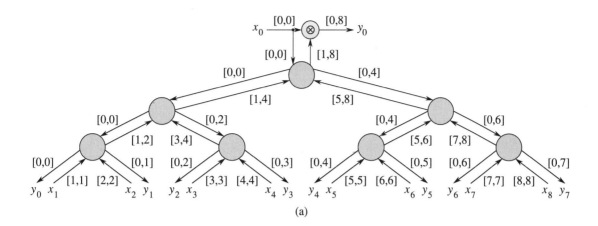

(a)

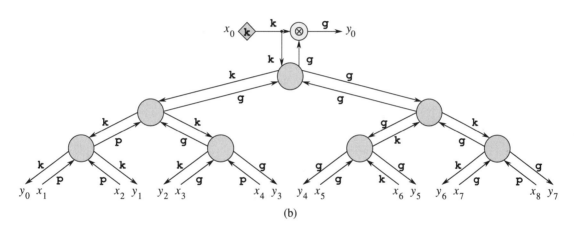

(b)

Figure 29.9 A parallel prefix circuit for $n = 8$. **(a)** The overall structure of the circuit, and the values carried on each wire. **(b)** The same circuit with values corresponding to Figures 29.3 and 29.7.

to k) and outputs $y_0, y_1, \ldots, y_n$. KPG box KPG_i takes external inputs a_i and b_i and produces sum bit s_i. (Input bits a_n and b_n are hardwired to 0.) Given a_{i-1} and b_{i-1}, box KPG_{i-1} computes $x_i \in \{k, p, g\}$ according to equation (29.3) and sends this value as the external input x_i of the parallel prefix circuit. (The value of x_{n+1} is ignored.) Computing all the x_i takes $\Theta(1)$ time. After a delay of $O(\lg n)$, the parallel prefix circuit produces $y_0, y_1, \ldots, y_n$. By Lemma 29.1, y_i is either k or g; it cannot be p. Each value y_i indicates the carry-in to full adder FA_i in the ripple-carry adder: $y_i = k$ implies $c_i = 0$, and $y_i = g$ implies $c_i = 1$. Thus, the value of y_i is fed into KPG_i to indicate the carry-in c_i, and the sum bit $s_i = \text{parity}(a_i, b_i, c_i)$ is produced in constant time. Thus, the carry-lookahead adder operates in $O(\lg n)$ time and has $\Theta(n)$ size.

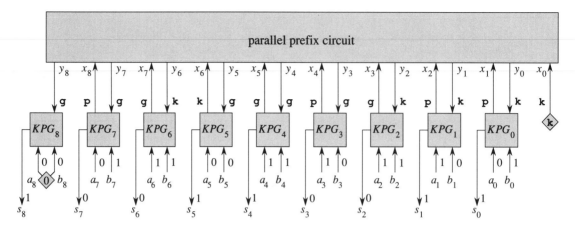

Figure 29.10   The construction of an n-bit carry-lookahead adder, shown here for $n = 8$. It consists of $n + 1$ KPG boxes KPG_i for $i = 0, 1, \ldots, n$. Each box KPG_i takes external inputs a_i and b_i (where a_n and b_n are hardwired to 0, as indicated by the diamond) and computes carry status x_{i+1}. These values are fed into the parallel prefix circuit, which returns the results y_i of the prefix computation. Each box KPG_i now takes y_i as input, interprets it as the carry-in bit c_i, and then outputs the sum bit $s_i = \mathrm{parity}(a_i, b_i, c_i)$. Sample values corresponding to those shown in Figures 29.3 and 29.9 are shown.

29.2.3   Carry-save addition

A carry-lookahead adder can add two n-bit numbers in $O(\lg n)$ time. Perhaps surprisingly, adding three n-bit numbers takes only a constant additional amount of time. The trick is to reduce the problem of adding three numbers to the problem of adding just two numbers.

Given three n-bit numbers $x = \langle x_{n-1}, x_{n-2}, \ldots, x_0 \rangle$, $y = \langle y_{n-1}, y_{n-2}, \ldots, y_0 \rangle$, and $z = \langle z_{n-1}, z_{n-2}, \ldots, z_0 \rangle$, an n-bit *carry-save adder* produces an n-bit number $u = \langle u_{n-1}, u_{n-2}, \ldots, u_0 \rangle$ and an $(n + 1)$-bit number $v = \langle v_n, v_{n-1}, \ldots, v_0 \rangle$ such that

$$u + v = x + y + z .$$

As shown in Figure 29.11(a), it does this by computing

$$
\begin{aligned}
u_i &= \mathrm{parity}(x_i, y_i, z_i) , \\
v_{i+1} &= \mathrm{majority}(x_i, y_i, z_i) ,
\end{aligned}
$$

for $i = 0, 1, \ldots, n - 1$. Bit v_0 always equals 0.

The n-bit carry-save adder shown in Figure 29.11(b) consists of n full adders $FA_0, FA_1, \ldots, FA_{n-1}$. For $i = 0, 1, \ldots, n - 1$, full adder FA_i takes inputs x_i, y_i, and z_i. The sum-bit output of FA_i is taken as u_i, and the carry-out of FA_i is taken as v_{i+1}. Bit v_0 is hardwired to 0.

Since the computations of all $2n + 1$ output bits are independent, they can be performed in parallel. Thus, a carry-save adder operates in $\Theta(1)$ time and has $\Theta(n)$ size. To sum three n-bit numbers, therefore, we need

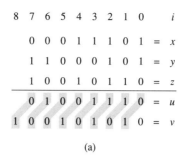

(a)

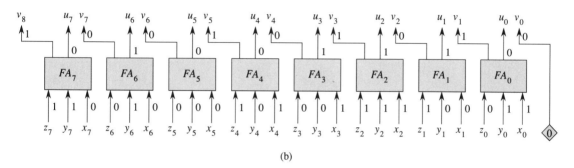

(b)

Figure 29.11 (a) Carry-save addition. Given three n-bit numbers x, y, and z, we produce an n-bit number u and an $(n+1)$-bit number v such that $x+y+z = u+v$. The ith pair of shaded bits are a function of x_i, y_i, and z_i. (b) An 8-bit carry-save adder. Each full adder FA_i takes inputs x_i, y_i, and z_i and produces sum bit u_i and carry-out bit v_{i+1}. Bit v_0 is hardwired to 0.

only perform a carry-save addition, taking $\Theta(1)$ time, and then perform a carry-lookahead addition, taking $O(\lg n)$ time. Although this method is not asymptotically better than the method of using two carry-lookahead additions, it is much faster in practice. Moreover, we shall see in Section 29.3 that carry-save addition is central to fast algorithms for multiplication.

Exercises

29.2-1
Let $a = \langle 01111111 \rangle$, $b = \langle 00000001 \rangle$, and $n = 8$. Show the sum and carry bits output by full adders when ripple-carry addition is performed on these two sequences. Show the carry statuses $x_0, x_1, \ldots, x_8$ corresponding to a and b, label each wire of the parallel prefix circuit of Figure 29.9 with the value it has given these x_i inputs, and show the resulting outputs $y_0, y_1, \ldots, y_8$.

29.2-2
Prove that the carry-status operator $\otimes$ given by Figure 29.5 is associative.

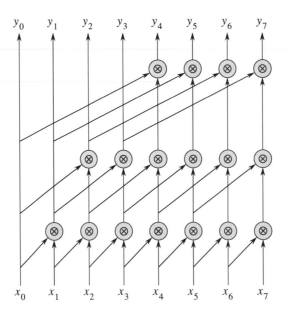

Figure 29.12   A parallel prefix circuit for use in Exercise 29.2-6.

29.2-3
Show by example how to construct an $O(\lg n)$-time parallel prefix circuit for values of n that are not exact powers of 2 by drawing a parallel prefix circuit for $n = 11$. Characterize the performance of parallel prefix circuits built in the shape of arbitrary binary trees.

29.2-4
Show the gate-level construction of the box KPG_i. Assume that each output x_i is represented by $\langle 00 \rangle$ if $x_i = \text{k}$, by $\langle 11 \rangle$ if $x_i = \text{g}$, and by $\langle 01 \rangle$ or $\langle 10 \rangle$ if $x_i = \text{p}$. Assume also that each input y_i is represented by 0 if $y_i = \text{k}$ and by 1 if $y_i = \text{g}$.

29.2-5
Label each wire in the parallel prefix circuit of Figure 29.9(a) with its depth. A **critical path** in a circuit is a path with the largest number of combinational elements on any path from inputs to outputs. Identify the critical path in Figure 29.9(a), and show that its length is $O(\lg n)$. Show that some node has $\otimes$ elements that operate $\Theta(\lg n)$ time apart. Is there a node whose $\otimes$ elements operate simultaneously?

29.2-6
Give a recursive block diagram of the circuit in Figure 29.12 for any number n of inputs that is an exact power of 2. Argue on the basis of your block diagram that the circuit indeed performs a prefix computation. Show that the depth of the circuit is $\Theta(\lg n)$ and that it has $\Theta(n \lg n)$ size.

29.2-7

What is the maximum fan-out of any wire in the carry-lookahead adder? Show that addition can still be performed in $O(\lg n)$ time by a $\Theta(n)$-size circuit even if we restrict gates to have $O(1)$ fan-out.

29.2-8

A **tally circuit** has n binary inputs and $m = \lceil \lg(n + 1) \rceil$ outputs. Interpreted as a binary number, the outputs give the number of 1's in the inputs. For example, if the input is $\langle 10011110 \rangle$, the output is $\langle 101 \rangle$, indicating that there are five 1's in the input. Describe an $O(\lg n)$-depth tally circuit having $\Theta(n)$ size.

29.2-9 ★

Show that n-bit addition can be accomplished with a combinational circuit of depth 4 and size polynomial in n if AND and OR gates are allowed arbitrarily high fan-in. (*Optional:* Achieve depth 3.)

29.2-10 ★

Suppose that two random n-bit numbers are added with a ripple-carry adder, where each bit is independently 0 or 1 with equal probability. Show that with probability at least $1 - 1/n$, no carry propagates farther than $O(\lg n)$ consecutive stages. In other words, although the depth of the ripple-carry adder is $\Theta(n)$, for two random numbers, the outputs almost always settle within $O(\lg n)$ time.

29.3 Multiplication circuits

The "grade-school" multiplication algorithm in Figure 29.13 can compute the $2n$-bit product $p = \langle p_{2n-1}, p_{2n-2}, \ldots, p_0 \rangle$ of two n-bit numbers $a = \langle a_{n-1}, a_{n-2}, \ldots, a_0 \rangle$ and $b = \langle b_{n-1}, b_{n-2}, \ldots, b_0 \rangle$. We examine the bits of b, from b_0 up to b_{n-1}. For each bit b_i with a value of 1, we add a into the product, but shifted left by i positions. For each bit b_i with a value of 0, we add in 0. Thus, letting $m^{(i)} = a \cdot b_i \cdot 2^i$, we compute

$$p = a \cdot b = \sum_{i=0}^{n-1} m^{(i)} \,.$$

Each term $m^{(i)}$ is called a **partial product**. There are n partial products to sum, with bits in positions 0 to $2n - 2$. The carry-out from the highest bit yields the final bit in position $2n - 1$.

In this section, we examine two circuits for multiplying two n-bit numbers. Array multipliers operate in $\Theta(n)$ time and have $\Theta(n^2)$ size. Wallace-tree multipliers also have $\Theta(n^2)$ size, but they operate in $\Theta(\lg n)$ time. Both circuits are based on the grade-school algorithm.

$$
\begin{array}{ccccccccc}
 & & & & 1 & 1 & 1 & 0 & = & a \\
 & & & & 1 & 1 & 0 & 1 & = & b \\
\hline
 & & & & 1 & 1 & 1 & 0 & = & m^{(0)} \\
 & & & 0 & 0 & 0 & 0 & & = & m^{(1)} \\
 & & 1 & 1 & 1 & 0 & & & = & m^{(2)} \\
 & 1 & 1 & 1 & 0 & & & & = & m^{(3)} \\
\hline
1 & 0 & 1 & 1 & 0 & 1 & 1 & 0 & = & p
\end{array}
$$

Figure 29.13 The "grade-school" multiplication method, shown here multiplying $a = \langle 1110 \rangle$ by $b = \langle 1101 \rangle$ to obtain the product $p = \langle 10110110 \rangle$. We add $\sum_{i=0}^{n-1} m^{(i)}$, where $m^{(i)} = a \cdot b_i \cdot 2^i$. Here, $n = 8$. Each term $m^{(i)}$ is formed by shifting either a (if $b_i = 1$) or 0 (if $b_i = 0$) i positions to the left. Bits that are not shown are 0 regardless of the values of a and b.

29.3.1   Array multipliers

An array multiplier consists conceptually of three parts. The first part forms the partial products. The second sums the partial products using carry-save adders. Finally, the third sums the two numbers resulting from the carry-save additions using either a ripple-carry or carry-lookahead adder.

Figure 29.14 shows an ***array multiplier*** for two input numbers $a = \langle a_{n-1}, a_{n-2}, \ldots, a_0 \rangle$ and $b = \langle b_{n-1}, b_{n-2}, \ldots, b_0 \rangle$. The a_j values run vertically, and the b_i values run horizontally. Each input bit fans out to n AND gates to form partial products. Full adders, which are organized as carry-save adders, sum partial products. The lower-order bits of the final product are output on the right. The higher-order bits are formed by adding the two numbers output by the last carry-save adder.

Let us examine the construction of the array multiplier more closely. Given the two input numbers $a = \langle a_{n-1}, a_{n-2}, \ldots, a_0 \rangle$ and $b = \langle b_{n-1}, b_{n-2}, \ldots, b_0 \rangle$, the bits of the partial products are easy to compute. Specifically, for $i, j = 0, 1, \ldots, n - 1$, we have

$$ m^{(i)}_{j+i} = a_j \cdot b_i . $$

Since the product of 1-bit values can be computed directly with an AND gate, all the bits of the partial products (except those known to be 0, which need not be explicitly computed) can be produced in one step using n^2 AND gates.

Figure 29.15 illustrates how the array multiplier performs the carry-save additions when summing the partial products in Figure 29.13. It starts by carry-save adding $m^{(0)}$, $m^{(1)}$, and 0, yielding an $(n + 1)$-bit number $u^{(1)}$ and an $(n + 1)$-bit number $v^{(1)}$. (The number $v^{(1)}$ has only $n + 1$ bits, not $n + 2$, because the $(n + 1)$st bits of both 0 and $m^{(0)}$ are 0.) Thus, $m^{(0)} + m^{(1)} = u^{(1)} + v^{(1)}$. It then carry-save adds $u^{(1)}$, $v^{(1)}$, and $m^{(2)}$, yielding an $(n + 2)$-bit number $u^{(2)}$ and an $(n + 2)$-bit number $v^{(2)}$. (Again,

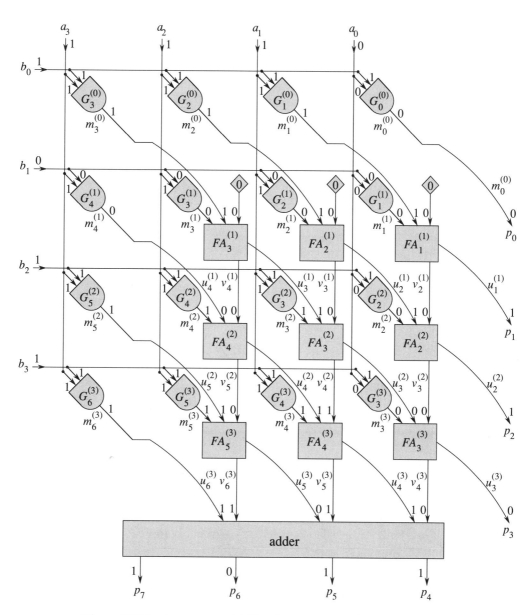

Figure 29.14   An array multiplier that computes the product $p = \langle p_{2n-1}, p_{2n-2}, \ldots, p_0 \rangle$ of two n-bit numbers $a = \langle a_{n-1}, a_{n-2}, \ldots, a_0 \rangle$ and $b = \langle b_{n-1}, b_{n-2}, \ldots, b_0 \rangle$, shown here for $n = 4$. Each AND gate $G_j^{(i)}$ computes partial-product bit $m_j^{(i)}$. Each row of full adders constitutes a carry-save adder. The lower n bits of the product are $m_0^{(0)}$ and the u bits coming out from the rightmost column of full adders. The upper n product bits are formed by adding the u and v bits coming out from the bottom row of full adders. Shown are bit values for inputs $a = \langle 1110 \rangle$ and $b = \langle 1101 \rangle$ and product $p = \langle 10110110 \rangle$, corresponding to Figures 29.13 and 29.15.

			0	0	0	0			=	0
			1	1	1	0			=	$m^{(0)}$
		0	0	0	0				=	$m^{(1)}$
		0	1	1	1	0			=	$u^{(1)}$
		0	0	0					=	$v^{(1)}$
	1	1	1	0					=	$m^{(2)}$
	1	1	0	1	1	0			=	$u^{(2)}$
	0	1	0						=	$v^{(2)}$
1	1	1	0						=	$m^{(3)}$
1	0	1	0	1	1	0			=	$u^{(3)}$
1	1	0							=	$v^{(3)}$
1	0	1	1	0	1	1	0		=	p

Figure 29.15 Evaluating the sum of the partial products by repeated carry-save addition. For this example, $a = \langle 1110 \rangle$ and $b = \langle 1101 \rangle$. Bits that are blank are 0 regardless of the values of a and b. We first evaluate $m^{(0)} + m^{(1)} + 0 = u^{(1)} + v^{(1)}$, then $u^{(1)} + v^{(1)} + m^{(2)} = u^{(2)} + v^{(2)}$, then $u^{(2)} + v^{(2)} + m^{(3)} = u^{(3)} + v^{(3)}$, and finally $p = m^{(0)} + m^{(1)} + m^{(2)} + m^{(3)} = u^{(3)} + v^{(3)}$. Note that $p_0 = m_0^{(0)}$ and $p_i = u_i^{(i)}$ for $i = 1, 2, \ldots, n - 1$.

$v^{(2)}$ has only $n + 2$ bits because both $u_{n+2}^{(1)}$ and $v_{n+2}^{(1)}$ are 0.) We then have $m^{(0)} + m^{(1)} + m^{(2)} = u^{(2)} + v^{(2)}$. The multiplier continues on, carry-save adding $u^{(i-1)}$, $v^{(i-1)}$, and $m^{(i)}$ for $i = 2, 3, \ldots, n-1$. The result is a $(2n-1)$-bit number $u^{(n-1)}$ and a $(2n-1)$-bit number $v^{(n-1)}$, where

$$
\begin{aligned}
u^{(n-1)} + v^{(n-1)} &= \sum_{i=0}^{n-1} m^{(i)} \\
&= p \, .
\end{aligned}
$$

In fact, the carry-save additions in Figure 29.15 operate on more bits than strictly necessary. Observe that for $i = 1, 2, \ldots, n - 1$ and $j = 0, 1, \ldots, i - 1$, we have $m_j^{(i)} = 0$ because of how we shift the partial products. Observe also that $v_j^{(i)} = 0$ for $i = 1, 2, \ldots, n - 1$ and $j = 0, 1, \ldots, i, i+n, i+n+1, \ldots, 2n-1$. (See Exercise 29.3-1.) Each carry-save addition, therefore, needs to operate on only $n - 1$ bits.

Let us now examine the correspondence between the array multiplier and the repeated carry-save addition scheme. Each AND gate is labeled by $G_j^{(i)}$ for some i and j in the ranges $0 \le i \le n - 1$ and $0 \le j \le 2n - 2$. Gate $G_j^{(i)}$ produces $m_j^{(i)}$, the jth bit of the ith partial product. For $i = 0, 1, \ldots, n-1$, the ith row of AND gates computes the n significant bits of the partial product $m^{(i)}$, that is, $\langle m_{n+i-1}^{(i)}, m_{n+i-2}^{(i)}, \ldots, m_i^{(i)} \rangle$.

Except for the full adders in the top row (that is, for $i = 2, 3, \ldots, n - 1$), each full adder $FA_j^{(i)}$ takes three input bits—$m_j^{(i)}$, $u_j^{(i-1)}$, and $v_j^{(i-1)}$—and produces two output bits—$u_j^{(i)}$ and $v_{j+1}^{(i)}$. (Note that in the leftmost column of full adders, $u_{i+n-1}^{(i-1)} = m_{i+n-1}^{(i)}$.) Each full adder $FA_j^{(1)}$ in the top row takes inputs $m_j^{(0)}$, $m_j^{(1)}$, and 0 and produces bits $u_j^{(1)}$ and $v_{j+1}^{(1)}$.

Finally, let us examine the output of the array multiplier. As we observed above, $v_j^{(n-1)} = 0$ for $j = 0, 1, \ldots, n - 1$. Thus, $p_j = u_j^{(n-1)}$ for $j = 0, 1, \ldots, n - 1$. Moreover, since $m_0^{(1)} = 0$, we have $u_0^{(1)} = m_0^{(0)}$, and since the lowest-order i bits of each $m^{(i)}$ and $v^{(i-1)}$ are 0, we have $u_j^{(i)} = u_j^{(i-1)}$ for $i = 2, 3, \ldots, n-1$ and $j = 0, 1, \ldots, i-1$. Thus, $p_0 = m_0^{(0)}$ and, by induction, $p_i = u_i^{(i)}$ for $i = 1, 2, \ldots, n - 1$. Product bits $\langle p_{2n-1}, p_{2n-2}, \ldots, p_n \rangle$ are produced by an n-bit adder that adds the outputs from the last row of full adders:

$$\langle p_{2n-1}, p_{2n-2}, \ldots, p_n \rangle =$$
$$\langle u_{2n-2}^{(n-1)}, u_{2n-3}^{(n-1)}, \ldots, u_n^{(n-1)} \rangle + \langle v_{2n-2}^{(n-1)}, v_{2n-3}^{(n-1)}, \ldots, v_n^{(n-1)} \rangle .$$

Analysis

Data ripple through an array multiplier from upper left to lower right. It takes $\Theta(n)$ time for the lower-order product bits $\langle p_{n-1}, p_{n-2}, \ldots, p_0 \rangle$ to be produced, and it takes $\Theta(n)$ time for the inputs to the adder to be ready. If the adder is a ripple-carry adder, it takes another $\Theta(n)$ time for the higher-order product bits $\langle p_{2n-1}, p_{2n-2}, \ldots, p_n \rangle$ to emerge. If the adder is a carry-lookahead adder, only $\Theta(\lg n)$ time is needed, but the total time remains $\Theta(n)$.

There are n^2 AND gates and $n^2 - n$ full adders in the array multiplier. The adder for the high-order output bits contributes only another $\Theta(n)$ gates. Thus, the array multiplier has $\Theta(n^2)$ size.

29.3.2 Wallace-tree multipliers

A *Wallace tree* is a circuit that reduces the problem of summing n n-bit numbers to the problem of summing two $\Theta(n)$-bit numbers. It does this by using $\lfloor n/3 \rfloor$ carry-save adders in parallel to convert the sum of n numbers to the sum of $\lceil 2n/3 \rceil$ numbers. It then recursively constructs a Wallace tree on the $\lceil 2n/3 \rceil$ resulting numbers. In this way, the set of numbers is progressively reduced until there are only two numbers left. By performing many carry-save additions in parallel, Wallace trees allow two n-bit numbers to be multiplied in $\Theta(\lg n)$ time using a circuit with $\Theta(n^2)$ size.

Figure 29.16 shows a Wallace tree[2] that adds 8 partial products $m^{(0)}$, $m^{(1)}, \ldots, m^{(7)}$. Partial product $m^{(i)}$ consists of $n + i$ bits. Each line represents an entire number, not just a single bit; next to each line is the number

---

[2]As you can see from the figure, a Wallace tree is not truly a tree, but rather a directed acyclic graph. The name is historical.

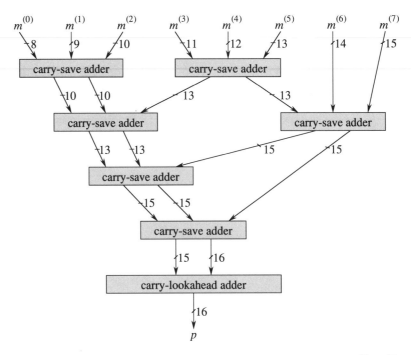

Figure 29.16   A Wallace tree that adds $n = 8$ partial products $m^{(0)}, m^{(1)}, \ldots, m^{(7)}$. Each line represents a number with the number of bits indicated. The left output of each carry-save adder represents the sum bits, and the right output represents the carry bits.

of bits the line represents (see Exercise 29.3-3). The carry-lookahead adder at the bottom adds a $(2n - 1)$-bit number to a $2n$-bit number to give the $2n$-bit product.

Analysis

The time required by an n-input Wallace tree depends on the depth of the carry-save adders. At each level of the tree, each group of 3 numbers is reduced to 2 numbers, with at most 2 numbers left over (as in the case of $m^{(6)}$ and $m^{(7)}$ at the top level). Thus, the maximum depth $D(n)$ of a carry-save adder in an n-input Wallace tree is given by the recurrence

$$D(n) = \begin{cases} 0 & \text{if } n \leq 2, \\ 1 & \text{if } n = 3, \\ D(\lceil 2n/3 \rceil) + 1 & \text{if } n \geq 4, \end{cases}$$

which has the solution $D(n) = \Theta(\lg n)$ by case 2 of the master theorem (Theorem 4.1). Each carry-save adder takes $\Theta(1)$ time. All n partial products can be formed in $\Theta(1)$ time in parallel. (The lowest-order $i - 1$ bits of $m^{(i)}$, for $i = 1, 2, \ldots, n-1$, are hardwired to 0.) The carry-lookahead adder takes $O(\lg n)$ time. Thus, the entire multiplication of two n-bit numbers takes $\Theta(\lg n)$ time.

A Wallace-tree multiplier for two n-bit numbers has $\Theta(n^2)$ size, which we can see as follows. We first bound the circuit size of the carry-save adders. A lower bound of $\Omega(n^2)$ is easy to obtain, since there are $\lfloor 2n/3 \rfloor$ carry-save adders at depth 1, and each one consists of at least n full adders. To get the upper bound of $O(n^2)$, observe that since the final product has $2n$ bits, each carry-save adder in the Wallace tree contains at most $2n$ full adders. We need to show that there are $O(n)$ carry-save adders altogether. Let $C(n)$ be the total number of carry-save adders in a Wallace tree with n input numbers. We have the recurrence

$$C(n) \leq \begin{cases} 1 & \text{if } n = 3, \\ C(\lceil 2n/3 \rceil) + \lfloor n/3 \rfloor & \text{if } n \geq 4, \end{cases}$$

which has the solution $C(n) = \Theta(n)$ by case 3 of the master theorem. We thus obtain an asymptotically tight bound of $\Theta(n^2)$ size for the carry-save adders of a Wallace-tree multiplier. The circuitry to set up the n partial products has $\Theta(n^2)$ size, and the carry-lookahead adder at the end has $\Theta(n)$ size. Thus, the size of the entire multiplier is $\Theta(n^2)$.

Although the Wallace-tree-based multiplier is asymptotically faster than the array multiplier and has the same asymptotic size, its layout when it is implemented is not as regular as the array multiplier's, nor is it as "dense" (in the sense of having little wasted space between circuit elements). In practice, a compromise between the two designs is often used. The idea is to use two arrays in parallel, one adding up half of the partial products and one adding up the other half. The propagation delay is only half of that incurred by a single array adding up all n partial products. Two more carry-save additions reduce the 4 numbers output by the arrays to 2 numbers, and a carry-lookahead adder then adds the 2 numbers to yield the product. The total propagation delay is a little more than half that of a full array multiplier, plus an additional $O(\lg n)$ term.

Exercises

29.3-1
Prove that in an array multiplier, $v_j^{(i)} = 0$ for $i = 1, 2, \ldots, n - 1$ and $j = 0, 1, \ldots, i, i + n, i + n + 1, \ldots, 2n - 1$.

29.3-2
Show that in the array multiplier of Figure 29.14, all but one of the full adders in the top row are unnecessary. You will need to do some rewiring.

29.3-3
Suppose that a carry-save adder takes inputs x, y, and z and produces outputs s and c, with n_x, n_y, n_z, n_s, and n_c bits respectively. Suppose also, without loss of generality, that $n_x \leq n_y \leq n_z$. Show that $n_s = n_z$ and that

$$n_c = \begin{cases} n_z & \text{if } n_y < n_z, \\ n_z + 1 & \text{if } n_y = n_z. \end{cases}$$

29.3-4
Show that multiplication can still be performed in $O(\lg n)$ time with $O(n^2)$ size even if we restrict gates to have $O(1)$ fan-out.

29.3-5
Describe an efficient circuit to compute the quotient when a binary number x is divided by 3. (*Hint:* Note that in binary, $.010101\ldots = .01 \times 1.01 \times 1.0001 \times \cdots$.)

29.3-6
A *cyclic shifter*, or *barrel shifter*, is a circuit that has two inputs $x = \langle x_{n-1}, x_{n-2}, \ldots, x_0 \rangle$ and $s = \langle s_{m-1}, s_{m-2}, \ldots, s_0 \rangle$, where $m = \lceil \lg n \rceil$. Its output $y = \langle y_{n-1}, y_{n-2}, \ldots, y_0 \rangle$ is specified by $y_i = x_{i+s \bmod n}$, for $i = 0, 1, \ldots, n-1$. That is, the shifter rotates the bits of x by the amount specified by s. Describe an efficient cyclic shifter. In terms of modular multiplication, what function does a cyclic shifter implement?

29.4   Clocked circuits

The elements of a combinational circuit are used only once during a computation. By introducing clocked memory elements into the circuit, we can reuse combinational elements. Because they can use hardware more than once, clocked circuits can often be much smaller than combinational circuits for the same function.

This section investigates clocked circuits for performing addition and multiplication. We begin with a $\Theta(1)$-size clocked circuit, called a bit-serial adder, that can add two n-bit numbers in $\Theta(n)$ time. We then investigate linear-array multipliers. We present a linear-array multiplier with $\Theta(n)$ size that can multiply two n-bit numbers in $\Theta(n)$ time.

29.4.1   Bit-serial addition

We introduce the notion of a clocked circuit by returning to the problem of adding two n-bit numbers. Figure 29.17 shows how we can use a single full adder to produce the $(n+1)$-bit sum $s = \langle s_n, s_{n-1}, \ldots, s_0 \rangle$ of two n-bit numbers $a = \langle a_{n-1}, a_{n-2}, \ldots, a_0 \rangle$ and $b = \langle b_{n-1}, b_{n-2}, \ldots, b_0 \rangle$. The external world presents the input bits one pair at a time: first a_0 and b_0, then a_1 and b_1, and so forth. Although we want the carry-out from one bit position to be the carry-in to the next bit position, we cannot just feed the full adder's c output directly into an input. There is a timing issue: the carry-in c_i entering the full adder must correspond to the appropriate

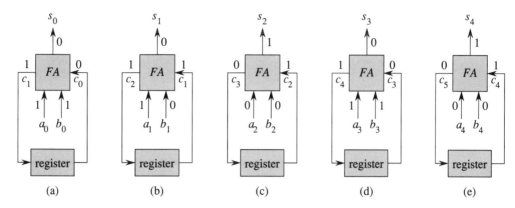

Figure 29.17 The operation of a bit-serial adder. During the ith clock period, for $i = 0, 1, \ldots, n$, the full adder *FA* takes input bits a_i and b_i from the outside world and a carry bit c_i from the register. The full adder then outputs sum bit s_i, which is provided externally, and carry bit c_{i+1}, which is stored back in the register to be used during the next clock period. The register is initialized with $c_0 = 0$. **(a)–(e)** The state of the circuit in each of the five clock periods during the addition of $a = \langle 1011 \rangle$ and $b = \langle 1001 \rangle$ to produce $s = \langle 10100 \rangle$.

inputs a_i and b_i. Unless these input bits arrive at exactly the same moment as the fed-back carry, the output may be incorrect.

As Figure 29.17 shows, the solution is to use a ***clocked circuit***, or ***sequential circuit***, consisting of combinational circuitry and one or more ***registers*** (clocked memory elements). The combinational circuitry has inputs from the external world or from the output of registers. It provides outputs to the external world and to the input of registers. As in combinational circuits, we prohibit the combinational circuitry in a clocked circuit from containing cycles.

Each register in a clocked circuit is controlled by a periodic signal, or ***clock***. Whenever the clock pulses, or ***ticks***, the register loads in and stores the value at its input. The time between successive clock ticks is a ***clock period***. In a ***globally clocked*** circuit, every register works off the same clock.

Let us examine the operation of a register in a little more detail. We treat each clock tick as a momentary pulse. At a given tick, a register reads the input value presented to it *at that moment* and stores it. This stored value then appears at the register's output, where it can be used to compute values that are moved into other registers at the next clock tick. In other words, the value at a register's input during one clock period appears on the register's output during the next clock period.

Now let us examine the circuit in Figure 29.17, which we call a ***bit-serial adder***. In order for the full adder's outputs to be correct, we require that the clock period be at least as long as the propagation delay of the full adder, so that the combinational circuitry has an opportunity to settle between clock ticks. During clock period 0, shown in Figure 29.17(a), the external world applies input bits a_0 and b_0 to two of the full adder's inputs. We assume that the register is initialized to store a 0; the initial carry-in bit, which is the register output, is thus $c_0 = 0$. Later in this clock period, sum bit s_0 and carry-out c_1 emerge from the full adder. The sum bit goes to the external world, where presumably it will be saved as part of the entire sum s. The wire from the carry-out of the full adder feeds into the register, so that c_1 is read into the register upon the next clock tick. At the beginning of clock period 1, therefore, the register contains c_1. During clock period 1, shown in Figure 29.17(b), the outside world applies a_1 and b_1 to the full adder, which, reading c_1 from the register, produces outputs s_1 and c_2. The sum bit s_1 goes out to the outside world, and c_2 goes to the register. This cycle continues until clock period n, shown in Figure 29.17(e), in which the register contains c_n. The external world then applies $a_n = b_n = 0$, so that we get $s_n = c_n$.

Analysis

To determine the total time t taken by a globally clocked circuit, we need to know the number p of clock periods and the duration d of each clock period: $t = pd$. The clock period d must be long enough for all combinational circuitry to settle between ticks. Although for some inputs it may settle earlier, if the circuit is to work correctly for all inputs, d must be at least proportional to the depth of the combinational circuitry.

Let us see how long it takes to add two n-bit numbers bit-serially. Each clock period takes $\Theta(1)$ time because the depth of the full adder is $\Theta(1)$. Since $n + 1$ clock ticks are required to produce all the outputs, the total time to perform bit-serial addition is $(n + 1)\,\Theta(1) = \Theta(n)$.

The size of the bit-serial adder (number of combinational elements plus number of registers) is $\Theta(1)$.

Ripple-carry addition versus bit-serial addition

Observe that a ripple-carry adder is like a replicated bit-serial adder with the registers replaced by direct connections between combinational elements. That is, the ripple-carry adder corresponds to a spatial "unrolling" of the computation of the bit-serial adder. The ith full adder in the ripple-carry adder implements the ith clock period of the bit-serial adder.

In general, we can replace any clocked circuit by an equivalent combinational circuit having the same asymptotic time delay if we know in advance how many clock periods the clocked circuit runs for. There is, of course, a trade-off involved. The clocked circuit uses fewer circuit elements (a factor of $\Theta(n)$ less for the bit-serial adder versus the ripple-carry adder), but the combinational circuit has the advantage of less control circuitry—we need no clock or synchronized external circuit to present input bits and store sum bits. Moreover, although the circuits have the same asymptotic time delay, the combinational circuit typically runs slightly faster in practice.

a	b		a	b
19	29		1 0 0 1 1	1 1 1 0 1
9	58		1 0 0 1	1 1 1 0 1 0
4	116		1 0 0	1 1 1 0 1 0 0
2	232		1 0	1 1 1 0 1 0 0 0
1	464		1	1 1 1 0 1 0 0 0 0
	551			1 0 0 0 1 0 0 1 1 1
(a)			(b)	

Figure 29.18   Multiplying 19 by 29 with the Russian peasant's algorithm. The a-column entry in each row is half of the previous row's entry with fractions ignored, and the b-column entries double from row to row. We add the b-column entries in all rows with odd a-column entries, which are shaded. This sum is the desired product. **(a)** The numbers expressed in decimal. **(b)** The same numbers in binary.

The extra speed is possible because the combinational circuit doesn't have to wait for values to stabilize during each clock period. If all the inputs stabilize at once, values just ripple through the circuit at the maximum possible speed, without waiting for the clock.

29.4.2   Linear-array multipliers

The combinational multipliers of Section 29.3 need $\Theta(n^2)$ size to multiply two n-bit numbers. We now present two multipliers that are linear, rather than two-dimensional, arrays of circuit elements. Like the array multiplier, the faster of these two linear-array multipliers runs in $\Theta(n)$ time.

The linear-array multipliers implement the ***Russian peasant's algorithm*** (so called because Westerners visiting Russia in the nineteenth century found the algorithm widely used there), illustrated in Figure 29.18(a). Given two input numbers a and b, we make two columns of numbers, headed by a and b. In each row, the a-column entry is half of the previous row's a-column entry, with fractions discarded. The b-column entry is twice the previous row's b-column entry. The last row is the one with an a-column entry of 1. We look at all the a-column entries that contain odd values and sum the corresponding b-column entries. This sum is the product $a \cdot b$.

Although the Russian peasant's algorithm may seem remarkable at first, Figure 29.18(b) shows that it is really just a binary-number-system implementation of the grade-school multiplication method, but with numbers expressed in decimal rather than in binary. Rows in which the a-column entry is odd contribute to the product a term of b multiplied by the appropriate power of 2.

A slow linear-array implementation

Figure 29.19(a) shows one way to implement the Russian peasant's algorithm for two n-bit numbers. We use a clocked circuit consisting of a linear array of $2n$ cells. Each cell contains three registers. One register holds a bit from an a entry, one holds a bit from a b entry, and one holds a bit of the product p. We use superscripts to denote cell values before each step of the algorithm. For example, the value of bit a_i before the jth step is $a_i^{(j)}$, and we define $a^{(j)} = \langle a_{2n-1}^{(j)}, a_{2n-2}^{(j)}, \ldots, a_0^{(j)} \rangle$.

The algorithm executes a sequence of n steps, numbered $0, 1, \ldots, n-1$, where each step takes one clock period. The algorithm maintains the invariant that before the jth step,

$$a^{(j)} \cdot b^{(j)} + p^{(j)} = a \cdot b \tag{29.6}$$

(see Exercise 29.4-2). Initially, $a^{(0)} = a$, $b^{(0)} = b$, and $p^{(0)} = 0$. The jth step consists of the following computations.

1. If $a^{(j)}$ is odd (that is, $a_0^{(j)} = 1$), then add b into p: $p^{(j+1)} \leftarrow b^{(j)} + p^{(j)}$. (The addition is performed by a ripple-carry adder that runs the length of the array; carry bits ripple from right to left.) If $a^{(j)}$ is even, then carry p through to the next step: $p^{(j+1)} \leftarrow p^{(j)}$.

2. Shift a right by one bit position:

$$a_i^{(j+1)} \leftarrow \begin{cases} a_{i+1}^{(j)} & \text{if } 0 \leq i \leq 2n-2 \text{,} \\ 0 & \text{if } i = 2n-1 \text{.} \end{cases}$$

3. Shift b left by one bit position:

$$b_i^{(j+1)} \leftarrow \begin{cases} b_{i-1}^{(j)} & \text{if } 1 \leq i \leq 2n-1 \text{,} \\ 0 & \text{if } i = 0 \text{.} \end{cases}$$

After running n steps, we have shifted out all the bits of a; thus, $a^{(n)} = 0$. Invariant (29.6) then implies that $p^{(n)} = a \cdot b$.

We now analyze the algorithm. There are n steps, assuming that the control information is broadcast to each cell simultaneously. Each step takes $\Theta(n)$ time in the worst case, because the depth of the ripple-carry adder is $\Theta(n)$, and thus the duration of the clock period must be at least $\Theta(n)$. Each shift takes only $\Theta(1)$ time. Overall, therefore, the algorithm takes $\Theta(n^2)$ time. Because each cell has constant size, the entire linear array has $\Theta(n)$ size.

A fast linear-array implementation

By using carry-save addition instead of ripple-carry addition, we can decrease the time for each step to $\Theta(1)$, thus improving the overall time to $\Theta(n)$. As Figure 29.19(b) shows, once again each cell contains a bit of an a entry and a bit of a b entry. Each cell also contains two more bits, from u and v, which are the outputs from carry-save addition. Using a carry-save

cell number

9	8	7	6	5	4	3	2	1	0	
0	0	0	0	0	1	0	0	1	1	$a^{(0)} = 19$
0	0	0	0	0	1	1	1	0	1	$b^{(0)} = 29$
0	0	0	0	0	0	0	0	0	0	$p^{(0)} = 0$

0	0	0	0	0	0	1	0	0	1	$a^{(1)} = 9$
0	0	0	0	1	1	1	0	1	0	$b^{(1)} = 58$
0	0	0	0	0	1	1	1	0	1	$p^{(1)} = 29$

0	0	0	0	0	0	0	1	0	0	$a^{(2)} = 4$
0	0	0	1	1	1	0	1	0	0	$b^{(2)} = 116$
0	0	0	1	0	1	0	1	1	1	$p^{(2)} = 87$

0	0	0	0	0	0	0	0	1	0	$a^{(3)} = 2$
0	0	1	1	1	0	1	0	0	0	$b^{(3)} = 232$
0	0	0	1	0	1	0	1	1	1	$p^{(3)} = 87$

0	0	0	0	0	0	0	0	0	1	$a^{(4)} = 1$
0	1	1	1	0	1	0	0	0	0	$b^{(4)} = 464$
0	0	0	1	0	1	0	1	1	1	$p^{(4)} = 87$

0	0	0	0	0	0	0	0	0	0	$a^{(5)} = 0$
1	1	1	0	1	0	0	0	0	0	$b^{(5)} = 928$
1	0	0	0	1	0	0	1	1	1	$p^{(5)} = 551$

(a)

cell number

9	8	7	6	5	4	3	2	1	0	
0	0	0	0	0	1	0	0	1	1	$a^{(0)} = 19$
0	0	0	0	0	1	1	1	0	1	$b^{(0)} = 29$
0	0	0	0	0	0	0	0	0	0	$u^{(0)} = 0$
0	0	0	0	0	0	0	0	0	0	$v^{(0)} = 0$

0	0	0	0	0	0	1	0	0	1	$a^{(1)} = 9$
0	0	0	0	1	1	1	0	1	0	$b^{(1)} = 58$
0	0	0	0	0	1	1	1	0	1	$u^{(1)} = 29$
0	0	0	0	0	0	0	0	0	0	$v^{(1)} = 0$

0	0	0	0	0	0	0	1	0	0	$a^{(2)} = 4$
0	0	0	1	1	1	0	1	0	0	$b^{(2)} = 116$
0	0	0	0	1	0	0	1	1	1	$u^{(2)} = 39$
0	0	0	0	1	1	0	0	0	0	$v^{(2)} = 48$

0	0	0	0	0	0	0	0	1	0	$a^{(3)} = 2$
0	0	1	1	1	0	1	0	0	0	$b^{(3)} = 232$
0	0	0	0	1	0	0	1	1	1	$u^{(3)} = 39$
0	0	0	0	1	1	0	0	0	0	$v^{(3)} = 48$

0	0	0	0	0	0	0	0	0	1	$a^{(4)} = 1$
0	1	1	1	0	1	0	0	0	0	$b^{(4)} = 464$
0	0	0	0	1	0	0	1	1	1	$u^{(4)} = 39$
0	0	0	0	1	1	0	0	0	0	$v^{(4)} = 48$

0	0	0	0	0	0	0	0	0	0	$a^{(5)} = 0$
1	1	1	0	1	0	0	0	0	0	$b^{(5)} = 928$
0	1	1	1	0	0	0	1	1	1	$u^{(5)} = 455$
0	0	0	1	1	0	0	0	0	0	$v^{(5)} = 96$

(b)

Figure 29.19 Two linear-array implementations of the Russian peasant's algorithm, showing the multiplication of $a = 19 = \langle 10011 \rangle$ by $b = 29 = \langle 11101 \rangle$, with $n = 5$. The situation at the beginning of each step j is shown, with the remaining significant bits of $a^{(j)}$ and $b^{(j)}$ shaded. **(a)** A slow implementation that runs in $\Theta(n^2)$ time. Because $a^{(5)} = 0$, we have $p^{(5)} = a \cdot b$. There are n steps, and each step uses a ripple-carry addition. The clock period is therefore proportional to the length of the array, or $\Theta(n)$, leading to $\Theta(n^2)$ time overall. **(b)** A fast implementation that runs in $\Theta(n)$ time because each step uses carry-save addition rather than ripple-carry addition, thus taking only $\Theta(1)$ time. There are a total of $2n - 1 = 9$ steps; after the last step shown, repeated carry-save addition of u and v yields $u^{(9)} = a \cdot b$.

representation to accumulate the product, we maintain the invariant that
before the jth step,

$$a^{(j)} \cdot b^{(j)} + u^{(j)} + v^{(j)} = a \cdot b \qquad (29.7)$$

(again, see Exercise 29.4-2). Each step shifts a and b in the same way as the
slow implementation, so that we can combine equations (29.6) and (29.7)
to yield $u^{(j)} + v^{(j)} = p^{(j)}$. Thus, the u and v bits contain the same information as the p bits in the slow implementation.

The jth step of the fast implementation performs carry-save addition
on u and v, where the operands depend on whether a is odd or even. If
$a_0^{(j)} = 1$, we compute

$$u_i^{(j+1)} \leftarrow \text{parity}(b_i^{(j)}, u_i^{(j)}, v_i^{(j)}) \qquad \text{for } i = 0, 1, \ldots, 2n - 1$$

and

$$v_i^{(j+1)} \leftarrow \begin{cases} \text{majority}(b_{i-1}^{(j)}, u_{i-1}^{(j)}, v_{i-1}^{(j)}) & \text{if } 1 \le i \le 2n - 1 \ , \\ 0 & \text{if } i = 0 \ . \end{cases}$$

Otherwise, $a_0^{(j)} = 0$, and we compute

$$u_i^{(j+1)} \leftarrow \text{parity}(0, u_i^{(j)}, v_i^{(j)}) \qquad \text{for } i = 0, 1, \ldots, 2n - 1$$

and

$$v_i^{(j+1)} \leftarrow \begin{cases} \text{majority}(0, u_{i-1}^{(j)}, v_{i-1}^{(j)}) & \text{if } 1 \le i \le 2n - 1 \ , \\ 0 & \text{if } i = 0 \ . \end{cases}$$

After updating u and v, the jth step shifts a to the right and b to the left
in the same manner as the slow implementation.

The fast implementation performs a total of $2n - 1$ steps. For $j \ge n$, we
have $a^{(j)} = 0$, and invariant (29.7) therefore implies that $u^{(j)} + v^{(j)} = a \cdot b$.
Once $a^{(j)} = 0$, all further steps serve only to carry-save add u and v.
Exercise 29.4-3 asks you to show that $v^{(2n-1)} = 0$, so that $u^{(2n-1)} = a \cdot b$.

The total time in the worst case is $\Theta(n)$, since each of the $2n - 1$ steps
takes $\Theta(1)$ time. Because each cell still has constant size, the total size
remains $\Theta(n)$.

Exercises

29.4-1
Let $a = \langle 101101 \rangle$, $b = \langle 011110 \rangle$, and $n = 6$. Show how the Russian
peasant's algorithm operates, in both decimal and binary, for inputs a
and b.

29.4-2
Prove the invariants (29.6) and (29.7) for the linear-array multipliers.

29.4-3
Prove that in the fast linear-array multiplier, $v^{(2n-1)} = 0$.

29.4-4
Describe how the array multiplier from Section 29.3.1 represents an "unrolling" of the computation of the fast linear-array multiplier.

29.4-5
Consider a data stream $\langle x_1, x_2, \ldots \rangle$ that arrives at a clocked circuit at the rate of 1 value per clock tick. For a fixed value n, the circuit must compute the value

$$y_t = \max_{t-n+1 \leq i \leq t} x_i$$

for $t = n, n + 1, \ldots$. That is, y_t is the maximum of the most recent n values received by the circuit. Give an $O(n)$-size circuit that on each clock tick inputs the value x_t and computes the output value y_t in $O(1)$ time. The circuit can use registers and combinational elements that compute the maximum of two inputs.

29.4-6 ★
Redo Exercise 29.4-5 using only $O(\lg n)$ "maximum" elements.

Problems

29-1 Division circuits
We can construct a division circuit from subtraction and multiplication circuits with a technique called *Newton iteration*. We shall focus on the related problem of computing a reciprocal, since we can obtain a division circuit by making one additional multiplication.

The idea is to compute a sequence $y_0, y_1, y_2, \ldots$ of approximations to the reciprocal of a number x by using the formula

$$y_{i+1} \leftarrow 2y_i - xy_i^2 \, .$$

Assume that x is given as an n-bit binary fraction in the range $1/2 \leq x \leq 1$. Since the reciprocal can be an infinite repeating fraction, we shall concentrate on computing an n-bit approximation accurate up to its least significant bit.

a. Suppose that $|y_i - 1/x| \leq \epsilon$ for some constant $\epsilon > 0$. Prove that $|y_{i+1} - 1/x| \leq \epsilon^2$.

b. Give an initial approximation y_0 such that y_k satisfies $|y_k - 1/x| \leq 2^{-2^k}$ for all $k \geq 0$. How large must k be for the approximation y_k to be accurate up to its least significant bit?

c. Describe a combinational circuit that, given an n-bit input x, computes an n-bit approximation to $1/x$ in $O(\lg^2 n)$ time. What is the size of your circuit? (*Hint:* With a little cleverness, you can beat the size bound of $\Theta(n^2 \lg n)$.)

29-2   *Boolean formulas for symmetric functions*

A n-input function $f(x_1, x_2, \ldots, x_n)$ is **symmetric** if

$$f(x_1, x_2, \ldots, x_n) = f(x_{\pi(1)}, x_{\pi(2)}, \ldots, x_{\pi(n)})$$

for any permutation π of $\{1, 2, \ldots, n\}$. In this problem, we shall show that there is a boolean formula representing f whose size is polynomial in n. (For our purposes, a boolean formula is a string comprised of the variables $x_1, x_2, \ldots, x_n$, parentheses, and the boolean operators $\vee$, $\wedge$, and $\neg$.) Our approach will be to convert a logarithmic-depth boolean circuit to an equivalent polynomial-size boolean formula. We shall assume that all circuits are constructed from 2-input AND, 2-input OR, and NOT gates.

a. We start by considering a simple symmetric function. The generalized **majority function** on n boolean inputs is defined by

$$\text{majority}_n(x_1, x_2, \ldots, x_n) = \begin{cases} 1 & \text{if } x_1 + x_2 + \cdots + x_n > n/2 \ , \\ 0 & \text{otherwise} \ . \end{cases}$$

Describe an $O(\lg n)$-depth combinational circuit for majority_n. (*Hint:* Build a tree of adders.)

b. Suppose that f is an arbitrary boolean function of the n boolean variables $x_1, x_2, \ldots, x_n$. Suppose further that there is a circuit C of depth d that computes f. Show how to construct from C a boolean formula for f of length $O(2^d)$. Conclude that there is polynomial-size formula for majority_n.

c. Argue that any symmetric boolean function $f(x_1, x_2, \ldots, x_n)$ can be expressed as a function of $\sum_{i=1}^{n} x_i$.

d. Argue that any symmetric function on n boolean inputs can be computed by an $O(\lg n)$-depth combinational circuit.

e. Argue that any symmetric boolean function on n boolean variables can be represented by a boolean formula whose length is polynomial in n.

Chapter notes

Most books on computer arithmetic focus more on practical implementations of circuitry than on algorithmic theory. Savage [173] is one of the few that investigates algorithmic aspects of the subject. The more hardware-oriented books on computer arithmetic by Cavanagh [39] and Hwang [108] are especially readable. Good books on combinational and sequential logic design include Hill and Peterson [96] and, with a twist toward formal language theory, Kohavi [126].

Aiken and Hopper [7] trace the early history of arithmetic algorithms. Ripple-carry addition is as at least as old as the abacus, which has been around for over 5000 years. The first mechanical calculator employing ripple-carry addition was devised by B. Pascal in 1642. A calculating machine adapted to repeated addition for multiplication was conceived by S. Morland in 1666 and independently by G. W. Leibnitz in 1671. The Russian peasant's algorithm for multiplication is apparently much older than its use in Russia in the nineteenth century. According to Knuth [122], it was used by Egyptian mathematicians as long ago as 1800 B.C.

The kill, generate, and propagate statuses of a carry chain were exploited in a relay calculator built at Harvard during the mid-1940's [180]. One of the first implementations of carry-lookahead addition was described by Weinberger and Smith [199], but their lookahead method requires large gates. Ofman [152] proved that n-bit numbers could be added in $O(\lg n)$ time using carry-lookahead addition with constant-size gates.

The idea of using carry-save addition to speed up multiplication is due to Estrin, Gilchrist, and Pomerene [64]. Atrubin [13] describes a linear-array multiplier of infinite length that can be used to multiply binary numbers of arbitrary length. The multiplier produces the nth bit of the product immediately upon receiving the nth bits of the inputs. The Wallace-tree multiplier is attributed to Wallace [197], but the idea was also independently discovered by Ofman [152].

Division algorithms date back to I. Newton, who around 1665 invented what has become known as Newton iteration. Problem 29-1 uses Newton iteration to construct a division circuit with $\Theta(\lg^2 n)$ depth. This method was improved by Beame, Cook, and Hoover [19], who showed that n-bit division can in fact be performed in $\Theta(\lg n)$ depth.

Algorithms for Parallel Computers

As parallel-processing computers have proliferated, interest has increased in *parallel algorithms*: algorithms that perform more than one operation at a time. The study of parallel algorithms has now developed into a research area in its own right. Indeed, parallel algorithms have been developed for many of the problems we have solved in this text using ordinary serial algorithms. In this chapter, we shall describe a few simple parallel algorithms that illustrate fundamental issues and techniques.

In order to study parallel algorithms, we must choose an appropriate model for parallel computing. The random-access machine, or RAM, which we have used throughout most of this book, is, of course, serial rather than parallel. The parallel models we have studied—sorting networks (Chapter 28) and circuits (Chapter 29)—are too restrictive for investigating, for example, algorithms on data structures.

The parallel algorithms in this chapter are presented in terms of one popular theoretical model: the parallel random-access machine, or PRAM (pronounced "PEE-ram"). Many parallel algorithms for arrays, lists, trees, and graphs can be easily described in the PRAM model. Although the PRAM ignores many important aspects of real parallel machines, the essential attributes of parallel algorithms tend to transcend the models for which they are designed. If one PRAM algorithm outperforms another PRAM algorithm, the relative performance is not likely to change substantially when both algorithms are adapted to run on a real parallel computer.

The PRAM model

Figure 30.1 shows the basic architecture of the *parallel random-access machine* (*PRAM*). There are p ordinary (serial) processors $P_0, P_1, \ldots, P_{p-1}$ that have as storage a shared, global memory. All processors can read from or write to the global memory "in parallel" (at the same time). The processors can also perform various arithmetic and logical operations in parallel.

The key assumption regarding algorithmic performance in the PRAM model is that running time can be measured as the number of parallel memory accesses an algorithm performs. This assumption is a straightforward generalization of the ordinary RAM model, in which the number

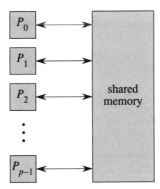

Figure 30.1 The basic architecture of the PRAM. There are p processors $P_0, P_1, \ldots, P_{p-1}$ connected to a shared memory. Each processor can access an arbitrary word of shared memory in unit time.

of memory accesses is asymptotically as good as any other measure of running time. This simple assumption will serve us well in our survey of parallel algorithms, even though real parallel computers cannot perform parallel accesses to global memory in unit time: the time for a memory access grows with the number of processors in the parallel computer.

Nevertheless, for parallel algorithms that access data in an arbitrary fashion, the assumption of unit-time memory operations can be justified. Real parallel machines typically have a communication network that can support the abstraction of a global memory. Accessing data through the network is a relatively slow operation in comparison with arithmetic and other operations. Thus, counting the number of parallel memory accesses executed by two parallel algorithms does, in fact, yield a fairly accurate estimate of their relative performances. The principal way in which real machines violate the unit-time abstraction of the PRAM is that some memory-access patterns are faster than others. As a first approximation, however, the unit-time assumption in the PRAM model is quite reasonable.

The running time of a parallel algorithm depends on the number of processors executing the algorithm as well as the size of the problem input. Generally, therefore, we must discuss both time and processor count when analyzing PRAM algorithms; this contrasts with serial algorithms, in whose analysis we have focused mainly on time. Typically, there is a trade-off between the number of processors used by an algorithm and its running time. Section 30.3 discusses these trade-offs.

Concurrent versus exclusive memory accesses

A *concurrent-read* algorithm is a PRAM algorithm during whose execution multiple processors can read from the same location of shared memory at the same time. An *exclusive-read* algorithm is a PRAM algorithm in which no two processors ever read the same memory location at the same time. We make a similar distinction with respect to whether or not multiple processors can write into the same memory location at the same time, dividing PRAM algorithms into *concurrent-write* and *exclusive-write* algorithms. Commonly used abbreviations for the types of algorithms we encounter are

- *EREW*: exclusive read and exclusive write,
- *CREW*: concurrent read and exclusive write,
- *ERCW*: exclusive read and concurrent write, and
- *CRCW*: concurrent read and concurrent write.

(These abbreviations are usually pronounced not as words but rather as strings of letters.)

Of these types of algorithms, the extremes—EREW and CRCW—are the most popular. A PRAM that supports only EREW algorithms is called an *EREW PRAM*, and one that supports CRCW algorithms is called a *CRCW PRAM*. A CRCW PRAM can, of course, execute EREW algorithms, but an EREW PRAM cannot directly support the concurrent memory accesses required in CRCW algorithms. The underlying hardware of an EREW PRAM is relatively simple, and therefore fast, because it needn't handle conflicting memory reads and writes. A CRCW PRAM requires more hardware support if the unit-time assumption is to provide a reasonably accurate measure of algorithmic performance, but it provides a programming model that is arguably more straightforward than that of an EREW PRAM.

Of the remaining two algorithmic types—CREW and ERCW—more attention has been paid in the literature to the CREW. From a practical point of view, however, supporting concurrency for writes is no harder than supporting concurrency for reads. In this chapter, we shall generally treat an algorithm as being CRCW if it contains either concurrent reads or concurrent writes, without making further distinctions. We discuss the finer points of this distinction in Section 30.2.

When multiple processors write to the same location in a CRCW algorithm, the effect of the parallel write is not well defined without additional elaboration. In this chapter, we shall use the *common-CRCW* model: when several processors write into the same memory location, they must all write a common (the same) value. There are several alternative types of PRAM's in the literature that handle this problem with a different assumption. Other choices include

- *arbitrary*: an arbitrary value from among those written is actually stored,
- *priority*: the value written by the lowest-indexed processor is stored, and
- *combining*: the value stored is some specified combination of the values written.

In the last case, the specified combination is typically some associative and commutative function such as addition (store the sum of all the values written) or maximum (store only the maximum value written).

Synchronization and control

PRAM algorithms must be highly synchronized to work correctly. How is this synchronization achieved? Also, the processors in PRAM algorithms must often detect termination of loop conditions that depend on the state of all processors. How is this control function implemented?

We won't discuss these issues extensively. Many real parallel computers employ a control network connecting the processors that helps with synchronization and termination conditions. Typically, the control network can implement these functions as fast as a routing network can implement global memory references.

For our purposes, it suffices to assume that the processors are inherently tightly synchronized. All processors execute the same statements at the same time. No processor races ahead while others are further back in the code. As we go through our first parallel algorithm, we shall point out where we assume that processors are synchronized.

For detecting the termination of a parallel loop that depends on the state of all processors, we shall assume that a parallel termination condition can be tested through the control network in $O(1)$ time. Some EREW PRAM models in the literature do not make this assumption, and the (logarithmic) time for testing the loop condition must be included in the overall running time (see Exercise 30.1-8). As we shall see in Section 30.2, CRCW PRAM's do not need a control network to test termination: they can detect termination of a parallel loop in $O(1)$ time through the use of concurrent writes.

Chapter outline

Section 30.1 introduces the technique of pointer jumping, which provides a fast way to manipulate lists in parallel. We show how pointer jumping can be used to perform prefix computations on lists and how fast algorithms on lists can be adapted for use on trees. Section 30.2 discusses the relative power of CRCW and EREW algorithms and shows that concurrent memory accessing provides increased power.

Section 30.3 presents Brent's theorem, which shows how combinational circuits can be efficiently simulated by PRAM's. The section also discusses the important issue of work efficiency and gives conditions under which a p-processor PRAM algorithm can be efficiently translated into a p'-processor PRAM algorithm for any $p' < p$. Section 30.4 reprises the problem of performing a prefix computation on a linked list and shows how a randomized algorithm can perform the computation in a work-efficient fashion. Finally, Section 30.5 shows how symmetry can be broken in parallel in much less than logarithmic time using a deterministic algorithm.

The parallel algorithms in this chapter have been drawn principally from the area of graph theory. They represent only a scant selection of the present array of parallel algorithms. The techniques introduced in this chapter, however, are quite representative of the techniques used for parallel algorithms in other areas of computer science.

30.1 Pointer jumping

Among the more interesting PRAM algorithms are those that involve pointers. In this section, we investigate a powerful technique called pointer jumping, which yields fast algorithms for operating on lists. Specifically, we introduce an $O(\lg n)$-time algorithm that computes the distance to the end of the list for each object in an n-object list. We then modify this algorithm to perform a "parallel prefix" computation on an n-object list in $O(\lg n)$ time. Finally, we investigate a technique that allows many problems on trees to be converted to list problems, which can then be solved by pointer jumping. All of the algorithms in this section are EREW algorithms: no concurrent accesses to global memory are required.

30.1.1 List ranking

Our first parallel algorithm operates on lists. We can store a list in a PRAM much as we store lists in an ordinary RAM. To operate on list objects in parallel, however, it is convenient to assign a "responsible" processor to each object. We shall assume that there are as many processors as list objects, and that the ith processor is responsible for the ith object. Figure 30.2(a), for example, shows a linked list consisting of the sequence of objects $\langle 3, 4, 6, 1, 0, 5 \rangle$. Since there is one processor per list object, every object in the list can be operated on by its responsible processor in $O(1)$ time.

Suppose that we are given a singly linked list L with n objects and wish to compute, for each object in L, its distance from the end of the list. More formally, if *next* is the pointer field, we wish to compute a value $d[i]$ for each object i in the list such that

$$d[i] = \begin{cases} 0 & \text{if } next[i] = \text{NIL} , \\ d[next[i]] + 1 & \text{if } next[i] \neq \text{NIL} . \end{cases}$$

We call the problem of computing the d values the *list-ranking problem*.

One solution to the list-ranking problem is simply to propagate distances back from the end of the list. This method takes $\Theta(n)$ time, since the kth object from the end must wait for the $k-1$ objects following it to determine

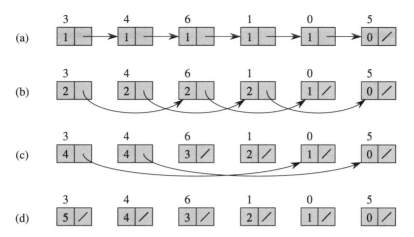

Figure 30.2   Finding the distance from each object in an *n*-object list to the end of the list in $O(\lg n)$ time using pointer jumping. **(a)** A linked list represented in a PRAM with *d* values initialized. At the end of the algorithm, each *d* value holds the distance of its object from the end of the list. Each object's responsible processor appears above the object. **(b)–(d)** The pointers and *d* values after each iteration of the **while** loop in the algorithm LIST-RANK.

their distances from the end before it can determine its own. This solution is essentially a serial algorithm.

An efficient parallel solution, requiring only $O(\lg n)$ time, is given by the following parallel pseudocode.

LIST-RANK(L)

```
1  for each processor i, in parallel
2      do if next[i] = NIL
3          then d[i] ← 0
4          else d[i] ← 1
5  while there exists an object i such that next[i] ≠ NIL
6      do for each processor i, in parallel
7          do if next[i] ≠ NIL
8              then d[i] ← d[i] + d[next[i]]
9                  next[i] ← next[next[i]]
```

Figure 30.2 shows how the algorithm computes the distances. Each part of the figure shows the state of the list before an iteration of the **while** loop of lines 5–9. Part (a) shows the list just after initialization. In the first iteration, the first 5 list objects have non-NIL pointers, so that lines 8–9 are executed by their responsible processors. The result appears in part (b) of the figure. In the second iteration, only the first 4 objects have non-NIL pointers; the result of this iteration is shown in part (c). In the third iteration, only the first 2 objects are operated on, and the final result, in which all objects have NIL pointers, appears in part (d).

The idea implemented by line 9, in which we set $next[i] \leftarrow next[next[i]]$ for all non-NIL pointers $next[i]$, is called ***pointer jumping***. Note that the pointer fields are changed by pointer jumping, thus destroying the structure of the list. If the list structure must be preserved, then we make copies of the *next* pointers and use the copies to compute the distances.

Correctness

LIST-RANK maintains the invariant that at the beginning of each iteration of the **while** loop of lines 5–9, for each object i, if we add the d values in the sublist headed by i, we obtain the correct distance from i to the end of the original list L. In Figure 30.2(b), for example, the sublist headed by object 3 is the sequence $\langle 3, 6, 0 \rangle$ whose d values 2, 2, and 1 sum to 5, its distance from the end of the original list. The reason the invariant is maintained is that when each object "splices out" its successor in the list, it adds its successor's d value to its own.

Observe that for this pointer-jumping algorithm to work correctly, the parallel memory accesses must be synchronized. Each execution of line 9 can update several *next* pointers. We rely on all the memory reads on the right-hand side of the assignment (reading $next[next[i]]$) occurring before any of the memory writes (writing $next[i]$) on the left-hand side.

Now let us see why LIST-RANK is an EREW algorithm. Because each processor is responsible for at most one object, every read and write in lines 2–7 is exclusive, as are the writes in lines 8–9. Observe that pointer jumping maintains the invariant that for any two distinct objects i and j, either $next[i] \neq next[j]$ or $next[i] = next[j] = $ NIL. This invariant is certainly true for the initial list, and it is maintained by line 9. Because all non-NIL *next* values are distinct, all reads in line 9 are exclusive.

We do need to assume that some synchronization is performed in line 8 if all reads are to be exclusive. In particular, we require that all processors i read $d[i]$ and then $d[next[i]]$. With this synchronization, if an object i has $next[i] \neq $ NIL and there is another object j pointing to i (that is, $next[j] = i$), then the first read fetches $d[i]$ for processor i and the second read fetches $d[i]$ for processor j. Thus, LIST-RANK is an EREW algorithm.

From here on, we ignore such details of synchronization and assume that the PRAM and its pseudocode programming environment act in a consistent, synchronized manner, with all processors executing reads and writes at the same time.

Analysis

We now show that if there are n objects in list L, then LIST-RANK takes $O(\lg n)$ time. Since the initialization takes $O(1)$ time and each iteration of the **while** loop takes $O(1)$ time, it suffices to show that there are exactly $\lceil \lg n \rceil$ iterations. The key observation is that each step of pointer jumping transforms each list into two interleaved lists: one consisting of the objects in even positions and the other consisting of objects in odd positions. Thus, each pointer-jumping step doubles the number of lists and halves their lengths. By the end of $\lceil \lg n \rceil$ iterations, therefore, all lists contain only one object.

We are assuming that the termination test in line 5 takes $O(1)$ time, presumably due to a control network in the EREW PRAM. Exercise 30.1-8 asks you to describe an $O(\lg n)$-time EREW implementation of LIST-RANK that performs the termination test explicitly in the pseudocode.

Besides parallel running time, there is another interesting performance measure for parallel algorithms. We define the **work** performed by a parallel algorithm as the product of its running time and the number of processors it requires. Intuitively, the work is the amount of computing that a serial RAM performs when it simulates the parallel algorithm.

The procedure LIST-RANK performs $\Theta(n \lg n)$ work, since it requires n processors and runs in $\Theta(\lg n)$ time. The straightforward serial algorithm for the list-ranking problem runs in $\Theta(n)$ time, indicating that more work is performed by LIST-RANK than is absolutely necessary, but only by a logarithmic factor.

We define a PRAM algorithm A to be **work-efficient** with respect to another (serial or parallel) algorithm B for the same problem if the work performed by A is within a constant factor of the work performed by B. We also say more simply that a PRAM algorithm A is **work-efficient** if it is work-efficient with respect to the best possible algorithm on a serial RAM. Since the best possible serial algorithm for list ranking runs in $\Theta(n)$ time on a serial RAM, LIST-RANK is not work-efficient. We shall present a work-efficient parallel algorithm for list ranking in Section 30.4.

30.1.2 Parallel prefix on a list

The technique of pointer jumping extends well beyond the application of list ranking. Section 29.2.2 shows how, in the context of arithmetic circuits, a "prefix" computation can be used to perform binary addition quickly. We now investigate how pointer jumping can be used to perform prefix computations. Our EREW algorithm for the prefix problem runs in $O(\lg n)$ time on n-object lists.

A **prefix computation** is defined in terms of a binary, associative operator $\otimes$. The computation takes as input a sequence $\langle x_1, x_2, \ldots, x_n \rangle$ and produces as output a sequence $\langle y_1, y_2, \ldots, y_n \rangle$ such that $y_1 = x_1$ and

$$
\begin{aligned}
y_k &= y_{k-1} \otimes x_k \\
&= x_1 \otimes x_2 \otimes \cdots \otimes x_k
\end{aligned}
$$

for $k = 2, 3, \ldots, n$. In other words, each y_k is obtained by "multiplying" together the first k elements of the sequence of x_k—hence, the term "prefix." (The definition in Chapter 29 indexes the sequences from 0, whereas this definition indexes from 1—an inessential difference.)

As an example of a prefix computation, suppose that every element of an n-object list contains the value 1, and let $\otimes$ be ordinary addition. Since the kth element of the list contains the value $x_k = 1$ for $k = 1, 2, \ldots, n$, a prefix computation produces $y_k = k$, the index of the kth element. Thus, another way to perform list ranking is to reverse the list (which can be done in $O(1)$ time), perform this prefix computation, and subtract 1 from each value computed.

We now show how an EREW algorithm can compute parallel prefixes in $O(\lg n)$ time on n-object lists. For convenience, we define the notation

$$[i, j] = x_i \otimes x_{i+1} \otimes \cdots \otimes x_j$$

for integers i and j in the range $1 \leq i \leq j \leq n$. Then, $[k, k] = x_k$ for $k = 1, 2, \ldots, n$, and

$$[i, k] = [i, j] \otimes [j + 1, k]$$

for $0 \leq i \leq j < k \leq n$. In terms of this notation, the goal of a prefix computation is to compute $y_k = [1, k]$ for $k = 1, 2, \ldots, n$.

When we perform a prefix computation on a list, we wish the order of the input sequence $\langle x_1, x_2, \ldots, x_n \rangle$ to be determined by how the objects are linked together in the list, and not by the index of the object in the array of memory that stores objects. (Exercise 30.1-2 asks for a prefix algorithm for arrays.) The following EREW algorithm starts with a value $x[i]$ in each object i in a list L. If object i is the kth object from the beginning of the list, then $x[i] = x_k$ is the kth element of the input sequence. Thus, the parallel prefix computation produces $y[i] = y_k = [1, k]$.

LIST-PREFIX(L)

```
1  for each processor i, in parallel
2      do y[i] ← x[i]
3  while there exists an object i such that next[i] ≠ NIL
4      do for each processor i, in parallel
5          do if next[i] ≠ NIL
6              then y[next[i]] ← y[i] ⊗ y[next[i]]
7                   next[i] ← next[next[i]]
```

The pseudocode and Figure 30.3 indicate the similarity between this algorithm and LIST-RANK. The only differences are the initialization and the updating of d or y values. In LIST-RANK, processor i updates $d[i]$—its own d value—whereas in LIST-PREFIX, processor i updates $y[next[i]]$—another processor's y value. Note that LIST-PREFIX is EREW for the same reason as LIST-RANK: pointer jumping maintains the invariant that for distinct objects i and j, either $next[i] \neq next[j]$ or $next[i] = next[j] = $ NIL.

Figure 30.3 shows the state of the list before each iteration of the **while** loop. The procedure maintains the invariant that at the end of the tth execution of the **while** loop, the kth processor stores $[\max(1, k - 2^t + 1), k]$,

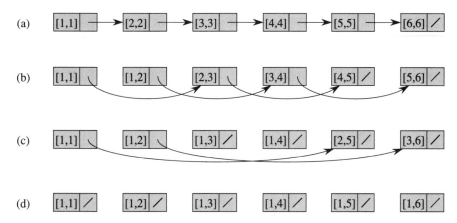

Figure 30.3   The parallel prefix algorithm LIST-PREFIX on a linked list. **(a)** The initial y value of the kth object in the list is $[k, k]$. The *next* pointer of the kth object points to the $(k + 1)$st object, or NIL for the last object. **(b)–(d)** The y and *next* values before each test in line 3. The final answer is in part **(d)**, in which the y value for the kth object is $[1, k]$ for all k.

for $k = 1, 2, \ldots, n$. In the first iteration, the kth list object points initially to the $(k + 1)$st object, except that the last object has a NIL pointer. Line 6 causes the kth object, for $k = 1, 2, \ldots, n - 1$, to fetch the value $[k + 1, k + 1]$ from its successor. It then performs the operation $[k, k] \otimes [k + 1, k + 1]$, yielding $[k, k + 1]$, which it stores back into its successor. The *next* pointers are then jumped as in LIST-RANK, and the result of the first iteration appears in Figure 30.3(b). We can view the second iteration similarly. For $k = 1, 2, \ldots, n - 2$, the kth object fetches the value $[k + 1, k + 2]$ from its successor (as defined by the new value in its field *next*), and then it stores $[k - 1, k] \otimes [k + 1, k + 2] = [k - 1, k + 2]$ into its successor. The result is shown in Figure 30.3(c). In the third and final iteration, only the first two list objects have non-NIL pointers, and they fetch values from their successors in their respective lists. The final result appears in Figure 30.3(d). The key observation that makes LIST-PREFIX work is that at each step, if we perform a prefix computation on each of the several existing lists, each object obtains its correct value.

Since the two algorithms use the same pointer-jumping mechanism, LIST-PREFIX has the same analysis as LIST-RANK: the running time is $O(\lg n)$ on an EREW PRAM, and the total work performed is $\Theta(n \lg n)$.

30.1.3   The Euler-tour technique

In this section, we shall introduce the Euler-tour technique and show how it can be applied to the problem of computing the depth of each node in an n-node binary tree. A key step in this $O(\lg n)$-time EREW algorithm is a parallel prefix computation.

To store binary trees in a PRAM, we use a simple binary-tree representation of the sort presented in Section 11.4. Each node i has fields *parent*[i], *left*[i], and *right*[i], which point to node i's parent, left child, and right child, respectively. Let us assume that each node is identified by a non-negative integer. For reasons that will soon become apparent, we associate not one but three processors with each node; we call these the node's A, B, and C processors. We should be able to map between a node and its three processors easily; for example, node i might be associated with processors $3i$, $3i + 1$, and $3i + 2$.

Computing the depth of each node in an n-node tree takes $O(n)$ time on a serial RAM. A simple parallel algorithm to compute depths propagates a "wave" downward from the root of the tree. The wave reaches all nodes at the same depth simultaneously, and thus by incrementing a counter carried along with the wave, we can compute the depth of each node. This parallel algorithm works well on a complete binary tree, since it runs in time proportional to the tree's height. The height of the tree could be as large as $n - 1$, however, in which case the algorithm would run in $\Theta(n)$ time—no better than the serial algorithm. Using the Euler-tour technique, however, we can compute node depths in $O(\lg n)$ time on an EREW PRAM, whatever the height of the tree.

An ***Euler tour*** of a graph is a cycle that traverses each edge exactly once, although it may visit a vertex more than once. By Problem 23-3, a connected, directed graph has an Euler tour if and only if for all vertices v, the in-degree of v equals the out-degree of v. Since each undirected edge (u, v) in an undirected graph maps to two directed edges (u, v) and (v, u) in the directed version, the directed version of any connected, undirected graph—and therefore of any undirected tree—has an Euler tour.

To compute the depths of nodes in a binary tree T, we first form an Euler tour of the directed version of T (viewed as an undirected graph). The tour corresponds to a walk of the tree and is represented in Figure 30.4(a) by a linked list running through the nodes of the tree. Its structure is as follows:

- A node's A processor points to the A processor of its left child, if it exists, and otherwise to its own B processor.

- A node's B processor points to the A processor of its right child, if it exists, and otherwise to its own C processor.

- A node's C processor points to the B processor of its parent if it is a left child and to the C processor of its parent if it is a right child. The root's C processor points to NIL.

Thus, the head of the linked list formed by the Euler tour is the root's A processor, and the tail is the root's C processor. Given the pointers composing the original tree, an Euler tour can be constructed in $O(1)$ time.

Once we have the linked list representing the Euler tour of T, we place a 1 in each A processor, a 0 in each B processor, and a -1 in each C processor, as shown in Figure 30.4(a). We then perform a parallel prefix

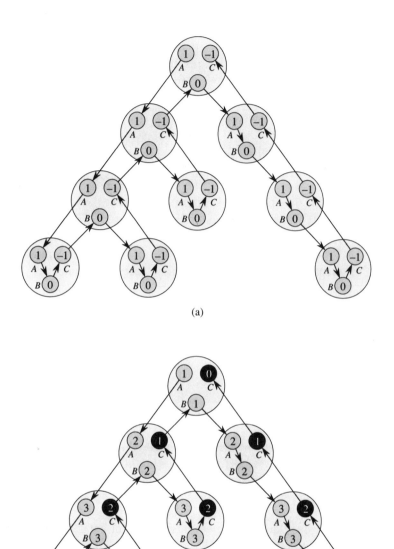

(a)

(b)

Figure 30.4   Using the Euler-tour technique to compute the depth of each node in a binary tree. **(a)** The Euler tour is a list corresponding to a walk of the tree. Each processor contains a number used by a parallel prefix computation to compute node depths. **(b)** The result of the parallel prefix computation on the linked list from (a). The C processor of each node (blackened) contains the node's depth. (You can verify the result of this prefix computation by computing it serially.)

computation using ordinary addition as the associative operation, as we did in Section 30.1.2. Figure 30.4(b) shows the result of the parallel prefix computation.

We claim that after performing the parallel prefix computation, the depth of each node resides in the node's C processor. Why? The numbers are placed into the A, B, and C processors in such a way that the net effect of visiting a subtree is to add 0 to the running sum. The A processor of each node i contributes 1 to the running sum in i's left subtree, reflecting the depth of i's left child being one greater than the depth of i. The B processor contributes 0 because the depth of node i's left child equals the depth of node i's right child. The C processor contributes -1, so that from the perspective of node i's parent, the entire visit to the subtree rooted at node i has no effect on the running sum.

The list representing the Euler tour can be computed in $O(1)$ time. It has $3n$ objects, and thus the the parallel prefix computation takes only $O(\lg n)$ time. Thus, the total amount of time to compute all node depths is $O(\lg n)$. Because no concurrent memory accesses are needed, the algorithm is an EREW algorithm.

Exercises

30.1-1
Give an $O(\lg n)$-time EREW algorithm that determines for each object in an n-object list whether it is the middle ($\lfloor n/2 \rfloor$th) object.

30.1-2
Give an $O(\lg n)$-time EREW algorithm to perform the prefix computation on an array $x[1 .. n]$. Do not use pointers, but perform index computations directly.

30.1-3
Suppose that each object in an n-object list L is colored either red or blue. Give an efficient EREW algorithm to form two lists from the objects in L: one consisting of the blue objects and one consisting of the red objects.

30.1-4
An EREW PRAM has n objects distributed among several disjoint circular lists. Give an efficient algorithm that determines an arbitrary representative object for each list and acquaints each object in the list with the identity of the representative. Assume that each processor knows its own unique index.

30.1-5
Give an $O(\lg n)$-time EREW algorithm to compute the size of the subtree rooted at each node of an n-node binary tree. (*Hint:* Take the difference of two values in a running sum along an Euler tour.)

30.1-6

Give an efficient EREW algorithm to compute preorder, inorder, and post-order numberings for an arbitrary binary tree.

30.1-7

Extend the Euler-tour technique from binary trees to ordered trees with arbitrary node degrees. Specifically, describe a representation for ordered trees that allows the Euler-tour technique to be applied. Give an EREW algorithm to compute the node depths of an n-node ordered tree in $O(\lg n)$ time.

30.1-8

Describe an $O(\lg n)$-time EREW implementation of LIST-RANK that performs the loop-termination test explicitly. (*Hint:* Interleave the test with the loop body.)

30.2 CRCW algorithms versus EREW algorithms

The debate about whether or not concurrent memory accesses should be provided by the hardware of a parallel computer is a messy one. Some argue that hardware mechanisms to support CRCW algorithms are too expensive and used too infrequently to be justified. Others complain that EREW PRAM's provide too restrictive a programming model. The answer to this debate probably lies somewhere in the middle, and various compromise models have been proposed. Nevertheless, it is instructive to examine what algorithmic advantage is provided by concurrent accesses to memory.

In this section, we shall show that there are problems on which a CRCW algorithm outperforms the best possible EREW algorithm. For the problem of finding the identities of the roots of trees in a forest, concurrent reads allow for a faster algorithm. For the problem of finding the maximum element in an array, concurrent writes permit a faster algorithm.

A problem in which concurrent reads help

Suppose we are given a forest of binary trees in which each node i has a pointer *parent*[i] to its parent, and we wish each node to find the identity of the root of its tree. Associating processor i with each node i in a forest F, the following pointer-jumping algorithm stores the identity of the root of each node i's tree in *root*[i].

FIND-ROOTS(F)

```
1  for each processor i, in parallel
2      do if parent[i] = NIL
3          then root[i] ← i
4  while there exists a node i such that parent[i] ≠ NIL
5      do for each processor i, in parallel
6          do if parent[i] ≠ NIL
7              then root[i] ← root[parent[i]]
8                   parent[i] ← parent[parent[i]]
```

Figure 30.5 illustrates the operation of this algorithm. After the initialization performed by lines 1–3, shown in Figure 30.5(a), the only nodes that know the identities of their roots are the roots themselves. The **while** loop of lines 4–8 performs the pointer jumping and fills in the *root* fields. Figures 30.5(b)–(d) show the state of the forest after the first, second, and third iterations of the loop. As you can see, the algorithm maintains the invariant that if *parent*[i] = NIL, then *root*[i] has been assigned the identity of the node's root.

We claim that FIND-ROOTS is a CREW algorithm that runs in $O(\lg d)$ time, where d is the depth of the maximum-depth tree in the forest. The only writes occur on lines 3, 7, and 8, and these are all exclusive because in each one, processor i writes into only node i. The reads in lines 7–8 are concurrent, however, because several nodes may have pointers to the same node. In Figure 30.5(b), for example, we see that during the second iteration of the **while** loop, *root*[4] and *parent*[4] are read by processors 18, 2, and 7.

The running time of FIND-ROOTS is $O(\lg d)$ for essentially the same reason as for LIST-RANK: the length of each path is halved in each iteration. Figure 30.5 shows this characteristic plainly.

How fast can n nodes in a forest determine the roots of their binary trees using only exclusive reads? A simple argument shows that $\Omega(\lg n)$ time is required. The key observation is that when reads are exclusive, each step of the PRAM allows a given piece of information to be copied to at most one other memory location; thus the number of locations that can contain a given piece of information at most doubles with each step. Looking at a single tree, we have initially that at most 1 memory location stores the identity of the root. After 1 step, at most 2 locations can contain the identity of the root; after k steps, at most 2^{k-1} locations can contain the identity of the root. If the size of the tree is $\Theta(n)$, we need $\Theta(n)$ locations to contain the root's identity when the algorithm terminates; thus, $\Omega(\lg n)$ steps are required in all.

Whenever the depth d of the maximum-depth tree in the forest is $2^{o(\lg n)}$, the CREW algorithm FIND-ROOTS asymptotically outperforms any EREW algorithm. Specifically, for any n-node forest whose maximum-depth tree is a balanced binary tree with $\Theta(n)$ nodes, $d = O(\lg n)$, in which case FIND-

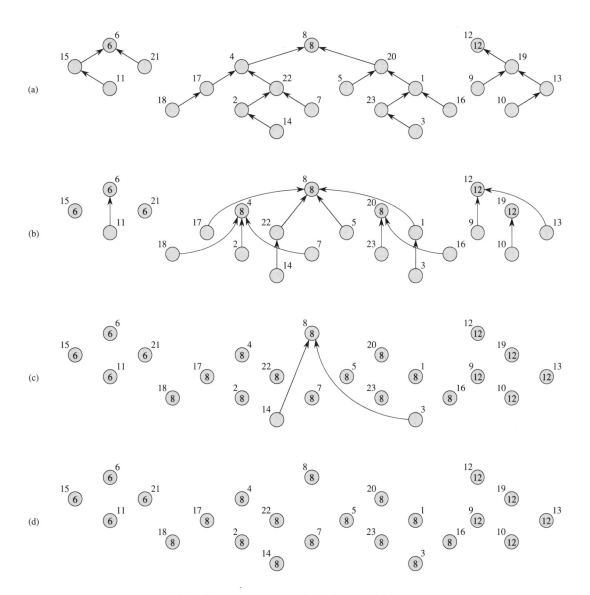

Figure 30.5 Finding the roots in a forest of binary trees on a CREW PRAM. Node numbers are next to the nodes, and stored *root* fields appear within nodes. The links represent *parent* pointers. **(a)–(d)** The state of the trees in the forest each time line 4 of FIND-ROOTS is executed. Note that path lengths are halved in each iteration.

ROOTS runs in $O(\lg \lg n)$ time. Any EREW algorithm for this problem must run in $\Omega(\lg n)$ time, which is asymptotically slower. Thus, concurrent reads help for this problem. Exercise 30.2-1 gives a simpler scenario in which concurrent reads help.

A problem in which concurrent writes help

To demonstrate that concurrent writes offer a performance advantage over exclusive writes, we examine the problem of finding the the maximum element in an array of real numbers. We shall see that any EREW algorithm for this problem takes $\Omega(\lg n)$ time and that no CREW algorithm does any better. The problem can be solved in $O(1)$ time using a common-CRCW algorithm, in which when several processors write to the same location, they all write the same value.

The CRCW algorithm that finds the maximum of n array elements assumes that the input array is $A[0 \mathinner{..} n-1]$. The algorithm uses n^2 processors, with each processor comparing $A[i]$ and $A[j]$ for some i and j in the range $0 \leq i, j \leq n - 1$. In effect, the algorithm performs a matrix of comparisons, and so we can view each of the n^2 processors as having not only a one-dimensional index in the PRAM, but also a two-dimensional index (i, j).

FAST-MAX(A)

```
 1   n ← length[A]
 2   for i ← 0 to n − 1, in parallel
 3       do m[i] ← TRUE
 4   for i ← 0 to n − 1 and j ← 0 to n − 1, in parallel
 5       do if A[i] < A[j]
 6             then m[i] ← FALSE
 7   for i ← 0 to n − 1, in parallel
 8       do if m[i] = TRUE
 9             then max ← A[i]
10   return max
```

Line 1 simply determines the length of the array A; it only needs to be executed on one processor, say processor 0. We use an array $m[0 \mathinner{..} n - 1]$, where processor i is responsible for $m[i]$. We want $m[i] = \text{TRUE}$ if and only if $A[i]$ is the maximum value in array A. We start (lines 2–3) by believing that each array element is possibly the maximum, and we rely on comparisons in line 5 to determine which array elements are not the maximum.

Figure 30.6 illustrates the remainder of the algorithm. In the loop of lines 4–6, we check each ordered pair of elements of array A. For each pair $A[i]$ and $A[j]$, line 5 checks whether $A[i] < A[j]$. If this comparison is TRUE, we know that $A[i]$ cannot be the maximum, and line 6 sets

$$A[j]$$

	5	6	9	2	9	m
5	F	T	T	F	T	F
6	F	F	T	F	T	F
9	F	F	F	F	F	T
2	T	T	T	F	T	F
9	F	F	F	F	F	T

$A[i]$

max 9

Figure 30.6 Finding the maximum of n values in $O(1)$ time by the CRCW algorithm FAST-MAX. For each ordered pair of the elements in the input array $A = \langle 5, 6, 9, 2, 9 \rangle$, the result of the comparison $A[i] < A[j]$ is shown in the matrix, abbreviated T for TRUE and F for FALSE. For any row that contains a TRUE value, the corresponding element of m, shown at the right, is set to FALSE. Elements of m that contain TRUE correspond to the maximum-valued elements of A. In this case, the value 9 is written into the variable *max*.

$m[i] \leftarrow$ FALSE to record this fact. Several (i, j) pairs may be writing to $m[i]$ simultaneously, but they all write the same value: FALSE.

After line 6 is executed, therefore, $m[i] =$ TRUE for exactly the indices i such that $A[i]$ achieves the maximum. Lines 7–9 then put the maximum value into the variable *max*, which is returned in line 10. Several processors may write into the variable *max*, but if they do, they all write the same value, as is consistent with the common-CRCW PRAM model.

Since all three "loops" in the algorithm are executed in parallel, FAST-MAX runs in $O(1)$ time. Of course, it is not work-efficient, since it requires n^2 processors, and the problem of finding the maximum number in an array can be solved by a $\Theta(n)$-time serial algorithm. We can come closer to a work-efficient algorithm, however, as Exercise 30.2-6 asks you to show.

In a sense, the key to FAST-MAX is that a CRCW PRAM is capable of performing a boolean AND of n variables in $O(1)$ time with n processors. (Since this capability holds in the common-CRCW model, it holds in the more powerful CRCW PRAM models as well.) The code actually performs several AND's at once, computing for $i = 0, 1, \ldots, n - 1$,

$$m[i] = \bigwedge_{j=0}^{n-1} (A[i] \geq A[j]) \,,$$

which can be derived from DeMorgan's laws (5.2). This powerful AND capability can be used in other ways. For example, the capability of a CRCW PRAM to perform an AND in $O(1)$ time obviates the need for a separate control network to test whether all processors are finished iterating a loop, such as we have assumed for EREW algorithms. The decision to finish the loop is simply the AND of all processors' desires to finish the loop.

The EREW model does not have this powerful AND facility. Any EREW algorithm that computes the maximum of n elements takes $\Omega(\lg n)$ time.

The proof is conceptually similar to the lower-bound argument for finding the root of a binary tree. In that proof, we looked at how many nodes can "know" the identity of the root and showed that it at most doubles for each step. For the problem of computing the maximum of n elements, we consider how many elements "think" that they might possibly be the maximum. Intuitively, with each step of an EREW PRAM, this number can at most halve, which leads to the $\Omega(\lg n)$ lower bound.

Remarkably, the $\Omega(\lg n)$ lower bound for computing the maximum holds even if we permit concurrent reading; that is, it holds for CREW algorithms. Cook, Dwork, and Reischuk [50] show, in fact, that any CREW algorithm for finding the maximum of n elements must run in $\Omega(\lg n)$ time, even with an unlimited number of processors and unlimited memory. Their lower bound also holds for the problem of computing the AND of n boolean values.

Simulating a CRCW algorithm with an EREW algorithm

We now know that CRCW algorithms can solve some problems more quickly than can EREW algorithms. Moreover, any EREW algorithm can be executed on a CRCW PRAM. Thus, the CRCW model is strictly more powerful than the EREW model. But how much more powerful is it? In Section 30.3, we shall show that a p-processor EREW PRAM can sort p numbers in $O(\lg p)$ time. We now use this result to provide a theoretical upper bound on the power of a CRCW PRAM over an EREW PRAM.

Theorem 30.1
A p-processor CRCW algorithm can be no more than $O(\lg p)$ times faster than the best p-processor EREW algorithm for the same problem.

Proof   The proof is a simulation argument. We simulate each step of the CRCW algorithm with an $O(\lg p)$-time EREW computation. Because the processing power of both machines is the same, we need only focus on memory accessing. We only present the proof for simulating concurrent writes here. Implementation of concurrent reading is left as Exercise 30.2-8.

The p processors in the EREW PRAM simulate a concurrent write of the CRCW algorithm using an auxiliary array A of length p. Figure 30.7 illustrates the idea. When CRCW processor P_i, for $i = 0, 1, \ldots, p - 1$, desires to write a datum x_i to a location l_i, each corresponding EREW processor P_i instead writes the ordered pair (l_i, x_i) to location $A[i]$. These writes are exclusive, since each processor writes to a distinct memory location. Then, the array A is sorted by the first coordinate of the ordered pairs in $O(\lg p)$ time, which causes all data written to the same location to be brought together in the output.

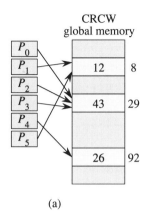

(a)

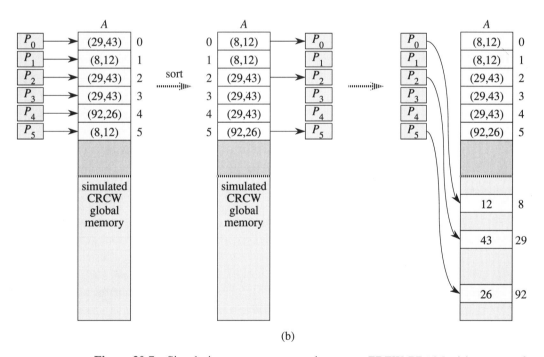

(b)

Figure 30.7 Simulating a concurrent write on an EREW PRAM. (a) A step of a common-CRCW algorithm in which 6 processors write concurrently to global memory. (b) Simulating the step on an EREW PRAM. First, ordered pairs containing location and data are written to an array A. The array is then sorted. By comparing adjacent elements in the array, we ensure that only the first of each group of identical writes into global memory is implemented. In this case, processors P_0, P_2, and P_5 perform the write.

Each EREW processor P_i, for $i = 1, 2, \ldots, p - 1$, now inspects $A[i] = (l_j, x_j)$ and $A[i - 1] = (l_k, x_k)$, where j and k are values in the range $0 \leq j, k \leq p-1$. If $l_j \neq l_k$ or $i = 0$, then processor P_i, for $i = 0, 1, \ldots, p - 1$, writes the datum x_j to location l_j in global memory. Otherwise, the processor does nothing. Since the array A is sorted by first coordinate, only one of the processors writing to any given location actually succeeds, and thus the write is exclusive. This process thus implements each step of concurrent writing in the common-CRCW model in $O(\lg p)$ time.   ∎

Other models for concurrent writing can be simulated as well. (See Exercise 30.2-9.)

The issue arises, therefore, of which model is preferable—CRCW or EREW—and if CRCW, which CRCW model. Advocates of the CRCW models point out that they are easier to program than the EREW model and that their algorithms run faster. Critics contend that hardware to implement concurrent memory operations is slower than hardware to implement exclusive memory operations, and thus the faster running time of CRCW algorithms is fictitious. In reality, they say, one cannot find the maximum of n values in $O(1)$ time.

Others say that the PRAM—either EREW or CRCW—is the wrong model entirely. Processors must be interconnected by a communication network, and the communication network should be part of the model. Processors should only be able to communicate with their neighbors in the network.

It is quite clear that the issue of the "right" parallel model is not going to be easily settled in favor of any one model. The important thing to realize, however, is that these models are just that: models. For a given real-world situation, the various models apply to differing extents. The degree to which the model matches the engineering situation is the degree to which algorithmic analyses in the model will predict real-world phenomena. It is important to study the various parallel models and algorithms, therefore, so that as the field of parallel computing grows, an enlightened consensus on which paradigms of parallel computing are best suited for implementation can emerge.

Exercises

30.2-1
Suppose we know that a forest of binary trees consists of only a single tree with n nodes. Show that with this assumption, a CREW implementation of FIND-ROOTS can be made to run in $O(1)$ time, independent of the depth of the tree. Argue that any EREW algorithm takes $\Omega(\lg n)$ time.

30.2-2

Give an EREW algorithm for FIND-ROOTS that runs in $O(\lg n)$ time on a forest of n nodes.

30.2-3

Give an n-processor CRCW algorithm that can compute the OR of n boolean values in $O(1)$ time.

30.2-4

Describe an efficient CRCW algorithm to multiply two $n \times n$ boolean matrices using n^3 processors.

30.2-5

Describe an $O(\lg n)$-time EREW algorithm to multiply two $n \times n$ matrices of real numbers using n^3 processors. Is there a faster common-CRCW algorithm? Is there a faster algorithm in one of the stronger CRCW models?

30.2-6 ⋆

Prove that for any constant $\epsilon > 0$, there is an $O(1)$-time CRCW algorithm using $O(n^{1+\epsilon})$ processors to find the maximum element of an n-element array.

30.2-7 ⋆

Show how to merge two sorted arrays, each with n numbers, in $O(1)$ time using a priority-CRCW algorithm. Describe how to use this algorithm to sort in $O(\lg n)$ time. Is your sorting algorithm work-efficient?

30.2-8

Complete the proof of Theorem 30.1 by describing how a concurrent read on a p-processor CRCW PRAM is implemented in $O(\lg p)$ time on a p-processor EREW PRAM.

30.2-9

Show how a p-processor EREW PRAM can implement a p-processor combining-CRCW PRAM with only $O(\lg p)$ performance loss. (*Hint:* Use a parallel prefix computation.)

30.3 Brent's theorem and work efficiency

Brent's theorem shows how we can efficiently simulate a combinational circuit by a PRAM. Using this theorem, we can adapt many of the results for sorting networks from Chapter 28 and many of the results for arithmetic circuits from Chapter 29 to the PRAM model. Readers unfamiliar with combinational circuits may wish to review Section 29.1.

A *combinational circuit* is an acyclic network of *combinational elements*. Each combinational element has one or more inputs, and in this section, we shall assume that each element has exactly one output. (Combinational elements with $k > 1$ outputs can be considered to be k separate elements.) The number of inputs is the *fan-in* of the element, and the number of places to which its output feeds is its *fan-out*. We generally assume in this section that every combinational element in the circuit has bounded ($O(1)$) fan-in. It may, however, have unbounded fan-out.

The *size* of a combinational circuit is the number of combinational elements that it contains. The number of combinational elements on a longest path from an input of the circuit to an output of a combinational element is the element's *depth*. The *depth* of the entire circuit is the maximum depth of any of its elements.

Theorem 30.2 (Brent's theorem)

Any depth-d, size-n combinational circuit with bounded fan-in can be simulated by a p-processor CREW algorithm in $O(n/p + d)$ time.

Proof   We store the inputs to the combinational circuit in the PRAM's global memory, and we reserve a location for each combinational element in the circuit to store its output value when it is computed. A given combinational element can then be simulated by a single PRAM processor in $O(1)$ time as follows. The processor simply reads the input values for the element from the values in memory corresponding to circuit inputs or element outputs that feed it, thereby simulating the wires in the circuit. It then computes the function of the combinational element and writes the result in the appropriate position in memory. Since the fan-in of each circuit element is bounded, each function can be computed in $O(1)$ time.

Our job, therefore, is to find a schedule of the p processors of the PRAM such that all combinational elements are simulated in $O(n/p + d)$ time. The main constraint is that an element cannot be simulated until the outputs from any elements that feed it have been computed. Concurrent reads are employed whenever several combinational elements being simulated in parallel require the same value.

Since all elements at depth 1 depend only on circuit inputs, they are the only ones that can be simulated initially. Once they have been simulated, all elements at depth 2 can be simulated, and so forth, until we finish with all elements at depth d. The key idea is that if all elements from depths 1 to i have been simulated, we can simulate any subset of elements at depth $i + 1$ in parallel, since their computations are independent of one another.

Our scheduling strategy, therefore, is quite naive. We simulate all the elements at depth i before proceeding to simulate those at depth $i + 1$. Within a given depth i, we simulate the elements p at a time. Figure 30.8 illustrates such a strategy for $p = 2$.

Let us analyze this simulation strategy. For $i = 1, 2, \ldots, d$, let n_i be the number of elements at depth i in the circuit. Thus,

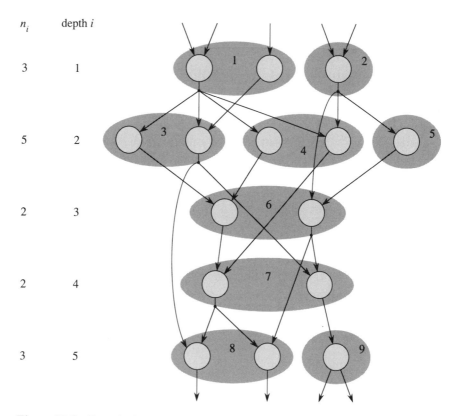

Figure 30.8   Brent's theorem. The combinational circuit of size 15 and depth 5 is simulated by a 2-processor CREW PRAM in $9 \leq 15/2 + 5$ steps. The simulation proceeds from top to bottom through the circuit. The shaded groups of circuit elements indicate which elements are simulated at the same time, and each group is labeled with a number corresponding to the time step when its elements are simulated.

$$\sum_{i=1}^{d} n_i = n \;.$$

Consider the n_i combinational elements at depth i. By grouping them into $\lceil n_i/p \rceil$ groups, where the first $\lfloor n_i/p \rfloor$ groups have p elements each and the leftover elements, if any, are in the last group, the PRAM can simulate the computations performed by these combinational elements in $O(\lceil n_i/p \rceil)$ time. The total simulation time is therefore on the order of

$$\sum_{i=1}^{d} \left\lceil \frac{n_i}{p} \right\rceil \;\; \leq \;\; \sum_{i=1}^{d} \left(\frac{n_i}{p} + 1 \right)$$
$$= \;\; \frac{n}{p} + d \;.$$

Brent's theorem can be extended to EREW simulations when a combinational circuit has $O(1)$ fan-out for each combinational element.

Corollary 30.3

Any depth-d, size-n combinational circuit with bounded fan-in and fan-out can be simulated on a p-processor EREW PRAM in $O(n/p + d)$ time.

Proof   We perform a simulation similar to that in the proof of Brent's theorem. The only difference is in the simulation of wires, which is where Theorem 30.2 requires concurrent reading. For the EREW simulation, after the output of a combinational element is computed, it is not directly read by processors requiring its value. Instead, the output value is copied by the processor simulating the element to the $O(1)$ inputs that require it. The processors that need the value can then read it without interfering with each other.   ∎

This EREW simulation strategy does not work for elements with unbounded fan-out, since the copying can take more than constant time at each step. Thus, for circuits having elements with unbounded fan-out, we need the power of concurrent reads. (The case of unbounded fan-in can sometimes be handled by a CRCW simulation if the combinational elements are simple enough. See Exercise 30.3-1.)

Corollary 30.3 provides us with a fast EREW sorting algorithm. As explained in the chapter notes of Chapter 28, the AKS sorting network can sort n numbers in $O(\lg n)$ depth using $O(n \lg n)$ comparators. Since comparators have bounded fan-in, there is an EREW algorithm to sort n numbers in $O(\lg n)$ time using n processors. (We used this result in Theorem 30.1 to show that an EREW PRAM can simulate a CRCW PRAM with at most logarithmic slowdown.) Unfortunately, the constants hidden by the O-notation are so large that this sorting algorithm has solely theoretical interest. More practical EREW sorting algorithms have been discovered, however, notably the parallel merge-sorting algorithm due to Cole [46].

Now suppose that we have a PRAM algorithm that uses at most p processors, but we have a PRAM with only $p' < p$ processors. We would like to be able to run the p-processor algorithm on the smaller p'-processor PRAM in a work-efficient fashion. By using the idea in the proof of Brent's theorem, we can give a condition for when this is possible.

Theorem 30.4

If a p-processor PRAM algorithm A runs in time t, then for any $p' < p$, there is an p'-processor PRAM algorithm A' for the same problem that runs in time $O(pt/p')$.

Proof   Let the time steps of algorithm A be numbered $1, 2, \ldots, t$. Algorithm A' simulates the execution of each time step $i = 1, 2, \ldots, t$ in time $O(\lceil p/p' \rceil)$. There are t steps, and so the entire simulation takes time $O(\lceil p/p' \rceil t) = O(pt/p')$, since $p' < p$.   ∎

The work performed by algorithm A is pt, and the work performed by algorithm A' is $(pt/p')p' = pt$; the simulation is therefore work-efficient. Consequently, if algorithm A is itself work-efficient, so is algorithm A'.

When developing work-efficient algorithms for a problem, therefore, one needn't necessarily create a different algorithm for each different number of processors. For example, suppose that we can prove a tight lower bound of t on the running time of any parallel algorithm, no matter how many processors, for solving a given problem, and suppose further that the best serial algorithm for the problem does work w. Then, we need only develop a work-efficient algorithm for the problem that uses $p = \Theta(w/t)$ processors in order to obtain work-efficient algorithms for all numbers of processors for which a work-efficient algorithm is possible. For $p' = o(p)$, Theorem 30.4 guarantees that there is a work-efficient algorithm. For $p' = \omega(p)$, no work-efficient algorithms exist, since if t is a lower bound on the time for any parallel algorithm, $p't = \omega(pt) = \omega(w)$.

Exercises

30.3-1
Prove a result analogous to Brent's theorem for a CRCW simulation of boolean combinational circuits having AND and OR gates with unbounded fan-in. (*Hint:* Let the "size" be the total number of inputs to gates in the circuit.)

30.3-2
Show that a parallel prefix computation on n values stored in an array of memory can be implemented in $O(\lg n)$ time on an EREW PRAM using $O(n/\lg n)$ processors. Why does this result not extend immediately to a list of n values?

30.3-3
Show how to multiply an $n \times n$ matrix A by an n-vector b in $O(\lg n)$ time with a work-efficient EREW algorithm. (*Hint:* Construct a combinational circuit for the problem.)

30.3-4
Give a CRCW algorithm using n^2 processors to multiply two $n \times n$ matrices. The algorithm should be work-efficient with respect to the normal $\Theta(n^3)$-time serial algorithm for multiplying matrices. Can you make the algorithm EREW?

30.3-5
Some parallel models allow processors to become inactive, so that the number of processors executing at any step varies. Define the work in this model as the total number of steps executed during an algorithm by active processors. Show that any CRCW algorithm that performs w

work and runs in t time can be run on a p-processor EREW PRAM in $O((w/p + t)\lg p)$ time. (*Hint:* The hard part is scheduling the active processors *while* the computation is proceeding.)

★ **30.4 Work-efficient parallel prefix computation**

In Section 30.1.2, we examined an $O(\lg n)$-time EREW algorithm LIST-RANK that can perform a prefix computation on an n-object linked list. The algorithm uses n processors and performs $\Theta(n \lg n)$ work. Since we can easily perform a prefix computation in $\Theta(n)$ time on a serial machine, LIST-RANK is not work-efficient.

This section presents a randomized EREW parallel prefix algorithm that is work-efficient. The algorithm uses $\Theta(n/\lg n)$ processors, and it runs in $O(\lg n)$ time with high probability. Thus, it is work-efficient with high probability. Moreover, by Theorem 30.4, this algorithm immediately yields work-efficient algorithms for any number $p = O(n/\lg n)$ of processors.

Recursive parallel prefix computation

The randomized parallel prefix algorithm RANDOMIZED-LIST-PREFIX operates on a linked list of n objects using $p = \Theta(n/\lg n)$ processors. During the algorithm, each processor is responsible for $n/p = \Theta(\lg n)$ of the objects in the original list. The objects are assigned to processors arbitrarily (not necessarily contiguously) before the recursion begins, and "ownership" of objects never changes. For convenience, we assume that the list is doubly linked, since doubly linking a single list takes $O(1)$ time.

The idea of RANDOMIZED-LIST-PREFIX is to eliminate some of the objects in the list, perform a recursive prefix computation on the resulting list, and then expand it by splicing in the eliminated objects to yield a prefix computation on the original list. Figure 30.9 illustrates the recursive process, and Figure 30.10 shows how the recursion unfolds. We shall show a little later that each stage of the recursion obeys two properties:

1. At most one object of those belonging to a given processor is selected for elimination.

2. No two adjacent objects are selected for elimination.

Before we show how to select objects that satisfy these properties, let us examine in more detail how the prefix computation is performed. Suppose that at the first step of the recursion, the kth object in the list is selected for elimination. This object contains the value $[k, k]$, which is fetched by the $(k + 1)$st object in the list. (Boundary situations, such as the one here when k is at the end of the list, can be handled straightforwardly and are not described.) The $(k + 1)$st object, which holds the value $[k + 1, k + 1]$,

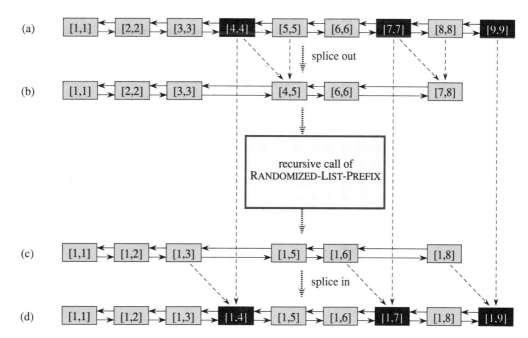

Figure 30.9 The work-efficient, randomized, recursive, parallel algorithm RAN-DOMIZED-LIST-PREFIX for performing prefix computations on a linked list of $n = 9$ objects. **(a)–(b)** A set of nonadjacent objects (blackened) are selected for elimination. The value in each black object is used to update the value in the next object in the list, and then the black object is spliced out. The algorithm is called recursively to compute a parallel prefix on the contracted list. **(c)–(d)** The resulting values are the correct final values for objects in the contracted list. The eliminated objects are then spliced back in, and each uses the value of the previous object to compute its final value.

then computes and stores $[k, k + 1] = [k, k] \otimes [k + 1, k + 1]$. The kth object is then eliminated from the list by splicing it out.

The procedure RANDOMIZED-LIST-PREFIX then calls itself recursively to perform a prefix computation on the "contracted" list. (The recursion bottoms out when the entire list is empty.) The key observation is that after returning from the recursive call, each object in the contracted list has the correct final value it needs for the parallel prefix computation on the original list. It remains only to splice back in the previously eliminated objects, such as the kth object, and update their values.

After the kth object is spliced in, its final prefix value can be computed using the value in the $(k - 1)$st object. After the recursion, the $(k - 1)$st object contains $[1, k - 1]$, and thus the kth object—which still has the value $[k, k]$—needs only to fetch the value $[1, k - 1]$ and compute $[1, k] = [1, k - 1] \otimes [k, k]$.

Because of property 1, each selected object has a distinct processor to perform the work needed to splice it out or in. Property 2 ensures that no confusion between processors arises when splicing objects out and in (see

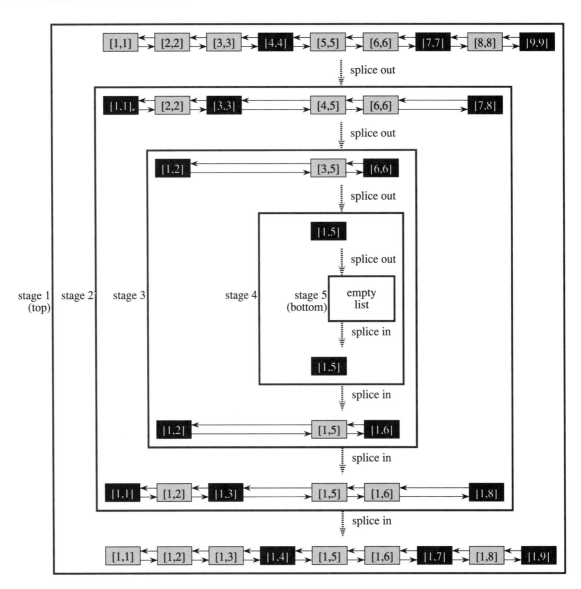

Figure 30.10   The recursive stages of RANDOMIZED-LIST-PREFIX, shown for $n = 9$ original objects. In each stage, the blackened objects are eliminated. The procedure recurses until the list is empty, and then the eliminated objects are spliced back in.

Exercise 30.4-1). The two properties together ensure that each step of the recursion can be implemented in $O(1)$ time in an EREW fashion.

Selecting objects for elimination

How does RANDOMIZED-LIST-PREFIX select objects for elimination? It must obey the two properties above, and in addition, we want the time to select objects to be short (and preferably constant). Moreover, we would like as many objects as possible to be selected.

The following method for randomized selection satisfies these conditions. Objects are selected by having each processor execute the following steps:

1. The processor picks an object i that has not previously been selected from among those it owns.

2. It then "flips a coin," choosing the values HEAD and TAIL with equal probability.

3. If it chooses HEAD, it marks object i as selected, unless $next[i]$ has been picked by another processor whose coin is also HEAD.

This randomized method takes only $O(1)$ time to select objects for elimination, and it does not require concurrent memory accesses.

We must show that this procedure obeys the two properties above. That property 1 holds can be seen easily, since only one object is chosen by a processor for possible selection. To see that property 2 holds, suppose to the contrary that two consecutive objects i and $next[i]$ are selected. This occurs only if both were picked by their processors, and both processors flipped HEAD. But object i is not selected if the processor responsible for $next[i]$ flipped HEAD, which is a contradiction.

Analysis

Since each recursive step of RANDOMIZED-LIST-PREFIX runs in $O(1)$ time, to analyze the algorithm we need only determine how many steps it takes to eliminate all the objects in the original list. At each step, a processor has at least probability $1/4$ of eliminating the object i it picks. Why? It flips HEAD with probability $1/2$, and the probability that it either does not pick $next[i]$ or picks it and flips TAIL is at least $1/2$. Since the two coin flips are independent events, we can multiply their probabilities, yielding the probability of at least $1/4$ of a processor eliminating the object it picks. Since each processor owns $\Theta(\lg n)$ objects, the expected time for a processor to eliminate all its objects is $\Theta(\lg n)$.

Unfortunately, this simple analysis does not show that the expected running time of RANDOMIZED-LIST-PREFIX is $\Theta(\lg n)$. For example, if most of the processors eliminate all their objects quickly and a few processors take much, much longer, the average time for a processor to eliminate all its objects might still be $\Theta(\lg n)$, but the running time of the algorithm could be large.

The expected running time of the procedure RANDOMIZED-LIST-PREFIX is indeed $\Theta(\lg n)$, even though the simple analysis does not show it. We shall use a high-probability argument to prove that with probability at least $1 - 1/n$, all objects are eliminated within $c \lg n$ stages of the recursion, for some constant c. Exercises 30.4-4 and 30.4-5 ask you to generalize this argument to prove the $\Theta(\lg n)$ bound on the expected running time.

Our high-probability argument is based on observing that the experiment of a given processor eliminating the objects it picks can be viewed as a sequence of Bernoulli trials (see Chapter 6). The experiment is a success if the object is selected for elimination, and it is a failure otherwise. Since we are interested in showing that the probability is small that very few successes are obtained, we can assume that successes occur with probability exactly $1/4$, rather than with probability at least $1/4$. (See Exercises 6.4-8 and 6.4-9 for a formal justification of similar assumptions.)

To further simplify the analysis, we assume that there are exactly $n/\lg n$ processors, each with $\lg n$ list objects. We are conducting $c \lg n$ trials, for some constant c that we shall determine, and we are interested in the event that fewer than $\lg n$ successes occur. Let X be the random variable denoting the total number of successes. By Corollary 6.3, the probability that a processor eliminates fewer than $\lg n$ objects in the $c \lg n$ trials is at most

$$
\begin{aligned}
\Pr\{X < \lg n\} &\leq \binom{c \lg n}{\lg n} \left(\frac{3}{4}\right)^{c \lg n - \lg n} \\
&\leq \left(\frac{ec \lg n}{\lg n}\right)^{\lg n} \left(\frac{3}{4}\right)^{(c-1)\lg n} \\
&= \left(ec \left(\frac{3}{4}\right)^{c-1}\right)^{\lg n} \\
&\leq \left(\frac{1}{4}\right)^{\lg n} \\
&= 1/n^2 ,
\end{aligned}
$$

as long as $c \geq 20$. (The second line follows from inequality (6.9).) Thus, the probability that all objects belonging to a given processor have not been eliminated after $c \lg n$ steps is at most $1/n^2$.

We now wish to bound the probability that all objects belonging to all processors have not been eliminated after $c \lg n$ steps. By Boole's inequality (6.22), this probability is at most the sum of the probabilities that each of processors has not eliminated its objects. Since there are $n/\lg n$ processors, and each has probability at most $1/n^2$ of not eliminating all its objects, the probability that any processor has not finished all its objects is at most

$$\frac{n}{\lg n} \cdot \frac{1}{n^2} \leq \frac{1}{n} \; .$$

We have thus proven that with probability at least $1 - 1/n$, every object is spliced out after $O(\lg n)$ recursive calls. Since each recursive call takes $O(1)$ time, RANDOMIZED-LIST-PREFIX takes $O(\lg n)$ time with high probability.

The constant $c \geq 20$ in the $c \lg n$ running time may seem a bit large for practicality. In fact, this constant is more an artifact of the analysis than a reflection of the algorithm's performance. In practice, the algorithm tends to be fast. The constant factors in the analysis are large because the event that one processor finishes eliminating all its list objects is dependent on the event that another processor finishes all its work. Because of these dependencies, we used Boole's inequality, which does not require independence but results in a weaker constant than would generally be experienced in practice.

Exercises

30.4-1
Draw figures to illustrate what can go wrong in RANDOMIZED-LIST-PREFIX if two adjacent list objects are selected for elimination.

30.4-2 $\star$
Suggest a simple change to make RANDOMIZED-LIST-PREFIX run in $O(n)$ worst-case time on a list of n objects. Use the definition of expectation to prove that with this modification, the algorithm runs in $O(\lg n)$ expected time.

30.4-3 $\star$
Show how to implement RANDOMIZED-LIST-PREFIX so that it uses at most $O(n/p)$ space per processor in the worst case, independent of how deep the recursion goes.

30.4-4 $\star$
Show that for any constant $k \geq 1$, RANDOMIZED-LIST-PREFIX runs in $O(\lg n)$ time with probability at least $1 - 1/n^k$. Show how the constant in the running-time bound is influenced by k.

30.4-5 $\star$
Using the result of Exercise 30.4-4, show that the expected running time of RANDOMIZED-LIST-PREFIX is $O(\lg n)$.

30.5   Deterministic symmetry breaking

Consider a situation in which two processors wish to acquire mutually exclusive access to an object. How can the processors determine which should acquire access first? We wish to avoid the scenario in which both are granted access, as well as the scenario in which neither is granted access. The problem of choosing one of the processors is an example of *symmetry breaking*. We have all seen the momentary confusion and diplomatic impasses that arise when two people attempt to go through a door simultaneously. Similar symmetry-breaking problems are pervasive in the design of parallel algorithms, and efficient solutions are extremely useful.

One method for breaking symmetry is to flip coins. On a computer, coin flipping can be implemented by means of a random-number generator. For the two-processor example, both processors can flip coins. If one obtains HEAD and the other TAIL, the one obtaining HEAD proceeds. If both flip the same value, they try again. With this strategy, symmetry is broken in constant expected time (see Exercise 30.5-1).

We saw the effectiveness of a randomized strategy in Section 30.4. In RANDOMIZED-LIST-PREFIX, adjacent list objects must not be selected for elimination, but as many picked objects as possible should be selected. In the midst of a list of picked objects, however, all objects look pretty much the same. As we saw, randomization provides a simple and effective way to break the symmetry between adjacent list objects while guaranteeing that, with high probability, many objects are selected.

In this section, we investigate a deterministic method for breaking symmetry. The key to the algorithm is to employ processor indices or memory addresses rather than random coin flips. For instance, in the two-processor example, we can break the symmetry by allowing the processor with smaller processor index to go first—clearly a constant-time process.

We shall use the same idea, but in a much more clever fashion, in an algorithm to break symmetry in an n-object linked list. The goal is to choose a constant fraction of the objects in the list but to avoid picking two adjacent objects. This algorithm can be performed with n processors in $O(\lg^* n)$ time by a deterministic EREW algorithm. Since $\lg^* n \leq 5$ for all $n \leq 2^{65536}$, the value $\lg^* n$ can be viewed as a small constant for all practical purposes (see page 36).

Our deterministic algorithm has two parts. The first part computes a "6-coloring" of the linked list in $O(\lg^* n)$ time. The second part converts the 6-coloring to a "maximal independent set" of the list in $O(1)$ time. The maximal independent set will contain a constant fraction of the n objects of the list, and no two objects in the set will be adjacent.

Colorings and maximal independent sets

A *coloring* of an undirected graph $G = (V, E)$ is a function $C : V \to \mathbf{N}$ such that for all $u, v \in V$, if $C(u) = C(v)$, then $(u, v) \notin E$; that is, no adjacent vertices have the same color. In a 6-coloring of a linked list, all colors are in the range $\{0, 1, 2, 3, 4, 5\}$ and no two consecutive vertices have the same color. In fact, any linked list has a 2-coloring, since we can color objects whose ranks are odd with color 0 and objects whose ranks are even with color 1. We can compute such a coloring in $O(\lg n)$ time using a parallel prefix computation, but for many applications, it suffices to compute only an $O(1)$-coloring. We shall show that a 6-coloring can be computed in $O(\lg^* n)$ time without using randomization.

An *independent set* of a graph $G = (V, E)$ is a subset $V' \subseteq V$ of vertices such that each edge in E is incident on at most one vertex in V'. A *maximal independent set*, or *MIS*, is an independent set V' such that for all vertices $v \in V - V'$, the set $V' \cup \{v\}$ is not independent—every vertex not in V' is adjacent to some vertex in V'. Do not confuse the problem of computing a *maximal* independent set—an easy problem—with the problem of computing a *maximum* independent set—a hard problem. The problem of finding an independent set of maximum size in a general graph is NP-complete. (See Chapter 36 for a discussion of NP-completeness. Problem 36-1 concerns maximum independent sets.)

For n-object lists, a maximum (and hence maximal) independent set can be determined in $O(\lg n)$ time by using a parallel prefix computation, as in the 2-coloring just mentioned, to identify the odd-ranked objects. This method selects $\lceil n/2 \rceil$ objects. Observe, however, that any maximal independent set of a linked list contains at least $n/3$ objects, since for any 3 consecutive objects, at least one must be in the set. We shall show, however, that a maximal independent set of a list can be determined in $O(1)$ time given an $O(1)$-coloring of the list.

Computing a 6-coloring

The algorithm SIX-COLOR computes a 6-coloring of a list. We won't give pseudocode for the algorithm, but we shall describe it in some detail. We assume that initially each object x in the linked list is associated with a distinct processor $P(x) \in \{0, 1, \dots, n-1\}$.

The idea of SIX-COLOR is to compute a sequence $C_0[x], C_1[x], \dots, C_m[x]$ of colors for each object x in the list. The initial coloring C_0 is an n-coloring. Each iteration of the algorithm defines a new coloring C_{k+1} based on the previous coloring C_k, for $k = 0, 1, \dots, m-1$. The final coloring C_m is a 6-coloring, and we shall prove that $m = O(\lg^* n)$.

The initial coloring is the trivial n-coloring in which $C_0[x] = P(x)$. Since no two list objects have the same color, no two adjacent list objects have the same color, and so the coloring is legal. Note that each of the initial colors can be described with $\lceil \lg n \rceil$ bits, which means that it can be stored in an ordinary computer word.

The subsequent colorings are obtained as follows. The kth iteration, for $k = 0, 1, \ldots, m - 1$, starts with a coloring C_k and ends with a coloring C_{k+1} using fewer bits per object, as the first part of Figure 30.11 shows. Suppose that at the start of an iteration, each object's color C_k takes r bits. We determine the new color of an object x by looking forward in the list at the color of $next[x]$.

To be more precise, suppose that for each object x, we have $C_k[x] = a$ and $C_k[next[x]] = b$, where $a = \langle a_{r-1}, a_{r-2}, \ldots, a_0 \rangle$ and $b = \langle b_{r-1}, b_{r-2}, \ldots, b_0 \rangle$ are r-bit colors. Since $C_k[x] \neq C_k[next[x]]$, there is some least index i at which the bits of the two colors differ: $a_i \neq b_i$. Because $0 \leq i \leq r - 1$, we can write i with only $\lceil \lg r \rceil$ bits: $i = \langle i_{\lceil \lg r \rceil - 1}, i_{\lceil \lg r \rceil - 2}, \ldots, i_0 \rangle$. We recolor x with the value of i concatenated with the bit a_i. That is, we assign

$$
\begin{aligned}
C_{k+1}[x] &= \langle i, a_i \rangle \\
&= \langle i_{\lceil \lg r \rceil - 1}, i_{\lceil \lg r \rceil - 2}, \ldots, i_0, a_i \rangle .
\end{aligned}
$$

The tail of the list gets the new color $\langle 0, a_0 \rangle$. The number of bits in each new color is therefore at most $\lceil \lg r \rceil + 1$.

We must show that if each iteration of SIX-COLOR starts with a coloring, the new "coloring" it produces is indeed a legal coloring. To do this, we prove that $C_k[x] \neq C_k[next[x]]$ implies $C_{k+1}[x] \neq C_{k+1}[next[x]]$. Suppose that $C_k[x] = a$ and $C_k[next[x]] = b$, and that $C_{k+1}[x] = \langle i, a_i \rangle$ and $C_{k+1}[next[x]] = \langle j, b_j \rangle$. There are two cases to consider. If $i \neq j$, then $\langle i, a_i \rangle \neq \langle j, b_j \rangle$, and so the new colors are different. If $i = j$, however, then $a_i \neq b_i = b_j$ by our recoloring method, and thus the new colors are once again different. (The situation at the tail of the list can be handled similarly.)

The recoloring method used by SIX-COLOR takes an r-bit color and replaces it with a $(\lceil \lg r \rceil + 1)$-bit color, which means that the number of bits is strictly reduced as long as $r \geq 4$. When $r = 3$, two colors can differ in bit position 0, 1, or 2. Each new color, therefore, is $\langle 00 \rangle$, $\langle 01 \rangle$, or $\langle 10 \rangle$ concatenated with either 0 or 1, thus leaving a 3-bit number once again. Only 6 of the 8 possible values for 3-bit numbers are used, however, so that SIX-COLOR indeed terminates with a 6-coloring.

Assuming that each processor can determine the appropriate index i in $O(1)$ time and perform a shift-left operation in $O(1)$ time—operations commonly supported on many actual machines—each iteration takes $O(1)$ time. The SIX-COLOR procedure is an EREW algorithm: for each object x, its processor accesses only x and $next[x]$.

Finally, let us see why only $O(\lg^* n)$ iterations are required to bring the initial n-coloring down to a 6-coloring. We have defined $\lg^* n$ as the number of times the logarithm function $\lg$ needs to be applied to n to reduce it to at most 1 or, letting $\lg^{(i)} n$ denote i successive applications of the lg function,

Figure 30.11 The algorithms Six-Color and List-MIS that break symmetry in a list. Together, the algorithms find a large set of nonadjacent objects in $O(\lg^* n)$ time using n processors. The initial list of $n = 20$ objects is shown on the left, running vertically. Each object has an initial, distinct 5-bit color. For these parameters, the algorithm Six-Color needs only the two iterations shown to recolor each object with a color in the range $\{0, 1, 2, 3, 4, 5\}$. White objects are placed into the MIS by List-MIS as the colors are processed, and black objects are killed.

$$\lg^* n = \min \left\{ i \geq 0 : \lg^{(i)} n \leq 1 \right\} .$$

Let r_i be the number of bits in the coloring just before the ith iteration. We shall prove by induction that if $\lceil \lg^{(i)} n \rceil \geq 2$, then $r_i \leq \lceil \lg^{(i)} n \rceil + 2$. Initially, we have $r_1 \leq \lceil \lg n \rceil$. The ith iteration brings the number of bits in the coloring down to $r_{i+1} = \lceil \lg r_i \rceil + 1$. Assuming that the inductive hypothesis holds for r_{i-1}, we obtain

$$
\begin{aligned}
r_i &= \lceil \lg r_{i-1} \rceil + 1 \\
&\leq \lceil \lg(\lceil \lg^{(i-1)} n \rceil + 2) \rceil + 1 \\
&\leq \lceil \lg(\lg^{(i-1)} n + 3) \rceil + 1 \\
&\leq \lceil \lg(2 \lg^{(i-1)} n) \rceil + 1 \\
&= \lceil \lg(\lg^{(i-1)} n) + 1 \rceil + 1 \\
&= \lceil \lg^{(i)} n \rceil + 2 .
\end{aligned}
$$

The fourth line follows from the assumption that $\lceil \lg^{(i)} n \rceil \geq 2$, which means that $\lceil \lg^{(i-1)} n \rceil \geq 3$. Therefore, after $m = \lg^* n$ steps, the number of bits in the coloring is $r_m \leq \lceil \lg^{(m)} n \rceil + 2 = 3$, since $\lg^{(m)} n \leq 1$ by definition of the $\lg^*$ function. Thus, at most one more iteration suffices to produce a 6-coloring. The total time of SIX-COLOR is therefore $O(\lg^* n)$.

Computing an MIS from a 6-coloring

Coloring is the hard part of symmetry breaking. The EREW algorithm LIST-MIS uses n processors to find a maximal independent set in $O(c)$ time given a c-coloring of an n-object list. Thus, once we have computed a 6-coloring of a list, we can find a maximal independent set of the linked list in $O(1)$ time.

The latter part of Figure 30.11 illustrates the idea behind LIST-MIS. We are given a c-coloring C. With each object x, we keep a bit $alive[x]$, which tells us whether x is still a candidate for inclusion in the MIS. Initially, $alive[x] = \text{TRUE}$ for all objects x.

The algorithm then iterates through each of the c colors. In the iteration for color i, each processor responsible for an object x checks whether $C[x] = i$ and $alive[x] = \text{TRUE}$. If both conditions hold, then the processor marks x as belonging to the MIS being constructed. All objects adjacent to those added into the MIS—those immediately preceding or following— have their $alive$ bits set to FALSE; they cannot be in the MIS because they are adjacent to an object in the MIS. After all c iterations, each object has either been "killed"—its $alive$ bit has been set to FALSE—or placed into the MIS.

We must show that the resulting set is independent and maximal. To see that it is independent, suppose that two adjacent objects x and $next[x]$ are placed into the set. Since they are adjacent, $C[x] \neq C[next[x]]$, because C is a coloring. Without loss of generality, we assume that $C[x] < C[next[x]]$, so that x is placed into the set before $next[x]$ is. But then *alive*[*next*[*x*]] has been set to FALSE by the time objects of color $C[next[x]]$ are considered, and *next*[*x*] could not have been placed into the set.

To see that the set is maximal, suppose that none of three consecutive objects x, y, and z has been placed into the set. The only way that y could have avoided being placed into the set, though, is if it had been killed when an adjacent object was placed into the set. Since, by our supposition, neither x nor z was placed into the set, the object y must have been still alive at the time when objects of color $C[y]$ were processed. It must have been placed into the MIS.

Each iteration of LIST-MIS takes $O(1)$ time on a PRAM. The algorithm is EREW since each object accesses only itself, its predecessor, and its successor in the list. Combining LIST-MIS with SIX-COLOR, we can break symmetry in a linked list in $O(\lg^* n)$ time deterministically.

Exercises

30.5-1
For the 2-processor symmetry-breaking example at the beginning of this section, show that symmetry is broken in constant expected time.

30.5-2
Given a 6-coloring of an n-object list, show how to 3-color the list in $O(1)$ time using n processors in an EREW PRAM.

30.5-3
Suppose that every nonroot node in an n-node tree has a pointer to its parent. Give a CREW algorithm to $O(1)$-color the tree in $O(\lg^* n)$ time.

30.5-4 ★
Give an efficient PRAM algorithm to $O(1)$-color a degree-3 graph. Analyze your algorithm.

30.5-5
A *k-ruling set* of a linked list is a set of objects (rulers) in the list such that no rulers are adjacent and at most k nonrulers (subjects) separate rulers. Thus, an MIS is a 2-ruling set. Show how an $O(\lg n)$-ruling set of an n-object list can be computed in $O(1)$ time using n processors. Show how an $O(\lg\lg n)$ ruling set can be computed in $O(1)$ time under the same assumptions.

30.5-6 ★
Show how to find a 6-coloring of an n-object linked list in $O(\lg(\lg^* n))$ time. Assume that each processor can store a precomputed table of size $O(\lg n)$. (*Hint:* In SIX-COLOR, upon how many values does the final color of an object depend?)

Problems

30-1   Segmented parallel prefix

Like an ordinary prefix computation, a ***segmented prefix computation*** is defined in terms of a binary, associative operator $\otimes$. It takes an input sequence $x = \langle x_1, x_2, \ldots, x_n \rangle$ whose elements are drawn from a domain S and a ***segment*** sequence $b = \langle b_1, b_2, \ldots, b_n \rangle$ whose elements are drawn from the domain $\{0, 1\}$, with $b_1 = 1$. It produces an output sequence $y = \langle y_1, y_2, \ldots, y_n \rangle$ over the domain S. The bits of b determine a partitioning of x and y into segments; a new segment begins wherever $b_i = 1$, and the current one continues if $b_i = 0$. The segmented prefix computation performs an independent prefix computation within each segment of x to produce the corresponding segment of y. Figure 30.12 illustrates a segmented prefix computation using ordinary addition.

a. Define the operator $\widehat{\otimes}$ on ordered pairs $(a, z), (a', z') \in \{0, 1\} \times S$ as follows:

$$(a, z) \widehat{\otimes} (a', z') = \begin{cases} (a, z \otimes z') & \text{if } a' = 0 , \\ (1, z') & \text{if } a' = 1 . \end{cases}$$

Prove that $\widehat{\otimes}$ is associative.

b. Show how to implement any segmented prefix computation on an n-element list in $O(\lg n)$ time on an EREW PRAM.

c. Describe an $O(k \lg n)$-time EREW algorithm to sort a list of n k-bit numbers.

30-2   Processor-efficient maximum algorithm

We wish to find the maximum of n numbers on a CRCW PRAM with $p = n$ processors.

a. Show that the problem of finding the maximum of $m \leq p/2$ numbers can be reduced to the problem of finding the maximum of at most m^2/p numbers in $O(1)$ time on a p-processor CRCW PRAM.

b. If we start with $m = \lfloor p/2 \rfloor$ numbers, how many numbers remain after k iterations of the algorithm in part (a)?

b =	1	0	0	1	0	1	1	0	0	0	0	0	1	0
x =	1	2	3	4	5	6	7	8	9	10	11	12	13	14
y =	1	3	6	4	9	6	7	15	24	34	45	57	13	27

Figure 30.12 A segmented prefix computation with segment sequence b, input sequence x, and output sequence y. There are 5 segments.

c. Show that the problem of finding the maximum of n numbers can be solved in $O(\lg \lg n)$ time on a CRCW PRAM with $p = n$ processors.

30-3 *Connected components*

In this problem, we investigate an arbitrary-CRCW algorithm for computing the connected components of an undirected graph $G = (V, E)$ that uses $|V + E|$ processors. The data structure used is a disjoint-set forest (see Section 22.3). Each vertex $v \in V$ maintains a pointer $p[v]$ to a parent. Initially, $p[v] = v$: the vertex points to itself. At the end of the algorithm, for any two vertices $u, v \in V$, we have $p[u] = p[v]$ if and only if $u \rightsquigarrow v$ in G. During the algorithm, the p pointers form a forest of rooted *pointer* trees. A *star* is a pointer tree in which $p[u] = p[v]$ for all vertices u and v in the tree.

The connected-components algorithm assumes that each edge $(u, v) \in E$ appears twice: once as (u, v) and once as (v, u). The algorithm uses two basic operations, HOOK and JUMP, and a subroutine STAR that sets $star[v] = \text{TRUE}$ if v belongs to a star.

HOOK(G)

```
1  STAR(G)
2  for each edge (u, v) ∈ E[G], in parallel
3       do if star[u] and p[u] > p[v]
4           then p[p[u]] ← p[v]
5  STAR(G)
6  for each edge (u, v) ∈ E[G], in parallel
7       do if star[u] and p[u] ≠ p[v]
8           then p[p[u]] ← p[v]
```

JUMP(G)

```
1  for each v ∈ V[G], in parallel
2       do p[v] ← p[p[v]]
```

The connected-components algorithm performs an initial HOOK, and then it repeatedly performs HOOK, JUMP, HOOK, JUMP, and so on, until no pointer is changed by a JUMP operation. (Note that two HOOK's are performed before the first JUMP.)

a. Give pseudocode for STAR(G).

b. Show that the p pointers indeed form rooted trees, with the root of a tree pointing to itself. Show that if u and v are in the same pointer tree, then $u \rightsquigarrow v$ in G.

c. Show that the algorithm is correct: it terminates, and when it terminates, $p[u] = p[v]$ if and only if $u \rightsquigarrow v$ in G.

To analyze the connected-components algorithm, let us examine a single connected component C, which we assume has at least two vertices. Suppose that at some point during the algorithm, C is made up of a set $\{T_i\}$ of pointer trees. Define the potential of C as

$$\Phi(C) = \sum_{T_i} \text{height}(T_i) \, .$$

The goal of our analysis is to prove that each iteration of hooking and jumping decreases $\Phi(C)$ by a constant factor.

d. Prove that after the initial HOOK, there are no pointer trees of height 0 and $\Phi(C) \le |V|$.

e. Argue that after the initial HOOK, subsequent HOOK operations never increase $\Phi(C)$.

f. Show that after every noninitial HOOK operation, no pointer tree is a star unless the pointer tree contains all vertices in C.

g. Argue that if C has not been collapsed into a single star, then after a JUMP operation, $\Phi(C)$ is at most 2/3 its previous value. Illustrate the worst case.

h. Conclude that the algorithm determines all the connected components of G in $O(\lg V)$ time.

30-4   *Transposing a raster image*

A raster-graphics frame buffer can be viewed as a $p \times p$ matrix M of bits. The raster-graphics display hardware makes the $n \times n$ upper left submatrix of M visible on the user's screen. A BITBLT operation (BLock Transfer of BITs) is used to move a rectangle of bits from one position to another. Specifically, BITBLT$(r_1, c_1, r_2, c_2, nr, nc, *)$ sets

$$M[r_2 + i, c_2 + j] \leftarrow M[r_2 + i, c_2 + j] * M[r_1 + i, c_1 + j]$$

for $i = 0, 1, \ldots, nr - 1$ and $j = 0, 1, \ldots, nc - 1$, where $*$ is any of the 16 boolean functions on two inputs.

We are interested in transposing the image $(M[i, j] \leftarrow M[j, i])$ in the visible portion of the frame buffer. We assume that the cost of copying the bits is less than that of calling the BITBLT primitive, and hence we are interested in using as few BITBLT operations as possible.

Show that any image on the screen can be transposed with $O(\lg n)$ BIT-BLT operations. Assume that p is sufficiently larger than n so that the nonvisible portion of the frame buffer provides enough working storage. How much additional storage do you need? (*Hint:* Use a parallel divide-and-conquer approach in which some of the BITBLT's are performed with boolean AND's.)

Chapter notes

Akl [9], Karp and Ramachandran [118], and Leighton [135] survey parallel algorithms for combinatorial problems. Various parallel machine architectures are described by Hwang and Briggs [109] and Hwang and DeGroot [110].

The theory of parallel computing began in the late 1940's when J. Von Neumann [38] introduced a restricted model of parallel computing called a cellular automaton, which is essentially a two-dimensional array of finite-state processors interconnected in meshlike fashion. The PRAM model was formalized in 1978 by Fortune and Wyllie [73], although many other authors had previously discussed essentially similar models.

Pointer jumping was introduced by Wyllie [204]. The study of parallel prefix computations arose from the work of Ofman [152] in the context of carry-lookahead addition. The Euler-tour technique is due to Tarjan and Vishkin [191].

Processor-time trade-offs for computing the maximum of a set of n numbers were provided by Valiant [193], who also showed that an $O(1)$-time work-efficient algorithm does not exist. Cook, Dwork, and Reischuk [50] proved that the problem of computing the maximum requires $\Omega(\lg n)$ time on a CREW PRAM. The simulation of a CRCW algorithm with an EREW algorithm is due to Vishkin [195].

Theorem 30.2 is due to Brent [34]. The randomized algorithm for work-efficient list ranking was discovered by Anderson and Miller [11]. They also have a deterministic, work-efficient algorithm for the same problem [10]. The algorithm for deterministic symmetry breaking is due to Goldberg and Plotkin [84]. It is based on a similar algorithm with the same running time due to Cole and Vishkin [47].

31 Matrix Operations

Operations on matrices are at the heart of scientific computing. Efficient algorithms for working with matrices are therefore of considerable practical interest. This chapter provides a brief introduction to matrix theory and matrix operations, emphasizing the problems of multiplying matrices and solving sets of simultaneous linear equations.

After Section 31.1 introduces basic matrix concepts and notations, Section 31.2 presents Strassen's surprising algorithm for multiplying two $n \times n$ matrices in $\Theta(n^{\lg 7}) = O(n^{2.81})$ time. Section 31.3 defines quasirings, rings, and fields, clarifying the assumptions required to make Strassen's algorithm work. It also contains an asymptotically fast algorithm for multiplying boolean matrices. Section 31.4 shows how to solve a set of linear equations using LUP decompositions. Then, Section 31.5 explores the close relationship between the problem of multiplying matrices and the problem of inverting a matrix. Finally, Section 31.6 discusses the important class of symmetric positive-definite matrices and shows how they can be used to find a least-squares solution to an overdetermined set of linear equations.

31.1 Properties of matrices

In this section, we review some basic concepts of matrix theory and some fundamental properties of matrices, focusing on those that will be needed in later sections.

Matrices and vectors

A *matrix* is a rectangular array of numbers. For example,

$$
\begin{aligned}
A &= \begin{pmatrix} a_{11} & a_{12} & a_{13} \\ a_{21} & a_{22} & a_{23} \end{pmatrix} \\
&= \begin{pmatrix} 1 & 2 & 3 \\ 4 & 5 & 6 \end{pmatrix}
\end{aligned}
\tag{31.1}
$$

is a 2×3 matrix $A = (a_{ij})$, where for $i = 1, 2$ and $j = 1, 2, 3$, the element of the matrix in row i and column j is a_{ij}. We use uppercase letters to denote matrices and corresponding subscripted lowercase letters to denote their elements. The set of all $m \times n$ matrices with real-valued entries is denoted $\mathbf{R}^{m \times n}$. In general, the set of $m \times n$ matrices with entries drawn from a set S is denoted $S^{m \times n}$.

The ***transpose*** of a matrix A is the matrix A^{T} obtained by exchanging the rows and columns of A. For the matrix A of equation (31.1),

$$A^{\mathrm{T}} = \begin{pmatrix} 1 & 4 \\ 2 & 5 \\ 3 & 6 \end{pmatrix} .$$

A ***vector*** is a one-dimensional array of numbers. For example,

$$x = \begin{pmatrix} 2 \\ 3 \\ 5 \end{pmatrix} \tag{31.2}$$

is a vector of size 3. We use lowercase letters to denote vectors, and we denote the ith element of a size-n vector x by x_i, for $i = 1, 2, \ldots, n$. We take the standard form of a vector to be as a ***column vector*** equivalent to an $n \times 1$ matrix; the corresponding ***row vector*** is obtained by taking the transpose:

$$x^{\mathrm{T}} = (\, 2 \quad 3 \quad 5 \,) .$$

The ***unit vector*** e_i is the vector whose ith element is 1 and all of whose other elements are 0. Usually, the size of a unit vector is clear from the context.

A ***zero matrix*** is a matrix whose every entry is 0. Such a matrix is often denoted 0, since the ambiguity between the number 0 and a matrix of 0's is usually easily resolved from context. If a matrix of 0's is intended, then the size of the matrix also needs to be derived from the context.

Square $n \times n$ matrices arise frequently. Several special cases of square matrices are of particular interest:

1. A ***diagonal matrix*** has $a_{ij} = 0$ whenever $i \neq j$. Because all of the off-diagonal elements are zero, the matrix can be specified by listing the elements along the diagonal:

$$\mathrm{diag}(a_{11}, a_{22}, \ldots, a_{nn}) = \begin{pmatrix} a_{11} & 0 & \ldots & 0 \\ 0 & a_{22} & \ldots & 0 \\ \vdots & \vdots & \ddots & \vdots \\ 0 & 0 & \ldots & a_{nn} \end{pmatrix} .$$

2. The $n \times n$ ***identity matrix*** I_n is a diagonal matrix with 1's along the diagonal:

$$I_n \quad = \quad \mathrm{diag}(1, 1, \ldots, 1)$$

$$
= \begin{pmatrix} 1 & 0 & \dots & 0 \\ 0 & 1 & \dots & 0 \\ \vdots & \vdots & \ddots & \vdots \\ 0 & 0 & \dots & 1 \end{pmatrix} .
$$

When I appears without a subscript, its size can be derived from context. The ith column of an identity matrix is the unit vector e_i.

3. A ***tridiagonal matrix*** T is one for which $t_{ij} = 0$ if $|i - j| > 1$. Nonzero entries appear only on the main diagonal, immediately above the main diagonal ($t_{i,i+1}$ for $i = 1, 2, \ldots, n - 1$), or immediately below the main diagonal ($t_{i+1,i}$ for $i = 1, 2, \ldots, n - 1$):

$$
T = \begin{pmatrix} t_{11} & t_{12} & 0 & 0 & \dots & 0 & 0 & 0 \\ t_{21} & t_{22} & t_{23} & 0 & \dots & 0 & 0 & 0 \\ 0 & t_{32} & t_{33} & t_{34} & \dots & 0 & 0 & 0 \\ \vdots & \vdots & \vdots & \vdots & \ddots & \vdots & \vdots & \vdots \\ 0 & 0 & 0 & 0 & \dots & t_{n-2,n-2} & t_{n-2,n-1} & 0 \\ 0 & 0 & 0 & 0 & \dots & t_{n-1,n-2} & t_{n-1,n-1} & t_{n-1,n} \\ 0 & 0 & 0 & 0 & \dots & 0 & t_{n,n-1} & t_{nn} \end{pmatrix} .
$$

4. An ***upper-triangular matrix*** U is one for which $u_{ij} = 0$ if $i > j$. All entries below the diagonal are zero:

$$
U = \begin{pmatrix} u_{11} & u_{12} & \dots & u_{1n} \\ 0 & u_{22} & \dots & u_{2n} \\ \vdots & \vdots & \ddots & \vdots \\ 0 & 0 & \dots & u_{nn} \end{pmatrix} .
$$

An upper-triangular matrix is ***unit upper-triangular*** if it has all 1's along the diagonal.

5. A ***lower-triangular matrix*** L is one for which $l_{ij} = 0$ if $i < j$. All entries above the diagonal are zero:

$$
L = \begin{pmatrix} l_{11} & 0 & \dots & 0 \\ l_{21} & l_{22} & \dots & 0 \\ \vdots & \vdots & \ddots & \vdots \\ l_{n1} & l_{n2} & \dots & l_{nn} \end{pmatrix} .
$$

A lower-triangular matrix is ***unit lower-triangular*** if it has all 1's along the diagonal.

6. A ***permutation matrix*** P has exactly one 1 in each row or column, and 0's elsewhere. An example of a permutation matrix is

$$
P = \begin{pmatrix} 0 & 1 & 0 & 0 & 0 \\ 0 & 0 & 0 & 1 & 0 \\ 1 & 0 & 0 & 0 & 0 \\ 0 & 0 & 0 & 0 & 1 \\ 0 & 0 & 1 & 0 & 0 \end{pmatrix} .
$$

Such a matrix is called a permutation matrix because multiplying a vector x by a permutation matrix has the effect of permuting (rearranging) the elements of x.

7. A **symmetric matrix** A satisfies the condition $A = A^{\mathrm{T}}$. For example,

$$\begin{pmatrix} 1 & 2 & 3 \\ 2 & 6 & 4 \\ 3 & 4 & 5 \end{pmatrix}$$

is a symmetric matrix.

Operations on matrices

The elements of a matrix or vector are numbers from a number system, such as the real numbers, the complex numbers, or integers modulo a prime. The number system defines how to add and multiply numbers. We can extend these definitions to encompass addition and multiplication of matrices.

We define **matrix addition** as follows. If $A = (a_{ij})$ and $B = (b_{ij})$ are $m \times n$ matrices, then their matrix sum $C = (c_{ij}) = A + B$ is the $m \times n$ matrix defined by

$$c_{ij} = a_{ij} + b_{ij}$$

for $i = 1, 2, \ldots, m$ and $j = 1, 2, \ldots, n$. That is, matrix addition is performed componentwise. A zero matrix is the identity for matrix addition:

$$\begin{aligned} A + 0 &= A \\ &= 0 + A \, . \end{aligned}$$

If λ is a number and $A = (a_{ij})$ is a matrix, then $\lambda A = (\lambda a_{ij})$ is the **scalar multiple** of A obtained by multiplying each of its elements by λ. As a special case, we define the **negative** of a matrix $A = (a_{ij})$ to be $-1 \cdot A = -A$, so that the ijth entry of $-A$ is $-a_{ij}$. Thus,

$$\begin{aligned} A + (-A) &= 0 \\ &= (-A) + A \, . \end{aligned}$$

Given this definition, we can define **matrix subtraction** as the addition of the negative of a matrix: $A - B = A + (-B)$.

We define **matrix multiplication** as follows. We start with two matrices A and B that are **compatible** in the sense that the number of columns of A equals the number of rows of B. (In general, an expression containing a matrix product AB is always assumed to imply that matrices A and B are compatible.) If $A = (a_{ij})$ is an $m \times n$ matrix and $B = (b_{jk})$ is an $n \times p$ matrix, then their matrix product $C = AB$ is the $m \times p$ matrix $C = (c_{ik})$, where

$$c_{ik} = \sum_{j=1}^{n} a_{ij} b_{jk} \tag{31.3}$$

for $i = 1, 2, \ldots, m$ and $k = 1, 2, \ldots, p$. The procedure MATRIX-MULTIPLY in Section 26.1 implements matrix multiplication in the straightforward manner based on equation (31.3), assuming that the matrices are square: $m = n = p$. To multiply $n \times n$ matrices, MATRIX-MULTIPLY performs n^3 multiplications and $n^2(n-1)$ additions, and its running time is $\Theta(n^3)$.

Matrices have many (but not all) of the algebraic properties typical of numbers. Identity matrices are identities for matrix multiplication:

$$I_m A = A I_n = A$$

for any $m \times n$ matrix A. Multiplying by a zero matrix gives a zero matrix:

$$A 0 = 0 \ .$$

Matrix multiplication is associative:

$$A(BC) = (AB)C \tag{31.4}$$

for compatible matrices A, B, and C. Matrix multiplication distributes over addition:

$$\begin{aligned} A(B + C) &= AB + AC \ , \\ (B + C)D &= BD + CD \ . \end{aligned} \tag{31.5}$$

Multiplication of $n \times n$ matrices is not commutative, however, unless $n = 1$. For example, if $A = \begin{pmatrix} 0 & 1 \\ 0 & 0 \end{pmatrix}$ and $B = \begin{pmatrix} 0 & 0 \\ 1 & 0 \end{pmatrix}$, then

$$AB = \begin{pmatrix} 1 & 0 \\ 0 & 0 \end{pmatrix}$$

and

$$BA = \begin{pmatrix} 0 & 0 \\ 0 & 1 \end{pmatrix} \ .$$

Matrix-vector products or vector-vector products are defined as if the vector were the equivalent $n \times 1$ matrix (or a $1 \times n$ matrix, in the case of a row vector). Thus, if A is an $m \times n$ matrix and x is a vector of size n, then Ax is a vector of size m. If x and y are vectors of size n, then

$$x^{\mathrm{T}} y = \sum_{i=1}^{n} x_i y_i$$

is a number (actually a 1×1 matrix) called the ***inner product*** of x and y. The matrix xy^{T} is an $n \times n$ matrix Z called the ***outer product*** of x and y, with $z_{ij} = x_i y_j$. The ***(euclidean) norm*** $\|x\|$ of a vector x of size n is defined by

$$\begin{aligned} \|x\| &= (x_1^2 + x_2^2 + \cdots + x_n^2)^{1/2} \\ &= (x^{\mathrm{T}} x)^{1/2} \ . \end{aligned}$$

Thus, the norm of x is its length in n-dimensional euclidean space.

Matrix inverses, ranks, and determinants

We define the *inverse* of an $n \times n$ matrix A to be the $n \times n$ matrix, denoted A^{-1} (if it exists), such that $AA^{-1} = I_n = A^{-1}A$. For example,

$$\begin{pmatrix} 1 & 1 \\ 1 & 0 \end{pmatrix}^{-1} = \begin{pmatrix} 0 & 1 \\ 1 & -1 \end{pmatrix}.$$

Many nonzero $n \times n$ matrices do not have inverses. A matrix without an inverse is is called *noninvertible*, or *singular*. An example of a nonzero singular matrix is

$$\begin{pmatrix} 1 & 0 \\ 1 & 0 \end{pmatrix}.$$

If a matrix has an inverse, it is called *invertible*, or *nonsingular*. Matrix inverses, when they exist, are unique. (See Exercise 31.1-4.) If A and B are nonsingular $n \times n$ matrices, then

$$(BA)^{-1} = A^{-1}B^{-1}. \tag{31.6}$$

The inverse operation commutes with the transpose operation:

$$(A^{-1})^{\mathrm{T}} = (A^{\mathrm{T}})^{-1}.$$

The vectors $x_1, x_2, \ldots, x_n$ are *linearly dependent* if there exist coefficients $c_1, c_2, \ldots, c_n$, not all of which are zero, such that $c_1 x_1 + c_2 x_2 + \cdots + c_n x_n = 0$. For example, the vectors $x_1 = (1 \quad 2 \quad 3)^{\mathrm{T}}$, $x_2 = (2 \quad 6 \quad 4)^{\mathrm{T}}$, and $x_3 = (4 \quad 11 \quad 9)^{\mathrm{T}}$ are linearly dependent, since $2x_1 + 3x_2 - 2x_3 = 0$. If vectors are not linearly dependent, they are *linearly independent*. For example, the columns of an identity matrix are linearly independent.

The *column rank* of a nonzero $m \times n$ matrix A is the size of the largest set of linearly independent columns of A. Similarly, the *row rank* of A is the size of the largest set of linearly independent rows of A. A fundamental property of any matrix A is that its row rank always equals its column rank, so that we can simply refer to the *rank* of A. The rank of an $m \times n$ matrix is an integer between 0 and $\min(m, n)$, inclusive. (The rank of a zero matrix is 0, and the rank of an $n \times n$ identity matrix is n.) An alternate, but equivalent and often more useful, definition is that the rank of a nonzero $m \times n$ matrix A is the smallest number r such that there exist matrices B and C of respective sizes $m \times r$ and $r \times n$ such that

$$A = BC.$$

A square $n \times n$ matrix has *full rank* if its rank is n. A fundamental property of ranks is given by the following theorem.

Theorem 31.1
A square matrix has full rank if and only if it is nonsingular. ∎

An $m \times n$ matrix has *full column rank* if its rank is n.

A *null vector* for a matrix A is a nonzero vector x such that $Ax = 0$. The following theorem, whose proof is left as Exercise 31.1-8, and its corollary relate the notions of column rank and singularity to null vectors.

Theorem 31.2
A matrix A has full column rank if and only if it does not have a null vector. ∎

Corollary 31.3
A square matrix A is singular if and only if it has a null vector. ∎

The ijth *minor* of an $n \times n$ matrix A, for $n > 1$, is the $(n-1) \times (n-1)$ matrix $A_{[ij]}$ obtained by deleting the ith row and jth column of A. The *determinant* of an $n \times n$ matrix A can be defined recursively in terms of its minors by

$$\det(A) = \begin{cases} a_{11} & \text{if } n = 1, \\ a_{11} \det(A_{[11]}) - a_{12} \det(A_{[12]}) \\ \qquad + \cdots + (-1)^{n+1} a_{1n} \det(A_{[1n]}) & \text{if } n > 1. \end{cases} \tag{31.7}$$

The term $(-1)^{i+j} \det(A_{[ij]})$ is known as the *cofactor* of the element a_{ij}.

The following theorems, whose proofs are omitted here, express fundamental properties of the determinant.

Theorem 31.4 (Determinant properties)
The determinant of a square matrix A has the following properties:

- If any row or any column of A is zero, then $\det(A) = 0$.
- The determinant of A is multiplied by λ if the entries of any one row (or any one column) of A are all multiplied by λ.
- The determinant of A is unchanged if the entries in one row (respectively, column) are added to those in another row (respectively, column).
- The determinant of A equals the determinant of A^{T}.
- The determinant of A is multiplied by -1 if any two rows (respectively, columns) are exchanged.

Also, for any square matrices A and B, we have $\det(AB) = \det(A)\det(B)$. ∎

Theorem 31.5
An $n \times n$ matrix A is singular if and only if $\det(A) = 0$. ∎

Positive-definite matrices

Positive-definite matrices play an important role in many applications. An $n \times n$ matrix A is *positive-definite* if $x^T A x > 0$ for all size-n vectors $x \neq 0$. For example, the identity matrix is positive-definite, since for any nonzero vector $x = (\, x_1 \quad x_2 \quad \cdots \quad x_n \,)^T$,

$$
\begin{aligned}
x^T I_n x &= x^T x \\
&= \|x\|^2 \\
&= \sum_{i=1}^{n} x_i^2 \\
&> 0 \, .
\end{aligned}
$$

As we shall see, matrices that arise in applications are often positive-definite due to the following theorem.

Theorem 31.6
For any matrix A with full column rank, the matrix $A^T A$ is positive-definite.

Proof We must show that $x^T (A^T A) x > 0$ for any nonzero vector x. For any vector x,

$$
\begin{aligned}
x^T (A^T A) x &= (Ax)^T (Ax) \qquad \text{(by Exercise 31.1-3)} \\
&= \|Ax\|^2 \\
&\geq 0 \, .
\end{aligned}
\tag{31.8}
$$

Note that $\|Ax\|^2$ is just the sum of the squares of the elements of the vector Ax. Therefore, if $\|Ax\|^2 = 0$, every element of Ax is 0, which is to say $Ax = 0$. Since A has full column rank, $Ax = 0$ implies $x = 0$, by Theorem 31.2. Hence, $A^T A$ is positive-definite. ∎

Other properties of positive-definite matrices will be explored in Section 31.6.

Exercises

31.1-1
Prove that the product of two lower-triangular matrices is lower-triangular. Prove that the determinant of a (lower- or upper-) triangular matrix is equal to the product of its diagonal elements. Prove that the inverse of a lower-triangular matrix, if it exists, is lower-triangular.

31.1-2
Prove that if P is an $n \times n$ permutation matrix and A is an $n \times n$ matrix, then PA can be obtained from A by permuting its rows, and AP can be

obtained from A by permuting its columns. Prove that the product of two permutation matrices is a permutation matrix. Prove that if P is a permutation matrix, then P is invertible, its inverse is P^T, and P^T is a permutation matrix.

31.1-3
Prove that $(AB)^T = B^T A^T$ and that $A^T A$ is always a symmetric matrix.

31.1-4
Prove that if B and C are inverses of A, then $B = C$.

31.1-5
Let A and B be $n \times n$ matrices such that $AB = I$. Prove that if A' is obtained from A by adding row j into row i, then the inverse B' of A' can be obtained by subtracting column i from column j of B.

31.1-6
Let A be a nonsingular $n \times n$ matrix with complex entries. Show that every entry of A^{-1} is real if and only if every entry of A is real.

31.1-7
Show that if A is a nonsingular symmetric matrix, then A^{-1} is symmetric. Show that if B is an arbitrary (compatible) matrix, then BAB^T is symmetric.

31.1-8
Show that a matrix A has full column rank if and only if $Ax = 0$ implies $x = 0$. (*Hint:* Express the linear dependence of one column on the others as a matrix-vector equation.)

31.1-9
Prove that for any two compatible matrices A and B,

$$\text{rank}(AB) \leq \min(\text{rank}(A), \text{rank}(B)) \, ,$$

where equality holds if either A or B is a nonsingular square matrix. (*Hint:* Use the alternate definition of the rank of a matrix.)

31.1-10
Given numbers $x_0, x_1, \ldots, x_{n-1}$, prove that the determinant of the **Vandermonde matrix**

$$V(x_0, x_1, \ldots, x_{n-1}) = \begin{pmatrix} 1 & x_0 & x_0^2 & \cdots & x_0^{n-1} \\ 1 & x_1 & x_1^2 & \cdots & x_1^{n-1} \\ \vdots & \vdots & \vdots & \ddots & \vdots \\ 1 & x_{n-1} & x_{n-1}^2 & \cdots & x_{n-1}^{n-1} \end{pmatrix}$$

is

$$\det(V(x_0, x_1, \ldots, x_{n-1})) = \prod_{0 \leq j < k \leq n-1} (x_k - x_j) \, .$$

(*Hint:* Multiply column i by $-x_0$ and add it to column $i + 1$ for $i = n - 1, n - 2, \ldots, 1$, and then use induction.)

31.2 Strassen's algorithm for matrix multiplication

This section presents Strassen's remarkable recursive algorithm for multiplying $n \times n$ matrices that runs in $\Theta(n^{\lg 7}) = O(n^{2.81})$ time. For sufficiently large n, therefore, it outperforms the naive $\Theta(n^3)$ matrix-multiplication algorithm MATRIX-MULTIPLY from Section 26.1.

An overview of the algorithm

Strassen's algorithm can be viewed as an application of a familiar design technique: divide and conquer. Suppose we wish to compute the product $C = AB$, where each of A, B, and C are $n \times n$ matrices. Assuming that n is an exact power of 2, we divide each of A, B, and C into four $n/2 \times n/2$ matrices, rewriting the equation $C = AB$ as follows:

$$\begin{pmatrix} r & s \\ t & u \end{pmatrix} = \begin{pmatrix} a & b \\ c & d \end{pmatrix} \begin{pmatrix} e & g \\ f & h \end{pmatrix} . \tag{31.9}$$

(Exercise 31.2-2 deals with the situation in which n is not an exact power of 2.) For convenience, the submatrices of A are labeled alphabetically from left to right, whereas those of B are labeled from top to bottom, in agreement with the way matrix multiplication is performed. Equation (31.9) corresponds to the four equations

$$r = ae + bf , \tag{31.10}$$
$$s = ag + bh , \tag{31.11}$$
$$t = ce + df , \tag{31.12}$$
$$u = cg + dh . \tag{31.13}$$

Each of these four equations specifies two multiplications of $n/2 \times n/2$ matrices and the addition of their $n/2 \times n/2$ products. Using these equations to define a straightforward divide-and-conquer strategy, we derive the following recurrence for the time $T(n)$ to multiply two $n \times n$ matrices:

$$T(n) = 8T(n/2) + \Theta(n^2) . \tag{31.14}$$

Unfortunately, recurrence (31.14) has the solution $T(n) = \Theta(n^3)$, and thus this method is no faster than the ordinary one.

Strassen discovered a different recursive approach that requires only 7 recursive multiplications of $n/2 \times n/2$ matrices and $\Theta(n^2)$ scalar additions and subtractions, yielding the recurrence

$$T(n) = 7T(n/2) + \Theta(n^2) \tag{31.15}$$

$$
\begin{aligned}
&= \ \Theta(n^{\lg 7}) \\
&= \ O(n^{2.81}) \ .
\end{aligned}
$$

Strassen's method has four steps:

1. Divide the input matrices A and B into $n/2 \times n/2$ submatrices, as in equation (31.9).

2. Using $\Theta(n^2)$ scalar additions and subtractions, compute 14 $n/2 \times n/2$ matrices $A_1, B_1, A_2, B_2, \ldots, A_7, B_7$.

3. Recursively compute the seven matrix products $P_i = A_i B_i$ for $i = 1, 2, \ldots, 7$.

4. Compute the desired submatrices r, s, t, u of the result matrix C by adding and/or subtracting various combinations of the P_i matrices, using only $\Theta(n^2)$ scalar additions and subtractions.

Such a procedure satisfies the recurrence (31.15). All that we have to do now is fill in the missing details.

Determining the submatrix products

It is not clear exactly how Strassen discovered the submatrix products that are the key to making his algorithm work. Here, we reconstruct one plausible discovery method.

Let us guess that each matrix product P_i can be written in the form

$$
\begin{aligned}
P_i &= \ A_i B_i \\
&= \ (\alpha_{i1}a + \alpha_{i2}b + \alpha_{i3}c + \alpha_{i4}d) \cdot (\beta_{i1}e + \beta_{i2}f + \beta_{i3}g + \beta_{i4}h) \ , \quad (31.16)
\end{aligned}
$$

where the coefficients α_{ij}, β_{ij} are all drawn from the set $\{-1, 0, 1\}$. That is, we guess that each product is computed by adding or subtracting some of the submatrices of A, adding or subtracting some of the submatrices of B, and then multiplying the two results together. While more general strategies are possible, this simple one turns out to work.

If we form all of our products in this manner, then we can use this method recursively without assuming commutativity of multiplication, since each product has all of the A submatrices on the left and all of the B submatrices on the right. This property is essential for the recursive application of this method, since matrix multiplication is not commutative.

For convenience, we shall use 4×4 matrices to represent linear combinations of products of submatrices, where each product combines one submatrix of A with one submatrix of B as in equation (31.16). For example, we can rewrite equation (31.10) as

$$
\begin{aligned}
r &= \ ae + bf \\
&= \ (a \ \ b \ \ c \ \ d)
\begin{pmatrix}
+1 & 0 & 0 & 0 \\
0 & +1 & 0 & 0 \\
0 & 0 & 0 & 0 \\
0 & 0 & 0 & 0
\end{pmatrix}
\begin{pmatrix}
e \\ f \\ g \\ h
\end{pmatrix}
\end{aligned}
$$

$$= \quad \begin{array}{c} a \\ b \\ c \\ d \end{array} \begin{matrix} e & f & g & h \\ \end{matrix} \left(\begin{matrix} + & \cdot & \cdot & \cdot \\ \cdot & + & \cdot & \cdot \\ \cdot & \cdot & \cdot & \cdot \\ \cdot & \cdot & \cdot & \cdot \end{matrix} \right) .$$

The last expression uses an abbreviated notation in which "+" represents $+1$, "·" represents 0, and "−" represents -1. (From here on, we omit the row and column labels.) Using this notation, we have the following equations for the other submatrices of the result matrix C:

$$s \;=\; ag + bh$$
$$= \; \left(\begin{matrix} \cdot & \cdot & + & \cdot \\ \cdot & \cdot & \cdot & + \\ \cdot & \cdot & \cdot & \cdot \\ \cdot & \cdot & \cdot & \cdot \end{matrix} \right) ,$$

$$t \;=\; ce + df$$
$$= \; \left(\begin{matrix} \cdot & \cdot & \cdot & \cdot \\ \cdot & \cdot & \cdot & \cdot \\ + & \cdot & \cdot & \cdot \\ \cdot & + & \cdot & \cdot \end{matrix} \right) ,$$

$$u \;=\; cg + dh$$
$$= \; \left(\begin{matrix} \cdot & \cdot & \cdot & \cdot \\ \cdot & \cdot & \cdot & \cdot \\ \cdot & \cdot & + & \cdot \\ \cdot & \cdot & \cdot & + \end{matrix} \right) .$$

We begin our search for a faster matrix-multiplication algorithm by observing that the submatrix s can be computed as $s = P_1 + P_2$, where P_1 and P_2 are computed using one matrix multiplication each:

$$P_1 \;=\; A_1 B_1$$
$$= \; a \cdot (g - h)$$
$$= \; ag - ah$$
$$= \; \left(\begin{matrix} \cdot & \cdot & + & - \\ \cdot & \cdot & \cdot & \cdot \\ \cdot & \cdot & \cdot & \cdot \\ \cdot & \cdot & \cdot & \cdot \end{matrix} \right) ,$$

$$P_2 \;=\; A_2 B_2$$
$$= \; (a + b) \cdot h$$
$$= \; ah + bh$$
$$= \; \left(\begin{matrix} \cdot & \cdot & \cdot & + \\ \cdot & \cdot & \cdot & + \\ \cdot & \cdot & \cdot & \cdot \\ \cdot & \cdot & \cdot & \cdot \end{matrix} \right) .$$

The matrix t can be computed in a similar manner as $t = P_3 + P_4$, where

$$
\begin{aligned}
P_3 &= A_3 B_3 \\
&= (c + d) \cdot e \\
&= ce + de \\
&= \begin{pmatrix} \cdot & \cdot & \cdot & \cdot \\ \cdot & \cdot & \cdot & \cdot \\ + & \cdot & \cdot & \cdot \\ + & \cdot & \cdot & \cdot \end{pmatrix}
\end{aligned}
$$

and

$$
\begin{aligned}
P_4 &= A_4 B_4 \\
&= d \cdot (f - e) \\
&= df - de \\
&= \begin{pmatrix} \cdot & \cdot & \cdot & \cdot \\ \cdot & \cdot & \cdot & \cdot \\ \cdot & \cdot & \cdot & \cdot \\ - & + & \cdot & \cdot \end{pmatrix} .
\end{aligned}
$$

Let us define an ***essential term*** to be one of the eight terms appearing on the right-hand side of one of the equations (31.10)–(31.13). We have now used 4 products to compute the two submatrices s and t whose essential terms are ag, bh, ce, and df. Note that P_1 computes the essential term ag, P_2 computes the essential term bh, P_3 computes the essential term ce, and P_4 computes the essential term df. Thus, it remains for us to compute the remaining two submatrices r and u, whose essential terms are the diagonal terms ae, bf, cg, and dh, without using more than 3 additional products. We now try the innovation P_5 in order to compute two essential terms at once:

$$
\begin{aligned}
P_5 &= A_5 B_5 \\
&= (a + d) \cdot (e + h) \\
&= ae + ah + de + dh \\
&= \begin{pmatrix} + & \cdot & \cdot & + \\ \cdot & \cdot & \cdot & \cdot \\ \cdot & \cdot & \cdot & \cdot \\ + & \cdot & \cdot & + \end{pmatrix} .
\end{aligned}
$$

In addition to computing both of the essential terms ae and dh, P_5 computes the inessential terms ah and de, which need to be cancelled somehow. We can use P_4 and P_2 to cancel them, but two other inessential terms then appear:

$$
\begin{aligned}
P_5 + P_4 - P_2 &= ae + dh + df - bh \\
&= \begin{pmatrix} + & \cdot & \cdot & \cdot \\ \cdot & \cdot & \cdot & - \\ \cdot & \cdot & \cdot & \cdot \\ \cdot & + & \cdot & + \end{pmatrix} .
\end{aligned}
$$

By adding an additional product

$$
\begin{aligned}
P_6 &= A_6 B_6 \\
&= (b - d) \cdot (f + h) \\
&= bf + bh - df - dh \\
&= \begin{pmatrix} \cdot & \cdot & \cdot & \cdot \\ \cdot & + & \cdot & + \\ \cdot & \cdot & \cdot & \cdot \\ \cdot & - & \cdot & - \end{pmatrix},
\end{aligned}
$$

however, we obtain

$$
\begin{aligned}
r &= P_5 + P_4 - P_2 + P_6 \\
&= ae + bf \\
&= \begin{pmatrix} + & \cdot & \cdot & \cdot \\ \cdot & + & \cdot & \cdot \\ \cdot & \cdot & \cdot & \cdot \\ \cdot & \cdot & \cdot & \cdot \end{pmatrix}.
\end{aligned}
$$

We can obtain u in a similar manner from P_5 by using P_1 and P_3 to move the inessential terms of P_5 in a different direction:

$$
\begin{aligned}
P_5 + P_1 - P_3 &= ae + ag - ce + dh \\
&= \begin{pmatrix} + & \cdot & + & \cdot \\ \cdot & \cdot & \cdot & \cdot \\ - & \cdot & \cdot & \cdot \\ \cdot & \cdot & \cdot & + \end{pmatrix}.
\end{aligned}
$$

By subtracting an additional product

$$
\begin{aligned}
P_7 &= A_7 B_7 \\
&= (a - c) \cdot (e + g) \\
&= ae + ag - ce - cg \\
&= \begin{pmatrix} + & \cdot & + & \cdot \\ \cdot & \cdot & \cdot & \cdot \\ - & \cdot & - & \cdot \\ \cdot & \cdot & \cdot & \cdot \end{pmatrix},
\end{aligned}
$$

we now obtain

$$
\begin{aligned}
u &= P_5 + P_1 - P_3 - P_7 \\
&= cg + dh \\
&= \begin{pmatrix} \cdot & \cdot & \cdot & \cdot \\ \cdot & \cdot & \cdot & \cdot \\ \cdot & \cdot & + & \cdot \\ \cdot & \cdot & \cdot & + \end{pmatrix}.
\end{aligned}
$$

The 7 submatrix products $P_1, P_2, \ldots, P_7$ can thus be used to compute the product $C = AB$, which completes the description of Strassen's method.

Discussion

The large constant hidden in the running time of Strassen's algorithm makes it impractical unless the matrices are large (n at least 45 or so) and dense (few zero entries). For small matrices, the straightforward algorithm is preferable, and for large, sparse matrices, there are special sparse-matrix algorithms that beat Strassen's in practice. Thus, Strassen's method is largely of theoretical interest.

By using advanced techniques beyond the scope of this text, one can in fact multiply $n \times n$ matrices in better than $\Theta(n^{\lg 7})$ time. The current best upper bound is approximately $O(n^{2.376})$. The best lower bound known is just the obvious $\Omega(n^2)$ bound (obvious because we have to fill in n^2 elements of the product matrix). Thus, we currently do not know how hard matrix multiplication really is.

Strassen's algorithm does not require that the matrix entries be real numbers. All that matters is that the number system form an algebraic ring. If the matrix entries do not form a ring, however, sometimes other techniques can be brought to bear to allow his method to apply. These issues are discussed more fully in the next section.

Exercises

31.2-1
Use Strassen's algorithm to compute the matrix product

$$\begin{pmatrix} 1 & 3 \\ 5 & 7 \end{pmatrix} \begin{pmatrix} 8 & 4 \\ 6 & 2 \end{pmatrix}.$$

Show your work.

31.2-2
How would you modify Strassen's algorithm to multiply $n \times n$ matrices in which n is not an exact power of 2? Show that the resulting algorithm runs in time $\Theta(n^{\lg 7})$.

31.2-3
What is the largest k such that if you can multiply 3×3 matrices using k multiplications (not assuming commutativity of multiplication), then you can multiply $n \times n$ matrices in time $o(n^{\lg 7})$? What would the running time of this algorithm be?

31.2-4
V. Pan has discovered a way of multiplying 68×68 matrices using 132,464 multiplications, a way of multiplying 70×70 matrices using 143,640 multiplications, and a way of multiplying 72×72 matrices using 155,424 multiplications. Which method yields the best asymptotic running time when

used in a divide-and-conquer matrix-multiplication algorithm? Compare it with the running time for Strassen's algorithm.

31.2-5
How quickly can you multiply a $kn \times n$ matrix by an $n \times kn$ matrix, using Strassen's algorithm as a subroutine? Answer the same question with the order of the input matrices reversed.

31.2-6
Show how to multiply the complex numbers $a + bi$ and $c + di$ using only three real multiplications. The algorithm should take a, b, c, and d as input and produce the real component $ac - bd$ and the imaginary component $ad + bc$ separately.

⋆ 31.3 Algebraic number systems and boolean matrix multiplication

The properties of matrix addition and multiplication depend on the properties of the underlying number system. In this section, we define three different kinds of underlying number systems: quasirings, rings, and fields. We can define matrix multiplication over quasirings, and Strassen's matrix-multiplication algorithm works over rings. We then present a simple trick for reducing boolean matrix multiplication, which is defined over a quasiring that is not a ring, to multiplication over a ring. Finally, we discuss why the properties of a field cannot naturally be exploited to provide better algorithms for matrix multiplication.

Quasirings

Let $(S, \oplus, \odot, \overline{0}, \overline{1})$ denote a number system, where S is a set of elements, $\oplus$ and $\odot$ are binary operations on S (the addition and multiplication operations, respectively), and $\overline{0}$ and $\overline{1}$ are distinct distinguished elements of S. This system is a **quasiring** if it satisfies the following properties:

1. $(S, \oplus, \overline{0})$ is a **monoid**:

   - S is **closed** under $\oplus$; that is, $a \oplus b \in S$ for all $a, b \in S$.
   - $\oplus$ is **associative**; that is, $a \oplus (b \oplus c) = (a \oplus b) \oplus c$ for all $a, b, c \in S$.
   - $\overline{0}$ is an **identity** for $\oplus$; that is, $a \oplus \overline{0} = \overline{0} \oplus a = a$ for all $a \in S$.

   Likewise, $(S, \odot, \overline{1})$ is a monoid.

2. $\overline{0}$ is an **annihilator**; that is, $a \odot \overline{0} = \overline{0} \odot a = \overline{0}$ for all $a \in S$.

3. The operator $\oplus$ is **commutative**; that is, $a \oplus b = b \oplus a$ for all $a, b \in S$.

4. The operator $\odot$ **distributes** over $\oplus$; that is, $a \odot (b \oplus c) = (a \odot b) \oplus (a \odot c)$ and $(b \oplus c) \odot a = (b \odot a) \oplus (c \odot a)$ for all $a, b, c \in S$.

Examples of quasirings include the ***boolean quasiring*** ($\{0, 1\}, \vee, \wedge, 0, 1$), where $\vee$ denotes logical OR and $\wedge$ denotes logical AND, and the natural number system ($\mathbf{N}, +, \cdot, 0, 1$), where $+$ and $\cdot$ denote ordinary addition and multiplication. Any closed semiring (see Section 26.4) is also a quasiring; closed semirings obey additional idempotence and infinite-sum properties.

We can extend $\oplus$ and $\odot$ to matrices as we did for $+$ and $\cdot$ in Section 31.1. Denoting the $n \times n$ identity matrix composed of $\overline{0}$ and $\overline{1}$ by $\overline{I}_n$, we find that matrix multiplication is well defined and the matrix system is itself a quasiring, as the following theorem states.

Theorem 31.7 (Matrices over a quasiring form a quasiring)
If $(S, \oplus, \odot, \overline{0}, \overline{1})$ is a quasiring and $n \geq 1$, then $(S^{n \times n}, \oplus, \odot, \overline{0}, \overline{I}_n)$ is a quasiring.

Proof   The proof is left as Exercise 31.3-3.   ∎

Rings

Subtraction is not defined for quasirings, but it is for a ***ring***, which is a quasiring $(S, \oplus, \odot, \overline{0}, \overline{1})$ that satisfies the following additional property:

5. Every element in S has an ***additive inverse***; that is, for all $a \in S$, there exists an element $b \in S$ such that $a \oplus b = b \oplus a = \overline{0}$. Such a b is also called the ***negative*** of a and is denoted $(-a)$.

Given that the negative of any element is defined, we can define subtraction by $a - b = a + (-b)$.

There are many examples of rings. The integers $(\mathbf{Z}, +, \cdot, 0, 1)$ under the usual operations of addition and multiplication form a ring. The integers modulo n for any integer $n > 1$—that is, $(\mathbf{Z}_n, +, \cdot, 0, 1)$, where $+$ is addition modulo n and $\cdot$ is multiplication modulo n—form a ring. Another example is the set $\mathbf{R}[x]$ of finite-degree polynomials in x with real coefficients under the usual operations—that is, $(\mathbf{R}[x], +, \cdot, 0, 1)$, where $+$ is polynomial addition and $\cdot$ is polynomial multiplication.

The following corollary shows that Theorem 31.7 generalizes naturally to rings.

Corollary 31.8 (Matrices over a ring form a ring)
If $(S, \oplus, \odot, \overline{0}, \overline{1})$ is a ring and $n \geq 1$, then $(S^{n \times n}, \oplus, \odot, \overline{0}, \overline{I}_n)$ is a ring.

Proof   The proof is left as Exercise 31.3-3.   ∎

Using this corollary, we can prove the following theorem.

Theorem 31.9
Strassen's matrix-multiplication algorithm works properly over any ring of matrix elements.

Proof Strassen's algorithm depends on the correctness of the algorithm for 2×2 matrices, which requires only that the matrix elements belong to a ring. Since the matrix elements do belong to a ring, Corollary 31.8 implies the matrices themselves form a ring. Thus, by induction, Strassen's algorithm works correctly at each level of recursion. ∎

Strassen's algorithm for matrix multiplication, in fact, depends critically on the existence of additive inverses. Out of the seven products $P_1, P_2, \ldots, P_7$, four involve differences of submatrices. Thus, Strassen's algorithm does not work in general for quasirings.

Boolean matrix multiplication

Strassen's algorithm cannot be used directly to multiply boolean matrices, since the boolean quasiring $(\{0, 1\}, \vee, \wedge, 0, 1)$ is not a ring. There are instances in which a quasiring is contained in a larger system that is a ring. For example, the natural numbers (a quasiring) are a subset of the integers (a ring), and Strassen's algorithm can therefore be used to multiply matrices of natural numbers if we consider the underlying number system to be the integers. Unfortunately, the boolean quasiring cannot be extended in a similar way to a ring. (See Exercise 31.3-4.)

The following theorem presents a simple trick for reducing boolean matrix multiplication to multiplication over a ring. Problem 31-1 presents another efficient approach.

Theorem 31.10
If $M(n)$ denotes the number of arithmetic operations required to multiply two $n \times n$ matrices over the integers, then two $n \times n$ boolean matrices can be multiplied using $O(M(n))$ arithmetic operations.

Proof Let the two matrices be A and B, and let $C = AB$ in the boolean quasiring, that is,

$$c_{ij} = \bigvee_{k=1}^{n} a_{ik} \wedge b_{kj} \, .$$

Instead of computing over the boolean quasiring, we compute the product C' over the ring of integers with the given matrix-multiplication algorithm that uses $M(n)$ arithmetic operations. We thus have

$$c'_{ij} = \sum_{k=1}^{n} a_{ik} b_{kj} \, .$$

Each term $a_{ik}b_{kj}$ of this sum is 0 if and only if $a_{ik} \wedge b_{kj} = 0$, and 1 if and only if $a_{ik} \wedge b_{kj} = 1$. Thus, the integer sum c'_{ij} is 0 if and only if every term is 0 or, equivalently, if and only if the boolean OR of the terms, which is c_{ij}, is 0. Therefore, the boolean matrix C can be reconstructed with $\Theta(n^2)$ arithmetic operations from the integer matrix C' by simply comparing each c'_{ij} with 0. The number of arithmetic operations for the entire procedure is then $O(M(n)) + \Theta(n^2) = O(M(n))$, since $M(n) = \Omega(n^2)$.   ∎

Thus, using Strassen's algorithm, we can perform boolean matrix multiplication in $O(n^{\lg 7})$ time.

The normal method of multiplying boolean matrices uses only boolean variables. If we use this adaptation of Strassen's algorithm, however, the final product matrix can have entries as large as n, thus requiring a computer word to store them rather than a single bit. More worrisome is that the intermediate results, which are integers, may grow even larger. One method for keeping intermediate results from growing too large is to perform all computations modulo $n+1$. Exercise 31.3-5 asks you to show that working modulo $n + 1$ does not affect the correctness of the algorithm.

Fields

A ring $(S, \oplus, \odot, \overline{0}, \overline{1})$ is a *field* if it satisfies the following two additional properties:

6. The operator $\odot$ is *commutative*; that is, $a \odot b = b \odot a$ for all $a, b \in S$.

7. Every nonzero element in S has a *multiplicative inverse*; that is, for all $a \in S - \{\overline{0}\}$, there exists an element $b \in S$ such that $a \odot b = b \odot a = \overline{1}$. Such an element b is often called the *inverse* of a and is denoted a^{-1}.

Examples of fields include the real numbers $(\mathbf{R}, +, \cdot, 0, 1)$, the complex numbers $(\mathbf{C}, +, \cdot, 0, 1)$, and the integers modulo a prime p: $(\mathbf{Z}_p, +, \cdot, 0, 1)$.

Because fields offer multiplicative inverses of elements, division is possible. They also offer commutativity. By generalizing from quasirings to rings, Strassen was able to improve the running time of matrix multiplication. Since the underlying elements of matrices are often from a field—the real numbers, for instance—one might hope that by using fields instead of rings in a Strassen-like recursive algorithm, the running time might be further improved.

This approach seems unlikely to be fruitful. For a recursive divide-and-conquer algorithm based on fields to work, the matrices at each step of the recursion must form a field. Unfortunately, the natural extension of Theorem 31.7 and Corollary 31.8 to fields fails badly. For $n > 1$, the set of $n \times n$ matrices *never* forms a field, even if the underlying number system is a field. Multiplication of $n \times n$ matrices is not commutative, and many $n \times n$ matrices do not have inverses. Better algorithms for matrix multiplication are therefore more likely to be based on ring theory than on field theory.

Exercises

31.3-1 ⋆
Does Strassen's algorithm work over the number system $(\mathbf{Z}[x], +, \cdot, 0, 1)$, where $\mathbf{Z}[x]$ is the set of all polynomials with integer coefficients in the variable x and $+$ and $\cdot$ are ordinary polynomial addition and multiplication?

31.3-2 ⋆
Explain why Strassen's algorithm doesn't work over closed semirings (see Section 26.4) or over the boolean quasiring $(\{0, 1\}, \vee, \wedge, 0, 1)$.

31.3-3 ⋆
Prove Theorem 31.7 and Corollary 31.8.

31.3-4 ⋆
Show that the boolean quasiring $(\{0, 1\}, \vee, \wedge, 0, 1)$ cannot be embedded in a ring. That is, show that it is impossible to add a "-1" to the quasiring so that the resulting algebraic structure is a ring.

31.3-5
Argue that if all computations in the algorithm of Theorem 31.10 are performed modulo $n + 1$, the algorithm still works correctly.

31.3-6
Show how to determine efficiently if a given undirected input graph contains a triangle (a set of three mutually adjacent vertices).

31.3-7 ⋆
Show that computing the product of two $n \times n$ boolean matrices over the boolean quasiring is reducible to computing the transitive closure of a given directed $3n$-vertex input graph.

31.3-8
Show how to compute the transitive closure of a given directed n-vertex input graph in time $O(n^{\lg 7} \lg n)$. Compare this result with the performance of the TRANSITIVE-CLOSURE procedure in Section 26.2.

31.4 Solving systems of linear equations

Solving a set of simultaneous linear equations is a fundamental problem that occurs in diverse applications. A linear system can be expressed as a matrix equation in which each matrix or vector element belongs to a field, typically the real numbers $\mathbf{R}$. This section discusses how to solve a system of linear equations using a method called LUP decomposition.

We start with a set of linear equations in n unknowns $x_1, x_2, \ldots, x_n$:

$$a_{11}x_1 + a_{12}x_2 + \cdots + a_{1n}x_n = b_1 ,$$
$$a_{21}x_1 + a_{22}x_2 + \cdots + a_{2n}x_n = b_2 ,$$
$$\vdots$$
$$a_{n1}x_1 + a_{n2}x_2 + \cdots + a_{nn}x_n = b_n . \qquad (31.17)$$

A set of values for $x_1, x_2, \ldots, x_n$ that satisfy all of the equations (31.17) simultaneously is said to be a *solution* to these equations. In this section, we only treat the case in which there are exactly n equations in n unknowns.

We can conveniently rewrite equations (31.17) as the matrix-vector equation

$$\begin{pmatrix} a_{11} & a_{12} & \cdots & a_{1n} \\ a_{21} & a_{22} & \cdots & a_{2n} \\ \vdots & \vdots & \ddots & \vdots \\ a_{n1} & a_{n2} & \cdots & a_{nn} \end{pmatrix} \begin{pmatrix} x_1 \\ x_2 \\ \vdots \\ x_n \end{pmatrix} = \begin{pmatrix} b_1 \\ b_2 \\ \vdots \\ b_n \end{pmatrix}$$

or, equivalently, letting $A = (a_{ij})$, $x = (x_j)$, and $b = (b_i)$, as

$$Ax = b . \qquad (31.18)$$

If A is nonsingular, it possesses an inverse A^{-1}, and

$$x = A^{-1}b \qquad (31.19)$$

is the solution vector. We can prove that x is the unique solution to equation (31.18) as follows. If there are two solutions, x and x', then $Ax = Ax' = b$ and

$$
\begin{aligned}
x &= (A^{-1}A)x \\
&= A^{-1}(Ax) \\
&= A^{-1}(Ax') \\
&= (A^{-1}A)x' \\
&= x' .
\end{aligned}
$$

In this section, we shall be concerned predominantly with the case in which A is nonsingular or, equivalently (by Theorem 31.1), the rank of A is equal to the number n of unknowns. There are other possibilities, however, which merit a brief discussion. If the number of equations is less than the number n of unknowns—or, more generally, if the rank of A is less than n—then the system is *underdetermined*. An underdetermined system typically has infinitely many solutions (see Exercise 31.4-9), although it may have no solutions at all if the equations are inconsistent. If the number of equations exceeds the number n of unknowns, the system is *overdetermined*, and there may not exist any solutions. Finding good approximate solutions to overdetermined systems of linear equations is an important problem that is addressed in Section 31.6.

Let us return to our problem of solving the system $Ax = b$ of n equations in n unknowns. One approach is to compute A^{-1} and then multiply both sides by A^{-1}, yielding $A^{-1}Ax = A^{-1}b$, or $x = A^{-1}b$. This approach suffers in practice from **numerical instability**: round-off errors tend to accumulate unduly when floating-point number representations are used instead of ideal real numbers. There is, fortunately, another approach—LUP decomposition—that is numerically stable and has the further advantage of being about a factor of 3 faster.

Overview of LUP decomposition

The idea behind LUP decomposition is to find three $n \times n$ matrices L, U, and P such that

$$PA = LU ,\tag{31.20}$$

where

- L is a unit lower-triangular matrix,
- U is an upper-triangular matrix, and
- P is a permutation matrix.

We call matrices L, U, and P satisfying equation (31.20) an **LUP decomposition** of the matrix A. We shall show that every nonsingular matrix A possesses such a decomposition.

The advantage of computing an LUP decomposition for the matrix A is that linear systems can be solved more readily when they are triangular, as is the case for both matrices L and U. Having found an LUP decomposition for A, we can solve the equation (31.18) $Ax = b$ by solving only triangular linear systems, as follows. Multiplying both sides of $Ax = b$ by P yields the equivalent equation $PAx = Pb$, which by Exercise 31.1-2 amounts to permuting the equations (31.17). Using our decomposition (31.20), we obtain

$$LUx = Pb .$$

We can now solve this equation by solving two triangular linear systems. Let us define $y = Ux$, where x is the desired solution vector. First, we solve the lower-triangular system

$$Ly = Pb\tag{31.21}$$

for the unknown vector y by a method called "forward substitution." Having solved for y, we then solve the upper-triangular system

$$Ux = y\tag{31.22}$$

for the unknown x by a method called "back substitution." The vector x is our solution to $Ax = b$, since the permutation matrix P is invertible (Exercise 31.1-2):

$$Ax \;=\; P^{-1}LUx$$

$$
\begin{aligned}
&= \ P^{-1}Ly \\
&= \ P^{-1}Pb \\
&= \ b \ .
\end{aligned}
$$

Our next step is to show how forward and back substitution work and then attack the problem of computing the LUP decomposition itself.

Forward and back substitution

Forward substitution can solve the lower-triangular system (31.21) in $\Theta(n^2)$ time, given L, P, and b. For convenience, we represent the permutation P compactly by an array $\pi[1 \mathinner{\ldotp\ldotp} n]$. For $i = 1, 2, \ldots, n$, the entry $\pi[i]$ indicates that $P_{i,\pi[i]} = 1$ and $P_{ij} = 0$ for $j \neq \pi[i]$. Thus, PA has $a_{\pi[i],j}$ in row i and column j, and Pb has $b_{\pi[i]}$ as its ith element. Since L is unit lower-triangular, equation (31.21) can be rewritten as

$$
\begin{aligned}
y_1 \qquad\qquad\qquad\qquad\qquad &= \ b_{\pi[1]} \ , \\
l_{21}y_1 + \quad y_2 \qquad\qquad\qquad &= \ b_{\pi[2]} \ , \\
l_{31}y_1 + l_{32}y_2 + \quad y_3 \qquad\qquad &= \ b_{\pi[3]} \ , \\
&\ \ \vdots \\
l_{n1}y_1 + l_{n2}y_2 + l_{n3}y_3 + \cdots + y_n &= \ b_{\pi[n]} \ .
\end{aligned}
$$

Quite apparently, we can solve for y_1 directly, since the first equation tells us that $y_1 = b_{\pi[1]}$. Having solved for y_1, we can substitute it into the second equation, yielding

$$
y_2 = b_{\pi[2]} - l_{21}y_1 \ .
$$

Now, we can substitute both y_1 and y_2 into the third equation, obtaining

$$
y_3 = b_{\pi[3]} - (l_{31}y_1 + l_{32}y_2) \ .
$$

In general, we substitute $y_1, y_2, \ldots, y_{i-1}$ "forward" into the ith equation to solve for y_i:

$$
y_i = b_{\pi[i]} - \sum_{j=1}^{i-1} l_{ij}y_j \ .
$$

Back substitution is similar to forward substitution. Given U and y, we solve the nth equation first and work backward to to the first equation. Like forward substitution, this process runs in $\Theta(n^2)$ time. Since U is upper-triangular, we can rewrite the system (31.22) as

$$
\begin{aligned}
u_{11}x_1 + u_{12}x_2 + \cdots + \quad u_{1,n-2}x_{n-2} + \quad u_{1,n-1}x_{n-1} + \quad u_{1n}x_n &= y_1 \ , \\
u_{22}x_2 + \cdots + \quad u_{2,n-2}x_{n-2} + \quad u_{2,n-1}x_{n-1} + \quad u_{2n}x_n &= y_2 \ , \\
&\ \ \vdots \\
u_{n-2,n-2}x_{n-2} + u_{n-2,n-1}x_{n-1} + u_{n-2,n}x_n &= y_{n-2} \ , \\
u_{n-1,n-1}x_{n-1} + u_{n-1,n}x_n &= y_{n-1} \ , \\
u_{n,n}x_n &= y_n \ .
\end{aligned}
$$

Thus, we can solve for $x_n, x_{n-1}, \ldots, x_1$ successively as follows:

$$
\begin{aligned}
x_n &= y_n/u_{nn} \, , \\
x_{n-1} &= (y_{n-1} - u_{n-1,n}x_n)/u_{n-1,n-1} \, , \\
x_{n-2} &= (y_{n-2} - (u_{n-2,n-1}x_{n-1} + u_{n-2,n}x_n))/u_{n-2,n-2} \, , \\
&\vdots
\end{aligned}
$$

or, in general,

$$
x_i = \left(y_i - \sum_{j=i+1}^{n} u_{ij}x_j \right) / u_{ii} \, .
$$

Given P, L, U, and b, the procedure LUP-SOLVE solves for x by combining forward and back substitution. The pseudocode assumes that the dimension n appears in the attribute *rows*[L] and that the permutation matrix P is represented by the array π.

LUP-SOLVE(L, U, π, b)
1 $n \leftarrow rows[L]$
2 **for** $i \leftarrow 1$ **to** n
3   **do** $y_i \leftarrow b_{\pi[i]} - \sum_{j=1}^{i-1} l_{ij}y_j$
4 **for** $i \leftarrow n$ **downto** 1
5   **do** $x_i \leftarrow \left(y_i - \sum_{j=i+1}^{n} u_{ij}x_j \right) / u_{ii}$
6 **return** x

Procedure LUP-SOLVE solves for y using forward substitution in lines 2–3, and then it solves for x using backward substitution in lines 4–5. Since there is an implicit loop in the summations within each of the **for** loops, the running time is $\Theta(n^2)$.

As an example of these methods, consider the system of linear equations defined by

$$
\begin{pmatrix} 1 & 2 & 0 \\ 3 & 5 & 4 \\ 5 & 6 & 3 \end{pmatrix} x = \begin{pmatrix} 0.1 \\ 12.5 \\ 10.3 \end{pmatrix} \, ,
$$

where

$$
A = \begin{pmatrix} 1 & 2 & 0 \\ 3 & 5 & 4 \\ 5 & 6 & 3 \end{pmatrix} \, ,
$$

$$
b = \begin{pmatrix} 0.1 \\ 12.5 \\ 10.3 \end{pmatrix} \, ,
$$

and we wish to solve for the unknown x. The LUP decomposition is

$$
L = \begin{pmatrix} 1 & 0 & 0 \\ 0.6 & 1 & 0 \\ 0.2 & 0.571 & 1 \end{pmatrix} \, ,
$$

$$U = \begin{pmatrix} 5 & 6 & 3 \\ 0 & 1.4 & 2.2 \\ 0 & 0 & -1.856 \end{pmatrix},$$

$$P = \begin{pmatrix} 0 & 0 & 1 \\ 0 & 1 & 0 \\ 1 & 0 & 0 \end{pmatrix}.$$

(The reader can verify that $PA = LU$.) Using forward substitution, we solve $Ly = Pb$ for y:

$$\begin{pmatrix} 1 & 0 & 0 \\ 0.6 & 1 & 0 \\ 0.2 & 0.571 & 1 \end{pmatrix} \begin{pmatrix} y_1 \\ y_2 \\ y_3 \end{pmatrix} = \begin{pmatrix} 10.3 \\ 12.5 \\ 0.1 \end{pmatrix},$$

obtaining

$$y = \begin{pmatrix} 10.3 \\ 6.32 \\ -5.569 \end{pmatrix}$$

by computing first y_1, then y_2, and finally y_3. Using back substitution, we solve $Ux = y$ for x:

$$\begin{pmatrix} 5 & 6 & 3 \\ 0 & 1.4 & 2.2 \\ 0 & 0 & -1.856 \end{pmatrix} \begin{pmatrix} x_1 \\ x_2 \\ x_3 \end{pmatrix} = \begin{pmatrix} 10.3 \\ 6.32 \\ -5.569 \end{pmatrix},$$

thereby obtaining the desired answer

$$x = \begin{pmatrix} 0.5 \\ -0.2 \\ 3.0 \end{pmatrix}$$

by computing first x_3, then x_2, and finally x_1.

Computing an LU decomposition

We have now shown that if an LUP decomposition can be computed for a nonsingular matrix A, forward and back substitution can be used to solve the system $Ax = b$ of linear equations. It remains to show how an LUP decomposition for A can be found efficiently. We start with the case in which A is an $n \times n$ nonsingular matrix and P is absent (or, equivalently, $P = I_n$). In this case, we must find a factorization $A = LU$. We call the two matrices L and U an ***LU decomposition*** of A.

The process by which we perform LU decomposition is called ***Gaussian elimination***. We start by subtracting multiples of the first equation from the other equations so that the first variable is removed from those equations. Then, we subtract multiples of the second equation from the third and subsequent equations so that now the first and second variables are removed from them. We continue this process until the system that is left has an upper-triangular form—in fact, it is the matrix U. The matrix L is made up of the row multipliers that cause variables to be eliminated.

Our algorithm to implement this strategy is recursive. We wish to construct an LU decomposition for an $n \times n$ nonsingular matrix A. If $n = 1$, then we're done, since we can choose $L = I_1$ and $U = A$. For $n > 1$, we break A into four parts:

$$
\begin{aligned}
A &= \left(\begin{array}{c|ccc}
a_{11} & a_{12} & \cdots & a_{1n} \\
\hline
a_{21} & a_{22} & \cdots & a_{2n} \\
\vdots & \vdots & \ddots & \vdots \\
a_{n1} & a_{n2} & \cdots & a_{nn}
\end{array} \right) \\
&= \left(\begin{array}{cc}
a_{11} & w^{\mathrm{T}} \\
v & A'
\end{array} \right) ,
\end{aligned}
$$

where v is a size-$(n-1)$ column vector, w^{T} is a size-$(n-1)$ row vector, and A' is an $(n-1) \times (n-1)$ matrix. Then, using matrix algebra (verify the equations by simply multiplying through), we can factor A as

$$
\begin{aligned}
A &= \left(\begin{array}{cc}
a_{11} & w^{\mathrm{T}} \\
v & A'
\end{array} \right) \\
&= \left(\begin{array}{cc}
1 & 0 \\
v/a_{11} & I_{n-1}
\end{array} \right) \left(\begin{array}{cc}
a_{11} & w^{\mathrm{T}} \\
0 & A' - vw^{\mathrm{T}}/a_{11}
\end{array} \right) .
\end{aligned}
$$

The 0's in the first and second matrices of the factorization are row and column vectors, respectively, of size $n - 1$. The term vw^{T}/a_{11}, formed by taking the outer product of v and w and dividing each element of the result by a_{11}, is an $(n-1) \times (n-1)$ matrix, which conforms in size to the matrix A' from which it is subtracted. The resulting $(n-1) \times (n-1)$ matrix

$$A' - vw^{\mathrm{T}}/a_{11} \tag{31.23}$$

is called the ***Schur complement*** of A with respect to a_{11}.

We now recursively find an LU decomposition of the Schur complement. Let us say that

$$A' - vw^{\mathrm{T}}/a_{11} = L'U' ,$$

where L' is unit lower-triangular and U' is upper-triangular. Then, using matrix algebra, we have

$$
\begin{aligned}
A &= \left(\begin{array}{cc}
1 & 0 \\
v/a_{11} & I_{n-1}
\end{array} \right) \left(\begin{array}{cc}
a_{11} & w^{\mathrm{T}} \\
0 & A' - vw^{\mathrm{T}}/a_{11}
\end{array} \right) \\
&= \left(\begin{array}{cc}
1 & 0 \\
v/a_{11} & I_{n-1}
\end{array} \right) \left(\begin{array}{cc}
a_{11} & w^{\mathrm{T}} \\
0 & L'U'
\end{array} \right) \\
&= \left(\begin{array}{cc}
1 & 0 \\
v/a_{11} & L'
\end{array} \right) \left(\begin{array}{cc}
a_{11} & w^{\mathrm{T}} \\
0 & U'
\end{array} \right) \\
&= LU ,
\end{aligned}
$$

thereby providing our LU decomposition. (Note that because L' is unit lower-triangular, so is L, and because U' is upper-triangular, so is U.)

Of course, if $a_{11} = 0$, this method doesn't work, because it divides by 0. It also doesn't work if the upper leftmost entry of the Schur complement $A' - vw^{\mathrm{T}}/a_{11}$ is 0, since we divide by it in the next step of the recursion. The elements by which we divide during LU decomposition are called ***pivots***, and they occupy the diagonal elements of the matrix U. The reason we include a permutation matrix P during LUP decomposition is that it allows us to avoid dividing by zero elements. Using permutations to avoid division by 0 (or by small numbers) is called ***pivoting***.

An important class of matrices for which LU decomposition always works correctly is the class of symmetric positive-definite matrices. Such matrices require no pivoting, and thus the recursive strategy outlined above can be employed without fear of dividing by 0. We shall prove this result, as well as several others, in Section 31.6.

Our code for LU decomposition of a matrix A follows the recursive strategy, except that an iteration loop replaces the recursion. (This transformation is a standard optimization for a "tail-recursive" procedure—one whose last operation is a recursive call to itself.) It assumes that the dimension of A is kept in the attribute *rows*[A]. Since we know that the output matrix U has 0's below the diagonal, and since LU-SOLVE does not look at these entries, the code does not bother to fill them in. Likewise, because the output matrix L has 1's on its diagonal and 0's above the diagonal, these entries are not filled in either. Thus, the code computes only the "significant" entries of L and U.

LU-DECOMPOSITION(A)

```
 1   n ← rows[A]
 2   for k ← 1 to n
 3        do u_{kk} ← a_{kk}
 4            for i ← k + 1 to n
 5                do l_{ik} ← a_{ik}/u_{kk}     ▷ l_{ik} holds v_i
 6                   u_{ki} ← a_{ki}            ▷ u_{ki} holds w_i^T
 7            for i ← k + 1 to n
 8                do for j ← k + 1 to n
 9                       do a_{ij} ← a_{ij} − l_{ik}u_{kj}
10   return L and U
```

The outer **for** loop beginning in line 2 iterates once for each recursive step. Within this loop, the pivot is determined to be $u_{kk} = a_{kk}$ in line 3. Within the **for** loop in lines 4–6 (which does not execute when $k = n$), the v and w^{T} vectors are used to update L and U. The elements of the v vector are determined in line 5, where v_i is stored in l_{ik}, and the elements of the w^{T} vector are determined in line 6, where w_i^{T} is stored in u_{ki}. Finally, the elements of the Schur complement are computed in lines 7–9 and stored back in the matrix A. Because line 9 is triply nested, LU-DECOMPOSITION runs in time $\Theta(n^3)$.

$$
\begin{array}{cccc}
2 & 3 & 1 & 5 \\
6 & 13 & 5 & 19 \\
2 & 19 & 10 & 23 \\
4 & 10 & 11 & 31
\end{array}
$$
(a)

$$
\begin{array}{c|ccc}
\mathbf{2} & 3 & 1 & 5 \\
\hline
3 & 4 & 2 & 4 \\
1 & 16 & 9 & 18 \\
2 & 4 & 9 & 21
\end{array}
$$
(b)

$$
\begin{array}{cc|cc}
2 & 3 & 1 & 5 \\
3 & \mathbf{4} & 2 & 4 \\
\hline
1 & 4 & 1 & 2 \\
2 & 1 & 7 & 17
\end{array}
$$
(c)

$$
\begin{array}{ccc|c}
2 & 3 & 1 & 5 \\
3 & 4 & 2 & 4 \\
1 & 4 & \mathbf{1} & 2 \\
\hline
2 & 1 & 7 & 3
\end{array}
$$
(d)

$$
\begin{pmatrix}
2 & 3 & 1 & 5 \\
6 & 13 & 5 & 19 \\
2 & 19 & 10 & 23 \\
4 & 10 & 11 & 31
\end{pmatrix}
=
\begin{pmatrix}
1 & 0 & 0 & 0 \\
3 & 1 & 0 & 0 \\
1 & 4 & 1 & 0 \\
2 & 1 & 7 & 1
\end{pmatrix}
\begin{pmatrix}
2 & 3 & 1 & 5 \\
0 & 4 & 2 & 4 \\
0 & 0 & 1 & 2 \\
0 & 0 & 0 & 3
\end{pmatrix}
$$
$$ \quad\quad A \quad\quad\quad\quad\quad\quad L \quad\quad\quad\quad\quad\quad U $$
(e)

Figure 31.1 The operation of LU-DECOMPOSITION. (**a**) The matrix A. (**b**) The element $a_{11} = 2$ in black is the pivot, the shaded column is v/a_{11}, and the shaded row is w^{T}. The elements of U computed thus far are above the horizontal line, and the elements of L are to the left of the vertical line. The Schur complement matrix $A' - vw^{\mathrm{T}}/a_{11}$ occupies the lower right. (**c**) We now operate on the Schur complement matrix produced from part (b). The element $a_{22} = 4$ in black is the pivot, and the shaded column and row are v/a_{22} and w^{T} (in the partitioning of the Schur complement), respectively. Lines divide the matrix into the elements of U computed so far (above), the elements of L computed so far (left), and the new Schur complement (lower right). (**d**) The next step completes the factorization. (The element 3 in the new Schur complement becomes part of U when the recursion terminates.) (**e**) The factorization $A = LU$.

Figure 31.1 illustrates the operation of LU-DECOMPOSITION. It shows a standard optimization of the procedure in which the significant elements of L and U are stored "in place" in the matrix A. That is, we can set up a correspondence between each element a_{ij} and either l_{ij} (if $i > j$) or u_{ij} (if $i \le j$) and update the matrix A so that it holds both L and U when the procedure terminates. The pseudocode for this optimization is obtained from the above pseudocode merely by replacing each reference to l or u by a; it is not difficult to verify that this transformation preserves correctness.

Computing an LUP decomposition

Generally, in solving a system of linear equations $Ax = b$, we must pivot on off-diagonal elements of A to avoid dividing by 0. Not only is division by 0 undesirable, so is division by any small value, even if A is nonsingular, because numerical instabilities can result in the computation. We therefore try to pivot on a large value.

The mathematics behind LUP decomposition is similar to that of LU decomposition. Recall that we are given an $n \times n$ nonsingular matrix A and wish to find a permutation matrix P, a unit lower-triangular matrix L, and an upper-triangular matrix U such that $PA = LU$. Before we partition the matrix A, as we did for LU decomposition, we move a nonzero element, say a_{k1}, from the first column to the $(1, 1)$ position of the matrix. (If the first column contains only 0's, then A is singular, because its determinant is 0, by Theorems 31.4 and 31.5.) In order to preserve the set of equations, we exchange row 1 with row k, which is equivalent to multiplying A by a permutation matrix Q on the left (Exercise 31.1-2). Thus, we can write QA as

$$QA = \begin{pmatrix} a_{k1} & w^{\mathrm{T}} \\ v & A' \end{pmatrix} ,$$

where $v = (a_{21}, a_{31}, \ldots, a_{n1})^{\mathrm{T}}$, except that a_{11} replaces a_{k1}; $w^{\mathrm{T}} = (a_{k2}, a_{k3}, \ldots, a_{kn})$; and A' is an $(n-1) \times (n-1)$ matrix. Since $a_{k1} \neq 0$, we can now perform much the same linear algebra as for LU decomposition, but now guaranteeing that we do not divide by 0:

$$\begin{aligned} QA &= \begin{pmatrix} a_{k1} & w^{\mathrm{T}} \\ v & A' \end{pmatrix} \\ &= \begin{pmatrix} 1 & 0 \\ v/a_{k1} & I_{n-1} \end{pmatrix} \begin{pmatrix} a_{k1} & w^{\mathrm{T}} \\ 0 & A' - vw^{\mathrm{T}}/a_{k1} \end{pmatrix} . \end{aligned}$$

The Schur complement $A' - vw^{\mathrm{T}}/a_{k1}$ is nonsingular, because otherwise the second matrix in the last equation has determinant 0, and thus the determinant of matrix A is 0; but this means that A is singular, which contradicts our assumption that A is nonsingular. Consequently, we can inductively find an LUP decomposition for the Schur complement, with unit lower-triangular matrix L', upper-triangular matrix U', and permutation matrix P', such that

$$P'(A' - vw^{\mathrm{T}}/a_{k1}) = L'U' .$$

Define

$$P = \begin{pmatrix} 1 & 0 \\ 0 & P' \end{pmatrix} Q ,$$

which is a permutation matrix, since it is the product of two permutation matrices (Exercise 31.1-2). We now have

$$\begin{aligned} PA &= \begin{pmatrix} 1 & 0 \\ 0 & P' \end{pmatrix} QA \\ &= \begin{pmatrix} 1 & 0 \\ 0 & P' \end{pmatrix} \begin{pmatrix} 1 & 0 \\ v/a_{k1} & I_{n-1} \end{pmatrix} \begin{pmatrix} a_{k1} & w^{\mathrm{T}} \\ 0 & A' - vw^{\mathrm{T}}/a_{k1} \end{pmatrix} \\ &= \begin{pmatrix} 1 & 0 \\ P'v/a_{k1} & P' \end{pmatrix} \begin{pmatrix} a_{k1} & w^{\mathrm{T}} \\ 0 & A' - vw^{\mathrm{T}}/a_{k1} \end{pmatrix} \\ &= \begin{pmatrix} 1 & 0 \\ P'v/a_{k1} & I_{n-1} \end{pmatrix} \begin{pmatrix} a_{k1} & w^{\mathrm{T}} \\ 0 & P'(A' - vw^{\mathrm{T}}/a_{k1}) \end{pmatrix} \end{aligned}$$

$$
\begin{aligned}
&= \begin{pmatrix} 1 & 0 \\ P'v/a_{k1} & I_{n-1} \end{pmatrix} \begin{pmatrix} a_{k1} & w^{\mathrm{T}} \\ 0 & L'U' \end{pmatrix} \\
&= \begin{pmatrix} 1 & 0 \\ P'v/a_{k1} & L' \end{pmatrix} \begin{pmatrix} a_{k1} & w^{\mathrm{T}} \\ 0 & U' \end{pmatrix} \\
&= LU \ ,
\end{aligned}
$$

yielding the LUP decomposition. Because L' is unit lower-triangular, so is L, and because U' is upper-triangular, so is U.

Notice that in this derivation, unlike the one for LU decomposition, both the column vector v/a_{k1} and the Schur complement $A' - vw^{\mathrm{T}}/a_{k1}$ must be multiplied by the permutation matrix P'.

Like LU-DECOMPOSITION, our pseudocode for LUP decomposition replaces the recursion with an iteration loop. As an improvement over a direct implementation of the recursion, we dynamically maintain the permutation matrix P as an array π, where $\pi[i] = j$ means that the ith row of P contains a 1 in column j. We also implement the code to compute L and U "in place" in the matrix A. Thus, when the procedure terminates,

$$
a_{ij} = \begin{cases} l_{ij} & \text{if } i > j \ , \\ u_{ij} & \text{if } i \le j \ . \end{cases}
$$

LUP-DECOMPOSITION(A)

```
 1   n ← rows[A]
 2   for i ← 1 to n
 3       do π[i] ← i
 4   for k ← 1 to n − 1
 5       do p ← 0
 6          for i ← k to n
 7              do if |a_ik| > p
 8                     then p ← |a_ik|
 9                          k' ← i
10          if p = 0
11             then error "singular matrix"
12          exchange π[k] ↔ π[k']
13          for i ← 1 to n
14              do exchange a_ki ↔ a_k'i
15          for i ← k + 1 to n
16              do a_ik ← a_ik/a_kk
17                 for j ← k + 1 to n
18                     do a_ij ← a_ij − a_ik a_kj
```

Figure 31.2 illustrates how LUP-DECOMPOSITION factors a matrix. The array π is initialized by lines 2–3 to represent the identity permutation. The outer **for** loop beginning in line 4 implements the recursion. Each time through the outer loop, lines 5–9 determine the element $a_{k'k}$ with largest absolute value of those in the current first column (column k) of the $(n-k+1) \times (n-k+1)$ matrix whose LU decomposition must be found.

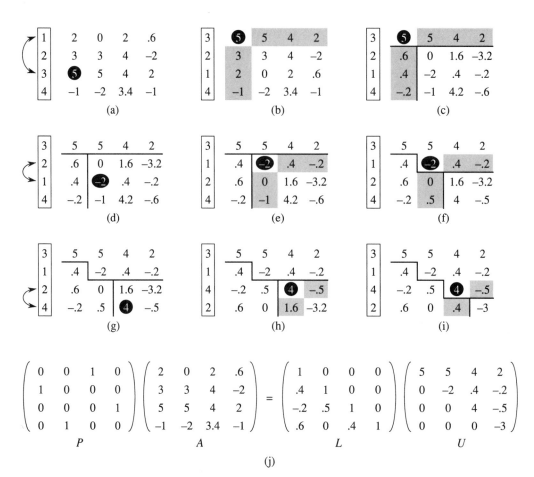

Figure 31.2 The operation of LUP-DECOMPOSITION. **(a)** The input matrix A with the identity permutation of the rows on the left. The first step of the algorithm determines that the element 5 in black in the third row is the pivot for the first column. **(b)** Rows 1 and 3 are swapped and the permutation is updated. The shaded column and row represent v and w^T. **(c)** The vector v is replaced by $v/5$, and the the lower right of the matrix is updated with the Schur complement. Lines divide the matrix into three regions: elements of U (above), elements of L (left), and elements of the Schur complement (lower right). **(d)–(f)** The second step. **(g)–(i)** The third step finishes the algorithm. **(j)** The LUP decomposition $PA = LU$.

If all elements in the current first column are zero, lines 10–11 report that the matrix is singular. To pivot, we exchange $\pi[k']$ with $\pi[k]$ in line 12 and exchange the kth and k'th rows of A in lines 13–14, thereby making the pivot element a_{kk}. (The entire rows are swapped because in the derivation of the method above, not only is $A' - vw^{\mathrm{T}}/a_{k1}$ multiplied by P', but so is v/a_{k1}.) Finally, the Schur complement is computed by lines 15–18 in much the same way as it is computed by lines 4–9 of LU-DECOMPOSITION, except that here the operation is written to work "in place."

Because of its triply nested loop structure, the running time of LUP-DECOMPOSITION is $\Theta(n^3)$, the same as that of LU-DECOMPOSITION. Thus, pivoting costs us at most a constant factor in time.

Exercises

31.4-1
Solve the equation

$$\begin{pmatrix} 1 & 0 & 0 \\ 4 & 1 & 0 \\ -6 & 5 & 1 \end{pmatrix} \begin{pmatrix} x_1 \\ x_2 \\ x_3 \end{pmatrix} = \begin{pmatrix} 3 \\ 14 \\ -7 \end{pmatrix}$$

by using forward substitution.

31.4-2
Find an LU decomposition of the matrix

$$\begin{pmatrix} 4 & -5 & 6 \\ 8 & -6 & 7 \\ 12 & -7 & 12 \end{pmatrix} .$$

31.4-3
Why does the **for** loop in line 4 of LUP-DECOMPOSITION run only up to $n-1$, whereas the corresponding **for** loop in line 2 of LU-DECOMPOSITION runs all the way to n?

31.4-4
Solve the equation

$$\begin{pmatrix} 1 & 5 & 4 \\ 2 & 0 & 3 \\ 5 & 8 & 2 \end{pmatrix} \begin{pmatrix} x_1 \\ x_2 \\ x_3 \end{pmatrix} = \begin{pmatrix} 12 \\ 9 \\ 5 \end{pmatrix}$$

by using an LUP decomposition.

31.4-5
Describe the LUP decomposition of a diagonal matrix.

31.4-6
Describe the LUP decomposition of a permutation matrix A, and prove that it is unique.

31.4-7

Show that for all $n \geq 1$, there exist singular $n \times n$ matrices that have LU decompositions.

31.4-8 ⋆

Show how we can efficiently solve a set of equations of the form $Ax = b$ over the boolean quasiring $(\{0, 1\}, \vee, \wedge, 0, 1)$.

31.4-9 ⋆

Suppose that A is an $m \times n$ real matrix of rank m, where $m < n$. Show how to find a size-n vector x_0 and an $m \times (n - m)$ matrix B of rank $n - m$ such that every vector of the form $x_0 + By$, for $y \in \mathbf{R}^{n-m}$, is a solution to the underdetermined equation $Ax = b$.

31.5   Inverting matrices

Although in practice we do not generally use matrix inverses to solve systems of linear equations, preferring instead to use more numerically stable techniques such as LUP decomposition, it is sometimes necessary to compute a matrix inverse. In this section, we show how LUP decomposition can be used to compute a matrix inverse. We also discuss the theoretically interesting question of whether the computation of a matrix inverse can be sped up using techniques such as Strassen's algorithm for matrix multiplication. Indeed, Strassen's original paper was motivated by the problem of showing that a set of a linear equations could be solved more quickly than by the usual method.

Computing a matrix inverse from an LUP decomposition

Suppose that we have an LUP decomposition of a matrix A in the form of three matrices L, U, and P such that $PA = LU$. Using LU-SOLVE, we can solve an equation of the form $Ax = b$ in time $\Theta(n^2)$. Since the LUP decomposition depends on A but not b, we can solve a second set of equations of the form $Ax = b'$ in additional time $\Theta(n^2)$. In general, once we have the LUP decomposition of A, we can solve, in time $\Theta(kn^2)$, k versions of the equation $Ax = b$ that differ only in b.

The equation

$$AX = I_n \tag{31.24}$$

can be viewed as a set of n distinct equations of the form $Ax = b$. These equations define the matrix X as the inverse of A. To be precise, let X_i denote the ith column of X, and recall that the unit vector e_i is the ith column of I_n. Equation (31.24) can then be solved for X by using the LUP decomposition for A to solve each equation

$$AX_i = e_i$$

separately for X_i. Each of the n X_i can be found in time $\Theta(n^2)$, and so the computation of X from the LUP decomposition of A takes time $\Theta(n^3)$. Since the LUP decomposition of A can be computed in time $\Theta(n^3)$, the inverse A^{-1} of a matrix A can be determined in time $\Theta(n^3)$.

Matrix multiplication and matrix inversion

We now show that the theoretical speedups obtained for matrix multiplication translate to speedups for matrix inversion. In fact, we prove something stronger: matrix inversion is equivalent to matrix multiplication, in the following sense. If $M(n)$ denotes the time to multiply two $n \times n$ matrices and $I(n)$ denotes the time to invert a nonsingular $n \times n$ matrix, then $I(n) = \Theta(M(n))$. We prove this result in two parts. First, we show that $M(n) = O(I(n))$, which is relatively easy, and then we prove that $I(n) = O(M(n))$.

Theorem 31.11 (Multiplication is no harder than inversion)
If we can invert an $n \times n$ matrix in time $I(n)$, where $I(n) = \Omega(n^2)$ and $I(n)$ satisfies the regularity condition $I(3n) = O(I(n))$, then we can multiply two $n \times n$ matrices in time $O(I(n))$.

Proof   Let A and B be $n \times n$ matrices whose matrix product C we wish to compute. We define the $3n \times 3n$ matrix D by

$$D = \begin{pmatrix} I_n & A & 0 \\ 0 & I_n & B \\ 0 & 0 & I_n \end{pmatrix} .$$

The inverse of D is

$$D^{-1} = \begin{pmatrix} I_n & -A & AB \\ 0 & I_n & -B \\ 0 & 0 & I_n \end{pmatrix} ,$$

and thus we can compute the product AB by taking the upper right $n \times n$ submatrix of D^{-1}.

We can construct matrix D in $\Theta(n^2) = O(I(n))$ time, and we can invert D in $O(I(3n)) = O(I(n))$ time, by the regularity condition on $I(n)$. We thus have

$$M(n) = O(I(n)) . \qquad \blacksquare$$

Note that $I(n)$ satisfies the regularity condition whenever $I(n)$ does not have large jumps in value. For example, if $I(n) = \Theta(n^c \lg^d n)$ for any constants $c > 0$, $d \geq 0$, then $I(n)$ satisfies the regularity condition.

Reducing matrix inversion to matrix multiplication

The proof that matrix inversion is no harder than matrix multiplication relies on some properties of symmetric positive-definite matrices that will be proved in Section 31.6.

Theorem 31.12 (Inversion is no harder than multiplication)
If we can multiply two $n \times n$ real matrices in time $M(n)$, where $M(n) = \Omega(n^2)$ and $M(n) = O(M(n + k))$ for $0 \leq k \leq n$, then we can compute the inverse of any real nonsingular $n \times n$ matrix in time $O(M(n))$.

Proof   We can assume that n is an exact power of 2, since we have

$$\begin{pmatrix} A & 0 \\ 0 & I_k \end{pmatrix}^{-1} = \begin{pmatrix} A^{-1} & 0 \\ 0 & I_k \end{pmatrix}$$

for any $k > 0$. Thus, by choosing k such that $n + k$ is a power of 2, we enlarge the matrix to a size that is the next power of 2 and obtain the desired answer A^{-1} from the answer to the enlarged problem. The regularity condition on $M(n)$ ensures that this enlargement does not cause the running time to increase by more than a constant factor.

For the moment, let us assume that the $n \times n$ matrix A is symmetric and positive-definite. We partition A into four $n/2 \times n/2$ submatrices:

$$A = \begin{pmatrix} B & C^{\mathrm{T}} \\ C & D \end{pmatrix} . \tag{31.25}$$

Then, if we let

$$S = D - CB^{-1}C^{\mathrm{T}} \tag{31.26}$$

be the Schur complement of A with respect to B, we have

$$A^{-1} = \begin{pmatrix} B^{-1} + B^{-1}C^{\mathrm{T}}S^{-1}CB^{-1} & -B^{-1}C^{\mathrm{T}}S^{-1} \\ -S^{-1}CB^{-1} & S^{-1} \end{pmatrix} , \tag{31.27}$$

since $AA^{-1} = I_n$, as can be verified by performing the matrix multiplication. The matrices B^{-1} and S^{-1} exist if A is symmetric and positive-definite, by Lemmas 31.13, 31.14, and 31.15 in Section 31.6, because both B and S are symmetric and positive-definite. By Exercise 31.1-3, $B^{-1}C^{\mathrm{T}} = (CB^{-1})^{\mathrm{T}}$ and $B^{-1}C^{\mathrm{T}}S^{-1} = (S^{-1}CB^{-1})^{\mathrm{T}}$. Equations (31.26) and (31.27) can therefore be used to specify a recursive algorithm involving 4 multiplications of $n/2 \times n/2$ matrices:

$C \cdot B^{-1}$,

$(CB^{-1}) \cdot C^{\mathrm{T}}$,

$S^{-1} \cdot (CB^{-1})$,

$(CB^{-1})^{\mathrm{T}} \cdot (S^{-1}CB^{-1})$.

Since we can multiply $n/2 \times n/2$ matrices using an algorithm for $n \times n$ matrices, matrix inversion of symmetric positive-definite matrices can be performed in time

$$
\begin{aligned}
I(n) &\leq 2I(n/2) + 4M(n) + O(n^2) \\
&= 2I(n/2) + O(M(n)) \\
&= O(M(n)) \, .
\end{aligned}
$$

It remains to prove that the asymptotic running time of matrix multiplication can be obtained for matrix inversion when A is invertible but not symmetric and positive-definite. The basic idea is that for any nonsingular matrix A, the matrix $A^T A$ is symmetric (by Exercise 31.1-3) and positive-definite (by Theorem 31.6). The trick, then, is to reduce the problem of inverting A to the problem of inverting $A^T A$.

The reduction is based on the observation that when A is an $n \times n$ nonsingular matrix, we have

$$
A^{-1} = (A^T A)^{-1} A^T \, ,
$$

since $((A^T A)^{-1} A^T)A = (A^T A)^{-1}(A^T A) = I_n$ and a matrix inverse is unique. Therefore, we can compute A^{-1} by first multiplying A^T by A to obtain $A^T A$, then inverting the symmetric positive-definite matrix $A^T A$ using the above divide-and-conquer algorithm, and finally multiplying the result by A^T. Each of these three steps takes $O(M(n))$ time, and thus any nonsingular matrix with real entries can be inverted in $O(M(n))$ time. ∎

The proof of Theorem 31.12 suggests a means of solving the equation $Ax = b$ without pivoting, so long as A is nonsingular. We multiply both sides of the equation by A^T, yielding $(A^T A)x = A^T b$. This transformation doesn't affect the solution x, since A^T is invertible, so we can factor the symmetric positive-definite matrix $A^T A$ by computing an LU decomposition. We then use forward and back substitution to solve for x with the right-hand side $A^T b$. Although this method is theoretically correct, in practice the procedure LUP-DECOMPOSITION works much better. LUP decomposition requires fewer arithmetic operations by a constant factor, and it has somewhat better numerical properties.

Exercises

31.5-1
Let $M(n)$ be the time to multiply $n \times n$ matrices, and let $S(n)$ denote the time required to square an $n \times n$ matrix. Show that multiplying and squaring matrices have essentially the same difficulty: $S(n) = \Theta(M(n))$.

31.5-2
Let $M(n)$ be the time to multiply $n \times n$ matrices, and let $L(n)$ be the time to compute the LUP decomposition of an $n \times n$ matrix. Show that multiplying matrices and computing LUP decompositions of matrices have essentially the same difficulty: $L(n) = \Theta(M(n))$.

31.5-3

Let $M(n)$ be the time to multiply $n \times n$ matrices, and let $D(n)$ denote the time required to find the determinant of an $n \times n$ matrix. Show that finding the determinant is no harder than multiplying matrices: $D(n) = O(M(n))$.

31.5-4

Let $M(n)$ be the time to multiply $n \times n$ boolean matrices, and let $T(n)$ be the time to find the transitive closure of $n \times n$ boolean matrices. Show that $M(n) = O(T(n))$ and $T(n) = O(M(n) \lg n)$.

31.5-5

Does the matrix-inversion algorithm based on Theorem 31.12 work when matrix elements are drawn from the field of integers modulo 2? Explain.

31.5-6 ⋆

Generalize the matrix-inversion algorithm of Theorem 31.12 to handle matrices of complex numbers, and prove that your generalization works correctly. (*Hint:* Instead of the transpose of A, use the ***conjugate transpose*** A^*, which is obtained from the transpose of A by replacing every entry with its complex conjugate. Instead of symmetric matrices, consider ***Hermitian*** matrices, which are matrices A such that $A = A^*$.)

31.6   Symmetric positive-definite matrices and least-squares approximation

Symmetric positive-definite matrices have many interesting and desirable properties. For example, they are nonsingular, and LU decomposition can be performed on them without our having to worry about dividing by 0. In this section, we shall prove several other important properties of symmetric positive-definite matrices and show an interesting application to curve fitting by a least-squares approximation.

The first property we prove is perhaps the most basic.

Lemma 31.13

Any symmetric positive-definite matrix is nonsingular.

Proof   Suppose that a matrix A is singular. Then by Corollary 31.3, there exists a nonzero vector x such that $Ax = 0$. Hence, $x^\mathrm{T} A x = 0$, and A cannot be positive-definite.   ■

The proof that we can perform LU decomposition on a symmetric positive-definite matrix A without dividing by 0 is more involved. We begin by proving properties about certain submatrices of A. Define the kth ***leading submatrix*** of A to be the matrix A_k consisting of the intersection of the first k rows and first k columns of A.

Lemma 31.14
If A is a symmetric positive-definite matrix, then every leading submatrix of A is symmetric and positive-definite.

Proof That each leading submatrix A_k is symmetric is obvious. To prove that A_k is positive-definite, let x be a nonzero column vector of size k, and let us partition A as follows:

$$A = \begin{pmatrix} A_k & B^T \\ B & C \end{pmatrix} .$$

Then, we have

$$\begin{aligned} x^T A_k x &= (x^T \quad 0) \begin{pmatrix} A_k & B^T \\ B & C \end{pmatrix} \begin{pmatrix} x \\ 0 \end{pmatrix} \\ &= (x^T \quad 0) A \begin{pmatrix} x \\ 0 \end{pmatrix} \\ &> 0 , \end{aligned}$$

since A is positive-definite, and hence A_k is also positive-definite. ∎

We now turn to some essential properties of the Schur complement. Let A be a symmetric positive-definite matrix, and let A_k be a leading $k \times k$ submatrix of A. Partition A as

$$A = \begin{pmatrix} A_k & B^T \\ B & C \end{pmatrix} . \tag{31.28}$$

Then, the ***Schur complement*** of A with respect to A_k is defined to be

$$S = C - BA_k^{-1}B^T . \tag{31.29}$$

(By Lemma 31.14, A_k is symmetric and positive-definite; therefore, A_k^{-1} exists by Lemma 31.13, and S is well defined.) Note that our earlier definition (31.23) of the Schur complement is consistent with definition (31.29), by letting $k = 1$.

The next lemma shows that the Schur-complement matrices of symmetric positive-definite matrices are themselves symmetric and positive-definite. This result was used in Theorem 31.12, and its corollary is needed to prove the correctness of LU decomposition for symmetric positive-definite matrices.

Lemma 31.15 (Schur complement lemma)
If A is a symmetric positive-definite matrix and A_k is a leading $k \times k$ submatrix of A, then the Schur complement of A with respect to A_k is symmetric and positive-definite.

Proof That S is symmetric follows from Exercise 31.1-7. It remains to show that S is positive-definite. Consider the partition of A given in equation (31.28).

For any nonzero vector x, we have $x^T A x > 0$ by assumption. Let us break x into two subvectors y and z compatible with A_k and C, respectively. Because A_k^{-1} exists, we have

$$
\begin{aligned}
x^T A x &= (y^T z^T) \begin{pmatrix} A_k & B^T \\ B & C \end{pmatrix} \begin{pmatrix} y \\ z \end{pmatrix} \\
&= y^T A_k y + y^T B^T z + z^T B y + z^T C z \\
&= (y + A_k^{-1} B^T z)^T A_k (y + A_k^{-1} B^T z) + z^T (C - B A_k^{-1} B^T) z , \quad (31.30)
\end{aligned}
$$

by matrix magic. (Verify by multiplying through.) This last equation amounts to "completing the square" of the quadratic form. (See Exercise 31.6-2.)

Since $x^T A x > 0$ holds for any nonzero x, let us pick any nonzero z and then choose $y = -A_k^{-1} B^T z$, which causes the first term in equation (31.30) to vanish, leaving

$$
z^T (C - B A_k^{-1} B^T) z = z^T S z
$$

as the value of the expression. For any $z \neq 0$, we therefore have $z^T S z = x^T A x > 0$, and thus S is positive-definite.   ∎

Corollary 31.16
LU decomposition of a symmetric positive-definite matrix never causes a division by 0.

Proof   Let A be a symmetric positive-definite matrix. We shall prove something stronger than the statement of the corollary: every pivot is strictly positive. The first pivot is a_{11}. Let e_1 be the first unit vector, from which we obtain $a_{11} = e_1^T A e_1 > 0$. Since the first step of LU decomposition produces the Schur complement of A with respect to $A_1 = (a_{11})$, Lemma 31.15 implies that all pivots are positive by induction.   ∎

Least-squares approximation

Fitting curves to given sets of data points is an important application of symmetric positive-definite matrices. Suppose that we are given a set of m data points

$$
(x_1, y_1), (x_2, y_2), \ldots, (x_m, y_m) ,
$$

where the y_i are known to be subject to measurement errors. We would like to determine a function $F(x)$ such that

$$
y_i = F(x_i) + \eta_i , \tag{31.31}
$$

for $i = 1, 2, \ldots, m$, where the approximation errors η_i are small. The form of the function F depends on the problem at hand. Here, we assume that it has the form of a linearly weighted sum,

$$F(x) = \sum_{j=1}^{n} c_j f_j(x) \, ,$$

where the number of summands n and the specific **basis functions** f_j are chosen based on knowledge of the problem at hand. A common choice is $f_j(x) = x^{j-1}$, which means that

$$F(x) = c_1 + c_2 x + c_3 x^2 + \cdots + c_n x^{n-1}$$

is a polynomial of degree $n - 1$ in x.

By choosing $n = m$, we can calculate each y_i *exactly* in equation (31.31). Such a high-degree F "fits the noise" as well as the data, however, and generally gives poor results when used to predict y for previously unseen values of x. It is usually better to choose n significantly smaller than m and hope that by choosing the coefficients c_j well, we can obtain a function F that finds the significant patterns in the data points without paying undue attention to the noise. Some theoretical principles exist for choosing n, but they are beyond the scope of this text. In any case, once n is chosen, we end up with an overdetermined set of equations that we wish to solve as well as we can. We now show how this can be done.

Let

$$A = \begin{pmatrix} f_1(x_1) & f_2(x_1) & \ldots & f_n(x_1) \\ f_1(x_2) & f_2(x_2) & \ldots & f_n(x_2) \\ \vdots & \vdots & \ddots & \vdots \\ f_1(x_m) & f_2(x_m) & \ldots & f_n(x_m) \end{pmatrix}$$

denote the matrix of values of the basis functions at the given points; that is, $a_{ij} = f_j(x_i)$. Let $c = (c_k)$ denote the desired size-n vector of coefficients. Then,

$$\begin{aligned} Ac &= \begin{pmatrix} f_1(x_1) & f_2(x_1) & \ldots & f_n(x_1) \\ f_1(x_2) & f_2(x_2) & \ldots & f_n(x_2) \\ \vdots & \vdots & \ddots & \vdots \\ f_1(x_m) & f_2(x_m) & \ldots & f_n(x_m) \end{pmatrix} \begin{pmatrix} c_1 \\ c_2 \\ \vdots \\ c_n \end{pmatrix} \\ &= \begin{pmatrix} F(x_1) \\ F(x_2) \\ \vdots \\ F(x_m) \end{pmatrix} \end{aligned}$$

is the size-m vector of "predicted values" for y. Thus,

$$\eta = Ac - y$$

is the size-m vector of **approximation errors**.

To minimize approximation errors, we choose to minimize the norm of the error vector η, which gives us a **least-squares solution**, since

$$\|\eta\| = \left(\sum_{i=1}^{m} \eta_i^2 \right)^{1/2} \, .$$

Since

$$\|\eta\|^2 = \|Ac - y\|^2 = \sum_{i=1}^{m} \left(\sum_{j=1}^{n} a_{ij} c_j - y_i \right)^2 ,$$

we can minimize $\|\eta\|$ by differentiating $\|\eta\|^2$ with respect to each c_k and then setting the result to 0:

$$\frac{d \|\eta\|^2}{dc_k} = \sum_{i=1}^{m} 2 \left(\sum_{j=1}^{n} a_{ij} c_j - y_i \right) a_{ik} = 0 . \tag{31.32}$$

The n equations (31.32) for $k = 1, 2, \ldots, n$ are equivalent to the single matrix equation

$$(Ac - y)^{\mathrm{T}} A = 0$$

or, equivalently (using Exercise 31.1-3), to

$$A^{\mathrm{T}}(Ac - y) = 0 ,$$

which implies

$$A^{\mathrm{T}} Ac = A^{\mathrm{T}} y . \tag{31.33}$$

In statistics, this is called the **normal equation**. The matrix $A^{\mathrm{T}} A$ is symmetric by Exercise 31.1-3, and if A has full column rank, then $A^{\mathrm{T}} A$ is positive-definite as well. Hence, $(A^{\mathrm{T}} A)^{-1}$ exists, and the solution to equation (31.33) is

$$\begin{aligned} c &= \left((A^{\mathrm{T}} A)^{-1} A^{\mathrm{T}} \right) y \\ &= A^{+} y , \end{aligned} \tag{31.34}$$

where the matrix $A^{+} = \left((A^{\mathrm{T}} A)^{-1} A^{\mathrm{T}} \right)$ is called the **pseudoinverse** of the matrix A. The pseudoinverse is a natural generalization of the notion of a matrix inverse to the case in which A is nonsquare. (Compare equation (31.34) as the approximate solution to $Ac = y$ with the solution $A^{-1} b$ as the exact solution to $Ax = b$.)

As an example of producing a least-squares fit, suppose that we have 5 data points

$$(-1, 2), (1, 1), (2, 1), (3, 0), (5, 3) ,$$

shown as black dots in Figure 31.3. We wish to fit these points with a quadratic polynomial

$$F(x) = c_1 + c_2 x + c_3 x^2 .$$

We start with the matrix of basis-function values

$$A = \begin{pmatrix} 1 & x_1 & x_1^2 \\ 1 & x_2 & x_2^2 \\ 1 & x_3 & x_3^2 \\ 1 & x_4 & x_4^2 \\ 1 & x_5 & x_5^2 \end{pmatrix} = \begin{pmatrix} 1 & -1 & 1 \\ 1 & 1 & 1 \\ 1 & 2 & 4 \\ 1 & 3 & 9 \\ 1 & 5 & 25 \end{pmatrix} ,$$

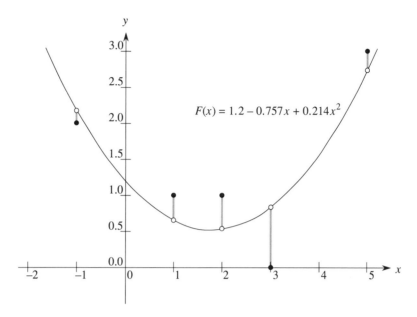

Figure 31.3 The least-squares fit of a quadratic polynomial to the set of data points $\{(-1, 2), (1, 1), (2, 1), (3, 0), (5, 3)\}$. The black dots are the data points, and the white dots are their estimated values predicted by the polynomial $F(x) = 1.2 - 0.757x + 0.214x^2$, the quadratic polynomial that minimizes the sum of the squared errors. The error for each data point is shown as a shaded line.

whose pseudoinverse is

$$A^+ = \begin{pmatrix} 0.500 & 0.300 & 0.200 & 0.100 & -0.100 \\ -0.388 & 0.093 & 0.190 & 0.193 & -0.088 \\ 0.060 & -0.036 & -0.048 & -0.036 & 0.060 \end{pmatrix} .$$

Multiplying y by A^+, we obtain the coefficient vector

$$c = \begin{pmatrix} 1.200 \\ -0.757 \\ 0.214 \end{pmatrix} ,$$

which corresponds to the quadratic polynomial

$$F(x) = 1.200 - 0.757x + 0.214x^2$$

as the closest-fitting quadratic to the given data, in a least-squares sense.

As a practical matter, we solve the normal equation (31.33) by multiplying y by A^{T} and then finding an LU decomposition of $A^{\mathrm{T}}A$. If A has full rank, the matrix $A^{\mathrm{T}}A$ is guaranteed to be nonsingular, because it is symmetric and positive-definite. (See Exercise 31.1-3 and Theorem 31.6.)

Exercises

31.6-1
Prove that every diagonal element of a symmetric positive-definite matrix is positive.

31.6-2
Let $A = \begin{pmatrix} a & b \\ b & c \end{pmatrix}$ be a 2×2 symmetric positive-definite matrix. Prove that its determinant $ac - b^2$ is positive by "completing the square" in a manner similar to that used in the proof of Lemma 31.15.

31.6-3
Prove that the maximum element in a symmetric positive-definite matrix lies on the diagonal.

31.6-4
Prove that the determinant of each leading submatrix of a symmetric positive-definite matrix is positive.

31.6-5
Let A_k denote the kth leading submatrix of a symmetric positive-definite matrix A. Prove that $\det(A_k)/\det(A_{k-1})$ is the kth pivot during LU decomposition, where by convention $\det(A_0) = 1$.

31.6-6
Find the function of the form

$$F(x) = c_1 + c_2 x \lg x + c_3 e^x$$

that is the best least-squares fit to the data points

$$(1, 1), (2, 1), (3, 3), (4, 8) .$$

31.6-7
Show that the pseudoinverse A^+ satisfies the following four equations:

$$
\begin{aligned}
AA^+A &= A , \\
A^+AA^+ &= A^+ , \\
(AA^+)^{\mathrm{T}} &= AA^+ , \\
(A^+A)^{\mathrm{T}} &= A^+A .
\end{aligned}
$$

Problems

31-1   Shamir's boolean matrix multiplication algorithm
In Section 31.3, we observed that Strassen's matrix-multiplication algorithm cannot be applied directly to boolean matrix multiplication because

the boolean quasiring $Q = (\{0, 1\}, \vee, \wedge, 0, 1)$ is not a ring. Theorem 31.10 showed that if we used arithmetic operations on words of $O(\lg n)$ bits, we could nevertheless apply Strassen's method to multiply $n \times n$ boolean matrices in $O(n^{\lg 7})$ time. In this problem, we investigate a probabilistic method that uses only bit operations to achieve nearly as good a bound but with some small chance of error.

a. Show that $R = (\{0, 1\}, \oplus, \wedge, 0, 1)$, where $\oplus$ is the XOR (exclusive-or) function, is a ring.

Let $A = (a_{ij})$ and $B = (b_{ij})$ be $n \times n$ boolean matrices, and let $C = (c_{ij}) = AB$ in the quasiring Q. Generate $A' = (a'_{ij})$ from A using the following randomized procedure:

- If $a_{ij} = 0$, then let $a'_{ij} = 0$.
- If $A_{ij} = 1$, then let $a'_{ij} = 1$ with probability $1/2$ and let $a'_{ij} = 0$ with probability $1/2$. The random choices for each entry are independent.

b. Let $C' = (c'_{ij}) = A'B$ in the ring R. Show that $c_{ij} = 0$ implies $c'_{ij} = 0$. Show that $c_{ij} = 1$ implies $c'_{ij} = 1$ with probability $1/2$.

c. Show that for any $\epsilon > 0$, the probability is at most ϵ/n^2 that a given c'_{ij} never takes on the value c_{ij} for $\lg(n^2/\epsilon)$ independent choices of the matrix A'. Show that the probability is at least $1 - \epsilon$ that all c'_{ij} take on their correct values at least once.

d. Give an $O(n^{\lg 7} \lg n)$-time randomized algorithm that computes the product in the boolean quasiring Q of two $n \times n$ matrices with probability at least $1 - 1/n^k$ for any constant $k > 0$. The only operations permitted on matrix elements are $\wedge$, $\vee$, and $\oplus$.

31-2 Tridiagonal systems of linear equations
Consider the tridiagonal matrix

$$A = \begin{pmatrix} 1 & -1 & 0 & 0 & 0 \\ -1 & 2 & -1 & 0 & 0 \\ 0 & -1 & 2 & -1 & 0 \\ 0 & 0 & -1 & 2 & -1 \\ 0 & 0 & 0 & -1 & 2 \end{pmatrix}.$$

a. Find an LU decomposition of A.

b. Solve the equation $Ax = (\, 1 \quad 1 \quad 1 \quad 1 \quad 1 \,)^{\mathrm{T}}$ by using forward and back substitution.

c. Find the inverse of A.

d. Show that for any $n \times n$ symmetric, positive-definite, tridiagonal matrix A and any n-vector b, the equation $Ax = b$ can be solved in $O(n)$ time by performing an LU decomposition. Argue that any method based on forming A^{-1} is asymptotically more expensive in the worst case.

e. Show that for any $n \times n$ nonsingular, tridiagonal matrix A and any n-vector b, the equation $Ax = b$ can be solved in $O(n)$ time by performing an LUP decomposition.

31-3   Splines

A practical method for interpolating a set of points with a curve is to use *cubic splines*. We are given a set $\{(x_i, y_i) : i = 0, 1, \ldots, n\}$ of $n + 1$ point-value pairs, where $x_0 < x_1 < \cdots < x_n$. We wish to fit a piecewise-cubic curve (spline) $f(x)$ to the points. That is, the curve $f(x)$ is made up of n cubic polynomials $f_i(x) = a_i + b_i x + c_i x^2 + d_i x^3$ for $i = 0, 1, \ldots, n - 1$, where if x falls in the range $x_i \leq x \leq x_{i+1}$, then the value of the curve is given by $f(x) = f_i(x - x_i)$. The points x_i at which the cubic polynomials are "pasted" together are called *knots*. For simplicity, we shall assume that $x_i = i$ for $i = 0, 1, \ldots, n$.

To ensure continuity of $f(x)$, we require that

$$
\begin{aligned}
f(x_i) &= f_i(0) = y_i \, , \\
f(x_{i+1}) &= f_i(1) = y_{i+1}
\end{aligned}
$$

for $i = 0, 1, \ldots, n - 1$. To ensure that $f(x)$ is sufficiently smooth, we also insist that there be continuity of the first derivative at each knot:

$$ f'(x_{i+1}) = f_i'(1) = f_{i+1}'(0) $$

for $i = 0, 1, \ldots, n - 1$.

a. Suppose that for $i = 0, 1, \ldots, n$, we are given not only the point-value pairs $\{(x_i, y_i)\}$ but also the first derivatives $D_i = f'(x_i)$ at each knot. Express each coefficient a_i, b_i, c_i, and d_i in terms of the values y_i, y_{i+1}, D_i, and D_{i+1}. (Remember that $x_i = i$.) How quickly can the $4n$ coefficients be computed from the point-value pairs and first derivatives?

The question remains of how to choose the first derivatives of $f(x)$ at the knots. One method is to require the second derivatives to be continuous at the knots:

$$ f''(x_{i+1}) = f_i''(1) = f_{i+1}''(0) $$

for $i = 0, 1, \ldots, n - 1$. At the first and last knots, we assume that $f''(x_0) = f_0''(0) = 0$ and $f''(x_n) = f_n''(1) = 0$; these assumptions make $f(x)$ a *natural* cubic spline.

b. Use the continuity constraints on the second derivative to show that for $i = 1, 2, \ldots, n - 1$,

$$ D_{i-1} + 4D_i + D_{i+1} = 3(y_{i+1} - y_{i-1}) \, . \tag{31.35} $$

c. Show that

$$
\begin{aligned}
2D_0 + D_1 &= 3(y_1 - y_0) \, , \tag{31.36} \\
D_{n-1} + 2D_n &= 3(y_n - y_{n-1}) \, . \tag{31.37}
\end{aligned}
$$

d. Rewrite equations (31.35)–(31.37) as a matrix equation involving the vector $D = \langle D_0, D_1, \ldots, D_n \rangle$ of unknowns. What attributes does the matrix in your equation have?

e. Argue that a set of $n + 1$ point-value pairs can be interpolated with a natural cubic spline in $O(n)$ time (see Problem 31-2).

f. Show how to determine a natural cubic spline that interpolates a set of $n + 1$ points (x_i, y_i) satisfying $x_0 < x_1 < \cdots < x_n$, even when x_i is not necessarily equal to i. What matrix equation must be solved, and how quickly does your algorithm run?

Chapter notes

There are many excellent texts available that describe numerical and scientific computation in much greater detail than we have room for here. The following are especially readable: George and Liu [81], Golub and Van Loan [89], Press, Flannery, Teukolsky, and Vetterling [161, 162], and Strang [181, 182].

The publication of Strassen's algorithm in 1969 [183] caused much excitement. Before then, it was hard to imagine that the naive algorithm could be improved upon. The asymptotic upper bound on the difficulty of matrix multiplication has since been considerably improved. The most asymptotically efficient algorithm for multiplying $n \times n$ matrices to date, due to Coppersmith and Winograd [52], has a running time of $O(n^{2.376})$. The graphical presentation of Strassen's algorithm is due to Paterson [155]. Fischer and Meyer [67] adapted Strassen's algorithm to boolean matrices (Theorem 31.10).

Gaussian elimination, upon which the LU and LUP decompositions are based, was the first systematic method for solving linear systems of equations. It was also one of the earliest numerical algorithms. Although it was known earlier, its discovery is commonly attributed to C. F. Gauss (1777–1855). In his famous paper [183], Strassen also showed that an $n \times n$ matrix can be inverted in $O(n^{\lg 7})$ time. Winograd [203] originally proved that matrix multiplication is no harder than matrix inversion, and the converse is due to Aho, Hopcroft, and Ullman [4].

Strang [182] has an excellent presentation of symmetric positive-definite matrices and on linear algebra in general. He makes the following remark on page 334: "My class often asks about *unsymmetric* positive definite matrices. I never use that term."

The straightforward method of adding two polynomials of degree n takes $\Theta(n)$ time, but the straightforward method of multiplying them takes $\Theta(n^2)$ time. In this chapter, we shall show how the Fast Fourier Transform, or FFT, can reduce the time to multiply polynomials to $\Theta(n \lg n)$.

Polynomials

A *polynomial* in the variable x over an algebraic field F is a function $A(x)$ that can be represented as follows:

$$A(x) = \sum_{j=0}^{n-1} a_j x^j \ .$$

We call n the **degree-bound** of the polynomial, and we call the values $a_0, a_1, \ldots, a_{n-1}$ the **coefficients** of the polynomial. The coefficients are drawn from the field F, typically the set $\mathbf{C}$ of complex numbers. A polynomial $A(x)$ is said to have **degree** k if its highest nonzero coefficient is a_k. The degree of a polynomial of degree-bound n can be any integer between 0 and $n-1$, inclusive. Conversely, a polynomial of degree k is a polynomial of degree-bound n for any $n > k$.

There are a variety of operations we might wish to define for polynomials. For *polynomial addition*, if $A(x)$ and $B(x)$ are polynomials of degree-bound n, we say that their *sum* is a polynomial $C(x)$, also of degree-bound n, such that $C(x) = A(x) + B(x)$ for all x in the underlying field. That is, if

$$A(x) = \sum_{j=0}^{n-1} a_j x^j$$

and

$$B(x) = \sum_{j=0}^{n-1} b_j x^j \ ,$$

then

$$C(x) = \sum_{j=0}^{n-1} c_j x^j \, ,$$

where $c_j = a_j + b_j$ for $j = 0, 1, \ldots, n-1$. For example, if $A(x) = 6x^3 + 7x^2 - 10x + 9$ and $B(x) = -2x^3 + 4x - 5$, then $C(x) = 4x^3 + 7x^2 - 6x + 4$.

For ***polynomial multiplication***, if $A(x)$ and $B(x)$ are polynomials of degree-bound n, we say that their ***product*** $C(x)$ is a polynomial of degree-bound $2n - 1$ such that $C(x) = A(x)B(x)$ for all x in the underlying field. You have probably multiplied polynomials before, by multiplying each term in $A(x)$ by each term in $B(x)$ and combining terms with equal powers. For example, we can multiply $A(x) = 6x^3 + 7x^2 - 10x + 9$ and $B(x) = -2x^3 + 4x - 5$ as follows:

$$
\begin{array}{r}
6x^3 + 7x^2 - 10x + 9 \\
\underline{-\ 2x^3 \qquad\qquad +\ 4x -\ 5} \\
-\ 30x^3 - 35x^2 + 50x - 45 \\
24x^4 + 28x^3 - 40x^2 + 36x \\
\underline{-\ 12x^6 - 14x^5 + 20x^4 - 18x^3 } \\
-\ 12x^6 - 14x^5 + 44x^4 - 20x^3 - 75x^2 + 86x - 45
\end{array}
$$

Another way to express the product $C(x)$ is

$$C(x) = \sum_{j=0}^{2n-2} c_j x^j \, , \tag{32.1}$$

where

$$c_j = \sum_{k=0}^{j} a_k b_{j-k} \, . \tag{32.2}$$

Note that $\text{degree}(C) = \text{degree}(A) + \text{degree}(B)$, implying

$$
\begin{aligned}
\text{degree-bound}(C) \ &= \ \text{degree-bound}(A) + \text{degree-bound}(B) - 1 \\
&\le \ \text{degree-bound}(A) + \text{degree-bound}(B) \, .
\end{aligned}
$$

We shall nevertheless speak of the degree-bound of C as being the sum of the degree-bounds of A and B, since if a polynomial has degree-bound k it also has degree-bound $k + 1$.

Chapter outline

Section 32.1 presents two ways to represent polynomials: the coefficient representation and the point-value representation. The straightforward methods for multiplying polynomials—equations (32.1) and (32.2)—take $\Theta(n^2)$ time when the polynomials are represented in coefficient form, but only $\Theta(n)$ time when they are represented in point-value form. We can, however, multiply polynomials using the coefficient representation in only $\Theta(n \lg n)$ time by converting between the two representations. To see why this works, we must first study complex roots of unity, which we do in Section 32.2. Then, we use the FFT and its inverse, also described in Section 32.2, to perform the conversions. Section 32.3 shows how to implement the FFT quickly in both serial and parallel models.

This chapter uses complex numbers extensively, and the symbol i will be used exclusively to denote $\sqrt{-1}$.

32.1   Representation of polynomials

The coefficient and point-value representations of polynomials are in a sense equivalent; that is, a polynomial in point-value form has a unique counterpart in coefficient form. In this section, we introduce the two representations and show how they can be combined to allow multiplication of two degree-bound n polynomials in $\Theta(n \lg n)$ time.

Coefficient representation

A *coefficient representation* of a polynomial $A(x) = \sum_{j=0}^{n-1} a_j x^j$ of degree-bound n is a vector of coefficients $a = (a_0, a_1, \ldots, a_{n-1})$. In matrix equations in this chapter, we shall generally treat vectors as column vectors.

The coefficient representation is convenient for certain operations on polynomials. For example, the operation of *evaluating* the polynomial $A(x)$ at a given point x_0 consists of computing the value of $A(x_0)$. Evaluation takes time $\Theta(n)$ using *Horner's rule*:

$$A(x_0) = a_0 + x_0(a_1 + x_0(a_2 + \cdots + x_0(a_{n-2} + x_0(a_{n-1}))\cdots)) .$$

Similarly, adding two polynomials represented by the coefficient vectors $a = (a_0, a_1, \ldots, a_{n-1})$ and $b = (b_0, b_1, \ldots, b_{n-1})$ takes $\Theta(n)$ time: we just output the coefficient vector $c = (c_0, c_1, \ldots, c_{n-1})$, where $c_j = a_j + b_j$ for $j = 0, 1, \ldots, n - 1$.

Now, consider the multiplication of two degree-bound n polynomials $A(x)$ and $B(x)$ represented in coefficient form. If we use the method described by equations (32.1) and (32.2), polynomial multiplication takes time $\Theta(n^2)$, since each coefficient in the vector a must be multiplied by each coefficient in the vector b. The operation of multiplying polynomials in coefficient form seems to be considerably more difficult than that of evaluating a polynomial or adding two polynomials. The resulting coefficient vector c, given by equation (32.2), is also called the *convolution* of the input vectors a and b, denoted $c = a \otimes b$. Since multiplying polynomials and computing convolutions are fundamental computational problems of considerable practical importance, this chapter concentrates on efficient algorithms for them.

Point-value representation

A *point-value representation* of a polynomial $A(x)$ of degree-bound n is a set of n *point-value pairs*

$$\{(x_0, y_0), (x_1, y_1), \ldots, (x_{n-1}, y_{n-1})\}$$

such that all of the x_k are distinct and

$$y_k = A(x_k) \tag{32.3}$$

for $k = 0, 1, \ldots, n - 1$. A polynomial has many different point-value representations, since any set of n distinct points $x_0, x_1, \ldots, x_{n-1}$ can be used as a basis for the representation.

Computing a point-value representation for a polynomial given in coefficient form is in principle straightforward, since all we have to do is select n distinct points $x_0, x_1, \ldots, x_{n-1}$ and then evaluate $A(x_k)$ for $k = 0, 1, \ldots, n - 1$. With Horner's method, this n-point evaluation takes time $\Theta(n^2)$. We shall see later that if we choose the x_k cleverly, this computation can be accelerated to run in time $\Theta(n \lg n)$.

The inverse of evaluation—determining the coefficient form of a polynomial from a point-value representation—is called *interpolation*. The following theorem shows that interpolation is well defined, assuming that the degree-bound of the interpolating polynomial equals the number of given point-value pairs.

Theorem 32.1 (Uniqueness of an interpolating polynomial)
For any set $\{(x_0, y_0), (x_1, y_1), \ldots, (x_{n-1}, y_{n-1})\}$ of n point-value pairs, there is a unique polynomial $A(x)$ of degree-bound n such that $y_k = A(x_k)$ for $k = 0, 1, \ldots, n - 1$.

Proof The proof is based on the existence of the inverse of a certain matrix. Equation (32.3) is equivalent to the matrix equation

$$
\begin{pmatrix}
1 & x_0 & x_0^2 & \cdots & x_0^{n-1} \\
1 & x_1 & x_1^2 & \cdots & x_1^{n-1} \\
\vdots & \vdots & \vdots & \ddots & \vdots \\
1 & x_{n-1} & x_{n-1}^2 & \cdots & x_{n-1}^{n-1}
\end{pmatrix}
\begin{pmatrix}
a_0 \\
a_1 \\
\vdots \\
a_{n-1}
\end{pmatrix}
=
\begin{pmatrix}
y_0 \\
y_1 \\
\vdots \\
y_{n-1}
\end{pmatrix}. \tag{32.4}
$$

The matrix on the left is denoted $V(x_0, x_1, \ldots, x_{n-1})$ and is known as a Vandermonde matrix. By Exercise 31.1-10, this matrix has determinant

$$\prod_{j<k}(x_k - x_j),$$

and therefore, by Theorem 31.5, it is invertible (that is, nonsingular) if the x_k are distinct. Thus, the coefficients a_j can be solved for uniquely given the point-value representation:

$$a = V(x_0, x_1, \ldots, x_{n-1})^{-1} y. \qquad \blacksquare$$

The proof of Theorem 32.1 describes an algorithm for interpolation based on solving the set (32.4) of linear equations. Using the LU decomposition algorithms of Chapter 31, we can solve these equations in time $O(n^3)$.

A faster algorithm for n-point interpolation is based on ***Lagrange's formula***:

$$A(x) = \sum_{k=0}^{n-1} y_k \frac{\prod_{j \neq k}(x - x_j)}{\prod_{j \neq k}(x_k - x_j)} . \tag{32.5}$$

You may wish to verify that the right-hand side of equation (32.5) is a polynomial of degree-bound n that satisfies $A(x_k) = y_k$ for all k. Exercise 32.1-4 asks you how to compute the coefficients of A using Lagrange's formula in time $\Theta(n^2)$.

Thus, n-point evaluation and interpolation are well-defined inverse operations that transform between the coefficient representation of a polynomial and a point-value representation.[1] The algorithms described above for these problems take time $\Theta(n^2)$.

The point-value representation is quite convenient for many operations on polynomials. For addition, if $C(x) = A(x) + B(x)$, then $C(x_k) = A(x_k) + B(x_k)$ for any point x_k. More precisely, if we have a point-value representation for A,

$$\{(x_0, y_0), (x_1, y_1), \ldots, (x_{n-1}, y_{n-1})\} ,$$

and for B,

$$\{(x_0, y_0'), (x_1, y_1'), \ldots, (x_{n-1}, y_{n-1}')\}$$

(note that A and B are evaluated at the *same* n points), then a point-value representation for C is

$$\{(x_0, y_0 + y_0'), (x_1, y_1 + y_1'), \ldots, (x_{n-1}, y_{n-1} + y_{n-1}')\} .$$

The time to add two polynomials of degree-bound n in point-value form is thus $\Theta(n)$.

Similarly, the point-value representation is convenient for multiplying polynomials. If $C(x) = A(x)B(x)$, then $C(x_k) = A(x_k)B(x_k)$ for any point x_k, and we can pointwise multiply a point-value representation for A by a point-value representation for B to obtain a point-value representation for C. We must face the problem, however, that the degree-bound of C is the sum of the degree-bounds for A and B. A standard point-value representation for A and B consists of n point-value pairs for each polynomial. Multiplying these together gives us n point-value pairs for C, but

---

[1] Interpolation is a notoriously tricky problem from the point of view of numerical stability. Although the approaches described here are mathematically correct, small differences in the inputs or round-off errors during computation can cause large differences in the result.

since the degree-bound of C is $2n$, Theorem 32.1 implies that we need $2n$ point-value pairs for a point-value representation of C. We must therefore begin with "extended" point-value representations for A and for B consisting of $2n$ point-value pairs each. Given an extended point-value representation for A,

$$\{(x_0, y_0), (x_1, y_1), \ldots, (x_{2n-1}, y_{2n-1})\} ,$$

and a corresponding extended point-value representation for B,

$$\{(x_0, y_0'), (x_1, y_1'), \ldots, (x_{2n-1}, y_{2n-1}')\} ,$$

then a point-value representation for C is

$$\{(x_0, y_0 y_0'), (x_1, y_1 y_1'), \ldots, (x_{2n-1}, y_{2n-1} y_{2n-1}')\} .$$

Given two input polynomials in extended point-value form, we see that the time to multiply them to obtain the point-value form of the result is $\Theta(n)$, much less than the time required to multiply polynomials in coefficient form.

Finally, we consider how to evaluate a polynomial given in point-value form at a new point. For this problem, there is apparently no approach that is simpler than converting the polynomial to coefficient form first, and then evaluating it at the new point.

Fast multiplication of polynomials in coefficient form

Can we use the linear-time multiplication method for polynomials in point-value form to expedite polynomial multiplication in coefficient form? The answer hinges on our ability to convert a polynomial quickly from coefficient form to point-value form (evaluate) and vice-versa (interpolate).

We can use any points we want as evaluation points, but by choosing the evaluation points carefully, we can convert between representations in only $\Theta(n \lg n)$ time. As we shall see in Section 32.2, if we choose "complex roots of unity" as the evaluation points, we can produce a point-value representation by taking the Discrete Fourier Transform (or DFT) of a coefficient vector. The inverse operation, interpolation, can be performed by taking the "inverse DFT" of point-value pairs, yielding a coefficient vector. Section 32.2 will show how the FFT performs the DFT and inverse DFT operations in $\Theta(n \lg n)$ time.

Figure 32.1 shows this strategy graphically. One minor detail concerns degree-bounds. The product of two polynomials of degree-bound n is a polynomial of degree-bound $2n$. Before evaluating the input polynomials A and B, therefore, we first double their degree-bounds to $2n$ by adding n high-order coefficients of 0. Because the vectors have $2n$ elements, we use "complex $(2n)$th roots of unity," which are denoted by the ω_{2n} terms in Figure 32.1.

Given the FFT, we have the following $\Theta(n \lg n)$-time procedure for multiplying two polynomials $A(x)$ and $B(x)$ of degree-bound n, where the

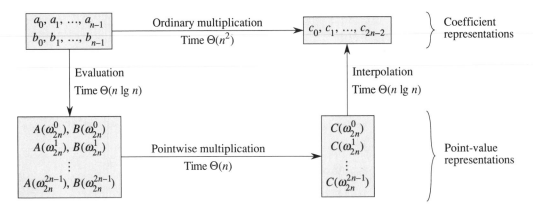

Figure 32.1   A graphical outline of an efficient polynomial-multiplication process. Representations on the top are in coefficient form, while those on the bottom are in point-value form. The arrows from left to right correspond to the multiplication operation. The ω_{2n} terms are complex $(2n)$th roots of unity.

input and output representations are in coefficient form. We assume that n is a power of 2; this requirement can always be met by adding high-order zero coefficients.

1. *Double degree-bound:* Create coefficient representations of $A(x)$ and $B(x)$ as degree-bound $2n$ polynomials by adding n high-order zero co-efficients to each.

2. *Evaluate:* Compute point-value representations of $A(x)$ and $B(x)$ of length $2n$ through two applications of the FFT of order $2n$. These representations contain the values of the two polynomials at the $(2n)$th roots of unity.

3. *Pointwise multiply:* Compute a point-value representation for the poly-nomial $C(x) = A(x)B(x)$ by multiplying these values together point-wise. This representation contains the value of $C(x)$ at each $(2n)$th root of unity.

4. *Interpolate:* Create the coefficient representation of the polynomial $C(x)$ through a single application of an FFT on $2n$ point-value pairs to com-pute the inverse DFT.

Steps (1) and (3) take time $\Theta(n)$, and steps (2) and (4) take time $\Theta(n \lg n)$. Thus, once we show how to use the FFT, we will have proven the following.

Theorem 32.2
The product of two polynomials of degree-bound n can be computed in time $\Theta(n \lg n)$, with both the input and output representations in coefficient form.   ∎

Exercises

32.1-1

Multiply the polynomials $A(x) = 7x^3 - x^2 + x - 10$ and $B(x) = 8x^3 - 6x + 3$ using equations (32.1) and (32.2).

32.1-2

Evaluating a polynomial $A(x)$ of degree-bound n at a given point x_0 can also be done by dividing $A(x)$ by the polynomial $(x - x_0)$ to obtain a quotient polynomial $q(x)$ of degree-bound $n - 1$ and a remainder r, such that

$$A(x) = q(x)(x - x_0) + r .$$

Clearly, $A(x_0) = r$. Show how to compute the remainder r and the coefficients of $q(x)$ in time $\Theta(n)$ from x_0 and the coefficients of A.

32.1-3

Derive a point-value representation for $A^{\text{rev}}(x) = \sum_{j=0}^{n-1} a_{n-1-j} x^j$ from a point-value representation for $A(x) = \sum_{j=0}^{n-1} a_j x^j$, assuming that none of the points is 0.

32.1-4

Show how to use equation (32.5) to interpolate in time $\Theta(n^2)$. (*Hint:* First compute $\prod_j (x - x_k)$ and $\prod_j (x_j - x_k)$ and then divide by $(x - x_k)$ and $(x_j - x_k)$ as necessary for each term. See Exercise 32.1-2.)

32.1-5

Explain what is wrong with the "obvious" approach to polynomial division using a point-value representation. Discuss separately the case in which the division comes out exactly and the case in which it doesn't.

32.1-6

Consider two sets A and B, each having n integers in the range from 0 to $10n$. We wish to compute the ***Cartesian sum*** of A and B, defined by

$$C = \{x + y : x \in A \text{ and } y \in B\} .$$

Note that the integers in C are in the range from 0 to $20n$. We want to find the elements of C and the number of times each element of C is realized as a sum of elements in A and B. Show that the problem can be solved in $O(n \lg n)$ time. (*Hint:* Represent A and B as polynomials of degree $10n$.)

32.2 The DFT and FFT

In Section 32.1, we claimed that if we use complex roots of unity, we can evaluate and interpolate in $\Theta(n \lg n)$ time. In this section, we define

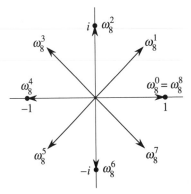

Figure 32.2 The values of $\omega_8^0, \omega_8^1, \ldots, \omega_8^7$ in the complex plane, where $\omega_8 = e^{2\pi i/8}$ is the principal 8th root of unity.

complex roots of unity and study their properties, define the DFT, and then show how the FFT computes the DFT and its inverse in just $\Theta(n \lg n)$ time.

Complex roots of unity

A *complex nth root of unity* is a complex number ω such that

$$\omega^n = 1 .$$

There are exactly n complex nth roots of unity; these are $e^{2\pi i k/n}$ for $k = 0, 1, \ldots, n - 1$. To interpret this formula, we use the definition of the exponential of a complex number:

$$e^{iu} = \cos(u) + i \sin(u) .$$

Figure 32.2 shows that the n complex roots of unity are equally spaced around the circle of unit radius centered at the origin of the complex plane. The value

$$\omega_n = e^{2\pi i/n} \tag{32.6}$$

is called *the principal nth root of unity*; all of the other complex nth roots of unity are powers of ω_n.

The n complex nth roots of unity,

$$\omega_n^0, \omega_n^1, \ldots, \omega_n^{n-1} ,$$

form a group under multiplication (see Section 33.3). This group has the same structure as the additive group $(\mathbf{Z}_n, +)$ modulo n, since $\omega_n^n = \omega_n^0 = 1$ implies that $\omega_n^j \omega_n^k = \omega_n^{j+k} = \omega_n^{(j+k) \bmod n}$. Similarly, $\omega_n^{-1} = \omega_n^{n-1}$. Essential properties of the complex nth roots of unity are given in the following lemmas.

Lemma 32.3 (Cancellation lemma)
For any integers $n \geq 0$, $k \geq 0$, and $d > 0$,

$$\omega_{dn}^{dk} = \omega_n^k \,. \tag{32.7}$$

Proof The lemma follows directly from equation (32.6), since

$$
\begin{aligned}
\omega_{dn}^{dk} &= \left(e^{2\pi i / dn}\right)^{dk} \\
&= \left(e^{2\pi i / n}\right)^{k} \\
&= \omega_n^k \,.
\end{aligned}
$$ ∎

Corollary 32.4
For any even integer $n > 0$,

$$\omega_n^{n/2} = \omega_2 = -1 \,.$$

Proof The proof is left as Exercise 32.2-1. ∎

Lemma 32.5 (Halving lemma)
If $n > 0$ is even, then the squares of the n complex nth roots of unity are the $n/2$ complex $(n/2)$th roots of unity.

Proof By the cancellation lemma, we have $(\omega_n^k)^2 = \omega_{n/2}^k$, for any non-negative integer k. Note that if we square all of the complex nth roots of unity, then each $(n/2)$th root of unity is obtained exactly twice, since

$$
\begin{aligned}
(\omega_n^{k+n/2})^2 &= \omega_n^{2k+n} \\
&= \omega_n^{2k} \omega_n^{n} \\
&= \omega_n^{2k} \\
&= (\omega_n^k)^2 \,.
\end{aligned}
$$

Thus, ω_n^k and $\omega_n^{k+n/2}$ have the same square. This property can also be proved using Corollary 32.4, since $\omega_n^{n/2} = -1$ implies $\omega_n^{k+n/2} = -\omega_n^k$, and thus $(\omega_n^{k+n/2})^2 = (\omega_n^k)^2$. ∎

As we shall see, the halving lemma is essential to our divide-and-conquer approach for converting between coefficient and point-value representations of polynomials, since it guarantees that the recursive subproblems are only half as large.

Lemma 32.6 (Summation lemma)
For any integer $n \geq 1$ and nonnegative integer k not divisible by n,

$$\sum_{j=0}^{n-1} \left(\omega_n^k\right)^j = 0 .$$

Proof   Because equation (3.3) applies to complex values,

$$
\begin{aligned}
\sum_{j=0}^{n-1} \left(\omega_n^k\right)^j
&= \frac{(\omega_n^k)^n - 1}{\omega_n^k - 1} \\
&= \frac{(\omega_n^n)^k - 1}{\omega_n^k - 1} \\
&= \frac{(1)^k - 1}{\omega_n^k - 1} \\
&= 0 .
\end{aligned}
$$

Requiring that k not be divisible by n ensures that the denominator is not 0, since $\omega_n^k = 1$ only when k is divisible by n.   ∎

The DFT

Recall that we wish to evaluate a polynomial

$$A(x) = \sum_{j=0}^{n-1} a_j x^j$$

of degree-bound n at $\omega_n^0, \omega_n^1, \omega_n^2, \ldots, \omega_n^{n-1}$ (that is, at the n complex nth roots of unity).[2] Without loss of generality, we assume that n is a power of 2, since a given degree-bound can always be raised—we can always add new high-order zero coefficients as necessary. We assume that A is given in coefficient form: $a = (a_0, a_1, \ldots, a_{n-1})$. Let us define the results y_k, for $k = 0, 1, \ldots, n - 1$, by

$$
\begin{aligned}
y_k &= A(\omega_n^k) \\
&= \sum_{j=0}^{n-1} a_j \omega_n^{kj} .
\end{aligned}
\tag{32.8}
$$

The vector $y = (y_0, y_1, \ldots, y_{n-1})$ is the **Discrete Fourier Transform (DFT)** of the coefficient vector $a = (a_0, a_1, \ldots, a_{n-1})$. We also write $y = \mathrm{DFT}_n(a)$.

---

[2]The length n is actually what we referred to as $2n$ in Section 32.1, since we double the degree-bound of the given polynomials prior to evaluation. In the context of polynomial multiplication, therefore, we are actually working with complex $(2n)$th roots of unity.

The FFT

By using a method known as the *Fast Fourier Transform (FFT)*, which takes advantage of the special properties of the complex roots of unity, we can compute $\text{DFT}_n(a)$ in time $\Theta(n \lg n)$, as opposed to the $\Theta(n^2)$ time of the straightforward method.

The FFT method employs a divide-and-conquer strategy, using the even-index and odd-index coefficients of $A(x)$ separately to define the two new degree-bound $n/2$ polynomials $A^{[0]}(x)$ and $A^{[1]}(x)$:

$$A^{[0]}(x) = a_0 + a_2 x + a_4 x^2 + \cdots + a_{n-2} x^{n/2-1} \,,$$
$$A^{[1]}(x) = a_1 + a_3 x + a_5 x^2 + \cdots + a_{n-1} x^{n/2-1} \,.$$

Note that $A^{[0]}$ contains all the even-index coefficients of A (the binary representation of the index ends in 0) and $A^{[1]}$ contains all the odd-index coefficients (the binary representation of the index ends in 1). It follows that

$$A(x) = A^{[0]}(x^2) + x A^{[1]}(x^2) \,, \tag{32.9}$$

so that the problem of evaluating $A(x)$ at $\omega_n^0, \omega_n^1, \ldots, \omega_n^{n-1}$ reduces to

1. evaluating the degree-bound $n/2$ polynomials $A^{[0]}(x)$ and $A^{[1]}(x)$ at the points

$$(\omega_n^0)^2, (\omega_n^1)^2, \ldots, (\omega_n^{n-1})^2 \,, \tag{32.10}$$

   and then

2. combining the results according to equation (32.9).

By the halving lemma, the list of values (32.10) consists not of n distinct values but only of the $n/2$ complex $(n/2)$th roots of unity, with each root occurring exactly twice. Therefore, the polynomials $A^{[0]}$ and $A^{[1]}$ of degree-bound $n/2$ are recursively evaluated at the $n/2$ complex $(n/2)$th roots of unity. These subproblems have exactly the same form as the original problem, but are half the size. We have now successfully divided an n-element DFT_n computation into two $n/2$-element $\text{DFT}_{n/2}$ computations. This decomposition is the basis for the following recursive FFT algorithm, which computes the DFT of an n-element vector $a = (a_0, a_1, \ldots, a_{n-1})$, where n is a power of 2.

RECURSIVE-FFT(a)

1 $n \leftarrow length[a]$ ▷ n is a power of 2.
2 **if** $n = 1$
3   **then return** a
4 $\omega_n \leftarrow e^{2\pi i/n}$
5 $\omega \leftarrow 1$
6 $a^{[0]} \leftarrow (a_0, a_2, \ldots, a_{n-2})$
7 $a^{[1]} \leftarrow (a_1, a_3, \ldots, a_{n-1})$
8 $y^{[0]} \leftarrow$ RECURSIVE-FFT($a^{[0]}$)
9 $y^{[1]} \leftarrow$ RECURSIVE-FFT($a^{[1]}$)
10 **for** $k \leftarrow 0$ **to** $n/2 - 1$
11   **do** $y_k \leftarrow y_k^{[0]} + \omega y_k^{[1]}$
12          $y_{k+(n/2)} \leftarrow y_k^{[0]} - \omega y_k^{[1]}$
13          $\omega \leftarrow \omega \omega_n$
14 **return** y ▷ y is assumed to be column vector.

The RECURSIVE-FFT procedure works as follows. Lines 2–3 represent the basis of the recursion; the DFT of one element is the element itself, since in this case

$$
\begin{aligned}
y_0 &= a_0 \omega_1^0 \\
&= a_0 \cdot 1 \\
&= a_0 \, .
\end{aligned}
$$

Lines 6–7 define the coefficient vectors for the polynomials $A^{[0]}$ and $A^{[1]}$. Lines 4, 5, and 13 guarantee that ω is updated properly so that whenever lines 11–12 are executed, $\omega = \omega_n^k$. (Keeping a running value of ω from iteration to iteration saves time over computing ω_n^k from scratch each time through the **for** loop.) Lines 8–9 perform the recursive $\text{DFT}_{n/2}$ computations, setting, for $k = 0, 1, \ldots, n/2 - 1$,

$$
\begin{aligned}
y_k^{[0]} &= A^{[0]}(\omega_{n/2}^k) \, , \\
y_k^{[1]} &= A^{[1]}(\omega_{n/2}^k) \, ,
\end{aligned}
$$

or, since $\omega_{n/2}^k = \omega_n^{2k}$ by the cancellation lemma,

$$
\begin{aligned}
y_k^{[0]} &= A^{[0]}(\omega_n^{2k}) \, , \\
y_k^{[1]} &= A^{[1]}(\omega_n^{2k}) \, .
\end{aligned}
$$

Lines 11–12 combine the results of the recursive $\text{DFT}_{n/2}$ calculations. For $y_0, y_1, \ldots, y_{n/2-1}$, line 11 yields

$$
\begin{aligned}
y_k &= y_k^{[0]} + \omega_n^k y_k^{[1]} \\
&= A^{[0]}(\omega_n^{2k}) + \omega_n^k A^{[1]}(\omega_n^{2k}) \\
&= A(\omega_n^k) \, ,
\end{aligned}
$$

where the last line of this argument follows from equation (32.9). For $y_{n/2}, y_{n/2+1}, \ldots, y_{n-1}$, letting $k = 0, 1, \ldots, n/2 - 1$, line 12 yields

$$
\begin{aligned}
y_{k+(n/2)} &= y_k^{[0]} - \omega_n^k y_k^{[1]} \\
&= y_k^{[0]} + \omega_n^{k+(n/2)} y_k^{[1]} \\
&= A^{[0]}(\omega_n^{2k}) + \omega_n^{k+(n/2)} A^{[1]}(\omega_n^{2k}) \\
&= A^{[0]}(\omega_n^{2k+n}) + \omega_n^{k+(n/2)} A^{[1]}(\omega_n^{2k+n}) \\
&= A(\omega_n^{k+(n/2)}) \ .
\end{aligned}
$$

The second line follows from the first since $\omega_n^{k+(n/2)} = -\omega_n^k$. The fourth line follows from the third because $\omega_n^n = 1$ implies $\omega_n^{2k} = \omega_n^{2k+n}$. The last line follows from equation (32.9). Thus, the vector y returned by RECURSIVE-FFT is indeed the DFT of the input vector a.

To determine the running time of procedure RECURSIVE-FFT, we note that exclusive of the recursive calls, each invocation takes time $\Theta(n)$, where n is the length of the input vector. The recurrence for the running time is therefore

$$
\begin{aligned}
T(n) &= 2T(n/2) + \Theta(n) \\
&= \Theta(n \lg n) \ .
\end{aligned}
$$

Thus, we can evaluate a polynomial of degree-bound n at the complex nth roots of unity in time $\Theta(n \lg n)$ using the Fast Fourier Transform.

Interpolation at the complex roots of unity

We now complete the polynomial multiplication scheme by showing how to interpolate the complex roots of unity by a polynomial, which enables us to convert from point-value form back to coefficient form. We interpolate by writing the DFT as a matrix equation and then looking at the form of the matrix inverse.

From equation (32.4), we can write the DFT as the matrix product $y = V_n a$, where V_n is a Vandermonde matrix containing the appropriate powers of ω_n:

$$
\begin{pmatrix}
y_0 \\
y_1 \\
y_2 \\
y_3 \\
\vdots \\
y_{n-1}
\end{pmatrix}
=
\begin{pmatrix}
1 & 1 & 1 & 1 & \cdots & 1 \\
1 & \omega_n & \omega_n^2 & \omega_n^3 & \cdots & \omega_n^{n-1} \\
1 & \omega_n^2 & \omega_n^4 & \omega_n^6 & \cdots & \omega_n^{2(n-1)} \\
1 & \omega_n^3 & \omega_n^6 & \omega_n^9 & \cdots & \omega_n^{3(n-1)} \\
\vdots & \vdots & \vdots & \vdots & \ddots & \vdots \\
1 & \omega_n^{n-1} & \omega_n^{2(n-1)} & \omega_n^{3(n-1)} & \cdots & \omega_n^{(n-1)(n-1)}
\end{pmatrix}
\begin{pmatrix}
a_0 \\
a_1 \\
a_2 \\
a_3 \\
\vdots \\
a_{n-1}
\end{pmatrix}
$$

The (k, j) entry of V_n is ω_n^{kj}, for $j, k = 0, 1, \ldots, n - 1$, and the exponents of the entries of V_n form a multiplication table.

For the inverse operation, which we write as $a = \mathrm{DFT}_n^{-1}(y)$, we proceed by multiplying y by the matrix V_n^{-1}, the inverse of V_n.

Theorem 32.7
For $j, k = 0, 1, \ldots, n - 1$, the (j, k) entry of V_n^{-1} is ω_n^{-kj}/n.

Proof   We show that $V_n^{-1}V_n = I_n$, the $n \times n$ identity matrix. Consider the (j, j') entry of $V_n^{-1}V_n$:

$$
\begin{aligned}
[V_n^{-1}V_n]_{jj'} &= \sum_{k=0}^{n-1}(\omega_n^{-kj}/n)(\omega_n^{kj'}) \\
&= \sum_{k=0}^{n-1}\omega_n^{k(j'-j)}/n \ .
\end{aligned}
$$

This summation equals 1 if $j' = j$, and it is 0 otherwise by the summation lemma (Lemma 32.6). Note that we rely on $-(n - 1) < j' - j < n - 1$, so that $j' - j$ is not divisible by n, in order for the summation lemma to apply.   ∎

Given the inverse matrix V_n^{-1}, we have that $\mathrm{DFT}_n^{-1}(y)$ is given by

$$
a_j = \frac{1}{n}\sum_{k=0}^{n-1}y_k\omega_n^{-kj} \tag{32.11}
$$

for $j = 0, 1, \ldots, n - 1$. By comparing equations (32.8) and (32.11), we see that by modifying the FFT algorithm to switch the roles of a and y, replace ω_n by ω_n^{-1}, and divide each element of the result by n, we compute the inverse DFT (see Exercise 32.2-4). Thus, DFT_n^{-1} can be computed in $\Theta(n \lg n)$ time as well.

Thus, by using the FFT and the inverse FFT, we can transform a polynomial of degree-bound n back and forth between its coefficient representation and a point-value representation in time $\Theta(n \lg n)$. In the context of polynomial multiplication, we have shown the following.

Theorem 32.8 (Convolution theorem)
For any two vectors a and b of length n, where n is a power of 2,

$$
a \otimes b = \mathrm{DFT}_{2n}^{-1}(\mathrm{DFT}_{2n}(a) \cdot \mathrm{DFT}_{2n}(b)) \ ,
$$

where the vectors a and b are padded with 0's to length $2n$ and $\cdot$ denotes the componentwise product of two $2n$-element vectors.   ∎

Exercises

32.2-1
Prove Corollary 32.4.

32.2-2
Compute the DFT of the vector $(0, 1, 2, 3)$.

32.2-3
Do Exercise 32.1-1 by using the $\Theta(n \lg n)$-time scheme.

32.2-4
Write pseudocode to compute DFT_n^{-1} in $\Theta(n \lg n)$ time.

32.2-5
Describe the generalization of the FFT procedure to the case in which n is a power of 3. Give a recurrence for the running time, and solve the recurrence.

32.2-6 $\star$
Suppose that instead of performing an n-element FFT over the field of complex numbers (where n is even), we use the ring $\mathbf{Z}_m$ of integers modulo m, where $m = 2^{tn/2} + 1$ and t is an arbitrary positive integer. Use $w = 2^t$ instead of ω_n as a principal nth root of unity, modulo m. Prove that the DFT and the inverse DFT are well defined in this system.

32.2-7
Given a list of values $z_0, z_1, \ldots, z_{n-1}$ (possibly with repetitions), show how to find the coefficients of the polynomial $P(x)$ of degree-bound n that has zeros only at $z_0, z_1, \ldots, z_{n-1}$ (possibly with repetitions). Your procedure should run in time $O(n \lg^2 n)$. (*Hint:* The polynomial $P(x)$ has a zero at z_j if and only if $P(x)$ is a multiple of $(x - z_j)$.)

32.2-8 $\star$
The *chirp transform* of a vector $a = (a_0, a_1, \ldots, a_{n-1})$ is the vector $y = (y_0, y_1, \ldots, y_{n-1})$, where $y_k = \sum_{j=0}^{n-1} a_j z^j$ and z is any complex number. The DFT is therefore a special case of the chirp transform, obtained by taking $z = \omega_n$. Prove that the chirp transform can be evaluated in time $O(n \lg n)$ for any complex number z. (*Hint:* Use the equation

$$y_k = z^{k^2/2} \sum_{j=0}^{n-1} \left(a_j z^{j^2/2} \right) \left(z^{-(k-j)^2/2} \right)$$

to view the chirp transform as a convolution.)

32.3 Efficient FFT implementations

Since the practical applications of the DFT, such as signal processing, demand the utmost speed, this section examines two efficient FFT implementations. First, we shall examine an iterative version of the FFT algorithm that runs in $\Theta(n \lg n)$ time but has a lower constant hidden in the Θ-notation than the recursive implementation in Section 32.2. Then, we shall use the insights that led us to the iterative implementation to design an efficient parallel FFT circuit.

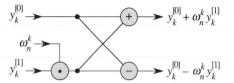

Figure 32.3   A butterfly operation. The two input values enter from the left, ω_n^k is multiplied by $y_k^{[1]}$, and the sum and difference are output on the right. The figure can be interpreted as a combinational circuit.

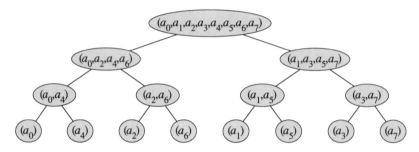

Figure 32.4   The tree of input vectors to the recursive calls of the RECURSIVE-FFT procedure. The initial invocation is for $n = 8$.

An iterative FFT implementation

We first note that the **for** loop of lines 10–13 of RECURSIVE-FFT involves computing the value $\omega_n^k y_k^{[1]}$ twice. In compiler terminology, this value is known as a ***common subexpression***. We can change the loop to compute it only once, storing it in a temporary variable t.

> **for** $k \leftarrow 0$ **to** $n/2 - 1$
>   **do** $t \leftarrow \omega y_k^{[1]}$
> $y_k \leftarrow y_k^{[0]} + t$
> $y_{k+(n/2)} \leftarrow y_k^{[0]} - t$
> $\omega \leftarrow \omega \, \omega_n$

The operation in this loop, multiplying ω (which is equal to ω_n^k) by $y_k^{[1]}$, storing the product into t, and adding and subtracting t from $y_k^{[0]}$, is known as a ***butterfly operation*** and is shown schematically in Figure 32.3.

We now show how to make the FFT algorithm iterative rather than recursive in structure. In Figure 32.4, we have arranged the input vectors to the recursive calls in an invocation of RECURSIVE-FFT in a tree structure, where the initial call is for $n = 8$. The tree has one node for each call of the procedure, labeled by the corresponding input vector. Each RECURSIVE-FFT invocation makes two recursive calls, unless it has received a 1-element vector. We make the first call the left child and the second call the right child.

Looking at the tree, we observe that if we could arrange the elements of the initial vector a into the order in which they appear in the leaves, we could mimic the execution of the RECURSIVE-FFT procedure as follows. First, we take the elements in pairs, compute the DFT of each pair using one butterfly operation, and replace the pair with its DFT. The vector then holds $n/2$ 2-element DFT's. Next, we take these $n/2$ DFT's in pairs and compute the DFT of the four vector elements they come from by executing two butterfly operations, replacing two 2-element DFT's with one 4-element DFT. The vector then holds $n/4$ 4-element DFT's. We continue in this manner until the vector holds two $(n/2)$-element DFT's, which we can combine using $n/2$ butterfly operations into the final n-element DFT.

To turn this observation into code, we use an array $A[0 .. n - 1]$ that initially holds the elements of the input vector a in the order in which they appear in the leaves of the tree of Figure 32.4. (We shall show later how to determine this order.) Because the combining has to be done on each level of the tree, we introduce a variable s to count the levels, ranging from 1 (at the bottom, when we are combining pairs to form 2-element DFT's) to $\lg n$ (at the top, when we are combining two $(n/2)$-element DFT's to produce the final result). The algorithm therefore has the following structure:

```
1  for s ← 1 to lg n
2      do for k ← 0 to n − 1 by 2ˢ
3          do combine the two 2ˢ⁻¹-element DFT's in
                 A[k .. k + 2ˢ⁻¹ − 1] and A[k + 2ˢ⁻¹ .. k + 2ˢ − 1]
                 into one 2ˢ-element DFT in A[k .. k + 2ˢ − 1]
```

We can express the body of the loop (line 3) as more precise pseudocode. We copy the **for** loop from the RECURSIVE-FFT procedure, identifying $y^{[0]}$ with $A[k .. k + 2^{s-1} - 1]$ and $y^{[1]}$ with $A[k + 2^{s-1} .. k + 2^s - 1]$. The value of ω used in each butterfly operation depends on the value of s; we use ω_m, where $m = 2^s$. (We introduce the variable m solely for the sake of readability.) We introduce another temporary variable u that allows us to perform the butterfly operation in place. When we replace line 3 of the overall structure by the loop body, we get the following pseudocode, which forms the basis of our final iterative FFT algorithm as well as the parallel implementation we shall present later.

FFT-BASE(a)
```
 1  n ← length[a]          ▷ n is a power of 2.
 2  for s ← 1 to lg n
 3      do m ← 2^s
 4          ω_m ← e^{2πi/m}
 5          for k ← 0 to n − 1 by m
 6              do ω ← 1
 7                  for j ← 0 to m/2 − 1
 8                      do t ← ω A[k + j + m/2]
 9                          u ← A[k + j]
10                          A[k + j] ← u + t
11                          A[k + j + m/2] ← u − t
12                          ω ← ω ω_m
```

We now present the final version of our iterative FFT code, which inverts the two inner loops to eliminate some index computation and uses the auxiliary procedure BIT-REVERSE-COPY(a, A) to copy vector a into array A in the initial order in which we need the values.

ITERATIVE-FFT(a)
```
 1  BIT-REVERSE-COPY(a, A)
 2  n ← length[a]          ▷ n is a power of 2.
 3  for s ← 1 to lg n
 4      do m ← 2^s
 5          ω_m ← e^{2πi/m}
 6          ω ← 1
 7          for j ← 0 to m/2 − 1
 8              do for k ← j to n − 1 by m
 9                  do t ← ω A[k + m/2]
10                      u ← A[k]
11                      A[k] ← u + t
12                      A[k + m/2] ← u − t
13                  ω ← ω ω_m
14  return A
```

How does BIT-REVERSE-COPY get the elements of the input vector a into the desired order in the array A? The order in which the leaves appear in Figure 32.4 is "bit-reverse binary." That is, if we let $\text{rev}(k)$ be the $\lg n$-bit integer formed by reversing the bits of the binary representation of k, then we want to place vector element a_k in array position $A[\text{rev}(k)]$. In Figure 32.4, for example, the leaves appear in the order $0, 4, 2, 6, 1, 5, 3, 7$; this sequence in binary is $000, 100, 010, 110, 001, 101, 011, 111$, and in bit-reverse binary we get the sequence $000, 001, 010, 011, 100, 101, 110, 111$. To see that we want bit-reverse binary order in general, we note that at the top level of the tree, indices whose low-order bit is 0 are placed in the left subtree and indices whose low-order bit is 1 are placed in the right subtree.

Stripping off the low-order bit at each level, we continue this process down the tree, until we get the bit-reverse binary order at the leaves.

Since the function rev(*k*) is easily computed, the BIT-REVERSE-COPY procedure can be written as follows.

BIT-REVERSE-COPY(*a, A*)

1 *n ← length[a]*
2 **for** *k ← 0* **to** *n − 1*
3   **do** *A*[rev(*k*)] *← a_k*

The iterative FFT implementation runs in time $\Theta(n \lg n)$. The call to BIT-REVERSE-COPY(*a, A*) certainly runs in $O(n \lg n)$ time, since we iterate *n* times and can reverse an integer between 0 and *n − 1*, with $\lg n$ bits, in $O(\lg n)$ time. (In practice, we usually know the initial value of *n* in advance, so we would probably code a table mapping *k* to rev(*k*), making BIT-REVERSE-COPY run in $\Theta(n)$ time with a low hidden constant. Alternatively, we could use the clever amortized reverse binary counter scheme described in Problem 18-1.) To complete the proof that ITERATIVE-FFT runs in time $\Theta(n \lg n)$, we show that $L(n)$, the number of times the body of the innermost loop (lines 9–12) is executed, is $\Theta(n \lg n)$. We have

$$
\begin{aligned}
L(n) &= \sum_{s=1}^{\lg n} \sum_{j=0}^{2^{s-1}-1} \frac{n}{2^s} \\
&= \sum_{s=1}^{\lg n} \frac{n}{2^s} \cdot 2^{s-1} \\
&= \sum_{s=1}^{\lg n} \frac{n}{2} \\
&= \Theta(n \lg n) \ .
\end{aligned}
$$

A parallel FFT circuit

We can exploit many of the properties that allowed us to implement an efficient iterative FFT algorithm to produce an efficient parallel algorithm for the FFT. (See Chapter 29 for a description of the combinational-circuit model.) The combinational circuit PARALLEL-FFT that computes the FFT on *n* inputs is shown in Figure 32.5 for *n* = 8. The circuit begins with a bit-reverse permutation of the inputs, followed by $\lg n$ stages, each stage consisting of *n/2* butterflies executed in parallel. The depth of the circuit is therefore $\Theta(\lg n)$.

The leftmost part of the circuit PARALLEL-FFT performs the bit-reverse permutation, and the remainder mimics the iterative FFT-BASE procedure. We take advantage of the fact that each iteration of the outermost **for** loop performs *n/2* independent butterfly operations that can be per-

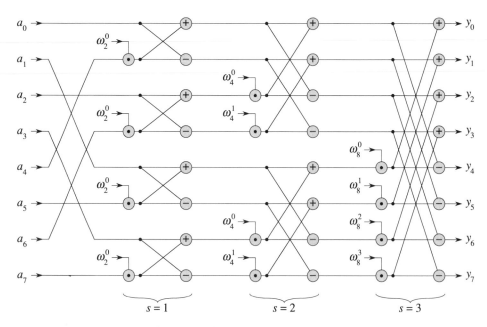

Figure 32.5 A combinational circuit PARALLEL-FFT that computes the FFT, here shown on $n = 8$ inputs. The stages of butterflies are labeled to correspond to iterations of the outermost loop of the FFT-BASE procedure. An FFT on n inputs can be computed in $\Theta(\lg n)$ depth with $\Theta(n \lg n)$ combinational elements.

formed in parallel. The value of s in each iteration within FFT-BASE corresponds to a stage of butterflies shown in Figure 32.5. Within stage s, for $s = 1, 2, \ldots, \lg n$, there are $n/2^s$ groups of butterflies (corresponding to each value of k in FFT-BASE), with 2^{s-1} butterflies per group (corresponding to each value of j in FFT-BASE). The butterflies shown in Figure 32.5 correspond to the butterfly operations of the innermost loop (lines 8–11 of FFT-BASE). Note also that the values of ω used in the butterflies correspond to those used in FFT-BASE: in stage s, we use $\omega_m^0, \omega_m^1, \ldots, \omega_m^{m/2-1}$, where $m = 2^s$.

Exercises

32.3-1
Show how ITERATIVE-FFT computes the DFT of the input vector $(0, 2, 3, -1, 4, 5, 7, 9)$.

32.3-2
Show how to implement an FFT algorithm with the bit-reversal permutation occurring at the end, rather than at the beginning, of the computation. (*Hint:* Consider the inverse DFT.)

32.3-3
To compute DFT_n, how many addition, subtraction, and multiplication elements, and how many wires, are needed in the PARALLEL-FFT circuit described in this section? (Assume that only one wire is needed to carry a number from one place to another.)

32.3-4 ⋆
Suppose that the adders in the FFT circuit sometimes fail in such a manner that they always produce a zero output, independent of their inputs. Suppose that exactly one adder has failed, but that you don't know which one. Describe how you can identify the failed adder by supplying inputs to the overall FFT circuit and observing the outputs. Try to make your procedure efficient.

Problems

32-1 Divide-and-conquer multiplication

a. Show how to multiply two linear polynomials $ax + b$ and $cx + d$ using only three multiplications. (*Hint:* One of the multiplications is $(a + b) \cdot (c + d)$.)

b. Give two divide-and-conquer algorithms for multiplying two polynomials of degree-bound n that run in time $\Theta(n^{\lg 3})$. The first algorithm should divide the input polynomial coefficients into a high half and a low half, and the second algorithm should divide them according to whether their index is odd or even.

c. Show that two n-bit integers can be multiplied in $O(n^{\lg 3})$ steps, where each step operates on at most a constant number of 1-bit values.

32-2 Toeplitz matrices
A *Toeplitz matrix* is an $n \times n$ matrix $A = (a_{ij})$ such that $a_{ij} = a_{i-1,j-1}$ for $i = 2, 3, \ldots, n$ and $j = 2, 3, \ldots, n$.

a. Is the sum of two Toeplitz matrices necessarily Toeplitz? What about the product?

b. Describe how to represent a Toeplitz matrix so that two $n \times n$ Toeplitz matrices can be added in $O(n)$ time.

c. Give an $O(n \lg n)$-time algorithm for multiplying an $n \times n$ Toeplitz matrix by a vector of length n. Use your representation from part (b).

d. Give an efficient algorithm for multiplying two $n \times n$ Toeplitz matrices. Analyze its running time.

32-3 *Evaluating all derivatives of a polynomial at a point*

Given a polynomial $A(x)$ of degree-bound n, its tth derivative is defined by

$$A^{(t)}(x) = \begin{cases} A(x) & \text{if } t = 0 , \\ \frac{d}{dx} A^{(t-1)}(x) & \text{if } 1 \leq t \leq n - 1 , \\ 0 & \text{if } t \geq n . \end{cases}$$

From the coefficient representation $(a_0, a_1, \ldots, a_{n-1})$ of $A(x)$ and a given point x_0, we wish to determine $A^{(t)}(x_0)$ for $t = 0, 1, \ldots, n - 1$.

a. Given coefficients $b_0, b_1, \ldots, b_{n-1}$ such that

$$A(x) = \sum_{j=0}^{n-1} b_j (x - x_0)^j ,$$

show how to compute $A^{(t)}(x_0)$, for $t = 0, 1, \ldots, n - 1$, in $O(n)$ time.

b. Explain how to find $b_0, b_1, \ldots, b_{n-1}$ in $O(n \lg n)$ time, given $A(x_0 + \omega_n^k)$ for $k = 0, 1, \ldots, n - 1$.

c. Prove that

$$A(x_0 + \omega_n^k) = \sum_{r=0}^{n-1} \left(\frac{\omega_n^{kr}}{r!} \sum_{j=0}^{n-1} f(j) g(r - j) \right) ,$$

where $f(j) = a_j \cdot j!$ and

$$g(l) = \begin{cases} x_0^{-l}/(-l)! & \text{if } -(n - 1) \leq l \leq 0 , \\ 0 & \text{if } 1 \leq l \leq (n - 1) . \end{cases}$$

d. Explain how to evaluate $A(x_0 + \omega_n^k)$ for $k = 0, 1, \ldots, n - 1$ in $O(n \lg n)$ time. Conclude that all nontrivial derivatives of $A(x)$ can be evaluated at x_0 in $O(n \lg n)$ time.

32-4 *Polynomial evaluation at multiple points*

We have observed that the problem of evaluating a polynomial of degree-bound $n - 1$ at a single point can be solved in $O(n)$ time using Horner's rule. We have also discovered that such a polynomial can be evaluated at all n complex roots of unity in $O(n \lg n)$ time using the FFT. We shall now show how to evaluate a polynomial of degree-bound n at n arbitrary points in $O(n \lg^2 n)$ time.

To do so, we shall use the fact that we can compute the polynomial remainder when one such polynomial is divided by another in $O(n \lg n)$ time, a result that we assume without proof. For example, the remainder of $3x^3 + x^2 - 3x + 1$ when divided by $x^2 + x + 2$ is

$$(3x^3 + x^2 - 3x + 1) \bmod (x^2 + x + 2) = 5x - 3 .$$

Given the coefficient representation of a polynomial $A(x) = \sum_{k=0}^{n-1} a_k x^k$ and n points $x_0, x_1, \ldots, x_{n-1}$, we wish to compute the n values $A(x_0)$, $A(x_1), \ldots, A(x_{n-1})$. For $0 \le i \le j \le n-1$, define the polynomials $P_{ij}(x) = \prod_{k=i}^{j}(x - x_k)$ and $Q_{ij}(x) = A(x) \bmod p_{ij}(x)$. Note that $Q_{ij}(x)$ has degree-bound at most $j - i$.

a. Prove that $A(x) \bmod (x - z) = A(z)$ for any point z.

b. Prove that $Q_{kk}(x) = A(x_k)$ and that $Q_{0,n-1}(x) = A(x)$.

c. Prove that for $i \le k \le j$, we have $Q_{ik}(x) = Q_{ij}(x) \bmod P_{ik}(x)$ and $Q_{kj}(x) = Q_{ij}(x) \bmod P_{kj}(x)$.

d. Give an $O(n \lg^2 n)$-time algorithm to evaluate $A(x_0), A(x_1), \ldots, A(x_{n-1})$.

32-5 *FFT using modular arithmetic*

As defined, the Discrete Fourier Transform requires the use of complex numbers, which can result in a loss of precision due to round-off errors. For some problems, the answer is known to contain only integers, and it is desirable to utilize a variant of the FFT based on modular arithmetic in order to guarantee that the answer is calculated exactly. An example of such a problem is that of multiplying two polynomials with integer coefficients. Exercise 32.2-6 gives one approach, using a modulus of length $\Omega(n)$ bits to handle a DFT on n points. This problem gives another approach that uses a modulus of the more reasonable length $O(\lg n)$; it requires that you understand the material of Chapter 33. Let n be a power of 2.

a. Suppose that we search for the smallest k such that $p = kn + 1$ is prime. Give a simple heuristic argument why we might expect k to be approximately $\lg n$. (The value of k might be much larger or smaller, but we can reasonably expect to examine $O(\lg n)$ candidate values of k on average.) How does the expected length of p compare to the length of n?

Let g be a generator of $\mathbf{Z}_p^*$, and let $w = g^k \bmod p$.

b. Argue that the DFT and the inverse DFT are well-defined inverse operations modulo p, where w is used as a principal nth root of unity.

c. Argue that the FFT and its inverse can be made to work modulo p in time $O(n \lg n)$, where operations on words of $O(\lg n)$ bits take unit time. Assume that the algorithm is given p and w.

d. Compute the DFT modulo $p = 17$ of the vector $(0, 5, 3, 7, 7, 2, 1, 6)$. Note that $g = 3$ is a generator of $\mathbf{Z}_{17}^*$.

Chapter notes

Press, Flannery, Teukolsky, and Vetterling [161, 162] have a good description of the Fast Fourier Transform and its applications. For an excellent introduction to signal processing, a popular FFT application area, see the text by Oppenheim and Willsky [153].

Cooley and Tukey [51] are widely credited with devising the FFT in the 1960's. The FFT had in fact been discovered many times previously, but its importance was not fully realized before the advent of modern digital computers. Press, Flannery, Teukolsky, and Vetterling attribute the origins of the method to Runge and König (1924).

33 Number-Theoretic Algorithms

Number theory was once viewed as a beautiful but largely useless subject in pure mathematics. Today number-theoretic algorithms are used widely, due in part to the invention of cryptographic schemes based on large prime numbers. The feasibility of these schemes rests on our ability to find large primes easily, while their security rests on our inability to factor the product of large primes. This chapter presents some of the number theory and associated algorithms that underlie such applications.

Section 33.1 introduces basic concepts of number theory, such as divisibility, modular equivalence, and unique factorization. Section 33.2 studies one of the world's oldest algorithms: Euclid's algorithm for computing the greatest common divisor of two integers. Section 33.3 reviews concepts of modular arithmetic. Section 33.4 then studies the set of multiples of a given number a, modulo n, and shows how to find all solutions to the equation $ax \equiv b \pmod{n}$ by using Euclid's algorithm. The Chinese remainder theorem is presented in Section 33.5. Section 33.6 considers powers of a given number a, modulo n, and presents a repeated-squaring algorithm for efficiently computing $a^b \bmod n$, given a, b, and n. This operation is at the heart of efficient primality testing. Section 33.7 then describes the RSA public-key cryptosystem. Section 33.8 describes a randomized primality test that can be used to find large primes efficiently, an essential task in creating keys for the RSA cryptosystem. Finally, Section 33.9 reviews a simple but effective heuristic for factoring small integers. It is a curious fact that factoring is one problem people may wish to be intractable, since the security of RSA depends on the difficulty of factoring large integers.

Size of inputs and cost of arithmetic computations

Because we shall be working with large integers, we need to adjust how we think about the size of an input and about the cost of elementary arithmetic operations.

In this chapter, a "large input" typically means an input containing "large integers" rather than an input containing "many integers" (as for sorting). Thus, we shall measure the size of an input in terms of the *number of bits* required to represent that input, not just the number of integers in the input. An algorithm with integer inputs $a_1, a_2, \ldots, a_k$ is a ***polynomial-time algorithm*** if it runs in time polynomial in $\lg a_1, \lg a_2, \ldots, \lg a_k$, that is, polynomial in the lengths of its binary-encoded inputs.

In most of this book, we have found it convenient to think of the elementary arithmetic operations (multiplications, divisions, or computing remainders) as primitive operations that take one unit of time. By counting the number of such arithmetic operations an algorithm performs, we have a basis for making a reasonable estimate of the algorithm's actual running time on a computer. Elementary operations can be time-consuming, however, when their inputs are large. It thus becomes convenient to measure how many ***bit operations*** a number-theoretic algorithm requires. In this model, a multiplication of two β-bit integers by the ordinary method uses $\Theta(\beta^2)$ bit operations. Similarly, the operation of dividing a β-bit integer by a shorter integer, or the operation of taking the remainder of a β-bit integer when divided by a shorter integer, can be performed in time $\Theta(\beta^2)$ by simple algorithms. (See Exercise 33.1-11.) Faster methods are known. For example, a simple divide-and-conquer method for multiplying two β-bit integers has a running time of $\Theta(\beta^{\lg_2 3})$, and the fastest known method has a running time of $\Theta(\beta \lg \beta \lg \lg \beta)$. For practical purposes, however, the $\Theta(\beta^2)$ algorithm is often best, and we shall use this bound as a basis for our analyses.

In this chapter, algorithms are generally analyzed in terms of both the number of arithmetic operations and the number of bit operations they require.

33.1   Elementary number-theoretic notions

This section provides a brief review of notions from elementary number theory concerning the set $\mathbf{Z} = \{\ldots, -2, -1, 0, 1, 2, \ldots\}$ of integers and the set $\mathbf{N} = \{0, 1, 2, \ldots\}$ of natural numbers.

Divisibility and divisors

The notion of one integer being divisible by another is a central one in the theory of numbers. The notation $d \mid a$ (read "d ***divides*** a") means that $a = kd$ for some integer k. Every integer divides 0. If $a > 0$ and $d \mid a$, then $|d| \le |a|$. If $d \mid a$, then we also say that a is a ***multiple*** of d. If d does not divide a, we write $d \nmid a$.

If $d \mid a$ and $d \ge 0$, we say that d is a ***divisor*** of a. Note that $d \mid a$ if and only if $-d \mid a$, so that no generality is lost by defining the divisors to be nonnegative, with the understanding that the negative of any divisor of a also divides a. A divisor of an integer a is at least 1 but not greater than $|a|$. For example, the divisors of 24 are 1, 2, 3, 4, 6, 8, 12, and 24.

Every integer a is divisible by the **trivial divisors** 1 and a. Nontrivial divisors of a are also called **factors** of a. For example, the factors of 20 are 2, 4, 5, and 10.

Prime and composite numbers

An integer $a > 1$ whose only divisors are the trivial divisors 1 and a is said to be a **prime** number (or, more simply, a **prime**). Primes have many special properties and play a critical role in number theory. The small primes, in order, are

$$2, 3, 5, 7, 11, 13, 17, 19, 23, 29, 31, 37, 41, 43, 47, 53, 59, \ldots .$$

Exercise 33.1-1 asks you to prove that there are infinitely many primes. An integer $a > 1$ that is not prime is said to be a **composite** number (or, more simply, a **composite**). For example, 39 is composite because $3 \mid 39$. The integer 1 is said to be a **unit** and is neither prime nor composite. Similarly, the integer 0 and all negative integers are neither prime nor composite.

The division theorem, remainders, and modular equivalence

Given an integer n, the integers can be partitioned into those that are multiples of n and those that are not multiples of n. Much number theory is based upon a refinement of this partition obtained by classifying the nonmultiples of n according to their remainders when divided by n. The following theorem is the basis for this refinement. The proof of this theorem will not be given here (see, for example, Niven and Zuckerman [151]).

Theorem 33.1 (Division theorem)
For any integer a and any positive integer n, there are unique integers q and r such that $0 \leq r < n$ and $a = qn + r$. ∎

The value $q = \lfloor a/n \rfloor$ is the **quotient** of the division. The value $r = a \bmod n$ is the **remainder** (or **residue**) of the division. We have that $n \mid a$ if and only if $a \bmod n = 0$. It follows that

$$a = \lfloor a/n \rfloor \, n + (a \bmod n) \tag{33.1}$$

or

$$a \bmod n = a - \lfloor a/n \rfloor \, n . \tag{33.2}$$

Given a well-defined notion of the remainder of one integer when divided by another, it is convenient to provide special notation to indicate equality of remainders. If $(a \bmod n) = (b \bmod n)$, we write $a \equiv b$ (mod n) and say that a is **equivalent** to b, modulo n. In other words, $a \equiv b$

(mod *n*) if *a* and *b* have the same remainder when divided by *n*. Equivalently, $a \equiv b \pmod{n}$ if and only if $n \mid (b - a)$. We write $a \not\equiv b \pmod{n}$ if *a* is not equivalent to *b*, modulo *n*. For example, $61 \equiv 6 \pmod{11}$. Also, $-13 \equiv 22 \equiv 2 \pmod{5}$.

The integers can be divided into *n* equivalence classes according to their remainders modulo *n*. The *equivalence class modulo n* containing an integer *a* is

$$[a]_n = \{a + kn : k \in \mathbf{Z}\} .$$

For example, $[3]_7 = \{\ldots, -11, -4, 3, 10, 17, \ldots\}$; other denotations for this set are $[-4]_7$ and $[10]_7$. Writing $a \in [b]_n$ is the same as writing $a \equiv b \pmod{n}$. The set of all such equivalence classes is

$$\mathbf{Z}_n = \{[a]_n : 0 \le a \le n - 1\} . \tag{33.3}$$

One often sees the definition

$$\mathbf{Z}_n = \{0, 1, \ldots, n - 1\} , \tag{33.4}$$

which should be read as equivalent to equation (33.3) with the understanding that 0 represents $[0]_n$, 1 represents $[1]_n$, and so on; each class is represented by its least nonnegative element. The underlying equivalence classes must be kept in mind, however. For example, a reference to -1 as a member of $\mathbf{Z}_n$ is a reference to $[n - 1]_n$, since $-1 \equiv n - 1 \pmod{n}$.

Common divisors and greatest common divisors

If *d* is a divisor of *a* and also a divisor of *b*, then *d* is a *common divisor* of *a* and *b*. For example, the divisors of 30 are 1, 2, 3, 5, 6, 10, 15, and 30, and so the common divisors of 24 and 30 are 1, 2, 3, and 6. Note that 1 is a common divisor of any two integers.

An important property of common divisors is that

$$d \mid a \text{ and } d \mid b \text{ implies } d \mid (a + b) \text{ and } d \mid (a - b) . \tag{33.5}$$

More generally, we have that

$$d \mid a \text{ and } d \mid b \text{ implies } d \mid (ax + by) \tag{33.6}$$

for any integers *x* and *y*. Also, if $a \mid b$, then either $|a| \le |b|$ or $b = 0$, which implies that

$$a \mid b \text{ and } b \mid a \text{ implies } a = \pm b . \tag{33.7}$$

The *greatest common divisor* of two integers *a* and *b*, not both zero, is the largest of the common divisors of *a* and *b*; it is denoted $\gcd(a, b)$. For example, $\gcd(24, 30) = 6$, $\gcd(5, 7) = 1$, and $\gcd(0, 9) = 9$. If *a* and *b* are not both 0, then $\gcd(a, b)$ is an integer between 1 and $\min(|a|, |b|)$. We define $\gcd(0, 0)$ to be 0; this definition is necessary to make standard properties of the gcd function (such as equation (33.11) below) universally valid.

The following are elementary properties of the gcd function:

$$\gcd(a, b) = \gcd(b, a) \,, \tag{33.8}$$

$$\gcd(a, b) = \gcd(-a, b) \,, \tag{33.9}$$

$$\gcd(a, b) = \gcd(|a|, |b|) \,, \tag{33.10}$$

$$\gcd(a, 0) = |a| \,, \tag{33.11}$$

$$\gcd(a, ka) = |a| \qquad \text{for any } k \in \mathbf{Z} \,. \tag{33.12}$$

Theorem 33.2

If a and b are any integers, not both zero, then $\gcd(a, b)$ is the smallest positive element of the set $\{ax + by : x, y \in \mathbf{Z}\}$ of linear combinations of a and b.

Proof   Let s be the smallest positive such linear combination of a and b, and let $s = ax + by$ for some $x, y \in \mathbf{Z}$. Let $q = \lfloor a/s \rfloor$. Equation (33.2) then implies

$$
\begin{aligned}
a \bmod s &= a - qs \\
&= a - q(ax + by) \\
&= a(1 - qx) + b(-qy) \,,
\end{aligned}
$$

and thus $a \bmod s$ is a linear combination of a and b as well. But, since $a \bmod s < s$, we have that $a \bmod s = 0$, because s is the smallest positive such linear combination. Therefore, $s \mid a$ and, by analogous reasoning, $s \mid b$. Thus, s is a common divisor of a and b, and so $\gcd(a, b) \geq s$. Equation (33.6) implies that $\gcd(a, b) \mid s$, since $\gcd(a, b)$ divides both a and b and s is a linear combination of a and b. But $\gcd(a, b) \mid s$ and $s > 0$ imply that $\gcd(a, b) \leq s$. Combining $\gcd(a, b) \geq s$ and $\gcd(a, b) \leq s$ yields $\gcd(a, b) = s$; we conclude that s is the greatest common divisor of a and b.   ■

Corollary 33.3

For any integers a and b, if $d \mid a$ and $d \mid b$ then $d \mid \gcd(a, b)$.

Proof   This corollary follows from equation (33.6), because $\gcd(a, b)$ is a linear combination of a and b by Theorem 33.2.   ■

Corollary 33.4

For all integers a and b and any nonnegative integer n,

$$\gcd(an, bn) = n \gcd(a, b) \,.$$

Proof   If $n = 0$, the corollary is trivial. If $n > 0$, then $\gcd(an, bn)$ is the smallest positive element of the set $\{anx + bny\}$, which is n times the smallest positive element of the set $\{ax + by\}$.   ■

Corollary 33.5
For all positive integers n, a, and b, if $n \mid ab$ and $\gcd(a, n) = 1$, then $n \mid b$.

Proof The proof is left as Exercise 33.1-4.   ∎

Relatively prime integers

Two integers a, b are said to be ***relatively prime*** if their only common divisor is 1, that is, if $\gcd(a, b) = 1$. For example, 8 and 15 are relatively prime, since the divisors of 8 are 1, 2, 4, and 8, while the divisors of 15 are 1, 3, 5, and 15. The following theorem states that if two integers are each relatively prime to an integer p, then their product is relatively prime to p.

Theorem 33.6
For any integers a, b, and p, if $\gcd(a, p) = 1$ and $\gcd(b, p) = 1$, then $\gcd(ab, p) = 1$.

Proof It follows from Theorem 33.2 that there exist integers x, y, x', and y' such that

$$
\begin{aligned}
ax + py &= 1 , \\
bx' + py' &= 1 .
\end{aligned}
$$

Multiplying these equations and rearranging, we have

$$ab(xx') + p(ybx' + y'ax + pyy') = 1 .$$

Since 1 is thus a positive linear combination of ab and p, an appeal to Theorem 33.2 completes the proof.   ∎

We say that integers $n_1, n_2, \ldots, n_k$ are ***pairwise relatively prime*** if, whenever $i \neq j$, we have $\gcd(n_i, n_j) = 1$.

Unique factorization

An elementary but important fact about divisibility by primes is the following.

Theorem 33.7
For all primes p and all integers a, b, if $p \mid ab$, then $p \mid a$ or $p \mid b$.

Proof Assume for the purpose of contradiction that $p \mid ab$ but that $p \nmid a$ and $p \nmid b$. Thus, $\gcd(a, p) = 1$ and $\gcd(b, p) = 1$, since the only divisors of p are 1 and p, and by assumption p divides neither a nor b. Theorem 33.6 then implies that $\gcd(ab, p) = 1$, contradicting our assumption that $p \mid ab$, since $p \mid ab$ implies $\gcd(ab, p) = p$. This contradiction completes the proof. ∎

A consequence of Theorem 33.7 is that an integer has a unique factorization into primes.

Theorem 33.8 (Unique factorization)
A composite integer a can be written in exactly one way as a product of the form

$$a = p_1^{e_1} p_2^{e_2} \cdots p_r^{e_r}$$

where the p_i are prime, $p_1 < p_2 < \cdots < p_r$, and the e_i are positive integers.

Proof The proof is left Exercise 33.1-10. ∎

As an example, the number 6000 can be uniquely factored as $2^4 \cdot 3 \cdot 5^3$.

Exercises

33.1-1
Prove that there are infinitely many primes. (*Hint:* Show that none of the primes $p_1, p_2, \ldots, p_k$ divide $(p_1 p_2 \cdots p_k) + 1$.)

33.1-2
Prove that if $a \mid b$ and $b \mid c$, then $a \mid c$.

33.1-3
Prove that if p is prime and $0 < k < p$, then $\gcd(k, p) = 1$.

33.1-4
Prove Corollary 33.5.

33.1-5
Prove that if p is prime and $0 < k < p$, then $p \mid \binom{p}{k}$. Conclude that for all integers a, b, and primes p,

$$(a + b)^p \equiv a^p + b^p \pmod{p}.$$

33.1-6
Prove that if a and b are any integers such that $a \mid b$ and $b > 0$, then

$$(x \bmod b) \bmod a = x \bmod a$$

for any x. Prove, under the same assumptions, that

$$x \equiv y \pmod{b} \quad \text{implies} \quad x \equiv y \pmod{a}$$

for any integers x and y.

33.1-7
For any integer $k > 0$, we say that an integer n is a ***kth power*** if there exists an integer a such that $a^k = n$. We say that $n > 1$ is a ***nontrivial power*** if it is a kth power for some integer $k > 1$. Show how to determine if a given β-bit integer n is a nontrivial power in time polynomial in β.

33.1-8
Prove equations (33.8)–(33.12).

33.1-9
Show that the gcd operator is associative. That is, prove that for all integers a, b, and c,

$$\gcd(a, \gcd(b, c)) = \gcd(\gcd(a, b), c) \ .$$

33.1-10 ⋆
Prove Theorem 33.8.

33.1-11
Give efficient algorithms for the operations of dividing a β-bit integer by a shorter integer and of taking the remainder of a β-bit integer when divided by a shorter integer. Your algorithms should run in time $O(\beta^2)$.

33.1-12
Give an efficient algorithm to convert a given β-bit (binary) integer to a decimal representation. Argue that if multiplication or division of integers whose length is at most β takes time $M(\beta)$, then binary-to-decimal conversion can be performed in time $\Theta(M(\beta) \lg \beta)$. (*Hint:* Use a divide-and-conquer approach, obtaining the top and bottom halves of the result with separate recursions.)

33.2 Greatest common divisor

In this section, we use Euclid's algorithm to compute the greatest common divisor of two integers efficiently. The analysis of running time brings up a surprising connection with the Fibonacci numbers, which yield a worst-case input for Euclid's algorithm.

We restrict ourselves in this section to nonnegative integers. This restriction is justified by equation (33.10), which states that $\gcd(a, b) = \gcd(|a|, |b|)$.

In principle, we can compute $\gcd(a, b)$ for positive integers a and b from the prime factorizations of a and b. Indeed, if

$$a \ = \ p_1^{e_1} p_2^{e_2} \cdots p_r^{e_r} \ , \tag{33.13}$$

$$b \ = \ p_1^{f_1} p_2^{f_2} \cdots p_r^{f_r} \ , \tag{33.14}$$

with zero exponents being used to make the set of primes $p_1, p_2, \ldots, p_r$ the same for both a and b, then

$$\gcd(a, b) = p_1^{\min(e_1, f_1)} p_2^{\min(e_2, f_2)} \cdots p_r^{\min(e_r, f_r)} \ . \tag{33.15}$$

As we shall show in Section 33.9, the best algorithms to date for factoring do not run in polynomial time. Thus, this approach to computing greatest common divisors seems unlikely to yield an efficient algorithm.

Euclid's algorithm for computing greatest common divisors is based on the following theorem.

Theorem 33.9 (GCD recursion theorem)
For any nonnegative integer a and any positive integer b,

$$\gcd(a, b) = \gcd(b, a \bmod b) \ .$$

Proof We shall show that $\gcd(a, b)$ and $\gcd(b, a \bmod b)$ divide each other, so that by equation (33.7) they must be equal (since they are both nonnegative).

We first show that $\gcd(a, b) \mid \gcd(b, a \bmod b)$. If we let $d = \gcd(a, b)$, then $d \mid a$ and $d \mid b$. By equation (33.2), $(a \bmod b) = a - qb$, where $q = \lfloor a/b \rfloor$. Since $(a \bmod b)$ is thus a linear combination of a and b, equation (33.6) implies that $d \mid (a \bmod b)$. Therefore, since $d \mid b$ and $d \mid (a \bmod b)$, Corollary 33.3 implies that $d \mid \gcd(b, a \bmod b)$ or, equivalently, that

$$\gcd(a, b) \mid \gcd(b, a \bmod b). \tag{33.16}$$

Showing that $\gcd(b, a \bmod b) \mid \gcd(a, b)$ is almost the same. If we now let $d = \gcd(b, a \bmod b)$, then $d \mid b$ and $d \mid (a \bmod b)$. Since $a = qb + (a \bmod b)$, where $q = \lfloor a/b \rfloor$, we have that a is a linear combination of b and $(a \bmod b)$. By equation (33.6), we conclude that $d \mid a$. Since $d \mid b$ and $d \mid a$, we have that $d \mid \gcd(a, b)$ by Corollary 33.3 or, equivalently, that

$$\gcd(b, a \bmod b) \mid \gcd(a, b). \tag{33.17}$$

Using equation (33.7) to combine equations (33.16) and (33.17) completes the proof. ∎

Euclid's algorithm

The following gcd algorithm is described in the *Elements* of Euclid (*circa* 300 B.C.), although it may be of even earlier origin. It is written as a recursive program based directly on Theorem 33.9. The inputs a and b are arbitrary nonnegative integers.

EUCLID(a, b)

1 **if** $b = 0$
2   **then return** a
3   **else return** EUCLID$(b, a \bmod b)$

As an example of the running of EUCLID, consider the computation of gcd$(30, 21)$:

$$
\begin{aligned}
\text{EUCLID}(30, 21) &= \text{EUCLID}(21, 9) \\
&= \text{EUCLID}(9, 3) \\
&= \text{EUCLID}(3, 0) \\
&= 3 .
\end{aligned}
$$

In this computation, there are three recursive invocations of EUCLID.

The correctness of EUCLID follows from Theorem 33.9 and the fact that if the algorithm returns a in line 2, then $b = 0$, so equation (33.11) implies that gcd$(a, b) = $ gcd$(a, 0) = a$. The algorithm cannot recurse indefinitely, since the second argument strictly decreases in each recursive call. Therefore, EUCLID always terminates with the correct answer.

The running time of Euclid's algorithm

We analyze the worst-case running time of EUCLID as a function of the size of a and b. We assume with little loss of generality that $a > b \geq 0$. This assumption can be justified by the observation that if $b > a \geq 0$, then EUCLID(a, b) immediately makes the recursive call EUCLID(b, a). That is, if the first argument is less than the second argument, EUCLID spends one recursive call swapping its arguments and then proceeds. Similarly, if $b = a > 0$, the procedure terminates after one recursive call, since $a \bmod b = 0$.

The overall running time of EUCLID is proportional to the number of recursive calls it makes. Our analysis makes use of the Fibonacci numbers F_k, defined by the recurrence (2.13).

Lemma 33.10
If $a > b \geq 0$ and the invocation EUCLID(a, b) performs $k \geq 1$ recursive calls, then $a \geq F_{k+2}$ and $b \geq F_{k+1}$.

Proof   The proof is by induction on k. For the basis of the induction, let $k = 1$. Then, $b \geq 1 = F_2$, and since $a > b$, we must have $a \geq 2 = F_3$. Since $b > (a \bmod b)$, in each recursive call the first argument is strictly larger than the second; the assumption that $a > b$ therefore holds for each recursive call.

Assume inductively that the lemma is true if $k - 1$ recursive calls are made; we shall then prove that it is true for k recursive calls. Since $k > 0$, we have $b > 0$, and EUCLID(a, b) calls EUCLID$(b, a \bmod b)$ recursively, which in turn makes $k - 1$ recursive calls. The inductive hypothesis then implies that $b \geq F_{k+1}$ (thus proving part of the lemma), and $(a \bmod b) \geq F_k$. We have

$$
\begin{aligned}
b + (a \bmod b) &= b + (a - \lfloor a/b \rfloor b) \\
&\leq a \,,
\end{aligned}
$$

since $a > b > 0$ implies $\lfloor a/b \rfloor \geq 1$. Thus,

$$
\begin{aligned}
a &\geq b + (a \bmod b) \\
&\geq F_{k+1} + F_k \\
&= F_{k+2} \,.
\end{aligned}
$$
∎

The following theorem is an immediate corollary of this lemma.

Theorem 33.11 (Lamé's theorem)
For any integer $k \geq 1$, if $a > b \geq 0$ and $b < F_{k+1}$, then the invocation EUCLID(a, b) makes fewer than k recursive calls. ∎

We can show that the upper bound of Theorem 33.11 is the best possible. Consecutive Fibonacci numbers are a worst-case input for EUCLID. Since EUCLID(F_3, F_2) makes exactly one recursive call, and since for $k \geq 2$ we have $F_{k+1} \bmod F_k = F_{k-1}$, we also have

$$
\begin{aligned}
\gcd(F_{k+1}, F_k) &= \gcd(F_k, (F_{k+1} \bmod F_k)) \\
&= \gcd(F_k, F_{k-1}) \,.
\end{aligned}
$$

Thus, EUCLID(F_{k+1}, F_k) recurses *exactly* $k - 1$ times, meeting the upper bound of Theorem 33.11.

Since F_k is approximately $\phi^k / \sqrt{5}$, where ϕ is the golden ratio $(1 + \sqrt{5})/2$ defined by equation (2.14), the number of recursive calls in EUCLID is $O(\lg b)$. (See Exercise 33.2-5 for a tighter bound.) It follows that if EUCLID is applied to two β-bit numbers, then it will perform $O(\beta)$ arithmetic operations and $O(\beta^3)$ bit operations (assuming that multiplication and division of β-bit numbers take $O(\beta^2)$ bit operations). Problem 33-2 asks you to show an $O(\beta^2)$ bound on the number of bit operations.

The extended form of Euclid's algorithm

We now rewrite Euclid's algorithm to compute additional useful information. Specifically, we extend the algorithm to compute the integer coefficients x and y such that

$$ d = \gcd(a, b) = ax + by \,. \tag{33.18} $$

Note that x and y may be zero or negative. We shall find these coefficients useful later for the computation of modular multiplicative inverses. The

a	b	$\lfloor a/b \rfloor$	d	x	y
99	78	1	3	−11	14
78	21	3	3	3	−11
21	15	1	3	−2	3
15	6	2	3	1	−2
6	3	2	3	0	1
3	0	—	3	1	0

Figure 33.1   An example of the operation of EXTENDED-EUCLID on the inputs 99 and 78. Each line shows for one level of the recursion: the values of the inputs a and b, the computed value $\lfloor a/b \rfloor$, and the values d, x, and y returned. The triple (d, x, y) returned becomes the triple (d', x', y') used in the computation at the next higher level of recursion. The call EXTENDED-EUCLID(99, 78) returns $(3, -11, 14)$, so $\gcd(99, 78) = 3$ and $\gcd(99, 78) = 3 = 99 \cdot (-11) + 78 \cdot 14$.

procedure EXTENDED-EUCLID takes as input an arbitrary pair of integers and returns a triple of the form (d, x, y) that satisfies equation (33.18).

EXTENDED-EUCLID(a, b)

1 **if** $b = 0$
2   **then return** $(a, 1, 0)$
3 $(d', x', y') \leftarrow$ EXTENDED-EUCLID($b, a \bmod b$)
4 $(d, x, y) \leftarrow (d', y', x' - \lfloor a/b \rfloor y')$
5 **return** (d, x, y)

Figure 33.1 illustrates the execution of EXTENDED-EUCLID with the computation of $\gcd(99, 78)$.

The EXTENDED-EUCLID procedure is a variation of the EUCLID procedure. Line 1 is equivalent to the test "$b = 0$" in line 1 of EUCLID. If $b = 0$, then EXTENDED-EUCLID returns not only $d = a$ in line 2, but also the coefficients $x = 1$ and $y = 0$, so that $a = ax + by$. If $b \neq 0$, EXTENDED-EUCLID first computes (d', x', y') such that $d' = \gcd(b, a \bmod b)$ and

$$d' = bx' + (a \bmod b)y'. \tag{33.19}$$

As for EUCLID, we have in this case $d = \gcd(a, b) = d' = \gcd(b, a \bmod b)$. To obtain x and y such that $d = ax + by$, we start by rewriting equation (33.19) using the equation $d = d'$ and equation (33.2):

$$
\begin{aligned}
d &= bx' + (a - \lfloor a/b \rfloor b)y' \\
  &= ay' + b(x' - \lfloor a/b \rfloor y').
\end{aligned}
$$

Thus, choosing $x = y'$ and $y = x' - \lfloor a/b \rfloor y'$ satisfies the equation $d = ax + by$, proving the correctness of EXTENDED-EUCLID.

Since the number of recursive calls made in EUCLID is equal to the number of recursive calls made in EXTENDED-EUCLID, the running times of EUCLID and EXTENDED-EUCLID are the same, to within a constant factor. That is, for $a > b > 0$, the number of recursive calls is $O(\lg b)$.

Exercises

33.2-1
Prove that equations (33.13)–(33.14) imply equation (33.15).

33.2-2
Compute the values (d, x, y) that are output by the invocation EXTENDED-EUCLID$(899, 493)$.

33.2-3
Prove that for all integers a, k, and n,

$$\gcd(a, n) = \gcd(a + kn, n) \ .$$

33.2-4
Rewrite EUCLID in an iterative form that uses only a constant amount of memory (that is, stores only a constant number of integer values).

33.2-5
If $a > b \geq 0$, show that the invocation EUCLID(a, b) makes at most $1 + \log_\phi b$ recursive calls. Improve this bound to $1 + \log_\phi(b / \gcd(a, b))$.

33.2-6
What does EXTENDED-EUCLID(F_{k+1}, F_k) return? Prove your answer correct.

33.2-7
Verify the output (d, x, y) of EXTENDED-EUCLID(a, b) by showing that if $d \mid a$, $d \mid b$, and $d = ax + by$, then $d = \gcd(a, b)$.

33.2-8
Define the gcd function for more than two arguments by the recursive equation $\gcd(a_0, a_1, \ldots, n) = \gcd(a_0, \gcd(a_1, \ldots, a_n))$. Show that gcd returns the same answer independent of the order in which its arguments are specified. Show how to find $x_0, x_1, \ldots, x_n$ such that $\gcd(a_0, a_1, \ldots, a_n) = a_0 x_0 + a_1 x_1 + \cdots + a_n x_n$. Show that the number of divisions performed by your algorithm is $O(n + \lg(\max_i a_i))$.

33.2-9
Define $\mathrm{lcm}(a_1, a_2, \ldots, a_n)$ to be the ***least common multiple*** of the integers $a_1, a_2, \ldots, a_n$, that is, the least nonnegative integer that is a multiple of each a_i. Show how to compute $\mathrm{lcm}(a_1, a_2, \ldots, a_n)$ efficiently using the (two-argument) gcd operation as a subroutine.

33.2-10
Prove that n_1, n_2, n_3, and n_4 are pairwise relatively prime if and only if $\gcd(n_1 n_2, n_3 n_4) = \gcd(n_1 n_3, n_2 n_4) = 1$. Show more generally that $n_1, n_2,$

$\ldots, n_k$ are pairwise relatively prime if and only if a set of $\lceil \lg k \rceil$ pairs of numbers derived from the n_i are relatively prime.

33.3   Modular arithmetic

Informally, we can think of modular arithmetic as arithmetic as usual over the integers, except that if we are working modulo n, then every result x is replaced by the element of $\{0, 1, \ldots, n - 1\}$ that is equivalent to x, modulo n (that is, x is replaced by $x \bmod n$). This informal model is sufficient if we stick to the operations of addition, subtraction, and multiplication. A more formal model for modular arithmetic, which we now give, is best described within the framework of group theory.

Finite groups

A ***group*** $(S, \oplus)$ is a set S together with a binary operation $\oplus$ defined on S for which the following properties hold.

1. **Closure:** For all $a, b \in S$, we have $a \oplus b \in S$.
2. **Identity:** There is an element $e \in S$ such that $e \oplus a = a \oplus e = a$ for all $a \in S$.
3. **Associativity:** For all $a, b, c \in S$, we have $(a \oplus b) \oplus c = a \oplus (b \oplus c)$.
4. **Inverses:** For each $a \in S$, there exists a unique element $b \in S$ such that $a \oplus b = b \oplus a = e$.

As an example, consider the familiar group $(\mathbf{Z}, +)$ of the integers $\mathbf{Z}$ under the operation of addition: 0 is the identity, and the inverse of a is $-a$. If a group $(S, \oplus)$ satisfies the ***commutative law*** $a \oplus b = b \oplus a$ for all $a, b \in S$, then it is an ***abelian group***. If a group $(S, \oplus)$ satisfies $|S| < \infty$, then it is a ***finite group***.

The groups defined by modular addition and multiplication

We can form two finite abelian groups by using addition and multiplication modulo n, where n is a positive integer. These groups are based on the equivalence classes of the integers modulo n, defined in Section 33.1.

To define a group on $\mathbf{Z}_n$, we need to have suitable binary operations, which we obtain by redefining the ordinary operations of addition and multiplication. It is easy to define addition and multiplication operations for $\mathbf{Z}_n$, because the equivalence class of two integers uniquely determines the equivalence class of their sum or product. That is, if $a \equiv a' \pmod{n}$ and $b \equiv b' \pmod{n}$, then

$$
\begin{aligned}
a + b &\equiv a' + b' \pmod{n}, \\
ab &\equiv a'b' \pmod{n}.
\end{aligned}
$$

$+_6$	0	1	2	3	4	5
0	0	1	2	3	4	5
1	1	2	3	4	5	0
2	2	3	4	5	0	1
3	3	4	5	0	1	2
4	4	5	0	1	2	3
5	5	0	1	2	3	4

(a)

$\cdot_{15}$	1	2	4	7	8	11	13	14
1	1	2	4	7	8	11	13	14
2	2	4	8	14	1	7	11	13
4	4	8	1	13	2	14	7	11
7	7	14	13	4	11	2	1	8
8	8	1	2	11	4	13	14	7
11	11	7	14	2	13	1	8	4
13	13	11	7	1	14	8	4	2
14	14	13	11	8	7	4	2	1

(b)

Figure 33.2 Two finite groups. Equivalence classes are denoted by their representative elements. **(a)** The group $(\mathbf{Z}_6, +_6)$. **(b)** The group $(\mathbf{Z}_{15}^*, \cdot_{15})$.

Thus, we define addition and multiplication modulo n, denoted $+_n$ and $\cdot_n$, as follows:

$$
\begin{aligned}
[a]_n +_n [b]_n &= [a+b]_n \,, \\
[a]_n \cdot_n [b]_n &= [ab]_n \,.
\end{aligned}
$$

(Subtraction can be similarly defined on $\mathbf{Z}_n$ by $[a]_n -_n [b]_n = [a-b]_n$, but division is more complicated, as we shall see.) These facts justify the common and convenient practice of using the least nonnegative element of each equivalence class as its representative when performing computations in $\mathbf{Z}_n$. Addition, subtraction, and multiplication are performed as usual on the representatives, but each result x is replaced by the representative of its class (that is, by $x \bmod n$).

Using this definition of addition modulo n, we define the ***additive group modulo n*** as $(\mathbf{Z}_n, +_n)$. This size of the additive group modulo n is $|\mathbf{Z}_n| = n$. Figure 33.2(a) gives the operation table for the group $(\mathbf{Z}_6, +_6)$.

Theorem 33.12
The system $(\mathbf{Z}_n, +_n)$ is a finite abelian group.

Proof Associativity and commutativity of $+_n$ follow from the associativity and commutativity of $+$:

$$
\begin{aligned}
([a]_n +_n [b]_n) +_n [c]_n &= [(a+b)+c]_n \\
&= [a+(b+c)]_n \\
&= [a]_n +_n ([b]_n +_n [c]_n) \,,
\end{aligned}
$$

$$
\begin{aligned}
[a]_n +_n [b]_n &= [a+b]_n \\
&= [b+a]_n \\
&= [b]_n +_n [a]_n \,.
\end{aligned}
$$

The identity element of $(\mathbf{Z}_n, +_n)$ is 0 (that is, $[0]_n$). The (additive) inverse of an element a (that is, $[a]_n$) is the element $-a$ (that is, $[-a]_n$ or $[n-a]_n$), since $[a]_n +_n [-a]_n = [a-a]_n = [0]_n$.   ∎

Using the definition of multiplication modulo n, we define the ***multiplicative group modulo n*** as $(\mathbf{Z}_n^*, \cdot_n)$. The elements of this group are the set $\mathbf{Z}_n^*$ of elements in $\mathbf{Z}_n$ that are relatively prime to n:

$$\mathbf{Z}_n^* = \{[a]_n \in \mathbf{Z}_n : \gcd(a, n) = 1\} \ .$$

To see that $\mathbf{Z}_n^*$ is well defined, note that for $0 \leq a < n$, we have $a \equiv (a+kn)$ (mod n) for all integers k. By Exercise 33.2-3, therefore, $\gcd(a, n) = 1$ implies $\gcd(a+kn, n) = 1$ for all integers k. Since $[a]_n = \{a + kn : k \in \mathbf{Z}\}$, the set $\mathbf{Z}_n^*$ is well defined. An example of such a group is

$$\mathbf{Z}_{15}^* = \{1, 2, 4, 7, 8, 11, 13, 14\} \ ,$$

where the group operation is multiplication modulo 15. (Here we denote an element $[a]_{15}$ as a.) Figure 33.2(b) shows the group $(\mathbf{Z}_{15}^*, \cdot_{15})$. For example, $8 \cdot 11 \equiv 13$ (mod 15), working in $\mathbf{Z}_{15}^*$. The identity for this group is 1.

Theorem 33.13
The system $(\mathbf{Z}_n^*, \cdot_n)$ is a finite abelian group.

Proof   Theorem 33.6 implies that $(\mathbf{Z}_n^*, \cdot_n)$ is closed. Associativity and commutativity can be proved for $\cdot_n$ as they were for $+_n$ in the proof of Theorem 33.12. The identity element is $[1]_n$. To show the existence of inverses, let a be an element of $\mathbf{Z}_n^*$ and let (d, x, y) be the output of EXTENDED-EUCLID(a, n). Then $d = 1$, since $a \in \mathbf{Z}_n^*$, and

$$ax + ny = 1$$

or, equivalently,

$$ax \equiv 1 \pmod{n} \ .$$

Thus, $[x]_n$ is a multiplicative inverse of $[a]_n$, modulo n. The proof that inverses are uniquely defined is deferred until Corollary 33.26.   ∎

When working with the groups $(\mathbf{Z}_n, +_n)$ and $(\mathbf{Z}_n, \cdot_n)$ in the remainder of this chapter, we follow the convenient practice of denoting equivalence classes by their representative elements and denoting the operations $+_n$ and $\cdot_n$ by the usual arithmetic notations $+$ and $\cdot$ (or juxtaposition) respectively. Also, equivalences modulo n may also be interpreted as equations in $\mathbf{Z}_n$. For example, the following two statements are equivalent:

$$ax \equiv b \pmod{n} \ ,$$
$$[a]_n \cdot_n [x]_n = [b]_n \ .$$

As a further convenience, we sometimes refer to a group $(S, \oplus)$ merely as S when the operation is understood from context. We may thus refer to the groups $(\mathbf{Z}_n, +_n)$ and $(\mathbf{Z}_n^*, \cdot_n)$ as $\mathbf{Z}_n$ and $\mathbf{Z}_n^*$, respectively.

The (multiplicative) inverse of an element a is denoted $(a^{-1} \bmod n)$. Division in $\mathbf{Z}_n^*$ is defined by the equation $a/b \equiv ab^{-1} \pmod{n}$. For example, in $\mathbf{Z}_{15}^*$ we have that $7^{-1} \equiv 13 \pmod{15}$, since $7 \cdot 13 \equiv 91 \equiv 1 \pmod{15}$, so that $4/7 \equiv 4 \cdot 13 \equiv 7 \pmod{15}$.

The size of $\mathbf{Z}_n^*$ is denoted $\phi(n)$. This function, known as *Euler's phi function*, satisfies the equation

$$\phi(n) = n \prod_{p \mid n} \left(1 - \frac{1}{p} \right) , \tag{33.20}$$

where p runs over all the primes dividing n (including n itself, if n is prime). We shall not prove this formula here. Intuitively, we begin with a list of the n remainders $\{0, 1, \ldots, n-1\}$ and then, for each prime p that divides n, cross out every multiple of p in the list. For example, since the prime divisors of 45 are 3 and 5,

$$
\begin{aligned}
\phi(45) &= 45 \left(1 - \frac{1}{3} \right) \left(1 - \frac{1}{5} \right) \\
&= 45 \left(\frac{2}{3} \right) \left(\frac{4}{5} \right) \\
&= 24 .
\end{aligned}
$$

If p is prime, then $\mathbf{Z}_p^* = \{1, 2, \ldots, p-1\}$, and

$$\phi(p) = p - 1 . \tag{33.21}$$

If n is composite, then $\phi(n) < n - 1$.

Subgroups

If $(S, \oplus)$ is a group, $S' \subseteq S$, and $(S', \oplus)$ is also a group, then $(S', \oplus)$ is said to be a *subgroup* of $(S, \oplus)$. For example, the even integers form a subgroup of the integers under the operation of addition. The following theorem provides a useful tool for recognizing subgroups.

Theorem 33.14 (A closed subset of a finite group is a subgroup)
If $(S, \oplus)$ is a finite group and S' is any subset of S such that $a \oplus b \in S'$ for all $a, b \in S'$, then $(S', \oplus)$ is a subgroup of $(S, \oplus)$.

Proof   The proof is left as Exercise 33.3-2.   ∎

For example, the set $\{0, 2, 4, 6\}$ forms a subgroup of $\mathbf{Z}_8$, since it is closed under the operation $+$ (that is, it is closed under $+_8$).

The following theorem provides an extremely useful constraint on the size of a subgroup.

Theorem 33.15 (Lagrange's theorem)

If $(S, \oplus)$ is a finite group and $(S', \oplus)$ is a subgroup of $(S, \oplus)$, then $|S'|$ is a divisor of $|S|$.   ∎

A subgroup S' of a group S is said to be a **proper** subgroup if $S' \neq S$. The following corollary will be used in our analysis of the Miller-Rabin primality test procedure in Section 33.8.

Corollary 33.16

If S' is a proper subgroup of a finite group S, then $|S'| \leq |S|/2$.   ∎

Subgroups generated by an element

Theorem 33.14 provides an interesting way to produce a subgroup of a finite group $(S, \oplus)$: choose an element a and take all elements that can be generated from a using the group operation. Specifically, define $a^{(k)}$ for $k \geq 1$ by

$$a^{(k)} = \bigoplus_{i=1}^{k} a = \underbrace{a \oplus a \oplus \cdots \oplus a}_{k} .$$

For example, if we take $a = 2$ in the group $\mathbf{Z}_6$, the sequence $a^{(1)}, a^{(2)}, \ldots$ is

$$2, 4, 0, 2, 4, 0, 2, 4, 0, \ldots .$$

In the group $\mathbf{Z}_n$, we have $a^{(k)} = ka \bmod n$, and in the group $\mathbf{Z}_n^*$, we have $a^{(k)} = a^k \bmod n$. The **subgroup generated by a**, denoted $\langle a \rangle$ or $(\langle a \rangle, \oplus)$, is defined by

$$\langle a \rangle = \{a^{(k)} : k \geq 1\} .$$

We say that a **generates** the subgroup $\langle a \rangle$ or that a is a **generator** of $\langle a \rangle$. Since S is finite, $\langle a \rangle$ is a finite subset of S, possibly including all of S. Since the associativity of $\oplus$ implies

$$a^{(i)} \oplus a^{(j)} = a^{(i+j)} ,$$

$\langle a \rangle$ is closed and therefore, by Theorem 33.14, $\langle a \rangle$ is a subgroup of S. For example, in $\mathbf{Z}_6$, we have

$$\begin{aligned}
\langle 0 \rangle &= \{0\} , \\
\langle 1 \rangle &= \{0, 1, 2, 3, 4, 5\} , \\
\langle 2 \rangle &= \{0, 2, 4\} .
\end{aligned}$$

Similarly, in $\mathbf{Z}_7^*$, we have

$$\begin{aligned}
\langle 1 \rangle &= \{1\} , \\
\langle 2 \rangle &= \{1, 2, 4\} , \\
\langle 3 \rangle &= \{1, 2, 3, 4, 5, 6\} .
\end{aligned}$$

The *order* of a (in the group S), denoted ord(a), is defined as the least $t > 0$ such that $a^{(t)} = e$.

Theorem 33.17
For any finite group $(S, \oplus)$ and any $a \in S$, the order of an element is equal to the size of the subgroup it generates, or ord(a) $= |\langle a \rangle|$.

Proof Let $t =$ ord(a). Since $a^{(t)} = e$ and $a^{(t+k)} = a^{(t)} \oplus a^{(k)} = a^{(k)}$ for $k \geq 1$, if $i > t$, then $a^{(i)} = a^{(j)}$ for some $j < i$. Thus, no new elements are seen after $a^{(t)}$, and $\langle a \rangle = \{a^{(1)}, a^{(2)}, \ldots, a^{(t)}\}$. To show that $|\langle a \rangle| = t$, suppose for the purpose of contradiction that $a^{(i)} = a^{(j)}$ for some i, j satisfying $1 \leq i < j \leq t$. Then, $a^{(i+k)} = a^{(j+k)}$ for $k \geq 0$. But this implies that $a^{(i+(t-j))} = a^{(j+(t-j))} = e$, a contradiction, since $i + (t - j) < t$ but t is the least positive value such that $a^{(t)} = e$. Therefore, each element of the sequence $a^{(1)}, a^{(2)}, \ldots, a^{(t)}$ is distinct, and $|\langle a \rangle| = t$. ∎

Corollary 33.18
The sequence $a^{(1)}, a^{(2)}, \ldots$ is periodic with period $t =$ ord(a); that is, $a^{(i)} = a^{(j)}$ if and only if $i \equiv j \pmod{t}$. ∎

It is consistent with the above corollary to define $a^{(0)}$ as e and $a^{(i)}$ as $a^{(i \bmod t)}$ for all integers i.

Corollary 33.19
If $(S, \oplus)$ is a finite group with identity e, then for all $a \in S$,

$$a^{(|S|)} = e .$$

Proof Lagrange's theorem implies that ord(a) $|$ $|S|$, and so $|S| \equiv 0$ $\pmod{t}$, where $t =$ ord(a). ∎

Exercises

33.3-1
Draw the group operation tables for the groups $(\mathbf{Z}_4, +_4)$ and $(\mathbf{Z}_5^*, \cdot_5)$. Show that these groups are isomorphic by exhibiting a one-to-one correspondence α between their elements such that $a + b \equiv c \pmod{4}$ if and only if $\alpha(a) \cdot \alpha(b) \equiv \alpha(c) \pmod{5}$.

33.3-2
Prove Theorem 33.14.

33.3-3
Show that if p is prime and e is a positive integer, then

$$\phi(p^e) = p^{e-1}(p-1) \ .$$

33.3-4
Show that for any $n > 1$ and for any $a \in \mathbf{Z}_n^*$, the function $f_a : \mathbf{Z}_n^* \to \mathbf{Z}_n^*$ defined by $f_a(x) = ax \bmod n$ is a permutation of $\mathbf{Z}_n^*$.

33.3-5
List all of the subgroups of $\mathbf{Z}_9$ and of $\mathbf{Z}_{13}^*$.

33.4   Solving modular linear equations

We now consider the problem of finding solutions to the equation

$$ax \equiv b \pmod{n} \ , \tag{33.22}$$

where $n > 0$, an important practical problem. We assume that a, b, and n are given, and we are to find the x's, modulo n, that satisfy equation (33.22). There may be zero, one, or more than one such solution.

Let $\langle a \rangle$ denote the subgroup of $\mathbf{Z}_n$ generated by a. Since $\langle a \rangle = \{a^{(x)} : x > 0\} = \{ax \bmod n : x > 0\}$, equation (33.22) has a solution if and only if $b \in \langle a \rangle$. Lagrange's theorem (Theorem 33.15) tells us that $|\langle a \rangle|$ must be a divisor of n. The following theorem gives us a precise characterization of $\langle a \rangle$.

Theorem 33.20
For any positive integers a and n, if $d = \gcd(a, n)$, then

$$\langle a \rangle = \langle d \rangle = \{0, d, 2d, \ldots, ((n/d) - 1)d\} \ , \tag{33.23}$$

and thus

$$|\langle a \rangle| = n/d \ .$$

Proof   We begin by showing that $d \in \langle a \rangle$. Observe that EXTENDED-EUCLID(a, n) produces integers x' and y' such that $ax' + ny' = d$. Thus, $ax' \equiv d \pmod{n}$, so that $d \in \langle a \rangle$.

Since $d \in \langle a \rangle$, it follows that every multiple of d belongs to $\langle a \rangle$, because a multiple of a multiple of a is a multiple of a. Thus, $\langle a \rangle$ contains every element in $\{0, d, 2d, \ldots, ((n/d) - 1)d\}$. That is, $\langle d \rangle \subseteq \langle a \rangle$.

We now show that $\langle a \rangle \subseteq \langle d \rangle$. If $m \in \langle a \rangle$, then $m = ax \bmod n$ for some integer x, and so $m = ax + ny$ for some integer y. However, $d \mid a$ and $d \mid n$, and so $d \mid m$ by equation (33.6). Therefore, $m \in \langle d \rangle$.

Combining these results, we have that $\langle a \rangle = \langle d \rangle$. To see that $|\langle a \rangle| = n/d$, observe that there are exactly n/d multiples of d between 0 and $n - 1$, inclusive.   ∎

Corollary 33.21
The equation $ax \equiv b \pmod{n}$ is solvable for the unknown x if and only if $\gcd(a, n) \mid b$. ∎

Corollary 33.22
The equation $ax \equiv b \pmod{n}$ either has d distinct solutions modulo n, where $d = \gcd(a, n)$, or it has no solutions.

Proof If $ax \equiv b \pmod{n}$ has a solution, then $b \in \langle a \rangle$. The sequence $ai \bmod n$, for $i = 0, 1, \ldots$ is periodic with period $|\langle a \rangle| = n/d$, by Corollary 33.18. If $b \in \langle a \rangle$, then b appears exactly d times in the sequence $ai \bmod n$, for $i = 0, 1, \ldots, n - 1$, since the length-(n/d) block of values $\langle a \rangle$ is repeated exactly d times as i increases from 0 to $n - 1$. The indices x of these d positions are the solutions of the equation $ax \equiv b \pmod{n}$. ∎

Theorem 33.23
Let $d = \gcd(a, n)$, and suppose that $d = ax' + ny'$ for some integers x' and y' (for example, as computed by EXTENDED-EUCLID). If $d \mid b$, then the equation $ax \equiv b \pmod{n}$ has as one of its solutions the value x_0, where

$$x_0 = x'(b/d) \bmod n \ .$$

Proof Since $ax' \equiv d \pmod{n}$, we have

$$
\begin{aligned}
ax_0 &\equiv ax'(b/d) && \pmod{n} \\
&\equiv d(b/d) && \pmod{n} \\
&\equiv b && \pmod{n} \ ,
\end{aligned}
$$

and thus x_0 is a solution to $ax \equiv b \pmod{n}$. ∎

Theorem 33.24
Suppose that the equation $ax \equiv b \pmod{n}$ is solvable (that is, $d \mid b$, where $d = \gcd(a, n)$) and that x_0 is any solution to this equation. Then, this equation has exactly d distinct solutions, modulo n, given by $x_i = x_0 + i(n/d)$ for $i = 1, 2, \ldots, d - 1$.

Proof Since $n/d > 0$ and $0 \le i(n/d) < n$ for $i = 0, 1, \ldots, d - 1$, the values $x_0, x_1, \ldots, x_{d-1}$ are all distinct, modulo n. By the periodicity of the sequence $ai \bmod n$ (Corollary 33.18), if x_0 is a solution of $ax \equiv b \pmod{n}$, then every x_i is a solution. By Corollary 33.22, there are exactly d solutions, so that $x_0, x_1, \ldots, x_{d-1}$ must be all of them. ∎

We have now developed the mathematics needed to solve the equation $ax \equiv b \pmod{n}$; the following algorithm prints all solutions to this equation. The inputs a and b are arbitrary integers, and n is an arbitrary positive integer.

MODULAR-LINEAR-EQUATION-SOLVER(a, b, n)

1   $(d, x', y') \leftarrow$ EXTENDED-EUCLID(a, n)
2   **if** $d \mid b$
3   **then** $x_0 \leftarrow x'(b/d) \bmod n$
4   **for** $i \leftarrow 0$ **to** $d - 1$
5   **do** print $(x_0 + i(n/d)) \bmod n$
6   **else** print "no solutions"

As an example of the operation of this procedure, consider the equation $14x \equiv 30 \pmod{100}$ (here, $a = 14$, $b = 30$, and $n = 100$). Calling EXTENDED-EUCLID in line 1, we obtain $(d, x, y) = (2, -7, 1)$. Since $2 \mid 30$, lines 3–5 are executed. In line 3, we compute $x_0 = (-7)(15) \bmod 100 = 95$. The loop on lines 4–5 prints the two solutions: 95 and 45.

The procedure MODULAR-LINEAR-EQUATION-SOLVER works as follows. Line 1 computes $d = \gcd(a, n)$ as well as two values x' and y' such that $d = ax' + ny'$, demonstrating that x' is a solution to the equation $ax' \equiv d \pmod{n}$. If d does not divide b, then the equation $ax \equiv b \pmod{n}$ has no solution, by Corollary 33.21. Line 2 checks if $d \mid b$; if not, line 6 reports that there are no solutions. Otherwise, line 3 computes a solution x_0 to equation (33.22), in accordance with Theorem 33.23. Given one solution, Theorem 33.24 states that the other $d - 1$ solutions can be obtained by adding multiples of (n/d), modulo n. The **for** loop of lines 4–5 prints out all d solutions, beginning with x_0 and spaced (n/d) apart, modulo n.

The running time of MODULAR-LINEAR-EQUATION-SOLVER is $O(\lg n + \gcd(a, n))$ arithmetic operations, since EXTENDED-EUCLID takes $O(\lg n)$ arithmetic operations, and each iteration of the **for** loop of lines 4–5 takes a constant number of arithmetic operations.

The following corollaries of Theorem 33.24 give specializations of particular interest.

Corollary 33.25
For any $n > 1$, if $\gcd(a, n) = 1$, then the equation $ax \equiv b \pmod{n}$ has a unique solution modulo n.   ∎

If $b = 1$, a common case of considerable interest, the x we are looking for is a ***multiplicative inverse*** of a, modulo n.

Corollary 33.26
For any $n > 1$, if $\gcd(a, n) = 1$, then the equation

$$ax \equiv 1 \pmod{n} \tag{33.24}$$

has a unique solution, modulo n. Otherwise, it has no solution.   ∎

Corollary 33.26 allows us to use the notation $(a^{-1} \bmod n)$ to refer to *the* multiplicative inverse of a, modulo n, when a and n are relatively prime. If $\gcd(a, n) = 1$, then one solution to the equation $ax \equiv 1 \pmod{n}$ is the integer x returned by EXTENDED-EUCLID, since the equation

$$\gcd(a, n) = 1 = ax + ny$$

implies $ax \equiv 1 \pmod{n}$. Thus, $(a^{-1} \bmod n)$ can be computed efficiently using EXTENDED-EUCLID.

Exercises

33.4-1
Find all solutions to the equation $35x \equiv 10 \pmod{50}$.

33.4-2
Prove that the equation $ax \equiv ay \pmod{n}$ implies $x \equiv y \pmod{n}$ whenever $\gcd(a, n) = 1$. Show that the condition $\gcd(a, n) = 1$ is necessary by supplying a counterexample with $\gcd(a, n) > 1$.

33.4-3
Consider the following change to line 3 of MODULAR-LINEAR-EQUATION-SOLVER:

3   **then** $x_0 \leftarrow x'(b/d) \bmod (n/d)$

Will this work? Explain why or why not.

33.4-4 $\star$
Let $f(x) \equiv f_0 + f_1 x + \cdots + f_t x^t \pmod{p}$ be a polynomial of degree t, with coefficients f_i drawn from $\mathbf{Z}_p$, where p is prime. We say that $a \in \mathbf{Z}_p$ is a ***zero*** of f if $f(a) \equiv 0 \pmod{p}$. Prove that if a is a zero of f, then $f(x) \equiv (x - a)g(x) \pmod{p}$ for some polynomial $g(x)$ of degree $t - 1$. Prove by induction on t that a polynomial $f(x)$ of degree t can have at most t distinct zeros modulo a prime p.

33.5 The Chinese remainder theorem

Around A.D. 100, the Chinese mathematician Sun-Tsŭ solved the problem of finding those integers x that leave remainders 2, 3, and 2 when divided by 3, 5, and 7 respectively. One such solution is $x = 23$; all solutions are of the form $23 + 105k$ for arbitrary integers k. The "Chinese remainder theorem" provides a correspondence between a system of equations modulo a set of pairwise relatively prime moduli (for example, 3, 5, and 7) and an equation modulo their product (for example, 105).

The Chinese remainder theorem has two major uses. Let the integer $n = n_1 n_2 \cdots n_k$, where the factors n_i are pairwise relatively prime. First, the Chinese remainder theorem is a descriptive "structure theorem" that describes the structure of $\mathbf{Z}_n$ as identical to that of the Cartesian product $\mathbf{Z}_{n_1} \times \mathbf{Z}_{n_2} \times \cdots \times \mathbf{Z}_{n_k}$ with componentwise addition and multiplication modulo n_i in the ith component. Second, this description can often be used to yield efficient algorithms, since working in each of the systems $\mathbf{Z}_{n_i}$ can be more efficient (in terms of bit operations) than working modulo n.

Theorem 33.27 (Chinese remainder theorem)
Let $n = n_1 n_2 \cdots n_k$, where the n_i are pairwise relatively prime. Consider the correspondence

$$a \leftrightarrow (a_1, a_2, \ldots, a_k) , \tag{33.25}$$

where $a \in \mathbf{Z}_n$, $a_i \in \mathbf{Z}_{n_i}$, and

$$a_i = a \bmod n_i$$

for $i = 1, 2, \ldots, k$. Then, mapping (33.25) is a one-to-one correspondence (bijection) between $\mathbf{Z}_n$ and the Cartesian product $\mathbf{Z}_{n_1} \times \mathbf{Z}_{n_2} \times \cdots \times \mathbf{Z}_{n_k}$. Operations performed on the elements of $\mathbf{Z}_n$ can be equivalently performed on the corresponding k-tuples by performing the operations independently in each coordinate position in the appropriate system. That is, if

$$
\begin{aligned}
a &\leftrightarrow (a_1, a_2, \ldots, a_k) , \\
b &\leftrightarrow (b_1, b_2, \ldots, b_k) ,
\end{aligned}
$$

then

$$(a + b) \bmod n \quad \leftrightarrow \quad ((a_1 + b_1) \bmod n_1, \ldots, (a_k + b_k) \bmod n_k) , \tag{33.26}$$
$$(a - b) \bmod n \quad \leftrightarrow \quad ((a_1 - b_1) \bmod n_1, \ldots, (a_k - b_k) \bmod n_k) , \tag{33.27}$$
$$(ab) \bmod n \quad \leftrightarrow \quad (a_1 b_1 \bmod n_1, \ldots, a_k b_k \bmod n_k) . \tag{33.28}$$

Proof Transforming between the two representations is quite straightforward. Going from a to $(a_1, a_2, \ldots, a_k)$ requires only k divisions. Computing a from inputs $(a_1, a_2, \ldots, a_k)$ is almost as easy, using the following formula. Let $m_i = n/n_i$ for $i = 1, 2, \ldots, k$. Note that $m_i = n_1 n_2 \cdots n_{i-1} n_{i+1} \cdots n_k$, so that $m_i \equiv 0 \pmod{n_j}$ for all $j \neq i$. Then, letting

$$c_i = m_i (m_i^{-1} \bmod n_i) \tag{33.29}$$

for $i = 1, 2, \ldots, k$, we have

$$a \equiv (a_1 c_1 + a_2 c_2 + \cdots + a_k c_k) \pmod{n} . \tag{33.30}$$

Equation 33.29 is well defined, since m_i and n_i are relatively prime (by Theorem 33.6), and so Corollary 33.26 implies that $(m_i^{-1} \bmod n_i)$ is defined. To verify equation (33.30), note that $c_j \equiv m_j \equiv 0 \pmod{n_i}$ if $j \neq i$, and that $c_i \equiv 1 \pmod{n_i}$. Thus, we have the correspondence

$$c_i \leftrightarrow (0, 0, \ldots, 0, 1, 0, \ldots, 0) \,,$$

a vector that has 0's everywhere except in the ith coordinate, where it has a 1. The c_i thus form a "basis" for the representation, in a certain sense. For each i, therefore, we have

$$
\begin{aligned}
a &\equiv a_i c_i && (\bmod\ n_i) \\
  &\equiv a_i m_i (m_i^{-1} \bmod n_i) && (\bmod\ n_i) \\
  &\equiv a_i && (\bmod\ n_i) \,.
\end{aligned}
$$

Since we can transform in both directions, the correspondence is one-to-one. Equations (33.26)–(33.28) follow directly from Exercise 33.1-6, since $x \bmod n_i = (x \bmod n) \bmod n_i$ for any x and $i = 1, 2, \ldots, k$. ∎

The following corollaries will be used later in this chapter.

Corollary 33.28
If $n_1, n_2, \ldots, n_k$ are pairwise relatively prime and $n = n_1 n_2 \cdots n_k$, then for any integers $a_1, a_2, \ldots, a_k$, the set of simultaneous equations

$$x \equiv a_i \ (\bmod\ n_i) \,,$$

for $i = 1, 2, \ldots, k$, has a unique solution modulo n for the unknown x. ∎

Corollary 33.29
If $n_1, n_2, \ldots, n_k$ are pairwise relatively prime and $n = n_1 n_2 \cdots n_k$, then for all integers x and a,

$$x \equiv a \ (\bmod\ n_i)$$

for $i = 1, 2, \ldots, k$ if and only if

$$x \equiv a \ (\bmod\ n) \,. \qquad\qquad ∎$$

As an example of the Chinese remainder theorem, suppose we are given the two equations

$$
\begin{aligned}
a &\equiv 2 \ (\bmod\ 5) \,, \\
a &\equiv 3 \ (\bmod\ 13) \,,
\end{aligned}
$$

so that $a_1 = 2$, $n_1 = m_2 = 5$, $a_2 = 3$, and $n_2 = m_1 = 13$, and we wish to compute $a \bmod 65$, since $n = 65$. Because $13^{-1} \equiv 2 \ (\bmod\ 5)$ and $5^{-1} \equiv 8 \ (\bmod\ 13)$, we have

$$
\begin{aligned}
c_1 &= 13(2 \bmod 5) &= 26 \,, \\
c_2 &= 5(8 \bmod 13) &= 40 \,,
\end{aligned}
$$

and

$$
\begin{aligned}
a &\equiv 2 \cdot 26 + 3 \cdot 40 && (\bmod\ 65) \\
  &\equiv 52 + 120 && (\bmod\ 65) \\
  &\equiv 42 && (\bmod\ 65) \,.
\end{aligned}
$$

	0	1	2	3	4	5	6	7	8	9	10	11	12
0	0	40	15	55	30	5	45	20	60	35	10	50	25
1	26	1	41	16	56	31	6	46	21	61	36	11	51
2	52	27	2	42	17	57	32	7	47	22	62	37	12
3	13	53	28	3	43	18	58	33	8	48	23	63	38
4	39	14	54	29	4	44	19	59	34	9	49	24	64

Figure 33.3 An illustration of the Chinese remainder theorem for $n_1 = 5$ and $n_2 = 13$. For this example, $c_1 = 26$ and $c_2 = 40$. In row i, column j is shown the value of a, modulo 65, such that $(a \bmod 5) = i$ and $(a \bmod 13) = j$. Note that row 0, column 0 contains a 0. Similarly, row 4, column 12 contains a 64 (equivalent to -1). Since $c_1 = 26$, moving down a row increases a by 26. Similarly, $c_2 = 40$ means that moving right a column increases a by 40. Increasing a by 1 corresponds to moving diagonally downward and to the right, wrapping around from the bottom to the top and from the right to the left.

See Figure 33.3 for an illustration of the Chinese remainder theorem, modulo 65.

Thus, we can work modulo n by working modulo n directly or by working in the transformed representation using separate modulo n_i computations, as convenient. The computations are entirely equivalent.

Exercises

33.5-1
Find all solutions to the equations $x \equiv 4 \pmod 5$ and $x \equiv 5 \pmod{11}$.

33.5-2
Find all integers x that leave remainders 1, 2, 3, 4, 5 when divided by 2, 3, 4, 5, 6, respectively.

33.5-3
Argue that, under the definitions of Theorem 33.27, if $\gcd(a, n) = 1$, then

$$(a^{-1} \bmod n) \leftrightarrow ((a_1^{-1} \bmod n_1), (a_2^{-1} \bmod n_2), \ldots, (a_k^{-1} \bmod n_k)) .$$

33.5-4
Under the definitions of Theorem 33.27, prove that the number of roots of the equation $f(x) \equiv 0 \pmod n$ is equal to the product of the number of roots of each the equations $f(x) \equiv 0 \pmod{n_1}$, $f(x) \equiv 0 \pmod{n_2}$, ..., $f(x) \equiv 0 \pmod{n_k}$.

33.6   Powers of an element

Just as it is natural to consider the multiples of a given element a, modulo n, it is often natural to consider the sequence of powers of a, modulo n, where $a \in \mathbf{Z}_n^*$:

$$a^0, a^1, a^2, a^3, \ldots, \tag{33.31}$$

modulo n. Indexing from 0, the 0th value in this sequence is $a^0 \bmod n = 1$, and the ith value is $a^i \bmod n$. For example, the powers of 3 modulo 7 are

i	0	1	2	3	4	5	6	7	8	9	10	11	$\cdots$
$3^i \bmod 7$	1	3	2	6	4	5	1	3	2	6	4	5	$\cdots$

whereas the powers of 2 modulo 7 are

i	0	1	2	3	4	5	6	7	8	9	10	11	$\cdots$
$2^i \bmod 7$	1	2	4	1	2	4	1	2	4	1	2	4	$\cdots$

In this section, let $\langle a \rangle$ denote the subgroup of $\mathbf{Z}_n^*$ generated by a, and let $\text{ord}_n(a)$ (the "order of a, modulo n") denote the order of a in $\mathbf{Z}_n^*$. For example, $\langle 2 \rangle = \{1, 2, 4\}$ in $\mathbf{Z}_7^*$, and $\text{ord}_7(2) = 3$. Using the definition of the Euler phi function $\phi(n)$ as the size of $\mathbf{Z}_n^*$ (see Section 33.3), we now translate Corollary 33.19 into the notation of $\mathbf{Z}_n^*$ to obtain Euler's theorem and specialize it to $\mathbf{Z}_p^*$, where p is prime, to obtain Fermat's theorem.

Theorem 33.30 (Euler's theorem)
For any integer $n > 1$,

$$a^{\phi(n)} \equiv 1 \pmod{n} \text{ for all } a \in \mathbf{Z}_n^* . \tag{33.32}$$

■

Theorem 33.31 (Fermat's theorem)
If p is prime, then

$$a^{p-1} \equiv 1 \pmod{p} \text{ for all } a \in \mathbf{Z}_p^* . \tag{33.33}$$

Proof By equation (33.21), $\phi(p) = p - 1$ if p is prime. ■

This corollary applies to every element in $\mathbf{Z}_p$ except 0, since $0 \notin \mathbf{Z}_p^*$. For all $a \in \mathbf{Z}_p$, however, we have $a^p \equiv a \pmod{p}$ if p is prime.

If $\text{ord}_n(g) = |\mathbf{Z}_n^*|$, then every element in $\mathbf{Z}_n^*$ is a power of g, modulo n, and we say that g is a ***primitive root*** or a ***generator*** of $\mathbf{Z}_n^*$. For example, 3 is a primitive root, modulo 7. If $\mathbf{Z}_n^*$ possesses a primitive root, we say that the group $\mathbf{Z}_n^*$ is ***cyclic***. We omit the proof of the following theorem, which is proven by Niven and Zuckerman [151].

Theorem 33.32
The values of $n > 1$ for which $\mathbf{Z}_n^*$ is cyclic are 2, 4, p^e, and $2p^e$, for all odd primes p and all positive integers e.   ∎

If g is a primitive root of $\mathbf{Z}_n^*$ and a is any element of $\mathbf{Z}_n^*$, then there exists a z such that $g^z \equiv a \pmod{n}$. This z is called the ***discrete logarithm*** or ***index*** of a, modulo n, to the base g; we denote this value as $\mathrm{ind}_{n,g}(a)$.

Theorem 33.33 (Discrete logarithm theorem)
If g is a primitive root of $\mathbf{Z}_n^*$, then the equation $g^x \equiv g^y \pmod{n}$ holds if and only if the equation $x \equiv y \pmod{\phi(n)}$ holds.

Proof   Suppose first that $x \equiv y \pmod{\phi(n)}$. Then, $x = y + k\phi(n)$ for some integer k. Therefore,

$$
\begin{aligned}
g^x &\equiv g^{y+k\phi(n)} &&\pmod{n} \\
    &\equiv g^y \cdot (g^{\phi(n)})^k &&\pmod{n} \\
    &\equiv g^y \cdot 1^k &&\pmod{n} \\
    &\equiv g^y &&\pmod{n} .
\end{aligned}
$$

Conversely, suppose that $g^x \equiv g^y \pmod{n}$. Because the sequence of powers of g generates every element of $\langle g \rangle$ and $|\langle g \rangle| = \phi(n)$, Corollary 33.18 implies that the sequence of powers of g is periodic with period $\phi(n)$. Therefore, if $g^x \equiv g^y \pmod{n}$, then we must have $x \equiv y \pmod{\phi(n)}$.   ∎

Taking discrete logarithms can sometimes simplify reasoning about a modular equation, as illustrated in the proof of the following theorem.

Theorem 33.34
If p is an odd prime and $e \geq 1$, then the equation

$$x^2 \equiv 1 \pmod{p^e} \tag{33.34}$$

has only two solutions, namely $x = 1$ and $x = -1$.

Proof   Let $n = p^e$. Theorem 33.32 implies that $\mathbf{Z}_n^*$ has a primitive root g. Equation (33.34) can be written

$$(g^{\mathrm{ind}_{n,g}(x)})^2 \equiv g^{\mathrm{ind}_{n,g}(1)} \pmod{n} . \tag{33.35}$$

After noting that $\mathrm{ind}_{n,g}(1) = 0$, we observe that Theorem 33.33 implies that equation (33.35) is equivalent to

$$2 \cdot \mathrm{ind}_{n,g}(x) \equiv 0 \pmod{\phi(n)} . \tag{33.36}$$

To solve this equation for the unknown $\mathrm{ind}_{n,g}(x)$, we apply the methods of Section 33.4. Letting $d = \gcd(2, \phi(n)) = \gcd(2, (p-1)p^{e-1}) = 2$, and noting that $d \mid 0$, we find from Theorem 33.24 that equation (33.36) has exactly $d = 2$ solutions. Therefore, equation (33.34) has exactly 2 solutions, which are $x = 1$ and $x = -1$ by inspection. ∎

A number x is a **nontrivial square root of 1, modulo n**, if it satisfies the equation $x^2 \equiv 1 \pmod{n}$ but x is equivalent to neither of the two "trivial" square roots: 1 or -1, modulo n. For example, 6 is a nontrivial square root of 1, modulo 35. The following corollary to Theorem 33.34 will be used in the correctness proof for the Miller-Rabin primality-testing procedure in Section 33.8.

Corollary 33.35
If there exists a nontrivial square root of 1, modulo n, then n is composite.

Proof This corollary is just the contrapositive to Theorem 33.34. If there exists a nontrivial square root of 1, modulo n, then n can't be a prime or a power of a prime. ∎

Raising to powers with repeated squaring

A frequently occurring operation in number-theoretic computations is raising one number to a power modulo another number, also known as **modular exponentiation**. More precisely, we would like an efficient way to compute $a^b \bmod n$, where a and b are nonnegative integers and n is a positive integer. Modular exponentiation is also an essential operation in many primality-testing routines and in the RSA public-key cryptosystem. The method of **repeated squaring** solves this problem efficiently using the binary representation of b.

Let $\langle b_k, b_{k-1}, \dots, b_1, b_0 \rangle$ be the binary representation of b. (That is, the binary representation is $k + 1$ bits long, b_k is the most significant bit, and b_0 is the least significant bit.) The following procedure computes $a^c \bmod n$ as c is increased by doublings and increments from 0 to b.

MODULAR-EXPONENTIATION(a, b, n)

```
 1   c ← 0
 2   d ← 1
 3   let ⟨b_k, b_{k-1}, ..., b_0⟩ be the binary representation of b
 4   for i ← k downto 0
 5       do c ← 2c
 6          d ← (d · d) mod n
 7          if b_i = 1
 8             then c ← c + 1
 9                  d ← (d · a) mod n
10   return d
```

Each exponent computed in a sequence is either twice the previous exponent or one more than the previous exponent; the binary representation

i	9	8	7	6	5	4	3	2	1	0
b_i	1	0	0	0	1	1	0	0	0	0
c	1	2	4	8	17	35	70	140	280	560
d	7	49	157	526	160	241	298	166	67	1

Figure 33.4 The results of MODULAR-EXPONENTIATION when computing a^b (mod n), where $a = 7$, $b = 560 = \langle 1000110000 \rangle$, and $n = 561$. The values are shown after each execution of the **for** loop. The final result is 1.

of b is read from right to left to control which operations are performed. Each iteration of the loop uses one of the identities

$$a^{2c} \bmod n = (a^c)^2 \bmod n \, ,$$
$$a^{2c+1} \bmod n = a \cdot (a^c)^2 \bmod n \, ,$$

depending on whether $b_i = 0$ or 1, respectively. The essential use of squaring in each iteration explains the name "repeated squaring." Just after bit b_i is read and processed, the value of c is the same as the prefix $\langle b_k, b_{k-1}, \ldots, b_i \rangle$ of the binary representation of b. As an example, for $a = 7$, $b = 560$, and $n = 561$, the algorithm computes the sequence of values modulo 561 shown in Figure 33.4; the sequence of exponents used is shown in row c of the table.

The variable c is not really needed by the algorithm but is included for explanatory purposes: the algorithm preserves the invariant that $d = a^c \bmod n$ as it increases c by doublings and incrementations until $c = b$. If the inputs a, b, and n are β-bit numbers, then the total number of arithmetic operations required is $O(\beta)$ and the total number of bit operations required is $O(\beta^3)$.

Exercises

33.6-1
Draw a table showing the order of every element in $\mathbf{Z}_{11}^*$. Pick the smallest primitive root g and compute a table giving $\operatorname{ind}_{11,g}(x)$ for all $x \in \mathbf{Z}_{11}^*$.

33.6-2
Give a modular exponentiation algorithm that examines the bits of b from right to left instead of left to right.

33.6-3
Explain how to compute $a^{-1} \bmod n$ for any $a \in \mathbf{Z}_n^*$ using the procedure MODULAR-EXPONENTIATION, assuming that you know $\phi(n)$.

33.7 The RSA public-key cryptosystem

A public-key cryptosystem can be used to encrypt messages sent between two communicating parties so that an eavesdropper who overhears the encrypted messages will not be able to decode them. A public-key cryptosystem also enables a party to append an unforgeable "digital signature" to the end of an electronic message. Such a signature is the electronic version of a handwritten signature on a paper document. It can be easily checked by anyone, forged by no one, yet loses its validity if any bit of the message is altered. It therefore provides authentication of both the identity of the signer and the contents of the signed message. It is the perfect tool for electronically signed business contracts, electronic checks, electronic purchase orders, and other electronic communications that must be authenticated.

The RSA public-key cryptosystem is based on the dramatic difference between the ease of finding large prime numbers and the difficulty of factoring the product of two large prime numbers. Section 33.8 describes an efficient procedure for finding large prime numbers, and Section 33.9 discusses the problem of factoring large integers.

Public-key cryptosystems

In a public-key cryptosystem, each participant has both a *public key* and a *secret key*. Each key is a piece of information. For example, in the RSA cryptosystem, each key consists of a pair of integers. The participants "Alice" and "Bob" are traditionally used in cryptography examples; we denote their public and secret keys as P_A, S_A for Alice and P_B, S_B for Bob.

Each participant creates his own public and secret keys. Each keeps his secret key secret, but he can reveal his public key to anyone or even publish it. In fact, it is often convenient to assume that everyone's public key is available in a public directory, so that any participant can easily obtain the public key of any other participant.

The public and secret keys specify functions that can be applied to any message. Let $\mathcal{D}$ denote the set of permissible messages. For example, $\mathcal{D}$ might be the set of all finite-length bit sequences. We require that the public and secret keys specify one-to-one functions from $\mathcal{D}$ to itself. The function corresponding to Alice's public key P_A is denoted $P_A()$, and the function corresponding to her secret key S_A is denoted $S_A()$. The functions $P_A()$ and $S_A()$ are thus permutations of $\mathcal{D}$. We assume that the functions $P_A()$ and $S_A()$ are efficiently computable given the corresponding key P_A or S_A.

The public and secret keys for any participant are a "matched pair" in that they specify functions that are inverses of each other. That is,

$$M = S_A(P_A(M)) , \tag{33.37}$$
$$M = P_A(S_A(M)) \tag{33.38}$$

for any message $M \in \mathcal{D}$. Transforming M with the two keys P_A and S_A successively, in either order, yields the message M back.

In a public-key cryptosystem, it is essential that no one but Alice be able to compute the function $S_A()$ in any practical amount of time. The privacy of mail that is encrypted and sent to Alice and the authenticity of Alice's digital signatures rely on the assumption that only Alice is able to compute $S_A()$. This requirement is why Alice keeps S_A secret; if she does not, she loses her uniqueness and the cryptosystem cannot provide her with unique capabilities. The assumption that only Alice can compute $S_A()$ must hold even though everyone knows P_A and can compute $P_A()$, the inverse function to $S_A()$, efficiently. The major difficulty in designing a workable public-key cryptosystem is in figuring out how to create a system in which we can reveal a transformation $P_A()$ without thereby revealing how to compute the corresponding inverse transformation $S_A()$.

In a public-key cryptosystem, encryption works as follows. Suppose Bob wishes to send Alice a message M encrypted so that it will look like unintelligible gibberish to an eavesdropper. The scenario for sending the message goes as follows.

- Bob obtains Alice's public key P_A (from a public directory or directly from Alice).

- Bob computes the **ciphertext** $C = P_A(M)$ corresponding to the message M and sends C to Alice.

- When Alice receives the ciphertext C, she applies her secret key S_A to retrieve the original message: $M = S_A(C)$.

Figure 33.5 illustrates this process. Because $S_A()$ and $P_A()$ are inverse functions, Alice can compute M from C. Because only Alice is able to compute $S_A()$, only Alice can compute M from C. The encryption of M using $P_A()$ has protected M from disclosure to anyone except Alice.

Digital signatures are similarly easy to implement in a public-key cryptosystem. Suppose now that Alice wishes to send Bob a digitally signed response M'. The digital-signature scenario proceeds as follows.

- Alice computes her **digital signature** σ for the message M' using her secret key S_A and the equation $\sigma = S_A(M')$.

- Alice sends the message/signature pair (M', σ) to Bob.

- When Bob receives (M', σ), he can verify that it originated from Alice using Alice's public key by verifying the equation $M' = P_A(\sigma)$. (Presumably, M' contains Alice's name, so Bob knows whose public key to use.) If the equation holds, then Bob concludes that the message M' was actually signed by Alice. If the equation doesn't hold, Bob concludes either that the message M' or the digital signature σ was corrupted by transmission errors or that the pair (M', σ) is an attempted forgery.

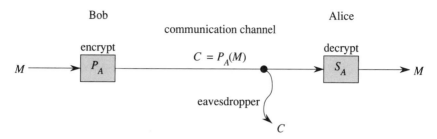

Figure 33.5 Encryption in a public key system. Bob encrypts the message M using Alice's public key P_A and transmits the resulting ciphertext $C = P_A(M)$ to Alice. An eavesdropper who captures the transmitted ciphertext gains no information about M. Alice receives C and decrypts it using her secret key to obtain the original message $M = S_A(C)$.

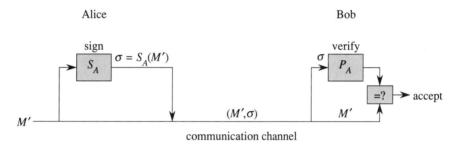

Figure 33.6 Digital signatures in a public-key system. Alice signs the message M' by appending her digital signature $\sigma = S_A(M')$ to it. She transmits the message/signature pair (M', σ) to Bob, who verifies it by checking the equation $M' = P_A(\sigma)$. If the equation holds, he accepts (M', σ) as a message that has been signed by Alice.

Figure 33.6 illustrates this process. Because a digital signature provides both authentication of the signer's identity and authentication of the contents of the signed message, it is analogous to a handwritten signature at the end of a written document.

An important property of a digital signature is that it is verifiable by anyone who has access to the signer's public key. A signed message can be verified by one party and then passed on to other parties who can also verify the signature. For example, the message might be an electronic check from Alice to Bob. After Bob verifies Alice's signature on the check, he can give the check to his bank, who can then also verify the signature and effect the appropriate funds transfer.

We note that a signed message is not encrypted; the message is "in the clear" and is not protected from disclosure. By composing the above protocols for encryption and for signatures, we can create messages that are both signed and encrypted. The signer first appends his digital signature to the message and then encrypts the resulting message/signature pair with the public key of the intended recipient. The recipient decrypts the received message with his secret key to obtain both the original message and its digital signature. He can then verify the signature using the public key of the signer. The corresponding combined process using paper-based systems is to sign the paper document and then seal the document inside a paper envelope that is opened only by the intended recipient.

The RSA cryptosystem

In the *RSA public-key cryptosystem*, a participant creates his public and secret keys with the following procedure.

1. Select at random two large prime numbers p and q. The primes p and q might be, say, 100 decimal digits each.

2. Compute n by the equation $n = pq$.

3. Select a small odd integer e that is relatively prime to $\phi(n)$, which, by equation (33.20), equals $(p - 1)(q - 1)$.

4. Compute d as the multiplicative inverse of e, modulo $\phi(n)$. (Corollary 33.26 guarantees that d exists and is uniquely defined.)

5. Publish the pair $P = (e, n)$ as his *RSA public key*.

6. Keep secret the pair $S = (d, n)$ as his *RSA secret key*.

For this scheme, the domain $\mathcal{D}$ is the set $\mathbf{Z}_n$. The transformation of a message M associated with a public key $P = (e, n)$ is

$$P(M) = M^e \pmod{n} . \tag{33.39}$$

The transformation of a ciphertext C associated with a secret key $S = (d, n)$ is

$$S(C) = C^d \pmod{n} . \tag{33.40}$$

These equations apply to both encryption and signatures. To create a signature, the signer applies his secret key to the message to be signed, rather than to a ciphertext. To verify a signature, the public key of the signer is applied to it, rather than to a message to be encrypted.

The public-key and secret-key operations can be implemented using the procedure MODULAR-EXPONENTIATION described in Section 33.6. To analyze the running time of these operations, assume that the public key (e, n) and secret key (d, n) satisfy $|e| = O(1)$, $|d| = |n| = \beta$. Then, applying a public key requires $O(1)$ modular multiplications and uses $O(\beta^2)$ bit operations. Applying a secret key requires $O(\beta)$ modular multiplications, using $O(\beta^3)$ bit operations.

Theorem 33.36 (Correctness of RSA)
The RSA equations (33.39) and (33.40) define inverse transformations of $\mathbf{Z}_n$ satisfying equations (33.37) and (33.38).

Proof From equations (33.39) and (33.40), we have that for any $M \in \mathbf{Z}_n$,

$$P(S(M)) = S(P(M)) = M^{ed} \pmod{n} \ .$$

Since e and d are multiplicative inverses modulo $\phi(n) = (p-1)(q-1)$,

$$ed = 1 + k(p-1)(q-1)$$

for some integer k. But then, if $M \not\equiv 0 \pmod{p}$, we have (using Theorem 33.31)

$$
\begin{aligned}
M^{ed} &\equiv M(M^{p-1})^{k(q-1)} && \pmod{p} \\
&\equiv M(1)^{k(q-1)} && \pmod{p} \\
&\equiv M && \pmod{p} \ .
\end{aligned}
$$

Also, $M^{ed} \equiv M \pmod{p}$ if $M \equiv 0 \pmod{p}$. Thus,

$$M^{ed} \equiv M \pmod{p}$$

for all M. Similarly,

$$M^{ed} \equiv M \pmod{q}$$

for all M. Thus, by Corollary 33.29 to the Chinese remainder theorem,

$$M^{ed} \equiv M \pmod{n}$$

for all M. ∎

The security of the RSA cryptosystem rests in large part on the difficulty of factoring large integers. If an adversary can factor the modulus n in a public key, then he can derive the secret key from the public key, using the knowledge of the factors p and q in the same way that the creator of the public key used them. So if factoring large integers is easy, then breaking the RSA cryptosystem is easy. The converse statement, that if factoring large integers is hard, then breaking RSA is hard, is unproven. After a decade of research, however, no easier method has been found to break the RSA public-key cryptosystem than to factor the modulus n. And as we shall see in Section 33.9, the factoring of large integers is surprisingly difficult. By randomly selecting and multiplying together two 100-digit primes, one can create a public key that cannot be "broken" in any feasible amount of time with current technology. In the absence of a fundamental breakthrough in the design of number-theoretic algorithms, the RSA cryptosystem is capable of providing a high degree of security in applications.

In order to achieve security with the RSA cryptosystem, however, it is necessary to work with integers that are 100–200 digits in length, since factoring smaller integers is not impractical. In particular, we must be able to find large primes efficiently, in order to create keys of the necessary length. This problem is addressed in Section 33.8.

For efficiency, RSA is often used in a "hybrid" or "key-management" mode with fast non-public-key cryptosystems. With such a system, the encryption and decryption keys are identical. If Alice wishes to send a long message M to Bob privately, she selects a random key K for the fast non-public-key cryptosystem and encrypts M using K, obtaining ciphertext C. Here, C is as long as M, but K is quite short. Then, she encrypts K using Bob's public RSA key. Since K is short, computing $P_B(K)$ is fast (much faster than computing $P_B(M)$). She then transmits $(C, P_B(K))$ to Bob, who decrypts $P_B(K)$ to obtain K and then uses K to decrypt C, obtaining M.

A similar hybrid approach is often used to make digital signatures efficiently. In this approach, RSA is combined with a public *one-way hash function* h—a function that is easy to compute but for which it is computationally infeasible to find two messages M and M' such that $h(M) = h(M')$. The value $h(M)$ is a short (say, 128-bit) "fingerprint" of the message M. If Alice wishes to sign a message M, she first applies h to M to obtain the fingerprint $h(M)$, which she then signs with her secret key. She sends $(M, S_A(h(M)))$ to Bob as her signed version of M. Bob can verify the signature by computing $h(M)$ and verifying that P_A applied to $S_A(h(M))$ as received equals $h(M)$. Because no one can create two messages with the same fingerprint, it is impossible to alter a signed message and preserve the validity of the signature.

Finally, we note that the use of *certificates* makes distributing public keys much easier. For example, assume there is a "trusted authority" T whose public key is known by everyone. Alice can obtain from T a signed message (her certificate) stating that "Alice's public key is P_A." This certificate is "self-authenticating" since everyone knows P_T. Alice can include her certificate with her signed messages, so that the recipient has Alice's public key immediately available in order to verify her signature. Because her key was signed by T, the recipient knows that Alice's key is really Alice's.

Exercises

33.7-1
Consider an RSA key set with $p = 11$, $q = 29$, $n = 319$, and $e = 3$. What value of d should be used in the secret key? What is the encryption of the message $M = 100$?

33.7-2
Prove that if Alice's public exponent e is 3 and an adversary obtains Alice's secret exponent d, then the adversary can factor Alice's modulus n in time polynomial in the number of bits in n. (Although you are not asked to prove it, you may be interested to know that this result remains true even if the condition $e = 3$ is removed. See Miller [147].)

33.7-3 ⋆

Prove that RSA is multiplicative in the sense that

$$P_A(M_1)P_A(M_2) \equiv P_A(M_1M_2) \pmod{n} .$$

Use this fact to prove that if an adversary had a procedure that could efficiently decrypt 1 percent of messages randomly chosen from $\mathbf{Z}_n$ and encrypted with P_A, then he could employ a probabilistic algorithm to decrypt every message encrypted with P_A with high probability.

⋆ 33.8 Primality testing

In this section, we consider the problem of finding large primes. We begin with a discussion of the density of primes, proceed to examine a plausible (but incomplete) approach to primality testing, and then present an effective randomized primality test due to Miller and Rabin.

The density of prime numbers

For many applications (such as cryptography), we need to find large "random" primes. Fortunately, large primes are not too rare, so that it is not too time-consuming to test random integers of the appropriate size until a prime is found. The ***prime distribution function*** $\pi(n)$ specifies the number of primes that are less than or equal to n. For example, $\pi(10) = 4$, since there are 4 prime numbers less than or equal to 10, namely, 2, 3, 5, and 7. The prime number theorem gives a useful approximation to $\pi(n)$.

Theorem 33.37 (Prime number theorem)
$$\lim_{n \to \infty} \frac{\pi(n)}{n/\ln n} = 1 .$$ ∎

The approximation $n/\ln n$ gives reasonably accurate estimates of $\pi(n)$ even for small n. For example, it is off by less than 6% at $n = 10^9$, where $\pi(n) = 50{,}847{,}478$ and $n/\ln n = 48{,}254{,}942$. (To a number theorist, 10^9 is a small number.)

We can use the prime number theorem to estimate the probability that a randomly chosen integer n will turn out to be prime as $1/\ln n$. Thus, we would need to examine approximately $\ln n$ integers chosen randomly near n in order to find a prime that is of the same length as n. For example, to find a 100-digit prime might require testing approximately $\ln 10^{100} \approx 230$ randomly chosen 100-digit numbers for primality. (This figure can be cut in half by choosing only odd integers.)

In the remainder of this section, we consider the problem of determining whether or not a large odd integer n is prime. For notational convenience, we assume that n has the prime factorization

$$n = p_1^{e_1} p_2^{e_2} \cdots p_r^{e_r} \;, \tag{33.41}$$

where $r \geq 1$ and $p_1, p_2, \ldots, p_r$ are the prime factors of n. Of course, n is prime if and only if $r = 1$ and $e_1 = 1$.

One simple approach to the problem of testing for primality is **trial division**. We try dividing n by each integer $2, 3, \ldots, \lfloor \sqrt{n} \rfloor$. (Again, even integers greater than 2 may be skipped.) It is easy to see that n is prime if and only if none of the trial divisors divides n. Assuming that each trial division takes constant time, the worst-case running time is $\Theta(\sqrt{n})$, which is exponential in the length of n. (Recall that if n is encoded in binary using β bits, then $\beta = \lceil \lg(n + 1) \rceil$, and so $\sqrt{n} = \Theta(2^{\beta/2})$.) Thus, trial division works well only if n is very small or happens to have a small prime factor. When it works, trial division has the advantage that it not only determines whether n is prime or composite but actually determines the prime factorization if n is composite.

In this section, we are interested only in finding out whether a given number n is prime; if n is composite, we are not concerned with finding its prime factorization. As we shall see in Section 33.9, computing the prime factorization of a number is computationally expensive. It is perhaps surprising that it is much easier to tell whether or not a given number is prime than it is to determine the prime factorization of the number if it is not prime.

Pseudoprimality testing

We now consider a method for primality testing that "almost works" and in fact is good enough for many practical applications. A refinement of this method that removes the small defect will be presented later. Let $\mathbf{Z}_n^+$ denote the nonzero elements of $\mathbf{Z}_n$:

$$\mathbf{Z}_n^+ = \{1, 2, \ldots, n - 1\} \;.$$

If n is prime, then $\mathbf{Z}_n^+ = \mathbf{Z}_n^*$.

We say that n is a **base-a pseudoprime** if n is composite and

$$a^{n-1} \equiv 1 \pmod{n} \;. \tag{33.42}$$

Fermat's theorem (Theorem 33.31) implies that if n is prime, then n satisfies equation (33.42) for every a in $\mathbf{Z}_n^+$. Thus, if we can find any $a \in \mathbf{Z}_n^+$ such that n does *not* satisfy equation (33.42), then n is certainly composite. Surprisingly, the converse *almost* holds, so that this criterion forms an almost perfect test for primality. We test to see if n satisfies equation (33.42) for $a = 2$. If not, we declare n to be composite. Otherwise, we output a guess that n is prime (when, in fact, all we know is that n is either prime or a base-2 pseudoprime).

The following procedure pretends in this manner to be checking the primality of n. It uses the procedure MODULAR-EXPONENTIATION from Section 33.6. The input n is assumed to be an integer larger than 2.

PSEUDOPRIME(n)

1 **if** MODULAR-EXPONENTIATION($2, n - 1, n$) $\not\equiv 1 \pmod{n}$
2   **then return** COMPOSITE   ▷ Definitely.
3   **else return** PRIME   ▷ We hope!

This procedure can make errors, but only of one type. That is, if it says that n is composite, then it is always correct. If it says that n is prime, however, then it makes an error only if n is a base-2 pseudoprime.

How often does this procedure err? Surprisingly rarely. There are only 22 values of n less than 10,000 for which it errs; the first four such values are 341, 561, 645, and 1105. It can be shown that the probability that this program makes an error on a randomly chosen β-bit number goes to zero as $\beta \to \infty$. Using more precise estimates due to Pomerance [157] of the number of base-2 pseudoprimes of a given size, we may estimate that a randomly chosen 50-digit number that is called prime by the above procedure has less than one chance in a million of being a base-2 pseudoprime, and a randomly chosen 100-digit number that is called prime has less than one chance in 10^{13} of being a base-2 pseudoprime.

Unfortunately, we cannot eliminate all the errors by simply checking equation (33.42) for a second base number, say $a = 3$, because there are composite integers n that satisfy equation (33.42) for *all* $a \in \mathbb{Z}_n^*$. These integers are known as **Carmichael numbers**. The first three Carmichael numbers are 561, 1105, and 1729. Carmichael numbers are extremely rare; there are, for example, only 255 of them less than 100,000,000. Exercise 33.8-2 helps explain why they are so rare.

We next show how to improve our primality test so that it won't be fooled by Carmichael numbers.

The Miller-Rabin randomized primality test

The Miller-Rabin primality test overcomes the problems of the simple test PSEUDOPRIME with two modifications:

- It tries several randomly chosen base values a instead of just one base value.

- While computing each modular exponentiation, it notices if a nontrivial square root of 1, modulo n, is ever discovered. If so, it stops and outputs COMPOSITE. Corollary 33.35 justifies detecting composites in this manner.

The pseudocode for the Miller-Rabin primality test follows. The input $n > 2$ is the odd number to be tested for primality, and s is the number of randomly chosen base values from $\mathbb{Z}_n^+$ to be tried. The code uses the

random-number generator RANDOM from Section 8.3: RANDOM$(1, n - 1)$
returns a randomly chosen integer a satisfying $1 \le a \le n-1$. The code uses
an auxiliary procedure WITNESS such that WITNESS(a, n) is TRUE if and
only if a is a "witness" to the compositeness of n—that is, if it is possible
using a to prove (in a manner that we shall see) that n is composite. The
test WITNESS(a, n) is similar to, but more effective than, the test

$$a^{n-1} \not\equiv 1 \pmod{n}$$

that formed the basis (using $a = 2$) for PSEUDOPRIME. We first present
and justify the construction of WITNESS, and then show how it is used in
the Miller-Rabin primality test.

WITNESS(a, n)

```
 1  let ⟨b_k, b_{k-1}, ..., b_0⟩ be the binary representation of n - 1
 2  d ← 1
 3  for i ← k downto 0
 4      do x ← d
 5         d ← (d · d) mod n
 6         if d = 1 and x ≠ 1 and x ≠ n - 1
 7             then return TRUE
 8         if b_i = 1
 9             then d ← (d · a) mod n
10  if d ≠ 1
11      then return TRUE
12  return FALSE
```

This pseudocode for WITNESS is based on the pseudocode of the procedure MODULAR-EXPONENTIATION. Line 1 determines the binary representation of $n - 1$, which will be used in raising a to the $(n - 1)$st power.
Lines 3–9 compute d as $a^{n-1} \bmod n$. The method used is identical to that
employed by MODULAR-EXPONENTIATION. Whenever a squaring step is
performed on line 5, however, lines 6–7 check to see if a nontrivial square
root of 1 has just been discovered. If so, the algorithm stops and returns
TRUE. Lines 10–11 return TRUE if the value computed for $a^{n-1} \bmod n$ is
not equal to 1, just as the PSEUDOPRIME procedure returns COMPOSITE in
this case.

We now argue that if WITNESS(a, n) returns TRUE, then a proof that n
is composite can be constructed using a.

If WITNESS returns TRUE from line 11, then it has discovered that $d =
a^{n-1} \bmod n \ne 1$. If n is prime, however, we have by Fermat's theorem
(Theorem 33.31) that $a^{n-1} \equiv 1 \pmod{n}$ for all $a \in Z_n^+$. Therefore, n
cannot be prime, and the equation $a^{n-1} \bmod 1 \ne 1$ is a proof of this fact.

If WITNESS returns TRUE from line 7, then it has discovered that x
is a nontrivial square root of 1, modulo n, since we have that $x \not\equiv \pm 1$
$\pmod{n}$ yet $x^2 \equiv 1 \pmod{n}$. Corollary 33.35 states that only if n is
composite can there be a nontrivial square root of 1 modulo n, so that a

demonstration that x is a nontrivial square root of 1 modulo n is a proof that n is composite.

This completes our proof of the correctness of WITNESS. If the invocation WITNESS(a, n) outputs TRUE, then n is surely composite, and a proof that n is composite can be easily determined from a and n. We now examine the Miller-Rabin primality test based on the use of WITNESS.

MILLER-RABIN(n, s)

```
1  for j ← 1 to s
2      do a ← RANDOM(1, n − 1)
3          if WITNESS(a, n)
4              then return COMPOSITE          ▷ Definitely.
5  return PRIME                                ▷ Almost surely.
```

The procedure MILLER-RABIN is a probabilistic search for a proof that n is composite. The main loop (beginning on line 1) picks s random values of a from Z_n^+ (line 2). If one of the a's picked is a witness to the compositeness of n, then MILLER-RABIN outputs COMPOSITE on line 4. Such an output is always correct, by the correctness of WITNESS. If no witness can be found in s trials, MILLER-RABIN assumes that this is because there are no witnesses to be found, and n is therefore prime. We shall see that this output is likely to be correct if s is large enough, but that there is a small chance that the procedure may be unlucky in its choice of a's and that witnesses do exist even though none has been found.

To illustrate the operation of MILLER-RABIN, let n be the Carmichael number 561. Supposing that $a = 7$ is chosen as a base, Figure 33.4 shows that WITNESS discovers a nontrivial square root of 1 in the last squaring step, since $a^{280} \equiv 67 \pmod{n}$ and $a^{560} \equiv 1 \pmod{n}$. Therefore, $a = 7$ is a witness to the compositeness of n, WITNESS($7, n$) returns TRUE, and MILLER-RABIN returns COMPOSITE.

If n is a β-bit number, MILLER-RABIN requires $O(s\beta)$ arithmetic operations and $O(s\beta^3)$ bit operations, since it requires asymptotically no more work than s modular exponentiations.

Error rate of the Miller-Rabin primality test

If MILLER-RABIN outputs PRIME, then there is a small chance that it has made an error. Unlike PSEUDOPRIME, however, the chance of error does not depend on n; there are no bad inputs for this procedure. Rather, it depends on the size of s and the "luck of the draw" in choosing base values a. Also, since each test is more stringent than a simple check of equation (33.42), we can expect on general principles that the error rate should be small for randomly chosen integers n. The following theorem presents a more precise argument.

Theorem 33.38

If n is an odd composite number, then the number of witnesses to the compositeness of n is at least $(n-1)/2$.

Proof   The proof shows that the number of nonwitnesses is no more than $(n-1)/2$, which implies the theorem.

We first observe that any nonwitness must be a member of $\mathbf{Z}_n^*$, since every nonwitness a satisfies $a^{n-1} \equiv 1 \pmod{n}$, yet if $\gcd(a, n) = d > 1$, then there are no solutions x to the equation $ax \equiv 1 \pmod{n}$, by Corollary 33.21. (In particular, $x = a^{n-2}$ is not a solution.) Thus every member of $\mathbf{Z}_n - \mathbf{Z}_n^*$ is a witness to the compositeness of n.

To complete the proof, we show that the nonwitnesses are all contained in a proper subgroup B of $\mathbf{Z}_n^*$. By Corollary 33.16, we then have $|B| \leq |\mathbf{Z}_n^*|/2$. Since $|\mathbf{Z}_n^*| \leq n-1$, we obtain $|B| \leq (n-1)/2$. Therefore, the number of nonwitnesses is at most $(n-1)/2$, so that the number of witnesses must be at least $(n-1)/2$.

We now show how to find a proper subgroup B of $\mathbf{Z}_n^*$ containing all of the nonwitnesses. We break the proof into two cases.

Case 1: There exists an $x \in \mathbf{Z}_n^*$ such that

$$x^{n-1} \not\equiv 1 \pmod{n} . \tag{33.43}$$

Let $B = \{b \in \mathbf{Z}_n^* : b^{n-1} \equiv 1 \pmod{n}\}$. Since B is closed under multiplication modulo n, we have that B is a subgroup of $\mathbf{Z}_n^*$ by Theorem 33.14. Note that every nonwitness belongs to B, since a nonwitness a satisfies $a^{n-1} \equiv 1 \pmod{n}$. Since $x \in \mathbf{Z}_n^* - B$, we have that B is a proper subgroup of $\mathbf{Z}_n^*$.

Case 2: For all $x \in \mathbf{Z}_n^*$,

$$x^{n-1} \equiv 1 \pmod{n} . \tag{33.44}$$

In this case, n cannot be a prime power. To see why, let $n = p^e$, where p is an odd prime and $e > 1$. Theorem 33.32 implies that $\mathbf{Z}_n^*$ contains an element g such that $\mathrm{ord}_n(g) = |\mathbf{Z}_n^*| = \phi(n) = (p-1)p^{e-1}$. But then equation (33.44) and the discrete logarithm theorem (Theorem 33.33, taking $y = 0$) imply that $n - 1 \equiv 0 \pmod{\phi(n)}$, or

$$(p-1)p^{e-1} \mid p^e - 1 .$$

This condition fails for $e > 1$, since the left-hand side is then divisible by p but the right-hand side is not. Thus, n is not a prime power.

Since n is not a prime power, we decompose it into a product $n_1 n_2$, where n_1 and n_2 are greater than 1 and relatively prime to each other. (There may be several ways to do this, and it doesn't matter which one we choose. For example, if $n = p_1^{e_1} p_2^{e_2} \cdots p_r^{e_r}$, then we can choose $n_1 = p_1^{e_1}$ and $n_2 = p_2^{e_2} p_3^{e_3} \cdots p_r^{e_r}$.)

Define t and u so that $n - 1 = 2^t u$, where $t \geq 1$ and u is odd. For any $a \in \mathbf{Z}_n^+$, consider the sequence

$$\widehat{a} = \langle a^u, a^{2u}, a^{2^2 u}, \ldots, a^{2^t u} \rangle \,, \tag{33.45}$$

where all elements are computed modulo n. Since $2^t \mid n - 1$, the binary representation of $n-1$ ends in t zeros, and the elements of $\widehat{a}$ are the last $t+1$ values of d computed by WITNESS during a computation of $a^{n-1} \bmod n$; the last t operations are squarings.

Now find a $j \in \{0, 1, \ldots, t\}$ such that there exists a $v \in \mathbf{Z}_n^*$ such that $v^{2^j u} \equiv -1 \pmod{n}$; j should be as large as possible. Such a j certainly exists since u is odd: we can choose $v = -1$ and $j = 0$. Fix v to satisfy the given condition. Let

$$B = \{x \in \mathbf{Z}_n^* : x^{2^j u} \equiv \pm 1 \pmod{n}\} \,.$$

Since B is closed under multiplication modulo n, it is a subgroup of $\mathbf{Z}_n^*$. Therefore, $|B|$ divides $|\mathbf{Z}_n^*|$. Every nonwitness must be a member of B, since the sequence (33.45) produced by a nonwitness must either be all 1's or else contain a -1 no later than the jth position, by the maximality of j.

We now use the existence of v to demonstrate that there exists a $w \in \mathbf{Z}_n^* - B$. Since $v^{2^j u} \equiv -1 \pmod{n}$, we have $v^{2^j u} \equiv -1 \pmod{n_1}$ by Corollary 33.29. By Corollary 33.28, there is a w simultaneously satisfying the equations

$$w \equiv v \pmod{n_1} \,,$$
$$w \equiv 1 \pmod{n_2} \,.$$

Therefore,

$$w^{2^j u} \equiv -1 \pmod{n_1} \,,$$
$$w^{2^j u} \equiv 1 \pmod{n_2} \,.$$

Together with Corollary 33.29, these equations imply that

$$w^{2^j u} \not\equiv \pm 1 \pmod{n} \,, \tag{33.46}$$

and so $w \notin B$. Since $v \in \mathbf{Z}_n^*$, we have that $v \in \mathbf{Z}_{n_1}^*$. Thus, $w \in \mathbf{Z}_n^*$, and so $w \in \mathbf{Z}_n^* - B$. We conclude that B is a proper subgroup of $\mathbf{Z}_n^*$.

In either case, we see that the number of witnesses to the compositeness of n is at least $(n - 1)/2$. ∎

Theorem 33.39

For any odd integer $n > 2$ and positive integer s, the probability that MILLER-RABIN(n, s) errs is at most 2^{-s}.

Proof Using Theorem 33.38, we see that if n is composite, then each execution of the loop of lines 1–4 has a probability of at least $1/2$ of discovering a witness x to the compositeness of n. MILLER-RABIN only makes an error if it is so unlucky as to miss discovering a witness to the compositeness of n on each of the s iterations of the main loop. The probability of such a string of misses is at most 2^{-s}. ∎

Thus, choosing $s = 50$ should suffice for almost any imaginable application. If we are trying to find large primes by applying MILLER-RABIN to *randomly chosen* large integers, then it can be argued (although we won't do so here) that choosing a small value of s (say 3) is very unlikely to lead to erroneous results. That is, for a randomly chosen odd composite integer n, the expected number of nonwitnesses to the compositeness of n is likely to be much smaller than $(n - 1)/2$. If the integer n is not chosen randomly, however, the best that can be proven is that the number of nonwitnesses is at most $(n - 1)/4$, using an improved version of Theorem 33.39. Furthermore, there do exist integers n for which the number of nonwitnesses is $(n - 1)/4$.

Exercises

33.8-1
Prove that if an integer $n > 1$ is not a prime or a prime power, then there exists a nontrivial square root of 1 modulo n.

33.8-2 ★
It is possible to strengthen Euler's theorem slightly to the form

$a^{\lambda(n)} \equiv 1 \pmod{n}$ for all $a \in \mathbf{Z}_n^*$,

where $\lambda(n)$ is defined by

$$\lambda(n) = \text{lcm}(\phi(p_1^{e_1}), \dots, \phi(p_r^{e_r})). \tag{33.47}$$

Prove that $\lambda(n) \mid \phi(n)$. A composite number n is a Carmichael number if $\lambda(n) \mid n - 1$. The smallest Carmichael number is $561 = 3 \cdot 11 \cdot 17$; here, $\lambda(n) = \text{lcm}(2, 10, 16) = 80$, which divides 560. Prove that Carmichael numbers must be both "square-free" (not divisible by the square of any prime) and the product of at least three primes. For this reason, they are not very common.

33.8-3
Prove that if x is a nontrivial square root of 1, modulo n, then $\gcd(x-1, n)$ and $\gcd(x + 1, n)$ are both nontrivial divisors of n.

★ **33.9   Integer factorization**

Suppose we have an integer n that we wish to *factor*, that is, to decompose into a product of primes. The primality test of the preceding section would tell us that n is composite, but it usually doesn't tell us the prime factors of n. Factoring a large integer n seems to be much more difficult than simply determining whether n is prime or composite. It is infeasible with today's supercomputers and the best algorithms to date to factor an arbitrary 200-decimal-digit number.

Pollard's rho heuristic

Trial division by all integers up to B is guaranteed to factor completely any number up to B^2. For the same amount of work, the following procedure will factor any number up to B^4 (unless we're unlucky). Since the procedure is only a heuristic, neither its running time nor its success is guaranteed, although the procedure is very effective in practice.

POLLARD-RHO(n)
```
 1  i ← 1
 2  x₁ ← RANDOM(0, n - 1)
 3  y ← x₁
 4  k ← 2
 5  while TRUE
 6      do i ← i + 1
 7          xᵢ ← (x²ᵢ₋₁ - 1) mod n
 8          d ← gcd(y - xᵢ, n)
 9          if d ≠ 1 and d ≠ n
10              then print d
11          if i = k
12              then y ← xᵢ
13                  k ← 2k
```

The procedure works as follows. Lines 1–2 initialize i to 1 and x_1 to a randomly chosen value in $\mathbf{Z}_n$. The **while** loop beginning on line 5 iterates forever, searching for factors of n. During each iteration of the **while** loop, the recurrence

$$x_i \leftarrow (x_{i-1}^2 - 1) \bmod n \qquad (33.48)$$

is used on line 7 to produce the next value of x_i in the infinite sequence

$$x_1, x_2, x_3, x_4, \ldots ; \qquad (33.49)$$

the value of i is correspondingly incremented on line 6. The code is written using subscripted variables x_i for clarity, but the program works the same if all of the subscripts are dropped, since only the most recent value of x_i need be maintained.

Every so often, the program saves the most recently generated x_i value in the variable y. Specifically, the values that are saved are the ones whose subscripts are powers of 2:

$$x_1, x_2, x_4, x_8, x_{16}, \ldots .$$

Line 3 saves the value x_1, and line 12 saves x_k whenever i is equal to k. The variable k is initialized to 2 in line 4, and k is doubled in line 13 whenever y is updated. Therefore, k follows the sequence $1, 2, 4, 8, \ldots$ and always gives the subscript of the next value x_k to be saved in y.

Lines 8–10 try to find a factor of n, using the saved value of y and the current value of x_i. Specifically, line 8 computes the greatest common divisor $d = \gcd(y - x_i, n)$. If d is a nontrivial divisor of n (checked in line 9), then line 10 prints d.

This procedure for finding a factor may seem somewhat mysterious at first. Note, however, that POLLARD-RHO never prints an incorrect answer; any number it prints is a nontrivial divisor of n. POLLARD-RHO may not print anything at all, though; there is no guarantee that it will produce any results. We shall see, however, that there is good reason to expect POLLARD-RHO to print a factor p of n after approximately $\sqrt{p}$ iterations of the **while** loop. Thus, if n is composite, we can expect this procedure to discover enough divisors to factor n completely after approximately $n^{1/4}$ updates, since every prime factor p of n except possibly the largest one is less than $\sqrt{n}$.

We analyze the behavior of this procedure by studying how long it takes a random sequence modulo n to repeat a value. Since $\mathbf{Z}_n$ is finite, and since each value in the sequence (33.49) depends only on the previous value, the sequence (33.49) eventually repeats itself. Once we reach an x_i such that $x_i = x_j$ for some $j < i$, we are in a cycle, since $x_{i+1} = x_{j+1}$, $x_{i+2} = x_{j+2}$, and so on. The reason for the name "rho heuristic" is that, as Figure 33.7 shows, the sequence $x_1, x_2, \ldots, x_{j-1}$ can be drawn as the "tail" of the rho, and the cycle $x_j, x_{j+1}, \ldots, x_i$ as the "body" of the rho.

Let us consider the question of how long it takes for the sequence of x_i to repeat. This is not exactly what we need, but we shall then see how to modify the argument.

For the purpose of this estimation, let us assume that the function $(x^2 - 1) \bmod n$ behaves like a "random" function. Of course, it is not really random, but this assumption yields results consistent with the observed behavior of POLLARD-RHO. We can then consider each x_i to have been independently drawn from $\mathbf{Z}_n$ according to a uniform distribution on $\mathbf{Z}_n$. By the birthday-paradox analysis of Section 6.6.1, the expected number of steps taken before the sequence cycles is $\Theta(\sqrt{n})$.

Now for the required modification. Let p be a nontrivial factor of n such that $\gcd(p, n/p) = 1$. For example, if n has the factorization $n = p_1^{e_1} p_2^{e_2} \cdots p_r^{e_r}$, then we may take p to be $p_1^{e_1}$. (If $e_1 = 1$, then p is just the smallest prime factor of n, a good example to keep in mind.) The sequence $\langle x_i \rangle$ induces a corresponding sequence $\langle x_i' \rangle$ modulo p, where

$$x_i' = x_i \bmod p$$

for all i. Furthermore, it follows from the Chinese remainder theorem that

$$x_{i+1}' = (x_i'^2 - 1) \bmod p \tag{33.50}$$

since

$$(x \bmod n) \bmod p = x \bmod p \ ,$$

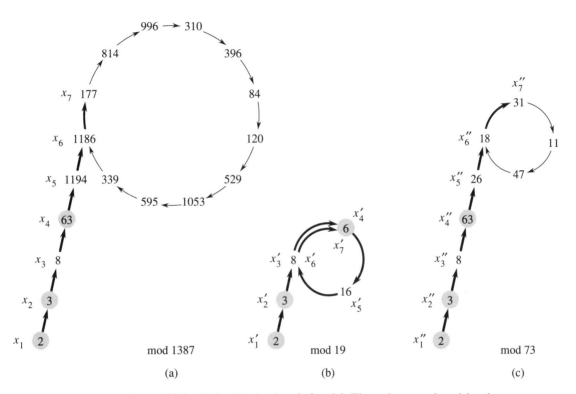

Figure 33.7 Pollard's rho heuristic. (a) The values produced by the recurrence $x_{i+1} \leftarrow (x_i^2 - 1) \bmod 1387$, starting with $x_1 = 2$. The prime factorization of 1387 is $19 \cdot 73$. The heavy arrows indicate the iteration steps that are executed before the factor 19 is discovered. The light arrows point to unreached values in the iteration, to illustrate the "rho" shape. The shaded values are the y values stored by POLLARD-RHO. The factor 19 is discovered after $x_7 = 177$ is reached, when $\gcd(63 - 177, 1387) = 19$ is computed. The first x value that would be repeated is 1186, but the factor 19 is discovered before this value is reached. (b) The values produced by the same recurrence, modulo 19. Every value x_i given in part (a) is equivalent, modulo 19, to the value x_i' shown here. For example, both $x_4 = 63$ and $x_7 = 177$ are equivalent to 6, modulo 19. (c) The values produced by the same recurrence, modulo 73. Every value x_i given in part (a) is equivalent, modulo 73, to the value x_i'' shown here. By the Chinese remainder theorem, each node in part (a) corresponds to a pair of nodes, one from part (b) and one from part (c).

by Exercise 33.1-6.

Reasoning as before, we find that the expected number of steps before the sequence $\langle x_i' \rangle$ repeats is $\Theta(\sqrt{p})$. If p is small compared to n, the sequence $\langle x_i' \rangle$ may repeat much more quickly than the sequence $\langle x_i \rangle$. Indeed, the $\langle x_i' \rangle$ sequence repeats as soon as two elements of the sequence $\langle x_i \rangle$ are merely equivalent modulo p, rather than equivalent modulo n. See Figure 33.7, parts (b) and (c), for an illustration.

Let t denote the index of the first repeated value in the $\langle x_i' \rangle$ sequence, and let $u > 0$ denote the length of the cycle that has been thereby produced. That is, t and $u > 0$ are the smallest values such that $x_{t+i}' = x_{t+u+i}'$ for all $i \geq 0$. By the above arguments, the expected values of t and u are both $\Theta(\sqrt{p})$. Note that if $x_{t+i}' = x_{t+u+i}'$, then $p \mid (x_{t+u+i} - x_{t+i})$. Thus, $\gcd(x_{t+u+i} - x_{t+i}, n) > 1$.

Therefore, once POLLARD-RHO has saved as y any value x_k such that $k \geq t$, then $y \bmod p$ is always on the cycle modulo p. (If a new value is saved as y, that value is also on the cycle modulo p.) Eventually, k is set to a value that is greater than u, and the procedure then makes an entire loop around the cycle modulo p without changing the value of y. A factor of n is then discovered when x_i "runs into" the previously stored value of y, modulo p, that is, when $x_i \equiv y \pmod{p}$.

Presumably, the factor found is the factor p, although it may occasionally happen that a multiple of p is discovered. Since the expected values of both t and u are $\Theta(\sqrt{p})$, the expected number of steps required to produce the factor p is $\Theta(\sqrt{p})$.

There are two reasons why this algorithm may not perform quite as expected. First, the heuristic analysis of the running time is not rigorous, and it is possible that the cycle of values, modulo p, could be much larger than $\sqrt{p}$. In this case, the algorithm performs correctly but much more slowly than desired. In practice, this seems not to be an issue. Second, the divisors of n produced by this algorithm might always be one of the trivial factors 1 or n. For example, suppose that $n = pq$, where p and q are prime. It can happen that the values of t and u for p are identical with the values of t and u for q, and thus the factor p is always revealed in the same gcd operation that reveals the factor q. Since both factors are revealed at the same time, the trivial factor $pq = n$ is revealed, which is useless. Again, this seems not to be a real problem in practice. If necessary, the heuristic can be restarted with a different recurrence of the form $x_{i+1} \leftarrow (x_i^2 - c) \bmod n$. (The values $c = 0$ and $c = 2$ should be avoided for reasons we won't go into here, but other values are fine.)

Of course, this analysis is heuristic and not rigorous, since the recurrence is not really "random." Nonetheless, the procedure performs well in practice, and it seems to be as efficient as this heuristic analysis indicates. It is the method of choice for finding small prime factors of a large number. To factor a β-bit composite number n completely, we only need to find all prime factors less than $\lfloor n^{1/2} \rfloor$, and so we expect POLLARD-RHO to require at most $n^{1/4} = 2^{\beta/4}$ arithmetic operations and at most $n^{1/4}\beta^3 = 2^{\beta/4}\beta^3$ bit operations. POLLARD-RHO's ability to find a small factor p of n with an expected number $\Theta(\sqrt{p})$ of arithmetic operations is often its most appealing feature.

Exercises

33.9-1
Referring to the execution history shown in Figure 33.7(a), when does POLLARD-RHO print the factor 73 of 1387?

33.9-2
Suppose that we are given a function $f : \mathbf{Z}_n \to \mathbf{Z}_n$ and an initial value $x_0 \in \mathbf{Z}_n$. Define $x_i = f(x_{i-1})$ for $i = 1, 2, \ldots$. Let t and $u > 0$ be the smallest values such that $x_{t+i} = x_{t+u+i}$ for $i = 0, 1, \ldots$. In the terminology of Pollard's rho algorithm, t is the length of the tail and u is the length of the cycle of the rho. Give an efficient algorithm to determine t and u exactly, and analyze its running time.

33.9-3
How many steps would you expect POLLARD-RHO to require to discover a factor of the form p^e, where p is prime and $e > 1$?

33.9-4 $\star$
One disadvantage of POLLARD-RHO as written is that it requires one gcd computation for each step of the recurrence. It has been suggested that we might batch the gcd computations by accumulating the product of several x_i in a row and then taking the gcd of this product with the saved y. Describe carefully how you would implement this idea, why it works, and what batch size you would pick as the most effective when working on a β-bit number n.

Problems

33-1 *Binary gcd algorithm*
On most computers, the operations of subtraction, testing the parity (odd or even) of a binary integer, and halving can be performed more quickly than computing remainders. This problem investigates the **binary gcd algorithm**, which avoids the remainder computations used in Euclid's algorithm.

a. Prove that if a and b are both even, then $\gcd(a, b) = 2 \gcd(a/2, b/2)$.

b. Prove that if a is odd and b is even, then $\gcd(a, b) = \gcd(a, b/2)$.

c. Prove that if a and b are both odd, then $\gcd(a, b) = \gcd((a - b)/2, b)$.

d. Design an efficient binary gcd algorithm for input integers a and b, where $a \geq b$, that runs in $O(\lg(\max(a, b)))$ time. Assume that each subtraction, parity test, and halving can be performed in unit time.

33-2   *Analysis of bit operations in Euclid's algorithm*

a. Show that using the ordinary "paper and pencil" algorithm for long division—dividing a by b, yielding a quotient q and remainder r—requires $O((1 + \lg q) \lg b)$ bit operations.

b. Define $\mu(a, b) = (1 + \lg a)(1 + \lg b)$. Show that the number of bit operations performed by EUCLID in reducing the problem of computing $\gcd(a, b)$ to that of computing $\gcd(b, a \bmod b)$ is at most $c(\mu(a, b) - \mu(b, a \bmod b))$ for some sufficiently large constant $c > 0$.

c. Show that EUCLID(a, b) requires $O(\mu(a, b))$ bit operations in general and $O(\beta^2)$ bit operations when applied to two β-bit inputs.

33-3   *Three algorithms for Fibonacci numbers*

This problem compares the efficiency of three methods for computing the nth Fibonacci number F_n, given n. Assume that the cost of adding, subtracting, or multiplying two numbers is $O(1)$, independent of the size of the numbers.

a. Show that the running time of the straightforward recursive method for computing F_n based on recurrence (2.13) is exponential in n.

b. Show how to compute F_n in $O(n)$ time using memoization.

c. Show how to compute F_n in $O(\lg n)$ time using only integer addition and multiplication. (*Hint:* Consider the matrix

$$\begin{pmatrix} 1 & 1 \\ 0 & 1 \end{pmatrix}$$

and its powers.)

d. Assume now that adding two β-bit numbers takes $\Theta(\beta)$ time and that multiplying two β-bit numbers takes $\Theta(\beta^2)$ time. What is the running time of these three methods under this more reasonable cost measure for the elementary arithmetic operations?

33-4   *Quadratic residues*

Let p be an odd prime. A number $a \in Z_p^*$ is a *quadratic residue* if the equation $x^2 = a \pmod{p}$ has a solution for the unknown x.

a. Show that there are exactly $(p - 1)/2$ quadratic residues, modulo p.

b. If p is prime, we define the ***Legendre symbol*** $(\frac{a}{p})$, for $a \in \mathbf{Z}_p^*$, to be 1 if a is a quadratic residue modulo p and -1 otherwise. Prove that if $a \in \mathbf{Z}_p^*$, then

$$\left(\frac{a}{p}\right) \equiv a^{(p-1)/2} \pmod{p} .$$

Give an efficient algorithm for determining whether or not a given number a is a quadratic residue modulo p. Analyze the efficiency of your algorithm.

c. Prove that if p is a prime of the form $4k + 3$ and a is a quadratic residue in $\mathbf{Z}_p^*$, then $a^{k+1} \bmod p$ is a square root of a, modulo p. How much time is required to find the square root of a quadratic residue a modulo p?

d. Describe an efficient randomized algorithm for finding a nonquadratic residue, modulo an arbitrary prime p. How many arithmetic operations does your algorithm require on average?

Chapter notes

Niven and Zuckerman [151] provide an excellent introduction to elementary number theory. Knuth [122] contains a good discussion of algorithms for finding the greatest common divisor, as well as other basic number-theoretic algorithms. Riesel [168] and Bach [16] provide more recent surveys of computational number theory. Dixon [56] gives an overview of factorization and primality testing. The conference proceedings edited by Pomerance [159] contains several nice survey articles.

Knuth [122] discusses the origin of Euclid's algorithm. It appears in Book 7, Propositions 1 and 2, of the Greek mathematician Euclid's *Elements*, which was written around 300 B.C. Euclid's description may have been derived from an algorithm due to Eudoxus around 375 B.C. Euclid's algorithm may hold the honor of being the oldest nontrivial algorithm; it is rivaled only by the Russian peasant's algorithm for multiplication (see Chapter 29), which was known to the ancient Egyptians.

Knuth attributes a special case of the Chinese remainder theorem (Theorem 33.27) to the Chinese mathematician Sun-Tsŭ, who lived sometime between 200 B.C. and A.D. 200—the date is quite uncertain. The same special case was given by the Greek mathematician Nichomachus around A.D. 100. It was generalized by Chhin Chiu-Shao in 1247. The Chinese remainder theorem was finally stated and proved in its full generality by L. Euler in 1734.

The randomized primality-testing algorithm presented here is due to Miller [147] and Rabin [166]; it is the fastest randomized primality-testing algorithm known, to within constant factors. The proof of Theorem 33.39 is a slight adaptation of one suggested by Bach [15]. A proof of a stronger result for MILLER-RABIN was given by Monier [148, 149]. Randomization appears to be necessary to obtain a polynomial-time primality-testing algorithm. The fastest deterministic primality-testing algorithm known is the Cohen-Lenstra version [45] of the primality test by Adleman, Pomerance, and Rumely [3]. When testing a number n of length $\lceil \lg(n + 1) \rceil$ for primality, it runs in $(\lg n)^{O(\lg \lg \lg n)}$ time, which is just slightly superpolynomial.

The problem of finding large "random" primes is nicely discussed in an article by Beauchemin, Brassard, Crépeau, Goutier, and Pomerance [20].

The concept of a public-key cryptosystem is due to Diffie and Hellman [54]. The RSA cryptosystem was proposed in 1977 by Rivest, Shamir, and Adleman [169]. Since then, the field of cryptography has blossomed. In particular, many new techniques have been developed for proving cryptosystems to be secure. For example, Goldwasser and Micali [86] show that randomization can be an effective tool in the design of secure public-key encryption schemes. For signature schemes, Goldwasser, Micali, and Rivest [88] present a digital-signature scheme for which every conceivable type of forgery is provably as difficult as factoring. Recently, Goldwasser, Micali, and Rackoff [87] introduced a class of "zero-knowledge" encryption schemes for which it can be proven (under certain reasonable assumptions) that no party learns more than he is supposed to learn from a communication.

The rho heuristic for integer factoring was invented by Pollard [156]. The version presented here is a variant proposed by Brent [35].

The best algorithms for factoring large numbers have a running time that grows roughly exponentially with the square root of the length of the number n to be factored. The quadratic-sieve factoring algorithm, due to Pomerance [158], is perhaps the most efficient such algorithm in general for large inputs. Although it is difficult to give a rigorous analysis of this algorithm, under reasonable assumptions we can derive a running-time estimate of $L(n)^{1+o(1)}$, where $L(n) = e^{\sqrt{\ln n \ln \ln n}}$. The elliptic-curve method due to Lenstra [137] may be more effective for some inputs than the quadratic-sieve method, since, like Pollard's rho method, it can find a small prime factor p quite quickly. With this method, the time to find p is estimated to be $L(p)^{\sqrt{2}+o(1)}$.

34 String Matching

Finding all occurrences of a pattern in a text is a problem that arises frequently in text-editing programs. Typically, the text is a document being edited, and the pattern searched for is a particular word supplied by the user. Efficient algorithms for this problem can greatly aid the responsiveness of the text-editing program. String-matching algorithms are also used, for example, to search for particular patterns in DNA sequences.

We formalize the *string-matching problem* as follows. We assume that the text is an array $T[1 \mathinner{.\,.} n]$ of length n and that the pattern is an array $P[1 \mathinner{.\,.} m]$ of length m. We further assume that the elements of P and T are characters drawn from a finite alphabet Σ. For example, we may have $\Sigma = \{0, 1\}$ or $\Sigma = \{a, b, \ldots, z\}$. The character arrays P and T are often called *strings* of characters.

We say that pattern P *occurs with shift s* in text T (or, equivalently, that pattern P *occurs beginning at position $s + 1$* in text T) if $0 \le s \le n - m$ and $T[s + 1 \mathinner{.\,.} s + m] = P[1 \mathinner{.\,.} m]$ (that is, if $T[s + j] = P[j]$, for $1 \le j \le m$). If P occurs with shift s in T, then we call s a *valid shift*; otherwise, we call s an *invalid shift*. The string-matching problem is the problem of finding all valid shifts with which a given pattern P occurs in a given text T. Figure 34.1 illustrates these definitions.

This chapter is organized as follows. In Section 34.1 we review the naive brute-force algorithm for the string-matching problem, which has worst-case running time $O((n - m + 1)m)$. Section 34.2 presents an interesting string-matching algorithm, due to Rabin and Karp. This algorithm also

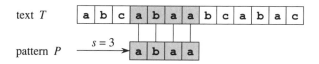

text T

pattern P $s = 3$

Figure 34.1 The string-matching problem. The goal is to find all occurrences of the pattern $P = \text{abaa}$ in the text $T = \text{abcabaabcabac}$. The pattern occurs only once in the text, at shift $s = 3$. The shift $s = 3$ is said to be a valid shift. Each character of the pattern is connected by a vertical line to the matching character in the text, and all matched characters are shown shaded.

has worst-case running time $O((n - m + 1)m)$, but it works much better on average and in practice. It also generalizes nicely to other pattern-matching problems. Section 34.3 then describes a string-matching algorithm that begins by constructing a finite automaton specifically designed to search for occurrences of the given pattern P in a text. This algorithm runs in time $O(n + m |\Sigma|)$. The similar but much cleverer Knuth-Morris-Pratt (or KMP) algorithm is presented in Section 34.4; the KMP algorithm runs in time $O(n + m)$. Finally, Section 34.5 describes an algorithm due to Boyer and Moore that is often the best practical choice, although its worst-case running time (like that of the Rabin-Karp algorithm) is no better than that of the naive string-matching algorithm.

Notation and terminology

We shall let Σ^* (read "sigma-star") denote the set of all finite-length strings formed using characters from the alphabet Σ. In this chapter, we consider only finite-length strings. The zero-length *empty string*, denoted ε, also belongs to Σ^*. The length of a string x is denoted $|x|$. The **concatenation** of two strings x and y, denoted xy, has length $|x| + |y|$ and consists of the characters from x followed by the characters from y.

We say that a string w is a **prefix** of a string x, denoted $w \sqsubset x$, if $x = wy$ for some string $y \in \Sigma^*$. Note that if $w \sqsubset x$, then $|w| \le |x|$. Similarly, we say that a string w is a **suffix** of a string x, denoted $w \sqsupset x$, if $x = yw$ for some $y \in \Sigma^*$. It follows from $w \sqsupset x$ that $|w| \le |x|$. The empty string ε is both a suffix and a prefix of every string. For example, we have ab $\sqsubset$ abcca and cca $\sqsupset$ abcca. It is useful to note that for any strings x and y and any character a, we have $x \sqsupset y$ if and only if $xa \sqsupset ya$. Also note that $\sqsubset$ and $\sqsupset$ are transitive relations. The following lemma will be useful later.

Lemma 34.1 (Overlapping-suffix lemma)
Suppose that x, y, and z are strings such that $x \sqsupset z$ and $y \sqsupset z$. If $|x| \le |y|$, then $x \sqsupset y$. If $|x| \ge |y|$, then $y \sqsupset x$. If $|x| = |y|$, then $x = y$.

Proof   See Figure 34.2 for a graphical proof.   ∎

For brevity of notation, we shall denote the k-character prefix $P[1 .. k]$ of the pattern $P[1 .. m]$ by P_k. Thus, $P_0 = \varepsilon$ and $P_m = P = P[1 .. m]$. Similarly, we denote the k-character prefix of the text T as T_k. Using this notation, we can state the string-matching problem as that of finding all shifts s in the range $0 \le s \le n - m$ such that $P \sqsupset T_{s+m}$.

In our pseudocode, we allow two equal-length strings to be compared for equality as a primitive operation. If the strings are compared from left to right and the comparison stops when a mismatch is discovered, we assume that the time taken by such a test is a linear function of the number of matching characters discovered. To be precise, the test "$x = y$" is assumed

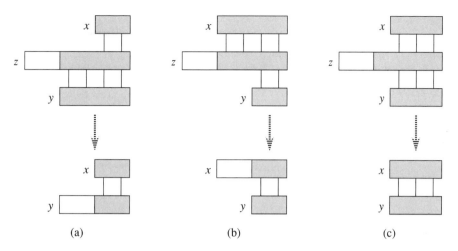

Figure 34.2   A graphical proof of Lemma 34.1. We suppose that $x \sqsupset z$ and $y \sqsupset z$. The three parts of the figure illustrate the three cases of the lemma. Vertical lines connect matching regions (shown shaded) of the strings. **(a)** If $|x| \leq |y|$, then $x \sqsupset y$. **(b)** If $|x| \geq |y|$, then $y \sqsupset x$. **(c)** If $|x| = |y|$, then $x = y$.

to take time $\Theta(t+1)$, where t is the length of the longest string z such that $z \sqsubset x$ and $z \sqsubset y$.

34.1   The naive string-matching algorithm

The naive algorithm finds all valid shifts using a loop that checks the condition $P[1 .. m] = T[s + 1 .. s + m]$ for each of the $n - m + 1$ possible values of s.

NAIVE-STRING-MATCHER(T, P)

1   $n \leftarrow length[T]$
2   $m \leftarrow length[P]$
3   **for** $s \leftarrow 0$ **to** $n - m$
4   **do if** $P[1 .. m] = T[s + 1 .. s + m]$
5   **then** print "Pattern occurs with shift" s

The naive string-matching procedure can be interpreted graphically as sliding a "template" containing the pattern over the text, noting for which shifts all of the characters on the template equal the corresponding characters in the text, as illustrated in Figure 34.3. The **for** loop beginning on line 3 considers each possible shift explicitly. The test on line 4 determines whether the current shift is valid or not; this test involves an implicit loop to check corresponding character positions until all positions match successfully or a mismatch is found. Line 5 prints out each valid shift s.

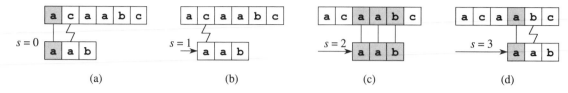

Figure 34.3   The operation of the naive string matcher for the pattern $P = $ aab and the text $T = $ acaabc. We can imagine the pattern P as a "template" that we slide next to the text. Parts (a)–(d) show the four successive alignments tried by the naive string matcher. In each part, vertical lines connect corresponding regions found to match (shown shaded), and a jagged line connects the first mismatched character found, if any. One occurrence of the pattern is found, at shift $s = 2$, shown in part (c).

Procedure NAIVE-STRING-MATCHER takes time $\Theta((n - m + 1)m)$ in the worst case. For example, consider the text string a^n (a string of n a's) and the pattern a^m. For each of the $n - m + 1$ possible values of the shift s, the implicit loop on line 4 to compare corresponding characters must execute m times to validate the shift. The worst-case running time is thus $\Theta((n - m + 1)m)$, which is $\Theta(n^2)$ if $m = \lfloor n/2 \rfloor$.

As we shall see, NAIVE-STRING-MATCHER is not an optimal procedure for this problem. Indeed, in this chapter we shall show an algorithm with a worst-case running time of $O(n+m)$. The naive string-matcher is inefficient because information gained about the text for one value of s is totally ignored in considering other values of s. Such information can be very valuable, however. For example, if $P = $ aaab and we find that $s = 0$ is valid, then none of the shifts 1, 2, or 3 are valid, since $T[4] = $ b. In the following sections, we examine several ways to make effective use of this sort of information.

Exercises

34.1-1
Show the comparisons the naive string matcher makes for the pattern $P = $ 0001 in the text $T = $ 000010001010001.

34.1-2
Show that the worst-case time for the naive string matcher to find the *first* occurrence of a pattern in a text is $\Theta((n - m + 1)(m - 1))$.

34.1-3
Suppose that all characters in the pattern P are different. Show how to accelerate NAIVE-STRING-MATCHER to run in time $O(n)$ on an n-character text T.

34.1-4

Suppose that pattern P and text T are *randomly* chosen strings of length m and n, respectively, from the d-ary alphabet $\Sigma_d = \{0, 1, \ldots, d - 1\}$, where $d \geq 2$. Show that the *expected* number of character-to-character comparisons made by the implicit loop in line 4 of the naive algorithm is

$$(n - m + 1)\frac{1 - d^{-m}}{1 - d^{-1}} \leq 2(n - m + 1) .$$

(Assume that the naive algorithm stops comparing characters for a given shift once a mismatch is found or the entire pattern is matched.) Thus, for randomly chosen strings, the naive algorithm is quite efficient.

34.1-5

Suppose we allow the pattern P to contain occurrences of a ***gap character*** $\diamond$ that can match an *arbitrary* string of characters (even one of zero length). For example, the pattern ab$\diamond$ba$\diamond$c occurs in the text cabccbacbacab as

$$\underbrace{c}_{}\underbrace{ab}_{ab}\underbrace{cc}_{\diamond}\underbrace{ba}_{ba}\underbrace{cba}_{\diamond}\underbrace{c}_{c}\underbrace{ab}_{}$$

and as

$$\underbrace{c}_{}\underbrace{ab}_{ab}\underbrace{ccbac}_{\diamond}\underbrace{ba}_{ba}\underbrace{}_{\diamond}\underbrace{c}_{c}\underbrace{ab}_{} .$$

Note that the gap character may occur an arbitrary number of times in the pattern but is assumed not to occur at all in the text. Give a polynomial-time algorithm to determine if such a pattern P occurs in a given text T, and analyze the running time of your algorithm.

34.2 The Rabin-Karp algorithm

Rabin and Karp have proposed a string-matching algorithm that performs well in practice and that also generalizes to other algorithms for related problems, such as two-dimensional pattern matching. The worst-case running time of the Rabin-Karp algorithm is $O((n - m + 1)m)$, but it has a good average-case running time.

This algorithm makes use of elementary number-theoretic notions such as the equivalence of two numbers modulo a third number. You may want to refer to Section 33.1 for the relevant definitions.

For expository purposes, let us assume that $\Sigma = \{0, 1, 2, \ldots, 9\}$, so that each character is a decimal digit. (In the general case, we can assume that each character is a digit in radix-d notation, where $d = |\Sigma|$.) We can then view a string of k consecutive characters as representing a length-k decimal number. The character string 31415 thus corresponds to the decimal number 31,415. Given the dual interpretation of the input characters as both graphical symbols and digits, we find it convenient in this section to denote them as we would digits, in our standard text font.

Given a pattern $P[1 .. m]$, we let p denote its corresponding decimal value. In a similar manner, given a text $T[1 .. n]$, we let t_s denote the decimal value of the length-m substring $T[s+1 .. s+m]$, for $s = 0, 1, \ldots, n - m$. Certainly, $t_s = p$ if and only if $T[s + 1 .. s + m] = P[1 .. m]$; thus, s is a valid shift if and only if $t_s = p$. If we could compute p in time $O(m)$ and all of the t_i values in a total of $O(n)$ time, then we could determine all valid shifts s in time $O(n)$ by comparing p with each of the t_s's. (For the moment, let's not worry about the possibility that p and the t_s's might be very large numbers.)

We can compute p in time $O(m)$ using Horner's rule (see Section 32.1):

$$p = P[m] + 10\left(P[m - 1] + 10(P[m - 2] + \cdots + 10(P[2] + 10P[1]) \cdots)\right) .$$

The value t_0 can be similarly computed from $T[1 .. m]$ in time $O(m)$.

To compute the remaining values $t_1, t_2, \ldots, t_{n-m}$ in time $O(n - m)$, it suffices to observe that t_{s+1} can be computed from t_s in constant time, since

$$t_{s+1} = 10(t_s - 10^{m-1}T[s + 1]) + T[s + m + 1] . \tag{34.1}$$

For example, if $m = 5$ and $t_s = 31415$, then we wish to remove the high-order digit $T[s + 1] = 3$ and bring in the new low-order digit (suppose it is $T[s + 5 + 1] = 2$) to obtain

$$
\begin{aligned}
t_{s+1} &= 10(31415 - 10000 \cdot 3) + 2 \\
&= 14152 .
\end{aligned}
$$

Subtracting $10^{m-1}T[s+1]$ removes the high-order digit from t_s, multiplying the result by 10 shifts the number left one position, and adding $T[s + m + 1]$ brings in the appropriate low-order digit. If the constant 10^{m-1} is precomputed (which can be done in time $O(\lg m)$ using the techniques of Section 33.6, although for this application a straightforward $O(m)$ method is quite adequate), then each execution of equation (34.1) takes a constant number of arithmetic operations. Thus, p and $t_0, t_1, \ldots, t_{n-m}$ can all be computed in time $O(n + m)$, and we can find all occurrences of the pattern $P[1 .. m]$ in the text $T[1 .. n]$ in time $O(n + m)$.

The only difficulty with this procedure is that p and t_s may be too large to work with conveniently. If P contains m characters, then assuming that each arithmetic operation on p (which is m digits long) takes "constant time" is unreasonable. Fortunately, there is a simple cure for this problem, as shown in Figure 34.4: compute p and the t_s's modulo a suitable modulus q. Since the computation of p, t_0, and the recurrence (34.1) can all be performed modulo q, we see that p and all the t_s's can be computed modulo q in time $O(n + m)$. The modulus q is typically chosen as a prime such that $10q$ just fits within one computer word, which allows all of the necessary computations to be performed with single-precision arithmetic.

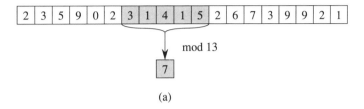

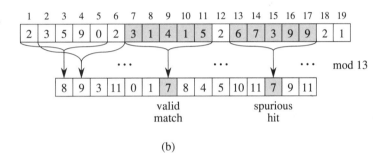

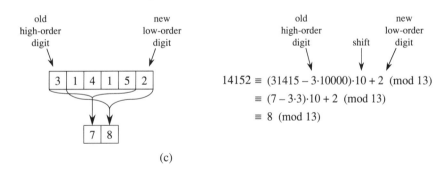

Figure 34.4 The Rabin-Karp algorithm. Each character is a decimal digit, and we compute values modulo 13. **(a)** A text string. A window of length 5 is shown shaded. The numerical value of the shaded number is computed modulo 13, yielding the value 7. **(b)** The same text string with values computed modulo 13 for each possible position of a length-5 window. Assuming the pattern $P = 31415$, we look for windows whose value modulo 13 is 7, since $31415 \equiv 7 \pmod{13}$. Two such windows are found, shown shaded in the figure. The first, beginning at text position 7, is indeed an occurrence of the pattern, while the second, beginning at text position 13, is a spurious hit. **(c)** Computing the value for a window in constant time, given the value for the previous window. The first window has value 31415. Dropping the high-order digit 3, shifting left (multiplying by 10), and then adding in the low-order digit 2 gives us the new value 14152. All computations are performed modulo 13, however, so the value for the first window is 7, and the value computed for the new window is 8.

In general, with a d-ary alphabet $\{0, 1, \ldots, d-1\}$, we choose q so that dq fits within a computer word and adjust the recurrence equation (34.1) to work modulo q, so that it becomes

$$t_{s+1} = (d(t_s - T[s+1]h) + T[s+m+1]) \bmod q , \qquad (34.2)$$

where $h \equiv d^{m-1} \pmod q$ is the value of the digit "1" in the high-order position of an m-digit text window.

The ointment of working modulo q now contains a fly, however, since $t_s \equiv p \pmod q$ does not imply that $t_s = p$. On the other hand, if $t_s \not\equiv p \pmod q$, then we definitely have that $t_s \neq p$, so that shift s is invalid. We can thus use the test $t_s \equiv p \pmod q$ as a fast heuristic test to rule out invalid shifts s. Any shift s for which $t_s \equiv p \pmod q$ must be tested further to see if s is really valid or we just have a ***spurious hit***. This testing can be done by explicitly checking the condition $P[1 .. m] = T[s+1 .. s+m]$. If q is large enough, then we can hope that spurious hits occur infrequently enough that the cost of the extra checking is low.

The following procedure makes these ideas precise. The inputs to the procedure are the text T, the pattern P, the radix d to use (which is typically taken to be $|\Sigma|$), and the prime q to use.

RABIN-KARP-MATCHER(T, P, d, q)

```
 1   n ← length[T]
 2   m ← length[P]
 3   h ← d^{m-1} mod q
 4   p ← 0
 5   t_0 ← 0
 6   for i ← 1 to m
 7       do p ← (dp + P[i]) mod q
 8           t_0 ← (dt_0 + T[i]) mod q
 9   for s ← 0 to n − m
10       do if p = t_s
11           then if P[1..m] = T[s+1..s+m]
12               then "Pattern occurs with shift" s
13           if s < n − m
14               then t_{s+1} ← (d(t_s − T[s+1]h) + T[s+m+1]) mod q
```

The procedure RABIN-KARP-MATCHER works as follows. All characters are interpreted as radix-d digits. The subscripts on t are provided only for clarity; the program works correctly if all the subscripts are dropped. Line 3 initializes h to the value of the high-order digit position of an m-digit window. Lines 4–8 compute p as the value of $P[1 .. m] \bmod q$ and t_0 as the value of $T[1 .. m] \bmod q$. The **for** loop beginning on line 9 iterates through all possible shifts s. The loop has the following invariant: whenever line 10 is executed, $t_s = T[s+1 .. s+m] \bmod q$. If $p = t_s$ in line 10 (a "hit"), then we check to see if $P[1 .. m] = T[s+1 .. s+m]$

in line 11 to rule out the possibility of a spurious hit. Any valid shifts found are printed out on line 12. If $s < n - m$ (checked in line 13), then the **for** loop is to be executed at least one more time, and so line 14 is first executed to ensure that the loop invariant holds when line 10 is again reached. Line 14 computes the value of $t_{s+1} \bmod q$ from the value of $t_s \bmod q$ in constant time using equation (34.2) directly.

The running time of RABIN-KARP-MATCHER is $\Theta((n - m + 1)m)$ in the worst case, since (like the naive string-matching algorithm) the Rabin-Karp algorithm explicitly verifies every valid shift. If $P = a^m$ and $T = a^n$, then the verifications take time $\Theta((n - m + 1)m)$, since each of the $n - m + 1$ possible shifts is valid. (Note also that the computation of $d^{m-1} \bmod q$ on line 3 and the loop on lines 6–8 take time $O(m) = O((n - m + 1)m)$.)

In many applications, we expect few valid shifts (perhaps $O(1)$ of them), and so the expected running time of the algorithm is $O(n + m)$ plus the time required to process spurious hits. We can base a heuristic analysis on the assumption that reducing values modulo q acts like a random mapping from Σ^* to $\mathbf{Z}_q$. (See the discussion on the use of division for hashing in Section 12.3.1. It is difficult to formalize and prove such an assumption, although one viable approach is to assume that q is chosen randomly from integers of the appropriate size. We shall not pursue this formalization here.) We can then expect that the number of spurious hits is $O(n/q)$, since the chance that an arbitrary t_s will be equivalent to p, modulo q, can be estimated as $1/q$. The expected amount of time taken by the Rabin-Karp algorithm is then

$$O(n) + O(m(v + n/q)) \, ,$$

where v is the number of valid shifts. This running time is $O(n)$ if we choose $q \geq m$. That is, if the expected number of valid shifts is small ($O(1)$) and the prime q is chosen to be larger than the length of the pattern, then we can expect the Rabin-Karp procedure to run in time $O(n + m)$.

Exercises

34.2-1
Working modulo $q = 11$, how many spurious hits does the Rabin-Karp matcher encounter in the text $T = 3141592653589793$ when looking for the pattern $P = 26$?

34.2-2
How would you extend the Rabin-Karp method to the problem of searching a text string for an occurrence of any one of a given set of k patterns?

34.2-3
Show how to extend the Rabin-Karp method to handle the problem of looking for a given $m \times m$ pattern in an $n \times n$ array of characters. (The

pattern may be shifted vertically and horizontally, but it may not be rotated.)

34.2-4

Alice has a copy of a long *n*-bit file $A = \langle a_{n-1}, a_{n-2}, \ldots, a_0 \rangle$, and Bob similarly has an *n*-bit file $B = \langle b_{n-1}, b_{n-2}, \ldots, b_0 \rangle$. Alice and Bob wish to know if their files are identical. To avoid transmitting all of A or B, they use the following fast probabilistic check. Together, they select a prime $q > 1000n$ and randomly select an integer x from $\{0, 1, \ldots, n-1\}$. Then, Alice evaluates

$$A(x) = \left(\sum_{i=0}^{n} a_i x^i \right) \bmod q$$

and Bob similarly evaluates $B(x)$. Prove that if $A \neq B$, there is at most one chance in 1000 that $A(x) = B(x)$, whereas if the two files are the same, $A(x)$ is necessarily the same as $B(x)$. (*Hint:* See Exercise 33.4-4.)

34.3   String matching with finite automata

Many string-matching algorithms build a finite automaton that scans the text string T for all occurrences of the pattern P. This section presents a method for building such an automaton. These string-matching automata are very efficient: they examine each text character *exactly once*, taking constant time per text character. The time used—after the automaton is built—is therefore $\Theta(n)$. The time to build the automaton, however, can be large if Σ is large. Section 34.4 describes a clever way around this problem.

We begin this section with the definition of a finite automaton. We then examine a special string-matching automaton and show how it can be used to find occurrences of a pattern in a text. This discussion includes details on how to simulate the behavior of a string-matching automaton on a given text. Finally, we shall show how to construct the string-matching automaton for a given input pattern.

Finite automata

A *finite automaton* M is a 5-tuple $(Q, q_0, A, \Sigma, \delta)$, where

- Q is a finite set of *states*,
- $q_0 \in Q$ is the *start state*,
- $A \subseteq Q$ is a distinguished set of *accepting states*,
- Σ is a finite *input alphabet*,
- δ is a function from $Q \times \Sigma$ into Q, called the *transition function* of M.

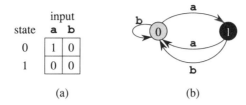

state	input a	b
0	1	0
1	0	0

(a)   (b)

Figure 34.5 A simple two-state finite automaton with state set $Q = \{0, 1\}$, start state $q_0 = 0$, and input alphabet $\Sigma = \{a, b\}$. **(a)** A tabular representation of the transition function δ. **(b)** An equivalent state-transition diagram. State 1 is the only accepting state (shown blackened). Directed edges represent transitions. For example, the edge from state 1 to state 0 labeled b indicates $\delta(1, b) = 0$. This automaton accepts those strings that end in an odd number of a's. More precisely, a string x is accepted if and only if $x = yz$, where $y = \varepsilon$ or y ends with a b, and $z = a^k$, where k is odd. For example, the sequence of states this automaton enters for input abaaa (including the start state) is $\langle 0, 1, 0, 1, 0, 1 \rangle$, and so it accepts this input. For input abbaa, the sequence of states is $\langle 0, 1, 0, 0, 1, 0 \rangle$, and so it rejects this input.

The finite automaton begins in state q_0 and reads the characters of its input string one at a time. If the automaton is in state q and reads input character a, it moves ("makes a transition") from state q to state $\delta(q, a)$. Whenever its current state q is a member of A, the machine M is said to have ***accepted*** the string read so far. An input that is not accepted is said to be ***rejected***. Figure 34.5 illustrates these definitions with a simple two-state automaton.

A finite automaton M induces a function ϕ, called the ***final-state function***, from Σ^* to Q such that $\phi(w)$ is the state M ends up in after scanning the string w. Thus, M accepts a string w if and only if $\phi(w) \in A$. The function ϕ is defined by the recursive relation

$$\phi(\varepsilon) = q_0 \,,$$
$$\phi(wa) = \delta(\phi(w), a) \qquad \text{for } w \in \Sigma^*, a \in \Sigma \,.$$

String-matching automata

There is a string-matching automaton for every pattern P; this automaton must be constructed from the pattern in a preprocessing step before it can be used to search the text string. Figure 34.6 illustrates this construction for the pattern $P = \text{ababaca}$. From now on, we shall assume that P is a given fixed pattern string; for brevity, we shall not indicate the dependence upon P in our notation.

In order to specify the string-matching automaton corresponding to a given pattern $P[1 \mathrel{..} m]$, we first define an auxiliary function σ, called the ***suffix function*** corresponding to P. The function σ is a mapping from Σ^* to $\{0, 1, \dots, m\}$ such that $\sigma(x)$ is the length of the longest prefix of P that is a suffix of x:

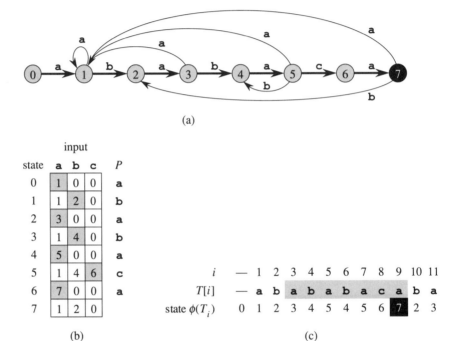

(a)

Figure 34.6 **(a)** A state-transition diagram for the string-matching automaton that accepts all strings ending in the string ababaca. State 0 is the start state, and state 7 (shown blackened) is the only accepting state. A directed edge from state i to state j labeled a represents $\delta(i, a) = j$. The right-going edges forming the "spine" of the automaton, shown heavy in the figure, correspond to successful matches between pattern and input characters. The left-going edges correspond to failing matches. Some edges corresponding to failing matches are not shown; by convention, if a state i has no outgoing edge labeled a for some $a \in \Sigma$, then $\delta(i, a) = 0$. **(b)** The corresponding transition function δ, and the pattern string $P =$ ababaca. The entries corresponding to successful matches between pattern and input characters are shown shaded. **(c)** The operation of the automaton on the text $T =$ abababacaba. Under each text character $T[i]$ is given the state $\phi(T_i)$ the automaton is in after processing the prefix T_i. One occurrence of the pattern is found, ending in position 9.

$$\sigma(x) = \max\{k : P_k \sqsupset x\} \ .$$

The suffix function σ is well defined since the empty string $P_0 = \varepsilon$ is a suffix of every string. As examples, for the pattern $P = \text{ab}$, we have $\sigma(\varepsilon) = 0$, $\sigma(\text{ccaca}) = 1$, and $\sigma(\text{ccab}) = 2$. For a pattern P of length m, we have $\sigma(x) = m$ if and only if $P \sqsupset x$. It follows from the definition of the suffix function that if $x \sqsupset y$, then $\sigma(x) \le \sigma(y)$.

We define the string-matching automaton corresponding to a given pattern $P[1 .. m]$ as follows.

- The state set Q is $\{0, 1, \ldots, m\}$. The start state q_0 is state 0, and state m is the only accepting state.

- The transition function δ is defined by the following equation, for any state q and character a:

$$\delta(q, a) = \sigma(P_q a) \ . \tag{34.3}$$

Here is an intuitive rationale for defining $\delta(q, a) = \sigma(P_q a)$. The machine maintains as an invariant of its operation that

$$\phi(T_i) = \sigma(T_i) \ ; \tag{34.4}$$

this result is proved as Theorem 34.4 below. In words, this means that after scanning the first i characters of the text string T, the machine is in state $\phi(T_i) = q$, where $q = \sigma(T_i)$ is the length of the longest suffix of T_i that is also a prefix of the pattern P. If the next character scanned is $T[i+1] = a$, then the machine should make a transition to state $\sigma(T_{i+1}) = \sigma(T_i a)$. The proof of the theorem shows that $\sigma(T_i a) = \sigma(P_q a)$. That is, to compute the length of the longest suffix of $T_i a$ that is a prefix of P, we can compute the longest suffix of $P_q a$ that is a prefix of P. At each state, the machine only needs to know the length of the longest prefix of P that is a suffix of what has been read so far. Therefore, setting $\delta(q, a) = \sigma(P_q a)$ maintains the desired invariant (34.4). This informal argument will be made rigorous shortly.

In the string-matching automaton of Figure 34.6, for example, we have $\delta(5, \text{b}) = 4$. This follows from the fact that if the automaton reads a b in state $q = 5$, then $P_q \text{b} = \text{ababab}$, and the longest prefix of P that is also a suffix of ababab is $P_4 = \text{abab}$.

To clarify the operation of a string-matching automaton, we now give a simple, efficient program for simulating the behavior of such an automaton (represented by its transition function δ) in finding occurrences of a pattern P of length m in an input text $T[1 .. n]$. As for any string-matching automaton for a pattern of length m, the state set Q is $\{0, 1, \ldots, m\}$, the start state is 0, and the only accepting state is state m.

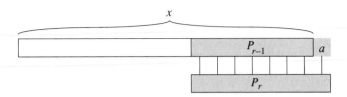

Figure 34.7   An illustration for the proof of Lemma 34.2. The figure shows that $r \leq \sigma(x) + 1$, where $r = \sigma(xa)$.

FINITE-AUTOMATON-MATCHER(T, δ, m)

```
1   n ← length[T]
2   q ← 0
3   for i ← 1 to n
4       do q ← δ(q, T[i])
5          if q = m
6             then s ← i − m
7                  print "Pattern occurs with shift" s
```

The simple loop structure of FINITE-AUTOMATON-MATCHER implies that its running time on a text string of length n is $O(n)$. This running time, however, does not include the time required to compute the transition function δ. We address this problem later, after proving that the procedure FINITE-AUTOMATON-MATCHER operates correctly.

Consider the operation of the automaton on an input text $T[1 .. n]$. We shall prove that the automaton is in state $\sigma(T_i)$ after scanning character $T[i]$. Since $\sigma(T_i) = m$ if and only if $P \sqsupset T_i$, the machine is in the accepting state m if and only if the pattern P has just been scanned. To prove this result, we make use of the following two lemmas about the suffix function σ.

Lemma 34.2 (Suffix-function inequality)
For any string x and character a, we have $\sigma(xa) \leq \sigma(x) + 1$.

Proof   Referring to Figure 34.7, let $r = \sigma(xa)$. If $r = 0$, then the conclusion $r \leq \sigma(x) + 1$ is trivially satisfied, by the nonnegativity of $\sigma(x)$. So assume that $r > 0$. Now, $P_r \sqsupset xa$, by the definition of σ. Thus, $P_{r-1} \sqsupset x$, by dropping the a from the end of P_r and from the end of xa. Therefore, $r - 1 \leq \sigma(x)$, since $\sigma(x)$ is largest k such that $P_k \sqsupset x$.   ∎

Lemma 34.3 (Suffix-function recursion lemma)
For any string x and character a, if $q = \sigma(x)$, then $\sigma(xa) = \sigma(P_q a)$.

Proof   From the definition of σ, we have $P_q \sqsupset x$. As Figure 34.8 shows, $P_q a \sqsupset xa$. If we let $r = \sigma(xa)$, then $r \leq q + 1$ by Lemma 34.2. Since

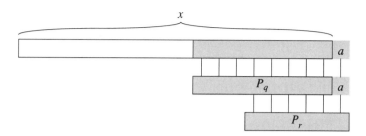

Figure 34.8 An illustration for the proof of Lemma 34.3. The figure shows that $r = \sigma(P_q a)$, where $q = \sigma(x)$ and $r = \sigma(xa)$.

$P_q a \sqsupset xa$, $P_r \sqsupset xa$, and $|P_r| \leq |P_q a|$, Lemma 34.1 implies that $P_r \sqsupset P_q a$. Therefore, $r \leq \sigma(P_q a)$, that is, $\sigma(xa) \leq \sigma(P_q a)$. But we also have $\sigma(P_q a) \leq \sigma(xa)$, since $P_q a \sqsupset xa$. Thus, $\sigma(xa) = \sigma(P_q a)$. ∎

We are now ready to prove our main theorem characterizing the behavior of a string-matching automaton on a given input text. As noted above, this theorem shows that the automaton is merely keeping track, at each step, of the longest prefix of the pattern that is a suffix of what has been read so far.

Theorem 34.4
If ϕ is the final-state function of a string-matching automaton for a given pattern P and $T[1..n]$ is an input text for the automaton, then

$$\phi(T_i) = \sigma(T_i)$$

for $i = 0, 1, \ldots, n$.

Proof The proof is by induction on i. For $i = 0$, the theorem is trivially true, since $T_0 = \varepsilon$. Thus, $\phi(T_0) = \sigma(T_0) = 0$.

Now, we assume that $\phi(T_i) = \sigma(T_i)$ and prove that $\phi(T_{i+1}) = \sigma(T_{i+1})$. Let q denote $\phi(T_i)$, and let a denote $T[i+1]$. Then,

$$
\begin{aligned}
\phi(T_{i+1}) &= \phi(T_i a) && \text{(by the definitions of } T_{i+1} \text{ and } a) \\
&= \delta(\phi(T_i), a) && \text{(by the definition of } \phi) \\
&= \delta(q, a) && \text{(by the definition of } q) \\
&= \sigma(P_q a) && \text{(by the definition (34.3) of } \delta) \\
&= \sigma(T_i a) && \text{(by Lemma 34.3 and induction)} \\
&= \sigma(T_{i+1}) && \text{(by the definition of } T_{i+1}) .
\end{aligned}
$$

By induction, the theorem is proved. ∎

By Theorem 34.4, if the machine enters state q on line 4, then q is the largest value such that $P_q \sqsupset T_i$. Thus, we have $q = m$ on line 5 if and only if an occurrence of the pattern P has just been scanned. We conclude that Finite-Automaton-Matcher operates correctly.

Computing the transition function

The following procedure computes the transition function δ from a given pattern $P[1 \ldots m]$.

COMPUTE-TRANSITION-FUNCTION(P, Σ)

```
1  m ← length[P]
2  for q ← 0 to m
3       do for each character a ∈ Σ
4              do k ← min(m + 1, q + 2)
5                 repeat k ← k - 1
6                 until Pₖ ⊐ Pqa
7                 δ(q, a) ← k
8  return δ
```

This procedure computes $\delta(q, a)$ in a straightforward manner according to its definition. The nested loops beginning on lines 2 and 3 consider all states q and characters a, and lines 4–7 set $\delta(q, a)$ to be the largest k such that $P_k \sqsupset P_q a$. The code starts with the largest conceivable value of k, which is $\min(m, q + 1)$, and decreases k until $P_k \sqsupset P_q a$.

The running time of COMPUTE-TRANSITION-FUNCTION is $O(m^3 |\Sigma|)$, because the outer loops contribute a factor of $m |\Sigma|$, the inner **repeat** loop can run at most $m + 1$ times, and the test $P_k \sqsupset P_q a$ on line 6 can require comparing up to m characters. Much faster procedures exist; the time required to compute δ from P can be improved to $O(m |\Sigma|)$ by utilizing some cleverly computed information about the pattern P (see Exercise 34.4-6). With this improved procedure for computing δ, the total running time to find all occurrences of a length-m pattern in a length-n text over an alphabet Σ is $O(n + m |\Sigma|)$.

Exercises

34.3-1
Construct the string-matching automaton for the pattern $P = \text{aabab}$ and illustrate its operation on the text string $T = \text{aaababaabaababaab}$.

34.3-2
Draw a state-transition diagram for a string-matching automaton for the pattern ababbabbababbabbabb over the alphabet $\Sigma = \{a, b\}$.

34.3-3
We call a pattern P **nonoverlappable** if $P_k \sqsupset P_q$ implies $k = 0$ or $k = q$. Describe the state-transition diagram of the string-matching automaton for a nonoverlappable pattern.

34.3-4 ⋆

Given two patterns P and P', describe how to construct a finite automaton that determines all occurrences of *either* pattern. Try to minimize the number of states in your automaton.

34.3-5

Given a pattern P containing gap characters (see Exercise 34.1-5), show how to build a finite automaton that can find an occurrence of P in a text T in $O(n)$ time, where $n = |T|$.

34.4 The Knuth-Morris-Pratt algorithm

We now present a linear-time string-matching algorithm due to Knuth, Morris, and Pratt. Their algorithm achieves a $\Theta(n + m)$ running time by avoiding the computation of the transition function δ altogether, and it does the pattern matching using just an auxiliary function $\pi[1 .. m]$ precomputed from the pattern in time $O(m)$. The array π allows the transition function δ to be computed efficiently (in an amortized sense) "on the fly" as needed. Roughly speaking, for any state $q = 0, 1, \ldots, m$ and any character $a \in \Sigma$, the value $\pi[q]$ contains the information that is independent of a and is needed to compute $\delta(q, a)$. (This remark will be clarified shortly.) Since the array π has only m entries, whereas δ has $O(m\,|\Sigma|)$ entries, we save a factor of Σ in the preprocessing by computing π rather than δ.

The prefix function for a pattern

The prefix function for a pattern encapsulates knowledge about how the pattern matches against shifts of itself. This information can be used to avoid testing useless shifts in the naive pattern-matching algorithm or to avoid the precomputation of δ for a string-matching automaton.

Consider the operation of the naive string matcher. Figure 34.9(a) shows a particular shift s of a template containing the pattern $P = \text{ababaca}$ against a text T. For this example, $q = 5$ of the characters have matched successfully, but the 6th pattern character fails to match the corresponding text character. The information that q characters have matched successfully determines the corresponding text characters. Knowing these q text characters allows us to determine immediately that certain shifts are invalid. In the example of the figure, the shift $s + 1$ is necessarily invalid, since the first pattern character, an a, would be aligned with a text character that is known to match with the second pattern character, a b. The shift $s + 2$ shown in part (b) of the figure, however, aligns the first three pattern characters with three text characters that must necessarily match. In general, it is useful to know the answer to the following question:

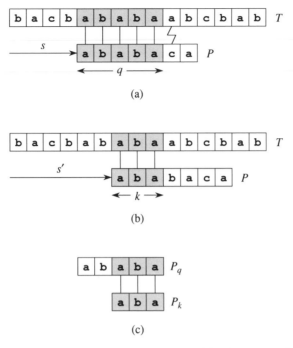

Figure 34.9 The prefix function π. **(a)** The pattern $P =$ ababaca is aligned with a text T so that the first $q = 5$ characters match. Matching characters, shown shaded, are connected by vertical lines. **(b)** Using only our knowledge of the 5 matched characters, we can deduce that a shift of $s + 1$ is invalid, but that a shift of $s' = s + 2$ is consistent with everything we know about the text and therefore is potentially valid. **(c)** The useful information for such deductions can be precomputed by comparing the pattern with itself. Here, we see that the longest prefix of P that is also a suffix of P_5 is P_3. This information is precomputed and represented in the array π, so that $\pi[5] = 3$. Given that q characters have matched successfully at shift s, the next potentially valid shift is at $s' = s + (q - \pi[q])$.

Given that pattern characters $P[1 \mathinner{.\,.} q]$ match text characters $T[s + 1 \mathinner{.\,.} s + q]$, what is the least shift $s' > s$ such that

$$P[1 \mathinner{.\,.} k] = T[s' + 1 \mathinner{.\,.} s' + k] \,, \tag{34.5}$$

where $s' + k = s + q$?

Such a shift s' is the first shift greater than s that is not necessarily invalid due to our knowledge of $T[s + 1 \mathinner{.\,.} s + q]$. In the best case, we have that $s' = s + q$, and shifts $s + 1, s + 2, \ldots, s + q - 1$ are all immediately ruled out. In any case, at the new shift s' we don't need to compare the first k characters of P with the corresponding characters of T, since we are guaranteed that they match by equation (34.5).

The necessary information can be precomputed by comparing the pattern against itself, as illustrated in Figure 34.9(c). Since $T[s' + 1 \mathinner{.\,.} s' + k]$ is part of the known portion of the text, it is a suffix of the string P_q. Equation (34.5) can therefore be interpreted as asking for the largest $k < q$

such that $P_k \sqsupset P_q$. Then, $s' = s + (q - k)$ is the next potentially valid shift. It turns out to be convenient to store the number k of matching characters at the new shift s', rather than storing, say, $s' - s$. This information can be used to speed up both the naive string-matching algorithm and the finite-automaton matcher.

We formalize the precomputation required as follows. Given a pattern $P[1..m]$, the **prefix function** for the pattern P is the function $\pi : \{1, 2, \ldots, m\} \to \{0, 1, \ldots, m-1\}$ such that

$$\pi[q] = \max \{k : k < q \text{ and } P_k \sqsupset P_q\} \ .$$

That is, $\pi[q]$ is the length of the longest prefix of P that is a proper suffix of P_q. As another example, Figure 34.10(a) gives the complete prefix function π for the pattern abababca.

The Knuth-Morris-Pratt matching algorithm is given in pseudocode below as the procedure KMP-MATCHER. It is mostly modeled after FINITE-AUTOMATON-MATCHER, as we shall see. KMP-MATCHER calls the auxiliary procedure COMPUTE-PREFIX-FUNCTION to compute π.

KMP-MATCHER(T, P)

```
 1   n ← length[T]
 2   m ← length[P]
 3   π ← COMPUTE-PREFIX-FUNCTION(P)
 4   q ← 0
 5   for i ← 1 to n
 6       do while q > 0 and P[q + 1] ≠ T[i]
 7              do q ← π[q]
 8          if P[q + 1] = T[i]
 9             then q ← q + 1
10          if q = m
11             then print "Pattern occurs with shift" i − m
12                 q ← π[q]
```

COMPUTE-PREFIX-FUNCTION(P)

```
 1   m ← length[P]
 2   π[1] ← 0
 3   k ← 0
 4   for q ← 2 to m
 5       do while k > 0 and P[k + 1] ≠ P[q]
 6              do k ← π[k]
 7          if P[k + 1] = P[q]
 8             then k ← k + 1
 9          π[q] ← k
10   return π
```

We begin with an analysis of the running times of these procedures. Proving these procedures correct will be more complicated.

Running-time analysis

The running time of COMPUTE-PREFIX-FUNCTION is $O(m)$, using an amortized analysis (see Chapter 18). We associate a potential of k with the current state k of the algorithm. This potential has an initial value of 0, by line 3. Line 6 decreases k whenever it is executed, since $\pi[k] < k$. Since $\pi[k] \geq 0$ for all k, however, k can never become negative. The only other line that affects k is line 8, which increases k by at most one during each execution of the **for** loop body. Since $k < q$ upon entering the **for** loop, and since q is incremented in each iteration of the **for** loop body, $k < q$ always holds. (This justifies the claim that $\pi[q] < q$ as well, by line 9.) We can pay for each execution of the **while** loop body on line 6 with the corresponding decrease in the potential function, since $\pi[k] < k$. Line 8 increases the potential function by at most one, so that the amortized cost of the loop body on lines 5–9 is $O(1)$. Since the number of outer-loop iterations is $O(m)$, and since the final potential function is at least as great as the initial potential function, the total actual worst-case running time of COMPUTE-PREFIX-FUNCTION is $O(m)$.

The Knuth-Morris-Pratt algorithm runs in time $O(m + n)$. The call of COMPUTE-PREFIX-FUNCTION takes $O(m)$ time as we have just seen, and a similar amortized analysis, using the value of q as the potential function, shows that the remainder of KMP-MATCHER takes $O(n)$ time.

Compared to FINITE-AUTOMATON-MATCHER, by using π rather than δ, we have reduced the time for preprocessing the pattern from $O(m |\Sigma|)$ to $O(m)$, while keeping the actual matching time bounded by $O(m + n)$.

Correctness of the prefix-function computation

We start with an essential lemma showing that by iterating the prefix function π, we can enumerate all the prefixes P_k that are suffixes of a given prefix P_q. Let

$$\pi^*[q] = \{q, \pi[q], \pi^2[q], \pi^3[q], \ldots, \pi^t[q]\} \,,$$

where $\pi^i[q]$ is defined in terms of functional composition, so that $\pi^0[q] = q$ and $\pi^{i+1}[q] = \pi[\pi^i[q]]$ for $i > 1$, and where it is understood that the sequence in $\pi^*[q]$ stops when $\pi^t[q] = 0$ is reached.

Lemma 34.5 (Prefix-function iteration lemma)

Let P be a pattern of length m with prefix function π. Then, for $q = 1, 2, \ldots, m$, we have $\pi^*[q] = \{k : P_k \sqsupset P_q\}$.

Proof   We first prove that

$$i \in \pi^*[q] \text{ implies } P_i \sqsupset P_q \,. \tag{34.6}$$

If $i \in \pi^*[q]$, then $i = \pi^u[q]$ for some u. We prove equation (34.6) by induction on u. For $u = 0$, we have $i = q$, and the claim follows since

i	1	2	3	4	5	6	7	8	9	10
$P[i]$	a	b	a	b	a	b	a	b	c	a
$\pi[i]$	0	0	1	2	3	4	5	6	0	1

(a)

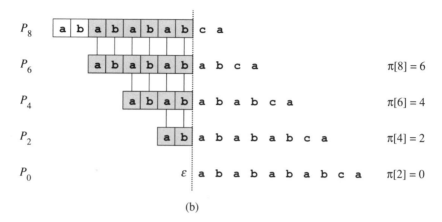

(b)

Figure 34.10   An illustration of Lemma 34.5 for the pattern $P = $ ababababca and $q = 8$. **(a)** The π function for the given pattern. Since $\pi[8] = 6$, $\pi[6] = 4$, $\pi[4] = 2$, and $\pi[2] = 0$, by iterating π we obtain $\pi^*[8] = \{8, 6, 4, 2, 0\}$. **(b)** We slide the template containing the pattern P to the right and note when some prefix P_k of P matches up with some proper suffix of P_8; this happens for $k = 6, 4, 2$, and 0. In the figure, the first row gives P, and the dotted vertical line is drawn just after P_8. Successive rows show all the shifts of P that cause some prefix P_k of P to match some suffix of P_8. Successfully matched characters are shown shaded. Vertical lines connect aligned matching characters. Thus, $\{k : P_k \sqsupset P_q\} = \{8, 6, 4, 2, 0\}$. The lemma claims that $\pi^*[q] = \{k : P_k \sqsupset P_q\}$ for all q.

$P_q \sqsupset P_q$. Using the relation $P_{\pi[i]} \sqsupset P_i$ and the transitivity of $\sqsupset$ establishes the claim for all i in $\pi^*[q]$. Therefore, $\pi^*[q] \subseteq \{k : P_k \sqsupset P_q\}$.

We prove that $\{k : P_k \sqsupset P_q\} \subseteq \pi^*[q]$ by contradiction. Suppose to the contrary that there is an integer in the set $\{k : P_k \sqsupset P_q\} - \pi^*[q]$, and let j be the largest such value. Because q is in $\{k : P_k \sqsupset P_q\} \cap \pi^*[q]$, we have $j < q$, and so we let j' denote the smallest integer in $\pi^*[q]$ that is greater than j. (We can choose $j' = q$ if there is no other number in $\pi^*[q]$ that is greater than j.) We have $P_j \sqsupset P_q$ because $j \in \{k : P_k \sqsupset P_q\}$, $P_{j'} \sqsupset P_q$ because $j' \in \pi^*[q]$; thus, $P_j \sqsupset P_{j'}$ by Lemma 34.1. Moreover, j is the largest such value with this property. Therefore, we must have $\pi[j'] = j$ and thus $j \in \pi^*[q]$. This contradiction proves the lemma.   ∎

Figure 34.10 illustrates this lemma.

The algorithm COMPUTE-PREFIX-FUNCTION computes $\pi[q]$ in order for $q = 1, 2, \ldots, m$. The computation of $\pi[1] = 0$ in line 2 of COMPUTE-PREFIX-FUNCTION is certainly correct, since $\pi[q] < q$ for all q. The following lemma and its corollary will be used to prove that COMPUTE-PREFIX-FUNCTION computes $\pi[q]$ correctly for $q > 1$.

Lemma 34.6

Let P be a pattern of length m, and let π be the prefix function for P. For $q = 1, 2, \ldots, m$, if $\pi[q] > 0$, then $\pi[q] - 1 \in \pi^*[q - 1]$.

Proof   If $k = \pi[q] > 0$, then $P_k \sqsupset P_q$, and thus $P_{k-1} \sqsupset P_{q-1}$ (by dropping the last character from P_k and P_q). By Lemma 34.5, therefore, $k - 1 \in \pi^*[q - 1]$.   ∎

For $q = 2, 3, \ldots, m$, define the subset $E_{q-1} \subseteq \pi^*[q - 1]$ by

$$E_{q-1} = \{k : k \in \pi^*[q - 1] \text{ and } P[k + 1] = P[q]\} \ .$$

The set E_{q-1} consists of the values k for which $P_k \sqsupset P_{q-1}$ (by Lemma 34.5); because $P[k + 1] = P[q]$, it is also the case that for these values of k, $P_{k+1} \sqsupset P_q$. Intuitively, E_{q-1} consists of those values $k \in \pi^*[q - 1]$ such that we can extend P_k to P_{k+1} and get a suffix of P_q.

Corollary 34.7

Let P be a pattern of length m, and let π be the prefix function for P. For $q = 2, 3, \ldots, m$,

$$\pi[q] = \begin{cases} 0 & \text{if } E_{q-1} = \emptyset \ , \\ 1 + \max\{k \in E_{q-1}\} & \text{if } E_{q-1} \neq \emptyset \ . \end{cases}$$

Proof   If $r = \pi[q]$, then $P_r \sqsupset P_q$, and so $r \geq 1$ implies $P[r] = P[q]$. By Lemma 34.6, therefore, if $r \geq 1$, then

$$r = 1 + \max\{k \in \pi^*[q - 1] : P[k + 1] = P[q]\} \ .$$

But the set maximized over is just E_{q-1}, so that $r = 1 + \max\{k \in E_{q-1}\}$ and E_{q-1} is nonempty. If $r = 0$, there is no $k \in \pi^*[q - 1]$ for which we can extend P_k to P_{k+1} and get a suffix of P_q, since then we would have $\pi[q] > 0$. Thus, $E_{q-1} = \emptyset$.   ∎

We now finish the proof that COMPUTE-PREFIX-FUNCTION computes π correctly. In the procedure COMPUTE-PREFIX-FUNCTION, at the start of each iteration of the **for** loop of lines 4–9, we have that $k = \pi[q - 1]$. This condition is enforced by lines 2 and 3 when the loop is first entered, and it remains true in each successive iteration because of line 9. Lines 5–8 adjust k so that it now becomes the correct value of $\pi[q]$. The loop on lines 5–6 searches through all values $k \in \pi^*[q - 1]$ until one is found for which $P[k + 1] = P[q]$; at that point, we have that k is the largest value in the set E_{q-1}, so that, by Corollary 34.7, we can set $\pi[q]$ to $k + 1$. If no such k is found, $k = 0$ in lines 7–9, and $\pi[q]$ is set to 0. This completes our proof of the correctness of COMPUTE-PREFIX-FUNCTION.

Correctness of the KMP algorithm

The procedure KMP-MATCHER can be viewed as a reimplementation of the procedure FINITE-AUTOMATON-MATCHER. Specifically, we shall prove that the code on lines 6–9 of KMP-MATCHER is equivalent to line 4 of FINITE-AUTOMATON-MATCHER, which sets q to $\delta(q, T[i])$. Instead of using a stored value of $\delta(q, T[i])$, however, this value is recomputed as necessary from π. Once we have argued that KMP-MATCHER simulates the behavior of FINITE-AUTOMATON-MATCHER, the correctness of KMP-MATCHER follows from the correctness of FINITE-AUTOMATON-MATCHER (though we shall see in a moment why line 12 in KMP-MATCHER is necessary).

The correctness of KMP-MATCHER follows from the claim that either $\delta(q, T[i]) = 0$ or else $\delta(q, T[i]) - 1 \in \pi^*[q]$. To check this claim, let $k = \delta(q, T[i])$. Then, $P_k \sqsupset P_q T[i]$ by the definitions of δ and σ. Therefore, either $k = 0$ or else $k \geq 1$ and $P_{k-1} \sqsupset P_q$ by dropping the last character from both P_k and $P_q T[i]$ (in which case $k - 1 \in \pi^*[q]$). Therefore, either $k = 0$ or $k - 1 \in \pi^*[q]$, proving the claim.

The claim is used as follows. Let q' denote the value of q when line 6 is entered. We use the equivalence $\pi^*[q] = \{k : P_k \sqsupset P_q\}$ to justify the iteration $q \leftarrow \pi[q]$ that enumerates the elements of $\{k : P_k \sqsupset P_{q'}\}$. Lines 6–9 determine $\delta(q', T[i])$ by examining the elements of $\pi^*[q']$ in decreasing order. The code uses the claim to begin with $q = \phi(T_{i-1}) = \sigma(T_{i-1})$ and perform the iteration $q \leftarrow \pi[q]$ until a q is found such that $q = 0$ or $P[q+1] = T[i]$. In the former case, $\delta(q', T[i]) = 0$; in the latter case, q is the maximum element in $E_{q'}$, so that $\delta(q', T[i]) = q + 1$ by Corollary 34.7.

Line 12 is necessary in KMP-MATCHER to avoid a possible reference to $P[m+1]$ on line 6 after an occurrence of P has been found. (The argument that $q = \sigma(T_{i-1})$ upon the next execution of line 6 remains valid by the hint given in Exercise 34.4-6: $\delta(m, a) = \delta(\pi[m], a)$ or, equivalently, $\sigma(Pa) = \sigma(P_{\pi[m]}a)$ for any $a \in \Sigma$.) The remaining argument for the correctness of the Knuth-Morris-Pratt algorithm follows from the correctness of FINITE-AUTOMATON-MATCHER, since we now see that KMP-MATCHER simulates the behavior of FINITE-AUTOMATON-MATCHER.

Exercises

34.4-1
Compute the prefix function π for the pattern ababbabbababbababbabb when the alphabet is $\Sigma = \{a, b\}$.

34.4-2
Give an upper bound on the size of $\pi^*[q]$ as a function of q. Give an example to show that your bound is tight.

34.4-3
Explain how to determine the occurrences of pattern P in the text T by examining the π function for the string PT (the string of length $m + n$ that is the concatenation of P and T).

34.4-4
Show how to improve KMP-MATCHER by replacing the occurrence of π in line 7 (but not line 12) by π', where π' is defined recursively for $q = 1, 2, \ldots, m$ by the equation

$$\pi'[q] = \begin{cases} 0 & \text{if } \pi[q] = 0 \text{ ,} \\ \pi'[\pi[q]] & \text{if } \pi[q] \neq 0 \text{ and } P[\pi[q] + 1] = P[q + 1] \text{ ,} \\ \pi[q] & \text{if } \pi[q] \neq 0 \text{ and } P[\pi[q] + 1] \neq P[q + 1] \text{ .} \end{cases}$$

Explain why the modified algorithm is correct, and explain in what sense this modification constitutes an improvement.

34.4-5
Give a linear-time algorithm to determine if a text T is a cyclic rotation of another string T'. For example, arc and car are cyclic rotations of each other.

34.4-6 ⋆
Give an efficient algorithm for computing the transition function δ for the string-matching automaton corresponding to a given pattern P. Your algorithm should run in time $O(m \, |\Sigma|)$. (*Hint:* Prove that $\delta(q, a) = \delta(\pi[q], a)$ if $q = m$ or $P[q + 1] \neq a$.)

⋆ 34.5   The Boyer-Moore algorithm

If the pattern P is relatively long and the alphabet Σ is reasonably large, then an algorithm due to Robert S. Boyer and J. Strother Moore is likely to be the most efficient string-matching algorithm.

BOYER-MOORE-MATCHER(T, P, Σ)

```
 1   n ← length[T]
 2   m ← length[P]
 3   λ ← COMPUTE-LAST-OCCURRENCE-FUNCTION(P, m, Σ)
 4   γ ← COMPUTE-GOOD-SUFFIX-FUNCTION(P, m)
 5   s ← 0
 6   while s ≤ n − m
 7       do j ← m
 8          while j > 0 and P[j] = T[s + j]
 9              do j ← j − 1
10          if j = 0
11             then print "Pattern occurs at shift" s
12                  s ← s + γ[0]
13             else s ← s + max(γ[j], j − λ[T[s + j]])
```

Aside from the mysterious-looking λ's and γ's, this program looks remarkably like the naive string-matching algorithm. Indeed, suppose we comment out lines 3–4 and replace the updating of s on lines 12–13 with simple incrementations as follows:

```
12                  s ← s + 1
13             else s ← s + 1
```

The modified program now acts exactly like the naive string matcher: the **while** loop beginning on line 6 considers each of the $n - m + 1$ possible shifts s in turn, and the **while** loop beginning on line 8 tests the condition $P[1 . . m] = T[s + 1 . . s + m]$ by comparing $P[j]$ with $T[s + j]$ for $j = m, m - 1, \ldots, 1$. If the loop terminates with $j = 0$, a valid shift s has been found, and line 11 prints out the value of s. At this level, the only remarkable features of the Boyer-Moore algorithm are that it compares the pattern against the text *from right to left* and that it increases the shift s on lines 12–13 by a value that is not necessarily 1.

The Boyer-Moore algorithm incorporates two heuristics that allow it to avoid much of the work that our previous string-matching algorithms performed. These heuristics are so effective that they often allow the algorithm to skip altogether the examination of many text characters. These heuristics, known as the "bad-character heuristic" and the "good-suffix heuristic," are illustrated in Figure 34.11. They can be viewed as operating independently in parallel. When a mismatch occurs, each heuristic proposes an amount by which s can safely be increased without missing a valid shift. The Boyer-Moore algorithm chooses the larger amount and increases s by that amount: when line 13 is reached after a mismatch, the bad-character heuristic proposes increasing s by $j - \lambda[T[s + j]]$, and the good-suffix heuristic proposes increasing s by $\gamma[j]$.

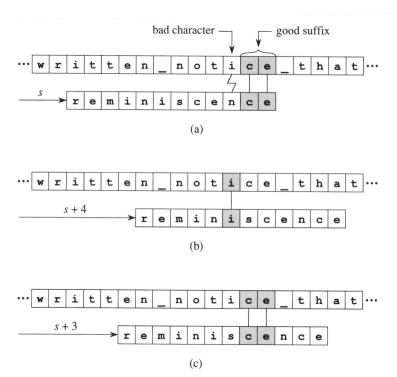

Figure 34.11 An illustration of the Boyer-Moore heuristics. **(a)** Matching the pattern reminiscence against a text by comparing characters in a right-to-left manner. The shift s is invalid; although a "good suffix" ce of the pattern matched correctly against the corresponding characters in the text (matching characters are shown shaded), the "bad character" i, which didn't match the corresponding character n in the pattern, was discovered in the text. **(b)** The bad-character heuristic proposes moving the pattern to the right, if possible, by the amount that guarantees that the bad text character will match the rightmost occurrence of the bad character in the pattern. In this example, moving the pattern 4 positions to the right causes the bad text character i in the text to match the rightmost i in the pattern, at position 6. If the bad character doesn't occur in the pattern, then the pattern may be moved completely past the bad character in the text. If the rightmost occurrence of the bad character in the pattern is to the right of the current bad character position, then this heuristic makes no proposal. **(c)** With the good-suffix heuristic, the pattern is moved to the right by the least amount that guarantees that any pattern characters that align with the good suffix ce previously found in the text will match those suffix characters. In this example, moving the pattern 3 positions to the right satisfies this condition. Since the good-suffix heuristic proposes a movement of 3 positions, which is smaller than the 4-position proposal of the bad-character heuristic, the Boyer-Moore algorithm increases the shift by 4.

The bad-character heuristic

When a mismatch occurs, the bad-character heuristic uses information about where the bad text character $T[s + j]$ occurs in the pattern (if it occurs at all) to propose a new shift. In the best case, the mismatch occurs on the first comparison ($P[m] \neq T[s + m]$) and the bad character $T[s + m]$ does not occur in the pattern at all. (Imagine searching for a^m in the text string b^n.) In this case, we can increase the shift s by m, since any shift smaller than $s + m$ will align some pattern character against the bad character, causing a mismatch. If the best case occurs repeatedly, the Boyer-Moore algorithm examines only a fraction $1/m$ of the text characters, since each text character examined yields a mismatch, thus causing s to increase by m. This best-case behavior illustrates the power of matching right-to-left instead of left-to-right.

In general, the ***bad-character heuristic*** works as follows. Suppose we have just found a mismatch: $P[j] \neq T[s + j]$ for some j, where $1 \leq j \leq m$. We then let k be the largest index in the range $1 \leq k \leq m$ such that $T[s + j] = P[k]$, if any such k exists. Otherwise, we let $k = 0$. We claim that we may safely increase s by $j - k$. We must consider three cases to prove this claim, as illustrated by Figure 34.12.

- $k = 0$: As shown in Figure 34.12(a), the bad character $T[s + j]$ didn't occur in the pattern at all, and so we can safely increase s by j without missing any valid shifts.

- $k < j$: As shown in Figure 34.12(b), the rightmost occurrence of the bad character is in the pattern to the left of position j, so that $j - k > 0$ and the pattern must be moved $j - k$ characters to the right before the bad text character matches any pattern character. Therefore, we can safely increase s by $j - k$ without missing any valid shifts.

- $k > j$: As shown in Figure 34.12(c), $j - k < 0$, and so the bad-character heuristic is essentially proposing to decrease s. This recommendation will be ignored by the Boyer-Moore algorithm, since the good-suffix heuristic will propose a shift to the right in all cases.

The following simple program defines $\lambda[a]$ to be the index of the rightmost position in the pattern at which character a occurs, for each $a \in \Sigma$. If a does not occur in the pattern, then $\lambda[a]$ is set to 0. We call λ the ***last-occurrence function*** for the pattern. With this definition, the expression $j - \lambda[T[s + j]]$ on line 13 of Boyer-Moore Matcher implements the bad-character heuristic. (Since $j - \lambda[T[s + j]]$ is negative if the rightmost occurrence of the bad character $T[s + j]$ in the pattern is to the right of position j, we rely on the positivity of $\gamma[j]$, proposed by the good-suffix heuristic, to ensure that the algorithm makes progress at each step.)

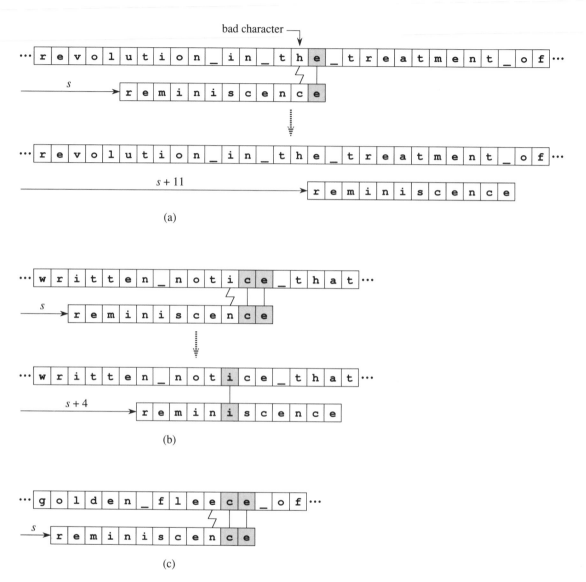

Figure 34.12 The cases of the bad-character heuristic. **(a)** The bad character h occurs nowhere in the pattern, and so the pattern can be advanced $j = 11$ characters until it has passed over the bad character. **(b)** The rightmost occurrence of the bad character in the pattern is at position $k < j$, and so the pattern can be advanced $j - k$ characters. Since $j = 10$ and $k = 6$ for the bad character i, the pattern can be advanced 4 positions until the i's line up. **(c)** The rightmost occurrence of the bad character in the pattern is at position $k > j$. In this example, $j = 10$ and $k = 12$ for the bad character e. The bad-character heuristic proposes a negative shift, which is ignored.

COMPUTE-LAST-OCCURRENCE-FUNCTION(P, m, Σ)

```
1  for each character a ∈ Σ
2      do λ[a] = 0
3  for j ← 1 to m
4      do λ[P[j]] ← j
5  return λ
```

The running time of procedure COMPUTE-LAST-OCCURRENCE-FUNCTION is $O(|\Sigma| + m)$.

The good-suffix heuristic

Let us define the relation $Q \sim R$ (read "Q is similar to R") for strings Q and R to mean that $Q \sqsupset R$ or $R \sqsupset Q$. If two strings are similar, then we can align them with their rightmost characters matched, and no pair of aligned characters will disagree. The relation "$\sim$" is symmetric: $Q \sim R$ if and only if $R \sim Q$. We also have, as a consequence of Lemma 34.1, that

$$Q \sqsupset R \text{ and } S \sqsupset R \text{ imply } Q \sim S . \tag{34.7}$$

If we find that $P[j] \neq T[s + j]$, where $j < m$, then the **good-suffix heuristic** says that we can safely advance s by

$$\gamma[j] = m - \max \{k : 0 \le k < m \text{ and } P[j + 1 .. m] \sim P_k\} .$$

That is, $\gamma[j]$ is the least amount we can advance s and not cause any characters in the "good suffix" $T[s + j + 1 .. s + m]$ to be mismatched against the new alignment of the pattern. The function γ is well defined for all j, since $P[j + 1 .. m] \sim P_0$ for all j: the empty string is similar to all strings. We call γ the **good-suffix function** for the pattern P.

We now show how to compute the good-suffix function γ. We first observe that $\gamma[j] \le m - \pi[m]$ for all j, as follows. If $w = \pi[m]$, then $P_w \sqsupset P$ by the definition of π. Furthermore, since $P[j + 1 .. m] \sqsupset P$ for any j, we have $P_w \sim P[j + 1 .. m]$, by equation (34.7). Therefore, $\gamma[j] \le m - \pi[m]$ for all j.

We can now rewrite our definition of γ as

$$\gamma[j] = m - \max \{k : \pi[m] \le k < m \text{ and } P[j + 1 .. m] \sim P_k\} .$$

The condition that $P[j + 1 .. m] \sim P_k$ holds if either $P[j + 1 .. m] \sqsupset P_k$ or $P_k \sqsupset P[j + 1 .. m]$. But the latter possibility implies that $P_k \sqsupset P$ and thus that $k \le \pi[m]$, by the definition of π. This latter possibility cannot reduce the value of $\gamma[j]$ below $m - \pi[m]$. We can therefore rewrite our definition of γ still further as follows:

$$\gamma[j] = m - \max (\{\pi[m]\} \cup \{k : \pi[m] < k < m \text{ and } P[j + 1 .. m] \sqsupset P_k\}) .$$

(The second set may be empty.) It is worth observing that the definition implies that $\gamma[j] > 0$ for all $j = 1, 2, \ldots, m$, which ensures that the Boyer-Moore algorithm makes progress.

To simplify the expression for γ further, we define P' as the reverse of the pattern P and π' as the corresponding prefix function. That is, $P'[i] = P[m - i + 1]$ for $i = 1, 2, \ldots, m$, and $\pi'[t]$ is the largest u such that $u < t$ and $P'_u \sqsupset P'_t$.

If k is the largest possible value such that $P[j + 1 \mathinner{.\,.} m] \sqsupset P_k$, then we claim that

$$\pi'[l] = m - j \,, \tag{34.8}$$

where $l = (m - k) + (m - j)$. To see that this claim is well defined, note that $P[j + 1 \mathinner{.\,.} m] \sqsupset P_k$ implies that $m - j \leq k$, and thus $l \leq m$. Also, $j < m$ and $k \leq m$, so that $l \geq 1$. We prove this claim as follows. Since $P[j + 1 \mathinner{.\,.} m] \sqsupset P_k$, we have $P'_{m-j} \sqsupset P'_l$. Therefore, $\pi'[l] \geq m - j$. Suppose now that $p > m - j$, where $p = \pi'[l]$. Then, by the definition of π', we have $P'_p \sqsupset P'_l$ or, equivalently, $P'[1 \mathinner{.\,.} p] = P'[l - p + 1 \mathinner{.\,.} l]$. Rewriting this equation in terms of P rather than P', we have $P[m - p + 1 \mathinner{.\,.} m] = P[m - l + 1 \mathinner{.\,.} m - l + p]$. Substituting for $l = 2m - k - j$, we obtain $P[m - p + 1 \mathinner{.\,.} m] = P[k - m + j + 1 \mathinner{.\,.} k - m + j + p]$, which implies $P[m-p+1 \mathinner{.\,.} m] \sqsupset P_{k-m+j+p}$. Since $p > m-j$, we have $j+1 > m-p+1$, and so $P[j+1 \mathinner{.\,.} m] \sqsupset P[m-p+1 \mathinner{.\,.} m]$, implying that $P[j+1 \mathinner{.\,.} m] \sqsupset P_{k-m+j+p}$ by the transitivity of $\sqsupset$. Finally, since $p > m - j$, we have $k' > k$, where $k' = k - m + j + p$, contradicting our choice of k as the largest possible value such that $P[j+1 \mathinner{.\,.} m] \sqsupset P_k$. This contradiction means that we can't have $p > m - j$, and thus $p = m - j$, which proves the claim (34.8).

Using equation (34.8), and noting that $\pi'[l] = m - j$ implies that $j = m - \pi'[l]$ and $k = m - l + \pi'[l]$, we can rewrite our definition of γ still further:

$$
\begin{aligned}
\gamma[j] &= m - \max(\{\pi[m]\} \\
&\qquad \cup \{m - l + \pi'[l] : 1 \leq l \leq m \text{ and } j = m - \pi'[l]\}) \\
&= \min(\{m - \pi[m]\} \\
&\qquad \cup \{l - \pi'[l] : 1 \leq l \leq m \text{ and } j = m - \pi'[l]\}) \,. \tag{34.9}
\end{aligned}
$$

Again, the second set may be empty.

We are now ready to examine the procedure for computing γ.

COMPUTE-GOOD-SUFFIX-FUNCTION(P, m)

```
 1   π ← COMPUTE-PREFIX-FUNCTION(P)
 2   P' ← reverse(P)
 3   π' ← COMPUTE-PREFIX-FUNCTION(P')
 4   for j ← 0 to m
 5       do γ[j] ← m − π[m]
 6   for l ← 1 to m
 7       do j ← m − π'[l]
 8          if γ[j] > l − π'[l]
 9             then γ[j] ← l − π'[l]
10   return γ
```

The procedure COMPUTE-GOOD-SUFFIX-FUNCTION is a straightforward implementation of equation (34.9). Its running time is $O(m)$.

The worst-case running time of the Boyer-Moore algorithm is clearly $O((n-m+1)m+|\Sigma|)$, since COMPUTE-LAST-OCCURRENCE-FUNCTION takes time $O(m+|\Sigma|)$, COMPUTE-GOOD-SUFFIX-FUNCTION takes time $O(m)$, and the Boyer-Moore algorithm (like the Rabin-Karp algorithm) spends $O(m)$ time validating each valid shift s. In practice, however, the Boyer-Moore algorithm is often the algorithm of choice.

Exercises

34.5-1
Compute the λ and γ functions for the pattern $P = 0101101201$ and the alphabet $\Sigma = \{0, 1, 2\}$.

34.5-2
Give examples to show that by combining the bad-character and good-suffix heuristics, the Boyer-Moore algorithm can perform much better than if it used just the good-suffix heuristic.

34.5-3 ⋆
An improvement to the basic Boyer-Moore procedure that is often used in practice is to replace the γ function by γ', defined by

$$\gamma'[j] = m - \max\{k : 0 \le k < m \text{ and } P[j+1..m] \sim P_k \text{ and } \\ (k - m + j > 0 \text{ implies } P[j] \ne P[k - m + j])\} .$$

In addition to ensuring that the characters in the good suffix will be mismatched at the new shift, the γ' function also guarantees that the same pattern character will not be matched up against the bad text character. Show how to compute the γ' function efficiently.

Problems

34-1 *String matching based on repetition factors*
Let y^i denote the concatenation of string y with itself i times. For example, $(ab)^3 = ababab$. We say that a string $x \in \Sigma^*$ has *repetition factor* r if $x = y^r$ for some string $y \in \Sigma^*$ and some $r > 0$. Let $\rho(x)$ denote the largest r such that x has repetition factor r.

a. Give an efficient algorithm that takes as input a pattern $P[1..m]$ and computes $\rho(P_i)$ for $i = 1, 2, \ldots, m$. What is the running time of your algorithm?

b. For any pattern $P[1 .. m]$, let $\rho^*(P)$ be defined as $\max_{1 \le i \le m} \rho(P_i)$. Prove that if the pattern P is chosen randomly from the set of all binary strings of length m, then the expected value of $\rho^*(P)$ is $O(1)$.

c. Argue that the following string-matching algorithm correctly finds all occurrences of pattern P in a text $T[1 .. n]$ in time $O(\rho^*(P)n + m)$.

REPETITION-MATCHER(P, T)

```
 1  m ← length[P]
 2  n ← length[T]
 3  k ← 1 + ρ*(P)
 4  q ← 0
 5  s ← 0
 6  while s ≤ n − m
 7      do if T[s + q + 1] = P[q + 1]
 8          then q ← q + 1
 9              if q = m
10                  then print "Pattern occurs with shift" s
11          if q = m or T[s + q + 1] ≠ P[q + 1]
12              then s ← s + max(1, ⌈q/k⌉)
13                  q ← 0
```

This algorithm is due to Galil and Seiferas. By extending these ideas greatly, they obtain a linear-time string-matching algorithm that uses only $O(1)$ storage beyond what is required for P and T.

34-2 *Parallel string matching*

Consider the problem of string matching on a parallel computer. Assume that for a given pattern, we have a string-matching automaton M with state set Q. Let ϕ be the final-state function for M. Suppose that our input text is $T[1 .. n]$. We wish to compute $\phi(T_i)$ for $i = 1, 2, \ldots, n$; that is, we wish to compute the final state for each prefix. Our strategy is to use the parallel prefix computation described in Section 30.1.2.

For any input string x, define the function $\delta_x : Q \to Q$ such that if M starts in state q and reads input x, then M ends in state $\delta_x(q)$.

a. Prove that $\delta_y \circ \delta_x = \delta_{xy}$, where $\circ$ denotes functional composition:

$$(\delta_y \circ \delta_x)(q) = \delta_y(\delta_x(q)) .$$

b. Argue that $\circ$ is an associative operation.

c. Argue that δ_{xy} can be computed from tabular representations of δ_x and δ_y in $O(1)$ time on a CREW PRAM. Analyze how many processors are needed in terms of $|Q|$.

d. Prove that $\phi(T_i) = \delta_{T_i}(q_0)$, where q_0 is the start state for M.

e. Show how to find all occurrences of a pattern in a text of length n in $O(\lg n)$ time on a CREW PRAM. Assume that the pattern is supplied in the form of the corresponding string-matching automaton.

Chapter notes

The relation of string matching to the theory of finite automata is discussed by Aho, Hopcroft, and Ullman [4]. The Knuth-Morris-Pratt algorithm [125] was invented independently by Knuth and Pratt and by Morris; they published their work jointly. The Rabin-Karp algorithm was proposed by Rabin and Karp [117], and the Boyer-Moore algorithm is due to Boyer and Moore [32]. Galil and Seiferas [78] give an interesting deterministic linear-time string-matching algorithm that uses only $O(1)$ space beyond that required to store the pattern and text.

35   Computational Geometry

Computational geometry is the branch of computer science that studies algorithms for solving geometric problems. In modern engineering and mathematics, computational geometry has applications in, among other fields, computer graphics, robotics, VLSI design, computer-aided design, and statistics. The input to a computational-geometry problem is typically a description of a set of geometric objects, such as a set of points, a set of line segments, or the vertices of a polygon in counterclockwise order. The output is often a response to a query about the objects, such as whether any of the lines intersect, or perhaps a new geometric object, such as the convex hull (smallest enclosing convex polygon) of the set of points.

In this chapter, we look at a few computational-geometry algorithms in two dimensions, that is, in the plane. Each input object is represented as a set of points $\{p_i\}$, where each $p_i = (x_i, y_i)$ and $x_i, y_i \in \mathbf{R}$. For example, an n-vertex polygon P is represented by a sequence $\langle p_0, p_1, p_2, \ldots, p_{n-1} \rangle$ of its vertices in order of their appearance on the boundary of P. Computational geometry can also be performed in three dimensions, and even in higher-dimensional spaces, but such problems and their solutions can be very difficult to visualize. Even in two dimensions, however, we can see a good sample of computational-geometry techniques.

Section 35.1 shows how to answer simple questions about line segments efficiently and accurately: whether one segment is clockwise or counter-clockwise from another that shares an endpoint, which way we turn when traversing two adjoining line segments, and whether two line segments intersect. Section 35.2 presents a technique called "sweeping" that we use to develop an $O(n \lg n)$-time algorithm for determining whether there are any intersections among a set of n line segments. Section 35.3 gives two "rotational-sweep" algorithms that compute the convex hull (smallest enclosing convex polygon) of a set of n points: Graham's scan, which runs in time $O(n \lg n)$, and Jarvis's march, which takes $O(nh)$ time, where h is the number of vertices of the convex hull. Finally, Section 35.4 gives an $O(n \lg n)$-time divide-and-conquer algorithm for finding the closest pair of points in a set of n points in the plane.

35.1   Line-segment properties

Several of the computational-geometry algorithms in this chapter will require answers to questions about the properties of line segments. A *convex*
combination of two distinct points $p_1 = (x_1, y_1)$ and $p_2 = (x_2, y_2)$ is any
point $p_3 = (x_3, y_3)$ such that for some α in the range $0 \leq \alpha \leq 1$, we
have $x_3 = \alpha x_1 + (1 - \alpha) x_2$ and $y_3 = \alpha y_1 + (1 - \alpha) y_2$. We also write that
$p_3 = \alpha p_1 + (1 - \alpha) p_2$. Intuitively, p_3 is any point that is on the line passing through p_1 and p_2 and is on or between p_1 and p_2 on the line. Given
two distinct points p_1 and p_2, the *line segment* $\overline{p_1 p_2}$ is the set of convex
combinations of p_1 and p_2. We call p_1 and p_2 the *endpoints* of segment
$\overline{p_1 p_2}$. Sometimes the ordering of p_1 and p_2 matters, and we speak of the *di-*
rected segment $\overrightarrow{p_1 p_2}$. If p_1 is the *origin* $(0, 0)$, then we can treat the directed
segment $\overrightarrow{p_1 p_2}$ as the *vector* p_2.

In this section, we shall explore the following questions:

1. Given two directed segments $\overrightarrow{p_0 p_1}$ and $\overrightarrow{p_0 p_2}$, is $\overrightarrow{p_0 p_1}$ clockwise from $\overrightarrow{p_0 p_2}$
   with respect to their common endpoint p_0?

2. Given two line segments $\overline{p_1 p_2}$ and $\overline{p_2 p_3}$, if we traverse $\overline{p_1 p_2}$ and then
   $\overline{p_2 p_3}$, do we make a left turn at point p_2?

3. Do line segments $\overline{p_1 p_2}$ and $\overline{p_3 p_4}$ intersect?

There are no restrictions on the given points.

We can answer each question in $O(1)$ time, which should come as no sur-
prise since the input size of each question is $O(1)$. Moreover, our methods
will use only additions, subtractions, multiplications, and comparisons.
We need neither division nor trigonometric functions, both of which can
be computationally expensive and prone to problems with round-off error.
For example, the "straightforward" method of determining whether two
segments intersect—compute the line equation of the form $y = mx + b$ for
each segment (m is the slope and b is the y-intercept), find the point of intersection of the lines, and check whether this point is on both segments—
uses division to find the point of intersection. When the segments are
nearly parallel, this method is very sensitive to the precision of the division operation on real computers. The method in this section, which
avoids division, is much more accurate.

Cross products

Computing cross products is at the heart of our line-segment methods.
Consider vectors p_1 and p_2, shown in Figure 35.1(a). The *cross product*
$p_1 \times p_2$ can be interpreted as the signed area of the parallelogram formed
by the points $(0, 0)$, p_1, p_2, and $p_1 + p_2 = (x_1 + x_2, y_1 + y_2)$. An equivalent,
but more useful, definition gives the cross product as the determinant of

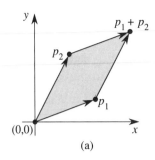
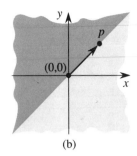

(a)   (b)

Figure 35.1 (a) The cross product of vectors p_1 and p_2 is the signed area of the parallelogram. (b) The lightly shaded region contains vectors that are clockwise from p. The darkly shaded region contains vectors that are counterclockwise from p.

a matrix:[1]

$$
\begin{aligned}
p_1 \times p_2 &= \det \begin{pmatrix} x_1 & x_2 \\ y_1 & y_2 \end{pmatrix} \\
&= x_1 y_2 - x_2 y_1 \\
&= -p_2 \times p_1 \ .
\end{aligned}
$$

If $p_1 \times p_2$ is positive, then p_1 is clockwise from p_2 with respect to the origin $(0,0)$; if this cross product is negative, then p_1 is counterclockwise from p_2. Figure 35.1(b) shows the clockwise and counterclockwise regions relative to a vector p. A boundary condition arises if the cross product is zero; in this case, the vectors are ***collinear***, pointing in either the same or opposite directions.

To determine whether a directed segment $\overrightarrow{p_0 p_1}$ is clockwise from a directed segment $\overrightarrow{p_0 p_2}$ with respect to their common endpoint p_0, we simply translate to use p_0 as the origin. That is, we let $p_1 - p_0$ denote the vector $p_1' = (x_1', y_1')$, where $x_1' = x_1 - x_0$ and $y_1' = y_1 - y_0$, and we define $p_2 - p_0$ similarly. We then compute the cross product

$$(p_1 - p_0) \times (p_2 - p_0) = (x_1 - x_0)(y_2 - y_0) - (x_2 - x_0)(y_1 - y_0) \ .$$

If this cross product is positive, then $\overrightarrow{p_0 p_1}$ is clockwise from $\overrightarrow{p_0 p_2}$; if negative, it is counterclockwise.

Determining whether consecutive segments turn left or right

Our next question is whether two consecutive line segments $\overline{p_0 p_1}$ and $\overline{p_1 p_2}$ turn left or right at point p_1. Equivalently, we want a method to determine

---

[1]Actually, the cross product is a three-dimensional concept. It is a vector that is perpendicular to both p_1 and p_2 according to the "right-hand rule" and whose magnitude is $|x_1 y_2 - x_2 y_1|$. In this chapter, however, it will prove convenient to treat the cross product simply as the value $x_1 y_2 - x_2 y_1$.

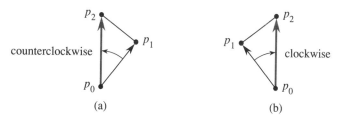

Figure 35.2 Using the cross product to determine how consecutive line segments $\overline{p_0p_1}$ and $\overline{p_1p_2}$ turn at point p_1. We check whether the directed segment $\overrightarrow{p_0p_2}$ is clockwise or counterclockwise relative to the directed segment $\overrightarrow{p_0p_1}$. **(a)** If counterclockwise, the points make a left turn. **(b)** If clockwise, they make a right turn.

which way a given angle $\angle p_0p_1p_2$ turns. Cross products allow us to answer this question without computing the angle. As shown in Figure 35.2, we simply check whether directed segment $\overrightarrow{p_0p_2}$ is clockwise or counterclockwise relative to directed segment $\overrightarrow{p_0p_1}$. To do this, we compute the cross product $(p_2 - p_0) \times (p_1 - p_0)$. If the sign of this cross product is negative, then $\overrightarrow{p_0p_2}$ is counterclockwise with respect to $\overrightarrow{p_0p_1}$, and thus we make a left turn at p_1. A positive cross product indicates a clockwise orientation and a right turn. A cross product of 0 means that points p_0, p_1, and p_2 are collinear.

Determining whether two line segments intersect

We use a two-stage process to determine whether two line segments intersect. The first stage is ***quick rejection***: the line segments cannot intersect if their bounding boxes do not intersect. The ***bounding box*** of a geometric figure is the smallest rectangle that contains the figure and whose segments are parallel to the x-axis and y-axis. The bounding box of line segment $\overline{p_1p_2}$ is represented by the rectangle $(\widehat{p}_1, \widehat{p}_2)$ with lower left point $\widehat{p}_1 = (\widehat{x}_1, \widehat{y}_1)$ and upper right point $\widehat{p}_2 = (\widehat{x}_2, \widehat{y}_2)$, where $\widehat{x}_1 = \min(x_1, x_2)$, $\widehat{y}_1 = \min(y_1, y_2)$, $\widehat{x}_2 = \max(x_1, x_2)$, and $\widehat{y}_2 = \max(y_1, y_2)$. Two rectangles, represented by lower left and upper right points $(\widehat{p}_1, \widehat{p}_2)$ and $(\widehat{p}_3, \widehat{p}_4)$, intersect if and only if the conjunction

$$(\widehat{x}_2 \geq \widehat{x}_3) \wedge (\widehat{x}_4 \geq \widehat{x}_1) \wedge (\widehat{y}_2 \geq \widehat{y}_3) \wedge (\widehat{y}_4 \geq \widehat{y}_1)$$

is true. The rectangles must intersect in both dimensions. The first two comparisons above determine whether the rectangles intersect in x; th second two comparisons determine whether the rectangles intersect ir

The second stage in determining whether two line segments int decides whether each segment "straddles" the line containing the oth segment $\overline{p_1p_2}$ ***straddles*** a line if point p_1 lies on one side of the line point p_2 lies on the other side. If p_1 or p_2 lies on the line, then we say th the segment straddles the line. Two line segments intersect if and only

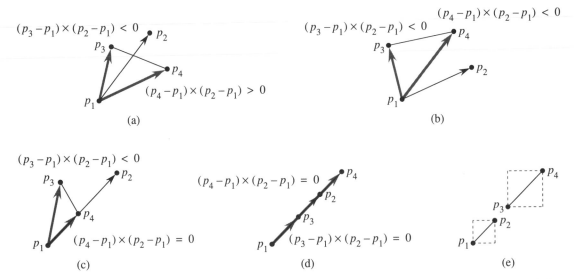

Figure 35.3 Determining whether line segment $\overline{p_3p_4}$ straddles the line containing segment $\overline{p_1p_2}$. **(a)** If it does straddle, then the signs of the cross products $(p_3 - p_1) \times (p_2 - p_1)$ and $(p_4 - p_1) \times (p_2 - p_1)$ differ. **(b)** If it does not straddle, then the signs of the cross products are the same. **(c)–(d)** Boundary cases in which at least one of the cross products is zero and the segment straddles. **(e)** A boundary case in which the segments are collinear but do not intersect. Both cross products are zero, but they would not be computed by our algorithm because the segments fail the quick rejection test—their bounding boxes do not intersect.

if they pass the quick rejection test and each segment straddles the line containing the other.

We can use the cross-product method to determine whether line segment $\overline{p_3p_4}$ straddles the line containing points p_1 and p_2. The idea, as shown in Figures 35.3(a) and (b), is to determine whether directed segments $\overrightarrow{p_1p_3}$ and $\overrightarrow{p_1p_4}$ have opposite orientations relative to $\overrightarrow{p_1p_2}$. If so, then the segment straddles the line. Recalling that we can determine relative orientations with cross products, we just check whether the signs of the cross products $(p_3 - p_1) \times (p_2 - p_1)$ and $(p_4 - p_1) \times (p_2 - p_1)$ are different. A boundary condition occurs if either cross product is zero. In this case, either p_3 or p_4 lies on the line containing segment $\overline{p_1p_2}$. Because the two segments have already passed the quick rejection test, one of the points p_3 and p_4 must in fact lie on segment $\overline{p_1p_2}$. Two such situations are shown in Figures 35.3(c) and (d). The case in which the two segments are collinear but do not intersect, shown in Figure 35.3(e), is eliminated by the quick rejection test. A final boundary condition occurs if one or both of the segments has zero length, that is, if its endpoints are coincident. If both segments have zero length, then the quick rejection test suffices. If just one segment, say $\overline{p_3p_4}$, has zero length, then the segments intersect if and only if the cross product $(p_3 - p_1) \times (p_2 - p_1)$ is zero.

Other applications of cross products

Later sections of this chapter will introduce additional uses for cross products. In Section 35.3, we shall need to sort a set of points according to their polar angles with respect to a given origin. As Exercise 35.1-2 asks you to show, cross products can be used to perform the comparisons in the sorting procedure. In Section 35.2, we shall use red-black trees to maintain the vertical ordering of a set of nonintersecting line segments. Rather than keeping explicit key values, we shall replace each key comparison in the red-black tree code by a cross-product calculation to determine which of two segments that intersect a given vertical line is above the other.

Exercises

35.1-1
Prove that if $p_1 \times p_2$ is positive, then vector p_1 is clockwise from vector p_2 with respect to the origin $(0, 0)$ and that if this cross product is negative, then p_1 is counterclockwise from p_2.

35.1-2
Write pseudocode to sort a sequence $\langle p_1, p_2, \ldots, p_n \rangle$ of n points according to their polar angles with respect to a given origin point p_0. Your procedure should take $O(n \lg n)$ time and use cross products to compare angles.

35.1-3
Show how to determine in $O(n^2 \lg n)$ time whether any three points in a set of n points are collinear.

35.1-4
Professor Amundsen proposes the following method to determine whether a sequence $\langle p_0, p_1, \ldots, p_{n-1} \rangle$ of n points forms the consecutive vertices of a convex polygon. (See Section 16.4 for definitions pertaining to polygons.) Output "yes" if the set $\{\angle p_i p_{i+1} p_{i+2} : i = 0, 1, \ldots, n - 1\}$, where subscript addition is performed modulo n, does not contain both left turns and right turns; otherwise, output "no." Show that although this method runs in linear time, it does not always produce the correct answer. Modify the professor's method so that it always produces the correct answer in linear time.

35.1-5
Given a point $p_0 = (x_0, y_0)$, the ***right horizontal ray*** from p_0 is the set points $\{p_i = (x_i, y_i) : x_i \geq x_0 \text{ and } y_i = y_0\}$, that is, it is the set of point. right of p_0 along with p_0 itself. Show how to determine whether a g. right horizontal ray from p_0 intersects a line segment $\overline{p_1 p_2}$ in $O(1)$ tir. by reducing the problem to that of determining whether two line segment. intersect.

35.1-6

One way to determine whether a point p_0 is in the interior of a simple, but not necessarily convex, polygon P is to look at any ray from p_0 and check that the ray intersects the boundary of P an odd number of times but that p_0 itself is not on the boundary of P. Show how to compute in $\Theta(n)$ time whether a point p_0 is in the interior of an n-vertex polygon P. (*Hint*: Use Exercise 35.1-5. Make sure your algorithm is correct when the ray intersects the polygon boundary at a vertex and when the ray overlaps a side of the polygon.)

35.1-7

Show how to compute the area of an n-vertex simple, but not necessarily convex, polygon in $\Theta(n)$ time.

35.2   Determining whether any pair of segments intersects

This section presents an algorithm for determining whether any two line segments in a set of segments intersect. The algorithm uses a technique known as "sweeping," which is common to many computational-geometry algorithms. Moreover, as the exercises at the end of this section show, this algorithm, or simple variations of it, can be used to solve other computational-geometry problems.

The algorithm runs in $O(n \lg n)$ time, where n is the number of segments we are given. It determines only whether or not any intersection exists; it does not print all the intersections. (By Exercise 35.2-1, it takes $\Omega(n^2)$ time in the worst case to find *all* the intersections in a set of n line segments.)

In *sweeping*, an imaginary vertical *sweep line* passes through the given set of geometric objects, usually from left to right. The spatial dimension that the sweep line moves across, in this case the x-dimension, is treated as a dimension of time. Sweeping provides a method for ordering geometric objects, usually by placing them into a dynamic data structure, and for taking advantage of relationships among them. The line-segment-intersection algorithm in this section considers all the line-segment endpoints in left-to-right order and checks for an intersection each time it encounters an endpoint.

Our algorithm for determining whether any two of n line segments intersect makes two simplifying assumptions. First, we assume that no input segment is vertical. Second, we assume that no three input segments intersect at a single point. (Exercise 35.2-8 asks you to describe an implementation that works even if these assumptions fail to hold.) Indeed, removing such simplifying assumptions and dealing with boundary conditions is often the most difficult part of programming computational-geometry algorithms and proving their correctness.

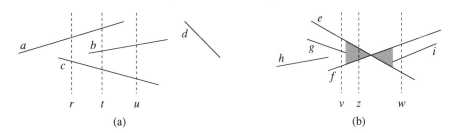

Figure 35.4 The ordering among line segments at various vertical sweep lines. **(a)** We have $a >_r c$, $a >_t b$, $b >_t c$, $a >_t c$, and $b >_u c$. Segment d is comparable with no other segment shown. **(b)** When segments e and f intersect, their orders are reversed: we have $e >_v f$ but $f >_w e$. Any sweep line (such as z) that passes through the shaded region has e and f consecutive in its total order.

Ordering segments

Since we assume that there are no vertical segments, any input segment that intersects a given vertical sweep line intersects it at a single point. We can thus order the segments that intersect a vertical sweep line according to the y-coordinates of the points of intersection.

To be more precise, consider two nonintersecting segments s_1 and s_2. We say that these segments are ***comparable*** at x if the vertical sweep line with x-coordinate x intersects both of them. We say that s_1 is ***above*** s_2 at x, written $s_1 >_x s_2$, if s_1 and s_2 are comparable at x and the intersection of s_1 with the sweep line at x is higher than the intersection of s_2 with the same sweep line. In Figure 35.4(a), for example, we have the relationships $a >_r c$, $a >_t b$, $b >_t c$, $a >_t c$, and $b >_u c$. Segment d is not comparable with any other segment.

For any given x, the relation "$>_x$" is a total order (see Section 5.2) on segments that intersect the sweep line at x. The order may differ for differing values of x, however, as segments enter and leave the ordering. A segment enters the ordering when its left endpoint is encountered by the sweep, and it leaves the ordering when its right endpoint is encountered.

What happens when the sweep line passes through the intersection of two segments? As Figure 35.4(b) shows, their positions in the total order are reversed. Sweep lines v and w are to the left and right, respectively, of the point of intersection of segments e and f, and we have $e >_v f$ and $f >_w e$. Note that because we assume that no three segments intersect at the same point, there must be some vertical sweep line x for which intersecting segments e and f are *consecutive* in the total order $>_x$. Any sweep line that passes through the shaded region of Figure 35.4(b), such as z, has e and f consecutive in its total order.

Moving the sweep line

Sweeping algorithms typically manage two sets of data:

1. The *sweep-line status* gives the relationships among the objects intersected by the sweep line.

2. The *event-point schedule* is a sequence of x-coordinates, ordered from left to right, that defines the halting positions of the sweep line. We call each such halting position an *event point*. Changes to the sweep-line status occur only at event points.

For some algorithms (the algorithm asked for in Exercise 35.2-7, for example), the event-point schedule is determined dynamically as the algorithm progresses. The algorithm at hand, however, determines the event points statically, based solely on simple properties of the input data. In particular, each segment endpoint is an event point. We sort the segment endpoints by increasing x-coordinate and proceed from left to right. We insert a segment into the sweep-line status when its left endpoint is encountered, and we delete it from the sweep-line status when its right endpoint is encountered. Whenever two segments first become consecutive in the total order, we check whether they intersect.

The sweep-line status is a total order T, for which we require the following operations:

- INSERT(T, s): insert segment s into T.
- DELETE(T, s): delete segment s from T.
- ABOVE(T, s): return the segment immediately above segment s in T.
- BELOW(T, s): return the segment immediately below segment s in T.

If there are n segments in the input, we can perform each of the above operations in $O(\lg n)$ time using red-black trees. Recall that the red-black-tree operations in Chapter 14 involve comparing keys. We can replace the key comparisons by cross-product comparisons that determine the relative ordering of two segments (see Exercise 35.2-2).

Segment-intersection pseudocode

The following algorithm takes as input a set S of n line segments, returning the boolean value TRUE if any pair of segments in S intersects, and FALSE otherwise. The total order T is implemented by a red-black tree.

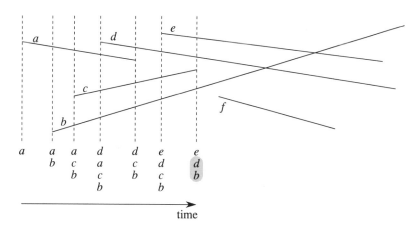

Figure 35.5 The execution of ANY-SEGMENTS-INTERSECT. Each dashed line is the sweep line at an event point, and the ordering of segment names below each sweep line is the total order T at the end of the **for** loop in which the corresponding event point is processed. The intersection of segments d and b is found when segment c is deleted.

ANY-SEGMENTS-INTERSECT(S)

```
 1   T ← ∅
 2   sort the endpoints of the segments in S from left to right,
                breaking ties by putting points with lower y-coordinates first
 3   for each point p in the sorted list of endpoints
 4       do if p is the left endpoint of a segment s
 5              then INSERT(T, s)
 6                   if (ABOVE(T, s) exists and intersects s)
                         or (BELOW(T, s) exists and intersects s)
 7                      then return TRUE
 8              if p is the right endpoint of a segment s
 9                  then if both ABOVE(T, s) and BELOW(T, s) exist
                            and ABOVE(T, s) intersects BELOW(T, s)
10                         then return TRUE
11                      DELETE(T, s)
12   return FALSE
```

Figure 35.5 illustrates the execution of the algorithm. Line 1 initializes the total order to be empty. Line 2 determines the event-point schedule by sorting the $2n$ segment endpoints from left to right, breaking ties by putting points with lower y-coordinates first. Note that line 2 can be performed by lexicographically sorting the endpoints on (x, y).

Each iteration of the **for** loop of lines 3–11 processes one event point p. If p is the left endpoint of a segment s, line 5 adds s to the total order, and lines 6–7 return TRUE if s intersects either of the segments it is consecutive with in the total order defined by the sweep line passing through p.

(A boundary condition occurs if p lies on another segment s'. In this case, we only require that s and s' be placed consecutively into T.) If p is the right endpoint of a segment s, then s is to be deleted from the total order. Lines 9–10 return TRUE if there is an intersection between the segments surrounding s in the total order defined by the sweep line passing through p; these segments will become consecutive in the total order when s is deleted. If these segments do not intersect, line 11 deletes segment s from the total order. Finally, if no intersections are found in processing all the $2n$ event points, line 12 returns FALSE.

Correctness

The following theorem shows that ANY-SEGMENTS-INTERSECT is correct.

Theorem 35.1
The call ANY-SEGMENTS-INTERSECT(S) returns TRUE if and only if there is an intersection among the segments in S.

Proof   The procedure can be incorrect only by returning TRUE when no intersection exists or by returning FALSE when there is at least one intersection. The former case cannot occur, because ANY-SEGMENTS-INTERSECT returns TRUE only if it finds an intersection between two of the input segments.

To show that the latter case cannot occur, let us suppose for the sake of contradiction that there is at least one intersection, yet ANY-SEGMENTS-INTERSECT returns FALSE. Let p be the leftmost intersection point, breaking ties by choosing the one with the lowest y-coordinate, and let a and b be the segments that intersect at p. Since no intersections occur to the left of p, the order given by T is correct at all points to the left of p. Because no three segments intersect at the same point, there exists a sweep line z at which a and b become consecutive in the total order.[2] Moreover, z is to the left of p or goes through p. There exists a segment endpoint q on sweep line z that is the event point at which a and b become consecutive in the total order. If p is on sweep line z, then $q = p$. If p is not on sweep line z, then q is to the left of p. In either case, the order given by T is correct just before q is processed. (Here we rely on p being the lowest of the leftmost intersection points. Because of the lexicographical order in which event points are processed, even if p is on sweep line z and there is another intersection point p' on z, event point $q = p$ is processed before the other intersection p' can interfere with the total order T.) There are only two possibilities for the action taken at event point q:

---

[2]If we allow three segments to intersect at the same point, there may be an intervening segment c that intersects both a and b at point p. That is, we may have $a <_w c$ and $c <_w b$ for all sweep lines w to the left of p for which $a <_w b$.

1. Either a or b is inserted into T, and the other segment is above or below it in the total order. Lines 4–7 detect this case.

2. Segments a and b are already in T, and a segment between them in the total order is deleted, making a and b become consecutive. Lines 8–11 detect this case.

In either case, the intersection p is found, contradicting the assumption that the procedure returns FALSE. ∎

Running time

If there are n segments in set S, then ANY-SEGMENTS-INTERSECT runs in time $O(n \lg n)$. Line 1 takes $O(1)$ time. Line 2 takes $O(n \lg n)$ time, using merge sort or heapsort. Since there are $2n$ event points, the **for** loop of lines 3–11 iterates at most $2n$ times. Each iteration takes $O(\lg n)$ time, since each red-black-tree operation takes $O(\lg n)$ time and, using the method of Section 35.1, each intersection test takes $O(1)$ time. The total time is thus $O(n \lg n)$.

Exercises

35.2-1
Show that there may be $\Theta(n^2)$ intersections in a set of n line segments.

35.2-2
Given two nonintersecting segments a and b that are comparable at x, show how to use cross products to determine in $O(1)$ time which of $a >_x b$ or $b >_x a$ holds.

35.2-3
Professor Maginot suggests that we modify ANY-SEGMENTS-INTERSECT so that instead of returning upon finding an intersection, it prints the segments that intersect and continues on to the next iteration of the **for** loop. The professor calls the resulting procedure PRINT-INTERSECTING-SEGMENTS and claims that it prints all intersections, left to right, as they occur in the set of line segments. Show that the professor is wrong on two counts by giving a set of segments for which the first intersection found by PRINT-INTERSECTING-SEGMENTS is not the leftmost one and a set of segments for which PRINT-INTERSECTING-SEGMENTS fails to find all the intersections.

35.2-4
Give an $O(n \lg n)$-time algorithm to determine whether an n-vertex polygon is simple.

35.2-5

Give an $O(n \lg n)$-time algorithm to determine whether two simple polygons with a total of n vertices intersect.

35.2-6

A ***disk*** consists of a circle plus its interior and is represented by its center point and radius. Two disks intersect if they have any point in common. Give an $O(n \lg n)$-time algorithm to determine whether any two disks in a set of n intersect.

35.2-7

Given a set of n line segments containing a total of k intersections, show how to output all k intersections in $O((n + k) \lg n)$ time.

35.2-8

Show how to implement the red-black-tree procedures so that ANY-SEG-MENTS-INTERSECT works correctly even if some segments are vertical or more than three segments intersect at the same point. Prove that your implementation is correct.

35.3   Finding the convex hull

The ***convex hull*** of a set Q of points is the smallest convex polygon P for which each point in Q is either on the boundary of P or in its interior. We denote the convex hull of Q by CH(Q). Intuitively, we can think of each point in Q as being a nail sticking out from a board. The convex hull is then the shape formed by a tight rubber band that surrounds all the nails. Figure 35.6 shows a set of points and its convex hull.

In this section, we shall present two algorithms that compute the convex hull of a set of n points. Both algorithms output the vertices of the convex

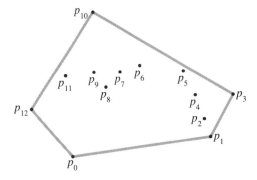

Figure 35.6   A set of points Q with its convex hull CH(Q) in gray.

hull in counterclockwise order. The first, known as Graham's scan, runs in $O(n \lg n)$ time. The second, called Jarvis's march, runs in $O(nh)$ time, where h is the number of vertices of the convex hull. As can be seen from Figure 35.6, every vertex of CH(Q) is a point in Q. Both algorithms exploit this property, deciding which vertices in Q to keep as vertices of the convex hull and which vertices in Q to throw out.

There are, in fact, several methods that compute convex hulls in $O(n \lg n)$ time. Both Graham's scan and Jarvis's march use a technique called "rotational sweep," processing vertices in the order of the polar angles they form with a reference vertex. Other methods include the following.

- In the ***incremental method***, the points are sorted from left to right, yielding a sequence $\langle p_1, p_2, \ldots, p_n \rangle$. At the ith stage, the convex hull CH($\{p_1, p_2, \ldots, p_{i-1}\}$) of the $i - 1$ leftmost points is updated according to the ith point from the left, thus forming CH($\{p_1, p_2, \ldots, p_i\}$). As Exercise 35.3-6 asks you to show, this method can be implemented to take a total of $O(n \lg n)$ time.

- In the ***divide-and-conquer method***, in $\Theta(n)$ time the set of n points is divided into two subsets, one of the leftmost $\lceil n/2 \rceil$ points and one of the rightmost $\lfloor n/2 \rfloor$ points, the convex hulls of the subsets are computed recursively, and then a clever method is used to combine the hulls in $O(n)$ time.

- The ***prune-and-search method*** is similar to the worst-case linear-time median algorithm of Section 10.3. It finds the upper portion (or "upper chain") of the convex hull by repeatedly throwing out a constant fraction of the remaining points until only the upper chain of the convex hull remains. It then does the same for the lower chain. This method is asymptotically the fastest: if the convex hull contains h vertices, it runs in only $O(n \lg h)$ time.

Computing the convex hull of a set of points is an interesting problem in its own right. Moreover, algorithms for some other computational-geometry problems start by computing a convex hull. Consider, for example, the two-dimensional ***farthest-pair problem***: we are given a set of n points in the plane and wish to find the two points whose distance from each other is maximum. As Exercise 35.3-3 asks you to prove, these two points must be vertices of the convex hull. Although we won't prove it here, the farthest pair of vertices of an n-vertex convex polygon can be found in $O(n)$ time. Thus, by computing the convex hull of the n input points in $O(n \lg n)$ time and then finding the farthest pair of the resulting convex-polygon vertices, we can find the farthest pair of points in any set of n points in $O(n \lg n)$ time.

Graham's scan

Graham's scan solves the convex-hull problem by maintaining a stack S of candidate points. Each point of the input set Q is pushed once onto the

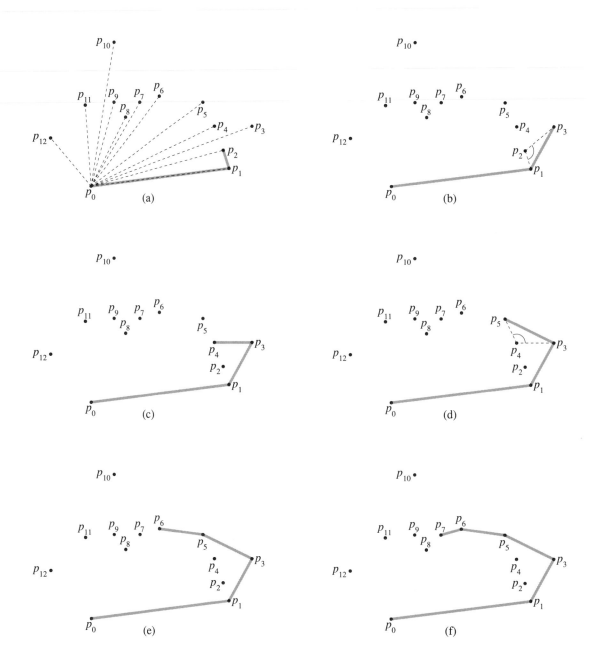

Figure 35.7 The execution of GRAHAM-SCAN on the set Q of Figure 35.6. The current convex hull contained in stack S is shown in gray at each step. **(a)** The ordered polar angles of $\langle p_1, p_2, \ldots, p_{12} \rangle$ relative to p_0 and the initial stack S containing p_0, p_1, and p_2. **(b)–(k)** Stack S after each iteration of the **for** loop of lines 7–10. Dashed lines show nonleft turns, which cause points to be popped from the stack. In part (h), for example, the right turn at angle $\angle p_7 p_8 p_9$ causes p_8 to be popped, and then the right turn at angle $\angle p_6 p_7 p_9$ causes p_7 to be popped. **(l)** The convex hull returned by the procedure, which matches that of Figure 35.6.

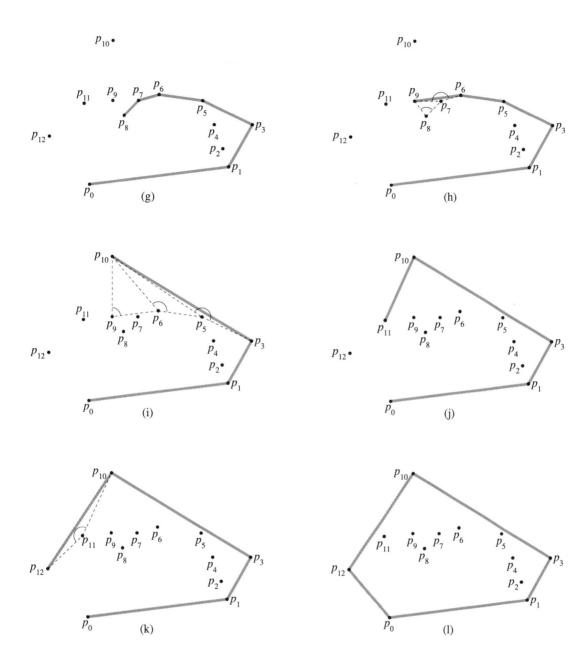

stack, and the points that are not vertices of CH(Q) are eventually popped from the stack. When the algorithm terminates, stack S contains exactly the vertices of CH(Q), in counterclockwise order of their appearance on the boundary.

The procedure GRAHAM-SCAN takes as input a set Q of points, where $|Q| \geq 3$. It calls the functions TOP(S), which returns the point on top of stack S without changing S, and NEXT-TO-TOP(S), which returns the point one entry below the top of stack S without changing S. As we shall prove in a moment, the stack S returned by GRAHAM-SCAN contains, from bottom to top, exactly the vertices of CH(Q) in counterclockwise order.

GRAHAM-SCAN(Q)

```
 1  let p₀ be the point in Q with the minimum y-coordinate,
           or the leftmost such point in case of a tie
 2  let ⟨p₁, p₂, ..., pₘ⟩ be the remaining points in Q,
           sorted by polar angle in counterclockwise order around p₀
           (if more than point has the same angle, remove all but
           the one that is farthest from p₀)
 3  top[S] ← 0
 4  PUSH(p₀, S)
 5  PUSH(p₁, S)
 6  PUSH(p₂, S)
 7  for i ← 3 to m
 8      do while the angle formed by points NEXT-TO-TOP(S),
                   TOP(S), and pᵢ makes a nonleft turn
 9              do POP(S)
10          PUSH(S, pᵢ)
11  return S
```

Figure 35.7 illustrates the progress of GRAHAM-SCAN. Line 1 chooses point p_0 as the point with the lowest y-coordinate, picking the leftmost such point in case of a tie. Since there is no point in Q that is below p_0 and any other points with the same y-coordinate are to its right, p_0 is a vertex of CH(Q). Line 2 sorts the remaining points of Q by polar angle relative to p_0, using the same method—comparing cross products—as in Exercise 35.1-2. If two or more points have the same polar angle relative to p_0, all but the farthest such point are convex combinations of p_0 and the farthest point, and so we remove them entirely from consideration. We let m denote the number of points other than p_0 that remain. The polar angle, measured in radians, of each point in Q relative to p_0 is in the half-open interval $[0, \pi/2)$. Since polar angles increase in a counterclockwise fashion, the points are sorted in counterclockwise order relative to p_0. We designate this sorted sequence of points by $\langle p_1, p_2, \ldots, p_m \rangle$. Note that points p_1 and p_m are vertices of CH(Q) (see Exercise 35.3-1). Figure 35.7(a) shows the points of Figure 35.6, with the ordered polar angles of $\langle p_1, p_2, \ldots, p_{12} \rangle$ relative to p_0.

The remainder of the procedure uses the stack S. Lines 3–6 initialize the stack to contain, from bottom to top, the first three points p_0, p_1, and p_2. Figure 35.7(a) shows the initial stack S. The **for** loop of lines 7–10 iterates once for each point in the subsequence $\langle p_3, p_4, \ldots, p_m \rangle$. The intent is that after processing point p_i, stack S contains, from bottom to top, the vertices of CH($\{p_0, p_1, \ldots, p_i\}$) in counterclockwise order. The **while** loop of lines 8–9 removes points from the stack if they are found not to be vertices of the convex hull. When we traverse the convex hull counterclockwise, we should make a left turn at each vertex. Thus, each time the **while** loop finds a vertex at which we make a nonleft turn, the vertex is popped from the stack. (By checking for a nonleft turn, rather than just a right turn, this test precludes the possibility of a straight angle at a vertex of the resulting convex hull. This is just what we want, since every vertex of a convex polygon must not be a convex combination of other vertices of the polygon.) After we pop all the vertices that have nonleft turns when heading toward point p_i, we push p_i onto the stack. Figures 35.7(b)–(k) show the state of the stack S after each iteration of the **for** loop. Finally, GRAHAM-SCAN returns the stack S in line 11. Figure 35.7(l) shows the corresponding convex hull.

The following theorem formally proves the correctness of GRAHAM-SCAN.

Theorem 35.2 (Correctness of Graham's scan)
If GRAHAM-SCAN is run on a set Q of points, where $|Q| \geq 3$, then a point of Q is on the stack S at termination if and only if it is a vertex of CH(Q).

Proof As noted above, a vertex that is a convex combination of p_0 and some other vertex in Q is not a vertex of CH(Q). Such a vertex is not included in the sequence $\langle p_1, p_2, \ldots, p_m \rangle$, and so it can never appear on stack S.

The crux of the proof lies in the two situations shown in Figure 35.8. Part (a) deals with nonleft turns, and part (b) deals with left turns.

We first show that each point popped from stack S is not a vertex of CH(Q). Suppose that point p_j is popped from the stack because angle $\angle p_k p_j p_i$ makes a nonleft turn, as shown in Figure 35.8(a). Because we scan the points in order of increasing polar angle relative to point p_0, there is a triangle $\triangle p_0 p_i p_k$ with point p_j either in the interior of the triangle or on line segment $\overline{p_i p_k}$. In either case, point p_j cannot be a vertex of CH(Q).

We now show that each point on stack S is a vertex of CH(Q) at termination. We start by proving the following claim: GRAHAM-SCAN maintains the invariant that the points on stack S always form the vertices of a convex polygon in counterclockwise order.

The claim holds immediately after the execution of line 6, since points p_0, p_1, and p_2 form a convex polygon. Now we examine how stack S changes during the course of GRAHAM-SCAN. Points are either popped or pushed. In the former case, we rely on a simply geometrical property: if a

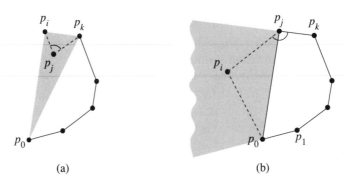

Figure 35.8   The two basic situations in the proof of correctness of GRAHAM-SCAN. **(a)** Showing that a point popped from the stack in GRAHAM-SCAN is not a vertex of CH(Q). If point p_j is popped from the stack because angle $\angle p_k p_j p_i$ makes a nonleft turn, then the shaded triangle $\triangle p_0 p_k p_i$ contains point p_j. Point p_j is therefore not a vertex of CH(Q). **(b)** If point p_i is pushed onto the stack, then there must be a left turn at angle $\angle p_k p_j p_i$. Because p_i follows p_j in the polar-angle ordering of points and because of how p_0 was chosen, p_i must be in the shaded region. If the points on the stack form a convex polygon before the push, then they must form a convex polygon afterward.

vertex is removed from a convex polygon, the resulting polygon is convex. Thus, popping a point from stack S preserves the invariant.

Before we consider the case in which a point is pushed onto the stack, let us examine another geometrical property, illustrated in Figures 35.9(a) and (b). Let P be a convex polygon, and choose any side $\overline{p_r p_t}$ of P. Consider the region bounded by $\overline{p_r p_t}$ and the extensions of the two adjacent sides. (Depending on the relative angles of the adjacent sides, the region may be either bounded, like the shaded region in part (a), or unbounded, like the shaded region in part (b).) If we add any point p_s in this region to P as a new vertex, with the sides $\overline{p_r p_s}$ and $\overline{p_s p_t}$ replacing side $\overline{p_r p_t}$, the resulting polygon is convex.

Now consider a point p_i that is pushed onto S. Referring back to Figure 35.8(b), let p_j be the vertex on the top of S just prior to pushing p_i, and let p_k be the predecessor of p_j on S. We claim that p_i must fall within the shaded region of Figure 35.8(b), which corresponds directly to the shaded regions of Figure 35.9. Because the angle $\angle p_k p_j p_i$ makes a left turn, p_i must be on the shaded side of the extension of $\overline{p_k p_j}$. Because p_i follows p_j in the polar-angle ordering, it must be on the shaded side of $\overline{p_0 p_j}$. Moreover, because of how we chose p_0, point p_i must be on the shaded side of the extension of $\overline{p_0 p_1}$. Thus, p_i is in the shaded region, and therefore after p_i has been pushed onto stack S, the points on S form a convex polygon. This completes the proof of the claim.

At the end of GRAHAM-SCAN, therefore, the points of Q that are on stack S form the vertices of a convex polygon. We have shown that all points not on S are not vertices of CH(Q) or, equivalently, that all vertices

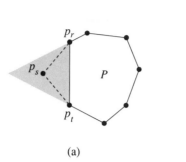 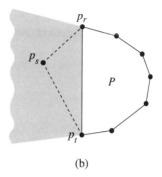

(a)   (b)

Figure 35.9 Adding a point in the shaded region to a convex polygon P yields another convex polygon. The shaded region is bounded by a side of $\overline{p_r p_t}$ and the extensions of the two adjacent sides. (**a**) The shaded region is bounded. (**b**) The shaded region is unbounded.

of CH(Q) are on S. Since S contains only vertices from Q and its points form a convex polygon, they must form CH(Q). ∎

We now show that the running time of GRAHAM-SCAN is $O(n \lg n)$, where $n = |Q|$. Line 1 takes $\Theta(n)$ time. Line 2 takes $O(n \lg n)$ time, using merge sort or heapsort to sort the polar angles and the cross-product method of Section 35.1 to compare angles. (Removing all but the farthest point with the same polar angle can be done in a total of $O(n)$ time.) Lines 3–6 take $O(1)$ time. Because $m \le n - 1$, the **for** loop of lines 7–10 is executed at most $n - 3$ times. Since PUSH takes $O(1)$ time, each iteration takes $O(1)$ time exclusive of the time spent in the **while** loop of lines 8–9, and thus overall the **for** loop takes $O(n)$ time exclusive of the nested **while** loop.

We use the aggregate method of amortized analysis to show that the **while** loop takes $O(n)$ time overall. For $i = 0, 1, \ldots, m$, each point p_i is pushed onto stack S exactly once. As in the analysis of the MULTIPOP procedure of Section 18.1, we observe that there is at most one POP operation for each PUSH operation. At least three points—p_0, p_1, and p_m—are never popped from the stack, so that in fact at most $m - 2$ POP operations are performed in total. Each iteration of the **while** loop performs one POP, and so there are at most $m - 2$ iterations of the **while** loop altogether. Since the test in line 8 takes $O(1)$ time, each call of POP takes $O(1)$ time, and $m \le n - 1$, the total time taken by the **while** loop is $O(n)$. Thus, the running time of GRAHAM-SCAN is $O(n \lg n)$.

Jarvis's march

Jarvis's march computes the convex hull of a set Q of points by a technique known as ***package wrapping*** (or ***gift wrapping***). The algorithm runs in time $O(nh)$, where h is the number of vertices of CH(Q). When h is $o(\lg n)$, Jarvis's march is asymptotically faster than Graham's scan.

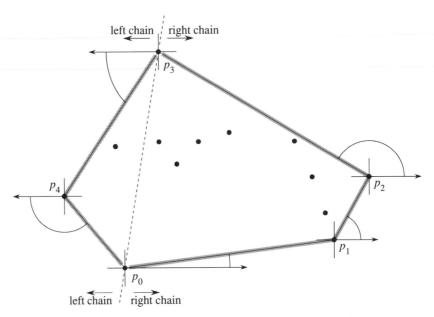

Figure 35.10   The operation of Jarvis's march. The first vertex chosen is the lowest point p_0. The next vertex, p_1, has the least polar angle of any point with respect to p_0. Then, p_2 has the least polar angle with respect to p_1. The right chain goes as high as the highest point p_3. Then, the left chain is constructed by finding least polar angles with respect to the negative x-axis.

Intuitively, Jarvis's march simulates wrapping a taut piece of paper around the set Q. We start by taping the end of the paper to the lowest point in the set, that is, to the same point p_0 with which we start Graham's scan. This point is a vertex of the convex hull. We pull the paper to the right to make it taut, and then we pull it higher until it touches a point. This point must also be a vertex of the convex hull. Keeping the paper taut, we continue in this way around the set of vertices until we come back to our original point p_0.

More formally, Jarvis's march builds a sequence $H = \langle p_0, p_1, \ldots, p_{h-1} \rangle$ of the vertices of CH(Q). We start with p_0. As Figure 35.10 shows, the next convex hull vertex p_1 has the least polar angle with respect to p_0. (In case of ties, we choose the point farthest from p_0.) Similarly, p_2 has the least polar angle with respect to p_1, and so on. When we reach the highest vertex, say p_k (breaking ties by choosing the farthest such vertex), we have constructed, as Figure 35.10 shows, the ***right chain*** of CH(Q). To construct the ***left chain***, we start at p_k and choose p_{k+1} as the point with the least polar angle with respect to p_k, but *from the negative x-axis*. We continue on, forming the left chain by taking polar angles from the negative x-axis, until we come back to our original vertex p_0.

We could implement Jarvis's march in one conceptual sweep around the convex hull, that is, without separately constructing the right and left chains. Such implementations typically keep track of the angle of the last convex-hull side chosen and require the sequence of angles of hull sides to be strictly increasing (in the range of 0 to 2π radians). The advantage of constructing separate chains is that we need not explicitly compute angles; the techniques of Section 35.1 suffice to compare angles.

If implemented properly, Jarvis's march has a running time of $O(nh)$. For each of the h vertices of $CH(Q)$, we find the vertex with the minimum polar angle. Each comparison between polar angles takes $O(1)$ time, using the techniques of Section 35.1. As Section 10.1 shows, we can compute the minimum of n values in $O(n)$ time if each comparison takes $O(1)$ time. Thus, Jarvis's march takes $O(nh)$ time.

Exercises

35.3-1
Prove that in the procedure GRAHAM-SCAN, points p_1 and p_m must be vertices of $CH(Q)$.

35.3-2
Consider a model of computation that supports addition, comparison, and multiplication and for which there is a lower bound of $\Omega(n \lg n)$ to sort n numbers. Prove that $\Omega(n \lg n)$ is a lower bound for computing, in order, the vertices of the convex hull of a set of n points in such a model.

35.3-3
Given a set of points Q, prove that the pair of points farthest from each other must be vertices of $CH(Q)$.

35.3-4
For a given polygon P and a point q on its boundary, the ***shadow*** of q is the set of points r such that the segment $\overline{qr}$ is entirely on the boundary or in the interior of P. A polygon P is ***star-shaped*** if there exists a point p in the interior of P that is in the shadow of every point on the boundary of P. The set of all such points p is called the ***kernel*** of P. (See Figure 35.11.) Given an n-vertex, star-shaped polygon P specified by its vertices in counterclockwise order, show how to compute $CH(P)$ in $O(n)$ time.

35.3-5
In the ***on-line convex-hull problem***, we are given the set Q of n points one point at a time. After receiving each point, we are to compute the convex hull of the points seen so far. Obviously, we could run Graham's scan once for each point, with a total running time of $O(n^2 \lg n)$. Show how to solve the on-line convex-hull problem in a total of $O(n^2)$ time.

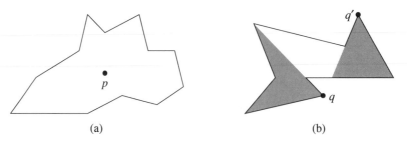

Figure 35.11   The definition of a star-shaped polygon, for use in Exercise 35.3-4. (**a**) A star-shaped polygon. The segment from point p to any point q on the boundary intersects the boundary only at q. (**b**) A non-star-shaped polygon. The shaded region on the left is the shadow of q, and the shaded region on the right is the shadow of q'. Since these regions are disjoint, the kernel is empty.

35.3-6 $\star$
Show how to implement the incremental method for computing the convex hull of n points so that it runs in $O(n \lg n)$ time.

35.4   Finding the closest pair of points

We now consider the problem of finding the closest pair of points in a set Q of $n \geq 2$ points. "Closest" refers to the usual euclidean distance: the distance between points $p_1 = (x_1, y_1)$ and $p_2 = (x_2, y_2)$ is $\sqrt{(x_1 - x_2)^2 - (y_1 - y_2)^2}$. Two points in set Q may be coincident, in which case the distance between them is zero. This problem has applications in, for example, traffic-control systems. A system for controlling air or sea traffic might need to know which are the two closest vehicles in order to detect potential collisions.

A brute-force closest-pair algorithm simply looks at all the $\binom{n}{2} = \Theta(n^2)$ pairs of points. In this section, we shall describe a divide-and-conquer algorithm for this problem whose running time is described by the familiar recurrence $T(n) = 2T(n/2) + O(n)$. Thus, this algorithm uses only $O(n \lg n)$ time.

The divide-and-conquer algorithm

Each recursive invocation of the algorithm takes as input a subset $P \subseteq Q$ and arrays X and Y, each of which contains all the points of the input subset P. The points in array X are sorted so that their x-coordinates are monotonically increasing. Similarly, array Y is sorted by monotonically increasing y-coordinate. Note that in order to attain the $O(n \lg n)$ time bound, we cannot afford to sort in each recursive call; if we did, the recurrence for the running time would be $T(n) = 2T(n/2) + O(n \lg n)$, whose solution is $T(n) = O(n \lg^2 n)$. We shall see a little later how to use "presorting" to maintain this sorted property without actually sorting in each recursive call.

A given recursive invocation with inputs P, X, and Y first checks whether $|P| \leq 3$. If so, the invocation simply performs the brute-force method described above: try all $\binom{|P|}{2}$ pairs of points and return the closest pair. If $|P| > 3$, the recursive invocation carries out the divide-and-conquer paradigm as follows.

Divide: It finds a vertical line l that bisects the point set P into two sets P_L and P_R such that $|P_L| = \lceil |P|/2 \rceil$, $|P_R| = \lfloor |P|/2 \rfloor$, all points in P_L are on or to the left of line l, and all points in P_R are on or to the right of l. The array X is divided into arrays X_L and X_R, which contain the points of P_L and P_R respectively, sorted by monotonically increasing x-coordinate. Similarly, the array Y is divided into arrays Y_L and Y_R, which contain the points of P_L and P_R respectively, sorted by monotonically increasing y-coordinate.

Conquer: Having divided P into P_L and P_R, it makes two recursive calls, one to find the closest pair of points in P_L and the other to find the closest pair of points in P_R. The inputs to the first call are the subset P_L and arrays X_L and Y_L; the second call receives the inputs P_R, X_R, and Y_R. Let the closest-pair distances returned for P_L and P_R be δ_L and δ_R, respectively, and let $\delta = \min(\delta_L, \delta_R)$.

Combine: The closest pair is either the pair with distance δ found by one of the recursive calls, or it is a pair of points with one point in P_L and the other in P_R. The algorithm determines if there is such a pair whose distance is less than δ. Observe that if there is a pair of points with distance less than δ, both points of the pair must be within δ units of line l. Thus, as Figure 35.12(a) shows, they both must reside in the 2δ-wide vertical strip centered at line l. To find such a pair, if one exists, the algorithm does the following.

1. It creates an array Y', which is the array Y with all points not in the 2δ-wide vertical strip removed. The array Y' is sorted by y-coordinate, just as Y is.

2. For each point p in the array Y', the algorithm tries to find points in Y' that are within δ units of p. As we shall see shortly, only the 7 points in Y' that follow p need be considered. The algorithm computes the distance from p to each of these 7 points and keeps track of the closest-pair distance δ' found over all pairs of points in Y'.

3. If $\delta' < \delta$, then the vertical strip does indeed contain a closer pair than was found by the recursive calls. This pair and its distance δ' are returned. Otherwise, the closest pair and its distance δ found by the recursive calls are returned.

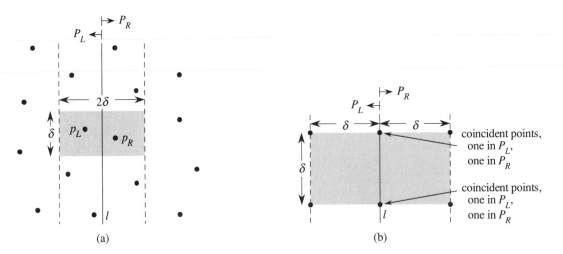

Figure 35.12 Key concepts in the proof that the closest-pair algorithm needs to check only 7 points following each point in the array Y'. (a) If $p_L \in P_L$ and $p_R \in P_R$ are less than δ units apart, they must reside within a $\delta \times 2\delta$ rectangle centered at line l. (b) How 4 points that are pairwise at least δ units apart can all reside within a $\delta \times \delta$ square. On the left are 4 points in P_L, and on the right are 4 points in P_R. There can be 8 points in the $\delta \times 2\delta$ rectangle if the points shown on line l are actually pairs of coincident points with one point in P_L and one in P_R.

The above description omits some implementation details that are necessary to achieve the $O(n \lg n)$ running time. After proving the correctness of the algorithm, we shall show how to implement the algorithm to achieve the desired time bound.

Correctness

The correctness of this closest-pair algorithm is obvious, except for two aspects. First, by bottoming out the recursion when $|P| \leq 3$, we ensure that we never try to divide a set of points with only one point. The second aspect is that we need only check the 7 points following each point p in array Y'; we shall now prove this property.

Suppose that at some level of the recursion, the closest pair of points is $p_L \in P_L$ and $p_R \in P_R$. Thus, the distance δ' between p_L and p_R is strictly less than δ. Point p_L must be on or to the left of line l and less than δ units away. Similarly, p_R is on or to the right of l and less than δ units away. Moreover, p_L and p_R are within δ units of each other vertically. Thus, as Figure 35.12(a) shows, p_L and p_R are within a $\delta \times 2\delta$ rectangle centered at line l. (There may be other points within this rectangle as well.)

We next show that at most 8 points of P can reside within this $\delta \times 2\delta$ rectangle. Consider the $\delta \times \delta$ square forming the left half of this rectangle. Since all points within P_L are at least δ units apart, at most 4 points can reside within this square; Figure 35.12(b) shows how. Similarly, at most

4 points in P_R can reside within the $\delta \times \delta$ square forming the right half of the rectangle. Thus, at most 8 points of P can reside within the $\delta \times 2\delta$ rectangle. (Note that since points on line l may be in either P_L or P_R, there may be up to 4 points on l. This limit is achieved if there are two pairs of coincident points, each pair consisting of one point from P_L and one point from P_R, one pair is at the intersection of l and the top of the rectangle, and the other pair is where l intersects the bottom of the rectangle.)

Having shown that at most 8 points of P can reside within the rectangle, it is easy to see that we need only check the 7 points following each point in the array Y'. Still assuming that the closest pair is p_L and p_R, let us assume without loss of generality that p_L precedes p_R in array Y'. Then, even if p_L occurs as early as possible in Y' and p_R occurs as late as possible, p_R is in one of the 7 positions following p_L. Thus, we have shown the correctness of the closest-pair algorithm.

Implementation and running time

As we have noted, our goal is to have the recurrence for the running time be $T(n) = 2T(n/2) + O(n)$, where $T(n)$ is, of course, the running time for a set of n points. The main difficulty is in ensuring that the arrays X_L, X_R, Y_L, and Y_R, which are passed to recursive calls, are sorted by the proper coordinate and also that the array Y' is sorted by y-coordinate. (Note that if the array X that is received by a recursive call is already sorted, then the division of set P into P_L and P_R is easily accomplished in linear time.)

The key observation is that in each call, we wish to form a sorted subset of a sorted array. For example, a particular invocation is given the subset P and the array Y, sorted by y-coordinate. Having partitioned P into P_L and P_R, it needs to form the arrays Y_L and Y_R, which are sorted by y-coordinate. Moreover, these arrays must be formed in linear time. The method can be viewed as the opposite of the MERGE procedure from merge sort in Section 1.3.1: we are splitting a sorted array into two sorted arrays. The following pseudocode gives the idea.

```
1  length[Y_L] ← length[Y_R] ← 0
2  for i ← 1 to length[Y]
3       do if Y[i] ∈ P_L
4            then length[Y_L] ← length[Y_L] + 1
5                 Y[length[Y_L]] ← Y[i]
6            else length[Y_R] ← length[Y_R] + 1
7                 Y[length[Y_R]] ← Y[i]
```

We simply examine the points in array Y in order. If a point $Y[i]$ is in P_L, we append it to the end of array Y_L; otherwise, we append it to the end of array Y_R. Similar pseudocode works for forming arrays X_L, X_R, and Y'.

The only remaining question is how to get the points sorted in the first place. We do this by simply ***presorting*** them; that is, we sort them once and

for all *before* the first recursive call. These sorted arrays are passed into
the first recursive call, and from there they are whittled down through the
recursive calls as necessary. The presorting adds an additional $O(n \lg n)$
to the running time, but now each step of the recursion takes linear time
exclusive of the recursive calls. Thus, if we let $T(n)$ be the running time of
each recursive step and $T'(n)$ be the running time of the entire algorithm,
we get $T'(n) = T(n) + O(n \lg n)$ and

$$T(n) = \begin{cases} 2T(n/2) + O(n) & \text{if } n > 3 , \\ O(1) & \text{if } n \le 3 . \end{cases}$$

Thus, $T(n) = O(n \lg n)$ and $T'(n) = O(n \lg n)$.

Exercises

35.4-1
Professor Smothers comes up with a scheme that allows the closest-pair
algorithm to check only 5 points following each point in array Y'. The
idea is always to place points on line l into set P_L. Then, there cannot be
pairs of coincident points on line l with one point in P_L and one in P_R.
Thus, at most 6 points can reside in the $\delta \times 2\delta$ rectangle. What is the flaw
in the professor's scheme?

35.4-2
Without increasing the asymptotic running time of the algorithm, show
how to ensure that the set of points passed to the very first recursive call
contains no coincident points. Prove that it then suffices to check the
points in the 6 (not 7) array positions following each point in the array Y'.
Why doesn't it suffice to check only the 5 array positions following each
point?

35.4-3
The distance between two points can be defined in ways other than eu-
clidean. In the plane, the L_m-***distance*** between points p_1 and p_2 is given by
$((x_1 - x_2)^m + (y_1 - y_2)^m)^{1/m}$. Euclidean distance, therefore, is L_2-distance.
Modify the closest-pair algorithm to use the L_1-distance, which is also
known as the ***Manhattan distance***.

35.4-4
Given two points p_1 and p_2 in the plane, the L_∞-distance between them
is $\max(|x_1 - x_2|, |y_1 - y_2|)$. Modify the closest-pair algorithm to use the
L_∞-distance.

Problems

35-1 Convex layers

Given a set Q of points in the plane, we define the ***convex layers*** of Q inductively. The first convex layer of Q consists of those points in Q that are vertices of $CH(Q)$. For $i > 1$, define Q_i to consist of the points of Q with all points in convex layers $1, 2, \ldots, i-1$ removed. Then, the ith convex layer of Q is $CH(Q_i)$ if $Q_i \neq \emptyset$ and is undefined otherwise.

a. Give an $O(n^2)$-time algorithm to find the convex layers of a set on n points.

b. Prove that $\Omega(n \lg n)$ time is required to compute the convex layers of a set of n points on any model of computation that requires $\Omega(n \lg n)$ time to sort n real numbers.

35-2 Maximal layers

Let Q be a set of n points in the plane. We say that point (x, y) ***dominates*** point (x', y') if $x \geq x'$ and $y \geq y'$. A point in Q that is dominated by no other points in Q is said to be ***maximal***. Note that Q may contain many maximal points, which can be organized into ***maximal layers*** as follows. The first maximal layer L_1 is the set of maximal points of Q. For $i > 1$, the ith maximal layer L_i is the set of maximal points in $Q - \bigcup_{j=1}^{i-1} L_j$.

Suppose that Q has k nonempty maximal layers, and let y_i be the y-coordinate of the leftmost point in L_i for $i = 1, 2, \ldots, k$. For now, assume that no two points in Q have the same x- or y-coordinate.

a. Show that $y_1 > y_2 > \cdots > y_k$.

Consider a point (x, y) that is to the left of any point in Q and for which y is distinct from the y-coordinate of any point in Q. Let $Q' = Q \cup \{(x, y)\}$.

b. Let j be the minimum index such that $y_j < y$, unless $y < y_k$, in which case we let $j = k + 1$. Show that the maximal layers of Q' are as follows.

- If $j \leq k$, then the maximal layers of Q' are the same as the maximal layers of Q, except that L_j also includes (x, y) as its new leftmost point.

- If $j = k + 1$, then the first k maximal layers of Q' are the same as for Q, but in addition, Q' has a nonempty $(k + 1)$st maximal layer: $L_{k+1} = \{(x, y)\}$.

c. Describe an $O(n \lg n)$-time algorithm to compute the maximal layers of a set Q of n points. (*Hint:* Move a sweep line from right to left.)

d. Do any difficulties arise if we now allow input points to have the same x- or y-coordinate? Suggest a way to resolve such problems.

35-3   *Ghostbusters and ghosts*

A group of n Ghostbusters is battling n ghosts. Each Ghostbuster is armed with a proton pack, which shoots a stream at a ghost, eradicating it. A stream goes in a straight line and terminates when it hits the ghost. The Ghostbusters decide upon the following strategy. They will pair off with the ghosts, forming n Ghostbuster-ghost pairs, and then simultaneously each Ghostbuster will shoot a stream at his or her chosen ghost. As we all know, it is *very* dangerous to let streams cross, and so the Ghostbusters must choose pairings for which no streams will cross.

Assume that the position of each Ghostbuster and each ghost is a fixed point in the plane and that no three positions are collinear.

a. Argue that there exists a line passing through one Ghostbuster and one ghost such the number of Ghostbusters on one side of the line equals the number of ghosts on the same side. Describe how to find such a line in $O(n \lg n)$ time.

b. Give an $O(n^2 \lg n)$-time algorithm to pair Ghostbusters with ghosts in such a way that no streams cross.

35-4   *Sparse-hulled distributions*

Consider the problem of computing the convex hull of a set of points in the plane that have been drawn according to some known random distribution. Sometimes, the convex hull of n points drawn from such a distribution has $O(n^{1-\epsilon})$ expected size for some constant $\epsilon > 0$. We call such a distribution *sparse-hulled*. Sparse-hulled distributions include the following:

- Points drawn uniformly from a unit-radius disk. The convex hull has $\Theta(n^{1/3})$ expected size.

- Points drawn uniformly from the interior of a convex polygon with k sides, for any constant k. The convex hull has $\Theta(\lg n)$ expected size.

- Points drawn according to a two-dimensional normal distribution. The convex hull has $\Theta(\sqrt{\lg n})$ expected size.

a. Given two convex polygons with n_1 and n_2 vertices respectively, show how to compute the convex hull of all $n_1 + n_2$ points in $O(n_1 + n_2)$ time. (The polygons may overlap.)

b. Show that the convex hull of a set of n points drawn independently according to a sparse-hulled distribution can be computed in $O(n)$ expected time. (*Hint:* Recursively find the convex hulls of the first $n/2$ points and the second $n/2$ points, and then combine the results.)

Chapter notes

This chapter barely scratches the surface of computational-geometry algorithms and techniques. Books on computational geometry include those by Preparata and Shamos [160] and Edelsbrunner [60].

Although geometry has been studied since antiquity, the development of algorithms for geometric problems is relatively new. Preparata and Shamos note that the earliest notion of the complexity of a problem was given by E. Lemoine in 1902. He was studying euclidean constructions—those using a ruler and a straightedge—and devised a set of five primitives: placing one leg of the compass on a given point, placing one leg of the compass on a given line, drawing a circle, passing the ruler's edge through a given point, and drawing a line. Lemoine was interested in the number of primitives needed to effect a given construction; he called this amount the "simplicity" of the construction.

The algorithm of Section 35.2, which determines whether any segments intersect, is due to Shamos and Hoey [176].

The original version of Graham's scan is given by Graham [91]. The package-wrapping algorithm is due to Jarvis [112]. Using a decision-tree model of computation, Yao [205] proved a lower bound of $\Omega(n \lg n)$ for the running time of any convex-hull algorithm. When the number of vertices h of the convex hull is taken into account, the prune-and-search algorithm of Kirkpatrick and Seidel [120], which takes $O(n \lg h)$ time, is asymptotically optimal.

The $O(n \lg n)$-time divide-and-conquer algorithm for finding the closest pair of points is by Shamos and appears in Preparata and Shamos [160]. Preparata and Shamos also show that the algorithm is asymptotically optimal in a decision-tree model.

All of the algorithms we have studied thus far have been ***polynomial-time algorithms***: on inputs of size n, their worst-case running time is $O(n^k)$ for some constant k. It is natural to wonder whether *all* problems can be solved in polynomial time. The answer is no. For example, there are problems, such as Turing's famous "Halting Problem," that cannot be solved by any computer, no matter how much time is provided. There are also problems that can be solved, but not in time $O(n^k)$ for any constant k. Generally, we think of problems that are solvable by polynomial-time algorithms as being tractable, and problems that require superpolynomial time as being intractable.

The subject of this chapter, however, is an interesting class of problems, called the "NP-complete" problems, whose status is unknown. No polynomial-time algorithm has yet been discovered for an NP-complete problem, nor has anyone yet been able to prove a superpolynomial-time lower bound for any of them. This so-called P ≠ NP question has been one of the deepest, most perplexing open research problems in theoretical computer science since it was posed in 1971.

Most theoretical computer scientists believe that the NP-complete problems are intractable. The reason is that if any single NP-complete problem can be solved in polynomial time, then *every* NP-complete problem has a polynomial-time algorithm. Given the wide range of NP-complete problems that have been studied to date, without any progress toward a polynomial-time solution, it would be truly astounding if all of them could be solved in polynomial time.

To become a good algorithm designer, you must understand the rudiments of the theory of NP-completeness. If you can establish a problem as NP-complete, you provide good evidence for its intractability. As an engineer, you would then do better spending your time developing an approximation algorithm (see Chapter 37) rather than searching for a fast algorithm that solves the problem exactly. Moreover, many natural and interesting problems that on the surface seem no harder than sorting, graph searching, or network flow are in fact NP-complete. Thus, it is important to become familiar with this remarkable class of problems.

This chapter studies the aspects of NP-completeness that bear most directly on the analysis of algorithms. In Section 36.1, we formalize our notion of "problem" and define the complexity class P of polynomial-time solvable decision problems. We also see how these notions fit into the framework of formal-language theory. Section 36.2 defines the class NP of decision problems whose solutions can be verified in polynomial time. It also formally poses the P ≠ NP question.

Section 36.3 shows how relationships between problems can be studied via polynomial-time "reductions." It defines NP-completeness and sketches a proof that one problem, called "circuit satisfiability," is NP-complete. Having found one NP-complete problem, we show in Section 36.4 how other problems can be proven to be NP-complete much more simply by the methodology of reductions. The methodology is illustrated by showing that two formula-satisfiability problems are NP-complete. A variety of other problems are shown to be NP-complete in Section 36.5.

36.1 Polynomial time

We begin our study of NP-completeness by formalizing our notion of polynomial-time solvable problems. These problems are generally regarded as tractable. The reason why is a philosophical, not a mathematical, issue. We can offer three supporting arguments.

First, although it is reasonable to regard a problem that requires time $\Theta(n^{100})$ as intractable, there are very few practical problems that require time on the order of such a high-degree polynomial. The polynomial-time computable problems encountered in practice typically require much less time.

Second, for many reasonable models of computation, a problem that can be solved in polynomial time in one model can be solved in polynomial time in another. For example, the class of problems solvable in polynomial time by the serial random-access machine used throughout most of this book is the same as the class of problems solvable in polynomial time on abstract Turing machines.[1] It is also the same as the class of problems solvable in polynomial time on a parallel computer, even if the number of processors grows polynomially with the input size.

Third, the class of polynomial-time solvable problems has nice closure properties, since polynomials are closed under addition, multiplication, and composition. For example, if the output of one polynomial-time algorithm is fed into the input of another, the composite algorithm is polynomial. If an otherwise polynomial-time algorithm makes a constant number

---

[1]See Hopcroft and Ullman [104] or Lewis and Papadimitriou [139] for a thorough treatment of the Turing-machine model.

of calls to polynomial-time subroutines, the running time of the composite algorithm is polynomial.

Abstract problems

To understand the class of polynomial-time solvable problems, we must first have a formal notion of what a "problem" is. We define an *abstract problem* Q to be a binary relation on a set I of problem *instances* and a set S of problem *solutions*. For example, consider the problem SHORTEST-PATH of finding a shortest path between two given vertices in an unweighted, undirected graph $G = (V, E)$. An instance for SHORTEST-PATH is a triple consisting of a graph and two vertices. A solution is a sequence of vertices in the graph, with perhaps the empty sequence denoting that no path exists. The problem SHORTEST-PATH itself is the relation that associates each instance of a graph and two vertices with a shortest path in the graph that connects the two vertices. Since shortest paths are not necessarily unique, a given problem instance may have more than one solution.

This formulation of an abstract problem is more general than is required for our purposes. For simplicity, the theory of NP-completeness restricts attention to *decision problems*: those having a yes/no solution. In this case, we can view an abstract decision problem as a function that maps the instance set I to the solution set $\{0, 1\}$. For example, a decision problem PATH related to the shortest-path problem is, "Given a graph $G = (V, E)$, two vertices $u, v \in V$, and a nonnegative integer k, does a path exist in G between u and v whose length is at most k?" If $i = \langle G, u, v, k \rangle$ is an instance of this shortest-path problem, then $\text{PATH}(i) = 1$ (yes) if a shortest path from u to v has length at most k, and $\text{PATH}(i) = 0$ (no) otherwise.

Many abstract problems are not decision problems, but rather *optimization problems*, in which some value must be minimized or maximized. In order to apply the theory of NP-completeness to optimization problems, we must recast them as decision problems. Typically, an optimization problem can be recast by imposing a bound on the value to be optimized. As an example, in recasting the shortest-path problem as the decision problem PATH, we added a bound k to the problem instance.

Although the theory of NP-completeness compels us to recast optimization problems as decision problems, this requirement does not diminish the impact of the theory. In general, if we can solve an optimization problem quickly, we can also solve its related decision problem quickly. We simply compare the value obtained from the solution of the optimization problem with the bound provided as input to the decision problem. If an optimization problem is easy, therefore, its related decision problem is easy as well. Stated in a way that has more relevance to NP-completeness, if we can provide evidence that a decision problem is hard, we also provide evidence that its related optimization problem is hard. Thus, even though it restricts attention to decision problems, the theory of NP-completeness applies much more widely.

Encodings

If a computer program is to solve an abstract problem, problem instances must must be represented in a way that the program understands. An *encoding* of a set S of abstract objects is a mapping e from S to the set of binary strings.[2] For example, we are all familiar with encoding the natural numbers $\mathbf{N} = \{0, 1, 2, 3, 4, \ldots\}$ as the strings $\{0, 1, 10, 11, 100, \ldots\}$. Using this encoding, $e(17) = 10001$. Anyone who has looked at computer representations of keyboard characters is familiar with either the ASCII or EBCDIC codes. In the ASCII code, $e(\mathtt{A}) = 1000001$. Even a compound object can be encoded as a binary string by combining the representations of its constituent parts. Polygons, graphs, functions, ordered pairs, programs—all can be encoded as binary strings.

Thus, a computer algorithm that "solves" some abstract decision problem actually takes an encoding of a problem instance as input. We call a problem whose instance set is the set of binary strings a *concrete problem*. We say that an algorithm *solves* a concrete problem in time $O(T(n))$ if, when it is provided a problem instance i of length $n = |i|$, the algorithm can produce the solution in at most $O(T(n))$ time. A concrete problem is *polynomial-time solvable*, therefore, if there exists an algorithm to solve it in time $O(n^k)$ for some constant k.

We can now formally define the *complexity class* **P** as the set of concrete decision problems that are solvable in polynomial time.

We can use encodings to map abstract problems to concrete problems. Given an abstract decision problem Q mapping an instance set I to $\{0, 1\}$, an encoding $e : I \to \{0, 1\}^*$ can be used to induce a related concrete decision problem, which we denote by $e(Q)$. If the solution to an abstract-problem instance $i \in I$ is $Q(i) \in \{0, 1\}$, then the solution to the concrete-problem instance $e(i) \in \{0, 1\}^*$ is also $Q(i)$. As a technicality, there may be some binary strings that represent no meaningful abstract-problem instance. For convenience, we shall assume that any such string is mapped arbitrarily to 0. Thus, the concrete problem produces the same solutions as the abstract problem on binary-string instances that represent the encodings of abstract-problem instances.

We would like to extend the definition of polynomial-time solvability from concrete problems to abstract problems using encodings as the bridge, but we would like the definition to be independent of any particular en-

---

[2]The codomain of e need not be *binary* strings; any set of strings over a finite alphabet having at least 2 symbols will do.

coding. That is, the efficiency of solving a problem should not depend on
how the problem is encoded. Unfortunately, it depends quite heavily. For
example, suppose that an integer k is to be provided as the sole input to
an algorithm, and suppose that the running time of the algorithm is $\Theta(k)$.
If the integer k is provided in ***unary***—a string of k 1's—then the running
time of the algorithm is $O(n)$ on length-n inputs, which is polynomial time.
If we use the more natural binary representation of the integer k, however,
then the input length is $n = \lceil \lg k \rceil$. In this case, the running time of the
algorithm is $\Theta(k) = \Theta(2^n)$, which is exponential in the size of the input.
Thus, depending on the encoding, the algorithm runs in either polynomial
or superpolynomial time.

The encoding of an abstract problem is therefore quite important to our
understanding of polynomial time. We cannot really talk about solving
an abstract problem without first specifying an encoding. Nevertheless,
in practice, if we rule out "expensive" encodings such as unary ones, the
actual encoding of a problem makes little difference to whether the problem
can be solved in polynomial time. For example, representing integers in
base 3 instead of binary has no effect on whether a problem is solvable in
polynomial time, since an integer represented in base 3 can be converted
to an integer represented in base 2 in polynomial time.

We say that a function $f : \{0, 1\}^* \rightarrow \{0, 1\}^*$ is ***polynomial-time computable*** if there exists a polynomial-time algorithm A that, given any input
$x \in \{0, 1\}^*$, produces as output $f(x)$. For some set I of problem instances,
we say that two encodings e_1 and e_2 are ***polynomially related*** if there exist
two polynomial-time computable functions f_{12} and f_{21} such that for any
$i \in I$, we have $f_{12}(e_1(i)) = e_2(i)$ and $f_{21}(e_2(i)) = e_1(i)$. That is, the encoding $e_2(i)$ can be computed from the encoding $e_1(i)$ by a polynomial-time
algorithm, and vice versa. If two encodings e_1 and e_2 of an abstract problem are polynomially related, which we use makes no difference to whether
the problem is polynomial-time solvable or not, as the following lemma
shows.

Lemma 36.1
Let Q be an abstract decision problem on an instance set I, and let e_1 and
e_2 be polynomially related encodings on I. Then, $e_1(Q) \in P$ if and only if
$e_2(Q) \in P$.

Proof   We need only prove the forward direction, since the backward
direction is symmetric. Suppose, therefore, that $e_1(Q)$ can be solved in
time $O(n^k)$ for some constant k. Further, suppose that for any problem
instance i, the encoding $e_1(i)$ can be computed from the encoding $e_2(i)$
in time $O(n^c)$ for some constant c, where $n = |e_1(i)|$. To solve problem
$e_2(Q)$, on input $e_2(i)$, we first compute $e_1(i)$ and then run the algorithm
for $e_1(Q)$ on $e_1(i)$. How long does this take? The conversion of encodings
takes time $O(n^c)$, and therefore $|e_1(i)| = O(n^c)$, since the output of a serial
computer cannot be longer than its running time. Solving the problem on

$e_1(i)$ takes time $O(|e_1(i)|^k) = O(n^{ck})$, which is polynomial since both c and k are constants.   ■

Thus, whether an abstract problem has its instances encoded in binary or base 3 does not affect its "complexity," that is, whether it is polynomial-time solvable or not, but if instances are encoded in unary, its complexity may change. In order to be able to converse in an encoding-independent fashion, we shall generally assume that problem instances are encoded in any reasonable, concise fashion, unless we specifically say otherwise. To be precise, we shall assume that the encoding of an integer is polynomially related to its binary representation, and that the encoding of a finite set is polynomially related to its encoding as a list of its elements, enclosed in braces and separated by commas. (ASCII is one such encoding scheme.) With such a "standard" encoding in hand, we can derive reasonable encodings of other mathematical objects, such as tuples, graphs, and formulas. To denote the standard encoding of an object, we shall enclose the object in angle braces. Thus, $\langle G \rangle$ denotes the standard encoding of a graph G.

As long as we implicitly use an encoding that is polynomially related to this standard encoding, we can talk directly about abstract problems without reference to any particular encoding, knowing that the choice of encoding has no effect on whether the abstract problem is polynomial-time solvable. Henceforth, we shall generally assume that all problem instances are binary strings encoded using the standard encoding, unless we explicitly specify the contrary. We shall also typically neglect the distinction between abstract and concrete problems. The reader should watch out for problems that arise in practice, however, in which a standard encoding is not obvious and the encoding does make a difference.

A formal-language framework

One of the convenient aspects of focusing on decision problems is that they make it easy to use the machinery of formal-language theory. It is worthwhile at this point to review some definitions from that theory. An *alphabet* Σ is a finite set of symbols. A *language* L over Σ is any set of strings made up of symbols from Σ. For example, if $\Sigma = \{0, 1\}$, the set $L = \{10, 11, 101, 111, 1011, 1101, 10001, \ldots\}$ is the language of binary representations of prime numbers. We denote the *empty string* by ε, and the *empty language* by $\emptyset$. The language of all strings over Σ is denoted Σ^*. For example, if $\Sigma = \{0, 1\}$, then $\Sigma^* = \{\varepsilon, 0, 1, 00, 01, 10, 11, 000, \ldots\}$ is the set of all binary strings. Every language L over Σ is a subset of Σ^*.

There are a variety of operations on languages. Set-theoretic operations, such as *union* and *intersection*, follow directly from the set-theoretic definitions. We define the *complement* of L by $\overline{L} = \Sigma^* - L$. The *concatenation* of two languages L_1 and L_2 is the language

$$L = \{x_1 x_2 : x_1 \in L_1 \text{ and } x_2 \in L_2\} \ .$$

The **closure** or **Kleene star** of a language L is the language

$$L^* = \{\varepsilon\} \cup L \cup L^2 \cup L^3 \cup \cdots,$$

where L^k is the language obtained by concatenating L to itself k times.

From the point of view of language theory, the set of instances for any decision problem Q is simply the set Σ^*, where $\Sigma = \{0, 1\}$. Since Q is entirely characterized by those problem instances that produce a 1 (yes) answer, we can view Q as a language L over $\Sigma = \{0, 1\}$, where

$$L = \{x \in \Sigma^* : Q(x) = 1\} \ .$$

For example, the decision problem PATH has the corresponding language

$$\begin{aligned}
\text{PATH} = \{\langle G, u, v, k \rangle : \ &G = (V, E) \text{ is an undirected graph,} \\
&u, v \in V, \\
&k \geq 0 \text{ is an integer, and} \\
&\text{there exists a path from } u \text{ to } v \text{ in } G \\
&\text{whose length is at most } k\} \ .
\end{aligned}$$

(Where convenient, we shall sometimes use the same name—PATH in this case—to refer to both a decision problem and its corresponding language.)

The formal-language framework allows us to express the relation between decision problems and algorithms that solve them concisely. We say that an algorithm A **accepts** a string $x \in \{0, 1\}^*$ if, given input x, the algorithm outputs $A(x) = 1$. The language **accepted** by an algorithm A is the set $L = \{x \in \{0, 1\}^* : A(x) = 1\}$, that is, the set of strings that the algorithm accepts. An algorithm A **rejects** a string x if $A(x) = 0$.

Even if language L is accepted by an algorithm A, the algorithm will not necessarily reject a string $x \notin L$ provided as input to it. For example, the algorithm may loop forever. A language L is **decided** by an algorithm A if every binary string is either accepted or rejected by the algorithm. A language L is **accepted in polynomial time** by an algorithm A if for any length-n string $x \in L$, the algorithm accepts x in time $O(n^k)$ for some constant k. A language L is **decided in polynomial time** by an algorithm A if for any length-n string $x \in \{0, 1\}^*$, the algorithm decides x in time $O(n^k)$ for some constant k. Thus, to accept a language, an algorithm need only worry about strings in L, but to decide a language, it must accept or reject every string in $\{0, 1\}^*$.

As an example, the language PATH can be accepted in polynomial time. One polynomial-time accepting algorithm computes the shortest path from u to v in G, using breadth-first search, and then compares the distance obtained with k. If the distance is at most k, the algorithm outputs 1 and halts. Otherwise, the algorithm runs forever. This algorithm does not decide PATH, however, since it does not explicitly output 0 for instances in which the shortest path has length greater than k. A decision algorithm for PATH must explicitly reject binary strings that do not belong to PATH. For a decision problem such as PATH, such a decision algorithm is easy to design. For other problems, such as Turing's Halting Problem, there exists an accepting algorithm, but no decision algorithm exists.

We can informally define a ***complexity class*** as a set of languages, membership in which is determined by a ***complexity measure***, such as running time, on an algorithm that determines whether a given string x belongs to language L. The actual definition of a complexity class is somewhat more technical—the interested reader is referred to the seminal paper by Hartmanis and Stearns [95].

Using this language-theoretic framework, wee can provide an alternative definition of the complexity class P:

$$\text{P} = \{L \subseteq \{0, 1\}^* : \text{there exists an algorithm } A$$
$$\text{that decides } L \text{ in polynomial time}\} \, .$$

In fact, P is also the class of languages that can be accepted in polynomial time.

Theorem 36.2
$\text{P} = \{L : L \text{ is accepted by a polynomial-time algorithm}\} \, .$

Proof Since the class of languages decided by polynomial-time algorithms is a subset of the class of languages accepted by polynomial-time algorithms, we need only show that if L is accepted by a polynomial-time algorithm, it is decided by a polynomial-time algorithm. Let L be the language accepted by some polynomial-time algorithm A. We shall use a classic "simulation" argument to construct another polynomial-time algorithm A' that decides L. Because A accepts L in time $O(n^k)$ for some constant k, there also exists a constant c such that A accepts L in at most $T = cn^k$ steps. For any input string x, the algorithm A' simulates the action of A for time T. At the end of time T, algorithm A' inspects the behavior of A. If A has accepted x, then A' accepts x by outputting a 1. If A has not accepted x, then A' rejects x by outputting a 0. The overhead of A' simulating A does not increase the running time by more than a polynomial factor, and thus A' is a polynomial-time algorithm that decides L. ∎

Note that the proof of Theorem 36.2 is nonconstructive. For a given language $L \in \text{P}$, we may not actually know a bound on the running time for the algorithm A that accepts L. Nevertheless, we know that such a bound exists, and therefore, that an algorithm A' exists that can check the bound, even though we may not be able to find the algorithm A' easily.

Exercises

36.1-1
Define the optimization problem LONGEST-PATH-LENGTH as the relation that associates each instance of a undirected graph and two vertices with the length of the longest simple path between the two vertices. Define the decision problem LONGEST-PATH = $\{\langle G, u, v, k \rangle : G = (V, E)$

is an undirected graph, $u, v \in V$, $k \geq 0$ is an integer, and there exists a simple path from u to v in G whose length is at least k}. Show that the optimization problem LONGEST-PATH-LENGTH can be solved in polynomial time if and only if LONGEST-PATH $\in$ P.

36.1-2
Give a formal definition for the problem of finding the longest simple cycle in an undirected graph. Give a related decision problem. Give the language corresponding to the decision problem.

36.1-3
Give a formal encoding of directed graphs as binary strings using an adjacency-matrix representation. Do the same using an adjacency-list representation. Argue that the two representations are polynomially related.

36.1-4
Is the dynamic-programming algorithm for the 0-1 knapsack problem that is asked for in Exercise 17.2-2 a polynomial-time algorithm? Explain your answer.

36.1-5
Suppose that a language L can accept any string $x \in L$ in polynomial time, but that the algorithm that does this runs in superpolynomial time if $x \notin L$. Argue that L can be decided in polynomial time.

36.1-6
Show that an algorithm that makes at most a constant number of calls to polynomial-time subroutines runs in polynomial time, but that a polynomial number of calls to polynomial-time subroutines may result in an exponential-time algorithm.

36.1-7
Show that the class P, viewed as a set of languages, is closed under union, intersection, concatenation, complement, and Kleene star. That is, if $L_1, L_2 \in$ P, then $L_1 \cup L_2 \in$ P, etc.

36.2 Polynomial-time verification

We now look at algorithms that "verify" membership in languages. For example, suppose that for a given instance $\langle G, u, v, k \rangle$ of the decision problem PATH, we are also given a path p from u to v. We can easily check whether the length of p is at most k, and if so, we can view p as a "certificate" that the instance indeed belongs to PATH. For the decision problem PATH, this certificate doesn't seem to buy us much. After all, PATH belongs to P—in fact, PATH can be solved in linear time—and so verifying

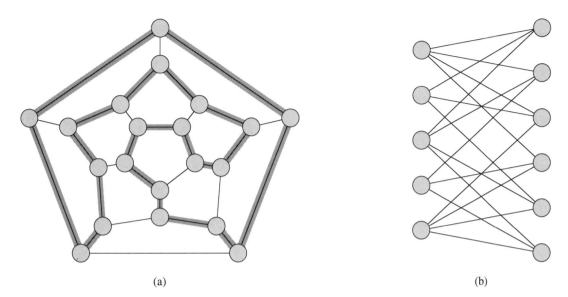

Figure 36.1 (**a**) A graph representing the vertices, edges, and faces of a dodecahedron, with a hamiltonian cycle shown by shaded edges. (**b**) A bipartite graph with an odd number of vertices. Any such graph is nonhamiltonian.

membership from a given certificate takes as long as solving the problem from scratch. We shall now examine a problem for which we know of no polynomial-time decision algorithm yet, given a certificate, verification is easy.

Hamiltonian cycles

The problem of finding a hamiltonian cycle in an undirected graph has been studied for over a hundred years. Formally, a **_hamiltonian cycle_** of an undirected graph $G = (V, E)$ is a simple cycle that contains each vertex in V. A graph that contains a hamiltonian cycle is said to be **_hamiltonian_**; otherwise, it is **_nonhamiltonian_**. Bondy and Murty [31] cite a letter by W. R. Hamilton describing a mathematical game on the dodecahedron (Figure 36.1(a)) in which one player sticks five pins in any five consecutive vertices and the other player must complete the path to form a cycle containing all the vertices. The dodecahedron is hamiltonian, and Figure 36.1(a) shows one hamiltonian cycle. Not all graphs are hamiltonian, however. For example, Figure 36.1(b) shows a bipartite graph with an odd number of vertices. (Exercise 36.2-2 asks you to show that all such graphs are nonhamiltonian.)

We can define the **_hamiltonian-cycle problem_**, "Does a graph G have a hamiltonian cycle?" as a formal language:

HAM-CYCLE $= \{\langle G \rangle : G \text{ is a hamiltonian graph}\}$.

How might an algorithm decide the language HAM-CYCLE? Given a problem instance $\langle G \rangle$, one possible decision algorithm lists all permutations of the vertices of G and then checks each permutation to see if it is a hamiltonian path. What is the running time of this algorithm? If we use the "reasonable" encoding of a graph as its adjacency matrix, the number m of vertices in the graph is $\Omega(\sqrt{n})$, where $n = |\langle G \rangle|$ is the length of the encoding of G. There are $m!$ possible permutations of the vertices, and therefore the running time is $\Omega(m!) = \Omega(\sqrt{n}!) = \Omega(2^{\sqrt{n}})$, which is not $O(n^k)$ for any constant k. Thus, this naive algorithm does not run in polynomial time, and in fact, the hamiltonian-cycle problem is NP-complete, as we shall prove in Section 36.5.

Verification algorithms

Consider a slightly easier problem, however. Suppose that a friend tells you that a given graph G is hamiltonian, and then offers to prove it by giving you the vertices in order along the hamiltonian cycle. It would certainly be easy enough to verify the proof: simply verify that the provided cycle is hamiltonian by checking whether it is a permutation of the vertices of V and whether each of the consecutive edges along the cycle actually exists in the graph. This verification algorithm can certainly be implemented to run in $O(n^2)$ time, where n is the length of the encoding of G. Thus, a proof that a hamiltonian cycle exists in a graph can be verified in polynomial time.

We define a ***verification algorithm*** as being a two-argument algorithm A, where one argument is an ordinary input string x and the other is a binary string y called a ***certificate***. A two-argument algorithm A ***verifies*** an input string x if there exists a certificate y such that $A(x, y) = 1$. The ***language verified*** by a verification algorithm A is

$$L = \{x \in \{0, 1\}^* : \text{there exists } y \in \{0, 1\}^* \text{ such that } A(x, y) = 1\} \ .$$

Intuitively, an algorithm A verifies a language L if for any string $x \in L$, there is a certificate y that A can use to prove that $x \in L$. Moreover, for any string $x \notin L$, there must be no certificate proving that $x \in L$. For example, in the hamiltonian-cycle problem, the certificate is the list of vertices in the hamiltonian cycle. If a graph is hamiltonian, the hamiltonian cycle itself offers enough information to verify this fact. Conversely, if a graph is not hamiltonian, there is no list of vertices that can fool the verification algorithm into believing that the graph is hamiltonian, since the verification algorithm carefully checks the proposed "cycle" to be sure.

The complexity class NP

The *complexity class* **NP** is the class of languages that can be verified by a polynomial-time algorithm.[3] More precisely, a language L belongs to NP if and only if there exists a two-input polynomial-time algorithm A and constant c such that

$$L = \{x \in \{0,1\}^* : \text{there exists a certificate } y \text{ with } |y| = O(|x|^c)$$
$$\text{such that } A(x,y) = 1\} .$$

We say that algorithm A *verifies* language L *in polynomial time*.

From our earlier discussion on the hamiltonian-cycle problem, it follows that HAM-CYCLE $\in$ NP. (It is always nice to know that an important set is nonempty.) Moreover, if $L \in$ P, then $L \in$ NP, since if there is a polynomial-time algorithm to decide L, the algorithm can be easily converted to a two-argument verification algorithm that simply ignores any certificate and accepts exactly those input strings it determines to be in L. Thus, P $\subseteq$ NP.

It is unknown whether P $=$ NP, but most researchers believe that P and NP are not the same class. Intuitively, the class P consists of problems that can be solved quickly. The class NP consists of problems for which a solution can be verified quickly. You may have learned from experience that it is often more difficult to solve a problem from scratch than to verify a clearly presented solution, especially when working under time constraints. Theoretical computer scientists generally believe that this analogy extends to the classes P and NP, and thus that NP includes languages that are not in P.

There is more compelling evidence that P $\neq$ NP—the existence of "NP-complete" languages. We shall study this class in Section 36.3.

Many other fundamental questions beyond the P $\neq$ NP question remain unresolved. Despite much work by many researchers, no one even knows if the class NP is closed under complement. That is, does $L \in$ NP imply $\overline{L} \in$ NP? We can define the *complexity class* **co-NP** as the set of languages L such that $\overline{L} \in$ NP. The question of whether NP is closed under complement can be rephrased as whether NP $=$ co-NP. Since P is closed under complement (Exercise 36.1-7), it follows that P $\subseteq$ NP $\cap$ co-NP. Once again, however, it is not known whether P $=$ NP $\cap$ co-NP or whether there is some language in NP $\cap$ co-NP $-$ P. Figure 36.2 shows the four possible scenarios.

Thus, our understanding of the precise relationship between P and NP is woefully incomplete. Nevertheless, by exploring the theory of NP-completeness, we shall find that our disadvantage in proving problems

---

[3]The name "NP" stands for "nondeterministic polynomial time." The class NP was originally studied in the context of nondeterminism, but this book uses the somewhat simpler yet equivalent notion of verification. Hopcroft and Ullman [104] give a good presentation of NP-completeness in terms of nondeterministic models of computation.

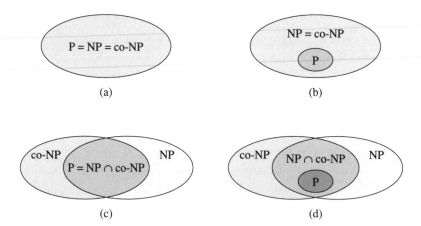

Figure 36.2 Four possibilities for relationships among complexity classes. In each diagram, one region enclosing another indicates a proper-subset relation. **(a)** P = NP = co-NP. Most researchers regard this possibility as the most unlikely. **(b)** If NP is closed under complement, then NP = co-NP, but it need not be the case that P = NP. **(c)** P = NP∩co-NP, but NP is not closed under complement. **(d)** NP ≠ co-NP and P ≠ NP∩co-NP. Most researchers regard this possibility as the most likely.

to be intractable is, from a practical point of view, not nearly so great as we might suppose.

Exercises

36.2-1
Consider the language GRAPH-ISOMORPHISM = $\{\langle G_1, G_2 \rangle : G_1$ and G_2 are isomorphic graphs$\}$. Prove that GRAPH-ISOMORPHISM $\in$ NP by describing a polynomial-time algorithm to verify the language.

36.2-2
Prove that if G is an undirected bipartite graph with an odd number of vertices, then G is nonhamiltonian.

36.2-3
Show that if HAM-CYCLE $\in$ P, then the problem of listing the vertices of a hamiltonian cycle, in order, is polynomial-time solvable.

36.2-4
Prove that the class NP of languages is closed under union, intersection, concatenation, and Kleene star. Discuss the closure of NP under complement.

36.2-5

Show that any language in NP can be decided by an algorithm running in time $2^{O(n^k)}$ for some constant k.

36.2-6

A **hamiltonian path** in a graph is a simple path that visits every vertex exactly once. Show that the language HAM-PATH $= \{\langle G, u, v\rangle :$ there is a hamiltonian path from u to v in graph $G\}$ belongs to NP.

36.2-7

Show that the hamiltonian-path problem can be solved in polynomial time on directed acyclic graphs. Give an efficient algorithm for the problem.

36.2-8

Let ϕ be a boolean formula constructed from the boolean input variables $x_1, x_2, \ldots, x_k$, negations ($\neg$), AND's ($\wedge$), OR's ($\vee$), and parentheses. The formula ϕ is a **tautology** if it evaluates to 1 for every assignment of 1 and 0 to the input variables. Define TAUTOLOGY as the language of boolean formulas that are tautologies. Show that TAUTOLOGY $\in$ co-NP.

36.2-9

Prove that P $\subseteq$ co-NP.

36.2-10

Prove that if NP $\neq$ co-NP, then P $\neq$ NP.

36.2-11

Let G be a connected, undirected graph with at least 3 vertices, and let G^3 be the graph obtained by connecting all pairs of vertices that are connected by a path in G of length at most 3. Prove that G^3 is hamiltonian. (*Hint:* Construct a spanning tree for G, and use an inductive argument.)

36.3 NP-completeness and reducibility

Perhaps the most compelling reason why theoretical computer scientists believe that P $\neq$ NP is the existence of the class of "NP-complete" problems. This class has the surprising property that if any *one* NP-complete problem can be solved in polynomial time, then *every* problem in NP has a polynomial-time solution, that is, P = NP. Despite years of study, though, no polynomial-time algorithm has ever been discovered for any NP-complete problem.

The language HAM-CYCLE is one NP-complete problem. If we could decide HAM-CYCLE in polynomial time, then we could solve every problem in NP in polynomial time. In fact, if NP $-$ P should turn out to be nonempty, we could say with certainty that HAM-CYCLE $\in$ NP $-$ P.

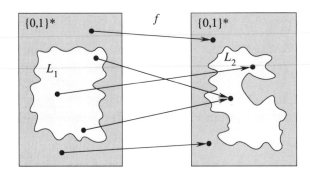

Figure 36.3   An illustration of a polynomial-time reduction from a language L_1 to a language L_2 via a reduction function f. For any input $x \in \{0,1\}^*$, the question of whether $x \in L_1$ has the same answer as the question of whether $f(x) \in L_2$.

The NP-complete languages are, in a sense, the "hardest" languages in NP. In this section, we shall show how to compare the relative "hardness" of languages using a precise notion called "polynomial-time reducibility." First, we formally define the NP-complete languages, and then we sketch a proof that one such language, called CIRCUIT-SAT, is NP-complete. In Section 36.5, shall use the notion of reducibility to show that many other problems are NP-complete.

Reducibility

Intuitively, a problem Q can be reduced to another problem Q' if any instance of Q can be "easily rephrased" as an instance of Q', the solution to which provides a solution to the instance of Q. For example, the problem of solving linear equations in an indeterminate x reduces to the problem of solving quadratic equations. Given an instance $ax + b = 0$, we transform it to $0x^2 + ax + b = 0$, whose solution provides a solution to $ax + b = 0$. Thus, if a problem Q reduces to another problem Q', then Q is, in a sense, "no harder to solve" than Q'.

Returning to our formal-language framework for decision problems, we say that a language L_1 is **_polynomial-time reducible_** to a language L_2, written $L_1 \leq_P L_2$, if there exists a polynomial-time computable function $f : \{0,1\}^* \rightarrow \{0,1\}^*$ such that for all $x \in \{0,1\}^*$,

$$x \in L_1 \text{ if and only if } f(x) \in L_2 . \tag{36.1}$$

We call the function f the **_reduction function_**, and a polynomial-time algorithm F that computes f is called a **_reduction algorithm_**.

Figure 36.3 illustrates the idea of a polynomial-time reduction from a language L_1 to another language L_2. Each language is a subset of $\{0,1\}^*$. The reduction function f provides a polynomial-time mapping such that if $x \in L_1$, then $f(x) \in L_2$. Moreover, if $x \notin L_1$, then $f(x) \notin L_2$. Thus, the reduction function maps any instance x of the decision problem repre-

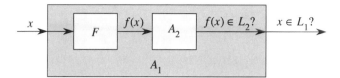

Figure 36.4 The proof of Lemma 36.3. The algorithm F is a reduction algorithm that computes the reduction function f from L_1 to L_2 in polynomial time, and A_2 is a polynomial-time algorithm that decides L_2. Illustrated is an algorithm A_1 that decides whether $x \in L_1$ by using F to transform any input x into $f(x)$ and then using A_2 to decide whether $f(x) \in L_2$.

sented by the language L_1 to an instance $f(x)$ of the problem represented by L_2. Providing an answer to whether $f(x) \in L_2$ directly provides the answer to whether $x \in L_1$.

Polynomial-time reductions give us a powerful tool for proving that various languages belong to P.

Lemma 36.3
If $L_1, L_2 \subseteq \{0, 1\}^*$ are languages such that $L_1 \leq_P L_2$, then $L_2 \in P$ implies $L_1 \in P$.

Proof Let A_2 be a polynomial-time algorithm that decides L_2, and let F be a polynomial-time reduction algorithm that computes the reduction function f. We shall construct a polynomial-time algorithm A_1 that decides L_1.

Figure 36.4 illustrates the construction of A_1. For a given input $x \in \{0, 1\}^*$, the algorithm A_1 uses F to transform x into $f(x)$, and then it uses A_2 to test whether $f(x) \in L_2$. The output of A_2 is the value provided as the output from A_1.

The correctness of A_1 follows from condition (36.1). The algorithm runs in polynomial time, since both F and A_2 run in polynomial time (see Exercise 36.1-6). ■

NP-completeness

Polynomial-time reductions provide a formal means for showing that one problem is at least as hard as another, to within a polynomial-time factor. That is, if $L_1 \leq_P L_2$, then L_1 is not more than a polynomial factor harder than L_2, which is why the "less than or equal to" notation for reduction is mnemonic. We can now define the set of NP-complete languages, which are the hardest problems in NP.

A language $L \subseteq \{0, 1\}^*$ is ***NP-complete*** if

1. $L \in$ NP, and
2. $L' \leq_P L$ for every $L' \in$ NP.

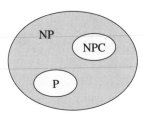

Figure 36.5 How most theoretical computer scientists view the relationships among P, NP, and NPC. Both P and NPC are wholly contained within NP, and $P \cap NPC = \emptyset$.

If a language L satisfies property 2, but not necessarily property 1, we say that L is ***NP-hard***. We also define NPC to be the class of NP-complete languages.

As the following theorem shows, NP-completeness is at the crux of deciding whether P is in fact equal to NP.

Theorem 36.4
If any NP-complete problem is polynomial-time solvable, then $P = NP$. If any problem in NP is not polynomial-time solvable, then all NP-complete problems are not polynomial-time solvable.

Proof   Suppose that $L \in P$ and also that $L \in NPC$. For any $L' \in NP$, we have $L' \leq_P L$ by property 2 of the definition of NP-completeness. Thus, by Lemma 36.3, we also have that $L' \in P$, which proves the first statement of the lemma.

To prove the second statement, suppose that there exists an $L \in NP$ such that $L \notin P$. Let $L' \in NPC$ be any NP-complete language, and for the purpose of contradiction, assume that $L' \in P$. But then, by Lemma 36.3, we have $L \leq_P L'$, and thus $L \in P$.   ■

It is for this reason that research into the $P \neq NP$ question centers around the NP-complete problems. Most theoretical computer scientists believe that $P \neq NP$, which leads to the relationships among P, NP, and NPC shown in Figure 36.5. But for all we know, someone may come up with a polynomial-time algorithm for an NP-complete problem, thus proving that $P = NP$. Nevertheless, since no polynomial-time algorithm for any NP-complete problem has yet been discovered, a proof that a problem is NP-compete provides excellent evidence for its intractability.

Circuit satisfiability

We have defined the notion of an NP-complete problem, but up to this point, we have not actually proved that any problem is NP-complete. Once we prove that at least one problem is NP-complete, we can use polynomial-

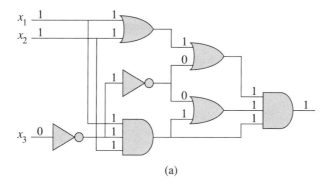

(a)

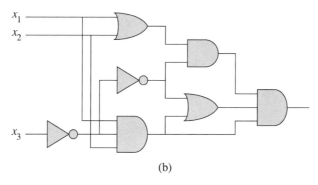

(b)

Figure 36.6 Two instances of the circuit-satisfiability problem. **(a)** The assignment $\langle x_1 = 1, x_2 = 1, x_3 = 0 \rangle$ to the inputs of this circuit causes the output of the circuit to be 1. The circuit is therefore satisfiable. **(b)** No assignment to the inputs of this circuit can cause the output of the circuit to be 1. The circuit is therefore unsatisfiable.

time reducibility as a tool to prove the NP-completeness of other problems. Thus, we now focus on demonstrating the existence of an NP-complete problem: the circuit-satisfiability problem.

Unfortunately, the formal proof that the circuit-satisfiability problem is NP-complete requires technical detail beyond the scope of this text. Instead, we shall informally describe a proof that relies on a basic understanding of boolean combinational circuits. This material is reviewed at the beginning of Chapter 29.

Figure 36.6 shows two boolean combinational circuits, each with three inputs and a single output. A ***truth assignment*** for a boolean combinational circuit is a set of boolean input values. We say that a one-output boolean combinational circuit is ***satisfiable*** if it has a ***satisfying assignment***: a truth assignment that causes the output of the circuit to be 1. For example, the circuit in Figure 36.6(a) has the satisfying assignment $\langle x_1 = 1, x_2 = 1, x_3 = 0 \rangle$, and so it is satisfiable. No assignment of values to x_1, x_2, and x_3 causes the circuit in Figure 36.6(b) to produce a 1 output; it always produces 0, and so it is unsatisfiable.

The ***circuit-satisfiability problem*** is, "Given a boolean combinational circuit composed of AND, OR, and NOT gates, is it satisfiable?" In order to pose this question formally, however, we must agree on a standard encoding for circuits. One can devise a graphlike encoding that maps any given circuit C into a binary string $\langle C \rangle$ whose length is not much larger than the size of the circuit itself. As a formal language, we can therefore define

CIRCUIT-SAT =

   $\{\langle C \rangle : C$ is a satisfiable boolean combinational circuit$\}$.

The circuit-satisfiability problem has great importance in the area of computer-aided hardware optimization. If a circuit always produces 0, it can be replaced by a simpler circuit that omits all logic gates and provides the constant 0 value as its output. A polynomial-time algorithm for the problem would have considerable practical application.

Given a circuit C, we might attempt to determine whether it is satisfiable by simply checking all possible assignments to the inputs. Unfortunately, if there are k inputs, there are 2^k possible assignments. When the size of C is polynomial in k, checking each one leads to a superpolynomial-time algorithm. In fact, as has been claimed, there is strong evidence that no polynomial-time algorithm exists that solves the circuit-satisfiability problem because circuit satisfiability is NP-complete. We break the proof of this fact into two parts, based on the two parts of the definition of NP-completeness.

Lemma 36.5
The circuit-satisfiability problem belongs to the class NP.

Proof   We shall provide a two-input, polynomial-time algorithm A that can verify CIRCUIT-SAT. One of the inputs to A is (a standard encoding of) a boolean combinational circuit C. The other input is a certificate corresponding to an assignment of boolean values to the wires in C.

The algorithm A is constructed as follows. For each logic gate in the circuit, it checks that the value provided by the certificate on the output wire is correctly computed as a function of the values on the input wires. Then, if the output of the entire circuit is 1, the algorithm outputs 1, since the values assigned to the inputs of C provide a satisfying assignment. Otherwise, A outputs 0.

Whenever a satisfiable circuit C is input to algorithm A, there is a certificate whose length is polynomial in the size of C and that causes A to output a 1. Whenever an unsatisfiable circuit is input, no certificate can fool A into believing that the circuit is satisfiable. Algorithm A runs in polynomial time: with a good implementation, linear time suffices. Thus, CIRCUIT-SAT can be verified in polynomial time, and CIRCUIT-SAT $\in$ NP.   ∎

The second part of proving that CIRCUIT-SAT is NP-complete is to show that the language is NP-hard. That is, we must show that every language in NP is polynomial-time reducible to CIRCUIT-SAT. The actual proof of this fact is full of technical intricacies, and so we shall settle for a sketch of the proof based on some understanding of the workings of computer hardware.

A computer program is stored in the computer memory as a sequence of instructions. A typical instruction encodes an operation to be performed, addresses of operands in memory, and an address where the result is to be stored. A special memory location, called the *program counter*, keeps track of which instruction is to be executed next. The program counter is automatically incremented whenever an instruction is fetched, thereby causing the computer to execute instructions sequentially. The execution of an instruction can cause a value to be written to the program counter, however, and then the normal sequential execution can be altered, allowing the computer to loop and perform conditional branches.

At any point during the execution of a program, the entire state of the computation is represented in the computer's memory. (We take the memory to include the program itself, the program counter, working storage, and any of the various bits of state that a computer maintains for book-keeping.) We call any particular state of computer memory a *configuration*. The execution of an instruction can be viewed as mapping one configuration to another. Importantly, the computer hardware that accomplishes this mapping can be implemented as a boolean combinational circuit, which we denote by M in the proof of the following lemma.

Lemma 36.6
The circuit-satisfiability problem is NP-hard.

Proof Let L be any language in NP. We shall describe a polynomial-time algorithm F computing a reduction function f that maps every binary string x to a circuit $C = f(x)$ such that $x \in L$ if and only if $C \in$ CIRCUIT-SAT.

Since $L \in$ NP, there must exist an algorithm A that verifies L in polynomial time. The algorithm F that we shall construct will use the two-input algorithm A to compute the reduction function f.

Let $T(n)$ denote the worst-case running time of algorithm A on length-n input strings, and let $k \geq 1$ be a constant such that $T(n) = O(n^k)$ and the length of the certificate is $O(n^k)$. (The running time of A is actually a polynomial in the total input size, which includes both an input string and a certificate, but since the length of the certificate is polynomial in the length n of the input string, the running time is polynomial in n.)

The basic idea of the proof is to represent the computation of A as a sequence of configurations. As shown in Figure 36.7, each configuration can be broken into parts consisting of the program for A, the program counter and auxiliary machine state, the input x, the certificate y, and working storage. Starting with an initial configuration c_0, each configuration c_i is mapped to a subsequent configuration c_{i+1} by the combinational circuit M

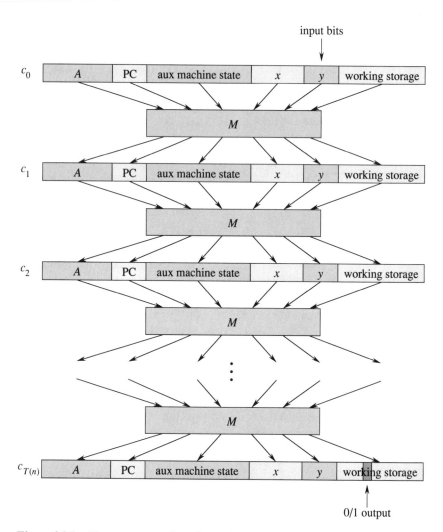

Figure 36.7   The sequence of configurations produced by an algorithm A running on an input x and certificate y. Each configuration represents the state of the computer for one step of the computation and, besides A, x, and y, includes the program counter (PC), auxiliary machine state, and working storage. Except for the certificate y, the initial configuration c_0 is constant. Each configuration is mapped to the next configuration by a boolean combinational circuit M. The output is a distinguished bit in the working storage.

implementing the computer hardware. The output of the algorithm A—0 or 1—is written to some designated location in the working storage when A finishes executing, and if we assume that thereafter A halts, the value never changes. Thus, if the algorithm runs for at most $T(n)$ steps, the output appears as one of the bits in $c_{T(n)}$.

The reduction algorithm F constructs a single combinational circuit that computes all configurations produced by a given initial configuration. The idea is to paste together $T(n)$ copies of the circuit M. The output of the ith circuit, which produces configuration c_i, is fed directly into the input of the $(i+1)$st circuit. Thus, the configurations, rather than ending up in a state register, simply reside as values on the wires connecting copies of M.

Recall what the polynomial-time reduction algorithm F must do. Given an input x, it must compute a circuit $C = f(x)$ that is satisfiable if and only if there exists a certificate y such that $A(x,y) = 1$. When F obtains an input x, it first computes $n = |x|$ and constructs a combinational circuit C' consisting of $T(n)$ copies of M. The input to C' is an initial configuration corresponding to a computation on $A(x,y)$, and the output is the configuration $c_{T(n)}$.

The circuit $C = f(x)$ that F computes is obtained by modifying C' slightly. First, the inputs to C' corresponding to the program for A, the initial program counter, the input x, and the initial state of memory are wired directly to these known values. Thus, the only remaining inputs to the circuit correspond to the certificate y. Second, all outputs to the circuit are ignored, except the one bit of $c_{T(n)}$ corresponding to the output of A. This circuit C, so constructed, computes $C(y) = A(x,y)$ for any input y of length $O(n^k)$. The reduction algorithm F, when provided an input string x, computes such a circuit C and outputs it.

Two properties remain to be proved. First, we must show that F correctly computes a reduction function f. That is, we must show that C is satisfiable if and only if there exists a certificate y such that $A(x,y) = 1$. Second, we must show that F runs in polynomial time.

To show that F correctly computes a reduction function, let us suppose that there exists a certificate y of length $O(n^k)$ such that $A(x,y) = 1$. Then, if we apply the bits of y to the inputs of C, the output of C is $C(y) = A(x,y) = 1$. Thus, if a certificate exists, then C is satisfiable. For the other direction, suppose that C is satisfiable. Hence, there exists an input y to C such that $C(y) = 1$, from which we conclude that $A(x,y) = 1$. Thus, F correctly computes a reduction function.

To complete the proof, we need only show that F runs in time polynomial in $n = |x|$. The first observation we make is that the number of bits required to represent a configuration is polynomial in n. The program for A itself has constant size, independent of the length of its input x. The length of the input x is n, and the length of the certificate y is $O(n^k)$. Since the algorithm runs for at most $O(n^k)$ steps, the amount of working storage required by A is polynomial in n as well. (We assume that this memory is contiguous; Exercise 36.3-4 asks you to extend the argument to the situation in which the locations accessed by A are scattered across a much larger region of memory and the particular pattern of scattering can differ for each input x.)

The combinational circuit M implementing the computer hardware has size polynomial in the length of a configuration, which is polynomial in $O(n^k)$ and hence is polynomial in n. (Most of this circuitry implements the logic of the memory system.) The circuit C consists of at most $t = O(n^k)$ copies of M, and hence it has size polynomial in n. The construction of C from x can be accomplished in polynomial time by the reduction algorithm F, since each step of the construction takes polynomial time. ∎

The language CIRCUIT-SAT is therefore at least as hard as any language in NP, and since it belongs to NP, it is NP-complete.

Theorem 36.7
The circuit-satisfiability problem is NP-complete.

Proof   Immediate from Lemmas 36.5 and 36.6 and the definition of NP-completeness. ∎

Exercises

36.3-1
Show that the $\leq_P$ relation is a transitive relation on languages. That is, show that if $L_1 \leq_P L_2$ and $L_2 \leq_P L_3$, then $L_1 \leq_P L_3$.

36.3-2
Prove that $L \leq_P \overline{L}$ if and only if $\overline{L} \leq_P L$.

36.3-3
Show that a satisfying assignment can be used as a certificate in an alternative proof of Lemma 36.5. Which certificate makes for an easier proof?

36.3-4
The proof of Lemma 36.6 assumes that the working storage for algorithm A occupies a contiguous region of polynomial size. Where in the proof is this assumption exploited? Argue that this assumption does not involve any loss of generality.

36.3-5
A language L is ***complete*** for a language class C with respect to polynomial-time reductions if $L \in C$ and $L' \leq_P L$ for all $L' \in C$. Show that $\emptyset$ and $\{0, 1\}^*$ are the only languages in P that are not complete for P with respect to polynomial-time reductions.

36.3-6
Show that L is complete for NP if and only if $\overline{L}$ is complete for co-NP.

36.3-7
The reduction algorithm F in the proof of Lemma 36.6 constructs the circuit $C = f(x)$ based on knowledge of x, A, and k. Professor Sartre observes that the string x is input to F, but only the existence of A and k is known to F (since the language L belongs to NP), not their actual values. Thus, the professor concludes that F can't possibly construct the circuit C and that the language CIRCUIT-SAT is not necessarily NP-hard. Explain the flaw in the professor's reasoning.

36.4 NP-completeness proofs

The NP-completeness of the circuit-satisfiability problem relies on a direct proof that $L \leq_P$ CIRCUIT-SAT for every language $L \in$ NP. In this section, we shall show how to prove that languages are NP-complete without directly reducing *every* language in NP to the given language. We shall illustrate this methodology by proving that various formula-satisfiability problems are NP-complete. Section 36.5 provides many more examples of the methodology.

The following lemma is the basis of our method for showing that a language is NP-complete.

Lemma 36.8
If L is a language such that $L' \leq_P L$ for some $L' \in$ NPC, then L is NP-hard. Moreover, if $L \in$ NP, then $L \in$ NPC.

Proof Since L' is NP-complete, for all $L'' \in$ NP, we have $L'' \leq_P L'$. By supposition, $L' \leq_P L$, and thus by transitivity (Exercise 36.3-1), we have $L'' \leq_P L$, which shows that L is NP-hard. If $L \in$ NP, we also have $L \in$ NPC. ∎

In other words, by reducing a known NP-complete language L' to L, we implicitly reduce every language in NP to L. Thus, Lemma 36.8 gives us a method for proving that a language L is NP-complete:

1. Prove $L \in$ NP.

2. Select a known NP-complete language L'.

3. Describe an algorithm that computes a function f mapping every instance of L' to an instance of L.

4. Prove that the function f satisfies $x \in L'$ if and only if $f(x) \in L$ for all $x \in \{0, 1\}^*$.

5. Prove that the algorithm computing f runs in polynomial time.

This methodology of reducing from a single known NP-complete language is far simpler than the more complicated process of providing reductions from every language in NP. Proving CIRCUIT-SAT ∈ NPC has given us a "foot in the door." Knowing that the circuit-satisfiability problem is NP-complete now allows us to prove much more easily that other problems are NP-complete. Moreover, as we develop a catalog of known NP-complete problems, applying the methodology will become that much easier.

Formula satisfiability

We illustrate the reduction methodology by giving an NP-completeness proof for the problem of determining whether a boolean formula, not a circuit, is satisfiable. This problem has the historical honor of being the first problem ever shown to be NP-complete.

We formulate the *(formula) satisfiability* problem in terms of the language SAT as follows. An instance of SAT is a boolean formula ϕ composed of

1. boolean variables: $x_1, x_2, \ldots$;

2. boolean connectives: any boolean function with one or two inputs and one output, such as ∧ (AND), ∨ (OR), ¬ (NOT), → (implication), ↔ (if and only if); and

3. parentheses.

As in boolean combinational circuits, a *truth assignment* for a boolean formula ϕ is a set of values for the variables of ϕ, and a *satisfying assignment* is a truth assignment that causes it to evaluate to 1. A formula with a satisfying assignment is a *satisfiable* formula. The satisfiability problem asks whether a given boolean formula is satisfiable; in formal-language terms,

$$\text{SAT} = \{\langle \phi \rangle : \phi \text{ is a satisfiable boolean formula}\} \ .$$

As an example, the formula

$$\phi = ((x_1 \rightarrow x_2) \vee \neg((\neg x_1 \leftrightarrow x_3) \vee x_4)) \wedge \neg x_2$$

has the satisfying assignment $\langle x_1 = 0, x_2 = 0, x_3 = 1, x_4 = 1 \rangle$, since

$$
\begin{aligned}
\phi &= ((0 \rightarrow 0) \vee \neg((\neg 0 \leftrightarrow 1) \vee 1)) \wedge \neg 0 & (36.2)\\
&= (1 \vee \neg(1 \vee 1)) \wedge 1 \\
&= (1 \vee 0) \wedge 1 \\
&= 1 \ ,
\end{aligned}
$$

and thus this formula ϕ belongs to SAT.

The naive algorithm to determine whether an arbitrary boolean formula is satisfiable does not run in polynomial time. There are 2^n possible assignments in a formula ϕ with n variables. If the length of $\langle \phi \rangle$ is polynomial in n, then checking every assignment requires superpolynomial time. As the following theorem shows, a polynomial-time algorithm is unlikely to exist.

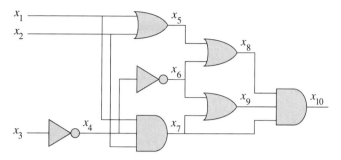

Figure 36.8 Reducing circuit satisfiability to formula satisfiability. The formula produced by the reduction algorithm has a variable for each wire in the circuit.

Theorem 36.9
Satisfiability of boolean formulas is NP-complete.

Proof   We shall argue first that SAT $\in$ NP. Then, we shall show that CIRCUIT-SAT $\leq_P$ SAT; by Lemma 36.8, this will prove the theorem.

To show that SAT belongs to NP, we show that a certificate consisting of a satisfying assignment for an input formula ϕ can be verified in polynomial time. The verifying algorithm simply replaces each variable in the formula with its corresponding value and then evaluates the expression, much as we did in equation (36.2) above. This task is easily doable in polynomial time. If the expression evaluates to 1, the formula is satisfiable. Thus, the first condition of Lemma 36.8 for NP-completeness holds.

To prove that SAT is NP-hard, we show that CIRCUIT-SAT $\leq_P$ SAT. In other words, any instance of circuit satisfiability can be reduced in polynomial time to an instance of formula satisfiability. Induction can be used to express any boolean combinational circuit as a boolean formula. We simply look at the gate that produces the circuit output and inductively express each of the gate's inputs as formulas. The formula for the circuit is then obtained by writing an expression that applies the gate's function to its inputs' formulas.

Unfortunately, this straightforward method does not constitute a polynomial-time reduction. Shared subformulas can cause the size of the generated formula to grow exponentially (see Exercise 36.4-1). Thus, the reduction algorithm must be somewhat more clever.

Figure 36.8 illustrates the basic idea of the reduction from CIRCUIT-SAT to SAT on the circuit from Figure 36.6(a). For each wire x_i in the circuit C, the formula ϕ has a variable x_i. The proper operation of a gate can now be expressed as a formula involving the variables of its incident wires. For example, the operation of the output AND gate is $x_{10} \leftrightarrow (x_7 \wedge x_8 \wedge x_9)$.

The formula ϕ produced by the reduction algorithm is the AND of the circuit-output variable with the conjunction of clauses describing the operation of each gate. For the circuit in the figure, the formula is

$$\phi = x_{10} \wedge (x_4 \leftrightarrow \neg x_3)$$
$$\wedge (x_5 \leftrightarrow (x_1 \vee x_2))$$
$$\wedge (x_6 \leftrightarrow \neg x_4)$$
$$\wedge (x_7 \leftrightarrow (x_1 \wedge x_2 \wedge x_4))$$
$$\wedge (x_8 \leftrightarrow (x_5 \vee x_6))$$
$$\wedge (x_9 \leftrightarrow (x_6 \vee x_7))$$
$$\wedge (x_{10} \leftrightarrow (x_7 \wedge x_8 \wedge x_9)) \ .$$

Given a circuit C, it is straightforward to produce such a formula ϕ in polynomial time.

Why is the circuit ϕ satisfiable exactly when the formula ϕ is satisfiable? If C has a satisfying assignment, each wire of the circuit has a well-defined value, and the output of the circuit is 1. Therefore, the assignment of wire values to variables in ϕ makes each clause of ϕ evaluate to 1, and thus the conjunction of all evaluates to 1. Conversely, if there is an assignment that causes ϕ to evaluate to 1, the circuit C is satisfiable by an analogous argument. Thus, we have shown that CIRCUIT-SAT $\leq_P$ SAT, which completes the proof.   ∎

3-CNF satisfiability

Many problems can be proved NP-complete by reduction from formula satisfiability. The reduction algorithm must handle any input formula, though, and this can lead to a huge number of cases that must be considered. It is often desirable, therefore, to reduce from a restricted language of boolean formulas, so that fewer cases need be considered. Of course, we must not restrict the language so much that it becomes polynomial-time solvable. One convenient language is 3-CNF satisfiability, or 3-CNF-SAT.

We define 3-CNF satisfiability using the following terms. A *literal* in a boolean formula is an occurrence of a variable or its negation. A boolean formula is in *conjunctive normal form*, or *CNF*, if it is expressed as an AND of clauses, each of which is the OR of one or more literals. A boolean formula is in *3-conjunctive normal form*, or *3-CNF*, if each clause has exactly three distinct literals.

For example, the boolean formula

$$(x_1 \vee \neg x_1 \vee \neg x_2) \wedge (x_3 \vee x_2 \vee x_4) \wedge (\neg x_1 \vee \neg x_3 \vee \neg x_4)$$

is in 3-CNF. The first of its three clauses is $(x_1 \vee \neg x_1 \vee \neg x_2)$, which contains the three literals x_1, $\neg x_1$, and $\neg x_2$.

In 3-CNF-SAT, we are asked whether a given boolean formula ϕ in 3-CNF is satisfiable. The following theorem shows that a polynomial-time algorithm that can determine the satisfiability of boolean formulas is unlikely to exist, even when they are expressed in this simple normal form.

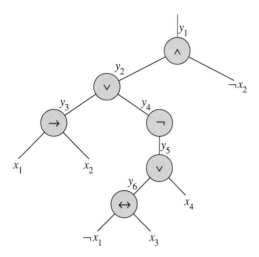

Figure 36.9 The tree corresponding to the formula

$$\phi = ((x_1 \rightarrow x_2) \vee \neg((\neg x_1 \leftrightarrow x_3) \vee x_4)) \wedge \neg x_2 \ .$$

Theorem 36.10

Satisfiability of boolean formulas in 3-conjunctive normal form is NP-complete.

Proof The argument we used in the proof of Theorem 36.9 to show that SAT $\in$ NP applies equally well here to show that 3-CNF-SAT $\in$ NP. Thus, we need only show that 3-CNF-SAT is NP-hard. We prove this by showing that SAT $\leq_P$ 3-CNF-SAT, from which the proof will follow by Lemma 36.8.

The reduction algorithm can be broken into three basic steps. Each step progressively transforms the input formula ϕ closer to the desired 3-conjunctive normal form.

The first step is similar to the one used to prove CIRCUIT-SAT $\leq_P$ SAT in Theorem 36.9. First, we construct a binary "parse" tree for the input formula ϕ, with literals as leaves and connectives as internal nodes. Figure 36.9 shows such a parse tree for the formula

$$\phi = ((x_1 \rightarrow x_2) \vee \neg((\neg x_1 \leftrightarrow x_3) \vee x_4)) \wedge \neg x_2 \ . \tag{36.3}$$

Should the input formula contain a clause such as the OR of several literals, associativity can be used to parenthesize the expression fully so that every internal node in the resulting tree has 1 or 2 children. The binary parse tree can now be viewed as a circuit for computing the function.

Mimicking the reduction in the proof of Theorem 36.9, we introduce a variable y_i for the output of each internal node. Then, we rewrite the original formula ϕ as the AND of the root variable and a conjunction of clauses describing the operation of each node. For the formula (36.3), the

y_1	y_2	x_2	$(y_1 \leftrightarrow (y_2 \wedge \neg x_2))$
1	1	1	0
1	1	0	1
1	0	1	0
1	0	0	0
0	1	1	1
0	1	0	0
0	0	1	1
0	0	0	1

Figure 36.10   The truth table for the clause $(y_1 \leftrightarrow (y_2 \wedge \neg x_2))$.

resulting expression is

$$
\begin{aligned}
\phi' = {} & y_1 \,\wedge\, (y_1 \leftrightarrow (y_2 \wedge \neg x_2)) \\
& \wedge\, (y_2 \leftrightarrow (y_3 \vee y_4)) \\
& \wedge\, (y_3 \leftrightarrow (x_1 \rightarrow x_2)) \\
& \wedge\, (y_4 \leftrightarrow \neg y_5) \\
& \wedge\, (y_5 \leftrightarrow (y_6 \vee x_4)) \\
& \wedge\, (y_6 \leftrightarrow (\neg x_1 \leftrightarrow x_3)) \,.
\end{aligned}
$$

Observe that the formula ϕ' thus obtained is a conjunction of clauses ϕ_i', each of which has at most 3 literals. The only additional requirement is that each clause be an OR of literals.

The second step of the reduction converts each clause ϕ_i' into conjunctive normal form. We construct a truth table for ϕ_i' by evaluating all possible assignments to its variables. Each row of the truth table consists of a possible assignment of the variables of the clause, together with the value of the clause under that assignment. Using the truth-table entries that evaluate to 0, we build a formula in *disjunctive normal form* (or *DNF*)—an OR of AND's—that is equivalent to $\neg\phi_i'$. We then convert this formula into a CNF formula ϕ_i'' by using DeMorgan's laws (5.2) to complement all literals and change OR's into AND's and AND's into OR's.

In our example, we convert the clause $\phi_1' = (y_1 \leftrightarrow (y_2 \wedge \neg x_2))$ into CNF as follows. The truth table for ϕ_1' is given in Figure 36.10. The DNF formula equivalent to $\neg\phi_1'$ is

$$(y_1 \wedge y_2 \wedge x_2) \vee (y_1 \wedge \neg y_2 \wedge x_2) \vee (y_1 \wedge \neg y_2 \wedge \neg x_2) \vee (\neg y_1 \wedge y_2 \wedge \neg x_2) \,.$$

Applying DeMorgan's laws, we get the CNF formula

$$
\begin{aligned}
\phi_1'' = {} & (\neg y_1 \vee \neg y_2 \vee \neg x_2) \wedge (\neg y_1 \vee y_2 \vee \neg x_2) \\
& \wedge (\neg y_1 \vee y_2 \vee x_2) \wedge (y_1 \vee \neg y_2 \vee x_2) \,,
\end{aligned}
$$

which is equivalent to the original clause ϕ_1'.

Each clause ϕ_i' of the formula ϕ' has now been converted into a CNF formula ϕ_i'', and thus ϕ' is equivalent to the CNF formula ϕ'' consisting of the conjunction of the ϕ_i''. Moreover, each clause of ϕ'' has at most 3 literals.

The third and final step of the reduction further transforms the formula so that each clause has *exactly* 3 distinct literals. The final 3-CNF formula ϕ''' is constructed from the clauses of the CNF formula ϕ''. It also uses two auxiliary variables that we shall call p and q. For each clause C_i of ϕ'', we include the following clauses in ϕ''':

- If C_i has 3 distinct literals, then simply include C_i as a clause of ϕ'''.

- If C_i has 2 distinct literals, that is, if $C_i = (l_1 \vee l_2)$, where l_1 and l_2 are literals, then include $(l_1 \vee l_2 \vee p) \wedge (l_1 \vee l_2 \vee \neg p)$ as clauses of $f(\phi)$. The literals p and $\neg p$ merely fulfill the syntactic requirement that there be exactly 3 distinct literals per clause: $(l_1 \vee l_2 \vee p) \wedge (l_1 \vee l_2 \vee \neg p)$ is equivalent to $(l_1 \vee l_2)$ whether $p = 0$ or $p = 1$.

- If C_i has just 1 distinct literal l, then include $(l \vee p \vee q) \wedge (l \vee p \vee \neg q) \wedge (l \vee \neg p \vee q) \wedge (l \vee \neg p \vee \neg q)$ as clauses of ϕ'''. Note that every setting of p and q causes the conjunction of these four clauses to evaluate to l.

We can see that the 3-CNF formula ϕ''' is satisfiable if and only if ϕ is satisfiable by inspecting each of the three steps. Like the reduction from CIRCUIT-SAT to SAT, the construction of ϕ' from ϕ in the first step preserves satisfiability. The second step produces a CNF formula ϕ'' that is algebraically equivalent to ϕ'. The third step produces a 3-CNF formula ϕ''' that is effectively equivalent to ϕ'', since any assignment to the variables p and q produces a formula that is algebraically equivalent to ϕ''.

We must also show that the reduction can be computed in polynomial time. Constructing ϕ' from ϕ introduces at most 1 variable and 1 clause per connective in ϕ. Constructing ϕ'' from ϕ' can introduce at most 8 clauses into ϕ'' for each clause from ϕ', since each clause of ϕ' has at most 3 variables, and the truth table for each clause has at most $2^3 = 8$ rows. The construction of ϕ''' from ϕ'' introduces at most 4 clauses into ϕ''' for each clause of ϕ''. Thus, the size of the resulting formula ϕ''' is polynomial in the length of the original formula. Each of the constructions can easily be accomplished in polynomial time.   ∎

Exercises

36.4-1

Consider the straightforward (nonpolynomial-time) reduction in the proof of Theorem 36.9. Describe a circuit of size n that, when converted to a formula by this method, yields a formula whose size is exponential in n.

36.4-2

Show the 3-CNF formula that results when we use the method of Theorem 36.10 on the formula (36.3).

36.4-3

Professor Jagger proposes to show that SAT $\leq_P$ 3-CNF-SAT by using only the truth-table technique in the proof of Theorem 36.10, and not the other steps. That is, the professor proposes to take the boolean formula ϕ, form a truth table for its variables, derive from the truth table a formula in 3-DNF that is equivalent to $\neg\phi$, and then negate and apply DeMorgan's laws to produce a 3-CNF formula equivalent to ϕ. Show that this strategy does not yield a polynomial-time reduction.

36.4-4

Show that the problem of determining whether a boolean formula is a tautology is complete for co-NP. (*Hint:* See Exercise 36.3-6.)

36.4-5

Show that the problem of determining the satisfiability of boolean formulas in disjunctive normal form is polynomial-time solvable.

36.4-6

Suppose that someone gives you a polynomial-time algorithm to decide formula satisfiability. Describe how to use this algorithm to find satisfying assignments in polynomial time.

36.4-7

Let 2-CNF-SAT be the set of satisfiable boolean formulas in CNF with exactly 2 literals per clause. Show that 2-CNF-SAT $\in$ P. Make your algorithm as efficient as possible. (*Hint:* Observe that $x \vee y$ is equivalent to $\neg x \rightarrow y$. Reduce 2-CNF-SAT to a problem on a directed graph that is efficiently solvable.)

36.5   NP-complete problems

NP-complete problems arise in diverse domains: boolean logic, graphs, arithmetic, network design, sets and partitions, storage and retrieval, sequencing and scheduling, mathematical programming, algebra and number theory, games and puzzles, automata and language theory, program optimization, and more. In this section, we shall use the reduction methodology to provide NP-completeness proofs for a variety of problems drawn from graph theory and set partitioning.

Figure 36.11 outlines the structure of the NP-completeness proofs in this section and Section 36.4. Each language in the figure is proved NP-complete by reduction from the language that points to it. At the root is CIRCUIT-SAT, which we proved NP-complete in Theorem 36.7.

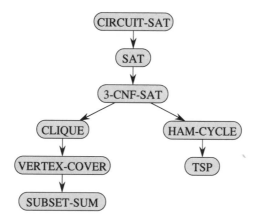

Figure 36.11 The structure of NP-completeness proofs in Sections 36.4 and 36.5. All proofs ultimately follow by reduction from the NP-completeness of CIRCUIT-SAT.

36.5.1 The clique problem

A *clique* in an undirected graph $G = (V, E)$ is a subset $V' \subseteq V$ of vertices, each pair of which is connected by an edge in E. In other words, a clique is a complete subgraph of G. The *size* of a clique is the number of vertices it contains. The *clique problem* is the optimization problem of finding a clique of maximum size in a graph. As a decision problem, we ask simply whether a clique of a given size k exists in the graph. The formal definition is

CLIQUE $= \{\langle G, k \rangle : G$ is a graph with a clique of size $k\}$.

A naive algorithm for determining whether a graph $G = (V, E)$ with $|V|$ vertices has a clique of size k is to list all k-subsets of V, and check each one to see whether it forms a clique. The running time of this algorithm is $\Omega(k^2 \binom{|V|}{k})$, which is polynomial if k is a constant. In general, however, k could be proportional to $|V|$, in which case the algorithm runs in superpolynomial time. As one might suspect, an efficient algorithm for the clique problem is unlikely to exist.

Theorem 36.11
The clique problem is NP-complete.

Proof To show that CLIQUE $\in$ NP, for a given graph $G = (V, E)$, we use the set $V' \subseteq V$ of vertices in the clique as a certificate for G. Checking whether V' is a clique can be accomplished in polynomial time by checking whether, for every pair $u, v \in V'$, the edge (u, v) belongs to E.

We next show that the clique problem is NP-hard by proving that 3-CNF-SAT $\leq_P$ CLIQUE. That we should be able to prove this result is

$$C_1 = x_1 \vee \neg x_2 \vee \neg x_3$$

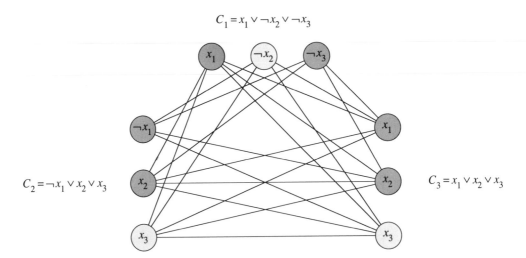

$C_2 = \neg x_1 \vee x_2 \vee x_3$

$C_3 = x_1 \vee x_2 \vee x_3$

Figure 36.12 The graph G derived from the 3-CNF formula $\phi = C_1 \wedge C_2 \wedge C_3$, where $C_1 = (x_1 \vee \neg x_2 \vee \neg x_3)$, $C_2 = (\neg x_1 \vee x_2 \vee x_3)$, and $C_3 = (x_1 \vee x_2 \vee x_3)$, in reducing 3-CNF-SAT to CLIQUE. A satisfying assignment of the formula is $\langle x_1 = 0, x_2 = 0, x_3 = 1 \rangle$. This satisfying assignment satisfies C_1 with $\neg x_2$, and it satisfies C_2 and C_3 with x_3, corresponding to the clique with lightly shaded vertices.

somewhat surprising, since on the surface logical formulas seem to have little to do with graphs.

The reduction algorithm begins with an instance of 3-CNF-SAT. Let $\phi = C_1 \wedge C_2 \wedge \cdots \wedge C_k$ be a boolean formula in 3-CNF with k clauses. For $r = 1, 2, \ldots, k$, each clause C_r has exactly three distinct literals l_1^r, l_2^r, and l_3^r. We shall construct a graph G such that ϕ is satisfiable if and only if G has a clique of size k.

The graph $G = (V, E)$ is constructed as follows. For each clause $C_r = (l_1^r \vee l_2^r \vee l_3^r)$ in ϕ, we place a triple of vertices v_1^r, v_2^r, and v_3^r in V. We put an edge between two vertices v_i^r and v_j^s if both of the following hold:

- v_i^r and v_j^s are in different triples, that is, $r \neq s$, and
- their corresponding literals are ***consistent***, that is, l_i^r is not the negation of l_j^s.

This graph can easily be computed from ϕ in polynomial time. As an example of this construction, if we have

$$\phi = (x_1 \vee \neg x_2 \vee \neg x_3) \wedge (\neg x_1 \vee x_2 \vee x_3) \wedge (x_1 \vee x_2 \vee x_3) \,,$$

then G is the graph shown in Figure 36.12.

We must show that this transformation of ϕ into G is a reduction. First, suppose that ϕ has a satisfying assignment. Then, each clause C_r contains at least one literal l_i^r that is assigned 1, and each such literal corresponds to a vertex v_i^r. Picking one such "true" literal from each clause yields a set of V' of k vertices. We claim that V' is a clique. For any two vertices

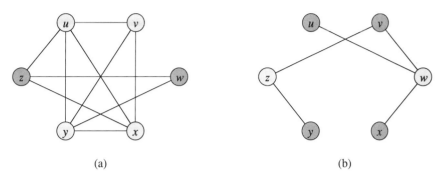

Figure 36.13 Reducing CLIQUE to VERTEX-COVER. **(a)** An undirected graph $G = (V, E)$ with clique $V' = \{u, v, x, y\}$. **(b)** The graph $\overline{G}$ produced by the reduction algorithm that has vertex cover $V - V' = \{w, z\}$.

$v_i^r, v_j^s \in V'$, where $r \neq s$, both corresponding literals l_i^r and l_j^s are mapped to 1 by the given satisfying assignment, and thus the literals cannot be complements. Thus, by the construction of G, the edge (v_i^r, v_j^s) belongs to E.

Conversely, suppose that G has a clique V' of size k. No edges in G connect vertices in the same triple, and so V' contains exactly one vertex per triple. We can assign 1 to each literal l_i^r such that $v_i^r \in V'$ without fear of assigning 1 to both a literal and its complement, since G contains no edges between inconsistent literals. Each clause is satisfied, and so ϕ is satisfied. (Any variables that correspond to no vertex in the clique may be set arbitrarily.)   ∎

In the example of Figure 36.12, a satisfying assignment of ϕ is $\langle x_1 = 0, x_2 = 0, x_3 = 1 \rangle$. A corresponding clique of size $k = 3$ consists of the vertices corresponding to $\neg x_2$ from the first clause, x_3 from the second clause, and x_3 from the third clause.

36.5.2 The vertex-cover problem

A ***vertex cover*** of an undirected graph $G = (V, E)$ is a subset $V' \subseteq V$ such that if $(u, v) \in E$, then $u \in V'$ or $v \in V'$ (or both). That is, each vertex "covers" its incident edges, and a vertex cover for G is a set of vertices that covers all the edges in E. The ***size*** of a vertex cover is the number of vertices in it. For example, the graph in Figure 36.13(b) has a vertex cover $\{w, z\}$ of size 2.

The ***vertex-cover problem*** is to find a vertex cover of minimum size in a given graph. Restating this optimization problem as a decision problem, we wish to determine whether a graph has a vertex cover of a given size k. As a language, we define

VERTEX-COVER $= \{\langle G, k \rangle : \text{graph } G \text{ has vertex cover of size } k\}$.

The following theorem shows that this problem is NP-complete.

Theorem 36.12
The vertex-cover problem is NP-complete.

Proof We first show that VERTEX-COVER ∈ NP. Suppose we are given a graph $G = (V, E)$ and an integer k. The certificate we choose is the vertex cover $V' \subseteq V$ itself. The verification algorithm affirms that $|V'| = k$, and then it checks, for each edge $(u, v) \in E$, whether $u \in V'$ or $v \in V'$. This verification can be performed straightforwardly in polynomial time.

We prove that the vertex-cover problem is NP-hard by showing that CLIQUE $\leq_P$ VERTEX-COVER. This reduction is based on the notion of the "complement" of a graph. Given an undirected graph $G = (V, E)$, we define the **complement** of G as $\overline{G} = (V, \overline{E})$, where $\overline{E} = \{(u, v) : (u, v) \notin E\}$. In other words, $\overline{G}$ is the graph containing exactly those edges that are not in G. Figure 36.13 shows a graph and its complement and illustrates the reduction from CLIQUE to VERTEX-COVER.

The reduction algorithm takes as input an instance $\langle G, k \rangle$ of the clique problem. It computes the complement $\overline{G}$, which is easily doable in polynomial time. The output of the reduction algorithm is the instance $\langle \overline{G}, |V| - k \rangle$ of the vertex-cover problem. To complete the proof, we show that this transformation is indeed a reduction: the graph G has a clique of size k if and only if the graph $\overline{G}$ has a vertex cover of size $|V| - k$.

Suppose that G has a clique $V' \subseteq V$ with $|V'| = k$. We claim that $V - V'$ is a vertex cover in $\overline{G}$. Let (u, v) be any edge in $\overline{E}$. Then, $(u, v) \notin E$, which implies that at least one of u or v does not belong to V', since every pair of vertices in V' is connected by an edge of E. Equivalently, at least one of u or v is in $V - V'$, which means that edge (u, v) is covered by $V - V'$. Since (u, v) was chosen arbitrarily from $\overline{E}$, every edge of $\overline{E}$ is covered by a vertex in $V - V'$. Hence, the set $V - V'$, which has size $|V| - k$, forms a vertex cover for $\overline{G}$.

Conversely, suppose that $\overline{G}$ has a vertex cover $V' \subseteq V$, where $|V'| = |V| - k$. Then, for all $u, v \in V$, if $(u, v) \in \overline{E}$, then $u \in V'$ or $v \in V'$ or both. The contrapositive of this implication is that for all $u, v \in V$, if $u \notin V'$ and $v \notin V'$, then $(u, v) \in E$. In other words, $V - V'$ is a clique, and it has size $|V| - |V'| = k$. ∎

Since VERTEX-COVER is NP-complete, we don't expect to find a polynomial-time algorithm for finding a minimum-size vertex cover. Section 37.1 presents a polynomial-time "approximation algorithm," however, which produces "approximate" solutions for the vertex-cover problem. The size of a vertex cover produced by the algorithm is at most twice the minimum size of a vertex cover.

Thus, we shouldn't give up hope just because a problem is NP-complete. There may be a polynomial-time approximation algorithm that obtains near-optimal solutions, even though finding an optimal solution is NP-complete. Chapter 37 gives several approximation algorithms for NP-complete problems.

36.5.3 The subset-sum problem

The next NP-complete problem we consider is arithmetic. In the **subset-sum problem**, we are given a finite set $S \subset \mathbf{N}$ and a **target** $t \in \mathbf{N}$. We ask whether there is a subset $S' \subseteq S$ whose elements sum to t. For example, if $S = \{1, 4, 16, 64, 256, 1040, 1041, 1093, 1284, 1344\}$ and $t = 3754$, then the subset $S' = \{1, 16, 64, 256, 1040, 1093, 1284\}$ is a solution.

As usual, we define the problem as a language:

SUBSET-SUM $=$

$\{\langle S, t \rangle$: there exists a subset $S' \subseteq S$ such that $t = \sum_{s \in S'} s\}$.

As with any arithmetic problem, it is important to recall that our standard encoding assumes that the input integers are coded in binary. With this assumption in mind, we can show that the subset-sum problem is unlikely to have a fast algorithm.

Theorem 36.13
The subset-sum problem is NP-complete.

Proof To show that SUBSET-SUM is in NP, for an instance $\langle S, t \rangle$ of the problem, we let the subset S' be the certificate. Checking whether $t = \sum_{s \in S'} s$ can be accomplished by a verification algorithm in polynomial time.

We now show that VERTEX-COVER $\leq_{\mathrm{P}}$ SUBSET-SUM. Given an instance $\langle G, k \rangle$ of the vertex-cover problem, the reduction algorithm constructs an instance $\langle S, t \rangle$ of the subset-sum problem such that G has a vertex cover of size k if and only if there is a subset of S whose sum is exactly t.

At the heart of the reduction is an incidence-matrix representation of G. Let $G = (V, E)$ be an undirected graph and let $V = \{v_0, v_1, \ldots, v_{|V|-1}\}$ and $E = \{e_0, e_1, \ldots, e_{|E|-1}\}$. The ***incidence matrix*** of G is a $|V| \times |E|$ matrix $B = (b_{ij})$ such that

$$b_{ij} = \begin{cases} 1 & \text{if edge } e_j \text{ is incident on vertex } v_i \text{ ,} \\ 0 & \text{otherwise .} \end{cases}$$

For example, Figure 36.14(b) shows the incidence matrix for the undirected graph of Figure 36.14(a). The incidence matrix is shown with lower-indexed edges on the right, rather than on the left as is conventional, in order to simplify the formulas for the numbers in S.

Given a graph G and an integer k, the reduction algorithm computes a set S of numbers and an integer t. To understand how the reduction algorithm works, let us represent numbers in a "modified base-4" fashion. The $|E|$ low-order digits of a number will be in base-4 but the high-order

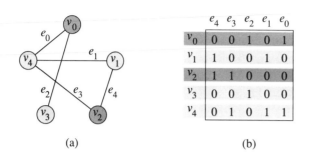

	e_4	e_3	e_2	e_1	e_0
v_0	0	0	1	0	1
v_1	1	0	0	1	0
v_2	1	1	0	0	0
v_3	0	0	1	0	0
v_4	0	1	0	1	1

(b)

			modified base 4					*decimal*
		e_4	e_3	e_2	e_1	e_0		
x_0 =	1	0	0	1	0	1	=	1041
x_1 =	1	1	0	0	1	0	=	1284
x_2 =	1	1	1	0	0	0	=	1344
x_3 =	1	0	0	1	0	0	=	1040
x_4 =	1	0	1	0	1	1	=	1093
y_0 =		0	0	0	0	1	=	1
y_1 =		0	0	0	1	0	=	4
y_2 =		0	0	1	0	0	=	16
y_3 =		0	1	0	0	0	=	64
y_4 =		1	0	0	0	0	=	256
t =	3	2	2	2	2	2	=	3754

(c)

Figure 36.14 The reduction of the vertex-cover problem to the subset-sum problem. **(a)** An undirected graph G. A vertex cover $\{v_1, v_3, v_4\}$ of size 3 is lightly shaded. **(b)** The corresponding incidence matrix. Shading of the rows corresponds to the vertex cover of part (a). Each edge e_j has a 1 in at least one lightly shaded row. **(c)** The corresponding subset-sum instance. The portion within the box is the incidence matrix. Here, the vertex cover $\{v_1, v_3, v_4\}$ of size $k = 3$ corresponds to the lightly shaded subset $\{1, 16, 64, 256, 1040, 1093, 1284\}$, which adds up to 3754.

digit can be as large as k. The set of numbers is constructed in such a way that no carries can be propagated from lower digits to higher digits.

The set S consists of two types of numbers, corresponding to vertices and edges respectively. For each vertex $v_i \in V$, we create a positive integer x_i whose modified base-4 representation consists of a leading 1 followed by $|E|$ digits. The digits correspond to v_i's row of the incidence matrix $B = (b_{ij})$ for G, as illustrated in Figure 36.14(c). Formally, for $i = 0, 1, \ldots, |V| - 1$,

$$x_i = 4^{|E|} + \sum_{j=0}^{|E|-1} b_{ij} 4^j \ .$$

For each edge $e_j \in E$, we create a positive integer y_j that is just a row of the "identity" incidence matrix. (The identity incidence matrix is the $|E| \times |E|$ matrix with 1's only in the diagonal positions.) Formally, for $j = 0, 1, \ldots, |E| - 1$,

$$y_j = 4^j \ .$$

The first digit of the target sum t is k, and all $|E|$ lower-order digits are 2's. Formally,

$$t = k4^{|E|} + \sum_{j=0}^{|E|-1} 2 \cdot 4^j \ .$$

All of these numbers have polynomial size when we represent them in binary. The reduction can be performed in polynomial time by manipulating the bits of the incidence matrix.

We must now show that graph G has a vertex cover of size k if and only if there is a subset $S' \subseteq S$ whose sum is t. First, suppose that G has a vertex cover $V' \subseteq V$ of size k. Let $V' = \{v_{i_1}, v_{i_2}, \ldots, v_{i_k}\}$, and define S' by

$$S' = \{x_{i_1}, x_{i_2}, \ldots, x_{i_k}\} \cup$$

$$\{y_j : e_j \text{ is incident on precisely one vertex in } V'\} \ .$$

To see that $\sum_{s \in S'} s = t$, observe that summing the k leading 1's of the $x_{i_m} \in S'$ gives the leading digit k of the modified base-4 representation of t. To get the low-order digits of t, each of which is a 2, consider the digit positions in turn, each of which corresponds to an edge e_j. Because V' is a vertex cover, e_j is incident on at least one vertex in V'. Thus, for each edge e_j, there is at least one $x_{i_m} \in S'$ with a 1 in the jth position. If e_j is incident on two vertices in V', then both contribute a 1 to the sum in the jth position. The jth digit of y_j contributes nothing, since e_j is incident on two vertices, which implies that $y_j \notin S'$. Thus, in this case, the sum of S' produces a 2 in the jth position of t. For the other case—when e_j is incident on exactly one vertex in V'—we have $y_j \in S'$, and the incident vertex and y_j each contribute 1 to the sum of the jth digit of t, thereby also producing a 2. Thus, S' is a solution to the subset-sum instance S.

Now, suppose that there is a subset $S' \subseteq S$ that sums to t. Let $S = \{x_{i_1}, x_{i_2}, \ldots, x_{i_m}\} \cup \{y_{j_1}, y_{j_2}, \ldots, y_{j_p}\}$. We claim that $m = k$ and that $V' = \{v_{i_1}, v_{i_2}, \ldots, v_{i_m}\}$ is a vertex cover for G. To prove this claim, we start by observing that for each edge $e_j \in E$, there are three 1's in set S in the e_j position: one from each of the two vertices incident on e_j, and one from y_j. Because we are working with a modified base-4 representation, there are no carries from position e_j to position e_{j+1}. Thus, for each of the $|E|$ low-order positions of t, at least one and at most two x_i must contribute to the sum. Since at least one x_i contributes to the sum for each edge, we see that V' is a vertex cover. To see that $m = k$, and thus that V' is a vertex cover of size k, observe that the only way the leading k in target t can be achieved is by including exactly k of the x_i in the sum. ■

In Figure 36.14, the vertex cover $V' = \{v_1, v_3, v_4\}$ corresponds to the subset $S' = \{x_1, x_3, x_4, y_0, y_2, y_3, y_4\}$. All of the y_j are included in S', with the exception of y_1, which is incident on two vertices in V'.

36.5.4 The hamiltonian-cycle problem

We now return to the hamiltonian-cycle problem defined in Section 36.2.

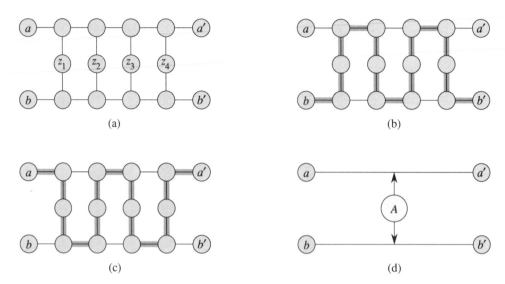

Figure 36.15 (a) Widget A, used in the reduction from 3-CNF-SAT to HAM-CYCLE. (b)–(c) If A is a subgraph of some graph G that contains a hamiltonian cycle and the only connections from A to the rest of G are through the vertices a, a', b, and b', then the shaded edges represent the only two possible ways in which the hamiltonian cycle may traverse the edges of subgraph A. (d) A compact representation of the A widget.

Theorem 36.14
The hamiltonian cycle problem is NP-complete.

Proof   We first show that HAM-CYCLE belongs to NP. Given a graph $G = (V, E)$, our certificate is the sequence of $|V|$ vertices that make up the hamiltonian cycle. The verification algorithm checks that this sequence contains each vertex in V exactly once and that with the first vertex repeated at the end, it forms a cycle in G. This verification can be performed in polynomial time.

We now prove that HAM-CYCLE is NP-complete by showing that 3-CNF-SAT $\leq_P$ HAM-CYCLE. Given a 3-CNF boolean formula ϕ over variables $x_1, x_2, \ldots, x_n$ with clauses $C_1, C_2, \ldots, C_k$, each containing exactly 3 distinct literals, we construct a graph $G = (V, E)$ in polynomial time such that G has a hamiltonian cycle if and only if ϕ is satisfiable. Our construction is based on ***widgets***, which are pieces of graphs that enforce certain properties.

Our first widget is the subgraph A shown in Figure 36.15(a). Suppose that A is a subgraph of some graph G and that the only connections between A and the remainder of G are through the vertices a, a', b, and b'. Furthermore, suppose that graph G has a hamiltonian cycle. Since any hamiltonian cycle of G must pass through vertices z_1, z_2, z_3, and z_4 in one of the ways shown in Figures 36.15(b) and (c), we may treat subgraph A as if it were simply a pair of edges (a, a') and (b, b') with the restriction that any hamiltonian cycle of G must include exactly one of these edges. We shall represent widget A as shown in Figure 36.15(d).

The subgraph B in Figure 36.16 is our second widget. Suppose that B is a subgraph of some graph G and that the only connections from B to the remainder of G are through vertices b_1, b_2, b_3, and b_4. A hamiltonian cycle of graph G cannot traverse *all* of the edges (b_1, b_2), (b_2, b_3), and (b_3, b_4), since then all vertices in the widget other than b_1, b_2, b_3, and b_4 would be missed. A hamiltonian cycle of G may, however, traverse any proper subset of these edges. Figures 36.16(a)–(e) show five such subsets; the remaining two subsets can be obtained by performing a top-to-bottom flip of parts (b) and (e). We represent this widget as in Figure 36.16(f), the idea being that at least one of the paths pointed to by the arrows must be taken by a hamiltonian cycle.

The graph G that we shall construct consists mostly of copies of these two widgets. The construction is illustrated in Figure 36.17. For each of the k clauses in ϕ, we include a copy of widget B, and we join these widgets together in series as follows. Letting b_{ij} be the copy of vertex b_j in the ith copy of widget B, we connect $b_{i,4}$ to $b_{i+1,1}$ for $i = 1, 2, \ldots, k-1$.

Then, for each variable x_m in ϕ, we include two vertices x'_m and x''_m. We connect these two vertices by means of two copies of the edge (x'_m, x''_m), which we denote by e_m and $\overline{e}_m$ to distinguish them. The idea is that if the hamiltonian cycle takes edge e_m, it corresponds to assigning variable x_m the value 1. If the hamiltonian cycle takes edge $\overline{e}_m$, the variable is assigned the value 0. Each pair of these edges forms a two-edge loop; we connect these small loops in series by adding edges (x'_m, x''_{m+1}) for $m = 1, 2, \ldots, n-1$. We connect the left (clause) side of the graph to the right (variable) side by means of two edges $(b_{1,1}, x'_1)$ and $(b_{k,4}, x''_n)$, which are the topmost and bottommost edges in Figure 36.17.

We are not yet finished with the construction of graph G, since we have yet to relate the variables to the clauses. If the jth literal of clause C_i is x_m, then we use an A widget to connect edge $(b_{ij}, b_{i,j+1})$ with edge e_m. If the jth literal of clause C_i is $\neg x_m$, then we instead put an A widget between edge $(b_{ij}, b_{i,j+1})$ and edge $\overline{e}_m$. In Figure 36.17, for example, because clause C_2 is $(x_1 \vee \neg x_2 \vee x_3)$, we place three A widgets as follows:

- between $(b_{2,1}, b_{2,2})$ and e_1,
- between $(b_{2,2}, b_{2,3})$ and $\overline{e}_2$, and
- between $(b_{2,3}, b_{2,4})$ and e_3.

Note that connecting two edges by means of A widgets actually entails replacing each edge by the five edges in the top or bottom of Figure 36.15(a) and, of course, adding the connections that pass through the z vertices as well. A given literal l_m may appear in several clauses ($\neg x_3$ in Figure 36.17, for example), and thus an edge e_m or $\overline{e}_m$ may be be influenced by several A widgets (edge $\overline{e}_3$, for example). In this case, we connect the A widgets in series, as shown in Figure 36.18, effectively replacing edge e_m or $\overline{e}_m$ by a series of edges.

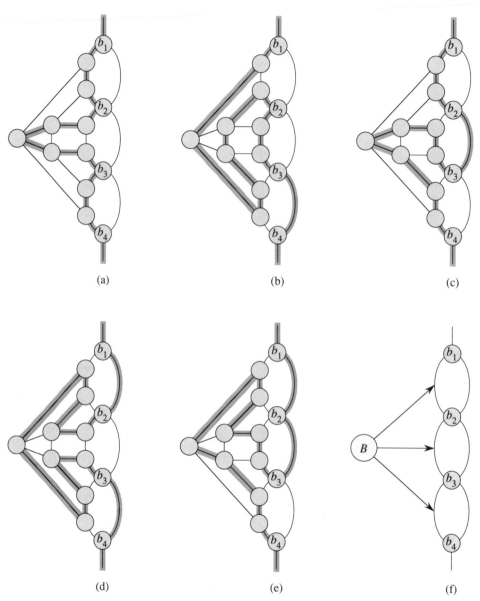

Figure 36.16 Widget B, used in the reduction from 3-CNF-SAT to HAM-CYCLE. No path from vertex b_1 to vertex b_4 containing all the vertices in the widget may use all three edges (b_1, b_2), (b_2, b_3), and (b_3, b_4). Any proper subset of these edges may be used, however. **(a)–(e)** Five such subsets. **(f)** A representation of this widget in which at least one of the paths pointed to by the arrows must be taken by a hamiltonian cycle.

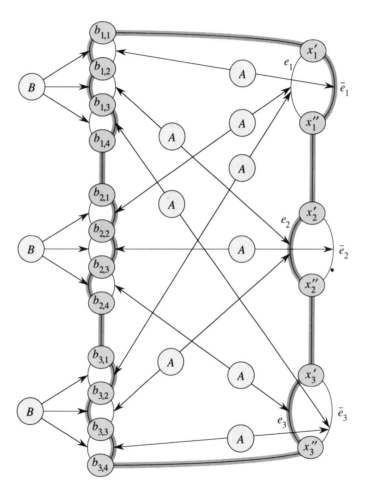

Figure 36.17 The graph G constructed from the formula $\phi = (\neg x_1 \vee x_2 \vee \neg x_3) \wedge (x_1 \vee \neg x_2 \vee x_3) \wedge (x_1 \vee x_2 \vee \neg x_3)$. A satisfying assignment s to the variables of ϕ is $s(x_1) = 0$, $s(x_2) = 1$, and $s(x_3) = 1$, which corresponds to the hamiltonian cycle shown. Note that if $s(x_m) = 1$, then edge e_m is in the hamiltonian cycle, and if $s(x_m) = 0$, then edge $\bar{e}_m$ is in the hamiltonian cycle.

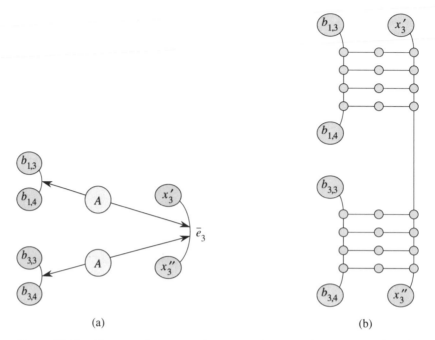

Figure 36.18 The actual construction used when an edge e_m or $\bar{e}_m$ is influenced by multiple A widgets. **(a)** A portion of Figure 36.17. **(b)** The actual subgraph constructed.

We claim that formula ϕ is satisfiable if and only if graph G contains a hamiltonian cycle. We first suppose that G has a hamiltonian cycle h and show that ϕ is satisfiable. Cycle h must take a particular form:

- First, it traverses edge $(b_{1,1}, x_1')$ to go from the top left to the top right.
- It then follows all of the x_m' and x_m'' vertices from top to bottom, choosing either edge e_m or edge $\bar{e}_m$, but not both.
- It next traverses edge $(b_{k,4}, x_n'')$ to get back to the left side.
- Finally, it traverses the B widgets from bottom to top on the left.

(It actually traverses edges within the A widgets as well, but we use these subgraphs to enforce the either/or nature of the edges it connects.)

Given the hamiltonian cycle h, we define a truth assignment for ϕ as follows. If edge e_m belongs to h, then we set $x_m = 1$. Otherwise, edge $\bar{e}_m$ belongs to h, and we set $x_m = 0$.

We claim that this assignment satisfies ϕ. Consider a clause C_i and the corresponding B widget in G. Each edge $(b_{i,j} b_{i,j+1})$ is connected by an A widget to either edge e_m or edge $\bar{e}_m$, depending on whether x_m or $\neg x_m$ is the jth literal in the clause. The edge $(b_{i,j}, b_{i,j+1})$ is traversed by h if and only if the corresponding literal is 0. Since each of the three edges $(b_{i,1}, b_{i,2}), (b_{i,2}, b_{i,3}), (b_{i,3}, b_{i,4})$ in clause C_i is also in a B widget, all three cannot be traversed by the hamiltonian cycle h. One of the three edges, therefore, must have a corresponding literal whose assigned value is 1, and

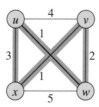

Figure 36.19 An instance of the traveling-salesman problem. Shaded edges represent a minimum-cost tour, with cost 7.

clause C_i is satisfied. This property holds for each clause C_i, $i = 1, 2, \ldots, k$, and thus formula ϕ is satisfied.

Conversely, let us suppose that formula ϕ is satisfied by some truth assignment. By following the rules from above, we can construct a hamiltonian cycle for graph G: traverse edge e_m if $x_m = 1$, traverse edge $\bar{e}_m$ if $x_m = 0$, and traverse edge $(b_{i,j}, b_{i,j+1})$ if and only if the jth literal of clause C_i is 0 under the assignment. These rules can indeed be followed, since we assume that s is a satisfying assignment for formula ϕ.

Finally, we note that graph G can be constructed in polynomial time. It contains one B widget for each of the k clauses in ϕ. There is one A widget for each instance of each literal in ϕ, and so there are $3k$ A widgets. Since the A and B widgets are of fixed size, the graph G has $O(k)$ vertices and edges and is easily constructed in polynomial time. Thus, we have provided a polynomial-time reduction from 3-CNF-SAT to HAM-CYCLE. ■

36.5.5 The traveling-salesman problem

In the ***traveling-salesman problem***, which is closely related to the hamiltonian-cycle problem, a salesman must visit n cities. Modeling the problem as a complete graph with n vertices, we can say that the salesman wishes to make a ***tour***, or hamiltonian cycle, visiting each city exactly once and finishing at the city he starts from. There is an integer cost $c(i, j)$ to travel from city i to city j, and the salesman wishes to make the tour whose total cost is minimum, where the total cost is the sum of the individual costs along the edges of the tour. For example, in Figure 36.19, a minimum-cost tour is $\langle u, w, v, x, u \rangle$, with cost 7. The formal language for the traveling-salesman problem is

$$\text{TSP} = \{ \langle G, c, k \rangle : G = (V, E) \text{ is a complete graph,}$$
$$c \text{ is a function from } V \times V \to \mathbf{Z},$$
$$k \in \mathbf{Z}, \text{ and}$$
$$G \text{ has a traveling-salesman tour with cost at most } k \} .$$

The following theorem shows that a fast algorithm for the traveling-salesman problem is unlikely to exist.

Theorem 36.15
The traveling-salesman problem is NP-complete.

Proof   We first show that TSP belongs to NP. Given an instance of the problem, we use as a certificate the sequence of n vertices in the tour. The verification algorithm checks that this sequence contains each vertex exactly once, sums up the edge costs, and checks whether the sum is at most k. This process can certainly be done in polynomial time.

To prove that TSP is NP-hard, we show that HAM-CYCLE $\leq_P$ TSP. Let $G = (V, E)$ be an instance of HAM-CYCLE. We construct an instance of TSP as follows. We form the complete graph $G' = (V, E')$, where $E' = \{(i, j) : i, j \in V\}$, and we define the cost function c by

$$c(i, j) = \begin{cases} 0 & \text{if } (i, j) \in E \text{ ,} \\ 1 & \text{if } (i, j) \notin E \text{ .} \end{cases}$$

The instance of TSP is then $(G', c, 0)$, which is easily formed in polynomial time.

We now show that graph G has a hamiltonian cycle if and only if graph G' has a tour of cost at most 0. Suppose that graph G has a hamiltonian cycle h. Each edge in h belongs to E and thus has cost 0 in G'. Thus, h is a tour in G' with cost 0. Conversely, suppose that graph G' has a tour h' of cost at most 0. Since the costs of the edges in E' are 0 and 1, the cost of tour h' is exactly 0. Therefore, h' contains only edges in E. We conclude that h is a hamiltonian cycle in graph G.   ∎

Exercises

36.5-1
The *subgraph-isomorphism problem* takes two graphs G_1 and G_2 and asks whether G_1 is a subgraph of G_2. Show that the subgraph-isomorphism problem is NP-complete.

36.5-2
Given an integer m-by-n matrix A and an integer m-vector b, the *0-1 integer-programming problem* asks whether there is an integer n-vector x with elements in the set $\{0, 1\}$ such that $Ax \leq b$. Prove that 0-1 integer programming is NP-complete. (*Hint:* Reduce from 3-CNF-SAT.)

36.5-3
Show that the subset-sum problem is solvable in polynomial time if the target value t is expressed in unary.

36.5-4
The *set-partition problem* takes as input a set S of numbers. The question is whether the numbers can be partitioned into two sets A and $\overline{A} = S - A$

such that $\sum_{x \in A} x = \sum_{x \in \overline{A}} x$. Show that the set-partition problem is NP-complete.

36.5-5
Show that the hamiltonian-path problem is NP-complete.

36.5-6
The *longest-simple-cycle problem* is the problem of determining a simple cycle (no repeated vertices) of maximum length in a graph. Show that this problem is NP-complete.

36.5-7
Professor Marconi proclaims that the subgraph used as widget A in the proof of Theorem 36.14 is more complicated than necessary: vertices z_3 and z_4 of Figure 36.15(a) and the vertices above and below them are not needed. Is the professor correct? That is, does the reduction work with this smaller version of the widget, or does the "either/or" property of the widget disappear?

Problems

36-1 *Independent set*
An *independent set* of a graph $G = (V, E)$ is a subset $V' \subseteq V$ of vertices such that each edge in E is incident on at most one vertex in V'. The *independent-set problem* is to find a maximum-size independent set in G.

a. Formulate a related decision problem for the independent-set problem, and prove that it is NP-complete. (*Hint:* Reduce from the clique problem.)

b. Suppose that you are given a subroutine to solve the decision problem you defined in part (a). Give an algorithm to find an independent set of maximum size. The running time of your algorithm should be polynomial in $|V|$ and $|E|$, where queries to the black box are counted as a single step.

Although the independent-set decision problem is NP-complete, certain special cases are polynomial-time solvable.

c. Give an efficient algorithm to solve the independent-set problem when each vertex in G has degree 2. Analyze the running time, and prove that your algorithm works correctly.

d. Give an efficient algorithm to solve the independent-set problem when G is bipartite. Analyze the running time, and prove that your algorithm works correctly. (*Hint:* Use the results of Section 27.3.)

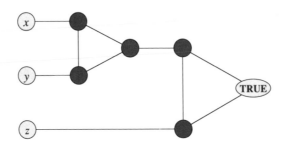

Figure 36.20   The widget corresponding to a clause $(x \lor y \lor z)$, used in Problem 36-2.

36-2 *Graph coloring*

A ***k-coloring*** of an undirected graph $G = (V, E)$ is a function $c : V \to \{1, 2, \ldots, k\}$ such that $c(u) \neq c(v)$ for every edge $(u, v) \in E$. In other words, the numbers $1, 2, \ldots, k$ represent the k colors, and adjacent vertices must have different colors. The ***graph-coloring problem*** is to determine the minimum number of colors needed to color a given graph.

a. Give an efficient algorithm to determine a 2-coloring of a graph if one exists.

b. Cast the graph-coloring problem as a decision problem. Show that your decision problem is solvable in polynomial time if and only if the graph-coloring problem is solvable in polynomial time.

c. Let the language 3-COLOR be the set of graphs that can be 3-colored. Show that if 3-COLOR is NP-complete, then your decision problem from part (b) is NP-complete.

To prove that 3-COLOR is NP-complete, we use a reduction from 3-CNF-SAT. Given a formula ϕ of m clauses on n variables $x_1, x_2, \ldots, x_n$, we construct a graph $G = (V, E)$ as follows. The set V consists of a vertex for each variable, a vertex for the negation of each variable, 5 vertices for each clause, and 3 special vertices: TRUE, FALSE, and RED. The edges of the graph are of two types: "literal" edges that are independent of the clauses and "clause" edges that depend on the clauses. The literal edges form a triangle on the special vertices and also form a triangle on x_i, $\neg x_i$, and RED for $i = 1, 2, \ldots, n$.

d. Argue that in any 3-coloring c of a graph containing the literal edges, exactly one of a variable and its negation is colored $c(\text{TRUE})$ and the other is colored $c(\text{FALSE})$. Argue that for any truth assignment for ϕ, there is a 3-coloring of the graph containing just the literal edges.

The widget shown in Figure 36.20 is used to enforce the condition corresponding to a clause $(x \lor y \lor z)$. Each clause requires a unique copy of the 5 vertices that are heavily shaded in the figure; they connect as shown to the literals of the clause and the special vertex TRUE.

e. Argue that if each of x, y, and z is colored $c(\text{TRUE})$ or $c(\text{FALSE})$, then the widget is 3-colorable if and only if at least one of x, y, or z is colored $c(\text{TRUE})$.

f. Complete the proof that 3-COLOR is NP-complete.

Chapter notes

Garey and Johnson [79] provide a wonderful guide to NP-completeness, discussing the theory at length and providing a catalogue of many problems that were known to be NP-complete in 1979. (The list of NP-complete problem domains at the beginning of Section 36.5 is drawn from their table of contents.) Hopcroft and Ullman [104] and Lewis and Papadimitriou [139] have good treatments of NP-completeness in the context of complexity theory. Aho, Hopcroft, and Ullman [4] also cover NP-completeness and give several reductions, including a reduction for the vertex-cover problem from the hamiltonian-cycle problem.

The class P was introduced in 1964 by Cobham [44] and, independently, in 1965 by Edmonds [61], who also introduced the class NP and conjectured that $P \neq NP$. The notion of NP-completeness was proposed in 1971 by Cook [49], who gave the first NP-completeness proofs for formula satisfiability and 3-CNF satisfiability. Levin [138] independently discovered the notion, giving an NP-completeness proof for a tiling problem. Karp [116] introduced the methodology of reductions in 1972 and demonstrated the rich variety of NP-complete problems. Karp's paper included the original NP-completeness proofs of the clique, vertex-cover, and hamiltonian-cycle problems. Since then, hundreds of problems have been proven to be NP-complete by many researchers.

The proof of Theorem 36.14 was adapted from Papadimitriou and Steiglitz [154].

37   Approximation Algorithms

Many problems of practical significance are NP-complete but are too important to abandon merely because obtaining an optimal solution is intractable. If a problem is NP-complete, we are unlikely to find a polynomial-time algorithm for solving it exactly, but this does not imply that all hope is lost. There are two approaches to getting around NP-completeness. First, if the actual inputs are small, an algorithm with exponential running time may be perfectly satisfactory. Second, it may still be possible to find *near-optimal* solutions in polynomial time (either in the worst case or on the average). In practice, near-optimality is often good enough. An algorithm that returns near-optimal solutions is called an ***approximation algorithm***. This chapter presents polynomial-time approximation algorithms for several NP-complete problems.

Performance bounds for approximation algorithms

Assume that we are working on an optimization problem in which each potential solution has a positive cost, and that we wish to find a near-optimal solution. Depending on the problem, an optimal solution may be defined as one with maximum possible cost or one with minimum possible cost; the problem may be a maximization or a minimization problem.

We say that an approximation algorithm for the problem has a ***ratio bound*** of $\rho(n)$ if for any input of size n, the cost C of the solution produced by the approximation algorithm is within a factor of $\rho(n)$ of the cost C^* of an optimal solution:

$$\max\left(\frac{C}{C^*}, \frac{C^*}{C}\right) \le \rho(n) . \tag{37.1}$$

This definition applies for both minimization and maximization problems. For a maximization problem, $0 < C \le C^*$, and the ratio C^*/C gives the factor by which the cost of an optimal solution is larger than the cost of the approximate solution. Similarly, for a minimization problem, $0 < C^* \le C$, and the ratio C/C^* gives the factor by which the cost of the approximate solution is larger than the cost of an optimal solution. Since all solutions are assumed to have positive cost, these ratios are always well defined. The ratio bound of an approximation algorithm is never less than 1, since $C/C^* < 1$ implies $C^*/C > 1$. An optimal algorithm has ratio bound 1, and an approximation algorithm with a large ratio bound may return a solution that is very much worse than optimal.

Sometimes, it is more convenient to work with a measure of relative error. For any input, the **relative error** of the approximation algorithm is defined to be

$$\frac{|C - C^*|}{C^*} ,$$

where, as before, C^* is the cost of an optimal solution and C is the cost of the solution produced by the approximation algorithm. The relative error is always nonnegative. An approximation algorithm has a **relative error bound** of $\epsilon(n)$ if

$$\frac{|C - C^*|}{C^*} \leq \epsilon(n) . \tag{37.2}$$

It follows from the definitions that the relative error bound can be bounded as a function of the ratio bound:

$$\epsilon(n) \leq \rho(n) - 1 . \tag{37.3}$$

(For a minimization problem, this is an equality, whereas for a maximization problem, we have $\epsilon(n) = (\rho(n) - 1)/\rho(n)$, which satisfies inequality (37.3) since $\rho(n) \geq 1$.)

For many problems, approximation algorithms have been developed that have a fixed ratio bound, independent of n. For such problems, we simply use the notation ρ or ϵ, indicating no dependence on n.

For other problems, computer scientists have been unable to devise any polynomial-time approximation algorithm having a fixed ratio bound. For such problems, the best that can be done is to let the ratio bound grow as a function of the input size n. An example of such a problem is the set-cover problem presented in Section 37.3.

Some NP-complete problems allow approximation algorithms that can achieve increasingly smaller ratio bounds (or, equivalently, increasingly smaller relative error bounds) by using more and more computation time. That is, there is a trade-off between computation time and the quality of the approximation. An example is the subset-sum problem studied in Section 37.4. This situation is important enough to deserve a name of its own.

An **approximation scheme** for an optimization problem is an approximation algorithm that takes as input not only an instance of the problem, but also a value $\epsilon > 0$ such that for any fixed ϵ, the scheme is an approximation algorithm with relative error bound ϵ. We say that an approximation scheme is a **polynomial-time approximation scheme** if for any fixed $\epsilon > 0$, the scheme runs in time polynomial in the size n of its input instance.

The running time of a polynomial-time approximation scheme should not increase too rapidly as ϵ decreases. Ideally, if ϵ decreases by a constant factor, the running time to achieve the desired approximation should not increase by more than a constant factor. In other words, we would like the running time to be polynomial in $1/\epsilon$ as well as in n.

We say that an approximation scheme is a ***fully polynomial-time approximation scheme*** if its running time is polynomial both in $1/\epsilon$ and in the size n of the input instance, where ϵ is the relative error bound for the scheme. For example, the scheme might have a running time of $(1/\epsilon)^2 n^3$. With such a scheme, any constant-factor decrease in ϵ can be achieved with a corresponding constant-factor increase in the running time.

Chapter outline

The first three sections of this chapter present some examples of polynomial-time approximation algorithms for NP-complete problems, and the last section presents a fully polynomial-time approximation scheme. Section 37.1 begins with a study of the vertex-cover problem, an NP-complete minimization problem that has an approximation algorithm with a ratio bound of 2. Section 37.2 presents an approximation algorithm with ratio bound 2 for the case of the traveling-salesman problem in which the cost function satisfies the triangle inequality. It also shows that without triangle inequality, an ϵ-approximation algorithm cannot exist unless P = NP. In Section 37.3, we show how a greedy method can be used as an effective approximation algorithm for the set-covering problem, obtaining a covering whose cost is at worst a logarithmic factor larger than the optimal cost. Finally, Section 37.4 presents a fully polynomial-time approximation scheme for the subset-sum problem.

37.1   The vertex-cover problem

The vertex-cover problem was defined and proved NP-complete in Section 36.5.2. A ***vertex cover*** of an undirected graph $G = (V, E)$ is a subset $V' \subseteq V$ such that if (u, v) is an edge of G, then either $u \in V'$ or $v \in V'$ (or both). The size of a vertex cover is the number of vertices in it.

The ***vertex-cover problem*** is to find a vertex cover of minimum size in a given undirected graph. We call such a vertex cover an ***optimal vertex cover***. This problem is NP-hard, since the related decision problem is NP-complete, by Theorem 36.12.

Even though it may be difficult to find an optimal vertex cover in a graph G, however, it is not too hard to find a vertex cover that is near-optimal. The following approximation algorithm takes as input an undirected graph G and returns a vertex cover whose size is guaranteed to be no more than twice the size of an optimal vertex cover.

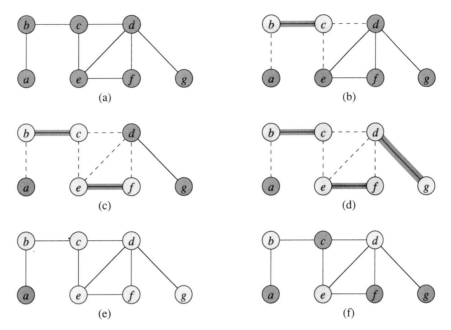

Figure 37.1 The operation of APPROX-VERTEX-COVER. (a) The input graph G, which has 7 vertices and 8 edges. (b) The edge (b, c), shown heavy, is the first edge chosen by APPROX-VERTEX-COVER. Vertices b and c, shown lightly shaded, are added to the set A containing the vertex cover being created. Edges (a, b), (c, e), and (c, d), shown dashed, are removed since they are now covered by some vertex in A. (c) Edge (e, f) is added to A. (d) Edge (d, g) is added to A. (e) The set A, which is the vertex cover produced by APPROX-VERTEX-COVER, contains the six vertices b, c, d, e, f, g. (f) The optimal vertex cover for this problem contains only three vertices: b, d, and e.

APPROX-VERTEX-COVER(G)

1 $C \leftarrow \emptyset$
2 $E' \leftarrow E[G]$
3 **while** $E' \neq \emptyset$
4   **do** let (u, v) be an arbitrary edge of E'
5          $C \leftarrow C \cup \{u, v\}$
6   remove from E' every edge incident on either u or v
7 **return** C

Figure 37.1 illustrates the operation of APPROX-VERTEX-COVER. The variable C contains the vertex cover being constructed. Line 1 initializes C to the empty set. Line 2 sets E' to be a copy of the edge set $E[G]$ of the graph. The loop on lines 3–6 repeatedly picks an edge (u, v) from E', adds its endpoints u and v to C, and deletes all edges in E' that are covered by either u or v. The running time of this algorithm is $O(E)$, using an appropriate data structure for representing E'.

Theorem 37.1
APPROX-VERTEX-COVER has a ratio bound of 2.

Proof   The set C of vertices that is returned by APPROX-VERTEX-COVER is a vertex cover, since the algorithm loops until every edge in $E[G]$ has been covered by some vertex in C.

To see that APPROX-VERTEX-COVER returns a vertex cover that is at most twice the size of an optimal cover, let A denote the set of edges that were picked in line 4 of APPROX-VERTEX-COVER. No two edges in A share an endpoint, since once an edge is picked in line 4, all other edges that are incident on its endpoints are deleted from E' in line 6. Therefore, each execution of line 5 adds two new vertices to C, and $|C| = 2|A|$. In order to cover the edges in A, however, any vertex cover—in particular, an optimal cover C^*—must include at least one endpoint of each edge in A. Since no two edges in A share an endpoint, no vertex in the cover is incident on more than one edge in A. Therefore, $|A| \leq |C^*|$, and $|C| \leq 2|C^*|$, proving the theorem.   ■

Exercises

37.1-1
Given an example of a graph for which APPROX-VERTEX-COVER always yields a suboptimal solution.

37.1-2
Professor Nixon proposes the following heuristic to solve the vertex-cover problem. Repeatedly select a vertex of highest degree, and remove all of its incident edges. Give an example to show that the professor's heuristic does not have a ratio bound of 2.

37.1-3
Give an efficient greedy algorithm that finds an optimal vertex cover for a tree in linear time.

37.1-4
From the proof of Theorem 36.12, we know that the vertex-cover problem and the NP-complete clique problem are complementary in the sense that an optimal vertex cover is the complement of a maximum-size clique in the complement graph. Does this relationship imply that there is an approximation algorithm with constant ratio bound for the clique problem? Justify your answer.

37.2 The traveling-salesman problem

In the traveling-salesman problem introduced in Section 36.5.5, we are given a complete undirected graph $G = (V, E)$ that has a nonnegative integer cost $c(u, v)$ associated with each edge $(u, v) \in E$, and we must find a hamiltonian cycle (a tour) of G with minimum cost. As an extension of our notation, let $c(A)$ denote the total cost of the edges in the subset $A \subseteq E$:

$$c(A) = \sum_{(u,v) \in A} c(u, v) .$$

In many practical situations, it is always cheapest to go directly from a place u to a place w; going by way of any intermediate stop v can't be less expensive. Putting it another way, cutting out an intermediate stop never increases the cost. We formalize this notion by saying that the cost function c satisfies the ***triangle inequality*** if for all vertices $u, v, w \in V$,

$$c(u, w) \leq c(u, v) + c(v, w) .$$

The triangle inequality is a natural one, and in many applications it is automatically satisfied. For example, if the vertices of the graph are points in the plane and the cost of traveling between two vertices is the ordinary euclidean distance between them, then the triangle inequality is satisfied.

As Exercise 37.2-1 shows, restricting the cost function to satisfy the triangle inequality does not alter the NP-completeness of the traveling-salesman problem. Thus, it is unlikely that we can find a polynomial-time algorithm for solving this problem exactly. We therefore look instead for good approximation algorithms.

In Section 37.2.1, we examine an approximation algorithm for the traveling-salesman problem with triangle inequality that has a ratio bound of 2. In Section 37.2.2, we show that without triangle inequality, an approximation algorithm with constant ratio bound does not exist unless $P = NP$.

37.2.1 The traveling-salesman problem with triangle inequality

The following algorithm computes a near-optimal tour of an undirected graph G, using the minimum-spanning-tree algorithm MST-PRIM from Section 24.2. We shall see that when the cost function satisfies the triangle inequality, the tour that this algorithm returns is no worse than twice as long as an optimal tour.

APPROX-TSP-TOUR(G, c)

1   select a vertex $r \in V[G]$ to be a "root" vertex
2   grow a minimum spanning tree T for G from root r
            using MST-PRIM(G, c, r)
3   let L be the list of vertices visited in a preorder tree walk of T
4   **return** the hamiltonian cycle H that visits the vertices in the order L

Recall from Section 13.1 that a preorder tree walk recursively visits every vertex in the tree, listing a vertex when it is first encountered, before any of its children are visited.

Figure 37.2 illustrates the operation of APPROX-TSP-TOUR. Part (a) of the figure shows the given set of vertices, and part (b) shows the minimum spanning tree T grown from root vertex a by MST-PRIM. Part (c) shows how the vertices are visited by a preorder walk of T, and part (d) displays the corresponding tour, which is the tour returned by APPROX-TSP-TOUR. Part (e) displays an optimal tour, which is about 23% shorter.

The running time of APPROX-TSP-TOUR is $\Theta(E) = \Theta(V^2)$, since the input is a complete graph (see Exercise 24.2-2). We shall now show that if the cost function for an instance of the traveling-salesman problem satisfies the triangle inequality, then APPROX-TSP-TOUR returns a tour whose cost is not more than twice the cost of an optimal tour.

Theorem 37.2
APPROX-TSP-TOUR is an approximation algorithm with a ratio bound of 2 for the traveling-salesman problem with triangle inequality.

Proof   Let H^* denote an optimal tour for the given set of vertices. An equivalent statement of the theorem is that $c(H) \le 2c(H^*)$, where H is the tour returned by APPROX-TSP-TOUR. Since we obtain a spanning tree by deleting any edge from a tour, if T is a minimum spanning tree for the given set of vertices, then

$$c(T) \le c(H^*) . \tag{37.4}$$

A ***full walk*** of T lists the vertices when they are first visited and also whenever they are returned to after a visit to a subtree. Let us call this walk W. The full walk of our example gives the order

$$a, b, c, b, h, b, a, d, e, f, e, g, e, d, a .$$

Since the full walk traverses every edge of T exactly twice, we have

$$c(W) = 2c(T) . \tag{37.5}$$

Equations (37.4) and (37.5) imply that

$$c(W) \le 2c(H^*) , \tag{37.6}$$

and so the cost of W is within a factor of 2 of the cost of an optimal tour.

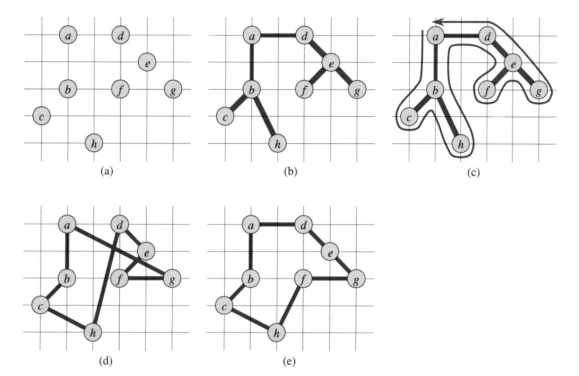

Figure 37.2 The operation of APPROX-TSP-TOUR. (**a**) The given set of points, which lie on vertices of an integer grid. For example, f is one unit to the right and two units up from h. The ordinary euclidean distance is used as the cost function between two points. (**b**) A minimum spanning tree T of these points, as computed by MST-PRIM. Vertex a is the root vertex. The vertices happen to be labeled in such a way that they are added to the main tree by MST-PRIM in alphabetical order. (**c**) A walk of T, starting at a. A full walk of the tree visits the vertices in the order $a, b, c, b, h, b, a, d, e, f, e, g, e, d, a$. A preorder walk of T lists a vertex just when it is first encountered, yielding the ordering a, b, c, h, d, e, f, g. (**d**) A tour of the vertices obtained by visiting the vertices in the order given by the preorder walk. This is the tour H returned by APPROX-TSP-TOUR. Its total cost is approximately 19.074. (**e**) An optimal tour H^* for the given set of vertices. Its total cost is approximately 14.715.

Unfortunately, W is generally not a tour, since it visits some vertices more than once. By the triangle inequality, however, we can delete a visit to any vertex from W and the cost does not increase. (If a vertex v is deleted from W between visits to u and w, the resulting ordering specifies going directly from u to w.) By repeatedly applying this operation, we can remove from W all but the first visit to each vertex. In our example, this leaves the ordering

a, b, c, h, d, e, f, g .

This ordering is the same as that obtained by a preorder walk of the tree T. Let H be the cycle corresponding to this preorder walk. It is a hamiltonian cycle, since every vertex is visited exactly once, and in fact it is the cycle computed by APPROX-TSP-TOUR. Since H is obtained by deleting vertices from the full walk W, we have

$$c(H) \leq c(W) .\tag{37.7}$$

Combining inequalities (37.6) and (37.7) completes the proof.   ∎

In spite of the nice ratio bound provided by Theorem 37.2, APPROX-TSP-TOUR is usually not the best practical choice for this problem. There are other approximation algorithms that typically perform much better in practice (see the references at the end of this chapter).

37.2.2   The general traveling-salesman problem

If we drop the assumption that the cost function c satisfies the triangle inequality, good approximate tours cannot be found in polynomial time unless P = NP.

Theorem 37.3
If P $\neq$ NP and $\rho \geq 1$, there is no polynomial-time approximation algorithm with ratio bound ρ for the general traveling-salesman problem.

Proof   The proof is by contradiction. Suppose to the contrary that for some number $\rho \geq 1$, there is a polynomial-time approximation algorithm A with ratio bound ρ. Without loss of generality, we assume that ρ is an integer, by rounding it up if necessary. We shall then show how to use A to solve instances of the hamiltonian-cycle problem (defined in Section 36.5.5) in polynomial time. Since the hamiltonian-cycle problem is NP-complete, by Theorem 36.14, solving it in polynomial time implies that P = NP, by Theorem 36.4.

Let $G = (V, E)$ be an instance of the hamiltonian-cycle problem. We wish to determine efficiently whether G contains a hamiltonian cycle by making use of the hypothesized approximation algorithm A. We turn G into an instance of the traveling-salesman problem as follows. Let $G' = (V, E')$ be the complete graph on V; that is,

$E' = \{(u, v) : u, v \in V \text{ and } u \neq v\}$.

Assign an integer cost to each edge in E' as follows:

$$c(u, v) = \begin{cases} 1 & \text{if } (u, v) \in E \text{,} \\ \rho |V| + 1 & \text{otherwise .} \end{cases}$$

Representations of G' and c can be created from a representation of G in time polynomial in $|V|$ and $|E|$.

Now, consider the traveling-salesman problem (G', c). If the original graph G has a hamiltonian cycle H, then the cost function c assigns to each edge of H a cost of 1, and so (G', c) contains a tour of cost $|V|$. On the other hand, if G does not contain a hamiltonian cycle, then any tour of G' must use some edge not in E. But any tour that uses an edge not in E has a cost of at least

$$(\rho |V| + 1) + (|V| - 1) > \rho |V| \text{ .}$$

Because edges not in G are so costly, there is a large gap between the cost of a tour that is a hamiltonian cycle in G (cost $|V|$) and the cost of any other tour (cost greater than $\rho |V|$).

What happens if we apply the approximation algorithm A to the traveling-salesman problem (G', c)? Because A is guaranteed to return a tour of cost no more than ρ times the cost of an optimal tour, if G contains a hamiltonian cycle, then A must return it. If G has no hamiltonian cycle, then A returns a tour of cost more than $\rho |V|$. Therefore, we can use A to solve the hamiltonian-cycle problem in polynomial time. ∎

Exercises

37.2-1
Show how in polynomial time we can transform one instance of the traveling-salesman problem into another instance whose cost function satisfies the triangle inequality. The two instances must have the same set of optimal tours. Explain why such a polynomial-time transformation does not contradict Theorem 37.3, assuming that $P \neq NP$.

37.2-2
Consider the following *closest-point heuristic* for building an approximate traveling-salesman tour. Begin with a trivial cycle consisting of a single arbitrarily chosen vertex. At each step, identify the vertex u that is not on the cycle but whose distance to any vertex on the cycle is minimum. Suppose that the vertex on the cycle that is nearest u is vertex v. Extend the cycle to include u by inserting u just after v. Repeat until all vertices are on the cycle. Prove that this heuristic returns a tour whose total cost is not more than twice the cost of an optimal tour.

37.2-3

The ***bottleneck traveling-salesman problem*** is the problem of finding the hamiltonian cycle such that the length of the longest edge in the cycle is minimized. Assuming that the cost function satisfies the triangle inequality, show that there exists a polynomial-time approximation algorithm with ratio bound 3 for this problem. (*Hint:* Show recursively that we can visit all the nodes in a minimum spanning tree exactly once by taking a full walk of the tree and skipping nodes, but without skipping more than 2 consecutive intermediate nodes.)

37.2-4

Suppose that the vertices for an instance of the traveling-salesman problem are points in the plane and that the cost $c(u, v)$ is the euclidean distance between points u and v. Show that an optimal tour never crosses itself.

37.3   The set-covering problem

The set-covering problem is an optimization problem that models many resource-selection problems. It generalizes the NP-complete vertex-cover problem and is therefore also NP-hard. The approximation algorithm developed to handle the vertex-cover problem doesn't apply here, however, and so we need to try other approaches. We shall examine a simple greedy heuristic with a logarithmic ratio bound. That is, as the size of the instance gets larger, the size of the approximate solution may grow, relative to the size of an optimal solution. Because the logarithm function grows rather slowly, however, this approximation algorithm may nonetheless give useful results.

An instance $(X, \mathcal{F})$ of the ***set-covering problem*** consists of a finite set X and a family $\mathcal{F}$ of subsets of X, such that every element of X belongs to at least one subset in $\mathcal{F}$:

$$X = \bigcup_{S \in \mathcal{F}} S \, .$$

We say that a subset $S \in \mathcal{F}$ ***covers*** its elements. The problem is to find a minimum-size subset $\mathcal{C} \subseteq \mathcal{F}$ whose members cover all of X:

$$X = \bigcup_{S \in \mathcal{C}} S \, . \tag{37.8}$$

We say that any $\mathcal{C}$ satisfying equation (37.8) ***covers*** X. Figure 37.3 illustrates the problem.

The set-covering problem is an abstraction of many commonly arising combinatorial problems. As a simple example, suppose that X represents a set of skills that are needed to solve a problem and that we have a given set of people available to work on the problem. We wish to form a committee, containing as few people as possible, such that for every

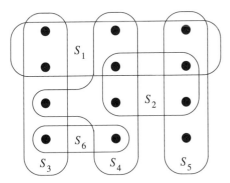

Figure 37.3   An instance $(X, \mathcal{F})$ of the set-covering problem, where X consists of the 12 black points and $\mathcal{F} = \{S_1, S_2, S_3, S_4, S_5, S_6\}$. A minimum-size set cover is $\mathcal{C} = \{S_3, S_4, S_5\}$. The greedy algorithm produces a cover of size 4 by selecting the sets S_1, S_4, S_5, and S_3 in order.

requisite skill in X, there is a member of the committee having that skill. In the decision version of the set-covering problem, we ask whether or not a covering exists with size at most k, where k is an additional parameter specified in the problem instance. The decision version of the problem is NP-complete, as Exercise 37.3-2 asks you to show.

A greedy approximation algorithm

The greedy method works by picking, at each stage, the set S that covers the most remaining uncovered elements.

GREEDY-SET-COVER$(X, \mathcal{F})$

```
1  U ← X
2  C ← ∅
3  while U ≠ ∅
4      do select an S ∈ F that maximizes |S ∩ U|
5          U ← U − S
6          C ← C ∪ {S}
7  return C
```

In the example of Figure 37.3, GREEDY-SET-COVER adds to $\mathcal{C}$ the sets S_1, S_4, S_5, S_3 in order.

The algorithm works as follows. The set U contains, at each stage, the set of remaining uncovered elements. The set $\mathcal{C}$ contains the cover being constructed. Line 4 is the greedy decision-making step. A subset S is chosen that covers as many uncovered elements as possible (with ties broken arbitrarily). After S is selected, its elements are removed from U, and S is placed in $\mathcal{C}$. When the algorithm terminates, the set $\mathcal{C}$ contains a subfamily of $\mathcal{F}$ that covers X.

The algorithm GREEDY-SET-COVER can easily be implemented to run in time polynomial in $|X|$ and $|\mathcal{F}|$. Since the number of iterations of the loop on lines 3–6 is at most $\min(|X|, |\mathcal{F}|)$, and the loop body can be implemented to run in time $O(|X||\mathcal{F}|)$, there is an implementation that runs in time $O(|X||\mathcal{F}|\min(|X|, |\mathcal{F}|))$. Exercise 37.3-3 asks for a linear-time algorithm.

Analysis

We now show that the greedy algorithm returns a set cover that is not too much larger than an optimal set cover. For convenience, in this chapter we denote the dth harmonic number $H_d = \sum_{i=1}^{d} 1/i$ (see Section 3.1) by $H(d)$.

Theorem 37.4
GREEDY-SET-COVER has a ratio bound

$H(\max\{|S| : S \in \mathcal{F}\})$.

Proof The proof proceeds by assigning a cost to each set selected by the algorithm, distributing this cost over the elements covered for the first time, and then using these costs to derive the desired relationship between the size of an optimal set cover $\mathcal{C}^*$ and the size of the set cover $\mathcal{C}$ returned by the algorithm. Let S_i denote the ith subset selected by GREEDY-SET-COVER; the algorithm incurs a cost of 1 when it adds S_i to $\mathcal{C}$. We spread this cost of selecting S_i evenly among the elements covered for the first time by S_i. Let c_x denote the cost allocated to element x, for each $x \in X$. Each element is assigned a cost only once, when it is covered for the first time. If x is covered for the first time by S_i, then

$$c_x = \frac{1}{|S_i - (S_1 \cup S_2 \cup \cdots \cup S_{i-1})|} .$$

The algorithm finds a solution $\mathcal{C}$ of total cost $|\mathcal{C}|$, and this cost has been spread out over the elements of X. Therefore, since the optimal cover $\mathcal{C}^*$ also covers X, we have

$$
\begin{aligned}
|\mathcal{C}| &= \sum_{x \in X} c_x \\
&\leq \sum_{S \in \mathcal{C}^*} \sum_{x \in S} c_x .
\end{aligned}
\tag{37.9}
$$

The remainder of the proof rests on the following key inequality, which we shall prove shortly. For any set S belonging to the family $\mathcal{F}$,

$$\sum_{x \in S} c_x \leq H(|S|) .\tag{37.10}$$

From inequalities (37.9) and (37.10), it follows that

$$
\begin{aligned}
|\mathcal{C}| &\leq \sum_{S \in \mathcal{C}^*} H(|S|) \\
&\leq |\mathcal{C}^*| \cdot H(\max\{|S| : S \in \mathcal{F}\}) ,
\end{aligned}
$$

proving the theorem. It thus remains only to prove inequality (37.10). For any set $S \in \mathcal{F}$ and $i = 1, 2, \ldots, |\mathcal{C}|$, let

$$u_i = |S - (S_1 \cup S_2 \cup \cdots \cup S_i)|$$

be the number of elements in S remaining uncovered after $S_1, S_2, \ldots, S_i$ have been selected by the algorithm. We define $u_0 = |S|$ to be the number of elements of S, which are all initially uncovered. Let k be the least index such that $u_k = 0$, so that every element in S is covered by at least one of the sets $S_1, S_2, \ldots, S_k$. Then, $u_{i-1} \geq u_i$, and $u_{i-1} - u_i$ elements of S are covered for the first time by S_i, for $i = 1, 2, \ldots, k$. Thus,

$$\sum_{x \in S} c_x = \sum_{i=1}^{k} (u_{i-1} - u_i) \cdot \frac{1}{|S_i - (S_1 \cup S_2 \cup \cdots \cup S_{i-1})|} \ .$$

Observe that

$$|S_i - (S_1 \cup S_2 \cup \cdots \cup S_{i-1})| \geq |S - (S_1 \cup S_2 \cup \cdots \cup S_{i-1})|$$
$$= u_{i-1} \ ,$$

because the greedy choice of S_i guarantees that S cannot cover more new elements than S_i does (otherwise, S would have been chosen instead of S_i). Consequently, we obtain

$$\sum_{x \in S} c_x \leq \sum_{i=1}^{k} (u_{i-1} - u_i) \cdot \frac{1}{u_{i-1}} \ .$$

For integers a and b, where $a < b$, we have

$$H(b) - H(a) = \sum_{i=a+1}^{b} 1/i$$
$$\geq (b - a)\frac{1}{b} \ .$$

Using this inequality, we obtain the telescoping sum

$$\sum_{x \in S} c_x \leq \sum_{i=1}^{k} (H(u_{i-1}) - H(u_i))$$
$$= H(u_0) - H(u_k)$$
$$= H(u_0) - H(0)$$
$$= H(u_0)$$
$$= H(|S|) \ ,$$

since $H(0) = 0$. This completes the proof of inequality (37.10). ∎

Corollary 37.5
GREEDY-SET-COVER has a ratio bound of $(\ln |X| + 1)$.

Proof Use inequality (3.12) and Theorem 37.4.   ∎

In some applications, max $\{|S| : S \in \mathcal{F}\}$ is a small constant, and so the solution returned by GREEDY-SET-COVER is at most a small constant times larger than optimal. One such application occurs when this heuristic is used to obtain an approximate vertex cover for a graph whose vertices have degree at most 3. In this case, the solution found by GREEDY-SET-COVER is not more than $H(3) = 11/6$ times as large as an optimal solution, a performance guarantee that is slightly better than that of APPROX-VERTEX-COVER.

Exercises

37.3-1
Consider each of the following words as a set of letters: {arid, dash, drain, heard, lost, nose, shun, slate, snare, thread}. Show which set cover GREEDY-SET-COVER produces when ties are broken in favor of the word that appears first in the dictionary.

37.3-2
Show that the decision version of the set-covering problem is NP-complete by reduction from the vertex-cover problem.

37.3-3
Show how to implement GREEDY-SET-COVER in such a way that it runs in time $O(\sum_{S \in \mathcal{F}} |S|)$.

37.3-4
Show that the following weaker form of Theorem 37.4 is trivially true:

$$|\mathcal{C}| \leq |\mathcal{C}^*| \max \{|S| : S \in \mathcal{F}\} \ .$$

37.3-5
Create a family of set-cover instances demonstrating that GREEDY-SET-COVER can return a number of different solutions that is exponential in the size of the instance. (Different solutions result from ties being broken differently in the choice of S in line 4.)

37.4 The subset-sum problem

An instance of the subset-sum problem is a pair (S, t), where S is a set $\{x_1, x_2, \ldots, x_n\}$ of positive integers and t is a positive integer. This decision problem asks whether there exists a subset of S that adds up exactly to the target value t. This problem is NP-complete (see Section 36.5.3).

The optimization problem associated with this decision problem arises in practical applications. In the optimization problem, we wish to find a subset of $\{x_1, x_2, \ldots, x_n\}$ whose sum is as large as possible but not larger than t. For example, we may have a truck that can carry no more than t pounds, and n different boxes to ship, the ith of which weighs x_i pounds. We wish to fill the truck as full as possible without exceeding the given weight limit.

In this section, we present an exponential-time algorithm for this optimization problem and then show how to modify the algorithm so that it becomes a fully polynomial-time approximation scheme. (Recall that a fully polynomial-time approximation scheme has a running time that is polynomial in $1/\epsilon$ as well as in n.)

An exponential-time algorithm

If L is a list of positive integers and x is another positive integer, then we let $L + x$ denote the list of integers derived from L by increasing each element of L by x. For example, if $L = \langle 1, 2, 3, 5, 9 \rangle$, then $L + 2 = \langle 3, 4, 5, 7, 11 \rangle$. We also use this notation for sets, so that

$$S + x = \{s + x : s \in S\} \ .$$

We use an auxiliary procedure MERGE-LISTS(L, L') that returns the sorted list that is the merge of its two sorted input lists L and L'. Like the MERGE procedure we used in merge sort (Section 1.3.1), MERGE-LISTS runs in time $O(|L| + |L'|)$. (We omit giving pseudocode for MERGE-LISTS.) The procedure EXACT-SUBSET-SUM takes an input set $S = \{x_1, x_2, \ldots, x_n\}$ and a target value t.

EXACT-SUBSET-SUM(S, t)

```
1  n ← |S|
2  L₀ ← ⟨0⟩
3  for i ← 1 to n
4       do Lᵢ ← MERGE-LISTS(Lᵢ₋₁, Lᵢ₋₁ + xᵢ)
5            remove from Lᵢ every element that is greater than t
6  return the largest element in Lₙ
```

Let P_i denote the set of all values that can be obtained by selecting a (possibly empty) subset of $\{x_1, x_2, \ldots, x_i\}$ and summing its members. For example, if $S = \{1, 4, 5\}$, then

$$P_1 \ = \ \{0, 1\} \ ,$$
$$P_2 \ = \ \{0, 1, 4, 5\} \ ,$$
$$P_3 \ = \ \{0, 1, 4, 5, 6, 9, 10\} \ .$$

Given the identity

$$P_i = P_{i-1} \cup (P_{i-1} + x_i) \ , \tag{37.11}$$

we can prove by induction on i (see Exercise 37.4-1) that the list L_i is a sorted list containing every element of P_i whose value is not more than t. Since the length of L_i can be as much as 2^i, EXACT-SUBSET-SUM is an exponential-time algorithm in general, although it is a polynomial-time algorithm in the special cases in which t is polynomial in $|S|$ or all of the numbers in S are bounded by a polynomial in $|S|$.

A fully polynomial-time approximation scheme

We can derive a fully polynomial-time approximation scheme for the subset-sum problem by "trimming" each list L_i after it is created. We use a trimming parameter δ such that $0 < \delta < 1$. To **trim** a list L by δ means to remove as many elements from L as possible, in such a way that if L' is the result of trimming L, then for every element y that was removed from L, there is an element $z \le y$ still in L' such that

$$\frac{y - z}{y} \le \delta$$

or, equivalently,

$$(1 - \delta)y \le z \le y .$$

We can think of such a z as "representing" y in the new list L'. Each y is represented by a z such that the relative error of z, with respect to y, is at most δ. For example, if $\delta = 0.1$ and

$$L = \langle 10, 11, 12, 15, 20, 21, 22, 23, 24, 29 \rangle ,$$

then we can trim L to obtain

$$L' = \langle 10, 12, 15, 20, 23, 29 \rangle ,$$

where the deleted value 11 is represented by 10, the deleted values 21 and 22 are represented by 20, and the deleted value 24 is represented by 23. It is important to remember that every element of the trimmed version of the list is also an element of the original version of the list. Trimming a list can dramatically decrease the number of elements in the list while keeping a close (and slightly smaller) representative value in the list for each element deleted from the list.

The following procedure trims an input list $L = \langle y_1, y_2, \ldots, y_m \rangle$ in time $\Theta(m)$, assuming that L is sorted into nondecreasing order. The output of the procedure is a trimmed, sorted list.

TRIM(L, δ)
```
1  m ← |L|
2  L' ← ⟨y₁⟩
3  last ← y₁
4  for i ← 2 to m
5      do if last < (1 − δ)yᵢ
6          then append yᵢ onto the end of L'
7              last ← yᵢ
8  return L'
```

The elements of L are scanned in increasing order, and a number is put into the returned list L' only if it is the first element of L or if it cannot be represented by the most recent number placed into L'.

Given the procedure TRIM, we can construct our approximation scheme as follows. This procedure takes as input a set $S = \{x_1, x_2, \ldots, x_n\}$ of n integers (in arbitrary order), a target integer t, and an "approximation parameter" ϵ, where $0 < \epsilon < 1$.

APPROX-SUBSET-SUM(S, t, ϵ)
```
1  n ← |S|
2  L₀ ← ⟨0⟩
3  for i ← 1 to n
4      do Lᵢ ← MERGE-LISTS(Lᵢ₋₁, Lᵢ₋₁ + xᵢ)
5          Lᵢ ← TRIM(Lᵢ, ε/n)
6          remove from Lᵢ every element that is greater than t
7  let z be the largest value in Lₙ
8  return z
```

Line 2 initializes the list L_0 to be the list containing just the element 0. The loop in lines 3–6 has the effect of computing L_i as a sorted list containing a suitably trimmed version of the set P_i, with all elements larger than t removed. Since L_i is created from L_{i-1}, we must ensure that the repeated trimming doesn't introduce too much inaccuracy. In a moment, we shall see that APPROX-SUBSET-SUM returns a correct approximation if one exists.

As an example, suppose we have the instance

$$L = \langle 104, 102, 201, 101 \rangle$$

with $t = 308$ and $\epsilon = 0.20$. The trimming parameter δ is $\epsilon/4 = 0.05$. APPROX-SUBSET-SUM computes the following values on the indicated lines:

line 2 : $L_0 = \langle 0 \rangle$,

line 4 : $L_1 = \langle 0, 104 \rangle$,
line 5 : $L_1 = \langle 0, 104 \rangle$,
line 6 : $L_1 = \langle 0, 104 \rangle$,

line 4 : $L_2 = \langle 0, 102, 104, 206 \rangle$,
line 5 : $L_2 = \langle 0, 102, 206 \rangle$,
line 6 : $L_2 = \langle 0, 102, 206 \rangle$,

line 4 : $L_3 = \langle 0, 102, 201, 206, 303, 407 \rangle$,
line 5 : $L_3 = \langle 0, 102, 201, 303, 407 \rangle$,
line 6 : $L_3 = \langle 0, 102, 201, 303 \rangle$,

line 4 : $L_4 = \langle 0, 101, 102, 201, 203, 302, 303, 404 \rangle$,
line 5 : $L_4 = \langle 0, 101, 201, 302, 404 \rangle$,
line 6 : $L_4 = \langle 0, 101, 201, 302 \rangle$.

The algorithm returns $z = 302$ as its answer, which is well within $\epsilon = 20\%$ of the optimal answer $307 = 104 + 102 + 101$; in fact, it is within 2%.

Theorem 37.6
APPROX-SUBSET-SUM is a fully polynomial-time approximation scheme for the subset-sum problem.

Proof The operations of trimming L_i in line 5 and removing from L_i every element that is greater than t maintain the property that every element of L_i is also a member of P_i. Therefore, the value z returned in line 8 is indeed the sum of some subset of S. It remains to show that it is not smaller than $1 - \epsilon$ times an optimal solution. (Note that because the subset-sum problem is a maximization problem, equation (37.2) is equivalent to $C^*(1 - \epsilon) \leq C$.) We must also show that the algorithm runs in polynomial time.

To show that the relative error of the returned answer is small, note that when list L_i is trimmed, we introduce a relative error of at most ϵ/n between the representative values remaining and the values before trimming. By induction on i, it can be shown that for every element y in P_i that is at most t, there is a $z \in L_i$ such that

$$(1 - \epsilon/n)^i y \leq z \leq y . \tag{37.12}$$

If $y^* \in P_n$ denotes an optimal solution to the subset-sum problem, then there is a $z \in L_n$ such that

$$(1 - \epsilon/n)^n y^* \leq z \leq y^* ; \tag{37.13}$$

the largest such z is the value returned by APPROX-SUBSET-SUM. Since it can be shown that

$$\frac{d}{dn}\left(1 - \frac{\epsilon}{n}\right)^n > 0 \,,$$

the function $(1 - \epsilon/n)^n$ increases with n, so that $n > 1$ implies

$$1 - \epsilon < (1 - \epsilon/n)^n \,,$$

and thus,

$$(1 - \epsilon)y^* \le z \,.$$

Therefore, the value z returned by APPROX-SUBSET-SUM is not smaller than $1 - \epsilon$ times the optimal solution y^*.

To show that this is a fully polynomial-time approximation scheme, we derive a bound on the length of L_i. After trimming, successive elements z and z' of L_i must have the relationship $z/z' > 1/(1 - \epsilon/n)$. That is, they must differ by a factor of at least $1/(1 - \epsilon/n)$. Therefore, the number of elements in each L_i is at most

$$\log_{1/(1-\epsilon/n)} t \quad = \quad \frac{\ln t}{-\ln(1 - \epsilon/n)}$$
$$\le \quad \frac{n \ln t}{\epsilon} \,,$$

using equation (2.10). This bound is polynomial in the number n of input values given, in the number of bits $\lg t$ needed to represent t, and in $1/\epsilon$. Since the running time of APPROX-SUBSET-SUM is polynomial in the length of the L_i, APPROX-SUBSET-SUM is a fully polynomial-time approximation scheme. ∎

Exercises

37.4-1
Prove equation (37.11).

37.4-2
Prove equations (37.12) and (37.13).

37.4-3
How would you modify the approximation scheme presented in this section to find a good approximation to the smallest value not less than t that is a sum of some subset of the given input list?

Problems

37-1 *Bin packing*
Suppose that we are given a set of n objects, where the the size s_i of the ith object satisfies $0 < s_i < 1$. We wish to pack all the objects into the

minimum number of unit-size bins. Each bin can hold any subset of the objects whose total size does not exceed 1.

a. Prove that the problem of determining the minimum number of bins required is NP-hard. (*Hint:* Reduce from the subset-sum problem.)

The ***first-fit*** heuristic takes each object in turn and places it into the first bin that can accommodate it. Let $S = \sum_{i=1}^{n} s_i$.

b. Argue that the optimal number of bins required is at least $\lceil S \rceil$.

c. Argue that the first-fit heuristic leaves at most one bin less than half full.

d. Prove that the number of bins used by the first-fit heuristic is never more than $\lceil 2S \rceil$.

e. Prove a ratio bound of 2 for the first-fit heuristic.

f. Give an efficient implementation of the first-fit heuristic, and analyze its running time.

37-2   *Approximating the size of a maximum clique*

Let $G = (V, E)$ be an undirected graph. For any $k \geq 1$, define $G^{(k)}$ to be the undirected graph $(V^{(k)}, E^{(k)})$, where $V^{(k)}$ is the set of all ordered k-tuples of vertices from V and $E^{(k)}$ is defined so that $(v_1, v_2, \ldots, v_k)$ is adjacent to $(w_1, w_2, \ldots, w_k)$ if and only if for some i, vertex v_i is adjacent to w_i in G.

a. Prove that the size of the maximum clique in $G^{(k)}$ is equal to the kth power of the size of the maximum clique in G.

b. Argue that if there is an approximation algorithm that has a constant ratio bound for finding a maximum-size clique, then there is a fully polynomial-time approximation scheme for the problem.

37-3   *Weighted set-covering problem*

Suppose that we generalize the set-covering problem so that each set S_i in the family $\mathcal{F}$ has an associated weight w_i and the weight of a cover $\mathcal{C}$ is $\sum_{S_i \in \mathcal{C}} w_i$. We wish to determine a minimum-weight cover. (Section 37.3 handles the case in which $w_i = 1$ for all i.)

Show that the greedy set-covering heuristic can be generalized in a natural manner to provide an approximate solution for any instance of the weighted set-covering problem. Show that your heuristic has a ratio bound of $H(d)$, where d is the maximum size of any set S_i.

Chapter notes

There is a wealth of literature on approximation algorithms. A good place to start is Garey and Johnson [79]. Papadimitriou and Steiglitz [154] also have an excellent presentation of approximation algorithms. Lawler, Lenstra, Rinnooy Kan, and Shmoys [133] provide an extensive treatment of the traveling-salesman problem.

Papadimitriou and Steiglitz attribute the algorithm APPROX-VERTEX-COVER to F. Gavril and M. Yannakakis. The algorithm APPROX-TSP-TOUR appears in an excellent paper by Rosenkrantz, Stearns, and Lewis [170]. Theorem 37.3 is due to Sahni and Gonzalez [172]. The analysis of the greedy heuristic for the set-covering problem is modeled after the proof published by Chvátal [42] of a more general result; this basic result as presented here is due to Johnson [113] and Lovász [141]. The algorithm APPROX-SUBSET-SUM and its analysis are loosely modeled after related approximation algorithms for the knapsack and subset-sum problem by Ibarra and Kim [111].

Bibliography

[1] Milton Abramowitz and Irene A. Stegun, editors. *Handbook of Mathematical Functions*. Dover, 1965.

[2] G. M. Adel'son-Vel'skiĭ and E. M. Landis. An algorithm for the organization of information. *Soviet Mathematics Doklady*, 3:1259–1263, 1962.

[3] Leonard M. Adleman, Carl Pomerance, and Robert S. Rumely. On distinguishing prime numbers from composite numbers. *Annals of Mathematics*, 117:173–206, 1983.

[4] Alfred V. Aho, John E. Hopcroft, and Jeffrey D. Ullman. *The Design and Analysis of Computer Algorithms*. Addison-Wesley, 1974.

[5] Alfred V. Aho, John E. Hopcroft, and Jeffrey D. Ullman. *Data Structures and Algorithms*. Addison-Wesley, 1983.

[6] Ravindra K. Ahuja, Kurt Mehlhorn, James B. Orlin, and Robert E. Tarjan. Faster algorithms for the shortest path problem. Technical Report 193, MIT Operations Research Center, 1988.

[7] Howard H. Aiken and Grace M. Hopper. The automatic sequence controlled calculator. In Brian Randell, editor, *The Origins of Digital Computers*, pages 203–222. Springer-Verlag, third edition, 1982.

[8] M. Ajtai, J. Komlós, and E. Szemerédi. An $O(n \log n)$ sorting network. In *Proceedings of the Fifteenth Annual ACM Symposium on Theory of Computing*, pages 1–9, 1983.

[9] Selim G. Akl. *The Design and Analysis of Parallel Algorithms*. Prentice-Hall, 1989.

[10] Richard J. Anderson and Gary L. Miller. Deterministic parallel list ranking. In John H. Reif, editor, *1988 Aegean Workshop on Computing*, volume 319 of *Lecture Notes in Computer Science*, pages 81–90. Springer-Verlag, 1988.

[11] Richard J. Anderson and Gary L. Miller. A simple randomized parallel algorithm for list-ranking. Unpublished manuscript, 1988.

[12] Tom M. Apostol. *Calculus*, volume 1. Blaisdell Publishing Company, second edition, 1967.

[13] A. J. Atrubin. A one-dimensional real-time iterative multiplier. *IEEE Transactions on Electronic Computers*, EC-14(1):394–399, 1965.

[14] Sara Baase. *Computer Algorithms: Introduction to Design and Analysis*. Addison-Wesley, second edition, 1988.

[15] Eric Bach. Private communication, 1989.

[16] Eric Bach. Number-theoretic algorithms. In *Annual Review of Computer Science*, volume 4, pages 119–172. Annual Reviews, Inc., 1990.

[17] R. Bayer. Symmetric binary B-trees: Data structure and maintenance algorithms. *Acta Informatica*, 1:290–306, 1972.

[18] R. Bayer and E. M. McCreight. Organization and maintenance of large ordered indexes. *Acta Informatica*, 1(3):173–189, 1972.

[19] Paul W. Beame, Stephen A. Cook, and H. James Hoover. Log depth circuits for division and related problems. *SIAM Journal on Computing*, 15(4):994–1003, 1986.

[20] Pierre Beauchemin, Gilles Brassard, Claude Crépeau, Claude Goutier, and Carl Pomerance. The generation of random numbers that are probably prime. *Journal of Cryptology*, 1:53–64, 1988.

[21] Richard Bellman. *Dynamic Programming*. Princeton University Press, 1957.

[22] Richard Bellman. On a routing problem. *Quarterly of Applied Mathematics*, 16(1):87–90, 1958.

[23] Michael Ben-Or. Lower bounds for algebraic computation trees. In *Proceedings of the Fifteenth Annual ACM Symposium on Theory of Computing*, pages 80–86, 1983.

[24] Jon L. Bentley. *Writing Efficient Programs*. Prentice-Hall, 1982.

[25] Jon L. Bentley. *Programming Pearls*. Addison-Wesley, 1986.

[26] Jon L. Bentley, Dorothea Haken, and James B. Saxe. A general method for solving divide-and-conquer recurrences. *SIGACT News*, 12(3):36–44, 1980.

[27] William H. Beyer, editor. *CRC Standard Mathematical Tables*. The Chemical Rubber Company, 1984.

[28] Patrick Billingsley. *Probability and Measure*. John Wiley & Sons, second edition, 1986.

[29] Manuel Blum, Robert W. Floyd, Vaughan Pratt, Ronald L. Rivest, and Robert E. Tarjan. Time bounds for selection. *Journal of Computer and System Sciences*, 7(4):448–461, 1973.

[30] Béla Bollobás. *Random Graphs*. Academic Press, 1985.

[31] J. A. Bondy and U. S. R. Murty. *Graph Theory with Applications*. American Elsevier, 1976.

[32] Robert S. Boyer and J. Strother Moore. A fast string-searching algorithm. *Communications of the ACM*, 20(10):762–772, 1977.

[33] Gilles Brassard and Paul Bratley. *Algorithmics: Theory and Practice*. Prentice-Hall, 1988.

[34] Richard P. Brent. The parallel evaluation of general arithmetic expressions. *Journal of the ACM*, 21(2):201–206, 1974.

[35] Richard P. Brent. An improved Monte Carlo factorization algorithm. *BIT*, 20(2):176–184, 1980.

[36] Mark R. Brown. *The Analysis of a Practical and Nearly Optimal Priority Queue*. PhD thesis, Computer Science Department, Stanford University, 1977. Technical Report STAN-CS-77-600.

[37] Mark R. Brown. Implementation and analysis of binomial queue algorithms. *SIAM Journal on Computing*, 7(3):298–319, 1978.

[38] Arthur W. Burks, editor. *Theory of Self-Reproducing Automata*. University of Illinois Press, 1966.

[39] Joseph J. F. Cavanagh. *Digital Computer Arithmetic*. McGraw-Hill, 1984.

[40] H. Chernoff. A measure of asymptotic efficiency for tests of a hypothesis based on the sum of observations. *Annals of Mathematical Statistics*, 23:493–507, 1952.

[41] Kai Lai Chung. *Elementary Probability Theory with Stochastic Processes*. Springer-Verlag, 1974.

[42] V. Chvátal. A greedy heuristic for the set-covering problem. *Mathematics of Operations Research*, 4(3):233–235, 1979.

[43] V. Chvátal, D. A. Klarner, and D. E. Knuth. Selected combinatorial research problems. Technical Report STAN-CS-72-292, Computer Science Department, Stanford University, 1972.

[44] Alan Cobham. The intrinsic computational difficulty of functions. In *Proceedings of the 1964 Congress for Logic, Methodology, and the Philosophy of Science*, pages 24–30. North-Holland, 1964.

[45] H. Cohen and H. W. Lenstra, Jr. Primality testing and jacobi sums. *Mathematics of Computation*, 42(165):297–330, 1984.

[46] Richard Cole. Parallel merge sort. In *Proceedings of the 27th Annual Symposium on Foundations of Computer Science*, pages 511–516. IEEE Computer Society, 1986.

[47] Richard Cole and Uzi Vishkin. Deterministic coin tossing with applications to optimal parallel list ranking. *Information and Control*, 70(1):32–53, 1986.

[48] D. Comer. The ubiquitous B-tree. *ACM Computing Surveys*, 11(2):121–137, 1979.

[49] Stephen Cook. The complexity of theorem proving procedures. In *Proceedings of the Third Annual ACM Symposium on Theory of Computing*, pages 151–158, 1971.

[50] Stephen Cook, Cynthia Dwork, and Rüdiger Reischuk. Upper and lower time bounds for parallel random access machines without simultaneous writes. *SIAM Journal on Computing*, 15(1):87–97, 1986.

[51] James W. Cooley and John W. Tukey. An algorithm for the machine calculation of complex Fourier series. *Mathematics of Computation*, 19(90): 297–301, April 1965.

[52] Don Coppersmith and Shmuel Winograd. Matrix multiplication via arithmetic progressions. In *Proceedings of the Nineteenth Annual ACM Symposium on Theory of Computing*, pages 1–6, 1987.

[53] George B. Dantzig. *Linear Programming and Extensions*. Princeton University Press, 1963.

[54] Whitfield Diffie and Martin E. Hellman. New directions in cryptography. *IEEE Transactions on Information Theory*, IT-22(6):644–654, 1976.

[55] E. W. Dijkstra. A note on two problems in connexion with graphs. *Numerische Mathematik*, 1:269–271, 1959.

[56] John D. Dixon. Factorization and primality tests. *The American Mathematical Monthly*, 91(6):333–352, 1984.

[57] Alvin W. Drake. *Fundamentals of Applied Probability Theory*. McGraw-Hill, 1967.

[58] James R. Driscoll, Harold N. Gabow, Ruth Shrairman, and Robert E. Tarjan. Relaxed heaps: An alternative to Fibonacci heaps with applications to parallel computation. *Communications of the ACM*, 31(11):1343–1354, 1988.

[59] James R. Driscoll, Neil Sarnak, Daniel D. Sleator, and Robert E. Tarjan. Making data structures persistent. In *Proceedings of the Eighteenth Annual ACM Symposium on Theory of Computing*, pages 109–121, 1986.

[60] Herbert Edelsbrunner. *Algorithms in Combinatorial Geometry*, volume 10 of *EATCS Monographs on Theoretical Computer Science*. Springer-Verlag, 1987.

[61] Jack Edmonds. Paths, trees, and flowers. *Canadian Journal of Mathematics*, 17:449–467, 1965.

[62] Jack Edmonds. Matroids and the greedy algorithm. *Mathematical Programming*, 1:126–136, 1971.

[63] Jack Edmonds and Richard M. Karp. Theoretical improvements in the algorithmic efficiency for network flow problems. *Journal of the ACM*, 19:248–264, 1972.

[64] G. Estrin, B. Gilchrist, and J. H. Pomerene. A note on high-speed digital multiplication. *IRE Transactions on Electronic Computers*, 5(3):140, 1956.

[65] Shimon Even. *Graph Algorithms*. Computer Science Press, 1979.

[66] William Feller. *An Introduction to Probability Theory and Its Applications*. John Wiley & Sons, third edition, 1968.

[67] M. J. Fischer and A. R. Meyer. Boolean matrix multiplication and transitive closure. In *Proceedings of the Twelfth Annual Symposium on Switching and Automata Theory*, pages 129–131. IEEE Computer Society, 1971.

[68] Robert W. Floyd. Algorithm 97 (SHORTEST PATH). *Communications of the ACM*, 5(6):345, 1962.

[69] Robert W. Floyd. Algorithm 245 (TREESORT). *Communications of the ACM*, 7:701, 1964.

[70] Robert W. Floyd and Ronald L. Rivest. Expected time bounds for selection. *Communications of the ACM*, 18(3):165–172, 1975.

[71] Lestor R. Ford, Jr., and D. R. Fulkerson. *Flows in Networks*. Princeton University Press, 1962.

[72] Lestor R. Ford, Jr., and Selmer M. Johnson. A tournament problem. *The American Mathematical Monthly*, 66:387–389, 1959.

[73] Steven Fortune and James Wyllie. Parallelism in random access machines. In *Proceedings of the Tenth Annual ACM Symposium on Theory of Computing*, pages 114–118, 1978.

[74] Michael L. Fredman and Michael E. Saks. The cell probe complexity of dynamic data structures. In *Proceedings of the Twenty First Annual ACM Symposium on Theory of Computing*, 1989.

[75] Michael L. Fredman and Robert E. Tarjan. Fibonacci heaps and their uses in improved network optimization algorithms. *Journal of the ACM*, 34(3):596–615, 1987.

[76] Harold N. Gabow and Robert E. Tarjan. A linear-time algorithm for a special case of disjoint set union. *Journal of Computer and System Sciences*, 30(2):209–221, 1985.

[77] Harold N. Gabow and Robert E. Tarjan. Faster scaling algorithms for network problems. *SIAM Journal on Computing*, 18(5):1013–1036, 1989.

[78] Zvi Galil and Joel Seiferas. Time-space-optimal string matching. *Journal of Computer and System Sciences*, 26(3):280–294, 1983.

[79] Michael R. Garey and David S. Johnson. *Computers and Intractability: A Guide to the Theory of NP-Completeness*. W. H. Freeman, 1979.

[80] Fănică Gavril. Algorithms for minimum coloring, maximum clique, minimum covering by cliques, and maximum independent set of a chordal graph. *SIAM Journal on Computing*, 1(2):180–187, 1972.

[81] Alan George and Joseph W-H Liu. *Computer Solution of Large Sparse Positive Definite Systems*. Prentice-Hall, 1981.

[82] Andrew V. Goldberg. *Efficient Graph Algorithms for Sequential and Parallel Computers*. PhD thesis, Department of Electrical Engineering and Computer Science, MIT, 1987.

[83] Andrew V. Goldberg, Éva Tardos, and Robert E. Tarjan. Network flow algorithms. Technical Report STAN-CS-89-1252, Computer Science Department, Stanford University, 1989.

[84] Andrew V. Goldberg and Serge A. Plotkin. Parallel $(\delta + 1)$ coloring of constant-degree graphs. *Information Processing Letters*, 25(4):241–245, 1987.

[85] Andrew V. Goldberg and Robert E. Tarjan. A new approach to the maximum flow problem. In *Proceedings of the Eighteenth Annual ACM Symposium on Theory of Computing*, pages 136–146, 1986.

[86] Shafi Goldwasser and Silvio Micali. Probabilistic encryption. *Journal of Computer and System Sciences*, 28(2):270–299, 1984.

[87] Shafi Goldwasser, Silvio Micali, and Charles Rackoff. The knowledge complexity of interactive proof systems. *SIAM Journal on Computing*, 18(1):186–208, 1989.

[88] Shafi Goldwasser, Silvio Micali, and Ronald L. Rivest. A digital signature scheme secure against adaptive chosen-message attacks. *SIAM Journal on Computing*, 17(2):281–308, 1988.

[89] Gene H. Golub and Charles F. Van Loan. *Matrix Computations*. The Johns Hopkins University Press, 1983.

[90] G. H. Gonnet. *Handbook of Algorithms and Data Structures*. Addison-Wesley, 1984.

[91] R. L. Graham. An efficient algorithm for determining the convex hull of a finite planar set. *Information Processing Letters*, 1:132–133, 1972.

[92] R. L. Graham and Pavol Hell. On the history of the minimum spanning tree problem. *Annals of the History of Computing*, 7(1):43–57, 1985.

[93] Leo J. Guibas and Robert Sedgewick. A diochromatic framework for balanced trees. In *Proceedings of the 19th Annual Symposium on Foundations of Computer Science*, pages 8–21. IEEE Computer Society, 1978.

[94] Frank Harary. *Graph Theory*. Addison-Wesley, 1969.

[95] J. Hartmanis and R. E. Stearns. On the computational complexity of algorithms. *Transactions of the American Mathematical Society*, 117:285–306, 1965.

[96] Frederick J. Hill and Gerald R. Peterson. *Introduction to Switching Theory and Logical Design*. John Wiley & Sons, second edition, 1974.

[97] C. A. R. Hoare. Algorithm 63 (partition) and algorithm 65 (find). *Communications of the ACM*, 4(7):321–322, 1961.

[98] C. A. R. Hoare. Quicksort. *Computer Journal*, 5(1):10–15, 1962.

[99] W. Hoeffding. On the distribution of the number of successes in independent trials. *Annals of Mathematical Statistics*, 27:713–721, 1956.

[100] Micha Hofri. *Probabilistic Analysis of Algorithms*. Springer-Verlag, 1987.

[101] John E. Hopcroft and Richard M. Karp. An $n^{5/2}$ algorithm for maximum matchings in bipartite graphs. *SIAM Journal on Computing*, 2(4):225–231, 1973.

[102] John E. Hopcroft and Robert E. Tarjan. Efficient algorithms for graph manipulation. *Communications of the ACM*, 16(6):372–378, 1973.

[103] John E. Hopcroft and Jeffrey D. Ullman. Set merging algorithms. *SIAM Journal on Computing*, 2(4):294–303, 1973.

[104] John E. Hopcroft and Jeffrey D. Ullman. *Introduction to Automata Theory, Languages, and Computation*. Addison-Wesley, 1979.

[105] Ellis Horowitz and Sartaj Sahni. *Fundamentals of Computer Algorithms*. Computer Science Press, 1978.

[106] T. C. Hu and M. T. Shing. Some theorems about matrix multiplication. In *Proceedings of the 21st Annual Symposium on Foundations of Computer Science*, pages 28–35. IEEE Computer Society, 1980.

[107] David A. Huffman. A method for the construction of minimum-redundancy codes. *Proceedings of the IRE*, 40(9):1098–1101, 1952.

[108] Kai Hwang. *Computer Arithmetic: Principles, Architecture, and Design*. John Wiley & Sons, 1979.

[109] Kai Hwang and Fayé A. Briggs. *Computer Architecture and Parallel Processing*. McGraw-Hill, 1984.

[110] Kai Hwang and Doug DeGroot. *Parallel Processing for Supercomputers and Artificial Intelligence*. McGraw-Hill, 1989.

[111] Oscar H. Ibarra and Chul E. Kim. Fast approximation algorithms for the knapsack and sum of subset problems. *Journal of the ACM*, 22(4):463–468, 1975.

[112] R. A. Jarvis. On the identification of the convex hull of a finite set of points in the plane. *Information Processing Letters*, 2:18–21, 1973.

[113] D. S. Johnson. Approximation algorithms for combinatorial problems. *Journal of Computer and System Sciences*, 9:256–278, 1974.

[114] Donald B. Johnson. Efficient algorithms for shortest paths in sparse networks. *Journal of the ACM*, 24(1):1–13, 1977.

[115] N. Karmarkar. A new polynomial-time algorithm for linear programming. *Combinatorica*, 4(4):373–395, 1984.

[116] Richard M. Karp. Reducibility among combinatorial problems. In Raymond E. Miller and James W. Thatcher, editors, *Complexity of Computer Computations*, pages 85–103. Plenum Press, 1972.

[117] Richard M. Karp and Michael O. Rabin. Efficient randomized pattern-matching algorithms. Technical Report TR-31-81, Aiken Computation Laboratory, Harvard University, 1981.

[118] Richard M. Karp and Vijaya Ramachandran. A survey of parallel algorithms for shared-memory machines. Technical Report UCB/CSD 88/408, Computer Science Division (EECS), University of California, Berkeley, 1988.

[119] A. V. Karzanov. Determining the maximal flow in a network by the method of preflows. *Soviet Mathematics Doklady*, 15:434–437, 1974.

[120] D. G. Kirkpatrick and R. Seidel. The ultimate planar convex hull algorithm? *SIAM Journal on Computing*, 15(2):287–299, 1986.

[121] Donald E. Knuth. *Fundamental Algorithms*, volume 1 of *The Art of Computer Programming*. Addison-Wesley, 1968. Second edition, 1973.

[122] Donald E. Knuth. *Seminumerical Algorithms*, volume 2 of *The Art of Computer Programming*. Addison-Wesley, 1969. Second edition, 1981.

[123] Donald E. Knuth. *Sorting and Searching*, volume 3 of *The Art of Computer Programming*. Addison-Wesley, 1973.

[124] Donald E. Knuth. Big omicron and big omega and big theta. *ACM SIGACT News*, 8(2):18–23, 1976.

[125] Donald E. Knuth, James H. Morris, Jr., and Vaughan R. Pratt. Fast pattern matching in strings. *SIAM Journal on Computing*, 6(2):323–350, 1977.

[126] Zvi Kohavi. *Switching and Finite Automata Theory*. McGraw-Hill, 1970.

[127] Bernhard Korte and László Lovász. Mathematical structures underlying greedy algorithms. In F. Gecseg, editor, *Fundamentals of Computation Theory*, number 117 in Lecture Notes in Computer Science, pages 205–209. Springer-Verlag, 1981.

[128] Bernhard Korte and László Lovász. Structural properties of greedoids. *Combinatorica*, 3:359–374, 1983.

[129] Bernhard Korte and László Lovász. Greedoids—a structural framework for the greedy algorithm. In W. Pulleybank, editor, *Progress in Combinatorial Optimization*, pages 221–243. Academic Press, 1984.

[130] Bernhard Korte and László Lovász. Greedoids and linear objective functions. *SIAM Journal on Algebraic and Discrete Methods*, 5(2):229–238, 1984.

[131] J. B. Kruskal. On the shortest spanning subtree of a graph and the traveling salesman problem. *Proceedings of the American Mathematical Society*, 7:48–50, 1956.

[132] Eugene L. Lawler. *Combinatorial Optimization: Networks and Matroids*. Holt, Rinehart, and Winston, 1976.

[133] Eugene L. Lawler, J. K. Lenstra, A. H. G. Rinnooy Kan, and D. B. Shmoys, editors. *The Traveling Salesman Problem*. John Wiley & Sons, 1985.

[134] C. Y. Lee. An algorithm for path connection and its applications. *IRE Transactions on Electronic Computers*, EC-10(3):346–365, 1961.

[135] F. Thomson Leighton. *Introduction to Parallel Algorithms and Architectures: Networks and Algorithms*. Morgan-Kaufmann, in preparation.

[136] Debra A. Lelewer and Daniel S. Hirschberg. Data compression. *ACM Computing Surveys*, 19(3):261–296, 1987.

[137] H. W. Lenstra, Jr. Factoring integers with elliptic curves. *Annals of Mathematics*, 126:649–673, 1987.

[138] L. A. Levin. Universal sorting problems. *Problemy Peredachi Informatsii*, 9(3):265–266, 1973. In Russian.

[139] Harry R. Lewis and Christos H. Papadimitriou. *Elements of the Theory of Computation*. Prentice-Hall, 1981.

[140] C. L. Liu. *Introduction to Combinatorial Mathematics*. McGraw-Hill, 1968.

[141] László Lovász. On the ratio of optimal integral and fractional covers. *Discrete Mathematics*, 13:383–390, 1975.

[142] Udi Manber. *Introduction to Algorithms: A Creative Approach*. Addison-Wesley, 1989.

[143] William J. Masek and Michael S. Paterson. A faster algorithm computing string edit distances. *Journal of Computer and System Sciences*, 20(1):18–31, 1980.

[144] Kurt Mehlhorn. *Sorting and Searching*, volume 1 of *Data Structures and Algorithms*. Springer-Verlag, 1984.

[145] Kurt Mehlhorn. *Graph Algorithms and NP-Completeness*, volume 2 of *Data Structures and Algorithms*. Springer-Verlag, 1984.

[146] Kurt Mehlhorn. *Multidimensional Searching and Computational Geometry*, volume 3 of *Data Structures and Algorithms*. Springer-Verlag, 1984.

[147] Gary L. Miller. Riemann's hypothesis and tests for primality. *Journal of Computer and System Sciences*, 13(3):300–317, 1976.

[148] Louis Monier. *Algorithmes de Factorisation D'Entiers*. PhD thesis, L'Université Paris-Sud, Centre D'Orsay, 1980.

[149] Louis Monier. Evaluation and comparison of two efficient probabilistic primality testing algorithms. *Theoretical Computer Science*, 12(1):97–108, 1980.

[150] Edward F. Moore. The shortest path through a maze. In *Proceedings of the International Symposium on the Theory of Switching*, pages 285–292. Harvard University Press, 1959.

[151] Ivan Niven and Herbert S. Zuckerman. *An Introduction to the Theory of Numbers*. John Wiley & Sons, fourth edition, 1980.

[152] Yu. Ofman. On the algorithmic complexity of discrete functions. *Soviet Physics Doklady*, 7(7):589–591, 1963. English translation.

[153] Alan V. Oppenheim and Alan S. Willsky, with Ian T. Young. *Signals and Systems*. Prentice-Hall, 1983.

[154] Christos H. Papadimitriou and Kenneth Steiglitz. *Combinatorial Optimization: Algorithms and Complexity*. Prentice-Hall, 1982.

[155] Michael S. Paterson, 1974. Unpublished lecture, Ile de Berder, France.

[156] J. M. Pollard. A Monte Carlo method for factorization. *BIT*, 15:331–334, 1975.

[157] Carl Pomerance. On the distribution of pseudoprimes. *Mathematics of Computation*, 37(156):587–593, 1981.

[158] Carl Pomerance. The quadratic sieve factoring algorithm. In T. Beth, N. Cot, and I. Ingemarrson, editors, *Advances in Cryptology*, volume 209 of *Lecture Notes in Computer Science*, pages 169–182. Springer-Verlag, 1984.

[159] Carl Pomerance, editor. *Proceedings of the AMS Symposia in Applied Mathematics: Computational Number Theory and Cryptography*. American Mathematical Society, to appear.

[160] Franco P. Preparata and Micheal Ian Shamos. *Computational Geometry: An Introduction*. Springer-Verlag, 1985.

[161] William H. Press, Brian P. Flannery, Saul A. Teukolsky, and William T. Vetterling. *Numerical Recipes: The Art of Scientific Computing*. Cambridge University Press, 1986.

[162] William H. Press, Brian P. Flannery, Saul A. Teukolsky, and William T. Vetterling. *Numerical Recipes in C*. Cambridge University Press, 1988.

[163] R. C. Prim. Shortest connection networks and some generalizations. *Bell System Technical Journal*, 36:1389–1401, 1957.

[164] Paul W. Purdom, Jr., and Cynthia A. Brown. *The Analysis of Algorithms.* Holt, Rinehart, and Winston, 1985.

[165] Michael O. Rabin. Probabilistic algorithms. In J. F. Traub, editor, *Algorithms and Complexity: New Directions and Recent Results*, pages 21–39. Academic Press, 1976.

[166] Michael O. Rabin. Probabilistic algorithm for testing primality. *Journal of Number Theory*, 12:128–138, 1980.

[167] Edward M. Reingold, Jürg Nievergelt, and Narsingh Deo. *Combinatorial Algorithms: Theory and Practice.* Prentice-Hall, 1977.

[168] Hans Riesel. *Prime Numbers and Computer Methods for Factorization.* Progress in Mathematics. Birkhäuser, 1985.

[169] Ronald L. Rivest, Adi Shamir, and Leonard M. Adleman. A method for obtaining digital signatures and public-key cryptosystems. *Communications of the ACM*, 21(2):120–126, 1978. See also U.S. Patent 4,405,829.

[170] D. J. Rosenkrantz, R. E. Stearns, and P. M. Lewis. An analysis of several heuristics for the traveling salesman problem. *SIAM Journal on Computing*, 6:563–581, 1977.

[171] Y. A. Rozanov. *Probability Theory: A Concise Course.* Dover, 1969.

[172] S. Sahni and T. Gonzalez. P-complete approximation problems. *Journal of the ACM*, 23:555–565, 1976.

[173] John E. Savage. *The Complexity of Computing.* John Wiley & Sons, 1976.

[174] Robert Sedgewick. Implementing quicksort programs. *Communications of the ACM*, 21(10):847–857, 1978.

[175] Robert Sedgewick. *Algorithms.* Addison-Wesley, second edition, 1988.

[176] Michael I. Shamos and Dan Hoey. Geometric intersection problems. In *Proceedings of the 16th Annual Symposium on Foundations of Computer Science*, pages 208–215. IEEE Computer Society, 1975.

[177] Daniel D. Sleator and Robert E. Tarjan. A data structure for dynamic trees. *Journal of Computer and System Sciences*, 26(3):362–391, 1983.

[178] Daniel D. Sleator and Robert E. Tarjan. Self-adjusting binary search trees. *Journal of the ACM*, 32(3):652–686, 1985.

[179] Joel Spencer. *Ten Lectures on the Probabilistic Method.* Regional Conference Series on Applied Mathematics (No. 52). SIAM, 1987.

[180] Staff of the Computation Laboratory. *Description of a Relay Calculator*, volume XXIV of *The Annals of the Computation Laboratory of Harvard University.* Harvard University Press, 1949.

[181] Gilbert Strang. *Introduction to Applied Mathematics.* Wellesley-Cambridge Press, 1986.

[182] Gilbert Strang. *Linear Algebra and Its Applications.* Harcourt Brace Jovanovich, third edition, 1988.

[183] Volker Strassen. Gaussian elimination is not optimal. *Numerische Mathematik*, 14(3):354–356, 1969.

[184] T. G. Szymanski. A special case of the maximal common subsequence problem. Technical Report TR-170, Computer Science Laboratory, Princeton University, 1975.

[185] Robert E. Tarjan. Depth first search and linear graph algorithms. *SIAM Journal on Computing*, 1(2):146–160, 1972.

[186] Robert E. Tarjan. Efficiency of a good but not linear set union algorithm. *Journal of the ACM*, 22(2):215–225, 1975.

[187] Robert E. Tarjan. A class of algorithms which require nonlinear time to maintain disjoint sets. *Journal of Computer and System Sciences*, 18(2): 110–127, 1979.

[188] Robert E. Tarjan. *Data Structures and Network Algorithms*. Society for Industrial and Applied Mathematics, 1983.

[189] Robert E. Tarjan. Amortized computational complexity. *SIAM Journal on Algebraic and Discrete Methods*, 6(2):306–318, 1985.

[190] Robert E. Tarjan and Jan van Leeuwen. Worst-case analysis of set union algorithms. *Journal of the ACM*, 31(2):245–281, 1984.

[191] Robert E. Tarjan and Uzi Vishkin. An efficient parallel biconnectivity algorithm. *SIAM Journal on Computing*, 14(4):862–874, 1985.

[192] George B. Thomas, Jr., and Ross L. Finney. *Calculus and Analytic Geometry*. Addison-Wesley, seventh edition, 1988.

[193] Leslie G. Valiant. Parallelism in comparison problems. *SIAM Journal on Computing*, 4(3):348–355, 1975.

[194] P. van Emde Boas. Preserving order in a forest in less than logarithmic time. In *Proceedings of the 16th Annual Symposium on Foundations of Computer Science*, pages 75–84. IEEE Computer Society, 1975.

[195] Uzi Vishkin. Implementation of simultaneous memory address access in models that forbid it. *Journal of Algorithms*, 4(1):45–50, 1983.

[196] Jean Vuillemin. A data structure for manipulating priority queues. *Communications of the ACM*, 21(4):309–315, 1978.

[197] C. S. Wallace. A suggestion for a fast multiplier. *IEEE Transactions on Electronic Computers*, EC-13(1):14–17, 1964.

[198] Stephen Warshall. A theorem on boolean matrices. *Journal of the ACM*, 9(1):11–12, 1962.

[199] A. Weinberger and J. L. Smith. A one-microsecond adder using one-megacycle circuitry. *IRE Transactions on Electronic Computers*, EC-5(2), 1956.

[200] Hassler Whitney. On the abstract properties of linear dependence. *American Journal of Mathematics*, 57:509–533, 1935.

[201] Herbert S. Wilf. *Algorithms and Complexity*. Prentice-Hall, 1986.

[202] J. W. J. Williams. Algorithm 232 (heapsort). *Communications of the ACM*, 7:347–348, 1964.

[203] S. Winograd. On the algebraic complexity of functions. In *Actes du Congrès International des Mathématiciens*, volume 3, pages 283–288, 1970.

[204] James C. Wyllie. *The Complexity of Parallel Computations*. PhD thesis, Department of Computer Science, Cornell University, 1979.

[205] Andrew C.-C. Yao. A lower bound to finding convex hulls. *Journal of the ACM*, 28(4):780–787, 1981.

Index

This index uses the following conventions. Numbers are alphabetized as if spelled out; for example, "2-3-4 tree" is indexed as if it were "two-three-four tree." When an entry refers to a place other than the main text, the page number is followed by a tag: ex. for exercise, pr. for problem, fig. for figure, and n. for footnote. A tagged page number often indicates the first page of an exercise, problem, figure, or footnote; this is not necessarily the page on which the reference actually appears. For example, "linear search" is defined on page 6 in an exercise that begins on page 5; hence, the corresponding index entry for linear search is "5 ex."

o-notation, 29–30
O-notation, 26–27
O'-notation, 39 pr.
$\widetilde{O}$-notation, 39 pr.
ω-notation, 30
Ω-notation, 27–28
$\overset{\infty}{\Omega}$-notation, 39 pr.
$\widetilde{\Omega}$-notation, 39 pr.
Θ-notation, 24–26
$\widetilde{\Theta}$-notation, 39 pr.
{ } (set), 77
$\in$ (set member), 77
$\notin$ (not a set member), 77
$\emptyset$ (empty set), 77
$\subseteq$ (subset), 77
$\subset$ (proper subset), 77
: (such that), 78
$\cap$ (set intersection), 78
$\cup$ (set union), 78
$-$ (set difference), 78
$| \ |$ (set cardinality), 79
$\times$
   (Cartesian product), 80
   (cross product), 887
$\langle \ \rangle$ (sequence), 84
$\binom{n}{k}$ (choose), 101
! (factorial), 35
$\lceil \ \rceil$ (ceiling), 32
$\lfloor \ \rfloor$ (floor), 32

$\sum$ (sum), 42
$\prod$ (product), 45
$\rightarrow$ (adjacency relation), 87
$\rightsquigarrow$ (reachability relation), 87
$\wedge$ (AND), 655, 746
$\neg$ (NOT), 655
$\vee$ (OR), 655, 746
$\oplus$
   (algebraic operator), 745
   (group operator), 814
   (summary operator for closed
     semirings), 570
   XOR (exclusive-or), 655
$\odot$
   (algebraic operator), 745
   (extension operator for closed
     semirings), 570
$\otimes$
   (carry-status operator), 663
   (convolution operator), 778
   (parallel-prefix operator), 695
* (closure operator), 573, 922
$|$ (divides relation), 802
$\equiv$ (equivalent modulo n), 83 ex., 803
$\not\equiv$ (not equivalent modulo n), 804
$[a]_n$ (equivalence class modulo n), 804
$+_n$ (addition modulo n), 815
$\cdot_n$ (multiplication modulo n), 815
$\left(\frac{a}{p}\right)$ (Legendre symbol), 850 pr.

ε (empty string), 854, 921
$\sqsubset$ (prefix relation), 854
$\sqsupset$ (suffix relation), 854
$\sim$ (similar relation), 881
$>_x$ (above relation), 893
$\triangleright$ (comment symbol), 4
$\leq_P$ (polynomial-time reducibility
  relation), 930

abelian group, 814
ABOVE, 894
absolutely convergent series, 43
absorption laws for sets, 78
abstract problem, 918
acceptance
  by an algorithm, 922
  by a finite automaton, 863
accepting state, 862
accounting method, 360–363
  for binary counters, 362
  for dynamic tables, 369
  for stack operations, 361–362,
    363 ex.
Ackermann's function, 451–453
activity-selection problem, 329–333
acyclic graph, 88
addition
  of binary integers, 6 ex.
  bit-serial, 678–680
  carry-lookahead, 662–667
  carry-save, 668–669
  circuits for, 660–671
  of matrices, 733
  modulo n ($+_n$), 815
  of polynomials, 776
  ripple-carry, 661–662
additive group modulo n, 815
additive inverse, 746
addressing, open, *see* open addressing
adjacency-list representation, 465
adjacency-matrix representation, 467
adjacent vertices, 87
admissible edge, 615
admissible network, 615–617
aggregate method, 357–360
  for binary counters, 358–360
  for disjoint-set data structures, 445,
    446 ex., 450 ex., 454–458
  for Fibonacci heaps, 435 ex.
  for Graham's scan, 905
  for stack operations, 357–358
AKS sorting network, 653
algorithm, 1
  correctness of, 2

running time of, 7
ALLOCATE-NODE, 388
ALLOCATE-OBJECT, 212
allocation of objects, 210–212
all-pairs shortest paths, 515, 550–578
  in ϵ-dense graphs, 576 pr.
  Floyd-Warshall algorithm, 558–562
  Johnson's algorithm, 565–570
  by matrix multiplication, 552–558
  by repeated squaring, 555–557
alphabet, 862, 921
amortized analysis, 356–377
  accounting method of, 360–363
  aggregate method of, 357–360
  for bit-reversal permutation, 375 pr.
  for CRCW connected-components
    algorithm, 727 pr.
  for disjoint-set data structures, 445,
    446 ex., 450 ex., 454–458
  for dynamic tables, 367–375
  for Fibonacci heaps, 422–426, 430,
    433–435, 435 ex.
  for generic preflow-push algorithm,
    613
  for Graham's scan, 905
  for Knuth-Morris-Pratt algorithm,
    872
  for making binary search dynamic,
    376 pr.
  potential method of, 363–367
  for stacks on secondary storage,
    398 pr.
  for weight-balanced trees, 376 pr.
amortized cost
  in the accounting method, 360
  in the aggregate method, 357
  in the potential method, 363
analysis of algorithms, 6–11
  see also amortized analysis,
    probabilistic analysis
ancestor, 93
  least common, 460 pr.
AND function ($\wedge$), 655, 746
  on a CRCW PRAM, 705
AND gate, 655
annihilator, 570, 745
antisymmetry, 82
ANY-SEGMENTS-INTERSECT, 895
approximation algorithm, 964–985
  for bin packing, 983 pr.
  for the maximum-clique problem,
    984 pr.
  for the set-covering problem,
    974–978

for the subset-sum problem,
    978–983
for the traveling-salesman problem,
    969–974
for the vertex-cover problem,
    966–968
for the weighted set-covering
    problem, 984 pr.
approximation by least squares,
    768–771
approximation scheme, 965–966
APPROX-SUBSET-SUM, 981
APPROX-TSP-TOUR, 970
APPROX-VERTEX-COVER, 967
arbitrage, 546 pr.
arc, *see* edge
area of a simple polygon, 892 ex.
argument of a function, 84
arithmetic, modular, 814–820
arithmetic circuits, 654–687
arithmetic series, 43
array, 4
array multiplier, 672–675
articulation point, 495 pr.
assignment
    multiple, 4
    satisfying, 933, 940
    truth, 933, 940
associative laws for sets, 78
associative operation, 570, 745, 814
asymptotically nonnegative, 24
asymptotically positive, 33
asymptotically tight bound, 24
asymptotic lower bound, 27
asymptotic notation, 23–32
    and graph algorithms, 463
    and linearity of summations, 43
asymptotic upper bound, 26
attribute of an object, 5
augmenting data structures, 281–296
augmenting path, 590–591
automaton
    cellular, 729
    finite, 862
    string-matching, 863–868
average-case running time, 10

back edge, 482, 486
back substitution, 752–753
bad-character heuristic, 879–881
balanced search tree
    B-trees, 381–399
    red-black trees, 263–280
    splay trees, 280, 380

2-3-4 trees, 385
2-3 trees, 280, 399
    weight-balanced trees, 376 pr.
balls and bins, 129–130, 132 ex.,
    133 pr.
barrel shifter, 678 ex.
Batcher's odd-even merging network,
    651 pr.
Bayes's theorem, 109
BELLMAN-FORD, 532
Bellman-Ford algorithm, 532–536
    in Johnson's algorithm, 569
    and objective functions, 545 ex.
    to solve systems of difference
        constraints, 543
    Yen's improvement to, 545 pr.
BELOW, 894
Bernoulli trial, 115
    and balls and bins, 129–130
    and height of a randomly built
        binary search tree, 256
    and streaks, 130–132
    and work-efficient parallel prefix,
        718
best-case running time, 11 ex., 28
BFS, 470
biconnected component, 495 pr.
bijective function, 85
binary character code, 337
binary counter
    analyzed by accounting method, 362
    analyzed by aggregate method,
        358–360
    analyzed by potential method,
        365–366
    and binomial heaps, 417 ex.
    bit-reversed, 375 pr.
binary entropy function, 103
binary gcd algorithm, 849 pr.
binary heap, *see* heap
binary relation, 81
binary search, 15 ex.
    with fast insertion, 376 pr.
    in insertion sort, 15 ex.
    in searching B-trees, 394 ex.
binary search tree, 244–262
    deletion from, 251–253
    with equal keys, 259 pr.
    insertion into, 250–251
    maximum key of, 248
    minimum key of, 248
    predecessor in, 248–249
    querying, 246–250
    randomly built, 254–259, 260 pr.

searching, 247–248
for sorting, 254 ex.
successor in, 248–249
see also red-black tree
binary-search-tree property, 245
vs. heap property, 246 ex.
binary tree, 94
finding the root of, on a CREW
PRAM, 708 ex.
full, 95
number of different ones, 262 pr.
representation of, 213
walk of, 215–216 ex.
binomial coefficient, 101–103
binomial distribution, 117–119
and balls and bins, 129
maximum value of, 120 ex.
tails of, 121–126
binomial expansion, 101
binomial heap, 400–419
and binary counter and binary
addition, 417 ex.
creating, 406
decreasing a key in, 415
deletion from, 415–416
extracting the minimum key from,
413–415
insertion into, 413
minimum key of, 406
properties of, 403
running times of operations on,
401 fig.
uniting, 407–413
BINOMIAL-HEAP-DECREASE-KEY, 415
BINOMIAL-HEAP-DELETE, 416, 417 ex.
BINOMIAL-HEAP-EXTRACT-MIN, 413
BINOMIAL-HEAP-INSERT, 413, 417 ex.
BINOMIAL-HEAP-MERGE, 408, 417 ex.
BINOMIAL-HEAP-MINIMUM, 406,
417 ex.
BINOMIAL-HEAP-UNION, 408
BINOMIAL-LINK, 407
binomial tree, 401–403
unordered, 423
bin packing, 983 pr.
bipartite graph, 89
corresponding flow network of, 601
determination of, 476 ex.
bipartite matching, 439, 600–604, 629
birthday paradox, 126–129, 132 ex.
bisection of a tree, 98 pr.
BITBLT, 728 pr.
bitonic euclidean traveling-salesman
problem, 324 pr.

bitonic sequence, 642
BITONIC-SORTER, 643
bitonic sorting network, 642–646
bitonic tour, 324 pr.
bit-reversal permutation, 375 pr.
BIT-REVERSE-COPY, 795
bit-reversed binary counter, 375 pr.
BIT-REVERSED-INCREMENT, 375 pr.
bit-serial addition, 678–680
bit vector, 221 ex.
black-height, 263
black vertex, 469, 477
block structure in pseudocode, 4
Boole's inequality, 109 ex.
boolean combinational element, 655
boolean connective, 940
boolean formula, 929 ex., 940, 946 ex.
boolean function, 103 ex.
boolean matrix multiplication
and transitive closure, 749 ex.,
766 ex.
using randomization, 772 pr.
using Strassen's algorithm, 747–748,
772 pr.
boolean quasiring, 746
bottleneck traveling-salesman
problem, 974 ex.
bottom of a stack, 200
bound
asymptotically tight, 24
asymptotic lower, 27
asymptotic upper, 26
on binomial coefficients, 102–103
on binomial distributions, 119
polylogarithmic, 35
ratio, 964
relative error, 965
on the tails of a binomial
distribution, 121–126
boundary of a polygon, 320
bounding a summation, 46–52
bounding box, 889
Boyer-Moore algorithm, 876–883
BOYER-MOORE-MATCHER, 877
breadth-first search, 469–477
and shortest paths, 472–475, 514
similarity to Dijkstra's algorithm,
531
breadth-first tree, 469, 475
Brent's theorem, 710–711, 713 ex.
bridge, 495 pr.
B-tree, 381–399
creating, 388
deletion from, 395–397

full node in, 385
height of, 385–386
insertion into, 390–392
minimum degree of, 385
minimum key of, 394 ex.
properties of, 384–387
searching, 387–388
splitting a node in, 389–390
2-3-4 trees, 385
B-TREE-CREATE, 388
B-TREE-DELETE, 395
B-TREE-INSERT, 391
B-TREE-INSERT-NONFULL, 392
B-TREE-SEARCH, 388, 394 ex.
B-TREE-SPLIT-CHILD, 390
bucket, 180
bucket sort, 180–183
BUCKET-SORT, 181
BUILD-HEAP, 145
BUILD-HEAP$'$, 152 pr.
butterfly operation, 792

calculus of paths in directed graphs,
    571–573
call by value, 5
cancellation lemma, 784
cancellation of flow, 583
capacity
    of a cut, 591
    of an edge, 580
    residual, 588, 590
capacity constraint, 580
cardinality of a set ($|\ |$), 79
Carmichael number, 839, 844 ex.
carry generate, 662
carry-in bit, 661
carry kill, 662
carry-lookahead addition, 662–667
carry-out bit, 661
carry propagate, 662
carry-save addition, 668–669, 677 ex.
carry status, 662
carry-status operator ($\otimes$), 663
Cartesian product ($\times$), 80
Cartesian sum, 783 ex.
cascading cut, 433, 438 ex.
CASCADING-CUT, 432
Catalan numbers, 262 pr., 304
ceiling function ($\lceil\ \rceil$), 32
cellular automaton, 729
certificate
    in a cryptosystem, 836
    for verification algorithms, 926
CHAINED-HASH-DELETE, 223

CHAINED-HASH-INSERT, 223
CHAINED-HASH-SEARCH, 223
chaining, 223–225, 241 pr.
chain of a convex hull, 906
changing a key in a Fibonacci heap,
    439 pr.
character code, 337
child, 93, 95
child list in a Fibonacci heap, 421
Chinese remainder theorem, 823–826
chirp transform, 791 ex.
choose ($\binom{n}{k}$), 101
chord of a polygon, 320
chromatic number, *see* coloring
ciphertext, 832
circuit
    for addition, 660–671, 678–680
    clocked, 678–685
    combinational, 655–660
    for division, 685 pr.
    for Fast Fourier Transform,
        795–796
    globally clocked, 679
    for multiplication, 671–678,
        681–684
    for parallel prefix, 665–666
    sequential, 678–685
    tally, 671 ex.
    see also comparison network
CIRCUIT-SAT, 934
circuit satisfiability, 932–938
circular linked list, 204
    see also linked list
class
    complexity, 923
    equivalence, 82
classification of edges
    in breadth-first search, 495 pr.
    in depth-first search, 482–483
classification of edges in depth-first
    search, 484 ex.
clean sequence, 642
clique, 947
CLIQUE, 947
clique problem, 947–949
    approximation algorithm for,
        984 pr.
    and vertex-cover problem, 968 ex.
clock, 679
clocked circuit, 678–685
clock period, 679
closed interval, 290
closed semiring, 570, 573–574
    for minimum spanning tree, 577 pr.

as a quasiring, 746
closest pair, finding, 908–912
closest-point heuristic, 973 ex.
closure
    group property, 814
    of a language, 922
    operator (*), 573
    transitive, *see* transitive closure
    under an operator, 570, 745
clustering, 235
CNF (conjunctive normal form), 942
code, 337–338
    Huffman, 337–345
codomain, 84
coefficient
    binomial, 101
    of a polynomial, 33, 776
coefficient representation, 778
    and fast multiplication, 781–782
cofactor, 736
coin changing, 353 pr.
collinearity, 888, 891 ex.
collision, 222
    resolution by chaining, 223–225
    resolution by open addressing,
        232–241
coloring, 97 pr., 721, 962 pr.
    on an EREW PRAM, 721–724
color of a red-black-tree node, 263
column rank, 735
column vector, 731
combination, 101
combinational circuit, 655–660, 710
    and equivalent clocked circuit, 680
    simulated by a CRCW PRAM,
        713 ex.
    simulated by a CREW PRAM,
        710–711
    simulated by an EREW PRAM,
        711–712
    see also circuit, comparison network
combinational element, 655, 710
comment in pseudocode (▷), 4
common-CRCW model, 690
common divisor, 804
    greatest, *see* greatest common
        divisor
common subsequence, 315
    longest, 314–320
commutative laws for sets, 78
commutativity under an operator,
    570, 745, 748, 814
COMPACTIFY-LIST, 213 ex.
compact list, 217 pr.

COMPACT-LIST-SEARCH, 217 pr.
comparable line segments, 893
comparator, 634, 638 ex., 648 ex.,
    650 ex.
comparison network, 634–639
comparison sort, 172
    and binary search trees, 246 ex.
    and mergeable heaps, 431 ex.
    and selection, 191
complement
    of an event, 105
    of a graph, 950
    of a language, 921
    Schur, 755, 767
    of a set, 79
complete graph, 89
complete k-ary tree, 95
completeness of a language, 938 ex.
complexity class, 923
    co-NP, 927
    NP, 927
    NPC, 932
    P, 919
complexity measure, 923
complex numbers, multiplication of,
    745 ex.
complex root of unity, 784
    interpolation at, 789–790
component
    biconnected, 495 pr.
    connected, 88
    strongly connected, 88
component graph, 494 ex.
composite number, 803
computational geometry, 886–915
computational problem, 1–2
COMPUTE-GOOD-SUFFIX-FUNCTION,
    882
COMPUTE-LAST-OCCURRENCE-
    FUNCTION, 881
COMPUTE-PREFIX-FUNCTION, 871
COMPUTE-SUMMARIES, 575, 576 ex.
COMPUTE-TRANSITION-FUNCTION, 868
concatenation
    of languages, 921
    of paths, 571
    of strings, 854
concrete problem, 919
concurrent-read, 689
concurrent-write, 690
conditional independence, 110 ex.
conditional probability, 107, 109
conjugate transpose, 766 ex.
conjunctive normal form, 942

connected component, 88
  identified on a CRCW PRAM,
    727 pr.
  identified using depth-first search,
    485 ex.
  identified using disjoint-set data
    structures, 441–442
CONNECTED-COMPONENTS, 441
connected graph, 88
connective, 940
co-NP, 927
conservation of flow, 580
consistency of literals, 948
CONSOLIDATE, 427
consolidating a Fibonacci-heap root
    list, 427, 431 ex.
constraint graph, 541–543
continuous uniform probability
    distribution, 107
contraction of a matroid, 349
convergent series, 43
convex combination of points, 887
convex hull, 898–908, 914 pr.
convex layers, 913 pr.
convex polygon, 320
convolution ($\otimes$), 778
convolution theorem, 790
corner of feasible region, 539 n.
correctness of an algorithm, 2
countably infinite set, 79
counter, *see* binary counter
counting, 99–104
  probabilistic, 134 pr.
counting sort, 175–178
  in radix sort, 179
COUNTING-SORT, 176
cover
  path, 626 pr.
  by a subset, 974
  vertex, 949, 966
CPU time, 383
CRCW (concurrent-read,
    concurrent-write), 690
  common, 690
  compared to EREW, 701–709
  finding connected components,
    727 pr.
  finding the maximum, 704–706,
    709 ex., 726 pr.
  AND function, 705
  matrix multiplication, 709 ex.
  merging two sorted arrays, 709 ex.
  OR function, 709 ex.
  simulated by EREW, 706–708

  simulation of, by EREW, 709 ex.,
    713 ex.
  simulation of a combinational
    circuit, 713 ex.
  work-efficient matrix multiplication,
    713 ex.
credit, in the accounting method, 360
CREW (concurrent-read,
    exclusive-write), 690
  finding roots in a forest, 701–704
  finding the root of a binary tree,
    708 ex.
  simulation of a combinational
    circuit, 710–711
  string matching, 884 pr.
critical edge, 598
critical path
  in a combinational circuit, 670 ex.
  in a directed acyclic graph, 538
cross edge, 482
crossing a cut, 501
cross product ($\times$), 887
cryptosystem, 831–837
cubic spline, 774 pr.
curve fitting, 768–771
cut
  cascading, 433
  of a flow network, 591–593
  of an undirected graph, 500
CUT, 432
cutting, in a Fibonacci heap, 432
cycle of a graph, 88
  detection of, 488 ex.
  hamiltonian, 925
  minimum mean-weight, 548 pr.
  negative-weight, *see* negative-weight
    cycle
cyclic group, 827
cyclic rotation, 876 ex.
cyclic shifter, 678 ex.

dag (directed acyclic graph), 89
  and back edges, 486
  and hamiltonian-path problem,
    929 ex.
  single-source shortest-paths
    algorithm for, 536–538
  topological sort of, 485–488
DAG-SHORTEST-PATHS, 536
d-ary heap, 152 pr.
  in shortest-paths algorithms, 576 pr.
data structure, 197–296, 379–461
  augmentation of, 281–296
  binary search trees, 244–262

binomial heaps, 400–419
B-trees, 381–399
deques, 203 ex.
dictionaries, 197
direct-address tables, 219–221
for disjoint sets, 440–461
dynamic trees, 380
Fibonacci heaps, 420–439
hash tables, 221–226
heaps, 140–152
interval trees, 290–295
linked lists, 204–209
order-statistic trees, 281–286
persistent, 278 pr., 380
potential of, 363
priority queues, 149–151
queues, 200–203
radix trees, 260 pr.
red-black trees, 263–280
relaxed heaps, 439
rooted trees, 213–216
on secondary storage, 382–384
splay trees, 280, 380
stacks, 200–201
2-3-4 heaps, 418 pr.
2-3 trees, 280, 399
van Emde Boas, 380
see also dynamic set
deallocation of objects, 210–212
decision by an algorithm, 922
decision problem, 918
decision tree, 173–174, 174 ex.
    zero-one principle for, 641 ex.
DECREASE-KEY, 400
decreasing a key
    in binomial heaps, 415
    in Fibonacci heaps, 431–434
    in 2-3-4 heaps, 418 pr.
DECREMENT, 360 ex.
degree
    of a binomial-tree root, 402
    maximum, of a Fibonacci heap,
        423, 431 ex., 435–438
    minimum, of a B-tree, 385
    of a node, 94
    of a polynomial, 33, 776
    of a vertex, 87
degree-bound, 776
DELETE, 198, 400
deletion
    from binary search trees, 251–253
    from binomial heaps, 415–416
    from B-trees, 395–397
    from chained hash tables, 223
    from direct-address tables, 220
    from dynamic tables, 372
    from Fibonacci heaps, 434–435,
        438 pr.
    from interval trees, 292
    from linked lists, 206
    from open-address hash tables, 234
    from order-statistic trees, 285
    from queues, 201
    from red-black trees, 272–277
    from stacks, 200
    from sweep-line statuses, 894
    from 2-3-4 heaps, 418 pr.
DeMorgan's laws, 78
dense graph, 465
    ϵ-dense, 576 pr.
density of prime numbers, 837
dependence
    linear, 735
    see also independence
depth
    average, of a node in a randomly
        built binary search tree, 260 pr.
    of a combinational circuit, 659, 710
    of a combinational element, 659,
        710
    of a comparison network, 637
    of a leaf in a decision tree, 174 ex.
    of a node in a red-black tree,
        267 ex., 289 ex.
    of a node in a rooted tree, 94
    of quicksort recursion tree, 160 ex.
    of SORTER, 650 ex.
    of a sorting network, 638 ex.
    of a stack, 169 pr.
depth-determination problem, 459 pr.
depth-first forest, 477
depth-first search, 477–485
    in finding articulation points,
        bridges, and biconnected
        components, 495 pr.
    in finding strongly connected
        components, 488–494
    in topological sorting, 485–488
depth-first tree, 477
deque, 203 ex.
DEQUEUE, 203
derivative of series, 44
descendant, 93
destination vertex, 515
det, *see* determinant
determinant, 736
    and matrix multiplication, 766 ex.

deterministic symmetry breaking, 720–725
DFS, 478
DFS-VISIT, 478
DFT (Discrete Fourier Transform), 786
diagonal matrix, 731
  LUP decomposition of, 761 ex.
diameter of a tree, 476 ex.
dictionary, 197
difference constraints, 539–545
difference equation, *see* recurrence
difference of sets (−), 78
differentiation of series, 44
digital signature, 832
digraph, *see* directed graph
DIJKSTRA, 527
Dijkstra's algorithm, 527–532
  implemented with a Fibonacci heap, 530
  implemented with a heap, 530
  with integer edge weights, 532 ex.
  in Johnson's algorithm, 569
  similarity to breadth-first search, 531
  similarity to Prim's algorithm, 505, 531
DIRECT-ADDRESS-DELETE, 220
direct addressing, 219–221
DIRECT-ADDRESS-INSERT, 220
DIRECT-ADDRESS-SEARCH, 220
direct-address table, 219–221
directed acyclic graph (dag), 89
  and back edges, 486
  and hamiltonian-path problem, 929 ex.
  single-source shortest-paths algorithm for, 536–538
  topological sort of, 485–488
directed graph, 86
  all-pairs shortest paths in, 550–578
  calculus of paths in, 571–573
  component graph, 494 ex.
  constraint graph, 541
  Euler tour of, 496 pr.
  path cover of, 626 pr.
  PERT chart, 538, 538 ex.
  semiconnected, 494 ex.
  shortest path in, 514
  single-source shortest paths in, 514–549
  singly connected, 485 ex.
  square of, 468 ex.
  transitive closure of, 562

transpose of, 468 ex.
  see also circuit, directed acyclic graph, graph, network
directed segment, 887–888
directed version of an undirected graph, 89
DISCHARGE, 617
discharge of an overflowing vertex, 617
discovered vertex, 469, 477
Discrete Fourier Transform, 786
discrete logarithm, 828
discrete logarithm theorem, 828
discrete probability distribution, 106
discrete random variable, 111–115
disjoint-set data structure, 440–461
  analysis of, 454–458
  in depth determination, 459 pr.
  disjoint-set-forest implementation of, 446–450
  in Kruskal's algorithm, 504
  linear-time special case of, 461
  linked-list implementation of, 443–446
  in off-line least common ancestors, 460 pr.
  in off-line minimum, 458 pr.
  in task scheduling, 354 pr.
disjoint-set forest, 446–450
  analysis of, 454–458
  rank properties of, 453–454
  see also disjoint-set data structure
disjoint sets, 79
disjunctive normal form, 944
disk, 898 ex.
  see also secondary storage
DISK-READ, 383
DISK-WRITE, 383
distance
  edit, 325 pr.
  euclidean, 908
  L_m, 912 ex.
  Manhattan, 193 pr., 912 ex.
  of a shortest path, 472
distribution
  binomial, 117–119
  geometric, 115–116
  of prime numbers, 837
  probability, 105–107
  sparse-hulled, 914 pr.
distributive laws for sets, 78
distributivity, 570, 745
divergent series, 43
divide-and-conquer method, 12–14

analysis of, 13–14
for binary search, 15 ex.
for conversion of binary to decimal,
    808 ex.
for Fast Fourier Transform,
    787–789
for finding the closest pair of points,
    908–912
for finding the convex hull, 899
for matrix inversion, 764–765
for merge sort, 12–15
for multiplication, 797 pr.
for quicksort, 153–171
and recursion trees, 59
relation to dynamic programming,
    301
for selection, 187–192
for Strassen's algorithm, 739–745
divides relation (|), 802
division circuit, 685 pr.
division method, 228
division theorem, 803
divisor, 802–803
    common, 804
    see also greatest common divisor
DNF (disjunctive normal form), 944
domain, 84
dominates relation, 913 pr.
double hashing, 235–237
doubly linked list, 204
    see also linked list
d-regular graph, 604 ex.
dynamic graph
    minimum-spanning-tree algorithm
        for, 510 ex.
    transitive closure of, 576 pr.
dynamic order statistics, 281–286
dynamic-programming method,
    301–328
    for activity selection, 333 ex.
    for all-pairs shortest paths, 552–562
    for bitonic euclidean
        traveling-salesman problem,
        324 pr.
    comparison with greedy algorithms,
        334–336
    for directed-path labels, 574–575
    for edit distance, 325 pr.
    elements of, 309–314
    for Floyd-Warshall algorithm,
        558–562
    for longest common subsequence,
        314–320

for matrix-chain multiplication,
    302–309
and memoization, 312–314
for minimum spanning tree, 577 pr.
for optimal polygon triangulation,
    320–324
optimal substructure in, 309–310
overlapping subproblems in,
    310–312
for printing neatly, 325 pr.
for transitive closure, 562–563
for Viterbi algorithm, 327 pr.
for 0-1 knapsack problem, 336 ex.
dynamic set, 197–198
    binary search trees, 244–262
    binomial heaps, 400–419
    bit-vectors, 221 ex.
    B-trees, 381–399
    deques, 203 ex.
    dictionaries, 197
    direct-address tables, 219–221
    disjoint-set data structure, 440–461
    Fibonacci heaps, 420–439
    hash tables, 221–226
    heaps, 140–152
    interval trees, 290–295
    linked lists, 204–209
    modifying operations on, 198
    order-statistic trees, 281–286
    persistent, 278 pr., 380
    priority queues, 197
    querying, 198
    queues, 201–203
    radix trees, 260 pr.
    red-black trees, 263–280
    relaxed heaps, 439
    rooted trees, 213–216
    splay trees, 280, 380
    stacks, 200–201
    2-3-4 heaps, 418 pr.
    2-3 trees, 280, 399
    van Emde Boas data structure, 380
dynamic table, 367–375
    analyzed by accounting method, 369
    analyzed by potential method,
        369–370, 372–374
    load factor of, 367
dynamic tree, 380

E[ ] (expected value), 112
edge, 86
    admissible, 615
    back, 482
    bridge, 495 pr.

capacity of, 580
classification in breadth-first search, 495 pr.
classification in depth-first search, 482–483
critical, 598
cross, 482
forward, 482
inadmissible, 615
label of, 571
light, 501
negative-weight, 515–516
residual, 588
safe, 499
saturated, 607
tree, 475, 477, 482
weight of, 466
edge connectivity, 600 ex.
edge set, 86
edit distance, 325 pr.
Edmonds-Karp algorithm, 596
elementary event, 104
element of a set ($\in$), 77
ellipsoid algorithm, 539, 549
elliptic-curve factorization method, 852
empty language ($\emptyset$), 921
empty set ($\emptyset$), 77
empty set laws, 78
empty stack, 200
empty string (ε), 854, 921
encoding of problem instances, 919–921
endpoint
  of an interval, 290
  of a line segment, 887
ENQUEUE, 202
entropy function, 103
ϵ-dense graph, 576 pr.
equality
  of functions, 84
  of sets, 77
equivalence, modular ($\equiv$), 83 ex., 803
equivalence class, 82
  modulo n ($[a]_n$), 804
equivalence relation, 82
  and modular equivalence, 83 ex.
ERCW (exclusive-read, concurrent-write), 690
EREW (exclusive-read, exclusive-write), 690
  coloring, 721–724
  compared to CRCW, 701–709

computing a maximal independent set from a 6-coloring, 724–725
deterministic symmetry breaking, 720–725
Euler-tour technique, 697–700
finding roots in a forest, 709 ex.
AND function, 705
list ranking, 692–695
matrix multiplication, 709 ex.
matrix-vector multiplication, 713 ex.
parallel prefix, 695–697, 714–719
pointer jumping, 692–701
segmented parallel prefix, 726 pr.
simulation of a combinational circuit, 711–712
simulation of CRCW, 706–708, 709 ex., 713 ex.
sorting, 712
escape problem, 625 pr.
EUCLID, 810
Euclid's algorithm, 808–814, 850 pr.
euclidean distance, 908
euclidean norm, 734
Euler's constant, 240 ex.
Euler's phi function, 817
Euler's theorem, 827, 844 ex.
Euler tour, 496 pr.
Euler-tour technique, 697–700
evaluation of a polynomial, 11 ex., 778, 783 ex.
  and its derivatives, 798 pr.
  at multiple points, 798 pr.
event, 105
event-point schedule, 894
EXACT-SUBSET-SUM, 979
excess flow, 605
exchange property, 345
exclusive-read, 689
exclusive-write, 690
expectation, *see* expected value
expected running time, 10
expected value, 112–113
  of a binomial distribution, 117
  of a geometric distribution, 115
explored vertex, 479
exponential function, 33–34
exponential series, 44
exponentiation
  modular, 829
  repeated, 450–451
EXTENDED-EUCLID, 812
EXTEND-SHORTEST-PATHS, 554
extension of a set, 346

extension operator for closed
    semirings (⊙), 570
exterior of a polygon, 320
external node, 93
external path length, 97 ex.
extracting the maximum key
    from *d*-ary heaps, 152 pr.
    from heaps, 150
extracting the minimum key
    from binomial heaps, 413–415
    from Fibonacci heaps, 426–430
    from 2-3-4 heaps, 418 pr.
EXTRACT-MAX, 149
EXTRACT-MIN, 400
extreme point, 539 n.

factor, 803
factorial function (!), 35
factorization, 844–849, 852
    unique, 807
failure in a Bernoulli trial, 115
fair coin, 106
fan-in, 657, 710
fan-out, 656, 710
farthest-pair problem, 899
FASTER-ALL-PAIRS-SHORTEST-PATHS,
    556, 558 ex.
Fast Fourier Transform (FFT)
    circuit for, 795–796
    iterative implementation of,
        792–795
    recursive implementation of,
        787–789
    using modular arithmetic, 799 pr.
FAST-MAX, 704
feasibility problem, 540
feasible region, 539 n.
feasible solution, 540
Fermat's theorem, 827
FFT, *see* Fast Fourier Transform
FFT-BASE, 794
FIB-HEAP-CHANGE-KEY, 439 pr.
FIB-HEAP-DECREASE-KEY, 432
FIB-HEAP-DELETE, 434
FIB-HEAP-EXTRACT-MIN, 426
FIB-HEAP-INSERT, 424
FIB-HEAP-LINK, 427
FIB-HEAP-PRUNE, 439 pr.
FIB-HEAP-UNION, 425
Fibonacci heap, 420–439
    changing a key in, 439 pr.
    creating, 424
    decreasing a key in, 431–434
    deletion from, 434–435, 438 pr.

in Dijkstra's algorithm, 530
extracting the minimum key from,
    426–430
insertion into, 424–425
in Johnson's algorithm, 569
maximum degree of, 423, 435–438
minimum key of, 425
potential function for, 422–423
in Prim's algorithm, 509
pruning, 439 pr.
running times of operations on,
    401 fig.
uniting, 425–426
Fibonacci numbers, 36–37, 74 pr., 436
    computation of, 850 pr.
field, algebraic, 748
field of an object, 5
FIFO (first-in, first-out), 200
    see also queue
final-state function, 863
FIND-DEPTH, 459 pr.
find path, 447
FIND-ROOTS, 702
FIND-SET, 441
    disjoint-set-forest implementation
        of, 449, 450 ex., 461
    linked-list implementation of, 443,
        446 ex.
finished vertex, 477
finite automaton, 862
    for string matching, 863–868
FINITE-AUTOMATON-MATCHER, 866
finite group, 814
finite sequence, 84
finite set, 79
first-fit heuristic, 983 pr.
first-in, first-out, 200
    see also queue
fixed-length code, 337
floor function (⌊ ⌋), 32
flow, 580–587
    excess, 605
    integer-valued, 601
    sum, 586 ex.
    value of, 580
flow conservation, 580
flow network, 580–587
    corresponding to a bipartite graph,
        601
    cut of, 591–593
    multicommodity, 587 ex.
    with upper and lower capacity
        bounds, 628 pr.
FLOYD-WARSHALL, 560

FLOYD-WARSHALL', 564 ex.
Floyd-Warshall algorithm, 558–562,
  563 ex., 576 ex.
FORD-FULKERSON, 594
Ford-Fulkerson method, 587–600
FORD-FULKERSON-METHOD, 588
forefather, 490
forest, 89, 91
  depth-first, 477
  disjoint-set, 446–450
  finding roots of, on a CREW
    PRAM, 701–704
  finding roots of, on an EREW
    PRAM, 709 ex.
formal power series, 74 pr.
formula-satisfiability problem,
  940–942
forward edge, 482
forward substitution, 752
fractional knapsack problem, 335,
  337 ex.
freeing of objects, 210–212
free list, 211
FREE-OBJECT, 212
free tree, 89, 91
full adder, 657
full binary tree, 95, 97 ex.
  relation to optimal code, 338
full node, 385
full rank, 735
full walk of a tree, 970
fully parenthesized, 302
fully polynomial-time approximation
  scheme, 966
  for the maximum-clique problem,
    984 pr.
  for the subset-sum problem,
    978–983
function, 84–86

Gabow's scaling algorithm for
  single-source shortest paths,
  547 pr.
gap character, 857 ex.
garbage collection, 140, 211
gate, 655
Gaussian elimination, 754
gcd, 804–806
  see also greatest common divisor
generate a carry bit, 662
generating function, 74 pr.
generator
  of a subgroup, 818
  of Z_n^*, 827

GENERIC-MST, 500
GENERIC-PREFLOW-PUSH, 609
generic preflow-push algorithm,
  608–614
geometric distribution, 115–116
  and balls and bins, 129
  and streaks, 130
geometric series, 44
gift wrapping, 905
globally clocked circuit, 679
global variable, 4
Goldberg's algorithm, *see*
  preflow-push algorithm
golden ratio (ϕ), 36, 74 pr.
good-suffix function, 881
good-suffix heuristic, 881–883
grade-school multiplication algorithm,
  671
GRAFT, 459 pr.
Graham's scan, 899–905
GRAHAM-SCAN, 902
graph, 86–90
  adjacency-list representation of, 465
  adjacency-matrix representation of,
    467
  algorithms for, 463–629
  breadth-first search of, 469–477
  complement of, 950
  dense, 465
  depth-first search of, 477–485
  ϵ-dense, 576 pr.
  hamiltonian, 925
  incidence matrix of, 354 pr., 468 ex.,
    951
  interval, 333 ex.
  nonhamiltonian, 925
  shortest path in, 472
  sparse, 465
  tour of, 959
  weighted, 466
  see also directed acyclic graph,
    directed graph, flow network,
    undirected graph, tree
graph-coloring problem, 962 pr.
graphic matroid, 345
GRAPH-ISOMORPHISM, 928 ex.
gray vertex, 469, 477
greatest common divisor (gcd),
  804–806
  computed by binary gcd algorithm,
    849 pr.
  computed by Euclid's algorithm,
    808–814

with more than two arguments,
813 ex.
recursion theorem for, 809
greedoid, 355
GREEDY, 348
GREEDY-ACTIVITY-SELECTOR, 330
greedy algorithm, 329–355
for activity selection, 329–333
for coin changing, 353 pr.
comparison with dynamic
programming, 334–336
Dijkstra's algorithm, 527–532
elements of, 333–337
for finding optimal vertex cover for
a tree, 968 ex.
for fractional knapsack problem,
335
greedy-choice property in, 334
for Huffman code, 337–345
Kruskal's algorithm, 504–505
for minimum spanning tree, 498
optimal substructure in, 334
Prim's algorithm, 505–510
for the set-covering problem,
974–978
for task scheduling, 350–353,
354 pr.
theoretical foundations of, 345–350
on a weighted matroid, 347–350
for the weighted set-covering
problem, 984 pr.
greedy-choice property, 334
of Huffman codes, 340–343
of a weighted matroid, 348
GREEDY-SET-COVER, 975
grid, 625 pr.
group, 814–820
cyclic, 827

HALF-CLEANER, 642
half-open interval, 290
Hall's theorem, 604 ex.
halting problem, 916
halving lemma, 785
HAM-CYCLE, 925
hamiltonian
cycle, 925
graph, 925
path, 929 ex.
hamiltonian-cycle problem, 925,
953–959
hamiltonian-path problem, 961 ex.
HAM-PATH, 929 ex.
handshaking lemma, 90 ex.

hardwired, 661
harmonic number, 44
harmonic series, 44, 240 ex.
HASH-DELETE, 240 ex.
hash function, 222, 226–232
division method, 228
multiplication method, 228–229
one-way, 836
hashing, 219–243
chaining, 223–225, 241 pr.
k-universal, 242 pr.
open addressing, 232–241
of static sets, 241 pr.
universal, 229–231
HASH-INSERT, 233, 240 ex.
HASH-SEARCH, 234, 240 ex.
hash table, 221–226
dynamic, 374 ex.
see also hashing
hash value, 222
head
of a linked list, 204
of a queue, 201
heap, 140–152
analyzed by potential method,
366 ex.
binomial, *see* binomial heap
building, 145–147, 152 pr.
d-ary, 152 pr., 576 pr.
in Dijkstra's algorithm, 530
extracting the maximum key from,
150
Fibonacci, *see* Fibonacci heap
as garbage-collected storage, 140
to implement a mergeable heap, 400
increasing a key in, 151 ex.
insertion into, 150
in Johnson's algorithm, 569
maximum key of, 150
mergeable, *see* mergeable heap
in Prim's algorithm, 509
as a priority queue, 149–151
relaxed, 439
running times of operations on,
401 fig.
2-3-4, 418 pr.
HEAP-DELETE, 151 ex.
HEAP-EXTRACT-MAX, 150
HEAPIFY, 143, 144 ex.
HEAP-INCREASE-KEY, 151 ex
HEAP-INSERT, 150
building a heap with, 152 pr.
heap-ordered, 403
heap property, 141

maintenance of, 142–144
vs. binary-search-tree property, 246 ex.
heapsort, 140–152
stability of, 180 ex.
HEAPSORT, 147
height
of a binomial tree, 402
black-, 263
of a B-tree, 385–386
of a *d*-ary heap, 152 pr.
of a decision tree, 174
of a Fibonacci heap, 438 ex.
of a heap, 141, 142 ex.
of a node in a heap, 141, 147 ex.
of a randomly built binary search tree, 258
of a red-black tree, 264
of a tree, 94, 141
height function, in preflow-push algorithms, 606
hereditary family of subsets, 345
Hermitian matrix, 766 ex.
HOOK, 727 pr.
Horner's rule, 11 ex., 778
HUFFMAN, 340
Huffman code, 337–345
hyperedge, 90
hypergraph, 89

idempotence under an operator, 570
idempotency laws for sets, 78
identity, 570, 745, 814
identity matrix, 731
image, 84
implicit summation notation, 585
inactive processor, 713 ex.
inadmissible edge, 615
incidence, 87
incidence matrix
and difference constraints, 541
of a directed graph, 354 pr., 468 ex.
of an undirected graph, 354 pr., 951
increasing a key in a heap, 151 ex.
INCREMENT, 359
incremental design method, 11
for finding the convex hull, 899
in-degree, 87
indentation in pseudocode, 4
independence, 107–108, 110 ex., 112
independent family of subsets, 345
independent set, 721, 961 pr.
index of an element of $\mathbf{Z}_n^*$, 828
induced subgraph, 88

infinite sequence, 84
infinite set, 79
infinite sum, 42
INITIALIZE-PREFLOW, 608
INITIALIZE-SINGLE-SOURCE, 520
injective function, 85
inner product, 734
inorder tree walk, 245, 246 ex., 250 ex., 284
INORDER-TREE-WALK, 245
input
to an algorithm, 1
to a combinational circuit, 656
to a logic gate, 655
size of, 7
input alphabet, 862
input sequence, 635
input wire, 635
INSERT, 149, 198, 400
insertion
into binary search trees, 250–251
into binomial heaps, 413
into B-trees, 390–392
into chained hash tables, 223
into *d*-ary heaps, 152 pr.
into direct-address tables, 220
into dynamic tables, 368
into Fibonacci heaps, 424–425
into heaps, 150
into interval trees, 292
into linked lists, 205
into open-address hash tables, 233
into order-statistic trees, 284–285
into queues, 201
into red-black trees, 268–272
into stacks, 200
into sweep-line statuses, 894
into 2-3-4 heaps, 418 pr.
insertion sort, 2–4, 7–9, 15 ex.
in bucket sort, 181
compared to merge sort, 17 ex.
in merge sort, 17 pr.
in quicksort, 167 ex.
sorting-network implementation of, 638 ex.
stability of, 180 ex.
using binary search, 15 ex.
INSERTION-SORT, 3, 8
instance
of an abstract problem, 918
of a problem, 2
integers ($\mathbf{Z}$), 77
integer-valued flow, 601
integrality theorem, 603

integration of series, 44
interior of a polygon, 320
intermediate vertex, 558
internal node, 93
internal path length, 97 ex.
interpolation by a cubic spline, 774 pr.
interpolation by a polynomial, 779
  at complex roots of unity, 789–790
intersection
  of chords, 286 ex.
  determining, for a set of line
    segments, 892–898
  determining, for two disks, 898 ex.
  determining, for two line segments,
    889–890
  determining, for two simple
    polygons, 898 ex.
  finding all, in a set of line segments,
    898 ex.
  of languages, 921
  of sets ($\cap$), 78
interval, 290
INTERVAL-DELETE, 290
interval-graph coloring problem,
  333 ex.
INTERVAL-INSERT, 290
INTERVAL-SEARCH, 292, 294 ex.
INTERVAL-SEARCH-EXACTLY, 295 ex.
interval tree, 290–295
interval trichotomy, 290
intractability, 916
invalid shift, 853
inverse
  additive, 746
  of a bijective function, 85
  in a group, 814
  of a matrix, 735
  of a matrix from an LUP
    decomposition, 762–763
  multiplicative, 231, 748
  multiplicative modulo n, 822
inverse Ackermann's function (α),
  452–453
inversion in a sequence, 18 pr.
inverter, 655
invertible matrix, 735
isomorphic graphs, 88
iterated function, 40 pr.
iterated logarithm function, 36, 451
iteration method, 58–61
ITERATIVE-FFT, 794
ITERATIVE-TREE-SEARCH, 248

Jarvis's march, 905–907

JOHNSON, 569
Johnson's algorithm, 565–570
joining
  of red-black trees, 278 pr.
  of 2-3-4 trees, 399 pr.
joint probability density function, 111
Josephus permutation, 296 pr.
JUMP, 727 pr.

Karmarkar's algorithm, 539, 549
Karp's minimum mean-weight cycle
    algorithm, 548 pr.
k-ary tree, 95
k-combination, 101
kernel of a polygon, 907 ex.
key, 137, 149, 197
  median, of a B-tree node, 389
  public, 831
  secret, 831
kill a carry bit, 662
Kleene star (*), 922
KMP algorithm, 869–876
KMP-MATCHER, 871
knapsack problem
  fractional, 335, 337 ex.
  0-1, 335, 336 ex., 924 ex.
knot, of a spline, 774 pr.
Knuth-Morris-Pratt algorithm,
  869–876
k-permutation, 100
KPG box, 666
Kraft inequality, 97 ex.
k-ruling set, 725 ex.
Kruskal's algorithm, 504–505
  with integer edge weights, 510 ex.
k-string, 100
k-subset, 80
k-substring, 100
kth power, 808 ex.
k-universal hashing, 242 pr.

labeling function in path calculus, 571
Lagrange's formula, 780
Lagrange's theorem, 817
Lamé's theorem, 811
language, 921
  completeness of, 938 ex.
  proving NP-completeness of,
    939–940
  verification of, 926
last-in, first-out, 200
  see also stack
last-occurrence function, 879
layers

convex, 913 pr.
maximal, 913 pr.
LCA, 461 pr.
lcm (least common multiple), 813 ex.
LCS (longest common subsequence),
   314–320
LCS-LENGTH, 317, 319 ex.
leading submatrix, 766
leaf, 93
least common ancestor, 460 pr.
least common multiple, 813 ex.
least-squares approximation, 768–771
LEFT, 141
left child, 95
left-child, right-sibling representation,
   214, 216 ex.
LEFT-ROTATE, 266, 277 ex., 294 ex.
left subtree, 94
Legendre symbol $\left(\frac{a}{p}\right)$, 850 pr.
length
   of a path, 87
   of a sequence, 84
   of a string, 100
length function, 347
lexicographic sorting, 260 pr.
lg (binary logarithm), 34
lg* (iterated logarithm function), 36
   and repeated exponentiation, 451
$\lg^k$ (exponentiation of logarithms), 34
lg lg (composition of logarithms), 34
LIFO (last-in, first-out), 200
   see also stack
LIFT, 608
lifted vertex, 608
lift operation, 607, 612
LIFT-TO-FRONT, 621
lift-to-front algorithm, 615–625
light edge, 501
linear-array multiplier, 681–684
linear dependence, 735
linear equations
   solving modular, 820–823
   solving systems of, 749–762
   solving tridiagonal systems of,
     773 pr.
linear function, 8
linear independence, 735
linearity of expectation, 112
   and balls and bins, 130
   and the birthday paradox, 128
linearity of summations, 43
linear order, 83
linear probing, 234–235
linear programming

and maximum flow, 587 ex.
and multicommodity flow, 587 ex.
and single-source shortest paths,
   539–545
linear search, 5 ex., 11 ex.
line segment, 887
   determining turn of, 888–889
   determining whether any intersect,
     892–898
   determining whether two intersect,
     889–890
   finding all intersections of, in a set,
     898 ex.
link
   of binomial trees, 401
   of Fibonacci-heap roots, 427
LINK, 449
linked list, 204–209
   compact, 213 ex., 217 pr.
   deletion from, 206
   to implement disjoint sets, 443–446
   insertion into, 205
   k-ruling set of, 725 ex.
   searching, 204–205, 231 ex.
list, *see* linked list
LIST-DELETE, 206
LIST-DELETE', 206
LIST-INSERT, 205
LIST-INSERT', 207
LIST-MIS, 724
LIST-PREFIX, 696
LIST-RANK, 693
list ranking in parallel, 692–695
LIST-SEARCH, 205
LIST-SEARCH', 207
literal, 942
L_m-distance, 912 ex.
ln (natural logarithm), 34
load factor
   of a dynamic table, 367
   of a hash table, 224
local variable, 4
logarithm function (log), 34–35
   discrete, 828
   iterated (lg*), 36
logic gate, 655
LOMUTO-PARTITION, 168 pr.
longest common subsequence,
   314–320, 327
LONGEST-PATH, 923 ex.
LONGEST-PATH-LENGTH, 923 ex.
longest-simple-cycle problem, 961 ex.
LOOKUP-CHAIN, 313
looping constructs in pseudocode, 4

lower bounds
    for convex hull, 907 ex.
    for sorting, 172–175
lower-triangular matrix, 732
LU decomposition, 754–757
LU-DECOMPOSITION, 756
LUP decomposition, 751
    computation of, 757–761
    of a diagonal matrix, 761 ex.
    in matrix inversion, 762–763
    and matrix multiplication, 765 ex.
    of a permutation matrix, 761 ex.
    use of, 751–754
LUP-DECOMPOSITION, 759
LUP-SOLVE, 753

main memory, 382
majority function, 657, 686 pr.
MAKE-BINOMIAL-HEAP, 406
MAKE-HEAP, 400
MAKE-SET, 440
    disjoint-set-forest implementation
        of, 448
    linked-list implementation of, 443,
        446 ex.
MAKE-TREE, 459 pr.
Manhattan distance, 193 pr., 912 ex.
marked node, 421, 432–433, 435 ex.
Markov's inequality, 114 ex.
master method for solving a
    recurrence, 61–64
master theorem, 62
    proof of, 64–72
matched vertex, 600
matching
    and maximum flow, 600–604
    of strings, 853–885
    weighted bipartite, 439
matric matroid, 345
matrix, 730–739
    adjacency, 467
    conjugate transpose of, 766 ex.
    Hermitian, 766 ex.
    incidence, 354 pr., 468 ex., 951
    predecessor, 551
    pseudoinverse of, 770
    and quasirings, 746
    and rings, 746–747
    symmetric positive-definite,
        766–768
    Toeplitz, 797 pr.
    transpose of, 467, 731
    see also matrix inversion, matrix
        multiplication

matrix-chain multiplication, 302–309
    correspondence to polygon
        triangulation, 321–323
MATRIX-CHAIN-MULTIPLY, 308
MATRIX-CHAIN-ORDER, 306
matrix inversion, 762–765
matrix multiplication
    for all-pairs shortest paths, 552–558
    boolean, 747–748, 749 ex., 766 ex.,
        772 pr.
    and computing the determinant,
        766 ex.
    on a CRCW PRAM, 709 ex.
    on an EREW PRAM, 709 ex.
    and LUP decomposition, 765 ex.
    and matrix inversion, 763–765
    Pan's method, 744 ex.
    Strassen's algorithm, 739–745
    by a work-efficient CRCW
        algorithm, 713 ex.
MATRIX-MULTIPLY, 303, 554
matrix-vector multiplication, 713 ex.
matroid, 345–350, 354 pr.
MAX-FLOW-BY-SCALING, 628 pr.
max-flow min-cut theorem, 593
maximal
    element of a partially ordered set,
        83
    layers, 913 pr.
    point, 913 pr.
    subset in a matroid, 346
maximal independent set, 721
    computed from a 6-coloring on an
        EREW PRAM, 724–725
maximum, 185
    in binary search trees, 248
    of a binomial distribution, 120 ex.
    finding, 185–187, 704–706, 709 ex.,
        726 pr.
    in heaps, 150
    in order-statistic trees, 289 ex.
    in red-black trees, 265
MAXIMUM, 149, 198
maximum bipartite matching,
    600–604, 614 ex., 629
maximum degree in a Fibonacci heap,
    423, 431 ex., 435–438
maximum flow, 579–629
    Ford-Fulkerson method, 587–600
    lift-to-front algorithm, 615–625
    and maximum bipartite matching,
        600–604
    preflow-push algorithms, 605–625
    scaling algorithm, 627 pr.

updating, 627 pr.
with upper and lower capacity
bounds, 628 pr.
mean, *see* expected value
mean weight of a cycle, 548 pr.
median, 185–194
of sorted lists, 192 ex.
weighted, 193 pr.
median key of a B-tree node, 389
median-of-3 method, 170 pr.
member of a set ($\in$), 77
memoization, 312–314
MEMOIZED-MATRIX-CHAIN, 313
merge
on a CRCW PRAM, 709 ex.
of k sorted lists, 151 ex.
of linked lists, 208 ex.
of two sorted arrays, 12
using a comparison network,
646–648
MERGE, 12, 15 ex.
mergeable heap, 400
linked-list implementation of,
217 pr.
in minimum-spanning-tree
algorithm, 418 pr.
relaxed heaps, 439
running times of operations on,
401 fig.
2-3-4 heaps, 418 pr.
see also binomial heap, Fibonacci
heap
MERGE-LISTS, 979
MERGER, 646
merge sort, 12–15
compared to insertion sort, 17 ex.
sorting-network implementation of,
648–650
stability of, 180 ex.
use of insertion sort in, 17 pr.
MERGE-SORT, 13
recursion tree for, 314 ex.
merging network, 646–648
odd-even, 651 pr.
MILLER-RABIN, 841
Miller-Rabin primality test, 839–844
MIN-GAP, 295 ex.
minimax weight, 577 pr.
minimum, 185
in binary search trees, 248
in binomial heaps, 406
in B-trees, 394 ex.
in Fibonacci heaps, 425
finding, 185–187

off-line, 458 pr.
in order-statistic trees, 289 ex.
in red-black trees, 265
MINIMUM, 186, 198, 400
minimum-cost spanning tree, *see*
minimum spanning tree
minimum degree of a B-tree, 385
minimum key
in 2-3-4 heaps, 418 pr.
minimum mean-weight cycle, 548 pr.
minimum node of a Fibonacci heap,
422
minimum path cover, 626 pr.
minimum spanning tree, 498–513
as a closed semiring, 577 pr.
constructed using mergeable heaps,
418 pr.
on dynamic graphs, 510 ex.
in finding a near-optimal
traveling-salesman tour, 969
generic algorithm, 499–504
Kruskal's algorithm, 504–505
Prim's algorithm, 505–510
relation to matroids, 347
second-best, 511 pr.
minor of a matrix, 736
MIS (maximal independent set), 721
computed from a 6-coloring on an
EREW PRAM, 724–725
modular arithmetic, 814–820
modular exponentiation, 829
MODULAR-EXPONENTIATION, 829
modular linear equations, 820–823
MODULAR-LINEAR-EQUATION-SOLVER,
822
monoid, 570, 745
monotonically decreasing, 32
monotonically increasing, 32
MST-KRUSKAL, 505
MST-MERGEABLE-HEAP, 419 pr.
MST-PRIM, 509
MST-REDUCE, 512 pr.
multicommodity flow network, 587 ex.
multigraph, 89
converting to equivalent undirected
graph, 468 ex.
multiple, 733, 802
of an element modulo n, 820–823
multiple assignment, 4
multiple sources and sinks, 584–585
multiplication
array multiplier, 672–675
circuits for, 671–678, 681–684
of complex numbers, 745 ex.

divide-and-conquer method for, 797 pr.
grade-school algorithm for, 671
linear-array multiplier, 681–684
of matrices, 733
of a matrix chain, *see* matrix-chain multiplication
modulo n ($\cdot_n$), 815
of polynomials, 777
Russian peasant's algorithm for, 681
Wallace-tree multiplier, 675–677
multiplication method, 228–229
multiplicative group modulo n, 816
multiplicative inverse, 748
    modulo n, 822
MULTIPOP, 357
MULTIPUSH, 360 ex.
mutually exclusive events, 105
mutually independent events, 108

N (set of natural numbers), 77
naive algorithm for string matching, 855–857
NAIVE-STRING-MATCHER, 855
NAND gate, 655
natural cubic spline, 774 pr.
natural numbers (N), 77
negative
    in an algebraic system, 746
    of a matrix, 733
negative-weight cycle
    detection of, by all-pairs shortest-paths algorithm, 558 ex.
    detection of, by Floyd-Warshall algorithm, 565 ex.
    and difference constraints, 542
    finding, 536 ex., 558 ex.
    and relaxation, 526 ex.
    and shortest paths, 515
negative-weight edge
    in Dijkstra's algorithm, 531 ex.
    and shortest paths, 515–516
neighbor, 89
neighborhood, 604 ex.
neighbor list, 617
nesting boxes, 546 pr.
net flow, 580–581
    across a cut, 591
network
    admissible, 615–617
    bitonic sorting, 642–646
    comparison, 634–639
    flow, *see* flow network
    for merging, 646–648

odd-even merging, 651 pr.
odd-even sorting, 651 pr.
permutation, 652 pr.
residual, 588–590
sorting, 634–653
transposition, 651 pr.
Newton iteration, 685 pr.
NEXT-TO-TOP, 902
NIL, 5
node, 93
see also vertex
nondeterministic polynomial time, 927 n.
see also NP
nonhamiltonian graph, 925
noninvertible matrix, 735
nonoverlappable string pattern, 868 ex.
nonsaturating push, 607, 613
nonsingular matrix, 735
nontrivial power, 808 ex.
nontrivial square root of 1, modulo n, 829
NOR gate, 655
normal equation, 770
norm of a vector, 734
NOT function ($\neg$), 655
NOT gate, 655
NP (complexity class), 927, 928 ex.
NPC (complexity class), 932
NP-complete, 931
NP-completeness, 916–963
    of the circuit-satisfiability problem, 932–938
    of the clique problem, 947–949
    of determining whether a boolean formula is a tautology, 946 ex.
    of the formula-satisfiability problem, 940–942
    of the graph-coloring problem, 962 pr.
    of the hamiltonian-cycle problem, 953–959
    of the hamiltonian-path problem, 961 ex.
    of the independent-set problem, 961 pr.
    of the longest-simple-cycle problem, 961 ex.
    proving, of a language, 939–940
    of the set-covering problem, 978 ex.
    of the set-partition problem, 960 ex.
    of the subgraph-isomorphism problem, 960 ex.
    of the subset-sum problem, 951–953

of the 3-CNF-satisfiability problem,
942–945
of the traveling-salesman problem,
959–960
of the vertex-cover problem,
949–951
of the 0-1 integer-programming
problem, 960 ex.
NP-hard, 932
n-set, 80
n-tuple, 80
null vector, 736
numerical instability, 751

o-notation, 29–30
O-notation, 26–27
O'-notation, 39 pr.
$\tilde{O}$-notation, 39 pr.
object, 5
allocation and freeing of, 210–212
array implementation of, 209–213
objective function, 539, 545 ex.
occurrence of a pattern, 853
odd-even merging network, 651 pr.
odd-even sorting network, 651 pr.
OFF-LINE-MINIMUM, 459 pr.
off-line problem
least common ancestors, 460 pr.
minimum, 458 pr.
$\bar{1}$, 570, 745
one-pass method, 461
one-to-one correspondence, 85
one-to-one function, 85
one-way hash function, 836
on-line convex-hull problem, 907 ex.
onto, 85
open-address hash table, 232–241
double hashing, 235–237
linear probing, 234–235
quadratic probing, 235, 242 pr.
open interval, 290
optimal polygon triangulation,
320–324
optimal subset of a matroid, 347
optimal substructure
in dynamic programming, 309–310
of the fractional knapsack problem,
335
in greedy algorithms, 334
of Huffman codes, 343
of longest common subsequences,
315–316
of matrix-chain multiplication, 304

of optimal polygon triangulation,
323
of shortest paths, 519–520,
552–553, 558–559
of weighted matroids, 349
of the 0-1 knapsack problem, 335
optimal vertex cover, 966
optimization problem, 301, 918
approximation algorithms for,
964–985
OR function ($\vee$), 655, 746
on a CRCW PRAM, 709 ex.
order
of a group, 819
linear, 83
partial, 83
total, 83
ordered pair, 80
ordered tree, 94
order statistics, 185–194
dynamic, 281–286
order-statistic tree, 281–286
querying, 289 ex.
OR gate, 655
origin, 887
OS-KEY-RANK, 286 ex.
OS-RANK, 283
OS-SELECT, 282, 286 ex.
out-degree, 87
outer product, 734
output
of an algorithm, 1
of a combinational circuit, 656
of a logic gate, 655
output sequence, 635
output wire, 635
overdetermined system of linear
equations, 750
overflow
of a queue, 202, 203 ex.
of a stack, 201
overflowing vertex, 605
overlapping intervals, 290
finding all, 295 ex.
point of maximum overlap, 295 pr.
overlapping rectangles, 295 ex.
overlapping subproblems, 310–312
overlapping-suffix lemma, 854

P (complexity class), 919, 923, 924 ex.
package wrapping, 905
page on a disk, 382, 398 pr.
pairwise disjoint sets, 79
pairwise independence, 108

pairwise relatively prime, 806
Pan's method for matrix
        multiplication, 744 ex.
parallel algorithm, 688–729
    see also arithmetic circuit,
        comparison network, CRCW,
        CREW, EREW, parallel
        random-access machine, sorting
        network
parallel combinational circuit
        operation, 655
parallel prefix
    on an array, 713 ex.
    circuit for, 665–666, 670 ex.
    on a list, 695–697
    segmented, 726 pr.
    used in Euler-tour technique, 698
    work-efficient parallel algorithm,
        714–719
parallel random-access machine,
        688–691, 712–713, 713 ex.
    see also CRCW, CREW, ERCW,
        EREW
parameter, 5
    costs of passing, 73 pr.
parent, 93
    in a breadth-first tree, 469
PARENT, 141
parenthesis theorem, 480
parenthesization of a matrix-chain
        product, 302
    correspondence to polygon
        triangulation, 321–323
parity function, 657
parse tree, 321, 943
partial order, 83
partial product, 671
PARTITION, 154, 168 pr.
partitioning algorithm, 154–155
    around median of 3 elements,
        168 ex.
    Lomuto version, 168 pr.
    randomized, 162
partition of a set, 79, 82
Pascal's triangle, 104 ex.
path, 87
    augmenting, 590–591
    calculus of, in directed graphs,
        571–573
    concatenation of, 571
    critical, 538, 670 ex.
    find, 447
    hamiltonian, 929 ex.
    label of, 571

shortest, 472, 514
    weight of, 514
PATH, 922
path compression, 447
path cover, 626 pr.
path length, of a tree, 97 ex.
pattern in string matching, 853
pattern matching, *see* string matching
perfect matching, 604 ex.
permutation, 85
    bit-reversal, 375 pr.
    Josephus, 296 pr.
    of a set, 100
permutation matrix, 732, 737 ex.
    LUP decomposition of, 761 ex.
permutation network, 652 pr.
persistent data structure, 278 pr., 380
PERSISTENT-TREE-INSERT, 278 pr.
PERT chart, 538, 538 ex.
phi function, 817
PISANO-DELETE, 438 pr.
pivot, 756
point
    in computational geometry,
        886–887
    extreme, 539 n.
pointer, 5
    array implementation of, 209–213
pointer jumping, 692–701
pointer tree, 727 pr.
point-value representation, 779
polar angle, sorting points by, 891 ex.
Pollard's rho heuristic, 845–849
POLLARD-RHO, 845
polygon, 320
    computing area of, 892 ex.
    determining whether two simple
        ones intersect, 898 ex.
    kernel of, 907 ex.
    simplicity testing, 897 ex.
    star-shaped, 907 ex.
    triangulation of, 320–324
polylogarithmically bounded, 35
polynomial, 33, 776
    addition of, 776
    asymptotic behavior of, 38 pr.
    coefficient representation of, 778
    evaluation of, 11 ex., 778, 783 ex.,
        798 pr.
    interpolation by, 779
    multiplication of, 777, 781–782,
        797 pr.
    point-value representation of, 779
polynomially bounded, 33

polynomially related, 920
polynomial-time
    acceptance, 922
    algorithm, 802, 916
    approximation scheme, 965–966
    computability, 920
    decision, 922
    reducibility ($\leq_P$), 930
    solvability, 919
    verification, 924–929
Pop, 201
positional tree, 95
positive-definite matrix, 737
positive net flow, 581
post-office location problem, 193 pr.
postorder tree walk, 245
potential function, 363
potential method, 363–367
    for binary counters, 365–366
    for CRCW connected-components
        algorithm, 727 pr.
    for dynamic tables, 369–370,
        372–374
    for Fibonacci heaps, 422–426, 430,
        433–435
    for generic preflow-push algorithm,
        613
    for heaps, 366 ex.
    for Knuth-Morris-Pratt algorithm,
        872
    for stack operations, 364–365
potential of a data structure, 363
power
    of an element modulo n, 827–830
    kth, 808 ex.
    nontrivial, 808 ex.
power series, 74 pr.
power set, 80
Pr { } (probability distribution), 105
PRAM (parallel random-access
        machine), 688–691, 712–713,
        713 ex.
    see also CRCW, CREW, ERCW,
        EREW
predecessor
    in binary search trees, 248–249
    in breadth-first trees, 469
    in B-trees, 394 ex.
    in linked lists, 204
    in order-statistic trees, 289 ex.
    in red-black trees, 265
    in shortest-paths trees, 516
Predecessor, 198
predecessor matrix, 551

predecessor subgraph
    in all-pairs shortest paths, 551
    in breadth-first search, 475
    in depth-first search, 477
    in single-source shortest paths, 517
prefix
    of a sequence, 315
    of a string ($\sqsubseteq$), 854
prefix code, 338
prefix computation
    in carry-lookahead addition, 663
    on an EREW PRAM, 695–697,
        713 ex.
    on a list, 695
    by a parallel prefix circuit, 665–666
    work-efficient version on an EREW
        PRAM, 714–719
prefix function, 869–871
prefix-function iteration lemma, 872
preflow, 605
preflow-push algorithm, 605–625, 629
    basic operations in, 606–608
    by discharging an overflowing vertex
        of maximum height, 625 ex.
    to find a maximum bipartite
        matching, 614 ex.
    generic algorithm, 608–614
    lift-to-front algorithm, 615–625
    with a queue of overflowing
        vertices, 625 ex.
preorder tree walk, 245
presorting, 911
Prim's algorithm, 505–510
    with an adjacency matrix, 510 ex.
    in finding a near-optimal
        traveling-salesman tour, 969
    implemented with a Fibonacci heap,
        509
    implemented with a heap, 509
    with integer edge weights, 510 ex.
    similarity to Dijkstra's algorithm,
        505, 531
    for sparse graphs, 511 pr.
primality testing, 837–844, 852
    Miller-Rabin test, 839–844
    pseudoprimality testing, 838–839
primary clustering, 235
primary memory, 382
prime distribution function, 837
prime number, 803
    density of, 837
prime number theorem, 837
primitive root of $\mathbf{Z}_n^*$, 827
principal root of unity, 784

principle of inclusion and exclusion, 81 ex.
PRINT-ALL-PAIRS-SHORTEST-PATH, 551
PRINT-INTERSECTING-SEGMENTS, 897 ex.
PRINT-LCS, 318
PRINT-OPTIMAL-PARENS, 308 ex.
PRINT-PATH, 476
priority queue, 149–151
  in constructing Huffman codes, 340
  in Dijkstra's algorithm, 530
  heap implementation of, 149–151
  in Prim's algorithm, 507, 509
  see also binary search tree, binomial heap, Fibonacci heap
probabilistic analysis, 126–132
  of average-case lower bound for sorting, 183 pr.
  of average node depth in a randomly built binary search tree, 260 pr.
  of balls and bins, 129–130, 132 ex.
  of birthday paradox, 126–129, 132 ex.
  of boolean matrix multiplication, 772 pr.
  of bucket sort, 181–182, 183 ex.
  of carry propagation in a ripple-carry adder, 671 ex.
  of collisions, 225 ex., 240 ex.
  of convex hull over a sparse-hulled distribution, 914 pr.
  of file comparison, 862 ex.
  of finding the maximum in an array, 133 pr.
  of hashing with chaining, 224–225
  of height of a randomly built binary search tree, 254–259
  of hiring problem, 134 pr.
  of insertion into a binary search tree with equal keys, 259 pr.
  of longest-probe bound for hashing, 241 pr.
  of Miller-Rabin primality test, 841–844
  of open-address hashing, 237–239, 240 ex.
  of partitioning, 161 ex., 164–165, 168 ex., 168 pr., 170 pr.
  of Pollard's rho heuristic, 846–849, 849 ex.
  of probabilistic counting, 134 pr.
  of quicksort, 164–167, 168 pr., 170 pr., 259 ex.
  of Rabin-Karp algorithm, 861
  of randomized selection, 188–189
  of searching a compact list, 217 pr.
  of slot-size bound for chaining, 241 pr.
  of sorting points by distance from origin, 183 ex.
  of streaks, 130–132, 132 ex.
  of universal hashing, 230–231
  of work-efficient parallel prefix algorithm, 717–719, 719 ex.
probabilistic counting, 134 pr.
probability, 104–111
probability density function, 111
probability distribution, 105
probability distribution function, 183 ex.
probe, 233, 241 pr.
problem
  abstract, 918
  computational, 1–2
  concrete, 919
  decision, 918
  intractable, 916
  optimization, 301, 918
  solution to, 2, 918–919
  tractable, 916
procedure, 2
product
  Cartesian, 80
  cross, 887
  inner, 734
  of matrices, 733
  outer, 734
  partial, 671
  of polynomials, 777
  rule of, 100
  scalar flow, 587 ex.
propagate a carry bit, 662
propagation delay, 655
proper ancestor, 93
proper descendant, 93
proper subgroup, 818
proper subset ($\subset$), 77
prune-and-search method, 899
pruning a Fibonacci heap, 439 pr.
pseudocode, 2, 4–5
pseudoinverse, 770
pseudoprime, 838–839
PSEUDOPRIME, 839
pseudorandom-number generator, 161
public key, 831, 834

public-key cryptosystem, 831–837

PUSH

  preflow-push operation, 607

  stack operation, 201

push operation (in preflow-push algorithms), 607

quadratic function, 9

quadratic probing, 235, 242 pr.

quadratic residue, 850 pr.

quadratic-sieve factorization algorithm, 852

quantile, 192 ex.

quasiring, 745–746

query, 198

queue, 200–203

  in breadth-first search, 470

  linked-list implementation of, 208 ex.

  in preflow-push algorithms, 625 ex.

  priority, *see* priority queue

quicksort, 153–171

  analysis of, 156–161, 163–168

  average-case analysis of, 164–167

  description of, 153–156

  good worst-case implementation of, 192 ex.

  with median-of-3 method, 170 pr.

  randomized versions of, 161–163

  stability of, 180 ex.

  stack depth of, 169 pr.

  tail-recursive version of, 169 pr.

  use of insertion sort in, 167 ex.

  worst-case analysis of, 163–164

QUICKSORT, 154, 168 pr.

QUICKSORT$'$, 170 pr.

quotient, 803

$\mathbf{R}$ (set of real numbers), 77

Rabin-Karp algorithm, 857–862

RABIN-KARP-MATCHER, 860

radix sort, 178–180

RADIX-SORT, 179

radix tree, 260 pr.

RAM, *see* random-access machine

RANDOM, 161, 163 ex.

random-access machine, 6

  parallel, 688–691, 712–713, 713 ex.

  vs. comparison networks, 634

randomized algorithm, 161

  for boolean matrix multiplication, 772 pr.

  coin-flipping in, 717

  for insertion into a binary search tree with equal keys, 259 pr.

  Miller-Rabin primality test, 839–844

  for partitioning, 162, 168 ex., 168 pr., 170 pr.

  for permutation, 163 ex.

  Pollard's rho heuristic, 845–849

  quicksort, 161–163, 168 ex., 168 pr., 170 pr.

  for searching a compact list, 217 pr.

  for selection, 187–189

  universal hashing, 229–231

  for work-efficient parallel prefix, 714–719

  worst-case performance of, 162 ex.

RANDOMIZED-LIST-PREFIX, 714

RANDOMIZED-PARTITION, 162

RANDOMIZED-QUICKSORT, 162, 168 pr., 259 ex.

  relation to randomly built binary search trees, 260 pr.

RANDOMIZED-SELECT, 187, 189 ex.

randomly built binary search tree, 254–259, 260 pr.

random-number generator, 161

random permutation, 163 ex.

random variable, 111–115

range, 85

rank

  column, 735

  full, 735

  of a matrix, 735

  of a node in a disjoint-set forest, 447, 453–454

  of a number in an ordered set, 164, 281

  in order-statistic trees, 283–284, 286 ex.

  row, 735

ratio bound, 964

RB-DELETE, 273

RB-DELETE-FIXUP, 274

RB-ENUMERATE, 289 ex.

RB-INSERT, 268

RB-JOIN, 278 pr.

reachability in a graph ($\rightsquigarrow$), 87

real numbers ($\mathbf{R}$), 77

record (data), 137

recurrence, 53–76

  recursion tree for, 59

  and sloppiness conditions, 74 pr.

  solution by iteration method, 58–61

  solution by master method, 61–64

solution by substitution method, 54–58
recurrence equation, *see* recurrence
recursion, 12
recursion tree, 59
  for merge sort, 314 ex.
  in proof of master theorem, 66
RECURSIVE-FFT, 788
RECURSIVE-MATRIX-CHAIN, 311
red-black tree, 263–280
  augmentation of, 288–289
  comparison with B-trees, 386
  deletion from, 272–277
  in determining whether any line segments intersect, 894
  enumerating keys in a range, 289 ex.
  height of, 264
  insertion into, 268–272
  joining, 278 pr.
  maximum key of, 265
  minimum key of, 265
  predecessor in, 265
  properties of, 263–265
  rotation in, 265–267
  searching in, 265
  successor in, 265
  and 2-3-4 trees, 387 ex.
  see also interval tree, order-statistic tree
reducibility, 930–931
reduction algorithm, 930
reduction function, 930
reflexive relation, 81
reflexivity of asymptotic notation, 30
register, 679
rejection
  by an algorithm, 922
  by a finite automaton, 863
relation, 81–84
relative error, 965
relative error bound, 965
relatively prime, 806
RELAX, 520
relaxation, 520–527
relaxed heap, 439
remainder, 803
repeated exponentiation, 450–451
repeated squaring
  for all-pairs shortest paths, 555–557
  for raising a number to a power, 829
repetition factor of a string, 883 pr.
REPETITION-MATCHER, 884 pr.
representative of a set, 440
RESET, 363 ex.

residual capacity, 588, 590
residual edge, 588
residual network, 588–590
residue, 803, 850 pr.
responsible processor, 692
reweighting
  in all-pairs shortest paths, 565
  in single-source shortest paths, 547 pr.
rho heuristic, 845–849
RIGHT, 141
right child, 95
RIGHT-ROTATE, 266
right subtree, 94
ring, 746–747
ripple-carry addition, 661–662
  compared to bit-serial addition, 680
root
  of a tree, 93
  of unity, 784
  of $\mathbf{Z}_n^*$, 827
rooted tree, 93
  representation of, 213–216
root list
  of a binomial heap, 405
  of a Fibonacci heap, 422
rotation
  cyclic, 876 ex.
  in a red-black tree, 265–267
rotational sweep, 899–907
row rank, 735
row vector, 731
RSA public-key cryptosystem, 831–837
rule of product, 100
rule of sum, 99
ruling set, 725 ex.
running time, 7
  average-case, 10
  best-case, 11 ex., 28
  of a combinational circuit, 659
  of a comparison network, 637
  expected, 10
  of a graph algorithm, 463
  worst-case, 9, 28
Russian peasant's algorithm, 681

safe edge, 499
SAME-COMPONENT, 442
sample space, 104
SAT, 940
satellite data, 137, 197
satisfiability, 933, 940–942
satisfiable formula, 940

satisfying assignment, 933, 940
saturated edge, 607
saturating push, 607, 612
scalar flow product, 587 ex.
scalar multiple, 733
scaling
    in maximum flow, 627 pr.
    in single-source shortest paths,
        547 pr.
Schur complement, 755, 767
Schur complement lemma, 767
SEARCH, 198
searching
    binary search, 15 ex.
    in binary search trees, 247–248
    in B-trees, 387–388
    in chained hash tables, 223
    in compact lists, 217 pr.
    in direct-address tables, 220
    for an exact interval, 295 ex.
    in interval trees, 292–294
    linear search, 5 ex., 11 ex.
    in linked lists, 204–205
    in open-address hash tables,
        233–234
    problem of, 5 ex.
    in red-black trees, 265
    of static sets, 241 pr.
search tree, *see* balanced search tree,
        binary search tree, B-tree, interval
        tree, order-statistic tree, red-black
        tree, splay tree, 2-3 tree, 2-3-4 tree
secondary clustering, 235
secondary storage
    search tree for, 381–399
    stacks on, 398 pr.
second-best minimum spanning tree,
        511 pr.
secret key, 831, 834
segment, *see* directed segment, line
        segment
segmented parallel prefix, 726 pr.
SELECT, 190, 191 ex.
selection
    of activities, *see* activity-selection
        problem
    and comparison sorts, 191
    in expected linear time, 187–189
    in order-statistic trees, 282–283
    problem of, 185
    in worst-case linear time, 189–192
selection sort, 10 ex.
self-loop, 86
semiconnected graph, 494 ex.

sentinel, 206–208, 208 ex., 272,
        277 ex., 282
sequence (⟨ ⟩), 84, 635, 642
    inversion in, 18 pr.
series, 43–44, 74 pr.
set ({ }), 77–81
    independent, 721, 961 pr.
    ruling, 725 ex.
    static, 241 pr.
set-covering problem, 974–978
    weighted, 984 pr.
set-partition problem, 960 ex.
settling of circuit values, 655
shadow of a point, 907 ex.
Shamir's boolean matrix
        multiplication algorithm, 772 pr.
Shell's sort, 19
shifter, 678 ex.
shift in string matching, 853
SHORTEST-PATH, 918
shortest paths, 514–578
    all-pairs, 550–578
    Bellman-Ford algorithm, 532–536
    and breadth-first search, 472–475,
        514
    and difference constraints, 539–545
    Dijkstra's algorithm, 527–532
    on a directed acyclic graph, 536–538
    in ϵ-dense graphs, 576 pr.
    estimate of, 520
    Floyd-Warshall algorithm, 558–562
    Gabow's scaling algorithm, 547 pr.
    Johnson's algorithm, 565–570
    by matrix multiplication, 552–558
    and negative-weight cycles, 515
    with negative-weight edges, 515–516
    optimal substructure of, 519–520
    problem variants, 515
    and relaxation, 520–523
    by repeated squaring, 555–557
    single-source, 514–549
    tree of, 517, 523–526
    in an unweighted graph, 472
    in a weighted graph, 514
sibling, 93
side of a polygon, 320
similar (∼), 881
simple cycle, 88
simple graph, 88
simple path, 87
simple polygon, 320
    determination of, 897 ex.
simple uniform hashing, 224
simplex, 539 n.

simplex algorithm, 539, 549
simulation, work-efficient, 712–713
single-destination shortest paths, 515
single-pair shortest path, 515, 544 ex.
single-source shortest paths, 514–549
    Bellman-Ford algorithm, 532–536
    and difference constraints, 539–545
    Dijkstra's algorithm, 527–532
    on a directed acyclic graph, 536–538
    in ϵ-dense graphs, 576 pr.
    Gabow's scaling algorithm, 547 pr.
singleton, 80
singly connected graph, 485 ex.
singly linked list, 204
    see also linked list
singular matrix, 735
sink, 468 ex., 580, 584–585
SIX-COLOR, 721
size
    of an algorithm's input, 7, 801–802,
        919–921
    of a binomial tree, 402
    of a clique, 947
    of a combinational circuit, 659, 710
    of a disjoint-set tree, 453
    of a set, 79
    of a subtree in a Fibonacci heap,
        436
    of a vertex cover, 949, 966
skew symmetry, 580
sloppiness conditions for recurrences,
    74 pr.
slot, 220
SLOW-ALL-PAIRS-SHORTEST-PATHS,
    555
solution
    to an abstract problem, 918
    to a computational problem, 2
    to a concrete problem, 919
    feasible, 540
    to a system of linear equations, 750
sorted linked list, 204
    see also linked list
SORTER, 648, 650 ex.
sorting, 137–184
    average-case lower bound for,
        183 pr.
    bucket sort, 180–183
    counting sort, 175–178
    on an EREW PRAM, 712
    heapsort, 140–152
    insertion sort, 2–4
    lexicographic, 260 pr.
    in linear time, 175–183, 184 pr.

lower bounds for, 172–175
merge sort, 12–15
    in place, 3, 138
    of points by polar angle, 891 ex.
    problem of, 137
    quicksort, 153–171
    radix sort, 178–180
    selection sort, 10 ex.
    Shell's sort, 19
    using a binary search tree, 254 ex.
    using networks, *see* sorting network
sorting network, 637, 638 ex.
    AKS, 653
    based on insertion sort, 638 ex.
    based on merge sort, 648–650
    bitonic, 642–646
    odd-even, 651 pr.
source, 469, 515, 580, 584–585
spanning tree, 345–346, 498
sparse graph, 465
sparse-hulled distribution, 914 pr.
splay tree, 280, 380
spline, 774 pr.
splitting
    of B-tree nodes, 389–390
    of 2-3-4 trees, 399 pr.
spurious hit, 860
square matrix, 731
square of a directed graph, 468 ex.
square root, modulo a prime, 850 pr.
squaring, repeated
    for all-pairs shortest paths, 555–557
    for raising a number to a power, 829
stability
    of circuit values, 655
    of sorting algorithms, 177, 177 ex.,
        180 ex.
stack, 200–201
    in Graham's scan, 899
    linked-list implementation of,
        208 ex.
    operations analyzed by accounting
        method, 361–362
    operations analyzed by aggregate
        method, 357–358
    operations analyzed by potential
        method, 364–365
    for procedure execution, 169 pr.
    on secondary storage, 398 pr.
STACK-EMPTY, 201
standard deviation, 114
STAR, 727 pr.
star-shaped polygon, 907 ex.
star tree, 727 pr.

start state, 862
state of a finite automaton, 862
static set, 241 pr.
Stirling's approximation, 35
STOOGE-SORT, 169 pr.
storage management, 140, 210–212,
    213 ex., 226 ex.
Strassen's algorithm, 739–745
  and boolean matrix multiplication,
    747–748, 772 pr.
streaks, 130–132, 132 ex.
strictly decreasing, 32
strictly increasing, 32
string, 100, 853
string matching, 853–885
  based on repetition factors, 883 pr.
  Boyer-Moore algorithm, 876–883
  on a CREW PRAM, 884 pr.
  by finite automata, 862–869
  with gap characters, 857 ex., 869 ex.
  Knuth-Morris-Pratt algorithm,
    869–876
  naive algorithm, 855–857
  Rabin-Karp algorithm, 857–862
string-matching automaton, 863–868,
    869 ex.
strongly connected component, 88
  decomposition into, 488–494
STRONGLY-CONNECTED-COMPONENTS,
    489
strongly connected graph, 88
subgraph, 88
subgraph-isomorphism problem,
    960 ex.
subgroup, 817–819
subpath, 88
subsequence, 314
subset
  hereditary family of, 345
  independent family of, 345
subset ($\subseteq$), 77
SUBSET-SUM, 951
subset-sum problem
  approximation algorithm for,
    978–983
  NP-completeness of, 951–953
  with unary target, 960 ex.
substitution method, 54–58
substring, 100
subtree, 93
  maintaining sizes of, in
    order-statistic trees, 284–285
success in a Bernoulli trial, 115
successor

in binary search trees, 248–249
finding ith, of a node in an
    order-statistic tree, 286 ex.
in linked lists, 204
in order-statistic trees, 289 ex.
in red-black trees, 265
SUCCESSOR, 198
suffix ($\sqsupset$), 854
suffix function, 863
suffix-function inequality, 866
suffix-function recursion lemma, 866
sum
  Cartesian, 783 ex.
  flow, 586 ex.
  infinite, 42
  of matrices, 733
  of polynomials, 776
  rule of, 99
  telescoping, 44
sum bit, 661
summary of path labels, 571
summary operator ($\oplus$), 570
summation, 42–52
  in asymptotic notation, 43
  bounding, 46–52
  formulas and properties of, 42–46
  implicit, 585
  linearity of, 43
summation lemma, 785
superpolynomial time, 916
supersink, 584
supersource, 584
surjection, 85
sweeping, 892–898, 913 pr.
sweep line, 892
sweep-line status, 894
symbol table, 219, 227, 230
symmetric function, 686 pr.
symmetric matrix, 733, 738 ex.
symmetric positive-definite matrix,
    766–768
symmetric relation, 81
symmetry breaking, 720–725
symmetry of Θ-notation, 30
systems of difference constraints,
    539–545
systems of linear equations, 749–762,
    773 pr.

TABLE-DELETE, 372
TABLE-INSERT, 368
tail
  of a binomial distribution, 121–126
  of a linked list, 204

of a queue, 201
tail recursion, 169 pr.
tally circuit, 671 ex.
Tarjan's off-line
      least-common-ancestors
      algorithm, 460 pr.
task scheduling, 350–353, 354 pr.
tautology, 929 ex., 946 ex.
Taylor series, 262 pr.
telescoping series, 44
telescoping sum, 44
text in string matching, 853
3-CNF, 942
3-CNF-SAT, 942
3-CNF satisfiability, 942–945
3-COLOR, 962 pr.
3-conjunctive normal form, 942
tick of a clock, 679
time, *see* running time
timestamp, 477, 484 ex.
Toeplitz matrix, 797 pr.
Top, 902
top of a stack, 200
topological sort, 485–488
   in computing single-source shortest
      paths on a dag, 536
Topological-Sort, 486
total order, 83
tour
   bitonic, 324 pr.
   Euler, 698
   of a graph, 959
tractability, 916
transition function, 862, 868, 876 ex.
transitive closure, 562–563, 749 ex.
   and boolean matrix multiplication,
      749 ex., 766 ex.
   of dynamic graphs, 576 pr.
Transitive-Closure, 563
transitive relation, 82
transitivity of asymptotic notation, 30
transpose
   conjugate, 766 ex.
   of a directed graph, 468 ex.
   of a matrix, 467, 731
transpose symmetry of asymptotic
      notation, 30
transposing a raster image, 728 pr.
transposition network, 651 pr.
traveling-salesman problem
   approximation algorithm for,
      969–974
   bitonic euclidean, 324 pr.
   bottleneck, 974 ex.

NP-completeness of, 959–960
   with triangle inequality, 969–972
   without triangle inequality, 972–973
traversal of a tree, *see* tree walk
tree, 91–97
   binary, *see* binary tree
   binomial, 401–403, 423
   bisection of, 98 pr.
   breadth-first, 469, 475
   decision, 173–174, 174 ex.
   depth-first, 477
   diameter of, 476 ex.
   dynamic, 380
   finding the root of, on a CREW
      PRAM, 708 ex.
   free, 89, 91
   full walk of, 970
   height of, 94, 141
   minimum spanning, 498–513
   optimal vertex cover of, 968 ex.
   parse, 321, 943
   pointer, 727 pr.
   recursion, 59
   rooted, 93, 213–216
   shortest-paths, 517, 523–526
   spanning, 345–346, 498
   splay, 280, 380
   star, 727 pr.
   2-3, 280, 399
   2-3-4, 385
Tree-Delete, 253, 273
tree edge, 475, 477, 482
Tree-Insert, 251, 253 ex., 268
Tree-Maximum, 248
Tree-Minimum, 248
Tree-Predecessor, 249
Tree-Search, 247, 388
Tree-Successor, 249
tree walk, 215–216 ex., 245, 284
trial division, 838
triangle, 320
   Pascal's, 104 ex.
   in an undirected graph, 749 ex.
triangle inequality, 969
triangular matrix, 732, 737 ex.
triangulation, 320–324
trichotomy property of real numbers,
      31
tridiagonal linear systems, 773 pr.
tridiagonal matrix, 732
Trim, 981
trimming of a list, 980
trivial divisor, 803
truth assignment, 933, 940

truth table, 655
TSP, 959
tuple, 80
2-CNF-SAT, 946 ex.
2-CNF satisfiability, 946 ex.
two-pass method, 449
2-3-4 heap, 418 pr.
2-3-4 tree, 385
  joining, 399 pr.
  and red-black trees, 387 ex.
  splitting, 399 pr.
2-3 tree, 280, 399

unary, 920
uncountable set, 80
underdetermined system of linear
  equations, 750
underflow
  of a queue, 203 ex.
  of a stack, 201
undirected graph, 86
  articulation point of, 495 pr.
  biconnected component of, 495 pr.
  bridge of, 495 pr.
  clique in, 947
  coloring of, 97 pr., 721, 962 pr.
  computing a minimum spanning
    tree in, 498–513
  converting to, from a multigraph,
    468 ex.
  d-regular, 604 ex.
  grid, 625 pr.
  independent set of, 721, 961 pr.
  matching of, 600
  vertex cover of, 949, 966
  see also graph
undirected version of a directed
  graph, 89
uniform hashing, 234
uniform probability distribution,
  106–107
union
  of dynamic sets, *see* uniting
  of languages, 921
  of sets ($\cup$), 78
UNION, 400, 440
  disjoint-set-forest implementation
    of, 448
  linked-list implementation of,
    443–445, 446 ex.
union by rank, 447
unique factorization of integers, 807
uniting
  of binomial heaps, 407–413

of Fibonacci heaps, 425–426
of heaps, 400
of linked lists, 208 ex.
of 2-3-4 heaps, 418 pr.
unit lower-triangular matrix, 732
unit upper-triangular matrix, 732
unit vector, 731
universal hashing, 229–231
universe, 79
unmatched vertex, 600
unordered binomial tree, 423
unsorted linked list, 204
  see also linked list
upper-triangular matrix, 732

valid shift, 853
value
  of a flow, 580
  of a function, 84
Vandermonde matrix, 738 ex.
van Emde Boas data structure, 380
Var[ ] (variance), 113
variable
  in pseudocode, 4
  random, 111–115
variable-length code, 338
variance, 113
  of a binomial distribution, 118
  of a geometric distribution, 116
vector, 731, 734–736
  convolution of, 778
  cross product of, 887
  in the plane, 887
Venn diagram, 79
verification, 924–929
vertex
  articulation point, 495 pr.
  in a graph, 86
  intermediate, 558
  of a polygon, 320
vertex cover, 949, 966
  for a tree, 968 ex.
VERTEX-COVER, 949
vertex-cover problem
  approximation algorithm for,
    966–968
  and clique problem, 968 ex.
  NP-completeness of, 949–951
vertex set, 86
Viterbi algorithm, 327 pr.
VLSI (very-large-scale integration),
  75 n.

walk of a tree, 215–216 ex., 245, 284

Wallace-tree multiplier, 675–677
weight
  of an edge, 466
  mean, 548 pr.
  minimax, 577 pr.
  of a path, 514
weight-balanced tree, 376 pr.
weighted bipartite matching, 439
weighted matroid, 346–350
weighted median, 193 pr.
weighted set-covering problem, 984 pr.
weighted-union heuristic, 445
weight function
  for a graph, 466
  for polygon triangulation, 320
  in a weighted matroid, 346
white-path theorem, 482
white vertex, 469, 477
widget, 954
wire, 635, 656
WITNESS, 840
witness to the compositeness of a
    number, 840
work, 695, 713 ex.
work-efficient PRAM algorithm, 695
  matrix multiplication on a CRCW
    PRAM, 713 ex.
  matrix-vector multiplication on an
    EREW PRAM, 713 ex.
  parallel prefix computation,
    714–719
work-efficient simulation, 712–713
worst-case running time, 9, 28

XOR (exclusive-or) function ($\oplus$), 655
XOR gate, 655

Yen's improvement to the
    Bellman-Ford algorithm, 545 pr.

$\mathbf{Z}$ (set of integers), 77
$\mathbf{Z}_n$ (equivalence classes modulo n),
  804
$\mathbf{Z}_n^*$ (elements of multiplicative group
    modulo n), 816
$\mathbf{Z}_n^+$ (nonzero elements of $\mathbf{Z}_n^*$), 838
$\overline{0}$, 570, 745
zero-knowledge encryption, 852
zero matrix, 731
zero of a polynomial modulo a prime,
  823 ex.
0-1 integer-programming problem,
  960 ex.
0-1 knapsack problem, 335, 336 ex.,
  924 ex.

zero-one principle, 639–642, 646 ex.,
  648 ex.